Sociology

It was a pleasure to read your work. I felt as though I became acquainted with you through your words.

Thanks for your dedication to making the field of sociology more exciting to learn about.

Thank you again for your fine book. My college education would not have been complete without this course.

I took Sociology courses in high school and none have made as much sense as this text.

I found it extremely fascinating, well organized, easy to read, and most of all, interesting.

D0164536

"Dear Professor Henslin . . ."

The following are excerpts from e-mails to the author from students who have used various versions and editions of *Sociology: A Down-to-Earth Approach.*

Hello Mr. Henslin,
I am a first semester sociology student at Valley College in San Bernadino, California. To be perfectly honest, I did not anticipate this class being so fascinating. Although we are just beginning your book I just thought I would write you a quick note to tell you I enjoy it very much. I think more textbooks should be written with your "down-to-earth approach." Thanks for a great book.

Cordially,
John Tornello

Mr. Henslin,
I am a 50(!) year old student. I am really enjoying using your book. I am a mom and a grandmother, so my time is limited. I have never written a letter like this, but I wanted to let you know how strongly I feel about this textbook.

Thank you for helping me realize my dream of going to college!!!

Sincerely,
Marsha Roberts
Shelton State Junior College
Tuscaloosa, Alabama

Your text *Essentials of Sociology* is amazing. I am a student at Tennessee State University and have decided to choose sociology as a second major. I have never been so intrigued with a text as I am with yours.

Jeannie Owen

Mr. Henslin,
I just wanted to say thank you, thank you, and THANK YOU for your incredible book. I have not read a more coherent sociology book in all my years of college. I really appreciate the time that you took in making your book interesting and thought-provoking.

It has been a long time since I wanted to read a textbook straight through from the first page to the finish, but I have to tell you that your book is a fascinating read equal to any paperback novel that I have just devoured.

Thank you for bringing the excitement back into the sociology class and thank you for making me think and wonder again.

Sincerely,
Brandi Altheide
Mott Community College
Flint, Michigan

Hello! My name is Kathy. I am taking a sociology class this summer, and I have already preread this whole textbook. I must say, this is the easiest to understand textbook that I have had so far in my college experience. Thanks!

Kathy Patton
Owens Community College
Findlay, Ohio

Hi Mr. Henslin,
I am a student at Greenville Technical College in Greenville, South Carolina. I am currently taking Introduction to Sociology here at Tech and I must tell you, your book rocks!!!! It is the most fun I have ever had reading any textbook in my life!

Sincerely,
Kim B

Dear Professor Henslin,
I am a student at Stony Brook University in New York and I'm working toward a major in Sociology. I just completed an introductory summer course in Sociology that was taught with your textbook. I found your book to be incredibly interesting—so much that I am now reading the chapters we skipped over in class.

Thanks again,
Anna Maria Huertas Kormoski

Hi, Prof. Henslin.

Your book was the required reading for the course and I purchased it on Tuesday . . . since then, I haven't been able to stop reading it. (I've covered all of the material up until midterm time, ha.) Besides that, I think I have discovered my major. I just wanted to thank you for putting such effort into this book because I have really, really enjoyed every part of it that I have read so far. It's always wonderful to find someone that loves a topic so much because it makes learning about it even more interesting. Thanks again . . .

Jessica King
University of Cincinnati

I am currently a freshman at Dordt College, a liberal arts college in Sioux City, Iowa. I really enjoy your book so far. It is very easy to read and understand. I especially appreciate the "down-to-earthiness" of this book. I have found that I can apply the things I have learned [from your text] to my Psychology 201 class also. Thanks for your dedication to making the field of sociology more exciting to learn about.

Joya Gerritsma

Dear James,

Hey there, my name is Leo Chagolla. I attend the University of Toledo and I am a Pharmacy major. When I registered for classes in the beginning of the fall semester, I was told I would either need to take sociology or psychology as an elective. To tell you the truth, I only took sociology because I had to—and it sounded easier than psychology. What I have discovered is that sociology has become one of the most interesting subjects I have ever studied.

Your book, *A Down-to-Earth Approach,* is marvelously well written and constructed. I seriously believe that reading your book has made me a better person. I am only one chapter away from completing the book—my class was only supposed to read on to chapter 9—but I just cannot stop reading.

Leo Chagolla

Dear Mr. Henslin,

I would like to take a minute to write you a brief letter expressing my gratitude for your most interesting and enlightening book. I have just begun my exploration into the world of sociology. With the help of your book, and my college professor, you have helped to educate me in a discipline that was foreign to me. I was unaware of the possibilities available to sociology majors, and after researching I have found this is definitely the field for me!

Sincerely,
Katie Bailey

Dr. James Henslin,

I had acquired *Essentials of Sociology: A Down-to-Earth Approach* as part of my required liberal arts core classes (Sociology 101) at Marquette University. I am now in the middle of my senior year and would like to tell you that I have used this text in most of the subsequent classes that I enrolled in after that class.

I want to thank you for helping the rest of my educational journey to be a pleasant one. It may also interest you to know that I am an adult learner at age 41, who returned to college after 18 years of factory work.

Doug Bulson
East Troy, WI
Marquette University

Dear Mr. Henslin,

I just finished a Sociology class using your text, the fourth edition of *Sociology, A Down-to-Earth Approach.* Tomorrow, I will take my final exam. I just wanted to commend you on this book. I found it extremely fascinating, well-organized, easy to read and most of all, interesting.

If you want a profile of some of your readers (students), I am 60 years old, a Catholic writer, author of four books, and a late bloomer who is just now getting her college education. I will graduate in August from Ottawa U. with a degree in Religion and a concentration on Psychology.

Thank you again for your fine book. My college education would not have been complete without this course.

Sincerely,
Judy Esway
Mesa, AZ

Sociology

Sociology

A DOWN-TO-EARTH APPROACH

SEVENTH EDITION

James M. Henslin
Southern Illinois University, Edwardsville

Boston New York San Francisco
Mexico City Montreal Toronto London Madrid Munich Paris
Hong Kong Singapore Tokyo Cape Town Sydney

Senior Series Editor: Jeff Lasser
Editorial Assistant: Sara Owen
Supplements Editor: Andrea Christie
Cover Administrator: Linda Knowles
Composition and Prepress Buyer: Linda Cox
Manufacturing Buyer: Megan Cochran
Senior Marketing Manager: Krista Groshong
Photo Researcher: Myrna Engler
Fine Art Researcher: Laurie Frankenthaler
Editorial-Production Service: The Book Company
Text Designer: Brigid Kavanagh
Electronic Composition: Omegatype Typography, Inc.

For related titles and support materials, visit our online catalog at www.ablongman.com

Cataloging-in-Publication Data not available at time of publication
ISBN 0-205-40735-8

Printed in the United States of America
10 9 8 7 6 5 6 5 4 3 2 VHP 07 06 05 04

Chapter Opener Art Credits:

Chapter 1: *Parts Equal the Whole I* by Diana Ong. Computer graphics. © Diana Ong/SuperStock.

Chapter 2: *Painted Clay Figure* by Chen Lian Xing, 2000. Watercolor, 14 × 14 in. © Red Lantern Folk Art/The Mukashi Collection/SuperStock.

Chapter 3: *Men Exist for the Sake of One Another, Teach Them Then or Bear With Them (Great Ideas of Western Man Series)* by Jacob Lawrence, 1958. Oil on prepared fiberboard, 20 ¾ in. × 16 ¾ in. © Smithsonian American Art Museum, Washington, DC/Art Resource, NY.

Chapter 4: *6 of Hearts* by Rosa Ibarra, 1993. Oil on canvas, 41 × 48 in. © **Rosa Ibarra**/Omni-Photo Communications.

Chapter 5: *Diverse Cross-Section* by Ivan Lee Sanford, 1991. Acrylic, 4 × 2.75 in. © Ivan Lee Sanford/Images.com, Inc.

Chapter 6: *Pushball* by Pavel Varfolomeevic Kusnezov, 1911. © Tretyakov Gallery, Moscow/SuperStock, © Estate of Pavel Kusnezov/RAO, Moscow/VAGA, New York.

Chapter 7: *Geometric Shapes on Face Figures (Digital)* by Noma & Jim Bliss, 1998. Digital and line art, 8 × 10 in. © Noma & Jim Bliss/Images.com, Inc.

Chapter 8: *Les Fetiches* by Lois Mailou Jones, 1938. Oil on canvas, 25 ½ × 21 ¼". Museum purchase made possible by N.H. Green, R. Harlan and F. Musgrave. © Smithsonian American Art Museum, Washington, DC/Art Resource, NY.

Chapter 9: *Hunger* by Francesco Clemente, 1980. © Philadelphia Museum of Art/CORBIS.

Chapter 10: *Apple Vendor* by Barbara Stevenson, ca. 1933-1934. Oil on canvas, 31 ¼ × 29 ⅛ in. (79.3 × 74.1 cm.). © Smithsonian American Art Museum, Washington, DC/Art Resource, NY.

Chapter 11: *Women in Burkah* by Pacita Abad, 1979. Oil on canvas, 125 × 88 cm. © Pacita Abad.

Chapter 12: *You have to blend in before you stand out* by Pacita Abad, 1995. Acrylic and oil, painted and printed cotton on stitched and padded canvas, 290 × 293 cm. © Pacita Abad.

Credits continue on page PC-1, which is a continuation of this copyright page.

To my fellow sociologists, who do such creative research on social life and who communicate the sociological imagination to generations of students.

With my sincere admiration and appreciation,

Brief Contents

Contents

THROUGH THE AUTHOR'S LENS

When a Tornado Strikes: Social Organization Following a Natural Disaster

When TV news announced that a tornado had ripped apart a town just hours from my own, not only destroying buildings but also taking lives, I wondered how the people were adjusting to their sudden loss. These photos, taken the next day, show a community in the process of rebuilding. (Page 118)

PART III Social Inequality

THROUGH THE AUTHOR'S LENS

The Dump People: Working and Living and Playing in the City Dump of Phnom Penh, Cambodia

I could hardly believe my ears when I learned that people were living in the city dump of Phnom Penh, the capital of Cambodia. This photo essay reveals their life far better than words ever could. These men, women, and children are not only scavenging trash, but also they are participating in a community. (Page 250)

THROUGH THE AUTHOR'S LENS

Work and Gender: Women at Work in India

Like women in the West, women in India are not limited to the home. Their work roles, however, stand in sharp contrast with those of women in the West. This photo essay illustrates some of the amazing differences I saw. (Page 296)

PART IV Social Institutions

18 Religion 510

THROUGH THE AUTHOR'S LENS

A Walk Through El Tiro in Medellin, Colombia

One of the most significant changes in the world is the global rush of poor, rural people to the cities of the Least Industrialized Nations. Some of these settlements are dangerous. I was fortunate to be escorted by an insider through this section of Medellin, Colombia. (Page 592)

THROUGH THE AUTHOR'S LENS

Social Movements and Propaganda: The Execution of Timothy McVeigh

When Timothy McVeigh, the Oklahoma bomber, was scheduled to be executed at the federal penitentiary in Terre Haute, Indiana, the media reported rumors that there was going to be a riot—and maybe even an insurrection. I couldn't resist going. This photo essay illustrates the use of propaganda by social movement activists. (Page 632)

Boxed Features

DOWN-TO-EARTH SOCIOLOGY

CULTURAL DIVERSITY AROUND THE WORLD

CULTURAL DIVERSITY IN THE UNITED STATES

MASS MEDIA IN SOCIAL LIFE

SOCIOLOGY AND THE NEW TECHNOLOGY

THINKING CRITICALLY

Guide to Social Maps

To the Student from the Author

Welcome to sociology! I've loved sociology since I was in my teens, and I hope you enjoy it, too. Sociology is fascinating because it holds the key to so much understanding of social life.

If you like to watch people and try to figure out why they do what they do, you will like sociology. Sociology pries open the doors of society so you can see what goes on behind them. *Sociology: A Down-to-Earth Approach* stresses how profoundly our society and the groups to which we belong influence us. Social class, for example, sets us on a path in life. For some, the path leads to better health, more education, and higher income, but for others it leads to poverty, dropping out of school, and even a higher risk of illness and disease. These paths are so significant that they affect our chances of making it to our first birthday, as well as of getting in trouble with the police. They even influence how our marriage will work out, the number of children we will have—and whether or not we will read this book in the first place.

When I took my first course in sociology, I was "hooked." Seeing how marvelously my life had been affected by these larger social influences opened my eyes to a new world, one that has been fascinating to explore. I hope that this will be your experience also.

From how people become homeless to how they become presidents, from why people commit suicide to why women are discriminated against in every society around the world—all are part of sociology. This breadth, in fact, is what makes sociology so intriguing. We can place the sociological lens on broad features of society, such as social class, gender, and race-ethnicity, and then immediately turn our focus on the small-scale level. If we look at two people interacting—whether quarreling or kissing—we see how these broad features of society are being played out in their lives.

We aren't born with instincts. Nor do we come into this world with preconceived notions of what life should be like. At birth, we have no ideas of race-ethnicity, gender, age, or social class. We have no idea, for example, that people "ought" to act in certain ways because they are male or female. Yet we all learn such things as we grow up in our society. Uncovering the "hows" and the "whys" of this process is also part of what makes sociology so fascinating.

One of sociology's many pleasures is that as we study life in groups (which can be taken as a definition of sociology), whether those groups be in some far-off part of the world or in some nearby corner of our own society, we constantly gain insights into our own selves. As we see how *their* customs affect *them,* the effects of our own society on us become more visible.

This book, then, can be part of an intellectual adventure, for it can lead you to a new way of looking at your social world—and in the process, help you to better understand both society and yourself.

I wish you the very best in college—and in your career afterward. It is my sincere hope that *Sociology: A Down-to-Earth Approach* will contribute to that success.

James M. Henslin
Department of Sociology
Southern Illinois University, Edwardsville

P.S. I enjoy communicating with students, so feel free to comment on your experiences with this text. Because I travel a lot, it is best to reach me by e-mail: henslin@aol.com

Also, you may want to look at the Website for this text: *www.ablongman.com/henslin7e*

To the Instructor from the Author

Remember when you first got "hooked" on sociology, how the windows of perception opened as you began to see life-in-society through the sociological perspective? For most of us, this was an eye-opening experience. This text is designed to open those windows onto social life, so students can see clearly the vital effects of group membership on their lives. Although few students will get into what Peter Berger calls "the passion of sociology," we at least can provide them the opportunity.

Sociology is like a huge jigsaw puzzle. Only very gradually do the intricate pieces start to fit together. As they do so, our perspective changes as we shift our eyes from the many small, disjointed pieces onto the whole that is being formed. Although this analogy is imperfect, it indicates a fascinating process of sociological discovery. Of all the endeavors we could have entered, we chose sociology because of the ways in which it joins together the "pieces" of society and the challenges it poses to "ordinary" thinking. To share the sociological perspective with students is our privilege.

As instructors of sociology, we have set ambitious goals for ourselves: to teach both social structure and social interaction, and to introduce students to the main sociological literature, to both the classic theorists and contemporary research. And we would like to accomplish this in ways that enliven the classroom, encourage critical thinking, and stimulate our students' sociological imagination. Although formidable, these goals are attainable. This book, based on many years of frontline (classroom) experience, is designed to help you reach these goals. Its subtitle, *A Down-to-Earth Approach,* is not proposed lightly. My goal is to share the fascination of sociology with students, and thereby make your teaching more rewarding.

Over the years, I have found the introductory course especially enjoyable. It is singularly satisfying to see students' faces light up as they begin to see how separate pieces of their world fit together. It is a pleasure to watch them gain insight into how their social experiences give shape to even their innermost desires. This is precisely what this text is designed to do—to stimulate your students' sociological imagination so they can better perceive how the "pieces" of society fit together—and what this means for their own lives.

Filled with examples from around the world as well as from our own society, this text helps make today's multicultural, global society come alive for students. From learning how the international elite carves up global markets to studying the intimacy of friendship and marriage, students can see how sociology is the key to explaining contemporary life—and their own place in it.

In short, this text is designed to make your teaching easier. There simply is no justification for students to have to wade through cumbersome approaches to sociology. I am firmly convinced that the introduction to sociology should be enjoyable, and that the introductory textbook can be an essential tool in sharing the discovery of sociology with students.

THE ORGANIZATION OF THIS TEXT

The text is laid out in five parts. Part I focuses on the sociological perspective, which I introduce in the first chapter. We then look at how culture influences us in Chapter 2, examine socialization in Chapter 3, and compare macrosociology and microsociology in Chapter 4. In Chapter 5, we look at how sociologists do research. Placing research methods in the fifth chapter is not usual, but doing so allows students to first become immersed in the captivating findings of sociology—then, after their interest is awakened, they learn how sociologists gather their data. This works very well, but if you prefer the more traditional order, simply teach this chapter as the second chapter. No content will be affected.

Part II, which focuses on groups and social control, adds to the students' understanding of how significantly social groups influence our lives. Chapter 6 opens this part with an overview of groups—from society, which encompasses us, to the smaller networks in which we are immersed. In this chapter, we also look at the fascinating area of group dynamics. In Chapter 7, we examine the impact of bureaucracy and formal organizations. Then in Chapter 8, we focus on how groups "keep us in line" and sanction those who violate their norms.

In Part III, we examine how social inequality pervades society and how those inequalities have an impact on our own lives. Because social stratification is so significant, I have written two chapters on this topic. The first (Chapter 9), with its global focus, presents an overview of the principles of stratification. The second (Chapter 10), with its emphasis on social class, focuses on stratification in U.S. society. After establishing this broader context of social inequality, in Chapter 11 we examine gender, the most global of the inequalities. Then in Chapter 12, we focus on inequalities of race and ethnicity, and in Chapter 13, those of age.

Part IV helps students become more aware of how social institutions encompass their lives. In Chapters 14 and 15, we look at how the economy and politics are our overarching social institutions. In Chapter 16, we examine the family, and in Chapter 17 we turn our focus on education. In Chapter 18, we look at the significance of religion, and, finally, in Chapter 19, that of medicine. Throughout, we look at how these social institutions are changing, and how their changes, in turn, influence our orientations to life.

With its focus on broad social change, Part V provides an appropriate conclusion for the book. Here we examine why our world is changing so rapidly, as well as catch a glimpse of what is yet to come. In Chapter 20, we analyze trends in population and urbanization, sweeping forces in our lives that ordinarily remain below our level of awareness. Our focus on collective behavior and social movements in Chapter 21, and social change and the environment in Chapter 22, takes us to the "cutting edge" of vital changes that engulf us all.

THEMES AND FEATURES

Six central themes run throughout this text: globalization, cultural diversity, down-to-earth sociology, critical thinking, the new technology, and the growing influence of the mass media on our lives. Let's look at these six themes.

Globalization

The first theme, globalization, explores the impact of global issues. The new global economy, for example, which has intertwined the fates of nations, vitally affects our lives. The globalization of capitalism influences the kinds of skills and knowledge we need, types of work available to us, costs of the goods and services we consume, and even whether our country is at war or peace. In addition to the strong emphasis on global issues that runs throughout this text, I have written a separate chapter on global stratification. I have also featured global issues in the chapters on social institutions and the final chapters on social change: population, urbanization, social movements, and the environment.

What occurs in Russia, Japan, and China, as well as in much smaller nations such as Afghanistan and Iraq, has direct and far-reaching consequences on our own lives. Consequently, in addition to the global focus that runs throughout the text, the second theme, Cultural Diversity, also has a strong global emphasis.

Cultural Diversity Around the World and in the United States

The second theme, cultural diversity, has two primary emphases. The first is cultural diversity around the world. Gaining an understanding of how social life is "done" in other parts of the world often challenges our taken-for-granted assumptions of social life. At times, learning about other cultures gives us an appreciation for the life of other peoples; at other times, we may be shocked or even disgusted at some aspect of another group's way of life (such as female circumcision) and come away with a renewed appreciation of our own customs.

To highlight this sub-theme, I have written a series of boxes called **Cultural Diversity Around the World.** The boxed features, here and throughout the text, are one of my favorite features of the book. They are especially valuable for introducing the provocative and controversial materials that make sociology

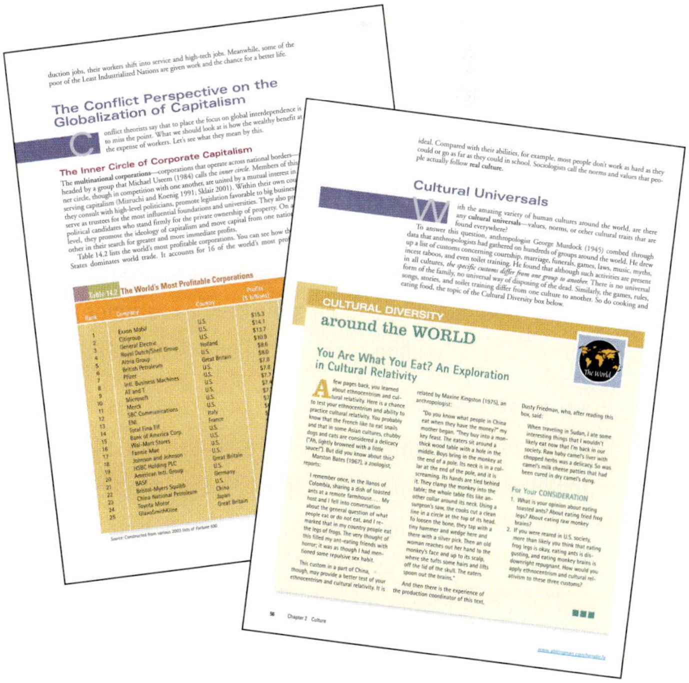

such a lively activity. Among the boxed features that stress this sub-theme of cultural diversity around the world are food customs that will likely test the limits of our cultural relativity (Chapter 2), apology specialists in Japan (Chapter 2), how Westerners and Easterners perceive the world differently (Chapter 3), human sexuality in Mexico and Kenya (Chapter 8), selling brides in China (Chapter 11), female circumcision in Africa (Chapter 11), love and arranged marriage in India (Chapter 16), female infanticide in China (Chapter 20), and the destruction of the rain forests and indigenous people in Brazil (Chapter 22).

The second emphasis is **cultural diversity in the United States.** In this sub-theme, we examine groups that make up the fascinating array of people who compose the United States. Among the boxes I have written with this sub-theme of cultural diversity in the United States are the significance of language—Spanish and English in Miami (Chapter 2), the terms people choose for their own racial-ethnic self-identification (Chapter 2), how the Amish resist social change (Chapter 4), how Tiger Woods represents a significant change in racial-ethnic identification (Chapter 12), discrimination against immigrants (Chapter 12), Islam as the new religious neighbor (Chapter 18), cultural confusion in the health care of Mexican immigrants (Chapter 19), and our shifting racial-ethnic mix (Chapter 20).

Looking at cultural diversity—whether it be in the United States or in other regions of the world—often challenges our own orientations to life. Seeing that there are so many varieties of "doing" social life highlights the arbitrariness of our own customs—and our taken-for-granted ways of thinking. These contrasts help students develop their sociological imagination. They are better able to see connections among key sociological concepts such as culture, socialization, norms, race-ethnicity, gender, and social class. As your students' sociological imagination grows, they can attain a new perspective on their own experiences—and a better understanding of the social structure of U.S. society.

Down-to-Earth Sociology

As many years of teaching have shown me, all too often textbooks are written to appeal to the adopters of texts rather than to the students who must learn from them. Thus, a central concern in writing this book has been to present sociology in a way that not only facilitates understanding but also shares its excitement. During the course of writing other texts, I often have been told that my explanations and

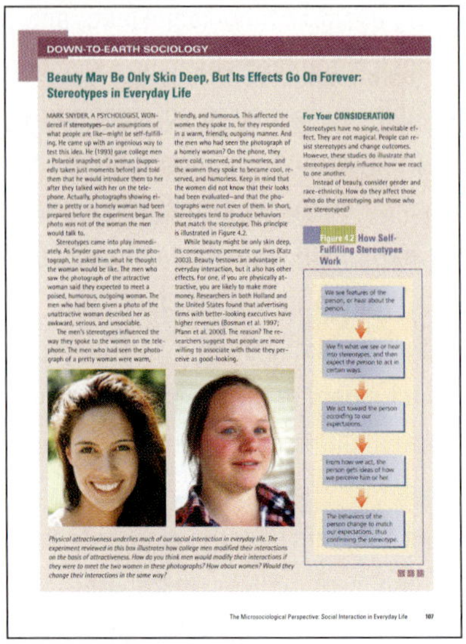

DOWN-TO-EARTH SOCIOLOGY

Beauty May Be Only Skin Deep, But Its Effects Go On Forever: Stereotypes in Everyday Life

MARK SNYDER, A PSYCHOLOGIST, WONdered if **stereotypes**—our assumptions of what people are like—might be self-fulfilling. He came up with an ingenious way to test this idea. He (1993) gave college men a Polaroid snapshot of a woman (supposedly taken just moments before) and told them that he would introduce them to her after they talked with her on the telephone. Actually, photographs showing either a pretty or a homely woman had been prepared before the experiment began. The photo was not of the woman the men would talk to.

Stereotypes came into play immediately. As Snyder gave each man the photograph, he asked him what he thought the woman would be like. The men who saw the photograph of the attractive woman said they expected to meet a poised, humorous, outgoing woman. The men who had been given a photo of the unattractive woman described her as awkward, serious, and unsociable.

The men's stereotypes influenced the way they spoke to the women on the telephone. The men who had seen the photograph of a pretty woman were warm, friendly, and humorous. This affected the women they spoke to, for they responded in a warm, friendly, outgoing manner. And the men who had seen the photograph of a homely woman? On the phone, they were cold, reserved, and humorless, and the women they spoke to became cool, reserved, and humorless. Keep in mind that the women did not know that their looks had been evaluated—and that the photographs were not even of them. In short, stereotypes tend to produce behaviors that match the stereotype. This principle is illustrated in Figure 4.2.

While beauty might be only skin deep, its consequences permeate our lives (Katz 2003). Beauty bestows an advantage in everyday interaction, but it also has other effects. For one, if you are physically attractive, you are likely to make more money. Researchers in both Holland and the United States found that advertising firms with better-looking executives have higher revenues (Bosman et al. 1997; Pfann et al. 2000). The reason? The researchers suggest that people are more willing to associate with those they perceive as good-looking.

Physical attractiveness underlies much of our social interaction in everyday life. The experiment reviewed in this box illustrates how college men modified their interactions on the basis of attractiveness. How do you think men would modify their interactions if they were to meet the two women in these photographs? How about women? Would they change their interactions in the same way?

For Your CONSIDERATION

Stereotypes have no single, inevitable effect. They are not magical. People can resist stereotypes and change outcomes. However, these studies do illustrate that stereotypes deeply influence how we react to one another.

Instead of beauty, consider gender and race-ethnicity. How do they affect those who do the stereotyping and those who are stereotyped?

Figure 4.2 How Self-Fulfilling Stereotypes Work

We see features of the person, or hear about the person.
We fit what we see or hear into stereotypes, and then expect the person to act in certain ways.
We act toward the person according to our expectations.
From how we act, the person gets ideas of how we perceive him or her.
The behaviors of the person change to match our expectations, thus confirming the stereotype.

The Microsociological Perspective: Social Interaction in Everyday Life 107

writing style are "down-to-earth," or accessible and inviting to students—so much so that I chose this phrase as the book's subtitle. The term is also featured in my introductory reader, *Down to Earth Sociology,* 12th edition (New York: Free Press, 2003).

This third theme is highlighted by a series of boxed features that explore sociological processes that underlie everyday life. In these **Down-to-Earth Sociology** boxes, we consider such topics as the relationship between heredity and environment (Chapter 3), beauty and success (Chapter 4), improper and fraudulent social research (Chapter 5), how the United States is being "McDonaldized" (Chapter 7), how hitting it big at the lottery changes people's lives (Chapter 10), lifestyles of the super-rich (Chapter 10), voice and racial discrimination in the rental market (Chapter 12), the "invisible knapsack" of cultural dominance (Chapter 12), the globalization of capitalism (Chapter 14), Big Brother and the new Homeland Security (Chapter 15), cohabitation (Chapter 16), when work becomes home and home becomes work (Chapter 16), why abused women don't pack up and leave (Chapter 16), home schooling (Chapter 17), terrorism and religion (Chapter 18), prayer and pregnancy (Chapter 18), the gentrification of Harlem (Chapter 20), mass hysteria (21), and corporate welfare (Chapter 22).

This third theme is actually a hallmark of the text, as my goal is to make sociology "down to earth." To help students grasp the fascination of sociology, I continuously stress sociology's relevance to their lives. To reinforce this theme, I avoid unnecessary jargon and use concise explanations and clear and simple (but not reductive) language. I often use student-relevant examples to illustrate key concepts, and I have based several of the chapters' opening vignettes on my own experiences in exploring social life. That this goal of sharing sociology's fascination is being reached is evident from the many comments I receive from instructors and students alike that the text helps make sociology "come alive."

Critical Thinking

The fourth theme, critical thinking, focuses on controversial social issues and engages students in examining the various sides of those issues. In these sections, titled **Thinking Critically,** as with the controversial materials presented in the boxed features, I present objective, fair portrayals of positions, and do not take a side—although I occasionally play the "devil's advocate" in the questions that close each of the topics. These sections can enliven your classroom with a vibrant exchange of ideas. Among the issues addressed are our tendency to conform to evil authority, as uncovered by the Milgram experiments (Chapter 6), bounties paid to kill homeless children in Brazil (Chapter 9), *maquiladoras* on the U.S.-Mexican border (Chapter 9), reparations for slavery (Chapter 12), our potential to increase our life span (Chapter 13), medically assisted suicide (Chapter 19), and abortion as a social movement (Chapter 21).

Because these *Thinking Critically* sections are based on controversial social issues that either affect the student's own life or are something that he or she is vitally interested in, they stimulate critical thinking and lively class discussion. They also lend themselves especially well to debates and small-group discussion.

Sociology and the New Technology

The fifth theme, sociology and the new technology, explores an aspect of social life that has come to be central to our existence. We welcome these new tools, for they help us to be more efficient at doing our tasks, from making a living to communicating with people on the other side of the globe. The significance of the new technology goes far beyond the tools and the ease and efficiency they bring to our tasks, however. The new technology also penetrates our being—it shapes our thinking, leading to changed ways of viewing life. The new technology has ushered us into a social revolution that will leave few aspects of our lives untouched.

This theme is introduced in Chapter 2, where technology is defined and presented as a major aspect of culture. It is then discussed throughout the text. Examples include how technology is being used to control workers in order to produce the "maximum security" workplace (Chapter 7), the implications of technology for maintaining global stratification (Chapter 9), and how the consequences of technology differ by social class (Chapter 10). The final chapter (22), "Social Change and the Environment," concludes the book with a focus on this theme.

To highlight this theme, I have written a series of boxes called **Sociology and the New Technology,** where the focus is on how technology is changing society and affecting our lives. Among these are the dilemmas of cloning (Chapter 6); electronic communities (Chapter 6), cyberloafing and cybersleuthing (Chapter

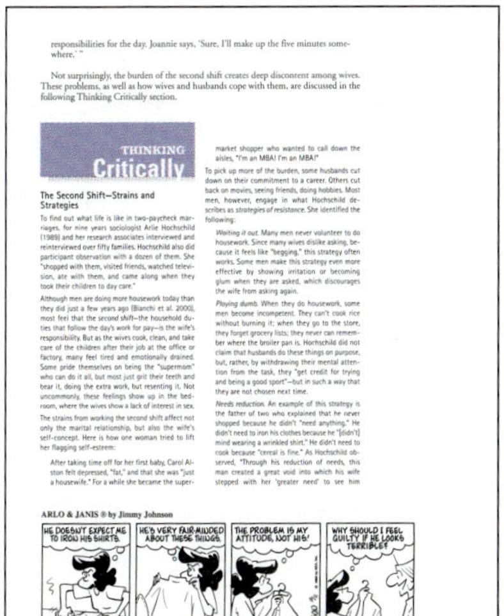
responsibilities for the day. Joannie says, 'Sure, I'll make up the five minutes somewhere.' "

Not surprisingly, the burden of the second shift creates deep discontent among wives. These problems, as well as how wives and husbands cope with them, are discussed in the following Thinking Critically section.

THINKING Critically

The Second Shift—Strains and Strategies

To find out what life is like in two-paycheck marriages, for nine years sociologist Arlie Hochschild (1989) and her research associates interviewed and reinterviewed over fifty families. Hochschild also did participant observation with a dozen of them. She "shopped with them, visited friends, watched television, ate with them, and came along when they took their children to day care."

Although men are doing more housework today than they did just a few years ago (Bianchi et al. 2000), most feel that the *second shift*—the household duties that follow the day's work for pay—is the wife's responsibility. But as the wives cook, clean, and take care of the children after their job at the office or factory, many feel tired and emotionally drained. Some pride themselves on being the "supermom" who can do it all, but most just grit their teeth and bear it, doing the extra work, but resenting it. Not uncommonly, these feelings show up in the bedroom, where the wives show a lack of interest in sex.

The strains from working the second shift affect not only the marital relationship, but also the wife's self-concept. Here is how one woman tried to lift her flagging self-esteem:

After taking time off for her first baby, Carol Alston felt depressed, "fat," and that she was "just a housewife." For a while she became the supermarket shopper who wanted to call down the aisles, "I'm an MBA! I'm an MBA!"

To pick up more of the burden, some husbands cut down on their commitment to a career. Others cut back on movies, seeing friends, doing hobbies. Most men, however, engage in what Hochschild describes as *strategies of resistance*. She identified the following:

Waiting it out. Many men never volunteer to do housework. Since many wives dislike asking, because it feels like "begging," this strategy often works. Some men make this strategy even more effective by showing irritation or becoming glum when they are asked, which discourages the wife from asking again.

Playing dumb. When they do housework, some men become incompetent. They can't cook rice without burning it; when they go to the store, they forget grocery lists; they never can remember where the broiler pan is. Hochschild did not claim that husbands do these things on purpose, but, rather, by withdrawing their mental attention from the task, they "get credit for trying and being a good sport"—but in such a way that they are not chosen next time.

Needs reduction. An example of this strategy is the father of two who explained that he never shopped because he didn't "need anything." He didn't need to iron his clothes because he "[didn't] mind wearing a wrinkled shirt." He didn't need to cook because "cereal is fine." As Hochschild observed, "Through his reduction of needs, this man created a great void into which his wife stepped with her 'greater need' to see him

ARLO & JANIS ® by Jimmy Johnson

HE DOESN'T EXPECT ME TO IRON HIS SHIRTS.
HE'S VERY FAIR-MINDED ABOUT THESE THINGS.
THE PROBLEM IS MY ATTITUDE, NOT HIS!
WHY SHOULD I FEEL GUILTY IF HE LOOKS TERRIBLE?

The cartoonist has beautifully captured the reduction of needs strategy discussed by Hochschild.

Marriage and Family in Theoretical Perspective 453

sociology and the NEW technology

Internet University: No Walls, No Ivy, No All Night Parties

Distance learning, courses taught to students who are not physically present with their instructor, is not new. For decades, we have had correspondence courses. Today, however, telecommunications have transformed distance learning. Satellites, computers, video conferencing, and streaming video are making cyber colleges part of mainstream education. Using video links, students are able to watch the professor on their screen. Clicking a little icon, they can "raise their hands" to ask questions. Eventually, computer-mounted cameras may allow everyone in the class to see everyone else simultaneously. Spider-web diagrams let the instructor know who is e-mailing others—and who is holding back. Tucked deeper in the software is a program to allow deans (supervisors) to scrutinize the instructors. The deans will get reports, for example, that let them know how long it takes instructors to answer e-mail from students.

Distance learning offers tremendous potential for increasing cultural diversity, to the benefit of both students and professors. It is possible to enjoy a stimulating international experience without ever leaving the country. For example, sociology professors at the State University of New York and the State University of Belarus (Minsk, Russia) jointly taught an online course on Social Control. With their political experiences so different from one another, the American and Russian students found that the course opened their eyes to different realities (Beaman 2003).

Why should formal education be limited to walled classrooms? Think of the possibilities of the Net. We could study human culture and compare notes on eating, dating, or burial customs with fellow students in Thailand, Iceland, South Africa, Germany, Egypt, China, and Australia. We could write a joint paper in which we compare our experiences with one another, within the context of theories taught in the text, and then submit our paper to our mutual instructor.

Will we eventually go from kindergarten to grad school with classmates from around the world? While this may sound intriguing, no walls also means no joking in the hallway or dorm, no flirting after class, no getting together over a cup of coffee. . . .

A different view of distance learning is presented in the Sociology and the New Technology box on the next page.

Problems in U.S. Education—and Their Solutions

To conclude this chapter, let's examine two problems facing U.S. education—and consider their potential solutions.

Problems: Mediocrity and Violence

The Rising Tide of Mediocrity All Arizona high school sophomores took a math test. It covered the math that sophomores should know. Seven of eight failed it. Meanwhile, in New York, to get its students to graduate, the state had to drop its passing

Problems in U.S. Education—and Their Solutions 501

7), social inequality and the digital divide (Chapter 10), how technology is restructuring work (Chapter 14), unusual reproduction (Chapter 16), capitalism and distance learning (Chapter 17), and the genetic revolution and genetic privacy (Chapter 19).

The Mass Media and Social Life

In the sixth theme, we stress how the mass media affect our behavior and permeate our thinking. We consider how they even penetrate our consciousness to such a degree that they influence how we perceive our own bodies. As your students consider this theme, they should begin to see the mass media in a different light, which should further stimulate their sociological imagination.

In addition to making this a recurring theme throughout the text, I have also written a series of boxed features called **Mass Media in Social Life** to make it more prominent for students. Among these are an analysis of why Native Americans like Western novels and movies even though Indians are usually portrayed as victims (Chapter 2), the influence of computer games on images of gender (Chapter 3), the worship of thinness—and how this affects our own body images (Chapter 4), the issue of censoring high-tech pornography (Chapter 8), slavery in today's world (Chapter 9), stimulating greed to stimulate the economy (Chapter 14), and God on the Net (Chapter 18).

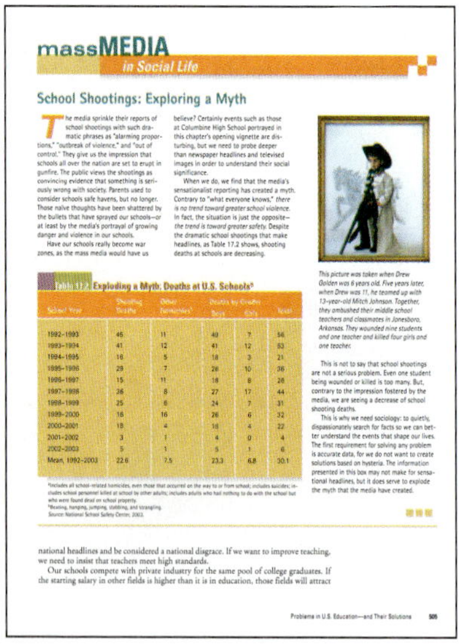
massMEDIA in Social Life

School Shootings: Exploring a Myth

The media sprinkle their reports of school shootings with such dramatic phrases as "alarming proportions," "outbreak of violence," and "out of control." They give us the impression that schools all over the nation are set to erupt in gunfire. The public views the shootings as convincing evidence that something is seriously wrong with society. Parents used to consider schools safe havens, but no longer. Those naive thoughts have been shattered by the bullets that have sprayed our schools—or at least by the media's portrayal of growing danger and violence in our schools.

Have our schools really become war zones, as the mass media would have us believe? Certainly events such as those at Columbine High School portrayed in this chapter's opening vignette are disturbing, but we need to probe deeper than newspaper headlines and televised images in order to understand their social significance.

When we do, we find that the media's sensationalist reporting has created a myth. Contrary to "what everyone knows," *there is no trend toward greater school violence.* In fact, the situation is just the opposite—*the trend is toward greater safety.* Despite the dramatic school shootings that make headlines, as Table 17.2 shows, shooting deaths at schools are decreasing.

This picture was taken when Drew Golden was 6 years old. Five years later, when Drew was 11, he teamed up with 13-year-old Mitch Johnson. Together, they ambushed their middle school teachers and classmates in Jonesboro, Arkansas. They wounded nine students and one teacher and killed four girls and one teacher.

Table 17.2 Exploding a Myth: Deaths at U.S. Schools[a]

School Year	Shooting Deaths	Other Homicides[b]	Deaths by Gender: Boys	Girls	Total
1992–1993	45	11	49	7	56
1993–1994	41	12	41	12	53
1994–1995	16	5	18	3	21
1995–1996	29	7	26	10	36
1996–1997	15	11	18	8	26
1997–1998	36	8	27	17	44
1998–1999	25	6	24	7	31
1999–2000	16	16	26	6	32
2000–2001	18	4	18	4	22
2001–2002	3	1	4	0	4
2002–2003	5	1	5	1	6
Mean, 1992–2003	22.6	7.5	23.3	6.8	30.1

[a]Includes all school-related homicides, even those that occurred on the way to or from school; includes suicides; includes school personnel killed at school by other adults; includes adults who had nothing to do with the school but who were found dead on school property.
[b]Beating, hanging, jumping, stabbing, and strangling.
Source: National School Safety Center, 2003.

This is not to say that school shootings are not a serious problem. Even one student being wounded or killed is too many. But, contrary to the impression fostered by the media, we are seeing a decrease of school shooting deaths.

This is why we need sociology: to quietly, dispassionately search for facts so we can better understand the events that shape our lives. The first requirement for solving any problem is accurate data, for we do not want to create solutions based on hysteria. The information presented in this box may not make for sensational headlines, but it does serve to explode the myth that the media have created.

national headlines and be considered a national disgrace. If we want to improve teaching, we need to insist that teachers meet high standards.

Our schools compete with private industry for the same pool of college graduates. If the starting salary in other fields is higher than it is in education, those fields will attract

Problems in U.S. Education—and Their Solutions 505

New Topics

Because sociology is about social life, as society changes and as sociologists report new research, the topics of this introductory text reflect those developments. Consequently, this edition contains numerous new topics. Among them are feminism and the conflict perspective (Chapter 1), food customs and culture (Chapter 2), social class and differing views of how children develop, and consequence for children's play (Chapter 3), differences in how Easterners and Westerners see the world (Chapter 3), role exit (Chapter 4), and an exposé on Milgram's research on the small world phenomenon (Chapter 6).

Also new are how groupthink helps explain the *Columbia* space shuttle disaster (Chapter 6), a new study on the recidivism of prisoners (Chapter 7), the decline of quality circles (Chapter 7), how NATO is an example of goal displacement and the perpetuation of bureaucracies (Chapter 7), social class bias in the death penalty (Chapter 8), the drop in crime rates (Chapter 8), how neocolonialism explains Saudi Arabia's oil prices (Chapter 9), how life changes for big lottery winners (Chapter 10), and a new study of intergenerational social mobility (Chapter 10).

New, too, are gender and the control of workers (Chapter 11), rape at the Air Force Academy and at West Point (Chapter 11), "honor" killings (Chapter 11), the "invisible knapsack" of taken-for-granted cultural dominance (Chapter 12), learning prejudice and the internalization of dominant norms (Chapter 12), racism as an everyday burden for minorities (Chapter 12), job discrimination because names are white-sounding and black-sounding (Chapter 12), the U.S. Supreme Court's decision on affirmative action practices at the University of Michigan (Chapter 12), adjusting to the death of a loved one (Chapter 13), and the new centenarians (Chapter 13).

In this edition, we also consider the new Homeland Security laws and the erosion of civil liberties (Chapter 15), grandparents who serve as parents (Chapter 16), the Wallerstein-Hetherington debate on the effects of divorce on children (Chapter 16), intimacy rape among lesbian couples (Chapter 16), the probability of remarrying after divorce (Chapter 16), the development of community colleges, (Chapter 17), capitalism and the marketing of education in cyberspace (Chapter 17), the low standards some states have for teachers (Chapter 17), the *No Child Left Behind* law (Chapter 17), and an evaluation of Milwaukee's voucher program (Chapter 17).

New in the final chapters are the interviewer effect in surveys on church attendance (Chapter 18), the new decennial survey of gains and losses in church membership (Chapter 18), terrorism and religion (Chapter 18), SARS

(Chapter 19), alternative medicine (Chapter 19), Federal Empowerment Zones (Chapter 20), the 1921 riot in Tulsa (Chapter 21), international terrorism as a social movement (Chapter 21), the Internet as a source of rumors (Chapter 21), G-8's changing views of Africa (Chapter 22), China's ascendancy as a threat to G-8 (Chapter 22), and implanted microchips for the political control of citizens (Chapter 22).

Some of the most interesting—and even fascinating—new topics are presented in a visual form. See the next section.

New and Expanded Features

Through the Author's Lens This edition features three new photo essays called *Through the Author's Lens.* Using this format, students are able to look over my shoulder as I experience other cultures or explore aspects of this one. What I found in India and Cambodia expanded my own sociological imagination, and I hope that these reports will do the same for your students. These photo essays should open your students' minds to other ways of doing social life, as well as stimulate enlightening class discussion.

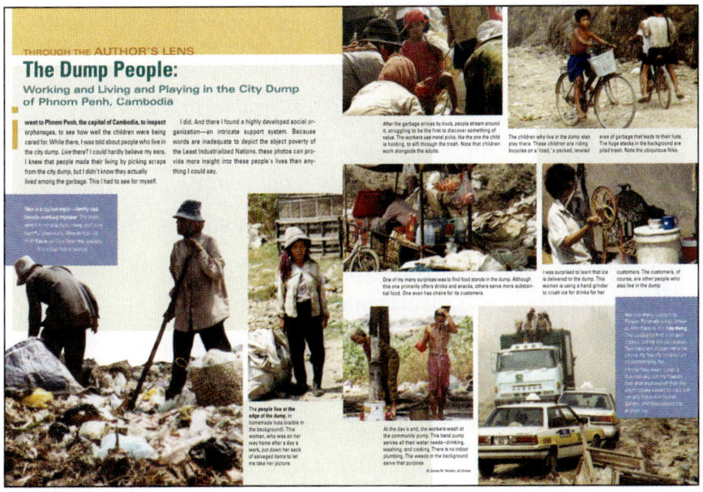

The Dump People of Phnom Penh, Cambodia Among the culture shocks I experienced in Cambodia was not to find out that people scavenge at Phnom Penh's huge city dump—this I knew—but that they also live there. With the aid of an interpreter, I was able to interview these people, as well as photograph them as they went about their everyday lives. An entire community lives in the city dump, complete with restaurants amidst the huge piles of garbage. This photo essay reveals not just their activities but also their social organization (Chapter 9).

Work and Gender: Women at Work in India As I traveled in India, I took photos of women at work in public places. The more that I traveled in this country and the more photos I took, the more insight I received into gender relations. Despite the general submissiveness of women to men in India, women are far from limited to family and home. They are found at work throughout the society. What is even more remarkable is how vastly different "women's work" is in India than it is in the United States. This, too, is an intellectually provocative photo essay (Chapter 11).

When a Tornado Strikes: Social Organization Following a Natural Disaster When a tornado hit a small town just several hours from where I live, I immediately drove there to see the aftermath of the disaster. The police let me in to view the neighborhood where the tornado had struck, destroying homes and killing several people. I was impressed by how quickly people were putting their lives back together, the topic of this third new photo essay in this edition (Chapter 4).

For this series, *Through the Author's Lens,* I have retained these two photo essays from the last edition:

A Walk through El Tiro in Medellin, Colombia: One of the most significant social changes in the world is taking place in the Least Industrialized Nations. There, in the search for a better life, people are abandoning rural areas. Fleeing poverty, they are flocking to the cities, only to find even more poverty. Some of these settlements of the new urban poor are dangerous. I was fortunate to be escorted by an insider through a section of Medellin, Colombia (Chapter 20).

Social Movements and Propaganda: The Execution of Timothy McVeigh: The national news piqued my interest. There were reports about a possible riot and perhaps even an insurrection. This was too much to resist, and I drove to Terra Haute, Indiana, where Timothy McVeigh was to be executed. I was able to interview and photograph activists on both sides of the death penalty issue, and to see how the police and military were handling the potential riot. Chapter 21 features my account of this media event, a study in propaganda and social movements.

Photo Essay on Subcultures To help students better understand subcultures, I have added a photo essay to Chapter 2. Because this photo essay consists of photos taken by others, it is not a part of the series, *Through the Author's Lens.* The variety of subcultures featured in this photo essay, however, should be instructive to your students.

Other Photos Sprinkled throughout this edition are photos that I took in travels I just completed. These photos illustrate sociological principles and topics better than photos available from commercial sources. As an example, the possibility of photographing and interviewing a feral child was one of the reasons that I made the trip to Cambodia. While in the United States, I was told about a feral child who had been discovered living with monkeys and who had been taken to an orphanage in Cambodia. That particular photo is on page 65. Another of my favorites is on page 200.

Thinking Critically About the Chapters In this edition, I close each chapter with three critical thinking questions. Each question focuses on some major feature of the chapter, asking students to reflect and consider some issue. Many of these questions ask the students to apply sociological findings and principles to their own lives. (The in-chapter Thinking Critically sections of previous editions have been retained.)

Special Pedagogical Features

In addition to chapter summaries and reviews, key terms, and a comprehensive glossary, I have included several special features to aid students in learning sociology. **In Sum** sections help students review important points within the chapter before going on to new materials. I have also developed a series of **Social Maps,** which illustrate how social conditions vary by geography.

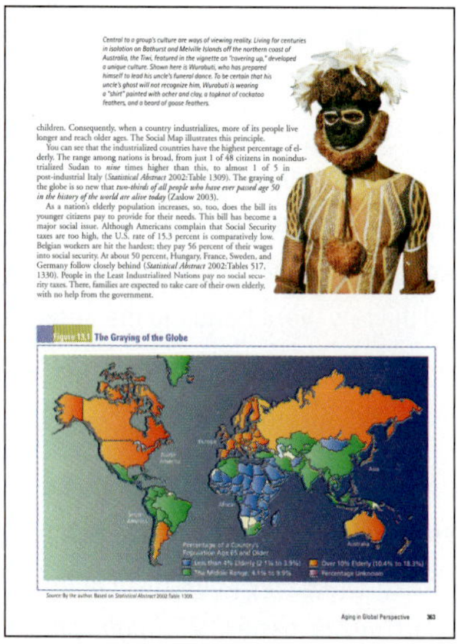
Central to a group's culture are ways of viewing reality. Living for centuries in isolation on Bathurst and Melville Islands off the northern coast of Australia, the Tiwi, featured in the vignette on "covering up," developed a unique culture. Shown here is Wurabuti, who has prepared himself to lead his uncle's funeral dance. To be certain that his uncle's ghost will not recognize him, Wurabuti is wearing a "shirt" painted with ocher and clay, a topknot of cockatoo feathers, and a beard of goose feathers.

children. Consequently, when a country industrializes, more of its people live longer and reach older ages. The Social Map illustrates this principle.

You can see that the industrialized countries have the highest percentage of elderly. The range among nations is broad, from just 1 of 48 citizens in nonindustrialized Sudan to *nine* times higher than this, to almost 1 of 5 in post-industrial Italy (*Statistical Abstract* 2002:Table 1309). The graying of the globe is so new that *two-thirds of all people who have ever passed age 50 in the history of the world are alive today* (Zaslow 2003).

As a nation's elderly population increases, so, too, does the bill its younger citizens pay to provide for their needs. This bill has become a major social issue. Although Americans complain that Social Security taxes are too high, the U.S. rate of 15.3 percent is comparatively low. Belgian workers are hit the hardest: they pay 56 percent of their wages into social security. At about 50 percent, Hungary, France, Sweden, and Germany follow closely behind (*Statistical Abstract* 2002:Tables 517, 1330). People in the Least Industrialized Nations pay no social security taxes. There, families are expected to take care of their own elderly, with no help from the government.

Figure 13.1 The Graying of the Globe

Source: By the author. Based on Statistical Abstract 2002:Table 1309.

Aging in Global Perspective 363

Chapter-Opening Vignettes feature down-to-earth illustrations of a major aspect of each chapter's content. Some of these are based on my own experiences. Several come from my research with the homeless, the time I spent with them on the streets and slept in their shelters (Chapters 1, 10, and 19). Others recount my travels in Africa (Chapters 2 and 11) and Mexico (Chapter 20). I also share my experiences when I spent a night with street people at DuPont Circle in Washington, D.C. (Chapter 4). Other vignettes are based on current and historical events (Chapters 5, 7, 12, 17, 18, 21, and 22), classic studies in the social sciences (Chapters 3, 8, and 13), and even a summary of role-playing on terrorism that our top politicians participated in (Chapter 15). Many students have told their instructors that they find these vignettes compelling, that they stimulate their interest in the chapter.

On Sources and Terms Sociological data are found in an amazingly wide variety of sources, and this text reflects that variety. Cited throughout this text are standard journals such as the *American Journal of Sociology, Social Problems, American Sociological Review,* and *Journal of Marriage and the Family,* as well as more esoteric journals such as the *Bulletin of the History of Medicine, Chronobiology International,* and *Western Journal of Black Studies.* I have also drawn heavily from standard news sources, especially the *New York Times* and *Wall Street Journal,* as well as more unusual sources such as *El País.* In addition, I cite unpublished papers by sociologists, such as the one new to this edition on job discrimination among applicants who used white-sounding and black-sounding names

Finally, a note on terms. Although some still use the terms First World, Second World, and Third World, these terms are biased. Even though unintentional, to say First World inevitably connotes superiority of some sort—a sort of coming in first place, with other nations trailing in lesser, inferior positions. Because the collapse of the Soviet Union's system of socialism/communism also made these terms outmoded, some have replaced them with Most Developed Countries, Less Developed Countries, and Least Developed Countries. These terms, too, carry the same ethnocentric burden. They indicate that our economic state is superior: *We* are "developed," but *they* are not—but maybe they'll be fortunate enough to become like us.

To overcome these problems of ethnocentric bias and misplaced cultural superiority, I have chosen neutrally descriptive terms: the Most Industrialized Nations, the Industrializing Nations, and the Least Industrialized Nations. These terms do not carry an ethnocentric value burden, for they indicate only that a nation's amount of industrialization is measurable and relative, without a connotation that industrialization is desirable.

ACKNOWLEDGMENTS

The gratifying response to earlier editions indicates that my efforts at making sociology down to earth have succeeded. The years that have gone into writing this text are a culmination of the many more years that preceded its writing—from graduate school to that equally demanding endeavor known as classroom teaching. No text, of course, comes solely from its author. Although I am responsible for the final words on the printed page, instructors who have taught from the first six editions have given me excellent feedback. In addition, I am especially grateful to

Reviewers of the Sixth Edition

Lada Gibson-Shreve, *Stark State College*
Paulina X. Ruf, *University of Tampa*
William Yoels, *University of Alabama Birmingham*
G. Kathleen Grant, *The University of Findlay*
Diane Levy, *The University of North Carolina, Wilmington*
Joseph A. Kotarba, *University of Houston*
Stephen L. Vassar, *Minnesota State University, Mankato*
Morten Ender, *U.S. Military Academy*
Brian W. Agnitsch, *Marshalltown Community College*
Howard R. Housen, *Broward Community College*
Richard Brunk, *Francis Marion University*
Brenda Blackburn, *California State University. Fullerton*
Lawrence Peck, *Erie Community College*
Remi Hajjar, *U.S. Military Academy*
Robert Ostrow, *Wayne State*
John Ehle, *Northern Virginia Community College*

Reviewers of the First through Fifth Editions

Francis O. Adeola, *University of New Orleans*
Sandra L. Albrecht, *The University of Kansas*
Richard Alman, *Sierra College*
Gabriel C. Alvarez, *Duquesne University*
Kenneth Ambrose, *Marshall University*
Alberto Arroyo, *Baldwin–Wallace College*
Karren Baird-Olsen, *Kansas State University*
Rafael Balderrama, *University of Texas—Pan American*
Linda Barbera-Stein, *The University of Illinois*
Ronnie J. Booxbaum, *Greenfield Community College*
Cecil D. Bradfield, *James Madison University*
Karen Bradley, *Central Missouri State University*
Francis Broouer, *Worcester State College*
Valerie S. Brown, *Cuyahoga Community College*
Sandi Brunette-Hill, *Carrol College*
Karen Bullock, *Salem State College*
Allison R. Camelot, *California State University at Fullerton*
Paul Ciccantell, *Kansas State University*
John K. Cochran, *The University of Oklahoma*
James M. Cook, *Duke University*
Joan Cook-Zimmern, *College of Saint Mary*
Russell L. Curtis, *University of Houston*
John Darling, *University of Pittsburgh—Johnstown*
Ray Darville, *Stephen F. Austin State University*
Jim David, *Butler County Community College*
Nanette J. Davis, *Portland State University*
Vincent Davis, *Mt. Hood Community College*
Lynda Dodgen, *North Harris Community College*
Terry Dougherty, *Portland State University*
Marlese Durr, *Wright State University*
Helen R. Ebaugh, *University of Houston*
Obi N. Ebbe, *State University of New York—Brockport*
Cy Edwards, Chair, *Cypress Community College*
Rebecca Susan Fahrlander, *Bellevue University*
Louis J. Finkle, *Horry-Georgetown Technical College*
Nicole T. Flynn, *University of South Alabama*
Lorna E. Forster, *Clinton Community College*
David O. Friedrichs, *University of Scranton*
Bruce Friesen, *Kent State University—Stark*
Norman Goodman, *State University of New York—Stony Brook*
Rosalind Gottfried, *San Joaquin Delta College*
Bill Grisby, *University of Northern Colorado*
Ramon Guerra, *University of Texas—Pan American*
Donald W. Hastings, *The University of Tennessee—Knoxville*
Lillian O. Holloman, *Prince George's Community College*
Michael Hoover, *Missouri Western State College*
James H. Huber, *Bloomsburg University*
Erwin Hummel, *Portland State University*
Charles E. Hurst, *The College of Wooster*
Nita Jackson, *Butler County Community College*
Jennifer A. Johnson, *Germanna Community College*
Kathleen R. Johnson, *Keene State College*

Tammy Jolley, *University of Arkansas Community College at Batesville*
David Jones, *Plymouth State College*
Ali Kamali, *Missouri Western State College*
Irwin Kantor, *Middlesex County College*
Mark Kassop, *Bergen Community College*
Myles Kelleher, *Bucks County Community College*
Mary E. Kelly, *Central Missouri State University*
Alice Abel Kemp, *University of New Orleans*
Diana Kendall, *Austin Community College*
Gary Kiger, *Utah State University*
Gene W. Kilpatrick, *University of Maine—Presque Isle*
Jerome R. Koch, *Texas Tech University*
Michele Lee Kozimor-King, *Pennsylvania State University*
Abraham Levine, *El Camino Community College*
Stephen Mabry, *Cedar Valley College*
David Maines, *Oakland University*
Ron Matson, *Wichita State University*
Armaund L. Mauss, *Washington State University*
Evelyn Mercer, *Southwest Baptist University*
Robert Meyer, *Arkansas State University*
Michael V. Miller, *University of Texas—San Antonio*
John Mitrano, *Central Connecticut State University*
W. Lawrence Neuman, *University of Wisconsin—Whitewater*
Charles Norman, *Indiana State University*
Patricia H. O'Brien, *Elgin Community College*
Laura O'Toole, *University of Delaware*
Mike K. Pate, *Western Oklahoma State College*
Ruth Pigott, *University of Nebraska—Kearney*
Phil Piket, *Joliet Junior College*
Trevor Pinch, *Cornell University*
Daniel Polak, *Hudson Valley Community College*
James Pond, *Butler Community College*
Deedy Ramo, *Del Mar College*
Adrian Rapp, *North Harris Community College*
Ray Rich, *Community College of Southern Nevada*
Barbara Richardson, *Eastern Michigan University*
Salvador Rivera, *State University of New York—Cobleskill*
Howard Robboy, *Trenton State College*
Michael Samano, *Portland Community College*
Michael L. Sanow, *Community College of Baltimore County*
Mary C. Sengstock, *Wayne State University*
Walt Shirley, *Sinclair Community College*
Marc Silver, *Hofstra University*
Roberto E. Socas, *Essex County College*
Susan Sprecher, *Illinois State University*
Mariella Rose Squire, *University of Maine at Fort Kent*
Randolph G. Ston, *Oakland Community College*
Vickie Holland Taylor, *Danville Community College*
Maria Jose Tenuto, *College of Lake County*
Gary Tiederman, *Oregon State University*
Kathleen Tiemann, *University of North Dakota*
Judy Turchetta, *Johnson & Wales University*
Steven Vassar, *Mankato State University*
William J. Wattendorf, *Adirondack Community College*
Jay Weinstein, *Eastern Michigan University*
Larry Weiss, *University of Alaska*
Douglas White, *Henry Ford Community College*
Stephen R. Wilson, *Temple University*
Anthony T. Woart, *Middlesex Community College*
Stuart Wright, *Lamar University*
Mary Lou Wylie, *James Madison University*
Diane Kholos Wysocki, *University of Nebraska—Kearney*
Stacey G. H. Yap, *Plymouth State College*
Joan Cook Zimmern, *College of Saint Mary*

I am also indebted to the fine staff of Allyn and Bacon. I wish to thank Jeff Lasser for his many fine suggestions and helpful consultation; Tom Pauken, whose unswerving efforts and outstanding attitude as he approached his task have been an encouragement; Karen Hanson, who first saw the merits of this project and gave it strong support; Hannah Rubenstein, who made vital contributions to earlier editions of the text on which this one is based; Judy Fiske, for constantly hovering over the many details—and for wholeheartedly supporting my many suggestions; Kathy Smith, for continuing her creative copy editing; Myrna Engler, for being so helpful in photo research—and for her willingness to "keep on looking"; Randi Slayton for checking references, and Dusty Friedman, who, so capable at overseeing the routine and the urgent, manages to exhibit an exemplary attitude. It is difficult to heap too much praise on such fine and capable people. Their efforts, often going "beyond the call of duty" as we faced pressing deadlines, have coalesced with mine in producing this text. Students, whom we constantly kept in mind as we prepared this edition, are the beneficiaries of this intricate teamwork.

Since this text is based on the contributions of many, I would count it a privilege if you would share your teaching experiences with this book, including any suggestions for improving the text. Both positive and negative comments are welcome. It is in this way that I learn.

I wish you the very best in your teaching. It is my sincere desire that *Sociology: A Down-to-Earth Approach* contributes to that success.

James M. Henslin
Department of Sociology
Southern Illinois University, Edwardsville

I welcome your correspondence. E-mail is the best way to reach me: henslin@aol.com

A NOTE FROM THE PUBLISHER ON SUPPLEMENTS

INSTRUCTOR'S SUPPLEMENTS

Instructor's Manual with Companion Website Teaching Tool

Anthony Zumpetta, West Chester University.

For each chapter in the text, the Instructor's Manual provides an At-a-Glance grid that coordinates use of the other supplements, a chapter summary, learning objectives, a lecture outline, key terms and people, classroom discussion topics. The manual also includes a section on how to incorporate the text's Web site into your course.

Test Bank

Anthony Zumpetta, West Chester University.

This heavily revised and expanded test bank contains a multitude of questions in multiple choice, true-false, short answer, and essay formats. A new section contains in-depth questions designed for open-book testing.

Computerized Test Bank

The Test Bank is also available on Windows or Macintosh CD-ROM through Allyn and Bacon's computerized testing system, TestGen EQ. This fully networkable test generating software is available on a multi-platform CD-ROM. The user-friendly interface allows you to view, edit, and add questions, transfer questions to tests, and print tests in a variety of fonts. Search and sort features allow you to locate questions quickly and to arrange them in whatever order you prefer.

Allyn & Bacon Transparencies for Introductory Sociology

Recently revised, this package includes more than 125 color acetates featuring illustrations from current Allyn and Bacon Sociology titles.

Online Course Management

CourseCompass, powered by Blackboard and hosted nationally, is Allyn and Bacon's own course management system. CourseCompass helps you manage all aspects of teaching your course. It features preloaded content to support the Introduction to Sociology course. (Your sales rep can give you additional information.) For colleges and universities with **WebCT**™ and **Blackboard**™ licenses, special course management packages are available in these formats as well.

Allyn and Bacon/ABC News Sociology Video Program

If you want to use footage and documentary-style programs to illustrate sociological themes, these videos are from *Nightline, World News Tonight,* and *20/20.* Each video comes with a user's guide. The themes of the first titles are Poverty and Stratification, Race and Ethnicity, Gender and Deviance. New videos for this edition include Aging, and Population and Urbanization. Other themes will be added.

Sociology Video Library

Videos are available on every major topic in sociology. Some of the videos are from Films for the Humanities and Sciences and Annenberg/CPB. Some restrictions apply. Contact your Allyn and Bacon representative for details.

The Blockbuster Approach: A Guide to Teaching Sociology with Video

By Casey Jordan, Western Connecticut State University

This electronic manual describes hundreds of commercially available videos that represent sociological ideas and themes. Included are samples of in-class discussions, homework assignments, and projects.

Text-Specific PowerPoint

Dan Cavanaugh

These PowerPoint presentations on CD-ROM, created for the Seventh Edition, feature lecture outlines for every chapter and artwork from the text. PowerPoint software is not required, as a PowerPoint viewer is included on the CD.

New to this edition: James Henslin narrates the photo essay feature new to this edition, *Through the Author's Lens.* This helps make the experience of doing sociology more personal to the students.

The Sociology Digital Media Archive III

Want more electronic presentations in your classroom? This CD-ROM contains hundreds of graphs, charts, and maps to supplement your lectures and illustrate key sociological concepts. It also includes 40 topical lectures with 20–50 PowerPoint slides each. If you have full multimedia capability, you can use the DMA's video segments and links to sociology Web sites.

Telecourse Support

Allyn and Bacon provides special assistance for instructors who use the video series from Dallas TeleLearning, *Exploring Society.* They also correlate the questions in their standard test bank with the videos. To help instructors give tests based on the video programs, Allyn and Bacon will also correlate every question in our standard Test Bank with the videos. These telecourse materials can be viewed at **www.ablongman.com/sociologytelecourse.**

STUDENT'S SUPPLEMENTS

New: Exploring Social Life: A Reader to Accompany Sociology: A Down-to-Earth Approach, Seventh Edition

James M. Henslin

This brief reader contains one reading for each chapter of the text, chosen and introduced by James M. Henslin. The reader can be packaged with the main text at a special discount.

New: Sociology Tutor Center

(Access Code Required)

Tutoring from qualified sociology instructors by phone, email, or fax is available free for your students during evening hours on all the material covered in the text. Access to the Sociology Tutor Center is available with every copy of the *Study Guide Plus* and the *Study Guide for Native Speakers of Spanish.* It is also available free upon request when packaged with a new copy of *Sociology: A Down-to-Earth Approach.*

Study Guide Plus with Tutor Center

Kathy Rowell, Sinclair Community College

This manual provides chapter summaries, learning objectives, key terms and key people, student projects, self-tests, and glossaries, plus Tutor Center Access.

Student Workbook with Practice Tests and PowerPoint Lecture Outlines

Anthony LaGreca, University of Florida

This free guide contains practice tests and exercises to help students prepare for quizzes and exams, plus lecture outlines that correspond to the PowerPoint presentation for this text. Packaged free upon request with the text.

Study Guide for Native Speakers of Spanish

This study guide is designed to help native Spanish speakers who are taking a course in English. It includes Spanish translations of chapter summaries and definitions of key terms, as well as practice tests in Spanish.

Companion Web Site with Online Study Guide

This Web site features practice tests, annotated Web resources, interactive maps activities, a detailed section on Census 2000, and a link to the research database ResearchNavigator™. The site also features an *eThemes of the Times* collection with the full text of thirty articles from the *New York Times,* as well as a bibliography of other recommended articles.

www.ablongman.com/henslin7e

Premium Resource CD

This CD contains over forty video clips, each with corresponding quiz questions, and provides access to the online chapter: *The Sociology of Human Sexuality.* Packaged free upon request with the text.

Research Navigator™

(Access Code Required)

This research database is available free to students when the text is packaged with the *Research Navigator Guide* for Sociology (see below). Searchable by keyword, it gives your students access to hundreds of full-text articles from scholarly journals and popular publications included in the *ContentSelect Research Database,* as well as a one-year archive of the *New York Times.*

ADDITIONAL SUPPLEMENTS

Research Navigator Guide: Sociology

This reference guide includes tips, resources, activities, and URLs to help students. The first part introduces students to the basics of the Internet and the World Wide Web. Part two includes over thirty Net activities that tie into the content of the text. Part three lists hundreds of WWW resources for sociologists. The guide also includes information on how to correctly cite research, a guide to building an online glossary, and an access code for the ResearchNavigator site. Packaged free upon request with the text.

Building Bridges: The Allyn & Bacon Guide to Service Learning

Doris Hamner

This manual offers practical advice for students who must complete a service-learning project as part of their required course work. Packaged free upon request with the text.

Careers in Sociology, 3e

W. Richard Stephens, Eastern Nazarene College

This supplement explains how sociology can help students prepare for careers in such fields as law, gerontology, social work, business, and computers. It also examines how sociologists entered the field. Packaged free upon request with the text.

Doing Sociology with Student CHIP: Data Happy!, 4e

By Gregg Lee Carter, Bryant College

This workbook with CHIP software is designed for classes with an empirical orientation. The computer exercises allow students to explore sociological issues using real data.

Breaking the Ice, 3e

By Daisy Kabagarama

This supplement aims to help students understand different cultures and people from other cultures, encouraging the reader to react and draw upon their experiences. Exercises are included in each chapter encourage readers to discover their own biases.

College and Society: An Introduction to the Sociological Imagination

By Stephen Sweet

This supplemental text uses examples from familiar surroundings—the patterns of interaction, social structures, and expectations of conduct on a typical college campus—to help students see the ways in which larger society also operates.

About the Author

James M. Henslin, who was born in Minnesota, graduated from high school and junior college in California and from college in Indiana. Awarded scholarships, he earned his Master's and doctorate degrees in sociology at Washington University in St. Louis, Missouri. After this, he was awarded a postdoctoral fellowship from the National Institute of Mental Health, and spent a year studying how people adjust to the suicide of a family member. His primary interests in sociology are the sociology of everyday life, deviance, and international relations. Among his many books is *Down to Earth Sociology: Introductory Readings* (Free Press), now in its twelfth edition. This book of readings reflects some of these sociological interests. He has also published widely in sociology journals, including *Social Problems* and *American Journal of Sociology.*

While a graduate student, Jim taught at the University of Missouri at St. Louis. After completing his doctorate, he joined the faculty at Southern Illinois University, Edwardsville, where he is Professor Emeritus of Sociology. He says, "I've always found the introductory course enjoyable to teach. I love to see students' faces light up when they first glimpse the sociological perspective and begin to see how society has become an essential part of how they view the world."

Henslin enjoys reading and fishing. His two favorite activities are writing and traveling. He especially enjoys visiting and living in other cultures, for this brings him face to face with behaviors and ways of thinking that he cannot take for granted, experiences that "make sociological principles come alive."

Sociology

Chapter

1

The Sociological Perspective

Diana Ong, *Parts Equal the Whole I*

e ven from the glow of the faded red-and-white exit sign, its faint light barely illuminating the upper bunk, I could see that the sheet was filthy. Resigned to another night of fitful sleep, I reluctantly crawled into bed, tucking my clothes around my body like a protective cocoon.

The next morning, I joined the long line of disheveled men leaning against the chain-link fence. Their faces were as downcast as their clothes were dirty. Not a glimmer of hope among them.

No one spoke as the line slowly inched forward. When my turn came, I was handed a cup of coffee, some plastic utensils, and a bowl of semiliquid that I couldn't identify. It didn't look like any food I had seen before. Nor did it taste like anything I had ever eaten.

My stomach fought the foul taste, every spoonful a battle. But I was determined. "I will experience what they experience," I kept telling myself. My stomach reluctantly gave in and accepted its morning nourishment.

The room was strangely silent. Hundreds of men were eating, each immersed in his own private hell, his head awash with disappointment, remorse, bitterness.

But I was determined.
"I will experience *what they experience,"*
I kept telling myself.

As I stared at the Styrofoam cup that held my coffee, grateful at least for this small pleasure, I noticed what looked like teeth marks. I shrugged off the thought, telling myself that my long weeks as a sociological observer of the homeless were finally getting to me. "That must be some sort of crease from handling," I concluded.

I joined the silent ranks of men turning in their bowls and cups. When I saw the man behind the counter swishing out Styrofoam cups in a washtub of water, I began to feel sick to my stomach. I knew then that the jagged marks on my cup really had come from a previous mouth.

How much longer did this research have to last? I felt a deep longing to return to my family—to a welcome world of clean sheets, healthy food, and "normal" conversations.

Chapter Outline

The Sociological Perspective

Why were these men so silent? Why did they receive such despicable treatment? What was I doing in that homeless shelter? After all, I hold a respectable, professional position, and I have a home and family.

Sociology offers a perspective, a view of the world. The *sociological perspective* (or imagination) opens a window onto unfamiliar worlds—and offers a fresh look at familiar worlds. In this text you will find yourself in the midst of Nazis in Germany, warriors in South America, and even, as I recently discovered, people who live in a city dump in Cambodia. But you will also find yourself looking at your own world in a different light. As you view other worlds—or your own—the sociological perspective enables you to gain a new vision of social life. In fact, this is what many find appealing about sociology.

The sociological perspective has been a motivating force in my own life. Ever since I took my first introductory course in sociology, I have been enchanted by the perspective that sociology offers. I have thoroughly enjoyed both observing other groups and questioning my own assumptions about life. I sincerely hope the same happens to you.

Seeing the Broader Social Context

The **sociological perspective** stresses the social contexts in which people live. It examines how these contexts influence people's lives. At the center of the sociological perspective is the question of how groups influence people, especially how people are influenced by their **society**—a group of people who share a culture and a territory.

To find out why people do what they do, sociologists look at **social location**, the corners in life that people occupy because of where they are located in a society. Sociologists look at jobs, income, education, gender, age, and race as significant. Consider, for example, how being identified with a group called *females* or with a group called *males* when we are growing up affects our ideas of who we are and what we should attain in life. Growing up as a male or a female influences not only our aspirations, but also how we feel about ourselves and the way we relate to others in dating and marriage and at work.

Sociologist C. Wright Mills (1959) put it this way: "The sociological perspective enables us to grasp the connection between history and biography." By *history,* Mills meant that each society is located in a broad stream of events. Because of this, each society has specific characteristics—such as its ideas about the proper roles of men and women. By *biography,* Mills referred to the individual's specific experiences. In short, people don't do what they do because of inherited internal mechanisms, such as instincts. Rather, *external* influences—our experiences—become part of our thinking and motivations. The society in which we grow up, and our particular location in that society, lie at the center of what we do and how we think.

Consider a newborn baby. If we were to take the baby away from its U.S. parents and place it with a Yanomamö Indian tribe in the jungles of South America, you know that when the child begins to speak, his or her words will not be in English. You also know that the child will not think like an American. He or she will not grow up wanting credit cards, for example, or designer jeans, a new car, and the latest video game. Equally, the child will unquestioningly take his or her place in Yanomamö society—perhaps as a food gatherer, a hunter, or a warrior—and he or she will not even know about the world left behind at birth. And, whether male or female, the child will grow up

Examining the broad social context in which people live is essential to the sociological perspective, *for this context shapes our beliefs and attitudes and sets guidelines for what we do. From this photo, you can see how distinctive those guidelines are for the Yanomamö Indians who live on the border of Brazil and Venezuela. How has this Yanomamö man been influenced by his group? How has your behavior been influenced by your groups?*

assuming that it is natural to want many children, not debating whether to have one, two, or three children.

People around the globe take their particular world for granted. Something inside us Americans tells us that hamburgers are delicious, small families are desirable, and designer clothing is attractive. Yet something inside some of the Sinai Desert Arab tribes tells them that warm, fresh camel's blood makes a fine drink and that everyone should have a large family and wear flowing robes (Murray 1935; McCabe and Ellis 1990). And that something certainly isn't an instinct. As sociologist Peter Berger (1963) phrased it, that "something" is "society within us."

Although obvious, this point frequently eludes us. We often think and talk about people's behavior as though it were caused by their sex, their race, or some other factor transmitted by their genes. The sociological perspective helps us escape from this cramped personal view by exposing the broader social context that underlies human behavior. It helps us see the links between what people do and the social settings that shape their behavior.

This brings us to *you*—to how *your* social groups have shaped *your* ideas and desires. Over and over in this text, you will see that the way you look at the world is the result of your exposure to human groups. I think you will enjoy the process of self-discovery that sociology offers.

The Growing Global Context

As is evident to all of us—from the labels on our clothing to the components in our cars—our world is becoming a global village. Our predecessors lived isolated on farms and in small towns; beyond the borders of their communities lay a world they only dimly perceived. Communications were so slow that in the War of 1812, the Battle of New Orleans was fought two weeks *after* the adversaries, the United States and Great Britain, had signed a peace treaty. The armed forces there had not yet heard that the war was over (Volti 1995).

Today, in contrast, communications connect us instantly with remote areas of the globe, and a vast economic system connects us not only with Canada and Mexico but also with Ireland, Taiwan, and India. At the same time that we are immersed in such global interconnections, however, we continue to occupy little corners of life, marked by differences in family background, religion, job, gender, race, and social class. In these corners, we learn distinctive ways of viewing the world.

One of the beautiful—and fascinating—aspects of sociology is that it is able to analyze both parts of our current reality: the changes that incorporate us into a global network and our unique experiences in our smaller corners of life. In this text, we shall examine both of these vital aspects of our lives.

Sociology and the Other Sciences

Just as humans today have an intense desire to unravel the mysteries around them, people in ancient times also attempted to understand their world. Their explanations, however, were not based only on observations, but were also mixed with magic and superstition.

To satisfy their basic curiosities about the world around them, humans gradually developed **science,** systematic methods used to study the social and natural worlds, as well as the knowledge obtained by those methods. **Sociology,** the scientific study of society and human behavior, is one of the sciences that modern civilization has developed.

A useful way of comparing these sciences—and of gaining a better understanding of sociology's place—is to divide them into the natural and the social sciences.

The Natural Sciences

The **natural sciences** are the intellectual and academic disciplines designed to explain and predict the events in our natural environment. The natural sciences are divided into specialized fields of research according to subject matter, such as biology, geology, chemistry,

sociological perspective understanding human behavior by placing it within its broader social context

society people who share a culture and a territory

social location the group memberships that people have because of their location in history and society

science the application of systematic methods to obtain knowledge and the knowledge obtained by those methods

sociology the scientific study of society and human behavior

natural sciences the intellectual and academic disciplines designed to comprehend, explain, and predict events in our natural environment and physics. These are further subdivided into even more highly specialized areas. Biology is divided into botany and zoology, geology into mineralogy and geomorphology, chemistry into its organic and inorganic branches, and physics into biophysics and quantum mechanics. Each area of investigation examines a particular "slice" of nature (Henslin 2003a).

The Social Sciences

People have not limited themselves to investigating nature. In the pursuit of a more adequate understanding of life, they have also developed fields of science that focus on the social world. The **social sciences** examine human relationships. Just as the natural sciences attempt to objectively understand the world of nature, the social sciences attempt to objectively understand the social world. Just as the world of nature contains ordered (or lawful) relationships that are not obvious but must be discovered through controlled observation, so the ordered relationships of the human or social world are not obvious, and must be revealed by means of repeated observations.

Like the natural sciences, the social sciences are divided into specialized fields based on their subject matter. These divisions are anthropology, economics, political science, psychology, and sociology. The social sciences are subdivided further into specialized fields. Thus, anthropology is divided into cultural and physical anthropology; economics has macro (large-scale) and micro (small-scale) specialties; political science has theoretical and applied branches; psychology may be clinical or experimental; and sociology has its quantitative and qualitative branches. Since our focus is sociology, let's contrast sociology with each of the other social sciences.

Anthropology *Anthropology* is the sister discipline of sociology. The chief concern of anthropologists is to understand *culture,* a people's total way of life. Culture includes a group's (1) *artifacts,* such as its tools, art, and weapons; (2) *structure,* that is, the patterns (such as positions that require respect) that determine how its members interact with one another; (3) *ideas and values,* especially how its belief system affects people's lives; and (4) *forms of communication,* especially language. The traditional focus of anthropology has been on tribal peoples. Anthropologists who are studying for their doctorate usually live with a group. In their reports, they emphasize the group's family (kin) relationships. As there are no "undiscovered" groups left in the world, this focus on tribal groups is giving way to the study of groups in industrialized settings. When anthropologists study the same groups that sociologists do, they place greater emphasis on artifacts, authority (hierarchy), and language, especially kinship terms.

Economics *Economics* concentrates on a single social institution. Economists study the production and distribution of the material goods and services of a society. They want to know what goods are being produced at what rate and at what cost, and how those goods are distributed. Economists also are interested in the choices that determine production and consumption; for example, they study what motivates people to buy a certain item instead of another.

Political Science *Political science* focuses on politics and government. Political scientists examine forms of government and how these forms are related to other institutions of society. Political scientists are especially interested in how people attain ruling positions in their society, how they maintain those positions, and the consequences of their actions for those they govern. In studying a constitutional government, such as that of the United States, political scientists also analyze voting behavior.

Psychology The focus of *psychology* is on processes that occur *within* the individual, inside what they call the "skin-bound organism." Psychologists focus primarily on mental processes (what occurs in the brain, or the mind). They examine intelligence, emotions, perception, memory, even dreams. Some study how personality is formed. Others focus on mental aberration (psychopathology or mental illness). Many psychologists work in private practice and as counselors in school and work settings, where they give personality tests, IQ tests, and vocational aptitude tests. As therapists, they focus on re-

social sciences the intellectual and academic disciplines designed to understand the social world objectively by means of controlled and repeated observations

generalization a statement that goes beyond the individual case and is applied to a broader group or situation

patterns recurring characteristics or events

solving personal problems, whether they involve the need to recover from trauma, such as abuse, or to be freed from addiction to drugs, alcohol, or gambling.

Sociology *Sociology* has many similarities to the other social sciences. Like anthropologists, sociologists also study culture; they, too, have an interest in group structure and belief systems, as well as in how people communicate with one another. Like economists, sociologists are also concerned with what happens to the goods and services of a society, but sociologists place their focus on the social consequences of inequality. Like political scientists, sociologists also study how people govern one another, especially how government affects people's lives. Like psychologists, sociologists are also concerned with how people adjust to the difficulties of life.

Given these overall similarities, then, what distinguishes sociology from the other social sciences? Unlike anthropologists, sociologists focus primarily on industrialized societies. Unlike political scientists and economists, sociologists do not concentrate on a single social institution. And unlike psychologists, sociologists stress factors *external* to the individual to determine what influences people. The Down-to-Earth Sociology box below revisits an old tale about how members of different disciplines perceive the same subject matter.

The Goals of Science

The first goal of each scientific discipline is to *explain* why something happens. The second goal is to make **generalizations,** that is, to go beyond the individual case and make statements that apply to a broader group or situation. For example, a sociologist wants to explain not only why Mary went to college or became an armed robber but also why people with her characteristics are more likely than others to go to college or to become armed robbers. To achieve generalizations, sociologists look for **patterns,** recurring characteristics or events. The third scientific goal is to *predict,* to specify what will happen in the future in the light of current knowledge.

DOWN-TO-EARTH SOCIOLOGY

An Updated Version of the Old Elephant Story

IT IS SAID THAT IN THE RECENT PAST FIVE wise men and women, all blindfolded, were led to an elephant and asked to explain what they "saw." The first, a psychologist, stroking the top of the elephant's head, said, "This is the only thing that counts. All feeling and thinking take place inside here. To understand this beast, study only this."

The second, an anthropologist, tenderly touched the trunk and the tusks, then smiled and said, "This is really primitive. I feel very comfortable here. Concentrate on these."

The third, a political scientist, feeling the gigantic ears, announced, "This is the power center. What goes in here controls the entire beast. Concentrate your studies here."

The fourth, an economist, feeling the mouth, said, "This is what counts. What goes in here is distributed throughout the body. Concentrate your studies on how it is distributed."

Then came the sociologist (of course!), who, after feeling the entire body, said, "You can't understand the beast by concentrating on only one part. Each is but part of the whole. The head, the trunk and tusks, the ears, the mouth—all are important. But so are the parts of the beast that you haven't mentioned. We must remove our blindfolds so we can see the larger picture. We have to see how everything works together to form the entire animal."

Pausing for emphasis, the sociologist added, "And we also need to understand how this creature interacts with similar creatures. How does its life in groups influence its behavior?"

I wish I could conclude this tale by saying that the psychologist, the anthropologist, the political scientist, and the economist were dazzled on hearing the wisdom of the sociologist, and, amid gasps of wonderment, they tore off their blindfolds, joined together, and began to examine the entire animal. But, alas and alack! On hearing this sage advice, the specialists stubbornly bound their blindfolds even tighter so they could concentrate all the more on their particular part. And if you listened very, very carefully, you could even hear them mutter, "The top of the head is mine—stay away from it." "Don't touch the tusks." "Take your hand off the ears." "Stay away from the mouth—that's my area."

To attain these goals, scientists do not rely on magic, superstition, or common beliefs, but, instead, they do systematic research. They explain exactly how they did their research so it can be checked by others. Secrecy, prejudice, and other biases go against the grain of science.

Sociologists and other scientists also move beyond **common sense**—the prevailing ideas in a society, the things that "everyone knows" are true. "Everyone" can be mistaken today just as easily as when common sense dictated that the world was flat or that no human could ever walk on the moon. As sociologists examine people's assumptions about the world, their findings may contradict commonsense notions about social life. To test your own "common sense," read the Down-to-Earth Sociology box on the next page.

Sometimes the explorations of sociologists take them into nooks and crannies that people would prefer remain unexplored. For example, a sociologist might study how people make decisions to commit a crime or to cheat on their spouses. Since sociologists want above all to understand social life, they cannot cease their studies because people feel uncomfortable. Sociologists consider all realms of human life legitimate avenues to explore, and their findings sometimes challenge cherished ideas.

As they examine how groups operate, sociologists often confront attempts to keep things secret. It seems that every organization, every group, nourishes a pet image that it presents to others. Sociologists are interested in knowing what is really going on behind the scenes, however, so they peer beneath the surface to get past that sugar-coated image (Berger 1963). This approach sometimes brings sociologists into conflict with people who feel threatened by that information—which is all part of the adventure, and risk, of being a sociologist.

Origins of Sociology

Tradition Versus Science

Just how did sociology begin? In some ways it is difficult to answer this question. Even ancient peoples tried to figure out social life. They asked questions about why war exists, why some people become more powerful than others, and why some become rich. However, they often based their answers on superstition, myth, or even the positions of the stars, and did not *test* their assumptions.

Science, in contrast, requires the development of theories that can be tested by systematic research. Measured by this standard, sociology only recently appeared on the human scene. It emerged about the middle of the 1800s, when social observers began to use scientific methods to test their ideas.

Sociology grew out of social upheaval. The Industrial Revolution had just begun. By the middle of the nineteenth century, the economy of Europe was changing from agriculture to factory production. Masses of people were moving to cities in search of work. Their ties to the land—and to a culture that provided them with ready answers—were broken. The city greeted them with horrible working conditions: low pay; long, exhausting hours; dangerous work. To survive, even children had to work in these conditions; some were even chained to factory machines to make certain they could not run away. Life no longer looked the same, and tradition, which had provided the answers to questions about social life, no longer could be counted on.

Tradition was to suffer further blows. The success of the American and French revolutions encouraged people to rethink social life. New ideas arose, including the conviction that individuals possess inalienable rights. As this new idea caught fire, many traditional Western monarchies gave way to more democratic forms of government. People found the ready answers of tradition, including religion, inadequate.

When tradition reigns, it provides ready answers: "We do this because it has always been done this way." Tradition discourages original thinking. Since the answers are already provided, why search for explanations? Sweeping change, however, does the opposite: By upsetting the existing order, it encourages questioning and demands new answers.

common sense those things that "everyone knows" are true

scientific method (the) using objective, systematic observations to test theories

positivism the application of the scientific approach to the social world

sociology the scientific study of society and human behavior

DOWN-TO-EARTH SOCIOLOGY

Enjoying A Sociology Quiz—Sociological Findings Versus Common Sense

SOME FINDINGS OF SOCIOLOGY SUPPORT commonsense understandings of social life, while others contradict them. Can you tell the difference? To enjoy this quiz, complete *all* the questions before turning the page to check your answers.

1. True/False More U.S. students are killed in school shootings now than ten or fifteen years ago.
2. True/False The earnings of U.S. women have just about caught up with those of U.S. men.
3. True/False When faced with natural disasters such as floods and earthquakes, people panic and social organization disintegrates.
4. True/False Most rapists are mentally ill.
5. True/False Most people on welfare are lazy and looking for a handout. They could work if they wanted to.
6. True/False Compared with women, men maintain more eye contact in face-to-face conversations.
7. True/False Couples who live together before marriage are usually more satisfied with their marriages than couples who do not live together before marriage.
8. True/False Most husbands of working wives who get laid off from work take up the slack and increase the amount of housework they do.
9. True/False Because bicyclists are much more likely to wear helmets now than just a few years ago, their rate of head injuries has dropped.
10. True/False Students in Japan are under such intense pressure to do well in school that their suicide rate is about double that of U.S. students.

Then there was the imperialism of the time. The Europeans had conquered many parts of the world, and their new colonial empires stretched from Asia and Africa to North and South America. This exposed them to radically different ways of life, and they began to ask why cultures differ.

Another impetus for the development of sociology was the success of the natural sciences. Just as tradition was breaking down and people were questioning fundamental aspects of life, **the scientific method**—using objective, systematic observations to test theories—was being tried out in chemistry and physics. Many secrets that had been concealed in nature were uncovered. With tradition no longer providing the answers to questions about social life, the logical step was to apply the scientific method to these questions. The result was the birth of sociology.

Auguste Comte and Positivism

This idea of applying the scientific method to the social world, known as **positivism,** apparently was first proposed by Auguste Comte (1798–1857). With the philosophical upheaval of the French Revolution still fresh in his mind, Comte left the small, conservative town in which he had grown up and moved to Paris. The changes he experienced in this move, combined with those France underwent in the revolution, led Comte to become interested in what holds society together. What creates social order, he wondered, instead of anarchy or chaos? And then, once society does become set on a particular course, what causes it to change?

***Auguste Comte** (1798–1857), who is credited as the founder of sociology, began to analyze the bases of the social order. Although he stressed that the scientific method should be applied to the study of society, he did not apply it himself.*

As Comte considered these questions, he concluded that the right way to answer them was to apply the scientific method to social life. Just as this method had revealed the law of gravity, so, too, it would uncover the laws that underlie society. Comte called this new science **sociology**—"the study of society" (from the Greek *logos,* "study of," and the Latin *socius,* "companion," or "being with others"). Comte stressed that this new science not only would discover social principles but also would apply them to social reform. Sociologists would reform the entire society, making it a better place to live.

To Comte, however, applying the scientific method to social life meant practicing what we might call "armchair philosophy"—drawing conclusions from informal observations

DOWN-TO-EARTH SOCIOLOGY

Sociological Findings Versus Common Sense—Answers to the Sociology Quiz

1. False. More students were shot to death at U.S. schools in the early 1990s than now. See page 505.
2. False. Over the years, the wage gap has narrowed, but only slightly. On average, full-time working women earn only 70 percent of what full-time working men earn. This low figure is actually an improvement over earlier years. See Figures 11.7 and 11.8 on pages 311 and 312.
3. False. Following natural disasters, people develop *greater* cooperation and social organization to deal with the catastrophe. For an example, see the photo essay on pages 118–119.
4. False. Sociologists compared the psychological profiles of prisoners convicted of rape and prisoners convicted of other crimes. Their profiles were similar. Like robbery, rape is a learned behavior. See pages 142–143.
5. False. Most people on welfare are children, the old, the sick, the mentally and physically handicapped, or young mothers with few skills. Less than 2 percent meet the common stereotype of an able-bodied man. See page 279.
6. False. Women maintain considerably more eye contact (Henley et al. 1985).
7. False. The opposite is true. The reason, researchers suggest, is that many couples who cohabit before marriage are less committed to marriage in the first place—and a key to marital success is a strong commitment to one another (Larson 1988).
8. False. Most husbands of working wives who get laid off from work *reduce* the amount of housework they do. See page 454 for an explanation.
9. False. The opposite is true. Bicyclists today are more likely to wear helmets, but their rate of head injuries is higher. Apparently, wearing helmets makes them feel safer, and they take more risks (Barnes 2001). (Unanticipated consequences of human action are studied by functionalists. See page 26.)
10. False. The suicide rate of U.S. students is about double that of Japanese students (Haynes and Chalker 1997).

of social life. He did not do what today's sociologists would call research, and his conclusions have been abandoned. Nevertheless, Comte's insistence that we must observe and classify human activities in order to uncover society's fundamental laws is well taken. Because he developed this idea and coined the term *sociology,* Comte often is credited with being the founder of sociology.

Herbert Spencer and Social Darwinism

***Herbert Spencer** (1820–1903), sometimes called the second founder of sociology, coined the term "survival of the fittest." Spencer thought that helping the poor was wrong, that this merely helped the "less fit" survive.*

Herbert Spencer (1820–1903), who grew up in England, is sometimes called the second founder of sociology. Spencer disagreed profoundly with Comte that sociology should guide social reform. Spencer thought that societies evolve from lower ("barbarian") to higher ("civilized") forms. As generations pass, the most capable and intelligent ("the fittest") members of a society survive, while the less capable die out. Thus, over time, societies improve. If you help the lower classes, you interfere with this natural process. The fittest members will produce a more advanced society—unless misguided do-gooders get in the way and help the less fit survive.

Spencer called this principle "the survival of the fittest." Although Spencer coined this phrase, it usually is attributed to his contemporary, Charles Darwin, who proposed that organisms evolve over time as they adapt to their environment. Because they are so similar to Darwin's ideas, Spencer's views of the evolution of societies became known as *social Darwinism.*

Spencer's ideas that charity and helping the poor were wrong appalled many. The wealthy industrialists of the time, however, who saw themselves as "the fittest"—and therefore superior—found Spencer's ideas attractive. Not coincidentally, Spencer's views helped them avoid feelings of guilt for living like royalty while people around them went hungry.

Like Comte, Spencer was more of a social philosopher than a sociologist. Also like Comte, Spencer did not conduct scientific studies. He simply developed ideas about so-

This eighteenth-century painting (artist unknown) depicts women from Paris joining the French Army on its way to Versailles on October 5, 1789. The French Revolution of 1789 not only overthrew the aristocracy but also upset the entire social order. This extensive change removed the past as a sure guide to the present. The events of this period stimulated Auguste Comte to analyze how societies change. His writings are often taken as the origin of sociology.

ciety. Spencer gained a wide following in England and the United States, where he was sought after as a speaker, but eventually social Darwinism was discredited.

Karl Marx and Class Conflict

Karl Marx (1818–1883) not only influenced sociology but also left his mark on world history. Marx's influence has been so great that even the *Wall Street Journal,* that staunch advocate of capitalism, has called him one of the three greatest modern thinkers (the other two being Sigmund Freud and Albert Einstein).

Like Comte, Marx thought that people should try to change society. Marx, who came to England after being exiled from his native Germany for proposing revolution, believed that the engine of human history is **class conflict.** He said that the **bourgeoisie** (boo-shwa-zee) (the *capitalists,* those who own the means to produce wealth—capital, land, factories, and machines) are locked in conflict with the **proletariat** (the exploited workers who do not own the means of production). This bitter struggle can end only when the workers unite in revolution and throw off their chains of bondage. The result will be a classless society, one free of exploitation, in which people will work according to their abilities and receive according to their needs (Marx and Engels 1848/1967).

Marxism is not the same as communism. Although Marx supported revolution as the only way that the workers could gain control of society, he did not develop the political system called *communism.* This is a later application of his ideas. Indeed, Marx himself felt disgusted when he heard debates about his insights into social life. After listening to some of the positions attributed to him, he shook his head and said, "I am not a Marxist" (Dobriner 1969b:222; Gitlin 1997:89).

Unlike Comte and Spencer, Marx did not think of himself as a sociologist. He spent years studying in the library of the British Museum in London, where he wrote widely on history, philosophy, and, of course, economics and political science. Because of his insights into the relationship between the social classes, especially the class struggle between the "haves" and the "have-nots," many sociologists claim Marx as a significant early sociologist. He also introduced one of the major perspectives in sociology, conflict theory, which is discussed on pages 28–29.

Emile Durkheim and Social Integration

The primary professional goal of Emile Durkheim (1858–1917) was to get sociology recognized as a separate academic discipline (Coser 1977). Up to this time, sociology was viewed as part of history and economics. Durkheim, who grew up in eastern France and

***Karl Marx** (1818–1883) believed that the roots of human misery lay in* class conflict, *the exploitation of the working classes by those who own the means of production. Social change, in the form of the overthrow of the capitalists by the proletariat, was inevitable from Marx's perspective. Although Marx did not consider himself a sociologist, his ideas have profoundly influenced many in the discipline, particularly conflict theorists.*

class conflict Marx's term for the struggle between capitalists and workers

bourgeoisie Karl Marx's term for capitalists, those who own the means of production

proletariat Marx's term for the exploited class, the mass of workers who do not own the means of production

The French sociologist ***Emile Durkheim*** *(1858–1917) contributed many important concepts to sociology. His systematic study comparing suicide rates among several countries revealed an underlying social factor: People are more likely to commit suicide if their ties to others in their communities are weak. Durkheim's identification of the key role of* social integration *in social life remains central to sociology today.*

was educated in both Germany and France, achieved his goal when he received the first academic appointment in sociology at the University of Bordeaux in 1887.

Durkheim also had another goal: to show how social forces affect people's behavior. To accomplish this, he conducted rigorous research. Comparing the suicide rates of several European countries, Durkheim (1897/1966) found that each country's suicide rate was different and that each remained remarkably stable year after year. He also found that different groups within a country had different suicide rates, and that these, too, remained stable from year to year. For example, Protestants, males, and the unmarried killed themselves at a higher rate than did Catholics, Jews, females, and the married. From this, Durkheim drew the insightful conclusion that suicide is not simply a matter of individuals here and there deciding to take their lives for personal reasons. Instead, *social factors underlie suicide,* and this is what keeps a group's rates fairly constant year after year.

Durkheim identified **social integration,** the degree to which people are tied to their social group, as a key social factor in suicide. He concluded that people who have weaker social ties are more likely to commit suicide. This factor, he said, explained why Protestants, males, and the unmarried have higher suicide rates. This is how it works, Durkheim said: Protestantism encourages greater freedom of thought and action; males are more independent than females; and the unmarried lack the connections and responsibilities that come with marriage. In other words, because their social integration is weaker, members of these groups have fewer of the social ties that keep people from committing suicide.

Although strong social bonds help protect people from suicide, Durkheim noted that in some instances strong bonds encourage suicide. An example is people who, torn apart by grief, kill themselves after their spouse dies. Their own feelings are so integrated with those of their spouse that they prefer death rather than life without the one who gave meaning to life.

Over a hundred years later, Durkheim's study is still quoted. His research was so thorough that the principle he uncovered still applies: People who are less socially integrated have higher rates of suicide. Even today, those same categories that Durkheim identified—Protestants, males, and the unmarried—are more likely to kill themselves.

social integration the degree to which people feel a part of social groups

From Durkheim's study of suicide, we see the principle that was central in his research: *Human behavior cannot be understood simply in individualistic terms; we must always examine the social forces that affect people's lives.* Suicide, for example, appears at first to be such an intensely individual act that psychologists should study it, not sociologists. Yet,

Durkheim believed that modern societies produce feelings of isolation, much of which comes from the division of labor. In contrast, members of traditional societies, who work alongside family and neighbors and participate in similar activities, experience a high degree of social integration. The photo on the right shows workers in Zinacantan, Mexico, cooking corn.

Figure 1.1 How Americans Commit Suicide

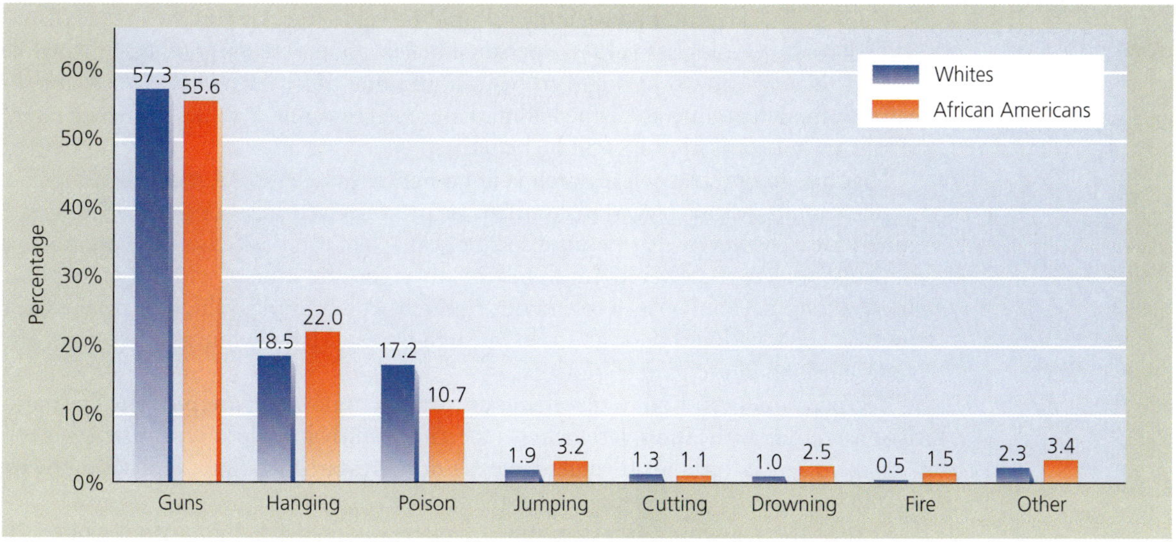

Note: The source lists no separate totals for Latinos.
Source: By the author. Based on Centers for Disease Disease Control, 2002.

as Durkheim illustrated, if we look at human behavior (such as suicide) only in individualistic terms, we miss its *social* basis. For a glimpse of what Durkheim meant, look at Figure 1.1. That African Americans and whites commit suicide in such similar ways indicates something that goes far beyond the individual. Since these patterns are similar year after year, they reflect conditions in society, such as the popularity and accessibility of guns.

Max Weber and the Protestant Ethic

Max Weber (Mahx VAY-ber) (1864–1920), a German sociologist and a contemporary of Durkheim, also held professorships in the new academic discipline of sociology. Like Durkheim and Marx, Weber is one of the most influential of all sociologists, and you will come across his writings and theories in the coming chapters. Let's look at two issues Weber raised that remain controversial today.

***Max Weber** (1864–1920) was another early sociologist who left a profound impression on sociology. He used cross-cultural and historical materials to trace the causes of social change and to determine how extensively social groups affect people's orientations to life.*

Religion and the Origin of Capitalism Weber disagreed with Marx's claim that economics is the central force in social change. That role, he said, belongs to religion. Weber (1904/1958) theorized that the Roman Catholic belief system encouraged followers to hold onto traditional ways of life, while the Protestant belief system encouraged its members to embrace change. Protestantism, he said, undermined people's spiritual security. Roman Catholics believed that because they were church members, they were on the road to heaven. But Protestants, who did not share this belief, looked for "signs" that they were in God's will. Financial success became the major sign that God was on their side. Consequently, Protestants began to live frugal lives, saving their money and investing the surplus in order to make even more. This, said Weber, brought about the birth of capitalism.

Weber called this self-denying approach to life the *Protestant ethic.* He termed the readiness to invest capital in order to make more money the *spirit of capitalism.* To test his theory, Weber compared the extent of capitalism in Roman Catholic and Protestant countries. In line with his theory, he found that capitalism was more likely to flourish in Protestant countries. Weber's conclusion that religion was the key factor in the rise of capitalism was controversial when he made it, and it continues to be debated today (Kaelber 2001). We'll explore these ideas in more detail in Chapter 7.

Values in Sociological Research

Weber raised another issue that remains controversial among sociologists. He said that sociology should be **value free.** By this, he meant that a sociologist's **values**—personal beliefs about what is good or worthwhile in life and the way the world ought to be—should not affect research. Weber wanted **objectivity**, total neutrality, to be the hallmark of social research. If values influence research, he said, sociological findings will be biased.

That bias has no place in research is not a matter of debate. All sociologists agree that no one should distort data to make them fit preconceived ideas or personal values. It is equally clear, however, that because sociologists—like everyone else—are members of a particular society at a given point in history, they, too, are infused with values of all sorts. These values inevitably play a role in our research. For example, values are part of the reason that one sociologist chooses to do research on the Mafia, while another turns a sociological eye on kindergarten students.

Because values can lead to unwitting distortions in how we interpret our findings, sociologists stress **replication**, researchers repeating a study in order to compare their results with the original findings. If values have distorted research findings, replication by other sociologists should uncover the bias and correct it.

Despite this consensus, however, values remain a hotly debated topic in sociology (Buraway 2003; Gans 2003). The disagreement centers on the proper purposes and uses of sociology. Regarding its *purpose,* some sociologists take the position that their goal should be simply to advance understanding of social life. They should gather data on any topic in which they are interested and then use the best theory available to interpret their findings. Others are convinced that sociologists have the responsibility to investigate the social arrangements that harm people—the causes of poverty, crime, war, and other forms of human exploitation.

Then, as Figure 1.2 illustrates, there is also the disagreement over the *uses* of sociology. Those who say that understanding is sociology's proper goal take the position that the knowledge gained by social research belongs to the scientific community and to the world. Accordingly, it can be used by anyone for any purpose. In contrast, those who say that sociologists should focus on harmful social conditions take the position that sociologists should spearhead social reform. They say that sociologists should use their studies to alleviate human suffering and make society a better place to live.

Although this debate is more complicated than the argument summarized here—few sociologists take such one-sided views—this sketch does identify its major issues. Perhaps sociologist John Galliher (1991) best expresses today's majority position:

> Some argue that social scientists, unlike politicians and religious leaders, should merely attempt to describe and explain the events of the world but should never make value judgments based on those observations. Yet a value-free and nonjudgmental social science has no place in a world that has experienced the Holocaust, in a world having had slavery, in a world with the ever-present threat of rape and other sexual assault, in a world with frequent, unpunished crimes in high places, including the production of products known by their manufacturers to cause death and injury as has been true of asbestos products and continues to be true of the cigarette industry, and in a world dying from environmental pollution by these same large multinational corporations.

value free the view that a sociologist's personal values or biases should not influence social research

values the standards by which people define what is desirable or undesirable, good or bad, beautiful or ugly

objectivity total neutrality

replication repeating a study in order to test its findings

Figure 1.2

The Debate Over Values in Sociological Research

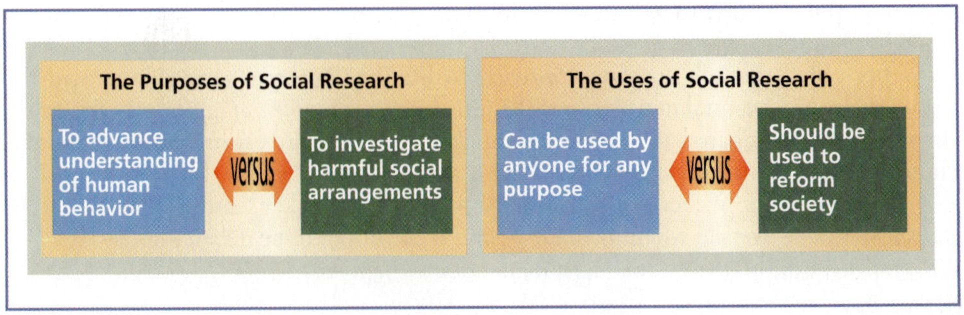

The Purposes of Social Research
To advance understanding of human behavior
versus
To investigate harmful social arrangements
The Uses of Social Research
Can be used by anyone for any purpose
versus
Should be used to reform society

Verstehen and Social Facts

Weber and *Verstehen*

Weber also stressed that to understand human behavior, we should use ***Verstehen*** (vare-shtay-in) (a German word meaning "to understand"). Perhaps the best translation of this term is "to grasp by insight." By emphasizing *Verstehen,* Weber meant that the best interpreter of human behavior is someone who "has been there," someone who can understand the feelings and motivations of the people being studied. In short, we must pay attention to what are called **subjective meanings,** the ways in which people interpret their own behavior. We can't understand what people do, Weber insisted, unless we look at how people view and explain their own behavior.

To better understand this term, let's return to the homeless in our opening vignette. Why were the men so silent? Why were they so unlike the noisy, sometimes boisterous college students who swarm dorms and cafeterias?

Verstehen can help explain this. When I interviewed men in the shelters (and, in other settings, homeless women), they revealed their despair. Because you know—at least on some level—what the human emotion of despair is, you can immediately apply your understanding to their situation. You know that people in despair feel a sense of hopelessness. The future looks bleak, hardly worth plodding toward. Consequently, why is it worth talking about? Who wants to hear another hard-luck story?

By applying *Verstehen*—your understanding of what it means to be human and to face some situation in life—you gain insight into people's behavior. In this case, you can understand their silence, their lack of communication in the shelter.

Verstehen a German word used by Weber that is perhaps best understood as "to have insight into someone's situation"

subjective meanings the meanings that people give their own behavior

social facts Durkheim's term for a group's patterns of behavior

Durkheim and Social Facts

In contrast to Weber's emphasis on *Verstehen* and subjective meanings, Durkheim stressed what he called **social facts.** By this term, he meant the patterns of behavior that characterize a social group. Examples of social facts in the United States include June being the most popular month for weddings, suicide rates being higher among the elderly, and more births occurring on Tuesdays than on any other day of the week.

Durkheim said that we must use social facts to interpret social facts. In other words, each pattern reflects some condition of society. People all over the country don't just coincidentally decide to do similar things, whether that be to get married or to commit suicide. If this were the case, in some years, middle-aged people would be the most likely to kill themselves, in other years, young people, and so on. *Patterns that hold true year after year indicate that as thousands and even millions of people make their individual decisions, they are responding to conditions in their society.* It is the job of the sociologist, then, to uncover social facts and to explain them through other social facts. In the following section, let's look at how the social facts I mentioned—of weddings, suicide, and births—are explained by other social facts.

Granted their deprivation, it is not surprising that the homeless are not brimming with optimism. This scene at the Bowery Mission in New York City is typical, reminiscent of the many meals I ate in soup kitchens with men who looked exactly like this.

How Social Facts and *Verstehen* Fit Together

Social facts and *Verstehen* go hand in hand. As a member of U.S. society, you know how June weddings are related to the end of the school year and how this month, locked in tradition, common sentiment, and advertising, carries its own momentum. As for suicide among the elderly (see Chapter 13), you probably already have a sense of the greater despair that many Americans of this age feel. This is your *verstehen* of the social facts.

But do you know why more Americans are born on Tuesday than on any other day of the week? One would expect Tuesday to be no more common than any other

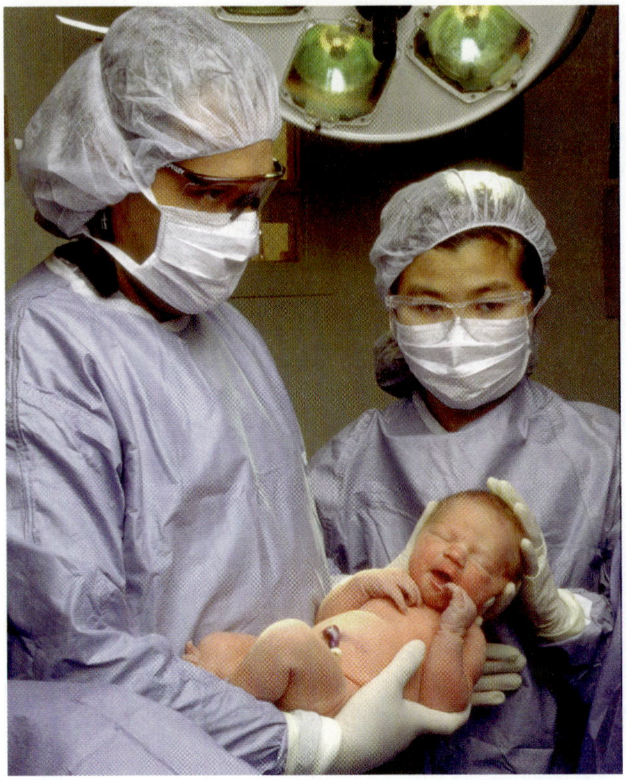

Cesarean deliveries used to be unusual, a last resort to prevent harm to the mother or to save the baby. Today, these deliveries have become routine in the United States. To understand this change, both social facts and Verstehen *are useful.*

day, and that is how it used to be. But no longer. To understand this change, we need a combination of social facts and *Verstehen.* Four social facts are relevant: First, due to technology, the hospital has become a dominating force in the U.S. medical system. Second, current technology has made delivery by cesarean section safer. Third, as discussed in Chapter 19 (page 549), doctors took over the delivery of babies. Fourth, profit is a top goal of practicing medicine in the United States. As a result of these social facts, an operation that used to be a last resort for emergencies has become so routine that almost one-fourth (23 percent) of all U.S. babies are now delivered in this manner (*Statistical Abstract* 2002:Table 79). This is the highest rate of such births in the world (Wolff et al. 1992).

If we add *Verstehen* to these social facts, we gain insight that goes far beyond the cold statistics. We can understand that most mothers-to-be prefer to give birth in a hospital and that, under the influence of physicians at a highly emotionally charged moment, alternatives appear quite dim. We can also understand that the services of physicians are in high demand and that they schedule deliveries for the time that is most convenient for themselves. Tuesday is the day that suits them best.

Sexism in Early Sociology

Attitudes of the Time

As you may have noticed, all the sociologists we have discussed are men. In the 1800s, sex roles were rigidly defined, with women assigned the roles of wife and mother. In the classic German phrase, women were expected to devote themselves to the four K's: *Kirche, Küchen, Kinder, und Kleider* (church, cooking, children, and clothes). Trying to break out of this mold meant risking severe disapproval.

Few people, male or female, received any education beyond basic reading and writing. Higher education, for the rare few who received it, was reserved for men. A handful of women from wealthy families, however, did pursue higher education. A few even managed to study sociology, although the sexism so deeply entrenched in the universities stopped them from obtaining advanced degrees or becoming professors. In line with the times, the writings of women were almost entirely ignored. Jane Frohock, Lucretia Mott, and Elizabeth Cady Stanton, for example, were little known beyond a small circle. Frances Perkins, a sociologist and the first woman to hold a cabinet position (as Secretary of Labor under President Franklin Roosevelt), is no longer remembered.

Harriet Martineau and Early Social Research

A classic example is Harriet Martineau (1802–1876), who was born into a wealthy family in England. When Martineau first began to analyze social life, she would hide her writing beneath her sewing when visitors arrived, for writing was "masculine" and sewing "feminine" (Gilman 1911:88). Martineau persisted in her interests, however, and eventually she studied social life in both Great Britain and the United States. In 1837, two or three decades before Durkheim and Weber were born, Martineau published *Society in America,* in which she reported on this new nation's customs—family, race, gender, politics, and religion. Despite her insightful examination of U.S. life, which is still worth reading today, Martineau's research met the same fate as the work of other early women sociologists and, until recently, has been ignored. Instead, she is known primarily for translating Comte's ideas into English. The Down-to-Earth Sociology box on the next page features selections from *Society in America.*

Sociology in North America

Early History: The Tension Between Social Reform and Sociological Analysis

Transplanted to U.S. soil in the late nineteenth century, sociology first took root at the University of Kansas in 1890, at the University of Chicago in 1892, and at Atlanta University, then an all-black school, in 1897. From there, academic specialties in sociology spread throughout North America. The growth was gradual, however. It was not until 1922 that McGill University gave Canada its first department of sociology. Harvard University did not open its department of sociology until 1930, and the University of California at Berkeley did not follow until the 1950s.

Initially, the department at the University of Chicago, which was founded by Albion Small (1854–1926), dominated sociology. (Small also founded the *American Journal of Sociology* and was its editor from 1895 to 1925.) Members of this early sociology department whose ideas continue to influence today's sociologists include Robert E. Park (1864–1944), Ernest Burgess (1886–1966), and George Herbert Mead (1863–1931). Mead developed the symbolic interactionist perspective, which we will examine later.

The situation of women in North America was similar to that of European women, and their contributions to sociology met a similar fate. Among the early women sociologists were Jane Addams, Emily Greene Balch, Isabel Eaton, Sophie Germain, Charlotte Perkins Gilman, Alice Hamilton, Florence Kelley, Elsie Clews Parsons, and Alice Paul. Denied faculty appointments in sociology, many turned to social activism (Young 1995).

Because some of these women worked with the poor rather than as professors of sociology, many sociologists classify them as social workers. Today's distinction between sociology and social work is fairly clear cut. There is a profession called social work; people train for it, they are hired to do it, and they call themselves social workers. They focus on aiding people in poverty and socially maladjusted members of society. They have jobs in hospitals and schools, and many work in the area of public aid. Others set up private practice and counsel patients. Earlier in the development of sociology, however, there often was little distinction between sociology and social work. This fuzziness lasted for generations, and many departments combined sociology and social work. Some still do.

DOWN-TO-EARTH SOCIOLOGY:

Listening to an Early Feminist

*Interested in social reform, **Harriet Martineau** (1802–1876) turned to sociology, where she discovered the writings of Comte. An active advocate for the abolition of slavery, she traveled widely and wrote extensively.*

IN SEPTEMBER OF 1834, Harriet Martineau, an early feminist sociologist from England, began a fascinating two-year journey around the United States. Traveling by stagecoach, she interviewed people living in poverty, as well as James Madison, the former President of the United States. She spoke with both slaveholders and abolitionists. She also visited prisons and attended sessions of the U.S. Supreme Court. Her observations on the status of U.S. women are taken from this research, published in her 1837 book, *Society in America.*

Concerning women not being allowed to vote:

One of the fundamental principles announced in the Declaration of Independence is that governments derive their just powers from the consent of the governed. How can the political condition of women be reconciled with this?

Governments in the United States have power to tax women who hold property . . . to fine, imprison, and execute them for certain offences. Whence do these governments derive their powers? They are not "just," as they are not derived from the consent of the women thus governed. . . .

The democratic principle condemns all this as wrong; and requires the equal political representation of all rational beings. Children, idiots, and criminals . . . are the only fair exceptions . . .

Concerning sex, slavery, and relations between white women and men in the South:

[White American women] are all married young . . . and there is ever present an unfortunate servile class of their own sex [female slaves] to serve the purposes of licentiousness [as sexual objects for white slaveholders]. . . . [When most] men carry secrets which their wives must be the last to know . . . there is an end to all wholesome confidence and sympathy, and woman sinks to be the ornament of her husband's house, the domestic manager of his establishment, instead of being his all-sufficient friend. . . . I have seen, with heart-sorrow, the kind politeness, the gallantry, so insufficient to the loving heart, with which the wives of the south are treated by their husbands. . . . I know the tone of conversation which is adopted towards women; different in its topics and its style from that which any man would dream of offering to any other man. I have heard the boast of chivalrous consideration in which women are held throughout their woman's paradise; and seen something of the anguish of crushed pride, of the conflict of bitter feelings with which such boasts have been listened to by those whose aspirations teach them the hollowness of the system . . .

Concerning women's education:

The intellect of woman is confined by an unjustifiable restriction . . . As women have none of the objects in life for which an enlarged education is considered requisite, the education is not given . . . [S]ome things [are] taught which . . . serve to fill up time . . . to improve conversation, and to make women something like companions to their husbands, and able to teach their children somewhat. . . . There is rarely or never a . . . promotion of clear intellectual activity. . . . [A]s long as women are excluded from the objects for which men are trained . . . intellectual activity is dangerous: or, as the phrase is, unfit. Accordingly marriage is the only object left open to woman.

Jane Addams and Social Reform

Although many North American sociologists combined the role of sociologist with that of social reformer, none was as successful as Jane Addams (1860–1935). Like Harriet Martineau, Addams came from a background of wealth and privilege. She attended The Women's Medical College of Philadelphia, but dropped out because of illness (Addams 1910/1981). On one of her many trips to Europe, Addams was impressed with work being done to help London's poor. From then on, she tirelessly worked for social justice.

In 1889, Addams co-founded Hull-House, located in Chicago's notorious slums. Hull-House was open to people who needed refuge—to immigrants, the sick, the aged, the poor. Sociologists from nearby University of Chicago were frequent visitors at Hull-House. With her piercing insights into the social classes, especially the ways workers were exploited and how peasant immigrants adjusted to city life, Addams strived to bridge the gap between the powerful and the powerless. She worked with others to win the eight-hour day and to pass laws against child labor. Her efforts at social reform were so outstanding that in 1931, she was a co-winner of the Nobel Peace Prize, the only sociologist to win this coveted award.

Jane Addams, *1860–1935, a recipient of the Nobel Peace Prize, worked on behalf of poor immigrants. With Ellen G. Starr, she founded Hull-House, a center to help immigrants in Chicago. She was also a leader in women's rights (women suffrage), as well as the peace movement of World War I.*

W.E.B. Du Bois and Race Relations

Confronted by the racism of this period, African American professionals also found life difficult. The most notable example is provided by W.E.B. Du Bois (1868–1963), who, after earning a bachelor's degree from Fisk University, became the first African American to earn a doctorate at Harvard. After completing his education at the University of Berlin, where he attended lectures by Max Weber, Du Bois taught Greek and Latin at Wilberforce University. He was hired by Atlanta University in 1897, where he remained for most of his career (Du Bois 1935/1966).

It is difficult to imagine the racism that Du Bois encountered. For example, he once saw the fingers of a lynching victim displayed in a Georgia butcher shop (Aptheker 1990). Although Du Bois was invited to present a paper at the 1909 meetings of the American Sociological Society, he was too poor to attend, despite his education, faculty position, and accomplishments. When he could afford to attend subsequent meetings, discrimination was so prevalent that restaurants and hotels would not allow him to eat or room with the white sociologists. Later in life, when Du Bois had the money to travel, the U.S. State Department feared that he would criticize the United States and refused to give him a passport (Du Bois 1968).

Each year between 1896 and 1914, Du Bois published a book on relations between African Americans and whites. Of his almost 2,000 writings, *The Philadelphia Negro* (1899/1967) stands out. In this analysis of how African Americans in Philadelphia coped with racism, Du Bois pointed out that some of the more successful African Americans were breaking their ties with other African Americans in order to win acceptance by

W(illiam) E(dward) B(urghardt) Du Bois *(1868–1963) spent his lifetime studying relations between African Americans and whites. Like many early North American sociologists, Du Bois combined the role of academic sociologist with that of social reformer. He was also the editor of* Crisis, *an influential journal of the time.*

In the 1940s, when this photo was taken, racial segregation was a taken-for-granted fact of life. Although many changes have occurred since then—and since W.E.B. Du Bois analyzed race relations—race remains a significant factor in the lives of Americans.

whites. This, he said, weakened the African American community by depriving it of their influence. One of Du Bois' most elegantly written books, which preserves a picture of race relations immediately after the Civil War, is *The Souls of Black Folk* (1903). The Down-to-Earth Sociology box below is taken from this book.

At first, Du Bois was content to collect and interpret objective data. Later, frustrated at the continued racism of his time, Du Bois turned to social action. Along with Jane Addams and others from Hull-House, he founded the National Association for the Advancement of Colored People (NAACP) (Deegan 1988). Continuing to battle racism both as a sociologist and as a journalist, Du Bois eventually embraced revolutionary Marxism. At age 93, dismayed that so little improvement had been made in race relations, he moved to Ghana, where he is buried (Stark 1989).

Until recently, W.E.B. Du Bois was neglected in sociology, his many contributions unrecognized. As a personal example, during my entire graduate program at Washington University, I was never introduced to Du Bois' books and thought. Today, however, sociologists are rediscovering Du Bois, and he is beginning to receive some long-deserved respect.

DOWN-TO-EARTH SOCIOLOGY

Early North American Sociology: Du Bois and Race Relations

THE WRITINGS OF W.E.B. DU BOIS, WHO expressed sociological thought more like an accomplished novelist than a sociologist, have been neglected in sociology. To help remedy this omission, I reprint the following excerpts from pages 66–68 of *The Souls of Black Folk* (1903). In this book, Du Bois analyzes changes that occurred in the social and economic conditions of African Americans during the thirty years following the Civil War.

For two summers, while he was a student at Fisk, Du Bois taught in a log-hut, segregated school "way back in the hills" of rural Tennessee. The following excerpts help us understand conditions at that time.

> It was a hot morning late in July when the school opened. I trembled when I heard the patter of little feet down the dusty road, and saw the growing row of dark solemn faces and bright eager eyes facing me. . . . There they sat, nearly thirty of them, on the rough benches, their faces shading from a pale cream to deep brown, the little feet bare and swinging, the eyes full of expectation, with here and there a twinkle of mischief, and the hands grasping Webster's blue-black spelling-book. I loved my school, and the fine faith the children had in the wisdom of their teacher was truly marvelous. We read and spelled together, wrote a little, picked flowers, sang, and listened to stories of the world beyond the hill. . . .
>
> On Friday nights I often went home with some of the children,—sometimes to Doc Burke's farm. He was a great, loud, thin Black, ever working, and trying to buy these seventy-five acres of hill and dale where he lived; but people said that he would surely fail and the "white folks would get it all." His wife was a magnificent Amazon, with saffron face and shiny hair, uncorseted and barefooted, and the children were strong and barefooted. They lived in a one-and-a-half-room cabin in the hollow of the farm near the spring. . . .
>
> Often, to keep the peace, I must go where life was less lovely; for instance, 'Tildy's mother was incorrigibly dirty, Reuben's larder was limited seriously, and herds of untamed insects wandered over the Eddingses' beds. Best of all I loved to go to Josie's, and sit on the porch, eating peaches, while the mother bustled and talked: how Josie had bought the sewing-machine; how Josie worked at service in winter, but that four dollars a month was "mighty little" wages; how Josie longed to go away to school, but that it "looked liked" they never could get far enough ahead to let her; how the crops failed and the well was yet unfinished; and, finally, how mean some of the white folks were.
>
> For two summers I lived in this little world. . . . I have called my tiny community a world, and so its isolation made it; and yet there was among us but a half-awakened common consciousness, sprung from common joy and grief, at burial, birth, or wedding; from common hardship in poverty, poor land, and low wages, and, above all, from the sight of the Veil* that hung between us and Opportunity. All this caused us to think some thoughts together; but these, when ripe for speech, were spoken in various languages. Those whose eyes twenty-five and more years had seen "the glory of the coming of the Lord," saw in every present hindrance or help a dark fatalism bound to bring all things right in His own good time. The mass of those to whom slavery was a dim recollection of childhood found the world a puzzling thing: it asked little of them, and they answered with little, and yet it ridiculed their offering. Such a paradox they could not understand, and therefore sank into listless indifference, or shiftlessness, or reckless bravado.

*"The Veil" is shorthand for the Veil of Race, referring to how race colors all human relations. Du Bois' hope was that "sometime, somewhere, men will judge men by their souls and not by their skins" (p. 261).

Talcott Parsons and C. Wright Mills: Theory Versus Reform

Like Du Bois, many early North American sociologists combined the role of sociologist with that of social reformer. They saw society, or parts of it, as corrupt and in need of reform. During the 1920s and 1930s, for example, Park and Burgess not only studied crime, drug addiction, juvenile delinquency, and prostitution, but also offered suggestions for how to alleviate these social problems.

During the 1940s, the emphasis shifted from social reform to social theory. Talcott Parsons (1902–1979), for example, developed abstract models of society that influenced a generation of sociologists. Parsons' detailed models of how the parts of society harmoniously work together did nothing to stimulate social activism.

C. Wright Mills (1916–1962) deplored the theoretical abstractions of this period, and he urged sociologists to get back to social reform. He saw the coalescing of interests on the part of a group he called the *power elite*—the top leaders of business, politics, and the military—as an imminent threat to freedom. Shortly after Mills' death, the United States entered the turbulent era of the 1960s and 1970s. This sparked interest in social activism, and Mills' ideas became popular among a new generation of sociologists.

C. Wright Mills was a controversial figure in sociology because of his analysis of the role of the power elite *in U.S. society. Today, his analysis is taken for granted by many sociologists and members of the public.*

The Continuing Tension and the Rise of Applied Sociology

The apparent contradiction of these two aims—analyzing society versus working toward its reform—created a tension in sociology that is still evident today. Some sociologists believe that their proper role is to analyze some aspect of society and to publish their findings in sociology journals. Others say this is not enough: Sociologists have an obligation to use their expertise to try to make society a better place in which to live and to help bring justice to the poor.

Somewhere between these extremes lies **applied sociology,** which uses sociology to solve problems. (See Figure 1.3, which contrasts basic and applied sociology.) One of the first attempts at applied sociology—and one of the most successful—was the founding of the National Association for the Advancement of Colored People. Today's applied sociologists work in a variety of settings (Dentler 2002; Stephens 2004). Some work for business firms to solve problems in the workplace. Others do research for the government, where they investigate social problems such as pornography, rape, environmental pollution, or the spread of AIDS. Still others work in high technology. The Down-to-Earth Sociology box on the next page gives an idea of the variety of settings in which applied sociologists work.

applied sociology the use of sociology to solve problems—from the micro level of family relationships to the macro level of crime and pollution

Figure 1.3 Comparing Basic and Applied Sociology

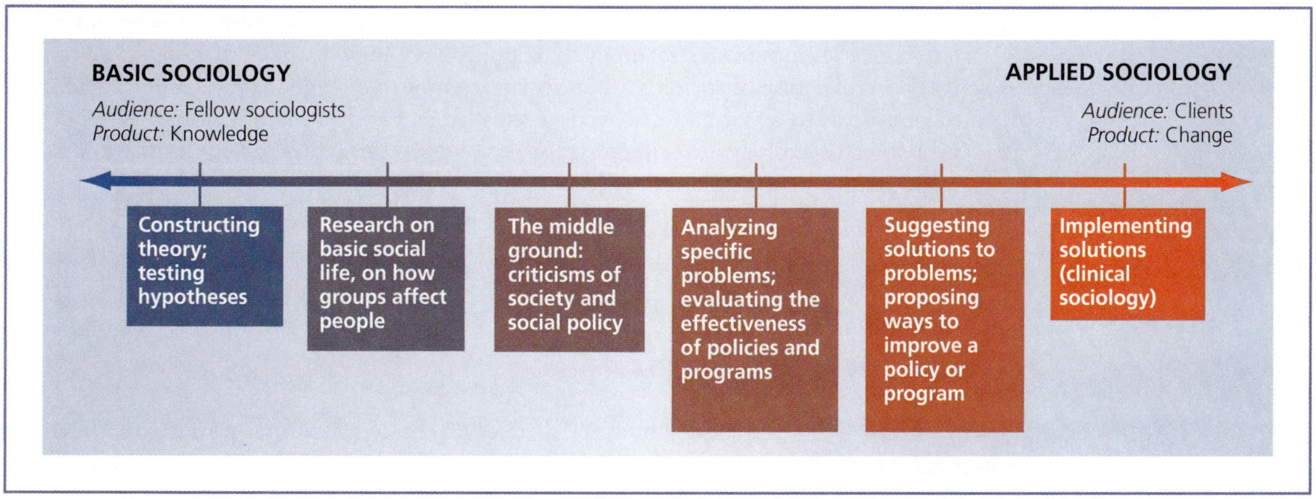

Source: By the author. Based on DeMartini 1982.

DOWN-TO-EARTH SOCIOLOGY

Careers in Sociology: What Applied Sociologists Do

MOST SOCIOLOGISTS TEACH IN COLLEGES and universities, sharing sociological knowledge with college students, as your instructor is doing with you in this course. Applied sociologists, in contrast, work in a wide variety of areas—from counseling children to studying how diseases are transmitted. Some even make software more "user friendly." (They study how people use new computer products and give feedback to the software engineers who design those products [Guice 1999].) To give you an idea of this variety, let's look over the shoulders of four applied sociologists.

Leslie Green, who does marketing research at Vanderveer Group in Philadelphia, Pennsylvania, earned her bachelor's degree in sociology at Shippensburg University. She helps develop strategies to get doctors to prescribe particular drugs. She sets up the meetings, locates moderators for the discussion groups, and arranges payments to the physicians who participate in the research. "My training in sociology," she says, "helps me in 'people skills.' It helps me to understand the needs of different groups, and to interact with them."

Stanley Capela, whose master's degree is from Fordham University, works as an applied sociologist at HeartShare Human Services in New York. He evaluates how children's programs—such as ones that focus on housing, AIDS, group homes, and preschool education—actually work, compared with how they are supposed to work. He spots problems and suggests solutions. One of his assignments was to find out why children had to wait so long to be adopted, even though there was a long list of eager adoptive parents. Capela pinpointed how the paperwork got bogged down as it was routed through the system and suggested ways to improve the flow of paperwork.

Laurie Banks, who received her master's degree in sociology from Fordham University, analyzes statistics for the New York City Health Department. As she examined death certificates, she noticed that a Polish neighborhood had very high rates of stomach cancer. She alerted the Centers for Disease Control, which conducted interviews in the neighborhood. They traced the cause to eating large amounts of sausage. In another case, Banks compared birth certificates with school records. She found that problems at birth—low birth weight, lack of prenatal care, and birth complications—were linked to low reading skills and behavior problems in school.

Joyce Miller Iutcovich, whose doctorate is from Kent State University, is president of Keystone University Research Corporation in Erie, Pennsylvania. She is also a past president of the Society for Applied Sociology. Iutcovich does research and consulting, primarily for government agencies. In one of her projects, she designed a training program for child care providers. She also did research on how well the caregivers did. Her research and program improved the quality of care given to children by the Pennsylvania Department of Public Welfare. Her organization also administers the Pennsylvania Substance Abuse and Health Information Clearinghouse, which mails over 300,000 pieces of literature a month.

From just these few examples, you can catch a glimpse of the variety of work that applied sociologists do. Some work for corporations, some are employed by government and private agencies, and others run their own businesses. You can also see that having a doctorate is not necessary in order to work as an applied sociologist.

Applied sociology is not the same as social reform. It is an application of sociology in some specific setting, not an attempt to rebuild society, as early sociologists envisioned. Consequently, a new tension has emerged in sociology. Sociologists who want the emphasis to be on social reform say that applied sociology doesn't even come close to this. It is an application of sociology, but not an attempt to change society. Others, who want the emphasis to remain on discovering knowledge, say that when sociology is applied, it is no longer sociology. If sociologists use sociological principles to help prostitutes escape from pimps, for example, is it still sociology?

At this point, let's consider how theory fits into sociology.

Theoretical Perspectives in Sociology

Facts never interpret themselves. In everyday life, we interpret what we observe by using common sense. We place our observations or "facts" into a framework of more-or-less related ideas. Sociologists do this, too, but they place their observations into a conceptual framework called a theory. A **theory** is a general statement about how some parts of the world fit together and how they work. It is an explanation of how two or more "facts" are related to one another.

Sociologists use three major theories: symbolic interactionism, functional analysis, and conflict theory. Let's first examine the main elements of these theories. Then let's see how each theory helps us to understand why the divorce rate in the United States is so high. As we do so, you will see how each theory, or perspective, provides a distinct interpretation of social life.

George Herbert Mead (1863–1931) is one of the founders of symbolic interactionism, a major theoretical perspective in sociology. He taught at the University of Chicago, where his lectures were popular. Although he wrote little, after his death students compiled his lectures into an influential book, Mind, Self, and Society.

Symbolic Interactionism

We can trace the origins of **symbolic interactionism** to the Scottish moral philosophers of the eighteenth century, who noted that individuals evaluate their own conduct by comparing themselves with others (Stryker 1990). In the United States, a long line of thinkers added to this analysis, including the pioneering psychologist William James (1842–1910) and the educator John Dewey (1859–1952), who analyzed how people use symbols to make sense out of their experiences. This theoretical perspective was brought to sociology by Charles Horton Cooley (1864–1929), William I. Thomas (1863–1947), and George Herbert Mead (1863–1931). Cooley's and Mead's analyses of how symbols lie at the basis of the self-concept are discussed on pages 68–70.

Symbols in Everyday Life Symbolic interactionists study how people use *symbols*—the things to which we attach meaning—to develop their views of the world and communicate with one another. Without symbols, our social life would be no more sophisticated than that of animals. For example, without symbols we would have no aunts or uncles, employers or teachers—or even brothers and sisters. I know that this sounds strange, but it is symbols that define for us what relationships are. There would still be reproduction, of course, but no symbols to tell us how we are related to whom. We would not know to whom we owe respect and obligations, or from whom we can expect privileges—the stuff that our relationships are made of.

Look at it like this: If you think of someone as your aunt or uncle, you behave in certain ways, but if you think of that person as a boyfriend or girlfriend, you behave quite differently. It is the symbol that tells you how you are related to others—and how you should act toward them.

To make this clearer, suppose that you are head-over-heels in love with someone and are going to marry this person tomorrow. The night before you are going to marry, your mother confides that she had a child before she married, a child she gave up for adoption. You then discover that the person you are going to marry is this child. You can see how the symbol will change overnight! And your behavior, too!

Symbols not only allow relationships to exist, but also society. Without symbols, we could not coordinate our actions with those of other people. We could not make plans for a future date, time, and place. Unable to specify times, materials, sizes, or goals, we could not build bridges and highways. Without symbols, there would be no movies or musical instruments. We would have no hospitals, no government, no religion. The class you are taking could not exist—nor could this book. On the positive side, there would be no war.

In short, symbolic interactionists analyze how our behaviors depend on the ways we define ourselves and others. They study face-to-face interaction, looking at how people work out their relationships and how they make sense out of life and their place in it. They point out that even the *self* is a symbol, for it consists of the ideas we have about who we are. And the self is a changing symbol: As we interact with others, we constantly adjust our views of who we are based on how we interpret the reactions of others. We'll get more into this later.

Applying Symbolic Interactionism To better understand symbolic interactionism, let's see how changing symbols (meanings) help to explain the high U.S. divorce rate. For background, you should understand that marriage used to be seen as a lifelong commitment. Divorce was viewed as an immoral act, a flagrant disregard for public opinion, and the abandonment of adult responsibilities.

1. *Emotional satisfaction.* Slowly, the meaning of marriage began to change. In 1933, sociologist William Ogburn observed that personality was becoming more important in mate selection. In 1945, sociologists Ernest Burgess and Harvey Locke noted

theory a general statement about how some parts of the world fit together and how they work; an explanation of how two or more facts are related to one another

symbolic interactionism a theoretical perspective in which society is viewed as composed of symbols that people use to establish meaning, develop their views of the world, and communicate with one another the growing importance of mutual affection, understanding, and compatibility in marriage. What these sociologists had observed was a fundamental shift in U.S. marriage: Husbands and wives were coming to expect—and demand—greater emotional satisfaction from one another.

As this trend intensified, intimacy became the core of marriage and Americans placed more importance on physical attractiveness in a spouse (Bus et al. 2001). At the same time, as society grew more complex and impersonal, Americans came to view marriage as a solution to the tensions that society produced (Lasch 1977). This new form, "companionate marriage," contributed to divorce, for it encouraged people to expect that their spouse would satisfy "each and every need." Consequently, sociologists say, marriage became an "overloaded institution."

2. *The love symbol.* Our symbol of love also helps to "overload" marriage. An expectation that "true love" will be a constant source of emotional satisfaction sets people up for crushed hopes, for when dissatisfactions enter marriage, as they inevitably do, spouses tend to blame one another for what they see as the other's failure. Their engulfment in the symbol of love at the time of marriage blinds them to the basic unreality of their expectations.
3. *The meaning of children.* Ideas about childhood have undergone a deep historical shift with far-reaching consequences for the U.S. family. In medieval Europe, children were seen as miniature adults, and there was no sharp separation between the worlds of adults and children (Ariés 1965). Boys were apprenticed at about age 7, while girls of the same age learned the homemaking duties associated with being a wife. In the United States, just three generations ago, children "became adults" when they graduated from eighth grade and went to work. Today's contrast is amazing: From miniature adults, children have been culturally fashioned into impressionable, vulnerable, and innocent beings.
4. *The meaning of parenthood.* These changed notions of childhood have had a deep impact on our ideas of good parenting. Today's parents are expected not only to provide unending amounts of love and tender care but also to ensure that their children "reach their potential." Today's child rearing lasts longer and is more demanding. These greater responsibilities place heavier burdens on today's couples, and with them, more strain on marriage.
5. *Marital roles.* In earlier generations, the responsibilities and privileges of husbands and wives were clearly defined. Newlyweds knew what they could legitimately expect from each other. In contrast, with today's much vaguer guidelines couples must work out more aspects of their respective roles on their own. Many struggle to figure out how to divide up responsibilities for work, home, and children.
6. *Perception of alternatives.* While these changes were taking place, society was making another major shift: More and more women began taking jobs outside the home. As they earned paychecks of their own, many wives began to see alternatives to remaining in unhappy marriages. Symbolic interactionists consider the perception of an alternative an essential first step to making divorce possible.
7. *The meaning of divorce.* As these factors came together—expecting more emotional satisfaction in marriage, changed marital and parental roles, and a new perception of alternatives to an unhappy marriage—divorce steadily increased. As Figure 1.4 shows, divorce went from practically zero in 1890 to our current 1.1 million divorces a year. (The plateau for both marriage and divorce since 1980 is probably due to increased cohabitation.)

   As divorce became common, its meaning changed. Once a symbol of failure—and of immorality and irresponsibility—divorce came to indicate freedom and new meanings. Removing the stigma from divorce shattered a strong barrier that had kept husbands and wives from breaking up, setting the stage for divorce on an even larger scale.
8. *Changes in the law.* As the law—itself a powerful symbol—began to reflect these changed ideas about divorce, it became an additional factor that encouraged di-

functional analysis a theoretical framework in which society is viewed as composed of various parts, each with a function that, when fulfilled, contributes to society's equilibrium; also known as functionalism and structural functionalism vorce. Divorce previously had been granted only for severe reasons, such as adultery, but then legislators made "incompatibility" grounds for divorce. States then pioneered "no-fault" divorce, in which a couple could dissolve their marriage without accusing each other of wrongdoing. Some states even began to provide do-it-yourself divorce kits.

Symbolic interactionists analyze how family relationships have changed over time, and how these changes are related to divorce. From its particular experiences, each family also develops unique perspectives. How do you think this family views its relationships?

IN SUM

Symbolic interactionists explain an increasing divorce rate in terms of the changing symbols (or meanings) associated with both marriage and divorce. Changes in people's ideas—about divorce, marital satisfaction, love, the nature of children and parenting, and the roles of husband and wife—have made marriage more fragile. No single change is *the* cause, but taken together, these changes provide a strong "push" toward divorce.

Are these changes good or bad? Central to symbolic interactionism is the position that to make a value judgment about change (or anything else) requires a value framework from which to view the change. Symbolic interactionism provides no such value framework. In short, symbolic interactionists, like other sociologists, can analyze social change, but they cannot pass judgment on that change.

Functional Analysis

The central idea of **functional analysis** is that society is a whole unit, made up of interrelated parts that work together. Functional analysis, also known as *functionalism* and *structural functionalism,* is rooted in the origins of sociology (Turner 1978). Auguste Comte and Herbert Spencer viewed society as a kind of living organism. Just as a person

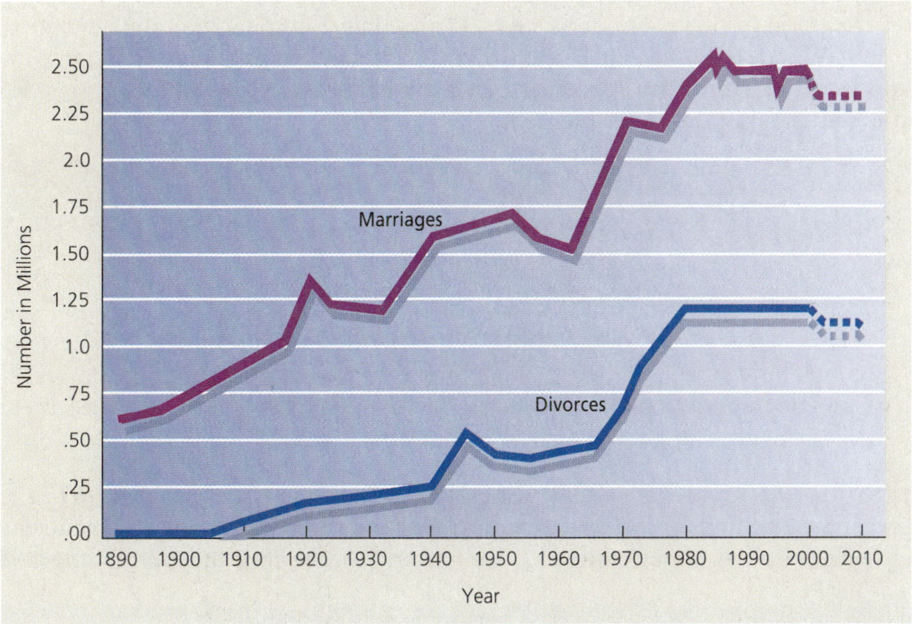

Figure 1.4

U.S. Marriage, U.S. Divorce

Sources: By the author. Based on *Statistical Abstract* 1998:Table 92; earlier editions for earlier years; "Population Update" 2000. The broken lines indicate the author's estimates.

Sociologists who use the functionalist perspective *stress how industrialization and urbanization undermined the traditional* functions *of the family. Before industrialization, members of the family worked together as an economic unit. As production moved away from the home, it took with it first the father and, more recently, the mother. One consequence is a major* dysfunction, *the weakening of family ties. This 19th century engraving depicts a carpenter at work while his mother tells stories to the children (and to the adults) and his wife cooks the evening meal.*

or animal has organs that function together, they wrote, so does society. Like an organism, if society is to function smoothly, its various parts must work together in harmony.

Emile Durkheim also saw society as being composed of many parts, each with its own function. When all the parts of society fulfill their functions, society is in a "normal" state. If they do not fulfill their functions, society is in an "abnormal" or "pathological" state. To understand society, then, functionalists say that we need to look at both *structure* (how the parts of a society fit together to make the whole) and *function* (what each part does, how it contributes to society).

Robert Merton and Functionalism

Robert Merton (1910–2003) dismissed the organic analogy, but he did maintain the essence of functionalism—the image of society as a whole composed of parts that work together. Merton used the term *functions* to refer to the beneficial consequences of people's actions: Functions help keep a group (society, social system) in equilibrium. In contrast, *dysfunctions* are consequences that harm a society: They undermine a system's equilibrium.

Functions can be either manifest or latent. If an action is *intended* to help some part of a system, it is a **manifest function.** For example, suppose that government officials become concerned about our slowing rate of childbirth. Congress offers a $10,000 bonus for every child born to a married couple. The intention, or manifest function, of the bonus is to increase childbearing. Merton pointed out that people's actions can also have **latent functions;** they can have *unintended* consequences that help a system adjust. Let's suppose that the bonus works and the birth rate jumps. As a result, the sale of diapers and baby furniture booms. Because the benefits to these businesses were not the intended consequences, they are *latent* functions of the bonus.

Of course, human actions can also hurt a system. Because such consequences usually are unintended, Merton called them *latent dysfunctions.* Let's assume that the government has failed to specify a "stopping point" with regard to its bonus system. To collect the bonus, some people keep on having children. The more children they have, however, the more they need the next bonus to survive. Large families become common, and poverty increases. Welfare is reinstated, taxes jump, and the nation erupts in protest. Because these results were not intended and because they harmed the social system, they represent latent dysfunctions of the bonus program.

IN SUM

From the perspective of functional analysis, then, the group is a functioning unit, with each part related to the whole. Whenever we examine a smaller part, we need to look for its functions and dysfunctions to see how it is related to the larger unit. This basic approach can be applied to any social group, whether an entire society, a college, or even a group as small as a family.

manifest functions the intended beneficial consequences of people's actions

latent functions unintended beneficial consequences of people's actions

Applying Functional Analysis Now let's apply functional analysis to the U.S. divorce rate. Functionalists stress that industrialization and urbanization undermined the traditional functions of the family. Let's see how each of the basic functions of the family has changed.

1. *Economic production.* Prior to industrialization, the family was an economic team. At that time, it was difficult to obtain the basic necessities of life, and to survive,

family members had to cooperate in producing what they needed. When industrialization moved production from home to factory, it disrupted this family team. This weakened the bonds that tied family members together. Especially significant was the transfer of the husband-father to the factory, for this isolated him from the family's daily routine. In addition, the wife-mother and children now contributed less to the family's economic survival.

2. *Socialization of children.* As these sweeping changes took place, the government was growing larger and more powerful. It then took over many family functions. To give just one example, schools took away from the family the education of children. In so doing, they assumed much of the responsibility for socializing children. To make certain that families went along with this change, states passed laws requiring school attendance and threatened parents with jail if they did not send their children to school.
3. *Care of the sick and elderly.* As medical training and technology improved, institutionalized medicine grew more powerful. Care of the sick gradually shifted from the family to outside medical specialists. As the central government expanded, its agencies multiplied, and care of the aged changed from a family concern to a government obligation.
4. *Recreation.* As more disposable income became available to Americans, businesses sprang up to compete for that income. This cost the family a good part of its recreational function, for much entertainment and "fun" moved from home-based, family-centered activities to attendance at paid events.
5. *Sexual control.* The vast changes that swept the country also affected the family's role in controlling human sexuality. Traditionally, only sexual relations within marriage were considered legitimate. Although this value was more ideal than real—even the Puritans had a lot of sex outside marriage (Smith and Hindus 1975)—the "sexual revolution" opened many alternatives to marital sex.
6. *Reproduction.* The only family function that seems to have been left untouched is reproduction. Yet even this seemingly inviolable function has not gone unchallenged.

In the 1800s, poverty was widespread in the United States. Most people were so poor that they expended their life energies on just getting enough food, fuel, and clothing to survive. Formal education beyond the first several grades was a luxury. This photo depicts the conditions of the people Du Bois worked with. (See the Down-to-Earth Sociology box on page 20.)

A prime example is the greater number of single women who bear children. One third of all U.S. babies are born to an unmarried mother (*Statistical Abstract* 2002:Table 74). Even schools and doctors have taken over some of the family's control over reproduction. A married woman, for example, can get an abortion without informing her husband, and some U.S. high schools distribute condoms.

A Glimpse of the Past To see how sharply family functions have changed, it may be useful to take a glimpse of family life in the 1800s.

> When Phil became sick, he was nursed by Ann, his wife. She cooked for him, fed him, changed the bed linen, bathed him, read to him from the Bible, and gave him his medicine. (She did this in addition to doing the housework and taking care of their six children.) Phil was also surrounded by the children, who shouldered some of his chores while he was sick.
>
> When Phil died, the male neighbors and relatives made the casket while Ann, her mother, and female friends washed and dressed the body. Phil was then "laid out" in the front parlor (the formal living room), where friends, neighbors, and relatives viewed him, paying their last respects. From there, friends moved his body to the church for the final message, and then to the grave they themselves had dug.

As you can see, the family used to have more functions. The family handled many aspects of life and death that we now assign to outside agencies. Not only did the care of the sick take place almost exclusively within the family, but also death was a family affair—from preparing the body to burying it. Today we assume that such functions *properly* belong to specialized agencies, and few of us can imagine ourselves preparing the body of a close relative for burial. Such an act may even seem grotesque, almost barbarous, for our current customs also guide our feelings, another fascinating aspect of social life. (On pages 73–75, we return to the topic of emotions.)

IN SUM

The family has lost many of its traditional functions, while others are presently under assault. Especially significant are changes in economic production. No longer is this a cooperative, home-based effort, with husbands and wives depending on one another for their interlocking contributions to a mutual endeavor. Husbands and wives today earn individual paychecks, and increasingly function as separate components of an impersonal, multinational, and even global system. When outside agencies take over family functions, this makes the family more fragile, and an increase in divorce becomes inevitable. The fewer functions that family members have in common, the fewer are their "ties that bind," and these ties are what help husbands and wives get through the inevitable problems they experience.

Conflict Theory

Conflict theory provides a third perspective on social life. Unlike the functionalists who view society as a harmonious whole, with its parts working together, conflict theorists stress that society is composed of groups that engage in fierce competition for scarce resources. Although alliances or cooperation may prevail on the surface, beneath that surface lies a struggle for power.

Karl Marx and Conflict Theory Karl Marx, the founder of conflict theory, witnessed the Industrial Revolution that transformed Europe. He saw that peasants who had left the land to seek work in cities had to work at wages that barely provided enough to eat. Things were so bad that the average worker died at age 30, the average wealthy person at age 50 (Edgerton 1992:87). Shocked by this suffering and exploitation, Marx began to analyze society and history. As he did so, he developed **conflict theory.** He concluded that the key to human history is class struggle. In each society, some small group

conflict theory a theoretical framework in which society is viewed as composed of groups competing for scarce resources controls the means of production and exploits those who are not in control. In industrialized societies, the struggle is between the *bourgeoisie,* the small group of capitalists who own the means to produce wealth, and the *proletariat,* the mass of workers who are exploited by the bourgeoisie. The capitalists also control politics, so that if workers rebel, the capitalists are able to call on the power of the state to subdue them (Angell 1965).

When Marx made his observations, capitalism was in its infancy and workers were at the mercy of their employers. Workers had none of what we take for granted today—the right to strike, minimum wages, eight-hour days, coffee breaks, five-day work weeks, paid vacations and holidays, medical benefits, sick leave, unemployment compensation, or Social Security. Marx's analysis reminds us that these benefits came not from generous hearts, but from workers forcing concessions from their employers.

Conflict Theory Today Some conflict sociologists use conflict theory in a much broader sense. They see conflict as inherent in all relations that involve authority. They point out that **authority,** or power that people consider legitimate, permeates every layer of society—whether that be a small group, an organization, a community, or the entire society. People in positions of authority try to enforce conformity, which, in turn, creates resentment and resistance. The result is a constant struggle throughout society to determine who has authority over what (Turner 1978; Bartos and Wehr 2002).

Sociologist Lewis Coser (b. 1913–2003) pointed out that conflict is most likely to develop among people who are in close relationships. They have worked out ways to distribute responsibilities and privileges, power and rewards. Any change in this arrangement can lead to hurt feelings, or bitterness and conflict. Even in intimate relationships, then, people are in a constant balancing act, with conflict lying uneasily just beneath the surface.

Feminists and Conflict Theory *Feminists* stress that men and women should have equal rights. As they view the relations between men and women, they see a conflict that goes back to the origins of history. Just as Marx stressed conflict between capitalists and workers, so many feminists stress a similar conflict between men and women. Feminists are not united by the conflict perspective, however. Although some feminists focus on the oppression of women by men and women's struggle against that oppression, feminists do research on all the topics of sociology and use whatever theories apply. (Feminism is discussed in Chapter 11.)

Applying Conflict Theory To explain why the U.S. divorce rate is high, conflict theorists focus on how men's and women's relationships have changed. For millennia, men dominated women. Women had few alternatives other than accepting their exploitation. Today, however, with industrialization, women can meet their basic survival needs outside of marriage. Industrialization has also fostered a culture in which females participate in social worlds beyond the home. Consequently, refusing to bear burdens that earlier generations accepted as inevitable, today's women are much more likely to dissolve a marriage that becomes intolerable—or even unsatisfactory.

IN SUM

Conflict theorists see marriage as reflecting society's basic inequalities between males and females. The traditional imbalance of power between men and women, which had been taken for granted, changed as women gained power, especially through the paycheck. One consequence is a higher divorce rate as wives strive for more equality and husbands resist their efforts. From the conflict perspective, then, the increase in divorce is not a sign that marriage has weakened, but, rather, a sign that women are making headway in their historical struggle with men.

Levels of Analysis: Macro and Micro

A major difference between these three theoretical perspectives is their level of analysis. Functionalists and conflict theorists focus on the **macro level;** that is, they examine large-scale patterns of society. In contrast, symbolic interactionists usually focus on the

authority power that people consider legitimate, as rightly exercised over them; also called *legitimate power*

macro-level analysis an examination of large-scale patterns of society

micro level, on **social interaction**—what people do when they are in one another's presence. See Table 1.1 below.

To make this distinction between micro and macro levels clearer, let's return to the example of the homeless, with which we opened this chapter. To study homeless people, symbolic interactionists would focus on the micro level. They would analyze what homeless people do when they are in shelters and on the streets. They would also analyze their communications, both their talk and their **nonverbal interaction** (gestures, silence, use of space, and so on). The observations I made at the beginning of this chapter about the silence in the homeless shelter, for example, would be of interest to symbolic interactionists.

This micro level, however, would not interest functionalists and conflict theorists. They would focus instead on the macro level. Functionalists would examine how changes in the parts of society have increased homelessness. They might look at how changes in the family (fewer children, more divorce) and economic conditions (higher rents, fewer unskilled jobs, loss of jobs overseas) cause homelessness among people who are unable to find jobs and have no family to fall back on. For their part, conflict theorists would stress the struggle between social classes, especially how the policies of the wealthy force certain groups into unemployment and homelessness. That, they point out, accounts for the disproportionate number of African Americans who are homeless. Chapter 4 focuses on the distinctions between macro and micro levels of analysis.

micro-level analysis an examination of small-scale patterns of society

social interaction what people do when they are in one another's presence

nonverbal interaction communication without words through gestures, use of space, silence, and so on

Putting the Theoretical Perspectives Together

Which theoretical perspective should we use to study human behavior? Which level of analysis is the correct one? As you have seen, these theoretical perspectives provide contrasting pictures of human life. In the case of divorce, these interpretations are quite different from the commonsense understanding that two people are simply "incompatible." *Because each theory focuses on different features of social life, each provides a distinctive interpretation. Consequently, it is necessary to use all three theoretical lenses to analyze human behavior. By combining their contributions, we gain a more comprehensive picture of social life.*

Table 1.1 Major Theoretical Perspectives in Sociology

Perspectives	Usual Level of Analysis	Focus of Analysis	Key Terms	Applying the Perspectives to the U.S. Divorce Rate
Symbolic Interactionism	Microsociological–examines small-scale patterns of social interaction	Face-to face interaction, how people use symbols to create social life	Symbols Interaction Meanings Definitions	Industrialization and urbanization changed marital roles and led to a redefinition of love, marriage, children, and divorce.
Functional Analysis (also called functionalism and structural functionalism)	Macrosociological–examines large-scale patterns of society	Relationships among the parts of society; how these parts are *functional* (have beneficial consequences) or *dysfunctional* (have negative consequences)	Structure Functions (manifest and latent) Dysfunctions Equilibrium	As social change erodes the traditional functions of the family, family ties weaken, and the divorce rate increases.
Conflict Theory	Macrosociological–examines large-scale patterns of society	The struggle for scarce resources by groups in a society; how the elites use their power to control the weaker groups	Inequality Power Conflict Competition Exploitation	When men control economic life, the divorce rate is low because women find few alternatives to a bad marriage; the high divorce rate reflects a shift in the balance of power between men and women.

Trends Shaping the Future of Sociology

Two major trends indicate changing directions in sociology. Let's look again at the relationship of sociology to the reforming of society, and then at globalization.

Sociology Full Circle: Reform Versus Research A tension between social reform and social analysis has always run through sociology. To better understand this tension, some sociologists find it useful to divide sociology into three major periods (Lazarsfeld and Reitz 1989). During the first phase, sociologists stressed the need to do research in order to improve society. One of the first presidents of the American Sociological Society, Albion Small, made this goal explicit. In 1912, Small said that the primary reason for sociology was its "practical application to the improvement of social life." He said that sociologists should use science to gain knowledge, and then use that knowledge to "realize visions" (Fritz 1989). This first phase of sociology lasted until the 1920s.

During the second phase, from the 1920s until World War II, the emphasis switched from making the world a better place to making sociology a respected field of knowledge. Sociologists emphasized **basic** or **pure sociology,** that is, research and theory aimed at making discoveries about life in human groups, but not at making changes within those groups. They achieved this goal within a generation, and almost every college and university in the United States added sociology to its course offerings. It is because of these efforts that you are taking this introductory course in sociology.

We are now in a third phase, which began around the end of World War II. In 1954, the U.S. Supreme Court based a major ruling partially on sociological research. The Court was deciding whether racially segregated public schools were constitutional. Up to this time, states followed a so-called "separate but equal" doctrine and had separate public schools for whites and blacks. (The schools, as many observers noted, were separate, but certainly not equal.) In this landmark ruling (*Brown v. the Board of Education of Topeka*), which banned segregated public schools, sociologists testified on the harmful effects of segregation.

This fundamental change in law had a direct impact on education across the country. It also made sociologists more aware of their potential to bring about social change. Just as sociologists switched from their initial concern with improving society to developing abstract knowledge, today they are seeking ways to apply their research findings. With the development of applied sociology, these efforts have gained momentum. Many sociology departments offer courses in applied sociology; some offer internships in applied sociology at both the graduate and undergraduate levels.

I want to stress that sociology is filled with diverse opinions. We do not move in lockstep toward a single goal. To divide sociology into three separate phases overlooks as much as it reveals. Even during the first phase, Durkheim and Weber did research for the purpose of gaining academic respectability for sociology. Similarly, during the second phase, many sociologists who wanted to reform society chafed at the emphasis on understanding. And today, many sociologists want the emphasis to remain on basic sociology. Some do not even acknowledge that applied sociology is "real" sociology. They say that it is actually social work or psychology masquerading as sociology.

Each particular period, however, does have basic emphases, and this division of sociology into three phases does pinpoint major trends. The tension that has run through sociology—between gaining knowledge and applying knowledge—will continue. During this current phase, the pendulum seems to be swinging toward applying sociological knowledge.

Globalization A second major trend, globalization, also seems destined to leave its mark on sociology. **Globalization** is the breaking down of national boundaries because of advances in communication, trade, and travel. Currently, the United States dominates sociology. As sociologists William Martin and Mark Beittel (1998) put it, U.S. sociology is the "unrivaled center of the discipline on a world scale." One consequence of this dominance is an emphasis on groups in the United States. We U.S. sociologists tend to look inward, concentrating on events and relationships that occur in our own country. We

pure or **basic sociology** sociological research whose purpose is to make discoveries about life in human groups, not to make changes in those groups

globalization the extensive interconnections among nations due to the expansion of capitalism

globalization of capitalism capitalism (investing to make profits within a rational system) becoming the globe's dominant economic system

even base most of our findings on U.S. samples. Globalization is likely to broaden our horizons, directing us to a greater consideration of global issues. This, in turn, is likely to motivate us to try more vigorously to identify universal principles.

Application of Globalization to This Text With each passing year, the world becomes smaller as we become more connected to the global village. What occurs elsewhere has a direct impact on our lives, and, increasingly, our welfare is tied to that of people in other nations. To help broaden our horizons, in this book we will visit many cultures around the world, examining what life is like for the people in those cultures. Seeing how *their* society affects their behavior and orientations to life will help us understand how *our* society influences what we do and how we feel about life.

Globalization is one of the most significant events in world history, and you and I are living through it. Throughout this text, I will stress the impact of globalization on your life, especially how it is likely to shape your future. We will also examine the **globalization of capitalism,** focusing on implications of the triumph of this economic system. From time to time, as you read the following pages, you will also confront the developing new world order, which appears destined to play a most significant role in your future.

SUMMARY and REVIEW

The Sociological Perspective

What is the sociological perspective?

The **sociological perspective** stresses that people's social experiences—the groups to which they belong and their experiences within these groups—underlie their behavior. C. Wright Mills referred to this as the intersection of biography (the individual) and history (social factors that influence the individual). Pp. 4–5.

Sociology and the Other Sciences

What is science, and where does sociology fit in?

Science is the application of systematic methods to obtain knowledge and the knowledge obtained by those methods. The sciences are divided into the **natural sciences,** which seek to explain and predict events in the natural environment; and the **social sciences,** which seek to understand the social world objectively by means of controlled and repeated observations. **Sociology** is the scientific study of society and human behavior. Pp. 5–8.

Origins of Sociology

When did sociology first appear as a separate discipline?

Sociology emerged as a separate discipline in the mid-1800s in western Europe, during the onset of the Industrial Revolution. Industrialization affected all aspects of human existence—where people lived, the nature of their work, how they viewed life, and their interpersonal relationships. Early sociologists who focused on these social changes include Auguste Comte, Herbert Spencer, Karl Marx, Emile Durkheim, Max Weber, Harriet Martineau, and W.E.B. Du Bois. Pp. 8–13.

Values in Sociological Research

Should the purpose of social research be only to advance human understanding or also to reform society?

Sociologists agree that research findings should be **value free,** that the researcher's values and beliefs should be set aside in order to permit objective conclusions. But sociologists do not agree on the uses and purposes of social research. Some believe its purpose should be only to advance understanding of human behavior; others, that its goal should be to reform harmful social arrangements. P. 14.

Verstehen and Social Facts

How do sociologists use *Verstehen* and social facts to study human behavior?

According to Max Weber, to understand why people act as they do, sociologists must try to put themselves in their shoes. He used the German verb ***Verstehen,*** "to grasp by insight," to describe this essentially subjective approach. Although not denying the importance of *Verstehen,* Emile Durkheim emphasized the importance of uncovering **social facts,** objective social conditions that influence how people behave. Contemporary sociology uses both approaches to understand human behavior. Pp. 15–16.

Sexism in Early Sociology

What was the position of women in early sociology?

Sociology appeared during a historical period of deep sexism. Consequently, the few women who received the education required to become sociologists, such as Harriet Martineau, were ignored. Pp. 16–17.

Sociology in North America

When was sociology established in the United States?

The earliest departments of sociology were established in the late 1800s at the universities of Kansas, Chicago, and Atlanta. During the 1940s, sociology was dominated by the University of Chicago. A tension between social reform and social research and theory ran through sociology, and in its early years, the contributions of women and minorities were largely ignored. Pp. 1–21.

What is the difference between basic (or pure) and applied sociology?

Basic (or **pure**) **sociology** is sociological research whose purpose is to make discoveries. In contrast, **applied sociology** is the use of sociology to solve problems. Pp. 21–22.

Theoretical Perspectives in Sociology

What is a theory?

A **theory** is a general statement about how facts are related to one another. A theory provides a conceptual framework for interpreting facts. Pp. 22–23.

What are sociology's major theoretical perspectives?

Sociologists use three primary theoretical frameworks to interpret social life. **Symbolic interactionism** examines how people use symbols to develop and share their views of the world. Symbolic interactionists usually focus on the **micro level**—on small-scale, face-to-face interaction. **Functional analysts,** in contrast, focus on the **macro level**—on large-scale patterns of society. Functional theorists stress that a social system is made up of many parts. When working properly, each part contributes to the stability of the whole, fulfilling a function that contributes to the system's equilibrium. **Conflict theorists** also focus on large-scale patterns of society. They stress that society is composed of competing groups that struggle for scarce resources.

With each perspective focusing on select features of social life and each providing a unique interpretation, no single theory is adequate. The combined insights of all three perspectives yield a more comprehensive picture of social life. Pp. 23–30.

Trends Shaping the Future of Sociology

What trends are likely to have an impact on sociology?

Sociology has gone through three phases: The first was an emphasis on reforming society; the second, an emphasis on basic sociology. In today's third phase, we are swinging full circle, coming closer to our roots of applying sociology to social change. Applied sociology is likely to continue its influence. A second major trend, **globalization,** is likely to broaden sociological horizons, refocusing research and theory away from its concentration on U.S. society. Pp. 31–32.

Where can I read more on this topic?

Suggested Readings for this chapter are at the back of this book.

THINKING Critically ABOUT CHAPTER 1

1. Do you think that sociologists should try to reform society, or dispassionately study it?
2. Of the three theoretical perspectives, which one would you prefer to use if you were a sociologist? Why?
3. Considering the macro and micro approaches in sociology, which one do you think best explains social life? Why?

ADDITIONAL RESOURCES for This Chapter

www.ablongman.com/henslin7e

- *Content Select* Research Database for Sociology, with suggested key terms and annotated references
- Link to 2000 Census, with activities
- Flashcards of key terms and concepts
- Practice Tests
- Weblinks
- Interactive Maps

Chapter 2

Culture

Chen Lian Xing, *Painted Clay Figure*, 2000

I had never felt heat like this before. This was *northern* Africa, and I wondered what it must be like closer to the equator. Sweat poured off me as the temperature climbed past 110 degrees Fahrenheit.

As we were herded into the building—which had no air conditioning—hundreds of people lunged toward the counter at the rear of the building. With body crushed against body, we waited as the uniformed officials behind the windows leisurely examined each passport. At times like this I wondered what I was doing in Africa.

When I first arrived in Morocco, I found the sights that greeted me exotic—not far removed from my memories of *Casablanca, Raiders of the Lost Ark,* and other movies that over the years had become part of my collective memory. The men, women, and even the children did wear those white robes that reached down to their feet. What was especially striking was that the women were almost totally covered. Despite the heat, they wore not only full-length gowns, but also head coverings that reached down over their foreheads, and veils that covered their faces from the nose down. All you could make out were their eyes—and every eye the same shade of brown.

And how short everyone was! The Arab women looked to be, on average, 5 feet, and the men only about three or four inches taller. As the only blue-eyed, blonde, 6-foot-plus person around, and the only one who was wearing jeans and a pullover shirt, in a world of white-robed short people I stood out like a sore thumb. Everyone stared. No matter where I went, they stared. Wherever I looked, I found brown eyes watching me intently. Even staring back at those many dark brown eyes had no effect. It was so different from home, where, if you caught someone staring at you, the person would immediately look embarrassed and glance away.

And lines? The concept apparently didn't even exist. Buying a ticket for a bus or train meant *pushing and shoving* toward the ticket man

Chapter Outline

And lines? The concept apparently didn't even exist. Buying a ticket for a bus or train meant pushing and shoving toward the ticket man (always a man—no women were visible in any public position), who took the money from whichever outstretched hand he decided on.

And germs? That notion didn't seem to exist here either. Flies swarmed over the food in the restaurants and the unwrapped loaves of bread in the stores. Shopkeepers would considerately shoo off the flies before handing me a loaf. They also offered home delivery. I still remember watching a bread vendor deliver an unwrapped loaf to a woman who stood on a second-floor balcony. She first threw her money to the bread vendor, and he then threw the bread up to her. Only, his throw was off. The bread bounced off the wrought-iron balcony railing and landed in the street, which was filled with people, wandering dogs, and the ever-present, defecating burros. The vendor simply picked up the unwrapped loaf and threw it again. This certainly wasn't his day, for he missed again. But he made it on his third attempt. The woman smiled as she turned back into her apartment, apparently to prepare the noon meal for her hungry family.

Now, standing in the oppressive heat on the Moroccan-Algerian border, the crowd once again became unruly. Another fight had broken out. And once again, the little man in uniform appeared, shouting and knocking people aside as he forced his way to a little wooden box nailed to the floor. Climbing onto this makeshift platform, he shouted at the crowd, his arms flailing about him. The people fell silent. But just as soon as the man left, the shouting and shoving began again.

The situation had become unbearable. His body pressed against mine, the man behind me decided that this was a good time to take a nap. Determining that I made a good support, he placed his arm against my back and leaned his head against his arm. Sweat streamed down my back at the point where his arm and head touched me.

Finally, I realized that I had to abandon U.S. customs. So I pushed my way forward, forcing my frame into every square inch of vacant space that I could create. At the counter, I shouted in English. The official looked up at the sound of this strange tongue, and I thrust my long arms over the heads of three people, shoving my passport into his hand.

What Is Culture?

What is culture? The concept is sometimes easier to grasp by description than by definition. For example, suppose you meet a young woman who has just arrived in the United States from India. That her culture is different from yours is immediately evident. You first see it in her clothing, jewelry, makeup, and hairstyle. Next you hear it in her speech. It then becomes apparent by her gestures. Later, you may hear her express unfamiliar beliefs about the world or about what is valuable in life. All these characteristics are indicative of **culture**—the language, beliefs, values, norms, behaviors, and even material objects that are passed from one generation to the next.

In northern Africa, I was surrounded by a culture quite alien to my own. It was evident in everything I saw and heard. The **material culture**—such things as jewelry, art, buildings, weapons, machines, and even eating utensils, hairstyles, and clothing—provided a sharp contrast to what I was used to seeing. There is nothing inherently "natural" about material culture. That is, it is no more natural (or unnatural) to wear gowns on the street than it is to wear jeans.

I also found myself immersed in a contrasting **nonmaterial culture**, that is, a group's ways of thinking (its beliefs, values, and other assumptions about the world) and doing (its common patterns of behavior, including language, gestures, and other forms of interaction). North African assumptions about crowding to buy a ticket and staring in public are examples of nonmaterial culture. So are U.S. assumptions about not doing either of these things. Like material culture, neither custom is "right." People simply become comfortable with the customs they learn during childhood, and—as in the case of my visit to northern Africa—uncomfortable when their basic assumptions about life are challenged.

Culture and Taken-for-Granted Orientations to Life

To develop a sociological imagination, it is essential to understand how culture affects people's lives. Meeting someone from a different culture may make us aware of culture's pervasive influence, but attaining the same level of awareness regarding our own culture is quite another matter. *Our* speech, *our* gestures, *our* beliefs, and *our* customs are usually taken for granted. We assume they are "normal" or "natural," and we almost always follow them without question. As anthropologist Ralph Linton (1936) said, "The last thing a fish would ever notice would be water." So also with people: Except in unusual circumstances, the effects of our own culture generally remain imperceptible to us.

Yet culture's significance is profound; it touches almost every aspect of who and what we are. We came into this life without a language, without values and morality, with no ideas about religion, war, money, love, use of space, and so on. We possessed none of these fundamental orientations that we take for granted and that are so essential in determining the type of people we become. Yet at this point in our lives we all have acquired them. Sociologists call this *culture within us.* These learned and shared ways of believing and of doing (another definition of culture) penetrate our beings at an early age and quickly become part of our taken-for-granted assumptions about what normal behavior is. *Culture becomes the lens through which we perceive and evaluate what is going on around us.* Seldom do we question these assumptions, for, like water to a fish, the framework from which we view life remains largely beyond our ordinary perception.

The rare instances in which these assumptions are challenged, however, can be upsetting. Although as a sociologist I should be able to look at my own culture "from the outside," my trip to Africa quickly revealed how fully I had internalized my own culture. My upbringing in Western society had given me strong assumptions about aspects of social life that had become deeply rooted in my being—staring, hygiene, and the use of space. But in this part of Africa these assumptions were useless in helping me get through daily life. No longer could I count on people to stare only surreptitiously, to take precautions against invisible microbes, or to stand in line in an orderly fashion, one behind the other.

As you can tell from the opening vignette, I found these assumptions upsetting, for they violated my basic expectations of "the way people *ought* to be"—although I did not know how firmly I held these expectations until they were so abruptly challenged. When my nonmaterial culture failed me—when it no longer enabled me to make sense out of the world—I experienced a disorientation known as **culture shock.** In the case of buying tickets, the fact that I was several inches taller than most Moroccans and thus able to outreach others helped me to adjust partially to their different ways of doing things. But I never did get used to the idea that pushing ahead of others was "right," and I always felt guilty when I used my size to receive preferential treatment.

An important consequence of culture within us is **ethnocentrism,** a tendency to use our own group's ways of doing things as the yardstick for judging others. All of us learn that the ways of our own group are good, right, proper, and even superior to other ways of life. As sociologist William Sumner (1906), who developed this concept, said, "One's own group is the center of everything, and all others are scaled and rated with reference to it." Ethnocentrism has both positive and negative consequences. On the positive side, it creates in-group loyalties. On the negative side, ethnocentrism can lead to discrimination against people whose ways differ from ours.

The many ways culture affects our lives fascinate sociologists. In this chapter, we'll examine how profoundly culture affects everything we are. This will serve as a basis from

culture the language, beliefs, values, norms, behaviors, and even material objects that are passed from one generation to the next

material culture the material objects that distinguish a group of people, such as their art, buildings, weapons, utensils, machines, hairstyles, clothing, and jewelry

nonmaterial culture (also called *symbolic culture*) a group's ways of thinking (including its beliefs, values, and other assumptions about the world) and doing (its common patterns of behavior, including language and other forms of interaction)

culture shock the disorientation that people experience when they come in contact with a fundamentally different culture and can no longer depend on their taken-for-granted assumptions about life

ethnocentrism the use of one's own culture as a yardstick for judging the ways of other individuals or societies, generally leading to a negative evaluation of their values, norms, and behaviors

cultural relativism not judging a culture but trying to understand it on its own terms

which you can start to analyze your own assumptions of reality. I should give you a warning at this point: This can result in a changed perspective on social life and your role in it. If so, life will never look the same.

IN SUM

To avoid losing track of the ideas under discussion, let's pause for a moment to summarize, and in some instances clarify, the principles we have covered.

1. There is nothing "natural" about material culture. Arabs wear gowns on the street and feel that it is natural to do so. Americans do the same with jeans.
2. There is nothing "natural" about nonmaterial culture. It is just as arbitrary to stand in line as it is to push and shove.
3. Culture penetrates deep into our thinking, becoming a taken-for-granted lens through which we see the world and obtain our perception of reality.
4. Culture provides implicit instructions that tell us what we ought to do in various situations. It provides a fundamental basis for our decision making.
5. Culture also provides a "moral imperative"; that is, the culture that we internalize becomes the "right" way of doing things. (I, for example, deeply believed that it was wrong to push and shove to get ahead of others.)
6. Coming into contact with a radically different culture challenges our basic assumptions of life. (I experienced culture shock when I discovered that my deeply ingrained cultural ideas about hygiene and the use of space no longer applied.)
7. Although the particulars of culture differ from one group of people to another, culture itself is universal. That is, all people have culture. There are no exceptions. A society cannot exist without developing shared, learned ways of dealing with the demands of life.
8. All people are ethnocentric, which has both positive and negative consequences.

Practicing Cultural Relativism

To counter our tendency to use our own culture as the standard by which we judge other cultures, we can practice **cultural relativism;** that is, we can try to understand a culture on its own terms. This means to look at how the elements of a culture fit together, without judging those elements as superior or inferior to our own way of life.

Because we tend to use our own culture to judge others, cultural relativism presents a challenge to ordinary thinking. For example, most U.S. citizens appear to have strong feelings against raising bulls for the purpose of stabbing them to death in front of crowds that shout "Olé!" According to cultural relativism, however, bullfighting must be viewed from the framework of the culture in which it takes place—*its* history, *its* folklore, *its* ideas of bravery, and *its* ideas of sex roles.

You may still regard bullfighting as wrong, of course, if your culture, which is deeply ingrained in you, has no history of bullfighting. We all possess culturally specific ideas about cruelty to animals, ideas that have evolved slowly and match other elements of our culture. In the United States, for example, practices that once were common in some areas—cock fighting, dog fighting, bear–dog fighting, and so on—have been gradually weeded out (Bryant 1993).

None of us can be entirely successful at practicing cultural relativism; we simply cannot help viewing a contrasting way of life

Many Americans perceive bullfighting, which is illegal in the United States, as a cruel activity that should be abolished everywhere. To Spaniards and those who have inherited Spanish culture, however, bullfighting is a beautiful, artistic sport in which matador and bull blend into a unifying image of power, courage, and glory. Cultural relativism *requires that we suspend our own perspectives in order to grasp the perspectives of others, something that is much easier described than attained.*

through the lens that our own culture provides. Cultural relativism, however, is an attempt to refocus that lens and thereby appreciate other ways of life rather than simply asserting, "Our way is right." As you view the photos below, try to appreciate the cultural differences. Also, see the Cultural Diversity box on the next page.

Although cultural relativism helps us avoid cultural smugness, this view has come under attack. In a provocative book, *Sick Societies* (1992), anthropologist Robert Edgerton points out that some cultures endanger their people's health, happiness, or survival. He suggests that we should develop a scale for evaluating cultures on their "quality of life," much as we do for U.S. cities. He also asks why we should consider cultures that practice female circumcision, gang rape, wife beating, or that sell little girls into prostitution as

Standards of beauty vary so greatly from one culture *to another that what one group finds attractive, another may not. Yet, in its* ethnocentrism, *each group thinks that its standards are the best—that their appearance reflects what beauty "really" is. As indicated by these photos, around the world men and women aspire to their group's standards of gender. To make themselves appealing to others, they make certain that their appearance reflects those standards.*

Tibet

Somalia

New Guinea

Thailand

Japan

India (Gypsy)

Peru

United States

CULTURAL DIVERSITY around the WORLD

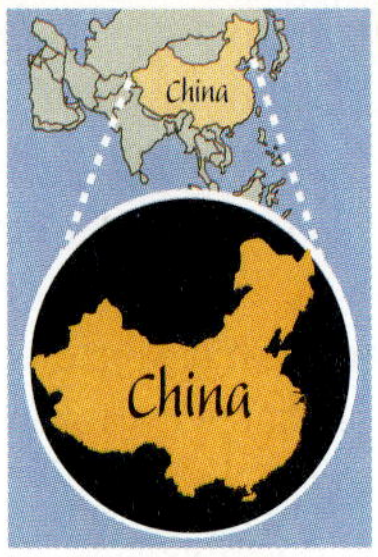

Do You Feel Sorry? Hire an Apology Specialist

Americans are often casual about apologies. "Sorry about that" and "Excuse me" slip easily from our lips.

It is not this easy for the Chinese and Japanese. For them, to make an apology means to lose face. This affects their sense of identity and understandings about relationships. Apologies are not taken lightly.

In China and Japan, apologies require just the right words, spoken in a precise tone of voice. They even require the right clothing. When the United States mistakenly took the Chinese embassy in Belgrade for a terrorist center and bombed it, President Clinton apologized on television. Chinese officials were outraged at the apology, and the Chinese media refused to broadcast the tape. Why? When Clinton made his statement, he was outdoors and wearing a polo shirt. This made things too casual to be a "real" apology.

So who ya gonna call? How about The Apology and Gift Center, a business in China? The company's 20 employees are somber, middle-aged men and women who have college degrees. They are lawyers, teachers, and social workers who have received additional training in counseling. They know how to say the right words in the right way.

People who feel too embarrassed or inadequate to make an apology themselves come to The Apology and Gift Center, where apology specialists study the details and decide on the best course of action. They write letters, deliver gifts, and make explanations in person.

Hiring someone to apologize for you may sound strange, but employing someone to plead your case in other matters was once a novel idea, too. Today we have lawyers on every street corner—or so it seems.

For Your CONSIDERATION

What is it about U.S. culture that makes it most unlikely that apology specialists will ever become common?

Source: Based on Rosenthal 2001a.

morally equivalent to those that do not. Cultural values that result in exploitation, he says, are inferior to those that enhance people's lives.

Edgerton's sharp questions and incisive examples bring us to a topic that comes up repeatedly in this text—the disagreements that arise among scholars as they confront contrasting views of reality. It is such questioning of assumptions that keeps sociology interesting.

Components of Symbolic Culture

Sociologists sometimes refer to nonmaterial culture as **symbolic culture,** because its central component is the symbols that people use. A **symbol** is something to which people attach meaning and that they then use to communicate. Symbols are the basis of nonmaterial culture. They include gestures, language, values, norms, sanctions, folkways, and mores. Let's look at each of these components of symbolic culture.

symbolic culture another term for nonmaterial culture

symbol something to which people attach meanings and then use to communicate with others

gestures the ways in which people use their bodies to communicate with one another

Gestures

Gestures, which involve using one's body to communicate with others, are useful shorthand ways to give messages without using words. Although people in every culture of the world use gestures, a gesture's meaning may change completely from one culture to another. North Americans, for example, communicate a succinct message by raising the middle finger in a short, upward stabbing motion. I wish to stress "North Americans," for that gesture does not convey the same message in South America or most other parts of the world.

I was once surprised to find that this particular gesture was not universal, having internalized it to such an extent that I thought everyone knew what it meant. When I was comparing gestures with friends in Mexico, however, this gesture drew a blank look from them. After I explained its intended meaning, they laughed and showed me their rudest gesture—placing the hand under the armpit and moving the upper arm up and down. To me, they simply looked as if they were imitating a monkey, but to them the gesture meant "Your mother is a whore"—absolutely the worst possible insult in that culture.

Gestures not only facilitate communication but also, because they differ around the world, can lead to misunderstanding, embarrassment, or worse. One time in Mexico, for example, I raised my hand to a certain height to indicate how tall a child was. My hosts began to laugh. It turned out that Mexicans use three hand gestures to indicate height: one for people, one for animals, and another for plants. They were amused because I had ignorantly used the plant gesture to indicate the child's height. (See Figure 2.1.)

To get along in another culture, then, it is important to learn the gestures of that culture. If you don't, not only will you fail to achieve the simplicity of communication that gestures allow, but also you will miss much of what is happening, run the risk of appearing foolish, and possibly offend people. In some cultures, for example, you would provoke deep offense if you were to offer food or a gift with your left hand, because the left hand is reserved for dirty tasks, such as wiping after going to the bathroom. Left-handed Americans visiting Arabs, please note!

Suppose for a moment that you are visiting southern Italy. After eating one of the best meals in your life, you are so pleased that when you catch the waiter's eye, you smile broadly and use the standard U.S. "A-OK" gesture of putting your thumb and forefinger together and making a large "O." The waiter looks horrified, and you are struck speechless when the manager asks you to leave. What have you done? Nothing on purpose, of course, but in that culture this gesture refers to a part of the human body that is not mentioned in polite company (Ekman et al. 1984).

Is it really true that there are no universal gestures? There is some disagreement on this point. Some anthropologists claim that no gesture is universal. They point out that even nodding the head up and down to indicate "yes" is not universal, because in some parts of the world, such as areas of Turkey, nodding the head up and down means "no" (Ekman et al. 1984). However, ethologists, researchers who study biological bases of behavior, claim that expressions of anger, pouting, fear, and sadness are built into our biology and are universal (Eibl-Eibesfeldt 1970:404). They point out that even infants who are born

Figure 2.1 Gestures to Indicate Height, Southern Mexico

blind and deaf, who have had no chance to *learn* these gestures, express themselves in the same way.

Although this matter is not yet settled, we can note that gestures tend to vary remarkably around the world. It is also significant that certain gestures can elicit emotions; some gestures are so associated with emotional messages that the gestures themselves summon up emotions. For example, my introduction to Mexican gestures took place at a dinner table. It was evident that my husband-and-wife hosts were trying to hide their embarrassment at using their culture's obscene gesture at their dinner table. And I felt the same way—not about *their* gesture, of course, which meant absolutely nothing to me—but about the one I was teaching them.

Although most gestures are learned, and therefore vary from culture to culture, some gestures that represent fundamental emotions such as sadness, anger, and fear appear to be inborn. This crying child whom I photographed in India differs little from a crying child in China—or the United States or anywhere else on the globe. In a few years, however, this child will demonstrate a variety of gestures highly specific to his Hindu culture.

Language

Gestures and words go hand in hand, as is evident when you watch people talking. We use gestures to supplement our words, to provide a deeper understanding of what we are communicating. In written language, we often miss the subtle cues that gestures provide. To help supply these cues in online communications, people have developed *emoticons,* a type of "written gestures," to help convey the feelings that go with their words. Emoticons are the topic of the Down-to-Earth Sociology box on the next page.

The primary way in which people communicate with one another is through **language**—symbols that can be combined in an infinite number of ways for the purpose of communicating abstract thought. Each word is actually a symbol, a sound to which we have attached a particular meaning. This allows us to use it to communicate with one another. Language itself is universal in the sense that all human groups have language, but there is nothing universal about the meanings given to particular sounds. Thus, like gestures, in different cultures the same sound may mean something entirely different—or may have no meaning at all.

The significance of language for human life is difficult to overstate. As will become apparent from the following discussion, *language allows culture to exist.*

Language Allows Human Experience to Be Cumulative

By means of language, we pass ideas, knowledge, and even attitudes on to the next generation, allowing it to build on experiences that it may never undergo. This building process enables humans to modify their behavior in light of what previous generations have learned. Hence the central sociological significance of language: *Language allows culture to develop by freeing people to move beyond their immediate experiences.*

Without language, human culture would be little more advanced than that of the lower primates. To communicate, we would be limited to grunts and gestures, which would minimize the temporal dimension of human life. Our communications would be limited to a small time span: events that are now taking place, those that have just taken place, or those that will take place immediately—a sort of "slightly extended present." You can grunt and gesture, for example, that you want a drink of water, but in the absence of language how could you share ideas concerning past or future events? There would be little or no way to communicate to others what event you had in mind, much less the greater complexities that humans communicate—ideas and feelings about events.

Language Provides a Social or Shared Past

Without language, our memories would be extremely limited, for we associate experiences with words and then use words to recall the experience. Such memories as would exist in the absence of language would be highly individualized, for only rarely and incompletely could we communicate them to others, much less discuss them and agree on something. By attaching words to an event, however, and then using those words to recall the event we are able to discuss the event. As we talk about past events, we develop shared understandings about what those events mean. In short, through talk, people develop a shared past.

language a system of symbols that can be combined in an infinite number of ways and can represent not only objects but also abstract thought

DOWN-TO-EARTH SOCIOLOGY

Emoticons: "Written Gestures" for Expressing Yourself Online

TALKING ONLINE HAS BECOME A FAVORITE activity of millions of people. Teenagers rehash the day's events with friends; grandparents keep in touch with grandchildren in different states; businesspeople seal their deals with the click of a "send" button. All of them love the speed of online communications. They send an e-mail or post a note in a chat room, and in an instant people across the country or in distant lands can read or respond to it.

There is something nagging about online talk, though. It leaves a dissatisfying taste because it is so one-dimensional. People miss the nuances of emotion and overlays of meaning that we transmit during face-to-face conversations. Lacking are the gestures and tones of voice that give color and life to our communications, the subtleties by which we monitor and communicate sub-messages.

To help fill this gap, computer users have developed a set of symbols to convey their humor, disappointment, sarcasm, and other moods and attitudes. Although these symbols are not as varied or spontaneous as the nonverbal cues of face-to-face interaction, they are useful. Here are some of them. If you tilt your head to the left as you view them, the symbols will be clearer.

:-)	Smile
:-))	Laugh
:-D	Laugh or big grin
:.)	Laughing tears
:-(	Frowning, or Sad
:-((	Very Sad
>:-(	Angry, annoyed
>:-)	Feeling in a devilish mood
:-X	My lips are sealed
;-)	-Wink, wink—know what I mean?
:-')	Tongue in cheek
:-P	Sticking out your tongue
:-0	WOW! (What a surprise!)
0:-)	Angel

Some correspondents also use abbreviations to add a touch of whimsy:

GMTA	Great Minds Think Alike
IAB	I Am Bored
ILY	I Love You
IMHO	In My Humble Opinion
J/K	Just Kidding
OIC	Oh, I see
LOL	Laughing Out Loud
OTF	On The Floor (laughing)
ROTF	Rolling On The Floor
ROFLWTIME	Rolling On Floor Laughing With Tears In My Eyes
UGG	You Go, Girl!
WTG	Way To Go!

With advancing technology, such shorthand may become unnecessary. Now that we can include video in our e-mail, recipients can see our image and hear our voice. As the cost of video transmitters drops, messages that include verbal and facial cues may replace much written e-mail. As long as written e-mail exists, however, some system of symbols to substitute for gestures will remain.

Language Provides a Social or Shared Future Language also extends our time horizons forward. Because language enables us to agree on times, dates, and places, it allows us to plan activities with one another. Think about it for a moment. Without language, how could you ever plan future events? How could you possibly communicate goals, times, and plans? Whatever planning could exist would be limited to rudimentary communications, perhaps to an agreement to meet at a certain place when the sun is in a certain position. But think of the difficulty, perhaps impossibility, of conveying just a slight change in this simple arrangement, such as "I can't make it tomorrow, but my neighbor can, if that's all right with you."

Language Allows Shared Perspectives Our ability to speak, then, provides us a social (or shared) past and future. This is vital for humanity. It is a watershed that distinguishes us from animals. But speech does much more than this. When we talk with one another, we are exchanging ideas about events; that is, we are sharing perspectives. Our words are the embodiment of our experiences, distilled into a readily exchangeable form, mutually understandable to people who have learned that language. Talking about events allows us to arrive at the shared understandings that form the basis of social life. To not share a language while living alongside one another, however, invites miscommunication and suspicion. This risk, which comes with a diverse society, is discussed in the Cultural Diversity box on the next page.

CULTURAL DIVERSITY in the UNITED STATES

Miami—Language in a Changing City

Since Castro seized power in Cuba, the city of Miami has been transformed from a quiet southern city to a Latin American mecca. Nothing reflects Miami's essential character today as much as its long-simmering feud over language: English versus Spanish. Half of the city's 360,000 residents have trouble speaking English. Only one-fourth of Miami residents speak English at home.

As this chapter stresses, language is a primary means by which people learn—and communicate—their social worlds. Consequently, language differences in Miami reflect not only cultural diversity but also people who live in separate social worlds.

Although its ethnic stew makes Miami culturally one of the richest cities in the United States, the language gap sometimes creates misunderstanding and anger. The aggravation felt by Anglos—which often seems tinged with hostility—is seen in the bumper stickers they used to parade, "Will the Last American Out Please Bring the Flag?"

But Latinos, now a majority in Miami, are similarly frustrated. Many feel that Anglos should be able to speak at least some Spanish. Nicaraguan immigrant Pedro Falcon, for example, is studying English and wonders why more people don't try to learn his language. "Miami is the capital of Latin America," he says. "The population speaks Spanish."

Language and cultural flare-ups sometimes make headlines in the city. Latinos were outraged when an employee at the Coral Gables Board of Realtors lost her job for speaking Spanish at the office. And protesters swarmed a Publix supermarket after a cashier was fired for chatting with a friend in Spanish.

What's happening in Miami, says University of Chicago sociologist Douglas Massey, is what happened in cities such as Chicago a hundred years ago. Then, as now, the rate of immigration exceeded the speed with which new residents learned English, creating a pile-up effect in the proportion of non-English speakers. "Becoming comfortable with English is a slow process," he points out, "whereas immigration is fast."

Massey expects Miami's percentage of non-English speakers to grow. But he says that this "doesn't mean that Miami is going to end up being a Spanish-speaking city." Instead, Massey believes that bilingualism will prevail. "Miami is the first truly bilingual city," he says. "The people who get ahead are not monolingual English speakers or monolingual Spanish speakers. They're people who speak both languages."

Source: Based on Sharp 1992; Usdansky 1992.

Language Allows Complex, Shared, Goal-Directed Behavior

Common understandings enable us to establish a *purpose* for getting together. Let's suppose you want to go on a picnic. You use speech not only to plan the picnic but also to decide on reasons for the picnic—which may be anything from "because it's a nice day and it shouldn't be wasted studying" to "because it's my birthday." Language permits you to blend individual activities into an integrated sequence. In other words, through discussion you decide where you will go; who will drive; who will bring the hamburgers, the potato chips, the soda; where you will meet; and so on. Only because of language can you participate in such a common yet complex event as a picnic—or build roads and bridges, or attend college classes.

IN SUM

The sociological significance of language is that it takes us beyond the world of apes and allows culture to develop. Language frees us from the present by providing a past and a future. It gives us the capacity to share understandings about the past and develop shared perceptions about the future, as well as to establish underlying pur-

Language is the basis of human culture around the world. The past few years have seen a major development in communication—the ease and speed with which we can "speak" to people across the globe. This development is destined to have vital effects on culture.

poses for our activities. Consequently, as in the case of planning a picnic, each individual is able to perform a small part of a larger activity, aware that others are carrying out related parts. In this way, language enables a series of separate activities to become united into a larger whole.

In short, *language is the basis of culture.* Like most aspects of culture, its linguistic base is usually invisible to us.

Language and Perception: The Sapir-Whorf Hypothesis In the 1930s, two anthropologists, Edward Sapir and Benjamin Whorf, became intrigued when they noted that the Hopi Indians of the southwestern United States had no words to distinguish among the past, the present, and the future. English, in contrast, as well as German, French, Spanish, and other languages, distinguishes carefully among these three time frames. From this observation, Sapir and Whorf concluded that the commonsense idea that words are merely labels that people attach to things was wrong. *Language, they concluded, has embedded within it ways of looking at the world.* Thus thinking and perception are not only expressed through language, but also shaped by language. When we learn a language, we learn not only words, but also particular ways of thinking and perceiving (Sapir 1949; Whorf 1956).

The implications of the **Sapir-Whorf hypothesis** are far-reaching. *The Sapir-Whorf hypothesis reverses common sense:* It indicates that rather than objects and events forcing themselves onto our consciousness, it is our language that determines our consciousness, and hence our perception, of objects and events. Sociologist Eviatar Zerubavel (1991) gives a good example. Hebrew, his native language, does not have separate words for jam and jelly. They are classified the same, and only when Zerubavel learned English could he "see" this difference, which is "obvious" to native English speakers. Similarly, if you learn to classify students as Jocks, Goths, Stoners, Skaters, and Preps, you will perceive students in an entirely different way from someone who does not know these classifications.

Although Sapir and Whorf's observation that the Hopi do not have tenses was incorrect (Edgerton 1992:27), they stumbled onto a major truth about social life. Learning a language means not only learning words but also acquiring the perceptions embedded in that language. In other words, language both reflects and shapes cultural experiences. The racial-ethnic terms that our culture provides, for example, influence how we see both ourselves and others, a point that is discussed in the Cultural Diversity box on the next page.

Sapir-Whorf hypothesis
Edward Sapir's and Benjamin Whorf's hypothesis that language creates ways of thinking and perceiving

CULTURAL DIVERSITY in the UNITED STATES

Race and Language: Searching for Self-Labels

The groups that dominate society often determine the names that are used to refer to racial-ethnic groups. If those names become associated with oppression, they take on negative meanings. For example, the terms *Negro* and *Colored People* came to be associated with submissiveness and low status. To overcome these meanings, those referred to by these terms began to identify themselves as *black* or *African American.* They infused these new terms with respect—a basic source of self-esteem which they felt the old terms denied them.

In a twist, African Americans—and to a lesser extent Latinos, Asian Americans, and Native Americans—have changed the rejected term *Colored People* to *People of Color.* Those who embrace this modified term are imbuing it with meanings that offer an identity of respect. The term also has political meanings. It indicates bonds that cross racial-ethnic lines, a growing sense of mutual ties and identity rooted in historical oppression.

There is *always* disagreement about racial-ethnic terms, and this one is no exception. Although most rejected the term *Colored People,* some found in it a sense of respect and claimed it for themselves. The NAACP, for example, stands for the National Association for the Advancement of Colored People. The new term, *People of Color,* arouses similar feelings. Some individuals that this term would include claim that it is inappropriate. They point out that this new label still makes color the primary identifier of people. They stress that humans transcend race-ethnicity, that what we have in common as human beings goes much deeper than what you see on the surface. They stress that we should avoid terms that focus on differences in the pigmentation of our skin.

The language of self-reference in a society so conscious of skin color is an ongoing issue. As long as our society continues to place high emphasis on such superficial differences, the search for adequate terms is not likely to ever be "finished." In this quest for terms that strike the right chord, the term *People of Color* may become a historical footnote. If it does, it will be replaced by another term that indicates a changing self-identification in a changing historical context.

values the standards by which people define what is desirable or undesirable, good or bad, beautiful or ugly

norms the expectations, or rules of behavior, that develop to reflect and enforce values

sanction expressions of approval or disapproval given to people for upholding or violating norms

positive sanction a reward or positive reaction for following norms, ranging from a smile to a prize

negative sanction an expression of disapproval for breaking a norm, ranging from a mild, informal reaction such as a frown to a formal reaction such as a prison sentence or an execution

Values, Norms, and Sanctions

To learn a culture is to learn people's **values,** their ideas of what is desirable in life. When we uncover people's values, we learn a great deal about them, for values are the standards by which people define what is good and bad, beautiful and ugly. Values underlie our preferences, guide our choices, and indicate what we hold worthwhile in life.

Every group develops expectations concerning the right way to reflect its values. Sociologists use the term **norms** to describe those expectations, or rules of behavior, that develop out of a group's values. The term **sanctions** refers to the reactions people get for following or breaking norms. A **positive sanction** expresses approval for following a norm, while a **negative sanction** reflects disapproval for breaking a norm. Positive sanctions can be material, such as a prize, a trophy, or money, but in everyday life they usually consist of hugs, smiles, a pat on the back, or even handshakes and "high fives." Negative sanctions can also be material—being fined in court is one example—but they, too, are more likely to be symbolic: harsh words, or gestures such as frowns, stares, clenched jaws, or raised fists. Getting a raise at work is a positive sanction, indicating that you have followed the norms clustering around work values. Getting fired, however, is a negative sanction, indicating that you have violated these norms. The North American finger gesture discussed earlier is, of course, a negative sanction.

Because people find norms stifling, some cultures relieve the pressure through *moral holidays,* specified times when people are allowed to break norms. Moral holidays often center around getting drunk and being rowdy. During moral holidays, such as Mardi Gras, many norms are loosened. Some activities for which people would otherwise be arrested are per-

Many societies relax their norms *during specified occasions. At these times, known as* moral holidays, *behavior that is ordinarily not permitted is allowed. From a functional standpoint,* moral holidays, *such as the Mardi Gras held at New Orleans, and spring break in Florida and Mexico, serve as safety valves, allowing a release of deviance. When the* moral holiday *is over, the usual enforcement of rules follows. The woman shown here on spring break is guzzling beer from a funnel (a "beer bong").*

folkways norms that are not strictly enforced

mores norms that are strictly enforced because they are thought essential to core values or the well-being of the group

mitted—and expected—including public drunkenness and some nudity. The norms are never completely dropped, however—just loosened a bit. Go too far, and the police step in.

Some societies have *moral holiday places,* locations where norms are expected to be broken. Red light districts of our cities are examples. There prostitutes are allowed to work the streets, bothered only when political pressure builds. If these same prostitutes attempt to solicit customers in adjacent areas, however, they are promptly arrested. Lake of the Ozarks in Missouri, a fairly straight-laced area, has "Party Cove." There, hundreds of boaters—from those operating cabin cruisers to jet skis—moor their vessels together in a highly publicized cove, where many get drunk and nude, and dance on the boats. In one of the more humorous incidents, boaters complained that a nude woman was riding a jet ski outside of the cove. The water patrol investigated but refused to arrest her because the woman was within the law—she had sprayed shaving cream on certain parts of her body. The Missouri Water Patrol even announced in the local newspaper that it will not enter this particular cove, supposedly because "there is so much traffic that they might not be able to get out in time to handle an emergency elsewhere."

The violation of mores *is usually a serious matter. In this case, it is serious enough that the police at this international rugby tournament have swung into action to protect the public from seeing a "disgraceful" sight—at least one so designated by this group. Yet, unlike most violations of* mores, *this scene also elicits barely suppressed laughter from the police.*

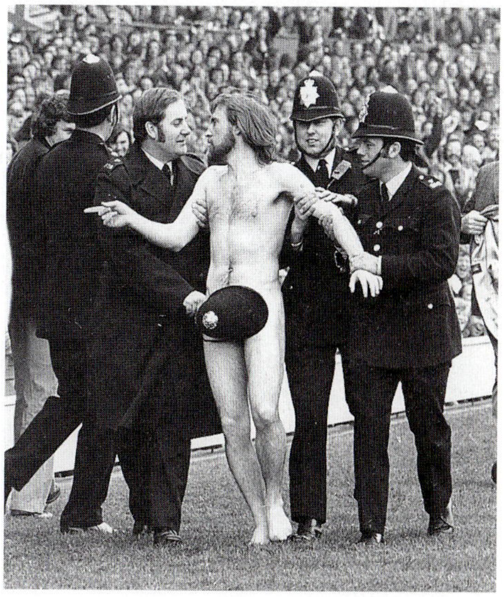

Folkways and Mores

Norms that are not strictly enforced are called **folkways.** We expect people to comply with folkways, but we are likely to shrug our shoulders and not make a big deal about it if they don't. If someone insists on passing you on the left side of the sidewalk, for example, you are unlikely to take corrective action although if the sidewalk is crowded and you must move out of the way, you might give the person a dirty look.

Other norms, however, are taken much more seriously. We think of them as essential to our core values, and we insist on conformity. These are called **mores** (MORE-rays). A person who steals, rapes, or kills has violated some of society's most important mores. As sociologist Ian Robertson (1987:62) put it,

> A man who walks down a street wearing nothing on the upper half of his body is violating a folkway; a man who walks down the street wearing nothing on the lower half of his body is violating one of our most important mores, the requirement that people cover their genitals and buttocks in public.

It should also be noted that one group's folkways may be another group's mores. Although a man walking down the street with the upper half of his body uncovered is deviating from a folkway, a woman doing the same thing is violating the mores. In addition, the folkways and mores of a subculture (the topic of the next section) may be the opposite of mainstream culture. For example, to walk down the sidewalk in a nudist camp with the entire body uncovered would conform to that subculture's folkways.

A **taboo** refers to a norm so strongly ingrained that even the thought of its violation is greeted with revulsion. Eating human flesh and having sex with one's parents are examples of such behaviors (Read 1974; Henslin 2003b). When someone breaks a taboo, the individual is usually judged unfit to live in the same society as others. The sanctions are severe, and may include prison, banishment, or death.

Many Cultural Worlds: Subcultures and Countercultures

What common condition do you think this doctor is describing? Here is what he said:

> [It accompanies] diaphragmatic pleurisy, pneumonia, uremia, or alcoholism . . . Abdominal causes include disorders of the stomach, and esophagus, bowel diseases, pancreatitis, pregnancy, bladder irritation, hepatic metastases, or hepatitis. Thoracic and mediastinal lesions or surgery may be responsible. Posterior fossa tumors or infarcts may stimulate centers in the medulla oblongata. (Chambliss 2003:443)

My best guess is that you don't have the slightest idea what this doctor was talking about. For most of us, he might as well be speaking Greek. Physicians who are lecturing students in medical school, however, talk like this. This doctor is describing hiccups!

Physicians form a **subculture,** *a world within the larger world of the dominant culture.* Subcultures consist of people whose experiences have led them to have distinctive ways of looking at life or some part of it. Even if we cannot understand the preceding quote, it makes us aware that the physician's view of life is not quite the same as ours.

U.S. society contains tens of thousands of subcultures. Some are as broad as the way of life we associate with teenagers, others as narrow as those we associate with body builders—or with doctors. Some U.S. ethnic groups also form subcultures: Their values, norms, and foods set them apart. So might their religion, language, and clothing. Occupational groups also form subcultures, as anyone who has hung out with cab drivers (Davis 1959; Henslin 1993), artists (McCall 1980), or construction workers (Haas 1972) can attest. Even sociologists form a subculture. As you are learning, they use a unique language for carving up the world.

Consider this quote from another subculture:

> If everyone applying for welfare had to supply a doctor's certificate of sterilization, if everyone who had committed a felony were sterilized, if anyone who had mental illness to any degree were sterilized—then our economy could easily take care of these people for the rest of their lives, giving them a decent living standard—but getting them out of the way. That way there would be no children abused, no surplus population, and, after a while, no pollution. . . .
>
> Now let's talk about stupidity. The level of intellect in this country is going down, generation after generation. The average IQ is always 100 because that is the accepted average. However, the kid with a 100 IQ today would have tested out at 70 when I was a lad. You get the concept . . . the marching morons. . . .
>
> When the . . . present world system collapses, it'll be good people like you who will be shooting people in the streets to feed their families. (Zellner 1995:58, 65)

Welcome to the world of the Survivalists, where the message is much clearer than that of physicians—and much more disturbing.

taboo a norm so strong that it often brings revulsion if violated

subculture the values and related behaviors of a group that distinguish its members from the larger culture; a world within a world

The values and norms of most subcultures blend in with mainstream society. In some cases, however, such as these survivalists, some of the group's values and norms place it at odds with the dominant culture. Sociologists use the term **counterculture** to refer to such groups. Another example would be Satanists. To better see this distinction, consider motorcycle enthusiasts and motorcycle gangs. Motorcycle enthusiasts—who emphasize personal freedom and speed *and* affirm cultural values of success—are members of a subculture. In contrast, the Hell's Angels not only stress freedom and speed, but also value dirtiness and contempt toward women and work. This makes them a counterculture (Watson 1988). For a visual depiction of this distinction, see the photo montage on the next two pages.

Countercultures do not have to be negative, however. Back in the 1800s, the Mormons were a counterculture that challenged the dominant culture's core value of monogamy.

An assault on core values is always met with resistance. To affirm their own values, members of the mainstream culture may ridicule, isolate, or even attack members of the counterculture. The Mormons, for example, were driven out of several states before they finally settled in Utah, which was then a wilderness. Even there the federal government would not let them practice polygyny (one man having more than one wife), and Utah's statehood was made conditional on its acceptance of monogamy (Anderson 1942/1966).

Values In U.S. Society

An Overview of U.S. Values

As you know, the United States is a **pluralistic society**, made up of many different groups. The United States has numerous religious and racial–ethnic groups, as well as countless interest groups that center around such divergent activities as collecting Barbie dolls and hunting deer. This state of affairs makes the job of specifying U.S. values difficult. Nonetheless, sociologists have tried to identify the underlying core values that are shared by the many groups that make up U.S. society. Sociologist Robin Williams (1965) identified the following:

1. *Achievement and success.* Americans place a high value on personal achievement, especially outdoing others. This value includes getting ahead at work and school, and attaining wealth, power, and prestige.
2. *Individualism.* Americans have traditionally prized success that comes from individual efforts and initiative. They cherish the ideal that an individual can rise from the bottom of society to its very top. If someone fails to "get ahead," Americans generally find fault with that individual, rather than with the social system for placing roadblocks in his or her path.
3. *Activity and work.* Americans expect people to work hard and to be busily engaged in some activity even when not at work. This value is becoming less important.
4. *Efficiency and practicality.* Americans award high marks for getting things done efficiently. Even in everyday life, Americans consider it important to do things fast, and they constantly seek ways to increase efficiency.
5. *Science and technology.* Americans have a passion for applied science, for using science to control nature—to tame rivers and harness winds—and to develop new technology, from motorized scooters to talking computers.
6. *Progress.* Americans expect rapid technological change. They believe that they should constantly build "more and better" gadgets that will help them move toward that vague goal called "progress."
7. *Material comfort.* Americans expect a high level of material comfort. This comfort includes not only good nutrition, medical care, and housing, but also late-model cars and recreational playthings—from boats to computer games.
8. *Humanitarianism.* Americans emphasize helpfulness, personal kindness, aid in mass disasters, and organized philanthropy.

counterculture a group whose values, beliefs, and related behaviors place its members in opposition to the broader culture

pluralistic society a society made up of many different groups

Looking at Subcultures

Subcultures can form around any interest or activity. Each subculture has its own values and norms that its members share, giving them a common identity. Each also has special terms that pinpoint the group's corner of life and that its members use to communicate with one another. Some of us belong to several subcultures simultaneously.

As you can see from these photos, most subcultures are compatible with the values of the dominant or mainstream culture. They represent specialized interests around which its members have chosen to build tiny worlds. Some subcultures, however, conflict with the mainstream culture. Sociologists give the name contracutlture to subcultures whose values (such as those of outlaw motorcyclists) or activities and goals (such as those of terrorists) are opposed to the mainstream culture. Contracultures, however, are exceptional, and few of us belong to them.

Membership in this subculture is not easily awarded. Not only must workers prove that they are able to work at great heights but also that they fit into the group socially, that they, for example, can take joking without offense.

This Native American also represents a subculture within this subculture, for many Mohawk Native Americans specialize in this occupation.

Truckers participate in a huge subculture, one with its own values and language combined with an emphasis on hyper-masculinity. Can you identify other subcultures that truckers are also likely to participate in?

"Showing" dogs is a highly specialized subculture. To be a member in good standing, intricate rules must be followed.

Almost anyone who has visited a carnival recognizes that there is something different about the people who work there. The values and norms of **"carnies"** have been studied by sociologists and folklorists.

▲ The **motorcyclist clubs** and groups that students and workers participate in on weekends are subcultures. Those that outlaw motorcyclists participate in are contracultures. Can you see why sociologists make this distinction?

◀ Why would people decorate themselves like this? Among the many reasons, one is to show their solidarity with the **football subculture**.

The **cabbies'** subculture, centering on their occupational activities and interests, is also broken into smaller subcultures that reflect their experiences of race-ethnicity.

Participants in the **rodeo** subculture "advertise" their membership by wearing special clothing. The clothing symbolizes a set of values that unites its members. Among those values is the awarding of hyper-masculine status through the conquest of animals.

Each subculture provides its members with values and distinctive ways of viewing the world. What values and perceptions do you think are common among **body builders**?

9. *Freedom.* This core value pervades U.S. life. It underscored the American Revolution, and Americans pride themselves on their personal freedom. The Down-to-Earth Sociology box below highlights an interesting study on how this core value applies to Native Americans.

DOWN-TO-EARTH SOCIOLOGY

Why Do Native Americans Like Westerns?

U.S. AUDIENCES (AND EVEN GERMAN, French, and Japanese ones) devour westerns. In the United States, it is easy to see why Anglos might like westerns, for it is they who seemingly defy the odds and emerge victorious. It is they who are portrayed as heroes who tame the savage wilderness and defend themselves from cruel, barbaric Indians who are intent on their destruction. But why would Indians like westerns?

Sociologist JoEllen Shively, a Chippewa who grew up on Indian reservations in Montana and North Dakota, observed that westerns are so popular that Native Americans bring bags of paperbacks into taverns to trade with one another. They even call one another "cowboy."

Intrigued, Shively decided to investigate the matter by showing a western movie to adult Native Americans and Anglos in a reservation town. The groups were matched in terms of education, age, income, and percentage of unemployment. To select the movie, Shively (1991, 1992) previewed more than seventy westerns. She chose a John Wayne movie, *The Searchers,* because it not only focuses on conflict between Indians and cowboys but also shows the cowboys defeating the Indians. After the movie, the viewers filled out questionnaires, and she interviewed them.

Shively found something surprising: *All* Native Americans and Anglos identified with the cowboys; *none* identified with the Indians. Anglos and Native Americans, however, identified with the cowboys in quite different ways. Each projected a different fantasy onto the story. While Anglos saw the movie as an accurate portrayal of the Old West and a justification of their own status in society, Native Americans saw it as embodying a free, natural way of life. In fact, Native Americans said that they were the "real cowboys." They said, "Westerns relate to the way I wish I could live"; "He's not tied down to an eight-to-five job, day after day"; "He's his own man."

Although John Wayne often portrayed an Anglo who kills Indians, Wayne is popular among Indian men. The men tend to identify with cowboys, who reflect their values of bravery, autonomy, and toughness.

Shively (1991) adds,

> What appears to make Westerns meaningful to Indians is the fantasy of being free and independent like the cowboy. . . . Indians . . . find a fantasy in the cowboy story in which the important parts of their ways of life triumph and are morally good, validating their own cultural group in the context of a dramatically satisfying story. (1992)
>
> To express their real identity—a combination of marginality on the one hand, with a set of values which are about the land, autonomy, and being free—they (use) a cultural vehicle (that is) written for Anglos about Anglos, but it is one in which Indians invest a distinctive set of meanings that speak to their own experience, which they can read in a manner that affirms a way of life they value, or a fantasy they hold to.

In other words, values, not ethnicity, are the central issue. If a Native American film industry were to portray Native Americans with the same values that the Anglo movie industry projects onto cowboys, then Native Americans would identify with their own group. Thus, says Shively, Native American viewers make cowboys "honorary Indians," for the cowboys express their values of bravery, autonomy, and toughness.

10. *Democracy.* By this term, Americans refer to majority rule, to the right of everyone to express an opinion, and to representative government.

11. *Equality.* It is impossible to understand Americans without being aware of the central role that the value of equality plays in their lives. Equality of opportunity (part of the ideal culture discussed later), has significantly influenced U.S. history and continues to mark relations between the groups that make up U.S. society.

12. *Racism and group superiority.* Although it contradicts freedom, democracy, and equality, Americans value some groups more than others and have done so throughout their history. The slaughter of Native Americans and the enslaving of Africans are the most notorious examples.

value cluster values that fit together to form a larger whole

In an earlier publication (Henslin 1975), I updated Williams' analysis by adding these three values.

13. *Education.* Americans are expected to go as far in school as their abilities and finances allow. Over the years, the definition of an "adequate" education has changed, and today a college education is considered an appropriate goal for most Americans. Those who have an opportunity for higher education and do not take it are sometimes viewed as doing something "wrong"—not merely as making a bad choice, but as somehow being involved in an immoral act.

14. *Religiosity.* There is a feeling that "every true American ought to be religious." This does not mean that everyone is expected to join a church, synagogue, or mosque, but that everyone ought to acknowledge a belief in a Supreme Being and follow some set of matching precepts. This value is so pervasive that Americans stamp "In God We Trust" on their money and declare in their national pledge of allegiance that they are "one nation under God."

15. *Romantic love.* Americans feel that the only proper basis for marriage is romantic love. Songs, literature, mass media, and "folk beliefs" all stress this value. They especially love the theme that "love conquers all."

Value Clusters

As you can see, values are not independent units; some cluster together to form a larger whole. In the **value cluster** surrounding success, for example, we find hard work, education, efficiency, material comfort, and individualism bound up together. Americans are expected to go far in school, to work hard afterward, to be efficient, and then to attain a high level of material comfort, which, in turn, demonstrates success. Success is attributed to the individual's efforts; lack of success is blamed on his or her faults.

The many groups that compose the United States contribute to its culture. The increasing numbers of Latinos in the United States, for example, are making an impact on music, art, and literature. This is also true of other areas of everyday life, such as this car-hopping contest in California. Cars are outfitted with bionic hydraulic systems, and contestants compete to see whose car can hop the highest or shimmy the most erratically from tire to tire.

value contradiction values that contradict one another; to follow the one means to come into conflict with the other

Value Contradictions and Social Change

Not all values fall into neat, integrated packages. Some even contradict one another. The value of group superiority contradicts freedom, democracy, and equality, producing a **value contradiction.** There simply cannot be full expression of freedom, democracy, and equality, along with racism and sexism. Something has to give. One way in which Americans sidestepped this contradiction in the past was to say that freedom, democracy, and equality applied only to some groups. The contradiction was bound to surface over time, however, and so it did with the Civil War and the women's liberation movement. *It is precisely at the point of value contradictions, then, that one can see a major force for social change in a society.*

Emerging Values

A value cluster of four interrelated core values—leisure, self-fulfillment, physical fitness, and youthfulness is emerging in the United States. A fifth core value—concern for the environment—is also emerging.

1. *Leisure.* The emergence of leisure as a value is reflected in a huge recreation industry—from computer games, boats, and motor homes to sports arenas, vacation homes, and travel and vacation services.
2. *Self-fulfillment.* This value is reflected in the "human potential" movement, which involves becoming "all one can be," and in books and talk shows that focus on "self-help," "relating," and "personal development."
3. *Physical fitness.* Physical fitness is not a new U.S. value, but increased emphasis is moving it into this emerging cluster. This trend is evident in the "natural" foods craze; obsessive concerns about weight and diet; the joggers, cyclists, and backpackers who take to the trails; and the many health clubs and physical fitness centers.
4. *Youthfulness.* While valuing youth and disparaging old age is not new, some note a new sense of urgency. They attribute this to the huge number of aging baby boomers, who, aghast at the changes in their bodies, attempt to deny their biological fate. An extreme view is represented by a physician who claims that "aging is not a normal life event, but a disease" (Cowley 1996). It is not surprising, then, that techniques for enhancing and maintaining a youthful appearance—from cosmetics to Botox injections—have become popular.

A value cluster *that centers around youthfulness, physical fitness, self-fulfillment, and leisure is becoming central to life in industrial and postindustrial societies. A major reason for the emergence of this value cluster is the greater abundance of material goods, which has freed people from the need to concentrate on survival.*

This emerging value cluster is a response to fundamental changes in U.S. society. Americans used to be preoccupied with forging a nation and fighting for economic survival. They now have come to a point in their economic development where millions of people are freed from long hours of work, and millions more are able to retire from work at an age when they anticipate decades of life ahead of them. This value cluster centers around helping people to maintain their health and vigor during their younger years and enabling them to enjoy their years of retirement.

5. *Concern for the environment.* During most of U.S. history, the environment was viewed as something to be exploited—a wilderness to be settled, forests to be chopped down, rivers and lakes to be fished, and animals to be hunted. One result was the near extinction of the bison and the extinction in 1915 of the passenger pigeon, a bird previously so numerous that its annual migration would darken the skies for days. Today, Americans have developed a genuine and (we can hope) long-term concern for the environment.

This emerging value of environmental concern is also related to the current stage of U.S. economic development, a point that becomes clearer when we note that people act on

Values, both those held by individuals and those that represent a nation or people, can undergo deep shifts. It is difficult for many of us to grasp the pride with which earlier Americans destroyed trees that took thousands of years to grow, are located only on one tiny speck of the globe, and that we today consider part of the nation's and world's heritage. But this is a value statement, representing current views. The pride expressed on these woodcutters' faces represents another set of values entirely.

environmental concerns only after basic needs are met. At this point in their development, for example, the world's poor nations have a difficult time "affording" this value.

Culture Wars: When Values Clash

Changes in core values are met with strong resistance by people who hold them dear. They see the change as a threat to their way of life, an undermining of both their present and their future. Efforts to change gender roles, for example, arouse intense controversy, as does support of alternative family forms and changes in sexual behavior. Alarmed at such onslaughts to their values, traditionalists fiercely defend historical family relationships and the gender roles they grew up with. The issue of socialist economic principles versus profit and private property is also at the center of controversy. Today's clash in values is so severe that the term *culture wars* has been coined to refer to it. Compared with the violence directed against the Mormons, however, today's reactions to such controversies are mild.

Values as Blinders

Just as values and their supporting beliefs paint a unique picture of reality, so they also form a view of what life *ought* to be like. Americans value individualism so highly, for example, that they tend to see everyone as free to pursue the goal of success. This value blinds them to the many circumstances that impede people's efforts. The dire consequences of family poverty, parents' low education, and dead-end jobs tend to drop from sight. Instead, Americans cling to the notion that everyone can make it—if they put out enough effort. And they "know" they are right, for every day, dangling before their eyes are enticing success stories—individuals who have succeeded despite huge handicaps.

"Ideal" Versus "Real" Culture

Many of the norms that surround cultural values are only partially followed. Differences always exist between a group's ideals and what its members actually do. Consequently, sociologists use the term **ideal culture** to refer to the values, norms, and goals that a group considers ideal, worth aspiring to. Success, for example, is part of ideal culture. Americans glorify academic progress, hard work, and the display of material goods as signs of individual achievement. What people actually do, however, usually falls short of the cultural

ideal culture the ideal values and norms of a people; the goals held out for them ideal. Compared with their abilities, for example, most people don't work as hard as they could or go as far as they could in school. Sociologists call the norms and values that people actually follow **real culture.**

Cultural Universals

With the amazing variety of human cultures around the world, are there any **cultural universals**—values, norms, or other cultural traits that are found everywhere?

To answer this question, anthropologist George Murdock (1945) combed through data that anthropologists had gathered on hundreds of groups around the world. He drew up a list of customs concerning courtship, marriage, funerals, games, laws, music, myths, incest taboos, and even toilet training. He found that although such activities are present in all cultures, *the specific customs differ from one group to another.* There is no universal form of the family, no universal way of disposing of the dead. Similarly, the games, rules, songs, stories, and toilet training differ from one culture to another. So do cooking and eating food, the topic of the Cultural Diversity box below.

CULTURAL DIVERSITY around the WORLD

You Are What You Eat? An Exploration in Cultural Relativity

A few pages back, you learned about ethnocentrism and cultural relativity. Here is a chance to test your ethnocentrism and ability to practice cultural relativity. You probably know that the French like to eat snails and that in some Asian cultures, chubby dogs and cats are considered a delicacy ("Ah, lightly browned with a little sauce!"). But did you know about this?

Marston Bates (1967), a zoologist, reports:

> I remember once, in the llanos of Colombia, sharing a dish of toasted ants at a remote farmhouse. . . . My host and I fell into conversation about the general question of what people eat or do not eat, and I remarked that in my country people eat the legs of frogs. The very thought of this filled my ant-eating friends with horror; it was as though I had mentioned some repulsive sex habit.

This custom in a part of China, though, may provide a better test of your ethnocentrism and cultural relativity. It is related by Maxine Kingston (1975), an anthropologist:

> "Do you know what people in China eat when they have the money?" my mother began. "They buy into a monkey feast. The eaters sit around a thick wood table with a hole in the middle. Boys bring in the monkey at the end of a pole. Its neck is in a collar at the end of the pole, and it is screaming. Its hands are tied behind it. They clamp the monkey into the table; the whole table fits like another collar around its neck. Using a surgeon's saw, the cooks cut a clean line in a circle at the top of its head. To loosen the bone, they tap with a tiny hammer and wedge here and there with a silver pick. Then an old woman reaches out her hand to the monkey's face and up to its scalp, where she tufts some hairs and lifts off the lid of the skull. The eaters spoon out the brains."

And then there is the experience of the production coordinator of this text, Dusty Friedman, who, after reading this box, said:

> When traveling in Sudan, I ate some interesting things that I wouldn't likely eat now that I'm back in our society. Raw baby camel's liver with chopped herbs was a delicacy. So was camel's milk cheese patties that had been cured in dry camel's dung.

For Your CONSIDERATION

1. What is your opinion about eating toasted ants? About eating fried frog legs? About eating raw monkey brains?
2. If you were reared in U.S. society, more than likely you think that eating frog legs is okay, eating ants is disgusting, and eating monkey brains is downright repugnant. How would you apply ethnocentrism and cultural relativism to these three customs?

Even incest is defined differently from group to group. For example, the Mundugumors of New Guinea extend the incest taboo so far that for each man, seven of every eight women are ineligible marriage partners (Mead 1935/1950). Other groups go in the opposite direction and allow some men to marry their own daughters (La Barre 1954). In certain circumstances, some groups *require* that brothers and sisters marry one another (Beals and Hoijer 1965). The Burundi of Africa even insist that, in order to remove a certain curse, a son must have sexual relations with his mother (Albert 1963). Such sexual relations are usually allowed only for special people (royalty) or in extraordinary situations (such as when a lion hunter faces a dangerous hunt), and no society permits generalized incest for its members.

In short, although there are universal human activities (speech, music, storytelling, marrying, disposing of the dead, preparing food, and so on), there is no universally accepted way of doing any of them. Humans have no biological imperative that results in one particular form of behavior throughout the world. As indicated in the following Thinking Critically section, a few sociologists do take the position that genes significantly influence human behavior, although almost all sociologists reject this view.

real culture the norms and values that people actually follow

cultural universal a value, norm, or other cultural trait that is found in every group

sociobiology a framework of thought that views human behavior as the result of natural selection and considers biological factors to be the fundamental cause of human behavior

THINKING Critically

Are We Prisoners of Our Genes? Sociobiology and Human Behavior

A controversial view of human behavior, called **sociobiology** (also known as neo-Darwinism), provides a sharp contrast to the perspective of this chapter, that human behavior is primarily due to culture. Sociobiologists (and their close cousins, evolutionary psychologists) believe that because of natural selection, the basic cause of human behavior is biology.

Charles Darwin (1859), who developed the idea of natural selection, pointed out that the genes of a species—the units that contain the individual's traits—are not distributed evenly among the offspring. The characteristics passed on to some members make it easier for them to survive their environment, increasing the likelihood that they will pass their genetic traits to the next generation. Over thousands of generations, the genetic traits that aid survival tend to become common in a species, while those that do not tend to disappear.

Natural selection explains not only the physical characteristics of animals, but also their behavior, for over countless generations, instincts emerged. Edward Wilson (1975), an insect specialist, claims that human behavior is also the result of natural selection. Human behavior, he said, is no different from the behavior of cats, dogs, rats, bees, or mosquitoes—it has been bred into *Homo sapiens* through evolutionary principles.

Wilson deliberately set out to create a storm of protest, and he succeeded. He went on to claim that religion, competition and cooperation, slavery and genocide, war and peace, envy and altruism—all can be explained by sociobiology. He provocatively added that because human behavior can be explained in terms of genetic programming, sociobiology will eventually absorb sociology—as well as anthropology and psychology.

Obviously, most sociologists find Wilson's position unacceptable. Not only is it a direct attack on their discipline, but also it bypasses the essence of what sociologists focus on: humans developing their own cultures, their own unique ways of life. Sociologists do not deny that biology underlies human behavior—at least not in the sense that it takes a highly developed brain to develop human culture and abstract thought, and that there would be no speech if humans had no tongue or larynx.

But most sociologists find ludicrous the claim that genetic programming causes human behavior (Howe et al. 1992). Pigs act like pigs because they don't have a cerebral cortex, and instincts control their behavior. So it is for spiders, elephants, and so on. But humans possess a self and have abstract thought. They discuss the reasons that underlie what they do. They develop purposes and goals. They immerse themselves in a world of symbols which allow them to consider, reflect, and make reasoned choices.

This controversy has turned into much more than simply an academic debate among scientists. Homosexuals, for example, have a personal interest in its outcome. If homosexuality is a lifestyle *choice*, then those who consider that lifestyle to be immoral will use this as a basis for excluding homosexuals from full social participation. If, however, homosexuality has a genetic basis, then choice as a reason for social exclusion is eliminated. Sociologist Peter Conrad (1997) expresses the dominant sociological position when he points out that not all homosexuals have Xq28, the so-called "gay gene," and some people who have this gene are not homosexual. This gene, then, does not determine behavior. Instead, we must look for *social* causes.

In short, sociobiologists and sociologists stand on opposite sides, the one looking at human behavior as determined by genetics, the other looking at human behavior as determined by social learning, by experiences in the human group. Sociologists point out that if humans were prisoners of their genes, we would not have developed such a variety of fascinating ways of life around the world—we would live in a monoculture of some sort.

Technology in the Global Village

The New Technology

The gestures, language, values, folkways, and mores that we have discussed—all are part of symbolic or nonmaterial culture. Culture, as you recall, also has a material aspect: a group's *things,* from its houses to its toys. Central to a group's material culture is its technology. In its simplest sense, **technology** can be equated with tools. In its broader sense, technology also includes the skills or procedures necessary to make and use those tools.

We can use the term **new technology** to refer to the emerging technologies that have a significant impact on social life. People develop minor technologies all the time. Most are slight modifications of existing technologies. Occasionally, however, they develop technologies that make a major impact on human life. It is primarily to these that the term *new technology* refers. For people 500 years ago, the new technology was the printing press. For us, the new technology consists of computers, satellites, and the electronic media.

The sociological significance of technology goes far beyond the tool itself. *Technology sets the framework for a group's nonmaterial culture.* If a group's technology changes, so do people's ways of thinking and how they relate to one another. An example is gender relations. Through the centuries and throughout the world, it has been the custom (the nonmaterial culture of a group) for men to dominate women. Today, with instantaneous communications (the material culture), this custom has become much more difficult to maintain. For example, when women from many nations gathered in Beijing for a U.N. conference in 1995, satellites instantly transmitted their grievances around the globe. Such communications both convey and create discontent, as well as a feeling of sisterhood, motivating women to agitate for social change.

In today's world, the long-accepted idea that it is proper to withhold rights on the basis of someone's sex can no longer hold. What is usually invisible in this revolutionary change is the role of the new technology, which joins the world's nations into a global communication network.

The adoption of new forms of communication by people who not long ago were cut off from events in the rest of the world is bound to change their nonmaterial culture. *How do you think this man's thinking and view of the world is changing?*

Cultural Lag and Cultural Change

About three generations ago, sociologist William Ogburn (1922/1938), a functional analyst, coined the term **cultural lag.** By this, Ogburn meant that not all parts of a culture change at the same pace. When some part of a culture changes, other parts lag behind.

Ogburn pointed out that *a group's material culture usually changes first, with the nonmaterial culture lagging behind,* playing a game of catch up. For example, when we get sick, we could type our symptoms into a computer and get a printout of our diagnosis and a recommended course of treatment. In fact, in some tests, computers outperform physicians (Waldholz 1991). Yet our customs have not caught up with our technology, and we continue to visit the doctor's office.

Sometimes nonmaterial culture never does catch up. Instead, we rigorously hold on to some outmoded form—one that once was needed, but was long ago bypassed by new technology. A striking example is our nine-month school year. Have you ever wondered why it is nine months long, and why we take summers off? For most of us, this is "just the way it's always been," and we've never questioned it. But there is more to this custom than meets the eye, for it is an example of cultural lag.

"COOL! A KEYBOARD THAT WRITES WITHOUT A PRINTER."

Technological advances are now so rapid that the technology of one generation is practically unrecognizable by the next generation.

technology in its narrow sense, tools; its broader sense includes the skills or procedures necessary to make and use those tools

new technology the emerging technologies of an era that have a significant impact on social life

cultural lag Ogburn's term for human behavior lagging behind technological innovations

cultural diffusion the spread of cultural characteristics from one group to another

In the late 1800s, when universal schooling came about, the school year matched the technology of the time, which was labor-intensive. For survival, parents needed their children's help at the crucial times of planting and harvesting. Although the invention of highly productive farm machinery eliminated the need for the school year to be so short, generations later we still live with this cultural lag.

Technology and Cultural Leveling

For most of human history, communication was limited and travel slow. Consequently, in their relative isolation, human groups developed highly distinctive ways of life as they responded to the particular situations they faced. The unique characteristics they developed that distinguished one culture from another tended to change little over time. The Tasmanians, who lived on a remote island off the coast of Australia, provide an extreme example. For thousands of years, they had no contact with other people. They were so isolated that they did not even know how to make clothing or fire (Edgerton 1992).

Except in such rare instances, humans always had *some* contact with other groups. During these contacts, people learned from one another, adopting some part of the other's way of life. In this process, called **cultural diffusion,** groups are most open to changes in their technology or material culture. They usually are eager, for example, to adopt superior weapons and tools. In remote jungles in South America one can find metal cooking pots, steel axes, and even bits of clothing spun in mills in South Carolina. Although the direction of cultural diffusion today is primarily from the West to other parts of the world, cultural diffusion is not a one-way street—as bagels, woks, hammocks, and sushi bars in the United States attest.

Shown here is a Masai Barbie Doll. Mattel Toys, the U.S. manufacturer, has modified Barbie to match Masai (Kenya) culture by dressing her in a traditional "shuka" dress, beads, shawl, headdress, and anklets. As objects diffuse from one culture to another, they are modified to meet the tastes of the adoptive culture. In this instance, the modification has been done intentionally as part of the globalization of capitalism. Now that Barbie is a Masai, can a Masai Ken be far behind?

With today's sophisticated technology in travel and communications, cultural diffusion is occurring rapidly. Air travel has made it possible to journey around the globe in a matter of hours. In the not-so-distant past, a trip from the United States to Africa was so unusual that only a few hardy people made it, and newspapers would herald their feat. Today, hundreds of thousands make the trip each year.

The changes in communication are no less vast. Communication used to be limited to face-to-face speech, to written messages that were passed from hand to hand, and to visual signals such as smoke or light that was reflected from mirrors. Despite newspapers, people in some parts of the United States did not hear that the Civil War had ended until weeks and even months after it was over. Today's electronic communications transmit messages across the globe in a matter of

cultural leveling the process by which cultures become similar to one another; especially refers to the process by which U.S. culture is being exported and diffused into other nations

seconds, and we learn almost instantaneously what is happening on the other side of the world. During Gulf War II, reporters were "embedded" with U.S. soldiers, and for the first time in history, they transmitted live video reports of battles and deaths as they occurred.

Travel and communication unite us to such an extent that there is almost no "other side of the world" anymore. One result is **cultural leveling,** a process in which cultures become similar to one another. The globalization of capitalism is bringing not only technology but also Western culture to the rest of the world. Japan, for example, has adopted not only capitalism but also Western forms of dress and music. These changes, which have been "superimposed" on Japanese culture, have turned Japan into a blend of Western and Eastern cultures.

Cultural leveling is occurring rapidly around the world, as is apparent to any traveler. The Golden Arches of McDonald's welcome today's visitors to Tokyo, Paris, London, Madrid, Moscow, Hong Kong, and Beijing. In Mexico, the most popular piñatas are no longer donkeys but, rather, Mickey Mouse and Fred Flintstone (Beckett 1996). In a jungle village in India—no electricity, no running water, and so remote that the only entrance was by a footpath—I saw a young man sporting a cap with the Nike emblem.

Although the bridging of geography and culture by electronic signals and the exportation of Western icons do not in and of themselves mark the end of traditional cultures, the inevitable result is some degree of *cultural leveling,* some blander, less distinctive way of life—U.S. culture with French, Japanese, and Brazilian accents, so to speak. Although the "cultural accent" remains, something vital is lost forever.

SUMMARY and REVIEW

What Is Culture?

All human groups possess **culture**—language, beliefs, values, norms, and material objects that are passed from one generation to the next. **Material culture** consists of objects (art, buildings, clothing, tools). **Nonmaterial** (or **symbolic**) **culture** is a group's ways of thinking and patterns of behavior. **Ideal culture** is a group's ideal values, norms, and goals. **Real culture** is their actual behavior, which often falls short of their cultural ideals. Pp. 36–37.

What are cultural relativism and ethnocentrism?

People are naturally **ethnocentric;** that is, they use their own culture as a yardstick for judging the ways of others. In contrast, those who embrace **cultural relativism** try to understand other cultures on those cultures' own terms. Pp. 37–40.

Components of Symbolic Culture

What are the components of nonmaterial culture?

The central component is **symbols,** anything to which people attach meaning and that they use to communicate with others. Universally, the symbols of nonmaterial culture are **gestures, language, values, norms, sanctions, folkways,** and **mores.** Pp. 40–48.

Why is language so significant to culture?

Language allows human experience to be goal-directed, cooperative, and cumulative. It also lets humans move beyond the present and share a past, future, and other common perspectives. According to the **Sapir-Whorf hypothesis,** language even shapes our thoughts and perceptions. Pp. 42–46.

How do values, norms, sanctions, folkways, and mores reflect culture?

All groups have **values,** standards by which they define what is desirable or undesirable, and **norms,** rules or expectations about behavior. Groups use **positive sanctions** to show approval of those who follow their norms, and **negative sanctions** to show disapproval of those who do not. Norms that are not strictly enforced are called **folkways,** while **mores** are norms to which groups demand conformity because they reflect core values. Pp. 46–48.

Many Cultural Worlds: Subcultures and Countercultures

How do subcultures and countercultures differ?

A **subculture** is a group whose values and related behaviors distinguish its members from the general culture. A **counterculture** holds some values that stand in opposition to those of the dominant culture. Pp. 48–49.

Values in U.S. Society

What are the core U.S. values?

Although the United States is a **pluralistic society,** made up of many groups, each with its own set of values, certain values dominate: achievement and success, individualism, activity and work, efficiency and practicality, science and technology, progress, material comfort, equality, freedom, democracy, humanitarianism, racism and group superiority, education, religiosity, and romantic love. Some values cluster together (**value clusters**) to form a larger whole. **Value contradictions** (such as equality and racism) indicate areas of social tension, which are likely points of social change. Leisure, self-fulfillment, physical fitness, youthfulness, and concern for the environment are emerging core values. Core values do not change without opposition. Pp. 49–56.

Cultural Universals

Do cultural universals exist?

Cultural universals are values, norms, or other cultural traits that are found in all cultures. Although all human groups have customs concerning cooking, funerals, weddings, and so on, because the forms these customs take vary from one culture to another, there are no cultural universals. Pp. 56–57.

Technology in the Global Village

How is technology changing culture?

William Ogburn coined the term **cultural lag** to describe how a group's nonmaterial culture lags behind its changing technology. With today's technological advances in travel and communications, **cultural diffusion** is occurring rapidly. This leads to **cultural leveling,** whereby many groups are adopting Western culture in place of their own customs. Much of the richness of the world's diverse cultures is being lost in the process. Pp. 58–60.

Where can I read more on this topic?

Suggested Readings for this chapter are at the back of this book.

THINKING Critically ABOUT CHAPTER 2

1. Do you favor ethnocentrism or cultural relativism? Explain your position.
2. Do you think that the language change in Miami, Florida, (discussed on page 45) is an indicator of the future of the United States? Why or why not?
3. Are you a member of any subcultures? Which one(s)? Why do you think that your group is a subculture? What is the relationship of your group to the mainstream culture?

ADDITIONAL RESOURCES for This Chapter

www.ablongman.com/henslin7e

- *Content Select* Research Database for Sociology, with suggested key terms and annotated references
- Link to 2000 Census, with activities
- Flashcards of key terms and concepts
- Practice Tests
- Weblinks
- Interactive Maps

Chapter 3

Socialization

Jacob Lawrence, *Men Exist for the Sake of One Another, Teach Them Then or Bear With Them*, 1958

The old man was horrified when he found out. Life never had been good since his daughter lost her hearing when she was just 2 years old. She couldn't even talk—just fluttered her hands around trying to tell him things. Over the years, he had gotten used to that. But now . . . he shuddered at the thought of her being pregnant. No one would be willing to marry her; he knew that. And the neighbors, their tongues would never stop wagging. Everywhere he went, he could hear people talking behind his back.

If only his wife were still alive, maybe she could come up with something. What should he do? He couldn't just kick his daughter out into the street.

After the baby was born, the old man tried to shake his feelings, but they wouldn't let loose. Isabelle was a pretty name, but every time he looked at the baby he felt sick to his stomach.

He hated doing it, but there was no way out. His daughter and her baby would have to live in the attic.

Unfortunately, this is a true story. Isabelle was discovered in Ohio in 1938 when she was about 6-1/2 years old, living in a dark room with her deaf-mute mother. Isabelle couldn't talk, but she did use gestures to communicate with her mother. An inadequate diet and lack of sunshine had given Isabelle a disease called rickets. Her legs

> were so bowed that as she stood erect the soles of her shoes came nearly flat together, and she got about with a skittering gait. Her behavior toward strangers, especially men, was almost that of *a wild animal,* manifesting much fear and hostility. In lieu of speech she made only a strange croaking sound. (Davis 1940/2003:138–139)

Her behavior toward strangers, especially men, *was almost that of a wild animal,* manifesting much fear and hostility.

When the newspapers reported this case, sociologist Kingsley Davis decided to find out what happened to Isabelle after her discovery. We'll come back to that later, but first let's use the case of Isabelle to gain some insight into human nature.

Chapter Outline

What Is Human Nature?

For centuries, people have been intrigued with the question of what is human about human nature. How much of people's characteristics comes from "nature" (heredity) and how much from "nurture" (the **social environment,** contact with others)? One way to answer this question is to study identical twins who have been reared apart, such as those discussed in the Down-to-Earth Sociology box below. Another way is to examine people who have been reared without human contact. Let's consider such children.

Feral Children

Over the centuries, the discovery of **feral** (wild) **children** has been reported from time to time. Supposedly, these children were abandoned or lost by their parents at a very early

DOWN-TO-EARTH SOCIOLOGY

Heredity or Environment? The Case of Oskar and Jack, Identical Twins

IDENTICAL TWINS SHARE EXACT GENETIC heredity. One fertilized egg divides to produce two embryos. If heredity determines personality—or attitudes, temperament, skills, and intelligence—then identical twins should be identical not only in their looks but also in these characteristics.

The fascinating case of Jack and Oskar helps us unravel this mystery. From their experience, we can see the far-reaching effects of the environment—how social experiences override biology.

Jack Yufe and Oskar Stohr are identical twins born in 1932 to a Jewish father and a Catholic mother. They were separated as babies after their parents divorced. Oskar was reared in Czechoslovakia by his mother's mother, who was a strict Catholic. When Oskar was a toddler, Hitler annexed this area of Czechoslovakia, and Oskar learned to love Hitler and to hate Jews. He joined the Hitler Youth (a sort of Boy Scout organization, except that this one was designed to instill the "virtues" of patriotism, loyalty, obedience—and hatred).

Jack's upbringing was in almost total contrast to Oskar's. Reared in Trinidad by his father, he learned loyalty to Jews and hatred of Hitler and the Nazis. After the war, Jack and his father moved to Israel. At the age of 17, Jack joined a kibbutz, and later, served in the Israeli army.

In 1954, the two brothers met. It was a short meeting, and Jack had been warned not to tell Oskar that they were Jews. Twenty-five years later, in 1979, when

The question of the relative influence of heredity and the environment on human behavior has fascinated and plagued researchers. Identical twins reared apart provide an opportunity to examine this relationship. However, almost all identical twins, including these girls, are reared together, frustrating efforts to separate heredity and environment.

they were 47 years old, social scientists at the University of Minnesota brought them together again. These researchers figured that because Jack and Oskar had the same genes, any differences they showed would have to be due to the environment—to their different social experiences.

Not only did Oskar and Jack hold different attitudes toward the war, Hitler, and Jews, but also their basic orientations to life were different. In their politics, Oskar was conservative, while Jack was more liberal. Oskar enjoyed leisure, while Jack was a workaholic. And, as you can predict, Jack was very proud of being a Jew. Oskar, who by this time knew that he was a Jew, wouldn't even mention it.

That would seem to settle the matter. But there was another side. The researchers also found that Oskar and Jack both excelled at sports as children, but had difficulty with math. They also had the same rate of speech, and both liked sweet liqueur and spicy foods. Strangely, both flushed the toilet both before and after using it and enjoyed startling people by sneezing in crowded elevators.

For Your CONSIDERATION

Heredity or environment? How much influence does each one have? The question is not yet settled, but at this point it seems fair to conclude that the *limits* of certain physical and mental abilities are established by heredity (such as ability at sports and mathematics), while such basic orientations to life as attitudes are the result of the environment. We can put it this way: For some parts of life, the blueprint is drawn by heredity; but even here the environment can redraw those lines. For other parts, the individual is a blank slate, and it is up to the environment to determine what is written on that slate.

Sources: Based on Begley 1979, Chen 1979, Wright 1995, Stewart 2000.

age and then raised by animals. (See the photo on this page.) In the 1700s, a feral child known as "the wild boy of Aveyron" was studied by the scientists of his day (Itard 1962). This boy, who was found in the forests of France in 1798, walked on all fours and pounced on small animals, devouring them uncooked. He could not speak, and he gave no indication of feeling the cold. Other reports of feral children have claimed that on discovery, these children acted like wild animals: They could not speak; they bit, scratched, growled, and walked on all fours; they drank by lapping water, ate grass, tore ravenously at meat, and showed an insensitivity to pain and cold (Malson 1972).

Most social scientists today dismiss the significance of feral children, taking the position that children cannot be raised by animals and that children found in the woods were reared by their parents as infants but then abandoned, probably because they were retarded. But what if this were not the case? Could it be that, if we were untouched by society, we would all by nature be like feral children?

One of the reasons I went to Cambodia was to interview a feral child—the boy shown here—who supposedly had been raised by monkeys. When I arrived at the remote location where the boy was living, I was disappointed to find that the story was only partially true. During its reign of terror, the Khmer Rouge had shot and killed the boy's parents, leaving him, at about the age of two, abandoned on an island. Some months later, villagers found him in the care of monkeys. Not quite a feral child–but the closest I'll ever come to one.

Isolated Children

Cases like Isabelle, in our opening vignette, surface from time to time. What can they tell us about human nature? We can first conclude that humans have no natural language, for isolated children like Isabelle are unable to speak.

But maybe Isabelle was mentally impaired, as most scientists claim feral children are, and could not progress through the usual stages of development. When given an intelligence test, she scored practically zero. But after a few months of intensive language training, Isabelle was able to speak in short sentences. In about a year, she could write a few words, do simple addition, and retell stories after hearing them. Seven months later, she had a vocabulary of almost 2,000 words. In just two years, Isabelle reached the intellectual level that is normal for her age. She then went on to school, where she was "bright, cheerful, energetic . . . and participated in all school activities as normally as other children" (Davis 1940/2003:139).

As discussed in the previous chapter, language is the key to human development. Without language, people have no mechanism for developing thought. Unlike animals, humans have no instincts that take the place of language. If an individual lacks language, he or she lives in an isolated world, a world of internal silence, without shared ideas, without connections to others.

Without language, there can be no culture—no shared way of life—and culture is the key to what people become. Each of us possesses a biological heritage, but this heritage does not determine specific behaviors, attitudes, or values. It is our culture that superimposes the specifics of what we become onto our biological heritage.

Institutionalized Children

Other than language, what else is required for a child to develop into what we consider a healthy, balanced, intelligent human being? We find part of the answer in an intriguing experiment from the 1930s. Back then, life was shorter, and orphanages dotted the United States. Children reared in orphanages often had difficulty establishing close bonds with others—and they tended to have lower IQs. "Common sense" (which we noted in Chapter 1 is unreliable) told everyone that the cause of mental retardation is biological ("They're just born that way"). Two psychologists, H. M. Skeels and H. B. Dye (1939), however, began to suspect another cause. For background on their experiment, Skeels (1966) provides this account of a "good" orphanage in Iowa during the 1930s, where he and Dye were consultants:

> Until about six months, they were cared for in the infant nursery. The babies were kept in standard hospital cribs that often had protective sheeting on the sides, thus effectively limiting visual stimulation; no toys or other objects were hung in the infants' line of vision. Human interactions were limited to busy nurses who, with the speed born of practice and necessity, changed diapers or bedding, bathed and medicated the infants, and fed them efficiently with propped bottles.

social environment the entire human environment, including direct contact with others

feral children children assumed to have been raised by animals, in the wilderness, isolated from other humans

The treatment given these orphaned children in Romania will make it difficult for them to develop into fully functioning adults. If they survive, they will carry scars into adulthood. As explained in the text, it is also likely that their abuse has affected their ability to reason.

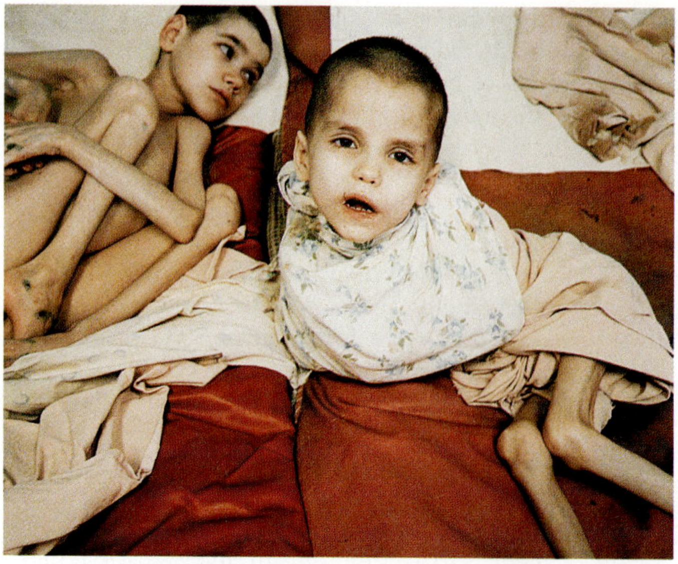

Perhaps, thought Skeels and Dye, the absence of stimulating social interaction was the problem, not some biological incapacity on the part of the children. To test their controversial idea, they selected thirteen infants whose mental retardation was so obvious that no one wanted to adopt them. They placed them in an institution for the mentally retarded. Each infant, then about 19 months old, was assigned to a separate ward of women ranging in mental age from 5 to 12 and in chronological age from 18 to 50. The women were pleased with this arrangement. They not only did a good job taking care of the infants' basic physical needs—diapering, feeding, and so on—but also they loved to play with the children, to cuddle them, and to shower them with attention. They even competed to see which ward would have "its baby" walking or talking first. Each child had one woman who became

> particularly attached to him [or her] and figuratively "adopted" him [or her]. As a consequence, an intense one-to-one adult-child relationship developed, which was supplemented by the less intense but frequent interactions with the other adults in the environment. Each child had some one person with whom he [or she] was identified and who was particularly interested in him [or her] and his [or her] achievements. (Skeels 1966)

The researchers left a control group of twelve infants at the orphanage. These infants were also retarded but were higher in intelligence than the other thirteen. They received the usual care. Two and a half years later, Skeels and Dye tested all the children's intelligence. Their findings were startling: Those assigned to the retarded women had gained an average of 28 IQ points while those who remained in the orphanage had lost 30 points.

What happened after these children were grown? Did these initial differences matter? Twenty-one years later, Skeels and Dye did a follow-up study. Those in the control group who had remained in the orphanage had, on average, less than a third-grade education. Four still lived in state institutions, while the others held low-level jobs. Only two had married. In contrast, the average level of education for the thirteen individuals in the experimental group was twelve grades (about normal for that period). Five had completed one or more years of college. One had even gone to graduate school. Eleven had married. All thirteen were self-supporting or were homemakers (Skeels 1966). Apparently, then, one characteristic we take for granted as being a basic "human" trait—high intelligence—depends on early, close relations with other humans.

Let's consider one other case, the story of Genie:

> In 1970, California authorities found Genie, a 13-year-old girl who had been locked in a small room and tied to a chair since she was 20 months old. Apparently

her father (70 years old when Genie was discovered) hated children, and probably had caused the death of two of Genie's siblings. Her 50-year-old mother was partially blind and frightened of her husband. Genie could not speak, did not know how to chew, was unable to stand upright, and could not straighten her hands and legs. On intelligence tests, she scored at the level of a 1-year-old. After intensive training, Genie learned to walk and use simple sentences (although they were garbled). As she grew up, her language remained primitive, she took anyone's property if it appealed to her, and she went to the bathroom wherever she wanted. At the age of 21, Genie went to live in a home for adults who cannot live alone. (Pines 1981)

From Genie's pathetic story, we can conclude that not only intelligence but also the ability to establish close bonds with others depends on early interaction. In addition, apparently there is a period prior to age 13 in which language and human bonding must occur for humans to develop high intelligence and the ability to be sociable and follow social norms.

Deprived Animals

Finally, let's consider animals that have been deprived of normal interaction. In a series of experiments with rhesus monkeys, psychologists Harry and Margaret Harlow demonstrated the importance of early learning. The Harlows (1962) raised baby monkeys in isolation. They gave each monkey two artificial mothers, shown in the photo on this page. One "mother" was only a wire frame with a wooden head, but it did have a nipple from which the baby could nurse. The frame of the other "mother," which had no bottle, was covered with soft terrycloth. To obtain food, the baby monkeys nursed at the wire frame.

When the Harlows (1965) frightened the babies with a large mechanical bear or dog, the babies did not run to the wire frame "mother." Instead, they would cling pathetically to their terrycloth "mother." The Harlows concluded that infant-mother bonding is due not to feeding but, rather, to what they termed "intimate physical contact." To most of us, this phrase means cuddling.

The monkeys raised in isolation were never able to adjust to monkey life. Placed with other monkeys when they were grown, they didn't know how to participate in "monkey interaction"—to play and to engage in pretend fights—and the other monkeys rejected them. Neither did they know how to have sexual intercourse, despite futile attempts to do so. The experimenters designed a special device, which allowed some females to become pregnant. After giving birth, however, these monkeys were "ineffective, inadequate, and brutal mothers . . . [who] . . . struck their babies, kicked them, or crushed the babies against the cage floor."

In one of their many experiments, the Harlows isolated baby monkeys for different lengths of time. They found that when monkeys were isolated for short periods (about three months), they were able to overcome the effects of their isolation. Those isolated for six months or more, however, were unable to adjust to normal monkey life. As mentioned, they could not play or engage in pretend fights, and the other monkeys rejected them. In other words, the longer the isolation, the more difficult it is to overcome. In addition, a critical learning stage may exist: If that stage is missed, it may be impossible to compensate for what has been lost. That may have been the case with Genie.

Because humans are not monkeys, we must be careful about extrapolating from animal studies to human behavior. The Harlow experiments, however, support what we know about children who are reared in isolation.

Like humans, monkeys need interaction to thrive. Those raised in isolation are unable to interact satisfactorily with others. In this photograph, we see one of the monkeys described in the text. Purposefully frightened by the experimenter, the monkey has taken refuge in the soft terrycloth draped over an artificial "mother."

IN SUM

Society Makes Us Human

Apparently, babies do not develop "naturally" into human adults. Although their bodies grow, if children are reared in isolation, they become little more than big animals. Without the concepts that language provides, they can't experience or even grasp relations between people (the "connections" we call brother, sister, parent, friend, teacher, and so on). And without warm, friendly interaction, they aren't "friendly" in the accepted sense of the term; nor do they cooperate with others. In short, it is through human contact that people learn to be members of the human community. This process by which we learn the ways of society (or of particular groups), called **socialization,** is what sociologists have in mind when they say "Society makes us human."

Socialization into the Self and Mind

At birth, we have no idea that we are separate beings. We don't even know that we are a he or she. How do we develop our ability to reason? Our personality? Our morality? Our emotions? How do we develop a **self,** the picture we have of how others see us, our image of who we are? Let's see how this occurs.

socialization the process by which people learn the characteristics of their group—the knowledge, skills, attitudes, values, and actions thought appropriate for them

self the unique human capacity of being able to see ourselves "from the outside"; the view we internalize of how others see us

looking-glass self a term coined by Charles Horton Cooley to refer to the process by which our self develops through internalizing others' reactions to us

taking the role of the other putting oneself in someone else's shoes; understanding how someone else feels and thinks and thus anticipating how that person will act

significant other an individual who significantly influences someone else's life

generalized other the norms, values, attitudes, and expectations of people "in general"; the child's ability to take the role of the generalized other is a significant step in the development of a self

Cooley and the Looking-Glass Self

Back in the 1800s, Charles Horton Cooley (1864–1929), a symbolic interactionist who taught at the University of Michigan, concluded that this unique aspect of "humanness" called the self is socially created. He said that *our sense of self develops from interaction with others.* Cooley (1902) coined the term **looking-glass self** to describe the process by which our sense of self develops. He summarized this idea in the following couplet:

> Each to each a looking-glass
> Reflects the other that doth pass.

The looking-glass self contains three elements:

1. *We imagine how we appear to those around us.* For example, we may think that others perceive us as witty or dull.
2. *We interpret others' reactions.* We come to conclusions about how others evaluate us. Do they like us for being witty? Do they dislike us for being dull?
3. *We develop a self-concept.* Based on our interpretations of how others react to us, we develop feelings and ideas about ourselves. A favorable reflection in this *social mirror* leads to a positive self-concept, a negative reflection to a negative self-concept.

Note that the development of the self does *not* depend on accurate evaluations. Even if we grossly misinterpret how others think about us, those misjudgments become part of our self-concept. Note also that *although the self-concept begins in childhood, its development is an ongoing, lifelong process.* The three steps of the looking-glass self are a part of our everyday lives: As we monitor how others react to us, we continually modify the self. The self, then, is never a finished product—it is always in process, even into old age.

Mead and Role Taking

Another symbolic interactionist, George Herbert Mead (1863–1931), who taught at the University of Chicago, added that play is crucial to the development of a self. In play, children learn to **take the role of the other,** that is, to put themselves in someone else's shoes—to understand how someone else feels and thinks and to anticipate how that person will act.

Only gradually do children attain this ability (Mead 1934; Coser 1977). Psychologist John Flavel (1968) asked 8- and 14-year-olds to explain a board game to some children who were blindfolded and to others who were not. The 14-year-olds gave more detailed instructions to those who were blindfolded, but the 8-year-olds gave the same instructions to everyone. The younger children could not yet take the role of the other, while the older children could.

Mead analyzed taking the role of the other *as an essential part of learning to be a full-fledged member of society. At first, we are able to take the role only of* significant others, *as this child is doing. Later we develop the capacity to take the role of* the generalized other, *which is essential not only for extended cooperation but also for the control of antisocial desires.*

As they develop this ability, at first children are able to take only the role of **significant others,** individuals who significantly influence their lives, such as parents or siblings. By assuming their roles during play, such as dressing up in their parents' clothing, children cultivate the ability to put themselves in the place of significant others.

As the self gradually develops, children internalize the expectations of more and more people. The ability to take on roles eventually extends to being able to take the role of "the group as a whole." Mead used the term **generalized other** to refer to our perception of how people in general think of us.

Taking the role of others is essential if we are to become cooperative members of human groups—whether they be our family, friends, or co-workers. This ability allows us to modify our behavior by anticipating how others will react—something Genie never learned.

Learning to take the role of the other entails three stages (see Figure 3.1):

1. *Imitation.* Children under 3 can only mimic others. They do not yet have a sense of self separate from others, and they can only imitate people's gestures and words. (This stage is actually not role taking, but it prepares the child for it.)
2. *Play.* During the second stage, from the age of about 3 to 6, children pretend to take the roles of specific people. They might pretend that they are a firefighter, a wrestler, the Lone Ranger, Supergirl, Xena, Spiderman, and so on. They also like costumes at this stage and enjoy dressing up in their parents' clothing, or tying a towel around their neck to "become" Superman or Wonder Woman.
3. *Games.* This third stage, organized play, or team games, coincides roughly with the early school years. The significance for the self is that to play these games the individual must be able to take multiple roles. One of Mead's favorite examples was that of a baseball game, in which each player must be able to take the role of all the other players. To play baseball, the child not only must know his or her own role but also must be able to anticipate who will do what when the ball is hit or thrown.

Figure 3.1 How We Learn to Take the Role of the Other: Mead's Three Stages

Stage 1: Imitation
Children under age 3
No sense of self
Imitate others

Stage 2: Play
Ages 3 to 6
Play "pretend" others
(Xena, Spiderman, etc.)

Stage 3: Games
After about age 6 or 7
Team games
("organized play")
Learn to take multiple roles

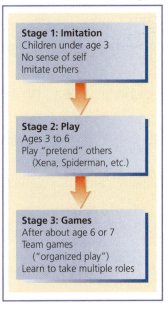

To help his students understand the term generalized other, *Mead used baseball as an illustration. Why are team sports and organized games such excellent examples to use in explaining this concept?*

Mead also said there were two parts of the self, the "I" and the "me." The "*I*" is *the self as subject,* the active, spontaneous, creative part of the self. In contrast, the "*me*" is *the self as object.* It is made up of attitudes we internalize from our interactions with others. Mead chose these pronouns because in English "I" is the active agent, as in "I shoved him," while "me" is the object of action, as in "He shoved me." Mead stressed that we are not passive in the socialization process. We are not like robots, passively absorbing the responses of others. Rather, our "I" is active. It evaluates the reactions of others and organizes them into a unified whole. Mead added that the "I" even monitors the "me," fine-tuning our actions to help us better match what others expect of us.

Mead also drew a conclusion that some find startling: *Not only the self but also the human mind is a social product.* Mead stressed that we cannot think without symbols. But where do these symbols come from? Only from society, which gives us our symbols by giving us language. If society did not provide the symbols, we would not be able to think, and thus would not possess what we call the mind. Mind, then, like language, is a product of society.

Piaget and the Development of Reasoning

An essential part of being human is the ability to reason. How do we learn this skill?

This question intrigued Jean Piaget (1896–1980), a Swiss psychologist who noticed that young children give similar wrong answers when they take intelligence tests. This might mean, he thought, that young children follow some sort of incorrect rule to figure out their answers. Perhaps children go through a natural process as they learn how to reason.

To find out, Piaget set up a laboratory where he could give children of different ages problems to solve (Piaget 1950, 1954; Flavel et al. 2002). After years of research, Piaget concluded that children go through four stages as they develop their ability to reason. (If you substitute "reasoning skills" for the term *operational* in the following explanations, Piaget's findings will be easier to understand.)

1. **The sensorimotor stage** (from birth to about age 2) During this stage, the infant's understanding is limited to direct contact with the environment—sucking, touching, listening, looking. Infants do not think in any sense that we understand. During the first part of this stage, they do not even know that their bodies are separate from the environment. Indeed, they have yet to discover that they have toes. Neither can infants recognize cause and effect. That is, they do not know that their actions cause something to happen.

2. **The preoperational stage** (from about age 2 to age 7) During this stage, children *develop the ability to use symbols.* However, they do not yet understand common concepts such as size, speed, or causation. Although they can count, they do not really understand what numbers mean. Nor do they yet have the ability to take the role of the other. Piaget asked preoperational children to describe a clay model of a mountain range. They did just fine. But when he asked them to describe how the mountain range looked from the perspective of a child who was sitting across from them, they couldn't do it. They could only repeat what they saw from their view.

3. **The concrete operational stage** (from the age of about 7 to 12) Although reasoning abilities are more developed, they remain *concrete.* Children can now understand numbers, causation, and speed, and they are able to take the role of the other and to participate in team games. Without concrete examples, however, they are unable to talk about concepts such as truth, honesty, or justice. They can explain why Jane's answer was a lie, but they cannot describe what truth itself is.

4. **The formal operational stage** (after the age of about 12) Children are now capable of abstract thinking. They can talk about concepts, come to conclusions based on general principles, and use rules to solve abstract problems. During this stage, children are likely to become young philosophers (Kagan 1984). If shown a photo of a slave, for example, a child at the concrete operational stage might have said, "That's wrong!" However, a child at the formal operational stage is more likely to ask, "If our county was founded on equality, how could people have owned slaves?"

Global Aspects of the Self and Reasoning

Cooley's conclusions about the looking-glass self appear to be universal. So do Mead's conclusions about role taking and the mind as a social product, although researchers are finding that the self may develop earlier than Mead indicated. The stages of reasoning that Piaget identified are also probably universal, but researchers have found that the ages at which individuals enter the stages differ from one person to another, and that the stages are not as distinct from one another as Piaget concluded (Flavel et al. 2002). Even during the sensorimotor stage, children show early signs of reasoning, which may indicate an innate ability that is wired into the brain. Although Piaget's theory is being refined, his contribution remains: *A basic structure underlies the way we develop reasoning, and children all over the world begin with the concrete and move to the abstract.*

Interestingly, some people seem to get stuck in the concreteness of the third stage and never reach the fourth stage of abstract thinking (Kohlberg and Gilligan 1971; Case and Okamoto 1996). College, for example, nurtures the fourth stage, and most people without this experience apparently have less ability for abstract thought. Social experiences, then, can modify these stages. Also, there is much that we don't yet know about how culture influences the way we think, a topic explored in the Cultural Diversity box below.

CULTURAL DIVERSITY

around the WORLD

The World

Do You See What I See?: Differences in Eastern and Western Perception and Thinking

Which two of these items go together: a panda, a monkey, and a banana? Please answer before you read further.

You probably said the panda and the monkey. Both are animals, while the banana is a fruit. This is logical.

At least this is the logic of Westerners, and it is difficult for us to see how the answer could be anything else. Someone from Japan, however, is likely to reply that the monkey and the banana go together.

Why? Whereas Westerners typically see categories (animals and fruit), Asians typically see relationships (monkeys eat bananas).

In one study, Japanese and U.S. students were shown a picture of an aquarium that contained one big, fast-moving fish and several smaller fish, along with plants, a rock, and bubbles. Later, when the students were asked what they saw, the Japanese students were 60 percent more likely to remember background elements. They also referred more to relationships, such as the "the little pink fish was in front of the blue rock."

The students were also shown 96 objects and asked which of them had been in the picture. The Japanese students did much better at remembering when the object was shown in its original surroundings. Not so for the U.S. students. They had never noticed the background.

Westerners pay more attention to the focal object, in this case the fish, while Asians are more attuned to the overall surroundings. The implications of this difference run deep: Easterners attribute less causation to actors and more to context, while Westerners minimize the context and place greater emphasis on individual actors.

Differences in how Westerners and Easterners perceive and think are just being uncovered. We know practically nothing about how these differences originate. *Because these initial findings indicate deep, culturally-based, fundamental differences in perception and thinkng,* this should prove to be a fascinating area of research.

For Your CONSIDERATION

In our global village, differences in perception and thinking can be crucial. Consider a crisis between the United States and North Korea. How might Easterners and Westerners see the matter differently? How might they attribute cause differently and, without knowing it, "talk past one another"?

Source: Based on Nisbett 2003.

Learning Personality, Morality, and Emotions

Vital for what we become as humans are our personality, morality, and emotions. Let's look at how we learn these essential aspects of our being.

Freud and the Development of Personality

Along with the development of our mind and the self comes the development of our personality. A theory of the origin of personality that has had a major impact on Western thought was developed by Sigmund Freud (1856–1939). Freud was a physician in Vienna in the early 1900s who founded *psychoanalysis,* a technique for treating emotional problems through long-term, intensive exploration of the subconscious mind. Let's look at his theory.

Freud believed that personality consists of three elements. Each child is born with the first, an **id,** Freud's term for inborn drives that cause us to seek self-gratification. The id of the newborn is evident in its cries of hunger or pain. The pleasure-seeking id operates throughout life. It demands the immediate fulfillment of basic needs: attention, safety, food, sex, and so on.

The id's drive for immediate gratification, however, runs into a roadblock: primarily the needs of other people especially those of the parents. To adapt to these constraints, a second component of the personality emerges, which Freud called the ego. The **ego** is the balancing force between the id and the demands of society that suppress it. The ego also serves to balance the id and the **superego,** the third component of the personality, more commonly called the *conscience.*

The superego represents *culture within us,* the norms and values we have internalized from our social groups. As the *moral* component of the personality, the superego provokes feelings of guilt or shame when we break social rules, or pride and self-satisfaction when we follow them.

According to Freud, when the id gets out of hand, we follow our desires for pleasure and break society's norms. When the superego gets out of hand, we become overly rigid in following those norms, finding ourselves bound in a straitjacket of rules that inhibit our lives. The ego, the balancing force, tries to prevent either the superego or the id from dominating. In the emotionally healthy individual, the ego succeeds in balancing these conflicting demands of the id and the superego. In the maladjusted individual, however, the ego cannot control the inherent conflict between the id and the superego, and the result is internal confusion and problem behaviors.

Sociological Evaluation Sociologists appreciate Freud's emphasis on socialization—that the social group into which we are born transmits norms and values that restrain our biological drives. Sociologists, however, object to the view that inborn and subconscious motivations are the primary reasons for human behavior. *This denies the central principle of sociology:* that factors such as social class (income, education, and occupation) and people's roles in groups underlie their behavior (Epstein 1988; Bush and Simmons 1990).

Feminist sociologists have been especially critical of Freud. Although what we just summarized applies to both females and males, Freud assumed that what is "male" is "normal." He even said that females are inferior, castrated males (Chodorow 1990; Gerhard 2000). It is obvious that sociologists need to research how we develop personality.

id Freud's term for our inborn basic drives

ego Freud's term for a balancing force between the id and the demands of society

superego Freud's term for the conscience, the internalized norms and values of our social groups

Kohlberg, Gilligan, and the Development of Morality

If you have observed young children, you know that they focus on immediate gratification and show little or no concern for others. ("Mine!" a 2-year-old will shout, as she grabs a toy from another child.) Yet, at a later age this same child will become considerate of others and concerned with moral issues. How does this change happen?

Kohlberg's Theory Psychologist Lawrence Kohlberg (1975, 1984, 1986; Walsh 2000) concluded that we go through a sequence of stages as we develop morality. Building on Piaget's work, he found that children begin in the *amoral stage* I just described. For them, there is no right or wrong, just personal needs to be satisfied. From about ages 7 to 10, children are in what Kohlberg called a *preconventional stage.* They have learned rules, and they follow them to stay out of trouble. They view right and wrong as what pleases or displeases their parents, friends, and teachers. Their concern is to avoid punishment. At about age 10, they enter the *conventional stage.* At this stage, morality means to follow the norms and values they have learned. In the *postconventional stage,* which Kohlberg says most people don't reach, people reflect on abstract principles of right and wrong and judge a behavior according to these principles.

Gilligan and Gender Differences in Morality Carol Gilligan, another psychologist, grew uncomfortable with Kohlberg's conclusions. They didn't seem to match her own experience, and she noted that he had used only boys in his studies. More women had become social scientists by this point, and they were questioning an assumption of male researchers—that female subjects were not necessary, for the results of research with boys would apply to girls as well.

Gilligan (1982, 1990) decided to find out if there were differences in how men and women looked at morality. After interviewing about 200 men and women, she concluded that women are more likely to evaluate morality in terms of *personal relationships.* They want to know how an action affects others. They are more concerned with personal loyalties and with the harm that might come to loved ones. Men, in contrast, tend to think more along the lines of *abstract principles* that define what is right or wrong. An act either matches or violates a code of ethics, and personal relationships have little to do with the matter.

Researchers tested Gilligan's conclusions. They found that *both* men and women use personal relationships and abstract principles when they make moral judgments (Wark and Krebs 1996). Because of this, Gilligan no longer supports her original position (Brannon 1999). The matter is not yet settled, however, for some researchers have found differences in how men and women make moral judgments (White 1999; Jaffee and Hyde 2000).

As with personality, in this vital area of human development, sociological research is also notably absent.

Socialization into Emotions

Emotions, too, are essential for what we become, and sociologists have recently begun to research this area of our "humanness." They find that emotions are also not simply the results of biology, but, like the mind, they, too, depend on socialization (Hochschild 1975; 1983; Reiser 1999; Turner 2000). This may sound strange. Don't all people get angry? Doesn't everyone cry? Don't we all feel guilt, shame, sadness, happiness, fear? What has socialization to do with emotions?

Global Emotions At first, it may look as though socialization is not relevant. Paul Ekman (1980), an anthropologist, studied emotions in several countries. He concluded that everyone experiences six basic emotions: anger, disgust, fear, happiness, sadness, and surprise—and we all show the same facial expressions when we feel these emotions. A person from Zimbabwe, for example, could tell from just the look on an American's face that she is angry, disgusted, or fearful, and we could tell from the Zimbabwean's face that he is happy, sad, or surprised. Because we all show the same facial expressions when we experience these six emotions, Ekman concluded that they are built into us biologically, "a product of our genes."

Expressing Emotions The existence of universal facial expressions for these basic emotions does *not* mean that socialization has no effect on how we express them. Facial expressions are only one way that we show emotions. Other ways vary with gender. For example, U.S. women are allowed to express their emotions more freely, while U.S. men are expected to be more reserved. To express sudden happiness, or a delightful surprise, for example, women are allowed to make "squeals of glee" in public places. Men are not. Such an expression would be a fundamental violation of their gender role.

Then there are culture, social class, and relationships. Consider culture. Two close Japanese friends who meet after a long separation don't shake hands or hug—they bow. Two Arab men will kiss. Social class is also significant, for it cuts across many other lines, even gender. Upon seeing a friend after a long absence, upper-class women and men are likely to be more reserved in expressing their delight than are lower-class women and men. Relationships also make a big difference. We express our emotions more openly if we are with close friends, more guardedly if we are at a staff meeting with the corporate CEO. A good part of childhood socialization centers on learning these "norms of emotion," how to express our emotions in a variety of settings.

What We Feel The matter goes deeper than this. Socialization not only leads to different ways of expressing emotions, but even affects *what* we feel (Clark 1991; 1997). People in one culture may learn to experience feelings that are unknown in another culture. For example, the Ifaluk, who live on the Western Caroline Islands of Micronesia, use the word *fago* to refer to the feelings they have when they see someone suffer. This comes close to what we call sympathy or compassion. But the Ifaluk also use this term to refer to what they feel when they are with someone who has high status, someone they highly respect or admire (Kagan 1984). To us, these are two distinct emotions, and they require separate terms. For a glimpse of a culture in which emotions, values, and behaviors are shockingly different from those we expect, see the Down-to-Earth Sociology box below.

DOWN-TO-EARTH SOCIOLOGY

Signs of the Times: Are We Becoming Ik?

ANTHROPOLOGIST COLIN TURNBULL (1972/1995) studied the Ik, a once-proud nomadic people in northern Uganda whose traditional hunting lands were seized by the government. Devastated by drought, hunger, and starvation, the Ik turned to extreme individualism in which selfishness, emotional numbness, and lack of concern for others reign supreme. The pursuit of food has become the only good; their society has been replaced by a passionless, numbed association of individuals.

Imagine, for a moment, that you are born into the Ik tribe. After your first three or four years of life, you are pushed out of the hut. From then on, you are on your own. You can sleep in the village courtyard, and, with permission, you can sit in the doorway of your parents' house, but you may not lie down or sleep there.

There is no school. No church. Nothing from this point in your life that even comes close to what we call family. You join a group of children aged 3 to 7. The weakest soon die, for only the strongest survive. Later, you join a band of 8- to 12-year-olds. At 12 or 13, you split off by yourself.

You learn from what you see going on around you, and here you see coldness. The men hunt, but game is scarce. If they get anything, they refuse to bring it back to their families. They say, "Each of them is seeing what he can get for himself. Do you think they will bring any back for me?"

You also see cruelty. When blind Lo'ono trips and rolls to the bottom of the ravine, the adults laugh as she lies on her back, feebly thrashing her arms and legs. When Lolim begs his son to let him in, pleading that he is going to die in a few hours, Longoli drives him away. Lolim dies alone.

The Ik children learn their lesson well: Selfishness is good, for your survival is all that counts. But the children add a childish glee to the adults' dispassionate coldness. When blind Lolim took ill, the children teased him, kneeling in front of him and laughing as he fell. His grandson crept up and drummed on the old man's bald head with a pair of sticks.

Then there was little Adupa, who managed, for a while, to maintain a sense of awe at what life had to offer. When Adupa found food, she would hold it in her hand, looking at it with wonder and delight. As she raised her hand to her mouth, the other children would jump on her, laughing as they beat her.

For Your CONSIDERATION

From the Ik, we learn that the values we take to be uniquely human are not inherent in humanity. Rather, they arise from society, and, as such, can be lost when the sense of identification that lies at the basis of society breaks down.

It is easy to criticize members of another society if you don't have to walk in their shoes, so let's turn the critical lens on our own society. Consider how people are treated like things—discarded when they are no longer needed. Corporations fire older workers because they can pay younger ones less—or they relocate a factory to a country where labor is cheaper. As they leave hundreds and even thousands of workers stranded, CEOs shrug their shoulders and say, "That's business." For the sake of higher salaries, people sever themselves from kin and community. Successful executives discard same-age spouses, the co-parent of their own children, in exchange for younger, more photogenic "trophy" mates.

Finally, consider how the values we would wish for in friends and family—kindness, generosity, patience, tolerance, cooperation, compassion—are undervalued. If a job requires such talents, it is low in pay and prestige (Maybury-Lewis 1995).

Research Needed Although Ekman identified only six basic emotions that are universal in feeling and facial expression, I suspect that other emotions are common to people around the world—and that everyone shows similar facial expressions when they experience them. I suggest that feelings of helplessness, despair, confusion, and shock are among these universal emotions. We need cross-cultural research to find out if this is so. We also need research into how children learn to feel and express emotions.

Western males are socialized to express less emotion than are females, but in recent years they have been allowed to more openly express emotions, even in ways that just a short time ago would have been considered feminine. Shown here is General Tommy Franks, who was the Commander of U.S. Central Command. He is hugging a soldier on the As Sayliyah base in Qatar, where the U.S. military was training for war with Iraq. The redefinition we are undergoing is from feminine to comradely.

The Self and Emotions as Social Control—Society Within Us

Much of our socialization is intended to turn us into conforming members of society. Socialization into the self and emotions is an essential part of this process, for both the self and our emotions mold our behavior. Although we like to think we are "free," consider for a moment just some of the factors that influence how we act: the expectations of friends and parents, of neighbors and teachers; classroom norms and college rules; city, state, and federal laws. For example, if in a moment of intense frustration, or out of a devilish desire to shock people, you wanted to tear off your clothes and run naked down the street, what would stop you?

The answer is your socialization—*society within you.* Your experiences in society have resulted in a self that thinks along certain lines and feels particular emotions. This helps keep you in line. Thoughts such as "Would I get kicked out of school?" and "What would my friends (parents) think if they found out?" represent an awareness of the self in relationship to others. So does the desire to avoid feelings of shame and embarrassment. Our *social mirror,* then—the result of being socialized into a self and emotions—sets up effective controls over our behavior. In fact, socialization into self and emotions is so effective that some people feel embarrassed just thinking about running nude in public!

IN SUM

Socialization is essential for our development as human beings. From interaction with others, we learn how to think, reason, and feel. The net result is to shape our behavior—including our thinking and emotions—according to cultural standards. This is what sociologists mean when they refer to "*society within us.*"

Socialization into Gender

To channel our behavior—including our thinking and emotions—along expected avenues, society also uses **gender socialization.** By expecting different attitudes and behaviors from us *because* we are male or female, the human group nudges boys and girls in separate directions in life. This foundation of contrasting attitudes and behaviors is so thorough that, as adults, most of us act, think, and even feel according to our culture's guidelines of what is appropriate for our sex.

How do we learn gender messages? The significance of gender is emphasized throughout this book, with a special focus in Chapter 11. For now, though, let's briefly consider the influence of the family and the mass media.

gender socialization the ways in which society sets children onto different courses in life *because* they are male or female

Gender Messages in the Family

Our parents are the first significant others who teach us our part in this fundamental symbolic division of the world. Sometimes they do so self-consciously, perhaps by bringing into play pink and blue, colors that have no meaning in themselves but that are now associated with gender. But our parents' own gender orientations have become so firmly embedded that they do much of this teaching without being aware of what they are doing.

This is illustrated by a classic study done by psychologists Susan Goldberg and Michael Lewis (1969), whose results have been confirmed by other researchers (Fagot et al. 1985; Connors 1996).

> Goldberg and Lewis asked mothers to bring their 6-month-old infants into their laboratory, supposedly to observe the infants' development. Covertly, however, they also observed the mothers. They found that the mothers kept their daughters closer to them. They also touched their daughters more and spoke to them more frequently than they did to their sons.
>
> By the time the children were 13 months old, the girls stayed closer to their mothers during play, and they returned to them sooner and more often than the boys did. When Goldberg and Lewis set up a barrier to separate the children from their mothers, who were holding toys, the girls were more likely to cry and motion for help; the boys, to try to climb over the barrier.

Goldberg and Lewis concluded that in our society, mothers subconsciously reward daughters for being passive and dependent, and sons for being active and independent.

These lessons continue throughout childhood. On the basis of their sex, children are given different kinds of toys. Boys are more likely to get guns and "action figures" that destroy enemies. Girls are more likely to get dolls and jewelry. Some parents try to choose "gender neutral" toys, but kids know what is popular, and they feel left out if they don't have what the other kids have. The significance of toys in gender socialization can be summarized this way: Almost all parents would be upset if someone gave their boy Barbie dolls.

Parents also let their preschool sons roam farther from home than their preschool daughters, and they subtly encourage them to participate in more rough-and-tumble play. They expect their sons to get dirtier and to be more defiant, their daughters to be daintier and more compliant (Gilman 1911/1971; Henslin 2003c). In large part, they get what they expect.

Such experiences in socialization lie at the heart of the sociological explanation of male-female differences. We should note, however, that some sociologists consider biology to be a cause of these differences. For example, were the infants in the Goldberg-Lewis study showing built-in biological predispositions, with the mothers merely reinforcing—not causing—those differences? We shall return to this controversial issue in Chapter 11.

Gender Messages from Peers

Sociologists stress how this sorting process that begins in the family is reinforced as the child is exposed to other aspects of society. Of those other influences, one of the most powerful is the peer group, individuals of roughly the same age who are linked by common interests. Examples of peer groups are friends, classmates, and "the kids in the neighborhood." Consider how girls and boys teach one another what it means to be a female or a male in U.S. society.

Let's eavesdrop on a conversation between two eighth-grade girls studied by sociologist Donna Eder (2003). You can see how these girls are reinforcing images of appearance and behavior that they think are appropriate for females:

> **CINDY:** The only thing that makes her look anything is all the makeup . . .
>
> **PENNY:** She had a picture, and she's standing like this. (Poses with one hand on her hip and one by her head)
>
> **CINDY:** Her face is probably this skinny, but it looks that big 'cause of all the makeup she has on it.
>
> **PENNY:** She's ugly, ugly, ugly.

Boys, of course, do the same thing. When sociologist Melissa Milkie (1994) studied junior high school boys, she found that much of their talk centered on movies and TV programs. Of the many images they saw, the boys would single out sex and violence. They would amuse one another by repeating lines, acting out parts, and joking and laughing at what they had seen.

mass media forms of communication, such as radio, newspapers, and television that are directed to mass audiences

gender role the behaviors and attitudes considered appropriate because one is a female or a male

SOON WE'LL GIVE UP DOLLS AND HOPSCOTCH---BUT THEY'LL BE INTO FOOTBALL FOREVER.
E-mail:BobThaves@aol.com ©2002 Thaves / Dist. by NEA, Inc. www.frankandernest.com
12-10 THAVES

The gender roles *that we learn during childhood become part of our basic orientations to life. Although we refine these roles as we grow older, they remain built around the framework established during childhood.*

If you know boys in their early teens, you've probably seen behavior like this. You may have been amused, or even have shaken your head in disapproval. As a sociologist, however, Milkie peered beneath the surface. She concluded that the boys were using media images to discover who they are as males. They had gotten the message: To be a "real" male is to be obsessed with sex and violence. Not to joke and laugh about murder and promiscuous sex would have marked a boy as a "weenie," a label to be avoided at all costs.

Gender Messages in the Mass Media

Another powerful influence is the **mass media,** forms of communication that are directed to large audiences. Let's look at how images in advertising, television, movies, and video games reinforce **gender roles,** the behaviors and attitudes considered appropriate for our sex.

Advertising Advertising bombards us, and the average U.S. child watches about 20,000 commercials a year (Witt 2000). Commercials aimed at children are more likely to show girls as cooperative and boys as aggressive. They also are more likely to show girls at home and boys at other locations (Larson 2001). Girls are also more likely to be portrayed as giggly and less capable at tasks (Browne 1998). When advertising directed at adults portrays men as dominant and rugged and women as sexy and submissive, it perpetuates similar stereotypes.

The result is a spectrum of stereotypical, culturally molded images. At one end of this spectrum are cowboys who roam the wide open spaces, while at the other end are scantily clad women, whose assets are intended to sell a variety of products, from automobiles to hamburgers. The portrayal of women with unrealistic physical assets makes women feel inadequate (Kilbourne 2003). This, of course, creates demand for an array of products that promise physical enhancement and romantic success.

Television and Movies Television and movies reinforce stereotypes of the sexes. In movies and on prime-time television, male characters still outnumber female characters. Male characters on television are also more likely to be portrayed in higher-status positions (Glascock 2001). Viewers get the message, for the more television people watch, the more they tend to have restrictive ideas about women's role in society (Signorielli 1989, 1990).

Stereotype-breaking characters are a sign of changing times. On comedies, females are more verbally aggressive than males (Glascock 2001). Buffy the Vampire Slayer saves her classmates from Evil, while, with tongue in cheek, the Powerpuff Girls are touted as "the most elite kindergarten crime-fighting force ever assembled." Perhaps the most stereotype-breaking of all is *Xena, Warrior Princess,* a television series imported from New Zealand. Portrayed as super dominant, Xena overcomes all obstacles and defeats all foes—whether men or women.

Video Games Many youths spend countless hours playing video games in arcades and at home. Even college students, especially men, relieve stress by escaping into video games (Jones 2003). Although sociologists have begun to study how the sexes are portrayed in these games, how the games affect their players' ideas of gender is unknown at present (Dietz 2000; Berger 2002). Because these games are on the cutting edge of society, they sometimes also reflect cutting-edge changes in sex roles, as examined in the Mass Media in Social Life box on the next page.

peer group a group of individuals of roughly the same age who are linked by common interests

massMEDIA in Social Life

From Xena, Warrior Princess, to Lara Croft, Tomb Raider: Changing Images of Women in the Mass Media

The mass media reflect women's changing role in society. Although media images that portray women as passive, as subordinate, or as mere background objects remain, a new image has broken through. Although this new image exaggerates changes, it does illustrate a fundamental change in social relations. As mentioned in the text, Xena, the Warrior Princess, is an outstanding example of this change.

Although it is unusual to call video games a form of the mass media, like books and magazines, they are made available to a mass audience. And with digital advances, they have crossed the line from what is traditionally thought of as games to something that more closely resembles interactive movies.

Sociologically, what is significant is that the *content* of video games socializes their users. As they play, gamers are exposed not only to action, but also to ideas and images. The gender images of video games communicate powerful messages, just as they do in other forms of the mass media.

Lara Croft, an adventure-seeking archeologist and star of *Tomb Raider* and its many sequels, is the essence of the new gender image. Lara is smart, strong, and able to utterly vanquish foes. With both guns blazing, she is the cowboy of the twenty-first century, the term *cowboy* being purposefully chosen, as Lara breaks stereotypical gender roles and assumes what previously was the domain of men. She is the first female protagonist in a field of muscle-rippling, gun-toting macho caricatures (Taylor 1999).

Yet, the old remains powerfully encapsulated in the new. As the photo on this page makes evident, Lara is a fantasy girl for young men of the digital generation. No matter her foe, no matter her predicament, Lara oozes sex. Her form-fitting outfits, which flatter her voluptuous physique, reflect the mental images of the men who fashioned this digital character. So successful has this effort been that boys and young men have bombarded corporate headquarters with questions about Lara's personal life.

The mass media not only reflect gender stereotypes but they also play a role in changing them. Sometimes they do both simultaneously. The images of Xena, Warrior Princess, and of Lara Croft not only reflect women's changing role in society, but also, by exaggerating the change, they mold new stereotypes.

Lara has caught young men's fancy to such an extent that more than 100 Web sites are devoted to her. Lara is also the star of two movies and a comic book. There is even a Lara Croft candy bar.

For Your CONSIDERATION

A sociologist who reviewed this text said, "It seems that for women to be defined as equal, we have to become symbolic males—warriors with breasts." Why is gender change mostly one-way—females adopting traditional male characteristics? Why aren't the media proclaiming a "new man," one with stereotypical female characteristics? To see why men get to keep their gender roles, these two questions should help: Who is moving into the traditional territory of the other? Do people prefer to imitate power or powerlessness?

Finally, consider just how far stereotypes have actually been left behind. The ultimate goal of the video game, after foes are vanquished, is to see Lara in a nightie.

IN SUM

All of us are born into a society in which "male" and "female" are significant symbols. Sorted into separate groups from childhood, girls and boys learn sharply different ideas of what to expect of themselves and of one another. These images begin in the family and are reinforced by other social institutions. Each of us learns the meaning that our society associates with the sexes. These images become integrated into our views of the world, forming a picture of "how" males and females "are," and forcing an interpretation of the world in terms of gender. Because gender serves as a primary basis for **social inequality**—giving privileges and obligations to one group of people while denying them to another—gender images are especially important to understand.

social inequality a social condition in which privileges and obligations are given to some but denied to others

agents of socialization people or groups that affect our self-concept, attitudes, behaviors, or other orientations toward life

Agents of Socialization

People and groups that influence our orientations to life—our self-concept, emotions, attitudes, and behavior—are called **agents of socialization.** We have already considered how two of these agents, the family and the mass media, influence our ideas of gender. Now we'll look more closely at how agents of socialization prepare us to take our place in society. We shall first consider the family, then the neighborhood, religion, day care, school and peers, sports, and the workplace.

The Family

Around the world, the first group to have a major impact on humans is the family. Unlike some animals, we cannot survive by ourselves, and as babies we are utterly dependent on our family. Our experiences in the family are so intense that they have a lifelong impact on us. They lay down our basic sense of self, establishing our initial motivations, values, and beliefs. The family gives us ideas about who we are and what we deserve out of life. It is in the family that we begin to think of ourselves as strong or weak, smart or dumb, good-looking or ugly—or somewhere in between. And as already noted, here we begin the lifelong process of defining ourselves as female or male.

Subtle Socialization To study this process, sociologists have observed parents and young children in public settings, where the act of observing does not interfere with the interaction. Researchers using this unobtrusive technique have noted what they call the *stroller effect* (Mitchell et al. 1992). When a child is in a stroller, the father is likely to be the one who pushes the stroller. If the child is out of the stroller, the mother is likely to push the empty stroller while the father carries the child. In this and countless ways, parents send their children subtle gender messages. Most of the ways that parents teach their children about expected differences between men and women involve nonverbal cues, not specific instruction.

This photo captures an extreme form of family socialization. The father seems to be more emotionally involved in the goal—and in more pain—than his daughter, as he pushes her toward the finish line in the Teen Tours of America Kid's Triathlon.

The Family and Social Class Sociologists have compared how working-class and middle-class parents rear their children. Melvin Kohn (1959, 1963, 1976, 1977; Kohn et al. 1986) found that working-class parents are mainly concerned that their children stay out of trouble. They also tend to use physical punishment. Middle-class parents, in contrast, focus more on developing their children's curiosity, self-expression, and self-control. They are more likely to reason with their children than to use physical punishment.

These findings were a sociological puzzle. Just why would working-class and middle-class parents rear their children so differently? Kohn knew that life experiences of some sort held the key, and he found that key in the world of work. Bosses usually tell blue-collar workers exactly what to do. Since they expect their children's lives to be like theirs, blue-collar parents stress obedience. At their work, in contrast, middle-class parents take more initiative. Expecting their children to work at similar jobs, middle-class parents socialize them into the qualities they have found valuable.

Kohn still felt puzzled, however, for some working-class parents act more like middle-class parents, and vice versa. As Kohn probed this puzzle, the pieces fell into place. The key was the parents' type of job. Middle-class office workers, for example, are closely supervised, and Kohn found that they follow the working-class pattern of child rearing, emphasizing conformity. And some blue-collar workers, such as those who do home repairs, have a good deal of freedom. These workers follow the middle-class model in rearing their children (Pearlin and Kohn 1966; Kohn and Schooler 1969).

Working-class and middle-class parents also have different views of how children develop, which has interesting consequences for children's play (Lareau 2002). Working-class parents think of children as developing naturally, while middle-class parents think that children need a lot of guidance to develop correctly. As a result, working-class parents see their job as providing food, shelter, and comfort, with the child's development taking care of itself. They set limits ("Don't go near the railroad tracks"), and let their children play as they wish. Middle-class parents, in contrast, want their children's play to develop knowledge and social skills. For example, they may want them to play baseball, not for the enjoyment of playing ball, but to help them learn how to be team players.

The Neighborhood

As all parents know, some neighborhoods are better for their children than others. Parents try to move to those neighborhoods—if they can afford them. Their commonsense evaluations are borne out by sociological research. Children from poor neighborhoods are more likely to get in trouble with the law, to become pregnant, to drop out of school, and to end up facing a disadvantaged life (Wilson 1987; Brooks-Gunn et al. 1997; Sampson et al. 2001).

Sociologists have also documented that the residents of more affluent neighborhoods watch out for the children more than do the residents of poor neighborhoods (Sampson et al. 1999). The adults are more likely to know the local children and their parents, and to help keep the children safe and out of trouble. It is one of the ironies of life that in those neighborhoods that are riskier for children (where there are more homicide and child abuse), adults watch out less for the children, and in neighborhoods where the children need less protection, the adults are more careful.

Religion

By influencing values, religion becomes a key component in people's ideas of right and wrong. Religion is so important to Americans that 68 percent belong to a local congregation, and during a typical week, two of every five Americans attend a religious service (*Statistical Abstract* 2002:Table 64). Religion is significant even for people reared in nonreligious homes—religious ideas pervade U.S. society, providing basic ideas of morality for us all.

The influence of religion extends to many areas of our lives. For example, participation in religious services teaches us not only beliefs about the hereafter but also ideas about what kinds of dress, speech, and manners are appropriate for formal occasions. Religion is so significant that we shall examine its influence in a separate chapter (Chapter 18).

Day Care

It is rare for social science research to make national news, but occasionally it does. One study on day care ignited a debate recently. Researchers followed 1,300 children in 10 cities from infancy into kindergarten. They observed the children at home and at day care. (Day care was defined as any care other than by the mother—including care by other relatives and the father.) They also videotaped and made detailed notes on the children's interaction with their mothers (National Institute of Child Health and Human Development 1999; Guensburg 2001). This is what caught the media's attention: Children who spend more hours in day care have weaker bonds with their mothers. In addition, these children are more likely to fight, to be cruel, and to be "mean." In contrast, children who spend less time in day care are more cooperative and more affectionate to their mothers. This holds true regardless of the quality of the day care, the family's social class, or whether the child is a girl or a boy.

This study was designed well, and its findings are without dispute. But how do we explain these findings? The cause could be time spent in day care. The researchers suggest that mothers who spend less time with their children are less responsive to their children's emotional needs because they are less familiar with their children's "signaling systems." But maybe the cause isn't day care. Perhaps mothers who put their children in day care for more hours are less sensitive to their children in the first place. Or perhaps employed mothers are less likely to meet their children's emotional needs because they are more tired and stressed than mothers who stay at home. From this study, we can't determine the cause of the weaker bonding and the behavioral problems.

These researchers also uncovered a positive side to day care. They found that children who spend more hours in day care have higher language skills (Guensburg 2001). Children whose language skills benefit the most are those from low-income homes and those from dysfunctional families—those with alcoholic, inept, or abusive parents (Scarr and Eisenberg 1993). As is obvious, we need more studies to be able to tease out the consequences of day care. While this longitudinal study is far from encouraging, it gives us no reason to conclude that day care is producing a generation of "mean but smart" children.

The School

Part of the **manifest function,** or *intended* purpose, of formal education, is to transmit knowledge and skills, such as reading, writing, and arithmetic. The transmission of such skills is certainly part of socialization, but so are the schools' **latent functions,** its *unintended* consequences that help the social system. Let's look at this less visible aspect of education.

At home, children learn attitudes and values that match their family's situation in life. At school, they learn a broader perspective that helps prepare them to take a role in the world beyond the family. At home, for example, a child may have been the almost exclusive focus of doting parents, but in school, the child learns *universality*—that the same rules apply to everyone, regardless of who their parents are or how special they may be at home. The Cultural Diversity box on the next page explores how these new values and ways of looking at the world sometimes even replace those the child learns at home.

Sociologists have also identified a *hidden curriculum* in our schools. This term refers to values that, although not explicitly taught, are part of a school's "message." For example, the stories and examples that are used to teach math and English may bring with them lessons in patriotism, democracy, justice, and honesty. There is also a *corridor curriculum,* what students teach one another outside the classroom. Unfortunately, the students' hidden curriculum seems to center on racism, sexism, illicit ways to make money, and coolness (Hemmings 1999). You can determine for yourself which of these is functional and dysfunctional.

Conflict theorists point out the significance of social class. Children born to wealthy parents go to private schools, where they learn skills and values that match their higher position. Children from poorer homes go to public schools, where they learn that not many of "their kind" will become professionals or leaders. Within public schools, social class is also significant, for children from blue-collar families are less likely to take college prep courses. In short, schools around the world reflect and reinforce their nation's social class, economic, and political systems. We will return to this topic in the chapter on education (Chapter 17).

Peer Groups

As a child's experiences with agents of socialization broaden, the influence of the family lessens. Entry into school marks only one of many steps in this transfer of allegiance. One of the most significant aspects of education is that it exposes children to peer groups that help them resist the efforts of parents and schools to socialize them.

manifest functions the intended beneficial consequences of people's actions

latent functions unintended beneficial consequences of people's actions

CULTURAL DIVERSITY in the UNITED STATES

Caught Between Two Worlds

It is a struggle to learn a new culture, for the behaviors and ways of thinking contrast with the ones already learned. This can lead to inner turmoil. One way to handle the conflict is to cut ties with your first culture. This, however, can create a sense of loss, perhaps one that is recognized only later in life.

Richard Rodriguez, a literature professor and essayist, was born to working-class Mexican immigrants. Wanting their son to be successful in their adopted land, his parents named him Richard instead of Ricardo. While his English-Spanish hybrid name indicates the parents' aspirations for their son, it was also an omen of the conflict that Richard would experience.

Like other children of Mexican immigrants, Richard's first language was Spanish—a rich mother tongue that introduced him to the world. Until the age of 5, when he began school, Richard knew only fifty words in English. He describes what happened when he began school:

> The change came gradually but early. When I was beginning grade school, I noted to myself the fact that the classroom environment was so different in its styles and assumptions from my own family environment that survival would essentially entail a choice between both worlds. When I became a student, I was literally "remade"; neither I nor my teachers considered anything I had known before as relevant. I had to forget most of what my culture had provided, because to remember it was a disadvantage. The past and its cultural values became detachable, like a piece of clothing grown heavy on a warm day and finally put away.

As happened to millions of immigrants before him, whose parents spoke German, Polish, Italian, and so on, learning English eroded family and class ties and ate away at his ethnic roots. For him, language and education were not simply devices that eased the transition to the dominant culture. Instead, they slashed at the roots that had given him life.

To face conflicting cultures is to confront a fork in the road. Some turn one way and withdraw from the new culture—a clue that helps explain why so many Latinos drop out of U.S. schools. Others go in the opposite direction. Cutting ties with their family and cultural roots, they wholeheartedly adopt the new culture.

Rodriguez took the second road. He excelled in his new language—so well, in fact, that he graduated from Stanford University and then became a graduate student in English at the University of California at Berkeley. He was even awarded a prestigious Fulbright fellowship to study English Renaissance literature at the British Museum.

But the past wouldn't let Rodriguez alone. Prospective employers were impressed with his knowledge of Renaissance literature. At job interviews, however, they would skip over the Renaissance training and would ask him if he would teach the Mexican novel and be an adviser to Latino students. Rodriguez was also haunted by the image of his grandmother, the warmth of the culture he had left behind, the language and thought to which he had become a stranger.

Richard Rodriguez represents millions of immigrants—not just those of Latino origin but those from other cultures, too—who want to be a part of the United States without betraying their past. They fear that to integrate into U.S. culture is to lose their roots. They are caught between two cultures, each beckoning, each offering rich rewards.

For Your CONSIDERATION

I have seen this conflict first hand with my father, who did not learn English until after the seventh grade (his last in school)—the broken English as German is left behind, awareness that the accent and awkward expressions remain, lingering emotional connections to old ways, and the suspicions, haughtiness, and slights of more assimilated Americans. A longing for security by grasping the past is combined with the everyday reality of the new culture. Have you seen anything similar?

Sources: Based on Richard Rodriguez 1975, 1982, 1990, 1991, 1995.

When sociologists Patricia and Peter Adler (1992, 1998), a husband and wife team, observed children at two elementary schools in Colorado, they saw how children separate themselves by sex and develop their own worlds with unique norms. The norms that made boys popular were athletic ability, coolness, and toughness. For girls, popularity was based on family background, physical appearance (clothing and use of makeup), and the ability to attract popular boys. In this children's subculture, academic achievement pulled in opposite directions: For boys, high grades lowered their popularity, but for girls, good grades increased their standing among peers.

Schools are one of the primary agents of socialization. *One of their chief functions is to sort young people into the adult roles thought appropriate for them, and to teach them the attitudes and skills that match those roles. What sorts of attitudes and adult roles do you think these junior high school girls in Santa Monica, California, are being socialized into? Is it a function or dysfunction—or both?*

You know from your own experience how compelling peer groups are. It is almost impossible to go against a peer group, whose cardinal rule seems to be "conformity or rejection." Anyone who doesn't do what the others want becomes an "outsider," a "nonmember," an "outcast." For preteens and teens just learning their way around in the world, it is not surprising that the peer group rules.

As a result, the standards of our peer groups tend to dominate our lives. If your peers, for example, listen to rap, heavy metal, rock and roll, country, or gospel, it is almost inevitable that you also prefer that kind of music. It is the same for other kinds of music, clothing styles, and dating standards. Peer influences also extend to behaviors that violate social norms. If your peers are college-bound and upwardly striving, that is most likely what you will be; but if they use drugs, cheat, and steal, you are likely to do so, too.

Sports and Competitive Success

Sports are another powerful socializing agent. Everyone recognizes that sports teach not only physical skills but also values. In fact, "teaching youngsters to be team players" is often given as the justification for financing organized sports.

The effects of sports on the self-image are not well understood. Boys learn that to achieve in sports is to gain stature in masculinity. The more successful a boy is in sports, the more masculine he is considered to be and the more he achieves prestige among his peers. Sociologist Michael Messner (1990) points out that this encourages boys to develop *instrumental* relationships—those based on what you can get out of them. Other aspects of boys' socialization into competitive success have the same effect, and boys tend to relate instrumentally to girls. Girls, in contrast, are more likely to be socialized to construct their identities on meaningful relationships, not on competitive success. As sports become more important in the formation of female identities, we will have to see what effects they have on women.

The Workplace

Another agent of socialization that comes into play somewhat later in life is the workplace. Those initial jobs that we take in high school and college are much more than just a way to earn a few dollars. From the people we rub shoulders with at work, we learn not only a set of skills but also a perspective on the world.

Most of us eventually become committed to some particular line of work, often after trying out many jobs. This may involve **anticipatory socialization,** learning to play a role before entering it. Anticipatory socialization is a sort of mental rehearsal for some future

anticipatory socialization
because one anticipates a future role, one learns parts of it now

Many adults who wish to reduce gender distinctions prefer that grade schoolers of both sexes participate in the same playground activities. Despite the sometimes not-so-subtle suggestions of teachers, however, grade school children insist on separating by sex, where they pursue different interests and activities and develop contrasting norms.

activity. We may talk to people who work in a particular career, read novels about that type of work, or take a summer internship. This allows us to gradually identify with the role, to become aware of what would be expected of us. Sometimes this helps people avoid committing themselves to an unrewarding career, as with some of my students who tried student teaching, found they couldn't stand it, and then moved on to other fields more to their liking.

An intriguing aspect of work as a socializing agent is that the more you participate in a line of work, the more the work becomes a part of your self-concept. Eventually you come to think of yourself so much in terms of the job that if someone asks you to describe yourself, you are likely to include the job in your self-description. You might say, "I'm a teacher." "I'm a nurse." "I'm a sociologist."

Resocialization

What does a woman who has just become a nun have in common with a man who has just divorced? The answer is that they both are undergoing **resocialization;** that is, they are learning new norms, values, attitudes, and behaviors to match their new situation in life. In its most common form, resocialization occurs each time we learn something contrary to our previous experiences. A new boss who insists on a different way of doing things is resocializing you. Most resocialization is mild, only a slight modification of things we have already learned.

Resocialization can be intense, however. People who join Alcoholics Anonymous (AA), for example, are surrounded by reformed drinkers who affirm the destructive effects of excessive drinking. Some students experience an intense period of resocialization when they leave high school and start college—especially during those initially scary days before they start to fit in and feel comfortable. To join a cult or to begin psychotherapy is even more profound, for these events expose people to ideas that conflict with their previous ways of looking at the world. If these ideas "take," not only does the individual's behavior change, but also he or she learns a fundamentally different way of looking at life.

resocialization the process of learning new norms, values, attitudes, and behaviors

total institution a place in which people are cut off from the rest of society and are almost totally controlled by the officials who run the place

Total Institutions

Relatively few of us experience the powerful agent of socialization that Erving Goffman (1961) called the **total institution.** He coined this term to refer to a place in which people are cut off from the rest of society and where they come under almost total control of the officials who run the place. Boot camp, prisons, concentration camps, convents, some religious cults, and some boarding schools, such as West Point, are total institutions.

A person entering a total institution is greeted with a **degradation ceremony** (Garfinkel 1956), an attempt to remake the self by stripping away the individual's current identity and stamping a new one in its place. This unwelcome greeting may involve fingerprinting, photographing, shaving the head, and banning the individual's *personal identity kit* (items such as jewelry, hairstyles, clothing, and other body decorations used to express individuality). Newcomers may be ordered to strip, undergo an examination (often in a humiliating, semi-public setting), and then to put on a uniform that designates their new status. (For prisoners, the public reading of the verdict and being led away in handcuffs by armed police are also part of the degradation ceremony.)

Total institutions are isolated from the public. The walls, bars, gates, guards, or other barriers not only keep the inmates in but also keep outsiders out. Total institutions suppress preexisting statuses: Inmates learn that their previous roles such as spouse, parent, worker, or student mean nothing. The only thing that counts is their current role. Staff members control information and replace the norms of "the outside world" with their own rules, values, and interpretation of life. This helps the institution shape the inmates' ideas and "picture" of the world. Staff members, who control the rewards and punishments, closely supervise the day-to-day lives of the residents. Eating, sleeping, showering, recreation—all are standardized. Under conditions of deprivation, simple rewards for compliance such as sleep, a television program, a letter from home, extra food, or even a cigarette, are powerful incentives in controlling behavior.

No one leaves a total institution unscathed, for the experience brands an indelible mark on the individual's self and colors the way he or she sees the world. Boot camp, as described in the Down-to-Earth Sociology box on the next page, is brutal but swift. Prison, in contrast, is brutal and prolonged. Neither recruit nor prisoner, however, has difficulty in pinpointing how the institution affected the self.

Socialization Through the Life Course

You are at a particular stage in your life now, and college is a good part of it. You know that you have more stages ahead of you as you go through life. These stages, from birth to death, are called the **life course** (Elder 1975; 1999). The sociological significance of the life course is twofold. First, as you pass through a stage, it affects your behavior and orientations. You simply don't think about life in the same way when you are 30, married, and have a baby and a mortgage, as you do when you are 18 or 20, single, and in college. (Actually, you don't see life the same as a freshman and as a senior.) Second, your life course differs by the historical period of your society. Finally, your social location makes a difference—your social class, race-ethnicity, and gender map out distinctive worlds of experience. Consequently, the typical life course differs for males and females, the rich and the poor, and so on. To emphasize this major sociological point, in the sketch that follows I will stress the *historical* setting of people's lives. Because of your particular social location, your own life course may differ from this sketch, which is a composite of stages others have suggested (Levinson 1978; Carr et al. 1995; Lee 2001).

Childhood (from birth to about age 12)

To begin, consider how different your childhood would have been if you had grown up during the Middle Ages. When historian Philippe Ariès (1965) examined European paintings from this period, he noticed that children were always dressed in adult clothing. If they were not depicted stiffly posed, as in a family portrait, they were shown doing adult activities. From this, Ariès drew a conclusion that sparked a debate among historians—that at that time and in that place, childhood was not regarded as a special

degradation ceremony a term coined by Harold Garfinkel to describe an attempt to remake the self by stripping away an individual's self-identity and stamping a new identity in its place

life course the stages of our life as we go from birth to death

DOWN-TO-EARTH SOCIOLOGY

Boot Camp as a Total Institution

THE BUS ARRIVES AT PARRIS ISLAND, South Carolina, at 3 A.M. The early hour is no accident. The recruits are groggy, confused. Up to a few hours ago, the young men were ordinary civilians. Now, as a sergeant sneeringly calls them "maggots," their heads are buzzed (25 seconds per recruit), and they are quickly thrust into the harsh world of Marine boot camp.

Buzzing their hair is just the first step in stripping away their identity so the Marines can stamp a new one in its place. The uniform serves the same purpose. There is a ban on using the first person "I." Even simple requests must be made in precise Marine style or they will not be acknowledged. ("Sir, Recruit Jones requests permission to make a head call, sir.")

Every intense moment of the next eleven weeks reminds the recruits that they are joining a subculture of self-discipline. Here pleasure is suspect and sacrifice is good. As they learn the Marine way of talking, walking, and thinking, they are denied the diversions they once took for granted: television, cigarettes, cars, candy, soft drinks, video games, music, alcohol, drugs, and sex.

Lessons are bestowed with fierce intensity. When Sgt. Carey checks brass belt buckles, Recruit Robert Shelton nervously blurts, "I don't have one." Sgt. Carey's face grows red as his neck cords bulge. "I?" he says, his face just inches from the recruit. With spittle flying from his mouth, he screams, " 'I' is gone!"

"Nobody's an individual" is the lesson that is driven home again and again. "You are a team, a Marine. Not a civilian. Not black or white—not Hispanic or any hyphenated American—but a Marine. You will live like a Marine, fight like a Marine, and, if necessary, die like a Marine."

Resocialization *is often a gentle process. Usually we are gradually exposed to different ways of thinking and doing. Sometimes, however,* resocialization *can be swift and brutal, as it is during boot camp in the Marines. This private at Parris Island is learning a world vastly unlike the civilian world he left behind.*

Each day begins before dawn with close order formations. The rest of the day is filled with training in hand-to-hand combat, marching, running, calisthenics, Marine history, and—always—following orders.

"An M-16 can blow someone's head off at 500 meters," Sgt. Norman says. "That's beautiful, isn't it?"

"Yes, sir!" shout the platoon's fifty-nine voices.

"Pick your nose!" Simultaneously 59 index fingers shoot into nostrils.

The pressure to conform is intense. Those sent packing for insubordination or suicidal tendencies are mocked in cadence during drills. ("Hope you like the sights you see / Parris Island casualty.") As lights go out at 9 P.M., the exhausted recruits perform the day's last task: The entire platoon, in unison, chants the virtues of the Marines.

Recruits are constantly scrutinized. Subperformance is not accepted, whether it be a dirty rifle or a loose thread on a uniform. The subperformer is shouted at, derided, humiliated. The group suffers for the individual. If a recruit is slow, the entire platoon is punished.

The system works.

One of the new Marines (until graduation, they are recruits, not Marines) says, "I feel like I've joined a new society or religion."

He has.

For Your CONSIDERATION

Of what significance is the recruits' degradation ceremony? Why are recruits not allowed video games, cigarettes, or calls home? Why are the Marines so unfair as to punish an entire platoon for the failure of an individual? Use concepts in this chapter to explain why the system works.

Sources: Based on Garfinkel 1956; Goffman 1961; "Anybody's Son Will Do," 1983; Ricks 1995; Dyer 2003.

time of life. He said that adults viewed children as miniature adults, and put them to work at very early ages. At the age of 7, for example, a boy might leave home for good to learn to be a jeweler or a stonecutter. A girl, in contrast, stayed home until she married, but by the age of 7 she was expected to assume her daily share of the household tasks. Historians do not deny that these were the customs of that time, but some say that Aries' conclusion is ridiculous. They say that other evidence of that period indicates that childhood was viewed as a special time of life (Orme 2002).

Such practices did not disappear with the Middle ages. It is still common for children in the Least Industrialized Nations to work alongside adults. The photo essay on pages 250–251 provides a startling example of this practice—reflecting not just different activities but also a view of children different from the one common in the Most Industrialized Nations.

In earlier centuries, parents and teachers also considered it their moral duty to terrorize children to keep them in line. They would lock children in dark closets, frighten them with bedtime stories of death and hellfire, and force them to witness gruesome events. Consider this:

> A common moral lesson involved taking children to visit the gibbet [an upraised post on which executed bodies were left hanging from chains], where they were forced to inspect rotting corpses hanging there as an example of what happens to bad children when they grow up. Whole classes were taken out of school to witness hangings, and parents would often whip their children afterwards to make them remember what they had seen. (DeMause 1975)

Industrialization transformed the way we perceive children. When children have the leisure to go to school, they come to be thought of as tender and innocent, as needing more adult care, comfort, and protection. Over time, such attitudes of dependency grow, and today we view children as needing gentle guidance if they are to develop emotionally, intellectually, morally, even physically. We take our view for granted—after all, it is only "common sense." Yet, as you can see, our view is not "natural," but is rooted in geography and history.

Technology can also change the nature of childhood. When television contains adult images of murder, rape, war, and other violence, children of a tender age learn about a world they never knew existed, one that used to be kept secret from them (Lee 2001).

In contemporary Western societies such as the United States, children are viewed as innocent and in need of protection from adult responsibilities such as work and self-support. Ideas of childhood vary historically and cross-culturally. From paintings, such as this 1605 portrait of Lady Tasburgh and her children, some historians conclude that Europeans once viewed children as miniature adults who assumed adult roles at the earliest opportunity.

IN SUM

Childhood is more than biology. Everyone's childhood occurs at some point in history, and is embedded in particular social locations, especially social class and gender. *These social factors are as vital as our biology,* for they determine what childhood will be like for us. Although a child's *biological* characteristics (such as being small and dependent) are universal, the child's *social* experiences (what happens to that child because of what others expect of him or her) are not. Thus sociologists say that childhood varies from culture to culture.

Adolescence (ages 13–17)

Adolescence is not a "natural" age division. It is a social invention. In earlier centuries, people simply moved from childhood into young adulthood, with no stopover in between. The Industrial Revolution brought such an abundance of material surpluses, however, that for the first time in history millions of teenagers were able to remain outside the labor force. At the same time, education became more important for success. The convergence of these two forces in industrialized societies created a gap between childhood and adulthood. In the early 1900s, the term *adolescence* was coined to indicate this new stage in life (Hall 1904), one that has become renowned for inner turmoil.

To ground the self-identity and mark the passage of children into adulthood, tribal societies hold *initiation rites.* In the industrialized world, however, adolescents must "find" themselves on their own. As they attempt to carve out an identity that is distinct from both the "younger" world being left behind and the "older" world still out of range, adolescents develop their own subcultures, with distinctive clothing, hairstyles, language, gestures, and music. We usually fail to realize that contemporary society, not biology, created the period of inner turmoil that we call *adolescence.*

In many societies, manhood is not bestowed upon males simply because they reach a certain age. Manhood, rather, signifies a standing in the community that must be achieved. Shown here is an initiation ceremony in Indonesia, where boys, to lay claim to the status of manhood, must jump over this barrier.

Young Adulthood (ages 18–29)

If society invented adolescence, can it also invent other periods of life? Historian Kenneth Keniston suggests that this is happening now. He notes that industrialized societies are adding a period of prolonged youth to the life course, in which people postpone adult responsibilities past adolescence. For millions, the end of high school marks a period of extended education characterized by continued freedom from the need to support oneself. During this time, people are "neither psychological adolescents nor sociological adults" (Keniston 1971). Somewhere during this period of extended youth, young adults gradually ease into adult responsibilities. They finish school, take a full-time job, engage in courtship rituals, get married—and go into debt.

The Middle Years (ages 30–65)

The Early Middle Years (ages 30–49) During their early middle years, most people are more sure of themselves and of their goals in life. As with any point in the life course, however, the self can receive severe jolts—in this case from such circumstances as divorce or being fired. It may take years for the self to stabilize after such ruptures.

The early middle years pose a special challenge for many U.S. women, who have been given the message, especially by the media, that they can "have it all." They can be superworkers, superwives, and supermoms—all rolled into one. The reality, however, often consists of conflicting pressures, of too little time and too many demands. Something has to give. Attempts to resolve this dilemma are often compounded by another hard reality—that during gender socialization their husbands learned that child care and housework are not "masculine." In short, adjustments continue in this and all phases of life.

The Later Middle Years (ages 50–65) During the later middle years, health and mortality begin to loom large as people feel their bodies change, especially if they watch their parents become frail, fall ill, and die. The consequence is a fundamental reorientation in thinking—*from time since birth to time left to live* (Neugarten 1976). With this changed orientation, people attempt to evaluate the past and come to terms with what lies ahead. They compare what they have accomplished with how far they had hoped to go. Many people also find themselves caring for not only their own children but also their aging parents. Because of this often crushing set of burdens, people in the later middle years sometimes are called the "sandwich generation."

Life during this stage isn't always stressful. Many people find late middle age to be the most comfortable period of their lives. They enjoy job security and a standard of living higher than ever before; they have a bigger house (one that may even be paid for), newer cars, and more exotic vacations. The children are grown, the self is firmly planted, and fewer upheavals are likely to occur.

As they anticipate the next stage of life, however, most people do not like what they see.

The Older Years (about age 65 on)

The Early Older Years In industrialized societies, the older years begin around the mid-60s. This, too, is recent, for in agricultural societies, when most people died early, old age was thought to begin at around age 40. With its improved nutrition, public health, and medical care, industrialization prolonged life. Today, for those in good health, being over 65 is often experienced not as old age, but as an extension of the middle years. People who continue to work or to do things they enjoy are less likely to perceive themselves as old (Neugarten 1977). Although frequency of sex declines, most men and women in their 60s and 70s are sexually active (Denney and Quadagno 1992).

Because we have a self and can reason abstractly, we can contemplate death. Initially death is a vague notion, a remote possibility. But as people see their friends die and their own bodies no longer functioning as before, death becomes less abstract. Increasingly during this stage in the life course, people feel that "time is closing in" on them.

The Later Older Years As with the preceding periods of life except the first one, there is no precise beginning point to this last stage. For some, the 75th birthday may mark entry into this period of life. For others, that marker may be the 80th or even the 85th birthday. For most, this stage is marked by growing frailty and illness; for all who reach this stage, it is ended by death. For some, the physical decline is slow, and a rare few manage to see their 100th birthday mentally alert and in good physical health.

This January 1937 photo from Sneedville, Tennessee, shows Eunice Johns, age 9, and her husband, Charlie Johns, age 22. The groom gave his wife a doll as a wedding gift. The new husband and wife planned to build a cabin, and, as Charlie Johns phrased it, "go to housekeepin'." This photo illustrates the cultural relativity of life stages, which we sometimes mistake as fixed. It also is interesting from a symbolic interactionist perspective—that of changing definitions—for while our sensibilities are shocked by such marriages, even though they were not common, they once were taken for granted.

The Sociological Significance of the Life Course

The sociological significance of the life course is that it does not merely represent biology, things that naturally occur to all of us as we add years to our lives. Rather, *social* factors influence our life course. As you just saw, *when* you live makes a huge difference in the course that your life takes. And the difference in time does not have to be vast. Being born just ten years earlier or later may mean that you experience war or peace, an expanding economy or a depression—and those factors vitally affect what happens to you not just during childhood but throughout your life.

Your *social location,* such as social class, gender, and race, is also highly significant. Your experience of society's events will be similar to that of people who share your location, but different from that of people who do not. If you are poor, for example, you likely will feel older faster than most wealthy people for whom life is much less demanding. The life course is also influenced by individual factors—such as your health, or marrying early or entering college late—that may make your life course "out of sequence" or atypical.

For all these reasons, this sketch of the life course may not adequately reflect your own past, present, and future. As sociologist C. Wright Mills (1959) would say, because employers are beating a path to your door, or failing to do so, you are more inclined to marry, to buy a house, and to start a family—or to postpone these life course events, perhaps indefinitely. In short, changing times change lives, steering the life course into different directions.

Are We Prisoners of Socialization?

From our discussion of socialization, you might conclude that sociologists think of people as robots: The socialization goes in, and the behavior comes out. People cannot help what they do, think, or feel, for everything is simply a result of their exposure to socializing agents.

Sociologists do *not* think of people in this way. Although socialization is powerful, and profoundly affects us all, we each have a self. Established in childhood and continually modified by later experience, the self is dynamic. It is not a sponge that passively absorbs influences from the environment, but, rather, a vigorous, essential part of our being that allows us to act on our environment.

Indeed, it is precisely because individuals are not robots that their behavior is so hard to predict. The countless reactions of other people merge in each of us. As discussed earlier, even identical twins do not receive identical reactions from others. As the self develops, we internalize or "put together" these innumerable reactions, producing a unique whole that we call the *individual.* Each unique individual uses his or her own mind to reason and to make choices in life.

In this way, *each of us is actively involved in the construction of the self.* For example, although our experiences in the family lay down the basic elements of our personality, including fundamental orientations to life, we are not doomed to keep those orientations if we do not like them. We can purposely expose ourselves to groups and ideas that we prefer. Those experiences, in turn, will have their own effects on our self. In short, although socialization is powerful, within the limitations of the framework laid down by our social location we can change even the self. And that self—along with the options available within society—is the key to our behavior.

SUMMARY and REVIEW

What Is Human Nature?

How much of our human characteristics come from "nature" (heredity) and how much from "nurture" (the social environment)?

Observations of isolated, institutionalized, and **feral children** help answer this question, as do experiments with monkeys that were raised in isolation. Language and intimate social interaction—aspects of "nurture"—are essential to the development of what we consider to be human characteristics. Pp. 64–68.

Socialization into the Self and Mind

How do we acquire a self?

Humans are born with the *capacity* to develop a **self,** but the self must be socially constructed; that is, its contents depend on social interaction. According to Charles Horton Cooley's concept of the **looking-glass self,** our self develops as we internalize others' reactions to us. George Herbert Mead identified the ability to **take the role of the other** as essential to the development of the self. Mead concluded that even the mind is a social product. Pp. 68–70.

How do children develop reasoning skills?

Jean Piaget identified four stages that children go through as they develop the ability to reason: (1) *sensorimotor,* in which understanding is limited to sensory stimuli such as touch and sight; (2) *preoperational,* the ability to use symbols; (3) *concrete operational,* in which reasoning ability is more complex but not yet capable of complex abstractions; and (4) *formal operational,* or abstract thinking. Pp. 70–71.

How do sociologists evaluate Freud's psychoanalytic theory of personality development?

Freud viewed personality development as the result of our **id** (inborn, self-centered desires) clashing with the demands of society. The **ego** develops to balance the id and the **superego,** the conscience. Sociologists, in contrast, do not examine inborn or subconscious motivations, but, instead, how social factors—social class, gender, religion, education, and so forth—underlie personality development. P. 72.

How do people develop morality?

Children are born without morality, and, according to Kohlberg, they go through four stages in learning it: amoral, preconventional, conventional, and postconventional. As they make moral decisions, both men and women use personal relationships and abstract principles. Pp. 72–73.

How does socialization influence emotions?

Socialization influences not only *how we express our emotions,* but also *what emotions we feel.* Socialization into emotions is one of the means by which society produces conformity. Pp. 73–75.

Socialization into Gender

How does gender socialization affect our sense of self?

Gender socialization—sorting males and females into different roles—is a primary means of controlling human behavior. Children receive messages about gender even in infancy. A society's ideals of sex-linked behaviors are reinforced by its social institutions. Pp. 75–79.

Agents of Socialization

What are the main agents of socialization?

The **agents of socialization** include family, the neighborhood, religion, day care, school, **peer groups,** sports, the **mass media,** and the workplace. Each has its particular influences in socializing us into becoming full-fledged members of society. Pp. 79–84.

Resocialization

What is resocialization?

Resocialization is the process of learning new norms, values, attitudes, and behavior. Most resocialization is voluntary, but some, as with prisoners in **total institutions,** is involuntary. Pp. 84–85.

Socialization Through the Life Course

Does socialization end when we enter adulthood?

Socialization occurs throughout the life course. In industrialized societies, the **life course** can be divided into childhood, adolescence, young adulthood, the middle years, and the older years. Typical Western patterns include obtaining education, becoming independent from parents, building a career, finding a mate, rearing children, and confronting aging. Life course patterns vary by social location such as history, gender, race-ethnicity, and social class, as well as by individual experiences such as health and age at marriage. Pp. 85–89.

Are We Prisoners of Socialization?

Although socialization is powerful, we are not merely the sum of our socialization experiences. Just as socialization influences human behavior, so humans act on their environment and influence even their self concept. Pp. 89–90.

Where can I read more on this topic?

Suggested readings for this chapter are at the back of this book.

THINKING Critically ABOUT CHAPTER 3

1. What two agents of socialization have influenced you the most? Can you pinpoint their influence on your attitudes, beliefs, values, or other orientations to life?
2. Summarize your views of gender. What in your gender socialization has led you to have these views?
3. What is your position in the life course? How does the text's summary of that position match your experiences? Explain the similarities and differences.

ADDITIONAL RESOURCES for This Chapter

www.ablongman.com/henslin7e

- *Content Select* Research Database for Sociology, with suggested key terms and annotated references
- Link to 2000 Census, with activities
- Flashcards of key terms and concepts
- Practice Tests
- Weblinks
- Interactive Maps

Chapter 4

Social Structure and Social Interaction

Rosa Ibarra, *6 of Hearts,* 1993

Chapter Outline

My curiosity had gotten the better of me. When the sociology convention finished, I climbed aboard the first city bus that came along. I didn't know where the bus was going, and I didn't know where I was going to spend the night.

"Maybe I overdid it this time," I thought as the bus began winding down streets I had never seen before. Actually, this was my first visit to Washington, D.C., so I hadn't seen any of the streets before. I had no destination, no plans, not even a map. I carried no billfold, just a driver's license shoved into my jeans for emergency identification, some pocket change, and a $10 bill tucked into my socks. My goal was simple: If I saw something interesting, I'd get off and check it out.

"Nothing but the usual things," I mused, as we passed row after row of apartment buildings and stores. I could see myself riding buses the entire night. Then something caught my eye. Nothing spectacular—just groups of people clustered around a large circular area where several streets intersected.

I climbed off the bus and made my way to what turned out to be Dupont Circle. I took a seat on a sidewalk bench and began to observe. As the scene came into focus, I noted several street corner men drinking and joking with one another. One of the men broke from his companions and sat down next to me. As we talked, I mostly listened.

Suddenly one of the men jumped up, smashed the emptied bottle *against the sidewalk, and* thrust the jagged neck outward

As night fell, the men said that they wanted to get another bottle of wine. I contributed. They counted their money and asked if I wanted to go with them.

Although I felt my stomach churning—a combination of hesitation and fear—I heard a confident "Sure!" come out of my mouth. As we left the circle, the three men began to cut through an alley. "Oh, no," I thought. "This isn't what I had in mind."

I had but a split second to make a decision. I found myself continuing to walk with the men, but holding back half a step so that none of the three was behind me. As we walked, they passed around the remnants of their bottle.

When my turn came, I didn't know what to do. I shuddered to think about the diseases lurking within that bottle. I made another quick decision. In the semidarkness I faked it, letting only my thumb and forefinger touch my lips and nothing enter my mouth.

When we returned to Dupont Circle, the men finished their new bottle of Thunderbird. I couldn't fake it in the light, so I passed, pointing at my stomach to indicate that I was having digestive problems.

Suddenly one of the men jumped up, smashed the emptied bottle against the sidewalk, and thrust the jagged neck outward in a menacing gesture. He glared straight ahead at another bench, where he had spotted someone with whom he had some sort of unfinished business. As the other men told him to cool it, I moved slightly to one side of the group—ready to flee, just in case.

Levels of Sociological Analysis

In this sociological adventure, I almost got myself in over my head. Fortunately, it turned out all right. The man's "enemy" didn't look our way, the broken bottle was set down next to the bench "just in case he needed it," and my introduction to a life that up until then I had only read about continued until dawn.

Sociologists Elliot Liebow (1967/1999), Mitchell Duneier (1999), and Elijah Anderson (1978, 1990, 1999, 2001) have written fascinating accounts about men like these. Although streetcorner men may appear to be disorganized—simply coming and going as they please and doing whatever feels good at the moment—Liebow and Anderson analyzed how, like us, these men are influenced by the norms and beliefs of our society. This will become more apparent as we examine the two levels of analysis that sociologists use.

Macrosociology and Microsociology

The first level, **macrosociology**, places the focus on broad features of society. Sociologists who use this approach analyze such things as social class and how groups are related to

Sociologists use both macro and micro levels of analysis to study social life. Those who use macrosociology *to analyze the homeless—or any human behavior—focus on broad aspects of society, such as the economy and social classes. Sociologists who use the* microsociological approach *analyze how people interact with one another. This photo illustrates social structure: The disparities between power and powerlessness are amply evident. It also illustrates the micro level—the isolation of this homeless person.*

one another. If macrosociologists were to analyze streetcorner men, for example, they would stress that these men are located at the bottom of the U.S. social class system. Their low status means that many opportunities are closed to them: The men have few job skills, little education, hardly anything to offer an employer. As "able-bodied" men, however, they are not eligible for welfare, even for a two-year limit, so they hustle to survive. As a consequence, they spend their lives on the streets.

Conflict theory and functionalism, both of which focus on the broader picture, are examples of this macrosociological approach. In these theories, the goal is to examine the large-scale social forces that influence people.

In the second level, **microsociology,** sociologists examine **social interaction,** what people do when they come together. Sociologists who use this approach to study streetcorner men are likely to focus on the men's rules or "codes" for getting along; their survival strategies ("hustles"); how they divide up money, wine, or whatever other resources they have; their relationships with girlfriends, family, and friends; where they spend their time and what they do there; their language; their pecking order; and so on. With its focus on face-to-face interaction, symbolic interactionism is an example of microsociology.

Because each approach has a different focus, macrosociology and microsociology yield distinctive perspectives, and both are needed to gain a fuller understanding of social life. We cannot adequately understand street-corner men, for example, without using *macrosociology.* It is essential that we place the men within the broad context of how groups in U.S. society are related to one another—for, just as with ourselves, the social class of these men helps to shape their attitudes and behavior. Nor can we adequately understand these men without *microsociology,* for their everyday situations also form a significant part of their lives.

To see how these two approaches help us to understand social life, let's examine each one. As we do so, you may find yourself feeling more comfortable with one approach than the other. This is what happens with sociologists. For reasons of personal background and professional training, sociologists find themselves more comfortable with one approach and tend to use it in their research. Both approaches, however, are necessary for a full understanding of life in society.

The Macrosociological Perspective: Social Structure

Why did the street people in the opening vignette act as they did, staying up all night drinking wine and ready to use a lethal weapon? Why don't *we* act like this? Social structure helps us answer such questions.

The Sociological Significance of Social Structure

To better understand human behavior, we need to understand *social structure,* the framework of society that was already laid out before you were born. **Social structure** refers to the typical patterns of a group, such as its usual relationships between men and women or students and teachers. *The sociological significance of social structure is that it guides our behavior.*

Because this term may seem vague, let's consider how you experience social structure in your own life. As I write this, I do not know your race-ethnicity. I do not know your religion. I do not know if you are young or old, tall or short, male or female. I do not know if you were reared on a farm, in the suburbs, or in the inner city. I do not know if you went to a public high school or an exclusive prep school. But I do know that you are in college. And this, alone, tells me a great deal about you.

From this one piece of information, I can assume that the social structure of your college is now shaping what you do. For example, let's suppose that today you felt euphoric over some great news. I can be fairly certain (not absolutely, mind you, but relatively certain) that when you entered the classroom, social structure overrode your mood. That is,

macrosociology analysis of social life that focuses on broad features of society, such as social class and the relationships of groups to one another; an approach usually used by functionalists and conflict theorists

microsociology analysis of social life that focuses on social interaction; an approach usually used by symbolic interactionists

social interaction what people do when they are in one another's presence

social structure the framework that surrounds us, consisting of the relationships of people and groups to one another, which give direction to and set limits on behavior instead of shouting at the top of your lungs and joyously throwing this book into the air, you entered the classroom in a fairly subdued manner and took your seat.

The same social structure influences your instructor, even if, on the one hand, he or she is facing a divorce or has a child dying of cancer, or, on the other, has just been awarded a promotion or a million-dollar grant. The instructor may feel like either retreating into seclusion or celebrating wildly, but most likely he or she will conduct class in the usual manner. In short, social structure tends to override personal feelings and desires.

Just as social structure influences you and your instructor, so it also establishes limits for street people. They, too, find themselves in a specific social location in the U.S. social structure—although it is quite different from yours or your instructor's. Consequently, they are affected differently. Nothing about their social location leads them to take notes or to lecture. Their behaviors, however, are as logical an outcome of where they find themselves in the social structure as are your own. In their position in the social structure, it is just as "natural" to drink wine all night as it is for you to stay up studying all night for a crucial examination. It is just as "natural" for you to nod and say, "Excuse me," when you enter a crowded classroom late and have to claim a desk on which someone has already placed books as it is for them to break off the head of a wine bottle and glare at an enemy.

In short, people learn their behaviors and attitudes because of their location in the social structure (whether they be privileged, deprived, or in between), and they act accordingly. This is equally true of street people and of ourselves. *The differences in behavior and attitudes are not due to biology (race, sex, or any other supposed genetic factors), but to people's location in the social structure.* Switch places with street people and watch your behaviors and attitudes change!

To better understand social structure, read the Down-to-Earth Sociology box on football below. Because social structure so crucially affects who we are and what we are like, let's look more closely at its major components: culture, social class, social status, roles, groups, and social institutions.

DOWN-TO-EARTH SOCIOLOGY

College Football as Social Structure

TO GAIN A BETTER IDEA OF WHAT *SOCIAL structure* is, think of college football (see Dobriner 1969a). You probably know the various positions on the team: center, guards, tackles, ends, quarterback, running backs, and the like. Each is a *status;* that is, each is a social position. For each of these statuses, there is a *role;* that is, each of these positions has certain expectations attached to it. The center is expected to snap the ball, the quarterback to pass it, the guards to block, the tackles to tackle or block, the ends to receive passes, and so on. Those role expectations guide each player's actions; that is, the players try to do what their particular role requires.

Let's suppose that football is your favorite sport and you never miss a home game at your college. Let's also suppose that you graduate, get a great job, and move across the country. Five years later, you return to your campus for a nostalgic visit. The climax of your visit is the biggest football game of the season. When you get to the game, you might be surprised to see a different coach, but you are not surprised that each playing position is occupied by people you don't know, for all the players you knew have graduated, and their places have been filled by others.

This scenario mirrors *social structure,* the framework around which a group exists. In this football example, that framework consists of the coaching staff and the eleven playing positions. The game does not depend on any particular individual, but, rather, on *social statuses,* the positions that the individuals occupy. When someone leaves a position, the game can go on because someone else takes over that position or status and plays the role. The game will continue even though not a single individual remains from one period of time to the next. Notre Dame's football team endures today even though Knute Rockne, the Gipper, and his teammates are long dead.

Even though you may not play football, you nevertheless live your life within a clearly established social structure. The statuses you occupy and the roles you play were already in place before you were born. You take your particular positions in life, others do the same, and society goes about its business. Although the specifics change with time, the game—whether of life or of football—goes on.

Culture

In Chapter 2, we considered culture's far-reaching effects on our lives. At this point, let's simply summarize its main impact. Sociologists use the term *culture* to refer to a group's language, beliefs, values, behaviors, and even gestures. Culture also includes the material objects that a group uses. Culture is the broadest framework that determines what kind of people we become. If we are reared in Eskimo, Arabian, Russian, or U.S. culture, we will grow up to be like most Eskimos, Arabs, Russians, or Americans. On the outside, we will look and act like them; and on the inside, we will think and feel like them.

Social Class

To understand people, we must examine the social locations that they hold in life. Especially significant is *social class,* which is based on income, education, and occupational prestige. Large numbers of people who have similar amounts of income and education and who work at jobs that are roughly comparable in prestige make up a **social class.** It is hard to overemphasize this aspect of social structure, for our social class influences not only our behaviors, but even our ideas and attitudes. We have this in common, then, with the street people described in the opening vignette—both they and we are influenced by our location in the social class structure. Theirs may be a considerably less privileged position, but it has no less influence on their lives. Social class is so significant that we shall spend an entire chapter (Chapter 10) on this topic.

Social Status

When you hear the word *status,* you are likely to think of prestige. These two words are welded together in people's minds. Sociologists, however, use **status** in a different way—to refer to the *position* that someone occupies. That position may carry a great deal of prestige, as in the case of a judge or an astronaut, or it may bring little prestige, as in the case of a convenience store clerk or a hamburger flipper at a fast-food restaurant. The status may also be looked down on, as in the case of a streetcorner man, an ex-convict, or a thief.

All of us occupy several positions at the same time. Simultaneously you may be a son or daughter, a worker, a date, and a student. Sociologists use the term **status set** to refer to all the statuses or positions that you occupy. Obviously your status set changes as your particular statuses change. For example, if you graduate from college and take a full-time job, get married, buy a home, have children, and so on, your status set changes to include the positions of worker, spouse, homeowner, and parent.

Like other aspects of social structure, statuses are part of our basic framework of living in society. The example given earlier of students and teachers who come to class and do what others expect of them despite their particular moods illustrates how statuses affect our actions—and those of the people around us. Our statuses—whether daughter or son, worker or date—serve as guides for our behavior.

Ascribed and Achieved Statuses

An **ascribed status** is involuntary. You do not ask for it, nor can you choose it. Some you inherit at birth such as your race-ethnicity, sex, and the social class of your parents, as well as your statuses as female or male, daughter or son, niece or nephew, and granddaughter or grandson. Others, such as teenager and senior citizen, are related to the life course discussed in Chapter 3, and are given to you later in life.

Achieved statuses, in contrast, are voluntary. These you earn or accomplish. As a result of your efforts you become a student, a friend, a spouse, a rabbi, minister, priest, or nun. Or, for lack of effort (or efforts that others fail to appreciate), you become a school dropout, a former friend, an ex-spouse, or a defrocked rabbi, priest, or nun. In other words, achieved statuses can be either positive or negative; both college president and bank robber are achieved statuses.

Each status provides guidelines for how we are to act and feel. Like other aspects of social structure, statuses set limits on what we can and cannot do. Because social statuses are an essential part of the social structure, they are found in all human groups.

social class according to Weber, a large group of people who rank close to one another in wealth, power, and prestige; according to Marx, one of two groups: capitalists who own the means of production or workers who sell their labor

status social ranking; the position that someone occupies in society or a social group

status set all the statuses or positions that an individual occupies

ascribed statuses positions an individual either inherits at birth or receives involuntarily later in life

achieved statuses positions that are earned, accomplished, or involve at least some effort or activity on the individual's part

Master statuses *are those that overshadow our other statuses. Shown here is Christopher Reeve, who was paralyzed when he was thrown from a horse. Before his accident, Reeve was a top Hollywood actor, celebrating worldwide success with his role as Superman. Today, his* master status *is that of a person with a disability. He has accepted this status and is a spokesperson for people suffering from spinal cord injuries. Reeve is shown here at a fundraiser for the Christopher Reeve Paralysis Foundation.*

Status Symbols People who are pleased with their particular social status may want others to recognize that they occupy that status. To elicit this recognition, they use **status symbols,** signs that identify a status. For example, people wear wedding rings to announce their marital status; uniforms, guns, and badges to proclaim that they are police officers (and to not so subtly let you know that their status gives them authority over you); and "backward" collars to declare that they are Lutheran ministers or Roman Catholic or Episcopal priests.

Some social statuses are negative, and so, therefore, are their status symbols. The scarlet letter in Nathaniel Hawthorne's book by the same title is one example. Another is the CONVICTED DUI (Driving Under the Influence) bumper sticker that some U.S. courts require convicted drunk drivers to display if they wish to avoid a jail sentence.

All of us use status symbols to announce our statuses to others and to help smooth our interactions in everyday life. You might consider your own status symbols. For example, how does your clothing announce your statuses of sex, age, and college student?

Master Statuses A **master status** is one that cuts across the other statuses that you hold. Some master statuses are ascribed. An example is your sex. Whatever you do, people perceive you as a male or as a female. If you are working your way through college by flipping burgers, people see you not only as a burger flipper and a student, but as a *male* or *female* burger flipper and a *male* or *female* college student. Other master statuses are race and age.

Some master statuses are achieved. If you become very, very wealthy (and it doesn't matter if your wealth comes from an invention or from the lottery—it is still *achieved* as far as sociologists are concerned), your wealth is likely to become a master status. For example, people might say, "She is a very rich burger flipper"—or more likely, "She's very rich, and she used to flip burgers!"

Similarly, people who become disfigured find, to their dismay, that their condition becomes a master status. For example, a person whose face is scarred from severe burns will be viewed through this unwelcome master status regardless of his or her occupation or accomplishments. It is the same for people with disabilities. Those who are confined to wheelchairs can attest to how their handicap overrides all their other statuses and determines others' perceptions of everything they do.

Although our statuses usually fit together fairly well, some people have a contradiction or mismatch between their statuses. This is known as **status inconsistency** (or discrepancy). A 14-year-old college student is an example. So is a 40-year-old married woman who is dating a 19-year-old college sophomore.

These examples reveal an essential aspect of social statuses: Like other components of social structure, they come with built-in *norms* (that is, expectations) that guide our behavior. When statuses mesh well, as they usually do, we know what to expect of people. This helps social interaction to unfold smoothly. Status inconsistency, however, upsets our expectations. If you met someone mentioned in the preceding examples, how should you act? Are you supposed to treat the 14-year-old as you would a young teenager, or as you would your college classmate? Do you react to the married woman as you would to the mother of your friend, or as you would to a classmate's date?

status symbols items used to identify a status

master status a status that cuts across the other statuses that an individual occupies

status inconsistency ranking high on some dimensions of social class and low on others

Roles

All the world's a stage
And all the men and women merely players.
They have their exits and their entrances;
And one man in his time plays many parts . . .
(William Shakespeare, *As You Like It,* Act II, Scene 7)

Like Shakespeare, sociologists see roles as essential to social life. When you were born, **roles**—the behaviors, obligations, and privileges attached to a status—were already set up for you. Society was waiting with outstretched arms to teach you how it expected you to act as a boy or a girl. And whether you were born poor, rich, or somewhere in between, that, too, attached certain behaviors, obligations, and privileges to your statuses.

The difference between role and status is that you *occupy* a status, but you *play* a role (Linton 1936). For example, being a son or daughter is your status, but your expectation of receiving food and shelter from your parents—as well as their expectation that you show respect to them—is your role. Or, again, your status is student, but your role is to attend class, take notes, do homework, and take tests.

The sociological significance of roles is that they lay out what is expected of people. They are like a fence. They allow us a certain amount of freedom, but for most of us that freedom doesn't go very far. Suppose a woman decides that she is not going to wear dresses—or a man that he will not wear suits and ties—regardless of what anyone says. In most situations, they'll stick to their decision. When a formal occasion comes along, however, such as a family wedding or a funeral, they are likely to cave in to norms that they find overwhelming. Almost all of us stay within the fences that mark out what is "appropriate" for our roles. Most of us are little troubled by such constraints, for our socialization is so thorough that we usually *want* to do what our roles indicate is appropriate.

Not all roles are forever. Some end at prescribed times, such as graduation from college. Others end even though we may not want them to, such as an unwelcome divorce. **Role exit** is the term sociologists use to refer to the ending of a role. Role exit always involves adjustments, for you have to get used to not "being" what you formerly were (Ebaugh 1988). Role exit also signals the beginning of another role, which may be welcome, such as the position you hope to get when you exit college. Or it may be unwelcome, even loathed, such as "divorced person," *if* you really wanted the marriage to continue and didn't want to again enter the dating scene. The *if* is important, for someone who looks forward to a divorce sees it differently from someone who does not.

Groups

A **group** consists of people who regularly and consciously interact with one another. Ordinarily, the members of a group share similar values, norms, and expectations. Just as social class, statuses, and roles influence our actions, so, too, the groups to which we belong are powerful forces in our lives. In fact, *to belong to a group is to yield to others the right to make certain decisions about our behavior.* If we belong to a group, we assume an obligation to act according to the expectations of other members of that group.

Although this principle holds true for all groups, some groups wield influence over only small segments of our behavior. If you belong to a stamp collector's club, for example, the group's influence may center around your display of knowledge about stamps, and perhaps your attendance at meetings. Other groups, however, such as the family, control many aspects of our behavior. When parents say to their 15-year-old daughter, "As long as you are living under my roof, you had better be home by midnight," they show their expectation that their children, as members of the family, will conform to their ideas about many aspects of life, including their views on curfew. They are saying that as long as the daughter wants to remain a member of the household, her behavior must conform to their expectations.

Social Institutions

At first glance, the term *social institution* may seem to have little relevance to your personal life. The term seems so cold and abstract. In fact, however, **social institutions**—the organized means that each society develops to meet its basic needs—vitally affect your life. By weaving the fabric of society, social institutions shape your behavior. They even color your thoughts. How can this be? Look at what social institutions are: the family, religion, education, economics, medicine, politics, law, science, the military, and the mass media.

role the behaviors, obligations, and privileges attached to a status

role exit refers to the ending of a role, including the adjustments people make when they face not "being" what they formerly were

group people who have something in common and who believe that what they have in common is significant; also called a social group

social institution the organized, usual, or standard ways by which society meets its basic needs

In industrialized societies, social institutions tend to be more formal, in tribal societies more informal. Education in industrialized societies, for example, is highly structured, while in tribal societies it usually consists of informally learning what adults do. Figure 4.1 below summarizes the basic social institutions. Note that each institution has its own

Figure 4.1 **Social Institutions in Industrial and Postindustrial Societies**

Social Institution	Basic Needs	Some Groups or Organizations	Some Statuses	Some Values	Some Norms
Family	Regulate reproduction, socialize and protect children	Relatives, kinship groups	Daughter, son, father, mother, brother, sister, aunt, uncle, grandparent	Sexual fidelity, providing for your family, keeping a clean house, respect for parents	Have only as many children as you can afford, be faithful to your spouse
Religion	Concerns about life after death, the meaning of suffering and loss; desire to connect with the Creator	Congregation, synagogue, mosque, denomination, charitable association	Priest, minister, rabbi, worshipper, teacher, disciple, missionary, prophet, convert	Reading and adhering to holy texts such as the Bible, the Koran, and the Torah; honoring God	Attend worship services, contribute money, follow the teachings
Education	Transmit knowledge and skills across the generations	School, college, student senate, sports team, PTA, teachers' union	Teacher, student, dean, principal, football player, cheerleader	Academic honesty, good grades, being "cool"	Do homework, prepare lectures, don't snitch on classmates
Economics	Produce and distribute goods and services	Credit unions, banks, credit card companies, buying clubs	Worker, boss, buyer, seller, creditor, debtor, advertiser	Making money, paying bills on time, producing efficiently	Maximize profits, "the customer is always right," work hard
Medicine	Heal the sick and injured, care for the dying	AMA, hospitals, pharmacies, insurance companies, HMOs	Doctor, nurse, patient, pharmacist, medical insurer	Hippocratic oath, staying in good health, following doctor's orders	Don't exploit patients, give best medical care available
Politics	Establish a hierarchy of power and authority	Political parties, congresses, parliaments, monarchies	President, senator, lobbyist, voter, candidate, spin doctor	Majority rule, the right to vote as a sacred trust	One vote per person, voting as a privilege and a right
Law	Maintain social order	Police, Courts, Prisons	Judge, police officer, lawyer, defendant, prison guard	Trial by one's peers, innocence until proven guilty	Give true testimony, follow the rules of evidence
Science	Master the environment	Local, state, regional, national, and international associations	Scientist, researcher, technician, administrator, journal editor	Unbiased research, open dissemination of research findings, don't plagiarize	Follow scientific method, be objective, fully disclose research findings
Military	Protection from enemies, support of national interests	Army, navy, air force, marines, coast guard, national guard	Soldier, recruit, enlisted person, officer, prisoner, spy	To die for one's country is an honor, obedience unto death	Be ready to go to war, obey superior officers, don't question orders
Mass Media (an emerging institution)	Disseminate information, mold public opinion, report events	Television networks, radio stations, publishers	Journalist, newscaster, author, editor, publisher	Timeliness, accuracy, large audiences, freedom of the press	Be accurate, fair, timely, and profitable

values, roles, and norms. Social institutions are so significant that Part IV of this book focuses on them.

The Sociological Significance of Social Institutions

To understand social institutions is to realize how profoundly social structure affects our lives. Much of their influence lies beyond our ordinary awareness. For example, because of our economic institution, it is common to work eight hours a day for five days every week. There is nothing normal or natural about this pattern, however. Its regularity is only an arbitrary arrangement for dividing work and leisure. Yet this one aspect of a single social institution has far-reaching effects, not only in terms of how people structure their time and activities but also in terms of how they deal with family and friends, and how they meet their personal needs.

Each of the other social institutions also has far-reaching effects on our lives. Our social institutions establish the context in which we live, shaping our behavior and coloring our thoughts. Social institutions are so significant that if they were different, we would be different people. We certainly could not remain the same, for social institutions influence our orientations to the social world, and even to life itself.

An Example: The Mass Media as an Emerging Social Institution

Far beyond serving simply as sources of information, the mass media influence our attitudes toward social issues, other people, and even our self-concept. Because the media significantly shape public opinion, all totalitarian governments attempt to maintain tight control over them.

The mass media are relatively new in human history, owing their origins to the invention of the printing press in the 1400s. This invention had immediate and profound consequences on virtually all other social institutions. The printing of the Bible altered religion, for instance, while the publication of political broadsides and newspapers altered politics. From these beginnings, a series of inventions—from radio and movies to television and, more recently, the microchip—has made the media an increasingly powerful force.

One of the most significant questions we can ask about this social institution is: Who controls it? That control, which in totalitarian countries is obvious, is much less visible in democratic nations. Functionalists might conclude that the media in a democratic nation represent the varied interests of the many groups that make up that nation. Conflict theorists, in contrast, see the matter quite differently: The mass media—at least a country's most influential newspapers and television stations—represent the interests of the political elite. The wealthy and powerful use the media to mold public opinion and to help preserve their places of privilege.

Since the mass media are so influential in our lives today, the answer to this question of who controls the media is of more than passing interest. This matter is vital to our understanding of contemporary society.

The mass media are a major influence in contemporary life. Until 1436, when Johann Gutenberg invented movable type, printing was a slow process, and printed materials were expensive. Today printed materials are common and often cheap. "Cheap" has a double meaning, with its second meaning illustrated in this photo.

Comparing Functionalist and Conflict Perspectives

Just as the functionalist and conflict perspectives of the mass media differ, so do their views of the nature of social institutions. Let's compare these views.

The Functionalist Perspective

Functionalists stress that no society is without social institutions. This is because social institutions perform vital functions for society. A group may be too small to have people who specialize in education, but it will have its own established ways of teaching skills and ideas to the young. It may be too small to have a military, but it will have some mechanism of self-defense. To

functional requisites the major tasks that a society must fulfill if it is to survive

survive, every society must meet its basic needs (or **functional requisites**). According to functionalists, that is the purpose of social institutions.

What are those basic needs? Functionalists identify five functional requisites that each society must fulfill if it is to survive (Aberle et al. 1950; Mack and Bradford 1979).

1. *Replacing members.* If a society does not replace its members, it cannot continue to exist. Because reproduction is so fundamental to a society's existence, and because every society has a vital need to protect infants and children, all groups have developed some version of the family. The family gives the newcomer to society a sense of belonging by providing a "lineage," an account of how he or she is related to others. The family also functions to control people's sex drive and to maintain orderly reproduction.
2. *Socializing new members.* Each baby must be taught what it means to be a member of the group into which it is born. To accomplish this, each human group develops devices to ensure that its newcomers learn the group's basic expectations. As the primary "bearer of culture," the family is essential to this process, but other social institutions, such as religion and education, also help meet this basic need.
3. *Producing and distributing goods and services.* Every society must produce and distribute basic resources, from food and clothing to shelter and education. Consequently, every society establishes an *economic* institution, a means of producing goods and services along with routine ways of distributing them.
4. *Preserving order.* Societies face two threats of disorder: one internal, the potential for chaos, and the other external, the possibility of attack. To defend themselves against external conquest, they develop a means of defense, some form of the military. To protect themselves from internal threat, they develop a system of policing themselves, ranging from formal organizations of armed groups to informal systems of gossip.
5. *Providing a sense of purpose.* For people to cooperate with one another and willingly give up personal gains in favor of working with and for others, they need a sense of purpose. They need to be convinced that it is worth sacrificing for the common good. Human groups develop many ways to instill such beliefs, but a primary one is religion, which attempts to answer questions about ultimate meaning. Actually, all of a society's institutions are involved in meeting this functional requisite; the family provides one set of answers about the sense of purpose, the school another, and so on. All of the answers are interrelated.

Functionalist theorists have identified five functional requisites *for the survival of a society. One, providing a sense of purpose, is often met through religious groups. To most people, snake handling, as in this church service in Jolo, West Virginia, is nonsensical. From a functional perspective, however, it makes a great deal of sense. Can you identify its sociological meanings?*

The Conflict Perspective Although conflict theorists agree that social institutions were originally designed to meet basic survival needs, they do not view social institutions as working harmoniously for the common good. On the contrary, conflict theorists stress that powerful groups control society's institutions, manipulating them in order to maintain their own privileged position of wealth and power (Useem 1984; Domhoff 1967, 1998, 1999b).

As evidence of their position, conflict theorists point out that a fairly small group of people has garnered the lion's share of the nation's wealth. Members of this elite sit on the boards of major corporations and the country's most prestigious universities. They make strategic campaign contributions to influence (or control) the nation's lawmakers, and it is they who make the major decisions in this society: to go to war or to refrain from war; to increase or to decrease taxes; to raise or to lower interest rates; and to pass laws that favor or impede moving capital, technology, and jobs out of the country.

Feminist sociologists (both women and men) have used conflict theory to gain a better understanding of how social institutions affect gender relations. Their basic insight is that gender is also an element of social structure, not simply a characteristic of individuals. In other words, throughout the world, social institutions divide males and females into separate groups, each with unequal access to society's resources.

IN SUM

Conflict theorists regard our social institutions as having a single primary purpose—to preserve the social order. They interpret this as preserving the wealthy and powerful in their privileged positions. Functionalists, in contrast, view social institutions as working together to meet universal human needs.

Changes in Social Structure

As you can see, this enveloping system that we call social structure powerfully affects our lives. This means that as social structure changes, so, too, do our orientations to life. Consider how culture changes as it responds to evolving values and new technology, and to innovative ideas from home and abroad. Our new era of "globalization" puts us in contact with the customs of many other people. As globalization causes our economy to grow or to stagnate, it opens or closes opportunities and changes our lives, sometimes brutally so. Groups that did not exist, such as the IRS, come into being, and afterward wield extraordinary power over us. The corner in life that we occupy is not independent of these forces, but is pushed and pulled in different directions as social structure changes.

What Holds Society Together?

With its many, often conflicting, groups and its extensive social change, how does society manage to hold together? Let's examine two answers that sociologists have proposed.

Mechanical and Organic Solidarity

Sociologist Emile Durkheim (1893/1933) found the key to **social cohesion**—the degree to which members of a society feel united by shared values and other social bonds—in what he called **mechanical solidarity.** By this term, Durkheim meant that people who perform similar tasks develop a shared consciousness, a sense of similarity that unites them into a common whole. Think of an agricultural society in which everyone is involved in planting, cultivating, and harvesting. Members of this group have so much in common that they know how most others feel about life. Societies with mechanical solidarity tolerate little diversity in thinking and attitudes, for their unity depends on similar thinking.

As societies get larger, their **division of labor** (how they divide up work) becomes more specialized. Some people mine gold, others turn it into jewelry, while still others sell it. This division of labor makes people depend on one another—for the work of each person contributes to the welfare of the whole.

Because this form of solidarity is based on interdependence, Durkheim called it **organic solidarity.** To see why he used this term, think about how you depend on your teacher to guide you through this introductory course in sociology. At the same time, your teacher needs you and other students in order to have a job. The two of you are *like organs in the same body.* (The "body" in this case is the college or university.) Although each of you performs different tasks, you depend on one another. This creates a form of unity.

The change to organic solidarity meant a new basis for solidarity—not similar views, but separate activities that contribute to the overall welfare of the group. As a result, modern societies can tolerate many differences among people and still manage to work as a whole. Both past and present societies are based on social solidarity, but the types of solidarity differ remarkably.

Gemeinschaft and *Gesellschaft*

Ferdinand Tönnies (1887/1988) also analyzed this major change. Tönnies used the term *Gemeinschaft* (Guh-MINE-shoft), or "intimate community," to describe village life, the type of society in which everyone knows everyone else. He noted that in the society that was emerging, the village's personal ties, family connections, and lifelong friendships were being crowded out by short-term relationships, individual accomplishments, and self-interest. Tönnies called this new type

social cohesion the degree to which members of a group or a society feel united by shared values and other social bonds

mechanical solidarity Durkheim's term for the unity (a shared consciousness) that people feel as a result of performing the same or similar tasks

division of labor the splitting of a group's or a society's tasks into specialties

organic solidarity solidarity based on the interdependence that results from the division of labor; people needing others to fulfill their jobs

Gemeinschaft a type of society in which life is intimate; a community in which everyone knows everyone else and people share a sense of togetherness

Warm, ongoing relationships of Gemeinschaft *society are apparent in this restaurant in Munich, Germany, while the more impersonal relationships of* Gesellschaft *society are evident in the Cybernet cafe in Seattle where people ignore one another in favor of electronic interaction via the Internet. Internet interactions do not easily fit standard sociological models—another instance of cultural lag.*

of society ***Gesellschaft*** (Guh-ZELL-shoft), or "impersonal association." He did not mean that we no longer have intimate ties to family and friends, but, rather, that these ties have shrunk in importance. Contracts, for example, replace handshakes, and work doesn't center around friends and family, but strangers and short-term acquaintances.

How Relevant Are These Concepts Today? I know that *Gemeinschaft, Gesellschaft,* and *mechanical* and *organic solidarity* are strange terms and that Durkheim's and Tönnies' observations must seem like a dead issue. The concern these sociologists expressed, however—that their world was changing from a community in which people are united by shared ideas and feelings to an anonymous association built around impersonal, short-term contacts—is still very real. In large part, this same concern explains the rise of Islamic fundamentalism (Volti 1995). Islamic leaders fear that Western values will uproot their traditional culture, that cold rationality will replace warm, personal relationships among families and clans. They fear, rightly so, that this will change even their views on life and morality. Although the terms may sound strange, even obscure, you can see that the ideas remain a vital part of today's world.

IN SUM

Gesellschaft a type of society that is dominated by impersonal relationships, individual accomplishments, and self-interest

Whether the terms are *Gemeinschaft* and *Gesellschaft* or *mechanical solidarity* and *organic solidarity,* they indicate that as societies change, so do people's orientations to life. *The sociological point is that social structure sets the context for what we do, feel, and think, and ultimately, then, for the kind of people we become.* As you read the Cultural Diversity box on the next page, which describes one of the few remaining *Gemeinschaft* societies in the United States, think of how fundamentally different you would be had you been reared in an Amish family.

CULTURAL DIVERSITY
in the UNITED STATES

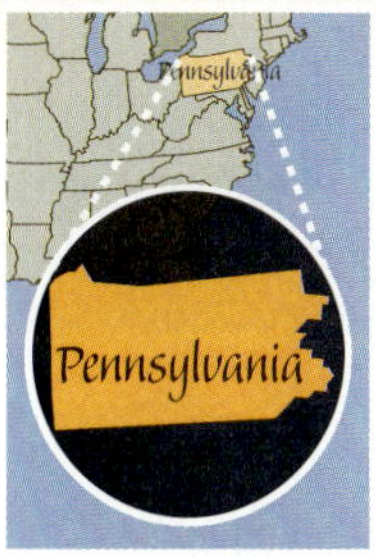

The Amish—*Gemeinschaft* Community in a *Gesellschaft* Society

In Ferdinand Tönnies' term, the United States is a *Gesellschaft* society. Impersonal associations pervade our everyday life. Local, state, and federal governments regulate many activities. Impersonal corporations hire and fire people not on the basis of personal relationships, but on the basis of the bottom line. And, perhaps even more significantly, millions of Americans do not even know their neighbors.

Within the United States, a handful of small communities exhibits characteristics that depart from those of the mainstream society. One such community is the Old Order Amish, followers of a sect that broke away from the Swiss-German Mennonite church in the 1600s, and settled in Pennsylvania around 1727. Today, about 150,000 Old Order Amish live in the United States. About 75 percent live in just three states: Pennsylvania, Ohio, and Indiana. The largest concentration, about 22,000, reside in Lancaster County, Pennsylvania. The Amish, who believe that birth control is wrong, have doubled in population in just the past two decades.

Because these farmers use horses instead of tractors, most Amish farms are one hundred acres or less. To the five million tourists who pass through Lancaster County each year, the rolling green pastures, white farmhouses, simple barns, horse-drawn buggies, and clotheslines hung with somber-colored garments convey a sense of peace and innocence reminiscent of another era. Although just sixty-five miles from Philadelphia, "Amish country" is a world away.

Amish life is based on separation from the world—an idea taken from Christ's

Sermon on the Mount—and obedience to the church's teachings and leaders. This rejection of worldly concerns, writes sociologist Donald Kraybill in *The Riddle of Amish Culture* (1989), "provides the foundation of such Amish values as humility, faithfulness, thrift, tradition, communal goals, joy of work, a slow-paced life, and trust in divine providence."

The *Gemeinschaft* of village life that Tönnies regretted as being lost to industrialization is still alive among the Amish. The Amish make their decisions in weekly meetings, where, by consensus, they follow a set of rules, or *Ordnung,* to guide their behavior. Religion and discipline are the glue that holds the Amish together. Brotherly love and the welfare of the community are paramount values. In times of birth, sickness, and death, neighbors pitch in with the chores. In these ways, they maintain the bonds of intimate community.

The Amish are bound by other ties, including language (a dialect of German known as Pennsylvania Dutch), black clothing whose style has remained unchanged for almost 300 years, and church-sponsored schools. Nearly all Amish marry, and divorce is forbidden. The family is a vital ingredient in Amish life; all major events take place in the home, including weddings, births, funerals, and church services. Amish children attend church schools, but only until the age of 13. (In 1972, the Supreme Court ruled that Amish parents had the right to take their children out of school after the eighth grade.) To go to school beyond the eighth grade would expose them to values and "worldly concerns" that would drive a wedge between them and their community. The Amish believe that violence is bad, even personal self-defense, and they register as conscientious objectors during times of war. They pay no social security, and they collect none.

The Amish cannot resist all change, of course. Instead, they try to adapt to change in ways that will least disrupt their core values. Because urban sprawl has driven up the price of farmland, about half of Amish men work at jobs other than farming, most in farm-related businesses or in woodcrafts. They go to great lengths to avoid leaving the home. The Amish believe that when a husband works away from home, all aspects of life change—from the marital relationship to the care of the children—certainly an astute sociological insight. They also believe that if a man receives a paycheck, he will think that his work is of more value than his wife's. For the Amish, intimate, or *Gemeinschaft,* society is essential for maintaining their way of life.

Sources: Hostetler 1980; Bender 1990; Kephart and Zellner 2001; Aeppel 1996; Savells 2003; Kraybill 2002.; Dawley 2003.

The Microsociological Perspective: Social Interaction in Everyday Life

Whereas the macrosociological approach stresses the broad features of society, the microsociological approach has a narrower focus. Microsociologists examine *face-to-face interaction,* what people do when they are in one another's presence. Let's examine some of the areas of social life that microsociologists study.

Symbolic Interaction

For symbolic interactionists, the most significant part of life in society is social interaction. Symbolic interactionists are especially interested in the symbols that people use. They want to know how people look at things and how this, in turn, affects their behavior and orientations to life. Of the many areas of social life that microsociologists study, let's look at stereotyping, personal space, touching, and eye contact.

Stereotypes in Everyday Life You are familiar with how strong first impressions are and the way they "set the tone" for interaction. When you first meet someone, you cannot help but notice certain highly visible and distinctive features, especially the person's sex, race, age, and physical appearance. Despite your best intentions, your assumptions about these characteristics shape your first impressions. They also affect how you act toward that person—and, in turn, how that person acts toward you. These fascinating aspects of our social interaction are discussed in the Down-to-Earth Sociology box on the next page.

Personal Space We all surround ourselves with a "personal bubble" that we go to great lengths to protect. We open the bubble to intimates—to our friends, children, parents, and so on—but we're careful to keep most people out of this space. In the hall, we might walk with our books clasped in front of us (a strategy often chosen by females). We carefully line up at the drinking fountain, making certain there is space between us so we don't touch the person in front of us and we aren't touched by the person behind us.

At times we extend our personal space. In the library, for example, you may place your coat on the chair next to you—claiming that space for yourself even though you aren't using it. If you want to really extend your space, you might even spread books in front of the other chairs, keeping the whole table to yourself by giving the impression that others have just stepped away.

The amount of space people prefer varies from one culture to another. South Americans, for example, like to be closer when they speak to others than do people reared in the United States. Anthropologist Edward Hall (1959; Hall and Hall 2003) recounts a conversation with a man from South America who had attended one of his lectures.

> He came to the front of the class at the end of the lecture. . . . We started out facing each other, and as he talked I became dimly aware that he was standing a little too close and that I was beginning to back up. Fortunately I was able to suppress my first impulse and remain stationary because there was nothing to communicate aggression in his behavior except the conversational distance. . . .
>
> By experimenting I was able to observe that as I moved away slightly, there was an associated shift in the pattern of interaction. He had more trouble expressing himself. If I shifted to where I felt comfortable (about twenty-one inches), he looked somewhat puzzled and hurt, almost as though he were saying, "Why is he acting that way? Here I am doing everything I can to talk to him in a friendly manner and he suddenly withdraws. Have I done anything wrong? Said something I shouldn't?" Having ascertained that distance had a direct effect on his conversation, I stood my ground, letting him set the distance.

As you can see, despite Hall's extensive knowledge of other cultures, he still felt uncomfortable in this conversation. He first interpreted the invasion of his personal space

stereotype assumptions of what people are like, whether true or false

DOWN-TO-EARTH SOCIOLOGY

Beauty May Be Only Skin Deep, But Its Effects Go On Forever: Stereotypes in Everyday Life

MARK SNYDER, A PSYCHOLOGIST, WONdered if **stereotypes**—our assumptions of what people are like—might be self-fulfilling. He came up with an ingenious way to test this idea. He (1993) gave college men a Polaroid snapshot of a woman (supposedly taken just moments before) and told them that he would introduce them to her after they talked with her on the telephone. Actually, photographs showing either a pretty or a homely woman had been prepared before the experiment began. The photo was not of the woman the men would talk to.

Stereotypes came into play immediately. As Snyder gave each man the photograph, he asked him what he thought the woman would be like. The men who saw the photograph of the attractive woman said they expected to meet a poised, humorous, outgoing woman. The men who had been given a photo of the unattractive woman described her as awkward, serious, and unsociable.

The men's stereotypes influenced the way they spoke to the women on the telephone. The men who had seen the photograph of a pretty woman were warm, friendly, and humorous. This affected the women they spoke to, for they responded in a warm, friendly, outgoing manner. And the men who had seen the photograph of a homely woman? On the phone, they were cold, reserved, and humorless, and the women they spoke to became cool, reserved, and humorless. Keep in mind that the women did not know that their looks had been evaluated—and that the photographs were not even of them. In short, stereotypes tend to produce behaviors that match the stereotype. This principle is illustrated in Figure 4.2.

While beauty might be only skin deep, its consequences permeate our lives (Katz 2003). Beauty bestows an advantage in everyday interaction, but it also has other effects. For one, if you are physically attractive, you are likely to make more money. Researchers in both Holland and the United States found that advertising firms with better-looking executives have higher revenues (Bosman et al. 1997; Pfann et al. 2000). The reason? The researchers suggest that people are more willing to associate with those they perceive as good-looking.

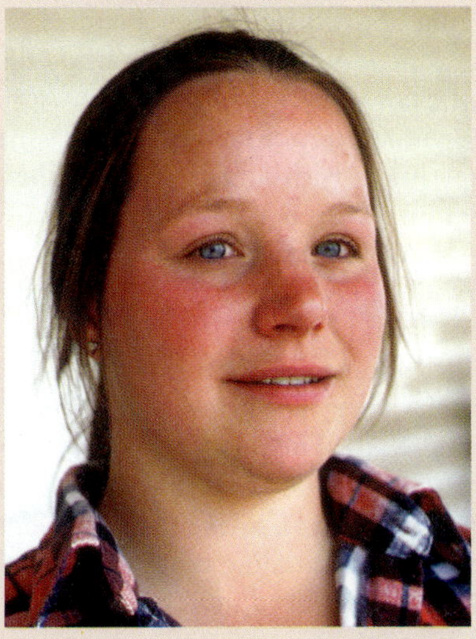

Physical attractiveness underlies much of our social interaction in everyday life. The experiment reviewed in this box illustrates how college men modified their interactions on the basis of attractiveness. How do you think men would modify their interactions if they were to meet the two women in these photographs? How about women? Would they change their interactions in the same way?

For Your CONSIDERATION

Stereotypes have no single, inevitable effect. They are not magical. People can resist stereotypes and change outcomes. However, these studies do illustrate that stereotypes deeply influence how we react to one another.

Instead of beauty, consider gender and race-ethnicity. How do they affect those who do the stereotyping and those who are stereotyped?

Figure 4.2 How Self-Fulfilling Stereotypes Work

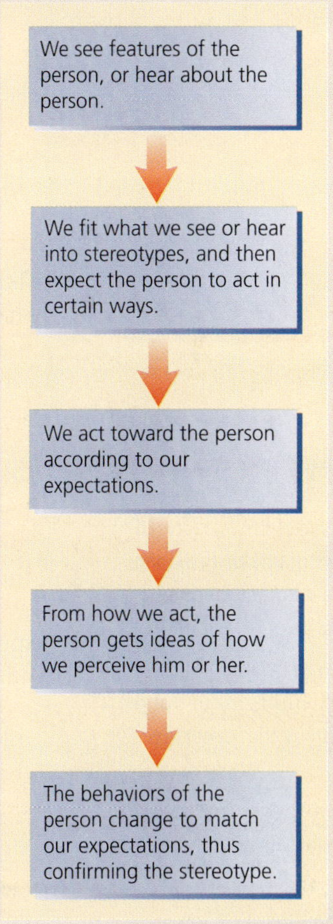
We see features of the person, or hear about the person.
We fit what we see or hear into stereotypes, and then expect the person to act in certain ways.
We act toward the person according to our expectations.
From how we act, the person gets ideas of how we perceive him or her.
The behaviors of the person change to match our expectations, thus confirming the stereotype.

Social space is one of the many aspects of social life studied by sociologists who have a micro-sociological focus. What do you see in common in these two photos?

as possible aggression, for people get close (and jut out their chins and chests) when they are hostile. But when he realized that was not the case, Hall resisted his impulse to move.

After Hall (1969; Hall and Hall 2003) analyzed situations like this, he observed that North Americans use four different "distance zones."

1. *Intimate distance.* This is the zone that the South American unwittingly invaded. It extends to about 18 inches from our bodies. We reserve this space for lovemaking, comforting, protecting, wrestling, hugging, and intimate touching.
2. *Personal distance.* This zone extends from 18 inches to 4 feet. We reserve it for friends and acquaintances and ordinary conversations. This is the zone in which Hall would have preferred speaking with the South American.
3. *Social distance.* This zone, extending out from us about 4 to 12 feet, marks impersonal or formal relationships. We use this zone for such things as job interviews.
4. *Public distance.* This zone, extending beyond 12 feet, marks even more formal relationships. It is used to separate dignitaries and public speakers from the general public.

Touching Not only does frequency of touching differ across cultures, but so does the meaning of touching within a culture. In general, higher-status individuals do more touching. Thus you are much more likely to see teachers touch students and bosses touch secretaries than the other way around. Apparently it is considered unseemly for lower-status individuals to put their hands on superiors.

An experiment with surgery patients illustrates how touching can have different meanings. The nurse, whose job it was to tell patients about their upcoming surgery, purposely touched the patients twice, once briefly on the arm when she introduced herself, and then for a full minute on the arm during the instruction period. When she left, she also shook the patient's hand (Thayer 1988).

Men and women reacted differently. For the women patients, the touching was soothing. It lowered their blood pressure and anxiety both before the surgery and for more than an hour afterward. The touching upset the men, however. Their blood pressure and anxiety increased. No one knows the reason for this difference. The experimenters suggest that the men found it harder to acknowledge dependency and fear. Instead of a comfort, the touch was a threatening reminder of their vulnerability. Perhaps. We don't know that answer. For this, we need more research.

Eye Contact One way we protect our personal bubble is by controlling eye contact. Letting someone gaze into our eyes—unless the person is our eye doctor—can easily be taken as a sign that we are attracted to that person, and even as an invitation to intimacy. A chain of supermarkets in Illinois, wanting to become "the friendliest store in town," ordered their checkout clerks to make direct eye contact with each customer. Women clerks complained that men customers were taking their eye contact the wrong

dramaturgy an approach, pioneered by Erving Goffman, in which social life is analyzed in terms of drama or the stage; also called *dramaturgical analysis*

impression management people's efforts to control the impressions that others receive of them

front stage where performances are given

back stage where people rest from their performances, discuss their presentations, and plan future performances

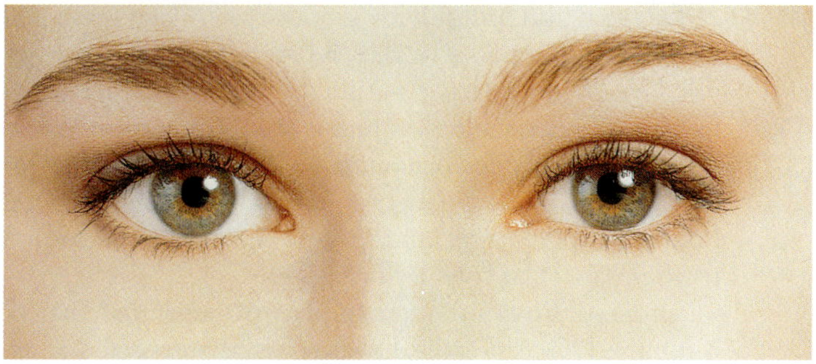

"Eye encounters" are a fascinating aspect of everyday life. We use fleeting eye contact for most of our interactions, such as those with clerks or people we pass in the hall between classes. Just as we reserve our close personal space for intimates, so, too, we reserve lingering eye contact for them.

way, as an invitation to intimacy. Management said they were exaggerating. The clerk's reply was, "We know the kind of looks we're getting back from men," and they refused to make direct eye contact with them.

Let's now turn to dramaturgy, a special area of symbolic interactionism.

Dramaturgy: The Presentation of Self in Everyday Life

> It was their big day, two years in the making. Jennifer Mackey wore a white wedding gown adorned with an 11-foot train and 24,000 seed pearls that she and her mother had sewn onto the dress. Next to her at the altar in Lexington, Kentucky, stood her intended, Jeffrey Degler, in black tie. They said their vows, then turned to gaze for a moment at the four hundred guests. That's when groomsman Daniel Mackey collapsed. As the shocked organist struggled to play Mendelssohn's "Wedding March," Mr. Mackey's unconscious body was dragged away, his feet striking—loudly—every step of the altar stairs.
>
> "I couldn't believe he would die at my wedding," the bride said. (Hughes 1990)

Sociologist Erving Goffman (1922–1982) added a new twist to microsociology when he developed **dramaturgy** (or dramaturgical analysis). By this term he (1959) meant that social life is like a drama or a stage play: Birth ushers us onto the stage of everyday life, and our socialization consists of learning to perform on that stage. The self that we studied in the previous chapter lies at the center of our performances. We have ideas of how we want others to think of us, and we use our roles in everyday life to communicate those ideas. Goffman called these efforts to manage the impressions that others receive of us **impression management.**

In dramaturgy, *a specialty within sociology, social life is viewed as similar to the theater. In our everyday lives, we all are actors like those in this cast of* The George Lopez Show. *We, too, perform roles, use props, and deliver lines to fellow actors—who, in turn, do the same.*

Everyday life, said Goffman, involves playing our assigned roles. We have **front stages** on which to perform them, as did Jennifer and Jeffrey. (By the way, Daniel Mackey didn't really die—he had just fainted.) But we don't have to look at weddings to find front stages. Everyday life is filled with them. Where your teacher lectures is a front stage. And if you make an announcement at the dinner table, you are using a front stage. In fact, you spend most of your time on front stages, for a front stage is wherever you deliver your lines. We also have **back stages,** places where we can retreat and let our hair down. When you close the bathroom or bedroom door for privacy, for example, you are entering a back stage.

The same setting can serve as both a back and a front stage. For example, when you get into your car and look over your hair in the mirror or check your makeup, you are using the car as a back stage. But when you wave at friends or if you give that familiar gesture to someone who has just cut in front of you in traffic, you are using your car as a front stage.

Role performance *refers to how we play our roles. One of the main roles we are assigned in life is gender. We learn our initial "gender lessons" early in life, and we are careful to project images that match cultural stereotypes. Shown here is "Pat," a former character on* Saturday Night Live. *The humor centered around people who didn't know whether to react to Pat as a male or as a female.*

Everyday life brings with it many roles. The same person may be a student, a teenager, a shopper, a worker, a date, as well as a daughter or a son. Although a role lays down the basic outline for a performance, it also allows a great deal of freedom. The particular emphasis or interpretation that we give a role, our "style," is known as **role performance.** Consider your role as son or daughter. You may play the role of ideal daughter or son, being very respectful, coming home at the hours your parents set, and so forth. Or this description may not even come close to your particular role performance.

Ordinarily our roles are sufficiently separated that conflict between them is minimized. Occasionally, however, what is expected of us in one role is incompatible with the expectations of another role. This problem, known as **role conflict,** makes us uncomfortable, as illustrated in Figure 4.3, in which family, friendship, student, and work roles come crashing together. Usually, however, we manage to avoid role conflict by segregating our roles, which in some instances may require an intense juggling act.

Sometimes the *same* role presents inherent conflict, a problem known as **role strain.** Suppose you are exceptionally well prepared for a particular class assignment. Although the instructor asks an unusually difficult question, you find yourself knowing the answer when no one else does. If you want to raise your hand, yet don't want to make your fellow students look bad, you will experience role strain. As illustrated in Figure 4.3, the difference between role conflict and role strain is that role conflict is conflict *between roles,* while role strain is conflict *within* a role.

A fascinating characteristic of roles is that *we tend to become the roles we play.* That is, roles become incorporated into the self-concept, especially those for which we prepare long and hard and that become part of our everyday lives. When sociologist Helen Ebaugh (1988), who had been a nun, studied *role exit,* she interviewed people who had left marriages, police work, the military, medicine, and religious vocations. She found that the role had become so intertwined with the individual's self-concept that leaving it threatened the person's identity. The question these people struggled with was "Who am I, now that I am not a nun (or physician, wife, colonel, and so on)?" Even years after leaving these roles, many continued to perform them in their dreams.

Figure 4.3 Role Strain and Role Conflict

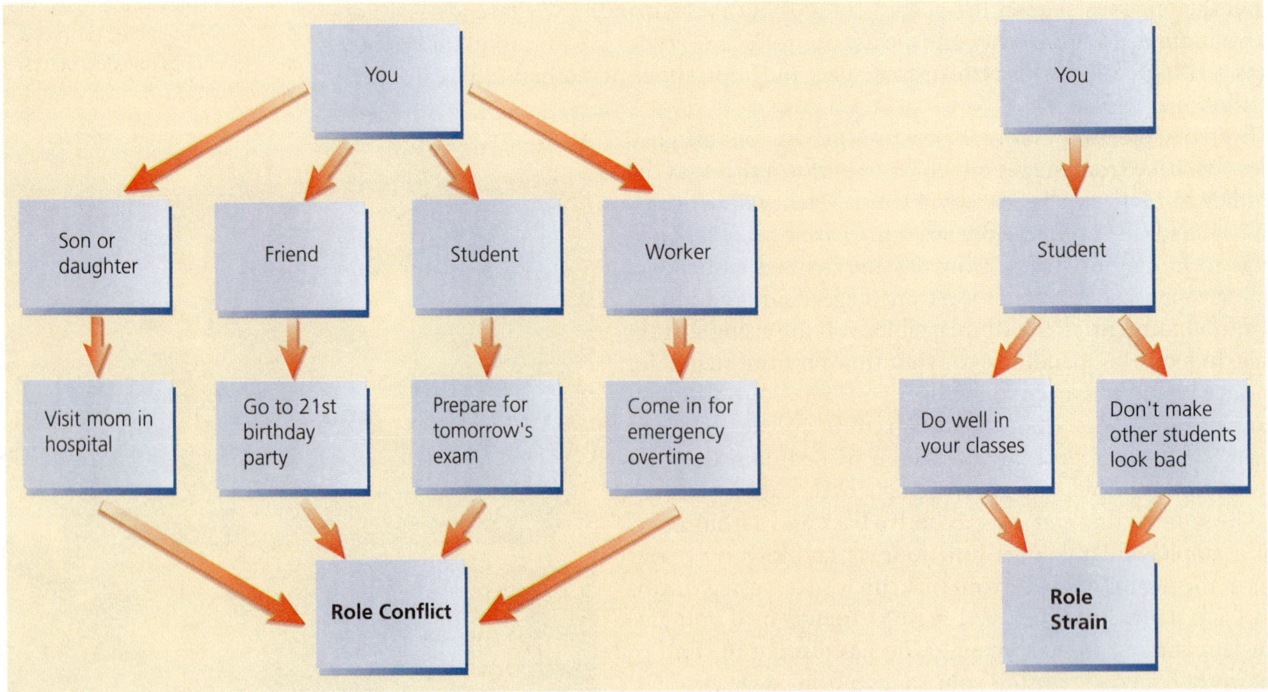

Having become such a part of the person, these roles linger after the individual has left them. This is illustrated by one of my own respondents, who said:

> After I left the (Protestant) ministry, I felt like a fish out of water. *Wearing that backward collar had become a part of me.* It was especially strange on Sunday mornings when I'd listen to someone else give the sermon. I knew that I should be up there preaching. I felt as though I had left God.

To communicate information about the self, we use three types of **sign-vehicles:** the social setting, our appearance, and our manner. The *social setting* is the place where the action unfolds. This is where the curtain goes up on your performance, where you find yourself on stage playing parts and delivering lines. A social setting might be an office, dorm, living room, church, gym, or bar. It is wherever you interact with others. Your social setting includes *scenery,* the furnishings you use to communicate messages, such as desks, blackboards, scoreboards, couches, and so on.

The second sign-vehicle is *appearance,* or how we look when we play our roles. Appearance includes *props,* which are like scenery except that they decorate the person rather than the setting. The teacher has books, lecture notes, and chalk, while the football player wears a special costume called a uniform. Although few of us carry around a football, we all use makeup, hairstyles, and clothing to communicate messages about ourselves. Props and other aspects of appearance give us cues that help us get through everyday life: By letting us know what to expect from others, props tell us how we should react. Think of the messages that props communicate. Some people use clothing to say they are college students, others to say they are older adults. Some use clothing to say they are clergy, others to say they are prostitutes. Similarly, people choose brands of cigarettes, liquor, and automobiles to convey messages about the self.

Even our body is a prop, its shape proclaiming messages about the self. The messages that are attached to various shapes change over time, but, as explored in the Mass Media box on the next page, currently thinness screams desirability.

The third sign-vehicle is *manner,* the attitudes we show as we play our roles. We use manner to communicate information about our feelings and moods. If we show anger or indifference, sincerity or good humor, for example, we indicate to others what they can expect of us as we play our roles.

We become so used to the roles we play in everyday life that we tend to think we are "just doing" things, not that we are like actors on a stage who manage impressions. Yet every time we dress for school, or for any other activity, we are preparing for impression management. Have you ever noticed how your very casually dressed classmates tend to change their appearance on the day they are scheduled to make a report to the class? No one asks them to do so, but their role has changed, and they dress for their slightly modified part. Similarly, you may have noticed that when teenagers begin to date, they take several showers a day, stand before a mirror for hours as they comb and recomb their hair, and then change and rechange their clothing until they "get it just right."

Despite our best efforts to manage impressions, however, we sometimes fail. One of my favorite television scenes took place on an old TV show, *The Days and Nights of Molly*

role performance the ways in which someone performs a role within the limits that the role provides; showing a particular "style" or "personality"

role conflict conflicts that someone feels *between* roles because the expectations attached to one role are incompatible with the expectations of another role

role strain conflicts that someone feels *within* a role

sign-vehicles the term used by Goffman to refer to how people use social setting, appearance, and manner to communicate information about the self

Both individuals and organizations do impression management, *trying to communicate messages about the self (or organization) that best meets their goals. At times, these efforts fail.*

mass MEDIA in Social Life

You Can't Be Thin Enough: Body Images and the Mass Media

An ad for Kellogg's Special K cereal shows an 18-month-old girl wearing nothing but a diaper. She has a worried look on her face. A bubble caption over her head has her asking, "Do I look fat?" (Krane et al. 2001)

When you stand before a mirror, do you like what you see? To make your body more attractive, do you watch your weight or work out? You have ideas about what you should look like. Where did you get them?

TV and magazine ads keep pounding home the message that our bodies aren't good enough, that we've got to improve them. The way to improve them, of course, is to buy the advertised products: wigs, hairpieces, hair transplants, padded brassieres, diet pills, and exercise equipment. Female movie stars effortlessly go through tough workouts without even breaking into a sweat. Muscular hulks show off machines that magically produce steel abs and incredible biceps—in just a few minutes a day. Women and men get the feeling that attractive members of the opposite sex will flock to them if they purchase that wonder-working workout machine.

All of us contrast the reality we see when we look in the mirror with our culture's ideal body types. Lara Flynn Boyle, a top U.S. actress, represents an ideal body type that has developed in some parts of Western culture. These cultural images often make it difficult for large people to maintain positive images of their bodies. These twins in Los Angeles, California have struggled against dominant cultural images.

Although we try to shrug off such messages, knowing they are designed to sell products, they still get our attention. They penetrate our thinking and feelings, helping to shape ideal images of how we "ought" to look. Those models so attractively clothed and coiffed as they walk down the runway, could they be any thinner? For women, the message is clear: You can't be thin enough. The men's message is also clear: You can't be strong enough.

Woman or man, your body isn't good enough. It sags where it should be firm. It bulges where it should be smooth. It sticks out where it shouldn't, and it doesn't stick out enough where it should.

Dodd. In this particular episode, Molly Dodd tried to impress a date. She went to the "powder room," a backstage fix-up place reserved for women, where she did the usual things. Satisfied that she looked good, she tried to make a grand entrance, walking confidently, an expectant smile on her face—all the while trailing a long piece of toilet paper from her shoe. The scene is humorous because it highlights an incongruity of elements, which creates *embarrassment.* In dramaturgical terms, embarrassment is a feeling we get when our performance fails.

If we show ourselves to be good role players, we get positive recognition from others. To accomplish this, said Goffman, we often use **teamwork**—two or more people working together to make certain that a performance goes off as planned. When a performance doesn't come off quite right, we use **face-saving behavior.** We may ignore flaws in someone's performance, which Goffman defines as *tact.* Suppose your teacher is about to make an important point. Suppose also that her lecturing has been outstanding and the class is hanging on every word. Just as she pauses for emphasis, her stomach lets out a loud growl. She might then use a *face-saving technique* by remarking, "I was so busy preparing for class that I didn't get breakfast this morning." It is more likely, however, that both class and

teamwork the collaboration of two or more people to manage impressions jointly

face-saving behavior techniques used to salvage a performance that is going sour

And—no matter what your weight—it's too much. You've got to be thinner.

Exercise takes time, and it's painful getting in shape. Once you do get in shape, if you slack off it seems to take only a few days for your body to return to its previous slothful, drab appearance. You can't let up, you can't exercise enough, and you can't diet enough.

But who can continue at such a torrid pace, striving for what are unrealistic cultural ideals? A few people, of course, but not many. So liposuction is appealing. Just lie there, put up with a little discomfort, and the doctor will suck the fat right out of you. Surgeons can transform flat breasts into super breasts overnight. They can lower receding hairlines and smooth furrowed brows. They remove lumps with their magical tummy tucks, and take off a decade with their rejuvenating skin peels and face lifts.

With the bosomy girls on *Baywatch* the envy of all, and the impossibly shaped models at *Victoria's Secret* the standard to which they hold themselves, even teens call the plastic surgeon. Anxious lest their child violate peer ideals and trail behind in her race for popularity, parents foot the bill. Some parents pay $25,000 just to give their daughters a flatter tummy (Gross 1998).

With peer pressure to alter the body already intense, surgeons keep stoking the fire. A sample ad: "No Ifs, Ands or Butts. You Can Change Your Bottom Line in Hours!" Some surgeons even offer gift certificates—so you can give your loved ones liposuction or botox injections along with their greeting card (Dowd 2002).

The thinness craze has moved to the East. Glossy magazines in Japan and China are filled with skinny models and crammed with ads touting diet pills and diet teas. In China, where famine used to abound, a little extra padding was valued as a sign of good health. Today, the obsession is thinness (Rosenthal 1999). Not-so-subtle ads scream that fat is bad. Some teas come with a package of diet pills. Weight-loss machines, with electrodes attached to acupuncture pressure points, not only reduce fat, but they also build breasts. Or so the advertisers claim.

Not limited by our rules, advertisers in Japan and China push a soap that supposedly "sucks up fat through the skin's pores" (Marshall 1995). What a dream product! After all, even though those TV models smile as they go through their paces, those exercise machines do look like a lot of hard work.

Then there is the other bottom line. Attractiveness does pay off. Economists studied physical attractiveness and earnings. The result? "Good-looking" men and women earn the most, "average-looking" men and women earn more than "plain" people., and the "ugly" are paid a "pittance" (Hamermesh and Biddle 1994). Consider obese women: Their net worth is less than half that of their slimmer sisters ("Fat is a Financial Issue" 2000). "Attractive" women have another cash advantage—they attract and marry higher earning men.

More popularity *and* more money? Maybe you can't be thin enough after all. Maybe those exercise machines are a good investment. If only we could catch up with the Japanese and develop a soap that would suck the fat right out of our pores. You can practically hear the jingle now.

For Your CONSIDERATION

What image do you have of your body? How do cultural expectations of "ideal" bodies underlie your image? Can you recall any advertisement or television program that has affected your body image?

Most advertising and television programs that focus on weight are directed at women. Women are more concerned than men about weight, more likely to have eating disorders, and more likely to express dissatisfaction with their bodies (Honeycutt 1995; Stinson 2001). Do you think that the targeting of women in advertising creates these attitudes and behaviors? Or do you think that these attitudes and behaviors would exist even if there were no such ads? Why?

teacher will simply ignore the sound, both giving the impression that no one heard a thing—a face-saving technique called *studied nonobservance.* This allows the teacher to make the point, or as Goffman would say, it allows the performance to go on.

Before closing this section, we should note that impression management is not limited to individuals. Families, businesses, colleges, sports teams, in fact probably all groups, try to manage impressions. So do governments. When on September 11, 2001, Arab terrorists hijacked four commercial airliners and flew three of them into the World Trade Center in New York City and the Pentagon in Washington, D.C., the president was in Florida, speaking at a grade school. For his safety, the Secret Service rushed him into hiding, first to a military base in Louisiana, then to another base in Nebraska. At first, Bush addressed the nation from these secluded locations. To assure the people that the government was still in control, it wouldn't do for the president to speak while in hiding. He had to get back to Washington. The perceived danger to the president was ruled less important than his presence in the White House. To reassure the public, Bush was flown to Washington, escorted by U.S. Air Force F-16 fighter jets, where that same evening he addressed the American people from within the symbol of power, the Oval office.

Ethnomethodology: Uncovering Background Assumptions

As discussed in Chapter 1, symbolic interactionists stress that the events of life do not come with built-in meanings. Rather, we give meaning to things by classifying them. When we place objects and events into the classifications provided by our culture, we are doing more than naming things—we are interpreting our world.

Certainly one of the strangest words in sociology is *ethnomethodology.* To better understand this term, consider the word's three basic components. *Ethno* means folk or people; *method* means how people do something; *ology* means "the study of." Putting them together, then, *ethno/method/ology* means "the study of how people do things." Specifically, **ethnomethodology** is the study of how people use commonsense understandings to make sense of life.

Let's suppose that during a routine office visit, your doctor remarks that your hair is rather long, then takes out a pair of scissors and starts to give you a haircut. You would feel strange about this—for your doctor has violated **background assumptions,** your ideas about the way life is and the way things ought to work. These assumptions, which lie at the root of everyday life, are so deeply embedded in our consciousness that we are seldom aware of them, and most of us fulfill them unquestioningly. Thus, your doctor does not offer you a haircut, even if he or she is good at cutting hair and you need one!

The founder of ethnomethodology, sociologist Harold Garfinkel, conducted some interesting exercises designed to uncover our background assumptions. Garfinkel (1967) asked his students to act as though they did not understand the basic rules of social life. Some tried to bargain with supermarket clerks; others would inch close to people and stare directly at them. They were met with surprise, bewilderment, even anger. In one exercise Garfinkel asked students to act as though they were boarders in their own homes. They addressed their parents as "Mr." and "Mrs.," asked permission to use the bathroom, sat stiffly, were courteous, and spoke only when spoken to. As you can imagine, the other family members didn't know what to make of this (Garfinkel 1967):

> They vigorously sought to make the strange actions intelligible and to restore the situation to normal appearances. Reports (by the students) were filled with accounts of astonishment, bewilderment, shock, anxiety, embarrassment, and anger, and with charges by various family members that the student was mean, inconsiderate, selfish, nasty, or impolite. Family members demanded explanations: What's the matter? What's gotten into you? . . . Are you sick? . . . Are you out of your mind or are you just stupid?

In another exercise, Garfinkel asked students to take words and phrases literally. When a student asked his girlfriend what she meant when she said that she had a flat tire, she said:

> What do you mean, "What do you mean?"? A flat tire is a flat tire. That is what I meant. Nothing special. What a crazy question!

Another conversation went like this:

> ACQUAINTANCE: How are you?
>
> STUDENT: How am I in regard to what? My health, my finances, my schoolwork, my peace of mind, my . . . ?
>
> ACQUAINTANCE (red in the face): look! I was just trying to be polite. Frankly, I don't give a damn how you are.

Students who are asked to break background assumptions can be highly creative. The young children of one of my students were surprised one morning when they came down for breakfast to find a sheet spread across the living room floor. On it were dishes, silverware, burning candles—and bowls of ice cream. They, too, wondered what was going on—but they dug eagerly into the ice cream before their mother could change her mind.

ethnomethodology the study of how people use background assumptions to make sense out of life

background assumptions deeply embedded common understandings, or basic rules, concerning our view of the world and of how people ought to act

All of us have background assumptions, *deeply ingrained expectations of how the world operates. They lay the groundwork for what we expect will happen in our interactions. How do you think the* background assumptions *of these two people differ?*

This is a risky assignment to give students, however, for breaking some background assumptions can make people suspicious. When a colleague of mine gave this assignment, a couple of his students began to wash dollar bills in a laundromat. By the time they put the bills in the dryer, the police were there.

IN SUM

Ethnomethodologists explore *background assumptions,* the taken-for-granted ideas about the world that underlie our behavior. These basic rules of social life are an essential part of the social structure and are violated only with risk. Deeply embedded in our minds, they give us basic directions for living everyday life.

The Social Construction of Reality

Symbolic interactionists stress how our ideas help determine our reality. In what has become known as *the definition of the situation,* or the **Thomas theorem**, sociologists W. I. and Dorothy S. Thomas said "If people define situations as real, they are real in their consequences." Consider the following incident:

> On a visit to Morocco, in northern Africa, I decided to buy a watermelon. When I indicated to the street vendor that the knife he was going to use to cut the watermelon was dirty (encrusted with filth would be more apt), he was very obliging. He immediately bent down and began to swish the knife in a puddle on the street. I shuddered as I looked at the passing burros that were freely urinating and defecating as they went by. Quickly, I indicated by gesture that I preferred my melon uncut after all.

For that vendor, germs did not exist. For me, they did. And each of us acted according to our definition of the situation. My perception and behavior did not come from the fact that germs are real but *because I grew up in a society that teaches they are real.* Microbes, of course, *objectively* exist, and whether or not germs are part of our thought world makes no difference to whether we are infected by them. Our behavior, however, does not depend on the *objective* existence of something but, rather, on our *subjective interpretation,*

Thomas theorem William I. and Dorothy S. Thomas' classic formulation of the definition of the situation: "If people define situations as real, they are real in their consequences."

on what sociologists call our *definition of reality.* In other words, it is not the reality of microbes that impresses itself on us, but society that impresses the reality of microbes on us.

Let's consider another example. Do you remember the identical twins, Oskar and Jack, who grew up so differently? As discussed on page 64, Jack was reared in Trinidad and learned to hate Hitler, while Oskar was reared in Germany and learned to love Hitler. Thus what Hitler meant to Oskar and Jack (and what he means to us) depends not on Hitler's acts, but, rather, on how we view his acts, that is, on our definition of the situation.

This is **the social construction of reality.** Our society, or the social groups to which we belong, have their particular views of life. From our groups (the *social* part of this process), we learn specific ways of looking at life—whether that be our view of Hitler (he's good, he's evil), germs (they exist, they don't exist), or *anything else in life.* In short, through our interaction with others, we *construct reality;* that is, we learn ways of interpreting our experiences in life.

Gynecological Examinations To better understand the social construction of reality, let's consider an extended example.

A gynecological nurse, Mae Biggs, and I did research on vaginal examinations. Reviewing about 14,000 cases, we looked at how the medical profession constructs social reality in order to define this examination as nonsexual (Henslin and Biggs 1971/2003). We found that the pelvic examination unfolds much as a stage play does. I will use "he" to refer to the physician because only male physicians participated in this study. Perhaps the results would be different with women gynecologists.

> **Scene 1 (the patient as person)** In this scene, the doctor maintains eye contact with his patient, calls her by name, and discusses her problems in a professional manner. If he decides that a vaginal examination is necessary, he tells a nurse, "Pelvic in room 1." By this statement, he is announcing that a major change will occur in the next scene.
>
> **Scene 2 (from person to pelvic)** This scene is the depersonalizing stage. In line with the doctor's announcement, the patient begins the transition from a "person" to a "pelvic." The doctor leaves the room, and a female nurse enters to help the patient make the transition. The nurse prepares the "props" for the coming examination and answers any questions the woman might have.

What occurs at this point is essential for the social construction of reality, for *the doctor's absence removes even the suggestion of sexuality.* To undress in front of him could suggest either a striptease or intimacy, thus undermining the reality so carefully being defined, that of nonsexuality.

The patient also wants to remove any hint of sexuality in the coming interaction, and during this scene she may express concern about what to do with her panties. Some mutter to the nurse, "I don't want him to see these." Most women solve the problem by either slipping their panties under their clothes or placing them in their purse.

> **Scene 3 (the person as pelvic)** This scene opens when the doctor enters the room. Before him is a woman lying on a table, her feet in stirrups, her knees tightly together, and her body covered by a drape sheet. The doctor seats himself on a low stool before the woman, tells her, "Let your knees fall apart" (rather than the sexually loaded "Spread your legs"), and begins the examination.

The drape sheet is crucial in this process of desexualization, for it *dissociates the pelvic area from the person:* Bending forward and with the drape sheet above his head, the physician can see only the vagina, not the patient's face. Thus dissociated from the individual, the vagina is dramaturgically transformed into an object of analysis. If the doctor examines the patient's breasts, he also dissociates them from her person by examining them one at a time, with a towel covering the unexamined breast. Like the vagina, each breast becomes an isolated item dissociated from the person.

social construction of reality the use of background assumptions and life experiences to define what is real

In this scene, the patient cooperates in being an object, becoming for all practical purposes a pelvis to be examined. She withdraws eye contact from the doctor, usually from the nurse as well, is likely to stare at the wall or at the ceiling, and avoids initiating conversation.

Scene 4 (from pelvic to person) In this scene, the patient becomes "repersonalized." The doctor has left the examining room; the patient dresses and fixes her hair and makeup. Her reemergence as a person is indicated by such statements to the nurse as, "My dress isn't too wrinkled, is it?" indicating a need for reassurance that the metamorphosis from "pelvic" back to "person" has been completed satisfactorily.

Scene 5 (the patient as person) In this scene, the patient is once again treated as a person rather than as an object. The doctor makes eye contact with her and addresses her by name. She, too, makes eye contact with the doctor, and the usual middle-class interaction patterns are followed. She has been fully restored.

IN SUM

To an outsider to our culture, the custom of women going to a male stranger for a vaginal examination might seem bizarre. But not to us. We learn that pelvic examinations are nonsexual. To sustain this definition requires teamwork—patients, doctors, and nurses working together to *socially construct reality.*

It is not just pelvic examinations or our views of microbes that make up our definitions of reality. Rather, *our behavior depends on how we define reality.* Our definitions (or constructions) provide the basis for what we do and how we feel about life. To understand human behavior, then, we must know how people define reality.

The Need for Both Macrosociology and Microsociology

As noted earlier, both microsociology and macrosociology make vital contributions to our understanding of human behavior.

Our understanding of social life would be vastly incomplete without one or the other. The photo essay on the next two pages should help make clear why we need *both* perspectives.

To illustrate this point, let's consider two groups of high school boys studied by sociologist William Chambliss (1973/2003). Both groups attended Hanibal High School. In one group were eight middle-class boys who came from "good" families and were perceived by the community as "going somewhere." Chambliss calls this group the "Saints." The other group consisted of six lower-class boys who were seen as headed down a dead-end road. Chambliss calls this group the "Roughnecks."

Both groups skipped school, got drunk, and did a lot of fighting and vandalism. The Saints were actually somewhat more delinquent, for they were truant more often and engaged in more vandalism. Yet the Saints had a good reputation, while the Roughnecks were seen by teachers, the police, and the general community as no good and headed for trouble.

These reputations carried crucial consequences. Seven of the eight Saints went on to graduate from college. Three studied for advanced degrees: One finished law school and became active in state politics, one finished medical school, and one went on to earn a Ph.D. The four other college graduates entered managerial or executive training programs with large firms. After his parents divorced, one Saint failed to graduate from high school on time and had to repeat his senior year. Although this boy tried to go to college by attending night school, he never finished. He was unemployed the last time Chambliss saw him.

THROUGH THE AUTHOR'S LENS

When a Tornado Strikes:

Social Organization Following A Natural Disaster

As I was watching television on March 20, 2003, I heard a report that a tornado had hit Camilla, Georgia. "Like a big lawn mower," the report said, it had cut a path of destruction through this little town. In its fury, the tornado had left behind six dead and about 200 injured.

From sociological studies of natural disasters I knew that immediately after the initial shock the survivors of natural disasters work together to try to restore order to their disrupted lives. I wanted to see this restructuring process first hand. The next morning, I took off for Georgia.

These photos, taken the day after the tornado struck, tell the story of people who are in the midst of trying to put their lives back together. I was impressed at how little time people spend commiserating about their misfortune and how quickly they take practical steps to restore their lives.

As you look at these photos, try to determine why you need both microsociology and macrosociology to understand what occurs after a natural disaster.

After making sure that their loved ones are safe, one of the next steps people take is to recover their possessions. The cooperation that emerges among people, as documented in the sociological literature on natural disasters, is illustrated here.

▲ In addition to the inquiring sociologist, television news teams also were interviewing survivors and photographing the damage. This was the second time in just three years that a tornado had hit this neighborhood.

◄ The owners of this house invited me inside to see what the tornado had done to their home. In what had been her dining room, this woman is trying to salvage whatever she can from the rubble. She and her family survived by taking refuge in the bathroom. They had been there only five seconds, she said, when the tornado struck.

No building or social institution escapes a tornado as it follows its path of destruction. Just the night before, members of this church had held evening worship service. After the tornado, someone mounted a U.S. flag on top of the cross, symbolic of the church members' patriotism and religiosity—and of their enduring hope.

Personal relationships are essential in putting lives together. Consequently, reminders of these relationships are one of the main possessions that people attempt to salvage. This young man, having just recovered the family photo album, is eagerly reviewing the photos.

Formal organizations also help the survivors of natural disasters recover. In this neighborhood, I saw representatives of insurance companies, the police, the fire department, and an electrical co-op. The Salvation Army brought meals to the neighborhood.

For children, family photos are not as important as toys. This girl has managed to salvage a favorite toy, which will help anchor her to her previous life.

A sign of the times. Like electricity and gas, cable television also has to be restored as soon as possible.

In contrast, only four of the Roughnecks finished even high school. Two of these boys did exceptionally well in sports and received athletic scholarships to college. They both graduated from college and became high school coaches. Of the two others who graduated from high school, one became a small-time gambler and the other disappeared "up north," where he was last reported to be driving a truck. The two who did not complete high school were sent to state penitentiaries for separate murders.

To understand what happened to the Saints and the Roughnecks, we need to grasp *both* social structure and social interaction. Using *macrosociology,* we can place these boys within the larger framework of the U.S. social class system. This reveals how opportunities open or close to people depending on their social class and how people learn different goals as they grow up in vastly different groups. We can then use *microsociology* to follow their everyday lives. We can see how the Saints manipulated their "good" reputations to skip classes repeatedly and how their access to automobiles allowed them to protect those reputations by transferring their troublemaking to different communities. In contrast, the Roughnecks, who did not have cars, were highly visible. Their lawbreaking, which was limited to a small area, readily came to the attention of the community. Microsociology also reveals how their respective reputations opened doors of opportunity to the first group of boys while closing them to the other.

Thus we need both kinds of sociology, and both are stressed in the following chapters.

SUMMARY and REVIEW

Levels of Sociological Analysis

What two levels of analysis do sociologists use?

Sociologists use macrosociological and microsociological levels of analysis. In **macrosociology,** the focus is placed on large-scale features of social life, while in **microsociology,** the focus is on **social interaction.** Functionalists and conflict theorists tend to use a macrosociological approach, while symbolic interactionists are more likely to use a microsociological approach. Pp. 94–95.

The Macrosociological Perspective: Social Structure

How does social structure influence our behavior?

The term **social structure** refers to the social envelope that surrounds us and establishes limits on our behavior. Social structure consists of culture, social class, social statuses, roles, groups, and social institutions. Together, these serve as foundations for how we view the world.

Our location in the social structure underlies our perceptions, attitudes, and behaviors. Culture lays the broadest framework, while **social class** divides people according to income, education, and occupational prestige. Each of us receives **ascribed statuses** at birth; later we add **achieved statuses.** Our behaviors and orientations are further influenced by the **roles** we play, the **groups** to which we belong, and our experiences with social institutions. These components of society work together to help maintain social order. Pp. 95–99.

Social Institutions

What are social institutions?

Social institutions are the standard means that a society develops to meet its basic needs. As summarized in Figure 4.1 (page 100), industrialized societies have ten social institutions—the family, religion, education, economics, medicine, politics, law, science, the military, and the mass media. From the functionalist perspective, social institutions meet universal group needs, or **functional requisites.** Conflict theorists stress how society's elite uses social institutions to maintain its privileged position. Pp. 99–103.

What holds society together?

According to Emile Durkheim, in agricultural societies people are united by **mechanical solidarity** (similar views and feelings). With industrialization comes **organic solidarity** (people depend on one another to do their jobs). Ferdinand Tönnies pointed out that the informal means of control of ***Gemeinschaft*** (small, intimate) societies are replaced by formal mechanisms in ***Gesellschaft*** (larger, more impersonal) societies. Pp. 103–105.

The Microsociological Perspective: Social Interaction in Everyday Life

What is the focus of symbolic interactionism?

In contrast to functionalists and conflict theorists, who as macrosociologists focus on the "big picture," symbolic interactionists tend to be microsociologists who focus on face-to-face social interaction. Symbolic interactionists analyze how people define their worlds, and how their definitions, in turn, influence their behavior. P. 106.

How do stereotypes affect social interaction?

Stereotypes are assumptions of what people are like. When we first meet people, we classify them according to our perceptions of their visible characteristics. Our ideas about those characteristics guide our behavior toward them. Our behavior, in turn, may influence them to behave in ways that reinforce our stereotypes. Pp. 106–107.

Do all human groups share a similar sense of personal space?

In examining how people use physical space, symbolic interactionists stress that we surround ourselves with a "personal bubble," one that we carefully protect. People from different cultures use "personal bubbles" of varying sizes, so the answer to the question is no. Americans typically use four different "distance zones"—intimate, personal, social, and public. Pp. 106, 108.

What is dramaturgy?

Erving Goffman developed **dramaturgy** (or dramaturgical analysis), in which everyday life is analyzed in terms of the stage. At the core of this analysis is **impression management,** our attempts to control the impressions we make on others. For this, we use the **sign-vehicles** of setting, appearance, and manner. Our performances often call for **teamwork** and **face-saving behavior.** Pp. 109–115.

What is the social construction of reality?

The phrase the **social construction of reality** refers to how we construct our views of the world, which, in turn, underlie our actions. **Ethnomethodology** is the study of how people make sense of everyday life. Ethnomethodologists try to uncover **background assumptions,** our basic ideas about the way life is. Pp. 115–117.

The Need for Both Macrosociology and Microsociology

Why are both levels of analysis important?

Because each focuses on different aspects of the human experience, both microsociology and macrosociology are necessary for us to understand social life. Pp. 117, 120.

Where can I read more on this topic?

Suggested Readings for this chapter are at the back of this book.

THINKING Critically ABOUT CHAPTER 4

1. The major components of social structure are culture, social class, social status, roles, and social institutions. Use social structure to explain why Native Americans have such a low rate of college graduation. (See Table 12.2 on page 345.)
2. Dramaturgy is a form of microsociology. Use dramaturgy to analyze a situation with which you are intimately familiar (such as interaction with your family or friends, or even in your sociology class).
3. To illustrate why we need both macrosociology and microsociology to understand social life, use some example from your own life.

ADDITIONAL RESOURCES for This Chapter

www.ablongman.com/henslin7e

- *Content Select* Research Database for Sociology, with suggested key terms and annotated references
- Link to 2000 Census, with activities
- Flashcards of key terms and concepts
- Practice Tests
- Weblinks
- Interactive Maps

Chapter 5

How Sociologists Do Research

Ivan Lee Sanford, *Diverse Cross-Section*, 1991

Cindy Hudo, a 21-year-old mother of two in Charleston, South Carolina, who was charged with the murder of her husband, Buba, said:

I start in the car, and I get down the road, and I see Buba walking, and he's real mad. . . . I pull over, you know, and [I said] "I didn't know to pick you up. You know, I'm sorry." And he didn't even say nothing to me. He just started hitting on me. And that's all I wanted to do, was just get home, because I was just self-conscious. I don't want nobody to see him hitting me, because I didn't want him to look bad.

I had to go to work in a half-hour, because I was working a double-shift. And he told me I had forty minutes to get all my furniture out of the house and get my clothes and be out or he was going to throw them out. And I was sitting there, because I could talk him down. You know, because I didn't want to leave him. I just talked to him. I said, "Buba, I don't want to leave." I said, "This is my house." And then he told me . . . (unclear) . . . "my kids." And I said, "No, you're not taking my kids from me. That's too much." And so I said, "Just let me leave. Just let me take the kids. And, you know I'll go, and you know, I won't keep the kids from you or nothing like that." And he said, "I'm going to take them, and you're getting out."

don't want nobody to see him hitting me, because I didn't want him to look bad.

[After they went inside their trailer, Buba threatened to shoot Cindy. He loaded a shotgun, pointed it at her, and said]: "The only way you're going to get out of this is if you kill me, and I'll—I'll kill you." [Buba gave me the shotgun and] turned around and walked right down the hall, because he knew I wouldn't do nothing. And I just sat there a minute. And I don't know what happened. I just, you know, I went to the bedroom, and I seen him laying there, and I just shot him. He moved. I shot him again because I thought he was going to get up again. . . .

I loved him too much. And I just wanted to help him.

Source: ABC Television, *20/20,* October 18, 1979

Chapter Outline

What Is a Valid Sociological Topic?

Sociologists do research on just about every area of human behavior. On the macro level, they study such broad matters as race relations (Wilson 2000), the military (Moscos and Butler 1997), and multinational corporations (Kanter et al. 1997). On the micro level, they study such individualistic matters as pelvic examinations (Henslin and Biggs 1971/2003), how people interact on street corners (Whyte 1989, 2001), and even how people decorate their homes at Christmas (Caplow 1991). In fact, no human behavior is ineligible for sociological scrutiny—whether that behavior is routine or unusual, respectable or reprehensible.

What happened to Cindy and Buba, then, is also a valid topic of sociological research. But exactly *how* would you research spouse abuse? As we look at how sociologists conduct their research, we shall try to answer this question.

Common Sense and the Need for Sociological Research

First, why do we need sociological research? Why can't we simply depend on common sense, on "what everyone knows"? As noted in Chapter 1 (pages 9–10), commonsense ideas may or may not be true. Common sense, for example, tells us that spouse abuse has a significant impact on the lives of the people who are abused.

Although this particular idea is accurate, we need research to test commonsense ideas, because not all such ideas are true. After all, common sense also tells us that if a woman is abused she will pack up and leave her husband. Research, however, shows that the reality of abuse is much more complicated than this. Some women do leave right away, some even after the first incident of abuse. For a variety of reasons, however, some women suffer abuse for years. The main reason is that they feel trapped and don't see viable alternatives.

This brings us to the need for sociological research, for we may want to know why some women put up with abuse, while others don't. Or we may want to know something entirely different, such as why men are more likely to be the abusers. Or why some people abuse the people they say they love.

In order to answer a question, we need to move beyond guesswork and common sense. We want to *know* what is really going on. To find out, sociologists do research on about every aspect of social life. Let's look at how they do their research.

A Research Model

As shown in Figure 5.1, scientific research follows eight basic steps. This is an ideal model, however, and in the real world of research some of these steps may run together. Some may even be omitted.

1. Selecting a Topic

The first step is to select a topic. What do you want to know more about? Many sociologists simply follow their curiosity, their drive to know. They become interested in a particular topic, and they pursue it, as I did in studying the homeless. Some sociologists choose a topic because funding is available for that topic, others because a social problem such as domestic violence is in the news and the sociologist wants to help people better understand it—and perhaps to help solve it. Let's use spouse abuse as our example.

2. Defining the Problem

The second step is to define the problem, to specify what you want to learn about the topic. My interest in the homeless increased until I wanted to learn about homelessness across the nation. Ordinarily, sociologists' interests are much more focused than this. They develop a researchable question that focuses on a specific area or problem. For example, they may want to compare the work experiences of homeless women and men. Or they may want to know what can be done to reduce spouse abuse.

Although sociologists study social problems such as homelessness and spouse abuse, they also conduct research on any aspect of social life that interests them. The "problem" can be as earth shattering as why nations would ever contemplate nuclear war or as simple as wanting to find out why Native Americans like Westerns (see the Mass Media in Social Life box on page 52).

3. Reviewing the Literature

The third step is to review the literature to see what has already been written about the problem. This helps the researcher narrow down the problem, identify areas that are already known, and pinpoint areas that need to be examined. Reviewing the literature may also provide ideas about what questions to ask. A researcher may even find out that the problem has been answered already. Then there is no need to do the research, for no one wants to reinvent the wheel.

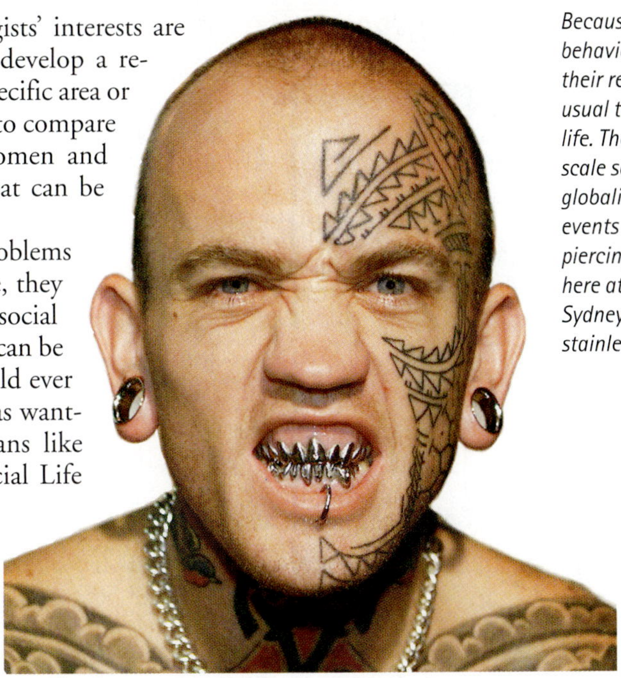

Because sociologists find all human behavior to be valid research topics, their research runs from the unusual to the routines of everyday life. Their studies range from broad scale social change, such as the globalization of capitalism, to such events as exhibitions of tattooing, piercing, and body painting. Shown here at the Australian Museum in Sydney is Lucky Rich, displaying his stainless steel teeth.

Figure 5.1 The Research Model

1. Select a topic.
2. Define the problem.
3. Review the literature.
4. Formulate a hypothesis.
5. Choose a research method.

| Survey | Participant observation | Secondary analysis | Documents | Experiment | Unobtrusive measures |

6. Collect the data.
7. Analyze the results.
8. Share the results.

Generates hypotheses

Stimulates ideas for more research

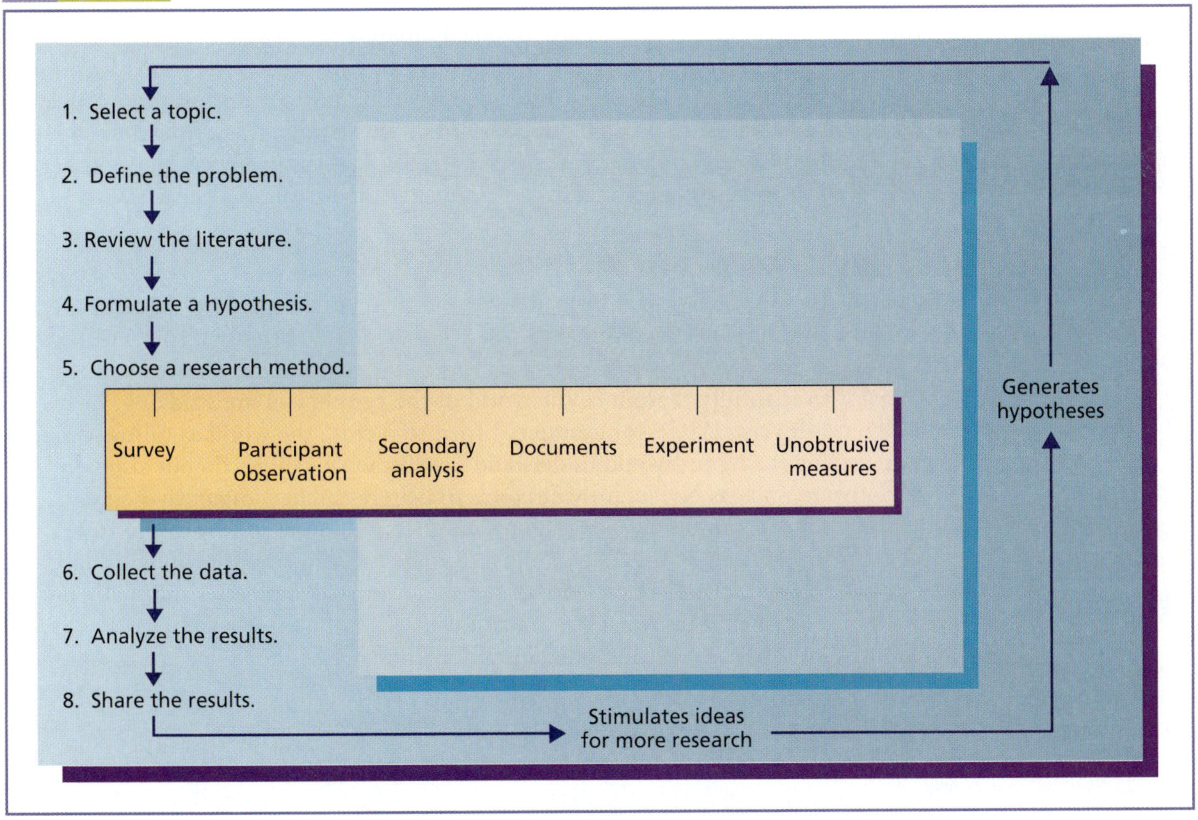

Source: Modification of Fig. 2.2 of Schaefer 1989.

THE FAR SIDE® By GARY LARSON

"Anthropologists! Anthropologists!"

A major concern of sociologists and other social scientists is that their research methods do not influence their findings. Respondents often change their behavior when they know they are being studied.

4. Formulating a Hypothesis

The fourth step is to formulate a **hypothesis,** a statement of what you expect to find according to predictions from a theory. A hypothesis predicts a relationship between or among **variables,** factors that change, or vary, from one person or situation to another. For example, the statement, "Men who are more socially isolated are more likely to abuse their wives than are men who are more socially integrated" is a hypothesis. Hypotheses need **operational definitions**—that is, precise ways to measure their variables. In this example, we would need operational definitions for three variables: social isolation, social integration, and spouse abuse.

5. Choosing a Research Method

The fifth step is to choose a **research method** (or research design), the means by which you will collect your data. Sociologists use six basic research methods, selecting the one that will best answer their particular questions. We'll examine these methods in the next section.

6. Collecting the Data

The next step is to gather the data. You have to take care to assure the **validity** of your data; that is, your operational definitions must measure what they are intended to measure. In this case, you must be certain that you really are measuring social isolation, social integration, and spouse abuse—and not something else. Spouse abuse, for example, seems to be obvious. Yet acts that some people consider to be abuse are not considered abuse by others. Which will you choose? In other words, your operational definitions must be so precise that no one has any question about what you are measuring.

You must also be sure your data are reliable. **Reliability** means that if other researchers use your operational definitions, their findings will be consistent with yours. If your operational definitions are sloppy, husbands who have committed the same act of violence might be included in some research but excluded in other studies. You would end up with erratic results. You might show a 10 percent rate of spousal violence, but another researcher finds it to be 30 percent. This would make your research unreliable.

hypothesis a statement of how variables are expected to be related to one another, often according to predictions from a theory

variable a factor thought to be significant for human behavior, which varies from one case to another

operational definition the way in which a researcher measures a variable

research method (or research design) one of six procedures that sociologists use to collect data: surveys, participant observation, secondary analysis, documents, experiments, and unobtrusive measures

7. Analyzing the Results

After you gather the data, it is time to analyze them. You can choose from qualitative and quantitative techniques. *Qualitative analysis* would include classifying novels, movies, television programs, and people's conversations in order to identify their main themes. The goal is to faithfully reproduce the world of the people you are studying. In my research on cabdrivers (1993), for example, I tried to picture the world as cabbies see it so anyone reading the report would understand not just what cabbies do but also why they do it. Software, such as Nvivo, provides tools to help researchers organize their data.

Quantitative analysis involves crunching numbers. Using today's software to test hypotheses, which is done at this stage, in just seconds you can run tests on your data that used to take days, or even weeks. Two basic programs that sociologists and many undergraduates use are Microcase and the Statistical Package for the Social Sciences (SPSS). Some software, such as the Methodologist's Toolchest, provides advice about collecting data and even about ethical issues.

8. Sharing the Results

The final step after analyzing the data is to wrap up the research (or, if it is a broad project, at least some part of it). At this point, you write a report to share your findings with the scientific community. To help others evaluate your research, the report includes a review of these first steps. It also reviews what has already been published on the topic, shows how your research is related to these earlier findings, and demonstrates how your research supports, refutes, or modifies the theories that apply to the topic.

When research is published, usually in a scientific journal or a book, it "belongs" to the scientific community. Table 5.1 below is an example of published research. These findings

validity the extent to which an operational definition measures what it was intended to measure

reliability the extent to which research produces consistent or dependable results

Table 5.1 How to Read a Table

Tables summarize information. Because sociological findings are often presented in tables, it is important to understand how to read them. Tables contain six elements: title, headnote, headings, columns, rows, and source. When you understand how these elements work together, you know how to read a table.

The **title** states the topic. It is located at the top of the table. What is the title of this table? Please determine your answer before looking at the correct answer at the bottom of the page.

The **headnote** is not always included in a table. When it is, it is located just below the title. Its purpose is to give more detailed information about how the data were collected or how data are presented in the table. What are the first seven words of the headnote of this table?

The **headings** tell what kind of information is contained in the table. There are three headings in this table. What are they? In the second heading, what does $n = 25$ mean?

Comparing Violent and Nonviolent Husbands

Based on interviews with 150 husbands and wives in a Midwestern city who were getting a divorce.

Husband's Achievement and Job Satisfaction	Violent Husbands $n = 25$	Nonviolent Husbands $n = 125$
He started but failed to complete high school or college.	44%	27%
He is very dissatisfied with his job.	44%	18%
His income is a source of constant conflict.	84%	24%
He has less education than his wife.	56%	14%
His job has less prestige than his father-in-law's.	37%	28%

Source: Modification of Table 1 in O'Brien 1975.

The **columns** present information arranged vertically. What is the fourth number in the second column and the second number in the third column?

The **rows** present information arranged horizontally. In the fourth row, which husbands are more likely to have less education than their wives?

The **source** of a table, usually listed at the bottom, provides information on where the data shown in the table originated. Often, as in this instance, the information is specific enough for you to consult the original source. What is the source for this table?

Some tables are much more complicated than this one, but all follow the same basic pattern. To apply these concepts to a table with more information, see page 345.

ANSWERS

1. Comparing Violent and Nonviolent Husbands
2. Based on interviews with 150 husbands and wives
3. Husband's Achievement and Job Satisfaction, Violent Husbands, Nonviolent Husbands. The *n* is an abbreviation for number, and $n = 25$ means that 25 violent husbands were in the sample.
4. 56%, 18%
5. Violent Husbands
6. A 1975 article by O'Brien (listed in the References section of this text).

are available for **replication**; that is, others can repeat the study to see if they come up with similar results. As finding is added to finding, scientific knowledge builds.

Let's look in greater detail at the fifth step to see what research methods sociologists use.

Research Methods

As we review the six research methods (or *research designs*) that sociologists use, we will continue our example of spouse abuse. As you will see, the method you choose will depend on the questions you want to answer. So you can have a yardstick for comparison, you will want to know what "average" is in your study. Table 5.2 discusses ways to measure average.

Surveys

Let's suppose that you want to know how many wives are abused each year. Some husbands are abused, of course, but let's assume that you are going to focus on wives. An appropriate method for this purpose would be the **survey**, in which you would ask individuals a series of questions. Before you begin your research, however, you must deal with practical matters that face all researchers. Let's look at these issues.

Selecting a Sample

Ideally, you might want to learn about all wives in the world. Obviously, your resources will not permit such a study, and you must narrow your **population**, the target group that you are going to study.

Let's assume that your resources (money, helpers, time) allow you to investigate spouse abuse only on your campus. Let's also assume that your college enrollment is large, so you won't be able to survey all the married women who are enrolled. Now you must select a **sample**, individuals from among your target population. How you choose a sample is cru-

Table 5.2 Three Ways to Measure "Average"

The Mean	The Median	The Mode
The term average seems clear enough. As you learned in grade school, to find the average you add a group of numbers and then divide the total by the number of cases that were added. For example, assume that the following numbers represent men convicted of battering their wives: 321 229 57 289 136 57 1,795 The total is 2,884. Divided by 7 (the number of cases), the average is 412. Sociologists call this form of average the *mean.* The mean can be deceptive because it is strongly influenced by extreme scores, either low or high. Note that six of the seven cases are less than the mean. Two other ways to compute averages are the median and the mode.	To compute the second average, the *median,* first arrange the cases in order—either from the highest to the lowest or the lowest to the highest. In this example, that arrangement will produce the following distribution: 57 1,795 57 321 136 289 229 or 229 289 136 321 57 1,795 57 Then look for the middle case, the one that falls halfway between the top and the bottom. That number is 229, for three numbers are lower and three numbers are higher. When there is an even number of cases, the median is the halfway mark between the two middle cases.	The third measure of average, the mode, is simply the cases that occur the most often. In this instance the mode is 57, which is way off the mark. Because the mode is often deceptive, and only by chance comes close to either of the other two averages, sociologists seldom use it. In addition, it is obvious that not every distribution of cases has a mode. And if two or more numbers appear with the same frequency, you can have more than one mode.

Because sociologists usually cannot interview or observe every member of a group they wish to study, such as the spectators and riot police at this soccer match in Belgrade, Serbia, they must select a sample that will let them generalize to the entire group. The text explains how samples are selected.

cial, for your choice will affect the results of your study. For example, to survey only women enrolled in introductory sociology courses, or only those in advanced physics classes, would produce skewed results.

Because you want to generalize your findings to your entire campus, you need a sample that is representative of the campus. How do you get a representative sample?

The best is a **random sample.** This does *not* mean that you stand on some campus corner and ask questions of any woman who happens to walk by. *In a random sample, everyone in your population has the same chance of being included in the study.* In this case, because your population is every married woman enrolled in your college, all married women—whether first-year or graduate students, full- or part-time—must have the same chance of being included in your sample.

How can you get a random sample? First, you need a list of all the married women enrolled in your college. Then you assign a number to each name on the list. Using a table of random numbers, you then determine which of these women become part of your sample. (Random numbers are available on tables in statistics books, or they can be generated by a computer.)

Because a random sample represents your study's population—in this case, married women enrolled at your college—you can generalize your findings to all the married women students on your campus, even if they were not included in your sample.

What if you want to know only about certain subgroups, such as freshmen and seniors? You could use a **stratified random sample.** You would need a list of the freshmen and senior married women. Then, using random numbers, you would select a sample from each group. This would allow you to generalize to all the freshmen and senior married women at your college, but you would not be able to draw any conclusions about the sophomores or juniors.

Asking Neutral Questions After you have decided on your population and sample, your next task is to make certain that your questions are neutral. Your questions must allow **respondents,** the people who answer your questions, to express their own opinions. Otherwise, you will end up with biased answers—which are worthless. For example, if you were to ask, "Don't you think that men who beat their wives should go to prison?" you would be tilting the answer toward agreement with a prison sentence. The *Doonesbury* cartoon on page 131 illustrates a more blatant example of biased questions. For examples of flawed research, see the Down-to-Earth Sociology box on the next page.

replication repeating a study in order to test its findings

survey the collection of data by having people answer a series of questions

population the target group to be studied

sample the individuals intended to represent the population to be studied

random sample a sample in which everyone in the target population has the same chance of being included in the study

stratified random sample a sample of specific subgroups of the target population and in which everyone in the subgroups has an equal chance of being included in the study

respondents people who respond to a survey, either in interviews or by self-administered questionnaires

DOWN-TO-EARTH SOCIOLOGY

Loading the Dice: How *Not* to Do Research

THE METHODS OF SCIENCE LEND themselves to distortion, misrepresentation, and downright fraud. Consider the following information. Surveys show that

> Americans overwhelmingly prefer Toyotas to Chryslers.
>
> Americans overwhelmingly prefer Chryslers to Toyotas.

> Americans think that cloth diapers are better for the environment than disposable diapers.
>
> Americans think that disposable diapers are better for the environment than cloth diapers.

Obviously these opposite conclusions cannot both be true. In fact, *both* sets of findings are misrepresentations, although each comes from surveys conducted by so-called independent researchers. These researchers, however, are biased, not independent and objective.

It turns out that some consumer researchers load the dice. Hired by firms that have a vested interest in the outcome of the research, they deliver the results their clients are looking for. There are six basic ways to load the dice.

1. **Choose a biased sample.** If you want to "prove" that Americans prefer Chryslers over Toyotas, interview unemployed union workers who trace their job loss to Japanese imports. The answer is predictable. You'll get what you're looking for.
2. **Ask biased questions.** Even if you choose an unbiased sample, you can phrase questions in such a way that most people see only one logical choice. The diaper study just cited is a case in point. When the disposable diaper companies paid for the survey, the researchers used an excellent sample, but they worded the question this way: "It is estimated that disposable diapers account for less than 2 percent of the trash in today's landfills. In contrast, beverage containers, third-class mail and yard waste are estimated to account for about 21 percent. Given this, in your opinion, would it be fair to ban disposable diapers?"

   Is it surprising, then, that 84 percent of the respondents said that disposable diapers are better for the environment than cloth diapers? Similarly, when the cloth diaper companies funded their survey, they worded the questions to load the dice in their favor.

   Consider the following finding, which is every bit as factual as those just cited:

   > 80 percent of Americans support foreign aid.

   It is difficult to get 80 percent of Americans to agree on anything, but as loaded as this question was it is surprising that there was *only* 80 percent agreement. Incredibly, the question was phrased this way: *"Should the U.S. share at least a small portion of its wealth with those in the world who are in great need?"*

   This question is obviously designed to channel people's thinking toward a predetermined answer—quite contrary to the standards of scientific research.
3. **List biased choices.** Another way to load the dice is to use closed-ended questions that push people into the answers you want. Consider this finding:

   > U.S. college students overwhelmingly prefer Levis 501 to the jeans of any competitor.

   Sound good? Before you rush out to buy Levis, note what these researchers did: In asking students which jeans would be the most popular in the coming year, their list of choices included *no other jeans* but Levis 501!
4. **Discard undesirable results.** Researchers can keep silent about results they find embarrassing, or they can continue to survey samples until they find one that matches what they are looking for.

   As stressed in this chapter, research must be objective if it is to be scientific. Obviously, none of the preceding results qualifies. The underlying problem with the research cited here—and with so many surveys bandied about in the media as fact—is that survey research has become big business. Simply put, the money offered by corporations has corrupted some researchers.

   The beginning of the corruption is subtle. Paul Light, dean at the University of Minnesota, put it this way: "A funder will never come to an academic and say, 'I want you to produce finding *X*, and here's a million dollars to do it.' Rather, the subtext is that if the researchers produce the right finding, more work—and funding—will come their way." He adds, "Once you're on that treadmill, it's hard to get off."

   The first four sources of bias are inexcusable, intentional fraud. The next two sources of bias reflect sloppiness—which is also inexcusable in science.
5. **Misunderstand the subjects' world.** This route can lead to errors every bit as great as those just cited. Even researchers who use an adequate sample, word their questions properly, and offer adequate choices can end up with skewed results. They may, for example, fail to anticipate that people may be embarrassed to express an opinion that isn't "politically correct." For example, surveys show that 80 percent of Americans are environmentalists. Most Americans, however, are probably embarrassed to tell a stranger otherwise. Today, that would be like going against the flag, motherhood, and apple pie.
6. **Analyze the data incorrectly.** Even when researchers strive for objectivity, the sample is good, the wording is neutral, and the respondents answer the questions honestly, the results can still be skewed. The researchers may make a mistake in their calculations, such as entering incorrect data into computers. This, too, of course, is inexcusable in science.

Sources: Based on Crossen 1991; Goleman 1993; Barnes 1995; Resnik 2000.

Improperly worded questions can steer respondents toward answers that are not their own, thus producing invalid results.

Questionnaires and Interviews Even if you have a representative sample and ask neutral questions, you can still end up with biased findings. **Questionnaires,** the list of questions to be asked, can be administered in ways that are flawed. There are two basic techniques for administering questionnaires. The first is to ask the respondents to fill them out. These **self-administered questionnaires** allow a larger number of people to be sampled at a lower cost, but the researchers lose control. They don't know the conditions under which people answered the questions. For example, others could have influenced their answers.

The second technique is the **interview.** Researchers ask people questions, often face to face, but even by telephone or e-mail. The advantage of this method is that the researchers can ask each question in precisely the same way. The main disadvantage is that interviews are time-consuming, and researchers end up with fewer respondents. Interviews can also create **interviewer bias;** that is, the presence of interviewers can affect what people say. For example, instead of saying what they really feel, respondents might give "socially acceptable" answers. Although they may be willing to write their true opinions on an anonymous questionnaire, they won't tell them to another person. Some even shape their answers to match what they think an interviewer wants to hear.

In some cases, **structured interviews** work best. This type of interview uses **closed-ended questions**—each question is followed by a list of possible answers. Structured interviews are faster to administer, and they make it easier to *code* (categorize) answers so they can be fed into a computer for analysis. As you can see from Table 5.3, the answers listed on a questionnaire may not include the respondent's opinions. Consequently, some researchers prefer **unstructured interviews.** Here the interviewer asks **open-ended questions,** which allow people to answer in their own words. Although open-ended questions allow you to tap the full range of people's opinions, they make it difficult to compare

questionnaires a list of questions

self-administered questionnaires questionnaires filled out by respondents

interview direct questioning of respondents

interviewer bias effects that interviewers have on respondents that lead to biased answers

structured interviews interviews that use closed-ended questions

closed-ended questions questions that are followed by a list of possible answers to be selected by the respondent

unstructured interviews interviews that use open-ended questions

open-ended questions questions that respondents are able to answer in their own words

Table 5.3 Closed and Open-Ended Questions

A. Closed-Ended Question	B. Open-Ended Question
Which of the following best fits your idea of what should be done to someone who has been convicted of spouse abuse? 1. probation 2. jail time 3. community service 4. counseling 5. divorce 6. nothing—it's a family matter	What do you think should be done to someone who has been convicted of spouse abuse?

rapport (ruh-pour) a feeling of trust between researchers and subjects

participant observation (or **fieldwork**) research in which the researcher participates in a research setting while observing what is happening in that setting

answers. For example, how would you compare these answers to the question "What do you think causes men to abuse their wives?"

"They're sick."

"I think they must have had problems with their mother."

"We ought to string them up!"

Establishing Rapport Research on spouse abuse brings up another significant issue. You may have been wondering if your survey would be worth anything even if you rigorously followed scientific procedures. Will women who have been abused really give honest answers to strangers?

If you were to walk up to a woman on the street and ask if her husband had ever beaten her, there would be little basis for taking your findings seriously. Researchers have to establish **rapport** ("ruh-pour"), a feeling of trust, with their respondents, especially when it comes to sensitive topics—those that elicit feelings of embarrassment, shame, or other deep emotions.

We know that once rapport is gained (for example, by first asking nonsensitive questions), victims will talk to researchers about personal, sensitive issues. A good example is rape. To go beyond police statistics, each year researchers conduct a national crime survey. They interview a random sample of 100,000 Americans, asking them if they have been victims of burglary, robbery, and so on. After establishing rapport, the researchers ask about rape. They find that rape victims will talk about their experiences. The national crime victimization survey shows that rape is *three* times as high as the official statistics indicate (*Statistical Abstract* 2002: page 180).

Participant Observation (Fieldwork)

In the second method, **participant observation,** the researcher *participates* in a research setting while *observing* what is happening in that setting. But how is it possible to study spouse abuse by participant observation? Obviously, this method does not mean that you would sit around and watch someone being abused. Spouse abuse, however, is a broad topic, and many questions about abuse cannot be answered adequately by any method other than participant observation.

Sociologists who enter a research setting to discover information are following a research method known as participant observation. *As discussed in the text, sociologists also conduct research in controversial settings such as this cockfight in Marigot, on the island of Saint Martin.*

Let's suppose that you are interested in learning how spouse abuse affects wives. You may want to know how the abuse has changed their relationship with their husbands. How has it changed their hopes and dreams? Or their ideas about men? Certainly it has affected their self-concept as well. But how? Participant observation may be able to provide insight into such questions.

For example, if your campus has a crisis intervention center, you may be able to observe victims of spouse abuse from the time they first report the attack through their participation in counseling. With good rapport, you may even be able to spend time with victims in other settings, observing other aspects of their lives. What the victims say and how they interact with others may be the keys that help you unlock answers about how the abuse has affected them. This, in turn, may allow you to make suggestions about how to improve college counseling services.

Participant observers face a problem with **generalizability,** being able to apply their findings to larger populations. Most of these studies are exploratory, documenting in detail the experiences of people in a particular setting. Although such research suggests that other people who face similar situations react in similar ways, it is difficult to know just how far the findings apply beyond their original setting. The results of participant observation, however, can stimulate hypotheses and theories that can be tested in other settings, using other research techniques.

generalizability the extent to which the findings from one group (or sample) can be generalized or applied to other groups (or populations)

secondary analysis the analysis of data that have been collected by other researchers

documents in its narrow sense, written sources that provide data; in its extended sense, archival material of any sort, including photographs, movies, CD disks, and so on

Secondary Analysis

In **secondary analysis,** a third research method, researchers analyze data that have already been collected by others. For example, if you were to examine the original data from a study of women who had been abused by their husbands, you would be doing secondary analysis. Ordinarily, researchers prefer to gather their own data, but lack of resources, especially money, may make this impossible. In addition, existing data may contain a wealth of information that wasn't pertinent to the goals of the original researchers, which you can analyze for your own purposes.

Like the other methods, secondary analysis also poses its own problems. How can a researcher who did not carry out the research be sure that the data were systematically gathered and accurately recorded, and that biases were avoided? This problem plagues researchers who do secondary analysis, especially if the original data have been gathered by a team of researchers, not all of whom were equally qualified.

Domestic abuse is one of the most common forms of violence. Until recently, it was treated by the police as a private family matter. Shown here are police pulling a woman from her bathrom window, where she had fled from her armed husband, who was threatening to shoot her.

Documents

The fourth method sociologists use is the study of **documents,** written sources. To investigate social life, they examine such diverse documents as books, newspapers, diaries, bank records, police reports, immigration files, and records kept by organizations.

To study spouse abuse, you might examine police reports and court records. These could reveal what proportion of complaints result in arrest and what proportion of the men arrested are charged, convicted, or put on probation. If these were your questions, police statistics would be valuable.

But for other questions, those records would be useless. If you want to know about the victims' social and emotional adjustment, for example, those records would tell you little. Other documents, however, might provide answers. For example, diaries kept by victims could yield insight into their reactions to abuse, showing how their attitudes and relationships change. If no diaries were available, you might ask victims to keep diaries. Perhaps the director of a crisis intervention center might ask clients to keep diaries for you—or get the victims' permission for you to examine records of their counseling sessions. To my knowledge, no sociologist has yet studied spouse abuse in this way.

Of course, I am presenting an ideal situation, a crisis intervention center that opens its arms to you. In actuality, the center might not cooperate at all. It might refuse to ask victims to keep diaries, and it might not even let you near its records. *Access,* then, is another problem researchers face. Simply put, you can't study a topic unless you can gain access to it.

Sociologists use different methods of research to answer different questions. One method that can be used to study spouse abuse is to examine the documents kept by shelters for battered women, which log the number of calls and visits made by victims. This woman is being counseled at a rape crisis center in Cambridge, Massachusetts.

Experiments

A lot of people say that abusers need therapy. But no one knows if therapy really works. Let's suppose that you want to find out. Frankly, no one knows how to change a wife abuser into a loving husband—which may be impossible—but knowing if therapy works would certainly be a step in the right direction. To find out, you may want to conduct an **experiment**, for experiments are useful for determining cause and effect. Causation has three necessary conditions, which are discussed in Table 5.4 on page 136.

Let's suppose that a judge likes your idea, and she gives you access to men who have been arrested for spouse abuse. You would randomly divide the men into two groups. (See Figure 5.2 on page 135.) This would help to ensure that their individual characteristics (attitudes, number of arrests, severity of crimes, jail time, education, race-ethnicity, age, and so on) are distributed evenly between the groups. You then would arrange for the men in the **experimental group** to receive some form of therapy. The men in the **control group** would not get therapy.

Your **independent variable,** something that causes a change in another variable, would be therapy. Your **dependent variable,** the variable that may change, would be the men's behavior: whether they abuse women after they get out of jail. To make that determination, you would need to rely on a sloppy operational definition: either reports from the wives or records indicating the men were rearrested for abuse. This is sloppy because some of the women will not report the abuse, and some of the men who abuse their wives will not be rearrested. Yet it may be the best you can do.

Let's assume that you choose rearrest as your operational definition. If you find that the men who received therapy are less likely to be rearrested for abuse, you can attribute the difference to the therapy. If you find no difference in rearrest rates, you can conclude that the therapy was ineffective. If you find that the men who received the therapy have a *higher* rearrest rate, you can conclude that the therapy backfired.

Ideally, you would test different types of therapy. Perhaps only some work. You might even want to test self-therapy by assigning articles, books, and videos.

As described in the Down-to-Earth Sociology box on page 136, some experiments are not conducted this rigorously. This increases the likelihood that cause and effect will be confused.

experiment the use of control and experimental groups and dependent and independent variables to test causation

experimental group the group of subjects exposed to the independent variable

control group the group of subjects not exposed to the independent variable

independent variable a factor that causes a change in another variable, called the dependent variable

dependent variable a factor that is changed by an independent variable

unobtrusive measures ways of observing people who do not know they are being studied

Unobtrusive Measures

Researchers sometimes use **unobtrusive measures,** observing the behavior of people who do not know they are being studied. For example, social researchers studied the level of whisky consumption in a town that was officially "dry" by counting empty bottles in trashcans. To study the degree of fear induced by ghost stories, they measured the shrinking diameter of a circle of seated children. Some sociologists even examined garbage. They found that more beef is wasted during a beef shortage—presumably because people buy more than they can store properly (Lee 2000). Researchers have also gone high-tech in their unobtrusive measures (Selingo 2001). They have outfitted shopping carts with infrared surveillance equipment to trace customers' paths through stores. Retailers use these findings to place items in their stores in more strategic locations (McCarthy 1993).

Figure 5.2 **The Experiment**

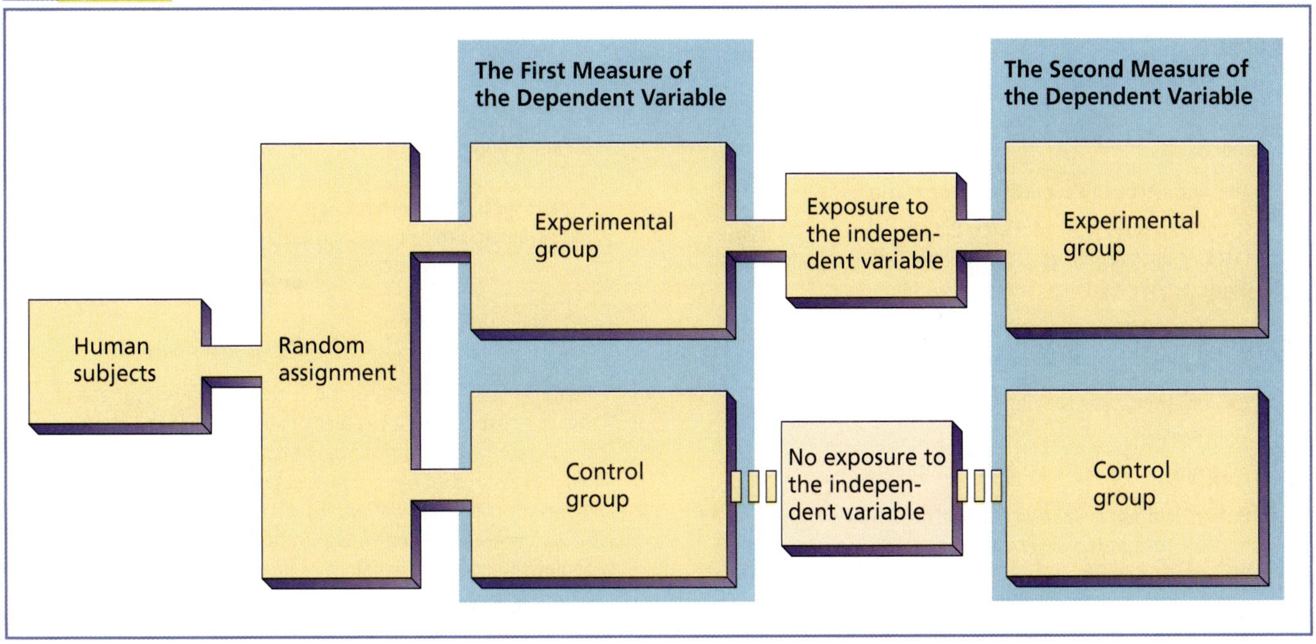

DOWN-TO-EARTH SOCIOLOGY

The Hawthorne Experiments

RESEARCH FROM THE 1920s, KNOWN AS the Hawthorne experiments, has become a classic in sociology. This research drives home how necessary it is to accurately identify independent and dependent variables.

The managers of the Hawthorne plant of the Western Electric Company near Chicago wanted to know if different levels of lighting would affect productivity. Several groups of women participated in what are known as the Relay Room Experiments. In the control room, the level of lighting was held constant, while in the experimental room, the lighting was varied. To everyone's surprise, output increased at *both* locations. In the experimental room, productivity remained high even when the lights were dimmed to about the level of moonlight—so low that workers could barely see what they were doing!

To solve this mystery, management called in a team of researchers headed by Elton Mayo of the University of Chicago. This team tested thirteen different work conditions. When they changed the women's' pay from hourly wages to piecework (paying them at a set rate for each unit they produce), productivity increased. When they served refreshments, output again went up. When they added two 5-minute rest periods, productivity jumped. When they changed the rest periods to two 10-minute periods, again output increased. When they let the workers go home early, they found the same result. Confused, the researchers restored the original conditions, offering none of these added benefits. The result? Even higher productivity.

The situation grew even more confusing when they observed men workers in what is known as the Bank Wiring Room Study. Here, the researchers didn't change the work conditions at all. They simply observed the men while they worked and interviewed them after work. They expected no change in productivity. What happened was that productivity *dropped.*

None of this made sense. Finally, Mayo concluded that the changes in productivity were due to the research itself. The women, pleased at the attention being paid to them, responded by increasing their efforts. The men, in contrast, became suspicious about why the researchers were observing them. They feared that if they had higher productivity, they would be expected to produce more each day, or that higher productivity might even cost some of them their jobs. Consequently, they decreased their output.

The Hawthorne research is important—not for its findings on worker productivity, but for what it revealed about the research process itself. Today, researchers carefully monitor the *Hawthorne effect,* the change in behavior that occurs when people know they are being studied.

Sources: Based on Roethlisberger and Dickson 1939; Mayo 1966; Baron and Greenberg 1990.

Table 5.4 Cause, Effect, and Spurious Correlations

Causation means that a change in one variable is caused by another variable. Three conditions are necessary for causation: correlation, temporal priority, and no spurious correlation. Let's apply each of these conditions to spouse abuse and alcohol abuse.

1. The first necessary condition is **correlation.**

   If two variables exist together, they are said to be correlated. If batterers have drunk alcohol, battering and alcohol abuse are correlated.

   Spouse Abuse + Alcohol Abuse

   People sometimes assume that correlation is causation. In this instance, they conclude that alcohol abuse causes spouse abuse.

   Alcohol Abuse → Spouse Abuse

   But *correlation never proves causation. Either* variable could be the cause of the other. Perhaps battering pushes men into getting drunk.

   Spouse Abuse → Alcohol Abuse

2. The second necessary condition is *temporal priority* (one variable must occur before the other).

   Temporal priority means that one thing happens before something else does. For a variable to be a cause (the *independent* variable), it must *precede* that which is changed (the *dependent* variable). If the men had not drunk alcohol until after they beat their wives, obviously alcohol abuse could not be the cause of the spouse abuse. Although the necessity of temporal priority is obvious, in many studies this is not easy to determine.

3. The third necessary condition is *no spurious correlation.*

   This is the necessary condition that really makes things difficult. Even if we identify correlation and can determine temporal priority, we still don't know that alcohol abuse is the cause. It is possible that we have a *spurious correlation;* that is, the cause may be some underlying third variable that is not easily visible. Some sociologists identify male culture as that underlying third variable.

   Male Culture → Spouse Abuse

   Socialized into dominance, some males learn to view women as objects on which to take out their frustration. In fact, this underlying third variable could be a cause of both spouse abuse and alcohol abuse.

   Male Culture → Spouse Abuse
   Male Culture → Alcohol Abuse

   But since only some men beat their wives, while all males are exposed to male culture, other variables must also be involved. Perhaps specific subcultures that promote violence and denigrate women lead to both spouse abuse and alcohol abuse.

   Male Subculture → Spouse Abuse
   Male Subculture → Alcohol Abuse

   If so, this does *not* mean that it is the only causal variable, for spouse abuse probably has many causes. Unlike the movement of amoebas or the action of heat on some object, human behavior is infinitely complicated. What is especially important is people's *definitions of the situation,* including their views of right and wrong. To explain spouse abuse, then, we need to add such variables as men's views of violence and their definitions of the relative rights of women and men. It is precisely to help unravel such complicating factors in human behavior that we need the experimental method.

More on Correlations

Correlation simply means that two or more variables are present together. The more often they are found together, the stronger their relationship. To indicate their strength, sociologists use a number called a *correlation coefficient.* If two variables are always related, that is, they are always present together, they have what is called a perfect positive correlation. The number 1.0 represents this correlation coefficient. Nature has some 1.0's, such as the lack of water and the death of trees. 1.0's also apply to the human physical state, such as the absence of nutrients and the absence of life. But social life is much more complicated than physical conditions, and there are no 1.0's in human behavior.

Two variables can also have a *perfect negative correlation.* This means that when one variable is present, the other is always absent. The number −1.0 represents this correlation coefficient.

Positive correlations of 0.1, 0.2, and 0.3 mean that one variable is associated with another only 1 time out of 10, 2 times out of 10, and 3 times out of 10. In other words, in most instances the first variable is *not* associated with the second, indicating a weak relationship. The greater the correlation coefficient, the stronger the relationship. A strong relationship *may* indicate causation, but not necessarily. Testing the relationship between variables is the goal of some sociological research.

It would be considered unethical to use most unobtrusive measures to research spouse abuse. You could, however, analyze 911 calls. If there were a *public* forum held by abused or abusing spouses on the Internet, you could also record and analyze the online conversations. Ethics are still a matter of dispute: To secretly record the behavior of people in public settings, such as a crowd, is generally considered acceptable, but to do so in private settings is not.

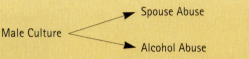

Deciding Which Method to Use

How do sociologists choose among these methods? Four primary factors affect their decision. First, *resources* are crucial. Sociologists must match methods with available resources. For example, although they may want to conduct a survey, they may find that finances won't permit it, and instead they turn to the study of documents. The second significant factor is *access to subjects.* If the people who comprise a sample live in remote parts of the country, researchers may have to mail them questionnaires or conduct a telephone survey even if they would prefer face-to-face interviews. The third factor concerns the *purpose of the research,* the questions that the sociologist wishes to investigate and answer. Each method is better for answering some questions than for others. Participant observation, for example, is good for uncovering people's attitudes, while experiments work better for resolving questions of cause and effect. Fourth, *the researcher's background or training* comes into play. In graduate school, sociologists study many methods, but they are able to practice only some of them. Consequently, after graduate school they generally use the methods in which they have had the most training.

Thus, sociologists who have been trained in **quantitative research methods,** which emphasize measurement, numbers, and statistics, are likely to use surveys. Sociologists who have been trained in **qualitative research methods,** which emphasize describing, observing, and interpreting people's behavior, lean toward participant observation. In the Down-to-Earth Sociology box, you can see how applied sociologists use a combination of quantitative and qualitative methods.

quantitative research methods research in which the emphasis is placed on precise measurement, the use of statistics and numbers

qualitative research methods research in which the emphasis is placed on observing, describing, and interpreting people's behavior

DOWN-TO-EARTH SOCIOLOGY

Applied Sociology: Marketing Research as a Blend of Quantitative and Qualitative Methods

IF A COMPANY IS GOING TO SURVIVE IN the highly competitive business world, it must figure out what consumers need and want, and then supply it—or else convince people that what they need or want is what the company is already producing.

What Marketing Research Is

To increase sales, manufacturers try to improve the position of their products. "Position" is marketing jargon for how customers think about a product.

This is where marketing researchers come into play. They find out what customers want, how they select products, how they use them, and what impressions they hold of a product or service. They also assess how the public will react to a new product or to a change in an established product.

Marketing researchers use both qualitative and quantitative methods. An example of a qualitative method is *focus groups.* Groups of about ten people are invited to discuss a product. A moderator leads a discussion while other team members observe or videotape the session from behind a one-way mirror. To control for regional variations, the researchers may hold other focus groups at the same time in other cities. Sociologist Roger Straus points out that his training in symbolic interactionism has been especially useful for interpreting these results.

Marketing researchers also use quantitative techniques. For example, they may conduct surveys to determine what the public thinks of a new product. They also gather sales data from the "bar codes" found on products. They use statistics to analyze the data, and they prepare tables and graphics to summarize the findings for clients.

A Sociological Controversy

Marketing research occupies a controversial position in sociology. Most of the results of marketing research are proprietary (owned by the client) and are therefore confidential. This means that the findings do not appear in sociology journals and are not used to create social theory. In addition, clients are usually interested in specific marketing problems, and they seldom commission research on important social issues. For such reasons, many sociologists do not consider marketing research a "legitimate" sociological activity. Some even scorn marketing researchers as wasting their sociological talents. They chide them for having "sold out"—for using sociological methods to help corporations exploit the public by convincing them to purchase unneeded goods and services.

Marketing researchers, of course, do not see things this way. They argue that marketing research is a neutral activity, that there is no reason to be against it on principle. They add that they do more than just help sell beer and soft drinks. They point out that they have helped colleges attract students and communities assess public needs. They argue that the decision to do research on any topic involves the researcher's own values. This applies to studying how to reduce juvenile delinquency as well as how to sell facial scrubs for acne. It is presumptuous, they say, for anyone to pass judgment on marketing research—as though other research were morally superior.

Sources: Based on Straus 1991 and communication with Straus 1993.

Sociologists sometimes find themselves in the hot seat because of their research. Some poke into private areas of life, which upsets people. Others investigate public matters, but their findings threaten those who have a stake in the situation. When a survey showed that if there were a peace settlement, most Palestinian refugees would be willing to accept compensation and not return to Israel, an enraged mob beat the researcher and trashed his office (Bennet 2003). From the following Thinking Critically section, you can see how using rigorous research methods on even such an innocuous topic as homelessness can land sociologists in the midst of controversy.

THINKING Critically

Doing Controversial Research—Counting the Homeless

What could be less offensive than counting the homeless? As sometimes occurs, however, even basic research lands sociologists in the midst of controversy. This is what happened to sociologist Peter Rossi and his associates.

There was a dispute between advocates for the homeless and the federal government. The advocates claimed that 3 to 7 million Americans were homeless; the government claimed that it was only one-twelfth to one-twenty-eighth that number, about a quarter of a million people. Each side accused the other of gross distortion—the one to place undue pressure on Congress, the other to keep the public from knowing how bad the situation really was.

Only an accurate count could clear up the picture, for both sides were only guessing at the numbers. Peter Rossi and the National Opinion Research Center decided to make an accurate count. They had no vested interest in supporting one side or the other, only in answering this question honestly.

The challenge was immense. The *population* was evident—the U.S. homeless. A *survey* would be appropriate, but how do you survey a *sample* of the homeless? No one has a list of the homeless, and only some of the homeless stay at shelters. As for *validity,* to make certain that they were counting only people who were really homeless, the researchers needed a good *operational definition* of homelessness. To include people who weren't really

As discussed on this page, research sometimes lands sociologists in the midst of controversy. An example is a study conducted to determine how many homeless people there are in the United States. Homeless advocates were not pleased with the results. These homeless men in New Haven, Connecticut, are guarding the belongings of other homeless people who are eating at a nearby soup kitchen.

homeless would destroy the study's *reliability.* The researchers wanted results that would be consistent if others were to *replicate,* or repeat, the study.

As an operational definition, the researchers used "literally homeless," people "who do not have access to a conventional dwelling and who would be homeless by any conceivable definition of the term." Because a national count would cost about $6 million, far beyond their resources, the researchers decided to count just the homeless in Chicago. The cost was still high, however—about $600,000.

By using a *stratified random sample,* the researchers were able to *generalize* to the entire city. How could they do this since there is no list of the homeless? For the homeless who sleep in shelters, they used a stratified random sample of the city's shelters. For the homeless who sleep in the streets, vacant buildings, and so forth, they used a stratified random sample of the city's blocks. To make doubly certain that their count was accurate, the researchers conducted two surveys. At night, trained teams visited the shelters and searched the alleys, bridges, and vacant houses.

They found that on an average night, Chicago has 2,722 homeless people. Because people move in and out of homelessness, between 5,000 and 7,000 are homeless at some point during the year. On warm nights, only two out of five sleep in the shelters, and even in winter only three out of four do so. The median age is 40; 75 percent are men, and 60 percent are African Americans. One in four is a former mental patient, one in five a former prisoner. A homeless person's income from all sources is less than $6 a day. Projecting these findings to the United States resulted in a national total of about 350,000 homeless people, a figure that was much closer to the government's estimate of 250,000 than to the advocates' estimate of 3 to 7 million.

The reactions were predictable. Government officials rubbed their hands in glee. The stunned homeless advocates denied the findings and began a sniping campaign at the researchers.

Remember that Rossi and his associates had no interest in proving which side in the debate was right, only in getting reliable figures. Using impeccable methods, this they did.

The researchers had no intention of minimizing the problem of homelessness. They stressed that 350,000 Americans are so poor that they sleep in city streets, live in shelters, eat out of garbage cans, and suffer from severe health problems. In short, these people live hopeless, desperate lives.

It is good to *know* how many Americans are homeless. Guesses aren't worth much. Even though the number is far less than what the homeless advocates had estimated, this information can still serve their cause: Having fewer homeless people makes the problem more manageable. It means that if we choose to do so, we can put our resources to work with greater certainty of success.

Those whose positions are not supported by research, however, are never pleased, and they tend to take potshots at the researchers. This is one of the risks of doing sociological research, for sociologists never know whose toes they will step on.

Sources: Based on Anderson 1986; Rossi et al. 1986; Rossi et al. 1987; Coughlin 1988; Rossi 1989; Rossi 1991; De Parle 1994; Rossi 1999.

Gender in Sociological Research

You know how significant gender is, how it affects your orientations and your attitudes. You may also be aware that it opens and closes doors to you, a topic that we will explore in Chapter 11. Gender can also be significant in social research, and researchers take steps to prevent gender from biasing their findings. For example, sociologists Diana Scully and Joseph Marolla (1984, 2003) interviewed convicted rapists in prison. They were concerned that their gender might lead to *interviewer bias*—that the prisoners might shift their answers, sharing certain experiences or expressing certain attitudes to Marolla, but saying something else to Scully. To prevent gender bias, each interviewed half the sample. Later in this chapter, we'll look at what they found out.

Gender certainly can be a major impediment in research. In our imagined research on spouse abuse, for example, could a man even do participant observation of women who have been beaten by their husbands? Technically, the answer is yes. But because the women have been victimized by men, they might be less likely to share their experiences and feelings with men. If so, women would be better suited to conduct this research, more likely to achieve valid results. The supposition that these victims will be more open with women than with men, however, is just that—a supposition. Research alone will verify or refute this assumption.

Gender is significant in other ways, too. As feminist sociologists point out, it is a mistake to assume that what applies to one sex is also relevant to the other (Bird and Rieker 1999; Neuman 2000). Women's and men's lives differ significantly, and if we do research on just half of humanity, our research will be vastly incomplete. With today's huge numbers of women sociologists, there is little risk of ignoring women in contemporary research. In the past, however, when almost all sociologists were men, women's experiences were neglected.

Gender pops up in unexpected ways in sociological research. I vividly recall an incident in San Francisco.

> The streets were getting dark, and I was still looking for homeless people. When I saw someone lying down, curled up in a doorway, I approached the individual. As I got close, I began my opening research line, "Hi, I'm Dr. Henslin from. . . ." The individual began to scream and started to thrash wildly. Startled by this sudden, high-pitched scream and by the rapid movements, I quickly backed away. When I later analyzed what had happened, I concluded that I had intruded into a woman's bedroom.

Of course, one can draw another lesson from this incident. Researchers do their best, but they make mistakes. Sometimes these mistakes are minor, and even humorous. The woman sleeping in the doorway wasn't frightened. It was only just getting dark, and there were many people on the street. She was just assertively marking her territory and letting me know in no uncertain terms that I was an intruder. If we make a mistake in research, we pick up and go on. As we do so, we take ethical considerations into account, which is the topic of our next section.

Ethics in Sociological Research

In addition to choosing an appropriate research method, then, we must also follow the ethics of sociology, which center on assumptions of science and morality (American Sociological Association 1997). Research ethics require openness (sharing findings with the scientific community), honesty, and truth. Ethics clearly forbid the falsification of results. They also condemn plagiarism—that is, stealing someone else's work. Another ethical guideline is that research subjects should generally be informed that they are being studied and never be harmed by the research. Ethics also require that sociologists protect the anonymity of those who provide information. Sometimes people reveal things that are intimate, potentially embarrassing, or otherwise harmful to themselves. Finally, although not all sociologists agree, it generally is considered unethical for researchers to misrepresent themselves.

Sociologists take these ethical standards seriously. To illustrate the extent to which they will go to protect their respondents, consider the research conducted by Mario Brajuha.

Protecting the Subjects: The Brajuha Research

Mario Brajuha, a graduate student at the State University of New York at Stony Brook, was doing participant observation of restaurant work. He lost his job as a waiter when the restaurant where he was working burned down—due to a fire of "suspicious origin," as the police said. When detectives learned that Brajuha had taken field notes (Brajuha and Hallowell 1986), they asked to see them. Because he had promised to keep the information confidential, Brajuha refused. The district attorney then subpoenaed the notes. Brajuha still refused to hand them over. The district attorney threatened to put Brajuha in jail. By this time, Brajuha's notes had become rather famous, and unsavory characters—perhaps those who had set the fire—also wanted to know what was in them. They accompanied their demands with threats of a different nature. Brajuha found himself between a rock and a hard place.

For two years Brajuha refused to hand over his notes, even though he grew anxious and had to appear at several court hearings. Finally, the district attorney dropped the subpoena. When the two men under investigation for setting the fire died, so did the threats to Brajuha, his wife, and their children.

Misleading the Subjects: The Humphreys Research

Sociologists agree on the necessity to protect respondents, and they applaud the professional manner in which Brajuha handled himself. Although there is less agreement that researchers should not misrepresent themselves, sociologists who violate this norm can become embroiled in ethical controversy. Let's look at the case of Laud Humphreys, whose research forced sociologists to rethink and refine their ethical stance.

Laud Humphreys, a classmate of mine at Washington University in St. Louis, was an Episcopal priest who decided to become a sociologist. For his Ph.D. dissertation, Humphreys (1970, 1971, 1975) studied social interaction in "tearooms," public restrooms where some men go for quick, anonymous oral sex with other men.

Humphreys found that some restrooms in Forest Park, just across from our campus, were tearooms. He began a participant observation study by hanging around these restrooms. He found that in addition to the two men having sex, a third man—called a "watchqueen"—served as a lookout for police and other unwelcome strangers. Humphreys took on the role of watchqueen, not only watching for strangers but also observing and systematically recording what the men did.

Humphreys decided he wanted to know more about the regular lives of these men. For example, what was the significance of the wedding rings that many of the men wore? He hit on an ingenious technique. Many of the men parked their cars near the tearooms, and Humphreys recorded their license numbers. A friend in the St. Louis police department gave Humphreys each man's address. About a year later, Humphreys arranged for these men to be included in a medical survey conducted by some of the sociologists on our faculty.

Disguising himself with a different hairstyle and clothing, and driving a different car, Humphreys visited their homes. He interviewed the men, supposedly for the medical study. He found that they led conventional lives. They voted, mowed their lawns, and

Ethics in social research are of vital concern to sociologists. As discussed in the text sociologists may disagree on some of the issue's finer points, but none would approve of slipping LSD to unsuspecting subjects like these Marine recruits at basic training in Miami, Florida. This was done to U.S. servicemen in the 1960s under the guise of legitimate testing—just "to see what would happen."

took their kids to Little League games. Many reported that their wives were not aroused sexually or were afraid of getting pregnant because their religion did not allow them to use birth control. Humphreys concluded that heterosexual men were also using the tearooms for a form of quick sex.

This study stirred controversy among sociologists and nonsociologists alike. Humphreys was criticized by many sociologists, and a national columnist even wrote a scathing denunciation of "sociological snoopers" (Von Hoffman 1970). As the controversy grew more heated and a court case loomed, Humphreys feared that his list of respondents might be subpoenaed. He gave me the list to take from Missouri to Illinois, where I had begun teaching. When he called and asked me to destroy it, I burned it in my backyard.

Was this research ethical? This question is not decided easily. Although many sociologists sided with Humphreys—and his book reporting the research won a highly acclaimed award—the criticisms mounted. At first, Humphreys vigorously defended his position, but five years later, in a second edition of his book (1975), he stated that he should have identified himself as a researcher.

How Research and Theory Work Together

Research cannot stand alone. Nor can theory. As sociologist C. Wright Mills (1959) so forcefully argued, research without theory is simply a collection of unrelated "facts." But theory without research, Mills added, is abstract and empty—it can't represent the way life really is.

Research and theory, then, are both essential for sociology. Every theory must be tested, which requires research. And as sociologists do research, they often come up with surprising findings. Those findings must be explained, and for that we need theory. As sociologists study social life, then, they combine research and theory.

The Real World: When the Ideal Meets the Real

Although we can list the ideals of research, real-life situations often force sociologists to settle for something that falls short of the ideal. Let's look at how two sociologists confronted the ideal and the real in the following Thinking Critically section.

THINKING Critically

Are Rapists Sick? A Close-Up View of Research

Two sociologists, Diana Scully and Joseph Marolla, were not satisfied with the typical explanation that rapists are "sick," psychologically disturbed, or different from other men. They developed the hypothesis that rape is like most human behavior—it is learned through interaction with others. That is, some men learn to think of rape as appropriate behavior.

To test this hypothesis, it would be best to interview a random sample of rapists. But this is impossible. There is no list of all rapists, so there is no way to give them all the same chance of being included in a sample. You can't even use prison populations to select a random sample, for many rapists have never been caught, some who were caught were found not guilty, and some who were found guilty were given probation. Some, too, who were convicted of rape are innocent. Consequently, Scully and Marolla confronted the classic dilemma of sociologists—

either to not do the study or to do it under less than ideal conditions.

They chose to do the study. When they had the opportunity to interview convicted rapists in prison, they jumped at it. They knew that whatever they learned would be more than we already knew. They sent out 3,500 letters to men serving time in seven prisons in Virginia, the state where they were teaching. About 25 percent of the prisoners agreed to be interviewed. They matched these men on the basis of age, education, race, severity of offense, and previous criminal record. This resulted in a sample of 98 prisoners who were convicted of rape and a control sample of 75 men convicted of other offenses.

As noted earlier, because the sex of the interviewer can bias research results, Scully and Marolla each interviewed half the sample. It took them 600 hours to gather information on the prisoners, including their psychological, criminal, and sexual history. To guard against lies, they checked what the individuals said against their institutional records. They used twelve scales to measure the men's attitudes about women, rape, and themselves. In order to find out what circumstances the men defined as rape or when they viewed the victim as responsible, they also gave the men nine vignettes of forced sexual encounters and asked them to determine responsibility in each one.

Scully and Marolla discovered something that goes against common sense—that most rapists are not sick, and that they are not overwhelmed by uncontrollable urges. The psychological histories of the rapists and the nonrapists were similar. Rapists, they concluded, are emotionally average men who have learned to view rape as appropriate in certain situations. Some rape spontaneously, while others plan their rapes. For some, rape is a form of recreation, and they rape with friends on weekends. Others use rape as a form of revenge, to get even with someone, not necessarily the woman.

Scully and Marolla also found support for what feminists had been pointing out for years, that power is a major element in rape. Here is what one man said:

> Rape gave me the power to do what I wanted to do without feeling I had to please a partner or respond to a partner. I felt in control, dominant. Rape was the ability to have sex without caring about the woman's response. I was totally dominant.

To discover that most rape is calculated behavior—that rapists are not "sick"; that the motivating force is power, not passion; that the behavior stems from the criminal pursuit of pleasure, not from mental illness—is significant. It makes the sociological quest worthwhile.

In comparing their sample of rapists with their control group of nonrapists, Scully and Marolla also made another significant finding: The rapists are more likely to believe "rape myths." They are more likely to believe that women cause their own rape by the way they act and the clothes they wear, that a woman who charges rape has simply changed her mind after participating in consensual sex, and that most men accused of rape are innocent.

Connecting Research and Theory

Such findings go far beyond simply adding to our storehouse of "facts." As indicated in Figure 5.1 on page 125, research stimulates both the development of theory and the need for more research. Scully and Marolla suggest that rape myths act as neutralizers, that they allow "potential rapists to turn off social prohibitions against injuring others."

This hypothesis, in turn, pinpoints the need to determine how such myths are transmitted. Which male subcultures perpetuate them? Do the mass media contribute to these myths? Do family, religion, and education create respect for females and help keep males from learning such myths? Or do they somehow contribute to these myths? If so, how?

Sociologists have begun to build on this pathbreaking research, which was done, as usual, under less than ideal conditions. The resulting theorizing and research may provide the basis for making changes that reduce the incidence of rape in our society.

Sources: Marolla and Scully 1986; Scully 1990; Hale 2003; Scully and Marolla 1984, 2003.

Sociology needs more of this type of research—imaginative and sometimes daring investigations conducted in an imperfect world under less than ideal conditions. This is really what sociology is all about. Sociologists study what people do—whether their behaviors are conforming or deviant, whether they please others or disgust them and arouse intense anger. No matter the behavior that is studied, systematic research methods and the application of social theory take us beyond common sense. They allow us to penetrate surface realities so we can better understand human behavior—and, in the ideal case, make changes to help improve social life.

SUMMARY and REVIEW

What Is a Valid Sociological Topic?

Any human behavior is a valid sociological topic, even disreputable behavior. Spouse abuse is an example. Sociological research is based on the sociologist's interests, access to subjects, appropriate methods, and ethical considerations. P. 124.

Common Sense and the Need for Sociological Research

Why isn't common sense adequate?

Common sense doesn't provide reliable knowledge. When subjected to scientific research, commonsense ideas often are found to be very limited or false. P. 124.

A Research Model

What are the eight basic steps of scientific research?

1. Selecting a topic, 2. Defining the problem, 3. Reviewing the literature, 4. Formulating a **hypothesis,** 5. Choosing a research method, 6. Collecting the data, 7. Analyzing the results, 8. Sharing the results. These steps are explained in detail on pp. 124–128.

Research Methods

How do sociologists gather data?

To gather data, sociologists use six **research methods** (or research designs): **surveys, participant observation** (fieldwork), **secondary analysis, documents, experiments,** and **unobtrusive measures.** Pp. 128–136.

How do sociologists choose a research method?

Sociologists choose their research method based on questions to be answered, their access to potential subjects, the resources available, their training, and ethical considerations. Pp. 137–138.

Gender in Sociological Research

What is the relationship between gender and research?

There are two aspects. First, sociologists used to study men and assume that their findings applied equally to women. As more women became sociologists, this changed. Second, in some kinds of research, such as studying rapists in prison, the gender of the researcher could affect findings. Pp. 139–140.

Ethics in Sociological Research

How important are ethics in sociological research?

Ethics are of fundamental concern to sociologists, who are committed to openness, honesty, truth, and protecting their subjects from harm. The Brajuha research on restaurants and the Humphreys research on "tearooms" were cited to illustrate ethical issues of concern to sociologists. Pp. 140–142.

How Research and Theory Work Together

What is the relationship between theory and research?

Theory and research depend on one another. Sociologists use theory to interpret the data they gather. Theory also generates questions that need to be answered by research. Research, in turn, helps to generate theory: When findings don't match what is expected, this indicates the need for new thinking. Pp. 142–143.

Where can I read more on this topic?

Suggested readings for this chapter are listed at the back of this book.

THINKING Critically ABOUT CHAPTER 5

1. Why do we need sociological research?
2. What factors make for *bad* sociological research? How can these be avoided?
3. What ethics govern sociological research?

ADDITIONAL RESOURCES for This Chapter

www.ablongman.com/henslin7e

- *Content Select* Research Database for Sociology, with suggested key terms and annotated references
- Link to 2000 Census, with activities
- Flashcards of key terms and concepts
- Practice Tests
- Weblinks
- Interactive Maps

Chapter 6

Societies to Social Networks

Pavel Varfolomeevic Kusnezov, *Pushball,* 1911

Chapter Outline

When Cody Scott joined the L. A. Crips, his initiation had two parts. Here's the first:

> "How old is you now anyway?"
>
> "Eleven, but I'll be twelve in November."
>
> I never saw the blow to my head come from Huck. Bam! And I was on all fours . . . Kicked in the stomach, I was on my back counting stars in the blackness. Grabbed by the collar, I was made to stand again. A solid blow to my chest exploded pain on the blank screen that had now become my mind. Bam! Another, then another. Blows rained on me from every direction . . .
>
> Up until this point not a word had been spoken. . . . Then I just started swinging, with no style or finesse, just anger and the instinct to survive. . . . (This) reflected my ability to represent the set [gang] in hand-to-hand combat. The blows stopped abruptly . . . My ear was bleeding, and my neck and face were deep red . . .

Scott's beating was followed immediately by the second part of his initiation. For this, he received the name *Monster,* which he so proudly carried:

> "Give Cody the pump" [12-gauge pump action shotgun] . . . Tray Ball spoke with the calm of a football coach. "Tonight we gonna rock they world." . . . Hand slaps were passed around the room . . . "Cody, you got eight shots, you don't come back to the car unless they all are gone."
>
> "Righteous," I said, eager to show my worth. . . .
>
> Hanging close to buildings, houses, and bushes, we made our way, one after the other, to within spitting distance of the Bloods. . . . Huck and Fly stepped from the shadows simultaneously and were never noticed until it was too late. Boom! Boom! Heavy bodies hitting the ground, confusion, yells of dismay, running, . . . By my sixth shot I had advanced past the first fallen bodies and into the street in pursuit of those who had sought refuge behind cars and trees. . . .
>
> Back in the shack we smoked more pot and drank more beer. I was the center of attention for my acts of aggression. . . .
>
> Tray Ball said. "You got potential, 'cause you eager to learn. Bangin' [being a gang member] ain't no part-time thang, it's full-time, it's a career. It's bein' down

's bein' down when
ain't nobody else
own with you.

when ain't nobody else down with you. It's gettin' caught and not tellin'. Killin' and not caring, and dyin' without fear. It's love for your set and hate for the enemy. You hear what I'm sayin'?"

Cody adds this insightful remark:

Though never verbally stated, death was looked upon as a sort of reward, a badge of honor, especially if one died in some heroic capacity for the hood . . . The supreme sacrifice was to "take a bullet for a homie" [fellow gang member]. The set functioned as a religion. Nothing held a light to the power of the set. If you died on the trigger you surely were smiled upon by the Crip God.

Excerpts from Scott 1994:8–13, 103.

Groups are the essence of life in society. We become who we are because of our membership in human groups. As we saw in Chapter 3, even our minds are a product of society, or, more specifically phrased, of the groups to which we belong.

In this chapter, we'll consider how groups influence our lives—and even the power that groups wield over us. Although none of us wants to think that we could participate in killings such as those recounted in our opening vignette, don't bet on it. You are going to read some surprising things about groups in this chapter.

Societies and Their Transformation

To better understand **groups**—people who interact with one another and who think of themselves as belonging together—let's first look at the big picture. The largest and most complex group that sociologists study is **society**, which consists of people who share a culture and a territory. Society, which surrounds us, sets the stage for our life experiences. Not only does it lay the broad framework for our behavior but also it influences the ways we think and feel. Since our society is so significant in our lives, let's look at how it developed. In Figure 6.1, you can see that technology is the key for understanding the broad, sweeping changes that have produced our society. As we summarize these changes, picture yourself as a member of each society. Consider how your life—even your thoughts and values—would be different in each society.

As society*—the largest and most complex type of* group*—changes, so, too, do the groups, activities, and, ultimately, the type of people who form that society. This photo of Trish Stratus of World Wrestling Entertainment captures some of the changes that U.S. society has been undergoing in recent years. What social changes can you identify from this photo?*

Figure 6.1 The Social Transformations of Society

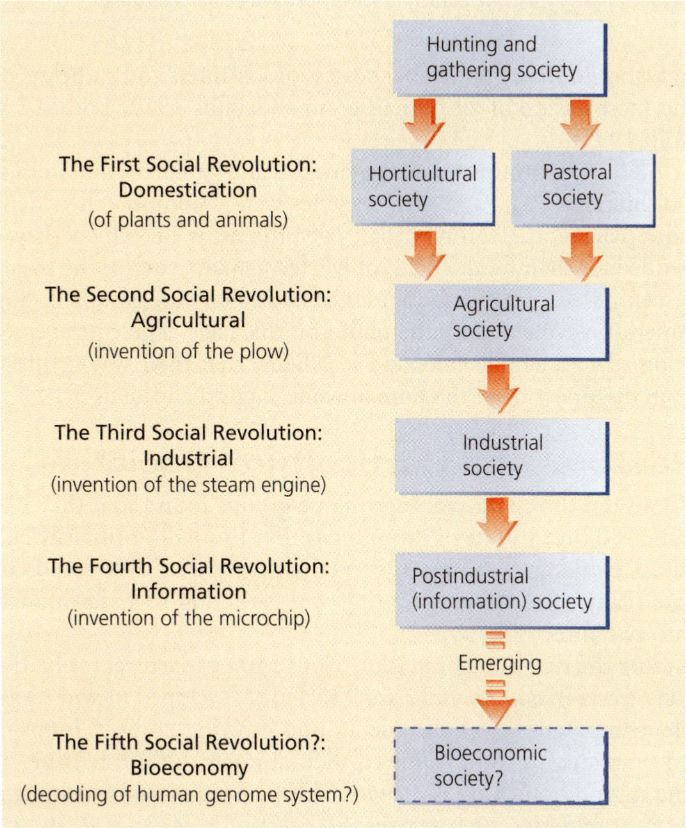

Hunting and Gathering Societies

Societies with the fewest social divisions are called **hunting and gathering societies.** As the name implies, these groups depend on hunting animals and gathering plants for their survival. In some, the men do the hunting, and the women the gathering. In others, both men and women (and children) gather plants, the men hunt large animals, and both men and women hunt small animals. Beyond this basic division of labor by sex, there are few social divisions. The groups usually have a **shaman,** an individual thought to be able to influence spiritual forces, but shamans, too, must help obtain food. Although these groups give greater prestige to the men hunters, the women gatherers contribute more food to the group, perhaps even four-fifths of their total food supply (Bernard 1992).

In addition to gender, the major unit of organization is the family. Most group members are related by ancestry or marriage. Because the family is the only distinct social institution in these societies, it fulfills functions that are divided among modern society's many specialized institutions. The family distributes food to its members, educates its children (especially in survival skills), nurses its sick, and provides for virtually all other needs.

Because an area cannot support a large number of people who hunt animals and gather plants (they do not plant—they only gather what is already there), hunting and gathering societies are small. They usually consist of only twenty-five to forty people. These groups are nomadic, moving from one place to another as the food supply of an area gives out. They place high value on sharing food, which is essential to their survival. Because of disease, drought, and pestilence, children have only about a fifty-fifty chance of surviving childhood (Lenski and Lenski 1987).

Of all societies, hunters and gatherers are the most egalitarian. Because what they hunt and gather is perishable and they have no money, the people accumulate few personal possessions. Consequently, no one becomes wealthier than anyone else. There are no rulers, and most decisions are arrived at through discussion. Because their needs are basic and they do

group people who have something in common and who believe that what they have in common is significant; also called a social group

society people who share a culture and a territory

hunting and gathering society a human group dependent on hunting and gathering for its survival

shaman the healing specialist of tribal groups who attempts to control the spirits thought to cause a disease or injury; commonly called a witch doctor

The simplest forms of societies are called hunting and gathering societies. *Members of these societies face severe hardships but have adapted well to their environments. They have the most leisure of any type of society. The man shown here is a member of a hunting and gathering society in the Brazilian Amazon.*

not work to store up material possessions, hunters and gatherers have the most leisure of all human groups (Sahlins 1972; Lorber 1994; Volti 1995).

All human groups were once hunters and gatherers, and until several hundred years ago such societies were common. Their demise came when other groups took over the areas on which they depended for their food. Today, only a few remain, such as the pygmies of central Africa, the aborigines of Australia, and groups in South America represented by the photo on this page. These groups seem doomed to a similar fate, and it is likely that their way of life will soon disappear from the human scene (Lenski and Lenski 1987).

Pastoral and Horticultural Societies

About ten thousand years ago, some groups found that they could tame and breed some of the animals they hunted—primarily goats, sheep, cattle, and camels. Others discovered that they could cultivate plants. As a result, hunting and gathering societies branched into two directions.

The key to understanding the first branching is the word *pasture;* **pastoral** (or herding) **societies** are based on the *pasturing of animals.* Pastoral societies developed in arid regions, where low rainfall made it impractical to build life around growing crops. Groups that took this turn remained nomadic, for they followed their animals to fresh pasture. The key to understanding the second branching is the word *horticulture,* or plant cultivation. **Horticultural** (or gardening) **societies** are based on the *cultivation of plants by the use of hand tools.* Because they no longer had to abandon an area as the food supply gave out, these groups developed permanent settlements.

We can call the domestication of animals and plants the *first social revolution.* As shown in Figure 6.1, it transformed human society. Although the **domestication revolution** was gradual, occurring over thousands of years, it represented a fundamental break with the past and changed human history. The more dependable food supply ushered in changes that touched almost every aspect of human life. Groups became larger because the more dependable food supply supported more people. With more food than was essential for survival, no longer was it necessary for everyone to produce food. This allowed groups to develop a division of labor, and some people began to specialize in making jewelry, tools, weapons, and so on. This led to a surplus of objects, which, in turn, stimulated trade. With trading, groups began to accumulate objects they prized, such as gold, jewelry, and utensils.

As Figure 6.2 illustrates, these changes set the stage for *social inequality.* Some families (or clans) acquired more goods than others. This led to feuds and war, for groups now possessed animals, pastures, croplands, jewelry, and other material goods to fight about. War, in turn, opened the door to slavery, for people found it convenient to let their captives do their drudge work. Social inequality remained limited, however, for the surplus itself was limited. As individuals passed on their possessions to their descendants, wealth grew more concentrated. So did power. At some point during this period, some individuals became chiefs, leaders of groups.

Note the primary pattern that runs through this transformation of group life: the change *from fewer to more possessions and from greater to lesser equality.* Where people were located *within* a society became vital for determining what happened to them in life. Again, Figure 6.2 summarizes how these changes led to social inequality.

pastoral society a society based on the pasturing of animals

horticultural society a society based on cultivating plants by the use of hand tools

domestication revolution the first social revolution, based on the domestication of plants and animals, which led to pastoral and horticultural societies

agricultural revolution the second social revolution, based on the invention of the plow, which led to agricultural society

agricultural society a society based on large-scale agriculture, dependent on plows drawn by animals

Industrial Revolution the third social revolution, occurring when machines powered by fuels replaced most animal and human power

industrial society a society based on the harnessing of machines powered by fuels

Agricultural Societies

When the plow was invented about five or six thousand years ago, social life was once again changed forever. Compared with hoes and digging sticks, the use of animals to pull plows was immensely efficient. As the earth was plowed, more nutrients were returned to the soil, making the land more productive. The food surplus of the **agricultural revolution** was unlike anything ever seen in human history. It allowed even more people to engage in activities other than farming. In this new **agricultural society**, people developed cities and what is popularly known as "culture," such as philosophy, art, literature, and architecture. Accompanied by the inventions of the wheel, writing, and numbers, the changes were so profound that this period is sometimes referred to as "the dawn of civilization."

The tendency toward social inequality of previous societies was only a forerunner of what was to come. *Inequality became a fundamental feature of life in society.* Some people managed to gain control of the growing surplus resources. To protect their expanding privileges and power, this elite surrounded itself with armed men. They even levied taxes on others, who now had become their "subjects." As conflict theorists point out, this concentration of resources and power—along with the oppression of people not in power—was the forerunner of the state.

No one knows exactly how it happened, but during this period females also became subject to males. Sociologist Elise Boulding (1976) theorizes that this change occurred because men were in charge of plowing and the cows. She suggests that when metals were developed, men took on the new job of attaching the metal as tips to the wooden plows and doing the plowing. As a result,

> the shift of the status of the woman farmer may have happened quite rapidly, once there were two male specializations relating to agriculture: plowing and the care of cattle. This situation left women with all the subsidiary tasks, including weeding and carrying water to the fields. The new fields were larger, so women had to work just as many hours as they did before, but now they worked at more secondary tasks. . . . This would contribute further to the erosion of the status of women.

This explanation, however, creates more questions than it answers. Why, for example, did men take over metal work and plowing? Why didn't women? It also does not account for why men control societies in which women are in charge of the cattle. In short, we are left in the dark as to why and how men became dominant, a reason likely to remain lost in human history.

Industrial Societies

In the 1700s, another invention turned society upside down. The **Industrial Revolution** began in 1765 when the steam engine was first used to run machinery in Great Britain. Before this, people used a few machines (such as wind and water mills) to harness nature, but most machines depended on human and animal power. The resulting **industrial society** is defined by sociologist Herbert Blumer (1990) as a society in which goods are produced by machines powered by fuels, instead of by the brute force of humans or animals.

With the steam engine, social inequality took another leap. This new technology was far more efficient than anything before it. Just as its surplus was greater, so were its effects on social life. Those who first used the steam engine accumulated such wealth that in many instances their riches outran the imagination of royalty. Gaining an early position in the markets, they were able not only to control the means of production (factories, machinery, tools), but also to dictate people's working conditions. The breakdown of feudal society helped them to control the workers. Masses of people were thrown off the lands that they and their ancestors had farmed as tenants for centuries. Having become homeless, these landless peasants moved to the cities. There they faced the choice of stealing, starving, or working for starvation wages (Chambliss 1964; Michalowski 1985).

Workers had no legal right to safe working conditions, nor the right to unionize. Employment was a private contract between the employer and the individual worker. If workers banded together to protest or to ask for higher wages, they were fired. If they returned to the factory, they were arrested for trespassing on

Figure 6.2 Fundamental Consequences of Animal Husbandry and Plant Cultivation

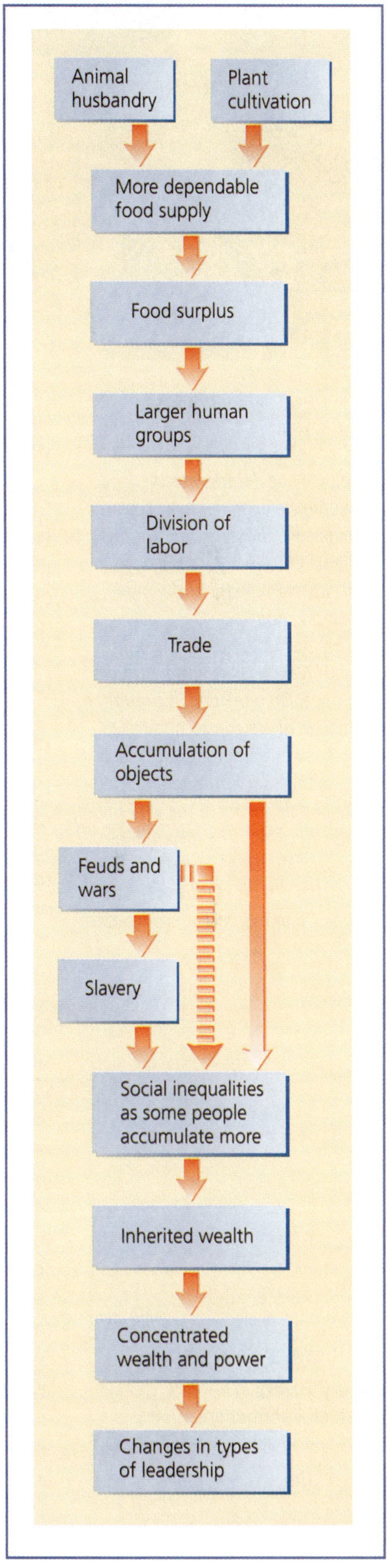

The sociological significance of the social revolutions discussed in the text is that the type of society in which we live determines the kind of people we become. It is obvious, for example, that the orientations to life of this worker would differ markedly from those of the man shown on page 150.

The machinery that ushered in industrial society was met with ambivalence. On one hand, it brought a multitude of welcomed goods. On the other hand, factory time clocks and the incessant production line made people slaves to the very machines they built. The idea of machines dominating workers is illustrated by this classic scene of Charlie Chaplin's in Modern Times.

private property. Strikes were illegal, and strikers were savagely beaten by the employer's private security force. On some occasions during the early 1900s, U.S. strikers were shot by private police, and even by the National Guard.

Against these odds, workers gradually won their fight for better working conditions. Wealth then spread to larger segments of society. Eventually, home ownership became common, as did the ownership of automobiles and an incredible variety of consumer goods. Today's typical worker in advanced industrial societies enjoys a high standard of living in terms of material conditions, health care, longevity, and access to libraries and education. Such gains go far beyond what early social reformers could have imagined.

As industrialization progressed, it reversed the pattern set earlier, and equality increased. Indicators of greater equality include better housing and a vast increase in consumer goods, the abolition of slavery, the shift from monarchies to more representative political systems, the right to be tried by a jury of one's peers and to cross-examine witnesses, the right to vote, the right to travel, and greater rights for women and minorities.

It is difficult to overstate the sociological principle that the type of society we live in is the fundamental reason for why we become who we are. To see how industrial society affects your life, note that you would not be taking this course if it were not for industrialization. Clearly you would not have a computer, car, telephone, DVD player, television, or your type of clothing or home. You wouldn't even have electric lights. And on a much deeper level, you would not feel the same about life, or have your particular aspirations for the future. Actually, no aspect of your life would be the same; you would be locked into the attitudes and views that come with an agricultural or horticultural way of life.

Postindustrial (Information) Societies

If you were to choose one word that characterizes our society, what would it be? Of the many candidates, the word *change* would have to rank high among them. The primary source of the sweeping changes that are transforming our lives is the new technology centering around the microchip. The change is so vast that sociologists say that a new type of society has emerged. They call it the **postindustrial** (or **information**) **society.**

What are the main characteristics of this new society? Unlike the industrial society, its hallmark is not raw materials and manufacturing. Rather, its basic component is *information.* Teachers pass on knowledge to students, while lawyers, physicians, bankers, pilots, and interior decorators sell their specialized knowledge of law, the body, money, aerodynamics, and color schemes to clients. Unlike the factory workers of an industrial society, these individuals don't *produce* anything. Rather, they transmit or use information to provide services that others are willing to pay for.

The United States was the first country to have more than 50 percent of its work force in service industries such as education, health, research, the government, counseling, banking, investments, insurance, sales, law, and the mass media. Australia, New Zealand, western Europe, and Japan soon followed. This basic trend away from manufacturing to selling information and services shows no sign of letting up.

The changes have been so profound that they have led to a *fourth social revolution.* The microchip is transforming established ways of life, uprooting old perspectives and replacing them with new ones. This new technology allows us to work at home, and while we ride in cars, trucks, and airplanes, to talk to others in distant cities and even to people on the other side of the globe. This tiny device lets us peer farther into the remote recesses of space than ever before. It is changing our shopping patterns as we spend billions of dollars on Internet purchases. And because of it, millions of children spend countless hours struggling against video enemies, at home and in the arcades. For a review of other changes, see the section on the computer in Chapter 22 (pages 652–657).

postindustrial (information) society a society based on information, services, and high technology, rather than on raw materials and manufacturing

Bioeconomic Societies: Is a New Type of Society Emerging?

The coming products are incredible (Elias 2001). Tobacco that fights cancer. ("Yes, smoke your way to health!") Corn that fights herpes and is a contraceptive. (You can make up your own jingle for that one.) Already we have goats whose milk contains spider silk (to make fishing lines and body armor), and animals that are part human (human genes have been inserted into their genes) so they produce medicines—and creamier mozzarella cheese (Kristoff 2002; Osborne 2002).

The changes are so revolutionary that a new type of society may be emerging already (Davis and Meyer 2000; Holloway 2002). If so, the chief distinguishing characteristic of the **bioeconomic society** will be an economy that centers around the application of genetic structures—both plant and animal—for the production of food and medicine. The natural sciences will be reconstituted. Already we see biotechnology replacing botany, and biochemistry replacing chemistry (Manavalan 2001). No longer will the transmission of information be limited to numbers, words, sounds, and images, but it will also include smell, taste, and touch (Davis 2001).

If we are witnessing the birth of a new type of society, just when did it begin? There are no firm edges on such momentous changes, and each type of new society overlaps the one it is replacing. We could trace the starting point of the bioeconomic society to 1953, however, when Francis Crick and James Watson identified the double-helix structure of DNA. Certainly the decoding of the human genome in 2001 also was a significant moment in the emergence of this new society—and perhaps may even mark its beginning.

Projecting a new type of society so soon after the arrival of the postindustrial or information society is risky and abounds in controversy. The wedding of genetics and economics may turn out to be simply another part of our information society. But we may be witnessing the birth of a new type of society, one destined to replace the information society. In either case, we can anticipate revolutionary changes in health care (prevention, instead of treating disease), and, with cloning and bioengineering, perhaps even changes in the human species. The Sociology and the New Technology box on the next page examines implications of cloning.

Although the full implications of the changes swirling around us are unknown—and whether they are part of a new type of society is not the main point. *The sociological significance of these changes is that just as the larger group called society always profoundly affects people's thinking and behavior, so, too, these recent developments will do the same for us.* As society is transformed, we will be swept along with it. The changes will be so extensive that they will transform even the ways we think about the self and life.

IN SUM

Our society sets boundaries around our lives. It establishes the values and beliefs that prevail and also determines the type and extent of social inequality. These factors, in turn, set the stage for relationships between men and women, the young and the elderly, racial and ethnic groups, the rich and the poor, and so on.

It is difficult to overstate the sociological principle that the type of society in which we live is the fundamental reason why we become who we are—why we feel about things the way we do, and even why we think our particular thoughts. On the obvious level, if you lived in a hunting and gathering society you would not be listening to your favorite music, watching your favorite TV programs, or playing your favorite video games. On a deeper level, you would not feel the same about life or hold your particular aspirations for the future.

Finally, we should note that not all the world's societies will go through the transformations shown in Figure 6.1 (page 149). Whether any hunting and gathering societies survive, however, remains to be seen. Perhaps a few will be allowed to survive, kept on "small reserves" that will be off limits to developers—but open to guided ecotours at a hefty fee.

bioeconomic society an economy that centers around the application of genetics—human genetics for medicine, and plant and animal genetics for the production of food.

sociology and the NEW technology

"So, You Want to Be Yourself?" Cloning in the Coming Bioeconomy

No type of society ends abruptly. Instead, one always overlaps the other. As the information society matures in the years ahead, it may gradually be overtaken by a bioeconomy. Let's try to peer over the edge of our current society to glimpse the one that may be coming. What would life be like? There are too many issues to deal with in this limited space, so let's consider just one: cloning.

Consider this scenario:

> Your four-year-old daughter has drowned, and you can't get over your sorrow. You go to Cleta's Cloning Clinic, where you have stored DNA for all members of your family. You pay the fee, and the technicians use a salaried surrogate mother to bring your daughter back as a newborn.

Will cloning humans become a reality? It seems inevitable, and it already is being attempted in clandestine labs ("Couple Plan . . . " 2002). Currently, scientists are plagued by the problem that clones are often deformed. Let's suppose that this problem has been solved, and the cloning of humans becomes routine. Consider these scenarios:

> Suppose that a couple can't have children. Testing shows that the husband is sterile. The couple talk about their dilemma, and the wife agrees to have her husband's genetic material implanted. Would this woman, in effect, be rearing her husband as a little boy?
>
> Or suppose that you love your mother dearly, and she is dying. With her permission, you decide to clone her. Who is the clone? Would you be rearing your own mother?
>
> What if a woman gave birth to her own clone? Would the clone be her daughter or her sister?

When genetic duplicates appear, the questions of what humans are, what their relationship is to their "parents," and indeed what parents and children are, will be brought up at every kitchen table.

For Your CONSIDERATION

As these scenarios show, cloning leads to profound issues, perhaps the most weighty being the future of society itself. Let's suppose that mass cloning becomes possible.

Many object that cloning is immoral, but some will argue the opposite. They will ask why we should leave human reproduction to people who have inferior traits—genetic diseases, low IQs, perhaps even the propensity for crime and violence. They will suggest that we select people with the finer characteristics—high creative ability, high intelligence, compassion, and a propensity for peace.

Let's assume that scientists have traced these characteristics—as well as the ability and appreciation for poetry, music, mathematics, architecture, and love—to genetics. Do you think that it should be our moral obligation to populate society with people like this? To try to build a society that is better for all—one without terrorism, war, violence, and greed? Could this perhaps even be our evolutionary destiny?

Source: Based on Davis and Meyer 2000; Kaebnick 2000; McGee 2000; Bjerklie et al. 2001; Davis 2001.

Now that we have reviewed the major historical shifts in societies, let's turn to groups within society. Just how do they affect our lives?

Groups Within Society

Sociologist Emile Durkheim (1933) wondered what could be done to prevent *anomie* (AN-uh-mee), that bewildering sense of not belonging. Durkheim found the answer in small groups. He said that small groups stand as a buffer between the individual and the larger society. If it weren't for these groups, we would feel oppressed by that huge, amorphous entity known as society. By providing intimate relationships, small groups give us a sense of meaning and purpose, helping to prevent anomie.

Before we examine groups in more detail, we should distinguish some terms. Two terms sometimes confused with "group" are *aggregate* and *category.* An **aggregate** consists of individuals who temporarily share the same physical space but who do not see themselves as belonging together. People waiting in a checkout line or drivers parked at a red light are an aggregate. A **category** is a statistic. It consists of people who share similar characteristics, such as all college women who wear glasses or all men over 6 feet tall. Unlike groups, the individuals who make up a category neither interact with one another nor take one another into account. The members of a *group,* in contrast, think of themselves as belonging together, and they interact with one another.

Groups affect your life so extensively that they determine just who you are. If you think this an exaggeration, read on. Let's begin by looking at the types of groups that make up our society.

aggregate individuals who temporarily share the same physical space but who do not see themselves as belonging together

category people who have similar characteristics

primary group a group characterized by intimate, long-term, face-to-face association and cooperation

Primary Groups

Our first group, the family, gives us our basic orientation to life. Later, among friends, we find more intimacy and an additional sense of belonging. These groups are what sociologist Charles Cooley called **primary groups.** By providing intimate, face-to-face interaction, they give us an identity, a feeling of who we are. As Cooley (1909) put it,

> By primary groups I mean those characterized by intimate face-to-face association and cooperation. They are primary in several senses, but chiefly in that they are fundamental in forming the social nature and ideals of the individual.

Producing a Mirror Within

It is significant that Cooley calls primary groups the "springs of life." By this, he means that primary groups are essential to our emotional well-being. You can see this in your own life with your family and friends. As humans, we have an intense need for face-to-face interaction that generates feelings of self-esteem. By offering a sense of belonging and a feeling of being appreciated—and sometimes even loved—primary groups are uniquely equipped to meet this basic human need. From our opening vignette, you can see that gangs are also primary groups.

Primary groups are also "springs of life" because their values and attitudes become fused into our identity. We internalize their views, which become the lenses through

Primary groups *such as the family play a key role in the development of the self. As a small group, the family also serves as a buffer from the often-threatening larger group known as society. The family has been of primary significance in forming the basic orientations of this Latino couple, as it will be for their children.*

secondary group compared with a primary group, a larger, relatively temporary, more anonymous, formal, and impersonal group based on some interest or activity, whose members are likely to interact on the basis of specific roles

in-groups groups toward which one feels loyalty

out-groups groups toward which one feels antagonism

which we view life. Even as adults—no matter how far we may have come from our childhood roots—early primary groups remain "inside" us, where they continue to form part of the perspective from which we look out onto the world. Ultimately, then, it is difficult, if not impossible, for us to separate the self from our primary groups, for the self and our groups merge into a "we."

Secondary Groups

Compared with primary groups, **secondary groups** are larger, more anonymous, formal, and impersonal. Secondary groups are based on some interest or activity, and their members are likely to interact on the basis of specific roles, such as president, manager, worker, or student. Examples are a college class, the American Sociological Association, and the Democratic Party.

In hunting and gathering and horticultural societies, the entire society forms a primary group. In industrial and postindustrial societies, secondary groups have become essential to our welfare. They are part of the way we get our education, make our living, and spend our money and leisure time.

As necessary as secondary groups are for contemporary life, they often fail to satisfy our deep needs for intimate association. Consequently, *secondary groups tend to break down into primary groups.* At school and work, we form friendship cliques. Our interaction with them is so important that we sometimes feel that if it weren't for our friends, school or work "would drive us crazy." The primary groups we form within secondary groups, then, serve as a buffer between us and the demands that secondary groups place on us.

In-Groups and Out-Groups

Groups toward which we feel loyalty are called **in-groups;** those toward which we feel antagonism, **out-groups.** For Monster Cody in our opening vignette, the gang was an in-group, while the Bloods and all other "enemies" were out-groups. That they—and we—make such a fundamental division of the world has far-reaching consequences for our lives.

How our participation in social groups shapes our self-concept is a focus of symbolic interactionists. In this process, knowing who we are not is as significant as knowing who we are.

Producing Loyalty, a Sense of Superiority, and Rivalries

Identification with a group can generate not only a sense of belonging, but also loyalty and feelings of superiority. These, in turn, often produce rivalries. Usually the rivalries are mild, such as sports rivalries between neighboring towns, where the most extreme act is likely to be the furtive invasion of the out-group's territory in order to steal a mascot, paint a rock, or uproot a goal post. The consequences of in-group membership can also be discrimination, hatred, and, as we saw in our opening vignette, even participation in murder.

"So long, Bill. This is my club. You can't come in."

Implications for a Socially Diverse Society

It is not surprising that in-group membership leads to discrimination, for, with our strong identifications and loyalties, we all favor members of our in-groups. This aspect of in- and out-groups is, of course, the basis of many problems in society. It underlies many gender and racial-ethnic divisions. As sociologist Robert Merton (1968) observed, this leads to a fascinating double standard. We view the traits of our in-group as virtues, while we see those *same* traits in out-groups as vices. Men may perceive an aggressive man as assertive, but an aggressive woman as pushy. They may think of a male employee who doesn't speak up as "knowing when to keep his mouth shut," but perceive a quiet woman as too timid to make it in the business world.

To divide the world into "we" and "them" poses a danger for a pluralistic society. As the Jews did for the Nazis, an out-group can come to symbolize evil, arousing fear, contempt, and hatred. After the terrorist bombings of New York and Washington, for some,

Arabs became this type of out-group. They saw Arabs as a sinister "them," as untrustworthy, bloodthirsty villains—certainly the opposite of how we evaluate "our" group (no matter what group that may be). Such extreme views often seem to justify attacking the out-group. Many Germans defended the Holocaust as necessary "dirty work." Following the terrorist attacks of 9/11, some Americans defended the sporadic attacks on Arab Americans—and even people who looked like them. The refusal of some airline pilots to leave the ground until "Arab looking" passengers had been forced to get off the plane also fits this pattern. Economic downturns also help to produce out-groups. Immigrants, for example, may be seen as people who "steal" jobs from friends and family. There may be attacks on immigrants, a national anti-immigration policy, or a resurgence of neo-Nazi groups or the Ku Klux Klan.

In short, to divide the world into in-groups and out-groups is a natural part of social life. But in addition to bringing functional consequences, it can also bring dysfunctional ones.

All of us have reference groups*—the groups we use as standards to evaluate ourselves. How do you think the reference groups of these members of the KKK who are demonstrating in Jaspar, Texas, differ from those of the police officer who is protecting their right of free speech? Although the KKK and this police officer use different groups to evaluate their attitudes and behaviors, the process is the same.*

Reference Groups

Suppose you have just been offered a good job. It pays double what you hope to make even after you graduate from college. You have just two days to make up your mind. If you accept it, you will have to drop out of college. As you consider the matter, thoughts like this may go through your mind: "My friends will say I'm a fool if I don't take the job . . . but Dad and Mom will practically go crazy. They've made sacrifices for me, and they'll be crushed if I don't finish college. They've always said I've got to get my education first, that good jobs will always be there. . . . But, then, I'd like to see the look on the faces of those neighbors who said I'd never amount to much!"

This is an example of how people use **reference groups,** the groups we use as standards to evaluate ourselves. Your reference groups may include your family, neighbors, teachers, classmates, co-workers, and the Scouts or the members of a church, synagogue, or mosque. If you were like Monster Cody in our opening vignette, the "set" would be your main reference group. Even a group you don't belong to can be a reference group. For example, if you are thinking about going to graduate school, graduate students or members of the profession you want to join may form a reference group. You would consider their standards as you evaluate your grades or writing skills.

Providing a Yardstick Reference groups exert tremendous influence over our lives. For example, if you want to become a corporate executive, you might start to dress more formally, try to improve your vocabulary, read the *Wall Street Journal,* and change your major to business or law. In contrast, if you want to become a rock musician, you might wear jewelry in several places where you have pierced your body, including your tongue, have many tattoos, dress in ways your parents and many of your peers consider extreme, read *Rolling Stone,* drop out of college, and hang around clubs and rock groups.

Exposure to Contradictory Standards in a Socially Diverse Society From these examples, you can see that the yardsticks provided by reference groups operate as a form of social control. When we see ourselves as measuring up to the yardstick, we feel no conflict. If our behavior, or even aspirations, do not match the standards held by a reference group, however, the mismatch can lead to inner turmoil. For example, to want to become a corporate executive would create no inner turmoil for most

reference group Herbert Hyman's term for the groups we use as standards to evaluate ourselves

We all use reference groups *to evaluate our accomplishments, failures, values, and attitudes. We compare what we see in ourselves with what we perceive as normative in our reference groups. As is evident in these two photos, the reference groups these youths are using are not likely to lead them to the same social destination.*

of us, but it would if we had grown up in an Amish home, for the Amish strongly disapprove of such aspirations for their children. They ban high school and college education, three-piece suits, and corporate employment. Similarly, if you wanted to become a soldier and your parents were dedicated pacifists, you likely would feel deep conflict, as your parents would hold quite different aspirations for you.

Given the social diversity of our society as well as our social mobility, many of us are exposed to contradictory ideas and standards from the many groups that become significant to us. The "internal recordings" that play contradictory messages from these reference groups, then, are one cost of social mobility.

Social Networks

If you are a member of a large group, you probably regularly associate with a few people within that group. In a sociology class I was teaching at a commuter campus, six women who didn't know one another chose to work together on a project. They got along well, and they began to sit together. Eventually they planned a Christmas party at one of their homes. These clusters, or internal factions, are called **cliques.** The links between people—their cliques, as well as their family, friends, acquaintances, and even "friends of friends"—are called **social networks.** Think of a social network as lines that extend outward from yourself, gradually encompassing more and more people.

The Small World Phenomenon Although we live in a huge society, we don't experience social life as a sea of nameless, strange faces. Instead, we interact within social networks that connect us to the larger society. Social scientists have wondered just how extensive the connections are between social networks (Watts 2003). If you list everyone you know, and each of those individuals lists everyone he or she knows, and you keep doing this, would almost everyone in the United States eventually be included on those lists?

It would be too cumbersome to test this hypothesis by drawing up such lists, but psychologist Stanley Milgram (1933–1984) came up with an interesting idea. In a classic study known as "the small world phenomenon," Milgram (1967) addressed a letter to "targets," the wife of a divinity student in Cambridge and a stockbroker in Boston. He sent the letter to "starters," who did not know these people. He asked them to send the letter to someone they knew on a first-name basis, someone they thought might know the "target." They, in turn, were asked to mail the letter to someone they knew who might

clique a cluster of people within a larger group who choose to interact with one another; an internal faction

social network the social ties radiating outward from the self that link people together

Why do people get ahead in life? Is it because of their abilities? Although personal abilities and efforts are important for success, so are social networks, *which open and close doors of opportunity. Despite the official program of sociology conventions, for example, much of the "real" business centers around renewing and extending social networks.*

know the "target," and so on. The question was, Would the letters ever reach the "target"? If so, how long would the chain be?

Think of yourself as part of this study. What would you do if you were a "starter," but the "target" lived in a state in which you know no one? You would send the letter to someone you knew who you think might know someone in that state. And this, Milgram reported, is just what happened. None of the senders knew the receivers, and the letters reached the designated individual in an average of just six jumps.

Milgam's study caught the public's fancy, leading to the phrase, "six degrees of separation." This means that, on average, everyone in the United States is separated by just six individuals. Milgram's conclusions have become so popular that even an Internet game, "Six Degrees of Kevin Bacon," is built around it.

Is the Small World Phenomenon an Academic Myth? But things are not this simple. There is a problem with Milgram's research, as psychologist Judith Kleinfeld (2002a, b) discovered when she decided to replicate Milgram's study. When she went to the archives at Yale University Library to get more details, she found that Milgram had stacked the deck in favor of finding a small world. He had used mailing lists to recruit the "starters," who in 1967 were likely to have higher incomes, and, therefore, were not representative of common people. In addition, he had made one of the "targets" a stockbroker and that person's "starters" investors in Blue Chip stocks. Kleinfeld also unearthed another huge discrepancy—on average, only 30 percent of the letters reached their "target." In one of Milgram's studies, it was just 5 percent.

Since most letters did *not* reach their targets, even with the deck stacked in favor of success, we can draw the *opposite* conclusion from the one that Milgram reported. People who don't know one another are dramatically separated by social barriers. From other studies, we know that besides geography, these barriers are primarily those of social class and race-ethnicity. As Kleinfeld says, "Rather than living in a small world, we may live in a world that looks a lot like a bowl of lumpy oatmeal, with many small worlds loosely connected and perhaps some small worlds not connected at all."

Implications for a Socially Diverse Society Unlike Milgram's conclusions, then, his study may actually be another indication of the barriers that separate us into distinct small worlds. One reason that overcoming the divisions that separate us is

electronic community individuals who regularly interact with one another on the Internet and who think of themselves as belonging together

networking using one's social networks for some gain

so difficult is that even our own social networks contribute to social inequality, a topic we explore in the Cultural Diversity box below.

Implications for Science Kleinfeld's revelations of Milgram's research reinforce the need of replication, a topic discussed in the previous chapter. For our knowledge of social life, we cannot depend on single studies, for there may be problems of generalizability on the one hand, or those of negligence or even fraud on the other. Replication by objective researchers is essential to build and advance solid social knowledge.

A New Group: Electronic Communities

In the 1990s, a new type of human group, the **electronic community**, made its appearance. On the Internet hundreds of thousands of people meet online in chat rooms and "news groups" to communicate about almost any conceivable topic, from donkey racing and bird-watching to sociology and quantum physics. Most news groups are simply an

CULTURAL DIVERSITY

in the UNITED STATES

How Our Own Social Networks Perpetuate Social Inequality

Consider some of the principles we have reviewed. People tend to form in-groups with which they identify; they use reference groups to evaluate their attitudes and behavior; and they interact in social networks. Our in-groups, reference groups, and social networks are likely to consist of people whose backgrounds are similar to our own. This means that, for most of us, just as social inequality is built into society, so it is built into our own relationships. One consequence is that we tend to perpetuate social inequality.

To see why, suppose that an outstanding job—great pay, interesting work, with opportunity for advancement—has just opened up where you work. Who are you going to tell? Most likely it will be someone you know, someone you like, or someone to whom you owe a favor. And most likely your social network is made up of people who look much like yourself—especially their race-ethnicity, age, social class, and probably also, gender. This tends to keep good jobs moving in the direction of people whose characteristics are similar to those of the people already in an organization. You can see how our social networks both reflect the inequality that characterizes our society and help to perpetuate it.

Consider a network of white men who are established in an organization. As they learn of opportunities (jobs, investments, real estate, and so on), they share this information with their networks. Opportunities and good jobs flow to people who have characteristics similar to their own. Those who benefit from this information, in turn, reciprocate with similar information when they learn of it. This bypasses people who have different characteristics, such as women and minorities, while it perpetuates the "good old boys'" network. No intentional discrimination need be involved.

To overcome this barrier, women and minorities do **networking.** They try to meet people who can help advance their careers. Like the "good old boys," they, too, go to parties, join clubs, churches, synagogues, mosques, and political parties. Women cultivate a network of women, and African American leaders cultivate a network of African American leaders. As a result, the network of African American leaders is so tight that one-fifth of the entire national African American leadership are personal acquaintances. Add some "friends of a friend," and *three-fourths* of the entire leadership belong to the same network (Taylor 1992). Women who reach top positions end up in a circle so tight that the term "new girl" network is being used, especially in the field of law. Remembering those who helped them and sympathetic to those who are trying to get ahead, these women tend to steer their business to other women. Like the "good old boys" who preceded them, the new insiders also justify their exclusionary practice (Jacobs 1997).

For Your CONSIDERATION

The perpetuation of social inequality does not require purposeful discrimination. Just as social inequality is built into society, so it is built into our personal relationships. How do you think your own social network helps to perpetuate social inequality? How do you think we can break this cycle? (The key must center on creating diversity in social networks.)

interesting way of communicating. Some, however, meet our definition of *group,* people who interact with one another and who think of themselves as belonging together.

Some of these groups pride themselves on the distinctive nature of their interest and knowledge—factors that give them a common identity and bind them together. This new form of group is explored in the Sociology and the New Technology box on the next page.

group dynamics the ways in which individuals affect groups and the ways in which groups influence individuals

small group a group small enough for everyone to interact directly with all the other members

dyad the smallest possible group, consisting of two persons

triad a group of three people

Group Dynamics

As you know from personal experience, the lively interaction *within* groups—who does what with whom—has profound consequences for how you adjust to life. Sociologists use the term **group dynamics** to refer to how groups influence us and how we affect groups. Let's consider how the size of a group makes a difference, and then examine leadership, conformity, and decision making.

Before doing this, we should see how sociologists define the term *small group.* In a **small group,** there are few enough members that each one can interact directly with all the other members. Small groups can be either primary or secondary. A wife, husband, and children, as well as workers who take their breaks together, are primary small groups, while bidders at an auction and guests at a cocktail party are secondary small groups.

Effects of Group Size on Stability and Intimacy

Writing in the early 1900s, sociologist Georg Simmel (1858–1918) noted the significance of group size. He used the term **dyad** for the smallest possible group, which consists of two people. Dyads, which include marriages, love affairs, and close friendships, show two distinct qualities. First, they are the most intense or intimate of human groups. Because only two people are involved, the interaction is focused on them. Second, because dyads require that both members participate and be committed, they are the most unstable of social groups. If one member loses interest, the dyad collapses. In larger groups, in contrast, even if one member withdraws, the group can continue, for its existence does not depend on any single member (Simmel 1950).

A **triad** is a group of three people. As Simmel noted, the addition of a third person fundamentally changes the group. With three people, interaction between the first two decreases. This can create strain. For example, with the birth of a child, hardly any aspect of a couple's relationship goes untouched. Attention focuses on the baby, and interaction

Japanese who work for the same firm think of themselves more as a group or team, Americans more as individuals. Japanese corporations use many techniques to encourage group identity, such as making group exercise a part of the work day. Similarity of appearance and activity helps to fuse group identity and company loyalty.

Electronic Communities and Online Posses

Jason Smith, a 21-year-old sophomore, had been supporting himself by selling computers on eBay. Jason made just enough to pay the rent and have a little left over. His online business went smoothly until he sold an Apple Powerbook to Steve Matthews of Chicago, who said he was buying the computer for his son in college.

Matthews sent a cashier's check for $3,052, and Jason shipped the computer. After paying his rent and buying a space heater, Jason went on Christmas break, where he spent more of the money. On his return to school, he got the bad news: a message from his bank that the cashier's check was a phony.

Jason was besides himself. He was out the computer, and his checking account was overdrawn. He called the Chicago police department, but they told him they were so busy they couldn't even talk to him about such a small matter for another week or so.

Jason turned to other Mac users. He posted his story at MacRumors, and people he didn't know began to help. They found Matthews' real address, took photos of his street, his

THE FAR SIDE® By GARY LARSON

© 1982 FarWorks, Inc. All Rights Reserved/Dist. by Creators Syndicate
Larson

In the days before television

between the husband and wife diminishes. Despite the difficulty that this presents—including in many instances the husband's jealousy that he is getting less attention from his wife—the marriage usually becomes stronger. Although the intensity of interaction is less in triads, they are inherently stronger and give greater stability to a relationship.

coalition the alignment of some members of a group against others

Yet, as Simmel noted, triads, too, are inherently unstable. For example, two members may feel stronger bonds with one another and form a **coalition.** A coalition occurs when some group members align themselves against others. In the case of the triad, two members act as a dyad, leaving the third member feeling hurt and excluded. Another characteristic of triads is that they often produce an arbitrator or mediator, someone who tries house, and even his car—with the license number visible.

Matthews actually lived in a town outside Chicago, and this police department turned out to be eager to solve the crime. Jason posted another ad on e-Bay, and Matthews took the bait. Jason shipped him a package, but this time the man in the FedEx uniform was a detective. He arrested Matthews when he signed for the package.

Jason was able to keep his apartment and stay in school—a bit wiser, and greatly encouraged by the help given by his online buddies (Hafner 2002).

In the past few years, a type of group unknown in human history has come into existence. *Electronic* (or *online*) *communities* consist of people who regularly "meet" on the Internet. They focus on some shared interest, whether it be antique cars, radical politics, or deviant sex. Some communities offer support. When people who suffer from cancer share their experiences with fear, pain, surgery, radiation, and chemotherapy, they break the depressing isolation that hems them in. Those who suffer from other debilitating diseases do the same. In Jason's case, the online posse came from Macintosh users, who already think of themselves as different, and as somehow belonging together because they share a passion for this particular kind of computer.

This form of communication has even led to the creation of *electronic* (or *online*) primary groups, people who regularly share and care although they have never met one another. As people communicate online, they come to identify with one another, develop a sense of intimacy, and share personal information. For some, online friends become so significant that they build their lives around each other. The first thing in the morning, they rush to their computer, where they eagerly read e-mail from their Net friends, and visit "chat rooms," where they discuss the latest development in their "real" (not online) relationships. Only then do they dress and go to work. After work, they rush back to their virtual world. For them, their Net friends are as real as their family—and sometimes have a greater impact on their lives.

With online social intimacy, people who never physically meet forge social bonds (Chayko 2002). They experience closeness without permanence, and depth without commitment (Cerulo et al. 1992). As this form of social intimacy becomes more common, it may affect not only our social interactions, but also our culture, and even our sense of self.

For Your CONSIDERATION

Social researchers first reported that the longer people were online, the more their relationships with family and friends declined. More recent studies indicate that gregarious people remain outgoing in both their virtual and real worlds. Eighty-five percent of Net users report no change in the time they spend with family and friends (Guernsey 2001). And it seems that teenagers are using the Net to explore their identities (Turkle 1995; Goldsborough 2001). Have you experienced Internet intimacy?

to settle disagreements between the other two. In one-child families, you can often observe both of these characteristics of triads—coalitions and arbitration.

The general principle is this: *As a small group grows larger, it becomes more stable, but its intensity, or intimacy, decreases.* To see why, look at Figure 6.3. As each new person comes into a group, the connections among people multiply. In a dyad, there is only 1 relationship; in a triad, 3; in a group of four, 6; in a group of five, 10. If we expand the group to six, we have 15 relationships, while a group of seven yields 21 relationships. If we continue adding members, we soon are unable to follow the connections: A group of eight has 28 possible relationships; a group of nine, 36 relationships; a group of ten, 45; and so on.

It is not only the number of relationships that makes larger groups more stable. As groups grow, they also tend to develop a more formal structure to accomplish their goals. For example, leaders emerge and more specialized roles come into play. This often results in such familiar offices as president, secretary, and treasurer. This structure provides a framework that helps the group survive over time.

Effects of Group Size on Attitudes and Behavior

> Imagine that your social psychology professors have asked you to join a few students to discuss your adjustment to college life. When you arrive, they tell you that to make the discussion anonymous they want you to sit unseen in a booth. You will participate in the discussion over an intercom, talking when your microphone comes on. The professors say they will not listen to the conversation, and they leave.
>
> You find the format somewhat strange, to say the least, but you go along with it. You have not seen the other students in their booths, but when they talk about their experiences, you find yourself becoming wrapped up in the problems they begin to share. One student even mentions how frightening he has found college because of his history of epileptic seizures. Later, you hear this individual breathe heavily into the microphone. Then he stammers and cries for help. A crashing noise follows, and you imagine him lying helpless on the floor.
>
> Nothing but an eerie silence follows. What do you do?

Your professors, John Darley and Bibb Latané (1968), staged the whole thing, but you don't know this. No one had a seizure. In fact, no one was even in the other booths. Everything, except your comments, was on tape.

Some participants were told they would be discussing the topic with just one other student, others with two, others with three, and so on. Darley and Latané found that all students who thought they were part of a dyad rushed out to help. If they thought they were part of a triad, only 80 percent went to help—and they were slower in leaving the booth. In six-person groups, only 60 percent went to see what was wrong—and they were even slower.

Figure 6.3 **The Effects of Group Size on Relationships**

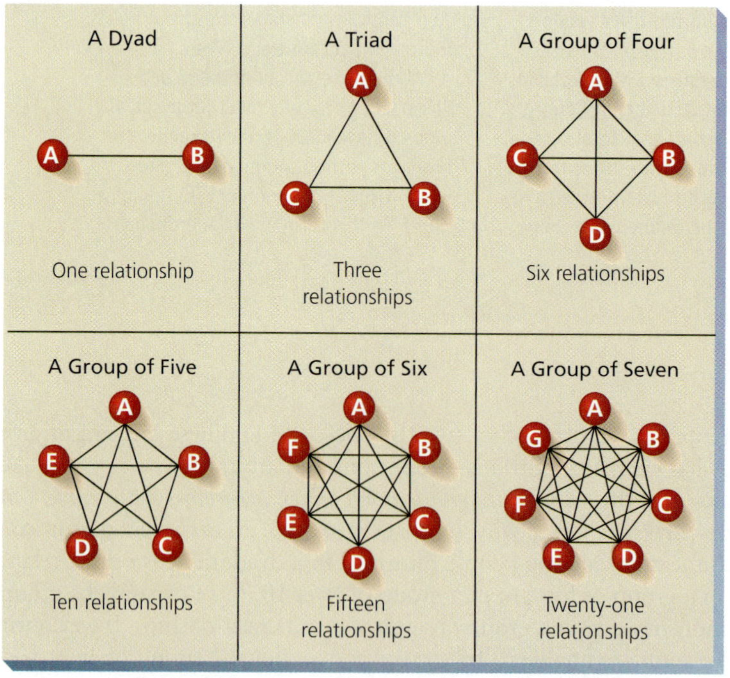

Group size has a significant influence on how people interact. When a group changes from a dyad *(two people) to a* triad *(three people), the relationships among the participants undergo a shift. How do you think the birth of this girl affected the relationship between her mother and father?*

Groups also mold our orientation to life. What assumptions of the world do you think this girl is growing up with?

This experiment demonstrates how deeply group size influences our attitudes and behavior—it even affects our willingness to help one another. Students in the dyad knew it was up to them to help the other student. The professor was gone, and if they didn't help there was no one else. In the larger groups, including the triad, students felt *a diffusion of responsibility:* Giving help was no more their responsibility than anyone else's.

You probably have observed the second consequence of group size firsthand. When a group is small, its members are informal, but as the group grows, they lose their sense of intimacy and become more formal. No longer can the members assume that the others are "insiders" in sympathy with what they say. Now they must take a "larger audience" into consideration, and instead of merely "talking," they begin to "address" the group. Their speech becomes more formal, and their body language stiffens.

You probably have observed a third aspect of group dynamics, too. In the early stages of a party, when only a few people are present, almost everyone talks with everyone else. But as others arrive, the guests break into several smaller groups. Some hosts, who want their guests to mix together, make a nuisance of themselves trying to achieve *their* idea of what a group should be like. The division into small groups is inevitable, however, for it follows the basic sociological principles we have just reviewed. Because the addition of each person rapidly increases connections (in this case, "talk lines"), conversation becomes more difficult. The guests break into smaller groups where they can see each other and comfortably interact directly with one another.

Leadership

All of us are influenced by leaders, so it is important to understand leadership. Let's look at how people become leaders, the types of leaders there are, and their different styles of leadership. Before we do this, though, we need to understand that leaders don't necessarily hold formal positions in a group. **Leaders** are simply people who influence the behaviors, opinions, or attitudes of others. Even a group of friends has leaders.

Who Becomes a Leader? Are leaders born with characteristics that propel them to the forefront of a group? No sociologist would agree with such an idea. In general, people who become leaders are perceived by group members as strongly representing their values, or as able to lead a group out of a crisis (Trice and Beyer 1991). Leaders also tend to be more talkative and to express determination and self-confidence.

leader someone who influences other people

Adolf Hitler was voted the most influential person of the twentieth century. He also was among the most evil. Why did so many people follow Hitler? That question stimulated the research by Stanley Milgram. Shown here is Hitler in Nuremberg, Germany; 1934. (Because this city was so closely connected with Nazism, to symbolize the defeat of the Nazis and to publicize the evil of their tyranny, the Allies chose it as the site of their war trials.)

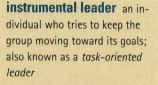

These findings may not be surprising, as such traits appear related to leadership. Researchers, however, have also discovered traits that seem to have no bearing on the ability to lead. For example, taller people and those judged better looking are more likely to become leaders (Stodgill 1974; Crosbie 1975). The taller and more attractive are also likely to earn more, but that is another story (Deck 1968; Feldman 1972; Katz 2003).

Many other factors underlie people's choice of leaders, most of which are quite subtle. A simple experiment performed by social psychologists Lloyd Howells and Selwyn Becker (1962) uncovered one of these factors. They formed groups of five people who did not know one another, seating them at a rectangular table, three on one side and two on the other. Each group discussed a topic for a set period of time, and then chose a leader. The findings are startling: Although only 40 percent of the people sat on the two-person side, 70 percent of the leaders emerged from that side. The explanation is that we tend to direct more interactions to people facing us than to people to the side of us.

instrumental leader an individual who tries to keep the group moving toward its goals; also known as a *task-oriented leader*

expressive leader an individual who increases harmony and minimizes conflict in a group; also known as a socioemotional leader

leadership styles ways in which people express their leadership

authoritarian leader a leader who leads by giving orders

democratic leader a leader who leads by trying to reach a consensus

laissez-faire leaders an individual who leads by being highly permissive

Types of Leaders Groups have two types of leaders (Bales 1950, 1953; Cartwright and Zander 1968). The first is easy to recognize. This person, called an **instrumental leader** (or *task-oriented leader*), tries to keep the group moving toward its goals. These leaders try to keep group members from getting sidetracked, reminding them of what they are trying to accomplish. The **expressive leader** (or *socioemotional leader*), in contrast, usually is not recognized as a leader, but he or she certainly is. This person is likely to crack jokes, to offer sympathy, or to do other things that help lift the group's morale. Both types of leadership are essential: the one to keep the group on track, the other to increase harmony and minimize conflicts.

It is difficult for the same person to be both an instrumental and an expressive leader, for these roles contradict one another. Because instrumental leaders are task oriented, they sometimes create friction as they prod the group to get on with the job. Their actions often cost them popularity. Expressive leaders, in contrast, who stimulate personal bonds and reduce friction, are usually more popular (Olmsted and Hare 1978).

Leadership Styles Let's suppose that the president of your college has asked you to head a task force to determine how the college can improve race relations on campus. Although this position requires you to be an instrumental leader, you can adopt a number of **leadership styles,** or ways of expressing yourself as a leader. The three basic styles are those of **authoritarian leader,** one who gives orders; **democratic leader,** one who tries to gain a consensus; and **laissez-faire leader,** one who is highly permissive. Which should you choose?

Social psychologists Ronald Lippitt and Ralph White (1958) carried out a classic study of these leadership styles. Boys matched for IQ, popularity, physical energy, and leadership were assigned to "craft clubs" made up of five boys each. The experimenters trained adult men in the three leadership styles. As the researchers peered through peepholes, taking notes and making movies, each adult rotated among the clubs, playing all three styles to control possible effects of their individual personalities.

The *authoritarian* leaders assigned tasks to the boys and told them exactly what to do. They also praised or condemned their work arbitrarily, giving no explanation for why it was good or bad. The *democratic* leaders held discussions with the boys, outlining the steps that would help them reach their goals. They also suggested alternative approaches and let the boys work at their own pace. When they evaluated the projects, they gave "facts" as the bases for their decisions. The *laissez-faire* leaders were passive. They gave the boys almost total freedom to do as they wished. They offered help when asked, but made few suggestions. They did not evaluate the boys' projects, either positively or negatively.

The results? The boys who had authoritarian leaders grew dependent on their leader and showed a high degree of internal solidarity. They also became either aggressive or apathetic, with the aggressive boys growing hostile toward their leader. In contrast, the boys who had democratic leaders were friendlier, and looked to one another for mutual approval. They did less scapegoating, and when the leader left the room they continued to work at a steadier pace. The boys with laissez-faire leaders asked more questions, but they made fewer decisions. They were notable for their lack of achievement. The researchers concluded that the democratic style of leadership works best. Their conclusion, however, may have been biased, as the researchers favored a democratic style of leadership in the first place, and they did the research during a highly charged political period (Olmsted and Hare 1978). Apparently, this same bias in studies of leadership continues (Cassel 1999).

You may have noted that only boys and men were involved in this experiment. It is interesting to speculate how the results might differ if we were to repeat the experiment with all-girl groups and with mixed groups of girls and boys—and if we used both men and women as leaders. Perhaps you will become the sociologist to study such variations of this classic experiment.

Leadership Styles in Changing Situations Different situations require different styles of leadership. Suppose, for example, that you are leading a dozen backpackers in California's Sierra Madre mountains, and it is time to make dinner. A laissez-faire style would be appropriate if the backpackers had brought their own food—or perhaps a democratic style if everyone were supposed to pitch in. Authoritarian leadership—you telling all the hikers how to prepare their meals—would create resentment. This, in turn, would likely interfere with meeting the primary goal of the group, which in this case is to have a good time while enjoying nature.

Now assume the same group but a different situation: One of your party is lost, and a blizzard is on its way. This situation calls for you to take charge and be authoritarian. To simply shrug your shoulders and say, "You figure it out," would invite disaster—and probably a lawsuit.

The Power of Peer Pressure: The Asch Experiment

How influential are groups in our lives? To answer this, let's look first at *conformity* in the sense of going along with our peers. Our peers have no authority over us, only the influence that we allow.

> Imagine that you are taking a course in social psychology with Dr. Solomon Asch and you have agreed to participate in an experiment. As you enter his laboratory, you see seven chairs, five of them already filled by other students. You are given the sixth. Soon the seventh person arrives. Dr. Asch stands at the front of the room next to a covered easel. He explains that he will first show a large card with a vertical line on it, then another card with three vertical lines. Each of you is to tell him which of the three lines matches the line on the first card (see Figure 6.4).
>
> Dr. Asch then uncovers the first card with the single line and the comparison card with the three lines. The correct answer is easy, for two of the lines are obviously

Figure 6.4 Asch's Cards

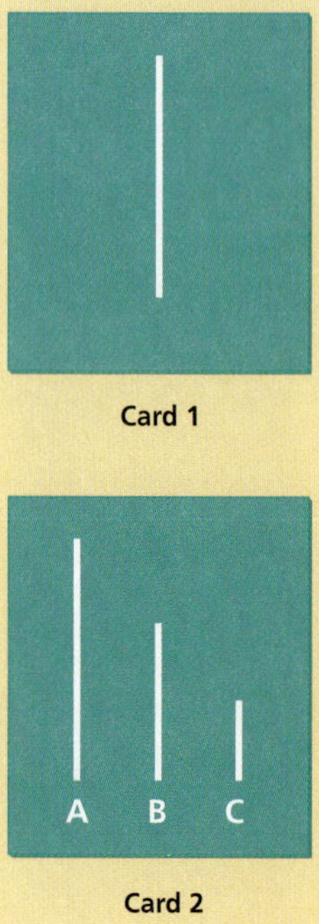

The cards used by Solomon Asch in his classic experiment on group conformity

Source: Asch 1952:452–453.

wrong, and one exactly right. Each person, in order, states his or her answer aloud. You all answer correctly. The second trial is just as easy, and you begin to wonder why you are there.

Then on the third trial something unexpected happens. Just as before, it is easy to tell which lines match. The first student, however, gives a wrong answer. The second gives the same incorrect answer. So do the third and the fourth. By now you are wondering what is wrong. How will the person next to you answer? You can hardly believe it when he, too, gives the same wrong answer. Then it is your turn, and you give what you know is the right answer. The seventh person also gives the same wrong answer.

On the next trial, the same thing happens. You know the choice of the other six is wrong. They are giving what to you are obviously wrong answers. You don't know what to think. Why aren't they seeing things the same way you are? Sometimes they do, but in twelve trials they don't. Something is seriously wrong, and you are no longer sure what to do.

When the eighteenth card is finished, you heave a sigh of relief. The experiment is finally over, and you are ready to bolt for the door. Dr. Asch walks over to you with a big smile on his face, and thanks you for participating in the experiment. He explains that you were the only real subject in the experiment! "The other six were stooges. I paid them to give those answers," he says. Now you feel real relief. Your eyes weren't playing tricks on you after all.

What were the results? Asch (1952) tested fifty people. One-third (33 percent) gave in to the group half the time, giving what they knew to be wrong answers. Another two of five (40 percent) gave wrong answers, but not as often. One of four (25 percent) stuck to their guns and always gave the right answer. I don't know how I would do on this test (if I knew nothing about it in advance), but I like to think that I would be part of the 25 percent. You probably feel the same way about yourself. But why should we feel that we wouldn't be like *most* people?

The results are disturbing, and more researchers have replicated Asch's experiment than any other study (Levine 1999). In our "land of individualism," the group is so powerful that most people are willing to say things that they know are not true. And this was a group of strangers! How much more conformity can we expect when our group consists of friends, people we value highly and depend on for getting along in life? Again, maybe you will become the sociologist to run that variation of Asch's experiment, perhaps using female subjects.

The Power of Authority: The Milgram Experiment

Even more disturbing are the results of the experiment described in the following Thinking Critically section.

THINKING Critically

If Hitler Asked You to Execute a Stranger, Would You? The Milgram Experiment

Imagine that you are taking a course with Dr. Stanley Milgram (1963, 1965), a former student of Dr. Asch. Assume that you do not know about the Asch experiment and have no reason to be wary. You arrive at the laboratory to participate in a study on punishment and learning. You and a second student draw lots for the roles of "teacher" and "learner." You are to be the teacher. When you see that the learner's chair has protruding electrodes, you are glad that you are the teacher. Dr. Milgram shows you the machine you will run. You see that one side of the control panel is marked "Mild Shock, 15 volts," while the center says "Intense Shock, 350 Volts," and the far right side reads "DANGER: SEVERE SHOCK."

"As the teacher, you will read aloud a pair of words," explains Dr. Milgram. "Then you will repeat the first word, and the learner will reply with the second word. If the learner can't remember the word, you press this lever on the shock generator. The shock will serve as punishment, and we can then determine if punishment improves memory." You nod, now very relieved that you haven't been designated the learner.

"Every time the learner makes an error, increase the punishment by 15 volts," instructs Dr. Milgram. Then, seeing the look on your face, he adds, "The shocks can be extremely painful, but they won't cause any permanent tissue damage." He pauses, and then says, "I want you to see." You then follow him to the "electric chair," and Dr. Milgram gives you a shock of 45 volts. "There. That wasn't too bad, was it?" "No," you mumble.

The experiment begins. You hope for the learner's sake that he is bright, but unfortunately he turns out to be rather dull. He gets some answers right, but you have to keep turning up the dial. Each turn makes you more and more uncomfortable. You find yourself hoping that the learner won't miss another answer. But he does. When he received the first shocks, he let out some moans and groans, but now he is screaming in agony. He even protests that he suffers from a heart condition.

How far do you turn that dial?

By now, you probably have guessed that there was no electricity attached to the electrodes and the "learner" was a stooge who only pretended to feel pain. The purpose of the experiment was to find out at what point people refuse to participate. Does anyone actually turn the lever all the way to "DANGER: SEVERE SHOCK"?

Milgram wanted the answer because of the Nazi slaughter of Jews, gypsies, Slavs, homosexuals, people with disabilities, and others whom they designated as "inferior." That millions of ordinary people did nothing to stop the deaths seemed bizarre, and Milgram wanted to see how ordinary, intelligent Americans might react in an analogous situation.

Milgram was upset by what he found. Many "teachers" broke into a sweat and protested to the experimenter that this was inhuman and should be stopped. But when the experimenter calmly replied that the experiment must go on, this assurance from an "authority" ("scientist, white coat, university laboratory") was enough for most "teachers" to continue, even though the "learner" screamed in agony. Even "teachers" who were "reduced to twitching, stuttering wrecks" continued to follow orders.

Milgram varied the experiments (Miller 1986). He used both men and women and put some "teachers" and "learners" in the same room, where the "teacher" could clearly see the suffering. He had some "learners" pound and kick the wall during the first shocks and then go silent. The results varied. When there was no verbal feedback from the "learner," 65 percent of the "teachers" pushed the lever all the way to 450 volts. Of those who could see the "learner," 40 percent turned the lever all the way. When Milgram added a second "teacher," a

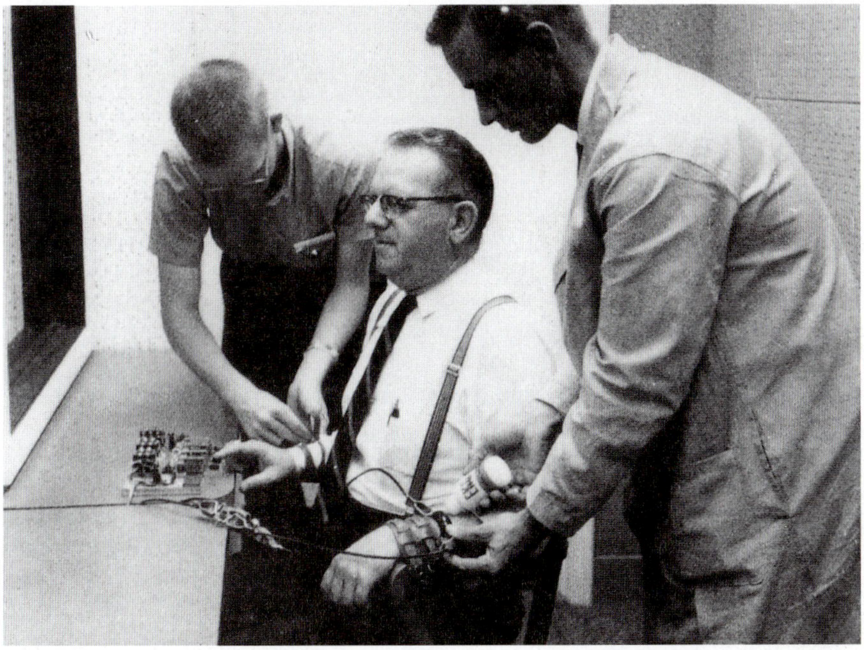

In the 1960s, U.S. social psychologists ran a series of creative but controversial experiments. Among these were Stanley Milgram's experiments, described in these pages. From this photo of the "learner" being prepared for the experiment, you can get an idea of how convincing the situation would be for the "teacher."

stooge who refused to go along with the experiment, only 5 percent of the "teachers" turned the lever all the way, a result that bears out some of Asch's findings.

A stormy discussion about research ethics erupted. Not only were researchers surprised and disturbed by what Milgram found, but also they were alarmed at his methods. Universities began to require that subjects be informed of the nature and purpose of social research. Researchers agreed that to reduce subjects to "twitching, stuttering wrecks" was unethical, and almost all deception was banned.

For Your CONSIDERATION

What is the connection between Milgram's experiment and the actions of Monster Cody in our opening vignette? Considering how significant these findings are, do you think that the scientific community overreacted to Milgram's experiments? Should we allow such research? Consider both the Asch and Milgram experiments, and use symbolic interactionism, functionalism, and conflict theory to explain why groups have such influence over us.

Global Consequences of Group Dynamics: Groupthink

Suppose you are a member of the President's inner circle. It is midnight, and the President has just called an emergency meeting to deal with a terrorist attack. At first, various options are presented. Eventually, these are narrowed to only a few choices, and at some point everyone seems to agree on what now appears to be "the only possible course of action." To express doubts at that juncture will bring you into conflict with *all* the other important people in the room. To criticize will mark you as not being a "team player." So you keep your mouth shut, with the result that each step commits you—and them—more and more to the "only" course of action.

What happened is called **groupthink.** Sociologist Irving Janis (1972, 1982) coined this term to refer to the collective tunnel vision that group members sometimes develop. As they begin to think alike, they become convinced that there is only one "right" viewpoint and course of action. They take any suggestion of alternatives as a sign of disloyalty. With their view so narrowed, they tend to show overconfidence and a disregard for risk. Becoming so convinced of their position, they may even put aside moral judgments (Hart 1991; Flippen 1999). The Asch and Milgram experiments help us see how groupthink can develop.

To better understand groupthink, consider two events.

The first occurred in 1986. The night before NASA was to launch the *Challenger,* subtropical Florida was hit by freezing weather. Ice covered the launch pad, and icicles hung like stalactites from the pad's service structure. Should they launch? NASA officials needed a stunning success because congressional support for the space program had weakened. Public interest was also running high because the first civilian, Christa McAuliffe, was to be on the *Challenger.* She would perform little experiments in space for schoolchildren to watch in their classrooms. Delaying the launch would bring a public relations nightmare. In the face of these pressures, NASA officials determined that the ice did not pose a risk. Disregarding all contrary evidence, they stuck to this conclusion. The *Challenger* exploded within seconds of being launched.

groupthink Irving Janis' term for a narrowing of thought by a group of people, leading to the perception that there is only one correct answer, in which to even suggest alternatives becomes a sign of disloyalty

Unfortunately, this didn't teach NASA to avoid groupthink. During *Columbia's* launch in 2003, foam broke loose on takeoff. Engineers were concerned that the foam had damaged tiles on the left wing, presenting a danger for reentry. They warned officials, sending them e-mails about the risk. One engineer even suggested that the crew do a "space walk" to examine the tiles (Vartabedian and Gold 2003). The team disregarded the warnings. Convinced that a piece of foam weighing less than two pounds could not seriously harm the shuttle, they refused to even consider the possibility (Wald and Schwartz 2003). The fiery results of their mental closure in this second instance were also transmitted around the globe.

As the space shuttle tragedies indicate, groupthink can bring serious consequences. Sometimes there are even greater consequences. In 1941, despite evidence that the Japanese were preparing to attack Pearl Harbor, President Franklin D. Roosevelt and his chiefs of staff refused to believe that the Japanese posed a danger. Their decision to continue naval operations as usual allowed the destruction of the U.S. naval fleet, ushering the United States into World War II. United States involvement in Vietnam and the resulting huge loss of life also involved groupthink, with U.S. officials steadfastly denying the strength of the North Vietnamese military, despite ample evidence to the contrary. Watergate is another noteworthy example, for it, too, plunged the United States into political crisis, for the first time in history forcing a U.S. president to resign.

In each of these cases, options closed as officials committed themselves to a single course of action. Questioning the decisions would have indicated disloyalty and disregard for "team playing." Those in power plunged ahead, no longer able to see alternative perspectives. No longer did they try to objectively weigh evidence as it came in, but, instead, interpreted everything as supporting their one "correct" decision.

Groupthink can also lead to a reevaluation of morals. Consider targeted killings. Until recently, U.S. officials had defined targeted killings as morally reprehensible. Now the CIA uses an approved, official "hit list," naming individuals their agents are authorized to hunt down and kill (Risen and Johnston 2002). Another example occurred after 9/11, when journalists and politicians openly discussed the option of torturing Arab suspects who wouldn't talk. They even defended torture as moral—"the lesser of two evils." Fortunately, there was open discussion and groupthink didn't win out.

Preventing Groupthink Groupthink is a danger that faces government leaders, who tend to surround themselves with an inner circle that closely reflects their own views. Isolated at the top, they can become cut off from information that does not support their own opinions. It is obvious that the extreme emotions that follow a terrorist attack can provide fertile ground for groupthink. Perhaps the key to preventing the mental captivity and intellectual paralysis known as groupthink is the widest possible circulation—especially among a nation's top government officials—of research that has been freely conducted by social scientists and information that has been freely gathered by media reporters.

If this conclusion comes across as an unabashed plug for sociological research and the free exchange of ideas, it is. Giving free rein to diverse opinions can effectively curb groupthink, which—if not prevented—can lead to the destruction of a society and, in today's world of sophisticated nuclear, biological, and chemical weapons, the obliteration of the earth's inhabitants.

SUMMARY and REVIEW

Social Groups and Societies

What is a group?

Sociologists use many definitions of groups, but, in general, **groups** consist of people who interact with one another and think of themselves as belonging together. **Societies** are the largest and most complex group that sociologists study. Pp. 148–149.

The Transformation of Societies

What inventions are linked to the change from one type of society to another?

On their way to postindustrial society, humans passed through four types of societies. Each emerged from a social revolution that was linked to new technology. The **domestication revolution**, which brought the pasturing of animals and the cultivation of plants, transformed **hunting and gathering societies** into **pastoral** and **horticultural societies.** Then the invention of the plow ushered in the **agricultural society,** while the **Industrial Revolution,** brought about by machines that were powered by fuels, led to the **industrial society.** The computer chip ushered in a new type of society called **postindustrial** (or **information**) **society.** Another new type of society, the **bioeconomic society,** may be emerging. Pp. 148–153.

How is social inequality linked to the transformation of societies?

Social equality was greatest in hunting and gathering societies, but over time social inequality grew. The root of the transition to social inequality was the accumulation of a food surplus, made possible through the domestication revolution. This surplus stimulated the division of labor, trade, accumulation of material goods, the subordination of females by males, the emergence of leaders, and the development of the state. Pp. 150–152.

Groups Within Society

How do sociologists classify groups?

Sociologists divide groups into primary groups, secondary groups, in-groups, out-groups, reference groups, and networks. The cooperative, intimate, long-term, face-to-face relationships provided by **primary groups** are fundamental to our sense of self. **Secondary groups** are larger, relatively temporary, and more anonymous, formal, and impersonal than primary groups. **In-groups** provide members with a strong sense of identity and belonging. **Out-groups** also foster identity by showing in-group members what they are *not.* **Reference groups** are groups whose standards we mentally refer to as we evaluate ourselves. **Social networks** consist of social ties that link people together. The new technology has given birth to a new type of group, the **electronic community.** Pp. 154–161.

Group Dynamics

How does a group's size affect its dynamics?

The term **group dynamics** refers to how individuals affect groups and how groups influence individuals. In a **small group,** everyone can interact directly with everyone else. As a group grows larger, its intensity decreases but its stability increases. A **dyad,** consisting of two people, is the most unstable of human groups, but it provides the most intense or intimate relationships. The addition of a third person, forming a **triad,** fundamentally alters relationships. Triads are unstable, as **coalitions** (the alignment of some members of a group against others) tend to form. Pp. 161–165.

What characterizes a leader?

A **leader** is someone who influences others. **Instrumental leaders** try to keep a group moving toward its goals, even though this causes friction and they lose popularity. **Expressive leaders** focus on creating harmony and raising group morale. Both types are essential to the functioning of groups. Pp. 165–166.

What are the three main leadership styles?

Authoritarian leaders give orders, **democratic leaders** try to lead by consensus, and **laissez-faire leaders** are highly permissive. An authoritarian style appears to be more effective in emergency situations, a democratic style works best for most situations, and a laissez-faire style is usually ineffective. Pp. 166–167.

How do groups encourage conformity?

The Asch experiment was cited to illustrate the power of peer pressure, the Milgram experiment to illustrate the influence of authority. Both experiments demonstrate how easily we can succumb to **groupthink,** a kind of collective tunnel vision. Preventing groupthink requires the free circulation of contrasting ideas. Pp. 167–171.

Where can I read more on this topic?

Suggested readings for this chapter are at the back of this book.

THINKING Critically ABOUT CHAPTER 6

1. How would your orientations to life (your ideas, attitudes, values, goals) be different if you had been reared in an agricultural society?
2. Identify your in-groups and your out-groups. How have your in-groups influenced the way you see the world?
3. Asch's experiment illustrates the power of peer pressure. How has peer pressure operated in your life? Think about something that you did not want to do, but did anyway because of peer pressure.

ADDITIONAL RESOURCES for This Chapter

www.ablongman.com/henslin7e

- *Content Select* Research Database for Sociology, with suggested key terms and annotated references
- Link to 2000 Census, with activities
- Flashcards of key terms and concepts
- Practice Tests
- Weblinks
- Interactive Maps

Chapter 7

Bureaucracy and Formal Organizations

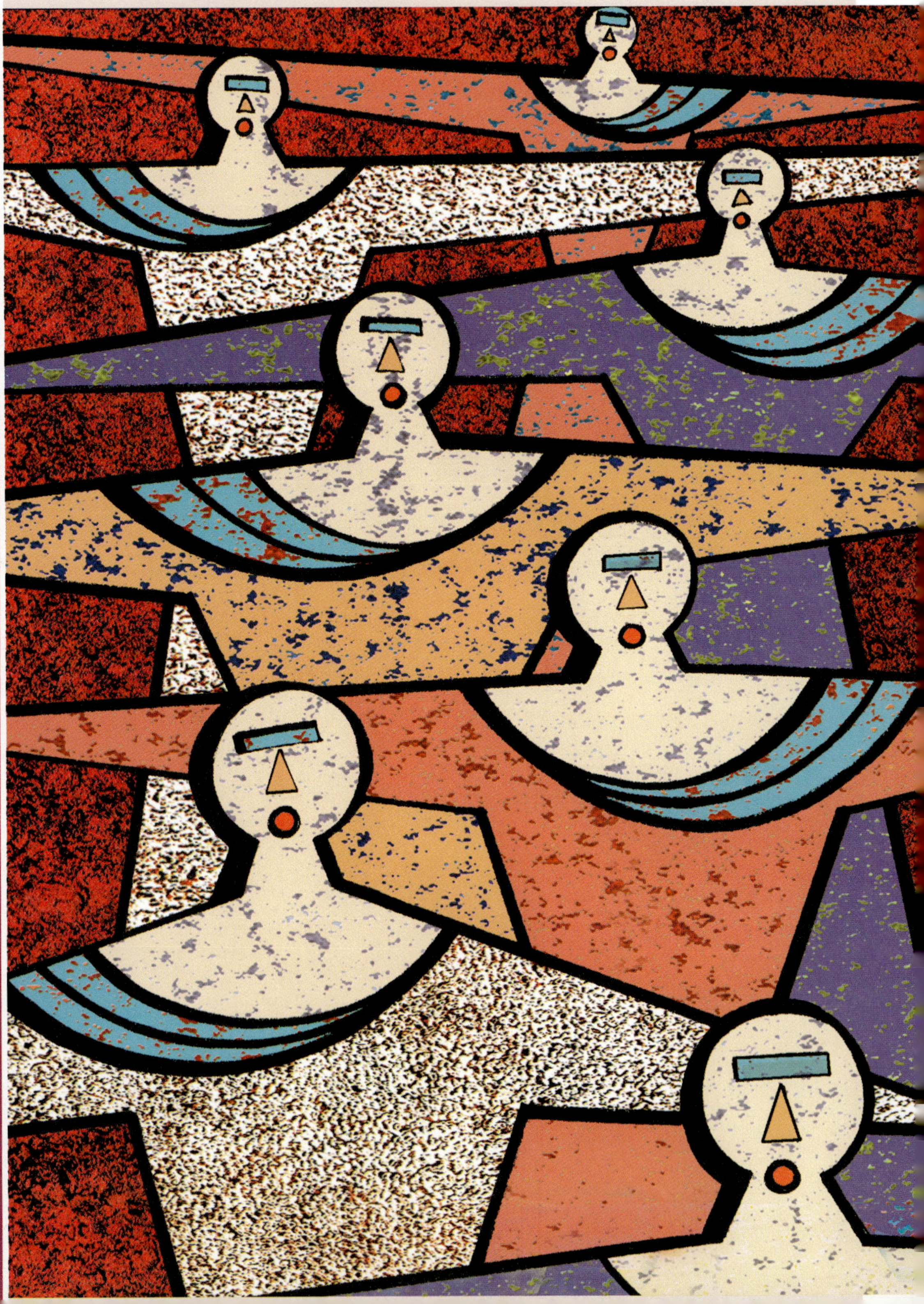

Noma & Jim Bliss, *Geometric Shapes on Face Figures (Digital)*, 1998

Chapter Outline

Imagine for a moment that you are a high school senior and you have applied to Cornell University. It's a long shot, you know, since you aren't in the top of your class—but what the heck? It's worth the extra hour it takes to fill out the application—since you have everything together for the other applications you've already sent to your state universities and regional colleges.

Now imagine the unthinkable. Like betting on the 75-to-1 long shot at the racetrack, your horse comes in! There is the letter from Cornell. You knew it would be a polite and cursory refusal, but, instead, as you hold it in your shaking hands and feel tears of joy welling up within you, the first words are: "Greetings from Cornell, your future alma mater!" and, below this, "Cornell is pleased to welcome you to its incoming freshman class."

You don't know whether to laugh, scream, cry, or what. You shout to your parents, who come running in to see what the problem is. They, too, are flabbergasted. While your Dad and Mom are proudly saying that they knew you could do it, you are already rushing to the phone to call your friends.

The next day, you are the talk of your class at school. Hardly anyone can believe it, for you are just an average student. "They must be trying for diversity of ability," jealously mumbles someone (who just took a sociology course), whom you *used* to count as a friend.

…ust too good

to be true,

…ou keep telling yourself,

…s you imagine yourself on the ivied campus.

"This is just too good to be true," you keep telling yourself, as you imagine yourself on the ivied campus.

And it is.

The call from the solemn Cornell admissions counselor explains that they had sent the wrong letter to 550 students. "We apologize for any confusion and distress this has caused," she says.

Confusion? How about shattered dreams?

—Based on Arenson 2003.

Some colleges admit thousands of students. To make the job manageable, they have broken down the admissions process into separate steps. Each step is an integrated part of the entire procedure. Computer software has facilitated this process, but, as this true event at Cornell indicates, things don't always go as planned. In this case, a low-level bureaucrat simply downloaded the wrong letter.

Despite their flaws, we need bureaucracies, and in this chapter we'll look at how society is organized to "get its job done." As you read it, you may be able to trace the source of some of your frustrations to this social organization—as well as see how your welfare depends on it.

The Rationalization of Society

In the previous chapter, we discussed how societies have undergone transformations so extensive that whole new types of societies have emerged. We also saw that we are now in the midst of one of those earth-shattering transformations. Underlying our information society (which may be merging into a bioeconomic society) is an emphasis on **rationality**, the idea that efficiency and practical results should dominate human affairs. Let's examine how this approach to life—which today we take for granted—came about.

Why Did Society Change?

Until recently, people were immersed in a **traditional orientation** to life—the idea that the past is the best guide for the present. In this view, what exists is good because it has passed the test of time. Customs—and relationships based on them—have served people well, and they should not be abandoned lightly. A central orientation of a traditional society is to protect the status quo. Change is viewed with suspicion and comes about slowly, if at all.

The traditional orientation to life stands in the way of industrialization. As Table 7.1 shows, the traditional orientation is based on personal relationships. Deep obligation and responsibility, which are often lifelong, permeate society. What counts in production is not who is best at doing something, but the relationships that people have with one another. Based on origins that are lost in history, everyone—even children—has an established role to play. The past is prized, and it rules the present.

Capitalism requires an entirely different way of looking at life. If a society is to industrialize, a deep shift must occur in people's thinking. Tradition ("This is the way we've always done it") must be replaced with *rationality* ("Let's find the most efficient way to do it"). As Table 7.1 shows, personal relationships are replaced by impersonal, short-term contracts. The "bottom line" (results) becomes the primary concern, and rule-of-thumb methods give way to explicit ways of measuring results.

It is difficult to overstate the significance of the change from a traditional orientation to one based on rationality, for it flies in the face of human history. We take this new view of *rationality*—judging things according to the bottom line instead of by personal relationships—so for granted that it is difficult to grasp how fundamentally different this orientation is. This may help. It is like a wife saying to her husband, "I'm going to evaluate how much you've contributed to the family budget and how much time you've put in on household tasks—and I'll keep or replace you on that basis."

As college registration illustrates, bureaucracies break tasks down into their component parts and have specialists handle each part. The efficiency of this procedure is sometimes lost on the clientele being served. Shown here is registration at University of Southern California.

Table 7.1 A Model of Production in Traditional and Nontraditional Societies

Traditional Societies (Horticultural, Agricultural)	Nontraditional Societies (Industrial, Postindustrial)
1. Production is done by family members and same-sex groups (men's and women's groups).	1. Production is done by workers hired for the job.
2. Production takes place in the home, or in fields and other areas adjacent to the home.	2. Production takes place in a centralized location set up for this purpose. (Some decentralization is occurring in the information society.)
3. Tasks are assigned according to personal relationships (men, women, and children do specific tasks based on custom).	3. Tasks are assigned according to agreements and training.
4. Relationships are based on history ("the way it's always been").	4. Relationships are based on contracts, which change as the situation changes.
5. Relationships are diffuse (vague, covering many areas of life).	5. Relationships are specific; contracts (even if not written) specify conditions.
6. Relationships are long-term, often lifelong.	6. Relationships are short-term, for the length of the contract.
7. The "how" of production is not evaluated; the issue is, "We want to keep doing it the way we've always done it."	7. The "how" of production is evaluated; the issue is, "How can we make this more efficient?"
8. It is assumed that arrangements will continue indefinitely.	8. Arrangements are evaluated periodically, to decide whether to continue or to change them.
9. People are evaluated according to how they fulfill their traditional roles.	9. People are evaluated according to the "bottom line" (the organization's goals).

Note: This model is an ideal type. Rationality is never totally absent from any society, and no society (or organization) is based entirely on rationality. Even the most rational organizations (those that most carefully and even ruthlessly compute the "bottom line") have traditional components. To properly understand this table, consider these nine characteristics as being "more" or "less" present.

You can see that this would be a fundamental change. And this is what going from tradition to rationality is like. How did the **rationalization of society**—the widespread acceptance of rationality and the construction of a social organization largely built around this idea—come about?

Marx: Capitalism Broke Tradition

An early sociologist, Karl Marx (1818–1883), was one of the first to note how tradition had given way to rationality. As he thought about why this change had taken place, he concluded that capitalism had broken the bonds of tradition. As people who had money experimented with capitalism, they saw that it was more efficient. They were impressed that it produced things they wanted in much greater abundance and yielded high profits. This encouraged them to invest capital in manufacturing. As capitalism spread, traditional thinking receded. Gradually, the rationality of capitalism replaced the traditional approach to life. Marx's conclusion: The change to capitalism changed the way people thought about life.

Weber: Religion Broke Tradition

To sociologist Max Weber (1864–1920), this problem was as intriguing as an unsolved murder is to a detective. Weber wasn't satisfied with Marx's answer, and he kept searching for the solution. He found the clue when he noted that capitalism thrived only in certain parts of Europe. "There has be a reason for this," he mused. As Weber pursued the matter, he noted that capitalism flourished in Protestant countries, while Roman Catholic countries held on to tradition and were relatively untouched by capitalism. "Somehow, then, religion holds the key," he thought.

But why did Roman Catholics cling to the past, while Protestants embraced change? Weber's answer to this puzzle has been the source of controversy ever since he first proposed it in his influential book, *The Protestant Ethic and the Spirit of Capitalism* (1904–1905). Weber concluded that Roman Catholic doctrine emphasized the acceptance of present arrangements, not change: "God wants you where you are. You owe allegiance to the Church, to your family, and to your king. Accept your lot in life and remain rooted." Weber argued that Protestant theology, in contrast, opened its followers to change. Weber was intimately familiar with Calvinism, his mother's religion. Calvinists (followers of the

rationality using rules, efficiency, and practical results to determine human affairs

traditional orientation the idea that the past is the best guide for the present; characteristic of tribal, peasant, and feudal societies

(the) rationalization of society a widespread acceptance of rationality and social organizations that are built largely around this idea

In traditional societies, religion was a dominant force. In this photo of Victoria, Malta, the cathedral makes it evident how tradition dominated village life. Max Weber and Karl Marx disagreed about why societies changed from a traditional orientation to a rational one.

teachings of John Calvin, 1509–1564) believed that people are destined before birth for either heaven or hell—and they do not know their destiny until after they die. Weber said that this teaching filled Calvinists with anxiety. Salvation became their chief concern—they wanted to know *now* where they were going after death.

To resolve their spiritual dilemma, Calvinists hit upon an ingenious solution: God surely did not want those chosen for heaven to be ignorant of their destiny. Therefore, those who were in God's favor would know it—they would receive a sign from God. But what sign? The answer, claimed Calvinists, was found not in mystical, spiritual experiences, but in things that people could see and measure. The sign of God's approval was success: Those whom God had predestined for heaven would be blessed with visible success in this life.

This idea transformed the lives of Calvinists. It motivated them to work hard, and because Calvinists also believed that thrift is a virtue, their dedication to work led to an accumulation of money. They could not spend this money on themselves, however, for to purchase items beyond the basic necessities was considered sinful. **Capitalism,** the investment of capital in the hope of producing profits, became an outlet for their excess money. The success of those investments, in turn, became a further sign of God's approval. In this way, Calvinists transformed worldly success into a spiritual virtue. Other branches of Protestantism, although not in agreement with the notion of predestination, also adopted the creed of thrift and hard work. Consequently, said Weber, Protestant countries embraced capitalism.

But what has this to do with rationalization? Simply put, capitalism demands rationalization, the careful calculation of practical results. If profits are your goal, you must keep track of your income and expenses. You must calculate inventories and wages, the cost of producing goods and how much they bring in. You must determine "the bottom line." Efficiency, then, not tradition, becomes the drumbeat to which you march. If traditional ways of doing things are inefficient, they are replaced, for what counts are the results. Weber's equation: A changed way of thinking (God will give a sign to the elect) produced capitalism.

Who is correct? Weber, who concluded that Protestantism produced rationality, which then paved the way for capitalism? Or Marx, who concluded that capitalism produced rationality? No analyst has yet reconciled these two opposing answers to the satisfaction of sociologists: The two views still remain side by side.

Formal Organizations and Bureaucracy

Regardless of whether Marx or Weber was right about its cause, rationality was a totally different way of approaching life. As this new orientation came to permeate society, it led to new types of organizations. One result was **formal organizations,** secondary groups designed to achieve explicit objectives. Formal organizations have become a central feature of our lives. Although they are fairly new to the human scene, today most of us are born within them, we are educated in them, we spend our working lives in them, and we are buried by them.

Formal Organizations

Prior to industrialization, there were few formal organizations. The guilds of western Europe during the twelfth century are an example. People who performed the same type of work organized to control their craft in a local area. They set prices and standards of workmanship (Bridgwater 1953; Volti 1995). Much like modern unions, guilds also prevented outsiders (nonmembers of the guild) from working at the particular craft. Another example of an early formal organization is the army, with its hierarchical structure of senior officers, junior officers, and ranks. Formal armies, of course, go back to early history.

With industrialization, secondary groups became common. Today we take their existence for granted and, beginning with grade school, all of us spend a good deal of time in them. Formal organizations tend to develop into bureaucracies, and in general, the larger the formal organization, the more likely it is to be bureaucratic.

capitalism an economic system characterized by the private ownership of the means of production, the pursuit of profit, and market competition

formal organization a secondary group designed to achieve explicit objectives

bureaucracy a formal organization with a hierarchy of authority, a clear division of labor; emphasis on written rules, communications, and records; and impersonality of positions

The Characteristics of Bureaucracies

What do the Soviet army, the Mormon Church, and your college have in common? The sociological answer is that they all are **bureaucracies.** As Weber (1913/1947) pointed out, bureaucracies have

1. *Clear levels, with assignments flowing downward and accountability flowing upward.* Each level assigns responsibilities to the level beneath it, while each lower level is accountable to the level above it for fulfilling those assignments. The bureaucratic structure of a typical university is shown in Figure 7.1 on the following page.
2. *A division of labor.* Each worker has a specific task to fulfill, and all the tasks are coordinated to accomplish the purpose of the organization. In a college, for example,

Figure 7.1 The Typical Bureaucratic Structure of a Medium-Sized University

This is a scaled-down version of a university's bureaucratic structure. The actual lines of a university are likely to be much more complicated than those depicted here. A large university may have a chancellor and several presidents under the chancellor, with each president responsible for a particular campus. Although in this figure extensions of authority are shown only for the vice president for administration and the College of Social Sciences, each of the other vice presidents and colleges has similar positions. If the figure were to be extended, departmental secretaries would be shown, and eventually, somewhere, even students.

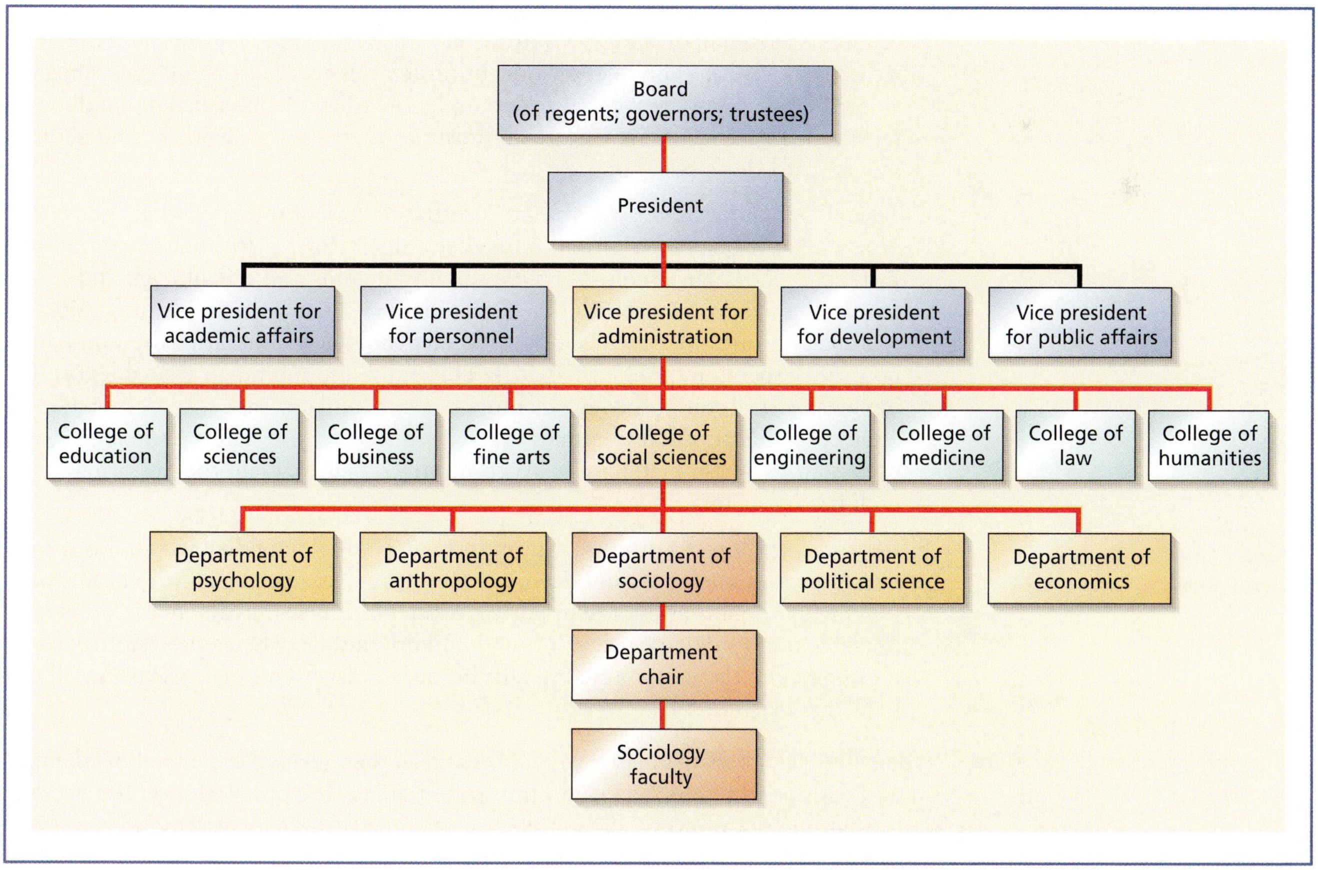

The division of labor, a central characteristic of formal organizations, is not new. In this painting of Italian farm life by Francesco Bassano (1549–1592), you can see the intricate division of labor that farm production required in the 1500s. Note the many specialized tasks these people are doing. Can you identify what is different about today's division of labor?

a teacher does not run the heating system, the president does not teach, and a secretary does not evaluate textbooks. These tasks are distributed among people who have been trained to do them.

3. *Written rules.* In their attempt to become efficient, bureaucracies stress written procedures. In general, the longer a bureaucracy exists, the larger it grows, and the more written rules it has. The rules of some bureaucracies cover just about every imaginable situation. In my university, for example, the rules are published in handbooks: separate ones for faculty, students, administrators, civil service workers, and perhaps others that I don't even know exist.

4. *Written communications and records.* Records are kept of much of what occurs in a bureaucracy ("Be sure to CC all immediate supervisors."). In some organizations, workers spend a fair amount of time sending memos and e-mail back and forth. Sometimes, workers must detail their activities in written reports. My university, for example, requires that each semester, faculty members summarize the number of hours they spent on specified activities. They must also submit an annual report listing what they accomplished in teaching, research, and service—all accompanied by copies of publications, testimonies to service, and written teaching evaluations from each course. These materials go to committees that evaluate the performance of each faculty member.

5. *Impersonality.* It is the office that is important, not the individual who holds the office. You work for the organization, not for the replaceable person who heads some post in the organization. Each worker is a replaceable unit, for many others are available to fulfill each particular function. For example, when a professor retires or dies, someone else is appointed to take his or her place. This makes you a small cog in a large machine.

These five characteristics help bureaucracies reach their goals. They also allow them to grow and endure. One bureaucracy in the United States, the postal service, has become so large that one out of every 150 employed Americans works for it (*Statistical Abstract*

2002:573, 1095). If the head of a bureaucracy dies, retires, or resigns, the organization continues without skipping a beat, for unlike a "mom and pop" operation, its functioning does not depend on the individual who heads it. The expansion (some would say domination) of bureaucracies in contemporary society is illustrated by the Down-to-Earth Sociology box on the following page.

This 1907 photo indicates one way that technology has changed our lives. The walls of little drawers that the women are searching contain customer records of the Metropolitan Life Insurance Company. Today, this entire bank of records could be stored on a personal computer. We also could use the computer to search or modify the records, infinitesimally faster—and certainly much easier on the legs—than standing on the ladder.

"Ideal" Versus "Real" Bureaucracy

Just as people often act differently from the way the norms say they should, so it is with bureaucracies. The characteristics of bureaucracies identified by Weber are *ideal types;* that is, they are a composite of characteristics based on many specific examples. Think of the judges at a dog show. They have a mental image of how each particular breed of dog should look and behave, and they judge each individual dog according to that mental image. Each dog will rank high on some of these characteristics, and lower on others. In the same way, a particular organization will rank higher or lower on the traits of a bureaucracy, yet still qualify as a bureaucracy. Instead of labeling a particular organization as a "bureaucracy" or "not a bureaucracy," it probably makes more sense to think in terms of the *extent* to which it is bureaucratized (Udy 1959; Hall 1963).

As with culture, then, a bureaucracy often differs from its ideal image. The actual lines of authority ("going through channels"), for example, may be different from those portrayed on organizational charts such as the one shown in Figure 7.1. For example, suppose that before being promoted, the university president taught in the history department. As a result, friends from that department may have direct access to him or her. If they wish to provide "input" (ranging from opinions about how to solve problems to personal grievances or even gossip), these individuals may skip their chairperson or even the dean of their college, and go directly to the president.

Today's armies, no matter what country they are from, are bureaucracies. They have a strict hierarchy of rank, division of labor, impersonality (an emphasis on the office, not the person holding it), and they stress written records, rules, and communications—essential characteristics identified by Max Weber. Though its outward appearance may differ from Western standards, this army in India is no exception to this principle.

DOWN-TO-EARTH SOCIOLOGY

The McDonaldization of Society

THE THOUSANDS OF MCDONALD'S restaurants that dot the U.S. landscape—and increasingly, the world—have a significance that goes far beyond the convenience of ready-made hamburgers and milk shakes. As sociologist George Ritzer (1993, 1998, 2001) says, our everyday lives are being "McDonaldized." Let's see what he means by this.

The McDonaldization of society—the standardization of everyday life—does not refer just to the robotlike assembly of food. As Ritzer points out, this process is occurring throughout society—and it is transforming our lives. Want to do some shopping? Shopping malls offer one-stop shopping in controlled environments. Planning a trip? Travel agencies offer "package" tours. They will transport middle-class Americans to ten European capitals in fourteen days. All visitors experience the same hotels, restaurants, and other scheduled sites—and no one need fear meeting a "real" native. Want to keep up with events? *USA Today* spews out McNews—short, bland, unanalytic pieces that can be digested between gulps of the McShake or the McBurger.

McDonald's in Tokyo, Japan

Efficiency brings dependability. You can expect your burger and fries to taste the same whether you buy them in Los Angeles or Beijing. Efficiency also lowers prices. But efficiency does come at a cost. Predictability washes away spontaneity, changing the quality of our lives. It produces a sameness, a bland version of what used to be unique experiences. In my own travels, for example, had I taken packaged tours I never would have had the enjoyable, eye-opening experiences that have added so much to my appreciation of human diversity.

For good or bad, our lives are being McDonaldized, and the predictability of packaged settings seems to be our social destiny. When education is rationalized, no longer will our children have to put up with real professors, who insist on discussing ideas endlessly, who never come to decisive answers, and who come saddled with idiosyncrasies. Our programmed education will eliminate the need for discussion of social issues—we will have packaged solutions to social problems, definitive answers like those we find in mathematics and engineering—and on television. Computerized courses will teach the same answers to everyone—the approved, "politically correct" ways to think about social issues. Mass testing will assure that students regurgitate the programmed responses.

Our coming prepackaged society will be efficient, of course. But it also means that we will be trapped in the "iron cage" of bureaucracy—just as Weber warned would happen.

Dysfunctions of Bureaucracies

Although in the long run no other form of social organization is more efficient, as Weber recognized, bureaucracies also have a dark side. Let's look at some of their dysfunctions.

Red Tape: A Rule Is a Rule Bureaucracies can be so bound by red tape that their rules impede the purpose of the organization. Some rules (or "correct procedures" in bureaucratic jargon) are enough to try the patience of a saint.

> In the Bronx, Mother Teresa spotted a structurally sound abandoned building and wanted to turn it into a homeless shelter. But she ran head on into a rule: The building must have an elevator for people with disabilities. Not having the funds for the elevator, Mother Teresa struggled to get permission to bypass this rule. Two frustrating years later, she gave up. The abandoned building is still rotting way. (Tobias 1995)

Obviously this rule about elevators was not intended to stop Mother Teresa from ministering to the down and out. But, hey, rules is rules!

Lack of Communication Between Units Each unit within a bureaucracy performs specialized tasks, which are designed to contribute to the organization's goals. At times, units fail to communicate with one another and end up working at cross purposes. In Granada, Spain, for example, the local government was concerned about the

the McDonaldization of society the process by which ordinary aspects of life become rationalized and efficiency comes to rule them, including such things as food preparation run-down appearance of buildings along one of its main streets. Consequently, one unit of the government fixed the fronts of these buildings, repairing concrete, iron, and stonework. The results were impressive, and the unit was proud of what it had accomplished. The only problem was that another unit of the government had slated these same buildings for demolition (Arías 1993). Because neither unit of this bureaucracy knew what the other was doing, one beautified the buildings while the other made sure they ended up as a heap of rubble.

Bureaucracies have become a powerful and overwhelming force in social life. Even Mother Teresa, one of the most famous religious figures of the late twentieth century, was unable to overcome bureaucratic red tape in her attempt to help New York City's homeless.

Bureaucratic Alienation Treated in terms of roles, rules, and functions rather than as individuals, many workers begin to feel more like objects than people. Marx termed these reactions **alienation,** which he said comes from being cut off from the finished product of one's labor. He pointed out that before industrialization, workers used their own tools to produce an entire product, such as a chair or table. Now the capitalists own the tools (machinery), and assign each worker only a single step or two in the entire production process. Relegated to repetitive tasks that seem remote from the final product, workers lose a sense of identity with what they produce. They come to feel estranged not only from their products but also from their work environment.

Resisting Alienation Because workers need to feel valued and want to have a sense of control over their work, they resist alienation. Forming primary groups at work is a major form of that resistance. Workers band together in informal settings—at lunch, around desks, or for a drink after work. There they give one another approval for jobs well done and express sympathy for the shared need to put up with cantankerous bosses, meaningless routines, and endless rules. They relate to one another not just as workers, but as people who value one another. They flirt, laugh and tell jokes, and talk about their families and goals. Adding this multidimensionality to their work relationships maintains their sense of being individuals rather than mere cogs in a machine.

Consider a common sight. While visiting an office, you see work areas that are decorated with family and vacation photos. The sociological implication is that of workers striving to resist alienation. By staking a claim to individuality, the workers are rejecting an identity as machines that exist to perform functions.

The Alienated Bureaucrat Not all workers succeed in resisting alienation. Some who become alienated remain in the organization either because they see no viable alternative or because they have "only so many years until retirement." They hate every minute of work, and it shows—in their attitudes toward clients, toward fellow workers, and toward authority in the organization. The alienated bureaucrat does not take initiative, will not do anything for the organization beyond what is absolutely required, and uses rules to justify doing as little as possible.

Despite poor attitude and performance, alienated workers often retain their jobs. Some keep their jobs because of seniority, while others threaten expensive, time-consuming, and embarrassing legal action if anyone tries to fire them. Some alienated workers are shunted off into small bureaucratic corners, where they spend the day doing trivial tasks and have little chance of coming in contact with the public. This treatment, of course, only alienates them further.

Bureaucratic Incompetence In a tongue-in-cheek analysis of bureaucracies, Laurence Peter proposed what has become known as the **Peter principle:** Each employee of a bureaucracy is promoted to his or her *level of incompetence* (Peter and Hull 1969). People who perform well in a bureaucracy come to the attention of those higher up the chain of command and are promoted. If they continue to perform well, they are again promoted. This process continues *until* they are promoted to a level at which they can no longer handle the responsibilities well—their level of incompetence. There they hide

alienation Marx's term for workers' lack of connection with the product of their labor; caused by their being assigned repetitive tasks on a small part of a product: this leads to a sense of powerlessness and normlessness; also used in the general sense of not feeling a part of something

Peter principle a tongue-in-cheek "law" according to which the members of an organization are promoted for good work until they reach their level of incompetence, the level at which they can no longer do good work

goal displacement the adoption of new goals by an organization; also known as goal replacement

behind the work of others, taking credit for the accomplishments of employees under their direction. In our opening vignette, the employee who sent the wrong mail has already reached his or her level of incompetence.

Although the Peter principle contains a grain of truth, if it were generally true, bureaucracies would be staffed by incompetents, and these organizations would not succeed. In reality, bureaucracies are remarkably successful. Sociologists Peter Evans and James Rauch (1999) examined the government bureaucracies of 35 developing countries. They found that prosperity comes to the countries that have central bureaucracies that hire workers on the basis of merit and offer them rewarding careers.

Goal Displacement and the Perpetuation of Bureaucracies

Bureaucracies have become a standard feature of our lives because they are a powerful form of social organization. They harness people's energies in order to reach specific goals. Once in existence, however, bureaucracies tend to take on a life of their own. In a process called **goal displacement,** even after the organization achieves its goal and no longer has a reason to continue, continue it does.

A classic example is the National Foundation for the March of Dimes, organized in the 1930s to fight polio (Sills 1957). At that time, the origin of polio was a mystery. The public was alarmed and fearful, for overnight a healthy child could be stricken with this crippling disease. To raise money to find a cure, the March of Dimes placed posters of children on crutches near cash registers in almost every store in the United States. (See the photo below.) They raised money beyond their wildest dreams. When Dr. Jonas Salk developed a vaccine for polio in the 1950s, the threat was wiped out almost overnight.

The staff that ran the March of Dimes did not quietly fold up their tents and slip away. Instead, they found a way to keep their jobs by targeting a new enemy—birth defects. But then in 2001, researchers finished mapping the human genome system. On the alert and perceiving that some day this information could help eliminate birth defects—and their jobs—officials of the March of Dimes came up with a new slogan, "Breakthroughs for Babies." This latest goal should ensure the organization's existence forever: It is so vague that we are not likely to ever run out of the need for "breakthroughs."

Then there is NATO (North Atlantic Treaty Organization), founded during the Cold War to prevent Russia from invading Western Europe. When the Cold War ended, removing the organization's purpose, the Western powers tried to find a reason to continue their organization. I mean, why waste a perfectly good bureaucracy? They appear to have

"I'm Winning
Because of You"
JOIN
THE MARCH OF
DIMES
FIGHT
INFANTILE
PARALYSIS
The National Foundation for Infantile Paralysis
FRANKLIN D. ROOSEVELT, Founder

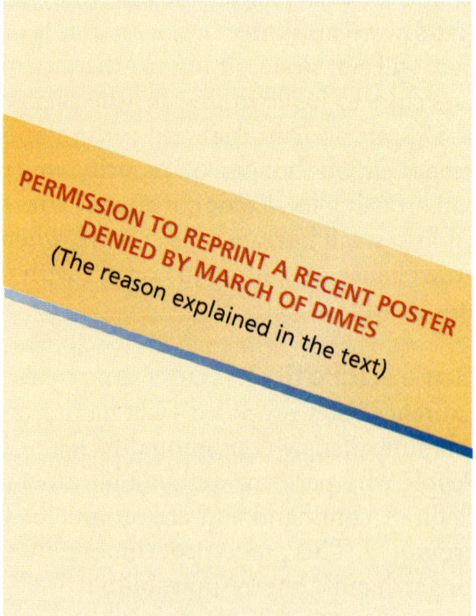

The March of Dimes was founded by President Franklin Roosevelt in the 1930s to fight polio. When a vaccine for polio was discovered in the 1950s, the organization did not declare victory and disband. Instead, it kept the organization intact by creating new goals—fighting birth defects. Sociologists use the term goal displacement to refer to this process of adopting new goals. "Fighting birth defects" is now being replaced by an even vaguer goal, "Breakthroughs for Babies." This new goal displacement may guarantee the organization's existence forever, for it is a goal so elusive it can never be reached. (Can we ever run out of the need for "breakthroughs"?)

hit upon one—to create "rapid response forces" to combat terrorism and "rogue nations" (Tyler 2002). To keep this bureaucracy going, they even allowed Russia to become a junior partner.

On a side note: Bureaucracies are sensitive about sociologists analyzing their activities. When I tried to get permission from the March of Dimes to reprint a copy of their current poster, I was denied that permission—*unless I changed my analysis to make it more favorable to the organization.* As you can see from the missing photo on the previous page, I refused to do so. Sociologists regularly confront such obstacles in their work.

The Sociological Significance of Bureaucracies

Perhaps the main sociological significance of bureaucracies is that they represent a fundamental change in how people relate to one another (see Table 7.1 on page 177). When work is rooted in personal relationships, much more is at stake than performing tasks efficiently and keeping an eye on the bottom line. Seeing that all relatives and friends have jobs, for example, was once the determining factor in making decisions. Bureaucracies, or the rationalization of society, changed this (Volti 1995).

Voluntary Associations

Although bureaucracies have become the dominant form of organization for large, task-oriented groups, even more common are voluntary associations. Let's examine their characteristics.

Back in the 1830s, Alexis de Tocqueville, a Frenchman, traveled across the United States, observing the customs of this new nation. His report, *Democracy in America* (1835), was widely read both in Europe and in the United States. It is still quoted for its insights into the American character. One of de Tocqueville's observations was that Americans joined a lot of **voluntary associations,** groups made up of volunteers who organize on the basis of some mutual interest.

Over the years, Americans have maintained this pattern and are very proud of it. A visitor entering one of the thousands of small towns that dot the U.S. landscape is often greeted with a highway sign proclaiming some of the town's volunteer associations: Girl Scouts, Boy Scouts, Kiwanis, Lions, Elks, Eagles, Knights of Columbus, Chamber of Commerce, American Legion, Veterans of Foreign Wars, and perhaps a host of others. One type of voluntary association is so prevalent that a separate sign sometimes indicates which varieties are present in the town: Roman Catholic, Baptist, Lutheran, Methodist, Episcopalian, and so on. Not listed on these signs are many other voluntary associations, such as political parties, unions, health clubs, the National Right to Life, the National Organization for Women, Alcoholics Anonymous, Gamblers Anonymous, Association of Pinto Racers, and Citizens United For or Against This and That.

Americans love voluntary associations, and use them to express a wide variety of interests. Some groups are local, consisting of only a few volunteers; others are national, with a paid professional staff. Some are temporary, organized to accomplish some specific task, such as arranging for Fourth of July fireworks. Others, such as the Scouts and political parties, are permanent—large, secondary organizations with clear lines of command—and they are also bureaucracies.

Functions of Voluntary Associations

Whatever their form, voluntary associations are numerous because they meet people's basic needs. People do not *have* to belong to these organizations. They join because they obtain benefits from their participation. Functionalists have identified seven functions of voluntary associations.

1. Voluntary organizations advance particular interests. For example, adults who are concerned about children's welfare volunteer for the Scouts because they think kids are better off joining this group than hanging out on the street. In short, voluntary

voluntary association a group made up of people who voluntarily organize on the basis of some mutual interest; also known as voluntary memberships associations get things done, whether that means arranging for the fireworks to go off on time or making people familiar with the latest legislation on abortion.

2. Voluntary groups offer people an identity. Some even provide a sense of purpose in life. As in-groups, they give their members a feeling of togetherness, of belonging. In many cases, they give them a sense of doing something worthwhile. This function is so important for some individuals that their participation in voluntary associations becomes the center of their lives.
3. Voluntary associations help govern the nation and maintain social order. Groups that help "get out the vote" or assist the Red Cross in coping with disasters are obvious examples.

The first two functions apply to all voluntary associations. In a general sense, so does the third. Although few organizations focus on politics, voluntary associations help to incorporate individuals into society, which helps to maintain social order.

Sociologist David Sills (1968) identified four other functions, which apply only to some voluntary associations.

4. Some voluntary groups mediate between the government and the individual. For example, some provide a way for people to put pressure on lawmakers.
5. By providing training in organizational skills, some groups help individuals climb the occupational ladder.
6. Other groups help bring people into the political mainstream. The National Association for the Advancement of Colored People (NAACP) is an example of such a group.
7. Finally, some voluntary associations pave the way to social change. Groups such as Greenpeace oppose the taken-for-granted definitions of "normal" when it comes to the environment. Their challenges to established boundaries often indicate the direction of social change.

Shared Interests

Voluntary associations, then, represent no single interest or purpose. They can be reactionary, resisting new ways of doing things, or they can be visionary, standing at the vanguard of social change. Despite their diversity, however, a common thread runs through voluntary associations. That thread is mutual interest. Although the particular interest varies from group to group, shared interest in some view or activity is the tie that binds their members together.

Motivations for joining these groups differ. Some people join because they hold strong convictions concerning the stated purpose of the organization, others simply because membership helps them politically or professionally. Some may even join because they have romantic interests in a group member.

With so many motivations for joining, and because the commitment of some members is fleeting, voluntary associations often have high turnover. Some people move in and out of groups almost as fast as they change clothes. Within each organization, however, is an inner circle—individuals who actively promote the group, who stand firmly behind the group's goals, and who are committed to maintaining the organization itself. If this inner circle loses its commitment, the group is likely to fold.

The Problem of Oligarchy

An interesting, and disturbing, aspect of voluntary associations is that the leaders often grow distant from their members and become convinced that they can trust only the inner circle to make the group's important decisions. To see this principle at work, let's look at the Veterans of Foreign Wars (VFW).

Sociologists Elaine Fox and George Arquitt (1985) studied three local posts of the VFW, a national organization of former U.S. soldiers who have served in foreign wars.

They found that although the leaders conceal their attitudes from the other members, they view the rank and file as a bunch of ignorant boozers. Because the leaders can't stand the thought that such people might represent them in the community and at national meetings, a curious situation arises. Although the VFW constitution makes rank-and-file members eligible for top leadership positions, they never become leaders. In fact, the leaders are so effective in controlling these top positions that even before an election they can tell you who is going to win. "You need to meet Jim," the sociologists were told. "He's the next post commander after Sam does his time."

In a process called the iron law of oligarchy, a small, self-perpetuating elite tends to take control of formal organizations. Veterans' organizations are no exception to this principle, as sociological studies have shown.

At first, the researchers found this puzzling. The election hadn't been held yet. As they investigated further, they found that leadership is actually decided behind the scenes. The elected leaders appoint their favored people to chair the key committees. This makes the members aware of their accomplishments, and they elect them as leaders. The inner circle, then, maintains control over the entire organization simply by appointing members of their inner circle to highly visible positions.

Like the VFW, most organizations are run by only a few of their members (Cnaan 1991). Building on the term *oligarchy,* a system in which many are ruled by a few, sociologist Robert Michels (1876–1936) coined the term **the iron law of oligarchy** to refer to how organizations come to be dominated by a small, self-perpetuating elite (Michels 1911). The majority of members are passive, and an elite inner circle keeps itself in power by passing the leadership positions from one clique member to another.

What many find disturbing about the iron law of oligarchy is that people are excluded from leadership because they don't represent the inner circle's values—or perhaps their background. This is true even of organizations that are strongly committed to democratic principles. For example, U.S. political parties—supposedly the backbone of the nation's representative government—have fallen prey to it. Run by an inner circle, they pass their leadership positions from one elite member to another. With their control of political machinery, access to free mailing, and even tax dollars to produce videos that can be sent by e-mail, a whopping 98 percent of U.S. Representatives who choose to run are reelected. For the U.S. Senate, that figure is 80 to 90 percent (*Statistical Abstract* 2002:Table 381).

The iron law of oligarchy is not without its limitations, of course. Members of the inner circle must remain attuned to the opinions of the other members, regardless of their personal feelings. If the oligarchy gets too far out of line, it runs the risk of a grassroots rebellion that would throw the elite out of office. This threat often softens the iron law of oligarchy by making the leadership responsive to the membership. In addition, because not all organizations become captive to an elite, this is a tendency, not an inevitability (Fisher 1994; Jarley et al. 2000).

Working for the Corporation

Since you are likely to end up working in a bureaucracy, let's look at how its characteristics may affect your career.

the iron law of oligarchy
Robert Michels' term for the tendency of formal organizations to be dominated by a small, self-perpetuating elite

Stereotypes and the "Hidden" Corporate Culture

Who gets ahead in large corporations? Although we might like to think that success comes from intelligence and hard work, many factors other than merit underlie salary increases and promotions. As sociologist Rosabeth Moss Kanter (1977, 1983) stresses, the

corporate culture contains "hidden values." These values create a self-fulfilling prophecy that affects people's careers.

It works like this: Corporate and department heads have stereotypes about what good workers are like and who will make good colleagues. Not surprisingly, people who match their stereotype have backgrounds similar to their own—and they even look like them. They give these workers better access to information, networking, and "fast track" positions. These people then perform better and become more committed to the organization—thus confirming the initial expectation or stereotype. In contrast, those judged to be outsiders are thought to have lesser abilities. Because of this, they are given fewer opportunities and challenges. Working at a level beneath their capacity, they come to think poorly of themselves, become less committed to the organization, and don't perform as well—thus confirming the stereotypes the bosses had of them. (You may want to review the discussion of stereotypes on page 107.)

The hidden values and stereotypes that created this self-fulfilling prophecy remain invisible. What people see are the promotions of workers with superior performances and greater commitment to the company, not higher and lower expectations and the open and closed opportunities that produced these attitudes and accomplishments.

You can see how these hidden values contribute to the iron law of oligarchy we just reviewed. Because of this self-fulfilling prophecy, the inner circle reproduces itself by favoring people who "look" like its own members, generally white and male. Women and minorities, who don't match the stereotype, are often "showcased"—placed in highly visible positions with little power in order to demonstrate how progressive the company is. There, however, they often hold "slow-track" positions, where accomplishments seldom come to the attention of top management.

Kanter found that the level people reach in an organization shapes their behavior, and even their attitudes. In general, the higher people go, the higher their morale. "This is a good company," they say to themselves. "They recognize my abilities." With their greater satisfaction, people in higher office also tend to be more helpful to subordinates and more flexible in their style of leadership. In contrast, people who don't get very far in the organization are frustrated and tend to have lower morale. They are also likely to be rigid supervisors and strong defenders of whatever privileges they have.

A significant part of bureaucracies lies below the surface. Because workers tend to see only the level that is readily visible, they usually ascribe differences in people's behaviors and attitudes to their personalities. Sociologists probe beneath the surface, however, to examine how corporate culture shapes people's attitudes, and, by extension, the quality of their work.

As corporations grapple with growing diversity, the hidden corporate culture and its stereotypes are likely to give way, but only slowly and grudgingly. In the following Thinking Critically section, we'll consider other aspects of diversity in the workplace.

corporate culture the orientations that characterize corporate work settings

THINKING Critically

Managing Diversity in the Workplace

Times have changed. The San Jose, California, electronic phone book lists *eight* times more *Nguyens* than *Joneses* (Pauken 2003). More than half of U.S. workers are minorities, immigrants, and women. Diversity in the workplace is much more than skin color. Diversity includes ethnicity, gender, age, religion, social class, and sexual orientation.

In the past, the idea was for people to join the "melting pot," to give up their distinctive traits and become like the dominant group. Today, with the successes of the civil rights and women's movements, people are more likely to prize their distinctive traits. Realizing that assimilation (being absorbed into the dominant culture) is probably not the wave of the future, three of four Fortune 500 companies have "diversity training." They hold lectures and workshops so employees can learn to work with colleagues of diverse cultures and racial-ethnic backgrounds.

Coors Brewery is a prime example of this change. Coors went into a financial tailspin after one of the Coors brothers gave a racially charged speech in the 1980s. Today, Coors offers diversity workshops, has sponsored a gay dance, and has paid for a corporate-wide mammography program. The company even had rabbis certify its suds as kosher. Its proud new slogan: "Coors cares" (Cloud 1998). Now, that's quite a change.

What Coors cares about, of course, is the bottom line. It's the same with the other corporations. Blatant racism and sexism once made no difference to profitability. Today, they do. To promote profitability, companies must promote diversity—or at least pretend to. The sincerity of corporate heads is not what's important; diversity in the workplace is.

Diversity training has the potential to build bridges, but it can backfire. Directors of these programs can be so incompetent that they create antagonisms and reinforce stereotypes. At a diversity training session at the U.S. Department of Transportation, for example, women groped men as the men ran by. Blacks and whites were encouraged to insult one another and to call one another names (Reibstein 1996). The intention may have been good (understanding the other through role reversal and getting hostilities "out in the open"), but the approach was moronic. Instead of healing, these behaviors wound and leave scars.

For Your CONSIDERATION . . .

Do you think that corporations and government agencies should offer diversity training? If so, how can we develop diversity training that fosters mutual respect? Can you suggest practical ways to develop workplaces that are not divided by gender and race-ethnicity?

Humanizing the Corporate Culture

Bureaucracies have transformed society by harnessing people's energies to reach specific goals and monitoring progress to achieve those goals. Weber (1946) predicted that because bureaucracies were so efficient and had the capacity to replace themselves, they would come to dominate social life. More than any prediction in sociology, this one has withstood the test of time (Rothschild and Whitt 1986; Perrow 1991).

Attempts to Humanize the Work Setting

Bureaucracies appear likely to remain our dominant form of social organization, and most of us, like it or not, are destined to spend our working lives in bureaucracies. Many people have become concerned about the negative side of bureaucracies, and would like to make them more humane. **Humanizing a work setting** means organizing work in such a way that it develops rather than impedes human potential. Humanized work settings offer access to opportunities on the basis of ability and contributions rather than personal characteristics. They distribute power more equally and have fewer rigid rules and more open decision making.

Can bureaucracies adapt to such a model? Contrary to some images, not all bureaucracies are unyielding, unwieldy monoliths. There is nothing in the nature of bureaucracies that makes them *inherently* insensitive to people's needs or that prevents them from fostering a corporate culture that maximizes human potential.

But what about the cost of such changes? The United States faces formidable economic competitors—Japan, western Europe, and now China. Humanizing corporate culture, however, does not require huge expense. Sociologist Rosabeth Moss Kanter (1983) compared forty-seven companies that were rigidly bureaucratic with competitors of the same size that were more flexible. Kanter found that the more flexible companies were more profitable—probably because their greater flexibility encouraged greater creativity, productivity, and company loyalty.

In light of such findings, many corporations have experimented with humanizing their work settings. As we look at them, keep in mind that they are not motivated by some

humanizing a work setting organizing a workplace in such a way that it develops rather than impedes human potential altruistic urge to make life better for workers, but by the same motivation as always—the bottom line. It is in management's self-interest to make their company more competitive.

Work Teams Work teams are used by one in five U.S. companies. It is a wonder that they are not more common. These self-managed teams, which encourage creative ideas and solutions to problems, instill a greater sense of loyalty to the company. Employees work harder, are absent less, and are more productive. Workers in these groups also react more quickly to threats posed by technological change and competitors' advances. No less a behemoth than IBM has found that people work more effectively in small groups than in a centralized command structure (Drucker 1992).

The concepts we discussed in the last chapter help to explain these results. In small work groups, people form primary relationships, and their identities become intertwined with their group. This reduces alienation, for rather than being lost in a bureaucratic maze, their individuality is appreciated and their contributions more readily recognized. The group's successes become the individual's successes—as do its failures. As a consequence of their expanded personal ties, workers make more of an effort. The results have been so good that, in what is known as "worker empowerment," some self-managed teams even replace bosses as the ones who control everything from schedules to hiring and firing (Lublin 1991).

Corporate Day Care Some companies help to humanize the work setting by offering on-site child care facilities. This eases the strain on parents. While they are at work, they can keep in touch with a baby or toddler, and observe the care their child is receiving. They are able to spend time with their children during breaks and lunch hours, and mothers can even nurse their children at the child care center.

Most U.S. companies, however, offer no child care at all. In the face of global competition, especially cheap labor in the Least Industrialized Nations, can U.S. firms afford child care? Surprisingly, providing child care can reduce labor costs. When the Union Bank of Monterey, California, decided to measure the cost of its day care center, they found that the annual turnover of employees who used the center was just one-fourth that of employees who did not use it. Users of the center were also absent from work less, and they took shorter maternity leaves. The net cost? After subtracting the center's costs from these savings, the bank saved more than $200,000 (Solomon 1988).

Providing back-up child care falls somewhere in between offering on-site child care and no child care at all. With this approach, parents use their own babysitter, but if the sitter can't make it, parents can use the center's back-up services, allowing them to get to work—and to work without worry (Narayan 1994).

Humanizing the work setting *means to make the work site a more pleasant place in order to better meet the needs of workers. You can see how on-site day care simplifies life for this father—both he and his son go to the same place at the same time. You can also see how this keeps the day care workers on their toes, for the parents are popping in and out throughout the day. Such services cost companies less than they appear to, for they reduce worker turnover.*

As the number of women in management increases, it is likely that more U.S. firms will offer child care services as part of a benefits package designed to attract and hold capable workers.

Employee Stock Ownership Plans If workers are shareholders, it is thought that their loyalty and productivity will increase. Consequently, many companies let their employees buy the firm's stock either at a discount or as part of their salary. About ten million U.S. workers own part of 11,000 companies. What are the results? Some studies show that these companies are more profitable than other firms (White 1991; Logue and Yates 2000). Other studies, in contrast, report that their profits are about the same, although their productivity may be higher (Blassi and Conte 1996). We need more definitive research on this matter.

If the employees own *all* the company stock, it should eliminate problems between workers and management. This should be obvious—after all, the workers and owners are the same people. But this is not the case. United Airline pilots, for example, who own the largest stake in their airline, staged a work slowdown during their 2001 contract negotiations, forcing the cancellation of thousands of flights. The machinists, who are also owners, followed suit. The machinists' union even threatened to strike. As passengers fled the airline, United racked up huge losses, and its stock plummeted (Zuckerman 2001). The irony is that the company's losses were the worker-owners' losses.

Profitability, not ownership, appears to be the key to reducing worker-management conflict. Unprofitable firms put more pressure on their employee-owners, while profitable companies are quicker to resolve problems.

Quality Circles Business practices are subject to fads, and something that is hot one day may be cold the next. Quality circles are an excellent example. *Quality circles* consist of workers and a manager or two who meet regularly to try to improve the quality of both working conditions and the company's products. Tens of thousands of U.S. firms adopted quality circles because they were used in Japan, and U.S. managers thought they had discovered the secret of Japanese success. At its height of popularity in 1983, 60 consultants specialized in quality circles. In just ten years, 55 of these consultants had switched to other business fads (Strang and Macy 2001), and today the term has been relegated to dictionaries.

The Conflict Perspective

Conflict theorists point out that it does not matter how work is structured. The basic relationship between workers and owners is always confrontational (Edwards 1979; Derber and Schwartz 1988). Workers and owners walk different paths in life, with owners exploiting workers to extract greater profits and workers trying to resist that exploitation. Because their basic interests are fundamentally opposed, critics argue, attempts by employers to humanize the work setting (or to manage diversity) are mere window dressing, efforts to conceal their fundamental goal of exploiting workers. It is just another attempt to manipulate workers into cooperating in their own exploitation.

Technology and the Control of Workers

The microchip has brought us higher quality manufactured goods and has reduced drudgery. Records are much easier to keep, and we can type just one letter and let the computer print it out and address it to ten individuals—or to ten thousand. Working on my computer, I can modify this sentence, this paragraph, or any section of this book with ease. The other side of the computer is its potential for abuse. Computers make it easier for governments to operate a police state by monitoring our every move. The Big Brother in Orwell's classic novel, *1984,* may turn out to be a computer.

Perhaps, as Orwell suggests, our destiny is to be oppressed by technology, to become servants to a master computer. We'll know shortly. In the meantime, we can see that the computer has allowed managers to increase surveillance without face-to-face supervision. For example, sitting in their office, managers know the exact number of keystrokes workers make each minute. They know precisely how long each worker takes for each telephone call. Workers who fall below the average are singled out for discipline. It doesn't matter that the slower workers may be more polite or more helpful, only that the computer reports slower performance.

Then there are the surveillance cameras mounted in the workplace, allowing bosses in remote locations to peer over the shoulders of workers. As sociologist Gary Marx (1995) says, we may be moving to a *maximum-security workplace.* Computers are able to measure motion, air currents, vibrations, odors, pressure changes, and voice stress. To prevent employees from punching in someone else's time card, a leading hotel uses a device to scan their workers' eyes. It compares these images with computerized data on file.

The maximum-security workplace seems an apt term, but with computers and surveillance cameras, the workplace may be just one aspect of a coming "maximum-security society" (Marx 1995). The Sociology and the New Technology box on the next page discusses how computers are being used to monitor workers who think that their actions have gone unnoticed.

U.S. and Japanese Corporations

How were the Japanese able to recover from the defeat of World War II—including the nuclear devastation of two of their major cities—to become a giant in today's global economy? Some analysts trace part of the answer to the way their corporations are organized.

How the Corporations Differ

One analyst, William Ouchi (1981), pinpointed five ways in which Japanese corporations differ from those of the United States. You will be surprised at how different they are. But are these differences in handling executives myth or reality?

Hiring and Promoting Teams In *Japan,* teamwork is central. College graduates who join a corporation are all paid about the same starting salary. They also get raises as a team. To learn about the company, they are rotated as a team through the various levels of the organization. They develop intense loyalty to one another and to their company, for the welfare of one represents the welfare of all. Only in later years are individuals singled out for recognition. When there is an opening in the firm, outsiders are not even considered.

In the *United States,* personal achievement is central. A worker is hired on the basis of what the firm thinks that individual can contribute. Employees try to outperform each other, and they strive for raises and promotions as signs of personal success. The individual's loyalty is to himself or herself, not to the company. Outsiders are considered for openings in the firm.

Lifetime Security In *Japan,* lifetime security is taken for granted. Employees can expect to work for the same firm for the rest of their lives. In return for not being laid off or fired, the firm expects them to be loyal to the company, to stick with it through good and bad times. Workers do not go job shopping, for their careers—and many aspects of their lives—are wrapped up in this one firm.

In the *United States,* lifetime security is unusual. It is limited primarily to teachers and some judges, who receive what is called *tenure.* Companies lay off workers in slow times. To remain competitive, they even reorganize and fire entire divisions. Workers, too, "look out for number one." They seek better pay and opportunities elsewhere. Job shopping and job hopping are common.

Almost Total Involvement In *Japan,* work is like a marriage: The worker and the company are committed to each other. The employee supports the company with loyalty and long hours at work, while the company supports its workers with lifetime secu-

sociology and the NEW technology

Cyberloafers and Cybersleuths: Surfing at Work

Few people work constantly at their jobs. Most of us take breaks and, at least once in a while, goof off. We meet fellow workers at the water cooler, and we talk in the hallway. Much of this interaction is good for the company, for it bonds us to fellow workers and ties us to our jobs.

Our personal lives may even cross over into our workday. Some of us make personal calls from the office. Bosses know that we need to check in with our child's preschool or make arrangements for a babysitter. They expect such calls. Some even wink as we make a date or nod as we arrange to have our car worked on. And most bosses make personal calls of their own from time to time. It's the abuse that bothers bosses, and it's not surprising that they fire anyone who talks on the phone all day for personal reasons.

The latest wrinkle at work is *cyberloafing,* using computers at work for personal purposes. Most workers fritter away some of their workday online (Greengard 2000). Many exchange jokes and send personal e-mail. Some trade stocks, download music, gamble, and even operate their own online businesses. Others read books, shop, and visit online red-light districts. Playing games is common, and some cyberloafers spend most of their "working" hours battling virtual enemies. One computer programmer became a national champion playing Starcraft at work.

Some workers defend their cyberloafing. They argue that since their work invades their homes—forcing them to work in the evening and on weekends—employers should accommodate their personal lives. Some Web sites protect cyberloafers: They feature a panic button in case the boss pokes her head in your office. Click the button and a phony spreadsheet pops onto your screen while typing sounds emerge from your speakers.

And then there is the *cybersleuth.* With specialized software, cybersleuths can examine everything employees read online, everything they write, and every Web site they visit (Nusbaum 2003). They can bring up every file they've deleted, even every word they've erased. What some workers don't know (and what some of us forget) is that "delete" does not mean erase. Our computers keep a hidden diary, even of what we've deleted. With a few clicks, the cybersleuth, like magic ink, makes our "deleted" information visible, exposing our hidden diary for anyone to read.

For Your CONSIDERATION

Do you think that cybersleuthing is an abuse of power? An invasion of privacy? Or do employers have a right to check on what their employees are doing with company computers on company time? Can you think of a less invasive solution to cyberloafing?

rity, health services, recreation, sports and social events, even a home mortgage. Involvement with the company does not stop when the workers leave the building. They join company study and exercise groups, and are likely to spend evenings with co-workers in bars and restaurants.

In the *United States,* work is a specific, often temporary contract. Workers are hired to do a certain job. When they have done that job, they have fulfilled their obligation to the company. Their after-work hours are their own. They go home to their private lives, which usually are separate from the firm.

Broad Training In *Japan,* workers move from one job to another within the company. Not only are they not stuck doing the same thing for years on end, but also they gain a broader picture of the corporation and how the specific jobs they are assigned fit into the bigger picture.

In the *United States,* workers are expected to perform one job, do it well, and then be promoted upward to a job with more responsibility. Their understanding of the company is largely tied to the particular corner they occupy, often making it difficult for them to see how their job fits into the overall picture.

Decision Making by Consensus In *Japan,* decision making is a lengthy process. Each person who will be affected by a decision is consulted. After lengthy deliberations, a consensus emerges, and everyone agrees on which suggestion is superior. This makes workers feel that they are an essential part of the organization, not simply cogs in a giant machine.

In the *United States,* the person in charge of the unit to be affected does as much consulting with others as he or she thinks is necessary and then makes the decision.

The Myth Versus Reality

Although these differences are *generally* true, if we peer beneath the surface we see that that a distorting myth has grown up around the Japanese corporation. Lifetime job security, for example, is elusive, and only about a third of Japanese workers find it. Most workers are also required by law to retire at age 60, whether they have the savings to support themselves or not (Clark and Ogawa 1997). Japanese corporations have begun to tie pay to productivity. They have found that paying the same wages to almost everyone in the same age group makes the company less competitive in the global market. Management by consensus is also a myth. This was not how decisions were made at Sony, one of Japan's most successful companies (Nathan 1999). Akio Morita, Sony's founder, was an entrepreneur from the same mold as Bill Gates. Morita didn't send memos up and down the line, as the myth would have you believe. Instead, he relied on his gut feeling about products. When he thought up the Walkman, Morita didn't discuss it until consensus emerged. Instead, he simply ordered it to be manufactured. And he made quick decisions. Over lunch, he decided to buy CBS Records. The cost was $2 billion. The Cultural Diversity box on the following page, with which we close this chapter, explores other aspects of the Japanese myth.

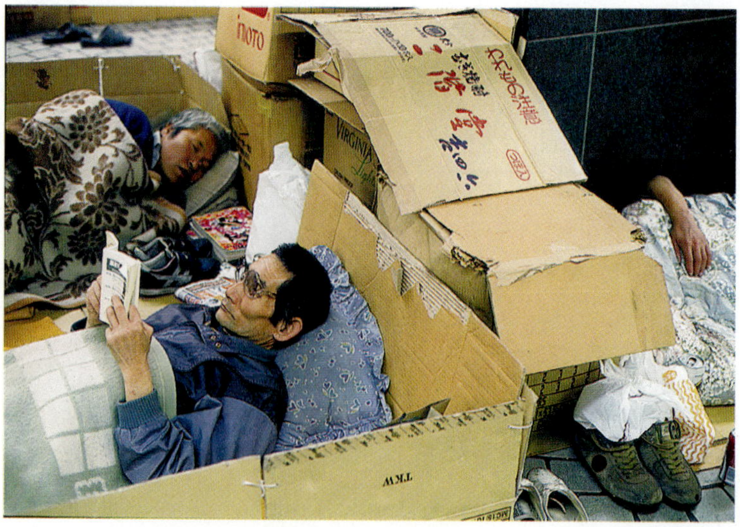

For a time, Americans stood in awe of the Japanese corporate model. The passage of time, however, has revealed serious flaws. Lifetime job security, for example, is a myth. These homeless men are living in the Shinjuko train station in Tokyo. Note how they have followed the Japanese custom of placing their shoes outside before entering their "home."

CULTURAL DIVERSITY

around the WORLD

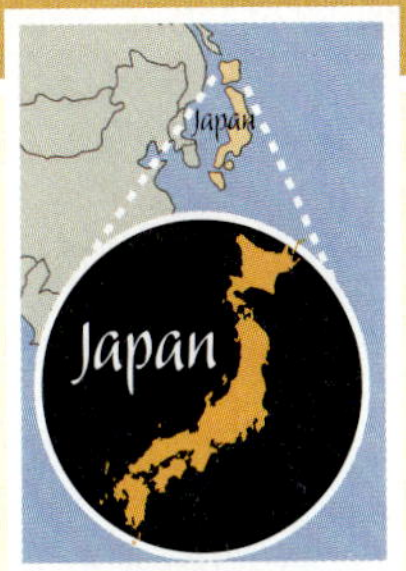

Japanese and U.S. Corporations in an Age of Greed

Do you know which of these statements is false?

The Japanese are more productive than Americans.

The living standard of Americans has fallen behind that of the Japanese.

Japanese workers enjoy lifetime job security.

The Japanese are paid less than Americans.

From what you just read, you know that the third one is false. So are the other three.

A while back, Japanese corporations seemed invincible. There was even talk that the United States had won World War II, but had lost the economic war. Impressed with Japan's success, many nations, including the United States, sent executives to Japan to study their companies. U.S. corporations then copied parts of that model.

Cracks in the facade soon appeared. Small at first, they grew, destroying some of Japan's major corporations. These companies had been built on personal relationships, on mutual obligations that transcend contracts. This had been a key to creating fierce loyalty, a corporate strength that turned out to be an Achilles heel. When Japan's economy went into a nose dive, companies refused to lay off workers. Layoffs were not part of their corporate culture. Costs mounted while profits disappeared, sinking companies in a sea of red ink.

In a surprise move, Japan studied U.S. corporations to see why they were more efficient. Flying in the face of their tradition, Japanese corporations began to lay off workers and to offer merit pay. Toyota and Honda began to give bonuses to managers who met their goals, a standard U.S. practice, but one that had been unthinkable in Japan (Schlesinger and Sapsford 1993; Reitman and Suris 1994; Shirouzu and Williams 1995; Kanabayashi 1996).

One of the biggest surprises was Ford's takeover of Mazda. With Mazda teetering on the edge of bankruptcy, its creditors decided that Ford knew more about building and marketing cars than Mazda and invited Ford to manage the company. In true U.S. fashion, Ford laid off workers and renegotiated contracts with suppliers. With its work force slashed from 46,000 to 36,000, Mazda again became profitable. The process isn't over: After Ford turned Mazda around, Renault took over Nissan Motor (Shirouzu 2000). A much leaner, meaner Japanese production machine is emerging.

The real bottom line is that we live in a global marketplace—of ideas as well as products. Companies from different countries learn from one another. Japanese corporations will learn how to compete more effectively in global capitalism's cutthroat production and marketing. It is not as apparent, however, that U.S. corporations will learn the cooperation that underlies the Japanese corporation—for it may not increase the bottom line.

SUMMARY and REVIEW

The Rationalization of Society

How did the rationalization of society come about?

The term **rationalization of society** refers to a transformation in people's thinking and behaviors—one that shifts the focus from following time-honored ways to being efficient in producing results. Max Weber, who developed this term, traced this change to Protestant theology, which he said brought about capitalism. Karl Marx attributed rationalization to capitalism itself. Pp. 176–178.

Formal Organizations and Bureaucracy

What are formal organizations?

Formal organizations are secondary groups designed to achieve specific objectives. Their dominant form is the

bureaucracy, which Weber said consists of a hierarchy, a division of labor, written rules and communications, and impersonality of positions—characteristics that make bureaucracies efficient and enduring. Pp. 178–181.

What dysfunctions are associated with bureaucracies?

The dysfunctions of bureaucracies include alienation, red tape, lack of communication between units, **goal displacement,** and incompetence (as seen in the **Peter principle**). In Weber's view, the impersonality of bureaucracies tends to produce **alienation** among workers—the feeling that no one cares about them and that they do not really fit in. Marx's view of alienation is somewhat different—workers do not identify with the product of their labor because they participate in only a small part of the production process. Pp. 182–185.

Voluntary Associations

What are the functions of voluntary associations?

Voluntary **associations** are groups made up of volunteers who organize on the basis of common interests. These associations further mutual interests, provide a sense of identity and purpose, help to govern and maintain order, mediate between the government and the individual, give training in organizational skills, help provide access to political power, and pave the way for social change. Pp. 185–186.

What is "the iron law of oligarchy"?

Sociologist Robert Michels noted that formal organizations have a tendency to become controlled by an inner circle that limits leadership to its own members. The dominance of a formal organization by an elite that keeps itself in power is called **the iron law of oligarchy.** Pp. 186–187.

Working for the Corporation

How does the corporate culture affect workers?

The term **corporate culture** refers to an organization's traditions, values, and unwritten norms. Much of corporate culture, such as its hidden values and stereotypes, is not readily visible. Often, a self-fulfilling prophecy is at work: People who match a corporation's hidden values tend to be put on tracks that enhance their chance of success, while those who do not match those values are set on a course that minimizes their performance. Pp. 187–189.

Humanizing the Corporate Culture

What does it mean to humanize the work setting?

Humanizing a work setting means to organize it in a way that develops rather than impedes human potential. Among the attempts to make bureaucracies more humane are work teams, corporate day care, and quality circles. Employee stock ownership plans give workers a greater stake in the outcomes of their work organizations, but they do not prevent worker-management conflict. Conflict theorists see attempts to humanize work as a way of manipulating workers. Pp. 189–193.

U.S. and Japanese Corporations

How do Japanese and U.S. corporations differ?

The Japanese corporate model contrasts sharply with the U.S. model in terms of hiring and promotion, lifetime security, interaction of workers after work, broad training of workers, and collective decision making. Much of this model is a myth, an idealization of reality, and does not reflect Japanese corporate life today. Pp. 193–195.

Where can I read more on this topic?

Suggested readings for this chapter are at the back of this book.

THINKING Critically ABOUT CHAPTER 7

1. How do bureaucracies affect your life?
2. Do you think the Peter principle is right? Why or why not?
3. Do you think U.S. corporations should have diversity training? If so, how should they go about it?

ADDITIONAL RESOURCES for This Chapter

www.ablongman.com/henslin7e

- *Content Select* Research Database for Sociology, with suggested key terms and annotated references
- Link to 2000 Census, with activities
- Flashcards of key terms and concepts
- Practice Tests
- Weblinks
- Interactive Maps

Chapter 8

Deviance and Social Control

Lois Maillou Jones, *Les Fetiches,* 1938

In just a few moments I was to meet my first Yanomamo, my first primitive man. What would it be like? . . . I looked up (from my canoe) and gasped when I saw a dozen burly, naked, filthy, hideous men staring at us down the shafts of their drawn arrows. Immense wads of green tobacco were stuck between their lower teeth and lips, making them look even more hideous, and strands of dark-green slime dripped or hung from their noses. We arrived at the village while the men were blowing a hallucinogenic drug up their noses. One of the side effects of the drug is a runny nose. The mucus is always saturated with the green powder, and the Indians usually let it run freely from their nostrils. . . . I just sat there holding my notebook, helpless and pathetic . . .

The whole situation was depressing, and I wondered why I ever decided to switch from civil engineering to anthropology in the first place. . . . (Soon) I was covered with red pigment, the result of a dozen or so complete examinations. . . . These examinations capped an otherwise grim day. The Indians would blow their noses into their hands, flick as much of the mucus off that would separate in a snap of the wrist, wipe the residue into their hair, and then carefully examine my face, arms, legs, hair, and the contents of my pockets. I said (in their language), "Your hands are dirty"; my comments were met by the Indians in the following way: they would "clean" their hands by spitting a quantity of slimy tobacco juice into them, rub them together, and then proceed with the examination.

They would "clean" their hands by spitting slimy tobacco juice into them

This is how Napoleon Chagnon describes his eye-opening introduction to the Yanomamo tribe of the rain forests of Brazil. His ensuing months of fieldwork continued to bring surprise after surprise, and often Chagnon (1977) could hardly believe his eyes—or his nose.

Chapter Outline

Where would we start if we were to list the deviant behaviors of these people? With the way they appear naked in public? Use hallucinogenic drugs? Let mucus hang from their noses? Or rubbing hands filled with mucus, spittle, and tobacco juice over a frightened stranger who doesn't dare to protest? Perhaps. But it isn't this simple, for as we shall see, deviance is relative.

What Is Deviance?

Sociologists use the term **deviance** to refer to any violation of norms, whether the infraction is as minor as driving over the speed limit, as serious as murder, or as humorous as Chagnon's encounter with the Yanomamo. This deceptively simple definition takes us to the heart of the sociological perspective on deviance, which sociologist Howard S. Becker (1966) described this way: *It is not the act itself, but the reactions to the act, that make something deviant.* Chagnon was frightened by what he saw, but to the Yanomamo those same behaviors represented normal, everyday life. What was deviant to Chagnon was *conformist* to the Yanomamo. From their viewpoint, you *should* check out strangers as they did, and nakedness is good, as are hallucinogenic drugs and letting mucus be "natural."

I took this photo on the outskirts of Hyderabad, India. Is this man deviant? If this were a U.S. street, he would be. But here? No houses have running water in his neighborhood, and the men, women, and children bathe at the neighborhood water pump. This man, then, would not be deviant in this culture. And yet, he is actually mugging for my camera, making the three bystanders laugh. Does this additional factor make this a scene of deviance?

Chagnon's abrupt introduction to the Yanomamo allows us to see the *relativity of deviance,* a major point made by symbolic interactionists. Because different groups have different norms, *what is deviant to some is not deviant to others.* (See the photo on this page.) This principle holds *within* a society as well as across cultures. Thus acts that are acceptable in one culture—or in one group within a society—may be considered deviant in another culture, or by another group within the same society. This idea is explored in the Cultural Diversity box on the next page.

This principle also applies to a specific form of deviance known as **crime,** the violation of rules that have been written into law. In the extreme, an act that is applauded by one group may be so despised by another group that it is punishable by death. Making a huge profit on a business deal is one example. Americans who do this are admired. Like Donald Trump, they may even write a book about it. In China, however, until recently this same act was a crime called *profiteering.* Anyone found guilty was hanged in a public square as a lesson to all.

Unlike the general public, sociologists use the term *deviance* nonjudgmentally, to refer to any act to which people respond negatively. When sociologists use this term, it does not mean they agree that an act is bad, just that people judge it negatively. To sociologists, then, all of us are deviants of one sort or another, for we all violate norms from time to time.

To be considered deviant, a person does not even have to *do* anything. Sociologist Erving Goffman (1963) used the term **stigma** to refer to characteristics that discredit people. These include violations of norms of ability (blindness, deafness, mental handicaps) and norms of appearance (a facial birthmark, obesity). They also include involuntary memberships, such as being a victim of AIDS or the brother of a rapist. The stigma can become a person's master status, defining him or her as deviant. Recall from Chapter 4 that a master status cuts across all other statuses that a person occupies.

How Norms Make Social Life Possible

No human group can exist without norms, for *norms make social life possible by making behavior predictable.* What would

CULTURAL DIVERSITY around the WORLD

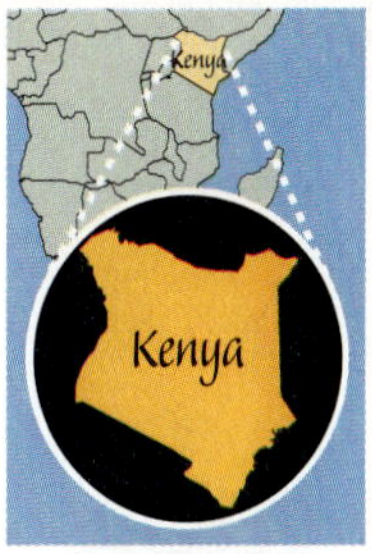

Human Sexuality in Cross-Cultural Perspective

Anthropologist Robert Edgerton (1976) reported how differently human groups react to similar behaviors. Of the many examples he cites, let's look at sexuality to illustrate how a group's definition of an act, not the act itself, determines whether or not it will be considered deviant.

Norms of sexual behavior vary so widely around the world that what is considered normal in one society may be considered deviant in another. The Pokot people of northwestern Kenya, for example, place high emphasis on sexual pleasure and expect that both a husband and his wife will reach orgasm. If a husband does not satisfy his wife, he is in trouble. Pokot men often engage in adulterous affairs, and should a husband's failure to satisfy his wife be attributed to adultery, his wife and her female friends will tie him up when he is asleep. The women will shout obscenities at him, beat him, and, as a final gesture of their utter contempt, slaughter and eat his favorite ox before releasing him. His hours of painful humiliation are intended to make him more dutiful concerning his wife's conjugal rights.

People can also become deviants for failing to understand that the group's ideal norms may not be its real norms. As with many groups, the Zapotec Indians of Mexico profess that sexual relations should take place exclusively between husband and wife. Yet the *only* person in one Zapotec community who had had no extramarital affairs was considered deviant. Evidently these people have an unspoken understanding that married couples will engage in affairs, but be discreet about them. When a wife learns that her husband is having an affair, she usually has one, too.

One Zapotec wife did not follow this covert norm. Instead, she would praise her own virtue to her husband—and then voice the familiar "headache" excuse. She also told other wives the names of the women their husbands were sleeping with. As a result, this virtuous woman was condemned by everyone in the village. Clearly, covert norms can conflict with formal norms—another illustration of the gap between ideal and real culture.

---

life be like if you could not predict what others would do? Imagine for a moment that you have gone to a store to purchase milk:

> Suppose the clerk says, "I won't sell you any milk. We're overstocked with soda, and I'm not going to sell anyone milk until our soda inventory is reduced."
>
> You don't like it, but you decide to buy a case of soda. At the checkout, the clerk says, "I hope you don't mind, but there's a $5 service charge on every fifteenth customer." You, of course, are the fifteenth.
>
> Just as you start to leave, another clerk stops you and says, "We're not working any more. We decided to have a party." Suddenly a CD player begins to blast, and everyone in the store begins to dance. "Oh, good, you've brought the soda," says a different clerk, who takes your package and passes sodas all around.

Life is not like this, of course. You can depend on grocery clerks to sell you milk. You can also depend on paying the same price as everyone else, and not being forced to attend a party in the store. Why can you depend on this? Because we are socialized to follow norms, to play the basic roles society assigns to us.

Without norms, we would have social chaos. Norms lay out the basic guidelines for how we should play our roles and interact with others. In short, norms bring about **social order,** a group's customary social arrangements. Our lives are based on these arrangements, which is why deviance often is perceived as so threatening: Deviance undermines predictability, the foundation of social life. Consequently, human groups develop a system of **social control,** formal and informal means of enforcing norms.

deviance the violation of rules or norms

crime the violation of norms written into law

stigma "blemishes" that discredit a person's claim to a "normal" identity

social order a group's usual and customary social arrangements, on which its members depend and on which they base their lives

social control a group's formal and informal means of enforcing its norms

Much of our interaction is based on background assumptions, *the unwritten, taken-for-granted "rules" that underlie our everyday lives. We don't have a "rule" that specifies, "Adults, don't shove a spike up your nose," yet we all know this rule exists. Shown here is Melvin Burkhart from Gibsonton, Florida, whose claim to fame is breaking this particular unspecified rule.*

Sanctions

As discussed in Chapter 2, people do not strictly enforce folkways, but they become very upset when someone breaks a more. Expressions of disapproval of deviance, called **negative sanctions,** range from frowns and gossip for breaking folkways to imprisonment and capital punishment for breaking mores. In general, the more seriously the group takes a norm, the harsher the penalty for violating it. In contrast, **positive sanctions**—from smiles to formal awards—are used to reward people for conforming to norms. Getting a raise is a positive sanction, being fired a negative sanction. Getting an *A* in intro to sociology is a positive sanction, getting an *F* a negative one.

Most negative sanctions are informal. You probably will merely stare when someone dresses in what you consider to be inappropriate clothing, or just gossip if a married person you know spends the night with someone other than his or her spouse. Whether you consider the breaking of a norm simply an amusing matter that warrants no severe sanctions or a serious infraction that does, however, depends on your perspective. If a woman appears at your college graduation ceremonies in a bikini, you may stare and laugh, but if this is *your* mother, you are likely to feel that different sanctions are appropriate. Similarly, if it is *your* father who spends the night with an 18-year-old college freshman, you are likely to do more than gossip.

Shaming and Degradation Ceremonies

Shaming is another sanction. Shaming is especially effective when members of a primary group use it. For this reason, it is often used to keep children in line. It is also effective in small communities, where the individual's reputation is at stake. As our society grew large and urban, it lost its sense of community, and shaming lost its effectiveness. Some are trying to bring shaming back. One Arizona sheriff, for example, makes the men in his jail wear pink underwear (Boxer 2001).

Shaming can be the centerpiece of public ritual, intended to mark the violator as a deviant and hold him or her up for all the world to see. In Nathaniel Hawthorne's *The Scarlet Letter,* town officials forced Hester Prynne to wear a scarlet A sewn on her dress. The A stood for *adulteress.* Wherever she went, Prynne had to wear this badge of shame, and the community expected her to wear it every day for the rest of her life.

Degradation ceremonies *are intended to humiliate norm violators and mark them as "not members" of the group. This photo was taken by the U.S. army in 1945 after U.S. troops liberated Cherbourg, France. Members of the French resistance shaved the heads of these women, who had "collaborated" (had sexual contact with) the occupying Nazis. They then marched the shamed women down the streets of the city, while the public shouted insults and spat on them.*

Sociologist Harold Garfinkel (1956) gave the name **degradation ceremony** to formal attempts to brand someone as an outsider. The individual is called to account before the group, witnesses denounce him or her, the offender is pronounced guilty, and steps are taken to strip the individual of his or her identity as a group member. In some court martials, officers who are found guilty stand at attention before their peers while the insignia of rank are ripped from their uniforms. This procedure dramatizes that the individual is no longer a member of the group. Although Hester Prynne was not banished from the group physically, she was banished morally; her degradation ceremony proclaimed her a *moral* outcast from the community. The scarlet A marked her as "not one" of them.

Although we don't use scarlet A's today, informal degradation ceremonies still occur. Consider what happened to Joseph Gray (Chivers 2001):

> Joseph Gray, a fifteen-year veteran of the New York City police force, was involved in a fatal accident. The *New York Times* and New York television stations reported that Gray had spent the afternoon drinking in a topless bar before plowing his car into a vehicle carrying a pregnant woman, her son, and her sister. All three died. Gray was accused of manslaughter and drunk driving (later convicted on both counts).
>
> The news media hammered this story to the public. Three weeks later, as Gray left police headquarters after resigning from his job, an angry crowd gathered around him. Gray hung his head in public disgrace as Victor Manuel Herrera, whose wife and son were killed in the crash, followed him, shouting, "You're a murderer!"

IN SUM

In sociology, the term *deviance* refers to all violations of social rules, regardless of their seriousness. The term is not a judgment about the behavior. Deviance is relative, for what is deviant in one group may be conformist in another. Consequently, we must consider deviance from *within* a group's own framework, for it is *their* meanings that underlie their behavior. The following Thinking Critically section focuses on this issue.

THINKING Critically

Is It Rape, Or Is It Marriage? A Study in Culture Clash

Surrounded by cornfields, Lincoln, Nebraska, is about as provincial as a state capital gets. Most of its residents have little experience with people from different ways of life. Their baptism into cultural diversity came as a shock.

The wedding was traditional and followed millennia-old Islamic practices (Annin and Hamilton 1996). A 39-year-old Iraqi refugee had arranged for his two eldest daughters, ages 13 and 14, to marry two fellow Iraqi refugees, ages 28 and 34. A Muslim cleric flew in from Ohio to perform the ceremony.

Nebraska went into shock. So did the refugees. What is marriage in Iraq is rape in Nebraska. The husbands were charged with rape, the girls' father with child abuse, and their mother with contributing to the delinquency of minors.

The event made front page news in Saudi Arabia, where people shook their heads in amazement at Americans. Nebraskans shook their heads in amazement, too.

In Fresno, California, a young Hmong refugee took a group of friends to a local college campus. There they picked up the girl he had selected to be his wife (Sherman 1988; Lacayo 1993). The young men brought her to his house, where he had sex with her. The young woman, however, was not in agreement with this plan.

The Hmong call this *zij poj niam*, marriage by capture. For them, this is an acceptable form of mate selection, one that mirrors Hmong courtship ideals of strong men and virtuous, resistant women. The Fresno District Attorney, however, called it kidnapping and rape.

negative sanction an expression of disapproval for breaking a norm, ranging from a mild, informal reaction such as a frown to a formal reaction such as a prison sentence or an execution

positive sanction a reward or positive reaction for following norms, ranging from a smile to a prize

degradation ceremony a term coined by Harold Garfinkel to describe an attempt to remake the self by stripping away an individual's self-identity and stamping a new identity in its place

For Your CONSIDERATION

To apply *symbolic interactionism* to these real-life dramas, ask how the perspectives of the people involved explain why they did what they did. To apply *functionalism*, ask how the U.S. laws that were violated are "functional" (that is, what are their benefits, and to whom?). To apply *conflict theory*, ask what groups are in conflict in these examples. (Do not focus on the individuals involved, but on the groups to which they belong.)

Understanding events in terms of different theoretical perspectives does not tell us what reaction is "right" when cultures clash. Remember that science can analyze causes and consequences, but it cannot determine what actions are right or wrong. Any sense of moral violation that you may feel about these cases comes from your values—which brings us, once again, to the initial issue—the relativity of deviance.

Competing Explanations of Deviance: Sociology, Sociobiology, and Psychology

Since norms are essential for society, why do people violate them? To better understand the reasons, it is useful to know how sociological explanations differ from biological and psychological ones.

Sociobiologists explain deviance by looking for answers *within* individuals. They assume that something in the individual's biological makeup leads him or her to become deviant. By contrast, *sociologists* look for answers in factors *outside* the individual. They assume that something in the environment influences people to become deviant.

Sociobiological explanations focus on **genetic predispositions** to such deviances as juvenile delinquency and crime (Lombroso 1911; Wilson and Herrnstein 1985; Hauser et al. 1995; Lalumiere and Quinsey 2000). Biological explanations include (but are not restricted to) the following three theories: (1) intelligence—low intelligence leads to crime; (2) the "XYY" theory—an extra Y chromosome in males leads to crime; and (3) body type—people with "squarish, muscular" bodies are more likely to commit **street crime**—acts such as mugging, rape, and burglary.

Unlike biology and psychology, which look within *individuals for explanations of human behavior, sociological explanations focus on* external *experiences, such as people's associations or group memberships. Sociological explanations of human behavior have become widely accepted and now permeate society, as illustrated by this teenager, whom I photographed as we were exiting the Staten Island Ferry in New York City.*

How have these theories held up? Not very well. Most people with these supposedly "causal" characteristics do not become criminals. Some criminals are very intelligent, and most people of low intelligence do not commit crimes. Most men who commit crimes have the normal "XY" chromosome combination, and most men with the "XYY" combination do not become criminals. In addition, no women have this combination of genes, so this explanation can't be applied to female criminals. Criminals also exhibit the full range of body types, and most people with "squarish, muscular" bodies do not become street criminals.

Psychologists, too, focus on abnormalities *within* the individual. They examine what are called **personality disorders.** Their supposition is that deviating individuals have deviating personalities (Heilbrun 1990; Krueger and Caspi 2000; Barnes 2001), and that subconscious motives drive people to deviance. No specific childhood experience, however, is invariably linked with deviance. For example, children who had "bad toilet training," "suffocating mothers," or "emotionally aloof fathers" may become embezzling bookkeepers—or good accountants. Just as students, teachers, and police officers represent a variety of bad—and good—childhood experiences, so do deviants. Similarly, people with "suppressed anger" can become freeway snipers or military heroes—or anything else. In short, there is no inevitable outcome of any childhood experience, and deviance is not associated with any particular personality.

In contrast with both sociobiologists and psychologists, *sociologists* search for factors *outside* the individual. They look for social influences that "recruit" people to break norms. To account for why people commit crimes, for example, sociologists examine such external influences as socialization, subcultural membership, and social class.

Social class, a concept discussed in depth in Chapter 10, refers to people's relative standing in terms of education, occupation, and especially income and wealth.

Knowing how relative deviance is, sociologists ask a crucial question: "Why should we expect to find something constant within people to account for a behavior that is conforming in one society and deviant in another?"

To see how sociologists explain deviance, let's contrast the three sociological perspectives—symbolic interactionism, functionalism, and conflict theory.

The Symbolic Interactionist Perspective

As we examine symbolic interactionism, it will become more evident why sociologists are not satisfied with explanations that are rooted in biology or personality. A basic principle of symbolic interactionism is this: We act according to how we interpret situations, not according to blind predisposition. Let's consider how our membership in groups influences our behaviors and our views of life.

Differential Association Theory

The Theory Contrary to theories built around biology and personality, sociologists stress that people *learn* deviance. Edwin Sutherland coined the term **differential association** to indicate that we learn to deviate or to conform to society's norms mostly by the *different* groups we *associate* with (Sutherland 1924, 1947; Sutherland et al. 1992). On the most obvious level, some boys and girls join Satan's Servants, while others join the Scouts. As sociologists have repeatedly demonstrated, what we learn influences us toward or away from deviance (Alarid et al. 2000; Erickson et al. 2000).

Sutherland's theory is actually more complicated than this, but he basically said that deviance is learned. This goes directly against the view that deviance is biological or is due to personality. Sutherland stressed that the different groups to which we belong (our "*differential* association") give us messages about conformity and deviance. We may receive mixed messages, but we end up with more of one than the other (an "excess of definitions," as Sutherland put it). The end result is an imbalance—attitudes that tilt us more in one direction than the other. Consequently, we conform or deviate.

Families Since our family is so important for teaching us attitudes, it probably is obvious to you that the family makes a big difference in whether we learn deviance or conformity. Researchers have confirmed this informal observation. They have found that delinquents are more likely to come from families that get in trouble with the law. They studied 25,000 delinquents who were locked up in high-security state institutions (Beck et al. 1988). They found that 25 percent had a father who had been in prison, 25 percent a brother or sister, 9 percent a mother, and 13 percent some other relative. Of all jail inmates across the United States, about half have a father, mother, brother, or sister who has served time (*Sourcebook of Criminal Justice Statistics* 1997:483). In short, families that are involved in crime tend to set their children on a lawbreaking path.

Friends, Neighborhoods, and Subcultures Most people don't know the term *differential association,* but they do know how it works. Most parents want to move out of "bad" neighborhoods because they know that if their kids have delinquent friends, they are likely to become delinquent, too. Sociological research supports this common observation (Miller 1958; Baskin and Sommers 1998; Sampson et al. 2001). Some neighborhoods even develop a subculture of violence. There, even a teasing remark can mean instant death. If the neighbors feel that a victim deserved killing, they refuse to testify because "he got what was coming to him" (Kubrin and Weitzer (2003).

Some neighborhoods even develop subcultures in which killing is considered an honorable act:

> Sociologist Ruth Horowitz (1983, 1987), who did participant observation in a lower-class Chicano neighborhood in Chicago, discovered how associating with

genetic predisposition inborn tendencies; in this context, to commit deviant acts

street crime crimes such as mugging, rape, and burglary

personality disorders the view that a personality disturbance of some sort causes an individual to violate social norms

differential association Edwin Sutherland's term to indicate that associating with some groups results in learning an "excess of definitions" of deviance, and, by extension, in a greater likelihood that one will become deviant

To experience a sense of belonging is a basic human need. Membership in groups, especially peer groups, is a primary way that people meet this need. Regardless of the orientation of the group—whether to conformity or to deviance—the process is the same. Shown here is a gang in Long Beach, California, "throwing signs." Gang membership helps provide a vital sense of identity.

> people who have a certain concept of "honor" propels young men to deviance. The formula is simple. "A real man has honor. An insult is a threat to one's honor. Therefore, not to stand up to someone is to be less than a real man."
>
> Now suppose you are a young man growing up in this neighborhood. You likely would do a fair amount of fighting, for you would interpret many things as attacks on your honor. You might even carry a knife or a gun, for words and fists wouldn't always be sufficient. Along with members of your group, you would define fighting, knifing, and shooting quite differently from the way most people do.

Members of the Mafia also intertwine ideas of manliness with violence. For them, *to kill is a measure of their manhood.* Not all killings are accorded the same respect, however, for "the more awesome and potent the victim, the more worthy and meritorious the killer" (Arlacchi 1980). Some killings are done to enforce norms. A member of the Mafia who gives information to the police, for example, has violated *omertá* (the Mafia's vow of secrecy). Such an offense can never be tolerated, for it threatens the very existence of the group. This example further illustrates just how relative deviance is. Although killing is deviant to mainstream society, for members of the Mafia, *not* to kill after certain rules are broken—such as when someone "squeals" to the cops—is the deviant act.

Prison or Freedom? An issue that comes up over and over again in sociology is whether we are prisoners of socialization. Symbolic interactionists stress that we are not mere pawns in the hands of others. We are not destined by our group memberships to think and act as our groups dictate. Rather, we *help produce our own orientations to life.* Our choice of membership (differential association), for example, helps to shape the self. For instance, one college student may join a feminist group that is trying to change the treatment of women in college; another may associate with a group of women who shoplift on weekends. Their choice of groups points them in two different directions. The one who associates with shoplifters may become even more oriented toward criminal activities, while the one who joins the feminist group may develop an even greater interest in producing social change.

Control Theory

Inside most of us, it seems, are strong desires to do things that would get us in trouble—inner drives, temptations, urges, hostilities, and so on. Yet most of us stifle these desires most of the time. Why?

The Theory Sociologist Walter Reckless (1973), who developed **control theory**, stresses that two control systems work against our motivations to deviate. Our *inner controls* include our internalized morality—conscience, religious principles, ideas of right and wrong. Inner controls also include fears of punishment, feelings of integrity, and the desire to be a "good" person (Hirschi 1969; Rogers 1977; Baron 2001). Our *outer controls* consist of people—such as family, friends, and the police—who influence us not to deviate.

The stronger our bonds are with society, the more effective our inner controls are (Hirschi 1969). Bonds are based on *attachments* (feeling affection and respect for people who conform to society's norms), *commitments* (having a stake in society that you don't want to risk, such as a respected place in your family, a good standing at college, a good job), *involvements* (putting time and energy into approved activities), and *beliefs* (believing that certain actions are morally wrong). This theory can be summarized as *self-control*, says sociologist Travis Hirschi. The key to learning high self-control is socialization, especially in childhood. Parents help their children develop self-control by supervising them and punishing their deviant acts (Gottfredson and Hirschi 1990).

control theory the idea that two control systems—inner controls and outer controls—work against our tendencies to deviate

Applying the Theory Consider drug use. Suppose that some friends have invited you to a night club. When you get there, you notice that everyone seems unusually happy, almost giddy would be a better word. They seem to be ecstatic in their animated conversations and dancing. Your friends tell you that almost everyone here has taken the drug Ecstasy, and they invite you to take some with them.

What do you do? Let's not explore the question of whether taking Ecstasy in this setting is a deviant or a conforming act. That is a separate issue. Instead, concentrate on the pushes and pulls you would feel. The pushes toward taking the drug: your friends, the setting, and your curiosity. Then there are the inner controls: the inner voices of your conscience and your parents, perhaps of your teachers, as well as your fears of arrest and of the dangers of illegal drugs. There are also the outer controls—perhaps the uniformed security guard looking in your direction.

So, what *did* you do? Which was stronger, your inner and outer controls or the pushes and pulls toward taking the drug? It is you who can best weigh these forces, for they differ with each of us.

Drugs and drug use are one of the more interesting areas of deviance. Drugs have social reputations. Sociologically, one of their more interesting aspects is that they go through fads. Shown here is one of those fads, a rave party in a Portland, Oregon, warehouse, where activities are based around the use of Ecstasy.

labeling theory the view, developed by symbolic interactionists, that the labels people are given affect their own and others' perceptions of them, thus channeling their behavior either into deviance or into conformity

techniques of neutralization ways of thinking or rationalizing that help people deflect (or neutralize) society's norms

Labeling Theory

Symbolic interactionists have developed **labeling theory**, which focuses on the significance of the labels (names, reputations) that we are given. Labels tend to become a part of our self-concept, which helps to set us on paths that either propel us into or divert us from deviance. Let's look at how people react to society's labels—from "whore" and "pervert" to "cheat" and "slob."

Rejecting Labels: How People Neutralize Deviance Most people resist the negative labels that others try to pin on them. Some are so successful that even though they persist in deviance, they still consider themselves conformists. For example, even though they beat up people and vandalize property, some delinquents consider themselves to be conforming members of society. How do they do it?

Sociologists Gresham Sykes and David Matza (1988) studied boys who were in this situation. They found that they used five **techniques of neutralization** to deflect society's norms.

Denial of Responsibility Some boys said, "I'm not responsible for what happened because . . . " and then were quite creative about the "becauses." They said that what happened was an "accident." Other boys saw themselves as "victims" of society. What else could you expect? They were like billiard balls shot around the pool table of life.

Denial of Injury Another favorite explanation of the boys was "What I did wasn't wrong because no one got hurt." They would define vandalism as "mischief," gang fights as a "private quarrel," and stealing cars as "borrowing." They might acknowledge that what they did was illegal, but claim that they were "just having a little fun."

Denial of a Victim Some boys thought of themselves as avengers. Vandalizing a teacher's car was done to get revenge for an unfair grade, while shoplifting was a way to even the score with "crooked" store owners. In short, even if the boys did accept responsibility and admit that someone had gotten hurt, they protected their self-concept by claiming that the people "deserved what they got."

Condemnation of the Condemners Another technique the boys used was to deny that others had the right to judge them. They might accuse people who pointed their fingers at them of being "a bunch of hypocrites": The police were "on the take," teachers had "pets," and parents cheated on their taxes. In short, they said, "Who are *they* to accuse *me* of something?"

The exhibit of deviants on The Jerry Springer Show *offers viewers a sense of being participants of hidden things. As Springer and others like him continue to parade deviants before the public, the shock and surprise wear off, making the deviance seem "more" normal. What is occurring is the* mainstreaming of deviance—*disapproved behaviors moving into the mainstream, or becoming more socially acceptable.*

Appeal to Higher Loyalties A final technique the boys used to justify antisocial activities was to consider loyalty to the gang more important than following the norms of society. They might say, "I had to help my friends. That's why I got in the fight." Not incidentally, the boy may have shot two members of a rival group, as well as a bystander!

IN SUM

These five techniques of neutralization have implications far beyond these boys, for it is not only delinquents who try to neutralize the norms of mainstream society. Look again at these five techniques—don't they sound familiar? (1)"I couldn't help myself"; (2)"Who really got hurt?"; (3)"Don't you think she deserved that, after what *she* did?"; (4)"Who are *you* to talk?"; and (5)"I had to help my friends—wouldn't you have done the same thing?" All of us attempt to neutralize the moral demands of society, for such neutralizations help us sleep at night.

Embracing Labels: The Example of Outlaw Bikers Although most of us resist attempts to label us as deviant, there are those who revel in a deviant identity. Some teenagers, for example, make certain by their clothing, choice of music, and hairstyles that no one misses their rejection of adult norms. Their status among fellow members of a subculture, within which they are almost obsessive conformists, is vastly more important than any status outside it.

One of the best examples of a group that embraces deviance is motorcycle gangs. Sociologist Mark Watson (1988) did participant observation with outlaw bikers. He rebuilt Harleys with them, hung around their bars and homes, and went on "runs" (trips) with them. He concluded that outlaw bikers see the world as "hostile, weak, and effeminate." They pride themselves on looking "dirty, mean, and generally undesirable" and take pleasure in provoking shocked reactions to their appearance. Holding the conventional world in contempt, they also pride themselves on getting into trouble, laughing at death, and treating women as lesser beings whose primary value is to provide them with services—especially sex. Outlaw bikers also regard themselves as losers, a factor that becomes woven into their unusual embrace of deviance.

The Power of Labels: The Saints and the Roughnecks We can see how powerful labeling is by referring back to the study of the "Saints" and the "Roughnecks" that was cited in Chapter 4 (pages 117, 120). As you recall, both groups of high school boys were "constantly occupied with truancy, drinking, wild parties, petty theft, and vandalism." Yet their teachers looked on the Saints as "headed for success" and the Roughnecks as "headed for trouble." By the time they finished high school, not one Saint had been arrested, while the Roughnecks had been in constant trouble with the police.

Why did the community see these boys so differently? Chambliss (1973/2003) concluded that this split vision was due to *social class.* As symbolic interactionists emphasize, social class vitally affects our perceptions and behavior. The Saints came from respectable, middle-class families, the Roughnecks from less respectable, working-class families. These backgrounds led teachers and the authorities to expect good behavior from the Saints but trouble from the Roughnecks. And, like the rest of us, teachers and police saw what they expected to see.

The boys' social class also affected their visibility. The Saints had automobiles, and they did their drinking and vandalism out of town. Without cars, the Roughnecks hung around their own street corners, where their boisterous behavior drew the attention of police and confirmed the ideas that the community already had of them.

The boys' social class also equipped them with distinct *styles of interaction.* When police or teachers questioned them, the Saints were apologetic. Their show of respect for authority elicited a positive reaction from teachers and police, allowing them to escape school and legal problems. The Roughnecks, said Chambliss, were "almost the polar opposite." When questioned, they were hostile. Even when they tried to assume a respectful attitude, everyone could see through it. Consequently, while teachers and police let the Saints off with warnings, they came down hard on the Roughnecks.

Although what happens in life is not determined by labels alone, the Saints and the Roughnecks did live up to the labels that the community gave them. As you recall, all but one of the Saints went on to college. One earned a doctorate, one became a lawyer, one a doctor, and the others business managers. In contrast, only two of the Roughnecks went to college. They earned athletic scholarships and became coaches. The other Roughnecks did not fare so well. Two of them dropped out of high school, later became involved in separate killings, and were sent to prison. One became a local bookie, and no one knows the whereabouts of the other.

How do labels work? Although the matter is complex, because it involves the self-concept and reactions that vary from one individual to another, we can note that labels open and close doors of opportunity. Unlike its use in sociology, in everyday usage, the label "deviant" is a way of judging people. This label can lock people out of conforming groups and push them into almost exclusive contact with people who have similar labels.

IN SUM

Symbolic interactionists examine how people's definitions of the situation underlie their deviation from or conformance to social norms. They focus on group membership (differential association), how people balance pressures to conform and to deviate (control theory), and the significance of the labels that are given to people (labeling theory).

The label *deviant* involves competing definitions and reactions to the same behavior. This central point of symbolic interactionism is explored in the Mass Media box on the next page.

The Functionalist Perspective

When we think of deviance, its dysfunctions are likely to come to mind. Functionalists, in contrast, are as likely to stress the functions of deviance as they are to emphasize its dysfunctions.

Can Deviance Really Be Functional for Society?

Most of us are upset by deviance, especially crime, and assume that society would be better off without it. The classic functionalist theorist Emile Durkheim (1893/1933, 1895/1964), however, came to a surprising conclusion. Deviance, he said, including crime, is functional for society, for it contributes to the social order. Its three main functions are:

1. *Deviance clarifies moral boundaries and affirms norms.* A group's ideas about how people should act and think mark its *moral boundaries.* Deviant acts challenge those boundaries. To call a deviant member into account is to say, in effect, "You broke an important rule, and we cannot tolerate that." To punish deviants affirms the group's norms and clarifies what it means to be a member of the group.
2. *Deviance promotes social unity.* To affirm the group's moral boundaries by punishing deviants fosters a "we" feeling among the group's members. In saying, "You can't get by with that," the group collectively affirms the rightness of its own ways.
3. *Deviance promotes social change.* Groups do not always agree on what to do with people who push beyond their accepted ways of doing things. Some group members may even approve of the rule-breaking behavior. Boundary violations that gain enough support become new, acceptable behaviors. Thus, deviance may force a group to rethink and redefine its moral boundaries, helping groups, and whole societies, to change their customary ways.

massMEDIA in Social Life

Pornography on the Internet: Freedom Versus Censorship

Pornography vividly illustrates one of the sociological principles discussed in this chapter—the relativity of deviance. It is not the act, but reactions to the act, that make something deviant. Consider one of today's major issues, pornography on the Internet.

Web surfers have a wide choice of pornography. Some sites are even indexed: heterosexual or gay, single or group, teenagers, cheerleaders, and older women who "still think they have it." Some offer only photographs, others video. Live sites are available, such as one that bills itself as "direct from Amsterdam." Sign on, and you can command your "model" to do anything your heart desires. Both male and female "models" are available, and the per minute charges are hefty.

What is the problem? Why can't people exchange nude photos electronically if they want to? Or watch others having sex online, if someone offers that service? Although some object to any kind of sex site, what disturbs many are the sites that feature bondage, torture, rape, bestiality (humans having sex with animals), and sex with children.

The Internet abounds with chat rooms, where people "meet" online to discuss some topic. No one is bothered by the chat rooms where the topic is Roman architecture or rap music or turtle racing. But those whose focus is how to torture women are another matter.

So are those that offer lessons on how to seduce grade school children—or that extol the delights of having sex with three-year-olds.

The state and federal governments have passed laws against child pornography, and the police seize computers and search them for illegal pictures. The courts levy fines and send some violators to prison. To exchange pictures of tortured and sexually abused women, however, remains legal.

For Your CONSIDERATION

Some feel that no matter how much they may disagree with a point of view or find it repugnant, communication about it (including photos) must be allowed. If we let the government censor these activities, it will censor other activities. Do you think it should be legal to exchange photos of women being sexually abused or tortured? Should it be legal to discuss ways to seduce children? If not, on what basis should they be banned? If we should make these activities illegal, then what other communications should we prohibit? On what basis?

In a 6-to-3 ruling, the U.S. Supreme Court upheld a federal law that requires public libraries that receive federal support to install pornography filters on all computers providing Internet access. Do you think that such filters violate the First Amendment's guarantee of free speech, as some of the Supreme Court justices declared? Or do you think that these filters are only a reasonable precaution to protect children?

Finally, can you disprove the central point of the symbolic interactionists—that an activity is deviant only because people decide that it is deviant? You may use examples cited in this box, or any others that you wish. You cannot invoke God or moral absolutes in your argument, however, as they are outside the field of sociology. As you will recall from the first chapter of this book, sociology cannot decide moral issues. This applies even to extreme cases.

Strain Theory: How Social Values Produce Deviance

Functionalists argue that crime is a *natural* part of society, not an aberration or some alien element in our midst. Indeed, they say, some mainstream values actually generate crime. To understand what they mean, consider what sociologists Richard Cloward and Lloyd Ohlin (1960) identified as the crucial problem of the industrialized world: the need to locate and train the most talented people of every generation—whether they were born into wealth or into poverty—so they can take over the key technical jobs of modern society. When children are born, no one knows which ones will have the ability to become dentists, nuclear physicists, or engineers. To get the most talented people to compete with one another, society tries to motivate *everyone* to strive for success. It does this by arousing discontent—making people feel dissatisfied with what they have so they will try to "better" themselves.

Most people, then, end up with strong desires to reach **cultural goals** such as wealth or high status, or to achieve whatever other objectives society holds out for them. However, not everyone has equal access to society's **institutionalized means,** the legitimate ways of

cultural goals the legitimate objectives held out to the members of a society

institutionalized means approved ways of reaching cultural goals

Social class divided people into distinct ways of life, so that even crimes differ by social class. Shown here is Martha Stewart, who, with her many products and television appearances, became a household name. In a previous edition of this text, Stewart was shown in happier times, as founder of her own company, Martha Stewart Onmimedia. Due to indictments for insider trading (trading stock on the basis of information gleaned from the "inside"), Stewart was forced to resign from the board of the New York Stock Exchange and the leadership of the company she founded. Obviously, the poor do not face the same opportunities for criminal acts as those Stewart is accused of.

achieving success. Some people find their path to education and good jobs blocked. These people experience *strain* or frustration, which may motivate them to take a deviant path.

This perspective, known as **strain theory,** was developed by sociologist Robert Merton (1956, 1968). People who experience strain, he said, are likely to feel *anomie,* a sense of normlessness. Because mainstream norms (such as work or education) don't seem to be getting them anywhere, they find it difficult to identify with these norms. They may even feel wronged by the system, and its rules may seem illegitimate (Anderson 1978).

Table 8.1 compares people's reactions to cultural goals and institutionalized means. The first reaction, which Merton said is the most common, is *conformity,* using socially acceptable means to try to reach cultural goals. In industrialized societies most people try to get good jobs, a good education, and so on. If well-paid jobs are unavailable, they take less desirable jobs. If they are denied access to Harvard or Stanford, they go to a state university. Others take night classes and go to vocational schools. In short, most people take the socially acceptable road.

Four Deviant Paths The remaining four responses, which are deviant, represent reactions to anomie. Let's look at each. *Innovators* are people who accept the goals of society but use illegitimate means to try to reach them. Drug dealers, for instance, accept the goal of achieving wealth, but they reject the legitimate avenues for doing so. Other examples are embezzlers, robbers, and con artists.

The second deviant path is taken by people who become discouraged and give up on achieving cultural goals. Yet they still cling to conventional rules of conduct. Merton called this response *ritualism.* Although ritualists have given up on excelling and advancing in position, they survive by following the rules of their job. Teachers whose idealism is shattered (who are said to suffer from "burnout"), for example, remain in the classroom, where they teach without enthusiasm. Their response is considered deviant because they cling to the job although they have abandoned the goal, which may have been to stimulate young minds or to make the world a better place.

People who choose the third deviant path, *retreatism,* reject both cultural goals and the institutionalized means of achieving them. Those who drop out of the pursuit of success by way of alcohol or drugs are retreatists. Such people even stop trying to appear as though they share the goals of their society.

The final type of deviant response is *rebellion.* Convinced that their society is corrupt, rebels, like retreatists, reject both society's goals and its institutionalized means. Unlike retreatists, however, they seek to replace existing goals with new ones. Revolutionaries are the most committed type of rebels.

Table 8.1 How People Match Their Goals to Their Means

Do They Feel the Strain That Leads to Anomie?	Mode of Adaptation	Cultural Goals	Institutionalized Means
No	Conformity	Accept	Accept
Yes	Innovation	Accept	Reject
	Ritualism	Reject	Accept
	Retreatism	Reject	Reject
	Rebellion	Reject/Replace	Reject/Replace

IN SUM

Strain theory underscores the sociological principle that deviants are the product of society. Due to their social location, some people experience greater pressures to deviate from society's norms, others much less. Simply put, if a society emphasizes the goal of material success, groups deprived of access to this goal will be more involved in property crime.

strain theory Robert Merton's term for the strain engendered when a society socializes large numbers of people to desire a cultural goal (such as success) but withholds from many the approved means to reach that goal; one adaptation to the strain is crime, the choice of an innovative means (one outside the approved system) to attain the cultural goal

illegitimate opportunity structure opportunities for crimes that are woven into the texture of life

Illegitimate Opportunity Structures: Social Class and Crime

One of the more interesting sociological findings in the study of deviance is that the social classes have distinct styles of crime. Let's see how unequal access to the institutionalized means to success helps to explain this.

Street Crime Functionalists point out that industrialized societies have no trouble socializing the poor into wanting to own things. Like others, the poor are bombarded with messages urging them to buy everything from designer jeans and DVD players to new cars. Television and movies show vivid images of middle-class people enjoying luxurious lives. These images reinforce the myth that all full-fledged Americans can afford society's many goods and services.

In contrast, the school system, the most common route to success, often fails the poor. The middle class runs it, and there the children of the poor confront a bewildering world, one at odds with their background. Their grammar and nonstandard language may be liberally sprinkled with what the middle class considers obscenities. Their ideas of punctuality and neatness, as well as their poor preparation in paper-and-pencil skills, are a mismatch with their new environment. Facing such barriers, the poor are more likely than their more privileged counterparts to drop out of school. Educational failure, in turn, closes the door on many legitimate avenues to financial success.

Not infrequently, however, a different door opens to the poor, one that sociologists Richard Cloward and Lloyd Ohlin (1960) called **illegitimate opportunity structures.** Woven into the texture of life in urban slums, for example, are robbery, burglary, drug dealing, prostitution, pimping, gambling, and other remunerative crimes, commonly

This 1871 wood engraving depicts children as they are being paid for their day's work in a London brickyard. In early capitalism, most street criminals came from the marginal working class, *as* did these children. *It is the same today.*

DOWN-TO-EARTH SOCIOLOGY

Islands in the Street: Urban Gangs in the United States

FOR MORE THAN TEN YEARS, SOCIOLOGIST Martín Sánchez Jankowski (1991) did participant observation of thirty-seven African American, Chicano, Dominican, Irish, Jamaican, and Puerto Rican gangs in Boston, Los Angeles, and New York City. The gangs earned money through gambling, arson, mugging, armed robbery, wholesaling drugs to pushers, and selling moonshine, guns, stolen car parts, and protection. Jankowski ate, slept, and sometimes fought with the gangs, but by mutual agreement he did not participate in drugs or other illegal activities. He was seriously injured twice during the study.

Contrary to stereotypes, Jankowski did not find that the motive for joining was to escape a broken home (there were as many members from intact as from broken homes) or to seek a substitute family (the same number of boys said they were close to their families as those that said they were not). Rather, the boys joined to gain access to money, to have recreation (including girls and drugs), to maintain anonymity in committing crimes, to get protection, and to help the community. This last reason may seem surprising, but in some neighborhoods gangs protect residents from outsiders. The boys also saw the gang as an alternative to the dead-end—and deadening—jobs held by their parents.

Neighborhood residents are ambivalent about gangs. On the one hand, they fear the violence. On the other hand, many adults once belonged to gangs, the gangs often provide better protection than the police, and gang members are the children of people who live in the neighborhood.

Particular gangs will come and go, but gangs will likely always remain part of the city. As functionalists point out, gangs fulfill needs of poor youth who live on the margins of society.

For Your CONSIDERATION

What are the functions that gangs fulfill (the needs they meet)? Suppose that you have been hired as an urban planner by the City of Los Angeles. How could you arrange to meet the needs that gangs fulfill in ways that minimize violence and encourage youth to follow mainstream norms?

called "hustles" (Liebow 1967/1997; Bourgois 1994; Anderson 1978, 1990, 2001). For many of the poor, the "hustler" is a role model—glamorous, in control, the image of "easy money," one of the few people in the area who comes close to attaining the cultural goal of success. For such reasons, then, these activities attract disproportionate numbers of the poor. As discussed in the Down-to-Earth Sociology box above, gangs are one way that the illegitimate opportunity structure beckons disadvantaged youth.

White-Collar Crime The more privileged social classes are not crime-free, of course, but for them different illegitimate opportunities beckon. They find *other forms* of crime to be functional. Physicians, for example, never hold up cabbies, but many do cheat Medicare. And you've heard about bookkeepers who embezzle from their employers. In other words, rather than mugging, pimping, and burglary, the more privileged encounter "opportunities" for evading income tax, bribing public officials, embezzling, and so on. Sociologist Edwin Sutherland (1949) coined the term **white-collar crime** to refer to crimes that people of respectable and high social status commit in the course of their occupations.

More than 200 people died from accidents involving Firestone tires. Shown here is Victor Rodriguez, whose 10-year-old son was killed when a Firestone tire on their Ford Explorer blew out in San Antonio, Texas. The fault may be Firestone's, for manufacturing defective tires; or it may lie with Ford, for equipping the vehicles with tires that were too small; or it may be a combination of the two. If so, this would be a case of white collar crime that kills. White-collar murderers are unlikely to ever spend a single day in jail for their crimes.

A special form of white-collar crime is **corporate crime,** crimes committed by executives in order to benefit their corporation. For example, in order to increase corporate profits, Sears executives systematically defrauded the poor of over $100 million. Their victims were so poor they had filed for bankruptcy. To avoid a criminal trial, Sears pleaded guilty. This frightened the parent companies of Macy's and Bloomingdale's, which had similar deceptive practices, and they settled with their debtors out of court (McCormick 1999). One of the most notorious corporate crimes was the decision by Firestone executives to let faulty tires remain on U.S. vehicles—even though they were recalling them in Saudi Arabia and Venezuela. As illustrated by the photo on this page, the consequences were devastating. These tires cost the lives of about 200 Americans (White et al. 2001).

Seldom is corporate crime taken seriously, even when it results in death. Consider this: Under federal law, causing the death of a worker by willfully violating safety rules is a misdemeanor punishable by up to six months in prison. Yet to harass a wild burro on federal lands is punishable by a year in prison (Barstow and Bergman 2003).

At $400 billion a year (Zeune 2001), "crime in the suites" actually costs more than "crime in the streets." This refers only to dollar costs. No one has yet figured out a way to compare, for example, the suffering experienced by a rape victim with the pain felt by an elderly couple who have lost their life savings to white-collar fraud.

The greatest concern of Americans, however, is street crime. They fear the violent stranger who will change their life forever. As the Social Map below shows, the chances of such an encounter depend on where you live. From this map, you can also see that some regions are safer than others. In general, the northern states are the safest, the southern states the most dangerous.

white-collar crime Edwin Sutherland's term for crimes committed by people of respectable and high social status in the course of their occupations; for example, bribery of public officials, securities violations, embezzlement, false advertising, and price fixing

corporate crime crimes committed by executives in order to benefit their corporation

Gender and Crime A major change in the nature of crime is the growing number of female offenders. As Table 8.2 on the next page shows, women are committing a larger proportion of almost all crimes—from car theft to burglary. The exceptions are murder and illegal gambling. As more women have joined the professions and corporate world, they, too, have been enticed by its illegitimate opportunities, and their involvement in embezzlement, fraud, and forgery has also increased.

Figure 8.1 Some States are Safer: Violent Crime in the United States

Violent crimes are murder, rape, robbery, and aggravated assault. The U.S. average is 506 per 100,000 people, but the chances of becoming a victim of these crimes varies widely among the states. One's chance of becoming a victim are *seven* times higher in some states. With a rate of 81, North Dakota is the safest state, while Florida, with a rate ten times higher, is the most dangerous state. Washington, D.C., a district, not a state, is even higher; its rate of 1,508 is three times the national average and over 18 times North Dakota's rate.

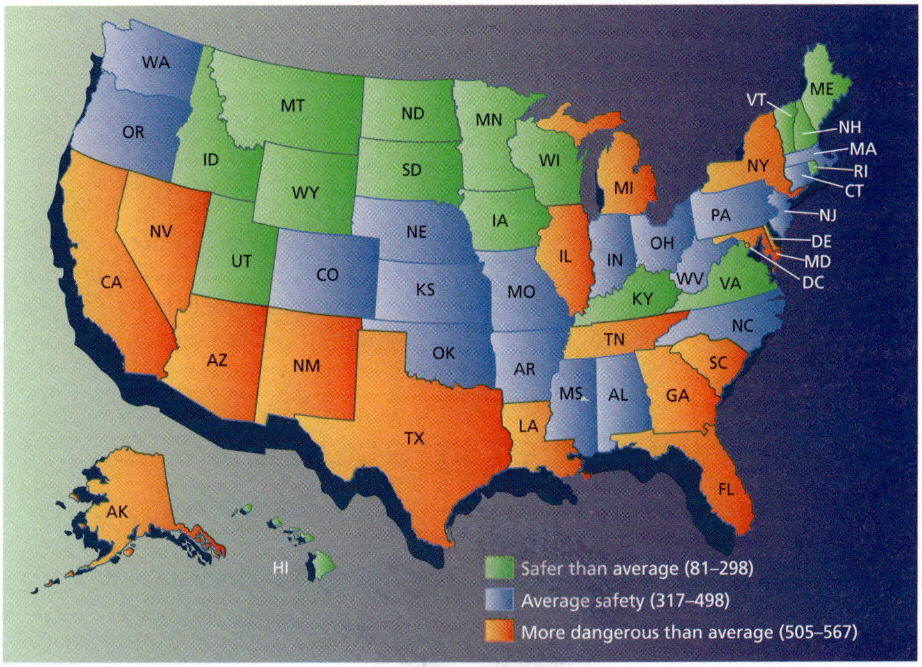

Source: By the author. Based on *Statistical Abstract* 2002:Table 285.

Table 8.2 Women and Crime: What a Difference 10 Years Makes

Of all those arrested, what percentage are women?

Crime	1990	2000[1]	Change
Car Theft	10.0%	15.7%	+57%
Aggravated Assault	13.3%	20.1%	+51%
Burglary	8.8%	13.3%	+51%
Possessing Stolen Property	12.0%	17.4%	+45%
Drunken Driving	12.8%	16.4%	+28%
Robbery	8.3%	10.1%	+22%
Embezzlement	41.2%	50.0%	+21%
Arson	13.0%	15.0%	+15%
Forgery and Counterfeiting	34.6%	39.0%	+13%
Larceny/Theft	32.0%	35.9%	+12%
Illegal Weapons	7.4%	8.0%	+8%
Murder	10.4%	10.3%	-1%
Illegal Gambling	13.8%	11.1%	-2%
OVERALL	18.4%	22.2%	+21%

[1]Latest year available

Source: Statistical Abstract 1992:Table 302; 2002:Table 299.

IN SUM

Functionalists conclude that much street crime is the consequence of socializing everyone into equating success with material possessions, while denying many in the lower social classes the means to attain that success. People from higher social classes encounter different opportunity structures to commit crimes.

The Conflict Perspective

Class, Crime, and the Criminal Justice System

Two leading U.S. aerospace companies, Hughes Electronics and Boeing Satellite Systems, were accused of illegally exporting missile technology to China. The technology allowed China to improve its delivery system for nuclear weapons, placing the United States at risk. The two companies pleaded guilty and paid fines. No executives went to jail. (Gerth 2003)

Contrast this corporate crime that places you in danger with stories you often read in newspapers about young men who are sentenced to several years in prison for stealing cars. How can a legal system that is supposed to provide "justice for all" be so inconsistent? According to conflict theorists, this question is central to the analysis of crime and the **criminal justice system**—the police, courts, and prisons that deal with people who are accused of having committed crimes. Let's see if conflict theorists have an answer.

Power and Inequality

Conflict theorists regard power and social inequality as the main characteristics of society. They stress that a group at the top, a power elite, controls the criminal justice system. This group makes certain that laws are passed that will protect its power. Other norms, such as those that govern informal behavior (chewing with a closed mouth, appearing in public with combed hair, and so on), may come from other sources, but they simply are not as important. Such norms influence our everyday behavior, but they do not determine who gets sent to prison and who does not.

Conflict theorists see the most fundamental division in capitalist society as that between the few who own the means of production and the many who do not, those who sell their labor and the privileged few who buy it. Those who buy labor, and thereby control workers, make up the **capitalist class;** those who sell their labor form the **working class.** Toward the most depressed end of the working class is the **marginal working class:** people with few skills who are subject to layoffs and whose jobs are low paying, part time, or seasonal. This class is marked by unemployment and poverty. From its ranks come most of the prison inmates in the United States. Desperate, these people commit street crimes, and because their crimes threaten the social order that keeps the elite in power, they are severely punished.

The Law as an Instrument of Oppression

According to conflict theorists, the idea that the law operates impartially and administers a code that is shared by all is a cultural myth promoted by the capitalist class. These theorists see the law as an instrument of oppression, a tool designed to maintain the powerful in their privileged position (Spitzer 1975; Chambliss 2000; Sheldon 2001). Because the working class has the potential to rebel and overthrow the current social order, when its members get out of line, they are arrested, tried, and imprisoned.

For this reason, the criminal justice system does not focus on the owners of corporations and the harm they do to the masses through unsafe products, wanton pollution, and price manipulations. Instead, it directs its energies against violations by the working class (Platt 1978; Chambliss 2000; Reiman 2001). The violations of the capitalist class cannot be totally ignored, however, for if they became too outrageous or oppressive, the working class might rise up and revolt. To prevent this, occasionally a flagrant violation by a member of the capitalist class is prosecuted. The publicity given to the case helps to stabilize the social system by providing visible evidence of the "fairness" of the criminal justice system.

Usually, however, the powerful are able to bypass the courts altogether, appearing instead before an agency that has no power to imprison (such as the Federal Trade Commission). These agencies are directed by people from wealthy backgrounds who sympathize with the intricacies of the corporate world. This means that most cases of illegal sales of stocks and bonds, price fixing, collusion, and so on are handled by "gentlemen overseeing gentlemen." Is it surprising, then, that the typical sanction is a token fine? In contrast, courts that do have the power to imprison handle the property crimes of the masses. Burglary, armed robbery, and theft committed by the poor threaten not only the sanctity of private property but, ultimately, the positions of the powerful.

When groups that have been denied access to power gain that access, we can expect to see changes in the legal system. This is precisely what is occurring now. Racial-ethnic minorities and homosexuals, for example, have more political power today than ever before. In line with conflict theory, a new category called *hate crime* has been formulated. We analyze this change in a different context on pages 222–223.

criminal justice system the system of police, courts, and prisons set up to deal with people who are accused of having committed a crime

capitalist class the wealthy who own the means of production and buy the labor of the working class

working class those people who sell their labor to the capitalist class

marginal working class the most desperate members of the working class, who have few skills, little job security, and are often unemployed

IN SUM

From the perspective of conflict theory, the small penalties imposed for crimes committed by the powerful are typical of a legal system that has been designed by the elite (capitalists) to control workers, to keep themselves in power, and, ultimately, to stabilize the social order. From this perspective, law enforcement is a cultural device through which the capitalist class carries out self-protective and repressive policies.

Reactions to Deviance

Whether it involves cheating on a sociology quiz or holding up a liquor store, any violation of norms invites reaction. Let's look at some of these reactions.

Figure 8.2 How Much Is Enough? The Explosion in the Number of U.S. Prisoners

To better understand how remarkable this change is, compare the prison growth with the growth of the U.S. population. Between 1970 and 2000, the U.S. population grew 38 percent, while the U.S. prison population grew *16 times* as fast (605 percent). If the U.S. prison population had grown at the same rate as the U.S. population, there would be about 270,000 prisoners, one fifth of the actual number. (Or if the U.S. population had increased at the same rate as that of U.S. prisoners, the U.S. population would be 1,423,000,000—more than the population of China.)

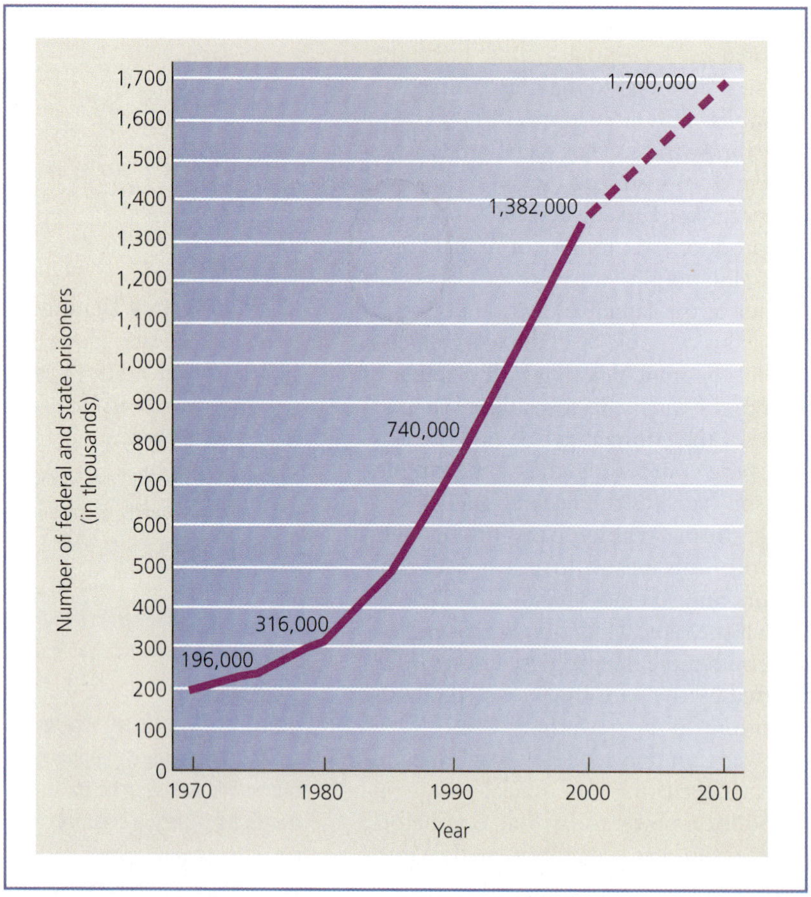

Source: By the author. Based on *Statistical Abstract* 1995:Table 349, 2002:Tables 1, 326. The broken line is the author's estimate.

Street Crime and Prisons

Today, we don't make people wear scarlet letters, but we do remove them from society and make them wear prison uniforms. And we still use degradation ceremonies—in this case, a public trial and the public pronouncement that someone is "unfit" to live among "decent, law-abiding people" for some specified period of time. Figure 8.2 illustrates the remarkable growth in the U.S. prison population. This huge number does *not* include jail inmates. If we add these, the total comes to over two million. The United States not only has more prisoners than any other nation, but a larger percentage of its population in prison as well ("Coming to . . . " 2001).

Who are these prisoners? To see how they compare with the U.S. population, look at Table 8.3. Several things may strike you. The prisoners tend to be much younger than the general U.S. population, and almost all of them are men. Then there is that remarkable statistic. Although African Americans make up just 11.5 percent of the U.S. population, almost half of all prisoners are African Americans. On any given day, about 1 of 8 African American men ages 20 to 34 are in jail or prison (Butterfield 2003). Finally, you might note how marriage—one of the major techniques society has of "anchoring" us—provides protection from prison.

As noted, social class funnels some people into the criminal justice system and others away from it. This becomes especially apparent if you look at the education totals on this table. You can see how people's chances of ending up in prison increase if they do not complete high school—and how unlikely it is for college graduates to have this unwelcome destination in life.

Table 8.3 Inmates in U.S. State Prisons

Characteristics	Percentage of Prisoners with These Characteristics	Percentage of U.S. Population with These Characteristics
Age		
17 and younger	0.5%	25.9%
18–24	19.3%	10.2%
25–34	38.1%	16.6%
35–44	29.4%	15.7%
45–54	9.8%	10.7%
55–64	2.2%	8.2%
65 and older	0.7%	12.7%
Race-Ethnicity		
African American	46.5%	12.2%
White	33.3%	68.2%
Latino	17.0%	13.5%
Others	3.2%	6.1%
Sex		
Male	93.7%	49.0%
Female	6.3%	51.0%
Marital Status		
Never Married	57.1%	23.5%
Divorced	18.6%	9.9%
Married	16.6%	59.7%
Education		
Less than high school	43.1%	15.8%
High school graduate	43.6%	33.1%
Some college	10.7%	25.4%
College graduate (BA or higher)	2.7%	25.6%

Sources: Sourcebook of Criminal Justice Statistics 2001:Table 6..29; *Statistical Abstract* 1998:Tables 16, 61, 262; 2002:Table 210; Figure 12.5 of this text.

For the past 15 years or so, the United States has followed a "get tough" policy. "Three strikes and you're out" laws (a mandatory sentence, sometimes life imprisonment, upon conviction for a third felony) have become common. While few of us would feel sympathy if a man convicted of a third rape or a third murder were sent to prison for life, as discussed in the following Thinking Critically section, these laws have had unanticipated consequences.

THINKING Critically

"Three Strikes and You're Out!" Unintended Consequences of Well-Intended Laws

In the 1980s, violent crime soared. Americans were fearful, and they demanded that their lawmakers do something. Politicians heard the message, and they responded by passing the "three strikes" law. Anyone convicted of a third felony receives an automatic mandatory sentence. Judges are not allowed to consider the circumstances. Some mandatory sentences carry life imprisonment.

In their haste to appease the public, the politicians did not limit these laws to *violent* crimes. And they did not consider that some minor crimes are considered felonies. As the functionalists would say, this has led to unanticipated consequences.

recidivism rate the proportion of released convicts who are rearrested

Here are some actual cases:

- In Los Angeles, a man was sentenced to 25 years for stealing a pizza (Cloud 1998).
- In New York City, a man who was about to be sentenced for selling crack said to the judge, "I'm only 19. This is terrible." He then hurled himself out of a courtroom window, plunging to his death sixteen stories below (Cloud 1998).
- In Los Angeles, a man who passed himself off as Tiger Woods to go on a $17,000 shopping spree was sentenced to 200 years in prison (Reuters 2001).
- In California, a man who stole 9 videotapes from K-Mart was sentenced to 50 years in prison without parole. He appealed to the U.S. Supreme Court, which upheld his sentence (Greenhouse 2003).

For Your CONSIDERATION

Apply the symbolic interactionist, functionalist, and conflict perspectives to mandatory sentencing. For *symbolic interactionism*, what do these laws represent to the public? How does your answer differ depending on what part of "the public" you are referring to? For *functionalism*, who benefits from these laws? What are some of their dysfunctions? For the *conflict perspective*, what groups are in conflict? Who has the power to enforce their will on others?

The Decline in Crime

As you saw in Figure 8.2, the courts have put more and more people in prison. In addition, legislators passed the three-strikes laws and reduced early releases. As these changes occurred, the crime rate dropped sharply. This drop has led to a controversy in sociology. Some sociologists conclude that the changes we discussed led to the drop in crime (Conklin 2003). Other sociologists, however, say that the reduction came about for different reasons, such as higher employment and a drop in drug use (Reiman 2001; Rosenfeld 2002). This matter is not yet settled, but both imprisonment and the economy seem to be important factors.

Recidivism

A major problem with prisons is that they fail to teach their clients to stay away from crime. Our **recidivism rate**—the percentage of former prisoners who are rearrested—is extremely high. If you were to survey the average prison, you would find that three out of every four prisoners have been in prison before. When prisoners convicted of violent crimes are released, in just three years half (52 percent) are back in prison (*Sourcebook of Criminal Justice* Statistics 2001:Table 6.44). Figure 8.3 shows recidivism by type of crime. It is safe to conclude that if—and this is a big if—the purpose of prisons is to teach people that crime doesn't pay, they are a colossal failure.

Charles Manson, shown here at a parole hearing, was arrested in 1969 and charged with ordering several murders, including that of Sharon Tate, an actress who was eight months pregnant. Manson was sentenced to death, but escaped this penalty when the death penalty was ruled unconstitutional as then administered. Manson is the poster boy for many people who, despairing of rehabilitation, call for retribution, deterrence, and incapacitation.

Figure 8.3 Recidivism of U.S. Prisoners

The individuals were not necessarily rearrested for the same crime for which they had originally been in prison.

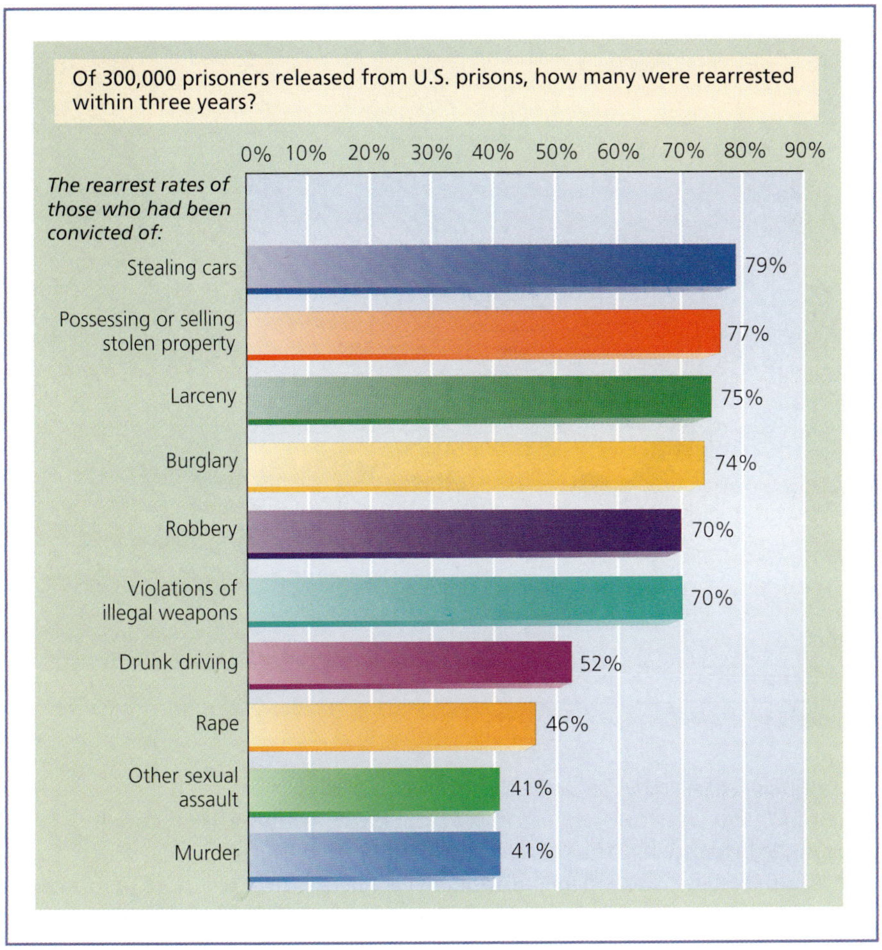

Source: Langan and Levin 2002.

capital punishment the death penalty

The Death Penalty and Bias

Capital punishment, the death penalty, is the most extreme and controversial measure the state takes. Apart from the moral and philosophical controversy surrounding the death penalty, people object to its biases. The death penalty is not administered evenly. Consider geography: Where people commit murder greatly affects their chances of being put to death. The Social Map on the next page shows this unevenness.

The death penalty also shows social class bias. As you know from news reports on murder and sentencing, it is rare for a rich person to be sentenced to death. Although the government does not collect statistics on social class and the death penalty, this common observation is borne out by the average education of the prisoners on death row. *Most* prisoners on death row (52%) have not finished high school (*Sourcebook of Criminal Justice Statistics* 2001:Table 6.77).

Table 8.4 shows gender and the death penalty. It is also almost unheard of for a woman to be sentenced to death. Although women commit 10.3 percent of the murders, they make up only 1.5 percent of death row inmates. It is likely that this statistic reflects the bias of more "tender feelings" toward women, but it could reflect the relative brutality of their murders.

The bias that once put an end to the death penalty, though, was flagrant. Donald Partington (1965), a Virginia lawyer, saw this bias first hand, so he decided to document it. He analyzed the executions for rape and attempted rape in Virginia between 1908 and 1963. He found that 2,798 men had been convicted for these crimes—56 percent whites

Table 8.4 Women and Men on Death Row

Women	1.5%
Men	98.5%

Source: Sourcebook of Criminal Justice Statistics 2001:Table 6.77.

Figure 8.4 Executions in the United States

Executions since 1977, when the death penalty was reinstated.

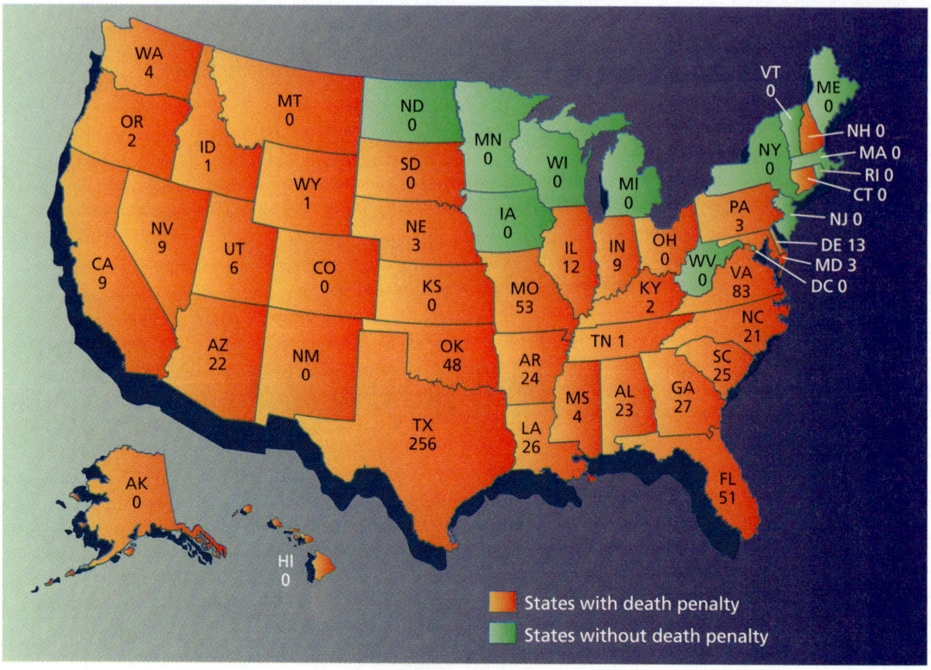

Source: By the author. Based on *Statistical Abstract* 2002:Table 331.

Table 8.5 The Racial-Ethnic Makeup of the 3,701 Prisoners on Death Row

46% Whites
43% African Americans
9% Latinos
1% Native Americans
1% Asian Americans

Source: Sourcebook of Criminal Justice Statistics 2001:Table 6.76.

and 44 percent blacks. For rape, 41 men had been executed. For attempted rape, 13 had been executed. *All those executed were black.* Not one of the whites was executed.

After listening to evidence like this, in 1972 the Supreme Court ruled in *Furman* v. *Georgia* that the death penalty was unconstitutionally applied. The execution of prisoners stopped—but not for long. The states wrote new laws, and in 1977 they again began to execute prisoners. Since then, 64 percent of those put to death have been white and 36 percent African American (*Statistical Abstract* 2002:Table 330). (Latinos are evidently counted as whites in this statistic.) Table 8.5 shows the race-ethnicity of the prisoners now on death row.

Legal Change

Did you know that it is a crime in Iran for women to wear makeup? A crime in Illinois to sell meat or alcohol before noon on Sundays? Or illegal in Wells, Maine, to advertise on tombstones? As stressed in this chapter, deviance, including the form called *crime,* is relative. It varies from one society to another, and from group to group within a society. It also varies from one time period to another, as opinions change or as different groups gain access to power.

Let's consider legal change.

THINKING Critically

Changing Views: Making Hate a Crime

Because crime consists of whatever acts authorities decide to assign that label, new crimes emerge from time to time. A prime example is juvenile delinquency, which Illinois lawmakers designated a separate type of crime in 1899. Juveniles committed crimes prior to this time, of course, but these youths were not considered to be a separate type of lawbreaker. They were just young people who committed crimes, and they were treated the same as adults who committed the same crime. New technology also leads to new crimes. Motor vehicle theft, a separate crime in the United States, obviously did not exist before the automobile was invented

In the 1980s, another new crime was born when state governments developed the classification **hate crime.** This is a crime that is motivated by *bias* (dislike, hatred) against someone's race-ethnicity, religion, sexual orientation, disability, or national origin. Prior to this, of course, people attacked others or destroyed their property out of these same motivations, but in those cases the motivation was not the issue. If someone injured or killed another person because of that person's race-ethnicity, religion, sexual orientation, national origin, or disability, he or she was charged with assault or murder. Today, motivation has become a central issue, and hate crimes carry more severe sentences than do crimes that involve the same act but without hatred as the motive. Table 8.6 summarizes the victims of hate crimes.

We can be certain that the "evolution" of crime is not yet complete. As society changes and as different groups gain access to power, we can expect the definitions of crime to change accordingly.

For Your CONSIDERATION

Why should we have a separate classification called hate crime? Why aren't the crimes of assault, robbery, and murder adequate? As one analyst (Sullivan 1999) said: "Was the brutal murder of gay college student Matthew Shepard [a hate crime] in Laramie, Wyoming, in 1998 worse than the abduction, rape, and murder an an eight-year-old Laramie girl [not a hate crime] by a pedophile that same year?" How do you think your social location (race-ethnicity, gender, social class, sexual orientation, or physical ability) affects your opinion?

Table 8.6 Hate Crimes

Directed Against	Number of Victims
Race-Ethnicity	
African Americans	3,609
Whites	1,125
Latinos	777
Asian Americans	347
Native Americans	66
Religion	
Jews	1,285
Catholics	64
Protestants	62
Muslims	37*
Sexual Orientation	
Male Homosexual	1,070
Female Homosexual	244
Homosexuals (general)	233
Heterosexuals	28
Disabilities	
Physical	20
Mental	18

*The latest year available is 2000; attacks against Muslims increased after 9/11.
Source: Statistical Abstract 2002:Table 292.

The Trouble with Official Statistics

Both the findings of symbolic interactionists (that stereotypes operate when authorities deal with groups such as the Saints and the Roughnecks) and the conclusion of conflict theorists (that the criminal justice system exists to serve the ruling elite) demonstrate the need for caution in interpreting official statistics. Crime statistics do

This graffiti was sprayed on the campus of Washington High School in Fremont, California. The suspects in this incident are also suspects in the vandalism of a Fremont synagogue.

hate crime crimes to which more severe penalties are attached because they are motivated by hatred (dislike, animosity) of someone's race-ethnicity, religion, sexual orientation, disability, or national origin

police discretion the practice of the police, in the normal course of their duties, to either arrest or ticket someone for an offense or to overlook the matter

medicalization of deviance to make deviance a medical matter, a symptom of some underlying illness that needs to be treated by physicians

not have an objective, independent existence. They are not like oranges that you pick out in a grocery store. Rather, crime statistics are a human creation. They are produced within a specific social and political context for some particular purpose. Change that context, and the statistics would change.

Consider this: According to official statistics, working-class boys are clearly more delinquent than middle-class boys. Yet, as we have seen, *who actually gets arrested for what* is affected by social class, a point that has far-reaching implications. As symbolic interactionists point out, the police follow a symbolic system as they enforce the law. Their ideas of "typical criminals" and "typical good citizens," for example, permeate their work. The more a suspect matches their mental "criminal profile," the more likely that person is to be arrested. **Police discretion,** the decision of whether to arrest someone or even to ignore a matter, is a routine part of police work. Consequently, official crime statistics always reflect these and many other biases.

IN SUM

Reactions to deviants vary from such mild sanctions as frowns and stares to such severe responses as imprisonment and death. Some sanctions are formal—court hearings, for example—although most are informal, as when friends refuse to talk to each other. One sanction is to label someone a deviant, which can have powerful consequences for the person's life, especially if the label closes off conforming activities and opens deviant ones. The degradation ceremony, in which someone is publicly labeled "not one of us," is a powerful sanction. So is imprisonment. Official statistics must be viewed with caution, for they reflect biases.

People whose behaviors violate norms often are called mentally ill. "Why else would they do such things?" is a common response to deviant behaviors that we don't understand. Mental illness is a label that contains the assumption that there is something wrong "within" people that "causes" their disapproved behavior. The surprise with this man, who changed his legal name to "Scary Guy," is that he speaks at schools across the country, where he promotes acceptance, awareness, love, and understanding.

The Medicalization of Deviance: Mental Illness

Another way in which society deals with deviance is to "medicalize" it. Let's look at what this entails.

Neither Mental Nor Illness?

To *medicalize* something is to make it a medical matter, to classify it as a form of illness that properly belongs in the care of physicians. For the past hundred years or so, especially since the time of Sigmund Freud (1856–1939), the Viennese physician who founded psychoanalysis, there has been a growing tendency toward the **medicalization of deviance.** In this view, deviance, including crime, is a sign of mental sickness. Rape, murder, stealing, cheating, and so on are external symptoms of internal disorders, consequences of a confused or tortured mind.

Thomas Szasz (1986, 1996, 1998), a renegade in his profession of psychiatry, argues that *mental illnesses are neither mental nor illness. They are simply problem behaviors.* Some forms of so-called mental illnesses have organic causes; that is, they are *physical* illnesses that result in unusual perceptions or behavior. Some depression, for example, is caused by a chemical imbalance in the brain, which can be treated by drugs. The depression, however, may show itself as crying, long-term sadness, and lack of interest in family, work, school, or one's appearance. When a person becomes deviant in ways that disturb others, *and* when these others cannot find a satisfying explanation for why the person is "like that," they conclude that a "sickness in the head" is causing the inappropriate, unacceptable behavior. For example, a new mental illness is "shopaholism" (compulsive shopping) (Chaker 2003).

All of us have troubles. Some of us face a constant barrage of problems as we go through life. Most of us continue the struggle, encouraged by relatives and friends, motivated by job, family responsibilities, and life goals. Even when the odds seem hopeless, we carry on, not perfectly, but as best we can.

Some people, however, fail to cope well with the challenges of daily life. Overwhelmed, they become depressed, uncooperative, or hostile. Some strike out at others, while some, in Merton's terms, become retreatists and withdraw into their apartments or homes, not wanting to come out. These are *behaviors, not mental illnesses,* stresses Szasz. They may be inappropriate coping devices, but they are coping devices, nevertheless, not mental illnesses. Thus, Szasz concludes that "mental illness" is a myth foisted on a naive public by a medical profession that uses pseudoscientific jargon in order to expand its area of control and force nonconforming people to accept society's definitions of "normal."

Szasz's extreme claim forces us to look anew at the forms of deviance that we usually refer to as mental illness. To explain behavior that people find bizarre, he directs our attention not to causes hidden deep within the "subconscious," but, instead, to how people learn such behaviors. To ask, "What is the origin of inappropriate or bizarre behavior?" then becomes similar to asking, "Why do some women steal?" "Why do some men rape?" "Why do some teenagers cuss their parents and stalk out of the room, slamming the door?" *The answers depend on those people's particular experiences in life, not on an illness in their mind.* In short, some sociologists find Szasz's renegade analysis refreshing because it indicates that *social experiences,* not some illness of the mind, underlie bizarre behaviors—as well as deviance in general.

The Homeless Mentally Ill

> Jamie was sitting on a low wall surrounding the landscaped courtyard of an exclusive restaurant. She appeared unaware of the stares that were elicited by her layers of mismatched clothing, her dirty face, and the shopping cart that overflowed with her meager possessions.
>
> Every once in a while Jamie would pause, concentrate, and point to the street, slowly moving her finger horizontally. I asked her what she was doing.
>
> "I'm directing traffic," she replied. "I control where the cars go. Look, that one turned right there," she said, now withdrawing her finger.
>
> "Really?" I said.
>
> After a while she confided that her cart talked to her.
>
> "Really?" I said again.
>
> "Yes," she replied. "You can hear it, too." At that, she pushed the shopping cart a bit.
>
> "Did you hear that?" she asked.
>
> When I shook my head, she demonstrated again. Then it hit me. She was referring to the squeaking wheels!
>
> I nodded.
>
> When I left, Jamie was pointing to the sky, for, as she told me, she also controlled the flight of airplanes.

This Los Angeles police officer is giving a ticket to a homeless woman for sleeping on the sidewalk. The supposed reason—as ridiculous as it sounds—that the L.A. police chief gave for cracking down on the homeless is because these "lawbreakers will graduate to bigger crimes if left unchecked." The real reason is that the slum area where this woman lives is slated for redevelopment for the upper middle class.

To most of us, Jamie's behavior and thinking are bizarre. They simply do not match any reality we know. Could you or I become like Jamie?

Suppose for a bitter moment that you are homeless and have to live on the streets. You have no money, no place to sleep, no bathroom. You do not know *if* you are going to eat, much less where. You have no friends or anyone you can trust, and you live in constant fear of rape and other violence. Do you think this might be enough to drive you over the edge?

Consider just the problems involved in not having a place to bathe. (Shelters are often so dangerous that many homeless prefer to sleep in public settings.) At first, you try to wash in the rest rooms of gas stations, bars, the bus station, or a shopping center. But you are dirty, and people stare when you enter and call the management when they see you wash your feet in the sink. You are thrown out and told in no uncertain terms never to come back. So you get dirtier and dirtier. Eventually you come to think of being dirty as a fact of life. Soon, maybe, you don't even care. The stares no longer bother you, at least not as much.

No one will talk to you, and you withdraw more and more into yourself. You begin to build a fantasy life. You talk openly to yourself. People stare, but so what? They stare anyway. Besides, they are no longer important to you.

Jamie might be mentally ill. Some organic problem, such as a chemical imbalance in her brain, might underlie her behavior. But perhaps not. How long would it take us to exhibit bizarre behaviors if we were homeless—and hopeless? The point is that *just being on the streets can cause mental illness*—or whatever we want to label socially inappropriate behaviors that we find difficult to classify. *Homelessness and mental illness are reciprocal:* Just as "mental illness" can cause homelessness, so the trials of being homeless, of living on cold, hostile streets, can lead to unusual and unacceptable thinking and behaviors.

The Need for a More Humane Approach

As Durkheim (1895/1964:68) pointed out, deviance is inevitable—even in a group of saints.

> Imagine a society of saints, a perfect cloister of exemplary individuals. Crimes, properly so called, will there be unknown; but faults which appear [invisible] to the layman will create there the same scandal that the ordinary offense does in ordinary [society].

With deviance inevitable, one measure of a society is how it treats its deviants. Our prisons certainly don't say much good about U.S. society. Filled with the poor, they are warehouses of the unwanted. They reflect patterns of broad discrimination in our larger society. White-collar criminals continue to get by with a slap on the wrist while street criminals are punished severely. Some deviants, who fail to meet current standards of admission to either prison or mental hospital, take refuge in shelters and cardboard boxes in city streets. Although no one has *the* answer, it does not take much reflection to see that there are more humane approaches than these.

Because deviance is inevitable, the larger issues are to find ways to protect people from deviant behaviors that are harmful to themselves or others, to tolerate those that are not harmful, and to develop systems of fairer treatment for deviants. In the absence of fundamental changes that would bring about a truly equitable social system, most efforts are, unfortunately, Band-Aid solutions. What we need is a more humane social system, one that would prevent the social inequalities that are the focus of the next four chapters.

SUMMARY and REVIEW

What Is Deviance?

From a sociological perspective, **deviance** (the violation of norms) is relative. What people consider deviant varies from one culture to another and from group to group within the same society. As symbolic interactionists stress, it is not the act itself, but the reactions to the act, that make something deviant. All groups develop systems of **social control** to punish **deviants**, those who violate its norms. Pp. 200–203.

How do sociological and individualistic explanations of deviance differ?

To explain why people deviate, sociobiologists and psychologists look for reasons *within* the individual, such as **genetic predispositions** or **personality disorders.** Sociologists, in contrast, look for explanations *outside* the individual, in social relations. Pp. 204–205.

The Symbolic Interactionist Perspective

How do symbolic interactionists explain deviance?

Symbolic interactionists have developed several theories to explain deviance such as **crime** (the violation of norms that are written into law). According to **differential association theory,** people learn to deviate by associating with others. According to **control theory,** each of us is propelled toward deviance, but most of us conform because of an effective system of inner and outer controls. People who have less effective controls deviate. Pp. 205–207.

Labeling theory focuses on how labels (names, reputations) help to funnel people into or away from deviance. People who commit deviant acts often use **techniques of neutralization** to continue to think of themselves as conformists. Pp. 208–210.

The Functionalist Perspective

How do functionalists explain deviance?

Functionalists point out that deviance, including criminal acts, is functional for society. Functions include affirming norms and promoting social unity and social change. According to **strain theory,** societies socialize their members into desiring **cultural goals.** Many people are unable to achieve these goals in socially acceptable ways—that is, by **institutionalized means.** *Deviants,* then, are people who either give up on the goals or use deviant means to attain them. Merton identified five types of responses to cultural goals and institutionalized means: conformity, innovation, ritualism, retreatism, and rebellion. **Illegitimate opportunity theory** stresses that some people have easier access to illegal means of achieving goals. Pp. 210–216.

The Conflict Perspective

How do conflict theorists explain deviance?

Conflict theorists take the position that the group in power (the **capitalist class**) imposes its definitions of deviance on other groups (the **working class** and the **marginal working class**). From the conflict perspective, the law is an instrument of oppression used to maintain the power and privilege of the few over the many. The marginal working class has little income, is desperate, and commits highly visible property crimes. The ruling class directs the **criminal justice system,** using it to punish the crimes of the poor while diverting its own criminal activities away from this punitive system. Pp. 216–218.

Reactions to Deviance

What are common reactions to deviance in the United States?

In following a "get-tough" policy, the United States has imprisoned millions of people. African Americans and Latinos comprise a disproportionate percentage of U.S. prisoners. The death penalty shows biases by geography, social class, race–ethnicity, and gender. In line with conflict theory, as groups gain political power, their views are reflected in the criminal code. **Hate crime** legislation was considered in this context. Pp. 218–223.

Are official statistics on crime reliable?

The conclusions of both symbolic interactionists (that the police operate with a large measure of discretion) and conflict theorists (that the legal system is controlled by the capitalist class) indicate that we must be cautious when using crime statistics. Pp. 223–224.

What is the medicalization of deviance?

The medical profession has attempted to **medicalize** many forms of **deviance,** claiming that they represent mental illnesses. Thomas Szasz disagrees, asserting that they are problem behaviors, not mental illnesses. Research on homeless people illustrates how problems in living can lead to bizarre behavior and thinking. Pp. 224–226.

What is a more humane approach?

Deviance is inevitable, so the larger issues are to find ways to protect people from deviance that harms themselves and others, to tolerate deviance that is not harmful, and to develop systems of fairer treatment for deviants. P. 226.

Where can I read more on this topic?

Suggested readings for this chapter are at the back of this book

THINKING Critically ABOUT CHAPTER 8

1. Select some deviance with which you are personally familiar. (It does not have to be your own—it can be something that someone you know did.) Which theoretical perspective best explains what happened?
2. As explained in the text, deviance can be mild. Recall some instance in which you broke a social rule in dress, etiquette, or speech. What was the reaction? Why do you think people reacted like that?
3. What do you think should be done about the U.S. crime problem? What sociological theories support your view?

ADDITIONAL RESOURCES for This Chapter

www.ablongman.com/henslin7e

- *Content Select* Research Database for Sociology, with suggested key terms and annotated references
- Link to 2000 Census, with activities
- Flashcards of key terms and concepts
- Practice Tests
- Weblinks
- Interactive Maps

Chapter 9

Global Stratification

Francesco Clemente, Hunger, 1980

et's contrast three "average" families from around the world:

For Getu Mulleta, 33, and his wife, Zenebu, 28, of rural Ethiopia, life is a constant struggle to keep themselves and their seven children from starving. They live in a 320-square-foot manure-plastered hut with no electricity, gas, or running water. They have a radio, but the battery is dead. Surviving on $130 a year, the family farms teff, a cereal grain.

The Mulletas' poverty is not due to a lack of hard work. Getu works about 80 hours a week, while Zenebu puts in even more hours. "Housework" for Zenebu includes fetching water, making fuel pellets out of cow dung for the open fire over which she cooks the family's food, and cleaning animal stables. Like other Ethiopian women, she eats after the men.

In Ethiopia, the average male can expect to live to 48, the average female to 50.

The Mulletas' most valuable possession is their oxen. Their wishes for the future: more animals, better seed, and a second set of clothing.

• • •

In Guadalajara, Mexico, Ambrosio and Carmen Castillo Balderas and their five children, ages 2 to 10, live in a four-room house. They also have a walled courtyard, where the family spends a good deal of time. They even have a washing machine, which is hooked up to a garden hose that runs to a public water main several hundred yards away. Like most Mexicans, they do not have a telephone, nor do they own a car.

hey own a recent
proud purchase
hat makes them the
envy of their neighbors, a television

Unlike many, however, they own a refrigerator, a stereo, and a recent proud purchase that makes them the envy of their neighbors, a television.

Ambrosio, 29, works full time as a wholesale distributor of produce. He also does welding on the side. The family's total annual income is $3,600. They spend 57 percent of their income on food. Carmen works about 60 hours a week taking care of their children and keeping their home spotless. The

Chapter Outline

neatness of their home stands in stark contrast to the neighborhood, which is lined with littered dirt roads. As in many other Mexican neighborhoods, public utilities and roadwork do not keep pace with people's needs.

The average life expectancy for males in Mexico is 70. For females, it is 76.

The Castillo Balderas' most valued possessions are their refrigerator and television. Their wish for the future: a truck.

• • •

Springfield, Illinois, is home to the Kellys—Rick, 36, Patti, 34, Julie, 10, and Michael, 7. The Kellys live in a four-bedroom, 2½ bath, 2,200-square-foot, carpeted ranch-style house, with a fireplace, central heating and air conditioning, a basement, and a two-car garage. Their home is equipped with a refrigerator, washing machine, clothes dryer, dishwasher, garbage disposal, vacuum cleaner, food processor, microwave, and toaster. They also own three radios, a CD player, five telephones (two cellular), three color televisions, a camcorder, VCR, DVD player, tape recorder, Gameboy, Nintendo, and a computer, printer, and scanner, not to mention two blow dryers, an answering machine, a blender, an electric can opener, and two electric toothbrushes. This doesn't count the stereo-radio-CD players in their pickup truck and car.

Rick works 40 hours a week as a cable splicer for a telephone company. Patti teaches school part time. Together they make $50,890, plus benefits. The Kellys can choose from among dozens of superstocked supermarkets. They spend $4,237 for food they eat at home, and another $2,875 eating out, a total of 14 percent of their annual income.

In the United States, the average life expectancy is 74 for males, 80 for females.

On the Kellys' wish list are a new SUV, an 80-gigabyte computer, a plasma screen TV, a digital video camera, a boat, a motor home, an ATV, and, oh yes, further down the road, a vacation cabin.

Sources: Menzel 1994; Population Reference Bureau 1995; *Statistical Abstract* 2002:Tables 91, 651, 657, 922.

"Worlds Apart" could be the title for these photos, which illustrate how life chances depend on global stratification. On the left is the Mulleta family of Ethiopia, featured in the opening vignette, standing in front of their home with all their material possessions. On the right is the Skeen family of Texas, surrounded by their possessions.

Systems of Social Stratification

social stratification the division of large numbers of people into layers according to their relative power, property, and prestige; applies to both nations and to people within a nation, society, or other group

slavery a form of social stratification in which some people own other people

Some of the world's nations are wealthy, others poor, and some in between. This layering of nations, and of groups of people within a nation, is called *social stratification.* Social stratification is one of the most significant topics we shall discuss in this book, for it affects our life chances—from our access to material possessions to the age at which we die as you saw in the opening vignette.

Social stratification also affects the way we think about life. If you had been born into the Ethiopian family in our opening vignette, for example, you would be illiterate and would expect your children to be the same. You also would expect hunger to be a part of life and would not be too surprised when people die young. To be born into either of the other two families, however, would give you quite a different picture of the world.

Social stratification is a system in which groups of people are divided into layers according to their relative power, property, and prestige. It is important to realize that social stratification does not refer to individuals. It is a *way of ranking large groups of people in a hierarchy that shows their relative privileges.*

It is also important to note that *every society stratifies its members.* Some, like agricultural societies, draw firm lines that separate group from group, while others, like hunting and gathering societies, show greater equality. Regardless of its forms, however, the existence of social stratification is universal. Let's look at four major systems of social stratification: slavery, caste, estate, and class.

Slavery

Slavery, whose essential characteristic is *ownership of some people by others,* has been common in world history. The Old Testament even lays out rules for how owners should treat their slaves. So does the Koran. The Romans had slaves, as did the Africans and Greeks. In classical Greece and Rome, slaves did the work, freeing citizens to engage in politics and the arts. Slavery was least common among nomads, especially hunters and gatherers, and most common in agricultural societies (Landtman 1938/1968). As we examine the major causes and conditions of slavery, you will see how remarkably it has varied around the world.

Causes of Slavery Contrary to popular assumption, slavery was not usually based on racism, but on one of three other factors. The first was debt. In some societies, creditors could enslave people who could not pay their debts. The second was crime. Instead of being killed, a murderer or thief might be enslaved by the family of the victim as compensation for their loss. The third was war and conquest. When one group of people conquered another, they often enslaved some of the vanquished (Starna and Watkins 1991). Historian Gerda Lerner (1986) notes that the first people enslaved through warfare were women. When tribal men raided a village or camp, they killed the men, raped the women, and then brought the women back as slaves. The women were valued for sexual purposes, for reproduction, and for their labor.

Roughly twenty-five hundred years ago, when Greece was but a collection of city-states, slavery was common. A city that became powerful and conquered another city would enslave some of the vanquished. Both slaves and slaveholders were Greek. Similarly, when Rome became the supreme power about two thousand years ago, following the custom of the time, the Romans enslaved some of the Greeks they had conquered. More educated than their conquerors, some of these slaves served as tutors in Roman homes. Slavery, then, was a sign of debt, of crime, or of defeat in battle. It was not a sign that the slave was inherently inferior.

As you can see from this 1864 photo taken on Whitehall Street in Atlanta, Georgia, under slavery, humans are bought and sold the same as commodities such as dishes. (Note the sign at the top of the building: China/Glass/Queensware.)

Conditions of Slavery The conditions of slavery have varied widely around the world. *In some cases, slavery was temporary.* Slaves of the Israelites were set free in the year of jubilee, which occurred every fifty years. Roman slaves ordinarily had the right to buy

bonded labor, or indentured service a contractual system in which someone sells his or her body (services) for a specified period of time in an arrangement very close to slavery, except that it is voluntarily entered into

themselves out of slavery. They knew what their purchase price was, and some were able to meet this price by striking a bargain with their owner and selling their services to others. In most instances, however, slavery was a lifelong condition. Some criminals, for example, became slaves when they were given life sentences as oarsmen on Roman war ships. There they served until death, which often came quickly to those in this exhausting service.

Slavery was not necessarily inheritable. In most places, the children of slaves were automatically slaves themselves. But in some instances, the child of a slave who served a rich family might even be adopted by that family, becoming an heir who bore the family name along with the other sons or daughters of the household. In ancient Mexico, the children of slaves were always free (Landtman 1938/1968:271).

Slaves were not necessarily powerless and poor. In almost all instances, slaves owned no property and had no power. Among some groups, however, slaves could accumulate property and even rise to high positions in the community. Occasionally, a slave might even become wealthy, loan money to the master, and, while still a slave, own slaves himself or herself (Landtman 1938/1968). This, however, was rare.

Slavery in the New World A gray area between a contract and slavery is **bonded labor,** also called **indentured service.** Many people who wanted to start a new life in the American colonies were unable to pay their passage. Ship captains would transport them on credit, and colonists would "buy their paper" when they arrived. This arrangement provided passage for the penniless, payment for the ship's captain, and, for wealthier colonists, servants for a set number of years. During that specified period, the servants were required by law to serve their master. If they ran away, they became outlaws and were captured and forcibly returned. At the end of the period of indenture, they became full citizens, able to live where they chose and free to sell their labor (Main 1965; Elkins 1968).

When there were not enough indentured servants to meet their growing need for labor, the colonists tried to enslave Native Americans. This attempt, however, failed miserably. One reason was that when Native Americans escaped they knew how to survive in the wilderness and were able to make their way back to their tribe. The colonists then turned to Africans, who were being brought to North and South America by the Dutch, English, Portuguese, and Spanish.

Because slavery has a broad range of causes, some analysts conclude that racism didn't lead to slavery, but, rather, slavery led to racism. Finding it profitable to make people slaves for life, U.S. slave owners developed an **ideology,** beliefs that justify social arrangements. Ideology leads to a picture of the world that makes current social arrangements seem inevitable, necessary, and fair. The colonists developed the view that the slaves were inferior. Some even said that they were not fully human. In short, the colonists developed elaborate justifications for slavery, built on the presumed superiority of their own group.

To make slavery even more profitable, slave states passed laws that made slavery *inheritable;* that is, the babies born to slaves became the property of the slave owners (Stampp 1956). These children could be sold, bartered, or traded. To strengthen their control, slave states passed laws making it illegal for slaves to hold meetings or to be away from the master's premises without carrying a pass (Lerner 1972). As sociologist W. E. B. Du Bois (1935/1966:12) noted, "gradually the entire white South became an armed camp to keep Negroes in slavery and to kill the black rebel."

Patterns of legal discrimination did not end after the Civil War. For example, until 1954 the states operated two separate school systems. Even until the 1950s, in order to keep the races from "mixing," it was illegal in Mississippi for a white and an African American to sit together on the same seat of a car! The reason there was no outright ban on blacks and whites being in the same car was to allow for African American chauffeurs.

During my research in India, I interviewed this 8 year-old girl. Mahashury is a bonded laborer *who was exchanged by her parents for a 2,000 rupee loan (about $14). To repay the loan, Mahashury must do construction work for one year. She will receive one meal a day and one set of clothing for the year. Because this centuries-old practice is now illegal, the master bribes Indian officials, who inform him when they are going to inspect the construction site. He then hides his bonded laborers. I was able to interview and photograph Mahashury because her master was absent the day I visited the construction site.*

Slavery Today Slavery has again reared its ugly head, this time in Sudan, Mauritania, and the Ivory Coast (Tandia 2001; Bales 2002; Del Castillo 2002). This region has a long history of slavery, and it was not until 1980 that slavery was officially abolished in Mauritania, and not until 1987 in Sudan (Ayittey 1998). Although officially abolished, slavery continues. Enslavement of members of the Dinka tribe in Sudan is the topic of the Mass Media box below.

ideology beliefs about the way things ought to be that justify social arrangements

massMEDIA in Social Life

What Price Freedom? Slavery Today

Children of the Dinka tribe in rural Sudan don't go to school. They work. Their families depend on them to tend the cattle that are so important to their way of life.

> On the morning of the raid, ten-year-old Adhieu had been watching the cattle. "We were very happy because we would soon leave the cattle camps and return home to our parents. But in the morning, there was shooting. There was yelling and crying everywhere. My uncle grabbed me by the hand, and we ran. We swam across the river. I saw some children drowning. We hid behind a rock."

By morning's end, 500 children were either dead or enslaved. Their attackers were their fellow countrymen—Arabs from northern Sudan. The children who were captured were forced to march hundreds of miles north. Some escaped on the way. Others tried to—and were shot (Akol 1998).

Tens of thousands of Dinkas have been killed or enslaved since civil war broke out in Sudan in the 1980s. Yet the Arab-led government—the National Islamic Front—insists that slavery does not exist. It claims it is an invention of foreign politicians, Christian humanitarians, and hostile foreign media (Akol 1998). But there are too many witnesses and too much documentation by human rights groups. There also are devastating accounts by journalists: Public television (PBS) has even run film footage of captive children in chains. And then there are the slaves who manage to escape, who recount their ordeal in horrifying detail (Dottridge 2001; Salopek 2003).

The United States bombed Kosovo into submission for its crimes against humanity, yet it has remained silent in the face of this outrage. A cynic might say that Kosovo was located at a politically strategic spot in Europe, whereas Sudan occupies an area of Africa in which the U.S. and European powers have little interest. A cynic might add that these powers fear Arab retaliation, which might take the form of oil embargoes and terrorism. A cynic might also suggest that outrages against black Africans are not as significant to these powers as those against white Europeans. Finally, a cynic might add that this will change as the oil below the surface of Sudan becomes more important.

In this photo, a representative of the Liason Agency Network (on the left) is buying the freedom of the Sudanese slaves (in the background).

Appalled by the lack of response on the part of the world's most powerful governments, private groups have stepped in. Christian Solidarity International (CSI), based in Zurich, Switzerland uses a controversial technique. Arab "retrievers" go to northern Sudan, where they either buy or abduct slaves. Walking by night and hiding by day, they elude security forces and bring the slaves south. There, CSI pays the retrievers $50 per slave (Mabry 1999).

> As CBS news cameras rolled, the rescuer paid the slave trader $50,000 in Sudanese pounds. At $50 per person, the bundle of bills was enough to free 1,000 slaves. The liberated slaves, mostly women and children, were then free to return to their villages. (Jacobs 1999)

Critics claim that buying slaves, even to free them, encourages slavery. The money provides motivation to enslave people in order to turn around and sell them. Fifty dollars is a lot of money in Sudan, where the average income for an entire year is $1,520 (Haub 2002). It is also the value of two or three goats (Gaviak 2000).

That is a bogus argument, replies CSI. What is intolerable is to leave women and children in slavery where they are deprived of their freedom and families, and beaten and raped by brutal masters.

CSI claims to have purchased the freedom of about 40,000 slaves (Dottridge 2001). No one knows how many people remain in slavery.

for your CONSIDERATION

What do you think about buying the freedom of slaves? Can you suggest a workable alternative? Why do you think the U.S. government has remained inactive about this issue for so long, when it invades other countries for human rights abuses? Do you think that, perhaps, its excursions into such places as Haiti and Kosovo were politically motivated, that they had little to do with human rights? If not, why the silence in the face of slavery?

The media coverage of this issue has motivated many Americans to become active in freeing slaves. High schools—and even grade schools—are raising money to participate in slave buy-back programs (Schaefer 1999). If you were a school principal, would you encourage this practice? Why or why not?

caste system a form of social stratification in which one's status is determined by birth and is lifelong

endogamy the practice of marrying within one's own group

Caste

The second system of social stratification is caste. In a **caste system,** status is determined by birth and is lifelong. Someone born into a low-status group will always have low status, no matter how much that person may accomplish in life. In sociological terms, the basis of a caste system is ascribed status (discussed on page 97). Achieved status cannot change an individual's place in this system.

Societies with this form of stratification try to make certain that the boundaries between castes remain firm. They practice **endogamy,** marriage within their own group, and prohibit intermarriage. To reduce contact between castes, they even develop elaborate rules about *ritual pollution,* teaching that contact with inferior castes contaminates the superior caste.

India's Religious Castes India provides the best example of a caste system. Based not on race but on religion, India's caste system has existed for almost three thousand years (Chandra 1993; Guru and Sidhva 2001). India's four main castes are depicted in Table 9.1. These four castes are subdivided into about two thousand subcastes, or *jati.* Each *jati* has an occupational specialty. For example, one subcaste washes clothes, another sharpens knives, and yet another repairs shoes.

The lowest group listed in Table 9.1, the Dalit, make up India's "untouchables." If a Dalit touches someone of a higher caste, that person becomes unclean. Even the shadow of an untouchable can contaminate. Early morning and late afternoons are especially risky, for the long shadows of these periods pose a danger to everyone higher up the caste system. Consequently, Dalits are not allowed in some villages during these times. Anyone who becomes contaminated must follow *ablution,* or washing rituals, to restore purity (Lannoy 1975).

Although the Indian government formally abolished the caste system in 1949, centuries-old practices cannot be so easily eliminated, and the caste system remains part of everyday life in India. The ceremonies people follow at births, marriages, and deaths, for example, are dictated by caste (Chandra 1993). The upper castes dread the upward mobility of the untouchables, whom they detest. On occasion, they even resist it with violence and ritual suicide (Crossette 1996; Filkins 1997; Deliege 2001).

Table 9.1 India's Caste System

Caste	Occupation
Brahman	Priests and teachers
Kshatriya	Rulers and soldiers
Vaishya	Merchants and traders
Shudra	Peasants and laborers
Dalit (untouchables)	The outcastes; degrading or polluting labor

In a caste system, status is determined by birth and is lifelong. At birth, these women received not only membership in a lower caste but also, because of their gender, a predetermined position in that caste. When I photographed these women, they were carrying sand to the second floor of a house being constructed in Andhra Pradesh, India.

An untouchable summed up his situation in life this way:

> At the tea stalls, we have separate cups to drink from, chipped and caked with dirt. We have to walk for 15 minutes to carry water to our homes, because we're not allowed to use the taps in the village that the upper castes use. We're not allowed into temples. When I attended school, my friends and I were forced to sit outside the classroom. The upper caste children would not allow us even to touch the football they played with. We played with stones instead. (Guru and Sidhva 2001)

apartheid the separation of racial-ethnic groups as was practiced in South Africa

estate stratification system the stratification system of medieval Europe, consisting of three groups or estates: the nobility, clergy, and commoners

South Africa Until recently, South Africa provided another example of social stratification based on caste. Europeans of Dutch descent, a numerical minority called Afrikaaners, controlled the government, the police, and the military. They used these sources of power to enforce a system called **apartheid** (ah-PAR-tate), the separation of the races. Everyone was classified by law into one of four groups: Europeans (whites), Africans (blacks), Coloureds (mixed races), and Asians. These classifications determined where people could live, work, and go to school. It also established where they could swim or see movies—for by law whites were not allowed to mix socially with the others.

After years of trade sanctions, sports boycotts, and other pressure, Afrikaaners reluctantly dismantled their caste system. Black Africans no longer carry special passes, public facilities are integrated, and all racial-ethnic groups have the right to vote and to hold office. Although apartheid has been dismantled, its legacy haunts South Africa. Whites still dominate the country's social institutions, and most blacks remain uneducated and poor. Many new rights—such as the right to higher education, to eat in restaurants, even to see a doctor—are of little use to people who can't afford them. Political violence has been replaced by old-fashioned crime. South Africa's murder rate, the highest in the world, runs *nine times* higher than the extraordinary U.S. rate ("South African . . . " 2001). Apartheid's legacy of prejudice, bitterness, and hatred is destined to fuel racial tensions for generations.

A U.S. Racial Caste System Before leaving the subject of caste, we should note that when slavery ended in the United States, it was replaced by a *racial caste system,* in which everyone was marked for life from the moment of birth (Berger 1963/2003). In this system, *all* whites, even if they were poor and uneducated, considered themselves to have a higher status than *all* African Americans. As in India and South Africa, the upper caste, fearing pollution from the lower caste, prohibited intermarriage and insisted on separate schools, hotels, restaurants, and even toilets and drinking fountains in public facilities. When any white met any African American on a southern sidewalk, the African American had to move aside—which the untouchables of India still must do when they meet someone of a higher caste (Deliege 2001).

Estate

During the middle ages, Europe developed the **estate stratification system.** There were three groups, or estates. The *first* estate was made up of the nobility, the wealthy families who ruled the country. They owned the land, which was the source of wealth at that time. The nobility did no farming themselves, or any "work" for that matter. Work was considered beneath their dignity, something to be done by servants. The nobility's responsibility was to administer their lands, and to live "genteel" lives worthy of their high position.

The *second* estate consisted of the clergy. The Roman Catholic Church was a political power at this time. It also owned vast amounts of land and collected taxes from everyone who lived within the boundaries of a parish. The church's power was so great that to be crowned, kings had to obtain the pope's permission.

To prevent its vast lands from being carved into smaller chunks, the nobility practiced *primogeniture,* allowing only firstborn sons to inherit land. The other sons had to find some way to support themselves, and joining the clergy was a favored way. (Other ways were becoming an officer in the military or practicing law.) The church was appealing because priests had a lifetime position and were guaranteed a comfortable living. At that time, the church sold offices, and the wealthy could buy the position of bishop, for example, which guaranteed a high income.

The *third* estate consisted of the commoners. Known as *serfs,* they belonged to the land. If someone bought or inherited land, the serfs came with it. Serfs were born into the third estate, and they died within it, too. The rare person who made it out of the third estate was a man who was knighted for extraordinary bravery in battle or someone "called" into a religious vocation.

class system a form of social stratification based primarily on the possession of money or material possessions

social mobility movement up or down the social class ladder

Women in the Estate System

Women belonged to the estate of their husbands. Women in the first estate had no occupation, for, like their husbands, work was considered beneath their dignity. Their responsibility was to administer the household, overseeing the servants. Women were not members of the second estate, as the Roman Catholic clergy did not marry. Women of the third estate shared the hard life of their husbands, including physical labor and food shortages. In addition, they faced the peril of rape by men of the first estate. A few commoners who caught the eye of men of the first estate did marry and join them in the first estate. This, however, was rare.

Class

As we have seen, stratification systems based on slavery, caste, and estate are rigid. The lines drawn between people are firm and there is little or no movement from one group to another. A **class system,** in contrast, is much more open, for it is based primarily on money or material possessions, which can be acquired. It, too, begins at birth, when individuals are ascribed the status of their parents, but, unlike these other systems, people can change their social class by what they achieve (or fail to achieve) in life. In addition, no laws specify people's occupations on the basis of birth or prohibit marriage between the classes.

A major characteristic of the class system, then, is its relatively fluid boundaries. A class system allows **social mobility,** movement up or down the class ladder. The potential for improving one's life—or for falling down the class ladder—is a major force that drives people to go far in school and to work hard. In the extreme, the family background that a child inherits at birth may present such obstacles that he or she has little chance of climbing very far—or it may provide such privileges that it makes it almost impossible to fall down the class ladder.

Global Stratification and the Status of Females

In every society of the world, gender is a basis for social stratification. In no society is gender the sole basis for stratifying people, but gender cuts across *all* systems of social stratification—whether slavery, caste, estate, or class (Huber 1990). In all these systems, on the basis of their gender, people are sorted into categories and given different access to the good things available in their society.

This cartoon of political protest appeared in London newspapers in 1843. It illustrates the severe exploitation of labor that occurred during early capitalism, which stimulated Marx to analyze relations between capitalists and workers.

Apparently these distinctions always favor males. It is remarkable, for example, that in *every* society of the world men's earnings are higher than women's. Men's dominance is even more evident when we consider female circumcision (see the box on page 300). That most of the world's illiterate are females drives home women's relative position. Of the several hundred million adults who cannot read, about 60 percent are women ("Fighting Illiteracy . . ." 2000). Because gender is so significant for what happens to us in life, we shall devote a separate chapter to this topic (Chapter 11).

What Determines Social Class?

In the early days of sociology, a disagreement arose about the meaning of social class. Let's compare how Marx and Weber analyzed the issue.

Taken at the end of the 1800s, these photos illustrate the contrasting worlds of social classes produced by capitalism. The sleeping boys shown in this classic 1890 photo by Jacob Riis sold newspapers in London. They did not go to school, and they had no home. The children on the right, Cornelius and Gladys Vanderbilt, are shown in front of their parents' estate. They went to school and did not work. You can see how the life situations illustrated in these photos would have produced different orientations to life—and, therefore, politics, ideas about marriage, values, and so on—the stuff of which life is made.

Karl Marx: The Means of Production

As discussed in Chapter 1, Karl Marx (1818–1883) witnessed the effects of societies in upheaval. When the feudal system broke up, masses of peasants were displaced from their traditional lands and occupations. Fleeing to cities, they competed for the few available jobs. Offered only a pittance for their labor, they dressed in rags, went hungry, and slept under bridges and in shacks. In contrast, the factory owners built mansions, hired servants, and lived in the lap of luxury. Seeing this great disparity between owners and workers, Marx concluded that social class depends on a single factor—the **means of production**—the tools, factories, land, and investment capital used to produce wealth (Marx 1844/1964; Marx and Engels 1848/1967).

Marx argued that the distinctions people often make among themselves—such as clothing, speech, education, income, or, today, even the car they drive—are superficial matters. These things camouflage the only dividing line that counts. There are just two classes of people, said Marx: the **bourgeoisie,** those who own the means of production, and the **proletariat,** those who work for the owners. In short, people's relationship to the means of production determines their social class.

Marx did recognize other groups: farmers and peasants; a *lumpenproletariat* (marginal people such as beggars, vagrants, and criminals); and a middle group of self-employed professionals. Marx did not consider these groups social classes, however, for they lacked **class consciousness**—a shared identity based on their position in the means of production. They did not perceive themselves as exploited workers whose plight could be solved by collective action. Consequently, Marx thought of these groups as insignificant in the coming workers' revolution destined to overthrow capitalism.

The capitalists will grow even wealthier, Marx said, and the hostilities will increase. When workers come to realize that capitalists are the source of their oppression, they will unite and throw off the chains of their oppressors. In a bloody revolution, they will seize the means of production and usher in a classless society, where no longer will the few grow rich at the expense of the many. What holds back the workers' unity and their revolution is **false consciousness,** workers mistakenly thinking of themselves as capitalists. For example, workers with a few dollars in the bank may forget that they are workers and instead see themselves as investors, or as capitalists who are about to launch a successful business.

The only distinction worth mentioning, then, is whether a person is an owner or a worker. This decides everything else, Marx stressed, for property determines people's lifestyles, shapes their ideas, and establishes their relationships with one another.

Max Weber: Property, Prestige, and Power

Max Weber (1864–1920) became an outspoken critic of Marx. Weber argued that property is only part of the picture. Social class, he said, is made up of three components—

means of production the tools, factories, land, and investment capital used to produce wealth

bourgeoisie Karl Marx's term for capitalists, those who own the means of production

proletariat Marx's term for the exploited class, the mass of workers who do not own the means of production

class consciousness Karl Marx's term for awareness of a common identity based on one's position in the means of production

false consciousness (or false class consciousness) Karl Marx's term to refer to workers identifying with the interests of capitalists property, prestige, and power (Gerth and Mills 1958; Weber 1922/1968). Some call these the three P's of social class. (Although Weber used the terms *class, status,* and *power,* some sociologists find *property, prestige,* and *power* to be clearer terms. To make them even clearer, you may wish to substitute *wealth* for *property.*)

Property (or wealth), said Weber, is certainly significant in determining a person's standing in society. On that point he agreed with Marx. But, added Weber, ownership is not the only significant aspect of property. For example, some powerful people, such as managers of corporations, *control* the means of production although they do not *own* them. If managers can control property for their own benefit—awarding themselves huge bonuses and magnificent perks—it makes no practical difference that they do not own the property that they so generously use for their own benefit.

Prestige, the second element in Weber's analysis, is often derived from property, for people tend to admire the wealthy. Prestige, however, can also be based on other factors. Olympic gold medalists, for example, may not own property, yet they have high prestige. Some are even able to exchange their prestige for property—such as those who are paid a small fortune for claiming that they start their day with "the breakfast of champions." In other words, property and prestige are not one-way streets: Although property can bring prestige, prestige can also bring property.

Power, the third element of social class, is the ability to control others, even over their objections. Weber agreed with Marx that property is a major source of power, but he added that it is not the only source. For example, prestige can be turned into power. Perhaps the best example is Ronald Reagan, an actor who became president of the most powerful country in the world. Figure 9.1 shows how property, prestige, and power are interrelated.

Figure 9.1 Weber's Three Components of Social Class: Interrelationships Among Them

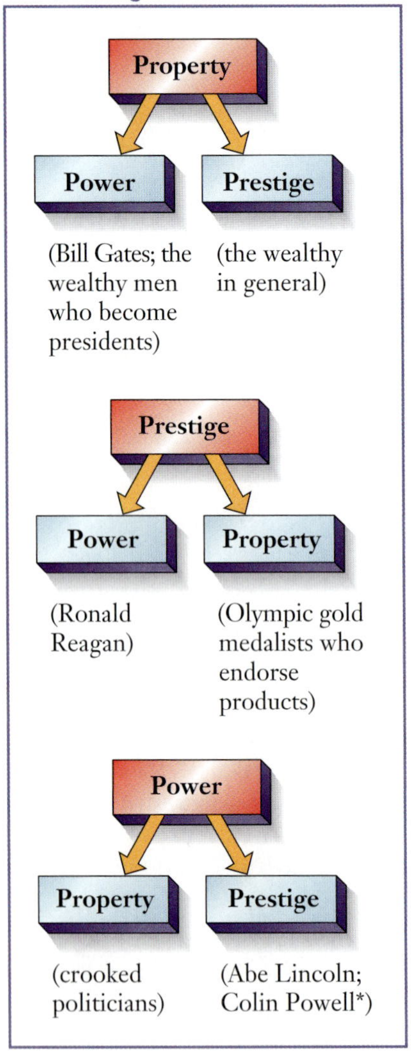

*Colin Powell illustrates the circularity of these components. Powell's power as Chairman of the Joint Chiefs of Staff led to prestige. Powell's prestige, in turn, led to power when he was called from retirement to serve as Secretary of State in the George W. Bush administration.

IN SUM

For Marx, social class was based solely on a person's relationship to the means of production. One is a member of either the bourgeoisie or the proletariat. Weber argued that social class is a combination of property, prestige, and power.

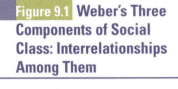

The text describes the many relationships among Weber's three components of social class: property, prestige, and power. Colin Powell is an example of power that was converted into prestige—which was then converted back into power.

Why Is Social Stratification Universal?

What is it about social life that makes all societies stratified? We shall first consider the explanation proposed by functionalists, which has aroused much controversy in sociology, and then explanations proposed by conflict theorists.

The Functionalist View: Motivating Qualified People

Functionalists take the position that the patterns of behavior that characterize a society exist because they are functional for that society. Because social inequality is universal, inequality must help societies survive. But how?

Davis and Moore's Explanation Two functionalists, Kingsley Davis and Wilbert Moore (1945, 1953), wrestled with this question. They concluded that stratification of society is inevitable because:

1. Society must make certain that its positions are filled.
2. Some positions are more important than others.
3. The more important positions must be filled by the more qualified people.
4. To motivate the more qualified people to fill these positions, society must offer them greater rewards.

Let's look at two examples to flesh out this functionalist argument. The position of college president is more important than that of a student because the president's decisions affect many more people. Any mistakes he or she makes carry implications for a large number of people, including many students. The same is true for an army general compared with a private. The decisions of a general affect careers and paychecks, and may even determine life and death.

Positions with greater responsibility also require greater accountability. College presidents and army generals are accountable for their performance—to boards of trustees and to the leader of a country, respectively. How can society motivate highly qualified people to enter its higher-pressure positions? What keeps people from avoiding them and seeking only less demanding jobs?

The answer, said Davis and Moore, is that society offers greater rewards for its more demanding and accountable positions. If these jobs didn't offer greater prestige, salaries, and benefits, why would anyone strive for them? Thus, a salary of $2 million, a country club membership, a private jet, and a chauffeured limousine may be necessary in order to get the most highly qualified people to compete with one another for some positions, while a $30,000 salary without fringe benefits is enough to get hundreds of less qualified people to compete for less demanding positions. It is the same with positions that require rigorous training. If you can get the same pay with a high school diploma, why suffer through the many tests and term papers that college requires?

The functionalist argument is simple and clear. Society works better if its most qualified people hold its most important positions. For example, to get highly talented people to become surgeons—to undergo many years of rigorous training and then cope with life-and-death situations on a daily basis, as well as withstand the Sword of Damocles known as malpractice suits—society must provide a high payoff.

Tumin's Critique of Davis and Moore Davis and Moore tried to explain *why* social stratification is universal, not justify social inequality. Nevertheless, their view makes many sociologists uncomfortable, for they see it as coming close to justifying the inequalities in society.

Melvin Tumin (1953) was the first sociologist to point out what he saw as major flaws in the functionalist position. Here are three of his arguments.

First, the functionalists say that the most important positions get the higher rewards. But how do we know that the positions with the highest rewards are the most important? Surgeons, for example, receive much higher incomes than garbage collectors, but this doesn't mean that garbage collectors are less important to society—since they help to prevent contagious diseases. We need independent ways to measure importance, and we don't have them.

Second, if stratification worked as Davis and Moore described it, society would be a **meritocracy;** that is, all positions would be awarded on the basis of merit. But what do we really have? Instead of ability being the best predictor of who goes to college, for example, the best predictor is income: The more a family earns, the more likely their children are to go to college. This isn't merit, but, rather, inequality built into society. Then there are those who inherit wealth and the opportunities that go with it—also a far cry from merit. Finally, consider gender. A stratification system that places most men above most women does not live up to the argument that talent and ability are the bases for holding important positions. In short, people hold positions in society for many reasons other than merit.

Third, if social stratification is so functional, it ought to benefit almost everyone. Yet social stratification is *dysfunctional* for many. Think of the people who could have made valuable contributions to society had they not been born in slums and dropped out of school to take menial jobs to help support the family. Then there are the many who, born female, are assigned "women's work," thus ensuring that they do not maximize their mental abilities.

The Conflict Perspective: Class Conflict and Scarce Resources

Conflict theorists don't just criticize details of the functionalist perspective. Rather, they attack its basic premise. Conflict, not function, they stress, is the reason we have social stratification. In every society, groups struggle with one another to gain a larger share of their society's resources. Whenever a group gains power, it uses that power to extract what it can from the groups beneath it. This elite group also uses the social institutions to keep itself in power.

Mosca's Argument

Italian sociologist Gaetano Mosca argued that every society will be stratified by power. This is inevitable, he said in an 1896 book titled *The Ruling Class,* because:

1. No society can exist unless it is organized. This requires leadership of some sort in order to coordinate people's actions and get society's work done.
2. Leadership (or political organization) means inequalities of power. Some people take leadership positions, while others follow.
3. Human nature is self-centered. Therefore, people in power will use their positions to seize greater rewards for themselves.

There is no way around these facts of life, added Mosca. They make social stratification inevitable, and every society will stratify itself along lines of power.

Marx's Argument

If he were alive to hear the functionalist argument, Karl Marx would be enraged. From his point of view, the people in power are not there because of superior traits, as the functionalists would have us believe. That view is simply an ideology the elite use to justify their being at the top—and to seduce the oppressed into believing that their welfare depends on keeping society stable. Human history is the history of class struggle, of those in power using society's resources to benefit themselves and to oppress those beneath them—and of oppressed groups trying to overcome their domination.

Marx predicted that the workers would revolt. The day will come, he said, when class consciousness will overcome the ideology that now blinds them. When the workers realize their common oppression, they will rebel against the capitalists. The struggle to con-

meritocracy a form of social stratification in which all positions are awarded on the basis of merit trol the means of production may be covert at first, taking the form of work slowdowns or industrial sabotage. Ultimately, however, resistance will break out into the open. The revolution will not be easy, for the bourgeoisie control the police, the military, and even education, where they implant ideas of false class consciousness in the minds of the workers' children.

Current Applications of Conflict Theory Just as Marx focused on overarching historic events—the accumulation of capital and power and the struggle between labor and capitalists—some of today's conflict sociologists are doing the same. Their focus is on the current capitalist triumph on a global level (Sklair 2001). They analyze the use of armed forces to keep capitalist nations dominant and the exploitation of workers as capital is moved from the Most Industrialized Nations to the Least Industrialized Nations.

Some conflict sociologists, in contrast, examine conflict wherever it is found, not just as it relates to capitalists and workers. They examine how groups *within the same class* compete with one another for a larger slice of the pie (Schellenberg 1996; Collins 1988, 1999). Even within the same industry, for example, union will fight against union for higher salaries, shorter hours, and more power. A special focus has been conflict between racial–ethnic groups as they compete for education, housing, and even prestige—whatever benefits society has to offer. Another focus has been relations between women and men, which they say is best understood as a conflict over power—the access and control of society's resources. Unlike functionalists, conflict theorists hold that just beneath the surface of what may appear to be a tranquil society lies conflict that is barely held in check.

Lenski's Synthesis

As you can see, functionalist and conflict theorists disagree sharply. Is it possible to reconcile their views? Sociologist Gerhard Lenski (1966) thought so. He suggested that surplus is the key. He said that the functionalists are right when it comes to groups that don't accumulate a surplus, such as hunting and gathering societies. These societies give a greater share of their resources to those who take on important tasks, such as warriors who risk their lives in battle. It is a different story, said Lenski, when it comes to societies that accumulate surpluses. In them, groups fight over the surplus, and the group that wins becomes an elite. It rules from the top, controlling the groups below it. In the resulting system of social stratification, where you are born in that society, not personal merit, becomes important.

How Do Elites Maintain Stratification?

Suppose that you are part of the ruling elite of your society. What can you do to make sure you don't lose your privileged position? The key lies in controlling ideas and information, and, in the least effective means of all, the use of force.

Ideology Versus Force

Medieval Europe provides a good example of the power of ideology. In the estate system that we reviewed, land was the primary source of wealth—and only the nobility and the church could own it. Almost everyone was a commoner (or serf) who worked for these powerful landowners. The serfs farmed the land, took care of the livestock, and built the roads and bridges. Each year, they had to turn over a designated portion of their crops to their feudal lord. Year after year, for centuries, they did so. Why?

Controlling Ideas Why didn't the serfs rebel and take over the land themselves? There were many reasons, not the least of which was that the nobility and church controlled the army. Coercion, however, only goes so far, for it breeds hostility and nourishes rebellion. How much more effective it is to get the masses to *want* to do what the ruling elite desires. This is where *ideology* (beliefs that justify the way things are) comes into play, and the nobility and clergy used it to great effect. They developed an ideology known as the **divine right of kings**—the idea that the king's authority comes directly from God. The king delegates authority to nobles, who as God's representatives must be obeyed. To disobey is a sin against God; to rebel means physical punishment on earth and eternal suffering in hell.

Controlling people's ideas can be remarkably more effective than using brute force. Although this particular ideology governs few peoples' minds today, the elite in every society develops ideologies to justify its position at the top. For example, around the world schools teach that their country's form of government—*no matter what form of government it is*—is the best. Religious leaders teach that we owe obedience to authority, that laws are to be obeyed. To the degree that their ideologies are accepted by the masses, the elite remains securely in power.

The divine right of kings *was an ideology that made the king God's direct representative on earth—to administer justice and punish evildoers. This theological-political concept was supported by the Roman Catholic Church, whose representatives crowned the king. Depicted here is Charlemagne, who, crowned by Pope Leo III in 800, established what is known as the Holy Roman Empire. This painting is by Jean Victor Schnetz (1787–1870).*

Controlling Information and Using Technology To maintain their positions of power, elites also try to control information. In dictatorships, this is accomplished through the threat of force. To muffle criticism, dictators control the press, and they imprison, torture, and kill reporters who dare to publish articles critical of their regime (Timerman 1981). Lacking such power, the ruling elites of democracies manipulate the media by selectively releasing information—and by withholding information "in the interest of national security."

The new technology is another tool for the elite. Telephones can be turned into microphones even when they are off the hook. Machines can read the entire contents of a computer in a second, without leaving a trace. Security cameras—"Little Brothers"—have sprouted almost everywhere. Face-recognition systems can scan a crowd of thousands, instantly matching the scans with digitized files of individuals. With these devices, the elite can monitor citizens' activities without anyone knowing that they are being observed. Dictatorships have few checks on how they employ such technology, but in democracies, checks and balances, such as asserting constitutional rights and requiring court orders for search and seizure, at least partially curb their abuse.

The new technology is a two-edged sword. Just as it gives the elite powerful tools for monitoring citizens, it also makes it more difficult for them to control information. The new technology of satellite communications, e-mail, and the Internet pays no respect to international borders. Whether government officials like it or not, on the Internet information flies around the globe in seconds. Internet users also have free access to PGP (Pretty Good Privacy), a code that no government has been able to break.

IN SUM

To maintain stratification within a society, the elite tries to dominate its society's institutions. In a dictatorship, the elite makes the laws. In a democracy, the elite influences the laws. In both, the legal establishment enforces the laws. The elite also controls the police and military and can give orders to crush a rebellion—or to run the post office or air traffic control if workers strike. Force has its limits, and a nation's elite generally finds it preferable to maintain its stratification system by peaceful means, especially by influencing the thinking of its people.

divine right of kings the idea that the king's authority comes directly from God

Comparative Social Stratification

Now that we have examined systems of social stratification, considered why stratification is universal, and looked at how elites keep themselves in power, let's compare social stratification in Great Britain and in the former Soviet Union. In the next chapter, we'll look at social stratification in the United States.

Social Stratification in Great Britain

Great Britain is often called England by Americans, but England is only one of the countries that make up the island of Great Britain. The others are Scotland and Wales. In addition, Northern Ireland is part of the United Kingdom of Great Britain and Northern Ireland.

Like other industrialized countries, Great Britain has a class system that can be divided into a lower, middle, and upper class. Great Britain's population is about evenly divided between the middle class and the lower (or working) class. A tiny upper class, perhaps 1 percent of the population, is wealthy, powerful, and highly educated.

Compared with Americans, the British are very class conscious. Like Americans, they recognize class distinctions on the basis of the type of car a person drives, or the stores someone patronizes. But the most striking characteristics of the British class system are language and education. This shows up in distinctive speech, which has a powerful impact on British life. Accent almost always betrays class. As soon as someone speaks, the listener is aware of that person's class—and treats him or her accordingly (Sullivan 1998).

Education is the primary way by which the British perpetuate their class system from one generation to the next. Almost all children go to neighborhood schools. Great Britain's richest 5 percent, however—who own half the nation's wealth—send their children to exclusive private boarding schools (contrastively known as "public" schools). There they are trained in subjects considered "proper" for members of the ruling class. An astounding 50 percent of the students at Oxford and Cambridge, the country's most prestigious universities, come from this 5 percent of the population. To illustrate how powerfully this system of stratified education affects the national life of Great Britain, sociologist Ian Robertson (1987) said,

> [E]ighteen former pupils of the most exclusive of them, Eton, have become prime minister. Imagine the chances of a single American high school producing eighteen presidents!

Social Stratification in the Former Soviet Union

Heeding Karl Marx's call for a classless society, Vladimir Ilyich Lenin (1870–1924) and Leon Trotsky (1879–1940) led a revolution in Russia. They, and the nations that followed their banner, never claimed to have achieved the ideal of communism, in which all contribute their labor to the common good and receive according to their needs. Instead, they used the term *socialism* to describe the intermediate step between capitalism and communism, in which social classes are abolished but some inequality remains.

To tweak the nose of Uncle Sam, the socialist countries would trumpet their equality and point a finger at glaring inequalities in the United States. They, too, however, were marked by huge disparities in privilege. Their major basis of stratification was membership in the Communist Party. This often decided who would gain admission to the better schools or obtain the more desirable jobs. The equally qualified son or daughter of a nonmember would be turned down, for such privileges came with demonstrated loyalty to the Party.

Even the Communist Party was highly stratified. Most members occupied a low level, where they fulfilled such tasks as spying on other workers. For this, they might get easier jobs in the factory or occasional access to special stores to purchase hard-to-find goods. The middle level consisted of bureaucrats who were given better than average access to resources and privileges. At the top level was a small elite: party members who enjoyed not only power but also limousines, imported delicacies, vacation homes, and even servants

Russia's reluctant embrace of capitalism has brought many changes. One is a new affluence—which is matched by a new poverty. Both are evident in this photo from Moscow.

and hunting lodges. As with other stratification systems around the world, women held lower positions in the Party. This was evident at each year's May Day celebration when the top members of the Party reviewed the latest weapons paraded in Moscow's Red Square. Photos of these events showed only men.

The leaders of the USSR became frustrated as they saw the West thrive. They struggled with a bloated bureaucracy, the inefficiencies of central planning, workers who did the minimum because they could not be fired, and a military so costly that it spent one of every eight of the nation's rubles (*Statistical Abstract* 1993:1432; table dropped in later editions). Their ideology did not call for their citizens to be deprived, and in an attempt to turn things around, the Soviet leadership initiated reforms. They allowed elections to be held in which more than one candidate ran for an office. (Prior to this, voters had a choice of only one candidate per office.) They also sold huge chunks of state-owned businesses to the public. Overnight, making investments to try to turn a profit changed from being a crime into a respectable goal.

Russia's transition to capitalism took a bizarre twist. As authority broke down, a powerful Mafia emerged. These criminal groups are headed by gangsters, corrupt government officials, and crooked businessmen. In some towns, they buy the entire judicial system—the police force, prosecutors, and judges (Tavernise 2002). They assassinate business leaders, reporters, and politicians who refuse to cooperate (Zarakhovich 2001; Wines 2002). They are amassing wealth and stashing it in offshore retreats, especially in such watering and wintering spots as Marbella on Spain's Costa del Sol.

Russia's "wild west" days are bound to disappear as the central government reestablishes its authority. At that time, this group of organized criminals will take its place as part of Russia's respectable capitalist class.

Global Stratification: Three Worlds

As noted at the beginning of this chapter, just as the people within a nation are stratified by power, prestige, and property, so are the world's nations. Until recently, a simple model consisting of First, Second, and Third Worlds was used to depict global stratification. *First World* referred to the industrialized capitalist nations, *Second World* to the communist nations, and *Third World* to any nation that did not fit into the first two categories. The breakup of the Soviet Union in 1989 made these terms outdated. In addition, although *first, second,* and *third* did not mean "best," "better," and "worst," they sounded like it. An alternative classification some now use—developed, developing, and undeveloped nations—has the same drawback. By calling ourselves "developed," it sounds as though we are mature and the "undeveloped" nations are somehow retarded.

Consequently, I have chosen more neutral, descriptive terms: *Most Industrialized, Industrializing,* and *Least Industrialized* nations. We can measure industrialization with no judgment implied as to whether a nation's industrialization represents "development," ranks it "first," or is even desirable at all.

The intention is to depict on a global level the three primary dimensions of social stratification: property, power, and prestige. The Most Industrialized Nations have much greater property (wealth), power (they get their way in international relations), and prestige (they are looked up to as world leaders). The three families sketched in the opening vignette illustrate the far-reaching effects of global stratification.

The Most Industrialized Nations

The Most Industrialized Nations are the United States and Canada in North America; Great Britain, France, Germany, Switzerland, and the other industrialized nations of western Europe; Japan in Asia; and Australia and New Zealand in the area of the world known as Oceania. Although there are variations in their economic systems, these nations are capitalistic. As Table 9.2 shows, although these nations have only 16 percent of the world's people, they have 31 percent of the earth's land. Their wealth is so enormous that even their poor live better and longer lives than do the average citizens of the Least Industrialized Nations. The Social Map on the next two pages shows the tremendous disparities in income among the world's nations.

The Industrializing Nations

The Industrializing Nations include most of the nations of the former Soviet Union and its former satellites in eastern Europe. As Table 9.2 shows, these nations account for 20 percent of the earth's land and 16 percent of its people.

The dividing points between the three "worlds" are soft, making it difficult to know how to classify some nations. This is especially the case with the Industrializing Nations. Exactly how much industrialization must a nation have to be in this category? Although soft, these categories do pinpoint essential differences among nations. Most people who live in the Industrializing Nations have much lower incomes and standards of living than those who live in the Most Industrialized Nations. Most, however, are better off than those who live in the Least Industrialized Nations. For example, on such measures as access to electricity, indoor plumbing, automobiles, telephones, and even food, citizens of the Industrializing Nations rank lower than those in the Most Industrialized Nations, but higher than those in the Least Industrialized Nations. As you saw in the opening vignette, this principle applies even to life expectancy.

Table 9.2 Distribution of the World's Land and Population

	Land	Population
Most Industrialized Nations	31%	16%
Industrializing Nations	20%	16%
Least Industrialized Nations	49%	68%

Sources: Computed from Kurian 1990, 1991, 1992.

Figure 9.2 Global Stratification: Income* of the World's Nations

The Most Industrialized Nations

	Nation	Income per Person
1	Luxembourg	$45,470
2	United States	$34,100
3	Switzerland	$30,450
4	Norway	$29,630
5	Iceland	$28,710
6	Belgium	$27,470
7	Denmark	$27,250
8	Japan	$27,080
9	Austria	$26,330
10	Netherlands	$25,850
11	Hong Kong	$25,590
12	Ireland	$25,520
13	Australia	$24,970
14	Germany	$24,920
15	Singapore	$24,910
16	Finland	$24,570
17	France	$24,420
18	Sweden	$23,970
19	United Kingdom	$23,550
20	Italy	$23,470
21	Canada	$21,170
22	Israel	$19,330
23	New Zealand	$18,530

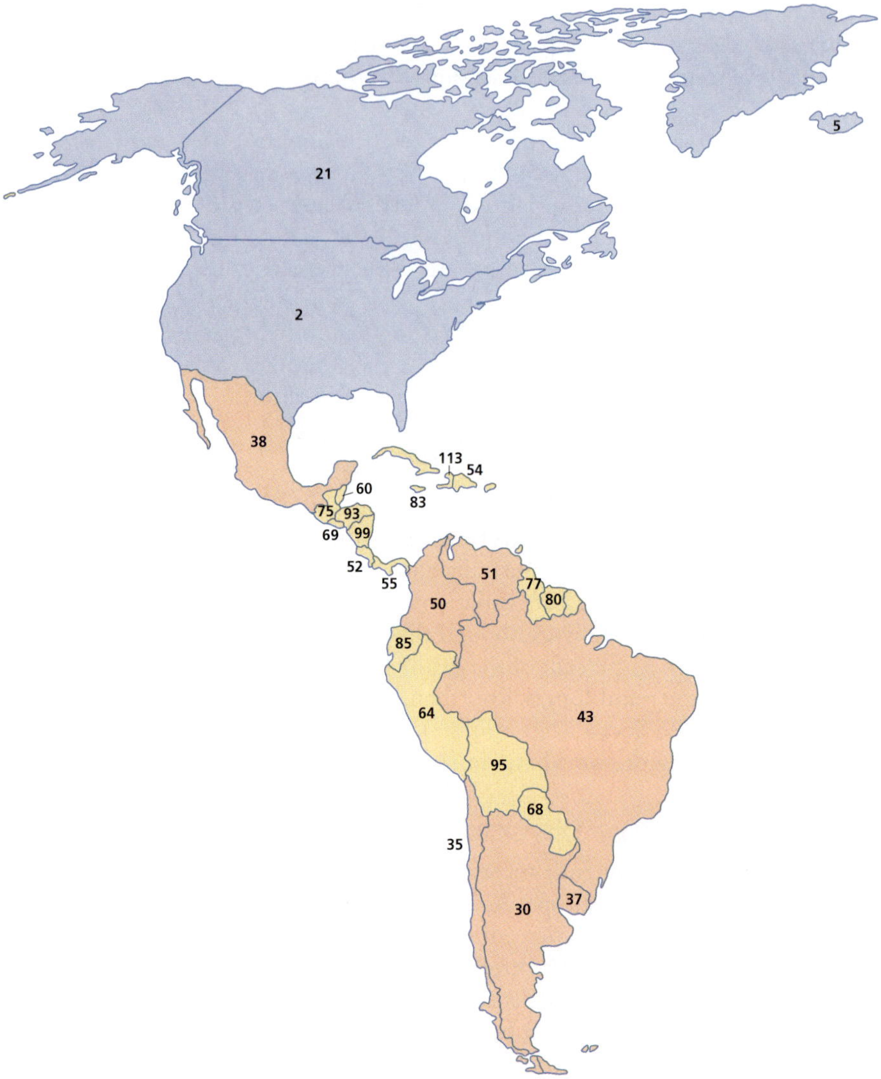

The Industrializing Nations

	Nation	Income per Person
24	Spain	$19,260
25	Slovenia	$17,310
26	Korea, South	$17,300
27	Portugal	$16,990
28	Greece	$16,860
29	Czech Republic	$13,780
30	Argentina	$12,050
31	Hungary	$11,990
32	Slovakia	$11,040
33	Estonia	$9,340
34	South Africa	$9,160
35	Chile	$9,100
36	Poland	$9,000
37	Uruguay	$8,880
38	Mexico	$8,790
39	Malaysia	$8,330
40	Russia	$8,010
41	Croatia	$7,960
42	Belarus	$7,550
43	Brazil	$7,300
44	Botswana	$7,170
45	Latvia	$7,070
46	Turkey	$7,030
47	Lithuania	$6,980
48	Romania	$6,360
49	Thailand	$6,320
50	Colombia	$6,060
51	Venezuela	$5,740

The Least Industrialized Nations

	Nation	Income per Person
52	Costa Rica	$7,980
53	Tunisia	$6,070
54	Dominican Republic	$5,710
55	Panama	$5,680
56	Equatorial Guinea	$5,600
57	Bulgaria	$5,560
58	Kazakhstan	$5,490
59	Gabon	$5,360
60	Belize	$5,240
61	Algeria	$5,040
62	Macedonia	$5,020
63	Cape Verde	$4,760
64	Peru	$4,660
65	Swaziland	$4,600

	Nation	Income per Person
66	Namibia	$4,500
67	Lebanon	$4,550
68	Paraguay	$4,450
69	El Salvador	$4,410
70	Maldives	$4,240
71	Philippines	$4,220
72	Jordan	$3,950
73	China	$3,920
74	Turkmenistan	$3,800
75	Guatemala	$3,770
76	Ukraine	$3,700
77	Guyana	$3,670
78	Egypt	$3,670
79	Albania	$3,600
80	Suriname	$3,480
81	Sri Lanka	$3,460

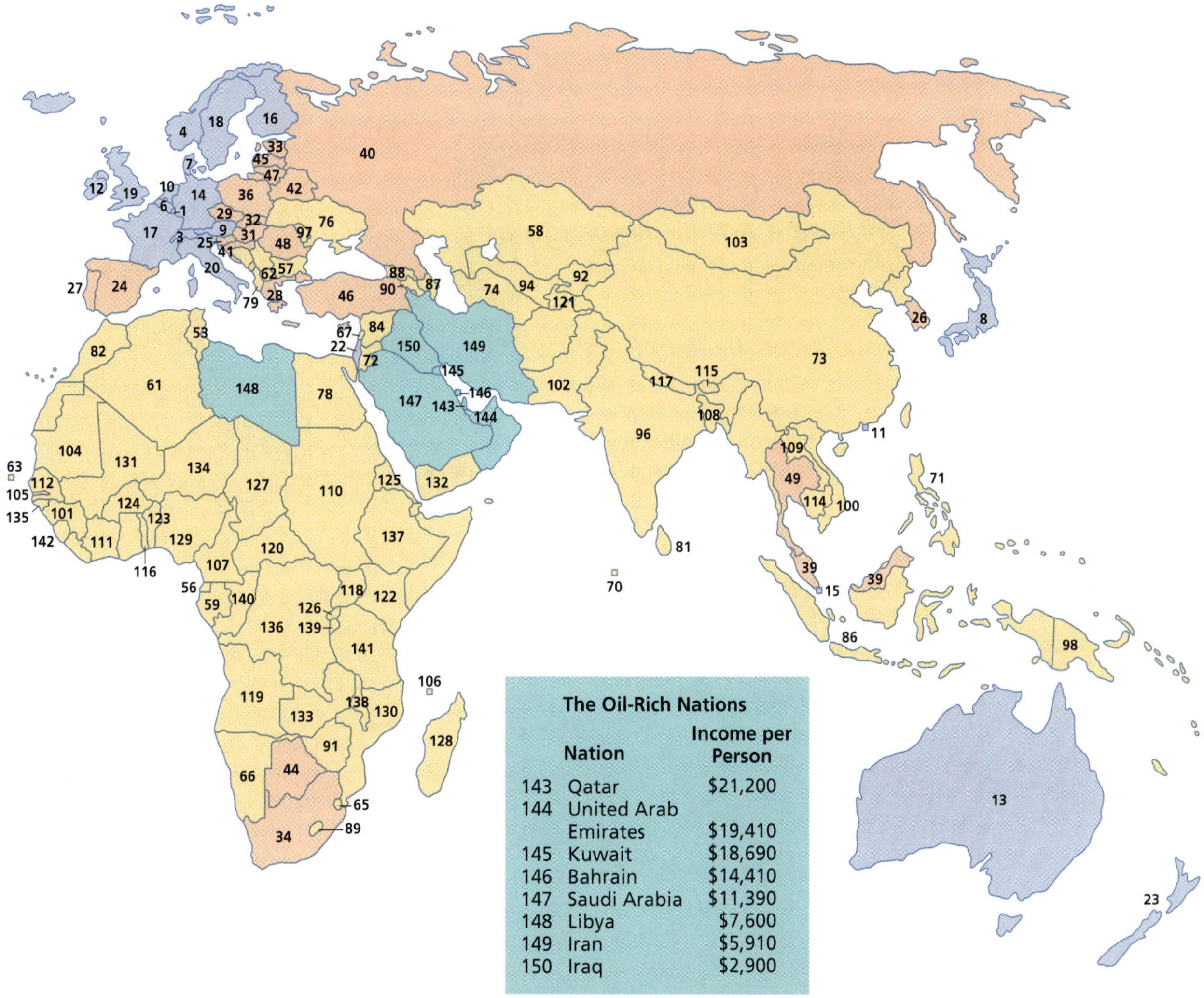

The Oil-Rich Nations

	Nation	Income per Person
143	Qatar	$21,200
144	United Arab Emirates	$19,410
145	Kuwait	$18,690
146	Bahrain	$14,410
147	Saudi Arabia	$11,390
148	Libya	$7,600
149	Iran	$5,910
150	Iraq	$2,900

The Least Industrialized Nations

	Nation	Income per Person
82	Morocco	$3,450
83	Jamaica	$3,440
84	Syria	$3,340
85	Ecuador	$2,910
86	Indonesia	$2,830
87	Azerbaijan	$2,740
88	Georgia	$2,680
89	Lesotho	$2,590
90	Armenia	$2,580
91	Zimbabwe	$2,550
92	Krygyzstan	$2,540
93	Honduras	$2,400
94	Uzbekistan	$2,360
95	Bolivia	$2,360
96	India	$2,340
97	Moldova	$2,230
98	Papua-New Guinea	$2,180
99	Nicaragua	$2,080
100	Vietnam	$2,000
101	Guinea	$1,930
102	Pakistan	$1,860
103	Mongolia	$1,760
104	Mauritania	$1,630
105	Gambia	$1,620
106	Comoros	$1,590
107	Cameroon	$1,590
108	Bangladesh	$1,590
109	Laos	$1,540
110	Sudan	$1,520
111	Cote d'Ivoire	$1,500
112	Senegal	$1,480
113	Haiti	$1,470
114	Cambodia	$1,440
115	Bhutan	$1,440
116	Togo	$1,410
117	Nepal	$1,370
118	Uganda	$1,210
119	Angola	$1,180
120	Central African Republic	$1,160
121	Tajikistan	$1,090
122	Kenya	$1,010
123	Benin	$980
124	Burkina Faso	$970
125	Eritrea	$960
126	Rwanda	$930
127	Chad	$870
128	Madagascar	$820
129	Nigeria	$800
130	Mozambique	$800
131	Mali	$780
132	Yemen	$770
133	Zambia	$750
134	Niger	$740
135	Guinea-Bissau	$710
136	Congo, Democratic Republic of	$680
137	Ethiopia	$660
138	Malawi	$600
139	Burundi	$580
140	Congo	$570
141	Tanzania	$520
142	Sierra Leone	$480

*Income is the country's per capita gross national product measured in U.S. dollars. Since some totals vary widely from year to year, they must be taken as approximate.

Sources: By the author. Based on Famighetti 1999, *Statistical Abstract* 2000:Table 1364, Haub and Cornelius 2001.

The benefits of industrialization are uneven. Large numbers of people in the Industrializing Nations remain illiterate and desperately poor. Conditions can be gruesome, as discussed in the following Thinking Critically section.

THINKING Critically

Open Season: Children As Prey

What is childhood like in the Industrializing Nations? The answer depends on who your parents are. If you are the son or daughter of rich parents, childhood can be pleasant—a world filled with luxuries, and even servants. If you are born into poverty, but living in a rural area where there is plenty to eat, life can still be good—although there may be no books, television, and little education. If you live in a slum, however, life can be horrible—worse even than in the slums of the Most Industrialized Nations. Let's take a glance at what is happening to children in the slums of Brazil.

There is not enough food—this you can take for granted—in addition to broken homes, alcoholism, drug abuse, and a lot of crime. From your knowledge of slums in the Most Industrialized Nations, you would expect these things. What you may not expect, however, are the brutal conditions in which Brazilian slum *(favela)* children live.

Sociologist Martha Huggins (1993; 2000) reports that poverty is so deep that children and adults swarm over garbage dumps to try to find enough decaying food to keep them alive. You might also be surprised to discover that in Brazil the owners of some of these dumps hire armed guards to keep the poor out—so they can sell the garbage for pig food. And you might be shocked to learn that the Brazilian police and death squads murder some of the children. Some associations of shop owners even hire hit men and auction designated victims off to the lowest bidder! The going rate is half a month's salary—figured at the low Brazilian minimum wage.

Life is cheap in the poor nations—but death squads for children? To understand this, we must first note that Brazil has a long history of violence. Brazil also has a high rate of poverty, has only a tiny middle class, and is controlled by a small group of families who, under a veneer of democracy, make the country's major decisions. Hordes of homeless children, with no schools or jobs, roam the streets. To survive, they shine shoes, beg, steal, and deliver drugs. These street children are viewed as dangerous, and as a threat to society.

To "respectable" storekeepers and shoppers, these children are nothing but trouble. They hurt business, for customers feel intimidated when they see a group of begging children clustered in front of stores. With no effective social institutions to care for these children, one solution is to kill them. As Huggins notes, murder sends a clear message—especially if it is accompanied by ritual torture—gouging out the eyes, ripping open the chest, cutting off the genitals, and raping the girls.

Not all life is bad in the Industrializing Nations, but this is about as bad as it gets.

For Your CONSIDERATION . . .

Do you think there is anything the Most Industrialized Nations can do about this situation? Or is it any of their business? Is it, though unfortunate, just an "internal" affair that is up to the Brazilians to handle as they wish?

The Least Industrialized Nations

In the Least Industrialized Nations, most people are peasant farmers living on farms or in villages. These nations account for 49 percent of the Earth's land and 68 percent of the world's people.

Poverty plagues the Least Industrialized Nations, as you can see from the photos on the next three pages. On pages 250–251 are photos I took of people who actually *live* in a city dump. Although wealthy nations have their pockets of poverty, *most* people in the Least Industrialized nations live on less than $1,000 a year, in many cases considerably less. *Most* of them have no running water, indoor plumbing, or access to trained physicians. Because modern medicine has cut infant mortality but not births, the population of most of these nations is mushrooming. This places even greater burdens on their limited resources, causing them to fall farther behind each year.

Modifying the Model

This classification of countries into Most Industrialized, Industrializing, and Least Industrialized is helpful in that it pinpoints gross differences among them. But it also presents problems. As mentioned, just how much industrialization does a nation need in order to be classified as Most Industrialized or Industrializing? Also, in Chapter 6 we noted that several nations have become "postindustrial." Does this new stage require a separate classification? Finally, the oil-rich nations of the Middle East are not industrialized, but by providing the oil and gasoline that fuel the machinery of the Most Industrialized Nations, some have become immensely wealthy. Consequently, to classify them simply as Least Industrialized glosses over significant distinctions, such as their modern hospitals, extensive prenatal care, pure water systems, abundant food and shelter, high literacy, and even computerized banking (see the Social Map on pages 246–247).

Kuwait, on whose formal behalf the United States and other Most Industrialized Nations fought Iraq in the first Gulf War, is an excellent example of the problem. Kuwait is so wealthy that almost none of its citizens works for a living. The government simply pays them a generous annual salary just for being citizens. Migrant workers from the poor nations do most of the onerous chores that daily life requires, while highly skilled workers from the Most Industrialized Nations run the specialized systems that keep Kuwait's economy going—and, as with the first Gulf War, apparently fight its wars for it as well. Table 9.3 reflects this significant distinction.

Homeless people sleeping on the streets is a common sight in India's cities. I took this photo in Chennai (formerly Madras).

Table 9.3 An Alternative Model of Global Stratification

Four Worlds of Development
1. Most Industrialized Nations
2. Industrializing Nations
3. Least Industrialized Nations
4. Oil-rich, nonindustrialized nations

How Did the World's Nations Become Stratified?

How did the globe become stratified into such distinct worlds? The commonsense answer is that the poorer nations have fewer resources than the richer nations. As with so many commonsense answers, however, this one, too, falls short. Many of the Industrializing and Least Industrialized Nations are rich in natural resources, while one Most Industrialized Nation, Japan, has few. Four theories explain how global stratification came about.

Colonialism

The first theory, **colonialism**, focuses on how the countries that industrialized first got the jump on the rest of the world. Beginning in Great Britain about 1750, industrialization spread throughout western Europe. Plowing some of their immense profits into powerful armaments and fast ships, these countries invaded weaker nations, making colonies out of them (Harrison 1993). After subduing these weaker nations, the more powerful countries left behind a controlling force in order to exploit the nations' labor and natural resources. At one point, there was even a free-for-all among the industrialized European

colonialism the process by which one nation takes over another nation, usually for the purpose of exploiting its labor and natural resources

THROUGH THE AUTHOR'S LENS

The Dump People:

Working and Living and Playing in the City Dump of Phnom Penh, Cambodia

I **went to Phnom Penh, the capital of Cambodia, to inspect** orphanages, to see how well the children were being cared for. While there, I was told about people who live in the city dump. *Live* there? I could hardly believe my ears. I knew that people made their living by picking scraps from the city dump, but I didn't know they actually lived among the garbage. This I had to see for myself.

I did. And there I found a highly developed social organization—an intricate support system. Because words are inadequate to depict the abject poverty of the Least Industrialized Nations, these photos can provide more insight into these people's lives than anything I could say.

This is a typical sight—family and friends working together. The trash, which is constantly burning, contains harmful chemicals. Why do they do this? Because they have few options. It is either this or starve.

The **people live at the edge of the dump**, in homemade huts (visible in the background). This woman, who was on her way home after a day's work, put down her sack of salvaged items to let me take her picture.

After the garbage arrives by truck, people stream around it, struggling to be the first to discover something of value. The workers use metal picks, like the one the child is holding, to sift through the trash. Note that children work alongside the adults.

The children who live in the dump also play there. These children are riding bicycles on a "road," a packed, leveled area of garbage that leads to their huts. The huge stacks in the background are piled trash. Note the ubiquitous Nike.

One of my many surprises was to find food stands in the dump. Although this one primarily offers drinks and snacks, others serve more substantial food. One even has chairs for its customers.

I was surprised to learn that ice is delivered to the dump. This woman is using a hand grinder to crush ice for drinks for her customers. The customers, of course, are other people who also live in the dump.

At the day's end, the workers wash at the community pump. This hand pump serves all their water needs–drinking, washing, and cooking. There is no indoor plumbing. The weeds in the background serve that purpose.

Not too many visitors to Phnom Penh tell a cab driver to take them to the **city dump**. The cabbie looked a bit perplexed, but he did as I asked. Two cabs are shown here because my friends insisted on accompanying me.

I know they were curious themselves, but my friends had also discovered that the destinations I want to visit are usually not in the tourist guides, and they wanted to protect me.

countries as they rushed to divide up an entire continent. As they sliced Africa into pieces, even tiny Belgium got into the act and acquired the Congo, which was *seventy-five* times larger than itself.

Whereas the more powerful European countries would plant their national flags in a colony and send their representatives to run the government, the United States usually chose to plant corporate flags in a colony and let these corporations dominate the territory's government. Central and South America are prime examples. There were exceptions, such as the conquest of the Philippines, which President McKinley said was "to educate the Filipinos, and uplift and civilize and Christianize them" (Krugman 2002). The purpose of colonialism was to establish *economic colonies*—to exploit the nation's people and resources for the benefit of the "mother" country.

Colonialism, then, shaped many of the Least Industrialized Nations. In some instances, the Most Industrialized Nations were so powerful that to divide their spoils, they drew lines across a map, creating new states without regard for tribal or cultural considerations (Kifner 1999). Britain and France did just this in North Africa and parts of the Middle East, which is why the national boundaries of Libya, Saudi Arabia, Kuwait, and other countries are so straight. This legacy of European conquests still erupts into racial-ethnic and tribal violence, because groups with no history of national identity were arbitrarily incorporated into the same political boundaries.

World System Theory

To explain how global stratification came about, Immanuel Wallerstein (1974, 1979, 1984, 1990) developed **world system theory.** He analyzed how industrialization led to four groups of nations. Those that industrialized first (Britain, France, Holland, and later Germany) grew rich and powerful. He calls these the *core nations.* The nations around the Mediterranean grew dependent on trade with these core nations, and their economies stagnated. Wallerstein calls this group the *semiperiphery.* The economies of the eastern European countries, which sold cash crops to the core nations, developed even less. This third group is the *periphery,* or fringe nations. A fourth group of nations was left out of the development of capitalism altogether. This *external area* includes most of Africa and Asia. As capitalism expanded, the relationships among these groups of nations changed. Most notably, Asia is no longer left out of capitalism.

The **globalization of capitalism**—the adoption of capitalism around the world—has created extensive ties among the world's countries. Production and trade are now so interconnected that events around the globe affect us all. Sometimes this is immediate, as happens when a revolution interrupts the flow of raw materials, or if terrorists managed to get their hands on nuclear weapons. At other times the effects are like a slow ripple, as when a government's policies impede its ability to compete in world markets. All of today's societies, then, no matter where they are located, are part of a *world system.*

This interconnection is more evident in some instances, especially in the case of Mexico and the United States. The following Thinking Critically section explores implications of Mexico's *maquiladoras.*

world system theory economic and political connections that tie the world's countries together

globalization of capitalism capitalism (investing to make profits) becoming the globe's dominant economic system

THINKING Critically

When Globalization Comes Home: *Maquiladoras* South of the Border

When Humberto drives his truck among Ciudad Juarez's shanties—patched together from packing crates, discarded tires, and cardboard—women and children flock around him. Humberto is the water man, and his truckload of water means life.

Two hundred thousand Mexicans are rushing to Juarez each year, fleeing the hopelessness of the rural areas in pursuit of a better life. They didn't have running water or plumbing in the country anyway, and here they have the possibility of a job, a weekly check that will buy food for the kids.

The pay is $10 a day.

This may not sound like much, but it is more than twice the minimum daily wage in Mexico.

Assembly-for-export plants, known as *maquiladoras,* dot the Mexican border. The North American

Free Trade Agreement (NAFTA) allows companies to import materials to Mexico without paying tax, and to then export the finished products into the United States, again without tax. It's a sweet deal—few taxes and $10 a day for workers starved for jobs. Some get an even sweeter deal. They pay their workers Mexico's minimum wage of $4—for 10-hour days with a 30 minute break (Darweesh 2000).

That these workers have to live in shacks, with no running water or means of sewage disposal, is not their concern.

Then there is the pollution. Juarez pumps 75 million gallons of untreated sewage into the Rio Grande—every day. Other *maquiladora* towns along the border do the same.

There is also the loss of jobs for U.S. workers. Along the sewage-infested Rio Grande sit 6 of the 15 poorest cities in the United States. NAFTA didn't bring poverty to these cities. They were poor before, but residents resent the jobs they've seen move across the border (Thompson 2001).

What if workers organize and demand better pay? The main obstacle is that even cheaper labor beckons. Guatemala and Honduras will gladly take the *maquiladoras.* So will China, where workers make $1 a day (Skiba 2001). Many *maquiladoras* are already moving farther south in Mexico, where the workers are even more desperate and will work for less (Thompson 2002).

Many Mexicans would say that this presentation is one-sided. "Sure there are problems," they say, "but that is always how it is when a country industrializes. Don't you realize that the *maquiladoras* bring jobs to people who have no work? They also bring roads, telephone lines, and electricity to undeveloped areas." "In fact," says Vicente Fox, the president of Mexico, "workers at the *maquiladoras* make more than the average salary in Mexico—and that's what we call fair wages" (Fraser 2001).

A photo taken inside a maquiladora *in Reynosa, Mexico. The worker is brazing mufflers onto copper pipes, which will be shipped backed to the United States.*

For Your CONSIDERATION . . .

Let's apply our three theoretical perspectives to see where reality lies. Conflict theorists say that capitalists weaken the bargaining power of workers by exploiting divisions among them. In what is known as the *split labor market,* to lower the cost of labor capitalists pit one group of workers against another. What examples of this do you see here?

When functionalists analyze a situation, they identity its functions and dysfunctions. What functions and dysfunctions of *maquiladoras* do you see?

Do *maquiladoras* represent exploitation or opportunity? As symbolic interactionists point out, reality is a perspective based on one's experience. What multiple realities do you see here?

This is where the workers live.

Culture of Poverty

An entirely different explanation of global stratification was proposed by economist John Kenneth Galbraith (1979). Galbraith claimed that the cultures of the Least Industrialized Nations hold them back. Building on the ideas of anthropologist Oscar Lewis (1966a, 1966b), Galbraith argued that some nations are crippled by a **culture of poverty,** a way of life that perpetuates poverty from one generation to the next. He explained it this way: Most of the world's poor live in rural areas, where they barely eke out a living from the land. Their marginal life offers little room for error or risk, so they stick closely to tried-and-true, traditional ways. To experiment with new farming techniques could be a disaster, for failure would lead to hunger and death.

Their religion also encourages them to accept their situation, for it teaches fatalism, that an individual's position in life is God's will. In India, the Dalits are taught that they must have done very bad things in a previous life to suffer so. They are supposed to submit to their situation—and in the next life maybe they'll come back in a more desirable state.

Evaluating the Theories

Most sociologists prefer colonialism and world system theory. To them, an explanation based on a culture of poverty places blame on the victim—the poor nations themselves. It points to characteristics of the poor nations, rather than to international political arrangements that benefit the Most Industrialized Nations at the expense of the poor nations. But even taken together, these theories yield only part of the picture. None of these theories, for example, would have led anyone to expect that after World War II, Japan—which had a religion that stressed fatalism, which had two major cities destroyed by atomic bombs, and which had been stripped of its colonies—would become an economic powerhouse.

Each theory, then, yields but a partial explanation, and the grand theorist who will put the many pieces of this puzzle together has yet to appear.

Maintaining Global Stratification

Regardless of how the world's nations became stratified, why do the same countries remain rich year after year, while the rest stay poor? Let's look at two explanations of how global stratification is maintained.

Neocolonialism

Sociologist Michael Harrington (1977) argued that colonialism fell out of style and was replaced by **neocolonialism.** When World War II changed public sentiment about sending soldiers and colonists to weaker countries, the Most Industrialized Nations turned to the international markets as a way to control the Least Industrialized Nations. These powerful nations determine how much they will pay for tin from Bolivia, copper from Peru, coffee from Brazil, and so forth. They also move hazardous industries into the Least Industrialized Nations.

As many of us to our sorrow learn, owing a large debt and falling behind on payments puts us at the mercy of our creditors. So it is with neocolonialism. The *policy* of selling weapons and other manufactured goods to the Least Industrialized Nations on credit turns those countries into eternal debtors. The capital they need to develop their own industries goes instead to the debt, which becomes bloated with mounting interest. Keeping these nations in debt makes them submit to trading terms dictated by the neocolonialists (Carrington 1993; S. Smith 2001).

The oil-rich Middle Eastern nations are a special case of neocolonialism. Because of significant events that recur in this area of the world—such as the two Gulf Wars and the terrorism that originates from this region—it is worth considering Saudi Arabia (*Strategic Energy Policy* 2001; Prashad 2002). This nation was founded under Great Britain's direction and named after the man (Ibn Saud) that Great Britain picked to lead it. To keep

culture of poverty the assumption that the values and behaviors of the poor make them fundamentally different from other people, that these factors are largely responsible for their poverty, and that parents perpetuate poverty across generations by passing these characteristics to their children

neocolonialism the economic and political dominance of the Least Industrialized Nations by the Most Industrialized Nations their factories running at a profit, the Most Industrialized Nations need low-priced oil. The Saudi's provide it. If other nations pump less—no matter the cause, whether revolution or a lowering of production in order to raise prices—the Saudis make up the shortfall. In return for stable oil prices, the United States supports the Saudi royal family, overlooks human rights violations, and, not insignificantly, furnishes the latest weapons.

Multinational Corporations

Multinational corporations, companies that operate across many national boundaries, also help to maintain the global dominance of the Most Industrialized Nations. In some cases, multinational corporations exploit the Least Industrialized Nations directly. A prime example is the United Fruit Company. For decades, this company controlled national and local politics in Central America. It ran these nations as fiefdoms for the company's own profit while the U.S. Marines waited in the wings in case the company's interests needed to be backed up.

Most commonly, however, multinational corporations help to maintain international stratification simply by doing business. A single multinational may manage mining operations in several countries, do manufacturing in many others, and run transportation and marketing networks around the globe. No matter where the profits are made, or where they are reinvested, the primary beneficiaries are the Most Industrialized Nations, especially the one in which the multinational corporation has its world headquarters. As Michael Harrington (1977) stressed, the real profits are made in processing the products and in controlling their distribution—and these profits are withheld from the Least Industrialized Nations. For more on multinational corporations, see pages 401–406.

Multinational corporations try to work closely with the elites of the Least Industrialized Nations (Sklair 2001; Wayne 2003). These elites, which live a sophisticated upper-class life in the major cities of their home country, send their children to prestigious universities, such as Oxford, the Sorbonne, and Harvard. The multinational corporations funnel investments to these small circles of power, whose members favor projects such as building laboratories and computer centers in the capital city, projects that do not help the vast majority of their people, who live in poor, remote villages where they eke out meager livings on small plots of land.

The end result is an informal partnership between multinational corporations and the elites of the Least Industrialized Nations. To gain access to the country's raw materials, labor, and market, the corporations pay off the elites. (These are politely called "subsidies" and "offsets," not bribes.) The elites use their payoffs not only to maintain their genteel lifestyle, but also to purchase advanced weapons from multinational corporations, which they use to oppress their people and preserve their dominance. Both elites and corporations benefit from political stability, which is necessary for keeping their diabolical partnership alive.

This, however, is not the full story. Multinational corporations also play a role in changing international stratification. This is an unintentional by-product of their worldwide search for cheap resources and labor. By moving manufacturing from the Most Industrialized Nations to the Least Industrialized Nations, they not only exploit cheap labor but also bring jobs and money to these nations. Although workers in the Least Industrialized Nations are paid a pittance, it is more than they can earn elsewhere. With new factories come opportunities to develop skills and a capital base.

This does not occur in all nations, but the Pacific Rim nations, nicknamed the "Asian tigers," are a remarkable case in point. They have developed such a strong capital base that they have begun to rival the older capitalist nations. As has become painfully apparent, these countries also are subject to capitalism's infamous "boom and bust" cycles. Many workers in the *maquiladoras* that you just read about will have their dreams smashed as capitalism moves into its next downturn.

multinational corporations companies that operate across national boundaries; also called *transnational corporations*

Technology and Global Domination

The race between the Most and Least Industrialized Nations to develop and apply the new technologies is like a race between a marathon runner and a one-legged man. Can the outcome be in doubt? The vast profits piled up by the multinational corporations allow the Most Industrialized Nations to invest huge sums in the latest technology. Gillette, for example, spent $100 million simply so it could adjust its production "on an hourly basis" (Zachary 1995). These millions came from just one U.S. company. Many Least Industrialized Nations would love to have $100 million to invest in their entire economy, much less to use for fine-tuning the production of razor blades. In short, in the quest to maintain global domination, the new technologies pile up even more advantages for the Most Industrialized Nations.

A Concluding Note

Let's return to the three families in our opening vignette. Remember that these families represent distinct worlds of money and power, that is, global stratification. Their life chances—from access to material possessions to the opportunity for education and even the likely age at which they will die—are profoundly affected by the global stratification we've looked at. This division of the globe into interconnected units of nations with more or less wealth and more or less power and prestige, then, is much more than a matter of theoretical interest. In fact, it is *your* life we are talking about.

SUMMARY and REVIEW

Systems of Social Stratification

What is social stratification?

Social stratification refers to a hierarchy of relative privilege based on power, property, and prestige. Every society stratifies its members, and in every society men as a group are placed above women as a group. P. 231.

What are four major systems of social stratification?

Four major stratification systems are slavery, caste, estate, and class. The essential characteristic of **slavery** is that some people own other people. Initially, slavery was based not on race but on debt, punishment, or defeat in battle. Slavery could be temporary or permanent, and was not necessarily passed on to one's children. North American slaves had no legal rights, and the system was gradually buttressed by a racist **ideology.** In a **caste system,** status is determined by birth and is lifelong. The **estate system** of feudal Europe consisted of the nobility, clergy, and commoners. A **class system** is much more open than these other systems, for it is based primarily on money or material possessions. Industrialization encourages the formation of class systems. Gender cuts across all forms of social stratification. Pp. 231–236.

What Determines Social Class?

Karl Marx argued that a single factor determines social class: If you own the means of production, you belong to the **bourgeoisie;** if you do not, you are one of the **proletariat.** Max Weber argued that three elements determine social class: *property, prestige,* and *power.* Pp. 236–238.

Why Is Social Stratification Universal?

To explain why stratification is universal, functionalists Kingsley Davis and Wilbert Moore argued that in order to attract the most capable people to fill its important positions, society must offer them greater rewards. Melvin Tumin said that if this view were correct, society would be a **meritocracy,** with all positions awarded on the basis of merit. Gaetano Mosca argued that stratification is inevitable because every society must have leadership, which by definition means inequality. Conflict theorists argue that stratification comes about because resources are limited, and an elite emerges as groups struggle against one another for them. Gerhard Lenski suggested a synthesis between the functionalist and conflict perspectives. Pp. 239–241.

How Do Elites Maintain Stratification?

To maintain social stratification within a nation, the ruling class uses an ideology that justifies current arrangements. It also controls information and uses technology, and, when all else fails, depends on brute force. Pp. 241–242.

Comparative Social Stratification

What are key characteristics of stratification systems in other nations?

The most striking features of the British class system are speech and education. In Britain, accent reveals social class, and almost all of the elite attend "public" schools (the equivalent of our private schools). In what is now the former Soviet Union, communism was supposed to abolish class distinctions. Instead, it merely ushered in a different set of classes. Pp. 243–244.

Global Stratification: Three Worlds

How are the world's nations stratified?

The model presented here divides the world's nations into three groups: the Most Industrialized, the Industrializing, and the Least Industrialized. This layering represents relative property, power, and prestige. The oil-rich nations are an exception. Pp. 244–249.

How the World's Nations Became Stratified

Why are some nations rich and others poor?

The main theories that seek to account for global stratification are **colonialism, world system theory,** and the **culture of poverty.** Pp. 249–254.

Maintaining Global Stratification

How do elites maintain global stratification?

There are two basic explanations for why the world's countries remain stratified. **Neocolonialism** is the ongoing dominance of the Least Industrialized Nations by the Most Industrialized Nations. The second explanation points to the influence of **multinational corporations.** The new technology gives further advantage to the Most Industrialized Nations. Pp. 254–256.

Where can I read more on this topic?

Suggested readings for this chapter are at the end of this book.

THINKING Critically ABOUT CHAPTER 9

1. How do slavery, caste, estate, and class systems of social stratification differ?
2. Why is social stratification universal?
3. Do you think that the low-wage factories of the multinational corporations located in such countries as Mexico represent exploitation or opportunity? Why?

ADDITIONAL RESOURCES for This Chapter

www.ablongman.com/henslin7e

- *Content Select* Research Database for Sociology, with suggested key terms and annotated references
- Link to 2000 Census, with activities
- Flashcards of key terms and concepts
- Practice Tests
- Weblinks
- Interactive Maps

Chapter 10

Social Class in the United States

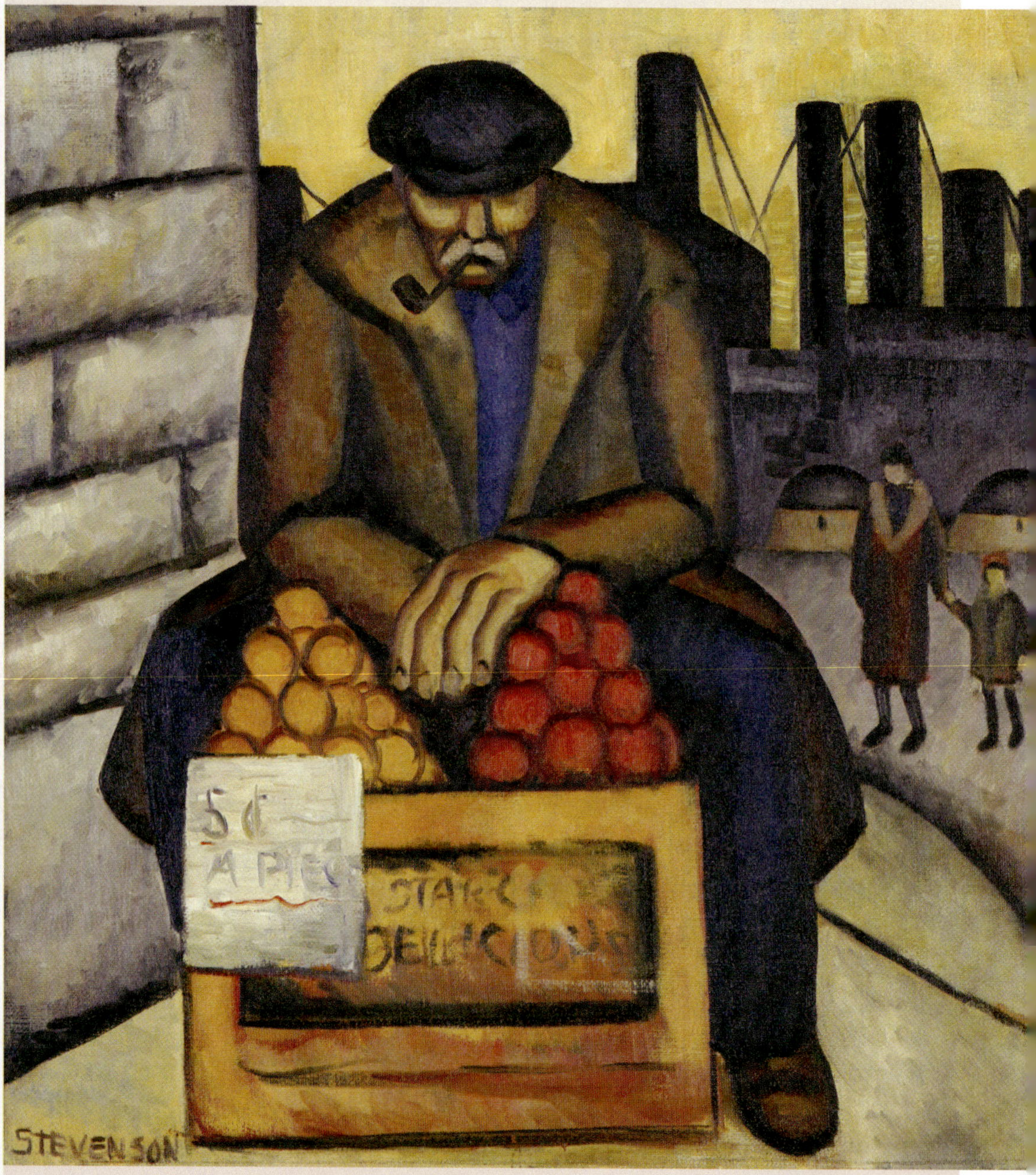

Barbara Stevenson, *Apple Vendor,* ca. 1933–1934

Ah, New Orleans, that fabled city on the Gulf. Images from its rich past floated through my head—pirates, wealth, intrigue. Memories from a pleasant vacation stirred my thoughts—the exotic French Quarter with its enticing aroma of Creole food and sounds of earthy jazz drifting through the air.

The shelter for the homeless, however, forced me back to an unwelcome reality. The shelter was the same as those I had visited in the North, West, and East—only dirtier. The dirt, in fact, was the worst that I had encountered during my research, and this shelter was the only one to insist on payment in exchange for sleeping in one of its filthy beds.

The men looked the same—disheveled and haggard, wearing that unmistakable expression of despair—just like the homeless anywhere in the country. Except for the accent, you wouldn't know what region you were in. Poverty wears the same tired face, I realized. The accent may differ, but the look remains the same.

The next morning, I felt indignation swell within me. I had grown used to the sights and smells of abject poverty. Those no longer surprised me. But now, just a block or so from the shelter, I was startled by a sight so out of step with the misery and despair I had just experienced that I stopped in midtrack.

I was startled by a sight so out of step with the misery and despair I had just experienced that I stopped in midtrack.

Confronting me were life-size, full-color photos mounted on the transparent plastic shelter that covered a bus stop. Staring back at me were finely dressed men and women proudly strutting about as they modeled elegant suits, dresses, diamonds, and furs.

A wave of disgust swept over me. "Something is cockeyed in this society," I thought, my mind refusing to stop juxtaposing these images with the suffering I had just witnessed. Occasionally the reality of social class hits home with brute force. This was one of those moments for me.

The disjunction that I felt in New Orleans was triggered by the ads, but it was not the first time that I had experienced this sensation. Whenever my

Chapter Outline

research abruptly transported me from the world of the homeless to one of another social class, I experienced a sense of disjointed unreality. Each social class has its own way of being, and because these fundamental orientations to the world contrast so sharply, the classes do not mix well.

What Is Social Class?

"There are the poor and the rich—and then there are you and I, neither poor nor rich." This is just about as far as most Americans' consciousness of social class goes. Let's try to flesh out this idea.

Our task is made somewhat difficult because sociologists have no clear-cut, agreed-on definition of social class. As noted in the last chapter, conflict sociologists (of the Marxist orientation) see only two social classes: those who own the means of production and those who do not. The problem with this view, say most sociologists, is that it lumps too many people together. Physicians and corporate executives with incomes of $500,000 a year are lumped together with hamburger flippers who work at McDonald's for $13,000 a year.

Most sociologists agree with Weber that there is more to social class than just a person's relationship to the means of production. Consequently, most sociologists use the components Weber identified and define **social class** as a large group of people who rank close to one another in wealth, power, and prestige. These three elements separate people into different lifestyles, give them different chances in life, and provide them with distinct ways of looking at the self and the world.

Let's look at how sociologists measure these three components of social class.

Wealth

The primary dimension of social class is **wealth,** the value of a person's property. *Property* comes in many forms, such as buildings, land, animals, machinery, cars, stocks, bonds, businesses, and bank accounts. **Income,** in contrast, is money received from a business or from wages, rent, interest, or royalties.

Distinction Between Wealth and Income

Wealth and income are sometimes confused, but they are not the same. Some people have much wealth and little income. For example, a farmer may own much land (a form of wealth), but bad weather, combined with the high cost of fertilizers and machinery, can cause the income to dry up. Others have much income and little wealth. An executive with a $250,000 annual income may be debt-ridden. Below the surface prosperity—the exotic vacations, country club membership, private schools for the children, sports cars, and an elegant home—the credit cards may be maxed out, the sports cars in danger of being repossessed, and the mortgage payments "past due." Typically, however, wealth and income go together.

Who owns the wealth in the United States? One answer, of course, is "everyone." Although this statement has some merit, it overlooks how the nation's wealth is divided among "everyone." Let's look at how the two forms of wealth—property and income—are distributed among Americans.

Distribution of Wealth

Overall, Americans are worth a hefty sum, about $30 trillion (*Statistical Abstract* 2002:Table 679). This includes all real estate, stocks, bonds, and business assets in the entire country. Figure 10.1 shows how highly concentrated this wealth is. Most wealth, 68 percent, is owned by only *10 percent* of the nation's families. And the higher up the income ladder we go, the more concentrated this wealth becomes. As you can see from Figure 10.1, this 1 percent owns 40 percent of all the wealth in the United States.

Distribution of Income

How is income distributed in the United States? Economist Paul Samuelson (Samuelson and Nordhaus 2000) put it this way: "If we made an income pyramid out of a child's blocks, with each layer portraying $500 of income, the

social class according to Weber, a large group of people who rank close to one another in wealth, power, and prestige; according to Marx, one of two groups: capitalists who own the means of production or workers who sell their labor

wealth property and income

income money received from a job, business, or assets

In the United States, a mere 0.5 percent of the population owns over a quarter of the nation's wealth. Very few minorities are numbered among this 0.5 percent. An exception is Oprah Winfrey, who has had an ultra-successful career in entertainment and investing. Worth $1 billion, she is one of the richest 500 people in the entire world. Winfrey, who has given millions of dollars to help minority children, is shown here as she interviews Arnold Schwarzenegger and his wife, Maria Shriver.

Figure 10.1
Distribution of Wealth of Americans

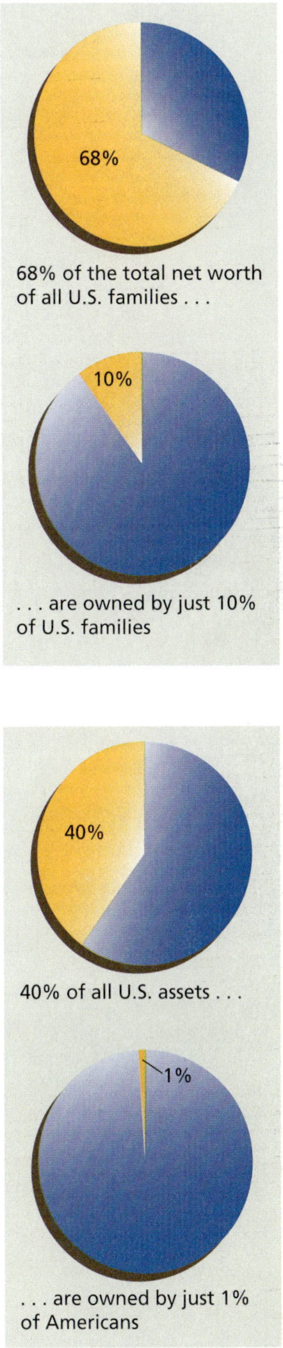

68%
68% of the total net worth of all U.S. families . . .
10%
. . . are owned by just 10% of U.S. families
40%
40% of all U.S. assets . . .
1%
. . . are owned by just 1% of Americans

Source: Western 2000.

peak would be far higher than Mount Everest, but most people would be within a few feet of the ground."

Actually, if each block were 1-½ inches tall, the typical American would be just 8 *feet off the ground,* for the average per capita income in the United States is about $30,000 per year. (This average income includes every American, even children.) The typical family climbs a little higher, for most families have more than one worker, and together they average about $51,000 a year. Yet compared with the few families who are on the mountain's peak, the average U.S. family would find itself only 13 feet off the ground (*Statistical Abstract* 2002:Tables 643, 660). Figure 10.2 portrays these differences.

The fact that some Americans enjoy the peaks of Mount Everest while most—despite their efforts—make it only 8 to 13 feet up the slope presents a striking image of income inequality in the United States. Another picture emerges if we divide the U.S. population into five equal groups and rank them from highest to lowest income. As Figure 10.3 shows, the top 20 percent of the population receives *almost half* (47.4 percent) of all income in the United States. In contrast, the bottom 20 percent of Americans receives only 4.3 percent of the nation's income.

Two features of Figure 10.3 are outstanding. First, notice how consistent income inequality remains through the years. Second, the changes that do occur indicate *growing inequality. The richest 20 percent of U.S. families have grown richer, while the poorest 20 percent have grown poorer.* Despite numerous antipoverty programs, the poorest 20 percent of Americans receive *less* of the nation's income today than they did in the 1940s (a drop from 5.4 percent to 4.3 percent). The richest 20 percent, in contrast, receive *more* than ever (an increase from about 41 percent to just over 47 percent).

The most affluent group in the United States is the chief executive officers (CEOs) of the nation's largest corporations. The *Wall Street Journal* surveyed the 350 largest U.S. companies to find out what they paid their CEOs ("Executive Pay," 2003). Their median compensation (including salaries, bonuses, and stock options) came to $3,022,000 a year. (Median means that half received more than this amount, and half less.) The CEOs' income—which does *not* include their interest payments, dividends, rents, and capital gains, or company-paid limousines and chauffeurs and private boxes at the opera and

Figure 10.2 Inequality of U.S. Income

Some U.S. incomes are higher than Mt. Everest
29,028 feet
If a 1½-inch child's block equals $500 of income, the average American is only 8 feet off the ground, the average family just 13 feet, while the income of some families propels them past the top of Mount Everest.
8 feet
13 feet
Average American
Average U.S. Family

Figure 10.3 Growing Inequality: The Percentage of the Nation's Income Received by Each Fifth of U.S. Families Since World War II

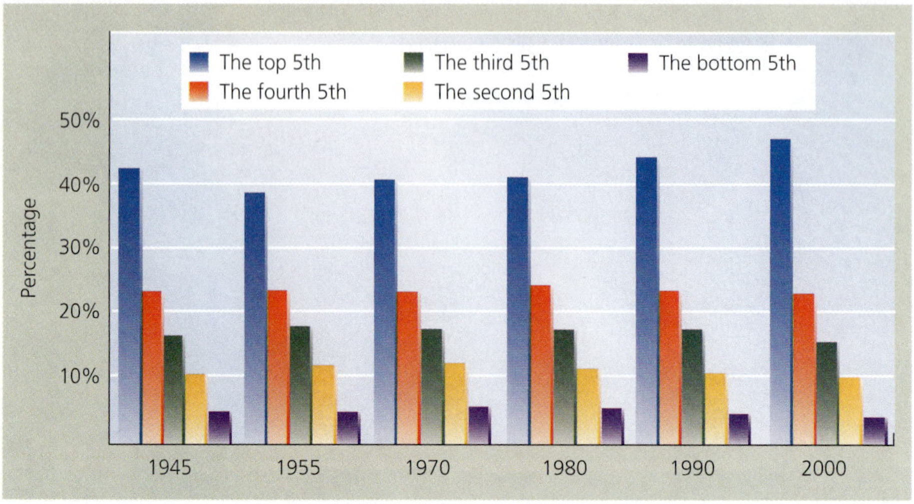

Note: The distribution of U.S. income—salaries, wages, and all other money received, except capital gains and government subsidies in the form of food stamps, health benefits, or subsidized housing.
Source: Statistical Abstract 1947; 2002:Table 659.

major league baseball games—is *85 times* higher than the average pay of U.S. workers (*Statistical Abstract* 2002: Table 611). To really see the disparity consider this: The average U.S. worker would have to work 3,671 years to earn the amount paid highest paid executive on Table 10.1 on the next page.

Imagine how you could live with an income like this. And this is precisely the point. Beyond cold numbers lies a dynamic reality that profoundly affects people's lives. The difference in wealth between those at the top and those at the bottom of the U.S. class structure means vastly different lifestyles. For example, a colleague of mine who was teaching at an exclusive eastern university piqued his students' curiosity when he lectured on poverty in Latin America. That weekend, one of his students borrowed his parents' corporate jet and pilot, and in class the next Monday he and his friends related their personal observations on poverty in Latin America. Americans who are at the low end of the in-

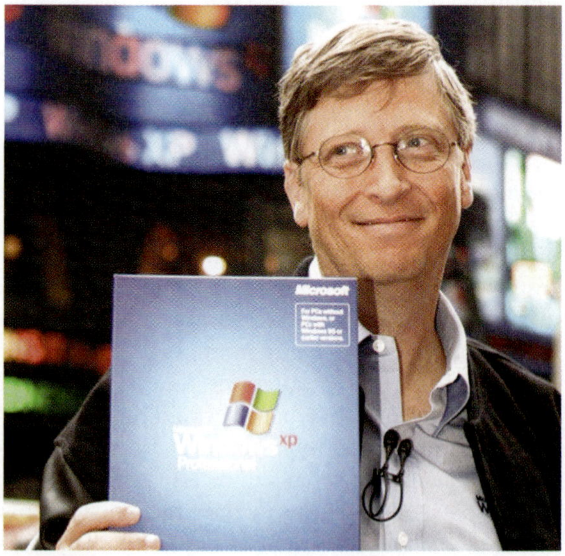

Bill Gates, a cofounder of Microsoft Corporation, is the wealthiest person in the world. His fortune runs between $50 billion and $100 billion, depending on the fluctuating value of his stock. His 40,000-square-foot home (sometimes called a "technopalace") in Seattle, Washington, is appraised at $110 million. In addition to being the wealthiest person in history, Gates is also the most generous. He has given more money to the poor and minorities than any individual in history.

come ladder, in contrast, lack the funds to travel even to a neighboring town for the weekend: Their choices revolve around whether to spend the little they have at the laundromat or on milk for the baby. In short, divisions of wealth represent not "mere" numbers, but choices that make vital differences in people's lives, a topic explored in the Down-to-Earth Sociology box below.

Table 10.1 Highest-Paid CEOs

Jeffrey C. Barbakow, Tenet Healthcare	$116.4 million
Irwin Mark Jacobs, Qualcomm	$63.2 million
Charles M. Cawley, MBNA	$48.3 million
Orin C. Smith, Starbucks	$38.8 million
Richard S. Fuld Jr., Lehman Brothers	$28.7 million
Scott G. McNealy, Sun Microsystems	$25.8 million
Vance D. Coffman, Lockheed Martin	$23.9 million

Source: "Executive Pay," 2003.

Power

Like many people, you may have said to yourself, "Sure, I can vote, but somehow the big decisions are always made despite what I might think. Certainly *I* don't make the decision to send soldiers to Afghanistan or Iraq. *I* don't launch missiles against Kosovo or Baghdad. *I* don't decide to raise taxes or lower interest rates. It isn't *I* who decides to change welfare benefits."

And then another part of you may say, "But I do participate in these decisions through my representatives in Congress, and by voting for president." True enough—as far as it goes. The trouble is, it just doesn't go far enough. Such views of being a participant in the nation's "big" decisions are a playback of the ideology we learn at an early age—an ideology that

DOWN-TO-EARTH SOCIOLOGY

How the Super-Rich Live

IT'S GOOD TO SEE HOW OTHER people live. It helps give us a different perspective for viewing life. Let's take a glimpse at the life of John Castle (his real name). After earning a degree in physics at MIT and an MBA at Harvard, John went into banking and securities, where he made more than $100 million (Lublin 1999).

Wanting to be close to someone famous, John bought President John F. Kennedy's "Winter White House," an oceanfront estate in Palm Beach, Florida. John spent $11 million to remodel the 13,000-square-foot house so it would be more to his liking. Among those changes: adding bathrooms numbers 14 and 15. He likes to show off John F. Kennedy's bed and also the dresser that has the drawer labeled "black underwear," carefully hand-lettered by Rose Kennedy.

If John gets bored at his beachfront estate—or tired of swimming in the Olympic-size pool where JFK swam the weekend before his assassination—he entertains himself by riding one of his thoroughbred horses at his nearby 10-acre ranch. If this fails to ease his boredom, he can relax aboard his custom-built 45-foot Hinckley yacht.

How do the super-rich live? It is difficult to even imagine their lifestyles, but this photo helps give you an idea of how different their lifestyles are from most of us. Shown here is Martha Stewart's home in East Hampton, Long Island. Many homes in the area are owned by celebrities and other wealthy residents.

The yacht is a real source of diversion. He once boarded it for an around-the-world trip. He didn't stay on board, though—just joined the cruise from time to time. A captain and crew kept the vessel on course, and whenever John felt like it he would fly in and stay a few days. Then he would fly back to the States to direct his business. He did this about a dozen times, flying perhaps 150,000 miles. An interesting way to go around the world.

How much does a custom-built Hinckley yacht cost? John can't tell you. As he says, "I don't want to know what anything costs. When you've got enough money, price doesn't make a difference. That's part of the freedom of being rich."

Right. And for John, being rich also means paying $1,000,000 to charter a private jet to fly Spot, his Appaloosa horse, back and forth to the vet. John didn't want Spot to have to endure a long trailer ride. Oh, and of course, there was the cost of Spot's medical treatment, another $500,000.

Other wealthy people put John to shame. Wayne Huizenga, the CEO of AutoNation, bought a 2,000-acre country club, complete with an 18-hole golf course, a 55,000-square foot clubhouse, and 68 slips for visiting vessels. The club is so exclusive that its only members are Wayne and his wife.

power the ability to carry out your will, even over the resistance of others

power elite C. Wright Mills' term for the top people in U.S. corporations, military, and politics that make the nation's major decisions

prestige respect or regard

Marx said is put forward by the elites to both legitimate and perpetuate their power. Sociologists Daniel Hellinger and Dennis Judd (1991) call this the "democratic facade" that conceals the real source of power in the United States.

Back in the 1950s, sociologist C. Wright Mills (1956) was criticized for insisting that **power**—the ability to carry out your will despite resistance—was concentrated in the hands of a few, for his analysis contradicted the dominant ideology of equality. As discussed in earlier chapters, Mills coined the term **power elite** to refer to those who make the big decisions in U.S. society.

Mills and others have stressed how wealth and power coalesce in a group of like-minded individuals who share ideologies and values. They belong to the same private clubs, vacation at the same exclusive resorts, and even hire the same bands for their daughters' debutante balls. These shared backgrounds and vested interests reinforce their view of the world and of their special place in it (Domhoff 1998, 1999a). This elite wields extraordinary power in U.S. society. Although there are exceptions, *most* U.S. presidents have come from this group—millionaire white men from families with "old money" (Baltzell and Schneiderman 1988).

Continuing in the tradition of Mills, sociologist William Domhoff (1990, 1998) argues that this group is so powerful that no major decision of the U.S. government is made without its approval. He analyzed how this group works behind the scenes with elected officials to determine both the nation's foreign and domestic policy—from setting Social Security taxes to imposing trade tariffs. Although Domhoff's conclusions are controversial—and alarming—they certainly follow logically from the principle that wealth brings power, and extreme wealth brings extreme power.

Prestige

Occupations and Prestige

What are you thinking about doing after college? Chances are you don't have the option of lolling under palm trees at the beach. Almost all of us have to choose an occupation and go to work. Look at Table 10.2 on the next page to see how the one you are considering stacks up in terms of **prestige** (respect or regard). Because we are moving toward a global society, this table also shows how the rankings given by Americans compare with those of the residents of sixty other countries.

Why do people give more prestige to some jobs than to others? If you look at Table 10.2, you will notice that the jobs at the top share four features:

1. They pay more.
2. They require more education.
3. They entail more abstract thought.
4. They offer greater autonomy (freedom, or self-direction).

Acceptable display of prestige and high social position varies over time and from one culture to another. Shown here is Elisabeth d'Autriche, queen of France from 1554 to 1592. It certainly would be difficult to outdress her at a party.

If we turn this around, we can see that people give less prestige to jobs that are low-paying, require less preparation or education, involve more physical labor, and are closely supervised. In short, the professions and white-collar jobs are ranked at the top of the list, with blue-collar jobs at the bottom.

One of the more interesting aspects of these rankings is how consistent they are across countries and over time. For example, people in every country rank college professors higher than nurses, nurses higher than social workers, and social workers higher than janitors. Similarly, the occupations that were ranked high 25 years ago still rank high today—and likely will rank high in the years to come.

Displaying Prestige

To get a sense of payoff, people want others to acknowledge their prestige. In times past, in some countries only the emperor and his family could wear purple—for it was the royal color. In France, only the nobility could wear lace. In England, no one could sit while the king was on his throne. Some kings and queens required that subjects walk backward as they left the room—so no one would "turn their back" on the "royal presence."

Table 10.2 Occupational Prestige: How the United States Compares with 60 Countries

Occupation	United States	Average of 60 Countries	Occupation	United States	Average of 60 Countries
Physician	86	78	Athletic coach	53	50
Supreme court judge	85	82	Social worker	52	56
College president	81	86	Electrician	51	44
Astronaut	80	80	Undertaker	49	34
Lawyer	75	73	Jazz musician	48	38
College professor	74	78	Real estate agent	48	49
Airline pilot	73	66	Mail carrier	47	33
Architect	73	72	Secretary	46	53
Biologist	73	69	Plumber	45	34
Dentist	72	70	Carpenter	43	37
Civil engineer	69	70	Farmer	40	47
Clergy	69	60	Bricklayer	36	34
Psychologist	69	66	Barber	36	30
Pharmacist	68	64	Store sales clerk	36	34
High school teacher	66	64	Truck driver	30	33
Registered nurse	66	54	Cab driver	28	28
Accountant	65	55	Garbage collector	28	13
Professional athlete	65	48	Waiter or waitress	28	23
Electrical engineer	64	65	Bartender	25	23
Author	63	62	Bellhop	25	14
Banker	63	67	Lives on public aid	25	16
Veterinarian	62	61	Bill collector	24	27
Police officer	61	40	Factory worker	24	29
Sociologist	61	67	Janitor	22	21
Journalist	60	55	Gas station attendant	21	25
Classical musician	59	56	Shoe shiner	17	12
Actor or actress	58	52	Street sweeper	11	13
Chiropractor	57	62			

Note: For five occupations not located in the 1994 source, the 1991 ratings were used: Supreme Court judge, astronaut, athletic coach, lives on public aid, and street sweeper.

Sources: Treiman 1977, Appendices A and D; Nakao and Treas 1991; 1994: Appendix D.

Concern with displaying prestige has not let up. For some, it is almost an obsession. Military manuals specify precisely who must salute whom. The U.S. president enters a room only after others are present (to show that *he* isn't the one waiting for *them*). They must also be standing when he enters. In the courtroom, bailiffs, sometimes armed, make certain that everyone stands when the judge enters.

The display of prestige permeates society. In Los Angeles, some people list their address as Beverly Hills and then add their correct ZIP code. When East Detroit changed its name to East Pointe to play off its proximity to swank Grosse Pointe, property values shot up (Fletcher 1997). Many pay more for clothing that bears a "designer" label. Prestige is often a primary factor in deciding which college to attend. Everyone knows how the prestige of a generic sheepskin from Regional State College compares with a degree from Harvard, Princeton, Yale, or Stanford.

Interestingly, status symbols vary with social class. Clearly, only the wealthy can afford certain items, such as yachts. But beyond affordability lies a class-based preference in status symbols. For example, Yuppies (young upwardly mobile professionals) are quick to flaunt labels, Hummers, and other material symbols to show that they have "arrived," while the rich, more secure in their status, often downplay such images. The wealthy see designer labels of the "common" classes as cheap and showy. They, of course, flaunt their own status symbols, such as $30,000 Rolex watches.

status consistency ranking high or low on all three dimensions of social class

status inconsistency ranking high on some dimensions of social class and low on others, also called *status discrepancy*

status social ranking; the position that someone occupies in society or a social group

anomie Durkheim's term for a condition of society in which people become detached from the norms that usually guide their behavior

Status Inconsistency

Ordinarily a person has a similar rank on all three dimensions of social class—wealth, power, and prestige. The homeless men in the opening vignette are an example. Such people are **status consistent.** Sometimes that match is not there, however, and someone has a mixture of high and low ranks, a condition called **status inconsistency.** This leads to some interesting situations.

Sociologist Gerhard Lenski (1954, 1966) pointed out that each of us tries to maximize our **status,** our social ranking. Thus individuals who rank high on one dimension of social class but lower on others expect people to judge them on the basis of their highest status. Others, however, who are trying to maximize their own position, may respond to them according to their lowest status.

A classic study of status inconsistency was done by sociologist Ray Gold (1952). He found that after apartment-house janitors unionized, they made more money than some of the tenants whose garbage they carried out. Tenants became upset when they saw their janitors driving more expensive cars than they did. Some attempted to "put the janitor in his place" by making "snotty" remarks to him. For their part, the janitors took secret delight in knowing "dirty" secrets about the tenants, gleaned from their garbage.

Individuals with status inconsistency, then, are likely to confront one frustrating situation after another. They claim the higher status, but are handed the lower one. The sociological significance of this condition is that such people tend to be more politically radical (Lenski 1954, Mateju and Kreidl 2001). An example is college professors. Their prestige is very high, as we saw in Table 10.2, but their incomes are relatively low. Hardly anyone in U.S. society is more educated, and yet college professors don't even come close to the top of the income pyramid. In line with Lenski's prediction, the politics of most college professors are left of center. This hypothesis may also hold true among academic departments; that is, the higher a department's average pay, the less radical are the members' politics. Teachers in departments of business and medicine, for example, are among the most highly paid in the university—and they also are the most politically conservative.

Instant wealth, the topic of the Down-to-earth Sociology box on the next page, provides an interesting case of status inconsistency.

Sociological Models of Social Class

The question of how many social classes there are is a matter of debate. Sociologists have proposed several models, but no model has gained universal support. There are two main models: one that builds on Marx, the other builds on Weber.

Figure 10.4 Marx's Model of the Social Classes

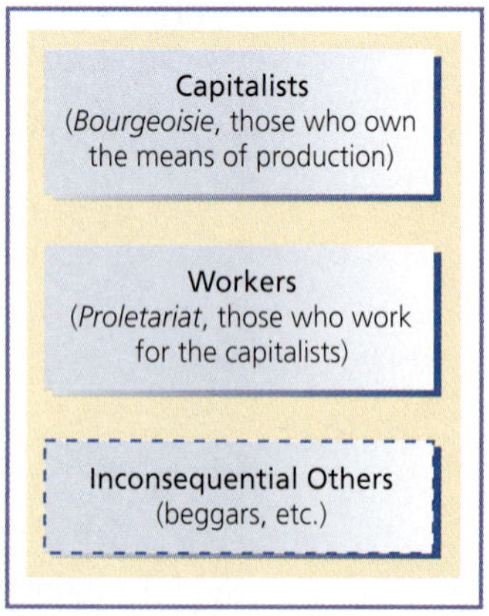

Updating Marx

Marx argued that there are just two classes—capitalists and workers—with membership based solely on a person's relationship to the means of production (see Figure 10.4). Sociologists have criticized this view because these categories are too broad. For example, because executives, managers, and supervisors don't own the means of production, they would be classified as workers. But what do these people have in common with assembly-line workers? Similarly, the category of "capitalist" takes in too many types. Some people employ a thousand workers, and their decisions directly affect a thousand families. Compare these people with a man I know in Godfrey, Illinois, who used to fix cars in his back yard. As Frank gained a following, he quit his regular job, and in a few years he put up a building with five bays and an office. Frank is now a capitalist, for he employs five or six mechanics and owns the tools and the building (the "means of production"). But what does he have in common with a factory owner who controls the lives of one thousand workers? Not only is Frank's work different, but so are his lifestyle and the way he looks at the world.

DOWN-TO-EARTH SOCIOLOGY

The Big Win: Life After the Lottery

"IF I JUST WIN THE LOTTERY, LIFE will be good. These problems I've got, they'll be gone. I can just see myself now."

So goes the dream. And many Americans shell out megabucks every week, with the glimmering hope that "Maybe this week, I'll hit it big."

Most are lucky to hit for $10, or maybe just win another scratch-off ticket.

But there are the big hits. What happens to these winners? Are their lives all roses and chocolate afterwards?

Unfortunately, we don't yet have any systematic studies of the big winners, so I can't tell you what life is like for the average winner. But several themes are apparent from reporters' interviews.

Status inconsistency *is common for lottery winners, whose new wealth is vastly greater than their education and occupational status. Shown here are John and Sandy Jarrell of Chicago, after they learned that they were one of 13 families to share a $295 million jackpot. How do you think their $22 million will affect their lives?*

The most common consequence of hitting it big is that life becomes topsy-turvy. All of us are rooted somewhere. We have connections with others that provide the basis for our orientations to life and how we feel about the world. Sudden wealth can rip these moorings apart, and the resulting *status inconsistency* can lead to a condition sociologists call **anomie.**

First comes the shock. As Mary Sanderson, a telephone operator in Dover, New Hampshire, who won $66 million, said, "I was afraid to believe it was real, and afraid to believe it wasn't." Mary says she never slept worse than her first night as a multimillionaire. "I spent the whole time crying—and throwing up" (Tresniowski 1999).

Reporters and TV cameras appear on your doorstep. "What are you going to do with all that money?" they demand. You haven't the slightest idea, but in a daze you mumble something.

Then come the calls. Some are welcome. Your Mom and Dad call to congratulate you. But long-forgotten friends and distant relatives suddenly remember how close they really are to you—and strangely enough, they all have emergencies that your money can solve. You even get calls from strangers who have sick mothers, sick kids, sick dogs . . .

You have to unplug the phone and get an unlisted number.

Some lottery winners are flooded with marriage proposals. These individuals certainly didn't become more attractive or sexy overnight—or did they? Maybe money makes people sexy.

You can no longer trust people. You don't know what their real motives are. Before, no one could be after your money because you didn't have any. You may even fear kidnappers. Before, this wasn't a problem—unless some kidnapper wanted the ransom of a seven-year-old car.

The normal becomes abnormal. Even picking out a wedding gift is a problem. If you give the usual toaster, everyone will think you're stingy. But should you write a check for $25,000? If you do, you'll be invited to every wedding in town—and everyone will expect the same.

Here is what happened to some lottery winners:

As a tip, a customer gave a lottery ticket to Tonda Dickerson, a waitress at the Waffle House in Grand Bay, Alabama. She won $10 million. (Yes, just like the Nicholas Cage movie, *It Could Happen to You.*) Her coworkers sued her, saying they had always agreed to split such winnings ("House Divided" 1999).

Then there is Michael Klinebiel of Rahwa, New Jersey. When he won $2 million, his mother, Phyllis, said they had pooled $20 a month for years to play the lottery. He said that was true, but his winning ticket wasn't from their pool. He bought this one on his own. Phyllis sued her son ("Sticky Ticket" 1998).

Frank Capaci, a retired electrician in Streamwood, Illinois, who won $195 million, is no longer welcome at his neighborhood bar, where he had hung out for years. Two bartenders had collected $5 from customers and driven an hour to Wisconsin to buy tickets. When Frank won, he gave $10,000 to each of them. They said he promised them more. Also, his former friends say that Capaci started to act "like a big shot," buying rounds of drinks but saying, "Except him," while pointing to someone he didn't like (Annin 1999).

Those who avoid *anomie* seem to be people who don't make sudden changes in their lifestyle or their behavior. They hold onto their old friends, routines, and other moorings in life that give them identity. Some even keep their old jobs—not for the money, of course, but because it anchors them to an identity with which they are familiar and comfortable.

Sudden wealth, in other words, poses a threat that has to be guarded against.

And I can just hear you say, "I'll take the risk!"

Table 10.3 Wright's Modification of Marx's Model of the Social Classes

1. Capitalists
2. Petty bourgeoisie
3. Managers
4. Workers

Sociologist Erik Wright (1985) resolved this problem by regarding some people as members of more than one class at the same time. They occupy what he called **contradictory class locations.** By this, Wright means that people's position in the class structure can generate contradictory interests. For example, the automobile-mechanic-turned-business-owner may want his mechanics to have higher wages since he, too, has experienced their working conditions. At the same time, his current interests—making profits and remaining competitive with other repair shops—lead him to resist pressures to raise wages.

Because of such contradictory class locations, Wright modified Marx's model. As summarized in Table 10.3, Wright identified four classes: (1) *capitalists,* business owners who employ many workers; (2) *petty bourgeoisie,* small business owners, (3) *managers,* who sell their own labor but also exercise authority over other employees; and (4) *workers,* who simply sell their labor to others. As you can see, this model allows finer divisions than the one Marx proposed, yet it maintains the primary distinction between employer and employee.

Problems persist, however. For example, in which category would we place college professors? And as you know, there are huge differences between managers. An executive at GM, for example, may manage a thousand workers, while a shift manager at McDonald's may be responsible for only a handful. They, too, have little in common.

Updating Weber

Sociologists Joseph Kahl and Dennis Gilbert (Gilbert and Kahl 1998; Gilbert 2003) developed a six-class model to portray the class structure of the United States and other capitalist countries. Think of their model—Figure 10.5 on the next page—as a ladder. Our discussion starts with the highest rung and moves downward. In line with Weber, on each lower rung you find less wealth, less power, and less prestige. Note that in this model education is also a primary measure of class.

The Capitalist Class Sitting on the top rung of the class ladder is a powerful elite that consists of just 1 percent of the U.S. population. As you saw in Figure 10.1, this capitalist class is so wealthy that it owns 40 percent of all U.S. assets. *This tiny 1 percent is worth more than the entire bottom 90 percent of the country* (Beeghley 2000).

Power and influence cling to this small elite. They have direct access to top politicians, and their decisions open or close jobs for millions of people. They even help to shape the consciousness of the nation: They own our major newspapers, magazines, and radio and television stations. They also control the boards of directors of our most influential colleges and universities. The super-rich perpetuate themselves in privilege by passing to their children their assets and social networks.

The capitalist class can be divided into "old" and "new" money. The longer that wealth has been in a family, the more it adds to the family's prestige. Their children seldom mingle with "common" folk—instead, they attend exclusive private schools where they learn views of life that support their privileged position. They don't work for wages; instead, many study business or enter the field of law so they can manage the family fortune. These old-money capitalists (also called "blue-bloods") wield vast power as they use their extensive political connections to protect their huge economic empires (Domhoff 1990, 1999b; Sklair 2001).

At the lower end of the capitalist class are the *nouveau riche,* those who have "new money." They are outsiders to this upper class. Although they have made fortunes in business, the stock market, inventions, entertainment, or sports, they have not attended the "right" schools, and they lack the influential social networks that come with old money. Not blue-bloods, they aren't trusted to have the right orientations to life (Burris 2000). Donald Trump, for example, is not listed in the *Social Register,* the "White Pages" of the blue-bloods that lists the most prestigious and wealthy one-tenth of 1 percent of the U.S. population. Trump says he "doesn't care," but he reveals his true feelings by adding that his heirs will be in it (Kaufman 1996). He probably is right, for the children of the new-

contradictory class locations Erik Wright's term for a position in the class structure that generates contradictory interests

Figure 10.5 The U.S. Social Class Ladder

Social Class	Education	Occupation	Income	Percentage of Population
Capitalist	Prestigious university	Investors and heirs, a few top executives	$500,000+	1%
Upper Middle	College or university, often with postgraduate study	Professionals and upper managers	$100,000+	15%
Lower Middle	High school or college; often apprenticeship	Semiprofessionals and lower managers, craftspeople, foremen	About $60,000	34%
Working	High school	Factory workers, clerical workers, low-paid retail sales, and craftspeople	About $35,000	30%
Working Poor	Some high school	Laborers, service workers, low-paid salespeople	About $17,000	16%
Underclass	Some high school	Unemployed and part-time, on welfare	Under $10,000	4%

Source: Based on Gilbert and Kahl 1998 and Gilbert 2003; income estimates are modified from Duff 1995.

moneyed can ascend into the top part of the capitalist class—if they go to the right schools *and* marry old money.

Many in the capitalist class are philanthropic. They establish foundations and give huge sums to "causes." Their motivations vary. Some feel guilty because they have so much while others have so little. Others feel a responsibility—even a sense of fate or purpose—to use their money for doing good. Still others seek prestige, acclaim, or fame.

The Upper Middle Class Of all the classes, the upper middle class is the one most shaped by education. Almost all members of this class have at least a bachelor's degree, and many have postgraduate degrees in business, management, law, or medicine. These people manage the corporations owned by the capitalist class or else operate their own business or profession. As Gilbert and Kahl (1998) say, these positions

> may not grant prestige equivalent to a title of nobility in the Germany of Max Weber, but they certainly represent the sign of having "made it" in contemporary America. . . . Their income is sufficient to purchase houses and cars and travel that become public symbols for all to see and for advertisers to portray with words and pictures that connote success, glamour, and high style.

Consequently, parents and teachers push children to prepare for upper-middle-class jobs. About 15 percent of the population belong to this class.

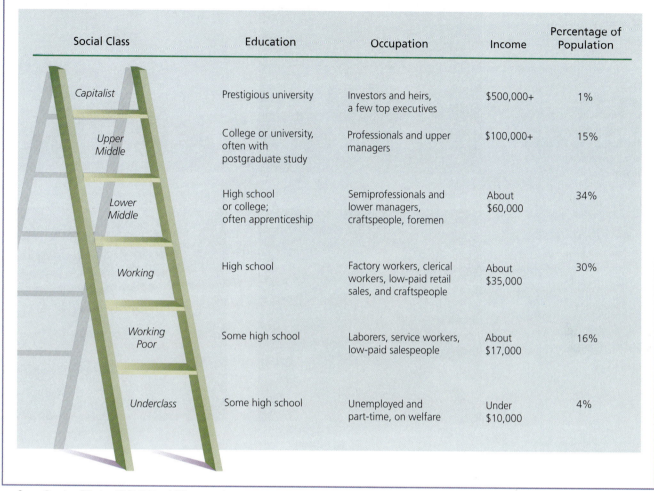

Sociologists use income, education, and occupational prestige to measure social class. For most people, this classification works well, but not for everyone. Entertainers sometimes are difficult to fit in. To what social class do Eminem, Lopez, Liu, and James belong? Eminem makes $35 million a year, Jennifer Lopez $29 million, and Lucy Liu around $5 million. When Lebron James got out of high school, he signed more than $100 million in endorsement contracts, as well as a $4 million contract to play basketball for the Cleveland Cavaliers.

Eminem

Jennifer Lopez

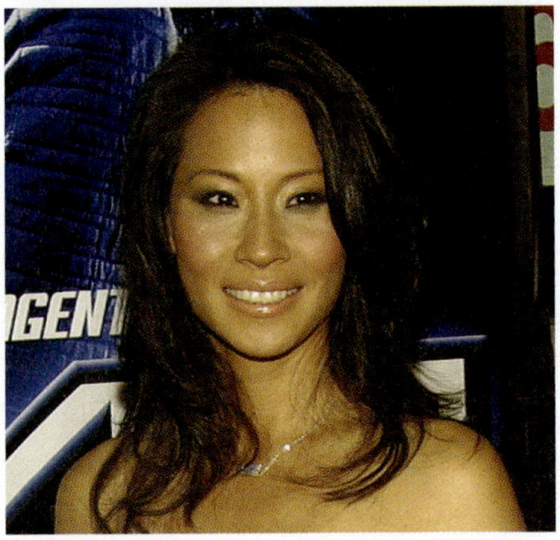

Lucy Liu

LeBron James

The Lower Middle Class About 34 percent of the population belong to the lower middle class. Members of this class have jobs that call for them to follow orders given by those who have upper-middle-class credentials. Their technical and lower-level management positions bring them a good living, although they feel threatened by taxes and inflation. They enjoy a comfortable, mainstream lifestyle, and many anticipate being able to move up the social class ladder.

The distinctions between the lower middle class and the working class on the next lower rung are more blurred than those between other classes. In general, however, members of the lower middle class work at jobs that have slightly more prestige, and their incomes are generally higher.

The Working Class About 30 percent of the U.S. population belong to this class of relatively unskilled blue-collar and white-collar workers. Compared with the lower middle class, they have less education and lower incomes. Their jobs are also less secure, more routine, and more closely supervised. One of their greatest fears is being laid off during a recession. With only a high school diploma, the average member of the working class has little hope of climbing up the class ladder. Job changes usually bring "more of the same," so most concentrate on getting ahead by achieving seniority on the job rather than by changing their type of work. They tend to think of themselves as having "real jobs," and the "suits" above them as paper pushers who have no practical experience (Gorman 2000).

The Working Poor Members of this class, about 16 percent of the population, work at unskilled, low-paying, temporary and seasonal jobs, such as sharecropping, migrant farm work, housecleaning, and day labor. Most are high school dropouts. Many are functionally illiterate, finding it difficult to read even the want ads. They are not likely to vote (Gilbert and Kahl 1998; Beeghley 2000), for they feel that no matter what party is elected to office, their situation won't change.

Although they work full time, millions of the working poor depend on help such as food stamps to supplement their meager incomes (O'Hare 1996b). It is easy to see how you can work full time and still be poor. Suppose that you are married and have a baby 3 months old and another child 3 years old. Your spouse stays home to care for them, so earning the income is up to you. But as a high-school dropout, all you can get is a minimum wage job. At $5.15 an hour, you earn $206 for 40 hours. In a year, this comes to $10,712—before deductions. Your nagging fear—and daily nightmare—is of ending up "on the streets."

The Underclass On the lowest rung, and with next to no chance of climbing anywhere, is the **underclass.** Concentrated in the inner city, this group has little or no connection with the job market. Those who are employed—and some are—do menial, low-paying, temporary work. Welfare, if it is available, along with food stamps and food pantries, is their main support. Most members of other classes consider these people the ne'er-do-wells of society. Life is the toughest in this class, and it is filled with despair. About 4 percent of the population fall into this class.

The homeless men described in the opening vignette of this chapter, and the women and children like them, are part of the underclass. These are the people whom most Americans wish would just go away. Their presence on our city streets bothers passersby from the more privileged social classes—which includes just about everyone. "What are those obnoxious, dirty, foul-smelling people doing here, cluttering up my city?" appears to be a common response. Some people react with sympathy and a desire to do something. But what? Almost all of us just shrug our shoulders and look the other way, despairing of a solution and somewhat intimidated by their presence.

The homeless are the "fallout" of our developing postindustrial economy. In another era, they would have had plenty of work. They would have tended horses, worked on farms, dug ditches, shoveled coal, and run the factory looms. Some would have explored and settled the West. Others would have been lured to California, Alaska, and Australia by the prospect of gold. Today, however, with no frontiers to settle, factory jobs scarce, and farms that are becoming technological marvels, we have little need for unskilled labor.

Social Class in the Automobile Industry

Let's use the automobile industry illustrates the social class ladder. The Fords, for example, own and control a manufacturing and financial empire whose net worth is truly staggering. Their power matches their wealth, for through their multinational corporation their decisions affect production and employment in many countries. The family's vast fortune, and its accrued power, are now several generations old. Consequently, Ford children go to the "right" schools, know how to spend money in the "right" way, and can be trusted to make family and class interests paramount in life. They are without question at the top level of the *capitalist* class.

Next in line come top Ford executives. Although they may have an income of several hundred thousand dollars a year (and some, with stock options and bonuses, earn several million dollars annually), most are new to wealth and power. Consequently, they would be classified at the lower end of the capitalist class.

A husband and wife who own a Ford agency are members of the *upper middle class.* Their income clearly sets them apart from the majority of Americans, and their reputation in the community is enviable. More than likely they also exert greater-than-average influence in their community, but their capacity to wield power is limited.

A Ford salesperson, as well as people who work in the dealership office, belongs to the *lower middle class.* Although there are some exceptional salespeople, even a few who make a lot of money selling prestigious, expensive cars to the capitalist class, those at a run-of-the-mill Ford agency are lower middle class. Compared with the owners of the agency, their income is less, their education is likely to be less, and their work is less prestigious.

Mechanics who repair customers' cars are members of the *working class.* A mechanic who is promoted to supervise the repair shop joins the lower middle class.

underclass a group of people for whom poverty persists year after year and across generations

Those who "detail" used cars (making them appear newer by washing and polishing the car, painting the tires, spraying "new car scent" into the interior, and so on) belong to the *working poor.* Their income and education are low, the prestige accorded their work minimal. They are laid off when selling slows down.

Ordinarily, the *underclass* is not represented in the automobile industry. It is conceivable, however, that the agency might hire a member of the underclass to do a specific job such as mowing the grass or cleaning up the used car lot. In general, however, personnel at the agency do not trust members of the underclass and do not want to associate with them—even for a few hours. They prefer to hire someone from the working poor for such jobs.

Consequences of Social Class

Each social class can be thought of as a broad subculture with distinct approaches to life. This means that social class affects people's health, family life, and education. It also influences their religion and politics, even their experiences with crime and the criminal justice system. Let's look at these consequences of social class, as well as how the new technology is related to social class.

Physical Health

Social class is so significant that it even affects our chances of living and dying. The principle is simple: The lower a person's class, the more likely that individual is to die before the expected age. This principle holds true at all ages. Infants born to the poor are more likely than other infants to die before their first birthday. In old age—whether 75 or 95—a larger proportion of the poor die each year than do the wealthy. The two primary reasons for this are lifestyle and medical care.

Social class shapes people's lifestyles, which, in turn, affect their health. Those in the lower social classes are more likely to smoke, eat more fats, abuse drugs and alcohol, exercise less, and practice unsafe sexual behavior (Chin et al. 2000; Navarro 2002). This, to understate the matter, does not increase people's health.

The photos of these two women were taken "at home." The woman in her home in Rio de Janeiro, Brazil, (above) and the wife of a coal miner in Novokuznetsk, Russia, (right) are both shown in their living rooms. From the contrast evident in these photos, can you see how social class makes such a vital difference in people's life chances? Can you see why these women are likely to see the world in highly distinctive ways, and why their politics and even their religions are likely to differ?

The second reason for the unequal death rates is unequal access to medical care. Consider this example:

> Terry Takewell (his real name) was a 21-year-old diabetic who lived in a trailer park in Somerville, Tennessee. When Zettie Mae Hill, Takewell's neighbor, found the unemployed carpenter drenched with sweat from a fever, she called an ambulance. Takewell was rushed to nearby Methodist Hospital. There he had an outstanding bill of $9,400. A notice had been posted in the emergency room telling staff members to alert supervisors if Takewell ever returned.
>
> By the time the hospital administrator was informed of the admission, Takewell was already in a hospital bed. The administrator went to Takewell's room, helped him to his feet, and escorted him to the parking lot. There, neighbors found him under a tree and took him home.
>
> Takewell died about twelve hours later.
>
> Zettie Mae Hill is still torn up about it. She wonders if Takewell would be alive today if she had directed his ambulance to a different hospital. She said, "I didn't think a hospital would just let a person die like that for lack of money." (Based on Ansberry 1988)

Why was Terry Takewell denied medical treatment and his life cut short? The fundamental reason is that health care in the United States is not a citizen's right. Instead, it is a commodity for sale. The result is a two-tier system of medical care—superior care for those who can afford the cost, and inferior care for those who cannot. Unlike the middle and upper classes, few poor people have a personal physician, and they often spend hours waiting in crowded public health clinics. After waiting most of a day, some don't even get to see a doctor; instead, they are told to come back the next day (Fialka 1993). And when the poor are hospitalized, they are likely to find themselves in understaffed and underfunded public hospitals, treated by rotating interns who do not know them and cannot follow up on their progress.

Mental Health

Social class also affects our mental health. From the 1930s until now, sociologists have found that the mental health of the lower classes is worse than that of the higher classes (Faris and Dunham 1939; Srole et al. 1978; Miller 1994; Lichter and Crowley 2002). Greater mental problems are part of the stress that accompanies poverty. Compared with middle- and upper-class Americans, the poor have less job security, lower wages, more unpaid bills, more divorce, more alcoholism, greater vulnerability to crime, and more physical illnesses—often accompanied by the threat of eviction hanging over their heads. Such conditions deal severe blows to people's emotional well-being.

People higher up the social class ladder experience stress, of course, but their stress is generally less and their coping resources greater. Not only can they afford vacations, psychiatrists, and counselors, but also *their class position gives them greater control over their lives, a key to good mental health.*

Family Life

Social class plays a significant role in family life. It even affects our choice of spouse, our chances of getting divorced, and how we rear our children.

Choice of Husband or Wife Members of the capitalist class place strong emphasis on family tradition. They stress the family's ancestors, history, and even a sense of purpose or destiny in life (Baltzell 1979; Aldrich 1989). Children of this class learn that their choice of husband or wife affects not just themselves but also the entire family, that their spouse will have an impact on the "family line." Because of these background expectations, the field of "eligible" marriage partners is much narrower than it is for the children of any other social class. In effect, parents in this class play a strong role in their children's mate selection.

Divorce The more difficult life of the lower social classes, especially the many tensions that come from insecure jobs and inadequate incomes, leads to higher marital friction and a greater likelihood of divorce. Consequently, children of the poor are more likely to grow up in broken homes.

Child Rearing As discussed on pages 79–80, sociologists have found significant class differences in child rearing. Lower-class parents focus on getting their children to obey authority figures, while middle-class parents focus on their children becoming creative. The reason for this difference appears to be the parents' occupation (Kohn (1977). Lower-class parents are closely supervised at work, and they anticipate that their children will have similar jobs. Consequently, they try to teach their children to defer to authority. Middle-class parents, in contrast, enjoy greater independence at work. Anticipating similar jobs for their children, they encourage them to be more creative. Out of these contrasting orientations arise different ways of disciplining children; lower-class parents are more likely to use physical punishment, while the middle classes rely more on verbal persuasion.

Working-class and middle-class parents also have different ideas about child development and children's play (Lareau 2002). Working-class parents think that children develop naturally, a sort of unfolding from within. If parents provide comfort, food, shelter, and other basic support, the child's development will take care of itself. Consequently, they set limits and let their children play as they wish. Middle-class parents, however, think that children need a lot of guidance to develop correctly, and they encourage play that will help develop the mind and social skills.

Education

As we saw in Figure 10.5, education increases as one goes up the social class ladder. It is not just the amount of education that changes, but also the type of education. Children of the capitalist class bypass public schools. They attend exclusive private schools where they are trained to take a commanding role in society. Prep schools such as Phillips Exeter Academy, Groton School, and Woodberry Forest School teach upper-class values and prepare their students for prestigious universities (Beeghley 2000; Higley 2003). Keenly sensitive to the significance of private schools, aspiring members of the upper middle class do their best to get their children into prestigious preschools—which cost up to $17,000 a year (Gross 2003). They even elicit letters of recommendation for their 2- and 3-year-olds. Such differences in parental expectations and resources are a major reason why children from the more privileged classes are more likely to enter and to graduate from college.

Religion

One area of social life that we might think would be unaffected by social class is religion. ("People are just religious, or they are not. What does social class have to do with it?") As we shall see in Chapter 18, however, the classes tend to cluster in different denominations. Episcopalians, for example, are more likely to attract the middle and upper classes. Baptists draw heavily from the lower classes, and Methodists are more middle class. Patterns of worship also follow class lines: The lower classes are attracted to more expressive worship services and louder music, while the middle and upper classes prefer more "subdued" worship.

Politics

As has been stressed throughout this text, symbolic interactionists emphasize that people perceive events from their own corner in life. Political views are no exception to this principle, and the rich and the poor walk different political paths. The higher that people are on the social class ladder, the more likely they are to vote for Republicans. In contrast, most members of the working class believe that the government should intervene in the economy to make citizens financially secure, and the majority of them are Democrats. Although the working class is more liberal on *economic* issues (policies that increase government spending), it is more conservative on *social* issues (such as opposing abortion and the Equal Rights Amendment) (Lipset 1959; Houtman 1995). People toward the bottom of the class structure are also less likely to be politically active—to campaign for candidates, or even to vote (Soss 1999; Beeghley 2000; Gilbert 2003).

Crime and the Criminal Justice System

If justice is supposed to be blind, it certainly is not when it comes to one's chances of being arrested (Henslin 2003a). In Chapter 8 (pages 213–215), we discussed how the upper and lower social classes have different styles of crime. The white-collar crimes of the more privileged classes are more likely to be dealt with outside the criminal justice system, while the police and courts deal with the street crimes of the lower classes. One consequence of this class standard is that members of the lower classes are more likely to be in prison, on probation, or on parole. In addition, since people tend to commit crimes in or near their own neighborhoods, the lower classes are more likely to be robbed, burglarized, or murdered.

Social Class and the New Technology

If the United States does not keep pace with global change and remain competitive by producing low-cost, quality goods, its economic position will decline. Opportunities will dwindle; there will be fewer jobs and shrinking paychecks. To compete in this global economic race, the United States is incorporating advanced technology in all spheres of life.

For the capitalist class, the new technology is a dream come true: By minimizing the obstacles of national borders, capitalists move factories to countries with cheaper labor. They produce components in one country, assemble them in another, and market the product throughout the world. Members of the upper middle class are well prepared for this change. Their higher education enables them to take a leading role in managing this global system for the capitalist class, or for using the new technology to advance in their professions.

Below these two most privileged classes, however, the new technology adds to the insecurity to life. As job markets shift, the skills of many in the lower middle class become outdated. This strikes fear in those who work at specialized crafts, for new technology can reduce or even eliminate the need for their specific skills. People in lower management are more secure, for they can transfer their skills from one job to another.

From this middle point on the ladder down, technology hits people the hardest. The working class is ill prepared to cope with the changes, and the threat of plant closings haunts them. The working poor are even more vulnerable, for they have even less to offer in the new job market. As unskilled jobs dry up, many workers are tossed into the industrial garbage bin.

The underclass, being technologically illiterate, is left behind. This point was driven home to me when I saw the homeless sitting dejected in the shelters. Of what value were these high school dropouts, our technological know-nothings, to this new society that is undergoing its piercing birth pains? With no productive place, their base of social belonging and self-esteem has been pulled out from under them.

In short, the new technology opens and closes opportunities for people largely by virtue of where they are located on the social class ladder, a topic discussed in the Sociology and the New Technology box on the next page.

Social Mobility

No aspect of life, then—from marriage to education—goes untouched by social class. Because life is so much more satisfying in the more privileged classes, people strive to climb the social class ladder. What affects their chances?

Three Types of Social Mobility

There are three basic types of social mobility: intergenerational, structural, and exchange. **Intergenerational mobility** refers to a change that occurs between generations—when grown-up children end up on a different rung of the social class ladder from the one their parents occupy. If the child of someone who sells used cars graduates from college and buys a Saturn dealership, that person experiences **upward social mobility.** Conversely, if a child of the dealership's owner parties too much, drops out of college, and ends up selling cars, he or she experiences **downward social mobility.**

intergenerational mobility the change that family members make in social class from one generation to the next

upward social mobility movement up the social class ladder

downward social mobility movement down the social class ladder

sociology and the **NEW technology**

Closing the Digital Divide: The Technology Gap Facing the Poor and Minorities

Consider this:

Ninety-three percent of children whose family has an annual income of $75,000 or more have computers at home, compared with about 32 percent of children in families with annual incomes less than $20,000 a year (*Statistical Abstract* 2002: Table 240).

> A high-income family is about seven times more likely to have Internet access than a low-income family (*Statistical Abstract* 2002: Table 240).
>
> A white child in a poor family is three or four times more likely to have Internet access than an African American or Latino child in a poor family (Lewin 2001a).
>
> Of all racial-ethnic groups, Native Americans have the least access to computers and the Internet. Only half have telephones at home (Romero 2000).

The term *digital divide* refers to this unequal access to computers and the Internet. As you can see from these examples, this technology gap marks the social classes and racial-ethnic groups.

Sociologists focus on the *structural* basis of wealth and poverty. That is, they examine how advantage and disadvantage are *built into society*—how birth forces some people to face many obstacles, while others face few. To level the playing field, the question is not how we can destroy the advantages that some have, but, rather, how we can reduce obstacles and increase opportunities for others.

If computers were only for playing cyber games, the digital divide would not be an issue. But in today's technological world, children who have less access to computers and the Internet face a major hurdle in life. To have weak computer skills means to be cut off from information and work opportunities.

For Your CONSIDERATION

What do you think can be done to overcome the digital divide? For example, should the government pay to connect every U.S. home to the Internet and buy a computer for every child, beginning in kindergarten? Why or why not?

Let's look at the problem this way: The Internet has become a gigantic library that spans the globe. Would we ever allow our city or school libraries to let some ethnic groups in more often than others? Would we allow them to let in the wealthy, but close the door on the poor? Finally, do you think that this analogy is fair, since libraries are funded by tax dollars but home computers and Internet access are paid for by individuals?

structural mobility movement up or down the social class ladder that is due to changes in the structure of society, not to individual efforts

We like to think that individual efforts are the reason people move up the class ladder—and their faults the reason they move down. In these examples, we can identify hard work, sacrifice, and ambition on the one hand, versus indolence and alcohol abuse on the other. Although individual factors such as these do underlie social mobility, sociologists consider **structural mobility** to be the crucial factor. This second basic type of mobility refers to changes in society that cause large numbers of people to move up or down the class ladder.

To better understand structural mobility, think of how opportunities abounded when computers were invented. New types of jobs appeared overnight. Huge numbers of people attended workshops and took crash courses, switching from blue-collar to white-collar work. Although individual effort certainly was involved—for some seized the opportunity while others did not—the underlying cause was a change in the *structure* of work. Consider the opposite—how opportunities disappear during a depression, and millions of people are forced downward on the class ladder. In this instance, too, their changed status is due less to individual behavior than to *structural* changes in society.

The third type of social mobility, **exchange mobility**, occurs when large numbers of people move up and down the social class ladder, but, on balance, the proportions of the social classes remain about the same. Suppose that a million or so working-class people are trained in computers, and they move up the class ladder. Suppose also that due to a surge in imports, about a million skilled workers have to take lower-status jobs. Although millions of people change their social class, there is, in effect, an *exchange* among them. The net result more or less balances out, and the class system remains basically untouched.

The term structural mobility *refers to changes in society that push large numbers of people either up or down the social class ladder. A remarkable example was the stock market crash of 1929, when tens of thousands of people suddenly lost immense amounts of wealth. People who once "had it made" found themselves standing on street corners selling apples or, as depicted here, selling their possessions at fire-sale prices.*

Women in Studies of Social Mobility

In classic studies, sociologists concluded that about half of sons passed their fathers; about one-third stayed at the same level, and only about one-sixth fell down the class ladder (Blau and Duncan 1967; Featherman and Hauser 1978; Featherman 1979).

Feminists pointed out that it wasn't good science to focus on sons and ignore women (Davis and Robinson 1988). They also objected that it was wrong to assume that women had no class position of their own and to assign wives the class of their husbands. The defense made by male sociologists of the time was that too few women were in the labor force to make a difference.

With huge numbers of women working for pay, more recent studies include women (Breen and Whelan 1995; Beeghley 2000). Sociologists Elizabeth Higginbotham and Lynn Weber (1992), for example, studied 200 women from working-class backgrounds who became professionals, managers, and administrators in Memphis. They found that almost without exception, the women's parents had encouraged them while they were still little girls to postpone marriage and get an education. This study confirms how important the family is in the socialization process and that the primary entry to the upper middle class is a college education. At the same time, note that if there had not been a *structural* change in society, the millions of new positions that women occupy would not exist.

Interpreting Statistics on Social Mobility

The United States is famous worldwide for its intergenerational mobility. That children can pass up their parents on the social class ladder is one of the attractions of this country. How much mobility is there? It turns out that most apples don't fall far from the tree. Of children who are born to the poorest 10 percent of Americans, about a third are still there when they are grown up—half end up in the poorest 20 percent. Similarly, of children who are born to the richest 10 percent of families, about a third stay there—two of five end up among the richest 20 percent (Krueger 2002). In short, the benefits that high-income parents enjoy tend to keep their children afloat, while the obstacles that low-income parents confront tend to weigh their children down.

But is the glass half empty or half full? We could also stress the other end of these findings: two-thirds of the very poorest kids move upward, and two-thirds of the very richest kids drop down. Remember that statistics don't lie, but liars use statistics. In this case, you can stress either part of these findings depending on what you are trying to prove.

exchange mobility about the same numbers of people moving up and down the social class ladder, such that, on balance, the social class system shows little change poverty line the official measure of poverty; calculated to include those incomes that are less than three times a low-cost food budget

The Pain of Social Mobility

You know that to be knocked down the social class ladder is painful, but were you aware that climbing it also brings pain? Sociologist Steph Lawler (1999) interviewed British women who had moved from the working class to the middle class. The women were caught between two worlds—their working-class background and their current middle-class life. Their relationship with their mothers had grown difficult. The mothers felt uncomfortable with their daughters' new tastes in furniture, food, and speech. Even how to rear children became a matter of dispute. Sociologists Richard Sennett and Jonathan Cobb (1972/1988) found something similar in Boston, where they studied working-class parents who had made deep sacrifices so their children could go to college. The parents expected their children to appreciate their sacrifice, but because the children's educated world was so distant from that of the parents, the children had grown aloof. The two had difficulty even talking to one another. As a result, the parents felt betrayed and were bitter.

In short, social class separates people into worlds so distinct that communication and mutual understanding become difficult. To change one's social class is to tear oneself from one's roots. As you may recall, Richard Rodriguez, featured in the Cultural Diversity box on page 82, found that his climb up the social class ladder had wrenching costs.

Poverty

Many Americans find the "limitless possibilities" on which the American dream is based to be elusive. As illustrated in Figure 10.5 on page 269, the working poor and underclass together form about one-fifth of the U.S. population. This translates into a huge number, almost 60 million people. Who are these people?

Drawing the Poverty Line

To determine who is poor, the U.S. government draws a **poverty line.** This measure was set in the 1960s, when poor people were thought to spend about one-third of their incomes on food. Based on this assumption, each year the government computes a low-cost food budget and multiplies it by 3. Families whose incomes are less than this amount are classified as poor; those whose incomes are higher—even by a dollar—are determined to be "not poor."

This official measure of poverty is grossly inadequate. Poor people actually spend only about 20 percent of their incomes on food, so to determine a poverty line we really ought to multiply their food budget by five instead of three (Uchitelle 2001). No political party in power wants to do this, as redrawing the line would make it appear that poverty increased under their watch. Another problem with the poverty line is that some mothers work and have to pay for child care, but they are treated the same as mothers who don't have this expense. The poverty line is also the same for everyone across the nation, even though the cost of living is much higher in New York than in Alabama. Nor, for some reason, does the government count food stamps as income.

That a change in the poverty line would instantly make millions of people poor—or take away their poverty—would be a laughable matter, if it weren't so serious. (The absurdity has not been lost on Parker and Hart, as you can see from this sarcastic cartoon.) Although this

By permission of Johnny Hart and Creators Syndicate

line is arbitrary, it is the official measure of poverty, and the government uses it to decide who will receive help and who will not. Based on this line, let's see who in the United States is poor. Before we do this, though, compare your ideas of the poor with the myths explored in the Down-to-Earth Sociology box below.

DOWN-TO-EARTH SOCIOLOGY

Exploring Myths About the Poor

Myth 1 Most poor people are lazy. They are poor because they do not want to work.
Half of the poor are either too old or too young to work: About 40 percent are under age 18, and another 10 percent are age 65 or older. About 30 percent of the working-age poor work at least half the year.

Myth 2 Poor people are trapped in a cycle of poverty that few escape.
The poverty population is dynamic. Most poverty lasts less than a year (Lichter and Crowley 2002). Only 12 percent remain in poverty for five or more consecutive years (O'Hare 1996a). Most children who are born in poverty are *not* poor as adults (Ruggles 1989).

Myth 3 Most of the poor are African Americans and Latinos.
As shown in Figure 10.6, the poverty rates of African Americans and Latinos are much higher than that of whites. Because there are so many more whites in the U.S. population, however, *most of the poor are white.* Of the 38 million U.S. poor, 56 percent are white, 21 percent African American, 19 percent Latino, 3 percent Asian American, and 1 percent Native American. (*Statistical Abstract* 2002: Table 668).

Myth 4 Most of the poor are single mothers and their children.
Although about 38 percent of the poor match this stereotype, 34 percent of the poor live in married-couple families, 22 percent live alone or with nonrelatives, and 6 percent live in other settings.

Myth 5 Most of the poor live in the inner city.
This one is close to fact, as about 42 percent do live in the inner city. But 36 percent live in the suburbs, and 22 percent live in small towns and rural areas.

Myth 6 The poor live on welfare.
About half of the income of poor adults comes from wages and pensions, about 25 percent from welfare, and about 22 percent from Social Security.

Sources: Primarily O'Hare 1996a and O'Hare 1996b, with other sources as indicated

Figure 10.6

Poverty in the United States, by Age and Race-Ethnicity

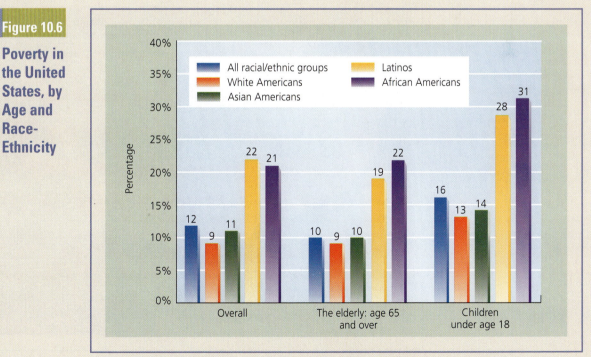

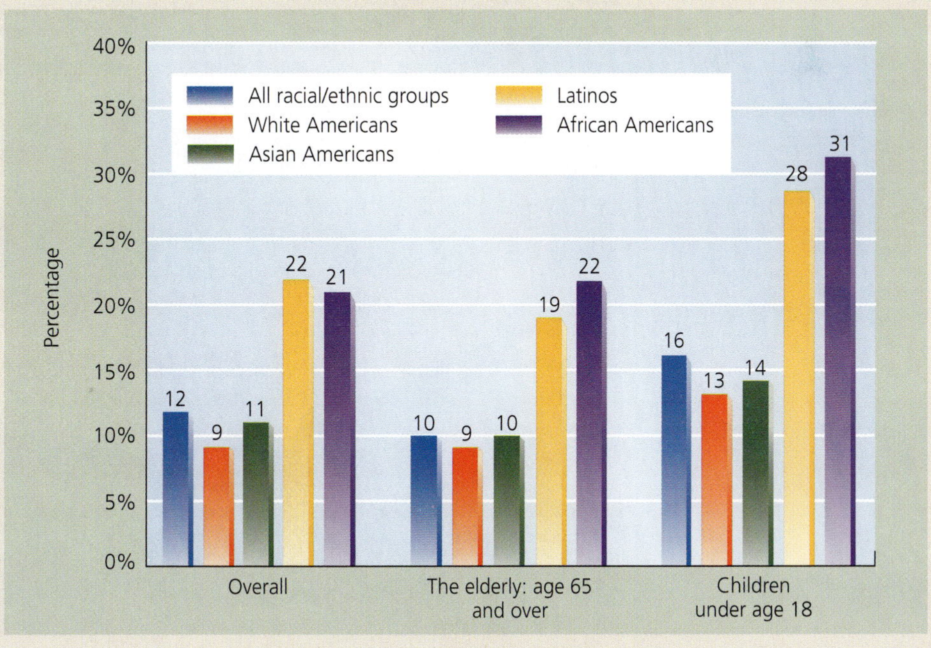

Note: The poverty line on which this figure is based is $18,194 for a family of four.

Source: By the author. Based on *Statistical Abstract* 2002:Tables 668, 671, 673.

Who Are the Poor?

Geography As you can see from the Social Map below, the poor are not evenly distributed among the states. This map shows a clustering of poverty in the South, a pattern that has prevailed for more than 100 years.

A second aspect of geography is also significant. About 59 million Americans live in rural areas. Of these, 9 million are poor. At 16 percent, their rate of poverty is higher than the national average of 12 percent. The rural poor are less likely to be single parents, and more likely to be married and to have jobs. Compared with urban Americans, the rural poor are less skilled and less educated, and the jobs available to them pay less than similar jobs in urban areas (Dudenhefer 1993; Lichter and Crowley 2002).

The greatest predictor of whether Americans are poor is not geography, however, but race-ethnicity, education, and the sex of the person who heads the family. Let's look at these three factors.

Race-Ethnicity One of the strongest factors in poverty is race-ethnicity. As Figure 10.6 on the previous page shows, only 9 percent of white Americans are poor, but 21 or 22 percent of African Americans and Latinos live in poverty. At 11 percent, the poverty rate of Asian Americans is close to that of white Americans. Although their poverty rate is the lowest, because there are so many more white Americans, most poor people are white.

Education You are aware that education is a vital factor in poverty, but you may not have known just how powerful it is. Figure 10.8 shows that only 2 of 100 people who finish college end up in poverty, but one of every five people who drop out of high school is poor. As you can see, the chances that someone will be poor become less with each higher

Figure 10.7 Patterns of Poverty

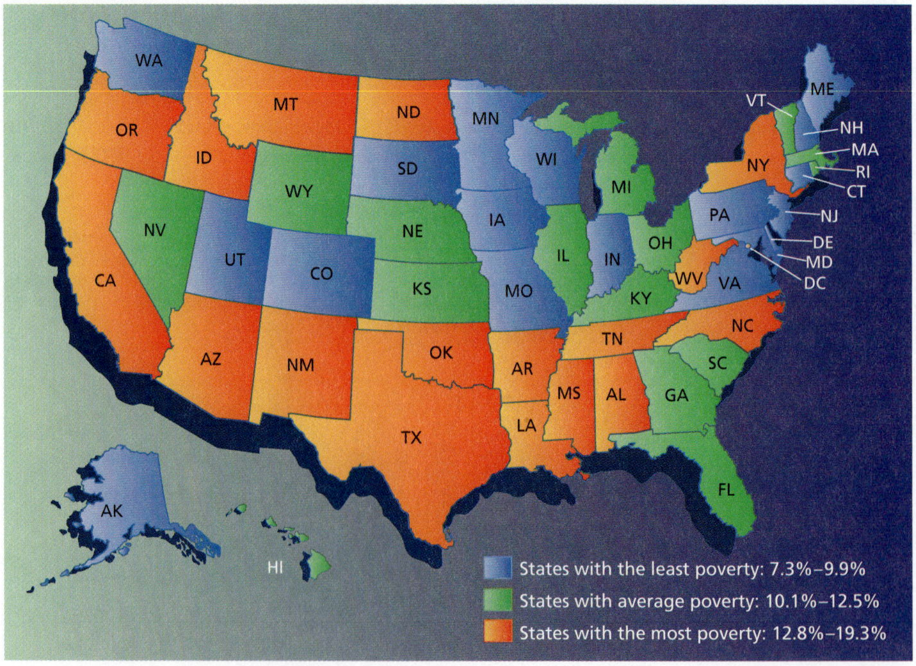

Note: Poverty varies tremendously from one state to another. In the extreme, poverty is almost three times as common in New Mexico (19.3%) than it is in Maryland (7.3%).
Source: By the author. Based on *Statistical Abstract* 2002:Table 673.

Figure 10.8 Who Ends Up Poor? Poverty by Education and Race-Ethnicity

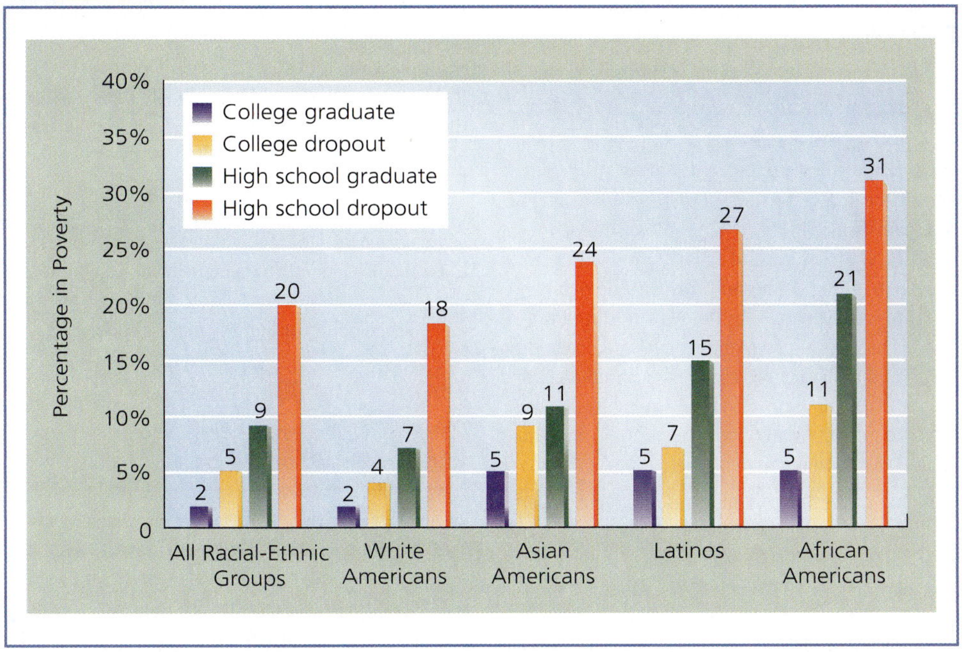

Source: Statistical Abstract 2002:Table 675.

(the) feminization of poverty a trend in U.S. poverty whereby most poor families are headed by women

level of education. This principle applies regardless of race-ethnicity, but this figure also shows that at every level of education race-ethnicity makes an impact.

The Feminization of Poverty The other major predictor of poverty is the sex of the person who heads the family. Women-headed families are *seven* times more likely to be poor than couple-headed families (Lichter and Crowley 2002). Women who head families average only two-thirds the income of men who head families (*Statistical Abstract* 2002: Table 662). Consequently, most poor families are headed by women. The three major causes of this phenomenon, called the **feminization of poverty**, are divorce, births to single women, and the lower wages paid to women.

Old Age As Figure 10.6 on page 279 shows, the elderly are less likely than the general population to be poor. This is quite a change. It used to be that growing old increased people's chances of being poor, but government policies to redistribute income—Social Security and subsidized housing, food, and medical care—slashed the rate of poverty among the elderly. This figure also shows how the prevailing racial-ethnic patterns carry over into old age. You can see how much more likely an elderly African American or Latino is to be poor than an elderly white or Asian American.

Beyond the awareness of most Americans are the rural poor, such as this family in Kentucky. This family is typical of the rural poor: white and headed by a woman. What do you think the future holds for these children?

Children of Poverty

Children are more likely to live in poverty than are adults or the elderly. This holds true regardless of race-ethnicity, but from Figure 10.6 you can see how much greater poverty is among Latino and African American children. That millions of U.S. children are reared in poverty is shocking when one considers the wealth of this country and the supposed concern for the well-being of children. This tragic aspect of poverty is the topic of the following Thinking Critically section.

Figure 10.9 How Many Births to Single Mothers?

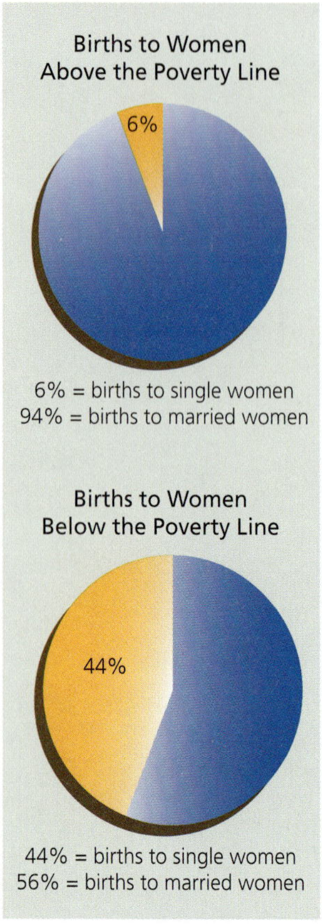

Note: Totals were available only for white women.
Source: Murray 1993.

Figure 10.10 How Long Does Poverty Last?

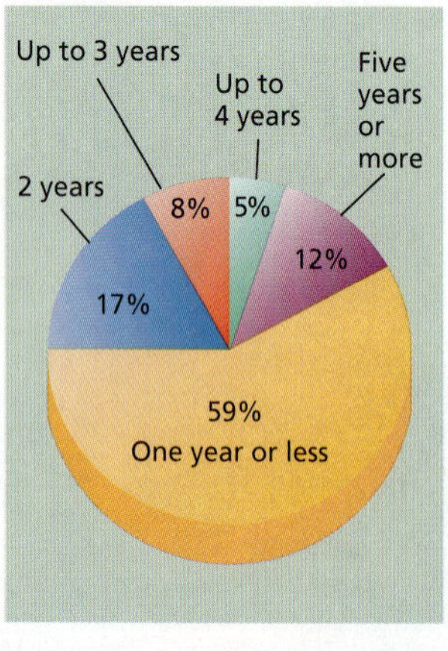

Source: Gottschalk et al. 1994:89.

THINKING Critically

The Nation's Shame: Children in Poverty

One of the most startling statistics in sociology is shown in Figure 10.6 on page 279: About one of seven or eight white and Asian American children and one of three Latino and African American children live in poverty. These figures translate into incredible numbers—approximately *15 million* children are poor: 7 million white children, 3½ million Latino children, 3½ million African American children, nearly ½ million Asian American children, and about 300,000 Native American children.

The main cause for this high rate of child poverty, said sociologist and former U.S. Senator Daniel Moynihan (1927–2003), is an increase in births outside marriage. In 1960, one of twenty U.S. children was born to a single woman. Today that total is *more than six times higher,* and single women now account for one of three (33 percent) of all U.S. births. Figure 10.9 shows the striking relationship between births to single women and social class. For women above the poverty line, only 6 percent of births are to single women; for women below the poverty line this rate is *seven* times higher.

Regardless of the causes of childhood poverty—and there are many—what is most significant is that these millions of children face all of the suffering and obstacles to a satisfying life that poverty entails. They are more likely to die in infancy, to go hungry, to be malnourished, to develop more slowly, and to have more health problems. They also are more likely to drop out of school, to become involved in criminal activities, and to have children while still in their teens—thus perpetuating the cycle of poverty.

For Your CONSIDERATION

Many social analysts—liberals and conservatives alike—are alarmed at this high rate of child poverty. They emphasize that it is time to stop blaming the victim, and, instead, to focus on the *structural* factors that underlie this problem. They say that we need three fundamental changes: (1) removing obstacles to employment; (2) improving education; and (3) strengthening the family. To achieve these changes, what specific programs would *you* recommend?

Sources: Moynihan 1991; Sandefur 1995; *Statistical Abstract* 1997: Table 1338; 2002: Tables 15, 75, 668, 671.

The Dynamics of Poverty

Some have suggested that the poor tend to get trapped in a **culture of poverty** (Harrington 1962; Lewis 1966a). They assume that the values and behaviors of the poor "make them fundamentally different from other Americans, and that these factors are largely responsible for their continued long-term poverty" (Ruggles 1989:7).

Lurking behind this concept is the idea that the poor are lazy people who bring poverty on themselves. Certainly some individuals and families match this stereotype—many of us have known them. But is a self-perpetuating culture—one that is transmitted across generations and that locks people in poverty—the basic reason for U.S. poverty?

Researchers who followed 5,000 U.S. families since 1968 uncovered some surprising findings. Contrary to common stereotypes, most poverty is short-lived, lasting only a year or less. This is because most poverty comes about due to a dramatic life change such as divorce, the loss of a job, or even the birth of a child (O'Hare 1996a). As Figure 10.10 shows, only 12 percent of poverty lasts five years or longer. Contrary to the stereotype of lazy people content to live off the government, few poor people enjoy poverty—and they do what they can to *not* be poor.

Yet from one year to the next, the number of poor people remains about the same. This means that the people who move out of poverty are replaced by people who move *into* poverty. Most of these newly poor will also move out of poverty within a year. Some people even bounce back and forth, never quite making it securely out of poverty. Poverty, then, is dynamic, touching a lot more people than the official totals indicate. Although 12 percent of Americans may be poor at any one time, twice that number, about one-fourth of the U.S. population, is or has been poor for at least a year.

Why Are People Poor?

Two explanations for poverty compete for our attention. The first, which sociologists prefer, focuses on *social structure.* Sociologists stress that *features of society* deny some people access to education or learning job skills. They emphasize racial, ethnic, age, and gender discrimination, as well as changes in the job market—the closing of plants, drying up of unskilled jobs, and an increase in marginal jobs that pay poverty wages. In short, some people find their escape routes to a better life blocked.

A competing explanation focuses on the *characteristics of individuals* that are assumed to contribute to poverty. Individualistic explanations that sociologists reject outright as worthless stereotypes are laziness and lack of intelligence. Individualistic explanations that sociologists reluctantly acknowledge include dropping out of school, bearing children in the teen years, and averaging more children than women in the other social classes. Most sociologists are reluctant to speak of such factors in this context, for they appear to blame the victim, something that sociologists bend over backward not to do.

The tension between these competing explanations is of more than just theoretical interest. Each explanation affects our perception and has practical consequences, as is illustrated in the following Thinking Critically section.

THINKING Critically

The Welfare Debate: The Deserving and the Undeserving Poor

Throughout U.S. history, Americans have divided the poor into two types: the deserving and the undeserving. The deserving poor are people who, in the public mind, are poor through no fault of their own. Most of the working poor, such as the Lewises, are considered deserving:

> Nancy and Ted Lewis are in their early 30s and have two children. Ted works three part-time jobs, earning $13,000 a year; Nancy takes care of the children and house and is not employed. To make ends meet, the Lewises rely on food stamps, Medicaid, and housing subsidies.

The undeserving poor, in contrast, are viewed as having brought on their own poverty. They are freeloaders who waste their lives in sloth, alcohol and drug abuse, and promiscuous sex. They don't deserve help, and, if given anything, will waste it on their dissolute lifestyles. Some would see Joan as an example:

> Joan, her mother, and her three brothers and two sisters lived on welfare. Joan started having sex at 13, bore her first child at 15, and, now, at 23, is expecting her fourth child. Her first two children have the same father, the third a different father, and Joan isn't sure who fathered her coming child. Joan parties most nights, using both alcohol and whatever drugs are available. Her house is filthy, the refrigerator usually empty, and social workers have threatened to take away her children.

This division of the poor into deserving and undeserving underlies the heated debate about welfare. "Why should we use *our* hard-earned money to help *them*? They are just going to waste it. Of course, there are others who want to get on their feet, and helping them is okay."

For Your CONSIDERATION

Why do people make a distinction between deserving and undeserving poor? Should we let some people starve because they "brought poverty upon themselves"? Should we let children go hungry because their parents are drug abusers? Does "unworthy" mean that we should not offer assistance to people who "squander" the help they are given?

In contrast to thinking of poor people as deserving or undeserving, use the sociological perspective to explain poverty without blaming the victim. What *social* conditions (conditions of society) create poverty? What *social* conditions produce the lifestyles that the middle class so despises?

Welfare Reform

After decades of criticism, U.S. welfare was restructured in 1996. A federal law—the Personal Responsibility and Work Opportunity Reconciliation Act—requires states to place a lifetime cap on welfare assistance and compels welfare recipients to look for work and to take available jobs. The maximum length of time someone can collect welfare is five years. In some states, it is less. Unmarried teen parents must attend school and live at home or in some other adult-supervised setting.

culture of poverty the assumption that the values and behaviors of the poor make them fundamentally different from other people, that these factors are largely responsible for their poverty, and that parents perpetuate poverty across generations by passing these characteristics to their children

This law set off a storm of criticism. Some called it an attack on the poor. Defenders replied that the new rules would rescue people from poverty. They would transform welfare recipients into self-supporting and hard-working citizens—and reduce welfare costs. National welfare rolls plummeted, dropping by 60 percent (Cancian et al. 2003). Two out of five who left welfare also moved out of poverty (Hofferth 2002).

This is only the rosy part of the picture, however. Three of five are still in poverty or are back on welfare. A third of those who were forced off welfare have no jobs (Lichter and Crowley 2002). Some can't work because they have health problems. Others lack transportation. Some are addicted to drugs and alcohol. Still others are trapped in economically depressed communities where there are no jobs. Then there are those who have jobs, but earn so little they remain in poverty. Consider one of the "success stories":

> JoAnne Sims, 37, lives in Erie, New York, with her 7-year-old daughter Jamine. JoAnne left welfare, and now earns \$6.75 an hour as a cook for Head Start. Her 37-hour week brings \$239.75 before deductions. With the help of medical benefits and a mother who provides child care, JoAnne "gets by." She says, "From what I hear, a lot of us who went off welfare are still poor . . . let me tell you, it's not easy." (Peterson 2000)

Conflict theorists have an interesting interpretation of welfare. They say that its purpose is not to help people, but, rather, to maintain an army of reserve workers. It is designed to keep the unemployed alive during economic downturns until they are needed during the next economic boom. Reducing the welfare rolls through the 1996 law fits this model, as it occurred during the longest economic boom in U.S. history. Recessions are inevitable, however, and just as inevitable is surging unemployment. In line with conflict theory, we can predict that during the coming recession welfare rules will be softened—in order to keep the reserve army of the unemployed ready for the next time they are needed.

Deferred Gratification

One consequence of a life of deprivation punctuated by emergencies—*and of seeing the future as more of the same*—is a lack of **deferred gratification,** giving up things in the present for the sake of greater gains in the future. It is difficult to practice this middle-class virtue if one does not have a middle-class surplus—or middle-class hope.

Back in 1967, sociologist Elliot Liebow noted that black streetcorner men did not defer gratification. Their jobs were low-paying and insecure, their lives pitted with emergencies. With the future looking exactly like the present, and any savings they did manage gobbled up by emergencies, saving for the future was pointless. The only thing that made sense from their perspective was to enjoy what they could at that moment. Immediate gratification, then, was not the cause of their poverty, but its consequence. Cause and consequence loop together, however, for their immediate gratification helped perpetuate their poverty. For another look at this "looping," see the Down-to-Earth Sociology box on the next page, in which I share my personal experiences with poverty.

If both causes are at work, why do sociologists emphasize the structural explanation? Reverse the situation for a moment. Suppose that members of the middle class drove old cars that broke down, faced threats from the utility company to shut off the electricity and heat, and had to make a choice between paying the rent or buying medicine and food and diapers. How long would they practice deferred gratification? Their orientations to life would likely make a sharp U-turn.

Sociologists, then, do not view the behaviors of the poor as the cause of their poverty, but, rather, as the result of their poverty. Poor people would welcome the middle-class opportunities that would allow them the chance to practice the middle-class virtue of deferred gratification. Without those opportunities, though, they just can't afford it.

deferred gratification forgoing something in the present in the hope of achieving greater gains in the future

Horatio Alger myth the belief that due to limitless possibilities anyone can get ahead if he or she tries hard enough

Where Is Horatio Alger? The Social Functions of a Myth

In the late 1800s, Horatio Alger was one of the country's most talked-about authors. The rags-to-riches exploits of his fictional boy heroes and their amazing successes in overcoming

DOWN-TO-EARTH SOCIOLOGY

Poverty: A Personal Journey

I WAS BORN IN POVERTY. MY PARENTS, who could not afford to rent a house or apartment, rented the tiny office in their minister's house. That is where I was born.

My father began to slowly climb the social class ladder. His fitful odyssey took him from laborer to truck driver to the owner of a series of small businesses (tire repair shop, bar, hotel), then to vacuum cleaner salesman, and back to bar owner. He converted a garage into a house. Although it had no indoor plumbing or insulation (in northern Minnesota!), it was a start. Later, he bought a house, and then he built a new home. After that we moved into a trailer, and then back to a house. My father's seventh grade education was always an obstacle. Although he never became wealthy, poverty eventually become a distant memory for him.

My social class took a leap—from working class to upper middle class—when, after attending college and graduate school, I became a university professor. I entered a world that was unknown to my parents, one much more pampered and privileged. I had opportunities to do research, to publish, and to travel to exotic places. My reading centered on sociological research, and I read books in Spanish as well as in English. My father, in contrast, never read a book in his life, and my mother read only detective stories and romance paperbacks. One set of experiences isn't "better" than the other, just significantly different in determining what windows of perception it opens onto the world.

My interest in poverty, which was rooted in my own childhood experiences, stayed with me. I traveled to a dozen or so skid rows across the United States and Canada, talking to homeless people and staying in their shelters. In my own town, I spent considerable time with people on welfare, observing how they lived. I constantly marveled at the connections between *structural* causes of poverty (low education and skills, undependable transportation, the lack of unskilled jobs) and its *personal* causes (the *culture of poverty*—alcohol and drug abuse, multiple out-of-wedlock births, frivolous spending, all-night partying, and a seeming incapacity to keep appointments—except to pick up the welfare check).

Sociologists haven't unraveled this connection, and as much as we might *like* for only the structural causes to apply, clearly *both* are at work (Duneier 1999: 122). The situation can be illustrated by looking at the perennial health problems I observed among the poor—the constant colds, runny noses, back aches, and injuries. The health problems stem from the *social structure* (less access to medical care, lesser trained or less capable physicians, drafty houses, lack of education regarding nutrition, and more dangerous jobs). At the same time, *personal* characteristics—hygiene, eating habits, and overdrinking—cause health problems. Which is the cause and which the effect? Both, of course, for one feeds into the other. The medical problems (which are based on both personal and structural causes) feed into the poverty these people experience, making them less able to perform their jobs successfully—or even to show up at work regularly. What an intricate puzzle for sociologists!

severe odds motivated thousands of boys of that period. Although Alger's characters have disappeared from U.S. literature, they remain alive and well in the psyche of Americans. From real-life examples of people from humble origins who climbed the social class ladder, Americans know that anyone can get ahead if they really try. In fact, they believe that most Americans, including minorities and the working poor, have an average or better-than-average chance of getting ahead—obviously a statistical impossibility (Kluegel and Smith 1986).

The accuracy of the **Horatio Alger myth** is less important than the belief that limitless possibilities exist for everyone. Functionalists would stress that this belief is functional for society. On the one hand, it encourages people to compete for higher positions, or, as the song says, "to reach for the highest star." On the other hand, it places blame for failure squarely on the individual. If you don't make it—in the face of ample opportunities to get ahead—the fault must be your own. The Horatio Alger myth helps to stabilize society, then, for since the fault is viewed as the individual's, not society's, current social arrangements can be regarded as satisfactory. This reduces pressures to change the system.

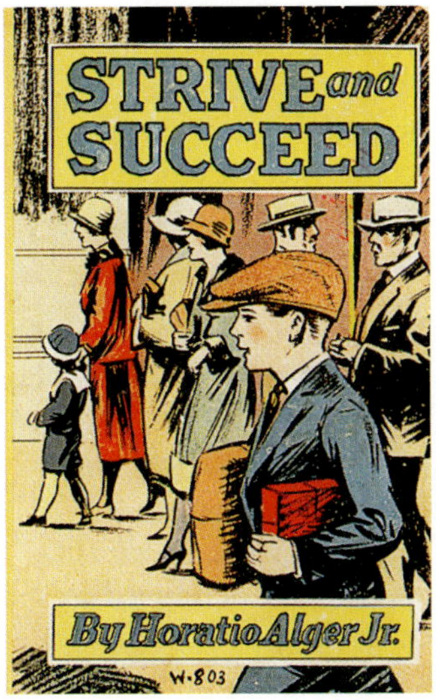

A culture's dominant ideology is reinforced in many ways, including in its literature. As discussed in the text, Horatio Alger provided inspirational heroes for thousands of boys. The central theme of these many novels, immensely popular in their time, was rags to riches. Through rugged determination and self-sacrifice, a boy could overcome seemingly insurmountable obstacles to reach the pinnacle of success. (Girls did not strive for financial success, but were dependent on fathers and husbands.)

As Marx and Weber pointed out, social class penetrates our consciousness, shaping our ideas of life and our "proper" place in society. When the rich look at the world around them, they sense superiority and anticipate control over their own destiny. When the poor look around them, they are more likely to sense defeat, and to anticipate that unpredictable forces will batter their lives. Both rich and poor know the dominant ideology, that their particular niche in life is due to their own efforts, that the reasons for success—or failure—lie solely with the self. Like the fish that don't notice the water, people tend not to perceive the effects of social class on their own lives.

SUMMARY and REVIEW

What Is Social Class?

What is meant by the term social class?

Most sociologists have adopted Weber's definition of **social class** as a large group of people who rank close to one another in terms of wealth, power, and prestige. **Wealth,** consisting of property and income, is concentrated in the upper classes. The distribution of wealth in the United States has changed little since World War II, but the changes that have occurred have been toward greater inequality. **Power** is the ability to get one's way even though others resist. C. Wright Mills coined the term **power elite** to refer to the small group that holds the reins of power in business, government, and the military. **Prestige** is linked to occupational status. Pp. 260–264.

People's rankings of occupational prestige have changed little over the decades and are similar from country to country. Globally, the occupations that bring greater prestige are those that pay more, require more education and abstract thought, and offer greater independence. Pp. 260–265.

What is meant by the term status inconsistency?

Status is social ranking. Most people are **status consistent;** that is, they rank high or low on all three dimensions of social class. People who rank higher on some dimensions than on others are status inconsistent. The frustrations of **status inconsistency** tend to produce political radicalism. Pp. 264–266.

Sociological Models of Social Class

What models are used to portray the social classes?

Erik Wright developed a four-class model based on Marx: (1) capitalists (owners of large businesses); (2) petty bourgeoisie (small business owners); (3) managers; and (4) workers. Kahl and Gilbert developed a six-class model based on Weber. At the top is the capitalist class. In descending order are the upper middle class, the lower middle class, the working class, the working poor, and the **underclass.** Pp. 266–272.

Consequences of Social Class

How does social class affect people's lives?

Social class leaves no aspect of life untouched. It affects our chances of benefiting from the new technology, dying early, becoming ill, receiving good health care, and getting divorced. Social class membership also affects child rearing, educational attainment, religious affiliation, political participation, and contact with the criminal justice system. Pp. 272–275.

Social Mobility

What are the three types of social mobility?

The term **intergenerational mobility** refers to changes in social class from one generation to the next. **Exchange mobility** is the movement of large numbers of people from one class to another, with the net result that the relative proportions of the population in the classes remain about the same. The term **structural mobility** refers to changes in society that lead large numbers of people to change their social class. Pp. 275–278.

Poverty

Who are the poor?

Poverty is unequally distributed in the United States. Minorities, children, women-headed households, and rural Americans are more likely than others to be poor. The poverty rate of the elderly is less than that of the general population. Pp. 278–282.

Why are people poor?

Some social analysts believe that characteristics of *individuals,* such as the desire for immediate gratification, cause poverty. Sociologists, in contrast, examine *structural* features of society, such as employment opportunities, to find the causes of poverty. Sociologists generally conclude that life orientations are a consequence, not the cause, of people's position in the social class structure. Pp. 282–284.

How is the Horatio Alger myth functional for society?

The **Horatio Alger myth**—the belief that anyone can get ahead if only he or she tries hard enough—encourages people to strive to get ahead. It also deflects blame for failure from society to the individual. Pp. 284–286.

Where can I read more on this topic?

Suggested readings for this chapter are at the end of this book.

THINKING Critically ABOUT CHAPTER 10

1. The belief that the United States is the land of opportunity draws millions of legal and illegal immigrants to the United States each year. How do the materials in this chapter support or undermine this ideal?
2. How does social class affect people's lives?
3. What social mobility has your own family experienced? How do you fit into this picture?

ADDITIONAL RESOURCES for This Chapter

www.ablongman.com/henslin7e

- *Content Select* Research Database for Sociology, with suggested key terms and annotated references
- Link to 2000 Census, with activities
- Flashcards of key terms and concepts
- Practice Tests
- Weblinks
- Interactive Maps

Chapter 11

Sex and Gender

Pacita Abad,
Women in Burkah

In Tunis, the capital of Tunisia, on Africa's northern coast, I met some U.S. college students, with whom I spent a couple of days. They wanted to see Tunis' red light district, and I wondered if it would be worth the trip. I already had seen other red light districts, including the unusual one in Amsterdam where the state licenses the women, requires medical checkups (certificates must be posted so customers can check them), sets the prices, and pays the prostitutes social security benefits upon retirement. The women sit behind lighted picture windows while customers stroll along the canal side streets and browse from the outside.

This time, the sight turned my stomach.

We ended up on a wharf that extended into the Mediterranean. Each side was lined with a row of one-room wooden shacks, each one crowded up against the next. In front of each open door stood a young woman. Peering from outside into the dark interiors, I could see that each door led to a tiny room with a well-worn bed.

n front of each open door
tood a young woman.
could see that . . .

The wharf was crowded with men who were eyeing the women. Many of them wore sailor uniforms from countries that I couldn't identify.

As I looked more closely, I could see that some of the women had runny sores on their legs. Incredibly, with such visible evidence of their disease, customers still entered. Evidently the $2 price was too low to resist.

With a sickening feeling in my stomach and the desire to vomit, I kept a good distance between the beckoning women and myself. One tour of the two-block area was more than sufficient.

Out of sight, I knew, was a group of men whose wealth derived from exploiting these women who were condemned to live short lives punctuated by fear and misery.

Chapter Outline

In this chapter, we examine **gender stratification**—males' and females' unequal access to power, prestige, and property. Gender is especially significant because it is a *master status;* that is, it cuts across *all* aspects of social life. No matter what we attain in life, we carry the label *male* or *female.* These labels carry images and expectations about how we should act. They not only guide our behavior, but they also serve as a basis of power and privilege.

In this chapter's fascinating journey, we shall look at inequality between the sexes around the world and in the United States. We shall explore whether it is biology or culture that makes us the way we are, and review sexual harassment, unequal pay, and violence against women. This excursion will provide a good context for understanding the power differences between men and women that lead to situations such as the one just described in our opening vignette. It should also give you insight into your own experiences with gender.

Issues of Sex and Gender

When we consider how females and males differ, the first thing that usually comes to mind is **sex,** the *biological characteristics* that distinguish males and females. *Primary sex characteristics* consist of a vagina or a penis and other organs related to reproduction. *Secondary sex characteristics* are the physical distinctions between males and females that are not directly connected with reproduction. Secondary sex characteristics become clearly evident at puberty when males develop more muscles and a lower voice, and gain more body hair and height, while females form more fatty tissue and broader hips, and develop breasts.

Gender, in contrast, is a *social,* not a biological characteristic. **Gender** consists of whatever behaviors and attitudes a group considers proper for its males and females. Consequently, gender varies from one society to another. Whereas *sex* refers to male or female, *gender* refers to masculinity or femininity. In short, you inherit your sex, but you learn your gender as you are socialized into the behaviors and attitudes your culture asserts are appropriate for your sex.

The expectations associated with gender vary around the world, as illustrated in the photo montage on the next page. They vary so greatly that some sociologists suggest we replace the terms *masculinity* and *femininity* with *masculinities* and *femininities* (Beynon 2002).

The sociological significance of gender is that it is a device by which society controls its members. Gender sorts us, on the basis of sex, into different life experiences. It opens and closes doors to power, property, and even prestige. Like social class, gender is a structural feature of society.

Before examining inequalities of gender, let's consider why the behaviors of men and women differ.

Gender Differences in Behavior: Biology or Culture?

Why are most males more aggressive than most females? Why do women enter "nurturing" occupations such as nursing in far greater numbers than men? To answer such questions, many people respond with some variation of "They're just born that way."

Is this the correct answer? Certainly biology plays a significant role in our lives. Each of us begins as a fertilized egg. The egg, or ovum, is contributed by our mother, the sperm that fertilizes the egg by our father. At the very moment the egg is fertilized, our sex is determined. Each of us receives twenty-three pairs of chromosomes from the ovum and twenty-three pairs from the sperm. The egg has an X chromosome. If the sperm that fertilizes the egg also has an X chromosome, we become a girl (XX). If the sperm has a Y chromosome, we become a boy (XY).

That's the biology. Now, the sociological question is: Does this biological difference control our behavior? Does it, for example, make females more nurturing and submissive and males more aggressive and domineering? Let's consider the positions that sociologists take.

gender stratification males' and females' unequal access to power, prestige, and property on the basis of their sex

sex biological characteristics that distinguish females and males, consisting of primary and secondary sex characteristics

gender the behaviors and attitudes that a society considers proper for its males and females; masculinity or femininity

To express their gender, people follow the guidelines of their culture. As you can see from these photos, the guidelines for demonstrating femininity and masculinity vary widely from one culture to another.

India

Brazil

Republic of Georgia

Mexico

Kenya

Chile

Ivory coast

Tibet

The Dominant Position in Sociology

The dominant sociological position is that social factors, not biology, are the reasons we behave the way we do. Our visible differences of sex do not come with meanings built into them. Rather, each human group makes its own interpretation of these physical differences and on this basis assigns males and females to separate groups. There, people learn what is expected of them and are given different access to their society's privileges.

Most sociologists find compelling the argument that if biology were the principal factor in human behavior, all around the world we would find women to be one sort of person and men another. In fact, however, ideas of gender vary greatly from one culture to another—and, as a result, so do male–female behaviors. This dominant position, that of culture, is presented in the Thinking Critically section.

Cynthia Fuchs Epstein, whose position in the ongoing "nature versus nurture" debate is summarized here.

THINKING Critically

Biology Versus Culture—Culture Is the Answer

For sociologist Cynthia Fuchs Epstein (1986, 1988, 1989), differences between the behavior of males and females are solely the result of social factors—specifically, socialization and social control. Her argument is as follows:

1. The anthropological record shows greater equality between the sexes in the past than we had thought. In earlier societies, women, as well as men, hunted small game, made tools, and gathered food. In hunting and gathering societies, the roles of both women and men are less rigid than those created by stereotypes. For example, the Agta and Mbuti are egalitarian. This proves that hunting and gathering societies exist in which women are not subordinate to men. Anthropologists claim that in these societies there is a separate but equal status of women at this level of development.
2. The types of work that men and women do in each society are determined not by biology but by social arrangements. Few people can escape these arrangements, and almost everyone works within his or her allotted narrow range. This gender division of work serves the interests of men, and both informal customs and formal laws enforce it. When these socially constructed barriers are removed, women's work habits are similar to those of men.
3. Biology "causes" some human behaviors, but these are limited to those involving reproduction or differences in body structure. These differences are relevant for only a few activities, such as playing basketball or "crawling through a small space."
4. Female crime rates are rising in many parts of the world. This indicates that aggression, which is often considered a biologically dictated male behavior, is related instead to social factors. When social conditions permit, such as when women become lawyers, they, too, become "adversarial, assertive, and dominant." Not incidentally, another form of this "dominant behavior" is the challenge women have made in scholarly journals to the biased views about human nature proposed by men.

In short, rather than "women's incompetence or inability to read a legal brief, perform brain surgery, [or] to predict a bull market," social factors—socialization, gender discrimination, and other forms of social control—create gender differences in behavior. Arguments that assign "an evolutionary and genetic basis" to explain differences in the behaviors of women and men are simplistic. They "rest on a dubious structure of inappropriate, highly selective, and poor data, oversimplification in logic and in inappropriate inferences by use of analogy."

Opening the Door to Biology

The matter of "nature" versus "nurture" is not so easily settled, however, and a number of sociologists acknowledge that biological factors are involved in some human behavior other than reproduction and childbearing (Udry 2000). The Thinking Critcally section on the next page presents this position. Alice Rossi, a feminist sociologist and former president of the American Sociological Association, has suggested that women are better prepared biologically for "mothering" than are men. She (1977, 1984) says that women are more sensitive to the infant's soft skin and to their nonverbal communications. Rossi stresses that the issue is not either biology or society. Instead, nature provides biological predispositions, which are then overlaid with culture.

To see why the door to biology is opening, just slightly, in sociology, let's consider a medical accident and a study of Vietnam veterans.

A Medical Accident The drama began in 1963, when 7-month-old male identical twins were taken to a doctor to be circumcised (Money and Ehrhardt 1972). The inept physician, who was using a heated needle, turned the electric current too high and accidentally burned off the penis of one of the boys. You can imagine the parents' disbelief—and then their horror—as the truth sank in.

What can be done in a situation like this? The damage was irreversible. The parents were told that their boy could never have sexual relations. After months of soul-searching

THINKING Critically

Biology Versus Culture— Biology Is the Answer

Sociologist Steven Goldberg (1974, 1986, 1993) finds it astonishing that anyone should doubt "the presence of core-deep differences in males and females, differences of temperament and emotion we call masculinity and femininity." Goldberg's argument—that it is not environment but inborn differences that "give masculine and feminine direction to the emotions and behaviors of men and women"—is as follows:

1. The anthropological record shows that all societies for which evidence exists are (or were) **patriarchies** (societies in which men dominate women). Stories about long-lost **matriarchies** (societies in which women dominate men) are myths.
2. In all societies, past and present, the highest statuses are associated with men. In every society, politics is ruled by "hierarchies overwhelmingly dominated by men."
3. Men dominate societies because they "have a lower threshold for the elicitation of dominance behavior . . . a greater tendency to exhibit whatever behavior is necessary in any environment to attain dominance in hierarchies and male-female encounters and relationships." Men are more willing "to sacrifice the rewards of other motivations—the desire for affection, health, family life, safety, relaxation, vacation and the like—in order to attain dominance and status."
4. Just as a 6-foot woman does not prove the social basis of height, so exceptional individuals, such as highly achieving and dominant women, do not refute "the physiological roots of behavior."

In short, there is only one valid interpretation of why every society from that of the Pygmy to that of the Swede associates dominance and attainment with men. Male dominance of society is "an inevitable resolution of the psychophysiological reality." Socialization and social institutions merely *reflect*—and sometimes exaggerate—inborn tendencies. Any interpretation other than inborn differences is "wrongheaded, ignorant, tendentious, internally illogical, discordant with the evidence, and implausible in the extreme." The argument that males are more aggressive because they have been socialized that way is equivalent to the claim that men can grow moustaches because boys have been socialized that way.

To acknowledge this reality is *not* to defend discrimination against women. Approval or disapproval of what societies have done with these basic biological differences is not the issue. The point is that biology leads males and females to different behaviors and attitudes—regardless of how we feel about this or whether we wish it were different.

Steven Goldberg, whose position in the ongoing "nature versus nurture" debate is summarized here.

and tearful consultations with experts, the parents decided that their son should have a sex change operation. When he was 22 months old, surgeons castrated the boy, using the skin to construct a vagina. They then gave the child a new name, Brenda, dressed him in frilly clothing, let his hair grow long, and began to treat him as a girl. Later, physicians gave Brenda female steroids to promote female pubertal growth (Colapinto 2001).

At first, the results were promising. When the twins were 4 years old, the mother said (remember that the children are biologically identical):

> One thing that really amazes me is that she is so feminine. I've never seen a little girl so neat and tidy. . . . She likes for me to wipe her face. She doesn't like to be dirty, and yet my son is quite different. I can't wash his face for anything. . . . She is very proud of herself, when she puts on a new dress, or I set her hair. . . . She seems to be daintier. (Money and Ehrhardt 1972)

About a year later, the mother described how their daughter imitated her while their son copied his father:

> I found that my son, he chose very masculine things like a fireman or a policeman. . . . He wanted to do what daddy does, work where daddy does, and carry a lunch kit. . . . [My daughter] didn't want any of those things. She wants to be a doctor or a teacher. . . . But none of the things that she ever wanted to be were like a policeman or a fireman, and that sort of thing never appealed to her. (Money and Ehrhardt 1972)

patriarchy a society or group in which men dominate women; authority is vested in males

matriarchy a society in which women as a group dominate men as a group

If the matter were this clear-cut, we could use this case to conclude that gender is entirely up to nurture. Seldom are things in life so simple, however, and a twist occurs in this story. Despite this promising start and her parents' coaching, Brenda did not adapt well to femininity. She preferred to mimic her father shaving, rather than her mother putting on makeup. She rejected dolls, favoring guns and her brother's toys. She liked rough and tumble games and insisted on urinating standing up. Classmates teased her and called her a "cavewoman" because she walked like a boy. At age 14, she was expelled from school for beating up a girl who teased her. Despite estrogen treatment, she was not attracted to boys, and at age 14, in despair over her inner turmoil, she was thinking of suicide. In a tearful confrontation, her father told her about the accident and her sex change.

"All of a sudden everything clicked. For the first time, things made sense, and I understood who and what I was," the twin says of this revelation. David (his new name) then had testosterone shots and, later, surgery to partially reconstruct a penis. At age 25, he married a woman and adopted her children (Diamond and Sigmundson 1997; Colapinto 2001.

The Vietnam Veterans Study Time after time, researchers have found that boys and men who have higher levels of testosterone tend to be more aggressive. In one study, researchers compared the testosterone levels of college men in a "rowdy" fraternity with those of men in a fraternity that had a reputation for academic success and social responsibility. Men in the "rowdy" fraternity had higher levels of testosterone (Dabbs et al. 1996). In another study, researchers found that prisoners who had committed sex crimes and acts of violence against people had higher levels of testosterone than those who had committed property crimes (Dabbs et al. 1995). The samples researchers used were small, however, leaving the nagging uncertainty that the findings of a particular study might be due to chance.

Then in 1985, the U.S. government began a health study of Vietnam veterans. To be certain the study was representative, the researchers chose a random sample of 4,462 men. Among the data they collected was a measurement of testosterone. Now, unexpectedly, sociologists had a large random sample available, and it is providing surprising clues about human behavior.

This sample supports earlier studies showing that men who have higher levels of testosterone tend to be more aggressive and to have more problems as a consequence. When the veterans with higher testosterone were boys, they were more likely to get in trouble with parents and teachers and to become delinquents. As adults, they are more likely to use hard drugs, to get into fights, to end up in lower-status jobs, and to have more sexual partners. Knowing this, you probably won't be surprised to learn that they also are less likely to marry—certainly their low-paying jobs and trouble with the police make them less appealing candidates for marriage. Those who do marry are more likely to have affairs, to hit their wives, and, it follows, to get divorced (Dabbs and Morris 1990; Booth and Dabbs 1993).

Fortunately for us sociologists, the Vietnam veterans study does not leave us with biology as the sole basis for behavior. Not all men with high testosterone get in trouble with the law, do poorly in school, or mistreat their wives. A chief difference, in fact, is social class. High-testosterone men from higher social classes are less likely to be involved in antisocial behaviors than are high-testosterone men from lower social classes (Dabbs and Morris 1990). *Social* factors (socialization, life goals, self-definitions), then, also play a part. In addition, conflict increases testosterone, so we can't be certain that high levels of testosterone are the cause or the consequence of conflict (Mazur and Michalek 1998). Uncovering the social factors and discovering how they work in combination with testosterone will be of great interest to sociologists.

Sociologists stress the social factors that underlie human behavior, the experiences that mold us, funneling us into different directions in life. The study of Vietnam veterans discussed in the text is one indication of how the sociological door is slowly opening to also consider biological factors in human behavior. Shown here are men of the 173rd Airborne Brigade in a "search and destroy" patrol in Tuy Province, Vietnam, in June 1966.

IN SUM

We shall have to await further studies, but the initial findings are intriguing. They indicate that some behavior that we sociologists usually assume to be due entirely to socialization is also influenced by biology. The findings are preliminary, but significant and provocative. In the years to come, this should prove to be an exciting—and controversial—area of sociological research. One level of research will be to determine if any behaviors are due only to biology. The second level will be to discover how social factors modify biology. The third level will be, in sociologist Janet Chafetz's (1990:30) phrase, to determine how "different" becomes translated into "unequal."

Anthropologist George Murdock surveyed 324 traditional societies worldwide. In all of them, some work was considered "men's work," while other tasks were considered "women's work." He found that almost universally cooking is considered women's work. This Navaho woman is making fry bread over an open fire in Monument Valley, Arizona.

Gender Inequality in Global Perspective

Some analysts speculate that in hunting and gathering societies women and men were social equals (Leacock 1981; Hendrix 1994). Apparently horticultural societies also had less gender discrimination than does our contemporary world (Collins et al. 1993). In these societies, women may have contributed about 60 percent of the group's total food. Yet, after reviewing the historical record, historian and feminist Gerda Lerner (1986) concluded that "there is not a single society known where women-as-a-group have decision-making power over men (as a group)."

Let's take a brief overview of some of this global inequality.

Sex Typing of Work

Anthropologist George Murdock (1937) surveyed 324 societies around the world. He found that in all of them activities are sex typed. In other words, every society associates activities with one sex or the other. He also found that activities that are considered "female" in one society may be considered "male" in another. In some groups, for example, taking care of cattle is women's work, while other groups assign this task to men.

Metalworking was the exception; it was considered men's work in all the societies Murdock examined. Three other pursuits—making weapons, pursuing sea mammals, and hunting—were almost universally the domain of men. In a few societies, however, women participated in these activities. Although Murdock found no specific work that was universally assigned to women only, he did find that making clothing, cooking, carrying water, and grinding grain were almost always female tasks. In a few societies, however, such activities were regarded as men's work.

From Murdock's cross-cultural survey, we can conclude that nothing about biology requires men and women to be assigned different work. Anatomy does not have to equal destiny when it comes to occupations, for as we have seen, pursuits that are considered feminine in one society may be deemed masculine in another, and vice versa. The photo essay on women at work in India underscores this point.

Throughout history, women have been denied the right to pursue various occupations on the basis of presumed biological characteristics. As society— and sex roles— have changed, women have increasingly entered occupations traditionally reserved for men.

THROUGH THE AUTHOR'S LENS

Work and Gender:

Women at Work in India

traveling through India was both a pleasant and an eye-opening experience. The country is incredibly diverse, the people friendly, and the land culturally rich. For this photo essay, wherever I went—whether city, village, or countryside—I took photos of women at work.

From these photos, you can see that Indian women work in a wide variety of occupations. Some of their jobs match traditional Western expectations, and some diverge sharply from our gender stereotypes. Although women in India remain subservient to men—with the women's movement hardly able to break the cultural surface—women's occupations are hardly limited to the home. I was surprised at some of the hard, heavy labor that Indian women do.

The villages of India have no indoor plumbing. Instead, each village has a well with a hand pump, and it is the women's job to fetch the water. This is backbreaking work, for, after pumping the water, the women wrestle the heavy buckets onto their heads and carry them home. This was one of the few occupations I saw that was limited to women.

Indian women are highly visible in public places. A storekeeper is as likely to be a woman as a man. This woman is selling glasses of water at a beach on the Bay of Bengal. The structure on which her glasses rest is built of sand.

Women also take care of livestock. It looks as though this woman dressed up and posed for her photo, but this is what she was wearing and doing when I saw her in the field and stopped to talk to her. While the sheep are feeding, her job is primarily to "be" there, to make certain the sheep don't wander off or that no one steals them.

Sweeping the house is traditional work for Western women. So it is in India, but the sweeping has been extended to areas outside the home. These women are sweeping a major intersection in Chennai. When the traffic light changes here, the women will continue sweeping, with the drivers swerving around them. This was one of the few occupations that seems to be limited to women.

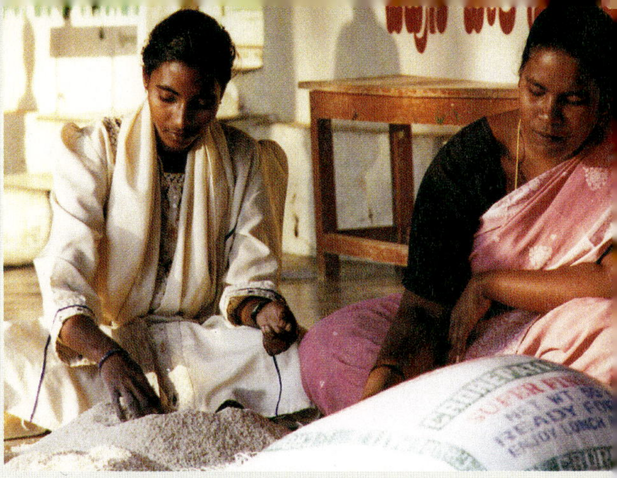

As in the West, food preparation in India is traditional women's work. Here, however, food preparation takes an unexpected twist. Having poured rice from the 60-pound sack onto the floor, these women in Chittoor search for pebbles or other foreign objects that might be in the rice.

When I saw this unusual sight, I had to stop and talk to the workers. From historical pictures, I knew that belt-driven machines were common on U.S. farms 100 years ago. This one in Tamil Nadu processes sugar cane. The woman feeds sugar cane into the machine, which disgorges the stalks on one side and sugar cane juice on the other.

I visited quarries in different parts of India, where I found men, women, and children hard at work in the tropical sun. This woman works 8 1/2 hours a day, six days a week. She earns 40 rupees a day (about ninety cents). Men make 60 rupees a day (about $1.35). Like many quarry workers, this woman is a bonded laborer. She must give half of her wages to her master.

This woman belongs to the Dobhy subcaste, whose occupation is washing clothes. She stands waist deep at this same spot doing the same thing day after day. The banks of this canal in Hyderabad are lined with men and women of her caste, who are washing linens for hotels and clothing for more well-to-do families.

A common sight in India is women working on construction crews. As they work on buildings and on highways, they mix cement, unload trucks, carry rubble, and, following Indian culture, carry heavy loads of bricks atop their heads. This photo was taken in Raipur, Chhattisgarh.

Prestige of Work

You might ask whether this division of labor really illustrates social inequality. Does it perhaps simply represent arbitrary forms of dividing up labor, not gender discrimination?

That could be the case, except for this finding: *Universally, greater prestige is given to male activities—regardless of what those activities are* (Linton 1936; Rosaldo 1974). If taking care of goats is men's work, then the care of goats is considered important and carries high prestige, but if it is women's work, it is considered less important and given less prestige. Or, to take an example closer to home, when delivering babies was "women's work" and was done by midwives, it was given low prestige. But when men took over this task, its prestige increased (Ehrenreich and English 1973). In short, it is not the work that provides the prestige, but the sex with which the work is associated.

Other Areas of Global Discrimination

Let's briefly consider four additional aspects of global gender discrimination. Later, when we focus on the United States, we shall examine these topics in greater detail.

Education Almost 1 billion adults around the world cannot read; two-thirds are women ("State of . . . " 2001). Table 11.1, which lists all the world's countries where less than half the women can read and write, illustrates this point further. In every one of these countries, a higher percentage of men are literate. This table also shows how illiteracy is clustered, for 22 of these 32 countries are in Africa.

Politics Around the world, women lack equal access to national decision making: No national legislature of any country has as many women as men. Women come closest to having equal representation in Sweden, where 43 percent of the legislators are women, but in some countries, such as Japan and Iran, the total is only 1 percent ("Women of . . . " 2002). In Kuwait and United Arab Emirates, women can't even vote (Crossette 1995a, b). In most nations, women hold only about 11 percent of the seats in parliaments and congress.

The Pay Gap In every nation, women average less pay than men. In the United States, full-time working women average only 65 percent of what men make (see Figure

Table 11.1 The Percentage of Women and Men Who Cannot Read and Write

Country	Women	Men	Country	Women	Men
Niger	92%	76%	Bhutan	66%	39%
Burkina Faso	86%	66%	Libya	64%	38%
Guinea-Bissau	81%	40%	Morocco	64%	38%
Pakistan	79%	40%	Liberia	62%	30%
Afghanistan	78%	48%	Cote d'Ivoire	61%	45%
Sierra Leone	77%	49%	Burundi	59%	43%
Nepal	76%	41%	Togo	59%	25%
Benin	75%	43%	Egypt	56%	33%
Yemen	75%	32%	Central African Republic	55%	40%
Senegal	72%	53%	Eritrea	55%	33%
Mozambique	71%	40%	India	55%	32%
Bangladesh	70%	48%	Iraq	54%	34%
Mauritania	68%	47%	Sudan	54%	30%
Ethiopia	67%	56%	Malawi	53%	25%
Laos	67%	36%	Haiti	52%	48%
Mali	66%	51%			
Chad	66%	48%			

Countries where less than half of the women are literate.
Source: "Women of Our World," 2002.

11.8 on page 312), while in South Korea women make half of what men earn (Monk-Turner and Turner 2000).

Violence Against Women A global human rights issue is violence against women. Historical examples are foot binding in China, witch burning in Europe, and *suttee* (burning the living widow with her dead husband's body) in India. Today we have rape, wife beating, female infanticide, and forced prostitution, which was probably the case in our opening vignette. One of today's most notorious examples is female circumcision, the topic of the Cultural Diversity box on the next page.

"Honor killings" are another form of violence against women. In some societies, such as Pakistan, Jordan, and Kurdistan, a woman who is thought to have brought disgrace on her family is killed by a male relative—usually a brother or husband, but often her father or uncles. What threat to the family's honor can be so severe that the daughter or the wife is killed? The usual reason is sex outside of marriage. In Iraq, even a woman who has been raped is in danger of becoming the victim of an honor killing (Banerjee 2003). Killing the girl or woman removes the "stain" she has brought to the family, restoring the family's honor in the community. The police generally ignore honor killings, viewing them as family matters.

Foot binding, a form of violence against women, was practiced in China. This photo of a woman in Canton, China, is from the early 1900s. The woman's tiny feet, which made it difficult for her to walk, were a status symbol, indicating that her husband was wealthy and did not need her labor. It also made her dependent on him.

How Females Became a Minority Group

Around the world, gender is *the* primary division between people. Every society sets up barriers to provide unequal access to power, property, and prestige on the basis of sex. Consequently, sociologists classify females as a *minority group*. In most countries females outnumber males, so you may find this strange. This term applies, however, because it refers to people who are discriminated against on the basis of physical or cultural characteristics, regardless of their numbers (Hacker 1951). For an overview of gender discrimination in a changing society, see the Cultural Diversity box on page 301.

Have females always been a minority group? As we just saw, some analysts speculate that in horticultural and hunting and gathering societies, women and men may have been social equals—or that at least there was much less gender discrimination than we have today. How did it happen, then, that around the world women came to be systematically discriminated against? Let's consider the primary theory that has been proposed.

The Origins of Patriarchy

The major theory of the origin of patriarchy—men dominating society—points to social consequences of human reproduction (Lerner 1986; Friedl 1990). In early human history, life was short, and in order to reproduce the human group, many children had to be born. Because only females get pregnant, carry a child for nine months, give birth, and nurse, women were limited in their activities for a considerable part of their lives. To survive, an infant needed a nursing mother. With a child at her breast or in her uterus, or one carried on her hip or on her back, women were physically encumbered. Consequently, around the world women assumed tasks that were associated with the home and child care, while men took over the hunting of large animals and other tasks that required greater speed and absence from the base camp for longer periods of time (Huber 1990).

As a consequence, men became dominant. It was they who left camp to hunt animals, who made contact with other tribes, who traded with these other groups, and who quarreled and waged war with them. It was also the men who made and controlled the instruments of death, the weapons used for hunting and warfare. It was they who

CULTURAL DIVERSITY
around the WORLD

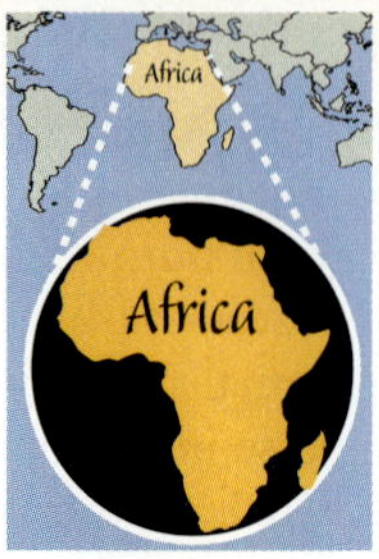

Female Circumcision

> "Lie down there," the excisor suddenly said to me [when she was 12], pointing to a mat on the ground. No sooner had I laid down than I felt my frail, thin legs grasped by heavy hands and pulled wide apart. . . . Two women on each side of me pinned me to the ground . . . I underwent the ablation of the labia minor and then of the clitoris. The operation seemed to go on forever. I was in the throes of agony, torn apart both physically and psychologically. It was the rule that girls of my age did not weep in this situation. I broke the rule. I cried and screamed with pain . . . !
>
> Afterwards they forced me, not only to walk back to join the other girls who had already been excised, but to dance with them. I was doing my best, but then I fainted. . . . It was a month before I was completely healed. When I was better, everyone mocked me, as I hadn't been brave, they said. (Walker and Parmar 1993:107–108)

Female circumcision is common in parts of Muslim Africa and in some parts of Malaysia and Indonesia. Often called female genital cutting by Westerners, this practice is also known as clitoral excision, clitoridectomy, infibulation, and labiadectomy, depending on how much of the tissue is removed. Worldwide, between 100 million and 200 million females have been circumcised. In Egypt, 97 percent of the women have been circumcised (Boyle et al. 2001).

In some cultures, only the girl's clitoris is cut off; in others, more is removed. In Sudan, the Nubia cut away most of the girl's genitalia, then sew together the remaining outer edges. They bind the girl's legs from ankles to waist for several weeks while scar tissue closes up the vagina. They leave a small opening the size of a pencil for the passage of urine and menstrual fluids.

Among most groups, the surgery takes place between the ages of 4 and 8. In some cultures, it occurs seven to ten days after birth. In others, it is not performed until girls reach adolescence. Because the surgery is usually done without anesthesia, the pain is so excruciating that adults must hold the girl down. In urban areas, physicians sometimes perform the operation; in rural areas, a neighborhood woman usually does it.

Shock, bleeding, infection, infertility, and death are among the risks. Common side-effects are vaginal spasms, painful intercourse, and lack of orgasms. Urinary tract infections also occur as urine and menstrual flow build up behind the tiny opening.

When a woman marries, the opening is cut wider to permit sexual intercourse. In some groups, this is the husband's responsibility. Before a woman gives birth, the opening is enlarged further. After birth, the vagina is again sutured shut, a cycle of surgically closing and opening that begins anew with each birth.

What are the reasons for this custom? Some groups believe that it reduces female sexual desire, making it more likely that a woman will be a virgin at marriage, and, afterward, remain faithful to her husband. Others think that it enhances fertility and vaginal cleanliness.

Feminists call female circumcision a form of ritual torture to control female sexuality. They point out that men dominate the societies that practice it. Mothers cooperate with the surgery because in these societies an uncircumcised woman is considered impure and is not allowed to marry. Grandmothers insist that the custom continue out of concern that their granddaughters marry well.

Change is coming. The first ladies of four countries—Burkina Faso, Guinea, Mali, and Nigeria—have condemned the practice (Lacey 2003). In Kenya, two girls obtained a court order stopping their father from having them circumcised. Their community was shocked, but an attorney reminded the court that Kenya had signed human rights agreements.

For Your CONSIDERATION

Do you think that the United States should try to make other nations stop this custom? Or would this be ethnocentric, the imposition of Western values on other cultures? As one Somali woman said, "The Somali woman doesn't need an alien woman telling her how to treat her private parts." What legitimate basis do you think there is for members of one culture to interfere with another?

Sources: Based on Mahran 1978, 1981; Ebomoyi 1987; Lightfoot-Klein 1989; Merwine 1993; Walker and Parmar 1993; Chalkley 1997; Collymore 2000; "Kenya . . ." 2001.

accumulated possessions in trade, and gained prestige by triumphantly returning with prisoners of war or with large animals to feed the tribe. In contrast, little prestige was given to the ordinary, routine, taken-for-granted activities of women—who were not seen as risking their lives for the group. Eventually, men took over society. Their weapons, items of trade, and knowledge gained from contact with other groups became sources of power. Women became second-class citizens, subject to men's decisions.

CULTURAL DIVERSITY

around the WORLD

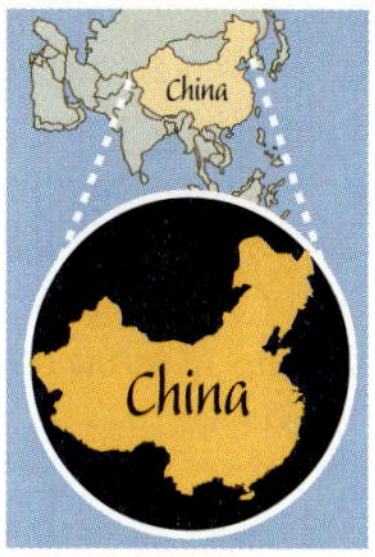

"Pssst. You Wanna Buy a Bride?" China in Transition

Nguyen Thi Hoan, age 22, thanked her lucky stars. A Vietnamese country girl, she had just arrived in Hanoi to look for work, and while she was still at the bus station a woman offered her a job in a candy factory.

It was a trap. After Nguyen had loaded a few sacks of sugar, the woman took her into the country to "get supplies." There some men took her to China, which was only 100 miles away. Nguyen was put up for auction, along with a 16-year-old Vietnamese girl. Each brought $350. Nguyen was traded from one bride dealer to another until she was taken to a Chinese village. There she was introduced to her new husband, who had paid $700 for her (Marshall 1999).

Why are tens of thousands of women kidnapped and sold as brides in China each year (Rosenthal 2001b)? First, parts of China have a centuries-long tradition of bride selling. Second, China has a shortage of women. The government enforces a "one couple-one child" policy. Since sons are preferred, female infanticide has become common. One result is a shortage of women of marriageable age. In some provinces, for every 100 women there are over 120 men. Yet all the men are expected to marry and produce heirs (Rosenthal 2001b).

Actually, Nguyen was lucky. Some kidnapped women are sold as prostitutes.

Bride selling and forced prostitution are millennia old practices. But China is also entering a new era, which is bringing with it new pressures for Chinese women. Ideas of beauty are changing, and blonde, blue-eyed women are becoming a fetish. As a consequence, Chinese women feel a pressure to "Westernize" their bodies. Surgeons promise to give them bigger breasts and Western-looking eyes. A Western style of advertising is gaining ground, too: Ads now show scantily clad women perched on top of sports cars (Chen 1995; Johansson 1999; Yat-ming Sin and Hon-ming Yau 2001).

China in transition . . . It is bringing back the old, bride selling, while moving toward the new, Western ideas of beauty and advertising. In both the old and new, women are commodities for the consumption of men.

Is this theory correct? Remember that the answer lies buried in human history, and there is no way of testing it. Male dominance may be due to some entirely different cause. For example, anthropologist Marvin Harris (1977) proposed that because most men are stronger than most women and hand-to-hand combat was necessary in tribal groups, men became the warriors and women the reward to entice them to do battle. Frederick Engels proposed that patriarchy developed with the origin of private property (Lerner 1986; Mezentseva 2001). He could not explain why private property should have produced male dominance, however. Gerda Lerner (1986) suggests that patriarchy may even have had different origins in different places.

Whatever its origins, a circular system of thought evolved. Men came to think of themselves as inherently superior—based on the evidence that they dominated society. They surrounded many of their activities with secrecy, and constructed elaborate rules and rituals to avoid "contamination" by females, whom they openly deemed inferior by that time.

A theory of how patriarchy originated centers on childbirth. Because only women give birth, they assumed tasks associated with home and child care, while men hunted and performed other survival tasks that required greater strength, speed, and absence from home. This woman, who is harvesting rice in Guizhou, China, also takes care of her child—just as her female ancestors have done for millennia.

The burqua worn by Arab women is viewed by many as a form of male domination, a way to suppress women's individuality, freedom, and sexuality. After the Taliban in Afghanistan were deposed by U.S. troops, one of the first things some women did was to throw off their burquas and veils.

Even today, patriarchy is always accompanied by cultural supports designed to justify male dominance—such as certain activities designated as "not appropriate" for women.

As tribal societies developed into larger groups, men, who enjoyed their power and privileges, maintained their dominance. Long after hunting and hand-to-hand combat ceased to be routine, and even after large numbers of children were no longer needed in order to reproduce the human group, men held on to their power. Male dominance in contemporary societies, then, is a continuation of a millennia-old pattern whose origin is lost in history.

Gender Inequality in the United States

Gender inequality is not some accidental, hit-or-miss affair. Rather, the institutions of each society work together to maintain the group's particular forms of inequality. Customs, often venerated throughout history, both justify and maintain these arrangements. Although men have resisted sharing their privileged positions with women, change has come.

Fighting Back: The Rise of Feminism

To see how far we have come, it is useful to see where we used to be. In early U.S. society, the second-class status of women was taken for granted. A husband and wife were legally one person—him (Chafetz and Dworkin 1986). Women could not serve on juries, nor could they vote, make legal contracts, or hold property in their own name. How could times have changed so much that these examples sound like fiction?

A central lesson of conflict theory is that power yields privilege; like a magnet, power draws society's best resources to the elite. Because men tenaciously held onto their privileges and used social institutions to maintain their position, basic rights for women came only through prolonged and bitter struggle.

feminism the philosophy that men and women should be politically, economically, and socially equal; organized activities on behalf of this principle

Feminism, the view that biology is not destiny and that stratification by gender is wrong and should be resisted, met with strong opposition—both by men who had privilege to lose and by women who accepted their status as morally correct. In 1894, for example, Jeannette Gilder said that women should not have the right to vote because "Politics is too public, too wearing, and too unfitted to the nature of women" (Crossen 2003).

The women's struggle for equal rights has been long and hard. Shown here is a 1919 photo from the "first wave" of the U.S. women's movement. Only against enormous opposition from men did U.S. women win the right to vote. They first voted in national elections in 1920.

Feminists, then known as suffragists, struggled against such views. In 1916, they founded the National Women's Party, and in 1917 they began to picket the White House. After picketing for six months, the women were arrested. Hundreds were sent to prison, including Lucy Burns and Alice Paul, two leaders of the National Women's Party. The extent to which these women had threatened male prerogatives is demonstrated by their treatment in prison.

> Two men brought in Dorothy Day [the editor of a periodical that espoused women's rights], twisting her arms above her head. Suddenly they lifted her and brought her body down twice over the back of an iron bench. . . . They had been there a few minutes when Mrs. Lewis, all doubled over like a sack of flour, was thrown in. Her head struck the iron bed and she fell to the floor senseless. As for Lucy Burns, they handcuffed her wrists and fastened the handcuffs over [her] head to the cell door. (Cowley 1969)

This *first wave* of the women's movement had a liberal branch that wanted to reform all the institutions of society, and a conservative branch whose concern was to win the vote for women (Freedman 2001). The conservative branch dominated, and after the vote was won in 1920 the movement basically dissolved.

The *second wave* began in the 1960s. Sociologist Janet Chafetz (1990) points out that up to this time most women thought of work as a temporary activity intended to fill the time between completing school and getting married. To see how children's books reinforced such thinking, see Figure 11.1. As more women took jobs, however, they began to regard them as careers. Women then started to compare their working conditions with those of men. This shift in their reference group changed the way they viewed their conditions at work. The result was a second wave of protest against gender inequalities. The goals of this second wave (which continues today) are broad; they range from raising women's pay to changing policies on violence against women.

This second wave of the women's movement also has its liberal and conservative branches. Although each holds a different view of what gender equality should look like, the two share several goals, including equality in job opportunities and pay. Both liberals and conservatives have a radical wing. On the liberal side, radicals call for hostility toward

Figure 11.1

By looking at the past we get an idea of how far we have come. This illustration from a 1970s children's book shows the mind-set of the day. You can see how children who grew up during this period were taught to view gender and work.

Source: Anthony Cortese, *Provocateur: Images of Women and Minorities in Advertising,* 2nd ed. Boulder, CO: Rowman and Little Publishers, 2003.

men; on the conservative side, radicals favor a return to traditional family roles. All factions—whether radical or conservative—claim to represent the "real" needs of today's women. It is from these claims and counterclaims that the women's movement will continue to take shape and affect public policy.

A *third wave* of feminism is emerging. Three main aspects are apparent. The first is a greater focus on the problems of women in the Least Industrialized Nations (Patel 1997; Spivak 2000). The second is a criticism of the values that dominate work and society. Some feminists argue that competition, emotional invulnerability, toughness, and independence represent "male" qualities and need to be replaced with cooperation, openness, connection, and interdependence (England 2000). A third aspect is the removal of impediments to women's love and pleasure (Gilligan 2002). As this third wave develops, we can assume that it, too, will have its liberal and conservative branches.

Although women enjoy fundamental rights today, gender inequality continues to play a central role in social life. Let's look at gender relations in health care, education, and everyday life, and then, in greater detail, at discrimination in the world of work.

Gender Inequality in Health Care

In Chapter 19, we will pursue the issue of sexism in medicine further, but for now let's consider how gender discrimination in health care can be a life-and-death matter. This is the topic of the Down-to-Earth Sociology box below.

Gender Inequality in Education

In education, too, a glimpse of the past sheds light on the present. Until 1832, women were not allowed to attend college with men. When women were admitted—first at Oberlin College in Ohio—they had to remain silent at public assemblies, do the men students' laundry, clean their rooms, and serve them their meals (Flexner 1971).

Educators thought that women didn't belong in higher education because their female organs dominated their minds. Referring to menstruation, Dr. Edward Clarke, of Harvard University, expressed the dominant sentiment this way:

> A girl upon whom Nature, for a limited period and for a definite purpose, imposes so great a physiological task, will not have as much power left for the tasks of school, as the boy of whom Nature requires less at the corresponding epoch. (Andersen 1988)

Because women were so much weaker, Clarke urged them to study only one-third as much as young men—and not to study at all during menstruation.

DOWN-TO-EARTH SOCIOLOGY

Subtle Sexism Can Be Deadly

Medical researchers were perplexed. Reports were coming in from all over the country: Women were twice as likely as men to die after coronary bypass surgery. Researchers at Cedars-Sinai Medical Center in Los Angeles checked their own records: Of 2,300 coronary bypass patients, 4.6 percent of the women died as a result of the surgery, compared with 2.6 percent of the men.

These findings presented a sociological puzzle. To solve it, researchers first turned to biology (Bishop 1990). In coronary bypass surgery, a blood vessel is taken from one part of the body and stitched to an artery on the surface of the heart. Perhaps this operation was more difficult to perform on women because they have smaller coronary arteries. To find out, researchers measured the amount of time that surgeons kept patients on the heart-lung machine while they operated. They were surprised to learn that women spent *less* time on the machine than men. This indicated that the operation was not more difficult to perform on women.

As the researchers probed, a surprising answer unfolded: unintended sexual discrimination. Physicians had not taken the chest pains of their women patients as seriously as they took the complaints of their men patients. They were *ten* times more likely to give men exercise stress tests and radioactive heart scans. They also sent men to surgery on the basis of abnormal stress tests, but waited until women showed clear-cut symptoms of heart disease before sending them to surgery. Having surgery after the disease is further along reduces the chances of survival.

As more women become physicians, perhaps this will change. We know that women doctors are more likely to order pap smears and mammograms (Lurie et al. 1993), so it is likely that they will be more responsive to the health complaints of women. If so, more women will choose women doctors. To be competitive, men doctors will have to become more responsive to women's health problems, too.

For Your CONSIDERATION

In short, gender bias is so pervasive that it operates beneath our level of awareness and is so severe that it can be a matter of life or death. It is important to note that the doctors in these studies had no intention of discriminating against anyone. In what ways does gender bias affect your own perceptions and behavior?

Figure 11.2 Changes in College Enrollment, by Sex

What percentages of U.S. college students are female and male?

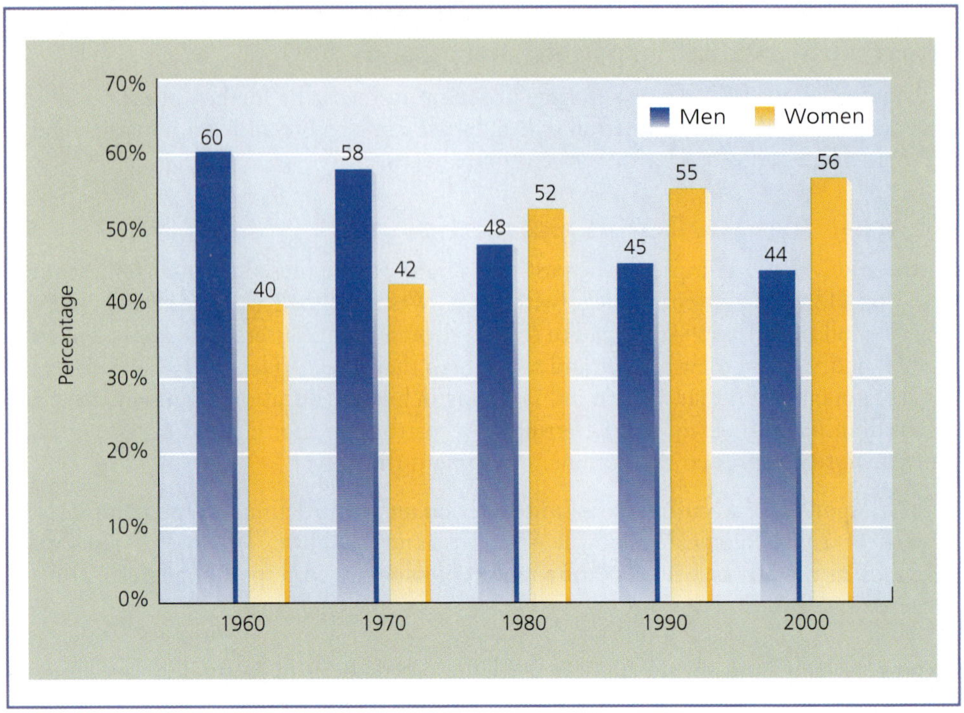

Source: Statistical Abstract 1991:Table 261; 2002:Table 260.

Like out-of-fashion clothing, these ideas were discarded, and women entered college in growing numbers. The change has been so great that of today's college students 56 percent are women (see Figure 11.2.). Women also earn 57 percent of all bachelor's degrees and 58 percent of all master's degrees (*Statistical Abstract* 2002: Table 276). Because men are now lagging behind, some have begun to call for *affirmative action for men*, especially for African American men (Kleinfeld 2002a). To see why, look at Figure 11.3.

Figure 11.4 illustrates another major change. From this figure, you can see how women have increased their share of professional degrees. The greatest change is in dentistry: In 1970 across the entire United States, only 34 women earned degrees in dentistry. Today, about 1,700 women become dentists each year.

Women earning more bachelor's and master's degrees than men and entering the professions in growing numbers are certainly major breaks with the past. If we probe beneath the surface, however, we still find old practices. Women's sports, for example, are usually considered less important than men's sports (Fisher 2002). And whenever I attend a high school football or basketball game, I still see a group of girls in short, brightly colored skirts wildly cheering the boys from the sidelines—but no such group of boys leading organized cheers for the girls when they play *their* sports.

Then there is the matter of *gender tracking;* that is, degrees tend to follow gender, which reinforces male-female distinctions. Here are two extremes: Men earn 81 percent of bachelor's degrees in the "masculine" field of engineering, while women are awarded 88 percent of bachelor's degrees in the "feminine" field of home economics (*Statistical Abstract* 2002:Table 279). Because gender socialization gives men and women different orientations to life, they enter college with gender-linked aspirations. It is their socialization—not some presumed innate characteristics—that channels men and women into different educational paths.

If we follow students into graduate school, we see that with each passing year the proportion of women drops. Table 11.2 on page 308 gives us a snapshot of doctoral programs in the sciences. Note how aspirations (enrollment) and accomplishments (doctorates earned) are sex linked. In five of these doctoral programs, men outnumber

Figure 11.3 Current College Students, by Sex and Race-Ethnicity

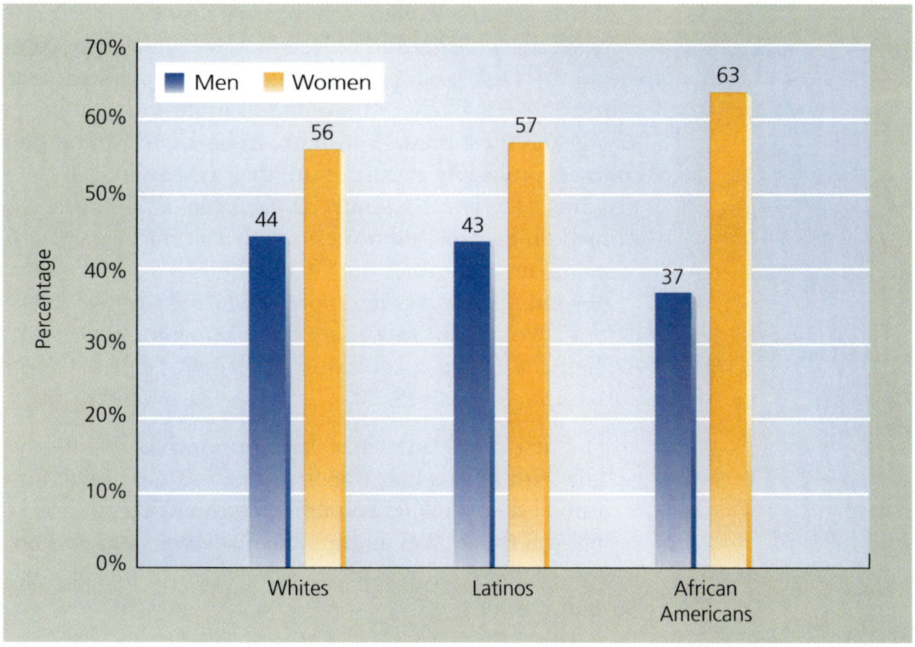

Source: Statistical Abstract 2002:Table 260.
Note: Only these groups are listed in the source.

Figure 11.4 Gender Changes in Professional Degrees

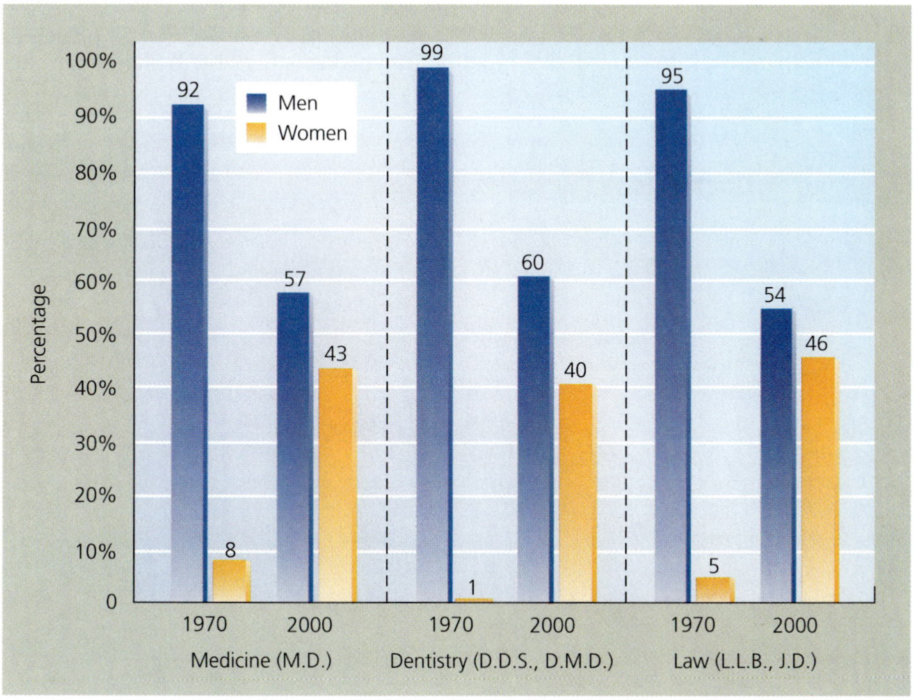

Source: Statistical Abstract 2002:Table 281.

women, and in three women outnumber men (in two by a very small margin). In *all* of them, however, women are less likely to complete the doctorate.

If we follow those who earn doctoral degrees to their teaching careers at colleges and universities, we find gender stratification in rank and pay. Throughout the United States, women are less likely to become full professors, the highest-paying and most prestigious rank. In both private and public colleges, professors average more than twice the salary of instructors (*Statistical Abstract* 2002:Table 272). Even when women do become full professors, they average less pay than men who are full professors (Wood 2001).

Beyond the pay gap lies more subtle and invasive discrimination. Women professors are not taken as seriously as men. As Barbara Grosz, a professor at Harvard, put it (Zernike 2001b).

> The first time you're mistaken for a secretary is funny. The 99th time is not. The first time the guys [men professors] don't include you in the conversation at a meeting, you think, "I'm not interested anyway." But a whole year of these conversations—there's this kind of constant erosion.

From grade school through college, male sports have been emphasized, and women's sports underfunded. Due to federal laws (Title IX), the funding gap has closed considerably, and there is an increasing emphasis on women's accomplishments in sports. Shown here is a Venus Williams, who took the tennis world by storm. Venus, who was coached by her father since she was 4 years old, turned professional at age 14.

Gender Inequality in Everyday Life

Of the many aspects of gender discrimination in everyday life that we could examine, we have space to look only at two: the general devaluation of femininity in U.S. society, and male dominance of conversation.

General Devaluation of Things Feminine

> Leaning against the water cooler, two men—both minor executives—are nursing their cups of coffee, discussing last Sunday's Giants game, postponing for as long as possible the moment when work must finally be faced.
>
> A [male] vice president walks by and hears them talking about sports. Does he stop and send them back to their desks? Does he frown? Probably not. Being a man, he

Table 11.2 Doctorates in Science, By Sex

	Students Enrolled		Doctorates Conferred		Completion Ratio* (Higher or Lower Than Expected)	
Field	Women	Men	Women	Men	Women	Men
Computer sciences	29%	71%	16%	84%	−44	+18
Engineering	20%	80%	16%	84%	−25	+5
Agriculture	42%	58%	29%	71%	−31	+22
Mathematics	35%	65%	25%	75%	−29	+15
Physical sciences	30%	70%	24%	76%	−20	+9
Social sciences	51%	49%	43%	57%	−16	+16
Biological sciences	52%	48%	46%	55%	−12	+15
Psychology	72%	28%	67%	33%	−7	+18

*The formula for the completion ratio is X minus Y divided by Y, where X is the doctorates conferred and Y is the proportion enrolled in a program.

Source: Statistical Abstract 2002:Tables 769, 771.

> is far more likely to pause and join in the conversation, anxious to prove that he, too, is "one of the boys," feigning an interest in football that he may very well not share at all. These men—all the men in the office—are his troops, his comrades-in-arms.
>
> Now, let's assume that two women are standing by the water cooler discussing whatever you please: women's liberation, clothes, work, any subject—except football, of course. The vice president walks by, sees them, and moves down the hall in a fury, cursing and wondering whether it is worth the trouble to complain—but to whom?—about all those bitches standing around gabbing when they should be working. "Don't they know," he will ask, in the words of a million men, "that this is an office?" (Korda 1973: 20–21)

As indicated in this scenario, women's interests, attitudes, and contributions are not taken as seriously as those of men. Masculinity is valued more highly, for it represents strength and success; femininity is devalued, for it is perceived as symbolizing weakness and lack of accomplishment.

Sociologist Samuel Stouffer produced a classic study of World War II combat soldiers. In *The American Soldier* (1949), he reported that officers used feminine terms as insults to motivate soldiers. To show less-than-expected courage or endurance was to risk the charge of not being a man. An officer might say, "Whatsa matter, Bud—got lace on your drawers?" A generation later, accusations of femininity were still used as motivating insults to prepare soldiers to fight in Vietnam. Drill sergeants would mock their troops by saying, "Can't hack it, little girls?" (Eisenhart 1975). The practice continues. Male soldiers who show hesitation during maneuvers are mocked by others, who call them girls (Miller 2001).

In sports, we see the same thing. Anthropologist Douglas Foley (2001) notes that football coaches insult boys who don't play well by saying that they are "wearing skirts," and sociologist Donna Eder (1995) notes that junior high boys call one another "girl" if they don't hit hard enough in football. Sociologists Jean Stockard and Miriam Johnson (1980), who observed boys playing basketball, heard boys who missed a basket being called a "woman." In professional hockey, players who are not rough enough on the ice are called "girls" (Gallmeier 1988:227).

These insults represent a devaluation of females. As Stockard and Johnson (1980:12) point out, "There is no comparable phenomenon among women, for young girls do not insult each other by calling each other 'man.'"

Gender Inequality in Conversation You may have noticed that men are more likely than women to interrupt conversations. They also are more likely to control changes in topics. Sociologists note that talk between a man and a woman is often more like talk between an employer and an employee than between social equals (West and Garcia 1988; Smith-Lovin and Brody 1989; Tannen 1990, 2003). In short, conversations between men and women mirror their relative positions of power in society.

Interrupting conversations and using "woman" and "girl" as terms of insult are only the tip of the iceberg. Underlying these aspects of everyday life is a structural inequality based on gender that runs throughout society. Let's look at this structural feature in the workplace.

Gender Inequality in the Workplace

To examine the work setting is to make visible basic relations between men and women. Let's begin with one of the most remarkable areas of gender inequality at work, the pay gap.

The Pay Gap

One of the chief characteristics of the U.S. work force is a steady growth in the numbers of women who work outside the home for wages. Figure 11.5 shows that in 1890 about

Figure 11.5 Women's and Men's Proportion of the U.S. Labor Force

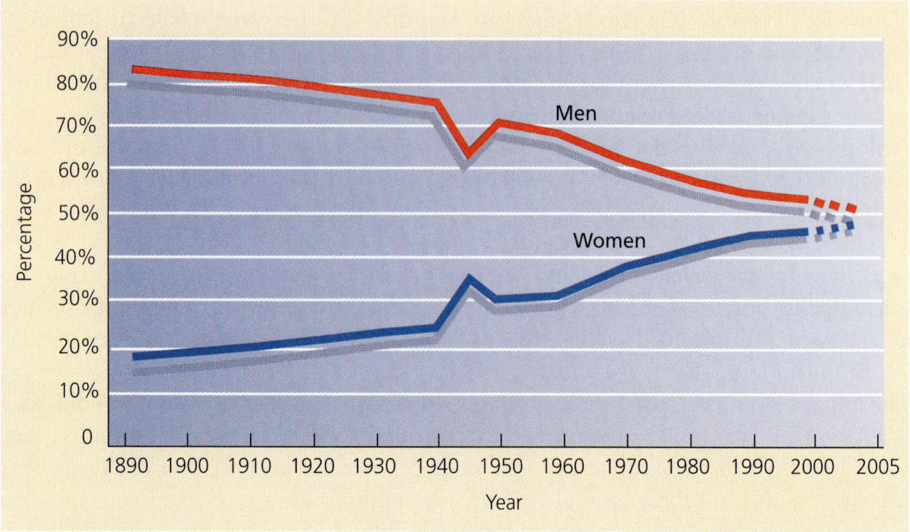

Note: Pre 1940 totals include women 14 and over: totals for 1940 and after are for women 16 and over. Broken lines are the author's projections.

Sources: By the author. Based on 1969 *Handbook on Women Workers,* 1969:10; *Manpower Report to the President,* 1971:203, 205; Mills and Palumbo, 1980:6, 45; *Statistical Abstract* 2002:Table 564.

one of every five workers was a woman. By 1940, this ratio had grown to one of four, by 1960 to one of three, and today it is almost one of two.

Women who work for wages are not evenly distributed throughout the United States. From the Social Map below, you can see that where a woman lives makes a difference in

Figure 11.6 Women in the Work Force

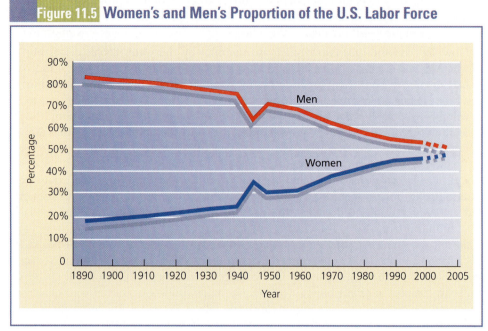

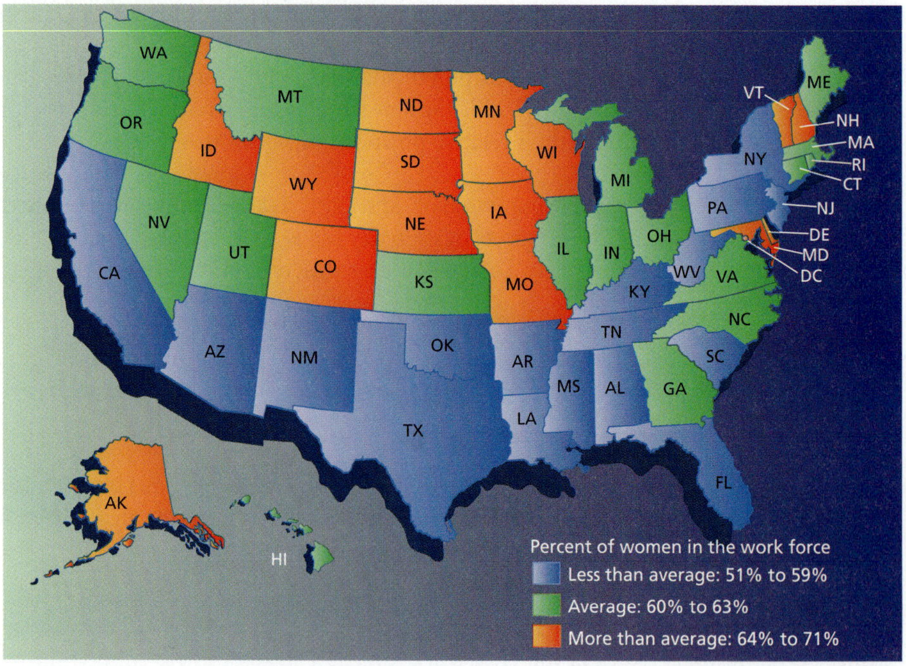

Source: By the author. Based on *Statistical Abstract* 2002:Table 565.

how likely she is to work outside the home. The geographical patterns evident in this map reflect regional-subcultural differences of which we currently have little understanding.

After college, you might like to take a few years off, travel a bit, and sit under a palm tree and drink piña coladas. But chances are, you are going to go to work instead. Since you have to work, how would you like to earn an extra $1,200,000 on your job? If this sounds appealing, read on. I'm going to reveal how you can make an extra $2,500 a month between the ages of 25 and 65.

Is this hard to do? Actually, it is simple for some, but impossible for others. As Figure 11.7 shows, all you have to do is be born a male and graduate from college. If we compare full-time workers, this is how much more the *average male* college graduate earns over the course of his career. Hardly any single factor pinpoints gender discrimination better than this million-plus dollars. But here is another. As you can see from this figure, the average woman who graduates from college earns about the same as the average man who drops out of college. You can also see that the pay gap shows up at *all* levels of education.

The pay gap is so great that U.S. women who work full time average *only 65 percent* of what men are paid. Figure 11.8 on the next page shows that the pay gap used to be even worse. You can see that the gap closed a bit during the 1980s, but then it grew during the 1990s. It is now back to where it was 15 years ago. The gender gap in pay occurs not only in the United States but also in *all* industrialized nations.

What logic can underlie the gender pay gap? Earlier we saw that college degrees are gender linked, so perhaps this gap is due to career choices. Maybe women are more likely to choose lower-paying jobs, such as teaching grade school, while men are more likely to go into better-paying fields, such as business and engineering. Actually, this is true, and researchers have found that about *half* the pay gap is due to such factors. And the balance? It consists of a combination of gender discrimination (Kemp 1990; Jacobs 2003) and what is called the "child penalty," women missing out on work experience while they care for children ("Redefining . . . " 2000; Hundley 2001).

Depending on your sex, then, you will either benefit from the pay gap or be its victim. Because the pay gap will be so important in your own work life, let's follow some college graduates to see how it actually comes about. Economists Rex Fuller and Richard

Figure 11.7 The Gender Pay Gap, by Education[1]

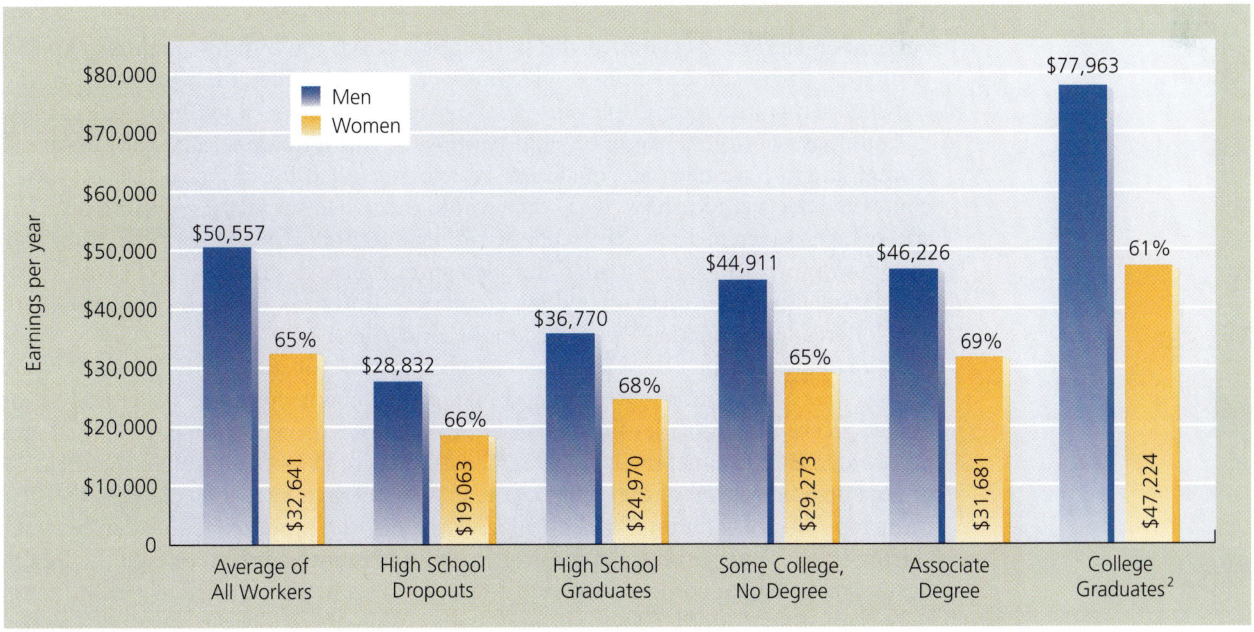

[1]Full-time workers in all fields.

[2]Bachelor's and all higher degrees, including professional degrees.

Source: By the author. Based on *Statistical Abstract* 2002:Table 666.

Figure 11.8 The Gender Gap Over Time: What Percentage of Men's Income Do Women Earn?

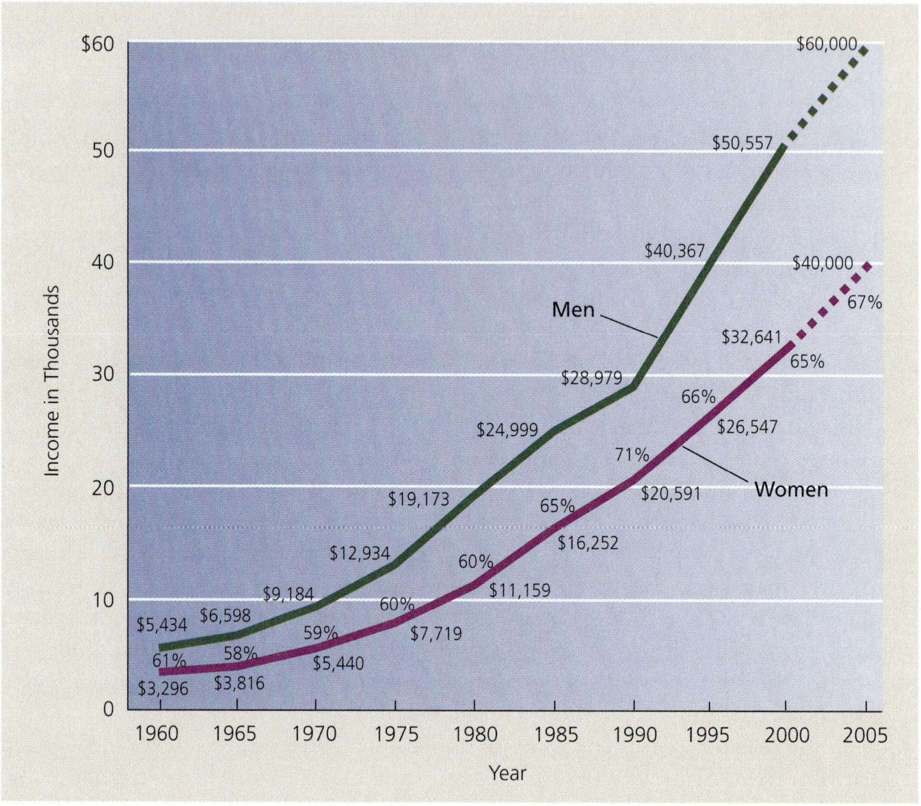

Note: The income jump from 1990 to 1995 could be due to a statistical procedure. The 1995 source (for 1990 income) uses "median income," while the 1997 source (for 1995 income) merely says "average earnings." How the "average" is computed is not stated. For a review of this distinction, see Table 5.2. Broken lines indicate the author's estimates.

Source: By the author. Based on *Statistical Abstract* 1995:Table 739; 2002:Table 666, and earlier years.

Schoenberger (1991) examined the starting salaries of the business majors at the University of Wisconsin, of whom 47 percent were women. They found that the women's starting salaries averaged 11 percent ($1,737) less than those of the men.

You might be able to think of valid reasons for this initial pay gap. For example, the women might have been less qualified. Perhaps they had lower grades. Or maybe they completed fewer internships. If so, they would deserve lower salaries. To find out, Fuller and Schoenberger reviewed the students' college records. To their surprise, they found that the women had *higher* grades and *more* internships. In other words, if women were equally qualified, they were offered lower salaries—and if they were more qualified, they were offered lower salaries—a classic lose-lose situation.

What happened after these graduates had been on the job a while? Did things even out, so that after a few years the women and men earned about the same? Fuller and Schoenberger checked their salaries five years later. Instead of narrowing, the pay gap had grown even wider. By this time, the women earned 14 percent ($3,615) less than the men.

As a final indication of the extent of the U.S. gender pay gap, consider this. Of the nation's top 500 corporations (the so-called "Fortune 500"), only 5 are headed by women (Hehir 2001). And 5 is a record-breaking number! I examined the names of the CEOs of the 350 largest U.S. corporations, and I found that your best chance to reach the top is to be named (in this order) John, Robert, James, William, or Charles. Edward, Lawrence, and Richard are also advantageous. Amber, Katherine, Leticia, and Maria, however, apparently draw a severe penalty. Naming your baby girl John or Robert might seem a little severe, but it could help her get to the top. (I say this only slightly tongue-in-cheek.)

The Glass Ceiling and the Glass Escalator

What keeps women from breaking through the **glass ceiling**, the mostly invisible barrier that keeps women from reaching the executive suite? Researchers have identified a "pipeline" that leads to the top—the marketing, sales, and production positions that directly affect the corporate bottom line (Reich 1995; Clarke 2000). Men, who dominate the executive suite, stereotype women as being less capable of leadership than men (Heilman 2001). Viewing women as good at "support," they steer women into human resources or public relations. There, successful projects are not appreciated in the same way as those that bring corporate profits—and bonuses for their managers.

Another reason the glass ceiling is so powerful is that women lack mentors, successful executives who take an interest in them and teach them the ropes. Lack of a mentor is no trivial matter, for mentors can provide opportunities to develop leadership skills that open the door to the executive suite (Heilman 2001).

The glass ceiling is cracking, however (Solomon 2000; Lane 2002). A look at women who've broken through reveals highly motivated individuals with a fierce competitive spirit who are willing to give up sleep and recreation for the sake of career advancement. They also learn to play by "men's rules," developing a style that makes men comfortable. Most of these women also have supportive husbands who share household duties and adapt their career to accommodate the needs of their executive wives (Lublin 1996).

Then there is the *glass escalator*. Sociologist Christine Williams (1995) interviewed men and women who worked in traditionally female jobs—as nurses, elementary school teachers, librarians, and social workers. Instead of bumping their heads against a glass ceiling, the men in these occupations found themselves aboard a **glass escalator.** They were given higher-level positions, more desirable work assignments, and higher salaries. The motor that drives the glass escalator is gender—the stereotype that because someone is male he is more capable.

glass ceiling the mostly invisible barrier that keeps women from advancing to the top levels at work

glass escalator the mostly invisible accelerators that push men into higher-level positions, more desirable work assignments, and higher salaries

The "Mommy Track"

Most women, even though employed full time, have the primary responsibility of taking care of the children and doing the housework. To help resolve this conflict, Felice

Nancy Pelosi has broken through two glass ceilings in politics. Not only is she a Representative from California, but also she is the first woman to be the minority leader (the head of the party that is not in the majority).

Schwartz (1989) suggested that corporations offer women a choice of two parallel career paths. The high-powered "fast track" would require out-of-town meetings and a briefcase jammed with work that has to be done at night and on weekends. Less would be expected of a woman in the "mommy track," which would emphasize both career and family,

The "mommy track" has met severe criticism. Critics say that it would encourage women to be satisfied with lower pay and fewer promotions, and relegate women to an inferior position in corporate life. And unless we have a "daddy track," it also assumes that child rearing is women's work (Starrels 1992). A better way to resolve the conflict between work and family, they say, is for men to take on greater responsibilities at home and for firms to provide on-site day care, flexible work schedules, and paid parental leave. Others maintain that the choice between family and career is artificial, that there are ample role models of family-oriented, highly successful women, from Sandra Day O'Connor and Ruth Bader Ginsberg, Justices of the U.S. Supreme Court, to Ann Fisher, astronaut and physician.

Gender and the Control of Workers

Conflict theorists analyze how capitalists exploit gender divisions among workers in order to control them. This does not come in an overt form, such as "Men, if you don't agree to what we are proposing, we'll hire women to take your place." Rather, owners and managers divide workers in subtle ways. For example, a Silicon Valley manufacturing firm specifies the color of the smocks that it requires its workers to wear. The color of the men's smocks depends on the particular job they do, but all the women wear the same color, regardless of their jobs.

Why should management have such a policy? According to sociologist Karen Hossfeld (2000), who studied these workers, the underlying message is: No matter what your job is, you are primarily a woman. Encouraging the women to think of themselves not as workers, but as *women* workers, makes them easier to control. For example, Hossfeld found that when their bosses flirted with them the women were less inclined to file grievances.

This same company has a "Ladies' Corner" in its newsletter. Because the newsletter has no "Men's Corner," the subtle message is that the newsletter is directed to men, with a little space for women. In other words, men are the *real* workers, but women are there, too.

Sexual Harassment and Worse

Sexual harassment—unwelcome sexual attention at work or at school, which may affect a person's job performance or create a hostile work environment—was not recognized as a problem until the 1970s. Before this, women considered unwanted sexual comments, touches, looks, and pressure to have sex to be a personal matter.

With the prodding of feminists, women began to perceive unwanted sexual advances at work and school as part of a *structural* problem. That is, they began to see them not simply as a man here and there doing obnoxious things because he was attracted to a woman, but, rather, as men abusing their positions of authority in order to force unwanted sexual activities on women. Since women have moved into positions of authority, they, too, have become sexual harassers (Wayne et al. 2001). With most authority vested in men, however, most sexual harassers are men.

As symbolic interactionists stress, terms affect our perception. Because we have the term *sexual harassment,* we perceive actions in a different light than did our predecessors. The meaning of sexual harassment is vague and shifting, however, and court cases constantly change what this term does and does not include. Originally sexual desire was an element of sexual harassment, but no longer. This changed when the U.S. Supreme Court considered the lawsuit of a homosexual who had been tormented by his supervisors and fellow workers. The Court ruled that sexual desire is not necessary and that sexual harassment laws also apply to homosexuals who are harassed by heterosexuals on the job (Felsenthal 1998).

Central to sexual harassment is the abuse of power, a topic that is explored in the following Thinking Critically section.

sexual harassment the abuse of one's position of authority to force unwanted sexual demands on someone

THINKING Critically

Sexual Harassment and Rape of Women in the Military

Women raped at West Point! Other women raped at the U.S. Air Force Academy!

So shrieked the headlines and the TV news teasers. For once, the facts turned out to be just as startling. Women cadets, who were studying to become officers in the U.S. military, had been sexually assaulted by their fellow cadets.

And when the women reported the attacks, *they* had been swiftly punished. The women found themselves charged with drinking alcohol and socializing with upperclassmen. For the most part, the women's charges against the men were ignored. The one man who faced a court martial was acquitted (Schemo 2003).

This got the attention of Congress. Hearings were held, and the commander of the Air Force Academy was replaced.

A few years earlier, several male Army sergeants at Aberdeen Proving Ground in Maryland had been accused of forcing sex on unwilling female recruits (McIntyre 1997). The drill sergeants, who claimed that the sex was consensual, were found guilty of rape. One married sergeant, who had pleaded guilty to having consensual sex with 11 trainees (adultery is a crime in the Army), was convicted of raping another 6 trainees a total of 18 times and was sentenced to 25 years in prison.

The Army appointed a blue-ribbon panel to investigate sexual harassment in its ranks. When Sgt. Major Gene McKinney, the highest-ranking of the Army's 410,000 noncommissioned officers, was appointed to this committee, former subordinates accused him of sexual harassment (Shenon 1997). McKinney was relieved of duties and court-martialed. Found not guilty of sexual harassment, but guilty of obstruction of justice, McKinney was reprimanded and demoted. His embittered accusers claimed the Army had sacrificed them for McKinney.

A civilian panel recommended that the services remain integrated, but that platoons (the smallest units, with fifty soldiers) be segregated by sex (Mersereau 1998). The Navy didn't like this recommendation, saying it wanted men and women to work together and to sleep in the same building, as they would on a ship. The Army and Navy continued as they were.

Although rape in the military has been covered up by military personnel, it is not an isolated event. Researchers who interviewed a random sample of women veterans found that 4 of 5 had experienced sexual harassment during their military service, and 30 percent had been victims of attempted or completed rape. Of the women who had been raped, one-third had been raped more than once. Three-fourths of the women who had been raped did not report their assault (Sadler et al 2003).

For Your CONSIDERATION . . .

How can we set up a structure to minimize sexual harassment and rape in the military? Can we do this and still train men and women together? Can we do this and still have men and women sleep in the same barracks and on the same ships? Be specific about the structure you would establish.

Gender and Violence

The high rate of violence in the United States shocks foreigners and frightens many Americans. Only a couple of generations ago, many Americans left their homes and cars unlocked. Today, fearful of carjackings, many lock their cars even while driving. Fearful of rape and kidnappings, many parents escort their children to school. Lurking behind these fears is the gender inequality of violence—the fact that females are much more likely to be victims of males, not the other way around. Let's briefly review this almost one-way street in gender violence.

Violence Against Women

In the Thinking Critically section above, we considered rape in the military; on pages 299 and 300, we examined violence against women in other cultures; and in Chapter 16 we shall review violence in the home. Here, due to space limitations, we can review only briefly some primary features of violence.

Forcible Rape Being raped is a common fear of U.S. women. As with rape in the military, which we just discussed, this fear is far from groundless. According to FBI statistics, each year 7 of every 10,000 females age 12 and older are raped. From the National

Crime Victimization Survey, however, we know that only about 32 percent of rape victims report this crime to the police (*Statistical* Abstract 2002:Table 290 and page 180). A more accurate total, then, is *three* times the official rate, or about 21 victims per 10,000 rather than 7. Despite these high numbers, women are safer now than they were just a few years ago, as rape has been declining for the past decade.

Although the victims of sexual assault include babies and very old, frail women, the typical victim is 12 to 24 years old. Contrary to stereotypes, most victims know their assailant. About two of five (38 percent) of rapes are committed by strangers (*Statistical Abstract* 2002:Tables 295, 296).

An aspect of rape that is usually overlooked is the rape of men in prison. With prison officials reluctant to let the public know about the horrible conditions behind bars, our studies are far from perfect. Those we have, however, indicate that about 15 to 20 percent of men in prison are raped. From court cases, we know that some guards even punish prisoners by placing them in cells with sexual predators (Donaldson 1993; Lewin 2001b).

Date (Acquaintance) Rape What has shocked so many about date rape (also known as *acquaintance rape*) is studies showing that it does not consist of a few isolated events (Collymore 2000; Goode 2001). Some researchers even report that most women students experience unwanted, forced, or coerced sex (Kalof 2000). Others report much smaller numbers. Researchers who used a representative sample of courses to survey the students at Marietta College, a private school in Ohio, found that 2.5 percent of the women had been physically forced to have sex (Felton et al. 2001). About as many men (23 percent) as women (24 percent) had given in to pressure to have sex when they didn't want to, but—and this is no surprise—none of the men had been physically forced to have sex.

Most date rapes go unreported. A primary reason is that the victim feels partially responsible because she knows the person and was with him voluntarily. However, as a physician who treats victims of date rape said, "Would you feel responsible if someone hit you over the head with a shovel—just because you knew the person?" (Carpenito 1999).

Murder Table 11.3 summarizes how gender fits into U.S. patterns of murder. Note that although females make up a little over 51 percent of the U.S. population, they don't even come close to making up 51 percent of the nation's killers. Note also that one-fourth of all murder victims are female—and nine times out of ten the killer is a male.

Violence in the Home Women are also the typical victims of family violence. Spouse battering, marital rape, and incest are discussed in Chapter 16, pages 000-000. A particular form of violence against women, genital circumcision, is the focus of the Cultural Diversity box on page 300.

Women in the Criminal Justice System There is another side to gender and violence. Although women are much less likely to kill, when they do kill, judges tend to be more lenient with them. As Table 11.4 shows, women are more likely to be given probation for murder (as well as for robbery, burglary, and all crimes listed on this table). Sexual stereotypes probably underlie these decisions—such as the idea that women are less of a menace than men and should be given another chance. It is also possible that women defendants have less of a criminal history ("rap sheet") when they are charged with crimes. We need research on this topic.

Table 11.3 Killers and Their Victims

The Victims	The Killers
Female 24% Male 76%	Female 10% Male 90%

Source: Statistical Abstract 2002:Tables 288, 299.

Feminism and Gendered Violence

Feminist sociologists have been especially effective in bringing violence against women to the public's attention. Some use symbolic interactionism, pointing out that to associate strength and virility with violence—as is done in many areas of U.S. culture—is to promote violence. Others use conflict theory. They argue that men are losing power, and that some men become violent against women as a way to reassert their declining power and status (Reiser 1999). Perhaps this is a reason for the violence featured in the Mass Media box on the next page.

Table 11.4 Going Easier on Women

When Men and Women Are Convicted of the Same Crime, Who Gets Off Easier?*

	Prison		Probation	
Crime	Men	Women	Men	Women
Murder	97%	89%	1%	5%
Robbery	78%	67%	9%	13%
Burglary	55%	43%	19%	23%
Aggravated Assault	54%	30%	18%	26%
Larceny	42%	28%	24%	34%
Fraud	39%	31%	28%	41%
Drug Dealing	50%	37%	20%	26%
Weapons	49%	28%	22%	30%

*This table examines the extremes of sentencing; totals do not add to 100 percent because of jail sentences and unspecified "other" dispositions.

Source: Sourcebook of Criminal Justice Statistics 1997:Table 5.50. (Table dropped in later editions.)

massMEDIA in Social Life

Beauty and Pain: How Much Is an Ad Worth?

The studio audience at *Super Jockey,* a popular television program in Japan, waits expectantly. They've seen it before, and they can't get enough. A young woman, clad in a revealing bikini, walks onto the stage. Cringing with fear, she is lowered into a glass tank of scalding hot water.

The studio audience eagerly watches the woman through the glass. The national audience watches at home. Both break into laughter as the girl writhes in pain.

To make sure the young woman gets the full treatment, a man ladles hot water over the woman's breasts—just as though he were basting a chicken. The television camera zooms in for a close-up shot of her reddening breasts.

Most women last only three or four seconds.

The camera follows as the young woman scrambles out of the tub, where she jumps up and down in pain and rubs ice all over her body.

The audience howls with glee.

Why do the women do it? For every second they stay in the hot water, they get one second on the program to advertise any product they wish. Most advertise their place of employment, their pain a favor to their boss (Strauss 1998).

It is often difficult to understand other cultures. *Super Jockey* wouldn't be tolerated in the United States. If some company tried to air a U.S. version, protests would erupt. The studio would be picketed, its sponsors boycotted.

Instead of trying to explain the intricacies of a culture that finds this behavior amusing (*Super Jockey* is a comedy show), we can turn the focus onto our own culture. Why do we find the rape of women a source of entertainment? How can I say that we do? It is apparent from *our* television—from our "dramas" and police shows in which the story line centers on women who are raped. Of course, in order to get the public's seal of approval, producers see to it that the rapist is apprehended and punished. As further evidence that this entertainment is meritorious, the rapist may commit suicide, get shot by the police, or get run down by a car as he tries to escape into his netherworld.

If you think that I've stretched things a bit, consider how entertaining our society finds the murder of women. The Halloween shocker-thriller-slasher films are outstanding examples. Audiences, simultaneously titillated and terror-stricken, watch crazed, masked killers hunt down college coeds with knives, axes, even chain saws. Audiences seem to find the screams of the victims especially entertaining. And the prettier, shapelier, and more skimpily clad the victim, the higher the entertainment value.

For Your CONSIDERATION

It is difficult to understand cultures—especially to explain why people find certain things amusing or entertaining. Why would Japanese and Americans find the victimization of women to be a scintillating source of entertainment?

Solutions

There is no magic bullet for this problem of gendered violence, but to be effective, any solution must break the connection between violence and masculinity. This would require an educational program that incorporates schools, churches, homes, and the media. Given the gun-slinging heroes of the Wild West and other American icons, as well as the violent messages so prevalent in today's mass media, it is difficult to be optimistic that a change will come any time soon.

Our next topic, women in politics, however, gives us much more reason for optimism.

The Changing Face of Politics

What do these nations have in common?

Canada in North America

Argentina, Bolivia, and Nicaragua in Latin America

Britain, Finland, France, Ireland, and Portugal in western Europe

The Philippines in Asia

Israel in the Mideast

Poland in eastern Europe

India, Pakistan, and Sri Lanka on the subcontinent

The answer is that all have had a woman president or prime minister. To this list, we can add even such bastions of male chauvinism as Haiti, Turkey, and Bangladesh (Harwood and Brooks 1993).

Then why not the United States? Why don't women, who outnumber men, take political control of the nation? Eight million more women than men are of voting age, and more women than men vote in U.S. national elections. As Table 11.5 shows, however, men greatly outnumber women in political office. Despite the gains women have made

Table 11.5 U.S. Women in Political Office

	Percentage of Offices Held by Women	Number of Offices Held by Women
National Office		
U.S. Senate	13%	13
U.S. House of Representatives	14%	60
State Office		
Governors	12%	6
Lt. Governors	36%	18
Attorneys general	14%	7
Secretaries of state	20%	10
Treasurers	16%	8
State auditors	14%	7
State legislators	23%	1,672

Sources: National Women's Political Caucus 1998; *Statistical Abstract* 2000:Tables 463, 471, 472; 2002:Tables 381, 389; 2002 election results.

in recent elections, since 1789 over 1,800 men have served in the U.S. Senate, but only 33 women have served, including 13 current senators. Not until 1992 was the first African American woman (Carol Moseley-Braun) elected to the U.S. Senate. No Latino or African American women have yet been elected to the Senate (National Women's Political Caucus 1998; *Statistical Abstract* 2002: Table 382).

Why are women underrepresented in U.S. politics? First, women are still underrepresented in law and business, the careers from which most politicians emerge. Then, too, most women find that the irregular hours kept by those who run for office are incompatible with their role as mother. Fathers, in contrast, whose ordinary roles are more likely to take them away from home, are less likely to feel this conflict. Women are also not as likely to have a supportive spouse who is willing to play an unassuming background role while providing solace, encouragement, child care, and voter appeal. Finally, preferring to hold on to their positions of power, men have been reluctant to incorporate women into centers of decision making or to present them as viable candidates.

These factors are changing, however, and we can expect more women to seek and gain political office. In 2002, for example, a watershed event occurred when Nancy Pelosi was elected by her colleagues as the first woman minority leader—the most powerful woman ever in the House of Representatives. There are other indicators. As we saw in Figure 11.4 (on page 307), more women are going into law. The same is true for business. In these professions, they are doing more traveling and making statewide and national contacts. Increasingly, child care is seen as a mutual responsibility of both mother and father. This generation, then, is likely to mark a fundamental change in women's political participation, and it appears to be only a matter of time until a woman occupies the Oval Office.

Glimpsing the Future—With Hope

By playing a fuller role in the decision-making processes of our social institutions, women are going against the stereotypes and role models that lock males into exclusively male activities and push females into roles that are considered feminine. As structural barriers fall and more activities are degendered, both males and females will be free to pursue activities that are more compatible with their abilities and desires as individuals.

As sociologists Janet Chafetz (1974), Janet Giele (1978), and Judith Lorber (1994) have pointed out, the ultimate possibility is a new conception of the human personality. At present, structural obstacles, accompanied by supporting socialization and stereotypes, cast most males and females into fairly rigid roles. Overcoming these obstacles and abandoning traditional stereotypes will give males and females new perceptions of themselves and one another. Females and males will then be free both to feel and to express needs and emotions that current social arrangements deny them. Females will likely perceive themselves as more in control of their environment and to explore this aspect of the human personality. Males will likely feel and express more emotional sensitivity—to be warmer, more affectionate and tender, and to give greater expression to anxieties and stresses that their gender now forces them to suppress. In the future, we may discover that such "greater wholeness" of males and females entails many other dimensions of the human personality.

As females and males develop a new consciousness both of themselves and their own potential, relationships will change. Certainly distinctions between the sexes will not disappear. There is no reason, however, for biological differences to be translated into social inequalities. The reasonable goal is to have an appreciation of sexual differences coupled with equality of opportunity—which may well lead to a transformed society (Gilman 1911/1971; Offen 1990). If this happens, as sociologist Alison Jaggar (1990) observed, gender equality can become less a goal than a background condition for living in society.

SUMMARY and REVIEW

Issues of Sex and Gender

What is gender stratification?

The term **gender stratification** refers to unequal access to power, prestige, and property on the basis of sex. Each society establishes a structure that, on the basis of sex and gender, opens and closes doors to its privileges. P. 290.

How do sex and gender differ?

Sex refers to biological distinctions between males and females. It consists of both primary and secondary sex characteristics. **Gender**, in contrast, is what a society considers proper behaviors and attitudes for its male and female members. Sex physically distinguishes males from females; gender defines what is "masculine" and "feminine." P. 290.

Why do the behaviors of males and females differ?

The "nature versus nurture" debate refers to whether differences in the behaviors of males and females are caused by inherited (biological) or learned (cultural) characteristics. Almost all sociologists take the side of nurture. In recent years, however, sociologists have begun to cautiously open the door to biology. Pp. 291–295.

Gender Inequality in Global Perspective

Is gender stratification universal?

George Murdock surveyed information on tribal societies and found that all of them have sex-linked activities and give greater prestige to male activities. **Patriarchy**, or male dominance, appears to be universal. Besides work, other areas of discrimination include education, politics, and violence. Pp. 295–299.

How Females Became a Minority Group

How did females become a minority group?

The main theory that attempts to explain how females became a **minority group** in their own societies focuses on the physical limitations imposed by childbirth. The origins of this discrimination, however, are lost in history, and no one knows how it began. Pp. 299–302.

Gender Inequality in the United States

Is the feminist movement new?

In what is called the "first wave," feminists made political demands for change in the early 1900s—and were met with hostility, and even violence. The "second wave" began in the 1960s and continues today. A "third wave" is emerging. Pp. 302–305.

What forms does gender stratification in education take?

Although more women than men attend college, each tends to select fields that are categorized as "feminine" or "masculine." Women are underrepresented in most doctoral programs in science, and they are less likely to complete these programs. Fundamental change is indicated by the growing numbers of women in law and medicine. Pp. 305–308.

Is there gender inequality in everyday life?

Two indications of gender inequality in everyday life are the devaluation of femininity and the male dominance of conversation. Pp. 308–309.

Gender Inequality in the Workplace

How does gender inequality show up in the workplace?

All occupations show a gender gap in pay. For college graduates, the lifetime pay gap runs over a million dollars in favor of men. **Sexual harassment** also continues to be a reality of the workplace. Pp. 309–315.

Gender and Violence

What is the relationship between gender and violence?

Overwhelmingly, the victims of rape and murder are females. Female circumcision is a special case of violence against females. Conflict theorists point out that men use violence to maintain their power and privilege. Pp. 315–318.

The Changing Face of Politics

What is the trend in gender inequality in politics?

A traditional division of gender roles—women as child care providers and homemakers, men as workers outside the home—used to keep women out of politics. Women continue to be underrepresented in politics, but the trend toward greater political equality is firmly in place. Pp. 318–319.

Glimpsing the Future—With Hope

How might changes in gender roles and stereotypes affect our lives?

In the United States, women are playing a fuller role in the decision-making processes of our social institutions. Men, too, are reexamining their traditional roles. A new conception of the human personality may develop, one that allows both males and females to pursue their individual interests unfettered by gender. P. 319.

Where can I read more on this topic?

Suggested Readings for this chapter are found at the back of this book.

THINKING Critically ABOUT CHAPTER 11

1. What is your position on the question of "nature versus nurture" (culture or biology)? Why do you hold that position?
2. Why do you think that the gender gap in pay exists all over the world?
3. What do you think can be done to reduce gender inequality?

ADDITIONAL RESOURCES for This Chapter

www.ablongman.com/henslin7e

- *Content Select* Research Database for Sociology, with suggested key terms and annotated references
- Link to 2000 Census, with activities
- Flashcards of key terms and concepts
- Practice Tests
- Weblinks
- Interactive Maps

Chapter 12

Race and Ethnicity

Pacita Abad, *You have to blend in before you stand out,* 1995

Chapter Outline

Imagine that you are an African American man living in Macon County, Alabama, during the Great Depression of the 1930s. Your home is a little country shack with a dirt floor. You have no electricity or running water. You never finished grade school, and you make a living, such as it is, by doing odd jobs. You haven't been feeling quite right lately, but you can't afford a doctor.

Then you rub your eyes in disbelief. It is just like winning the lottery. If you join *Miss Rivers' Lodge* (and it is free to join), you will get free physical examinations at Tuskegee University. You will even get free rides to and from the clinic, hot meals on examination days, and free treatment for minor ailments.

You eagerly join Miss Rivers' Lodge.

After your first physical examination, the doctor gives you the bad news. "You've got bad blood," he says. "That's why you've been feeling bad. Miss Rivers will give you some medicine and schedule you for your next exam. I've got to warn you, though. If you go to another doctor, there's no more free exams or medicine."

You can't afford another doctor anyway. You take your medicine and look forward to the next trip to the University.

ou have just become part of one of the most callous *xperiments of all time*

What has really happened? You have just become part of what is surely slated to go down in history as one of the most callous experiments of all time, outside of the infamous Nazi and Japanese experiments. With heartless disregard for human life, the U.S. Public Health Service told 399 African American men that they had joined a social club and burial society called "Miss Rivers' Lodge." What the men were *not* told was that they had syphilis. For forty years, the "Public Health Service" let these men's syphilis go untreated just "to see what happened." There was even a control group of 201 men free of the disease (Jones 1993).

By the way, you do get one further benefit—a free autopsy to determine the ravages of syphilis on your body.

Laying the Sociological Foundation

As unlikely as it seems, this is a true story. It really did happen to 399 men. Seldom do race and ethnic relations degenerate to this point, but troubled race relations are no stranger to us. Today's newspapers and TV news regularly report on racial problems. Sociology can contribute greatly to our understanding of this aspect of social life, and this chapter may be an eye-opener. To begin, let's consider to what extent race itself is a myth.

race physical characteristics that distinguish one group from another

genocide the systematic annihilation or attempted annihilation of a people based on their presumed race or ethnic group

Race: Myth and Reality

With its more than 6 billion people, the world offers a fascinating variety of human shapes and colors. People see one another as black, white, red, yellow, and brown. Eyes come in shades of blue, brown, and green. Lips are thick and thin. Hair is straight, curly, kinky, black, white, blonde, and red—and, of course, all shades of brown.

As humans spread throughout the world, their adaptations to diverse climates and other living conditions resulted in this profusion of complexions, colors, and shapes. Genetic mutations added distinct characteristics to the peoples of the globe. In this sense, the concept of **race**—a group of people with inherited physical characteristics that distinguish it from another group—is a reality. Humans do, indeed, come in a variety of colors and shapes.

In two senses, however, race is a myth, a fabrication of the human mind. The *first* myth is the idea that any race is superior to others. All races have their geniuses—and their idiots. As with language, one is not better than the others.

Ideas of racial superiority abound, however. They are not only false, but also dangerous. Adolf Hitler, for example, believed that the Aryans were a superior race, responsible for the cultural achievements of Europe. The Aryans, he said, were destined to establish a higher culture and usher in a new world order. This destiny required them to avoid the "racial contamination" that would come from breeding with inferior races; thus it was necessary to isolate or destroy races that might endanger Aryan culture.

When Hitler's views were put into practice, the world was left an appalling legacy—the Nazi slaughter of those they deemed inferior: Jews, Slavs, gypsies, homosexuals, and people with mental and physical disabilities. Dark images of gas ovens and emaciated bodies stacked like cordwood haunted the world's nations. At Nuremberg, the Allies, flush with victory, put the top Nazi officials on trial, exposing their heinous deeds to a shocked world. Their public executions, everyone assumed, marked the end of such grisly acts.

Obviously, they didn't. In the summer of 1994 in Rwanda, Hutus slaughtered about 800,000 Tutsis—mostly with machetes (Gourevitch 1995). A few years later, the Serbs in Bosnia systematically massacred thousands of Muslims, giving us the new term "ethnic cleansing." As these events sadly attest, **genocide,** the attempt to destroy a people because of their presumed race or ethnicity, remains alive and well. Although more recent killings may not be accompanied by swastikas and gas ovens, the perpetrators' goal is the same.

The *second* myth is that "pure" races exist. Humans show such a mixture of physical characteristics—in skin and eye color, hair texture, shape of nose and head, and so on—that there are no "pure" races. Instead of falling into distinct types that are clearly separate from one another, human characteristics flow endlessly together. The mapping of the human genome system shows that humans are strikingly homogenous, that so-called racial groups differ from one another only once in a thousand subunits of the genome (Angler 2000). As with Tiger Woods (discussed in the Cultural Diversity box on the next page), these minute gradations make any attempt to draw lines purely arbitrary.

Humans show such remarkable diversity that, as the text explains, there are no pure races. Shown here are Ming Yao, who weighs 296 pounds and is 7 feet 5 inches tall, and Verne Troyer, who weighs about 45 pounds and is 2 feet 8 inches short.

Although large groupings of people can be classified by blood type and gene frequencies, even these classifications do not uncover "race." Rather, they are so arbitrary that biologists and anthropologists cannot even agree on how many races there are. They have drawn up many lists, each containing a different number of "races." Ashley Montagu

CULTURAL DIVERSITY in the UNITED STATES

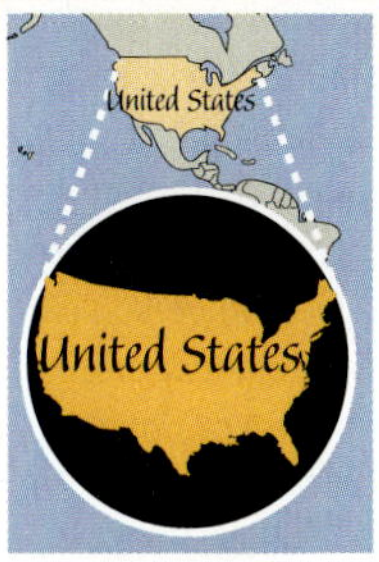

Tiger Woods and the Emerging Multiracial Identity: Mapping New Ethnic Terrain

Tiger Woods, perhaps the top golfer of all time, calls himself Cablinasian. Woods invented this term as a boy to try to explain to himself just who he was—a combination of Caucasian, Black, Indian, and Asian (Leland and Beals 1997; Hall 2001). Woods wants to embrace both sides of his family. To be known by a racial-ethnic identity that applies to just one of his parents is to deny the other parent.

Like many of us, Tiger Woods' heritage is difficult to specify. Analysts who like to quantify ethnic heritage put Woods at one-quarter Thai, one-quarter Chinese, one-quarter white, an eighth Native American, and an eighth African American. From this chapter, you know how ridiculous such computations are, but the sociological question is why many consider Tiger Woods an African American. The U.S. racial scene is indeed complex, but a good part of the reason is simply that this is the label the media chose. "Everyone has to fit somewhere" seems to be our attitude. If they don't, we grow uncomfortable. And for Tiger Woods, the media chose African American.

The United States once had a firm "color line"—barriers between racial-ethnic groups that you didn't dare cross, especially in dating or marriage. This invisible barrier has broken down, and today such marriages are common (*Statistical Abstract* 2002: Table 47). Several campuses have interracial student organizations. Harvard has two, one just for students who have one African American parent (Leland and Beals 1997).

As we march into unfamiliar ethnic terrain, our classifications are bursting at the seams. Kwame Anthony Appiah, of Harvard's Philosophy and Afro-American Studies Departments, says, "My mother is English; my father is Ghanaian. My sisters are married to a Nigerian and a Norwegian. I have nephews who range from blond-haired kids to very black kids. They are all first cousins. Now according to the American scheme of things, they're all black—even the guy with blond hair who skis in Oslo" (Wright 1994).

Tiger Woods, after making one of his marvelous shots, this one at Great Britain's Open Championship at St. George's in Sandwich, UK.

The U.S. census, which is taken every ten years, used to make everyone choose from Caucasian, Negro, Indian, and Oriental. Everyone was sliced and diced and packed into one of these restrictive classifications. After years of complaints, the list was expanded. In the 2000 census, everyone had to declare that they were or were not "Spanish/Hispanic/Latino." Then they had to mark "one or more races" that they "consider themselves to be." They could choose from White; Black, African American, or Negro; American Indian or Alaska Native; Asian Indian, Chinese, Filipino, Japanese, Korean, Vietnamese, Native Hawaiian, Guamanian or Chamorro, Samoan, and other Pacific Islander. Finally, if these didn't do it, you could check a box called "Some Other Race" and then write whatever you wanted.

Perhaps the census should list Cablinasian. Of course there should be GASH for the German-African-Swedish-Hispanic Americans, BITE for those of Botswanian-Indonesian-Turkish-English descent, and STUDY for the Swedish-Turkish-Uruguan-Danish-Yugoslavian Americans. As you read farther in this chapter, you will see why these terms make as much sense as the categories we currently use.

For Your CONSIDERATION

Just why do we count people by "race" anyway? Why not eliminate race from the U.S. census? (Race became a factor in the census during slavery when five blacks were counted the same as three whites to determine how many representatives a state could send to Congress!) Why is race so important to some people? Perhaps you can use the materials in this chapter to answer these questions.

(1964; 1999), a physical anthropologist, pointed out that some scientists have classified humans into only two "races," while others have found as many as two thousand. Montagu (1960) himself classified humans into forty "racial" groups. As the Down-to-Earth Sociology box on page 327 illustrates, even a plane ride can change our race!

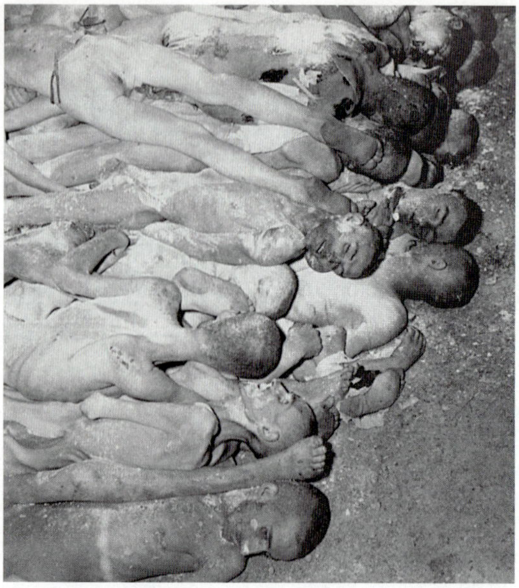

The reason I selected these photos is to illustrate how seriously we must take all preaching of hatred and of racial supremacy, even though it seems to come from harmless or even humorous sources. The strange-looking person on the left, who is wearing lederhosen, traditional clothing of Bavaria, Germany, is Adolf Hitler. He caused the horrific scene on the right, which greeted the British army when it liberated the concentration camp in Buchenwald, Germany. They found thousands of people dying of starvation and diseases amidst piles of rotting corpses awaiting mass burial.

The *idea* of race, of course, is far from a myth. Firmly embedded in our culture, it is a powerful force in our everyday lives. That no race is superior and that even experts cannot decide how people should be biologically classified into races is not what counts. "I know what I see, and you can't tell me any different" seems to be the common attitude. As noted in Chapter 4, sociologists W. I. and D. S. Thomas observed that "If people define situations as real, they are real in their consequences." In other words, people act on beliefs, not facts. As a result, we will always have people like Hitler, and, as in our opening vignette, officials like those in the U.S. Public Health Service who felt that it was fine to experiment with people they deemed inferior. While few people hold such extreme views, most people appear to be ethnocentric enough to believe, at least just a little, that their own race is superior to others.

IN SUM

Race, then, lies in the eye of the beholder. Humans show such a mixture of physical characteristics—in skin color, hair texture, nose shape, head shape, eye color, and so on—that there is no inevitable, much less universal, way to classify our many biological differences. Instead of falling into distinct types clearly separate from one another, human characteristics flow endlessly together. Because racial classifications are arbitrary, the categories people use differ from one society to another, and they change over time. In this sense, then, race and its accompanying idea of racial superiority are myths.

Ethnic Groups

Whereas people use the term *race* to refer to supposed biological characteristics that distinguish one people from another, **ethnicity** and **ethnic** apply to cultural characteristics. Derived from the word *ethnos* (a Greek word meaning "people" or "nation"), ethnicity and ethnic refer to people who identify with one another on the basis of common ancestry and cultural heritage. Their sense of belonging may center on their nation of origin, distinctive foods, dress, language, music, religion, or family names and relationships.

ethnicity (and ethnic) having distinctive cultural characteristics

DOWN-TO-EARTH SOCIOLOGY

Common Sense and Sociology: What Is Race?

AT THE BEGINNING OF THIS TEXT (pages 9–10), I mentioned that common sense and sociology often differ. This is especially so when it comes to race. According to common sense, our racial classifications represent biological differences between people. Sociologists, in contrast, stress that what we call races are *social* classifications, not biological categories.

Sociologists point out that *our "race" depends more on the society in which we live than on our biological characteristics.* For example, the racial categories common in the United States are merely one of *numerous* ways that people around the world classify physical appearances. Although groups around the world use different categories, each group assumes that its categories are natural, merely a response to visible biology.

To better understand this essential sociological point—that race is more social than it is biological—consider this: In the United States, children born to the same parents are all of the same race. "What could be more natural?" Americans assume. But in Brazil, children born to the same parents may be of different races—if their appearances differ. "What could be more natural?" assume Brazilians.

Consider how Americans usually classify a child born to a "black" mother and a "white" father. Why do they usually say that the child is "black"? Wouldn't it be equally as logical to classify the child as "white"? Similarly, if a child's grandmother is "black," but all her other ancestors are "white," the child is often considered "black." Yet she has much more "white blood" than "black blood." Why, then, is she considered "black"? Certainly not because of biology. Rather, such thinking is a legacy of slavery. Whites—in an attempt to preserve the "purity" of their "race" in the face of numerous children whose fathers were white slave masters and mothers were black slaves—classified anyone with even a "drop of black blood" as "not white."

Even a plane trip can change a person's race. In the city of Salvador in Brazil, people classify one another by color of skin and eyes, breadth of nose and lips, and color and curliness of hair. They use at least seven terms for what we call white and black. Consider again a U.S. child who has "white" and "black" parents. If she flies to Brazil, she is no longer "black"; she now belongs to one of their several "whiter" categories (Fish 1995).

On the flight just mentioned, did the girl's "race" actually change? Our common sense revolts at this, I know, but it actually did. We want to argue that because her biological characteristics remain unchanged, her race remains unchanged. This is because we think of race as biological, when *it really is a label we use to describe perceived biological characteristics.* Simply put, the race we "are" depends on *where* we are—on who is doing the classifying.

And our classifications are fluid, not fixed. You can see change occurring even now in the classifications used in the United States. The category "multiracial," for example, indicates changing thought.

For Your CONSIDERATION

How would you ever explain to "Joe Six-Pack" the sociological point that race is more a social classification than a biological one? Can you come up with any arguments to refute it? How do you think our racial-ethnic categories will change in the future?

People often confuse the terms *race* and *ethnic group.* For example, many people, including many Jews, consider the Jews a race. Jews, however, are more properly considered an ethnic group, for it is their cultural characteristics, especially their religion, that bind them together. Wherever Jews have lived in the world, they have intermarried. Consequently, Jews in China may look mongoloid, while some Swedish Jews are blue-eyed blonds. This matter is strikingly illustrated in the photo on the next page. Ethiopian Jews look so different from European Jews that when they immigrated to Israel many European Jews felt that they could not be *real* Jews.

Minority Groups and Dominant Groups

Sociologist Louis Wirth (1945) defined a **minority group** as people who are singled out for unequal treatment *and* who regard themselves as objects of collective discrimination. Either physical (racial) or cultural (ethnic) differences can serve as the basis of the unequal treatment. Wirth added that the discrimination excludes minorities from full participation in the life of their society.

minority group people who are singled out for unequal treatment and who regard themselves as objects of collective discrimination

Surprisingly, a minority group is not necessarily a *numerical* minority. For example, before India's independence in 1947, a handful of British colonial rulers discriminated against tens of millions of Indians. Similarly, when South Africa practiced apartheid, a smaller group of Dutch discriminated against a much larger number of blacks. And all

Because ideas of race and ethnicity *are such a significant part of society, all of us are classified according to those ideas. This photo illustrates the difficulty such assumptions posed for Israel. The Ethiopians, shown here as they arrived in Israel, although claiming to be Jews, looked so different from other Jews that it took several years for Israeli authorities to acknowledge this group's "true Jewishness."*

over the world, females are a minority group. Accordingly, sociologists refer to those who do the discriminating not as the *majority,* but, rather, as the **dominant group,** for they have the greater power, privileges, and social status.

Possessing political power and unified by shared physical and cultural traits, the dominant group uses its position to discriminate against those with different—and supposedly inferior—traits. The dominant group considers its privileged position to be the result of its own innate superiority.

Emergence of Minority Groups A group becomes a minority in one of two ways. The *first* is through the expansion of political boundaries. With the exception of females, tribal societies contain no minority groups. Everyone shares the same culture, including the same language, and belongs to the same group. When a group expands its political boundaries, however, it produces minority groups if it incorporates people with different customs, languages, values, and physical characteristics into the same political entity and discriminates against them. For example, after defeating Mexico in war, the United States took over the Southwest. The Mexicans living there, who had been the dominant group, were transformed into a minority group, a master status that has influenced their lives ever since. Referring to his ancestors, one Latino said, "We didn't move across the border—the border moved across us."

A *second* way in which a group becomes a minority is through migration. This can be voluntary, as with the millions of people who have chosen to move from Mexico to the United States, or involuntary, as with the millions of Africans who were brought in chains to the United States. (The way females became a minority group represents a third way, but, as discussed in the previous chapter, no one knows just how this occurred.)

Shared Characteristics Anthropologists Charles Wagley and Marvin Harris (1958) noted that no matter where they live in the world, minorities share these five characteristics:

1. Membership is an ascribed status; that is, it is not voluntary, but comes through birth.
2. The physical or cultural traits that distinguish minorities are held in low esteem by the dominant group.

dominant group the group with the most power, greatest privileges, and highest social status

3. Minorities are unequally treated by the dominant group.
4. Minorities tend to marry within their own group.
5. Minorities tend to feel strong group solidarity (a sense of "we-ness").

These conditions—especially when combined with collective discrimination—tend to create a shared sense of identity among minorities, and, in many instances, even a sense of common destiny.

How People Construct Their Racial-Ethnic Identity

Some of us have a greater sense of ethnicity than others. We feel firm boundaries between "us" and "them." Others have assimilated so extensively into the mainstream culture that they are only vaguely aware of their ethnic origins. With interethnic marrying common, some do not even know the countries from which their families originated—nor do they care. If asked to identify themselves ethnically, they respond with something like "I'm Heinz 57—German and Irish, with a little Italian and French thrown in—and I think someone said something about being one-sixteenth Indian, too."

Why do some people feel an intense sense of ethnic identity, while others feel hardly any? Figure 12.1 portrays four factors, identified by sociologist Ashley Doane, that heighten or reduce our sense of ethnic identity. From this figure, you can see that the keys are relative size, power, appearance, and discrimination. If your group is relatively small, has little power, looks different from most people in society, and is an object of discrimination, you will have a heightened sense of ethnic identity. In contrast, if you belong to the dominant group that holds most of the power, look like most people in the society, and feel no discrimination, you are likely to experience a sense of "belonging"—and to wonder why ethnic identity is such a big deal.

We can use the term **ethnic work** to refer to the way people construct their ethnicity. For people who have a strong ethnic identity, this term refers to how they enhance and maintain their group's distinctions—from clothing, food, and language to religion and holidays. For people whose ethnic identity is not as firm, it refers to attempts to recover their ethnic heritage, such as trying to trace family lines. Millions of Americans are engaged in ethnic work, which has confounded the experts who thought that the United States would be a **melting pot,** with most of its groups quietly blending into a sort of ethnic stew. In recent years, however, Americans have become fascinated with their "roots" and increasingly proud of their ethnic backgrounds. Consequently, some analysts think that "tossed salad" is more appropriate than "melting pot."

Figure 12.1 A Sense of Ethnicity

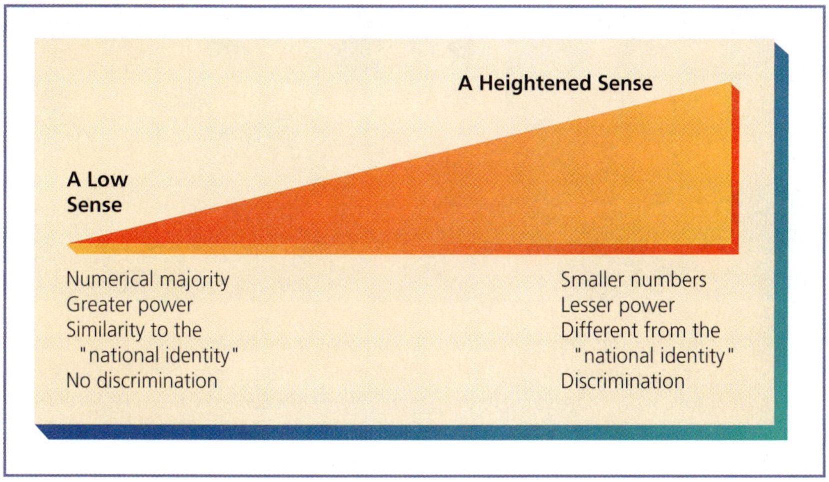

Source: By the author. Based on Doane 1997.

ethnic work activities designed to discover, enhance, or maintain ethnic and racial identification

melting pot the view that Americans of various backgrounds would blend into a sort of ethnic stew

discrimination *an act of unfair treatment directed against an individual or a group*

racism prejudice and discrimination on the basis of race

prejudice *an attitude or prejudging, usually in a negative way*

Prejudice and Discrimination

Prejudice and discrimination are common throughout the world. In Mexico, Hispanic Mexicans discriminate against Native American Mexicans; in Israel, Ashkenazi Jews, primarily of European descent, discriminate against Sephardi Jews from the Muslim world; and in Japan, the Japanese discriminate against just about anyone who isn't Japanese, especially immigrant Koreans and the descendants of the Eta caste. The Eta, now renamed the Burakumin, still bear a stigma because they used to do the society's dirty work—handling dead animals (stripping the hides and tanning the leather) and serving as Japan's executioners and prison guards (Deliege 2001). In some places the elderly discriminate against the young, in others the young against the elderly. And all around the world men discriminate against women.

As you can see from this list, **discrimination** is an *action*—unfair treatment directed against someone. When the basis of discrimination is race, it is known as **racism,** but discrimination can be based on many characteristics other than race—including age, sex, height, weight, income, education, marital status, sexual orientation, disease, disability, religion, and politics. Discrimination is often the result of an *attitude* called **prejudice**—a prejudging of some sort, usually in a negative way. There is also positive prejudice, which exaggerates the virtues of a group, as when people think that some group (usually their own) is more capable than others. Most prejudice, however, is negative and involves prejudging a group as inferior.

Two groups that base their existence on prejudice and discrimination are the neo-Nazis and the Ku Klux Klan. What would happen if a Jew attended the meetings of these groups that make hatred of Jews part of their identity? Would he or she survive? In the Down-to-Earth Sociology box on the next page, sociologist Raphael Ezekiel, a Jew, reveals some of the insights he gained during his remarkable study of these groups.

Learning Prejudice and the Internalization of Dominant Norms

As with our other attitudes, we are not born with prejudice. We can learn prejudice

In the 1920s and 1930s, the Ku Klux Klan was a powerful political force in the United States. To get a sense of the prevailing mood at the time, consider the caption that accompanied this photo of the Ku Klux Klan women from Freeport, New York, when it appeared in the papers: "Here's the Ladies in Their Natty Uniforms Marching in the Parade." Which theories would be most useful to explain this upsurge in racism among mainstream whites of the time?

DOWN-TO-EARTH SOCIOLOGY

The Racist Mind

SOCIOLOGIST RAPHAEL EZEKIEL WANTED to get a close look at the racist mind. As a Jew, he faced a unique problem. The best way to study racism from the inside is to do participant observation (see pp. 132–133). Would this be possible for him? Openly identifying himself as a Jew, Ezekiel asked Ku Klux Klan and neo-Nazi leaders if he could interview them and attend their meetings. Surprisingly, they agreed. Ezekiel published his path-breaking research in a book, *The Racist Mind* (1995). Here are some of the insights he gained during his fascinating sociological adventure:

> [The leader] builds on mass anxiety about economic insecurity and on popular tendencies to see an Establishment as the cause of economic threat; he hopes to teach people to identify that Establishment as the puppets of a conspiracy of Jews. [He has a] belief in exclusive categories. For the white racist leader, it is profoundly true . . . that the socially defined collections we call races represent fundamental categories. A man is black or a man is white; there are no in-betweens. Every human belongs to a racial category, and all the members of one category are radically different from all the members of other categories. Moreover, race represents the essence *of* the person. A truck is a truck, a car is a car, a cat is a cat, a dog is a dog, a black is a black, a white is a white. . . . These axioms have a rock-hard quality in the leaders' minds; *the world is made up of racial groups.* That is what exists for them.
>
> Two further beliefs play a major role in the minds of leaders. First, life is war. The world is made of distinct racial groups; life is about the war between these groups. Second, events have secret causes, are never what they seem superficially. . . . Any myth is plausible, as long as it involves intricate plotting. . . . It does not matter to him what others say. . . . He lives in his ideas and in the little world he has created where they are taken seriously. . . . Gold can be made from the tongues of frogs; Yahweh's call can be heard in the flapping swastika banner. (pp. 66–67)

Who is attracted to the neo-Nazis and Ku Klux Klan? Here is what Ezekiel discovered:

> [There is a] ready pool of whites who will respond to the racist signal. . . . This population [is] always hungry for activity—or for the talk of activity—that promises dignity and meaning to lives that are working poorly in a highly competitive world. . . . Much as I don't want to believe it, [this] movement brings a sense of meaning—at least for a while—to some of the discontented. To struggle in a cause that transcends the individual lends meaning to life, no matter how ill-founded or narrowing the cause. For the young men in the neo-Nazi group . . . membership was an alternative to atomization and drift; within the group they worked for a cause and took direct risks in the company of comrades. . . .
>
> When interviewing the young neo-Nazis in Detroit, I often found myself driving with them past the closed factories, the idled plants of our shrinking manufacturing base. The fewer and fewer plants that remain can demand better educated and more highly skilled workers. These fatherless Nazi youths, these high-school dropouts, will find little place in the emerging economy . . . a permanently underemployed white underclass is taking its place alongside the permanent black underclass. The struggle over race merely diverts youth from confronting the real issues of their lives. Not many seats are left on the train, and the train is leaving the station. (pp. 32–33)

For Your CONSIDERATION

Use functionalism, conflict theory, and symbolic interaction to explain (1) how the leaders and followers of these hate groups view the world, and (2) why some people are attracted to the message of hate.

through the mass media, but often we learn it through the people with whom we associate. In a fascinating study, sociologist Kathleen Blee (2002) interviewed women who were members of organized hate groups such as the KKK and Aryan Nations. Just as we would expect, most women were recruited by someone who already belonged to the group. But Blee also found something surprising: Some women learned racism *after* they joined the group. They were attracted to the group not because it matched their racist beliefs but because someone they liked belonged to it. Blee found that their intense racism was not the *cause* of their joining, but the *result* of their membership.

People can even learn to be prejudiced against their *own* group. A national survey of black Americans conducted by black interviewers found that African Americans think that lighter skinned African American women are more attractive than those with darker skin (Hill 2002). Sociologists call this *the internalization of the norms of the dominant group.*

The "Implicit Association Test" created by psychologist Anthony Greenwald confirms the internalization of dominant norms. In one version of this test, good and bad words are flashed on a screen along with photos of African Americans and whites. Subjects are quicker to associate positive words (such as love, peace, and baby) with whites and negative words (such as cancer, bomb, and devil) with blacks. Here's the clincher: This is true for *both* white and black subjects (Chamberlain 1998; Berreby 2000; Dasgupta et al. 2000). Apparently, we all carry around "ethnic maps" of our culture that lead to biased perception.

The Extent of Prejudice Social scientists have found that each racial-ethnic group views other groups as inferior in at least some ways. In a classic article, psychologist Eugene Hartley (1946) asked people how they felt about several groups. Besides blacks, Jews, and so on, he included the Wallonians, Pireneans, and Danireans—names he had made up. Most people who expressed dislike for Jews and blacks also expressed dislike for these three fictitious groups. Hartley's study shows that prejudice does not depend on negative experiences with others. It also reveals that people who are prejudiced against one racial or ethnic group tend to be prejudiced against other groups. People can be, and are, prejudiced against people they have never met—and even against groups that do not exist!

Sociologists Lawrence Bobo and James Kluegel (1991) found that older and less educated people are more prejudiced than are the younger and more educated. (See Figure 12.2.) Bobo and Kluegel interviewed whites, but other studies show that minority groups have their own prejudices (Brockerhoff 2000; Charles 2000).

Members of some groups are more prejudiced than others. At the University of Alabama, sociologist Donald Muir (1991) measured the attitudes of white students who belonged to fraternities and sororities and compared them to white students who did not belong to these organizations. He asked a variety of questions—from their ideas about dating African Americans to their view on attending classes together. On all measures, fraternity members were more prejudiced than the nonfrats. Research on other campuses supports this finding (Morris 1991). In the Thinking Critically section that follows, we'll take a close look at race relations on U.S. campuses.

Figure 12.2 A Measure of Preferred Social Distance

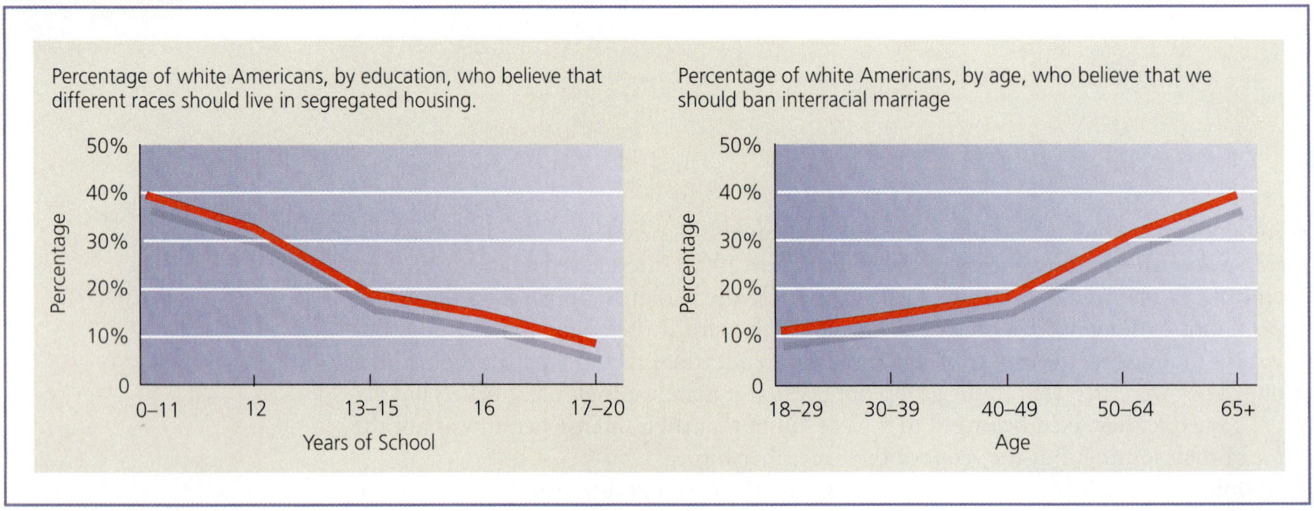

Source: Bobo and Kluegel 1991.

THINKING Critically

Self-Segregation: Help or Hindrance for Race Relations on Campus?

Only after a long, bitter, and violent struggle was federal civil rights legislation prohibiting racial segregation on college campuses passed in the 1960s. These laws did not mark the end of self-segregation, however. Certain practices continued, such as one area of a cafeteria or lounge being used almost exclusively by a particular group. Minority students often request separate dormitories (called *affinity houses*) and campus centers. At Brown University, an Ivy League school located in Providence, Rhode Island, the old rows of fraternity and sorority houses have been replaced by Harambee House (for African Americans), Hispanic House, Slavic House, East Asian House, and German House. Cornell University offers "theme dorms" for African Americans, Hispanics, and Native Americans.

Controversy surrounds this self-segregation of racial-ethnic groups. On one side is William H. Gray III, the head of the United Negro College Fund. Both African American and Latino students drop out of college at a much higher rate, Gray says, so colleges should do everything they can to make minority students feel welcome and accepted.

Critics call the trend toward separate housing a "separatist movement" that divides students into "small enclaves." When students self-segregate, they are deprived of the rich experiences that come through intercultural contacts. "We need to help students become 'culturally versatile' or 'culturally competent'," say officials at Dartmouth College, "to help prepare them for the new diverse society.

For this, they need to associate with one another, not separate themselves" (Rimer 2002).

Joshua Lehrer, a Brown University student who is white, says that some racial and ethnic groups "are separating themselves from everybody else, yet complain when society separates them. Can you really have it both ways?" he asks.

For Your CONSIDERATION . . .

Compare separate racial-ethnic housing on college campuses with three patterns discussed in this chapter: segregation, assimilation, and multiculturalism. Is self-segregation permissible if minority students desire it, but not if white students want it? Explain your position.

Sources: Bernstein 1993; Jordon 1996; Terry 2000; Rimer 2002.

Individual and Institutional Discrimination

Sociologists stress that we need to move beyond thinking in terms of **individual discrimination,** the negative treatment of one person by another. Although such behavior creates problems, it is primarily an issue between individuals. With their focus on the broader picture, sociologists encourage us to examine **institutional discrimination,** that is, to see how discrimination is woven into the fabric of society. Let's look at two examples.

Home Mortgages and Car Loans Bank lending provides an excellent illustration of institutional discrimination. As shown in Figure 12.3, race-ethnicity is a significant factor in getting a mortgage. When bankers looked at the statistics shown in this figure, they cried foul. It might *look* like discrimination, they said, but the truth is that whites have better credit histories. To see if this were true, researchers went over the data again, comparing the credit histories of applicants. The lending gap did narrow a bit, but the bottom line was that even when applicants were identical in all these areas, African Americans and Latinos were *60 percent* more likely to be rejected than whites (Thomas 1992; Passell 1996). Other studies show that African Americans are charged more than whites for their mortgages (Leonhardt 2002) and for car loans (Henriques 2001). In short, it is not a matter of a banker here or there discriminating according to personal prejudices; rather, discrimination is built into the country's financial institutions.

Health Care Discrimination does not have to be deliberate. It can occur without the awareness of either those doing the discriminating or those being discriminated against. An example is medical care for heart problems. White patients are more likely than either Latino or African American patients to receive coronary bypass surgery

individual discrimination the negative treatment of one person by another on the basis of that person's perceived characteristics

institutional discrimination negative treatment of a minority group that is built into a society's institutions; also called *systemic discrimination*

Figure 12.3 Race-Ethnicity and Mortgages: An Example of Institutional Discrimination

In 1990, the Federal Reserve Board gathered data on the loans made by 9,300 U.S. financial institutions (Thomas 1991). As shown here, loan applicants who had the same income did not receive the same treatment. Note how much more likely banks were to turn down minorities.

This figure illustrates institutional discrimination. (Because the discrimination is part of the social *system*, it is also called systemic discrimination.) As you can see, being turned down for a mortgage is not due to discrimination by an individual banker here and there, but, rather, is nationwide practice.

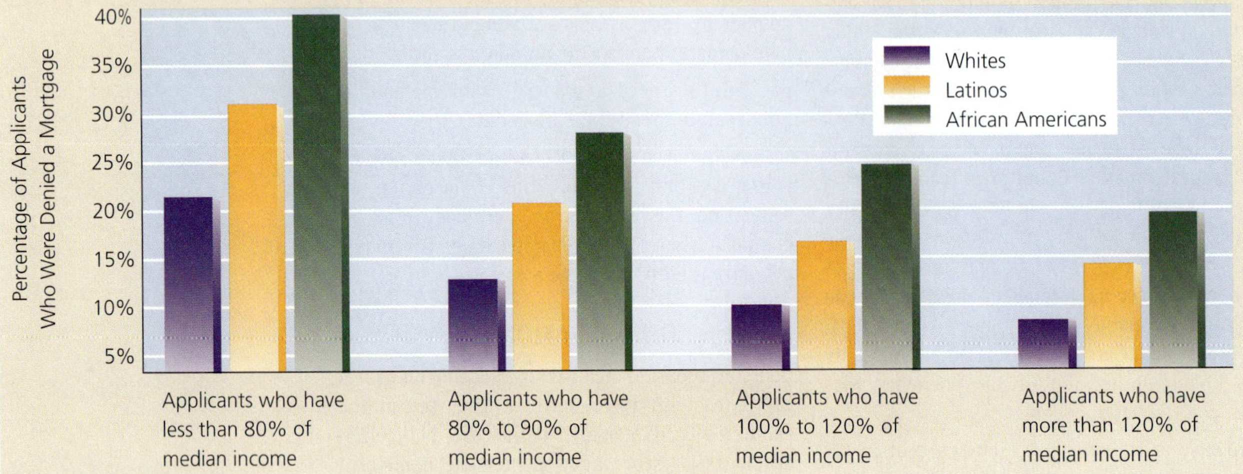

Source: By the author. Based on Thomas 1991.

(Smedley et al. 2003). Treatment after a heart attack follows a similar pattern. A study of 40,000 patients shows that whites are more likely than blacks to be given cardiac catheterization, a test to detect blockage of blood vessels. This study holds a surprise: Black *and* white doctors are both more likely to give this preventive care to whites (Stolberg 2001).

Researchers do not know why race is a factor in medical decisions. With both white and black doctors involved, we can be certain that physicians *do not intend* to discriminate. In ways we do not yet understand, discrimination is built into medicine. Race apparently works like gender. Just as women's higher death rates in coronary bypass surgery can be traced to attitudes about gender (see page 305), so also race serves as a subconscious reason for giving or denying access to advanced medical procedures.

Theories of Prejudice

Social scientists have developed several theories to explain prejudice. Let's look first at psychological explanations, then at sociological ones.

Psychological Perspectives

Frustration and Scapegoats In 1939, psychologist John Dollard suggested that prejudice is the result of frustration. People who cannot strike out at the real source of their frustration (such as low wages) look for someone to blame for their troubles. This **scapegoat**—often a racial, ethnic, or religious minority—becomes a target on which they vent their frustrations. Gender and age also provide common bases for scapegoating.

scapegoat an individual or group unfairly blamed for someone else's troubles

Even mild frustration can increase prejudice. A team of psychologists led by Emory Cowen (1959) measured the prejudice of a sample of students. They then gave the students two puzzles to solve, making sure they did not have enough time to solve them. After the students had worked furiously on the puzzles, the experimenters shook their heads in disgust and said they couldn't believe they hadn't finished such a simple task. They then retested the students and found that their scores on prejudice had increased. The students had directed their frustrations outward, onto people who had nothing to do with the contempt shown them for not completing the puzzles.

The Authoritarian Personality Have you ever wondered if personality is a cause of prejudice? Maybe some people are more inclined to be prejudiced, and others more fair-minded. For psychologist Theodor Adorno, who had fled from the Nazis, this was no idle speculation. With the horrors he had observed still fresh in his mind, Adorno wondered if there might be a certain type of person who is more likely to fall for the racist spewings of people like Hitler, Mussolini, and the Ku Klux Klan.

To find out, Adorno (1950) tested about two thousand people, ranging from college professors to prison inmates. He gave them three tests to measure ethnocentrism, anti-Semitism, and support for strong, authoritarian leaders. Adorno found that people who scored high on one test also scored high on the other two. For example, people who agreed with anti-Semitic statements also said that governments should be authoritarian and that foreign ways of life pose a threat to the "American" way.

Adorno concluded that highly prejudiced people are insecure conformists. They have deep respect for authority and are submissive to superiors. He termed this the **authoritarian personality.** These people believe that things are either right or wrong. Ambiguity disturbs them, especially in matters of religion or sex. They become anxious when they confront norms and values that differ from their own. To define people who differ from themselves as inferior assures them that their own positions are right.

Adorno's research stirred the scientific community, stimulating more than a thousand research studies. In general, the researchers found that people who are older, less educated, less intelligent, and from a lower social class are more likely to be authoritarian. Critics say that this doesn't indicate a particular personality, just that the less educated are more prejudiced—which we already knew (Yinger 1965; Ray 1991). Researchers, however, continue to study this concept (Whitley and Egisdottir 2000).

Sociological Perspectives

Sociologists find psychological explanations inadequate. They stress that the key to understanding prejudice is not something inside people, but factors *outside* them. Thus, sociologists focus on how some environments foster prejudice, while others discourage it. With this background, let's compare functionalist, conflict, and symbolic interactionist perspectives on prejudice.

Functionalism In a telling scene from a television documentary, journalist Bill Moyers interviewed Fritz Hippler, a Nazi intellectual who at age 29 was put in charge of the entire German film industry. Hippler said that when Hitler came to power the Germans were no more anti-Semitic than the French, probably less so. He was told to create anti-Semitism. Obediently, Hippler produced movies that contained vivid scenes comparing Jews to rats—their breeding threatening to infest the population.

Why was Hippler told to create hatred? Prejudice and discrimination were functional for the Nazis. The Jews provided a convenient scapegoat, a common enemy against which the Nazis could unite a Germany that had been brought to its knees by defeat in World War I and bled by war reparations and rampant inflation. In addition, the Jews owned businesses, bank accounts, art work, and other property that the Nazis could confiscate. They also held key positions (university professors, reporters, judges, and so on), which the Nazis could replace with their own flunkies. In the end, hatred also showed its dysfunctional side, as the Nazi officials who were hanged at Nuremberg discovered.

When state machinery is harnessed to hatred as it was by the Nazis—who exploited the schools, police, courts, mass media, and almost all aspects of the government—prejudice becomes practically irresistible. Recall the identical twins featured in the Down-to-Earth Sociology box on page 64. Oskar and Jack had been separated as babies. Jack was brought up as a Jew in Trinidad, while Oskar was reared as a Catholic in Czechoslovakia. Under the Nazi regime, Oskar learned to hate Jews, unaware that he himself was a Jew.

authoritarian personality
Theodor Adorno's term for people who are prejudiced and rank high on scales of conformity, intolerance, insecurity, respect for authority, and submissiveness to superiors

That prejudice is functional and is shaped by the social environment was demonstrated by psychologists Muzafer and Carolyn Sherif (1953). In a boys' summer camp, they assigned friends to different cabins and then had the cabins compete in sports. In just a few days, strong in-groups had formed, and even former lifelong friends were calling one another "crybaby" and "sissy" and showing intense dislike for one another.

The Sherif study teaches us several important lessons about social life. Note how it is possible to arrange the social environment so we generate either positive or negative feelings about people, and how prejudice arises when groups are pitted against one another in an "I win, you lose" situation. You can also see that prejudice is functional, how it creates in-group solidarity. And, of course, it is obvious how dysfunctional prejudice is, how it destroys human relationships.

Conflict Theory Conflict theorists also analyze how groups are pitted against one another, but they focus on how this arrangement benefits those with power. They begin by noting that workers want better food, health care, housing, and education. To attain these goals, workers need good jobs. If workers are united, they can demand higher wages and better working conditions. But if capitalists can keep workers divided, they can hold wages down. To do this, capitalists use two main weapons.

The first weapon is to keep workers insecure. The fear of unemployment works especially well. The unemployed serve as a **reserve labor force** for capitalists. They draw on this group to expand production during economic booms, and when the economy contracts, they release these workers to rejoin the ranks of the unemployed. The lesson is not lost on workers who still have jobs. They fear eviction and having their cars and furniture repossessed. Many know they are just one paycheck from ending up "on the streets." This helps keep workers docile.

The second weapon is to exploit racial and ethnic strife. Pitting worker against worker weakens their bargaining power. Sowing fear and suspicion among racial-ethnic groups—such as by letting whites know that blacks are waiting to take their jobs, or by getting blacks to view Latinos as a threat to theirs—also produces docile workers. The result is a **split labor market,** workers divided along racial-ethnic and gender lines (Du Bois 1935/1992; Minchin 1999; Roediger 2002).

The consequences are devastating, say conflict theorists. It is just like the boys in the Sherif experiment. African Americans, Latinos, whites, and others see themselves as able to make gains only at the expense of the others. This rivalry shows up along even finer racial-ethnic lines, such as that in Miami between Haitians and African Americans, who distrust each other as competitors. Divisions among workers deflect anger and hostility away from the power elite and direct these powerful emotions toward other racial and ethnic groups. Instead of recognizing their common class interests and working for their mutual welfare, workers learn to fear and distrust one another.

Symbolic Interactionism While conflict theorists focus on the role of the capitalist class in exploiting racial and ethnic divisions, symbolic interactionists examine how labels affect perception and create prejudice.

How Labels Create Prejudice Symbolic interactionists stress *that the labels we learn affect the way we see people.* Labels cause **selective perception;** that is, they lead us to see certain things while they blind us to others. If we apply a label to a group, we tend to see its members as all alike. We shake off evidence that doesn't fit (Simpson and Yinger 1972). Racial and ethnic labels are especially powerful. They are shorthand for emotionally charged stereotypes. The term nigger, for example, is not neutral. Nor are *honky, spic, mick, kike, limey, kraut, dago, guinea,* or any of the other scornful words people use to belittle ethnic groups. Such words overpower us with emotions, blocking out rational thought about the people to whom they refer (Allport 1954).

Stereotypes and Discrimination: The Self-Fulfilling Prophecy Some stereotypes not only justify prejudice and discrimination—they even produce the behavior depicted in the stereotype. Let's consider Group X. Negative stereotypes characterize Group X as lazy. If they are lazy, they don't deserve good jobs. ("They are lazy and undependable and wouldn't do well.") This attitude creates a *self-fulfilling prophecy.* Because they are denied

reserve labor force the unemployed; unemployed workers are thought of as being "in reserve"—capitalists take them "out of reserve" (put them back to work) during times of high production and then lay them off (put them back in reserve) when they are no longer needed

split labor market workers split along racial, ethnic, gender, age, or any other lines; this split is exploited by owners to weaken the bargaining power of workers

selective perception seeing certain features of an object or situation, but remaining blind to others jobs that require high dedication and energy, most members of Group X are limited to doing "dirty work," the kind of work thought appropriate for "that kind" of people. Since much dirty work is sporadic, members of Group X are often seen standing around street corners. The sight of their idleness reinforces the original stereotype of laziness. The discrimination that created the "laziness" in the first place passes unnoticed.

Global Patterns of Intergroup Relations

Sociologists have studied racial-ethnic relations around the world. They have found six basic patterns that characterize the relationship of dominant groups and minorities. These patterns are shown in Figure 12.4. Let's look at each.

Genocide

Last century's two most notorious examples of genocide occurred in Europe and Africa. In Germany during the 1930s and 1940s, Hitler and the Nazis attempted to destroy all Jews. In the 1990s, in Rwanda, the Hutus tried to destroy all Tutsis. One of the horrifying aspects of these slaughters was that those who participated did not crawl out from under a rock someplace. Rather, they were ordinary citizens whose participation was facilitated by labels that singled out the victims as enemies worthy of death (Huttenbach 1991; Browning 1993; Simmons 1998; Gross 2001).

To better understand how ordinary people can participate in genocide, let's look at an example from the 1800s. The U.S. government and white settlers chose the label "savages" to refer to Native Americans. To define the Native Americans as less than human made it easier to justify killing them in order to take over their resources, and to slaughter those who resisted their advance toward the West. Most Native Americans, however, did not die from bullets but from diseases that the whites brought with them. The Native Americans had no immunity against these diseases, such as measles, smallpox, and the flu (Dobyns 1983; Schaefer 2000). The settlers also ruthlessly destroyed the Native Americans' food supply (buffalos, crops). As a result, about *95 percent* of Native Americans died (Thornton 1987; Churchill 1997).

The same thing was happening in other places. In South Africa, the Boers, or Dutch settlers, viewed the native Hottentots as jungle animals and totally wiped them out. In

Figure 12.4 Global Patterns of Intergroup Relations: A Continuum

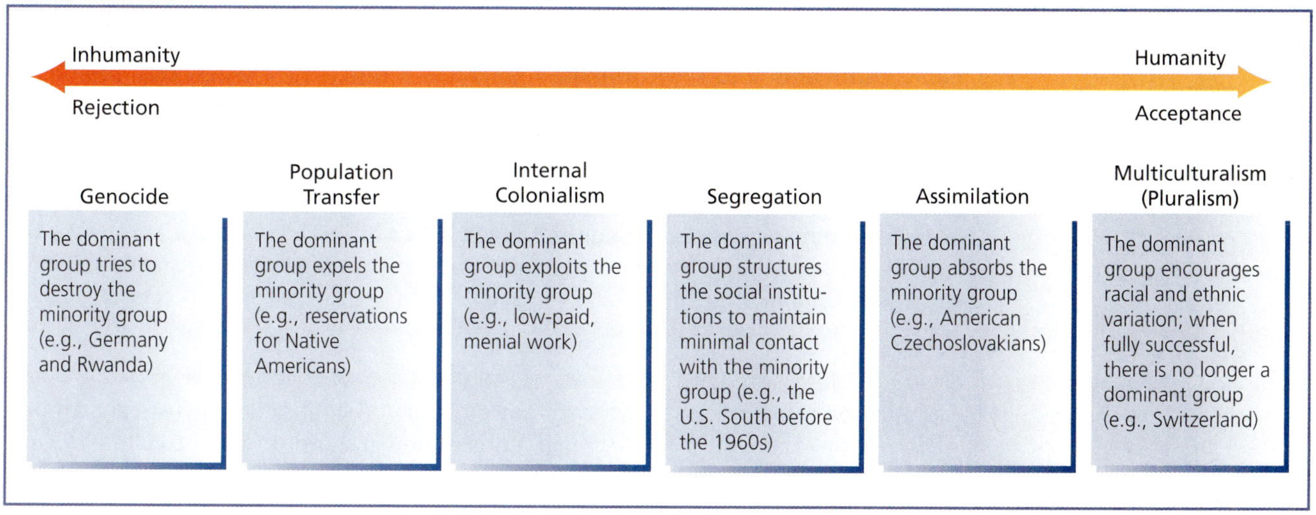

Inhumanity
Rejection
Humanity
Acceptance
Genocide
The dominant group tries to destroy the minority group (e.g., Germany and Rwanda)
Population Transfer
The dominant group expels the minority group (e.g., reservations for Native Americans)
Internal Colonialism
The dominant group exploits the minority group (e.g., low-paid, menial work)
Segregation
The dominant group structures the social institutions to maintain minimal contact with the minority group (e.g., the U.S. South before the 1960s)
Assimilation
The dominant group absorbs the minority group (e.g., American Czechoslovakians)
Multiculturalism (Pluralism)
The dominant group encourages racial and ethnic variation; when fully successful, there is no longer a dominant group (e.g., Switzerland)

Tasmania, the British settlers stalked the local aboriginal population, hunting them for sport and sometimes even for dog food.

Labels are powerful forces in human life. Labels that dehumanize others help people to **compartmentalize**—to separate their acts from their sense of being good and moral people. To regard members of some group as less than human means that it is okay to treat them inhumanely. Thus people can kill—and still retain a good self-concept (Bernard et al. 1971; Markhusen 1995). In short, *labeling the targeted group as less than fully human facilitates genocide.*

Population Transfer

There are two types of **population transfer:** indirect and direct. *Indirect* population transfer is achieved by making life so unbearable for members of a minority that they leave "voluntarily." Under the bitter conditions of czarist Russia, for example, millions of Jews made this "choice." *Direct transfer* occurs when a dominant group expels a minority. Examples include the relocation of Native Americans to reservations and the transfer of Americans of Japanese descent to internment camps during World War II.

In the 1990s, a combination of genocide and population transfer occurred in Bosnia and Kosovo, parts of the former Yugoslavia. A hatred nurtured for centuries had been kept under wraps during Tito's iron-fisted rule from 1944 to 1980. After Tito's death, these suppressed, smoldering hatreds soared to the surface and Yugoslavia split into warring factions. When the Serbs gained power, Muslims rebelled and began guerilla warfare. The Serbs vented their hatred by what they termed **ethnic cleansing:** They terrorized villages with killing and rape, forcing survivors to flee in fear.

Internal Colonialism

In Chapter 9, the term *colonialism* was used to refer to one way that the Most Industrialized Nations exploit the Least Industrialized Nations (pp. 249 and 252). Conflict theorists use the term **internal colonialism** to refer to the way a country's dominant group exploits minority groups for its economic advantage. The dominant group manipulates the social institutions to suppress minorities and deny them full access to the society's benefits. Slavery, reviewed in Chapter 9, is an extreme example of internal colonialism, as was the South African system of *apartheid.* Although the dominant Afrikaaners despised the minority, they found its presence necessary. As Simpson and Yinger (1972) put it, who else would do the hard work?

compartmentalize to separate acts from feelings or attitudes

population transfer forcing a minority group to move

ethnic cleansing a policy of population elimination, including forcible expulsion and genocide

internal colonialism the policy of economically exploiting minority groups

segregation the policy of keeping racial or ethnic groups apart

assimilation the process of being absorbed into the mainstream culture

Segregation

Internal colonialism is often accompanied by **segregation**—the separation of racial or ethnic groups. Segregation allows the dominant group to maintain social distance from the minority and yet to exploit their labor as cooks, cleaners, chauffeurs, housekeepers, nannies, factory workers, and so on. In the U.S. South until the 1960s, by law African Americans and whites had to use separate public facilities such as hotels, schools, swimming pools, bathrooms, and even drinking fountains. In thirty-eight states, laws prohibited marriage between blacks and whites. Violators could be sent to prison (Mahoney and Kooistra 1995). The last law of this type was repealed in 1967 (Spickard 1989). In Israel, Palestinians who work for the dominant Israelis have to carry passes and go through armed checkpoints in the morning and return to their own areas at the end of the day.

Racial-ethnic segregation in housing is still a fact of life for most Americans. In the Cultural Diversity box on the next page, you can see how residential segregation is related to internal colonialism.

Assimilation

Assimilation is the process by which a minority is absorbed into the mainstream culture. There are two types. In *forced assimilation* the dominant group refuses to allow the minority to practice its religion, speak its language, or follow its customs. Prior to the fall of

CULTURAL DIVERSITY in the UNITED STATES and around the WORLD

"You Can Work for Us, But You Can't Live Near Us"

Never before had so many people crowded in the city hall on Glen Cove, Long Island. What drew them was nothing less than the future of their community, which had become an ethnic and social class crucible. At the front sat the well-groomed Long Islanders in their designer clothing. At the back were men in soiled jeans and work boots whose calloused hands bespoke their occupations as landscape laborers and construction workers. Most of them had fled the civil war in El Salvador, seeking safety and jobs in the United States.

The meeting was called to order by the town mayor, the son of Italian immigrants, who had launched a campaign to rid the town of a day labor shape-up area. He had asked the Immigration and Naturalization Service to raid the area where men gathered on the sidewalks in the early mornings to look for day jobs. This evening he proposed an ordinance making it illegal for groups of five or more to assemble on city streets for the purpose of seeking work. City residents testified that the men made cat calls at women and urinated in public. They called the shape-up area an eyesore. Representatives of the immigrants countered by affirming the immigrants' constitutional right to freedom of assembly and argued that they were not loitering in the streets but waiting peacefully on the sidewalks.

The larger issue that haunted the Long Islanders, one they were reluctant to acknowledge publicly but that a few individuals admitted to me privately, was the fear that the immigrants gave the impression that the town was in decline. Such a perception in suburbia jeopardizes real estate values—the bedrock of U.S. middle-class security. Even the hint of racial or ethnic turnover frightens homeowners and potential buyers. In Glen Cove, this fear led to the campaign to get rid of the shape-up, the single most vivid image of the ethnically distinct people residing in the community.

What never was discussed in the town meeting nor came up in casual conversation was that the immigrants had been attracted to the area precisely because the suburbanites desired their inexpensive labor. Almost all the landscapers on Long Island are now Salvadoran, while many families depend on immigrant women to clean their houses and take care of their children and elderly. Immigrants, especially from El Salvador and other Latin American countries, toil in the island's restaurant kitchens, factories, industrial laundries, and in gleaming office buildings at night. They do the jobs that U.S. workers do not want to do or cannot afford to do because they pay too little to support their families.

When the Salvadorans and other immigrants arrived on Long Island, seeking their futures, they first lived in communities with high minority populations. But as the immigrants moved closer to their jobs, their numbers swelled in more traditional bedroom communities like Glen Cove. These other towns also began to adopt "not in my backyard" policies by passing new ordinances or enforcing old ones, even refusing to let undocumented immigrant children attend their public schools. Old timers felt that such measures could stem the decline in their way of life. What they overlooked was how immigrant labor is preserving their standard of living.

Sarah Maher
University of Vermont
Salvadorans in Suburbia

Day laborers lined up, soliciting offers for work.

the Soviet Union, for example, the dominant group, the Russians, required that Armenian children attend schools where they were taught in Russian. Armenians could honor only Russian, not Armenian, holidays. *Permissible assimilation,* in contrast, allows the minority to adopt the dominant group's patterns in its own way and at its own speed.

Multiculturalism (Pluralism)

A policy of **multiculturalism,** also called **pluralism,** permits or even encourages racial and ethnic variation. Minority groups are able to maintain their separate identities, yet freely participate in their country's social institutions, from education to politics. Switzerland provides an outstanding example of multiculturalism. The Swiss are made up of four ethnic groups—French, Italians, Germans, and Romansh. The groups have kept their own languages, and they live peacefully in political and economic unity. Multiculturalism has been so successful that none of these groups can properly be called a minority.

Race and Ethnic Relations in the United States

To write on race-ethnicity is like stepping into a minefield: One never knows where to expect the next explosion. Even basic terms are controversial. The term African American, for example, is rejected by some who ask why this term doesn't include white immigrants from South Africa. Some people classified as African Americans also reject this term because they identify themselves as blacks. Similarly, although some Latinos prefer the term *Hispanic American,* others reject it, saying that it ignores the Indian side of their heritage. Some would limit the term *Chicanos*—commonly used to refer to Americans from Mexico—to those who have a sense of oppression and ethnic unity; they say it does not apply to those who have assimilated.

No term that I use here, then, will satisfy everyone. Racial-ethnic identity is fluid, constantly changing, and all terms carry a risk as they take on newly-charged political meanings. Nevertheless, as part of everyday life we classify ourselves and one another as belonging to distinct racial-ethnic groups. Based on these self-identifications, whites make up 68 percent of the U.S. population, minorities (African Americans, Asian Americans, Latinos, and Native Americans) 31 percent. See Figure 12.5.

As you can see from the Social Map on page 342, the distribution of dominant and minority groups among the states seldom comes close to the national average. This is because minority groups tend to be clustered in regions. The extreme distributions are represented by Maine, which has only 3 percent minority, and by Hawaii, where minorities outnumber Anglos 76 percent to 29 percent. With this as background, let's review the major groups in the United States, going from the largest to the smallest.

White Europeans

Perhaps the event that best crystallizes the racial view of the nation's founders occurred at the first Continental Congress of the United States. There they passed the Naturalization Act of 1790, declaring that only white immigrants could apply for citizenship. The sense of superiority and privilege of **WASPs** (white Anglo-Saxon Protestants) was not limited to their views of race. They also viewed white Europeans from countries other than England as inferior. They greeted **white ethnics**—immigrants from Europe whose language and other customs differed from theirs—with negative stereotypes. They especially despised the Irish, viewing them as dirty, lazy drunkards, but they also painted Germans, Poles, Jews, Italians, and others with similarly broad brush strokes.

The cultural and political dominance of the WASPs placed pressure on immigrants to blend into the mainstream culture. The children of most immigrants embraced the new way of life and quickly came to think of themselves as Americans rather than as Germans, French, Hungarians, and so on. They dropped their distinctive customs, especially their language, often viewing them as symbols of shame. This second generation of immigrants

multiculturalism (also called **pluralism**) a philosophy or political policy that permits or encourages ethnic difference

WASP White Anglo-Saxon Protestant; narrowly, an American of English descent; broadly, an American of western European ancestry

white ethnics white immigrants to the United States whose cultures differ from that of WASPs

Figure 12.5 U.S. Racial-Ethnic Groups

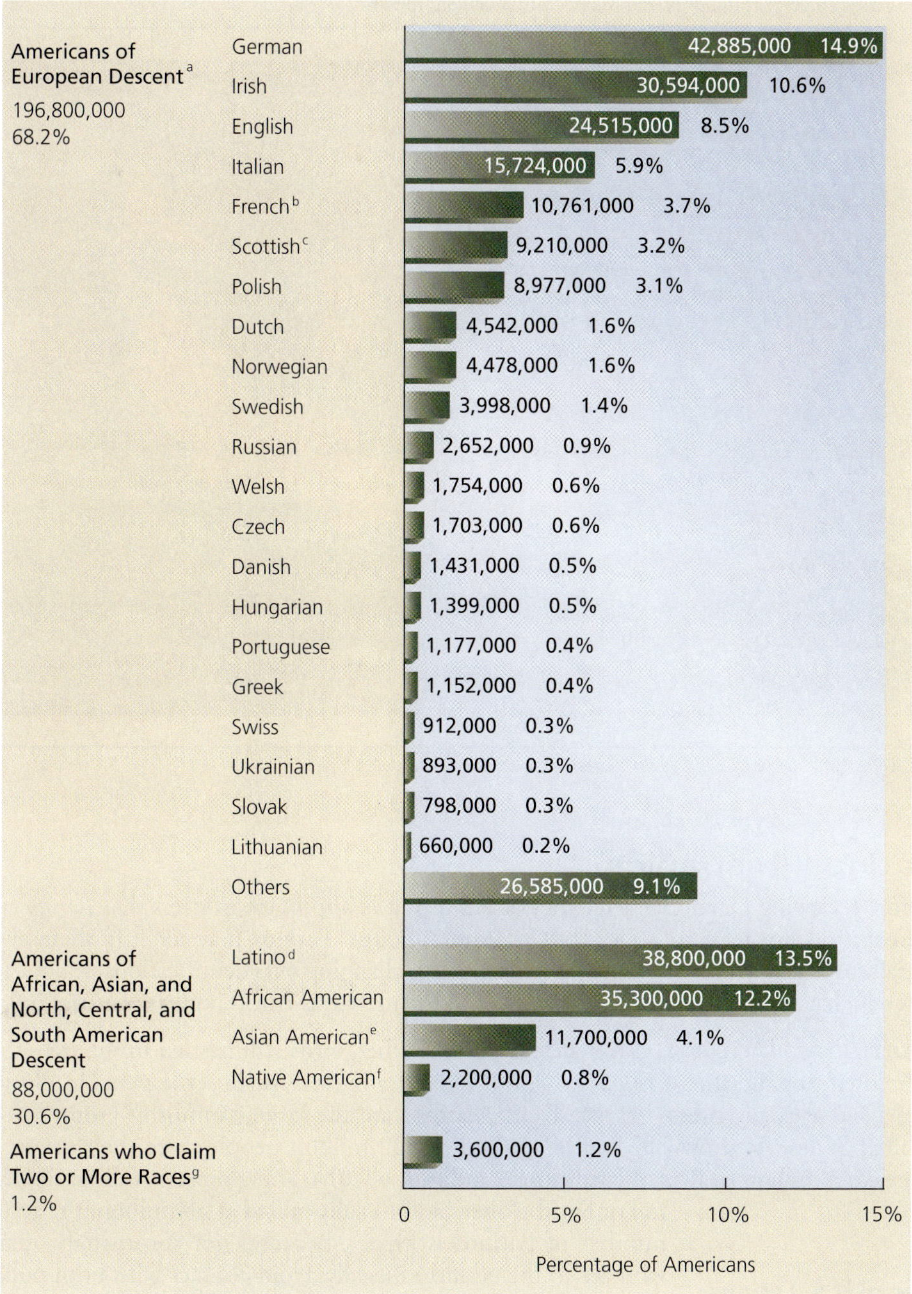

Notes:

[a]The totals in this figure should be taken as broadly accurate only. Table 1373 of the 2002 source lists 294,543,000 people in its various racial-ethnic categories, while the 2003 source lists 288,400,000. The 2003 source is used to compute percentages.

[b]Includes French Canadian.

[c]Includes "Scottish-Irish."

[d]Most Latinos trace at least part of their ancestry to Europe.

[e]In descending order, the largest groups of Asian Americans are from China, the Philippines, India, Japan, Korea, and Vietnam. See Figure 12.10. Also includes those who identify themselves as Native Hawaiian or Pacific Islander.

[f]Includes Native American, Eskimo, and Aleut.

[g]This is 1.2 million fewer people than in the year 2000 census.

Source: By the author. Based on *Statistical Abstract* 2002:Tables 36, 38, 1373; Bernstein and Bergman 2003.

was sandwiched between two worlds, that of their parents from "the old country" and their new home. Their children, the third generation, had an easier adjustment, for they had fewer customs to discard. As immigrants from other parts of Europe assimilated into this Anglo culture, the meaning of WASP expanded to include people of this descent.

In sum: Because protestant English immigrants settled the colonies, they established the culture—from the dominant language to the dominant religion. Highly ethnocentric, they regarded as inferior the customs of other groups. Because white Europeans took power, they determined the national agenda to which other ethnic groups had to react. Their institutional and cultural dominance still sets the stage for current ethnic relations, a topic explored in the Down-to-Earth Sociology box on page 343.

Figure 12.6 The Distribution of Dominant and Minority Groups

This social map indicates how unevenly distributed U.S. Minority groups are. The extremes are Hawaii with 75 percent minority and Maine with 3 percent minority.

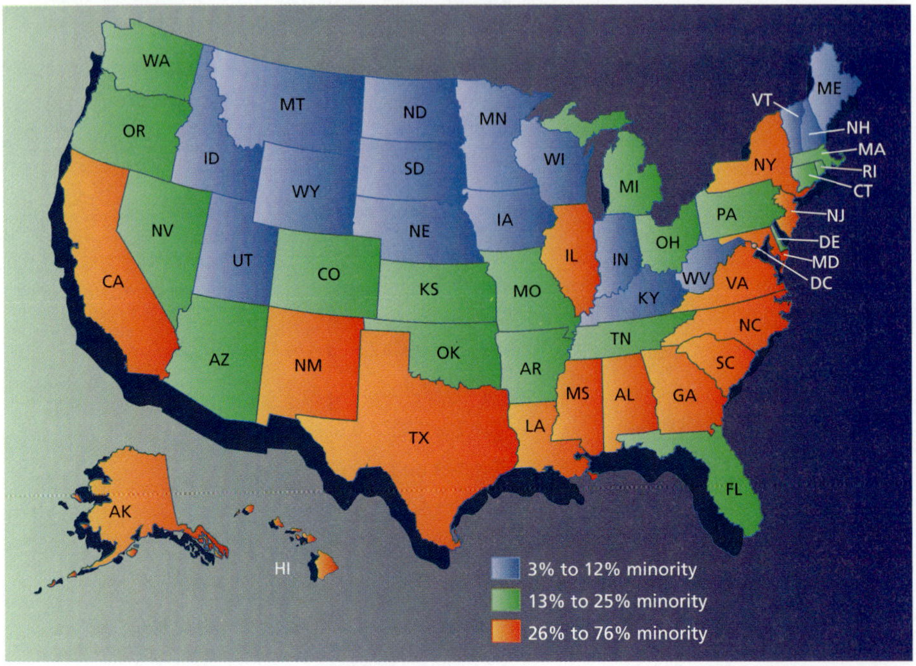

Source: By the author. Based on *Statistical Abstract* 2002:Table 22.

Latinos (Hispanics)

Before reviewing major characteristics of Latinos, it is important to stress that *Latino* and *Hispanic* do not refer to a race, but to ethnic groups. Latinos may identify themselves racially as black, white, or Native American. With changing self-identifications, some Latinos who have an African heritage even refer to themselves as Afro-Latinos (Navarro 2003).

Numbers, Origins, and Location When birds still nestled in the trees that were used to build the *Mayflower,* Latinos had already established settlements in Florida and New Mexico (Bretos 1994). Today, Latinos are the largest minority group in the United States. As shown in Figure 12.7, about 22 million people trace their origin to Mexico, 3 million to Puerto Rico, over 1 million to Cuba, and almost 5 million to Central or South America. Officially tallied at 35 million, the actual number of Latinos is higher, because, not surprisingly, many who are in the country illegally avoid contact with both public officials and census forms. Although most Latinos are legal residents, each year about *1.6 million* people are apprehended at the border or at points inland and are deported to Mexico (*Statistical Abstract* 2002:Table 301). Perhaps another million or so manage to enter the United States. Many migrate for temporary work and then return to their homes and families in Mexico.

To gain an understanding of how vast these numbers are, we can note that there are millions more Latinos in the United States than there are Canadians in Canada (32 million). To Midwesterners, such a comparison often comes as a surprise, for Latinos are absent from vast stretches of mid-America. As shown in Figure 12.8, 66 percent are concentrated in just four states: California, Texas, Florida, and New York.

Figure 12.7 Country of Origin of U.S. Latinos

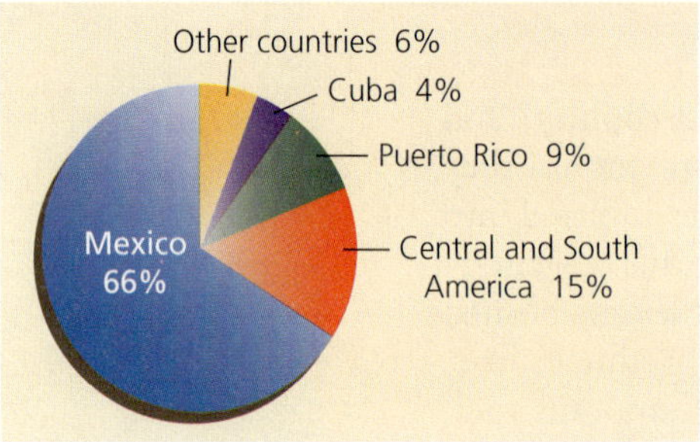

Source: By the author. Based on *Statistical Abstract* 2002:Table 40.

DOWN-TO-EARTH SOCIOLOGY

Unpacking the Invisible Knapsack: Exploring Cultural Privilege

OVERT RACISM IN THE UNITED STATES has dropped sharply, but doors still open and close on the basis of the color of our skin. Whites have a difficult time grasping the idea that good things come their way because they are white. They usually fail to perceive how "whiteness" operates in their own lives.

Peggy McIntosh, of Irish descent, began to wonder why she was so seldom aware of her race-ethnicity, while her African American friends were so conscious of theirs. She realized that people are not highly aware of things that they take for granted—and that "whiteness" is a "taken-for-granted" background feature of U.S. society. To explore this, she drew up a list of things that she can take for granted because of her "whiteness," what she calls her "invisible knapsack."

What is in this "knapsack"? What taken-for-granted-and-usually-unanalyzed privileges can most white people in U.S. society assume? Because she is white, McIntosh (1988) says:

1. If I don't do well as a leader, I can be sure people won't say that it is because of my race.
2. When I go shopping, store detectives won't follow me.
3. When I watch television or open the front page of the paper, I see people of my race widely and positively presented.
4. When I study our national heritage, I see people of my color and am taught that they made our country great.
5. When I cash a check or use a credit card, my skin color does not make the clerk think that I may be financially irresponsible.
6. To protect my children, I do not have to educate them to be aware of racism.
7. I can talk with my mouth full and not have people put this down to my color.
8. I can wear old clothes and not have people attribute this to the poverty of my race.
9. I can speak at a public meeting without putting my race on trial.
10. I can achieve at something and not be "a credit to my race."
11. I am never asked to speak for all the people of my race.
12. If a traffic cop pulls me over, I can be sure it isn't because I'm white.
13. I can take a job with an affirmative action employer without people thinking I got the job because of my race.
14. I can be late to a meeting without people thinking I was late because "That's how *they* are."

For Your CONSIDERATION

Can you think of other "unearned privileges" of everyday life that come to whites because of their skin color? (McIntosh's list contains 46 items.) Why are whites seldom aware that they carry this invisible knapsack?

Spanish Language The Spanish language distinguishes most Latinos from other U.S. ethnic groups. With 28 million people speaking Spanish at home, the United States has become one of the largest Spanish-speaking nations in the world (*Statistical Abstract* 2002:Table 1373). Because about half of Latinos are unable to speak English, or can do so only with difficulty, many millions face a major obstacle to getting good jobs.

The growing use of Spanish has become a matter of controversy. Perceiving the prevalence of Spanish as a threat, Senator S. I. Hayakawa of California initiated an "English only" movement in 1981. The constitutional amendment he sponsored never got off the ground, but 23 states have passed a law declaring English their official language (Schaefer 2000).

Diversity For Latinos, country of origin is highly significant. Those from Puerto Rico, for example, feel little in common with people from Mexico, Venezuela, or El Salvador—just as earlier immigrants from Germany, Sweden, and England felt they had little in common with one another. A sign of these divisions is the preference many have to refer to themselves in terms of their country of origin, such as Puerto Rican or Cuban American, rather than as Latino or Hispanic.

As with other ethnic groups, Latinos, too, are separated by social class. The half-million Cubans who fled Castro's rise to power in 1959,

Figure 12.8 Where U.S. Latinos Live

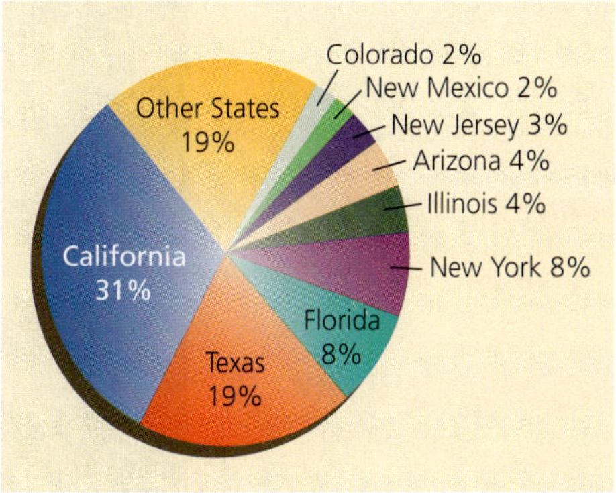

Source: By the author. Based on *Statistical Abstract* 2002:Table 23.

In reaction to the millions of recent Latino immigrants who speak Spanish, an "English-only" movement has developed in the United States. Twenty-three states have passed laws declaring that English is their official language. One wonders which version of English the legislators had in mind.

for example, were mostly well-educated, well-to-do professionals or businesspeople. In contrast, the "boat people" who fled later were mostly lower-class refugees, people with whom the earlier arrivals would not have associated in Cuba. The earlier arrivals, who are firmly established in Florida and in control of many businesses and financial institutions, distance themselves from the more recent immigrants.

These divisions of national origin and social class are a major obstacle to political unity. One consequence is a severe underrepresentation in politics. Because Latinos make up 13.5 percent of the U.S. population, we might expect 13 or 14 U.S. Senators to be Latino. How many are there? None. In addition, Latinos hold only 4 percent of the seats in the U.S. House of Representatives (*Statistical Abstract* 2002:Table 382).

When the U.S. government took control of what is now the southwestern United States, Mexicans living there were transformed from the dominant group into a minority group. To try to maintain their culture, Chicanos, Americans of Mexican origin, do ethnic work, such as this dance by Danza Teocalt at a Cinco de Mayo celebration in Los Angeles. (The Cinco de Mayo—Fifth of May—holiday marks the Mexican army's 1862 defeat of French troops at the city of Puebla.)

Fragmented among themselves, Latinos also find that a huge gulf separates them from African Americans (Flippen 2001). With highly distinct histories and cultures, the relationship of these two groups is often tinged with hostility. As Latinos have become more visible in U.S. society and more vocal in their demands for equality, they have come face to face with African Americans who fear that Latino gains in jobs and at the ballot box will come at their expense. Together, Latinos and African Americans make up one-fourth of the U.S. population. It is likely that these two groups will increasingly come to recognize that their unity will produce an unstoppable political force.

Comparative Conditions Table 12.1 shows how Latinos compare with other groups. You can see that compared with white Americans and Asian Americans, Latinos are worse off on all the indicators of well-being shown in this table. You can also see how similar their rankings on these indicators are to those of African Americans. This table also illustrates the significance of country of origin. You can see that Cuban Americans score the highest on these indicators of well-being, while Puerto Rican Americans score the lowest. Table 12.2 shows that one out of three Latinos does not complete high school, and only

Table 12.1 Race-Ethnicity and Comparative Well-Being

	Income		Unemployment		Poverty		Home Ownership	
	Median Family Income	Percentage of White Income	Percentage Unemployed	Percentage of White Unemployment	Percentage Below Poverty Line	Percentage of White Poverty	Percentage Owning Their Homes	Percentage of White Home Ownership
White Americans	$51,224	–	2.3%	–	9.8%	–	71%	–
Latinos	$31,663	62%	3.9%	170%	22.8%	233%	48%	65%
Country of origin								
Mexico	$31,123	61%	4.1%	178%	24.1%	246%	48%	68%
Puerto Rico	$30,129	59%	4.0%	174%	25.8%	263%	35%	49%
Cuba	$38,312	75%	2.7%	117%	17.3%	177%	59%	83%
Central and South America	$33,105	65%	3.5%	152%	16.7%	170%	38%	54%
African Americans	$31,778	62%	5.0%	217%	23.6%	241%	47%	66%
Asian Americans[a]	$54,500[c]	106%	2.6%	113%	10.8%	110%	53%	75%
Native Americans	$31,929	62%	20.2%	878%	28.4%	290%	NA[b]	NA

[a]Includes Pacific Islanders.
[b]Not available.
[c]Extrapolated from changes in income for other groups.

Sources: Statistical Abstract 2002:Tables 36, 37, 38, 40; and U.S. Bureau of the Census, *American Fact Finder*, 2003: Tables GCT-P12, P14.

Table 12.2 Education and Race-Ethnicity

	Less than High School Education	High School Education	1–3 Years of College	College Graduate	Number of Doctorates Awarded	Percentage of all Doctorates Awarded	Percentage of U.S. Population
White Americans	15%	33%	25%	26%	23,660	79%	68.2%
Latinos	32%	57%	NA%	11%	1,283	4%	13.5%
African Americans	22%	35%	27%	17%	1,760	6%	12.2%
Asian Americans	14%	22%	20%	44%	2,327	8%	4.1%
Native Americans	28%	59%	NA	13%	179	0.6%	0.8%

Note: NA = Not Available. Totals except for doctorates refer to persons 25 years and over.

Sources: Statistical Abstract 2000:Tables 42, 44; 2002:Tables 36, 37, 40, 771; U.S. Bureau of the Census, *American Fact Finder*, 2003: Table GCT-P11.

11 percent graduate from college. In a postindustrial society that increasingly requires advanced skills, these totals indicate that a large number of Latinos will be left behind.

African Americans

After slavery was abolished, in a practice known as *Jim Crow,* the South passed laws to segregate blacks and whites. In 1896, the Supreme Court ruled in *Plessy v. Ferguson* that state laws requiring "separate but equal" accommodations for blacks were a reasonable use of state power. Whites used this ruling to strip blacks of the political power they had gained after the Civil War. They prohibited blacks from voting in "white" primaries. It was not until 1944 that the Supreme Court ruled that African Americans could vote in southern primaries, and not until 1954 that they had the legal right to attend the same public schools as whites (Schaefer 2000). Well into the 1960s, the South was still openly—and legally—practicing segregation.

The Struggle for Civil Rights

It was 1955, in Montgomery, Alabama. As specified by law, whites took the front seats of the bus, while blacks went to the back. As the bus filled up, blacks had to give up their seats to whites.

When Rosa Parks, a 42-year-old African American woman and secretary of the Montgomery NAACP, was told she would have to stand so white folks could sit, she refused (Bray 1995). She stubbornly sat there while the bus driver raged and whites felt insulted. Her arrest touched off mass demonstrations, led fifty thousand blacks to boycott the city's buses for a year, and thrust an otherwise unknown preacher into a historic role.

Rev. Martin Luther King Jr., who had majored in sociology at Morehouse College in Atlanta, Georgia, took control. He organized car pools and preached nonviolence. Incensed at this radical organizer and at the stirrings in the normally compliant black community, segregationists also put their beliefs into practice—by bombing homes and dynamiting churches.

Until the 1960s, the South's public facilities were racially segregated. Some were reserved for whites only, others for blacks only. This apartheid was broken by blacks and whites who worked together and risked their lives to bring about a fairer society. Shown here is a 1963 sit-in at a Woolworth's lunch counter in Jackson, Mississippi. Sugar, ketchup, and mustard are being poured over the heads of the demonstrators.

Rising Expectations and Civil Strife The barriers came down, but they came down slowly. Not until 1964 did Congress pass the Civil Rights Act, making it illegal to discriminate in restaurants, hotels, theaters, and other public places. Then in 1965, Congress passed the Voting Rights Act, banning the fraudulent literacy tests that the South had used to keep African Americans from voting.

Encouraged by these gains, African Americans experienced what sociologists call **rising expectations;** that is, they believed better conditions would soon follow. The lives of the poor among them, however, changed little, if at all. Frustrations built, finally exploding in Watts in 1965, when African Americans in that Los Angeles ghetto took to the streets in the first of what have been termed "the urban revolts." When King was assassinated by a white supremacist on April 4, 1968, inner cities across the nation again erupted in fiery violence. Under threat of the destruction of U.S. cities, Congress passed the sweeping Civil Rights Act of 1968.

Continued Gains Since then, African Americans have made remarkable political, educational, and economic gains. At 9 percent, African Americans have *quadrupled* their membership in the U.S. House of Representatives in the past 30 years (Rich 1986; *Statistical Abstract* 2002:Table 382). As college enrollments increased, the middle class expanded. Today, half of all African American families make more than $35,000 a year. One in three makes more than $50,000 a year, and one of six more than $75,000 (*Statistical Abstract* 2002:Table 657). Although their poverty rate is among the highest (see Table 12.1), contrary to stereotypes, the average African American family is *not* poor.

The extent of African American political prominence was highlighted when Jesse Jackson (another sociology major) competed for the Democratic presidential nomination in 1984 and 1988. Political progress was further confirmed in 1989 when L. Douglas Wilder of Virginia became the nation's first elected African American governor. The political prominence of African Americans came to the nation's attention again in 2000 when Alan Keyes competed for the Republican presidential nomination.

Current Losses Despite these gains, African Americans continue to lag behind in politics, economics, and education. No U.S. Senator is African American, and based on the percentage of African Americans in the U.S. population we would expect about 12. As Tables 12.1 and 12.2 on page 345 show, African Americans average only 62 percent of white income, have much more unemployment and poverty, and are less likely to own their home or to have a college education. That half of African American families have an income over $35,000 is only part of the story. The other part is that about one of every five families makes less than $15,000 a year (*Statistical Abstract* 2002:Table 657).

Two worlds of African American experience have developed—one educated and affluent, the other uneducated and poor. Concentrated among the poor are those with the least hope, the highest despair, and the violence that so often dominates the evening news. Although homicide rates have dropped to their lowest point in 20 years, African American males are *seven* times as likely to be homicide victims as are white males. Compared with white females, African American females are more than *three* times as likely to be murdered (*Statistical Abstract* 2002:Table 289). Compared with whites, African Americans are also *eight* times more likely to die from AIDS (*Statistical Abstract* 2002:Table 109).

Race or Social Class? A Sociological Debate This division of African Americans into "haves" and "have-nots" has fueled a sociological controversy. Sociologist William Julius Wilson (1978, 1987, 2000) argues that social class has become more important than race in determining the life chances of African Americans. Prior to civil rights legislation, he says, the African American experience was dominated by race. Throughout the United States, African Americans were detoured from avenues of economic advancement—good schools and good jobs. When civil rights legislation opened new opportunities, African Americans seized them. Following the path taken by other ethnic groups, as African Americans advanced economically, they, too, moved out of the inner city. Just as legislation began to open doors to African Americans, however, manufacturing jobs dried up and many blue-collar jobs were moved to the suburbs. As a result, better-educated African Americans were able to obtain middle-class, white-collar jobs. In contrast, African Americans with poor education and few skills were left behind, trapped by poverty in the inner city.

rising expectations the sense that better conditions are soon to follow, which, if unfulfilled, increases frustration

As discussed in the text, sociologists disagree about the relative significance of race and social class in determining social and economic conditions of African Americans. William Julius Wilson, shown here, is an avid proponent of the social class side of this debate.

The result, says Wilson, is two worlds of African American experience. One group is stuck in the inner city, lives in poverty, attends poor schools, and faces dead-end jobs or welfare. This group is filled with hopelessness and despair, combined with apathy or hostility. In contrast, those who have moved up the social class ladder live in comfortable homes in secure neighborhoods. They work at jobs that provide decent incomes and send their children to good schools. Their middle-class experiences and lifestyle have changed their views on life, and their aspirations and values now have little in common with those of African Americans who remain poor. According to Wilson, then, social class—not race—has become the most significant factor in the lives of African Americans.

Some sociologists reply that this analysis overlooks the discrimination that continues to underlie the African American experience. They note that even when African Americans do the same work as whites they average less pay (Willie 1991; Herring 2002). This, they argue, points to racial discrimination, not to social class.

What is the answer to this debate? Wilson would reply that it is not an either-or question. My book is titled *The **Declining** Significance of Race,* he would say, not *The **Absence** of Race.* Certainly racism is still alive, he would add, but today social class is more central to the African American experience than is racial discrimination. For the poor in the inner city, we need to provide jobs—for the availability of work offers hope, and work provides an anchor to a responsible life (Wilson 1996, 2000).

Racism as an Everyday Burden Today's racism is much more subtle than it used to be, but it still walks among us. To study discrimination in the job market, researchers sent over 5,000 resumes in response to help wanted ads in the Boston and Chicago Sunday papers (Bertrand and Mullainathan 2002). The resumes were identical, but in some they used white-sounding names (Emily and Brandon), in others black-sounding names (Lakisha and Jamal). Although the qualifications of the supposed job applicants were identical, the white-sounding names elicited *50 percent* more callbacks than the black-sounding names. The Down-to-Earth Sociology box on the next page presents another study of subtle racism in more detail.

African Americans who occupy higher statuses enjoy greater opportunities, and they also face less discrimination. The discrimination they encounter, however, is no less painful—and, unlike whites, they feel discrimination's presence constantly hovering over them. Here is how an African American professor puts it:

> [One problem with] being black in America is that you have to spend so much time thinking about stuff that most white people just don't even have to think about. I worry when I get pulled over by a cop. . . . I worry what some white cop is going to think when he walks over to our car, because he's holding on to a gun. And I'm very aware of how many black folks accidentally get shot by cops. I worry when I walk into a store, that someone's going to think I'm in there shoplifting. . . . And I get resentful that I have to think about things that a lot of people, even my very close white friends whose politics are similar to mine, simply don't have to worry about. (Feagin 1999:398)

The following Thinking Critically section highlights a proposal to compensate for injustices to African Americans.

THINKING Critically

Reparations for Slavery: Justice or Foolishness?

The subtitle of this section, "Justice or Foolishness," is intended to frame the stark contrasts that surround the debate about reparations for slavery. The issue itself is simple. The enslavement of millions of Africans was a gross injustice. Since the slaves were never paid for 240 years of work, their descendants should be. This is both a moral and a legal issue.

The argument for reparations, or compensation, contains related matters. The first is that the greater wealth of today's white Americans is built on the

DOWN-TO-EARTH SOCIOLOGY

Stealth Racism in the Rental Market: What You Reveal by Your Voice

MOST BLATANT DISCRIMINATION HAS become a thing of the past. There was a time when whites could burn crosses with impunity at the homes of blacks. Some even lynched African Americans and Asian Americans without fear of the law. Today cross burning and lynching will be investigated and prosecuted. If local officials don't make an arrest, the FBI will step in. Similarly, discrimination in public accommodations was once standard. Today, no hotel, restaurant, or gas station would refuse service on the basis of race-ethnicity. This, too, has become a criminal matter.

With times so changed, some may think that racism is a thing of the past. Although overt racism has been relegated to the back shelves of social life, stealth racism is alive and well, as sociologist Douglas Massey of the University of Pennsylvania documents (Massey and Lundy 2001). In his undergraduate course in research methods were whites who spoke what is called White Middle Class English, African Americans who spoke a dialect known as Black English Vernacular, and other African Americans who spoke middle-class English with a black accent.

As you know, Americans often identify one another racially by their speech. Massey used this feature of everyday life to test discrimination in the housing market. He and his students designed standard identities for members of these linguistic groups (assigning them similar income, for example). They also developed a standard script, the one group translating it into Black English Vernacular. The students called on 79 apartments that were advertised for rent in newspapers. The study was done blindly, with the white and black students not knowing how the others were being treated.

Compared with whites, African Americans were less likely to speak to rental agents, who often used answering machines to screen calls. They also were less likely to be told that an apartment was available, more likely to have to pay an application fee, and more likely to have credit mentioned. Figure 12.9 shows the percentage of callers who were told that an apartment was available. Students who posed as lower-class blacks (speakers of Black English Vernacular) had the least access to apartments.

As you can see, although both men and women were discriminated against, the discrimination was worse for the women. This is sometimes referred to as the *double bind* that African American women experience—being discriminated against both because they are African Americans and because they are women.

Figure 12.9 Cloaked Discrimination in Apartment Rentals

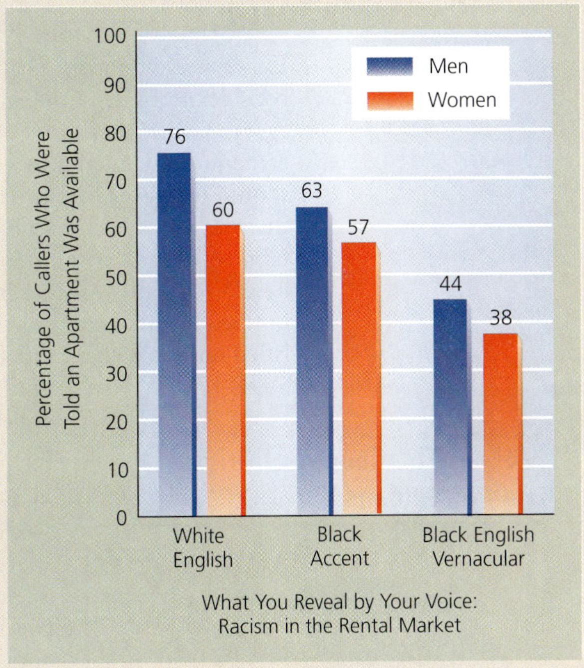

Source: Massey and Lundy 2001.

centuries of unpaid labor of black slaves. The second is that today's unequal conditions between African Americans and whites (the "racial deficit") in education, housing, and income are a legacy of slavery (Marable 2001; Conley 2002). Simply put, reparations are a form of back wages. These back wages should be paid either directly to the descendants of slaves or into a reparations trust fund targeted not to individuals but to black communities with the greatest need.

Opponents of reparations agree that slavery was a horrible crime against humanity. They stress that it occurred a long time ago, however, and that it is not a black and white issue. It was Africans who sold African prisoners to white slavers in the first place. And consider the problems in figuring who would get compensation. Would the descendants of free blacks get compensation? How about the descendants of free blacks who owned black slaves? Should reparations be given to the descendants of blacks who immigrated after slavery ended? Or to today's black immigrants?

Then there is the matter of who would pay the reparations. Most U.S. whites are descended from people who moved to the United States after slavery ended. Not only did they have nothing to do with slavery—neither did their ancestors. In addition, the money for reparations would come not only from taxes paid by whites but also from taxes paid by Latinos, Asian Americans, and Native Americans. Not incidentally, it would also come from taxes paid by African Americans.

For Your CONSIDERATION . . .

There are finer points on both sides of the argument, but these are the basic issues. What is your opinion of reparations?

Shelby Steele, a psychologist and an African American, argues that it is time to move beyond "thinking of ourselves as victims." He says that "we need to build a positive black identity, an identity built around ingenuity and personal responsibility. We should busy ourselves with the hard work of development, not try to manipulate white guilt" (Steele 2001). What do you think of his position?

Our opinions are not located in a social vacuum. They are rooted both in history and in our particular location in society. Can you identify how your social location underlies your opinions about this controversial topic? To do so, consider your racial-ethnic background, your social class, the ideas of your parents, the opinions of your friends, and when your ancestors arrived in the United States. How do these factors influence your views of what is both moral and logical in this issue?

Asian Americans

I have stressed in this chapter that our racial-ethnic categories are based more on social considerations than biological ones. This point is again obvious when we examine the category Asian American. As Figure 12.10 shows, those who are called Asian Americans came to the United States from many nations. With no unifying culture or "race," why should they ever be clustered together in a single category—except that others perceive them as a unit? Think about it. What culture or race-ethnicity do Samoans and Vietnamese have in common? Or Laotians and Pakistanis? Or Native Hawaiians and Chinese? Or people from India and those from Guam? Yet all these groups—and more—are lumped together and called Asian Americans. Apparently the U.S. government is not satisfied until it is able to pigeonhole everyone into a racial-ethnic category.

Since Asian American is a standard term, however, let's look at the characteristics of the nearly 11 million people who are lumped together and assigned this label.

Figure 12.10 The Country of Origin of Asian Americans

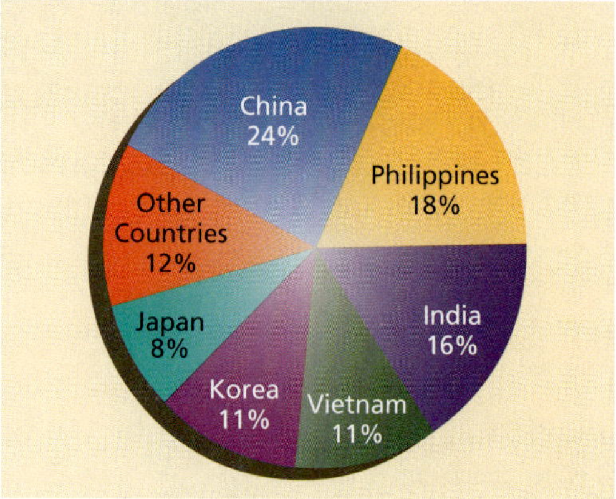

Source: By the author. Based on *Statistical Abstract* 2002: Table 24.

A Background of Discrimination

From the time they arrived on these shores, Asian Americans met discrimination. Lured by gold strikes in the West and a vast need for unskilled workers to build the railroads, 200,000 Chinese immigrated between 1850 and 1880. Feeling threatened by competing cheap labor, Anglos formed mobs and vigilante groups to intimidate these immigrants. In 1850, California passed the Foreign Miner's Act, which required Chinese (and Latinos) to pay a fee of $20 a month—when wages were a dollar a day. When the famous golden spike was driven at Promontory, Utah, in 1869 to mark the completion of the railroad to the west coast, white workers prevented Chinese workers from being in the photo—even though Chinese made up 90 percent of Central Pacific Railroad's labor force (Hsu 1971). The California Supreme Court ruled that Chinese testimony against whites was inadmissible in court (Carlson and Colburn 1972). In 1882, Congress passed the Chinese Exclusion Act, suspending all Chinese immigration for 10 years. Four years later,

Amid fears that Japanese Americans were "enemies within" who would sabotage industrial and military installations on the West Coast, in the early days of World War II Japanese Americans were transferred to "relocation camps." Many returned home after the war to find that their property had been vandalized.

the Statue of Liberty was dedicated. The tired, the poor, and the huddled masses it was intended to welcome were obviously not Chinese.

When immigrants from Japan arrived, they met *spillover bigotry,* a stereotype that lumped Asians together, depicting them as sneaky, lazy, and untrustworthy. After Japan attacked Pearl Harbor in 1941, conditions grew worse for the 110,000 Japanese Americans who called the United States their home. U.S. authorities feared that Japan would invade the United States and that the Japanese Americans would fight on Japan's side. They also feared that Japanese Americans would sabotage military installations on the West Coast. Although no Japanese American had been involved in even a single act of sabotage, on February 19, 1942, President Franklin D. Roosevelt ordered that everyone who was *one-eighth Japanese or more* be placed in special prisons (called "relocation camps"). They were charged with no crime, and they had no trials. Japanese ancestry was sufficient cause for being put in prison.

A World of Striking Contrasts As you can see from Table 12.1 on page 345, the annual income of Asian Americans has outstripped that of whites. This has led to an assumption that all Asian Americans are successful, a stereotype that masks huge ethnic differences. Look at the poverty rate of Asian Americans shown on Table 12.1. Although it is less than that of any other minority group shown on this table, it means that over a million Asian Americans live in poverty. Their poverty is not evenly distributed: Poverty is unusual among Chinese and Japanese Americans, but it clusters among Americans from Southeast Asia.

Reasons for Success The general success of Asian Americans can be traced to three major factors: family life, educational achievement, and assimilation into mainstream culture.

Of all ethnic groups, including whites, Asian American children are the most likely to grow up with two parents and the least likely to be born to a single mother (Lee 1998; *Statistical Abstract* 2002:Table 74). Most grow up in close-knit families that stress self-discipline, thrift, and hard work (Suzuki 1985; Bell 1991). This early socialization provides strong impetus for the other two factors.

The second factor is their high rate of college graduation. As Table 12.2 on page 345 shows, 44 percent of Asian Americans complete college. To realize how stunning this is, compare this with the other groups shown on this table. Their educational achievement, in turn, opens doors to economic success.

Assimilation, the third factor, is indicated by several measures. With about two of five marrying someone of another racial-ethnic group, Asian Americans have the highest intermarriage rate of any group. They also are the most likely to live in integrated neighborhoods (Lee 1998). Japanese Americans, the financially most successful of Asian Americans, are the most assimilated (Bell 1991; Schaefer 2000). About 73 percent say that their best friend is not a Japanese American.

Asian Americans are becoming more prominent in politics. With more than half of its citizens being Asian American, Hawaii has elected Asian American governors and sent several Asian American senators to Washington, including the two now serving there (Lee 1998, *Statistical Abstract* 2000:Table 25; 2002 election results). The first Asian American governor outside of Hawaii is Gary Locke, who in 1996 was elected governor of Washington, a state in which Asian Americans make up less than 6 percent of the population. Locke was re-elected in 2000.

Native Americans

> "I don't go so far as to think that the only good Indians are dead Indians, but I believe nine out of ten are—and I shouldn't inquire too closely in the case of the tenth. The most vicious cowboy has more moral principle than the average Indian."
>
> —Teddy Roosevelt, 1886
> President of the United States, 1901–1909

Diversity of Groups This quote provides insight into the rampant racism of previous generations. Yet, still today, thanks to countless grade B Westerns, some Americans hold stereotypes of Native Americans who lived on the frontier. They see them as wild, uncivilized savages, a single group of people subdivided into separate tribes. The European immigrants to the Colonies, however, encountered diverse groups of people with a variety of cultures—from nomadic hunters and gatherers to people living in wooden houses in settled agricultural communities. Altogether, they spoke over 700 languages (Schaefer 2000). Each group had its own norms and values—and the usual ethnocentric pride in its own culture. Consider what happened in 1744 when the colonists of Virginia offered college scholarships for "savage lads." The Iroquois replied:

> "Several of our young people were formerly brought up at the colleges of Northern Provinces. They were instructed in all your sciences. But when they came back to us, they were bad runners, ignorant of every means of living in the woods, unable to bear either cold or hunger, knew neither how to build a cabin, take a deer, or kill an enemy. . . . They were totally good for nothing."
>
> They added, "If the English gentlemen would send a dozen or two of their children to Onondaga, the great Council would take care of their education, bring them up in really what was the best manner and make men of them." (Nash 1974; in McLemore 1994)

Native Americans, who numbered between 5 and 10 million, had no immunity to the diseases the Europeans brought with them. With deaths due to disease—and warfare, a much lesser cause—their number was reduced to about *one-twentieth* its original size. A hundred years ago, the Native American population reached a low point of a half million. Native Americans, who now number about 2 million (see Figure 12.5 on page 341), speak 150 different languages. Like Latinos and Asian Americans, they do not think of themselves as a single people that justifies a single label.

From Treaties to Genocide and Population Transfer At first, relations between the European settlers and the Native Americans were by and large peaceful. The Native Americans accommodated the strangers, as there was plenty of land for both. As wave after wave of settlers continued to arrive, however, Pontiac, an Ottawa chief, saw the future—and didn't like it. He convinced several tribes to unite in an effort to push the Europeans into the sea. He almost succeeded, but failed when the English were reinforced by fresh troops (McLemore 1994).

The Native Americans stood in the way of the U.S. government's westward expansion. To seize their lands, the government followed a policy of genocide, *later replaced by* population transfer. *This woodcut by T. DeThulstrup, depicting an attack on a Sioux village by the U.S. Cavalry, appeared in* Harpers Weekly *in 1885.*

A pattern of deception evolved. The U.S. government would make treaties to buy some of a tribe's land, with the promise to honor forever the tribe's right to what it had not sold. European immigrants, who continued to pour into the United States, would disregard these boundaries. The tribes would resist, with death tolls on both sides. Washington would then intervene—not to enforce the treaty, but to force the tribe off its lands. In its relentless drive westward, the U.S. government embarked on a policy of genocide. It assigned the U.S. cavalry the task of "pacification," which translates as slaughtering Native Americans who "stood in the way" of this territorial expansion.

The acts of cruelty perpetrated by the Europeans against Native Americans appear endless, but two were especially grisly. The first was the distribution of blankets contaminated with smallpox—under the guise of a peace offering. The second was the Trail of Tears, a forced march of a thousand miles from the Carolinas and Georgia to Oklahoma. Fifteen thousand Cherokees were forced to make this midwinter march in light clothing. Conditions were so bad that 4,000 died. The symbolic end to Native American resistance came in 1890 with a massacre at Wounded Knee, South Dakota. Of 350 men, women, and children, the U.S. cavalry gunned down 300 and buried them in a mass grave (Thornton 1987; Lind 1995; Johnson 1998). These acts took place after the U.S. government changed its policy from genocide to population transfer and had begun to confine Native Americans to specified areas called *reservations.*

The Invisible Minority and Self-Determination Native Americans can truly be called the invisible minority. Because about half live in rural areas and one-third in just three states—Oklahoma, California, and Arizona—most other Americans are hardly conscious of a Native American presence in the United States. The isolation of about half of Native Americans on reservations further reduces their visibility (*Statistical Abstract* 2000:Table 43; 2002:Table 36).

The systematic attempts of European Americans to destroy the Native Americans' way of life and their resettlement onto reservations continue to have deleterious effects. Table 12.1 on page 345 shows their high rates of unemployment and of poverty. Their rate of suicide is the highest of any racial-ethnic group (Wallace et al. 1996), while their life expectancy is lower than that of the nation as a whole (U.S. Department of Health and Human Services 1990; Lester 1997). Table 12.2 on page 345 shows that their education also lags behind most groups; Only 13 percent graduate from college.

These negative conditions are the consequence of Anglo domination. In the 1800s, U.S. courts ruled that Native Americans did not own the land on which they had been

pan-Indianism a movement that focuses on common elements in the cultures of Native Americans in order to develop a cross-tribal self-identity and to work toward the welfare of all Native Americans

settled and had no right to develop its resources. Native Americans were made wards of the state and treated like children by the Bureau of Indian Affairs (Mohawk 1991). Then, in the 1960s, Native Americans won a series of legal victories that restored both their control over the land and their right to determine economic policy. As a result, many Native American tribes have opened businesses on their lands—ranging from industrial parks serving metropolitan areas to fish canneries.

It is the casinos, though, that have attracted the most attention. In 1988, the federal government passed a law that allowed Native Americans to operate gambling establishments on reservations. About half of the nation's 340 or so tribes opened casinos, which generate about $13 billion a year (Barlett and Steele 2002). Some tribes have struck it rich. The Oneida tribe of New York has only 1,000 members. Its casino nets $232,000 a year for each man, woman, and child (Peterson 2003). This huge amount, however, pales in comparison with that of the Pequot of Connecticut. With only 310 members, they bring in more than $2 million a day (Zielbauer 2000). Incredibly, one tribe has only *one* member: She has her own casino (Barlett and Steele 2002).

A highly controversial issue is *separatism.* Because Native Americans were independent peoples when the Europeans arrived and they never willingly joined the United States, many tribes maintain the right to remain separate from the U.S. government and U.S. society. The chief of the Onondaga tribe in New York, a member of the Iroquois Federation, summarizes the issue this way:

> For the whole history of the Iroquois, we have maintained that we are a separate nation. We have never lost a war. Our government still operates. We have refused the U.S. government's reorganization plans for us. We have kept our language and our traditions, and when we fly to Geneva to UN meetings, we carry Hau de no sau nee passports. We made some treaties that lost some land, but that also confirmed our separate-nation status. That the U.S. denies all this doesn't make it any less the case. (Mander 1992)

One of the most significant changes is **pan-Indianism.** This emphasis on common elements that run through Native American cultures is an attempt to develop an identity that goes beyond the tribe. Pan-Indianism ("We are all Indians") is a remarkable example of the plasticity of ethnicity. An identity originally imposed by Anglos replaces identities connected with tribes. As sociologist Irwin Deutscher (2002:61) puts it, "The peoples who have accepted the larger definition of who they are, have, in fact, little else in common with each other than the stereotypes of the dominant group which labels them."

Whether Native Americans wish to work together as in pan-Indianism or to stress separatism and to identify solely with their own tribe, to assimilate into the dominant culture or to remain apart from it, to move to cities or to remain on reservations, to operate casinos or to engage only in traditional activities—"Such decisions must be ours," say the Native Americans. "We are sovereign, and we will not take orders from the victors of past wars."

Looking Toward the Future

Back in 1903, sociologist W.E.B. Du Bois said, "The problem of the twentieth century is the problem of the color line—the relation of the darker to the lighter races of men." Incredibly, a hundred years later, the color line remains one of the most volatile topics facing the nation. From time to time, the color line takes on a different complexity, as with the war on terrorism and the corresponding discrimination directed against people of Middle Eastern descent.

In another hundred years, will yet another sociologist lament that the color of people's skin still affects human relationships? Given our past, it seems that although racial-ethnic walls will diminish, even crumble at some points, the color line is not likely to disappear. Two issues we are currently grappling with are immigration and affirmative action.

The Immigration Debate

Throughout its history, the United States has both welcomed immigration and feared its consequences. The gates opened wide (numerically, if not in attitude) for a wave of immigrants in the late 1800s and early 1900s. During the past 20 years, a second wave of immigration has brought close to a million new residents to the United States each year. Today, more immigrants (31 million) live in the United States than at any time in the country's history (*Statistical Abstract* 1989:Table 46; 2002:Tables 5, 41). Unlike the first wave, which was almost exclusively from western Europe, this second wave is more diverse. In fact, it is changing the U.S. racial-ethnic mix. If current trends in immigration (and birth) persist, in about 50 years the "average" American will trace his or her ancestry to Africa, Asia, South America, the Pacific Islands, the Middle East—to almost anywhere but white Europe. This change is discussed in the Cultural Diversity box on the next page.

In some states, the future is arriving much sooner than this. In California, racial-ethnic minorities already constitute the majority. California has 18 million minorities and 16 million whites (*Statistical Abstract* 2002:Table 23). Californians who request new telephone service from Pacific Bell can speak to customer service representatives in Spanish, Korean, Vietnamese, Mandarin, Cantonese—or in English.

As in the past, there is concern that "too many" immigrants will change the character of the United States. "Throughout the history of American immigration," write sociologists Alejandro Portés and Ruben Rumbaut (1990), "a consistent thread has been the fear that the 'alien element' would somehow undermine the institutions of the country and would lead it down the path of disintegration and decay." A hundred years ago, the widespread fear was that the immigrants from southern Europe, then arriving in huge numbers, would bring communism with them. Today, some fear that Spanish-speaking immigrants threaten the primacy of the English language. In addition, the age-old fear that immigrants will take jobs away from native-born Americans remains strong. Finally, minority groups that struggled for political representation fear that newer groups will gain political power at their expense.

Affirmative Action

The role of affirmative action in our multicultural society lies at the center of a national debate about race and ethnic relations. In this policy, initiated by President Kennedy in 1961, goals based on race (and sex) are used in hiring, promotion, and college admission. Sociologist Barbara Reskin (1998) examined the results of affirmative action. In agreement with earlier studies (Badgett and Hartmann 1995), she concluded that although it is difficult to separate the results of affirmative action from economic booms and busts and the greater numbers of women in the work force, affirmative action has had a modest impact.

The results may have been modest, but the reactions to this program have been anything but modest. Affirmative action has been at the center of controversy for more than a generation. Liberals, both white and minority, say that this program is the most direct way to level the playing field of economic opportunity. If whites are passed over, this is an unfortunate cost we must pay if we are to make up for past discrimination. Conservatives, in contrast, both white and minority, agree that opportunity should be open to all, but claim that putting race (or sex) ahead of an individual's training and ability to perform a job is reverse discrimination. Because of their race (or sex), qualified people who had nothing to do with past inequity are discriminated against. They add that affirmative action stigmatizes the people who benefit from it, because it suggests that they hold their jobs because of race (or sex), rather than merit.

CULTURAL DIVERSITY in the UNITED STATES

Glimpsing the Future: The Shifting U.S. Racial-Ethnic Mix

During the next twenty-five years, the population of the United States is expected to grow by about 22 percent. To see what the U.S. population will look like in twenty-five years, can we simply multiply the current racial-ethnic mix by 22 percent? The answer is a resounding no. As you can see from Figure 12.11, some groups will grow much more than others, giving us a different-looking United States. Some of the changes in the U.S. racial-ethnic mix will be dramatic. In twenty-five years, one of every nineteen Americans is expected to have an Asian background, and one of every six a Latino background.

Two basic causes underlie this fundamental shift: immigration and birth rates. By far, immigration is the more important. The racial-ethnic groups have different rates of immigration and birth rates, and this will change their proportions of the U.S. population. You can see how the proportion of non-Hispanic whites is expected to shrink, that of Native Americans to remain the same, and that of African Americans to increase slightly. With both vast immigration and higher-than-average birth rates, in fifty years almost one of four Americans is expected to be of Latino ancestry.

For Your CONSIDERATION

This shifting racial-ethnic mix is one of the most significant events occurring in the United States. To better understand its implications, apply the three theoretical perspectives.

Use the conflict perspective to identify the groups likely to be threatened by this change. Over what resources are struggles likely to develop? What impact do you think this changing mix might have on European Americans? On Latinos? On African Americans? On Asian Americans? On Native Americans? What changes in immigration laws (or their enforcement) can you anticipate?

To apply the symbolic interactionist perspective, consider how groups might perceive one another differently as their proportion of the population changes.

To apply the functionalist perspective, try to determine how each racial-ethnic group will benefit from this changing mix. How will other parts of society (such as businesses) benefit? What dysfunctions can you anticipate?

Figure 12.11 Projections of the Racial-Ethnic Makeup of the U.S. Population

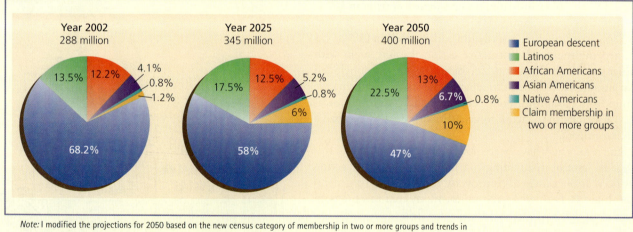

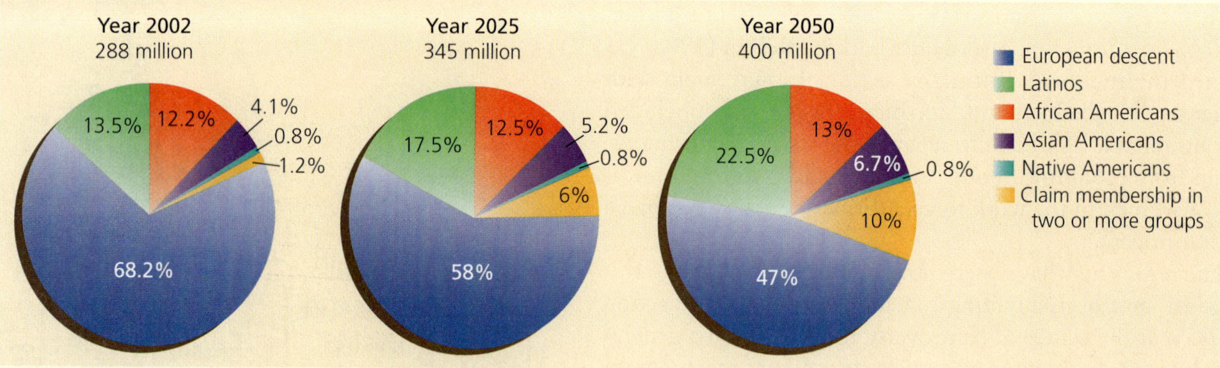

Note: I modified the projections for 2050 based on the new census category of membership in two or more groups and trends in interethnic marriage.

Sources: By the author. Based on *Statistical Abstract* 2002:Table 16; Bernstein and Bergman 2003.

This national debate crystallized with a series of controversial rulings. One of the most significant was *Proposition 209,* a 1996 amendment to the California state constitution. This amendment banned preferences to minorities and women in hiring, promotion, and college admissions. Despite appeals by a coalition of civil rights groups, the U.S. Supreme Court upheld this California law.

A second significant ruling was made in 2003, in response to complaints from white applicants who had been denied admission to the University of Michigan. They claimed that they were discriminated against because underrepresented minorities were given extra consideration. The Court's ruling was ambiguous. The goal of racial diversity in a student body is laudable, the Court ruled, and universities can give minorities an edge in admissions. Race, however, can only be a "plus factor." There must be, in the Court's words, "a meaningful individualized review of applicants." Mechanical systems, such as automatically giving extra points because of race, are unconstitutional.

Such a murky message leaves university officials—and, by extension, those in business and other public and private agencies—scratching their heads. Trying to bring about racial diversity is constitutional, but using quotas and mechanical systems is not. With the Court providing no specific guidelines to bring about affirmative action and its University of Michigan ruling open to different interpretations, we obviously have not yet heard the final word from the U.S. Supreme Court. This issue of the proper role of affirmative action in a multicultural society is likely to remain center stage for quite some time.

The United States is the most racially-ethnically diverse society in the world. This can be our central strength, with our many groups working together to build a harmonious society, a stellar example for the world. Or it can be our Achilles heel, with us breaking into feuding groups, a Balkanized society that marks an ill-fitting end to a grand social experiment. Our reality will probably fall somewhere between these extremes.

Toward a True Multicultural Society

The United States has the potential to become a society in which racial-ethnic groups not only coexist, but also respect one another—and thrive—as they work together for mutually beneficial goals. In a true multicultural society, the minority groups that make up the United States will participate fully in the nation's social institutions while maintaining their cultural integrity. To reach this goal will require that we understand that "the biological differences that divide one race from another add up to a drop in the genetic ocean." For a long time, we have given racial categories an importance they never merited. Now we need to figure out how to reduce them to the irrelevance they deserve. In short, we need to make real the abstraction called equality that we profess to believe (Cose 2000).

SUMMARY and REVIEW

Laying the Sociological Foundation

How is race both a reality and a myth?

In the sense that different groups inherit distinctive physical traits, race is a reality. There is, however, no agreement regarding what constitutes a particular race, or even how many races there are. In the sense of one race being superior to another and of there being pure races, race is a myth. The *idea* of race is powerful, shaping basic relationships among people. Pp. 324–326.

How do race and ethnicity differ?

Race refers to inherited biological characteristics; **ethnicity**, to cultural ones. Members of ethnic groups identify with one another on the basis of common ancestry and cultural heritage. Pp. 326–327.

What are minority and dominant groups?

Minority groups are people who are singled out for unequal treatment by members of the **dominant group**, the group with more power, privilege, and social status. Minorities originate with migration or the expansion of political boundaries. Pp. 327–329.

What heightens ethnic identity, and what is "ethnic work"?

A group's size, power, physical characteristics, and amount of discrimination heighten or reduce ethnic identity. **Ethnic work** is the process of constructing an ethnic identity. For people with strong ties to their culture of origin, ethnic work involves enhancing and maintaining group distinctions. For those without a firm ethnic identity, ethnic work is an attempt to recover one's ethnic heritage. P. 329.

Are prejudice and discrimination the same thing?

Prejudice is an attitude, **discrimination** an act. Prejudice is extensive, and even minorities tend to internalize the dominant racial-ethnic norms. Pp. 330–332.

How do individual and institutional discrimination differ?

Individual discrimination is the negative treatment of one person by another, while **institutional discrimination** is negative treatment that is built into social institutions. Institutional discrimination often occurs without the awareness of either the perpetrator or the object of discrimination. Health care after heart attacks is one example. Pp. 333–334.

Theories of Prejudice

How do psychologists explain prejudice?

Psychological theories of prejudice stress **authoritarian** personalities and frustration displaced toward **scapegoats.** Pp. 334–335.

How do sociologists explain prejudice?

Sociological theories focus on how different social environments increase or decrease prejudice. Functionalists stress the benefits and costs that come from discrimination. Conflict theorists look at how the groups in power exploit racial and ethnic divisions in order to hold down wages and otherwise maintain power. Symbolic interactionists stress how labels create **selective perception** and self-fulfilling prophecies. Pp. 335–337.

Global Patterns of Intergroup Relations

What are the major patterns of minority and dominant group relations?

Beginning with the least humane, they are **genocide, population transfer, internal colonialism, segregation, assimilation,** and **multiculturalism (pluralism).** Pp. 337–340.

Race and Ethnic Relations in the United States

What are the major ethnic groups in the United States?

From largest to smallest, the major ethnic groups are European Americans, Latinos, African Americans, Asian Americans, and Native Americans. P. 340.

What are some issues in race-ethnic relations and characteristics of minority groups today?

Latinos are divided by social class and country of origin. African Americans are increasingly divided into middle and lower classes, with two sharply contrasting worlds of experience. On many measures, Asian Americans are better off than white Americans, but their well-being varies with country of origin. For Native Americans, the primary issues are poverty, nationhood, and settling treaty obligations. The overarching issue for minorities is overcoming discrimination. Pp. 340–354.

Looking Toward the Future

What main issues dominate race-ethnic relations?

The main issues are immigration, affirmative action, and how to develop a true multicultural society. The answers affect our future. Pp. 354–357.

Where can I read more on this topic?

Suggested Readings for this chapter are at the back of this book.

THINKING Critically ABOUT CHAPTER 12

1. How many races do your friends think there are? Do they think that one race is superior to the others? What do you think their reaction would be to the sociological position that racial categories are primarily social?
2. A hundred years ago, sociologist W.E.B. Du Bois said, "The problem of the twentieth century is the problem of the color line—the relation of the darker to the lighter races of men." Why do you think that the color line remains one of the most volatile topics facing the nation?
3. If you were appointed head of the U.S. Civil Service Commission, what policies would you initiate in order to reduce racial-ethnic strife in the United States? Be ready to explain the sociological principles that might give your proposals a high chance of success.

ADDITIONAL RESOURCES for This Chapter

www.ablongman.com/henslin7e

- *Content Select* Research Database for Sociology, with suggested key terms and annotated references
- Link to 2000 Census, with activities
- Flashcards of key terms and concepts
- Practice Tests
- Weblinks
- Interactive Maps

Chapter

13

The Elderly

Alice Neel,
The Soyer Brothers, 1973

Chapter Outline

In 1928, while working on his Ph.D. in anthropology, Charles Hart did fieldwork with the Tiwi, who lived on an island off the northern coast of Australia. Because every Tiwi belonged to a clan, they assigned Hart to the bird (Jabijabui) clan and told him that a particular woman was his mother. Hart described the woman as "toothless, almost blind, withered." He added that she was "physically quite revolting and mentally rather senile." He then recounted this remarkable event:

> [T]oward the end of my time on the islands an incident occurred that surprised me because it suggested that some of them had been taking my presence in the kinship system much more seriously than I had thought. I was approached by a group of about eight or nine senior men, all of whom I knew. They were all senior members of the Jabijabui clan and they had decided among themselves that the time had come to get rid of the decrepit old woman who had first called me son and whom I now called mother. As I knew, they said, it was Tiwi custom, when an old woman became too feeble to look after herself, to "cover her up." This could only be done by her sons and brothers and all of them had to agree beforehand, since once it was done, they did not want any dissension among the brothers or clansmen, as that might lead to a feud. My "mother" was now completely blind, she was constantly falling over logs or into fires, and they, her senior clansmen, were in agreement that she would be better out of the way. Did I agree?
>
> I already knew about "covering up." The Tiwi, like many other hunting and gathering peoples, sometimes got rid of their ancient and decrepit females. The method was to dig a hole in the ground in some lonely place, put the old woman in the hole and fill it in with earth until only her head was showing. Everybody went away for a day or two and then went back to the hole to discover to their surprise, that the old woman was dead, having been too feeble to raise her arms from the earth. Nobody had "killed" her; her death in Tiwi eyes was a natural one. She had been alive when her relatives last saw her. I had never seen it done, though I knew it was the custom, so I asked my brothers if it was necessary for me to attend the "covering up."

The Tiwi, like many other hunting and gathering *peoples, sometimes got* rid of their ancient and decrepit females.

They said no and that they would do it, but only after they had my agreement. Of course I agreed, and a week or two later we heard in our camp that my "mother" was dead, and we wailed and put on the trimmings of mourning. (Hart and Pilling 1970:154)

Aging in Global Perspective

We won't deal with the question of whether it was moral or ethical for Hart to agree that the old woman should be "covered up." What is of interest for our purposes is how the Tiwi treated their frail elderly—or, more specifically, their frail *female* elderly. You probably noticed that the Tiwi "covered up" only old women. As noted in Chapter 11, females are discriminated against throughout the world. As this case makes evident, in some places that discrimination extends even to death.

Every society must deal with the problem of people growing old, and of some becoming very frail. Although few societies choose to bury old people alive, all societies must decide how to allocate limited resources among their citizens. As the percentage of the population that is elderly increases, which is happening in many nations, those decisions generate tensions between the generations.

The Social Construction of Aging

The way the Tiwi treated frail elderly women reflects one extreme of how societies cope with aging. Another extreme, one that reflects an entirely different attitude, is illustrated by the Abkhasians, an agricultural people who live in a mountainous region of Georgia, a republic of the former Soviet Union. Rather than "covering up" their elderly, the Abkhasians pay them high respect and look to them for guidance. They would no more dispense with one of their elderly in this manner than we would "cover up" a sick child in our culture.

The man riding the horse is Temir Tarba, who was 100 years old when the photo was taken. As discussed in the text, the Abkhasians have an extraordinarily large number of elderly, but due to a lack of records, there are questions about their exact age.

The Abkhasians may be the longest-lived people on earth. Many claim to live past 100—some beyond 120 and even 130 (Benet 1971). Although it is difficult to document the accuracy of these claims (Haslick 1974; Harris 1990), government records indicate that an extraordinary number of Abkhasians do live to a very old age.

Three main factors appear to account for their long lives. The first is their diet, which consists of little meat, much fresh fruit, vegetables, garlic, goat cheese, cornmeal, buttermilk, and wine. The second is their lifelong physical activity. They do slow down after age 80, but even after the age of 100 they still work about four hours a day. The third factor—a highly developed sense of community—goes to the very heart of the Abkhasian culture. From childhood, each individual is integrated into a primary group, and remains so throughout life. There is no such thing as a nursing home, nor do the elderly live alone. Because they continue to work and contribute to the group's welfare, the elderly aren't a burden to anyone. They don't vegetate, nor do they feel the need to "fill time" with bingo and shuffleboard. In short, the elderly feel no sudden rupture between what they "were" and what they "are."

The examples of the Tiwi and the Abkhasians reveal an important sociological principle—that, like gender, aging is *socially constructed.* That is, nothing in the nature of aging summons forth any particular set of attitudes. Rather, attitudes toward the aged are rooted in society and, therefore, differ from one social group to another. As we shall see, even the age at which people are considered old depends not on biology, but on culture.

Industrialization and the Graying of the Globe

As noted in previous chapters, industrialization is a worldwide trend. The higher standard of living that it brings includes more food, better public health practices (especially a purer water supply), and more effective ways of fighting the diseases that kill

Central to a group's culture are ways of viewing reality. Living for centuries in isolation on Bathurst and Melville Islands off the northern coast of Australia, the Tiwi, featured in the vignette on "covering up," developed a unique culture. Shown here is Wurabuti, who has prepared himself to lead his uncle's funeral dance. To be certain that his uncle's ghost will not recognize him, Wurabuti is wearing a "shirt" painted with ocher and clay, a topknot of cockatoo feathers, and a beard of goose feathers.

children. Consequently, when a country industrializes, more of its people live longer and reach older ages. The Social Map illustrates this principle.

You can see that the industrialized countries have the highest percentage of elderly. The range among nations is broad, from just 1 of 48 citizens in nonindustrialized Sudan to *nine* times higher than this, to almost 1 of 5 in post-industrial Italy (*Statistical Abstract* 2002:Table 1309). The graying of the globe is so new that *two-thirds of all people who have ever passed age 50 in the history of the world are alive today* (Zaslow 2003).

As a nation's elderly population increases, so, too, does the bill its younger citizens pay to provide for their needs. This bill has become a major social issue. Although Americans complain that Social Security taxes are too high, the U.S. rate of 15.3 percent is comparatively low. Belgian workers are hit the hardest; they pay 56 percent of their wages into social security. At about 50 percent, Hungary, France, Sweden, and Germany follow closely behind (*Statistical Abstract* 2002:Tables 517, 1330). People in the Least Industrialized Nations pay no social security taxes. There, families are expected to take care of their own elderly, with no help from the government.

Figure 13.1 The Graying of the Globe

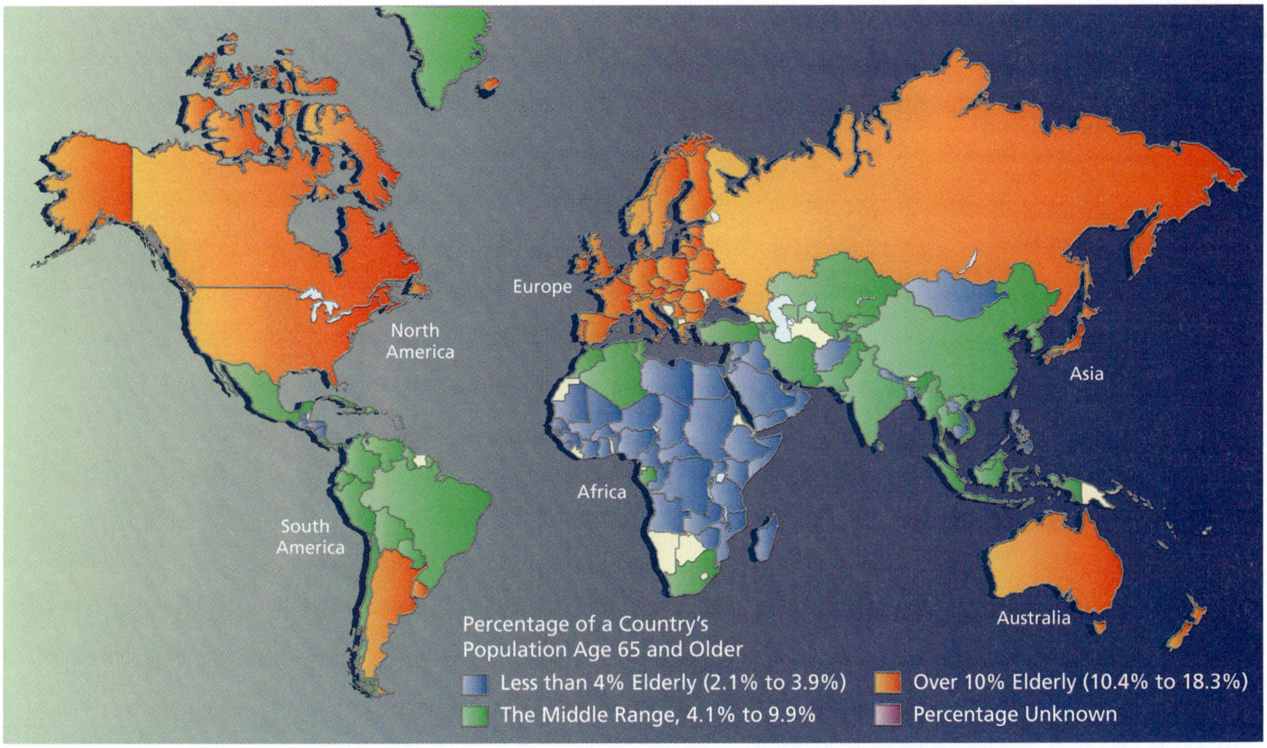

Source: By the author. Based on *Statistical Abstract* 2002:Table 1309.

life expectancy the number of years that an average person at any age, including newborns, can expect to live

graying of America refers to the growing percentage of older people in the U.S. population

With industrialization continuing without letup and with the proportion of the elderly population continuing to increase, future liabilities for care of the elderly have alarmed analysts. An outstanding case is Germany. By the year 2020, about 30 percent of Germans will be over the age of 60. In order to continue to furnish them the high level of care that they now receive, Germany will have to tax nearly *all* the income of its future workers (Wessel 1995). Obviously, this is impossible, but no one has yet come up with a workable solution to the problem.

The Graying of America

As Figure 13.2 illustrates, the United States is part of this global trend. This figure shows how U.S. **life expectancy**, the number of years people can expect to live, has increased since 1900. To me, and perhaps to you, it is startling to realize that a hundred years ago the average American could not even expect to see age 50. Since then, we've added about *30* years to our life expectancy, and Americans born today can expect to live into their 70s or 80s.

The term **graying of America** refers to this increasing percentage of older people in the U.S. population. As Figure 13.3 shows, in 1900 only 4 percent of Americans were age 65 and older. Today almost 13 percent are. The average 65-year-old can expect to live another eighteen years (*Statistical Abstract* 2002:Table 93). U.S. society has become so "gray" that, as Figure 13.4 shows, the median age has almost *doubled* since 1850. Today there are seven million *more* elderly Americans than there are teenagers (*Statistical Abstract* 2002:Table 12). Despite this change, as Table 13.1 shows, on a global scale Americans rank fifteenth in life expectancy.

As anyone who has ever visited Florida has noticed, the elderly population is not evenly distributed around the country. (As Jerry Seinfeld sardonically noted, "There's a law that when you get old you've got to move to Florida.") The Social Map on page 366 shows how uneven this distribution is expected to be in a couple of decades.

Race-Ethnicity and Aging

Just as the states have different percentages of elderly, so do the racial-ethnic groups that make up the United States. As you can see from

Figure 13.2 U.S. Life Expectancy by Year of Birth

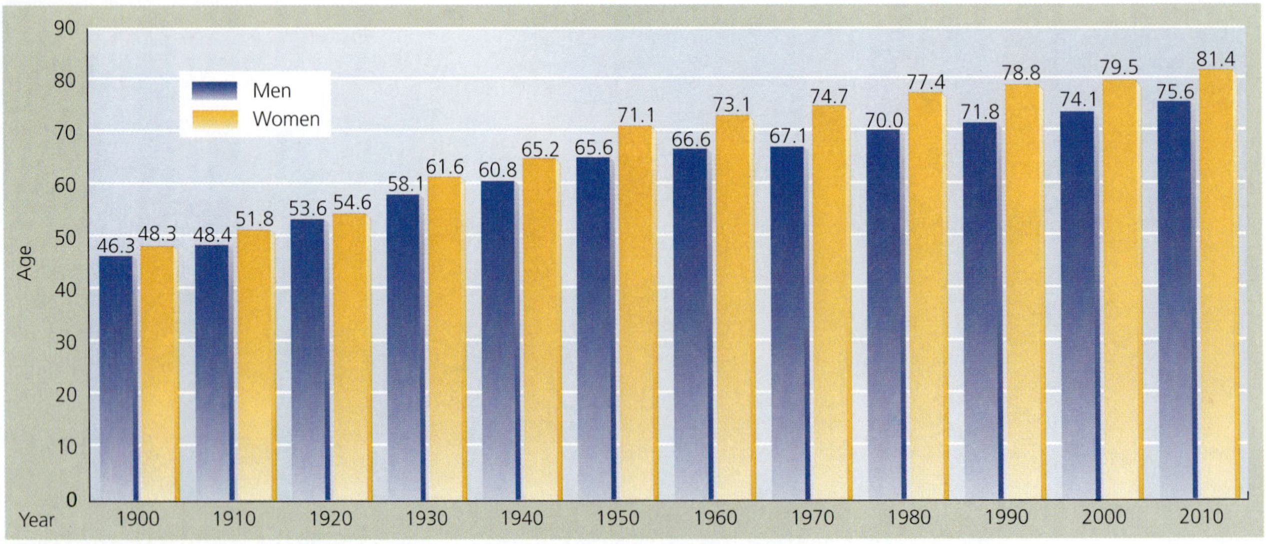

Sources: By the author. Based on *Historical Statistics of the United States, Colonial Times to 1970,* Bicentennial Edition, Part I, Series B, 107–115; *Statistical Abstract* 2002:Table 91.

Figure 13.3 The Graying of America: Americans Age 65 and Older

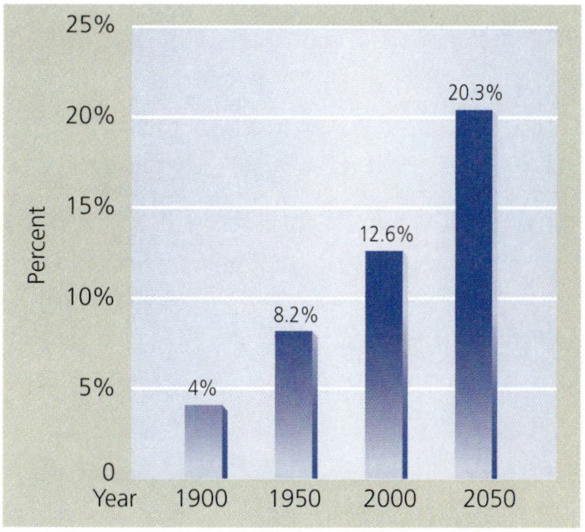

Source: By the author. Based on *Statistical Abstract* 2002:Table 13, and earlier years.

Figure 13.4 The Median Age of the U.S. Population

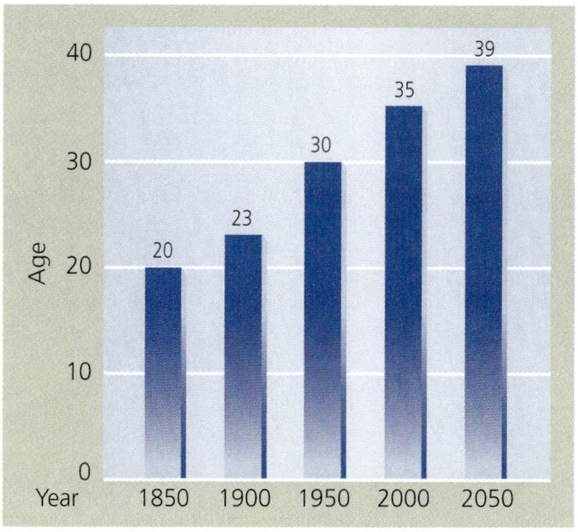

Source: By the author. Based on *Statistical Abstract* 2000:Table 14; 2002:Table 13, and earlier years.

Table 13.2, whites have the largest percentage of elderly and Latinos the smallest. The difference is so great that the proportion of elderly whites (13.6 percent) is more than twice that of Latinos (6.3 percent). The main reason that there is such a small percentage of older Latinos is the great numbers of younger Latinos who are migrating to the United States. Differences in cultural attitudes about aging, family relationships, work histories, and health practices will be important areas of sociological investigation in coming years.

Although more people are living to old age, the maximum length of life possible, the **life span,** has not increased. Experts disagree, however, on what that maximum is. It is at least 122, for this was the well-documented age of Jeanne Louise Calment of France at her death in 1998. If the reports on the Abkhasians are correct (and this is a matter of controversy), the human life span may exceed even this number by a comfortable margin. It is also likely that advances in genetics may extend the human life span. Some geneticists even think that we may be able to double it (Recer 2000).

Table 13.1 U.S. Life Expectancy in Global Perspective

World Rank	Country	Life Expectancy at Birth	World Rank	Country	Life Expectancy at Birth
1	Hong Kong	82.8	9	Sweden	78.5
2	Japan	80.8	10	Holland	78.4
3	Australia	79.9	11	Switzerland	78.1
4	Canada	79.6	12	Belgium	78.0
5	Italy	79.1	13	Great Britain	77.8
6	France	78.9	14	Germany	77.6
7	Spain	78.9	15	United States	77.3
8	Greece	78.6			

Source: Statistical Abstract 1997:Table 1336; 2002:Table 1312.

life span the maximum length of life of a species; for humans, the longest that a human has ever lived

Figure 13.5 As Florida Goes, So Goes the Nation: The Year 2025

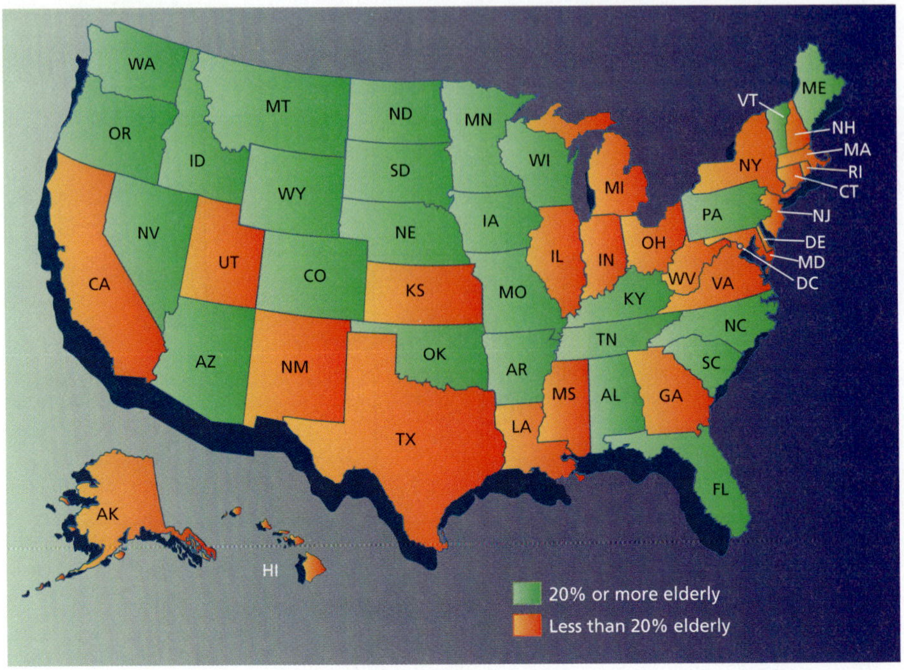

Note: The growing proportion of the elderly in the U.S. population is destined to have profound effects on U.S. society. By the year 2025, one-fifth of the population of 27 states is expected to be 65 or older. Today, at 18 percent, only Florida comes close to this.
Source: By the author. Based on U.S. Bureau of the Census, 1996, U.S. Department of Commerce, PPL-47; *Statistical Abstract* 2002:Table 21.

Table 13.2 Race-Ethnicity and Aging

What Percentage of These Groups Are Elderly?

	Age			
	65–74	75–84	85+	Total 65 and Over
Whites	6.8%	4.9%	1.9%	13.6%
African Americans	4.8%	2.7%	1.0%	8.5%
Asian Americans	4.7%	2.6%	0.8%	8.3%
Native Americans	4.0%	2.4%	1.1%	7.5%
Latinos	3.6%	2.0%	0.7%	6.3%
U.S. Average	6.4%	4.5%	1.7%	12.6%

Source: Statistical Abstract 2002:Table 19.

The Symbolic Interactionist Perspective

To better understand how aging is socially constructed, let's look beyond biology to some of the symbols associated with age. How does culture signal to us that we are "old"? How do stereotypes and the mass media affect our perceptions of aging?

Deciding When You Are Old

Charlotte Benkner of Lima, Ohio, who was born Nov. 16, 1889, in Germany, is the world's oldest living person whose age can be authenticated. She lives in a nursing home with her 99-year-old sister. The world's record for age that has been documented by a birth certificate was held by Jeanne Calment of France, who died in 1997 at the age of 122.

You probably can remember when you thought that a 12-year-old was "old"—and anyone older than that, beyond reckoning. You probably were 5 or 6 at the time. Similarly, to a 12-year-old, someone of 21 seems "old." To someone who is 21, 30 may mark the point at which one is no longer "young," and 40 may seem very old. As people add years, "old" gradually recedes further and further from the self. To people who turn 40, 50 seems old; at 50, the late 60s look old—not the early 60s, for the passing of years seems to accelerate as we age, and at 50 the 60s don't seem so far away.

In Western culture, most people have difficulty applying the label "old" to themselves. In the typical case, they have become used to what they see in the mirror. The changes have taken place gradually, and each change, if it has not exactly been taken in stride, has been accommodated. Consequently, it comes as a shock to meet a long-lost friend and see how much that person has changed. At class reunions, *each* person can hardly believe how much older *the others* appear!

If there is no single point at which people automatically cross a magical line and become "old," what, then, makes someone "old"? We can point to several factors that spur people to apply the label of old to themselves.

The first factor is *biology*. One person may experience "signs" of aging earlier than others: wrinkles, balding, aches, difficulty in doing something that he or she used to take for granted. Consequently, one person will *feel* "old" at an earlier or later age than others.

A second factor is *personal history* or biography. A woman who gave birth at 16 may have a daughter who in turn has a child at 18, making the woman a biological grandmother at age 34. It is most unlikely that she will begin to play any stereotypical role—spending the day in a rocking chair, for example—but *knowing* that she is a grandmother has an impact on her self-concept. At a minimum, she must *deny* that she is old. An accident that limits someone's mobility may also make that person feel old sooner than others.

Then there is **gender age**, the relative value that a culture places on men's and women's ages. For example, graying hair on men, even some wrinkles, may be seen as signs of "maturity"; on women, those same features may be interpreted as signs of being "old." "Mature" and "old," of course, carry different meanings in Western cultures; the first is desired, the second shunned. Similarly, around the world, most men are able to marry younger spouses than women can. Maria might be an exception and marry Bill, who is fourteen years younger than she. But in most marriages in which there is a fourteen-year age gap, the odds greatly favor the wife being the younger of the pair. Biology, of course, has nothing to do with this socially constructed reality of appearance and gender age.

The fourth factor in deciding when people label themselves as "old" is *timetables,* the signals societies use to inform their members that old age has begun. Since there is no automatic age at which people become "old," these timetables vary around the world. One group may choose a particular birthday, such as the 60th or 65th, to signal the onset of old age. Other groups do not even have birthdays, making such numbers meaningless. In the West, retirement is sometimes a cultural signal of the beginning of old age–which is one reason that some people resist retirement.

What Does Old Age Mean?

To help pinpoint how people's experiences of old age involve factors other than biology, let's look at three cross-cultural examples.

The first example is from the United States. The statement I just made about some groups not celebrating birthdays may have sounded like an exaggeration. Only after they moved to reservations, however, did Native Americans adopt the Anglo custom of counting

gender age the relative value placed on men's and women's ages

When does old age begin? And what activities are appropriate for the elderly? From this photo that I took of Munimah, a 65-year-old bonded laborer in Chennai, India, you can see how culturally relative these questions are. No one in Chennai thinks it is extraordinary that this woman makes her living by carrying heavy rocks all day in the burning, tropical sun. Working next to her in the quarry is her 18-year-old son, who breaks the rocks into the size that his mother carries.

birthdays. For traditional Native Americans today, the signal for old age remains more the inability to perform productive social roles than any particular birthday. Consequently, those unable to continue in these roles tend to think of themselves as old—regardless of their age. In one survey, for instance, a Native American woman who had many disabilities described herself as elderly. She was 37 (Kramer 1992).

Consider this fictionalized conversation between two Tiwi men:

> Bashti looked in envy at Masta. Masta strutted a bit as he noticed Bashti glance his way. He knew what Bashti was thinking. Had he not thought the same just twenty years earlier? Then he had no wife; now he has three. Then he had no grand hut. Now he does, plus one for each wife. Then he had no respect, no power, no wealth. Now he is looked up to by everyone. "Ah, the marvels and beauty of gray hair," Masta thought. Bashti hung his head as he slouched toward the fringe of the group. "But my turn will come. I, too, will grow old," he thought, finding some comfort in his present situation.

Why would a Tiwi man look forward to growing old, something that few people in the United States do? Traditional Tiwi society was a **gerontocracy**, a society run by the elderly. The old men held the power and controlled *everything*. Their power was so inclusive that the old men married *all* the women—both young and old—leaving none for the young men. Only at the age of 40 or so was a man able to marry (Hart and Pilling 1970). (In Tiwi society, females were the pawns, and aging was of no advantage to them. Indeed, in the opening vignette, we saw one of the disadvantages that old age brought to Tiwi women.)

A third example is traditional Eskimo society, which also provides a rich contrast to the postindustrial world.

> Shantu and Wishta fondly kissed their children and grandchildren farewell. Then, sadly, but with resignation at the sacrifice they knew they had to make for their family, they slowly climbed onto the ice floe. The painful goodbyes were made as the large slab of ice inched into the ocean currents. Shantu and Wishta would now starve. But they were old, and their death was necessary, for it reduced the demand on the small group's scarce food supply.
>
> As the younger relatives watched Shantu and Wishta recede into the distance, they knew that their turn to make this sacrifice would come. Each hoped to face it with similar courage.

Growing old in traditional Eskimo society meant a "voluntary" death. Survival in their harsh environment was so precarious that all, except very young children, had to pull their own weight. The food supply was so limited that nothing was left over to give to anyone who could not participate in the closely integrated tasks required for survival.

gerontocracy a society (or some other group) run by the elderly

IN SUM

Symbolic interactionists stress that, by itself, old age has no particular meaning. There is nothing about old age that automatically summons forth responses of honor and respect (as with the Abkhasians), envy (as with the Tiwi males), or resignation (as with the traditional Eskimo). This perspective helps us see the role of culture in the way we view the process of growing old—how the social modifies the biological.

ageism prejudice, discrimination, and hostility directed against people because of their age; can be directed against any age group, including youth

Changing Perceptions of the Elderly

> At first, the audience sat quietly as the developers explained their plans to build a high-rise apartment building. After a while, people began to shift uncomfortably in their seats. Then they began to show open hostility.
>
> "That's too much money to spend on those people," said one.
>
> "You even want them to have a swimming pool?" asked another incredulously.
>
> Finally, one young woman put their attitudes in a nutshell when she asked, "Who wants all those old people around?"

When physician Robert Butler (1975, 1980) heard these responses to plans to build apartments for senior citizens, he began to realize how deep antagonistic feelings against the elderly can run. He coined the term **ageism** to refer to prejudice, discrimination, and hostility directed against people because of their age. Let's see how ageism developed in U.S. society.

Shifting Meanings As we have seen, there is nothing inherent in old age to summon forth any particular attitude, negative or not. Old age may even have had positive meanings in early U.S. society (Cottin 1979; Kart 1990; Clair et al. 1993). In Colonial times, growing old was seen as an accomplishment because so few people made it to old age. With no pensions, the elderly continued to work at jobs that changed little over time. They were viewed as storehouses of knowledge about work skills and about how to live a long life.

The coming of industrialization, however, eroded these bases of respect. With better sanitation and medical care, more people reached old age. No longer was being elderly an honorable distinction. The new forms of mass production made young workers as productive as the elderly. Coupled with mass education, this stripped away the elderly's superior knowledge (Cowgill 1974). In the Cultural Diversity box on the next page, you can see how a similar process is now occurring in China as it, too, industrializes.

PEANUTS® by Charles M. Schulz

Stereotypes, which play such a profound role in social life, are a basic area of sociological investigation. In contemporary society, the mass media are a major source of stereotypes.

CULTURAL DIVERSITY

around the WORLD

China: Changing Sentiment About the Elderly

As she contemplates her future, Zhao Chunlan, a 71-year-old widow, smiles shyly, with evident satisfaction. She has heard about sons abandoning their aged parents. She has even heard whispering about abuse.

But Zhao has no such fears.

It is not that her son is so devoted that he would never swerve from his traditional duty to his mother. Rather, it is a piece of paper that has eased Zhao's mind. Her 51-year-old son has signed a support agreement: He will cook her special meals, take her to medical checkups, even give her the largest room in his house and put the family's color television in it (Sun 1990).

The high status of the elderly in China is famed around the world: They are considered a source of wisdom, given honored seating at both family and public gatherings—even venerated after death in ancestor worship.

Although this outline may represent more ideal than real culture, it appears to generally hold true. However, industrialization, by bringing a longer life expectancy, is tearing at the bonds between generations. So is a national policy that allows each married couple only one child. With fewer young people, the percentage of the population that is over 65 is mushrooming. Already numbering 88 million—7 percent of the population—China's elderly may soar to 40 percent in the next fifty years (Kinsella and Taeuber 1993; *Statistical Abstract* 2002:Tables 1308, 1309).

Because China has no national social security system, children must provide for their elders (Chang 2000). Alarmed by signs that parent-child bonds are weakening, many local officials require adult children to sign support agreements for their aged parents. One province has hit on an ingenious device: In order to get a marriage license, a couple must sign a contract pledging to support their parents after they reach age 60 (Sun 1990). "I'm sure he would do right by me, anyway," says Zhao, "but this way I know he will."

age cohort people born at roughly the same time who pass through the life course together

A basic principle of symbolic interactionism is that people perceive both themselves and others according to the symbols of their culture. Thus, as the meaning of old age was transformed—when it changed from an asset to a liability—not only did younger people come to view the elderly differently, but also the elderly began to perceive themselves in a new light. A sign of how they, too, internalized this shift in meanings is the way people lie about their age: They used to claim they were older than they were, but now they say they are younger than they are (Clair et al. 1993).

Because most U.S. elderly can take care of themselves financially—in fact, many are well-off—the meaning of old age is changing once again. In addition, members of the baby boom generation have now entered their 50s. With their vast numbers and better health and financial strength, they are destined to positively affect our images of the elderly. The next step in this symbolic shift, now in process, is to celebrate old age as a time of renewal—not simply as a period that precedes death, but, rather, as another stage of growth.

The Influence of the Mass Media

In Chapter 3 (pages 76–78), we noted that the mass media help to shape our ideas about both gender and relationships between men and women. As a powerful source of symbols, the media also influence our ideas of the elderly, a topic that is discussed in the Mass Media box on the next page.

The Functionalist Perspective

Functionalists analyze how the parts of society work together. Among the components of society are **age cohorts**, people who were born at roughly the same time and who pass through the life course together. Although

massMEDIA in Social Life

Shaping Our Perceptions of the Elderly

The mass media profoundly influence our lives. What we hear and see on television and in the movies, the songs we listen to, the books and magazines we read—all become part of our world view. Without our knowing it, the media shape our images of people. They influence how we view minorities, the dominant group, men, women, and children, people with disabilities, people from other cultures—and the elderly.

The shaping is subtle, so much so that it is usually beneath our awareness. The elderly, for example, are underrepresented on television and in most popular magazines. The covert message is that the elderly are of little consequence and can be safely ignored. Or consider how the media reflect and reinforce stereotypes of *gender age*. Older male news anchors are likely to be retained, while female anchors who turn the same age are more likely to be transferred to less visible positions. Similarly, in movies older men are more likely to play romantic leads—and opposite much younger rising stars.

Then there is advertising. The American Association of Retired Persons (AARP) points out that television ads often depict the elderly as being feeble or foolish, or as passing their time in rocking chairs (Goldman 1993). The reason for this, claims the AARP, is that younger people dominate advertising firms, and their ads reflect their negative images of older people. They pick out the "worst traits of the group, making everyone believe that old is something you don't want to be."

The message is not lost. As we add years, we go to great lengths to deny that we are growing old. This plays into advertisers' hands, who exploit our fears of losing our youth so they can sell us their hair dyes, skin creams, and other products that supposedly conceal even the appearance of old age. For the same reason, Americans visit plastic surgeons to remove telltale signs of aging.

As discussed in the text, the elderly's affluence is growing. This translates into economic power. It is inevitable, then, that the media's images of the elderly will change. An indication of that change is shown in the photo to the left.

Age is much more than biology. The point at which old age begins, for example, differs from one culture to another. In some cultures, Michael Douglas, 59, would be considered an old man, but he is still portrayed as the romantic lead opposite much younger actresses. Douglas is shown here with his wife, Catherine Zeta-Jones, age 34. Her two recent pregnancies, both occurring in the glare of media spotlight, serve as confirming symbols of her husband's vigor and a public and private denial that he has reached old age.

---

not visible to us, our age cohort affects our lives. For example, if the age cohort nearing retirement is large (a "baby boom" generation), many jobs open at roughly the same time. If it is small (a "baby bust" generation), however, fewer jobs open. Let's look at three theories that focus on how people adjust to retirement.

Disengagement Theory

Elaine Cumming and William Henry (1961) analyzed how society prevents disruption when the elderly leave their positions of responsibility. In what is called **disengagement theory,** they explained how it would be disruptive if the elderly left their positions only when they died or became incompetent. To avoid this, pensions are offered to entice the elderly to hand over their positions to younger people. Retirement (or disengagement), then, is a mutually beneficial agreement between two parts of society. It helps smooth the transition between the generations.

Cumming (1976) also examined disengagement from the individual's perspective. She pointed out that disengagement begins during middle age, long before retirement, when a person senses that the end of life is closer than its start. The individual does not immediately disengage, however, but, realizing that time is limited, begins to assign priority to goals and tasks. Disengagement begins in earnest when children leave home, then increases with retirement and eventually widowhood.

disengagement theory the view that society prevents disruption by having the elderly vacate (or disengage from) their positions of responsibility so the younger generation can step into their shoes

activity theory the view that satisfaction during old age is related to a person's amount and quality of activity

continuity theory the focus of this theory is how people adjust to retirement by continuing aspects of their earlier lives

Evaluation of the Theory Almost from the time it was formulated, disengagement theory came under attack (Hatch 2000). Anthropologist Dorothy Jerrome (1992) points out that it contains an implicit bias against older people—assumptions that the elderly disengage from productive social roles, and then sort of slink into oblivion. Her own research shows that instead of disengaging, the elderly *exchange* one set of roles for another. The new roles, which often center on friendship, are no less satisfying than the earlier roles. They are less visible to researchers, however, who tend to have a youthful orientation—and who show their bias by assuming that productivity is the measure of self-worth.

Retirement, too, is changing. Computers, the Internet, and the new types of work have blurred the dividing line between work and retirement. Less and less does retirement mean to hit a wall and to abruptly stop working. Many workers just slow down. Some continue at their jobs, but put in fewer hours. Others switch careers, even though they are in their 60s. Some may move to a warmer climate, but take their work with them. Many never "retire"—at least not in the sense of sinking into a recliner or being forever on the golf course. If disengagement theory is ever resurrected, it must come to grips with this fundamental change.

Activity Theory

Are retired people more satisfied with life? Are intimate activities more satisfying than formal ones? Such questions are the focus of **activity theory,** which assumes that the more activities elderly people engage in, the more they find life satisfying. Although we could consider this theory from other perspectives, because its focus is how disengagement is functional or dysfunctional, it can be considered from the functionalist perspective.

Evaluation of the Theory The results are mixed. In general, researchers have found that more active people are more satisfied. But not always. A study of retired people in France found that some people are happier when they are more active, others when they are less involved (Keith 1982). Similarly, most people find informal, intimate activities, such as spending time with friends, to be more satisfying than formal activities. But not everyone does. In one study, 2,000 retired U.S. men reported formal activities to be as important as informal ones. Even solitary activities, such as doing home repairs, had about the same impact as intimate activities on these men's life satisfaction (Beck and Page 1988). It is similarly the case with seeing adult children. The amount of interaction with adult children that increases satisfaction with life differs for each person—when, in their words, they see their children "frequently enough" (Hatch 2000).

In short, just counting the amount of interaction or activities of elderly people is simplistic, and this theory, too, has been rejected. If it is ever resurrected, researchers must take into account what activities *mean* to people.

As the numbers of U.S. elderly grow, a new emphasis is being placed on their well-being. Researchers are exploring the elderly's mental and social development, as well as the causes of physical well-being. As research progresses, do you think we will reach the point where the average old person will be in this man's physical condition?

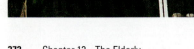

Continuity Theory

Another theory of how people adjust to growing old is **continuity theory.** As its name implies, the focus of this theory is how people adjust to change by continuing certain aspects of their lives, such as roles they are used to or their coping techniques. Researchers have found that people who have multiple roles (wife, author, mother, intimate friend, church member, etc.) are better equipped to handle the changes that growing old entails. They have also found that people from higher social classes have greater resources to meet the challenges of old age, and they adjust better to aging.

Evaluation of the Theory The basic criticism of continuity theory is that it is too broad (Hatch 2000). We all have anchor points based on our experiences, and we all rely on them to make adjustments to the changes we encounter in life. This applies to people of all ages beyond infancy. This theory is really a collection of loosely connected ideas, with no specific application to the elderly.

IN SUM

The *broader* perspective of the functionalists is how its components work together to keep society running smoothly. Although it is inevitable that younger workers replace the elderly, this transition could be disruptive. To entice the elderly out of their positions so younger people can take over, the elderly are offered pensions. Functionalists also use a *narrower* perspective to focus on how the elderly adjust to their retirement. The findings of this narrower perspective are too mixed to be of much value—except that people with better resources (including multiple roles) adjust better to old age.

The theories discussed here were developed when retirement at age 65 was required by law. Today, people can keep their jobs if they want to. Choice, then, needs to be factored into the theories–especially how people reconstruct their identities and come to terms with the new life they choose.

The Conflict Perspective

From the conflict perspective, the guiding principles of social life are power, competition, disequilibrium, and change. So it is with society's age groups. Regardless of whether the young and old recognize it, they are part of a basic struggle that threatens to throw society into turmoil. The passage of Social Security legislation is an example of this struggle.

Social Security Legislation

In the 1920s, before Social Security provided an income for the aged, two-thirds of all citizens over 65 had no savings and could not support themselves (Holtzman 1963; Hudson 1978). Only one-fifth of workers were able to retire before they died (O'Rand and Henretta 1999). The fate of workers sank even deeper during the Great Depression, and in 1930, Francis Townsend, a physician, started a movement to rally older citizens. He soon had one-third of all Americans over 65 enrolled in his Townsend clubs. They demanded that the federal government impose a national sales tax of 2 percent to provide $200 a month for every person over 65 ($2,025 a month in today's money). In 1934, the Townsend Plan went before Congress. Because it called for such high payments and many were afraid that it would destroy people's incentive to save for the future, members of Congress looked for a way to reject the plan without appearing to oppose the elderly. When President Roosevelt announced his own, more modest Social Security plan in 1934, Congress embraced it (Schottland 1963; Amenta et al. 1999).

To provide jobs for younger people, this legislation required that workers retire at 65. It did not matter how well people did their work, nor how much they needed the pay. For decades, the elderly protested. Finally, in 1986, Congress eliminated mandatory retirement. Today, almost 90 percent of Americans retire by age 65, but most do so voluntarily. No longer can they be forced out of their jobs simply because of their age.

Conflict theorists point out that Social Security did not come about because members of Congress had generous hearts. Rather, Social Security emerged from a struggle between competing interest groups. As conflict theorists stress, equilibrium is only a temporary balancing of social forces, one that can be upset at any time. Perhaps more direct conflict may emerge in the future. Let's consider that possibility.

Intergenerational Conflict

Will the future bring conflict between the elderly and the young? Although violence is not likely, if you listen closely, you can hear ripples of grumbling—complaints that the elderly are getting more than their fair share of society's resources. The huge costs of Social Security and Medicare have become a national concern. These two programs alone

Figure 13.6 Costs of Social Security

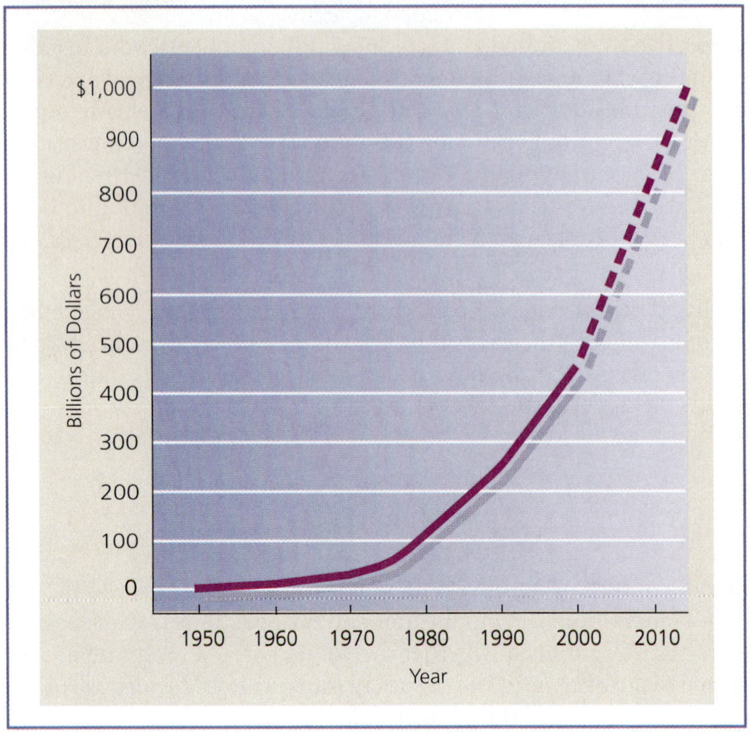

Source: By the author. Based on *Statistical Abstract* 1997:Table 518; 2002:Table 518. Broken line indicates the author's projections.

account for *one of every three* (35 percent) tax dollars (*Statistical Abstract* 2002:Table 453). As Figure 13.6 shows, Social Security taxes were $781 million in 1950; now they run about *600 times* higher. The Down-to-Earth Sociology box on page 376 examines stirrings of resentment that threaten to become widespread.

Some form of conflict seems inevitable. The graying of the United States leaves fewer workers to pay for the benefits received by the increasing millions who collect Social Security. This and other problems are discussed in the following Thinking Critically section.

THINKING Critically

Exploding the Myth of U.S. Budget Surpluses: Can We Pay the Elderly's Social Security Out of Thin Air?

Each month the Social Security Administration mails checks to 46 million people. Across the country, 187 million U.S. workers pay into the Social Security system, looking to it to provide for their basic necessities—and even a little more than that—in their old age (*Statistical Abstract* 2002:Tables 517, 519).

How dependable is Social Security? The short answer is "Don't bet your old age on it."

The first problem is well known. Social Security is not a bank account. The money taken from our checks is not deposited into our individual accounts. No money in the Social Security system is attached to anyone's name. At retirement, we don't withdraw the money we paid into Social Security. Instead, the government writes checks on money that it collects from current workers. When these workers retire, they, too, will be paid, not from their own savings, but from money collected from others who are still working.

The Social Security system is like a giant chain letter—it works as long as enough new people join the chain. If you join early enough, you'll collect more than you paid in—but if you join toward the end, you're simply out of luck. And, say some conflict theorists, we are nearing the end of the chain. The shift in the **dependency ratio**—the number of people who collect Social Security compared with the number of workers who contribute to it—is especially troubling. As Figure 13.7 shows, sixteen workers used to support each person who was collecting Social Security. Now the dependency ratio has dropped to four to one. In another generation, it should hit two to one. When this happens, Social Security taxes could be-

dependency ratio the number of workers required to support each dependent person—those 65 and older and those 15 and under

Figure 13.7 Fewer Workers Supporting a Larger Number of Retirees and Disabled Workers

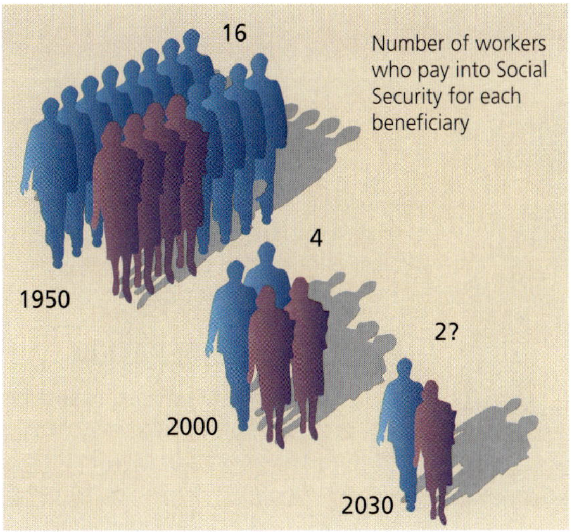

Source: By the author. Based on Social Security Administration; *Statistical Abstract* 2002:Tables 517, 519.

come so high that they stifle the country's economy. To prevent this, Congress raised Social Security taxes and established a Social Security trust fund. Supposedly, this fund has trillions of dollars. But does it? Let's look at the second problem.

The second problem with Social Security takes us to the root of the crisis, or, some say, fraud. In 1965, President Lyndon Johnson was bogged down in a war in Vietnam. To conceal the war's costs from the public, he hit on an ingenious solution: to prohibit the Social Security Administration from investing in anything but U.S. Treasury bonds, a form of government IOUs. This put the money collected for Social Security into the general fund, where Johnson could siphon it off to finance the war. Today's politicians still do this. They use the term "off budget" to refer to the Social Security money they spend. And each year, they spend it all.

Suppose that you buy a $10,000 U.S. Treasury bond. The government takes your $10,000 and hands you a document that says it owes you $10,000 plus interest. This is how Social Security works. The Social Security Administration (SSA) collects the money from workers, pays the retired, disabled, and survivors of deceased workers, and then hands the excess over to the U.S. government. The government, in turn, gives SSA gigantic IOUs in the form of U.S. Treasury bonds. The government spends the money on whatever it wants—whether that means building roads and schools or subsidizing tobacco crops.

Think of it this way: Suppose you are spending more money than you make, but you dip into Aunt Mary's bank account and put some of her money in your own account. If you don't count what you owe Aunt Mary, you have a surplus. The government simply does not count those huge IOUs it owes the elderly, and it sometimes reports a fraudulent surplus to the public.

This arrangement is a politician's dream. Each month the government wipes the Social Security trust fund clean. Politicians grab the money and hand out the IOUs.

The Gramm-Rudman law, which was designed to limit the amount of federal debt, does *not* count funds "borrowed" from Social Security. (In their terms, it is "off budget.") It is as though this government spending does not exist—and to politicians it doesn't. To them, Social Security is a money machine that produces billions from thin air. To them, those are just numbers on paper, not money that has been confiscated from workers.

As one analyst said, the Social Security trust fund isn't a fund and you shouldn't trust it (Sloan 2001).

For Your CONSIDERATION . . .

Here are three proposals to solve this problem.

1. Raise the retirement age to 70.
2. Each month, after paying beneficiaries apply all Social Security taxes that are left to the national debt. The debt could be paid off before the dependency ratio drops much further, making the money spent on interest (now $180 billion a year) available for Social Security payments. For this to work, the government could not increase its spending, almost an impossibility for politicians.
3. Change the entire system. Put what workers pay as Social Security taxes into their own individual retirement accounts. A board, independent of the government, would select money managers to invest these accounts in real estate, stocks, and bonds. Annually, the board would review the performance of the money managers, retaining those who do the best job and replacing the others. All investment results would be published and would be available for public inspection.

Think in terms of your own Social Security. Do you prefer to retain the current Social Security system? Do you prefer one of these three proposals? None is perfect. What problems might each have? Can you think of a better alternative?

Sources: Smith 1986; Smith 1987; Hardy 1991; Genetski 1993; Stevenson 1998, *Statistical Abstract* 2000. Government publications that list Social Security receipts as deficits can be found in *Monthly Treasury Statement of Receipts and Outlays*, the *Winter Treasury Bulletin*, and the *Statement of Liabilities and Other Financial Commitments of the United States Government.*

DOWN-TO-EARTH SOCIOLOGY

Changing Sentiment About the U.S. Elderly

MOST U.S. ELDERLY USED TO BE POOR. With Social Security, the elderly's rate of poverty dropped dramatically. As we saw in Figure 10.6 on page 279, today's elderly have a low rate of poverty. As you know, many elderly travel about the country in motor homes and spend a lot of money on recreation. Is their changed situation leading to a new sentiment about the elderly?

There are indications that it is. Senator Alan Simpson called the elderly "greedy geezers," and "oldsters in Bermuda shorts teeing off near their second homes in Florida" who demand government handouts (Duff 1995). Some people feel resentful when they pay more than the elderly for an identical room in the same hotel. Teresa Anderson (1985) said, "My parents work and own several pieces of property. Something is wrong when people are automatically entitled to a 'senior citizen discount' regardless of need."

Some even argue that we should ration medical care for the elderly (Perrin 1994). Considering costs, asks Daniel Callahan (1987), why should we perform open-heart surgery on people in their 80s? This only prolongs their life by two or three years. Doesn't it make more sense to use those same resources to give a kidney transplant to a child, whose life might be prolonged by fifty years?

Attitudes toward the elderly have undergone major shifts during the short history of the United States. As the economic circumstances of the elderly improve, attitudes are changing once again.

Robert Samuelson (1988) accuses the elderly's powerful lobby, the American Association of Retired Persons (AARP), of using misleading stereotypes. He says, "In the real world, the stereotypes of the elderly as sedentary, decrepit, and poor have long vanished, but in politics the cliché is promoted and perpetuated." He also accuses the AARP of hypocrisy: "They insist (rightfully) that age alone doesn't rob people of vitality and independence, while also arguing (wrongfully) that age alone entitles them to special treatment." They can't have it both ways, he says.

For Your CONSIDERATION

Use information in this chapter to analyze why perceptions of the elderly are changing. Note two sides of the coin. On the one side, our current 65-plus generation is enjoying the highest standard of living in U.S. history. One of three golfers is over 65, as are 60 percent of people who take ocean cruises. On the other side are the elderly who live in poverty—22 percent of African Americans, 19 percent of Latinos, 10 percent of Asian Americans, and 9 percent of whites (*Statistical Abstract* 2002:Table 671). Note also the contrasting images—on one hand, "blood-sucking vultures"; on the other hand, "pathetic creatures saving pennies to buy the best meal they can afford—dog food."

Figure 13.8 on the next page shows how medical costs for the elderly have soared. Because of this, some fear that children's health care will be shortchanged and that Congress will be forced to "choose between old people and kids." What especially alarms some are the data shown in Figure 13.9. You can see that until the early 1990s the condition of the elderly was improving, but that of children was getting worse. Fortunately, the poverty rate of the nation's children dropped sharply in the late 1990s—while that of the elderly stayed low. This was a period of prosperity, and without more social programs in place—the equivalent for children of Social Security for the elderly—it is likely that the rate of children's poverty will again increase during economic recession.

Fighting Back

Some organizations work to protect the hard-won gains of the elderly. Let's consider two.

The Gray Panthers The Gray Panthers, who claim 20,000 members, are aware that the working class can be split along age lines (Collins 2001). This organization, founded in 1970 by Margaret Kuhn (1905–1995), encourages people of all ages to work for the welfare of both the old and the young. On the micro level, the goal is to develop positive self-concepts (Kuhn 1990). On the macro level, the goal is to build a base so broad that it can challenge institutions that oppress the poor, whatever their age—and to fight attempts to pit people against one another along age lines. One indication of their

Figure 13.8 Health Care Costs for the Elderly and Disabled

Medicare is intended for the elderly and disabled, Medicaid for the poor. About 29 percent of Medicaid payments ($41 billion) goes to the elderly. (*Statistical Abstract* 2002:Table 131).

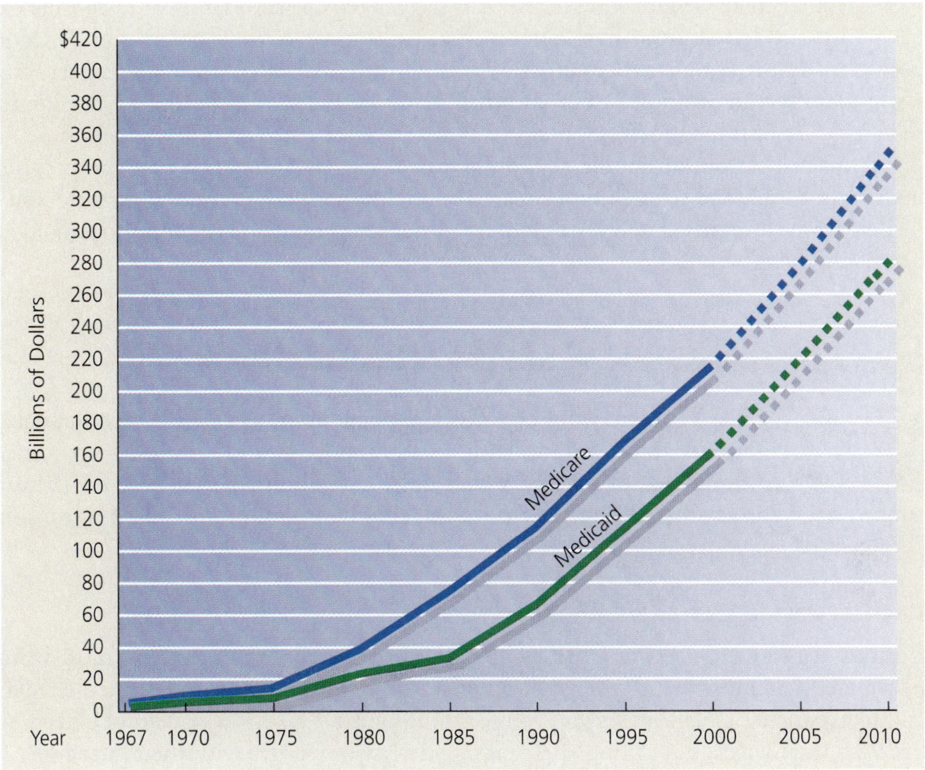

Note: Broken lines indicate the author's projections.
Source: By the author. Based on *Statistical Abstract*, various years, and 2002:Tables 128, 132.

Figure 13.9 Trends in Poverty

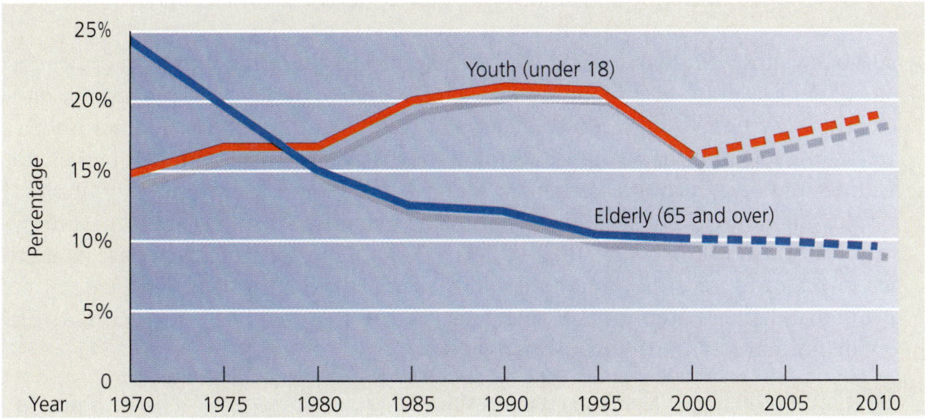

Note: For some years the government totals for youth refer to people under 18, for other years to people under 16 or 15. Broken lines indicate the author's projections.
Sources: By the author. Based on *Statistical Abstract* 1989:Table 738; 1992:Tables 718, 721; 1997:Table 739; 2002:Table 671.

effectiveness is that Gray Panthers frequently testify before congressional committees concerning pending legislation.

The American Association of Retired Persons The AARP also combats negative images of the elderly. This 35-million member organization is politically powerful. It monitors federal and state legislation and mobilizes its members to act on issues affecting their welfare. The AARP can trigger tens of thousands of telephone calls, telegrams, and letters from irate elderly citizens. To protect their chances of reelection, politicians know better than to cross swords with the AARP. As you can expect, critics claim that the organization is too powerful, that it is able to muster forces to claim more than its share of the nation's resources.

All this helps prove our point, say conflict theorists. Age groups are just one of society's many groups that are struggling for scarce resources, with conflict the inevitable result.

Before we close this chapter, let's look at problems of dependency and the sociology of death and dying.

Problems of Dependency

"When I get old, will I be able to take care of myself? Will I become frail and unable to get around? Will I end up poor and in some nursing home, in the hands of strangers who don't care about me?" These are common concerns. Let's examine the dependency of the elderly: isolation, nursing homes, abuse, and poverty.

Isolation and Gender

Contrary to some stereotypes, most U.S. elderly are *not* isolated. Because most women live longer than most men, however, women are more likely than men to lose their spouse and to experience isolation. As you can see from Figure 13.10, 73 percent of elderly men live with their wives, but only 41 percent of elderly women live with their husbands. The intense feelings of loss and isolation that widowhood brings, then, are more likely to be experienced by women. This difference in mortality also means that women are much more likely to take care of frail husbands than husbands are to care for frail wives. It also means that most patients in nursing homes are women.

Figure 13.10 Where Do the U.S. Elderly Live?

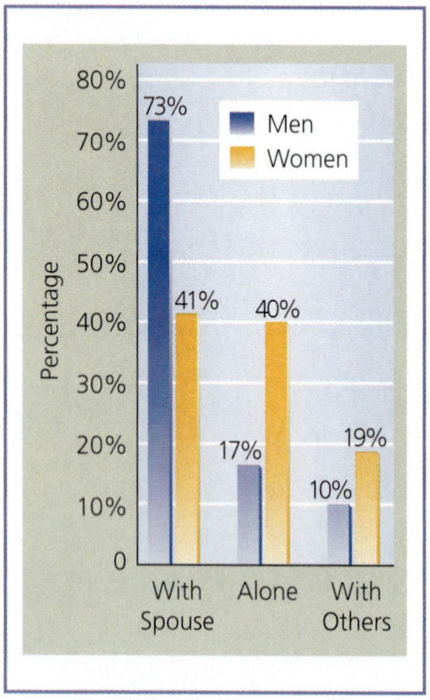

Source: By the author. Based on *Statistical Abstract* 2002:Table 39.

Nursing Homes

> In one nursing home, the nurses wrote in the patient's chart that she had a foot lesion. She actually had gangrene and maggots in her wounds (Rhone 2001). In another nursing home—supposedly a premier retirement home in Southern California—a woman suffered a stroke in her room. Her "caretakers" didn't discover her condition for 15 hours. She didn't survive (Morin 2001).

Although most elderly are cared for by their families, a million and a half Americans age 65 and over are in nursing homes. This comes to about 5 percent of the nation's elderly (*Statistical Abstract* 2002:Tables 11, 168). Some return home after only a few weeks or a few months. Others die after a short stay. Overall, about one half of elderly women and one-third of elderly men spend at least some time in nursing homes.

Nursing home residents are *not typical* of the elderly. Most (51.5 percent) are age 85 or older (*Statistical Abstract* 2002:Table 169). Those in nursing homes are likely to be widowed, or to never have married and thus are without family to take care of them. More than half are incontinent (unable to control their bladder), and most are disorientated or have memory loss (Treas 1995).

Understaffing, Dehumanization, and Death It is difficult to say good things about nursing homes. The literature on nursing homes, both popular and scientific, is filled with horror stories of neglected and abused patients. With events like those in the quotation that opens this section, Congress ordered a national study of nursing homes. They found that in nursing homes that are understaffed, patients are more likely to have bedsores and to be malnourished, underweight, and dehydrated. *Ninety percent* of nursing homes are understaffed (Pear 2002b).

It is easy to see why nursing homes are understaffed. Who willingly works for poverty-level wages in a place that smells of urine, where you have to clean up feces, and where you are surrounded by dying people? Forty to 100 percent of nursing home staff quit each year (DeFrancis 2002).

Even the few nursing homes with adequate staff have a tendency to strip away human dignity. Consider what sociologist Sharon Curtin (1976) found in one of these superior nursing homes:

> Miss Larson entered Montcliffe the last week of October. . . . Shortly after her admission, I arrived at 7 a.m. to find the night nurse indignant and angry. Miss Larson had climbed over the side rails during the night, and had been found in the bathroom. "She didn't ring or call out," said the nurse. . . . "Why, she might have been hurt, and she is so confused. I want the doctor to order me more sedation. We can't have her carrying on, and disturbing all the other patients."
>
> I walked in the room and Miss Larson was in restraints. . . . "Get me out of these!" she ordered. "How dare they try to stop me from getting out of bed. I always have to relieve myself at night; and they never answer my bell."
>
> Miss Larson was not confused; but in a place where all the patients are so sedated that they scarcely move a muscle during the night, she was counted a nuisance. I did not want them to increase her sedation; barbiturates frequently make old people confused and disoriented. Even if she was a pain in the neck, I like her better awake and making some sense. The problem was she had no rights. She was old, sick, feeble. Therefore she must shut up, lie still, take what little was offered and be grateful. And if she did that, she would be a "good girl."

The elderly resent being treated like children—in an institution or anywhere else. They resist, as did Miss Larson, but resistance is usually fruitless. We can add that such callous treatment doesn't come cheap. Nursing homes are big business. They have over a million employees and bring in $55 billion a year (*Statistical Abstract* 2002:Table 141). Nursing care is so expensive that 70 percent of residents without family go broke within just three months (Ruffenbach 1988; Treas 1995).

The residents of nursing homes are not typical of the elderly. They are in worse health and generally more isolated. In addition, as you may infer from this photo, they often are given drugs to keep them docile.

But all these criticisms of nursing homes pale in comparison with this finding, which is probably their single greatest indictment: Compared with the elderly who have similar conditions and remain in the community, those who are placed in nursing homes tend to get sicker and to die sooner (Wolinsky et al. 1997). Because of this, we can note—with only a trace of irony—that one of the major functions of nursing homes is to help dispose of the frail and unwanted elderly. In other words, we can consider them the equivalent of the Tiwi's practice of "covering up," which we reviewed in the chapter's opening vignette.

It doesn't have to be this way. For an example of an excellent system of institutionalized care, see the Cultural Diversity box.

CULTURAL DIVERSITY around the WORLD

Alzheimer's Disease: Lessons from Sweden

"I'm ready," Clay called from the bedroom.

"That was fast," thought Virginia, his wife of forty-eight years. "He never gets ready for church that fast."

Virginia walked into the bedroom, and there, smiling and ready to leave for church, stood Clay—absolutely naked except for three watches strapped to his left wrist. Virginia told me this story later that morning when I asked her how things were going.

As people grow old, among their fears is that of "losing their mind." By this they mean senility, or, more technically, Alzheimer's disease.

How do we care for people when they get like Clay?

Clay is in good hands. His wife is still healthy, and she lovingly makes certain that he eats nourishing meals, is included in social events—and wears more than watches when he goes out.

But what about the many who don't have close, caring relatives? For them, senility means institutionalization—which, even if it does not mirror the horror stories we all have heard, is certainly a far cry from the loving care that someone like Virginia gives.

Former president Ronald Reagan suffers from Alzheimer's disease. This disease devastates the thinking process, making its victims unable to carry out the ordinary routines on which everyday life depends. Reagan doesn't even remember that he was the president. As the percentage of the aged in our society increases, so will the number of people who suffer from this disease—and the caregiving that will become necessary.

Institutionalization, however, does not have to be a bad experience. To see the potential for positive care, we can turn to Sweden, which has been pioneering group homes for victims of Alzheimer's disease (Malmberg and Sundström 1996). The group homes consist of six to eight small apartments fanning outward from a shared kitchen and living room. Residents have their own accommodations, but a trained and well-paid staff is available around the clock. The goal is to mirror a home environment in which residents are lovingly cared for, where they are treated as individuals, and where they participate in everyday activities. The benefits go far beyond personalized care; secondary problems associated with Alzheimer's—depression, restlessness, and anxiety—apparently decrease.

For Your CONSIDERATION

The group home model pioneered by Sweden is exemplary, but expensive. In the United States, what chance do you think we have for providing group homes like this for victims of Alzheimer's? Suppose that we did provide such homes, but could not afford them for all Alzheimer's victims—how should they be rationed?

Technology and Nursing Homes You probably are aware of how important social interaction is for your well-being. It is the same for the elderly. Isolation can lead to their mental and physical deterioration. Researchers have found that an active social life helps to prevent the deterioration of the brain that can lead to Alzheimer's and Parkinson's diseases. Social isolation is not the cause of these brain conditions—which can strike anyone—but people who are socially isolated are more likely to come down with them (Ross 2000).

Social activity comes in many forms. Some residents of nursing homes find that the computer and Internet help them overcome isolation, loneliness, and depression. Sending and receiving e-mail helps them to keep in contact with relatives and friends, who may be dispersed throughout the country, and, in our emerging global society, throughout the world. With our capacity for video e-mail, this will become an even more important element in their mental and social well-being.

Elder Abuse

Stories of elder abuse abound—and so does the abuse itself. In interviews with a random sample of nursing home staff, 40 percent admitted that during the preceding year they had abused patients psychologically. Ten percent admitted to abusing patients physically (Pillemer and Hudson 1993). Most abuse of the elderly, however, takes place not in nursing homes but at home. Most abusers are not paid staff, but family members, who hit, verbally and emotionally abuse, or financially exploit their aged relatives (Pillemer and Wolf 1987; Shellenbarger 2003). The most likely abuser is the spouse (Nachman 1991; Pillemer and Suitor 1992).

Why do spouses, children, and other relatives abuse their own elderly? Sociologists Karl Pillemer and Jill Suitor (1992) interviewed more than 200 people who were caring for family members who suffered from Alzheimer's disease. One husband told them,

> Frustration reaches a point where patience gives out. I've never struck her, but sometimes I wonder if I can control myself. . . . This is . . . the part of her care that causes me the frustration and the loss of patience. What I tell her, she doesn't register. Like when I tell her, "You're my wife." "You're crazy," she says.

From this husband's statement, we can glean some insight into the stress that comes with caring for a person who is dependent, demanding, and uncomprehending. Since most people who care for the elderly undergo stress but are not violent toward those they care for, however, we do not have the answer to why some caregivers become violent. For this, we must await future research.

More important than understanding the causes of abuse, however, is preventing the elderly from being abused in the first place. There is little that can be done about abuse at home—except to enforce current laws when abuse comes to the attention of authorities. For nursing home workers, however, we can require background checks to screen out people who have been convicted of robbery, rape, and other violence. This is similar to requiring background checks of nursery school workers in order to screen out people who have been convicted of molesting children. Most states have passed such laws. These laws are only a first step to solving this problem. They will not prevent abuse, only avoid the obvious.

Figure 13.11 Gender and Poverty in Old Age

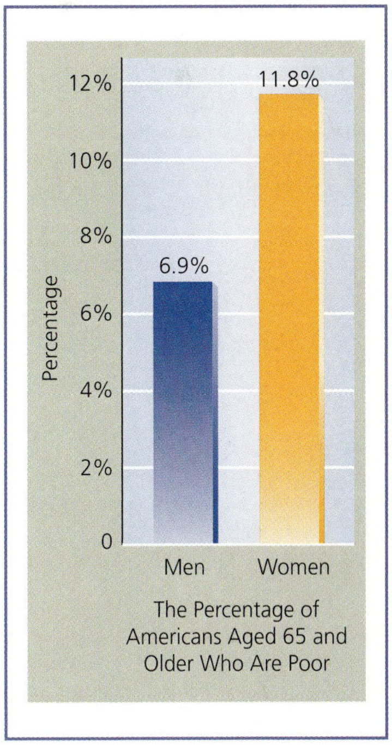

Source: By the author. Based on *Statistical Abstract* 2002:Table 39.

The Elderly Poor

Many elderly live in nagging fear of poverty. Since they do not know how long they will live, nor how much inflation there will be, they fear that they will outlive their savings. How realistic is this fear? Although we cannot speak to any individual case, we can look at the elderly as a group.

Gender and Poverty As reviewed in Chapter 11, during their working years most women earn less than men. Figure 13.11 shows that this pattern follows women

Figure 13.12 Poverty and Race-Ethnicity

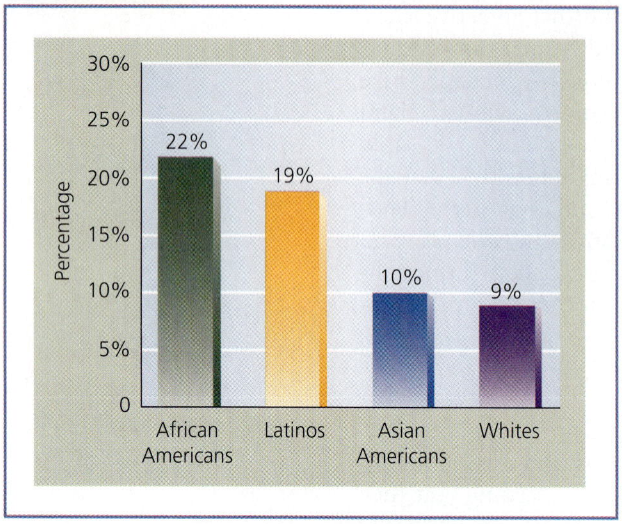

Source: By the author. Based on *Statistical Abstract* 2002:Table 671.

and men into their old age. As you can see, elderly women are about 70 percent more likely than elderly men to be poor.

Race—Ethnicity and Poverty The elderly also reflect the racial and ethnic patterns of the general society. As Figure 13.12 shows, elderly whites and Asian Americans are the least likely to be poor. Poverty is about twice as common among elderly African Americans and Latinos.

Back in the 1960s, poverty among the elderly was so severe that one of every three elderly Americans lived below the poverty line. In response to public demand, the federal government established anti-poverty programs and increased Social Security checks. Legislation also gave workers vested rights in their pension plans. (Employers had to put their retirement money in secure accounts.) This led to one of the few success stories in the government's campaign against poverty. As Figure 13.13 shows, this campaign has been so successful that, with the exception of those age 75 and over, today's elderly are less likely than the average American to be poor.

The Sociology of Death and Dying

Death and dying is a fascinating subfield of sociology. It is especially interesting how we use linguistic masks to try to distance ourselves from death. We have constructed an elaborate language of avoidance, ways to refer to death without using the word itself. Instead of dead, we use terms such as "gone," "passed on," "no longer with us," and "at peace now." We don't have space to explore this characteristic of social life, but we can take a brief look at why sociologists emphasize that, like old age, dying is more than a biological event. Let's look at how culture shapes the ways that we experience death.

Figure 13.13 Poverty and Age

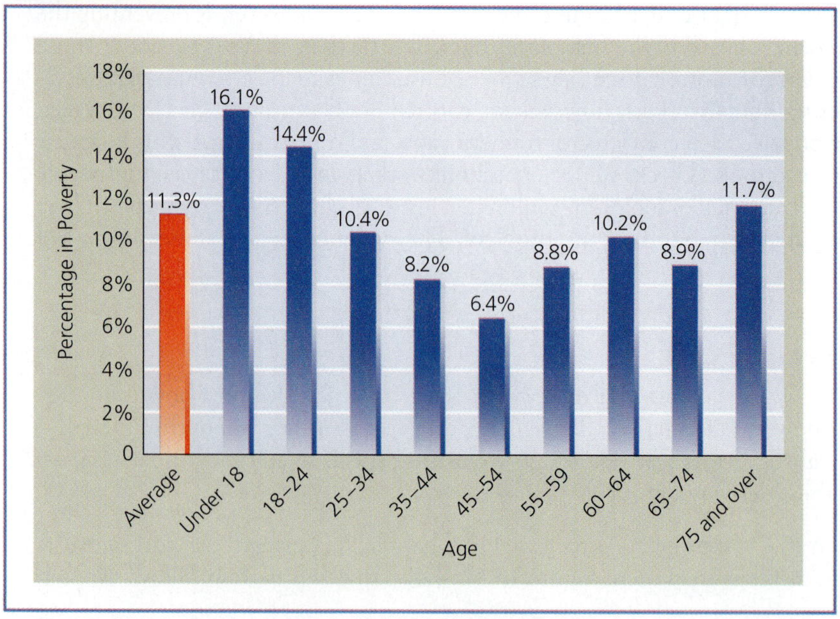

Source: By the author. Based on *Statistical Abstract* 2002:Table 671.

In old age, as in other stages in the life course, having enough money for one's needs and desires makes life more pleasant and satisfying. This elderly woman, who must live out of her car, is not likely to find this time of her life satisfying. Income, however, is hardly the sole determiner of satisfaction during old age. The elderly friends seen here enjoying a sauna in New York City get together regularly just to enjoy one another's company. Although far from welcoming old age, they are likely to find this time of life more satisfying than does the isolated homeless woman.

Industrialization and the New Technology

Before industrialization, death was no stranger. The family took care of the sick at home, and the sick died at home. Because life was short, *most* children saw a sibling or parent die (Blauner 1966). As noted in Chapter 1 (page 28), the family even prepared corpses for burial. Industrialization, however, made the process of dying strange and alien, transforming it into an event that is managed by professionals in hospitals. Dying now takes place behind closed doors—isolated, remote, and handled by strangers.

Not only did new technologies remove the dying from our presence, but also they created *technological life*—a form of existence that lies between life and death, but is neither (Cerulo and Ruane 1996). The "brain dead" in our hospitals have no self. Their "person" is gone—dead—yet our technology keeps the body alive. This muddles the boundary between life and death, which used to be firm.

For most of us, however, that boundary will remain firm and we will face a definite death. Some of us will even learn in advance that we will die shortly. Let's look at what researchers have found that indicate how we will probably cope with such knowledge.

Death as a Process

Psychologist Elisabeth Kübler-Ross (1969/1981) studied how people cope during the *living-dying interval,* that period between discovering they are going to die soon and death itself. After interviewing people who had been informed that they had an incurable disease, she concluded that people who come face to face with their own death go through five stages:

1. *Denial.* At first, people cannot believe that they are going to die. ("The doctor must have made a mistake. Those test results can't be right.") They avoid the topic of death and situations that remind them of it.
2. *Anger.* After a while, they acknowledge that they are going to die, but they see their death as unjust. ("I didn't do anything to deserve this. So-and-so is much worse than I am, and he's in good health. It isn't right that I should die.")
3. *Negotiation.* Next, the individual tries to get around death by making a bargain with God, with fate, or even with the disease itself. ("I need one more Christmas with my family. I never appreciated them as much as I should have. After Christmas, I'll be ready.")
4. *Depression.* During this stage, people become resigned to their death, but they grieve because their life is about to end, and they have no power to change the course of events.

5. *Acceptance.* In this final stage, people come to terms with their impending death. They put their affairs in order—make wills, pay bills, instruct their children to take care of the surviving parent. They also express regret at not having done certain things when they had the chance. Devout Christians are likely to talk about the hope of salvation and their desire to be in heaven with Jesus.

Dying is more individualized than this model indicates. Not everyone, for example, tries to make bargains. What is important sociologically is that death is a process, not just an event. People who expect to die soon face a different reality from the one experienced by those of us who expect to be alive years from now. Their impending death powerfully affects their thinking and behavior. Let me share an intimate event from my own life.

> When my mother was informed that she had inoperable cancer, she immediately went into a vivid stage of denial. If she later went through anger or negotiation, she kept it to herself. After a short depression, she experienced a longer period of questioning why this was happening to her. She then moved quickly into stage 5, which occurred very much as Kübler-Ross described it. After her funeral, my two brothers and I went to her apartment, as she had instructed us. There, to our surprise, attached to each item in every room—from the bed and the television to the boxes of dishes and knickknacks—was a piece of masking tape with one of our names on it. At first we found this strange. We knew she was an orderly person, but to this extent? As we sorted through her things, reflecting on why she had given certain items to whom, we began to appreciate the "closure" she had given to this aspect of her material life.

Hospices

In earlier generations, when life was short, death at an early age was taken for granted. Today, we take it for granted that most people will see old age. Due to advances in medical technology and better public health practices, *most* deaths in the United States (about 75 percent) occur after age 65. People want to die with dignity, in the comforting presence of friends and relatives, but hospitals, to put the matter bluntly, are awkward places in which to die. There people experience what sociologists call *institutional death*—they die surrounded by strangers in formal garb, in an organization that puts its routines ahead of patients' needs.

Hospices emerged as a way to reduce the emotional and physical burden of dying—and to lower the costs of death. Hospices are built around the idea that the control of dying

As discussed in the text, the number of elderly people is increasing, and older people are making up a larger proportion of our population. Because of medical advances and better nutrition, millions of the elderly enjoy good health. Rather than being considered a sequel to ill health and death, older age is being redefined as a period of opportunity to pursue interests and develop talents that provide new perspectives and a continued sense of satisfaction with life.

belongs to the people who are dying and their families. The term **hospice** originally referred to a place, but now it generally refers to home care. Services are brought into a dying person's home—from counseling to such down-to-earth help as providing babysitters or driving the person to a doctor or lawyer. At any one time, about 100,000 people are in hospice care in the United States (*Sociological Abstract* 2002:Table 166).

Whereas hospitals are dedicated to prolonging life, hospices are dedicated to providing dignity in death and making people comfortable during the *living-dying interval.* In the hospital, the focus is on the patient; in the hospice, the focus switches to both the dying person and his or her friends and family. In the hospital, the goal is to make the patient well; in the hospice, it is to relieve pain and suffering. In the hospital, the primary concern is the individual's physical welfare; in the hospice, although medical needs are met, the primary concern is the individual's social—and in some instances, spiritual—well-being.

Suicide and Age

We noted in Chapter 1 how Durkheim stressed that suicide has a *social* base. Suicide, he said, is much more than an individual act. Each country, for example, has its own suicide rate, which remains quite stable year after year. In the United States, we can predict that 30,000 people will commit suicide this year. If we are off by more than 1,000, it would be a surprise. As we saw in Figure 1.1. (page 13), we can also predict that Americans will choose firearms as the most common way to kill themselves, and that hanging will come in second. We can also be certain that this year men will be more likely than women to take their lives. It is this way year after year.

Statistics often fly in the face of the impressions we get from the mass media, and here we have such an example. Although the suicides of young people are given much publicity, such deaths are relatively rare. The suicide rate of adolescents is *lower* than that of almost all other ages. Because adolescents have such a low death rate, however, suicide does rank as their third leading cause of death—after accidents and homicide (*Statistical Abstract* 2002:Table 102).

These findings on suicide are an example of the primary sociological point stressed throughout this text: Recurring patterns of human behavior—whether education, marriage, work, crime, use of the Internet, or even suicide—represent underlying social forces. Consequently, if no basic change takes place in the social conditions under which the groups that make up U.S. society live, you can expect these same patterns of suicide five to ten years from now.

Adjusting to Death

As family members come to terms with a death, they may face conflicting feelings. While they might be grief stricken, they also may feel ambivalence, guilt, anger, or even relief. Their primary adjustment occurs during a period of mourning, which usually lasts one or two years. They also have to reorganize their family system to take account of the person who is now missing from it (Anderson and Sabatelli 2003).

In general, when death is expected, family members find it less stressful. They have dealt with the eventual death through a series of smaller losses, including getting used to the person's inability to fulfill his or her usual roles or to do specific tasks. They also have been able to say a series of goodbyes to their loved one. Unexpected deaths—accidents, suicide, and homicide—bring greater emotional shock. The family members have had no time to get used to the idea that the individual is going to die. One moment, the person is there; the next, he or she is gone. The sudden death gave them no chance to say goodbye or to bring any form of "closure" to their relationship.

Looking Toward the Future

We have reviewed several key issues in aging—from the social construction of "old" to problems with nursing homes. We also caught a glimpse of aging in other societies. To close the chapter, consider the new centenarians.

hospice a place, or services brought into someone's home, for the purpose of bringing comfort and dignity to a dying person

DOWN-TO-EARTH SOCIOLOGY

The New Centenarians

THE OXYMORON *NEW* CENTENARIANS may seem strange, since the word *centenarian* refers to someone who has reached age 100 or beyond. But apparently centenarians are new to the world. Some population experts think that before 1900 only one person a century made it to age 100 or beyond (Himes 2001).

Yet, while reaching 100 isn't exactly common today, it is frequent. On the 2000 census, about 50,000 Americans reported their age as 100 or more. Officials at the U.S. Census bureau think that people fudge a bit about their age when they get to be very old. They become proud of making it that far, and they tend to tack on a few years. Even if we lop off 10,000 people, this still leaves us with about 40,000 folks who have managed to reach age 100 or more.

As you probably would expect, more women than men reach 100. In fact, women centenarians outnumber men centenarians *four to one*. (The men have quite a choice of mates—but little interest.) Because the average woman outlives the average man, about 25 percent of men centenarians are married, but only about 4 percent of the women are. Then there is this surprising statistic: About 20 percent of centenarians report no disabilities (Himes 2001). They are still healthy and feeling good.

No one knows exactly why the "new" centenarians have appeared at this point in history, but our improved public health, modern medicines, and ample food supply certainly play a part. On the individual level—why Jane and Dick make it to 100 while Suzie and Fred do not—there appear to be three reasons: genetics, lifestyle, and luck. With regard to genetics, some people inherit physical problems that bring an earlier death. For lifestyle, some people take better care of their bodies, and some like to dive out of airplanes. Then there is the matter of luck—or the lack of it. You can simply be in the wrong place at the wrong time, such as visiting the World Trade Center on September 11, 2001, or Toronto in 2003 when SARS made world headlines.

Our new centenarians have arrived on the world scene because of natural causes. If the genetics researchers learn how to manipulate our aging genes, we may soon be talking about the new centenarians and a half—or even the double centenarians.

For Your CONSIDERATION

Centenarians are one of the fastest growing segments of our population. While still relatively rare today, they are socially destined to become more common. What do you think the consequences will be for society?

SUMMARY and REVIEW

Aging in Global Perspective

How are the elderly treated around the world?

No single set of attitudes, beliefs, or policies regarding the aged characterizes the world's nations. Rather, they vary from exclusion and killing to integration and honor. The global trend is for more people to live longer. P. 362.

What does the social construction of aging mean?

Nothing in the nature of aging summons forth any particular set of attitudes. Rather, attitudes toward the elderly are rooted in society and differ from one social group to another. Pp. 362–364.

What does the term "graying of America" mean?

The phrase **graying of America** refers to the growing proportion of Americans who reach old age. The costs of Social Security and health care for the elderly have become major social issues. Pp. 364–366.

The Symbolic Interactionist Perspective

What factors influence perceptions of aging?

Symbolic interactionists stress the social construction of aging, emphasizing that no age has any particular built-in meaning. They identify four factors that influence when people label themselves as "old": biological changes, biographical events, **gender age**, and cultural timetables. Cross-cultural comparisons—for example, the traditional Native Americans, Tiwi, and Eskimos—demonstrate the role of culture in determining how individuals experience aging. **Ageism**, negative reactions to the elderly, is based on stereotypes. Pp. 366–370.

The Functionalist Perspective

How is retirement functional for society?

Functionalists focus on how the withdrawal of the elderly from positions of responsibility benefits society.

Disengagement theory examines retirement as a device for ensuring that a society's positions of responsibility will be passed smoothly from one generation to the next. **Activity theory** examines how people adjust when they disengage from productive roles. **Continuity theory** focuses on how people adjust to growing old by continuing their roles and coping techniques. Pp. 370–373.

The Conflict Perspective

Is there conflict among different age groups?

Social Security legislation is an example of one generation making demands on another generation for limited resources. As the **dependency ratio,** the number of workers who support one retired person, drops, workers may become resentful. The Social Security Trust Fund may be a gigantic fraud perpetrated by the power elite on the nation's elderly. Organizations such as the Gray Panthers and the AARP watch out for the interests of the elderly. Pp. 373–378.

Problems of Dependency

What are some of the problems that today's elderly face?

Women are more likely to live alone and to be poor. At any one time, about 5 percent of the elderly live in nursing homes. Nursing homes are understaffed, and patients are often neglected and dehumanized. The most common abusers of the elderly are members of their own family. Poverty in old age, greatly reduced through government programs, reflects the gender and racial-ethnic patterns of poverty in the general society. Pp. 378–382.

The Sociology of Death and Dying

How does culture affect the meaning—and experience—of death and dying?

Like old age, death is much more than a biological event. Industrialization brought with it modern medicine, hospitals, and the custom of dying in a formal setting surrounded by strangers. Kübler-Ross identified five stages in the dying process, which, though insightful, do not characterize all people. **Hospices** are a cultural device designed to overcome the negative aspects of dying in hospitals. Suicide shows distinct patterns by age, sex, and method. It is possible that science will increase the human **life span.** Pp. 382–385.

Looking Toward the Future

What technological developments can be a wild card in social planning for the aged?

Technological breakthroughs may stretch the human life span. If so, it is difficult to see how younger workers would be able to support retired people for 100 years or so. Pp. 385–386.

Where can I read more on this topic?

Suggested Readings for this chapter are at the back of this book.

THINKING Critically ABOUT CHAPTER 13

1. How does culture influence people's ideas about when old age begins and what old age means?
2. How do the functionalist and conflict perspectives on the elderly differ?
3. If you were appointed to head the U.S. Department of Health and Human Services, how would you improve our nursing homes?

ADDITIONAL RESOURCES for This Chapter

www.ablongman.com/henslin7e

- *Content Select* Research Database for Sociology, with suggested key terms and annotated references
- Link to 2000 Census, with activities
- Flashcards of key terms and concepts
- Practice Tests
- Weblinks
- Interactive Maps

Chapter 14

The Economy

Douglass Crockwell, *Paperworkers*, 1934

If you are like most students, you are wondering how changes in the economy are going to affect your chances of getting a good job. Let's see if we can shed some light on this question. We'll begin with this story:

The sound of her alarm rang in Kim's ears. "Not Monday already," she groaned. "There must be a better way of starting the week." She pressed the snooze button on the clock (from Germany) to sneak another ten minutes' sleep. In what seemed like just thirty seconds, the alarm shrilly insisted she get up and face the week.

Still bleary-eyed after her shower, Kim peered into her closet and picked out a silk blouse (from China), a plaid wool skirt (from Scotland), and leather shoes (from India). She nodded, satisfied, as she added a pair of simulated pearls (from Taiwan). Running late, she hurriedly ran a brush (from Mexico) through her hair. As Kim wolfed down a bowl of cereal (from the United States) topped with milk (from the United States), bananas (from Costa Rica), and sugar (from the Dominican Republic), she turned on her kitchen television (from Korea) to listen to the weather forecast.

Gulping the last of her coffee (from Brazil), Kim grabbed her briefcase (from Wales), purse (from Spain), and jacket (from Malaysia), left her house, and quickly climbed into her car (from Japan). As she glanced at her watch (from Switzerland), she hoped the traffic would be in her favor. She muttered to herself as she pulled up at a stop light (from Great Britain) and eyed her gas gauge. She muttered again when she pulled into a station and paid for gas (from Saudi Arabia), for the price had risen over the weekend. "My paycheck never keeps up with prices," she moaned.

he said to herself. "If people were more like me, his country would be in better shape."

When Kim arrived at work, she found the office abuzz. Six months ago, the New York headquarters had put the company up for sale, but there had been no takers. The big news this Monday was that both a German and a Canadian corporation had put in bids over the weekend. No one got much work done that day, as the whole office speculated about how things might change.

As Kim walked to the parking lot after work, she saw a tattered "Buy American" bumper sticker on the car next to hers. "That's right," she said to herself. "If people were more like me, this country would be in better shape."

Chapter Outline

The Transformation of Economic Systems

Although this vignette may be slightly exaggerated, many of us are like Kim—we use a multitude of products from around the world, and yet we're concerned about our country's ability to compete in global markets. Today's **economy**—a system of producing and distributing goods and services—differs radically from those in all but our most recent past. The products Kim uses make it apparent that today's economy knows no national boundaries. To better understand how global forces affect the U.S. economy—and your life—let's begin with an overview of the sweeping historical changes that have taken place.

Preindustrial Societies: The Birth of Inequality

The earliest human groups, *hunting and gathering societies,* had a **subsistence economy.** Groups of perhaps twenty-five to forty people lived off the land. They gathered what they could and moved from place to place as their food supply ran low. Because there was little or no excess food or other items, they did little trading with other groups. With no excess to accumulate, everyone had the same amount of possessions—practically nothing.

Then people discovered how to breed animals and cultivate plants. This produced a surplus and ushered in social inequality. The more dependable food supply in *pastoral and horticultural societies* allowed humans to settle down in a single place. Human groups grew larger, and some individuals began to devote their energies to activities other than producing food. People began to focus on specialized tasks, such as working with leather or making weapons or jewelry. This new division of labor produced a surplus, and groups traded items with one another. The primary sociological significance of surplus and trade is this: They set the stage for *social inequality,* for some people accumulated more possessions than others. The effects of that change remain with us today.

economy a system of distribution of goods and services

subsistence economy a type of economy in which human groups live off the land and have little or no surplus

The invention of the plow ushered in the next major change. The plow multiplied food production, allowing *agricultural societies* to develop. As more people were freed from food production, more specialized divisions of labor followed. The result was an even greater surplus. As trade expanded, trading centers developed. Trading centers turned into cities, and power passed from the heads of families and clans to a ruling elite. The result was even greater social, political, and economic inequality.

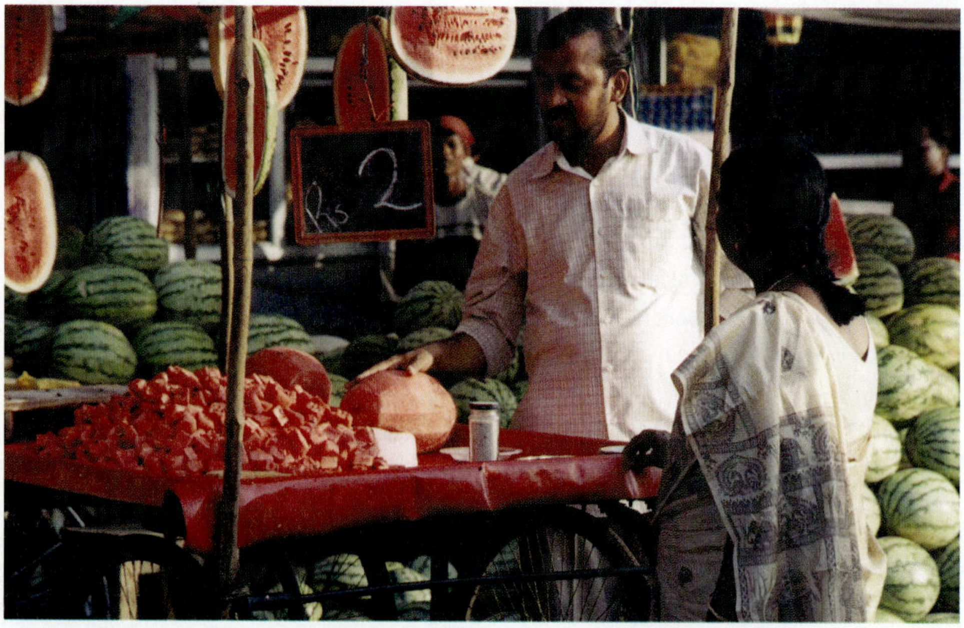

The common-sense meaning of market *is a place where people exchange or buy and sell goods. Such old-fashioned markets remain common in the Least Industrialized Nations, such as this one that I visited at Hyderabad, India. Here people find the social interaction every bit as rewarding as the goods and money that they exchange.*

One of the negative consequences of early industrialization in the West was the use of child labor. In the photo on the left, of the U.S. textile industry in the 1800s, you can see spindle boys at work in a Georgia cotton mill. Today's Least Industrialized Nations are experiencing the same negative consequence as they industrialize. The photo on the right shows boys at work in a contemporary textile factory in Varanas, India. About the only improvement is that the child workers in India are able to sit down as they exhaust their childhood.

Industrial Societies: The Birth of the Machine

In 1765, another invention changed the world. Machines powered by fuels, instead of by humans and animals, brought a surplus unlike anything in history. In the new *industrial society,* inequality increased even more. A handful of individuals opened factories, exploiting the labor of many. The owners became wealthy and were able to manipulate the political machinery for their own purposes. This set the stage for the bloody battles that followed, when workers unionized to improve their working conditions.

Then came more efficient machines. As the surpluses grew even greater, the emphasis slowly changed from producing goods to consuming them. In 1912, sociologist Thorstein Veblen coined the term **conspicuous consumption** to describe this change in people's orientations. Veblen noted that the Protestant ethic identified by Weber—an emphasis on hard work, savings, and a concern for salvation (discussed on pages 177–178)—was being replaced by an eagerness to show off wealth by the "elaborate consumption of goods."

Postindustrial Societies: The Birth of the Information Age

In 1973, sociologist Daniel Bell noted that a new type of society was emerging. This new society, which he called the *postindustrial society,* has six characteristics: (1) a service sector so large that *most* people work in it; (2) a vast surplus of goods; (3) even more extensive trade among nations; (4) a wider variety and quantity of goods available to the average person; (5) an information explosion; and (6) a *global village*—that is, the world's nations are linked by fast communications, transportation, and trade. The Sociology and the New Technology box on the next page discusses how interconnected the global village has become.

Bioeconomic Societies: The Merger of Biology and Economics

We may be on the verge of yet another new type of society, which is being ushered in by advances in biology, especially the deciphering of the human genome system in 2001. While the specifics of this new society have yet to be revealed, the marriage of biology and economics will yield even greater surpluses and more extensive trade. This new society

conspicuous consumption Thorstein Veblen's term for a change from the Protestant ethic to an eagerness to show off wealth by the consumption of goods

sociology and the NEW technology

"Your Name Is What? You Live Where? But You Sound Like You're Right Next Door."

"Hi. I'm Nancy Morrison from Chicago. May I help you?"

You are likely to be greeted with something like this when you call about your credit card or to inquire why something you ordered hasn't arrived yet. Or maybe you will talk to Susan Sanders from Newark, New Jersey.

Nothing surprising in this. It happens all the time. It just happens, however, that your call has been routed to a highly trained worker 8,000 miles away.

The individual who is greeting you is Nishara Hyderabad—or Narayana Ramdas. She doesn't live in Chicago or Newark. She lives in Bangalore, India. The accent is so perfect that even someone from Chicago or Newark couldn't tell the difference.

In training sessions, she and her fellow workers watch *Friends* and *Everybody Loves Raymond.* They must be able to reconstruct the dialogue, so they can master the nuances of English. They have to know, for example, that when a customer says, "No way, Jose" that there is no Jose.

In role playing sessions, their trainer poses as a caller and interrogates them on U.S. movies, TV programs, and sports. If a customer moves into unfamiliar territory, they are taught to say, "Can we get back to business?"

India is becoming "the back office for the world." Among other companies, General Electric and British Airways have set up huge phone banks in Bangalore to handle a daily barrage of customer inquiries. When I called AOL technical support, I jokingly asked the technician if he lived in India. He said that he lived in Bangalore, and then proudly told me how technically developed Bangalore is.

And what a competitive advantage the corporations find in India. The college graduates who handle the phones are paid a huge salary compared to most Indians. They earn somewhere between $1,600 and $2,100 a year.

For Your CONSIDERATION

How is technology shrinking the global village? Do you think that it is a fair business practice to have Indian telephone workers take on pseudo American identities? Are "Susan" and "Nancy" exploited by the multinational corporations? Or do they benefit from them?

Based on Landler 2001.

may also lead to longer and healthier lives. As history is our guide, it also may create even greater inequality between the rich and poor nations.

The broad changes in societies may seem to be abstract matters, but they are far from irrelevant to your life. Whenever society changes, so do our lives. Consider the information explosion. When you graduate from college, you will do some form of "knowledge work." Instead of working in a factory, you will manage information, or you may design, sell, or service products. The type of work you do has profound implications for your life. It produces social networks, nurtures attitudes, and even affects how you view yourself and the world.

It is the same with the global village. Think of the globe as being divided into three neighborhoods—the three worlds of industrialization and postindustrialization we reviewed in Chapter 9 (pages 244–249). Some nations are located in the poor part of the village. Their citizens barely eke out a living from menial work. Some of them even starve to death. Their fellow villagers in the rich neighborhood, in contrast, feast on the best that the globe has to offer. It's the same village, but what a difference the neighborhood makes.

Now visualize any one of the three neighborhoods. Again you will see gross inequalities. Not everyone who lives in the poor neighborhood is poor, and some areas of the rich neighborhood are packed with poor people. Because the United States is the global economic leader, occupying the most luxurious mansion in the best neighborhood and is spearheading the new bioeconomy, let's look at U.S. trends.

The Transformation of the Medium of Exchange

As each type of economy evolved, so, too, did the **medium of exchange,** the means by which people value and exchange goods and services. As we review this transformation, you'll see how the medium of exchange not only reflects a country's development but also contributes to it.

Earliest Mediums of Exchange

As noted, the lack of surplus in hunting and gathering and pastoral and horticultural societies meant that there was little to trade. Whatever trading did occur was by **barter,** directly exchanging one item for another. The surplus that stimulated trade in later societies led to new ways of valuing goods and services so people could exchange them. Let's look at how the medium of exchange was transformed.

Medium of Exchange in Agricultural Societies

Although bartering continued in agricultural societies, people increasingly came to use **money,** a medium of exchange that places a value on items. In most places, money consisted of gold and silver coins. A coin's weight and purity determined the amount of goods or services it could purchase. In some places people made purchases with **deposit receipts.** These receipts transferred ownership to a specified number of ounces of gold or bushels of grain, or to a specified amount of other goods that were on deposit in a warehouse or bank. Toward the end of the agricultural period, deposit receipts became formalized into **currency** (paper money). Each piece of paper represented a specific amount of gold or silver on deposit in a warehouse. Currency and deposit receipts represented **stored value.** No more currency or deposit receipts could be issued than the amount of gold or silver in the warehouse. Gold and silver coins continued to circulate alongside the deposit receipts and currency.

Medium of Exchange in Industrial Societies

With few exceptions, in industrial societies bartering became a thing of the past. Gold was replaced by paper currency, which, in the United States, could be exchanged for gold stored at Fort Knox. This policy was called the **gold standard.** As long as each dollar represented a specified amount of gold, the number of dollars that could be issued was limited. Toward the end of this period, U.S. paper money could no longer be exchanged for gold or silver. Instead, there was **fiat money,** currency issued by a government that is not backed by stored value.

When fiat money replaced stored value, coins made of precious metals disappeared from circulation. People considered these coins more valuable, and they were unwilling to part with them. Gold coins disappeared first, followed by the largest silver coin, the dollar. Then, as inferior metals (copper, zinc, and nickel) replaced the smaller silver coins, people began to hoard these silver coins, and they, too, disappeared from circulation.

Even without a gold standard that restrains the issuing of currency to stored value, governments have a practical limit on the amount of paper money they can issue. In general, prices increase if a government issues currency at a rate higher than the growth of its **gross domestic product** (GDP), the total goods and services that a country produces. This condition, **inflation,** means that each unit of currency will purchase fewer goods and services. Governments try to control inflation, for high inflation is a destabilizing influence.

As you can see from Figure 14.1 on the next page, as long as the gold standard limited the amount of currency, the purchasing power of the dollar remained relatively stable. When the United States left the gold standard in 1937, the dollar no longer represented stored value, and it plunged in value. Today, the dollar is but a shadow of its former self, retaining only about 7 percent of its original purchasing power.

In industrialized societies, checking accounts became common. A *check* is actually a type of deposit receipt, for it is a promise that the writer of the check has deposited

medium of exchange the means by which people place a value on goods and services in order to make an exchange, for example, currency, gold, and silver

barter the direct exchange of one item for another

money any item (from seashells to gold) that serves as a medium of exchange; today, currency is the most common form

deposit receipts a receipt stating that a certain amount of goods is on deposit in a warehouse or bank; the receipt is used as a form of money

currency paper money

stored value the goods that are stored and held in reserve that back up (or provide the value for) a currency

gold standard paper money backed by gold

fiat money currency issued by a government that is not backed by stored value

gross domestic product (GDP) the amount of goods and services produced by a nation

inflation an increase in prices

credit card a device that allows its owner to purchase goods and to be billed later

debit card a device that allows its owner to charge purchases against his or her bank account

e-cash digital money that is stored on computers

capitalism an economic system characterized by the private ownership of the means of production, the pursuit of profit, and market competition

Figure 14.1 Declining Value of the U.S. Dollar

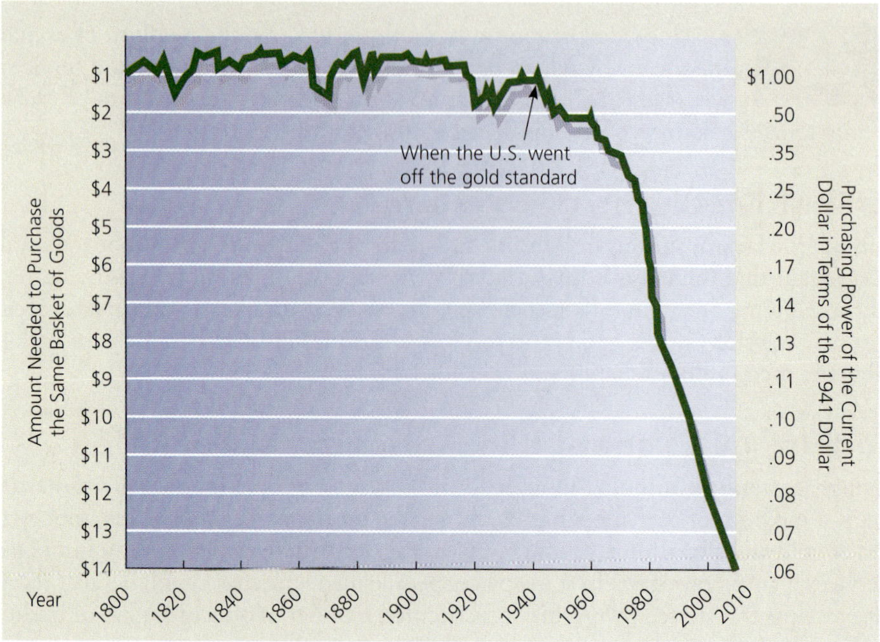

Source: Modified from "Alternative Investment Market Letter," November 1991.

enough currency in the warehouse (the bank or credit union) to cover the check. The latter part of the industrial period saw the invention of the **credit card.** This device allows its owner, who has been approved for a specified amount of credit, to purchase goods without an immediate exchange of money—either metal, currency, or check. The credit card owner is billed for the purchase.

Medium of Exchange in Postindustrial Societies

During the first part of the postindustrial (or information) society, paper money circulated freely. Paper money became less common, being gradually replaced by checks and credit cards. The next development was the **debit card,** a device that electronically withdraws the cost of an item from the cardholder's bank account. Like the check, the debit card is a type of deposit receipt, for it transfers ownership of currency on deposit.

The latest evolution of money is e-cash. **E-cash** consists of digital money that is stored on the owner's computer. E-cash can be encoded in e-mail and sent over the Internet. In effect, the new medium of exchange is itself a part of the information explosion.

World Economic Systems

Now that we have sketched the main economic changes in history, let's compare capitalism and socialism, the two main economic systems in force today. Table 14.1 presents a summary of this discussion.

Capitalism

People who live in a capitalist society may not understand its basic tenets, even though they see them reflected in their local shopping malls and fast-food chains. If we distill the many businesses of the United States to their basic components, we see that **capitalism** has three essential features: (1) *private ownership of the means of production* (individuals own the land, machines, and factories, and decide what they will produce); (2) *market competition* (an exchange of items between willing buyers and sellers); and (3) *the pursuit of profit* (selling something for more than it costs).

Table 14.1 Comparing Socialism and Capitalism

Socialism	Capitalism
1. The public owns the means of production. 2. Central committees plan production; no competition. 3. There is no profit motive in the distribution of goods and services.	1. Individuals own the means of production. 2. The owners determine production; based on competition. 3. The pursuit of profit is the reason for distributing goods and services.

laissez-faire capitalism unrestrained manufacture and trade (literally "hands off" capitalism)

welfare (or state) capitalism an economic system in which individuals own the means of production but the state regulates many economic activities for the welfare of the population

market restraints laws and regulations that limit the capacity to manufacture and sell products

Some people believe that the United States is an example of pure capitalism. Pure capitalism, however, known as **laissez-faire capitalism** (literally meaning "hands off"), means that the government doesn't interfere in the market. Such is not the case in the United States. The current form of U.S. capitalism is **welfare** or **state capitalism.** Private citizens own the means of production and pursue profits, but they do so within a vast system of laws designed to protect the welfare of the population. Consider this example:

> Suppose that you discover what you think is a miracle tonic: It will grow hair, erase wrinkles, and dissolve excess fat. If your product works, you will become an overnight sensation—not only a multimillionaire, but also the toast of television talk shows and the darling of Hollywood.
>
> But don't count your money or your fame yet. You still have to reckon with **market restraints,** the laws and regulations of welfare capitalism that limit your capacity to produce and sell. First, you must comply with local and state rules. You must obtain a business license and a state tax number that allows you to buy your ingredients without paying sales taxes. Then come the federal regulations. You cannot simply take your product to local stores and ask them to sell it; you first must seek approval from federal agencies that monitor compliance with the Pure Food and Drug Act. This means you must prove that your product will not cause harm to the public. In addition, you must be able to substantiate your claims—or else face being shut down by state and federal agencies that monitor the market for fraud. Your manufacturing process is also subject to federal, state, and local laws concerning hygiene and the disposal of hazardous wastes.
>
> Suppose that you overcome these obstacles, and your business prospers. Other federal agencies will monitor your compliance with laws concerning discrimination by race, sex, and disability, minimum wages, and Social Security taxes. State agencies will examine your records to see if you have paid unemployment taxes and sales taxes. Finally, the Internal Revenue Service will look over your shoulder and demand a share of your profits (about 35 percent).

To see how welfare or state capitalism developed in the United States, let's go back to an earlier era. When capitalism was in its infancy in the 1800s, you could have made your "magic" potion at home and sold it at any outlet willing to handle it. You could have advertised that it cured baldness, erased wrinkles, and dissolved fat, for no agency existed to monitor your product or your claims. (See the 1885 poster.) In fact, this is precisely what thousands of individuals did at that time. They made "elixirs" in their basements and gave them whimsical names such as "Granny's Miracle Medicine" and "Elixir of Health and Happiness." A single product could claim that it restored sexual potency, purged the intestines, and made people more intelligent. These tonics often made people feel better, for many elixirs were braced with alcohol—and even cocaine (Ashley 1975). (Coca-Cola was a "pick me up" during this period, for until 1903 it contained cocaine. This is what the *Coca* of Coca-Cola refers to.) To protect the public's health, in 1906 the federal government passed the Pure Food and Drug Act and began to regulate products.

This advertisement from 1885 represents an early stage of capitalism when individuals were free to manufacture and market products with little or no interference from the government. Today, the production and marketing of goods take place under detailed, complicated government laws and regulations.

As capitalism progressed, laws were developed to restrain it. Corporations often find ways to get around these laws, as Dilbert indicates tongue-in-cheek.

monopoly the control of an entire industry by a single company

socialism an economic system characterized by the public ownership of the means of production, central planning, and the distribution of goods without a profit motive

market forces the law of supply and demand

John D. Rockefeller's remarkable success in unregulated markets helps explain why the government began to regulate capitalism. After a ruthless drive to eliminate competition, Rockefeller managed to corner the U.S. oil and gasoline market. He would slash prices and then double them after driving out the competition. He would even sabotage competitors' pipelines and refineries (Josephson 1949). With his competitors crippled or eliminated, his company, Standard Oil, was able to dictate prices to the entire nation. Rockefeller had achieved the capitalist's dream, a **monopoly**, the control of an entire industry by a single company.

Rockefeller had played the capitalist game too well, however, for he had wiped out one of its essential components: competition. Consequently, to protect this cornerstone of capitalism, the federal government passed antimonopoly legislation and broke up Standard Oil. Today, the top firms in each industry—such as General Motors in automobiles and General Electric in household appliances—must obtain federal approval before acquiring another company in the same industry. If the government determines that one firm dominates a market, it can force that company to *divest* (sell off) some of its businesses.

Another characteristic of welfare capitalism is that although the government supports competition, it establishes its own monopoly over what it calls "common good" items. These are items presumed essential for the common good of the citizens, such as armed forces, war supplies, highways, and sewers.

Socialism

Socialism also has three essential components: (1) public ownership of the means of production; (2) central planning; and (3) the distribution of goods without a profit motive.

In socialist economies, the government owns the means of production. It owns not only the factories, but also the land, railroads, oil wells, and gold mines. Unlike capitalism, in which **market forces**—supply and demand—determine what will be produced and the prices that will be charged, a central committee decides on products and prices. The committee determines how many toothbrushes, toilets, and shoes the country needs. It also decides which factories will produce them, what price will be charged for the items, and where they will be distributed.

Socialism is designed to eliminate competition, for goods are sold at predetermined prices regardless of the demand for an item or the cost to produce it. Profit is not the goal, nor is encouraging consumption of goods in low demand (by lowering the price), nor limiting the consumption of hard-to-get goods (by raising the price). Rather, the goal is to produce goods for the general welfare and to distribute them according to people's needs, not their ability to pay.

In a socialist economy *everyone* works for the government. The members of the central committee who

Successful capitalists can buy most things in life. Donald Trump could be flashing a victory sign to signify that he can afford to sit in the front row at a title fight at Madison Square Garden in New York City. Or his victory sign could indicate that he is able to afford a trophy girlfriend. Sitting next to Trump, age 54, is his girlfriend, Melania Knauss, age 27.

set production goals are government employees, as are the supervisors who implement those goals, the factory workers who produce the merchandise, the truck drivers who move it, and the clerks who sell it. Those who buy the items may work at different jobs—in offices, on farms, or in day care centers—but they, too, are government employees.

Just as capitalism does not exist in a pure form, neither does socialism. Although the ideology of socialism calls for resources to be distributed according to need and not the ability to pay, in line with the functionalist argument of social stratification presented in Chapter 9 (pages 239–240), socialist countries found it necessary to offer higher salaries for some jobs. Only then could they entice capable people to take greater responsibilities. As a result, in socialist countries factory managers always earned more than factory workers. By narrowing the huge pay gaps that characterize capitalist nations, however, socialist nations established considerably greater equality of income.

Dissatisfied with the greed and exploitation of capitalism and the lack of freedom and individuality of socialism, Sweden and Denmark developed **democratic socialism** (also called *welfare socialism*). In this form of socialism, both the state and individuals produce and distribute goods and services. The government owns and runs the steel, mining, forestry, and energy concerns, as well as the country's telephones, television stations, and airlines. Remaining in private hands are the retail stores, farms, factories, and most service industries.

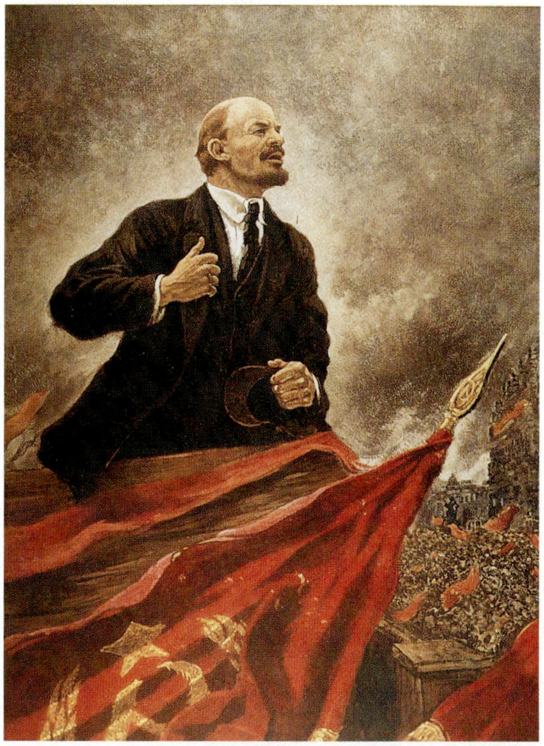

Throughout most of the twentieth century, capitalism and communism were pitted against one another in a deadly struggle. Each thought of itself as the correct economic form, and each viewed the other as an evil obstacle to be eradicated. In support of this view of essential goodness and evil, proponents of each system launched global propaganda campaigns. Shown here is a painting of Vladimir Lenin, leader of the worldwide workers' revolution. This 1930 painting by Alexander Gerassimow (1881–1963) hangs in the Tretyakov Gallery in Moscow.

Ideologies of Capitalism and Socialism

Not only do capitalism and socialism have different approaches to producing and distributing goods, but also they represent distinct ideologies. *Capitalists* believe that market forces should determine both products and prices. They also believe that greed is good. It is healthy for people to strive after profits, for this stimulates them to develop new products. The Mass Media box on the next page examines how capitalists create demand for their products.

Socialists, in contrast, believe that profit is immoral. Karl Marx said that an item's value is based on the work that goes into it. The only way there can be profit, he stressed, is by paying workers less than the value of their labor. Profit, then, is the *excess value* that has been withheld from workers. Socialists believe that the government should protect workers from this exploitation. To do so, it should own the means of production, using them not to produce profit, but to produce items that match people's needs, not their ability to pay.

Adherents to these ideologies paint each other in such stark colors that *each perceives the other as a system of exploitation.* Capitalists view socialists as violating basic human rights of freedom of decision and opportunity. Socialists see capitalists as violating the basic human right of freedom from poverty. With each side claiming moral superiority while viewing the other as a threat to its very existence, the last century witnessed the world split into two main blocs. In what was known as the *Cold War,* the West armed itself to defend capitalism, the East to defend socialism.

Criticisms of Capitalism and Socialism

The primary criticism leveled against capitalism is that it leads to social inequality. Capitalism, say its critics, produces a tiny top layer of wealthy, powerful people who exploit a vast bottom layer of poorly paid workers. Many of these workers are unemployed and underemployed (**underemployment** is having to work at a job beneath your training and abilities or being able to find only part-time work). Another criticism is that the tiny top layer wields vast political power. Those few who own the means of production reap huge profits, accrue power, and are able to get legislation passed that goes against the public good.

The primary criticism leveled against socialism is that it does not respect individual rights (Berger 1991). Others (in the form of some government body) control people's

democratic socialism a hybrid economic system in which capitalism is mixed with state ownership

underemployment the condition of having to work at a job beneath one's level of training and abilities, or of being able to find only part-time work

massMEDIA in Social Life

Greed Is Good—Selling the American Dream

Advertising is such an integral part of our lives that being deluged with ads almost appears to be our human destiny. When we open a newspaper or magazine, we expect to find pages that proclaim the virtues of products and firms. We turn on the television and are assailed with commercials for ten minutes of every half hour. Some social analysts even claim that the purpose of television is to round up an audience to watch the commercials—that the programs are mere diversions from the medium's real objective of selling products!

Advertising is so powerful that it can produce the desire to consume products for which we previously felt no need whatsoever. U.S. kitchens, filled with gadgets that slice and dice, attest to this power.

Advertising's power to turn people into gluttons goes beyond kitchen gadgets that are soon consigned to back drawers and garage sales. Many Americans would not think of going out in public without first shampooing, rinsing, conditioning, and blow-drying their hair. Many feel the need to apply an underarm deodorant so powerful that it overcomes the body's natural need to sweat. For many women, public appearance also demands the application of foundation, lipstick, eye shadow, mascara, rouge, powder, and perfume. For many men, after-shave lotion is essential. And only after covering the body with clothing that displays designer labels do Americans feel that they are presentable to the public.

Advertising influences not only what we put on our bodies, what we eat, and what we do for recreation, but also how we feel about ourselves. Our perceptions of whether we are too fat, too skinny, too hippy, or too buxom, whether our hair is too oily or too dry, our body too hairy, or our skin too rough are largely a consequence of advertising. As we weigh our self-image against the idealized images that bombard us in our daily fare of commercials, we conclude that we are lacking something. Advertising assures us that there is salvation—some new product that promises to deliver us from what we lack.

The approach is ingenious in its simplicity: Create discontent by presenting ideal images that are impossible to attain. And it works. We grow dissatisfied with ourselves. And we snatch the advertisers' solution: We strive to consume more of the never-ending products that the corporations offer us—those they have decided we need.

The American Dream . . . built on greed, discontent, enticing images, and the promise of redemption. Of course, dreams often juxtapose incompatible realities.

lives. They decide where people will live, where they will go to school, where they will work, and how much they will be paid. In China, they even decide how many children women may bear (Mosher 1983). Critics also argue that central planning is grossly inefficient and that socialism is not capable of producing much wealth. They say that its greater equality really amounts to giving almost everyone an equal chance to be poor.

The Convergence of Capitalism and Socialism

Regardless of the validity of these mutual criticisms, as nations industrialize they grow alike. They urbanize, produce similar divisions of labor (such as professionals and skilled technicians), and encourage higher education. Even similar values emerge (Kerr 1983). By itself, this tendency would make capitalist and socialist nations grow more alike, but another factor also brings them closer to one another (Form 1979): Despite their incompatible ideologies, both capitalist and socialist systems have adopted features of each other.

That capitalism and socialism are growing similar is known as **convergence theory.** This view points to a coming hybrid or mixed economy. A fundamental change in socialist countries gives evidence for convergence theory. Russia and China suffered from their production of shoddy goods, they were plagued by shortages, and their standard of living severely lagged behind that of the West. To try to catch up, in the 1980s and 1990s Russia and China reinstated market forces. They made the private ownership of property legal, and they auctioned off many of their state-owned industries. Making a profit—which had been a crime previously—was encouraged. They even invited their former archenemies, Western corporations, to open up shop. In China, capitalists have been invited to join the Communist Party (Kahn 2002). Even North Korea is setting up a commercial zone in which profit will be the goal (French 2002). For a glimpse of Russia's transition to capitalism, see the Cultural Diversity box on the next page.

convergence theory the view that as capitalist and socialist economic systems each adopt features of the other, a hybrid (or mixed) economic system will emerge

CULTURAL DIVERSITY around the WORLD

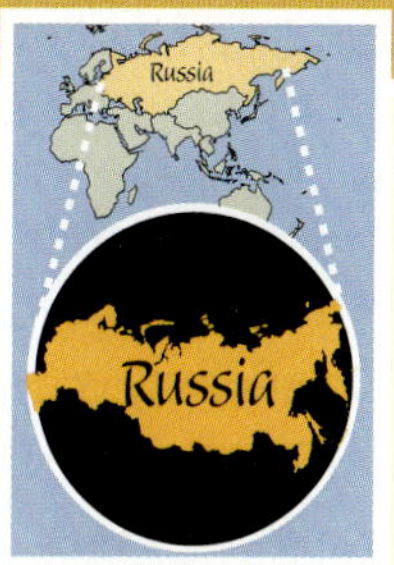

No Cash? No Problem! Barter in the Former Soviet Union

About 50 miles from the town of Bila Tserkva, you'll see a few tires piled alongside the highway. By the time you get to Bila Tserkva, the stacks of black tires have grown thicker and higher until they seem to line both sides of the road like thick rubber walls (Brzezinski 1997).

Welcome to Russia's transition to capitalism. This is payday at the tire plant in Bila Tserkva. With cash in short supply, workers are paid in tires. In other towns, workers get paid in airplanes, televisions, clothing, even tombstones, sex toys, and toilet bowls. Some laid-off workers get their unemployment benefits in manure (Paddock 1998; Schmemann 1998; Powell 1999). In Volgograd, workers are paid in brassieres. So many brassieres will get you into the latest Arnold Schwarzenegger movie—or buy you a hat, a pair of shoes, an ice cream cone. . . .

The new capitalism in Russia

In the cash-strapped former Soviet Union, it's not just individuals who use goods instead of cash. In Smolensk, the cannery pays its taxes in canned beef. It uses canned meat to pay for the cows and pigs it slaughters, the aluminum to make the cans, the equipment to can the meat, the electricity to run the equipment, and the cardboard boxes used for shipping the cans (Paddock 1998).

Barter chains have developed. Ukraine's electric utility company receives payment in goods ranging from military uniforms to steel tubing. The company passes the steel tubing on to the Russian company that supplies it with electricity, which, in turn, uses the tubing in its pipelines. The uniforms? It gives these to Russia's Ministry of Defense in lieu of taxes.

When city workers in Tatarstan arrived at city hall, they found 600 new trucks parked on the front lawn. The trucks were payment on the local truck maker's tax bill. The workers were lucky—they might have been greeted with piles of tires or brassieres.

Changes in capitalism also support this theory. The United States has adopted many socialist practices. One of the most obvious is extracting money from some individuals to pay for the benefits it gives to others. Examples include unemployment compensation (taxes paid by workers are distributed to those who no longer produce a profit); subsidized housing (shelter, paid for by the many, is given to the poor and elderly, with no motive of profit); welfare (taxes from the many are distributed to the needy); a minimum wage (the government, not the employer, determines the minimum that workers receive); and Social Security (the retired do not receive what they paid into the system, but, rather, money that the government collects from current workers). Such embracing of socialist principles means that the United States has produced its own version of a mixed type of economy.

Perhaps, then, convergence is unfolding before our very eyes. On the one hand, capitalists now assume that their system should provide workers at least minimal support during unemployment, illness, and old age. On the other hand, socialist leaders have reluctantly admitted that profit and private ownership do motivate people to work harder.

The matter, however, is not this simple. That each has adopted features of the other is only part of the picture. The systems remain far from "converged." Although it is muted

mechanical solidarity
Durkheim's term for the unity (or shared consciousness) that people feel as a result of performing the same or similar tasks

organic solidarity
Durkheim's term for the interdependence that results from the division of labor; people needing others to fulfill their jobs

compared to what it was in the heady days of the Cold War, the struggle between the systems continues. Russian and Polish citizens, for example, longing for greater stability, have voted Communists back into top government positions. In the United States, Republicans try to roll back socialistic measures and return to a purer capitalism, while Democrats resist. Meanwhile the Chinese, longing to transform themselves into the world's number one capitalist nation, await a "new-thinking" leadership.

The Functionalist Perspective on the Globalization of Capitalism

Sun Microsystems uses a single phone number to offer round-the-globe, round-the-clock technical service. The number is staffed by teams in California, England, and Australia. They electronically hand work off as a team when another country comes on line.

When the Turkish economy plunged, Goodyear didn't let its tire plant in Turkey sit idle. Instead, using flexible tire-making technology, Goodyear swiftly regeared its tire models and redirected output to the rest of Europe. (Zachary 1995)

The globalization of capitalism may be the most significant economic change in the past 100 years. Its impact on our lives may rival that of the Industrial Revolution itself. As Louis Gallambos, a historian of business, says, "This new global business system will change the way everyone lives and works" (Zachary 1995).

The New Global Division of Labor

To apply functionalism to the globalization of capitalism, we must first step back a moment and look at work itself. Work is functional for society. Only because people work do we have electricity, hospitals, schools, automobiles, and homes. Beyond this obvious point, however, lies a basic sociological principle: *Work binds us together.* As you may recall from Chapter 4, Emile Durkheim noted that in agricultural societies people do similar work and directly share most aspects of life. Because of this, they look at the world in similar ways. Durkheim used the term **mechanical solidarity** to refer to the sense of unity that comes from doing similar activities.

The industrialization of society, in contrast, brings a more extensive division of labor. Because people no longer share the same activity, they feel less solidarity with one another. Grape pickers in California, for example, may feel they have little in common with workers who make aircraft in Missouri. Yet, each worker performs a specific function and contributes to the welfare of the others. Because they are *like the separate organs that make up the same body,* Durkheim called this type of unity **organic solidarity.**

In their march toward globalization multinational companies locate their corporate headquarters in one country, manufacture their basic components in another country, assemble them in still another, and sell the finished product throughout the world. Shown here is a Nike assembly plant in Indonesia.

Durkheim observed the beginning of what has turned out to be a global process. Today, organic solidarity engulfs the world. We now have a *global division of labor,* and each of us depends on workers around the globe. People who live in California or New York—or even Michigan—depend on workers in Tokyo to produce cars. Tokyo workers, in turn, depend on Saudi Arabian workers for oil, South American workers to operate ships, and miners in South Africa for palladium for their catalytic converters. Although we do not feel a sense of unity with one another—in fact, we may feel threatened and hostile—interdependence links us all in the same global economic web. This process does not occur without cultural hurdles, of course, a topic of the Cultural Diversity box on the next page.

CULTURAL DIVERSITY

around the WORLD

Doing Business in the Global Village

The globalization of capitalism means that businesspeople face cultural hurdles as they sell products in other cultures. At times, even experienced firms don't manage to break through cultural barriers. General Motors, for example, was successful in marketing its automobile, the Nova, in the United States. When GM tried to export that success south of the border, Mexicans snickered, and few would buy the car. Finally, someone let the company in on the secret: In Spanish, "No va" is an entire sentence that means "It doesn't go" or "It doesn't work."

Ford did no better when it tried to sell its Pinto in Brazil. People there snickered, too. It turns out that pinto is Portuguese slang for "little penis." Ford changed the car's name to Corcel, "the horse" (Archbold and Harmon 2001).

Some companies, trying to market to Mexico's growing middle class and to Spanish-speaking Americans, have stumbled over their Spanish. When Parker Pen tried to translate "It won't leak in your pocket and embarrass you," it came out "It won't leak in your pocket and make you pregnant." Frank Perdue's cute chicken slogan, "It takes a strong man to make a tender chicken" didn't fare any better. It came out "It takes an aroused man to make a chicken affectionate."

Even Coca-Cola, with its many years of cross-cultural experience, stumbled when it first tried to market Coke in China. The name came out as "Bite the wax tadpole." And when American Airlines launched a "Fly in Leather" campaign to promote its leather seats in first class, the Mexican campaign stumbled just a bit. "Fly in Leather" (vuela en cuero), while literally correct, came out as Fly Naked. I suppose that slogan did appeal to some.

Some businesspeople have managed to avoid such problems. They have seized profit opportunities in cultural differences. For example, Japanese women are embarrassed by the sounds they make in public toilets. To drown out the offensive sounds, they flush the toilet an average of 2.7 times a visit (Iori 1988). This wastes a lot of water, of course. Seeing this cultural trait as an opportunity, a U.S. entrepreneur developed a battery-powered device that is mounted in the toilet stall. When a woman activates the device, it emits a 25-second flushing sound. A toilet-sound duplicator may be useless in our culture, but the Japanese have bought thousands of them.

Let's suppose that you decide to publish a magazine in Japan. Your market research shows that a magazine about sports heroes would be popular. It wouldn't surprise you to learn that your readers expect you to present details about their idol's vital statistics, career, and hobbies. But you would miss something essential if you didn't learn that the Japanese also expect to read about their hero's blood type. They view it as a sort of zodiac birth sign (Ono 1993). And you might learn that Japanese mothers save their baby's umbilical cord in a wooden box. If you could get hold of a sports hero's umbilical cord, you could make a small fortune (Shirouzu 1995).

If you opened a golf course in Japan, you would need to understand why golfers there fear shooting a hole-in-one. This obligates them to buy expensive gifts for their fellow players, throw a drinking party, and plant a commemorative tree to mark their "joy." Entrepreneurs have seized this cultural opportunity, too. To ward off such a catastrophe, they sell policies that for $100 provide $5,000 hole-in-one insurance (Hardy 1993).

Ownership and Management of Corporations

Capitalism is driving today's global interdependence. Its triumph as the world's dominant economic force can be traced to a social invention called the corporation. A **corporation** is a business that is treated legally as a person. A corporation can make contracts, incur debts, sue and be sued. Its liabilities and obligations, however, are separate from those of its owners. For example, each shareholder of Ford Motor Company—whether he or she has 1 or 100,000 shares—owns a portion of the company. However, Ford, not its individual owners, is responsible for fulfilling its contracts and paying its debts. To indicate how corporations now dominate the economy, sociologists use the term **corporate capitalism.**

One of the most surprising, but functional, aspects of corporations is their *separation of ownership and management.* Unlike most businesses, it is not the owners—those who own the company's stock—who run the day-to-day affairs of the company. Instead, managers run the corporation, and they are able to treat it *as though it were their own*

corporation the joint ownership of a business enterprise, whose liabilities and obligations are separate from those of its owners

corporate capitalism the domination of the economic system by giant corporations

In their search for profits, companies seek markets wherever they can find them. Mattel's stunning success with Barbie, bringing in over a billion dollars a year, has spawned numerous imitators. The Bratz dolls, much hipper and cooler than Barbie, with such names as Cloe, Jade, Sasha, and Yasmin, have proven such a success that Mattel came out with its own "street smart" Flava dolls. These two lines of dolls reflect fundamental changes in U.S. society. What changes do you think that they reflect?

(Walters 1995; Sklair 2001). The result is the "ownership of wealth without appreciable control, and control of wealth without appreciable ownership" (Berle and Means 1932). Sociologist Michael Useem (1984) put it this way:

> When few owners held all or most of a corporation's stock, they readily dominated its board of directors, which in turn selected top management and ran the corporation. Now that a firm's stock [is] dispersed among many unrelated owners, each holding a tiny fraction of the total equity, the resulting power vacuum allow[s] management to select the board of directors; thus management [becomes] self-perpetuating and thereby acquire[s] de facto control over the corporation.
>
> Management determines its own salaries, sets goals and awards itself bonuses for meeting them, authorizes market surveys, hires advertising agencies, determines marketing strategies, and negotiates with unions. The management's primary responsibility to the owners is to produce profits.

What makes this separation of ownership and management work is profits. When stock options and bonuses are tied to the company's performance, managers are highly motivated to make profits. At the annual stockholders' meeting, the owners consider broad company matters, including the selection of a board of directors and a firm to audit the company's books. As long as the managers report good profits, the stockholders rubber-stamp their recommendations. It is so unusual for this not to happen that when it doesn't take place it is called a **stockholders' revolt.** The irony of this term is generally lost, but remember that in such cases it is not the workers but the owners who are rebelling!

Functions on a Global Scale

The globalization of capitalism is leading to a new world structure. Three primary trading blocks are emerging: North and South America, dominated by the United States; Europe, dominated by Germany; and Asia, dominated by Japan. Functionalists stress not only how this new global division benefits the multinational giants, but also how it benefits the citizens of the world.

stockholders' revolt the refusal of a corporation's stockholders to rubber-stamp decisions made by its managers

Consider free trade. Free trade leads to greater competition, which, in turn, drives the search for greater productivity. This lowers prices and brings a higher standard of living. Free trade also has dysfunctions. As production moves to countries where labor costs are lower, millions of U.S., U.K., French, and German workers lose their jobs. Functionalists point out that this is merely a temporary dislocation. As the Most Industrialized Nations lose production jobs, their workers shift into service and high-tech jobs. Meanwhile, some of the poor of the Least Industrialized Nations are given work and the chance for a better life.

The Conflict Perspective on the Globalization of Capitalism

Conflict theorists say that to place the focus on global interdependence is to miss the point. What we should look at is how the wealthy benefit at the expense of workers. Let's see what they mean by this.

The Inner Circle of Corporate Capitalism

The **multinational corporations**—corporations that operate across national borders—are headed by a group that Michael Useem (1984) calls the *inner circle.* Members of this inner circle, though in competition with one another, are united by a mutual interest in preserving capitalism (Mizruchi and Koenig 1991; Sklair 2001). Within their own country, they consult with high-level politicians, promote legislation favorable to big business, and serve as trustees for the most influential foundations and universities. They also promote political candidates who stand firmly for the private ownership of property. On a global level, they promote the ideology of capitalism and move capital from one nation to another in their search for greater and more immediate profits.

Table 14.2 lists the world's most profitable corporations. You can see how the United States dominates world trade. It accounts for 16 of the world's most profitable 25

Table 14.2 The World's Most Profitable Corporations

Rank	Company	Country	Profits ($ billions)	Employees
1	Exxon Mobil	U.S.	$15.3	98,000
2	Citigroup	U.S.	$14.1	268,000
3	General Electric	U.S.	$13.7	310,000
4	Royal Dutch/Shell Group	Holland	$10.9	91,000
5	Altria Group	U.S.	$8.6	175,000
6	British Petroleum	Great Britain	$8.0	110,000
7	Pfizer	U.S.	$7.8	90,000
8	Intl. Business Machines	U.S.	$7.8	320,000
9	AT and T	U.S.	$7.7	118,000
10	Microsoft	U.S.	$7.4	48,000
11	Merck	U.S.	$7.3	78,000
12	SBC Communications	U.S.	$7.2	193,000
13	ENI	Italy	$6.9	71,000
14	Total Fina Elf	France	$6.9	122,000
15	Bank of America Corp.	U.S.	$6.8	143,000
16	Wal-Mart Stores	U.S.	$6.7	1,383,000
17	Fannie Mae	U.S.	$5.9	4,500
18	Johnson and Johnson	U.S.	$5.7	102,000
19	HSBC Holding PLC	Great Britain	$5.4	170,000
20	American Intl. Group	U.S.	$5.3	81,000
21	BASF	Germany	$5.2	93,000
22	Bristol-Myers Squibb	U.S.	$5.2	46,000
23	China National Petroleum	China	$5.0	1,167,000
24	Toyota Motor	Japan	$4.0	247,000
25	GlaxoSmithKline	Great Britain	$4.5	107,000

Source: Constructed from various 2003 lists of *Fortune 500.*

multinational corporations companies that operate across national boundaries; also called transnational corporations companies. No other country even comes close. The other 9 most profitable companies are spread among 7 other nations.

If the giant corporations cannot attain a monopoly, they strive for an **oligopoly**, where several large companies dominate a single industry, such as gasoline, breakfast cereal, or light bulbs. If they achieve this, then they can divide the market among themselves. They are also able to dictate the quality and prices of their products. To get legislation that gives them special tax breaks, oligopolies also cultivate political connections. (Some simply say that they "buy" politicians.)

One of the more significant, and to some, sinister, developments in capitalism is today's mergers of giant corporations from different nations. Merging, or one company buying another, reduces competition. This also makes it easier to set prices and quality and to trounce smaller competitors. In short, mergers consolidate the power of the multinational corporations and make it easier for them to dominate global markets.

Consolidation of power is one of the primary goals of these corporations. The inner circle looks for cooperative politicians and develops a cozy relationship with them. If they find hostility, some are not above plotting murder and overthrowing governments. In 1973, a U.S. multinational, the International Telephone & Telegraph Company (ITT), joined the CIA in a plot to unseat Chile's elected government. They first attempted to bring about the economic collapse of Chile. When this failed, they plotted a coup d'état, which led to the assassination of the Chilean president, Salvador Allende (Coleman 1995; Rohter 2002).

U.S. economic power is so integrated with politics that the inner circle can even get the U.S. president to pitch their products. If this sounds like an exaggeration, consider this report from the Associated Press (October 29, 1995):

> The White House celebrated Saudi Arabia's $6 billion purchase of U.S.-made airplanes Thursday, calling it a victory for both American manufacturers and the Clinton administration. . . . President Clinton helped broker the sale. . . . Prince Bandar bin Sultan, [Saudi Arabia's] minister of defense and aviation, credited Clinton for closing the purchase. *Clinton personally pitched the quality of the U.S. planes to Saudi King Fahd.* (Italics added.)
>
> . . . (T)he Clinton Administration worked this sale awfully damn hard because of the president's commitment to promoting U.S. business abroad. . . . He has done that routinely, instructed his ambassadors and his diplomats to put the economic interests of Americans forward as they conduct their diplomacy.

Although the president wasn't selling toothpaste, it was the same principle.

In short, the interests of the heads of the multinational corporations and those of the top political leaders converge. Together, they form a *power elite,* with top government leaders dedicated to promoting the interests of the country's economic leaders. To protect their far-flung resources and markets, they provide weapons to regimes that favor their interests and send armed forces against those that threaten them. We shall return to this topic in the next chapter.

Interlocking Directorates

Conflict theorists stress how the elite consolidate their power through **interlocking directorates** (Mizruchi and Koenig 1991; Sklair 2001). Members of the elite serve as directors of several companies. Their fellow members on those boards also sit on the boards of other companies, and so on. Like a spider's web that starts at the center and then fans out in all directions, the top companies are interlocked into a network (Mintz and Schwartz 1985). The chief executive officer of a firm in England, who sits on the board of directors of half a dozen other companies, said:

> If you serve on, say, six outside boards, each of which has, say, ten directors, and let's say out of the ten directors, five are experts in one or another subject, you have a built-in panel of thirty friends who are experts who you meet regularly, automatically each month, and you really have great access to ideas and information. You're joining a club, a very good club. (Useem 1984)

oligopoly the control of an entire industry by several large companies

interlocking directorates the same people serving on the board of directors of several companies

This concentration of power minimizes competition, for a director is not going to approve a plan that will be harmful to another company in which he or she (mostly he) has a stake. The top executives of the top U.S. companies are part of the powerful capitalist class described on pages 268-269. They even get together in recreational settings, where they renew their sense of solidarity, purpose, and destiny (Domhoff 1999b).

Global Investing

The two social maps that follow illustrate how corporations have outgrown their national boundaries. The world map below shows the investments that U.S. corporations have made in other countries. Cross-border investments are not a one-way street, however, as the U.S. map on the next page illustrates. If you buy a book from New York's Random House, you are making a purchase from Bertelsmann, a German company. Macy's (of the famous Macy's Thanksgiving Day parade) is owned by Campeau, a Canadian company. And if you buy a package of Tums, you are buying a product from an old-line U.S. company that is owned by Beecham Group, a British corporation.

Although we take the presence of multinational corporations for granted—as well as their cornucopia of products—their power and presence are new to the world scene. As multinational corporations do business across national borders, they become more and more detached from the interests and values of their country of origin. An executive of Colgate-Palmolive said, "The United States does not have an automatic call on our resources. There is no mindset that puts this country first" (Greider 2001). These corporate giants move investments and production from one part of the globe to another—with no concern for consequences other than profits. How their adding—or withdrawing—of investments affects workers is of no concern to them. With profit as their moral guide, the conscience of multinational corporations is dominated by dollar signs.

Figure 14.2 The Globalization of Capitalism: U.S. Ownership in Other Countries

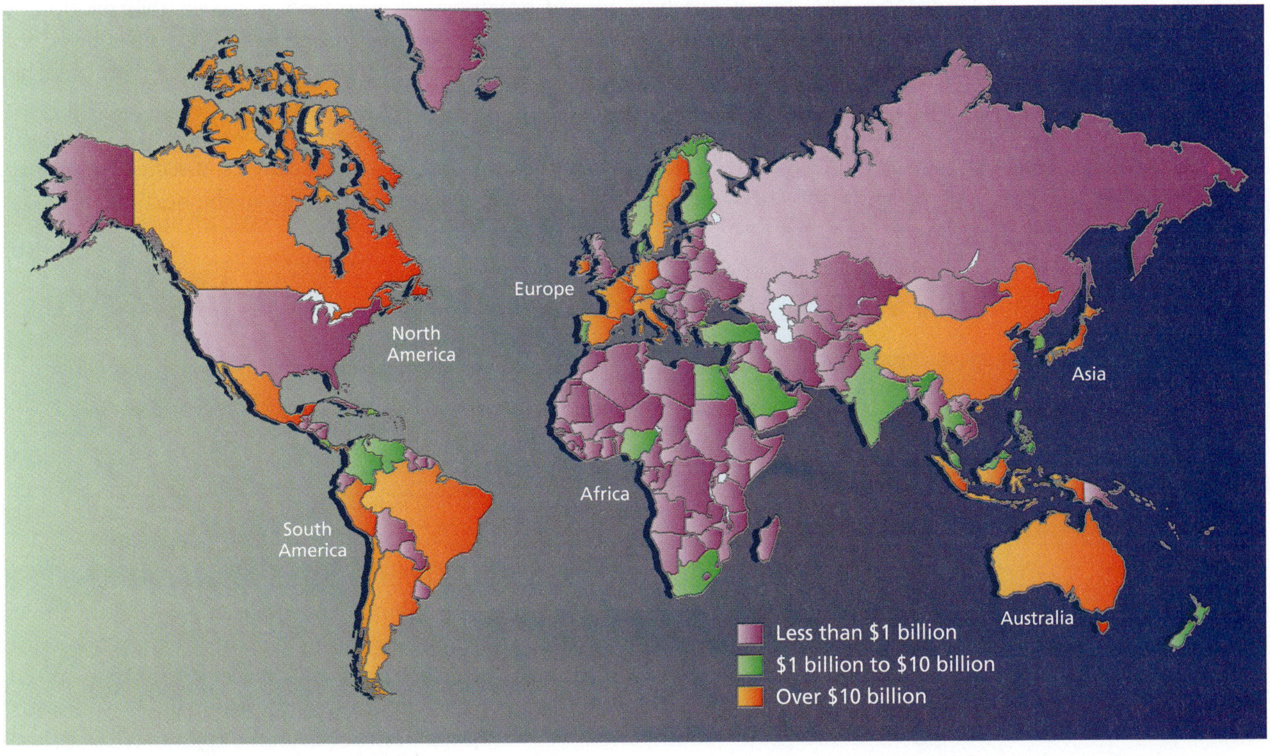

Source: By the author. Based on *Statistical Abstract* 2002:Table 1272.

Figure 14.3 The Globalization of Capitalism: Foreign Ownership of U.S. Business

Businesses in which at least 10 percent of the voting interest is controlled by a non-U.S. owner. Does not include banks.

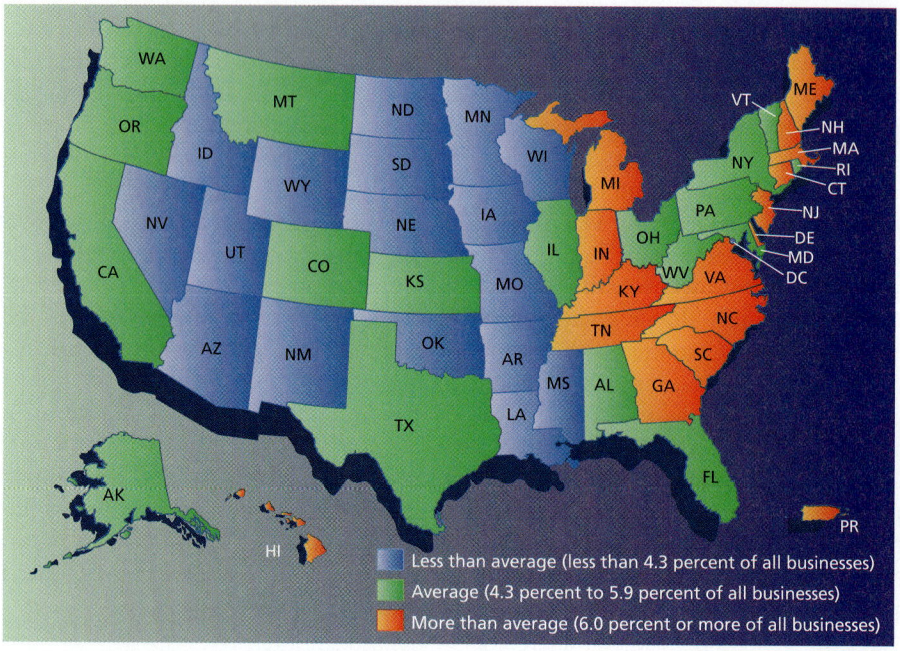

Source: By the author. Based on *Statistical Abstract* 2002:Table 1269.

This primary allegiance to profits and market share, rather than to any country, accompanied by a web of interconnections around the globe, is of high sociological significance. The shift in orientation and organization is so new, however, that we don't yet know its implications. But we can consider two stark contrasts. The first: Removed from tribal loyalties and national boundaries, the global interconnections of the multinational corporations may be a force for global peace. The second: They could create a New World Order dominated by a handful of corporate leaders. If so, we all may find ourselves at the mercy of a global elite in a system of interconnected societies, directed by the heads of the world's corporate giants. We will discuss this possibility in the next chapter.

Work in U.S. Society

With this broad, even global, background, let's turn our focus on work in U.S. society.

The Decline of Agriculture and the Transition to Postindustrial Society

At various times in this text, I have used the term *postindustrial society* to describe the United States. Figure 14.4 illustrates why this term is appropriate. This figure shows a change that is without parallel in human history. In the 1800s, most U.S. workers were farmers. Today, farmers make up about 2 percent of the work force. With the technology of the 1800s, a typical farmer produced enough food for only five people. With today's powerful machinery and hybrid seeds, he or she now feeds about eighty. In 1940, about half of U.S. workers wore a blue collar; then changing technology shrank the market for blue-collar jobs. White-collar work continued its ascent, reaching the dominant position it holds today. Figure 14.4 illustrates nothing less than the transition to a new society. Because of this change, your life is different—not just your work and your lifestyle, but also your attitudes and even the way you view the world.

Women and Work

One of the chief characteristics of the U.S. work force has been a steady increase in the numbers of women who work for wages outside the home. Over the past century, the number steadily increased, and today almost one of two U.S. workers is a woman. As you can see from Figure 14.5, the United States and Canada are tied for having the highest percentage of women in the work force, with Sweden following closely behind.

Researchers have found two primary distinctions between women and men in the world of work. First, women tend to be more concerned than men with maintaining a balance between their work and family lives (Statham et al. 1988). Second, men and women tend to follow different models for success: Men tend to emphasize individualism, power, and competition, while women are more likely to stress collaboration, persuasion, and helping (Miller-Loessi 1992). This creates a dilemma, with many women concerned about the extent to which they must adopt the male model in order to be successful in their careers. You should note that these findings represent tendencies. Although they seem to characterize the average woman or man, many people diverge from them.

Figure 14.4 The Revolutionary Change in the U.S. Work Force

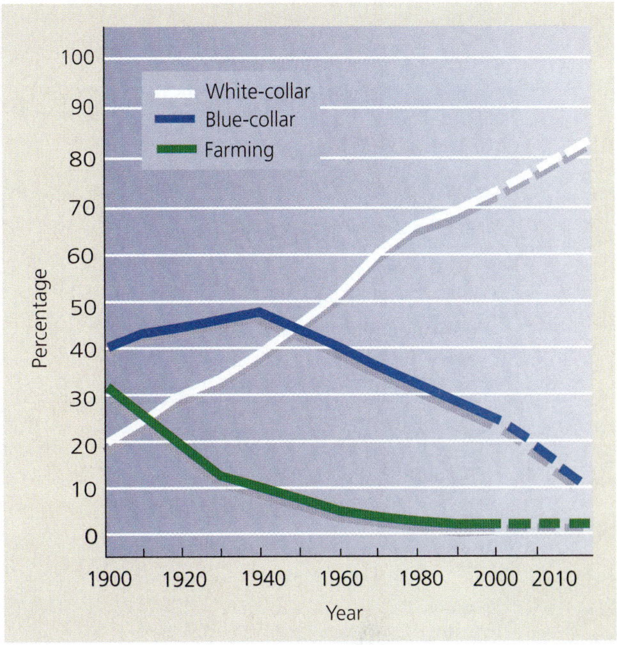

Note: From 1900 to 1940, "workers" refers to people age 14 and over, from 1970 to people age 16 and over. Broken lines are the author's projections.
Source: By the author. Based on *Statistical Abstract*, various years, and 2002:Table 590.

Figure 14.5 What Percentage of Women Are in the Labor Force?

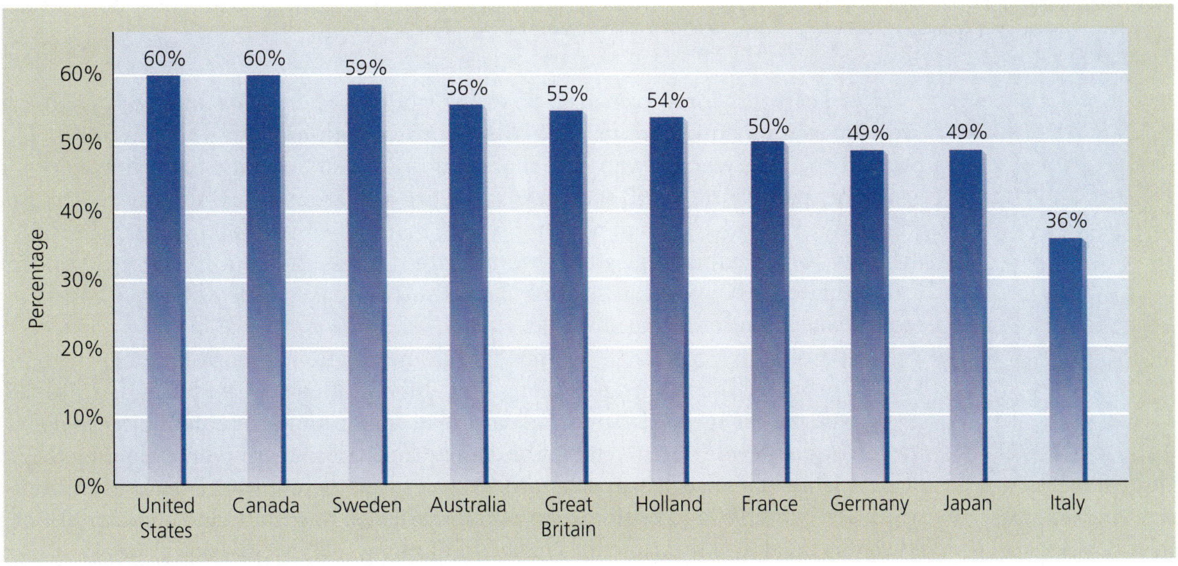

Source: By the author. Based on *Statistical Abstract* 2002:Table 1336.

Figure 14.6 Percentage of Women in the U.S. Labor Force

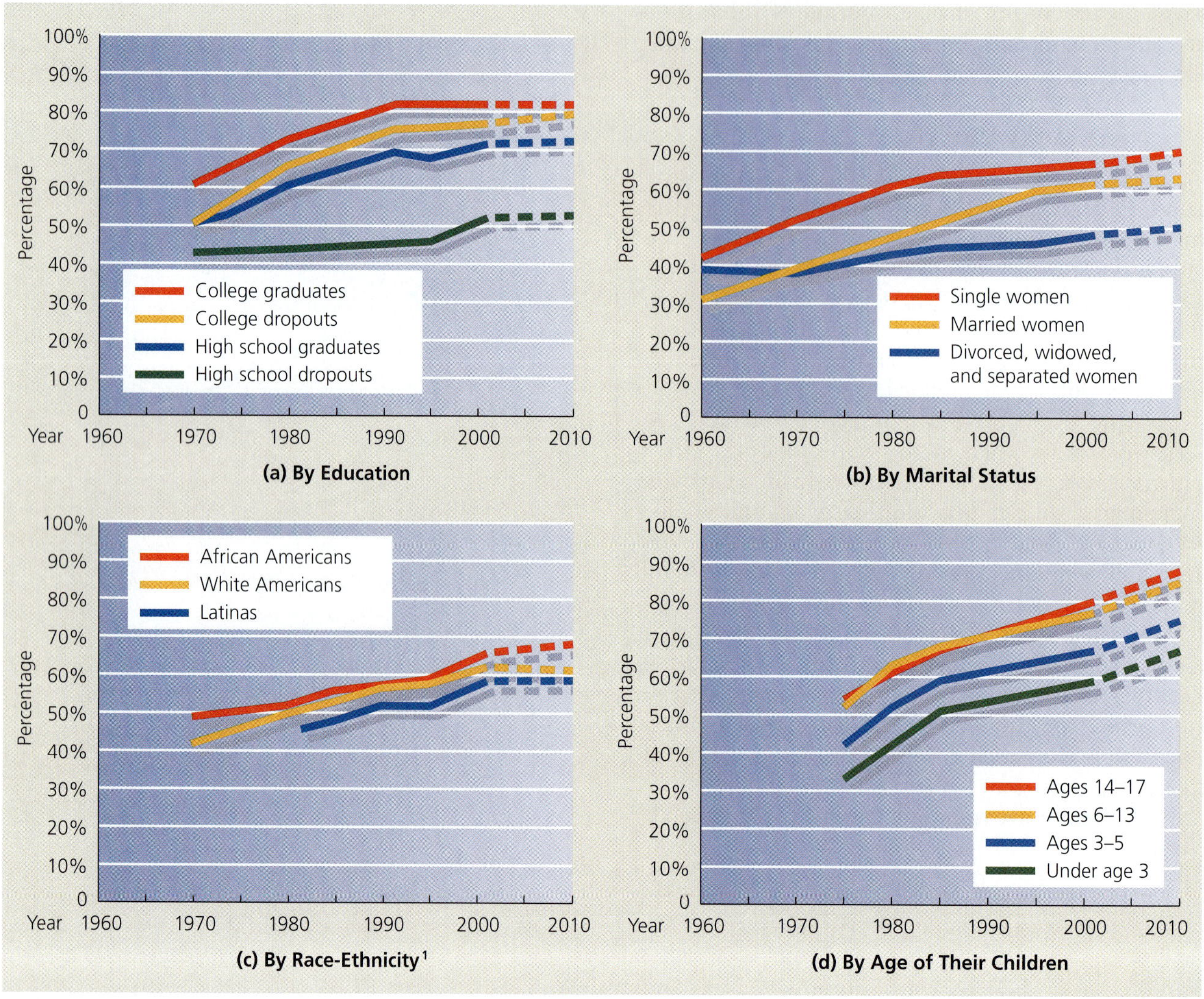

Note: Broken lines indicate the author's projections.
Source: By the author. Based on *Statistical Abstract* 1989:Table 640; 2002:Tables 501, 561, 564, 569, 570.

How likely it is for a woman to be in the labor force depends on several factors. Figure 14.6a shows how working for wages increases with each level of education. This is probably because women who have more education also find more satisfying work—and get higher pay. Figure 14.6b shows the influence of marital status. You can see that single women are the most likely to work for wages, married women follow closely behind, and divorced, widowed, and separated women are the least likely to be in the work force. From Figure 14.6c, you can see that race-ethnicity makes little difference and that the groups have been following a parallel course.

As discussed in Chapter 11, women face discrimination at work. The Down-to-Earth Sociology box on the next page explores how some women cope with this discrimination.

quiet revolution the fundamental changes in society that follow when vast numbers of women enter the work force

Because the change has been so gradual and its implications so profound, sociologists use the term **quiet revolution** to refer to the consequences of so many women joining the ranks of paid labor. This has led to a transformation in family consumer patterns, relations at work, self-concepts, and relationships with boyfriends, husbands, and children. All of this is accompanied by a fundamental change in thinking. I'll give just one example. It used to be considered most undesirable—perhaps immoral—for women with preschoolers to work for wages. These mothers did so only as a last resort. From Figure 14.6d above, you can see

DOWN-TO-EARTH SOCIOLOGY

Women in Business: Maneuvering the Male Culture

I WORK FOR A LARGE INSURANCE company. Of its twenty-five hundred employees, about 75 percent are women. Only 5 percent of the upper management positions, however, are held by women.

I am one of the more fortunate women, for I hold a position in middle management. I am also a member of the twelve-member junior board of directors, of whom nine are men and three are women.

Recently one of the female members of the board suggested that the company become involved in Horizons for Tomorrow, a program designed to provide internships for disadvantaged youth. Two other women and I spent many days developing a proposal for our participation.

The problem was how to sell the proposal to the company president. From past experiences, we knew that if he saw it as a "woman's project" it would be shelved into the second tier of "maybes." He hates what he calls "aggressive bitches."

We three decided, reluctantly, that the proposal had a chance only if it were presented by a man. We decided that Bill was the logical choice. We also knew that we had to "stroke" Bill if we were going to get his cooperation.

We first asked Bill if he would "show us how to present our proposal." (It is ridiculous to have to play the role of the "less capable female," but, unfortunately, the corporate culture sometimes dictates this strategy.) To clinch matters, we puffed up Bill even more by saying, "You're the logical choice for the next chairmanship of the board."

Bill, of course, came to our next planning session, where we "prepped" *him* on what to say.

At our meeting with the president, we had Bill give the basic presentation. We then backed *him* up, providing the background and rationale for why the president should endorse the project. As we answered the president's questions, we carefully deferred to Bill.

The president's response? "An excellent proposal," he concluded, "an appropriate project for our company."

To be successful, we had to maneuver through the treacherous waters of the "hidden culture" (actually not so "hidden" to women who have been in the company for a while). The proposal was not sufficient on its merits, for the "who" behind a proposal is at least as significant as the proposal itself.

"We shouldn't have to play these games," Laura said, summarizing our feelings.

But we all know that we have no choice. To become labeled "pushy" is to commit "corporate suicide"—and we're no fools.

Source: Written by an insurance executive in the author's introductory sociology class who, out of fear of retaliation at work, has chosen to remain anonymous.

how the proportion of women with preschoolers has steadily increased. From this figure, you can also see that more and more women enter the paid labor force as their children grow older. We discuss implications of these changes in Chapter 16.

The Underground Economy

> The underground economy. The term has a sinister ring—suggestive of dope deals struck in alleys and wads of bills hastily exchanged. The underground economy is this, but it is a lot more—and it is usually a lot more innocent. If you pay the plumber with a check made out to "cash," if you purchase a pair of sunglasses from a street vendor or a kitchen gadget at a yard sale, if you so much as hand a neighbor's kid a $20 bill to mow the lawn or to baby sit, you are participating in the underground economy. (Pennar and Farrell 1993)

Also known as the informal economy and the off-the-books economy, the **underground economy** consists of economic activities—whether legal or illegal—that people don't report to the government. What interests most of us is not unreported babysitting money, but the illegal activities that people cannot report even if they want to. As a 20-year-old child care worker in one of my classes who also works as a prostitute two or three nights a week told me, "Why do I do this? For the money! Where else can I make this kind of money in a few hours? And it's all tax free." Drug dealing is perhaps the largest single source of illegal income, for billions of dollars flow from users to sellers and their networks of growers, importers, processors, transporters, dealers, and enforcers. These

underground economy exchanges of goods and services that are not reported to the government and thereby escape taxation

The term underground economy *has a sinister ring to it. Part of the underground economy does consist of drug deals furtively transacted in back alleys, but the term refers to any unreported, untaxed commercial transaction. Most are as innocuous, and common, as that depicted in this photo taken at Union Square Market in New York City.*

particular networks are so huge that each year the police arrest more than a million Americans for illegal drug activities (*Statistical Abstract* 2002:Table 299).

The million or so illegal immigrants who enter the United States each year are also part of the underground economy. Often called *undocumented workers* (referred to as *los sin documentos* in Mexico), they work for employers who either pay no attention to their fake Social Security cards or pay them in cash. Of the 43 restaurant workers who were killed when terrorists struck the World Trade Center, 12 were working with fake Social Security cards (Cleeland 2001). Some illegal immigrants enter on their own, but smugglers bring in many (Henslin 2003d:272). Undocumented workers from China work primarily in Chinese restaurants and in New York's garment industry. Many from India and Pakistan work in fast food restaurants (Rosenbaum 1998). Those from Mexico and Central and South America are concentrated in California and Texas, but they disperse throughout the country. They do housework, pick lettuce on farms, sew garments in clandestine sweatshops, clean rooms in hotels, and serve food at restaurants. For the most part, they do the low-paying and dirty jobs that U.S. citizens try to avoid. The rest of us benefit from their labor, for they bring us cheaper goods and services.

Because of its subterranean nature, no one knows the size of the underground economy, but it probably runs at least 10 percent of the regular economy (Barber 2003). Since the official gross domestic product of the United States is about $10 trillion (*Statistical Abstract* 2002:Table 63), the underground economy probably totals over $1 trillion a year. It is so huge that it distorts the official statistics of the country's gross domestic product, and costs the IRS billions of dollars a year in lost taxes.

Stagnant and Shrinking Paychecks

U.S. workers are some of the most productive in the world (*Statistical Abstract* 2002:Table 1353). One might think, therefore, that their pay would be increasing. This brings us to a disturbing trend.

Look at Figure 14.7 on the next page. The gold bars show current dollars. These are the dollars the average worker finds in his or her paycheck. You can see that since 1970 the pay of U.S. workers has jumped from just over $3 an hour to over $14 an hour. Workers today are bringing home *four and a half* times as many dollars as workers used to. But let's strip away the illusion. Look at the green bars, which show the constant dollars, the *buying power* of those paychecks. They show how inflation has whittled away the value of

leisure time not taken up by work or required activities those dollars. Today's workers can buy only as much with their $14 an hour as workers in 1970 could with their "measly" $3 an hour. The question is not "How could workers live on just $3 an hour back then?" but, rather, "How can workers live on just $14 an hour today?"

Figure 14.7 Average Hourly Earnings of U.S. Workers in Current and Constant (1982) Dollars

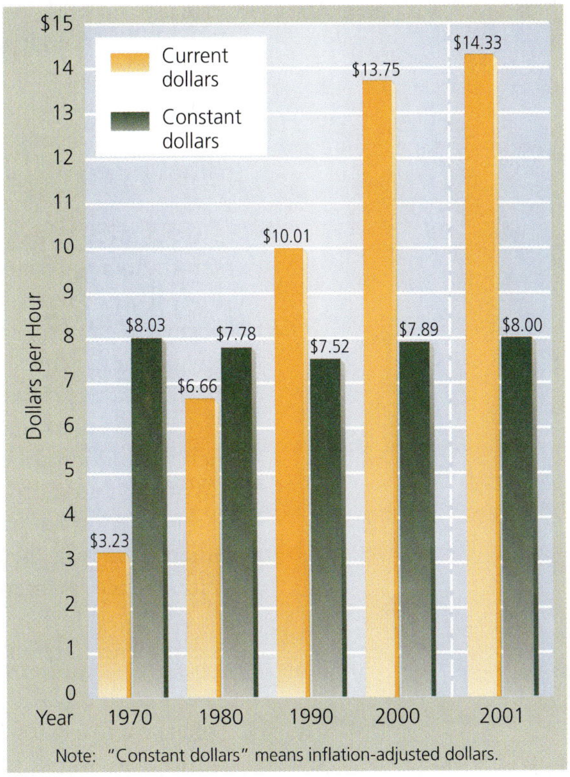

Source: By the author. Based on *Statistical Abstract* 1999:Table 698; 2002:Table 608.

Patterns of Work and Leisure

Suppose that it is 1860 and you work for a textile company in Lowell, Massachusetts. When you arrive at work one day, you find that the boss has posted a new work rule: All workers will have to come in at the same time and remain until quitting time. Like the other workers, you feel outrage. You join them as they shout, "This is slavery!" and march out of the plant, indignant at such a preposterous rule. (Zuboff 1991)

This is a true story. The workers were angry because up until then, they had been able to come and go when they wanted. Let's consider how patterns of work and leisure are related to the transformation of economies.

Effects of Industrialization

Hunting and gathering societies provided enormous amounts of **leisure,** time not taken up by work or required activities such as eating and sleeping. Assuming they didn't live in a barren place or have to deal with some unusual event, such as drought or pestilence, it did not take long for people to hunt and gather what they needed for the day. In fact, *most of their time was leisure,* and the rhythms of nature were an essential part of their lives. Agricultural economies also allowed much leisure, for, at least in the western hemisphere, work peaked with the spring planting, let up in the summer, and then peaked again with the fall harvest. During the winter work again receded, for by this time the harvest was in, animals had been slaughtered, food had been canned and stored, and a wood supply had been laid up.

Industrialization, however, broke this harnessing of work to seasonal rhythms. Going against all of human history, bosses and machines now dictated when work was to be done. Workers resisted these dictates, clinging to their traditional patterns. After working for several weeks—or even just days—a worker would disappear, only to reappear when money ran out. For most, enjoying leisure was considerably more important than amassing money (Weber 1958/1904–1905). Since regular, efficient production brought more profits, bosses began to insist that all workers start work at the same time. To workers of that period, this seemed like slavery. Today, in contrast, work patterns that are artificially imposed on us have become part of the taken-for-granted cultural rhythms that coordinate our lives.

Figure 14.8 Leisure and the Life Course: The "U" Curve of Leisure

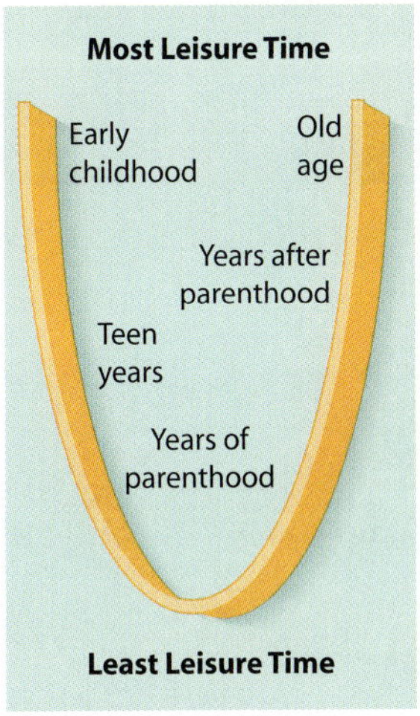

Source: By the author.

Trends in Leisure

It is not the activity itself that makes something leisure, but the purpose for which it is done. Consider driving a car. If you do it for pleasure, it is leisure, but if you are an on-duty police officer or if you must commute to the office, it is work. If done for enjoyment, horseback riding and reading a book are leisure—but these activities are work for jockeys and students.

Patterns of leisure change with the life course, following the U-curve shown on Figure 14.8. Young children enjoy the most leisure, but teenagers still have considerably more leisure than their parents. Parents with small children have the least leisure, but after the children leave home, leisure picks up again. After the age of 60 or so, the amount of leisure for adults peaks.

Compared with workers during early industrialization, today's workers have far more leisure. A hundred years ago the work week was half again as long as today's, for then workers had to be at their machines 60 hours a week. When workers unionized, they demanded a shorter work week. Over the years, the work week has gradually shrunk. In Germany the work week is 35 hours, with Friday afternoons usually off. Volkswagen was the world's first multinational corporation to adopt a 30-hour work week (Rifkin 1995). In addition, German workers get six weeks of paid vacation a year. A strange thing has happened in the United States, though. This trend toward more leisure has reversed course. U.S. workers now average 1,978 hours of work a year, the highest of any industrialized nation (DeGraaf 2003).

Telecommuting (Teleworking) Just as the Industrial Revolution took workers from home to factory, so our current technological revolution has allowed several million workers to return home (Wells 2001). There they do their work, while they "commute" electronically with their company. Corporations save office space, and workers avoid traffic jams. Productivity usually increases, but managers fret about a loss of control over workers. Many feel that if workers are out of sight, they aren't really working. For their part, workers often fear that their career will be sabotaged because they are out of touch with office politics.

Work is always more than work. The paycheck is the typical motivation for taking a job, but friendships with fellow workers are also valued. This creates a problem for teleworkers, who miss the camaraderie of their office mates. E-mail helps, but it isn't the same as face-to-face interaction, of seeing the look on Bob's and Mary's faces when they tell a joke or repeat the latest office gossip. Many teleworkers find work at home to be a soulless experience. Here is what a student who read this text reported:

> My husband is still working as a software engineer. His company "wired" most of their employees for home offices. So he now works from home and has a boss in another state whom he rarely sees in person. He misses his "community" at the office and often, out of the blue, will just go in for a few hours for no good reason. He's usually disappointed, though, because most everyone else works at home, and he finds few people to chat with. His company recognizes this as a big problem. It's hard to keep the team spirit, so they have tried to gently "mandate" once a week togetherness lunches. But it's not the same as everyday contact.

Facing the Future: Implications of Global Capitalism

We can catch a glimpse of the future by looking at two trends that are firmly in place: global trade and the new technology.

Global Trade: Inequalities and Conflict

The giant multinational corporations are carving up the world into major trading blocs and pushing for the reduction or elimination of tariffs. As a result, we can expect trade among nations to increase beyond anything the world has ever seen. U.S. corporations will continue to support an expansion of global trade, for world markets have become crucial for their success. For example, with the huge costs of making movies (the average movie now runs $50 million), the U.S. movie industry would go broke if it weren't for global distribution.

Not all nations will benefit equally, of course. The Most Industrialized Nations (even as they move through their postindustrial phase) will continue to garner the lion's share of the world's wealth. (You may want to look again at Table 14.2 on page 403.) A major concern is that economic inequality will increase between the richer and the poorer nations. The growing wealth of the nations that control global trade does not sit easily with the Least Industrialized Nations. Their poverty and powerlessness—illuminated by televised images of wealth and privilege beamed from the Most Industrialized Nations—breed discontent. So do growing pressures on their limited resources from their mushrooming populations. All this provides fertile ground for the recruitment of terrorists, who, if able, will vent their frustrations against those nations they perceive as exploiting them.

New Technologies and Downsizing: Utopia or Nightmare?

Computer-driven production will continue to reduce the number of workers who are needed to make the goods we use. As I wrote back in 1975,

> Although it may sound as though it is taken from some utopian scheme, it has been estimated that the day will come when only 2 percent of the population will be needed to produce all the manufactured goods our total population needs. That day may not be far off as Ford Motor Company now takes only six workers to produce a single car while it took 104 workers for the same task in 1910 . . . it is possible that a single plant with but a single worker can produce all the bread needed in southern California. . . . Whether such changes represent a utopian dream come true or not, for displaced workers it can well be a nightmare. (p. 341)

As capitalism globalizes, it is not just the products but also the cultures of the dominant capitalist nations that are exported around the world. As the premier producer and exporter of images, Hollywood makes a global impact. Shown here in Xian, China, is what has become a global icon.

Utopia or nightmare? From a symbolic interactionist standpoint, it all depends on your point of view. As conflict theorists stress, that point of view depends on where you stand in the production process. The jobs that the new technology destroys are not located at the top managerial levels of the multinationals, nor are they held by the capitalists who own the company stock. For the most part, these people are immune from such disruptions. Although they must modify their investment and management strategies to match changing markets, the new technology allows them to lower production costs, increase profits, and fatten their dividends and stock options. The people who bear the brunt of the change are low-level workers who live from paycheck to paycheck. It is they who suffer the ravages of uncertainty, the devastation of job loss, and, often, the wrenching adjustments that come from being forced from their jobs.

Let's close this chapter, then, with a Thinking Critically section that focuses on the far-reaching implications of this global transformation of our economy.

THINKING Critically

What Type of New Society? New Technology and the Restructuring of Work

The fear of being automated out of a job plagues many workers. They have seen machines displace people who worked at their side, the lucky ones getting "early retirement" and a pension, the others nothing.

But does technology actually take away jobs? On the one hand, there is no doubt that technology causes job after job to become obsolete. On this score, the workers' fears are not irrational. The automobile industry makes about as many cars as it did 30 years ago, but it employs less than half as many production workers. The number of workers at U.S. Steel has dropped from 120,000 to just 20,000—yet production remains the same (Volti

As conflict theorists stress, in order to keep labor costs low and profits high, capitalist economies use a reserve labor force *that pits one worker against another. This poorly paid gold miner in South Africa, working under the debilitating conditions you see in this photo, is an expendable part of the profit system that drives the economic machinery called* capitalism. *If this worker protests his working conditions, he will be fired immediately, for waiting in the wings are thousands of unemployed workers eager to take his place.*

1995). Computerized automation will continue to erase millions of U.S. manufacturing jobs.

But there is another side to the story, for technology also creates jobs. The automobile industry wiped out the livelihood of stable hands, but it put tens of thousands more to work in the new steel and gasoline industries. These jobs are in addition to mechanics, salespeople, and advertisers, as well as the work done in the body shops that dot our landscape.

Each new technology, then, both destroys old jobs and creates new ones. Some of these jobs—as with those in the many shops that do instant oil changes or sell tires—are readily visible. Others are less evident. The technology that went into airplanes, for example, not only spawned pilots, mechanics, and reservation clerks, but also stimulated global tourism. To put this in a nutshell: *Most* of us work at jobs that did not even exist 75 years ago.

And the future? New technologies are inevitable. The basic question is whether the new technologies will destroy jobs faster than they create them. For the millions of workers who find their jobs pulled out from under them, this question is of more than theoretical interest.

Consider two futures (Rifkin 1995). The one is a technoparadise of abundance and leisure. With few workers needed, work is spread around, and the work week is only 10 or 15 hours. Yet everyone is able to possess goods in abundance. Having restored the leisure that humans used to enjoy in their early days as hunters and gatherers, creative leisure becomes a chief characteristic of the new society. Some spend time in intellectual pursuits, studying the sciences, philosophy, languages. Some follow the arts—painting, poetry, the theater. Many travel. Parents spend much more time with their children. Others, of course, just watch more soap operas, play more video games, or sit transfixed, with a beer in one hand and the remote in the other, through endless hours of televised sports and reality shows.

The second future is a society split into factions. One group, smaller and affluent, lives among a larger group of impoverished workers and those dispossessed from the work force. The contrasts are so great that it is almost like a country inside a country. Millions, surviving in hopelessness and despair, accept meager handouts that are only grudgingly given. Displaced from job opportunities, the nation's youth produce a violent criminal subculture. Frightened and confused at the increasing violence, the affluent lock themselves behind gated communities.

We can't turn back the clock. New technology is here to stay, and, as always, it will continue to change the nature of work. The basic issue, then, is how we, as a society, react. The transformation of work is inevitable, but the consequences of that restructuring are not.

For Your CONSIDERATION . . .

Which of these futures appears to be more likely? In answering this question, refer to the discussion in this chapter about the effects of the new technolo-

Figure 14.9 The Inverted Income Pyramid: The Proportion of Income Received by Each Fifth of the U.S. Population

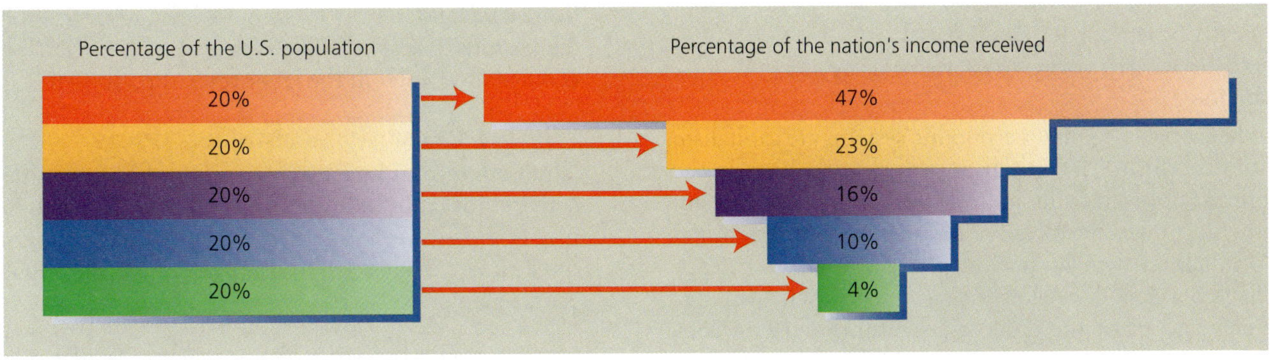

Source: By the author. Based on *Statistical Abstract* 2002:Table 659.

gies on work, the globalization of capitalism, and the growing power of multinational corporations.

The growing gap between the "haves" and the "have-nots" of our society reveals an ominous trend. Look at the inverted pyramid shown in Figure 14.9 above. This figure renders a snapshot of how the nation's income is divided. Each rectangle on the left represents a fifth of the U.S. population. The rectangles on the right represent the proportion of the nation's income that goes to each of these fifths. From this inverted pyramid, you can see that *47 percent* of the entire country's income goes to the richest fifth of Americans, while only *4 percent* goes to the poorest fifth. This gap is now greater than it has been in generations. Rather than bringing equality, then, the postindustrial economy is perpetuating and enlarging the income inequalities of the industrial economy. What implications of this division of the nation's wealth do you see for our future?

SUMMARY and REVIEW

The Transformation of Economic Systems

How are economic systems linked to types of societies?

The earliest societies, hunting and gathering, were **subsistence economies:** Small groups lived off the land and produced little or no surplus. Economic systems grew more complex as people discovered how to domesticate animals and grow plants (pastoral and horticultural societies), farm (agricultural societies), and manufacture (industrial societies). Each of these methods allowed people to produce a *surplus,* which fostered trade. Trade, in turn, brought social inequality as some people accumulated more than others. Service industries dominate the postindustrial societies. If a bioeconomic society is emerging, it is too early to know its consequences. Pp. 390–392.

The Transformation of the Medium of Exchange

How has the medium of exchange evolved?

A **medium of exchange** is any means by which people exchange goods and services. In hunting and gathering and pastoral and horticultural societies, people **bartered** goods and services. In agricultural societies, **money** came into use, which evolved into **currency,** or paper money, representing a specific amount of gold or silver on deposit. Postindustrial societies rely increasingly on electronic transfer of funds in the form of **credit cards, debit cards,** and **e-cash.** Pp. 393–394.

World Economic Systems

How do the major economic systems differ?

The world's two major economic systems are capitalism and socialism. In **capitalism,** private citizens own the means of production and pursue profits. In **socialism,** the state owns the means of production and determines production with no goal of profit. Adherents of each have developed ideologies that defend their own systems and paint the other as harmful. Following **convergence theory,** each system has adopted features of the other. Pp. 394–400.

The Functionalist Perspective on the Globalization of Capitalism

From the functionalist perspective, work is a basis of social solidarity. Traditional societies have **mechanical solidarity;** people perform similar tasks and identify with one another. Industrialization brings **organic solidarity,** interdependence based on the division of labor. This process has continued to the point that we now are developing a global division of labor. **Corporations,** with their separation of ownership and management, underlie the success of capitalism. Pp. 400–403.

The Conflict Perspective on the Globalization of Capitalism

Conflict theorists, who focus on power, note that global capitalism is a means by which capitalists exploit workers. At the top of the **multinational corporations** is an inner circle. While workers lose jobs to automation, the *inner circle* maintains its political power and profits from the new technology. The term **corporate capitalism** indicates that giant corporations dominate capitalism today. Pp. 403–406.

Work in U.S. Society

How has the workforce changed?

In the transition to a postindustrial society, the number of farm workers has plummeted, blue-collar work has decreased, and almost everyone works at service jobs. The United States and Canada have the highest percentage of women in the labor force. Pp. 406–409.

What is the underground economy?

The **underground economy** consists of any economic activity not reported to the government, from babysitting to prostitution. The size of the underground economy runs perhaps 10 to 15 percent of the regular economy. Pp. 409–410.

How have patterns of work and leisure changed?

In hunting and gathering societies, most time was leisure. In agricultural societies, work was dictated by the seasons. Industrialization reduced workers' leisure, but workers have now gained some leisure back. Americans work more hours per week than do the workers of any other industrialized nation. Pp. 411–412.

Facing the Future: Implications of Global Capitalism

What economic trends will affect our future?

Due to expanding global trade, new technologies, and downsizing, the nature of work will continue to be transformed. Choices made now can lead either to a better society or to a nightmare. Pp. 412–415.

Where can I read more on this topic?

Suggested Readings for this chapter are at the back of this book.

THINKING Critically ABOUT CHAPTER 14

1. What global forces are affecting the U.S. economy? What consequences are they having? How might they affect your own life?
2. What are the major characteristics and ideologies of capitalism and socialism? How are these related to the political and economic competition called the *Cold War*?
3. How can anyone say that the average U.S. worker hasn't gotten ahead in recent years, when the average hourly wage is now several times larger than it used to be? What implications does this have for your own future?

ADDITIONAL RESOURCES for This Chapter

www.ablongman.com/henslin7e

- *Content Select* Research Database for Sociology, with suggested key terms and annotated references
- Link to 2000 Census, with activities
- Flashcards of key terms and concepts
- Practice Tests
- Weblinks
- Interactive Maps

Chapter 15

Politics

Frederick Childe Hassam,
The Fourth of July, 1916

You may have missed this in the news:

A month before Christmas last year, three people, most likely men, walked into a crowded shopping mall in Oklahoma City. Dressed as maintenance workers and carrying plant sprayers, they strolled among the holiday shoppers, tending to the potted plants that decorated the corridors. A short time later, the three walked to the mall exits and vanished into the winter darkness. At that moment, two other teams were doing the same thing at malls in Atlanta and Philadelphia.

At 7 p.m. on December 9, the President of the United States summoned the National Security Council. He skipped preliminary remarks and somberly announced, "Three cases of smallpox have been confirmed in Oklahoma City. There may be 20 more. It looks like the disease has been deliberately introduced, that we are under a bioterrorist attack."

As the President spoke, a laboratory in Oklahoma confirmed 23 cases of smallpox, and said it suspected 30 more. Atlanta reported 17 cases, and Philadelphia 10.

The Department of Homeland Security confirmed that the only known sources of smallpox were at the Centers for Disease Control in Atlanta and the Vector Laboratory in Russia. Russian intelligence revealed that a former Vector scientist, an expert in smallpox, had disappeared. She was thought to be in Iran.

a former Vector scientist,
an expert in smallpox,
had disappeared.
She was thought to be in Iran.

Within a week, thousands of Americans were showing signs of smallpox and were overwhelming hospital emergency rooms. The nation quickly ran out of vaccine. Television news footage of tearful mothers holding sick babies and crowds demanding medical help alarmed the public. Out of fear of catching the disease, almost everyone stayed home, refusing to go out into the public. Businesses and public services across the country shut down.

By December 15, officials had confirmed 2,000 cases of smallpox in 15 states, with more in Canada and Mexico. There were 300 deaths. A week later, there were 16,000 cases, and the death toll had reached a thousand. Health authorities

Chapter Outline

projected several million cases of smallpox in just the Untied States and more than a million deaths. The disease had spread to a dozen more countries.

GAME OVER.

This really did happen—the game, that is. "Dark Winter" was played in June 2001 at Andrews Air Force Base, with a former U.S. Senator taking the role of the President. The results were dismaying. They showed just how unprepared we are to deal with bioterrorism.

Based on Simons 2002.

What does biological terrorism have to do with politics, the topic of this chapter? We'll come back to this matter, but for now let's consider power and politics.

Micropolitics and Macropolitics

The images that come to mind when we think of *politics* are those of government: kings, queens, coups, dictatorships, people running for office, voting. These are examples of politics, but the term actually has a much broader meaning. It refers to power relations wherever they exist, including those in your own life. As Weber (1922/1968) said, **power** is the ability to get your way even over the resistance of others. If two or three employees try to impress their new boss—who is going to decide which one of them will be promoted to manager—this is an example of jockeying for power, and of politics. So are parents' efforts to enforce a curfew despite protests from a reluctant daughter or son. Ever struggle over the TV remote control? This, too, is an attempt to gain power—and, thus, of politics. *Every group, then, is political, for in every group there is a power struggle of some sort.* Symbolic interactionists use the term **micropolitics** to refer to the exercise of power in everyday life (Schwartz 1990).

In contrast, **macropolitics**—the focus of this chapter—refers to the exercise of power over a large group. Governments, whether a dictatorship or the elected forms in the United States and Canada, are examples of macropolitics. Let's turn, then, to macropolitics, considering first the matter of authority.

Power, Authority, and Violence

To exist, every society must have a system of leadership. Some people must have power over others. As Max Weber (1913/1947) pointed out, we perceive power as either legitimate or illegitimate. Legitimate power is called **authority**. This is power that people accept as right. In contrast, illegitimate power—called **coercion**—is power that people do not accept as just.

power the ability to carry out your will, even over the resistance of others

micropolitics the exercise of power in everyday life, such as deciding who is going to do the housework or control the remote

Imagine that you are on your way to buy a digital, flat screen TV on sale for $250. As you are on your way to the store, a man jumps out of an alley and shoves a gun in your face. He demands your money. Frightened for your life, you hand over the $250. After filing a police report, you head back to college to take a sociology exam. You are running late, so you step on the gas. As the needle hits 85, you see flashing blue and red lights in your rearview mirror. Your explanation about the robbery doesn't faze the officer—nor the judge who hears your case a few weeks later. She first lectures you on safety and then orders you to pay $50 in court costs plus $10 for every mile an hour over 65. You pay the $250.

The mugger, the police officer, and the judge—each has power, and in each case you part with $250. What, then, is the difference? The difference is that the mugger has no authority. His power is illegitimate—he has no *right* to do what he did. In contrast, you acknowledge that the officer has the right to stop you and that the judge has the right to fine you. They have authority, or legitimate power.

Authority and Legitimate Violence

As sociologist Peter Berger observed, it makes little difference whether you willingly pay the fine that the judge levies against you, or refuse to pay it. The court will get its money one way or another.

> There may be innumerable steps before its application [of violence], in the way of warnings and reprimands. But if all the warnings are disregarded, even in so slight a matter as paying a traffic ticket, the last thing that will happen is that a couple of cops show up at the door with handcuffs and a Black Maria [billy club]. Even the moderately courteous cop who hands out the initial traffic ticket is likely to wear a gun—just in case. (Berger 1963)

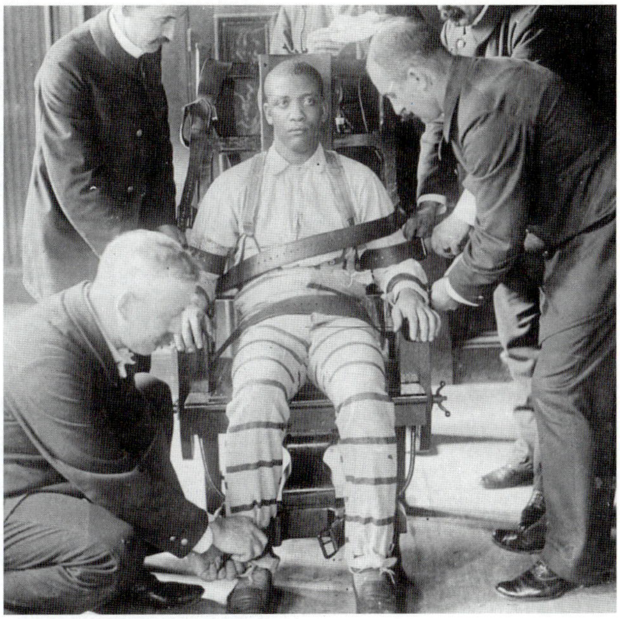

The ultimate foundation of any political order is violence. At no time is this more starkly demonstrated than when a government takes a human life. Shown in this 1910 photo from New York's Sing Sing Prison is a man who is about to be executed.

The *government,* then, also called the **state,** claims a monopoly on legitimate force or violence. This point, made by Max Weber (1946, 1922/1968)—that the state claims the exclusive right to use violence and the right to punish everyone else who does—is crucial to our understanding of politics. If someone owes you a debt, you cannot imprison that person or even forcibly take the money. The state, however, can. The ultimate proof of the state's authority is that you cannot kill someone because he or she has done something that you consider absolutely horrible—but the state can. As Berger (1963) summarized this matter, *"Violence is the ultimate foundation of any political order."*

Before we explore the origins of the modern state, let's first look at a situation in which the state loses legitimacy.

The Collapse of Authority

Sometimes the state oppresses its people, and they resist their government just as they do a mugger. The people cooperate reluctantly—with a smile if that is what is required—while they eye the gun in the hand of the government's representatives. But, as they do with a mugger, when they get the chance, they take up arms to free themselves. **Revolution,** armed resistance with the intent to overthrow and replace a government, is not only a people's rejection of a government's claim to rule over them but also their rejection of its monopoly on violence. In a revolution, people assert that right for themselves. If successful, they establish a new state in which they claim the right to monopolize violence.

What some see as coercion, however, others see as authority. Consequently, while some people are ready to take up arms against a government, others remain loyal to it, willingly defend it, and perhaps even die for it. *The more that its power is seen as legitimate, then, the more stable a government is.*

But just why do people accept power as legitimate? Max Weber (1922/1968) identified three sources of authority: traditional, rational-legal, and charismatic. Let's examine each.

Traditional Authority

Throughout history, the most common basis for authority has been tradition. **Traditional authority**, which is based on custom, is the hallmark of tribal groups. In these societies, custom dictates basic relationships. For example, birth into a particular family makes an individual the chief, king, or queen. As far as members of that society are concerned, this is the right way to determine who shall rule because "We've always done it this way."

Gender relations often open a window on traditional authority. For example, as shown in the photo on the next page, in the villages of Portugal widows are expected to wear only black until they remarry. This generally means that they wear black for the rest of their lives. By law, a widow is free to wear any color she wishes, but not by custom. Tradition,

macropolitics the exercise of large-scale power, the government being the most common example

authority power that people consider legitimate, as rightly exercised over them; also called *legitimate power*

coercion power that people do not accept as rightly exercised over them; also called *illegitimate power*

state a political entity that claims monopoly on the use of violence in some particular territory; commonly known as a country

revolution armed resistance designed to overthrow and replace a government

traditional authority authority based on custom

For centuries, widows in Mediterranean countries, such as these widows in Portugal, were expected to dress in black and to mourn for their husbands the rest of their lives. Their long dresses were matched by black stockings, black shoes, and black head coverings. Widows conformed to this expression of lifetime sorrow for their deceased husband not because of law, but because of custom. As industrialization erodes traditional authority, fewer widows follow this practice.

decreeing black, is so strong that if a widow were to violate this dress code, she would be perceived as having profaned the memory of her deceased husband and would be ostracized by the community.

When a traditional society industrializes, its transformation undermines traditional authority. Social change brings new experiences. This opens up new perspectives on life, and no longer does traditional authority go unchallenged. Thus, in Portugal you can still see old women dressed in black from head to toe—and you immediately know their marital status. Younger widows, however, are likely to be indistinguishable from other women.

Although traditional authority declines with industrialization, it never completely dies out. In postindustrial societies, for example, parents exercise authority over their children *because* parents always have had such authority. From generations past, we inherit the idea that parents should discipline their children, choose their doctors and schools, and teach them religion and morality.

Rational-Legal Authority

The second type of authority, **rational-legal authority**, is not based on custom but on written rules. *Rational* means reasonable, and *legal* means part of law. Thus *rational-legal* refers to matters agreed to by reasonable people and written into law (or regulations of some sort). The matters agreed to may be as broad as a constitution that specifies the rights of all members of a society or as narrow as a contract between two individuals. Because bureaucracies are based on written rules, rational-legal authority is sometimes called *bureaucratic authority.*

Rational-legal authority comes from the *position* that someone holds, not from the person who holds that position. In a democracy, for example, the president's authority comes from the office, as specified in a written constitution, not from custom or the individual's personal characteristics. In rational-legal authority, everyone—no matter how high the office—is subject to the organization's written rules. In governments based on traditional authority, the ruler's word may be law, but in those based on rational-legal authority, the ruler's word is subject to the law.

rational-legal authority authority based on law or written rules and regulations; also called *bureaucratic authority*

Charismatic Authority

A few centuries back, in 1429, the English controlled large parts of France. When they wouldn't allow the coronation of a new French king, a farmer's daughter heard a voice telling her that God had a special assignment for her—that she should put on men's clothing, recruit an army, and go to war against the English. Inspired, Joan of Arc raised an army, conquered cities, and defeated the English. Later that year, her visions were fulfilled as she stood next to Charles VII while he was crowned king of France. (Bridgwater 1953)

Joan of Arc is an example of **charismatic authority,** the third type of authority Weber identified. (*Charisma* is a Greek word that means a gift freely and graciously given [Arndt and Gingrich 1957].) A charismatic individual is someone people are drawn to because they believe that person has been touched by God or has been endowed by nature with exceptional qualities (Lipset 1993). The armies did not follow Joan of Arc because it was the custom to do so, as in traditional authority. Nor did they risk their lives alongside her because she held a position defined by written rules, as in rational-legal authority. Instead, people followed her because they were drawn to her outstanding traits. They saw her as a messenger of God, fighting on the side of justice, and they accepted her leadership because of these appealing qualities.

One of the best examples of charismatic authority *is Joan of Arc, shown here at the coronation of Charles VII, whom she was instrumental in making king. Uncomfortable at portraying Joan of Arc wearing only a man's coat of armor, the artist has made certain she is wearing plenty of makeup, and also has added a ludicrous skirt.*

The Threat Posed by Charismatic Leaders

A king owes allegiance to tradition, and a president to written laws. To what, however, does a charismatic leader owe allegiance? Because their authority is based on their personal ability to attract followers, charismatic leaders pose a threat to the established political system. They lead followers according to personal inclination, not according to the path of tradition or the regulations of law. Accordingly, they can inspire followers to disregard—or even to overthrow—traditional and rational-legal authorities.

This means that charismatic leaders pose a threat to the established order. Consequently, traditional and rational-legal authorities are often quick to oppose charismatic leaders. If they are not careful, however, their opposition may arouse even more positive sentiment in favor of the charismatic leader, causing him or her to be viewed as an underdog persecuted by the powerful. Occasionally the Roman Catholic Church faces such a threat, as when a priest claims miraculous powers that appear to be accompanied by amazing healings. As

Charismatic authorities *can be of any morality, from the saintly to the most bitterly evil. Like Joan of Arc, Adolf Hitler attracted throngs of people, providing the stuff of dreams and arousing them from disillusionment to hope. This poster from the 1930s, titled* Es Lebe Deutschland *("Long Live Germany"), illustrates the qualities of leadership that Germans of that period saw in Hitler.*

charismatic authority authority based on an individual's outstanding traits, which attract followers

routinization of charisma the transfer of authority from a charismatic figure to either a traditional or a rational-legal form of authority

people flock to this individual, they bypass parish priests and the formal ecclesiastical structure. This transfer of allegiance from the organization to an individual threatens the church hierarchy. Consequently, church officials may encourage the priest to withdraw from the public eye, perhaps to a monastery, to rethink matters. Thus the threat is defused, rational-legal authority reasserted, and the stability of the organization maintained.

Authority as Ideal Type

Weber's classifications—traditional, rational-legal, and charismatic—represent ideal types of authority. As noted on page 181, ideal type does not refer to what is ideal or desirable, but to a composite of characteristics found in many real-life examples. A particular leader, then, may show a combination of characteristics.

An example is John F. Kennedy, who combined rational-legal and charismatic authority. As the elected head of the U.S. government, Kennedy represented rational-legal authority. Yet his mass appeal was so great that his public speeches aroused large numbers of people to action. When in his inaugural address Kennedy said, "Ask not what your country can do for you; ask what you can do for your country," millions of Americans were touched. When Kennedy proposed a Peace Corps to help poorer countries, thousands of idealistic young people volunteered for challenging foreign service.

Charismatic and traditional authority can also overlap. The Ayatollah Khomeini of Iran, for example, was a religious leader, holding the traditional position of ayatollah. His embodiment of the Iranian people's dreams, however, as well as his austere life and devotion to principles of the Koran, gave him such mass appeal that he was also a charismatic leader. Khomeini's followers were convinced that he had been chosen by God, and his speeches aroused tens of thousands of followers to action.

In rare instances, then, traditional and rational-legal leaders possess charismatic traits. This is unusual, however, and most authority is clearly one type or another.

The Transfer of Authority

The orderly transfer of authority from one leader to another is crucial for social stability. Under traditional authority, people know who is next in line. Under rational-legal authority, people may not know who the next leader will be, but they do know how that person will be selected. South Africa provides a remarkable example of the orderly transfer of authority under a rational-legal organization. This country had been ripped apart by decades of racial strife, including horrible killings committed by each side. Yet, by maintaining its rational-legal authority, the country was able to peacefully transfer power from the dominant group led by President de Klerk to the minority group led by Nelson Mandela.

Crucial for society is the orderly transfer of power. One of the most remarkable transfers occurred in South Africa. Under this country's constitutional system, power was transferred from the white dominated government headed by Fredrik Willem de Klerk (on the left) to Nelson Mandela (on the right).

Charismatic authority has no such rules of succession, however. This makes it less stable than either traditional or rational-legal authority. Because charismatic authority is built around a single individual, the death or incapacitation of a charismatic leader can mean a bitter struggle for succession. To avoid this, some charismatic leaders make arrangements for an orderly transition of power by appointing a successor. This does not guarantee orderly succession, of course, for the followers may not perceive the designated heir in the same way as they did the charismatic leader. A second strategy is for the charismatic leader to build an organization. As the organization develops a system of rules or regulations, it transforms itself into a rational-legal organization. Weber used the term the **routinization of charisma** to refer to the transition of authority from a charismatic leader to either traditional or rational-legal authority.

Types of Government

How do the various types of government—monarchies, democracies, dictatorships, and oligarchies—differ? As we compare them, let's also look at how the institution of the state arose, and why the concept of citizenship was revolutionary.

city-state an independent city whose power radiates outward, bringing the adjacent area under its rule

monarchy a form of government headed by a king or queen

democracy a system of government in which authority derives from the people; the term comes from two Greek words that translate literally as "power to the people"

direct democracy a form of democracy in which the eligible voters meet together to discuss issues and make their decisions

representative democracy a form of democracy in which voters elect representatives to govern and make decisions on their behalf

Monarchies: The Rise of the State

Early societies were small and needed no extensive political system. They operated more like an extended family. As surpluses developed and societies grew larger, cities evolved—perhaps about 3500 B.C. (Fischer 1976). **City-states** then came into being, with power radiating outward from a city like a spider's web. Although the city controlled the immediate area around it, the areas between cities remained in dispute. Each city-state had its own **monarchy**, a king or queen whose right to rule was passed on to their children. If you drive through Spain, France, or Germany, you can still see evidence of former city-states. In the countryside, you will see only scattered villages. Farther on, your eye will be drawn to the outline of a castle on a faraway hill. As you get closer, you will see that the castle is surrounded by a city. Several miles farther, you will see another city, also dominated by a castle. Each city, with its castle, was once a center of power.

City-states often quarreled, and wars were common. The victors extended their rule, and eventually a single city-state was able to wield power over an entire region. As the size of these regions grew, the people slowly began to identify with the larger region. That is, they began to see distant inhabitants as "we" instead of "they." What we call the *state*—the political entity that claims a monopoly on the use of violence within a territory—came into being.

Democracies: Citizenship as a Revolutionary Idea

The United States had no city-states. Each colony, however, was small and independent like a city-state. After the American Revolution, the colonies united. With the greater strength and resources that came from political unity, they conquered almost all of North America, bringing it under the power of a central government.

The government formed in this new country was called a **democracy.** (Derived from two Greek words—*demos* [common people] and *kratos* [power]—*democracy* literally means "power to the people.") Because of the bitter antagonisms associated with the revolution against the British king, the founders of the new country were distrustful of monarchies. They wanted to put political decisions into the hands of the people. This was not the first democracy the world had seen, but such a system had been tried before only with smaller groups. Athens, a city-state of Greece, practiced democracy two thousand years ago, with each free male above a certain age having the right to be heard and to vote. Members of some Native American tribes, such as the Iroquois, also elected their chiefs, and in some, women were able to vote and to hold the office of chief. (The Incas and Aztecs of Mexico and Central America had monarchies.)

Because of their small size, tribes and cities were able to practice **direct democracy.** That is, they were small enough for the eligible voters to meet together, express their opinions, and then vote publicly—much like a town hall meeting today. As populous and spread out as the United States was, however, direct democracy was impossible, and **representative democracy** was invented. Certain citizens (at first only white male landowners) voted for men to represent them in

Democracy *was a heritage left by the British rule of India. The people take elections seriously, and the government transfers power peacefully from one party and candidate to another. Shown here are ballot boxes being delivered to remote areas of the northern Indian state of Assam.*

citizenship the concept that birth (and residence) in a country impart basic rights

Washington. Later the vote was extended to nonowners of property, to African American men, then to women, and to others. Our new communications technologies, which make "electronic town meetings" possible, may also allow a new form of direct democracy. This issue is explored in the Mass Media box below.

Today we take the concept of citizenship for granted. What is not evident to us is that this idea had to be conceived in the first place. There is nothing natural about citizenship—it is simply one way in which people choose to define themselves. Throughout most of human history, people were thought to *belong* to a clan, to a tribe, or even to a ruler. The idea of **citizenship**—that by virtue of birth and residence people have basic rights—is quite new to the human scene (Turner 1990; Eisenstadt 1999).

The concept of representative democracy based on citizenship—perhaps the greatest gift the United States has given to the world—was revolutionary. Power was to be vested in the people themselves, and government was to flow from the people. That this concept

massMEDIA in Social Life

Politics and Democracy in a Technological Society

"Politics is just like show business."—RONALD REAGAN

The new technology holds tremendous promise for democracy, but does it also pose a threat to democracy?

Certainly the new technology is a powerful tool for political campaigns. All major candidates are using the Internet to organize supporters and raise funds. Politicians also use computers, telephone link-ups, faxes, e-mail, and Web sites to take the pulse of the public—and to convey their platforms and their views.

And this use of technology is changing the way the public interacts with politicians. Instead of tuning in and passively listening to a politician's speech, we now can talk back to candidates and leaders via chat rooms, "electronic town meetings," and call-in radio and TV talk shows.

The Internet even holds the potential for transforming the way we vote and pass laws. If we used "televoting," voters would no longer have to travel to polling places in rain and snow. It is likely that more people would vote, for they could vote from the comfort of their own living rooms and offices. Eventually, when almost everyone owns a computer, televoting could even replace our representational democracy with a form of direct democracy.

The Internet also holds the potential of making politicians more responsive to our will. Voters will be able to circulate petitions online, and sign them with digital signatures. In fact, on many matters voters may be able to bypass politicians entirely, Online, they will be able to decide issues that politicians now resolve for them. They could even pass laws online.

Crucial for society is the orderly transfer of power. Under its constitutional system, the United States is remarkably stable: Power is transferred peacefully—even when someone of an unusual background wins an election. Arnold Schwarzenegger, shown here in his role in Terminator 3, was elected governor of California.

With all these potential benefits, how could the new technology pose a threat to democracy?

Some fear that the Internet isn't safe for voting. With no poll watchers, undue influence (threats, promises, or gifts in return for votes) would go undetected. Others raise a more fundamental issue: Direct democracy might detour the U.S. Constitution's system of checks and balances, which was designed to safeguard us from the "tyranny of the majority." To determine from a poll that 51 percent of adults hold a certain opinion on an issue is one thing—that information can guide our leaders. But to have 51 percent of televoters determine a law is not the same as having elected representatives publicly argue the merits of a proposal and then try to balance the interests of the many groups that make up their constituency.

Others counter that before televoting, the merits of a proposal would be vigorously debated in newspapers, on radio and television, and even on the Internet itself. Voters would certainly be no less informed than they now are. As far as balancing interest groups is concerned, that would take care of itself, for people from all interest groups would participate in televoting.

For Your CONSIDERATION

Do you think direct democracy would be superior to representative democracy? How about the issue of the "tyranny of the majority"? (This means that the interests of smaller groups—whether racial-ethnic, regional, or even an occupational group—are overwhelmed by the votes of the majority.) How can we use the mass media to improve government?

Sources: Diamond and Silverman 1995; Raney 1999; Seib 2000; Langley 2003.

was revolutionary is generally forgotten, but its implementation meant *the reversal of traditional ideas. It made the government responsive to the people's will, not the people responsive to the government's will.* To keep the government responsive to the needs of its citizens, people had not only the right, but also the obligation, to express dissent. In a widely quoted statement, Thomas Jefferson observed that

> a little rebellion now and then is a good thing. . . . It is a medicine necessary for the sound health of government. . . . God forbid that we should ever be twenty years without such a rebellion. . . . The tree of liberty must be refreshed from time to time with the blood of patriots and tyrants. It is its natural manure. (In Hellinger and Judd 1991)

The idea of **universal citizenship**—of *everyone* having the same basic rights by virtue of being born in a country (or by immigrating and becoming a naturalized citizen)—flowered very slowly, and came into practice only through fierce struggle. When the United States was founded, for example, this idea was still in its infancy. Today it seems inconceivable to Americans that anyone should be denied the right to vote, hold office, make a contract, testify in court, or own property on the basis of gender or race-ethnicity. For earlier generations of white Americans, however, it seemed just as inconceivable that women, racial–ethnic minorities, and the poor should be allowed such rights.

Over the years, then, rights have been extended, and in the United States citizenship and its privileges now apply to all. No longer do property, sex, or race-ethnicity determine the right to vote, testify in court, and so on. These characteristics, however, do influence whether one votes, as we shall see in a later section on voting patterns.

Dictatorships and Oligarchies: The Seizure of Power

If an individual seizes power and then dictates his will onto the people, the government is known as a **dictatorship**. If a small group seizes power, the government is called an **oligarchy**. The occasional coups in Central and South America and Africa, in which military leaders seize control of a country, are examples of oligarchies. Although one individual may be named president, often a group of high-ranking military officers is lurking behind the scenes, making the decisions. If their designated president becomes uncooperative, they remove him from office and appoint another.

Monarchies, dictatorships, and oligarchies vary in the amount of control they exert over their citizens. **Totalitarianism** is almost *total* control of a people by the government. In Nazi Germany, Hitler organized a ruthless secret police force, the Gestapo, which searched for any sign of dissent. Spies even watched how moviegoers reacted to newsreels, reporting those who did not respond "appropriately" (Hippler 1987). Saddam Hussein acted as ruthlessly toward Iraqis. Children who refused to join Saddam's Iraqi Youth were put in filthy prisons and beaten.

People around the world find great appeal in the freedom inherent in citizenship and representative democracy. Those who have no say in their government's decisions, or who face prison or even death for expressing dissent, find in these ideas the hope for a brighter future. With today's electronic communications, people no longer remain ignorant of whether they are more or less politically privileged than others. This knowledge produces pressure for greater citizen participation in government. As electronic communications develop further, this pressure will increase.

The U.S. Political System

With this global background, let's examine the U.S. political system. We shall consider the two major political parties and elections, compare the U.S. political system with other democratic systems, and examine voting patterns and the role of lobbyists and PACs.

universal citizenship the idea that everyone has the same basic rights by virtue of being born in a country (or by immigrating and becoming a naturalized citizen)

dictatorship a form of government in which power has been seized by an individual

oligarchy a form of government in which power is held by a small group of individuals; the rule of the many by the few

totalitarianism a form of government that exerts almost total control over people

Political Parties and Elections

After the founding of the United States, numerous political parties emerged, but by the time of the Civil War, two parties dominated U.S. politics (Burnham 1983): the Democrats, who in the public mind are associated with the working class, and the Republicans, who are associated with wealthier people. Each party nominates candidates, and in pre-elections, called *primaries,* the voters decide which candidates will represent their party. Each candidate then campaigns, trying to appeal to the most voters. The Social Map below shows how Americans align themselves with political parties.

Although the Democrats and Republicans represent different philosophical principles, each party appeals to a broad membership, and it is difficult to distinguish a conservative Democrat from a liberal Republican. The extremes are easy to discern, however. Deeply committed Democrats support legislation that transfers income from the richer to the poorer, or that controls wages, working conditions, and competition. Dyed-in-the-wool Republicans oppose such legislation.

Those elected to Congress may cross party lines. That is, some Democrats vote for legislation proposed by Republicans, and *vice versa.* This happens because officeholders support their party's philosophy, but not necessarily its specific proposals. Thus, when it comes to a particular bill, such as raising the minimum wage, some conservative Democrats may view the measure as unfair to small employers, or too costly, and vote with the Republicans against the bill. At the same time, liberal Republicans—feeling that the proposal is just, or sensing a dominant sentiment in voters back home—may side with its Democratic backers.

Regardless of their differences and their public quarrels, the Democrats and Republicans represent *different slices of the center.* Although each may ridicule its opposition and promote different legislation, each party firmly supports such fundamentals of U.S. political

Figure 15.1 U.S. Political Parties

Which party dominates, Democrat or Republican?

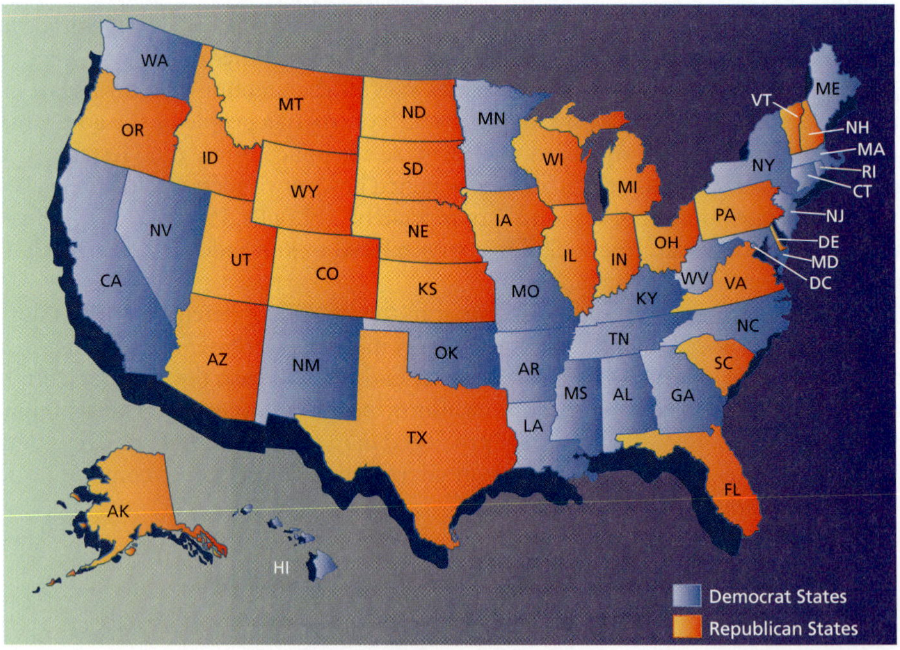

Note: Based on the composition of the states' upper and lower houses. Votes for President and Congress may differ. For states whose upper and lower houses are dominated by different parties, the total number of legislators was used. In case of ties, or as with Nebraska, no party designation, percentage vote for president was used.

Source: By the author. Based on *Statistical Abstract* 2002:Table 387.

philosophy as free public education; a strong military; freedom of religion, speech, and assembly; and, of course, capitalism—especially the private ownership of property.

Third parties also play a role in U.S. politics, but to gain power they, too, must support these centrist themes. Any party that advocates radical change is doomed to a short life. Because most Americans consider a vote for a third party a waste, third parties do notoriously poorly at the polls. Two exceptions are the Bull Moose party, whose candidate, Theodore Roosevelt, won more votes in 1912 than Taft, the Republican presidential candidate, and the United We Stand (now Reform) party, founded by billionaire Ross Perot, which won 19 percent of the vote in 1992. Amidst bickering, the Reform Party rapidly declined, winning only 8 percent in 1996, and less than 1 percent in 2000 (Bridgwater 1953; *Statistical Abstract* 1995:Table 437; 2000:Table 456; election 2000 reports).

As Latinos have grown in numbers, so has their political prominence. Shown here is Cruz Bustamante, the Lt. Governor of California. People have many reasons for voting the way they do, including the ethnicity of the candidate. When political parties select candidates, their race-ethnicity is always a consideration.

Contrast with Democratic Systems in Europe

We tend to take our political system for granted and assume that any other democracy looks like ours—even down to having two major parties. Such is not the case. To gain a comparative understanding, let's look at the European system.

Although both their system and ours are democracies, there are fundamental distinctions between the two (Domhoff 1979, 1983; Lind 1995). First, elections in most of Europe are not winner-take-all. In the United States, elections are determined by a simple majority. For example, if a Democrat wins 51 percent of the votes cast in an electoral district, he or she takes office. The Republican candidate, who may have won 49 percent, loses everything. In contrast, most European countries base their elections on a system of **proportional representation;** that is, the seats in the national legislature are divided according to the proportion of votes each political party receives. If one party wins 51 percent of the vote, for example, that party is awarded 51 percent of the seats; while a party with 49 percent of the votes receives 49 percent of the seats.

Second, proportional representation encourages minority parties, while the winner-take-all system discourages them. The proportional representation system of most European countries means that if a party gets 10 percent of the voters to support its candidate, it will get 10 percent of the seats. This system encourages the formation of **noncentrist parties,** those that propose less popular or even offbeat ideas. For example, a party may make its central platform a return to the gold standard, or the shutting down of nuclear power reactors. In the United States, in contrast, 10 percent of the votes means 0 seats. So does 49 percent of the votes. This pushes parties to the center, for to have any chance of "taking all," a party must strive to obtain broad support. For this reason, the United States has **centrist parties.**

In the proportional representation system, to win even just a few seats in the national legislature is important. It allows even a tiny party to gain access to the media throughout the year. This publicity helps keep its issues alive. Small parties also gain power beyond their numbers. Because votes are fragmented among the many parties that compete in national elections, seldom does a single party gain a majority of the seats in the legislature. To muster the required votes, the party with the most seats must align itself with one or more of the smaller parties and form a **coalition government.** A party with only 10 or 15 percent of the seats, then, may be able to trade its vote on some issues for the larger party's support on others. Because coalitions often fall apart, these governments tend to be less stable than that of the United States. Italy, for example, has had fifty-nine different governments since World War II, compared with the United States, which has had eleven presidents since then. Seeing the greater stability of the U.S. government, the Italians have voted that three-fourths of their Senate seats will be decided on the winner-take-all system (Melloan 1993b; D'Emilio 2000).

proportional representation an electoral system in which seats in a legislature are divided according to the proportion of votes each political party receives

noncentrist party a political party that represents marginal ideas

centrist party a political party that represents the center of political opinion

coalition government a government in which a country's largest party aligns itself with one or more smaller parties

Voting Patterns

Year after year, Americans show consistent voting patterns. From Table 15.1, you can see that the percentage of people who vote increases with age. The exception is those ages 21 to 24. This table also shows how significant race-ethnicity is. Non-Hispanic whites are more

Table 15.1 Who Votes for President?

	1980	1984	1988	1992	1996	2000
Overall						
Americans Who Vote	59%	60%	57%	61%	54%	55%
Age						
18–20	36	37	33	39	31	28
21–24	38	44	46	33	24	24
25–34	55	58	48	53	43	44
35–44	64	64	61	64	55	55
45–64	69	70	68	70	64	64
65 and up	65	68	69	70	67	68
Sex						
Male	59	59	56	60	53	53
Female	59	61	58	62	56	56
Race/Ethnicity[a]						
Whites	61	61	59	64	56	56
African Americans	51	56	52	54	51	54
Latinos	30	33	29	29	27	28
Education						
Grade school only	43	43	37	35	28	27
High school dropout	46	44	41	41	34	34
High school graduate	59	59	55	58	49	49
College dropout	67	68	65	69	61	60
College graduate	80	79	78	81	73	72
Marital Status						
Married	NA	NA	NA	NA	NA	50
Divorced	NA	NA	NA	NA	NA	38
Labor Force						
Employed	62	62	58	64	55	56
Unemployed	41	44	39	46	37	35
Income[c]						
Under $5,000	38	39	35	NA	NA	21[b]
$5,000 to $9,999	46	49	41	NA	NA	24
$10,000 to $19,999	54	55	48	NA	NA	30
$15,000 to $24,999	59	63	56	NA	NA	35
$25,000 to $34,999	67	74	64	NA	NA	40
$35,000 to $49,999	74	74	70	NA	NA	44
$50,000 to $74,999	NA	NA	NA	NA	NA	50
$75,000 and over	NA	NA	NA	NA	NA	57

[a]Only these racial-ethnic groups are listed in all sources.

[b]Because the breakdown of voting by income for the year 2002 is not contained in the 2002 source, data for 1998 from U.S. Census Bureau, *Current Population Report*, P20–523, 2000: Tables 1, 5, 7, 8, 9 is used.

[c]For years preceding 1998, the category $35,000 to $49,999 is $35,000 and over, except for 1998, which is an average of $35,000 to $49,900 and over $50,000.

Sources: as listed above and *Statistical Abstract* 1991:Table 450; 1997:Table 462; *Statistical Abstract* 2002:Table 393.

likely to vote than are African Americans, while Latinos are the least likely to vote. The significance of race-ethnicity is so great that Latinos are only half as likely to vote as are non-Hispanic whites. A crucial aspect of the socialization of newcomers to the United States is to learn the U.S. political system, the topic of the following Cultural Diversity box.

CULTURAL DIVERSITY in the UNITED STATES

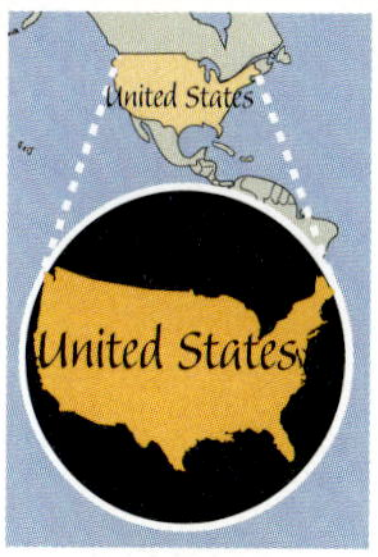

The Politics of Immigrants: Power, Ethnicity, and Social Class

That the United States is the land of immigrants is a truism. Every schoolchild knows that since the English Pilgrims landed on Plymouth Rock, successive groups have crossed the Atlantic Ocean to reach U.S. shores. Some, such as the Irish immigrants in the late 1800s and early 1900s, left to escape brutal poverty and famine. Others, such as the Jews of czarist Russia, fled persecution. Some sought refuge from lands ravaged by war. Others, called entrepreneurial immigrants, came for better economic opportunities. Still others were sojourners who planned to return home after a temporary stay. Some, not usually called immigrants, came in chains, held in bondage by early immigrants.

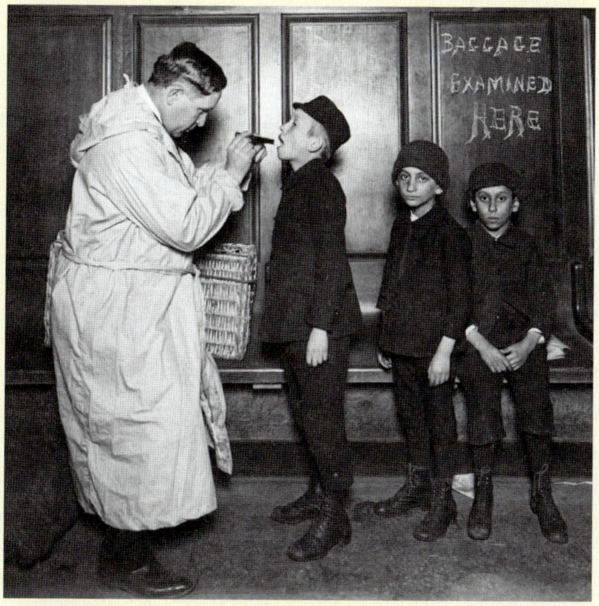

This photo, from 1911, shows immigrants arriving at Ellis Island, New York. They are being inspected for obvious signs of disease. If any disease is detected, they will be refused entry. Sociologists have studied the process by which immigrants are assimilated.

Today, the United States is in the midst of its second largest wave of immigration. In the first, in the early 1900s, immigrants accounted for 15 percent of the U.S. population. Almost all of those immigrants came from Europe. Today, immigrants make up about 11 percent of the U.S. population, and the mix is far more diverse (Martin and Midgley 2003). Only about 10 percent of legal immigrants come from Europe (see Table 20.2 on page 588). Most are from Asia, Mexico, and South and Central America. Since 1980, more than 15 million legal immigrants have settled in the United States. Another 7 to 9 million are here illegally.

In the last century, U.S.-born Americans feared that immigrants would bring socialism or communism with them. Today some fear that the millions of immigrants from Spanish-speaking countries threaten the primacy of the English language. As in the last century, the fear that immigrants will take jobs away from U.S.-born Americans remains strong. In addition, African Americans fear a loss of political power as immigrants from Mexico and Central and South America swell the Latino population.

After they are in the country, what path to political activity do immigrants take? In general, they first organize as a group on the basis of *ethnicity* rather than *class*. They respond to common problems, especially discrimination and those associated with adapting to a new way of life. This first step in political activity is a reaffirmation of their cultural identity. As sociologists Alejandro Portés and Ruben Rumbaut (1990) note, "By mobilizing the collective vote and by electing their own to office, immigrant minorities have learned the rules of the democratic game and absorbed its values in the process."

Irish immigrants to Boston illustrate this pattern of banding together on the basis of ethnicity. They built a power base that put the Irish in political control of the city and, ultimately, saw John F. Kennedy, one of their own, sworn in as president of the United States.

As Portés and Rumbaut observe, immigrants don't become "American" overnight. Instead, they begin by fighting for their own interests as a group—as Irish, Italians, and so on. Only after they attain enough political power to overcome discrimination do immigrant groups become "like everyone else"—that is, like those who have power. At this point of political power—when a group has representation somewhat proportionate to its numbers—a major change occurs. Social class then becomes more significant than race-ethnicity. This, then, is the typical path that immigrants follow in their socialization into the U.S. political system.

Sources: Portés and Rumbaut 1990; Salholz 1990; Prud'Homme 1991; James 1993; *Statistical Abstract* 1999:Table 10; 2002:Tables 7, 41.

Table 15.1 (on page 430) also shows that voting increases with education. College graduates are twice as likely to vote as those who don't complete high school. Employment and income are also significant. People who make more than $50,000 a year are twice as likely to vote as those who make less than $10,000. Finally, note that women are slightly more likely than men to vote.

Social Integration How can we explain the voting patterns shown in Table 15.1? Look at the extremes. Those most likely to vote are whites who are older, more educated, affluent, and employed. Those least likely to vote are Latinos who are poor, younger, less educated, and unemployed. From these extremes, we can draw this principle: *The more that people feel they have a stake in the political system, the more likely they are to vote.* They have more to protect, and they feel that voting can make a difference. In effect, people who have been rewarded more by the political and economic system feel more socially integrated. They vote because they perceive that elections directly affect their own lives and the type of society in which they and their children live.

Alienation and Apathy In contrast, those who gain less from the system—in terms of education, income, and jobs—are more likely to feel alienated from politics. Viewing themselves as outsiders, many feel hostile toward the government. Some feel betrayed, believing that politicians have sold out to special-interest groups. They are convinced that all politicians are liars. Minorities who feel that the U.S. political system is a "white" system are less likely to vote.

From Table 15.1, we see that many highly educated people with good incomes also stay away from the polls. Many people do not vote because of **voter apathy,** or indifference. Their view is that "next year will just bring more of the same, regardless of who is president." A common attitude of those who are apathetic is "What difference will my one vote make when there are millions of voters?" Many see little difference between the two major political parties.

Alienation and apathy are so common that *half* of the nation's eligible voters do not vote for president, and even more fail to vote for candidates for Congress (*Statistical Abstract* 2002:Table 396).

The Gender and Racial-Ethnic Gap in Voting Historically, men and women have voted the same way, but we now have a *political gender gap*. That is, when they go to the ballot box, men and women are somewhat more likely to vote for different presidential candidates. As you can see from Table 15.2, men are more likely to favor the Republican candidate, while women are more likely to favor the Democratic candidate. This table also illustrates the much larger racial-ethnic gap in politics. Note how few African Americans vote for a Republican presidential candidate.

As we saw in Table 15.1, voting patterns reflect life experiences, especially economic circumstances. On average, women earn less than men and African Americans earn less than whites. As a result, at this point in history women and African Americans tend to look more favorably on government programs that redistribute income.

Lobbyists and Special-Interest Groups

Suppose that you are president of the United States, and you want to make milk and bread more affordable for the poor. As you check into the matter, you find that prices are high because the government is paying farmers billions of dollars a year in price supports. You propose to eliminate these subsidies.

Immediately, large numbers of people leap into action. They contact their senators and representatives and hold news conferences. Your office is flooded with calls, faxes, and e-mail. Reuters and the Associated Press distribute pictures of farm families—their Holsteins grazing contentedly in the background—and inform readers that your harsh proposal will destroy these hard-working, healthy, happy good Americans who are struggling to make a living. President or not, you have little chance of getting your legislation passed.

What happened? The dairy industry went to work to protect its special interests. A **special-interest group** consists of people who think alike on a particular issue and who

voter apathy indifference and inaction on the part of individuals or groups with respect to the political process

special-interest group a group of people who support a particular issue and who can be mobilized for political action

Table 15.2 How the Two-Party Presidential Vote Is Split

	1988	1992	1996	2000
Women				
Democrat	50%	61%	65%	56%
Republican	50%	39%	35%	44%
Men				
Democrat	44%	55%	50%	47%
Republican	56%	45%	50%	53%
African Americans				
Democrat	92%	94%	99%	92%
Republican	8%	6%	1%	8%
Whites				
Democrat	41%	53%	54%	46%
Republican	59%	47%	46%	54%
Latinos				
Democrat	NA	NA	NA	61%
Republican	NA	NA	NA	39%
Asian Americans				
Democrat	NA	NA	NA	62%
Republican	NA	NA	NA	38%

Source: Gallup Poll 2000, *Los Angeles Times Exit Poll*, November 7, 2001; *Statistical Abstract* 1999:Table 464; 2002:Table 372.

can be mobilized for political action. The dairy industry is just one of thousands of such groups that employ **lobbyists,** people who are paid to influence legislation on behalf of their clients. Special-interest groups and lobbyists have become a major force in U.S. politics. Members of Congress who want to be re-elected must pay attention to them, for they represent blocs of voters who share a vital interest in the outcome of specific bills. Well financed and able to contribute huge sums, lobbyists can deliver votes to you—or to your opponent.

Some members of Congress who lose an election or retire become lobbyists. They know their way around Washington, and, unlike other lobbyists, they have access to the floor of the House and Senate. Those who headed powerful committees can demand over a million dollars a year. Those lower in the pecking order get $200,000 or so. *Half* of the President's top one hundred White House officials go to work for or advise the very companies that they regulated while they worked for the President (Ismail 2003).

What about the laws that prohibit office holders and White House officials from lobbying during the first year after they leave their jobs? They skirt these laws by calling themselves "strategic advisors," not lobbyists. They direct other lobbyists, and—drawing one of Washington's fine moral lines—supposedly do not make direct contacts for a year (Wayne 2000). After that year, they come out into the open and register as lobbyists.

Another law is also easily skirted. To prevent special-interest groups from unduly influencing legislation, the law limits the amount that any individual, corporation, or special-interest group can give a candidate, and requires all contributions over $1,000 to be reported. To get around this law, special-interest groups form **political action committees (PACs).** These organizations solicit contributions from many donors—each contribution being within the legal limit—and then use the large total to influence legislation.

PACs are powerful, for they bankroll lobbyists and legislators. To influence politics, about 4,000 PACs shell out $260 million a year directly to their candidates (*Statistical Abstract* 2002:Tables 399, 400). PACs also contribute millions in indirect ways. Some give

lobbyists people who influence legislation on behalf of their clients

political action committee (PAC) an organization formed by one or more special-interest groups to solicit and spend funds for the purpose of influencing legislation

Figure 15.2 Foreign Lobbyists: The Top 10 Spenders

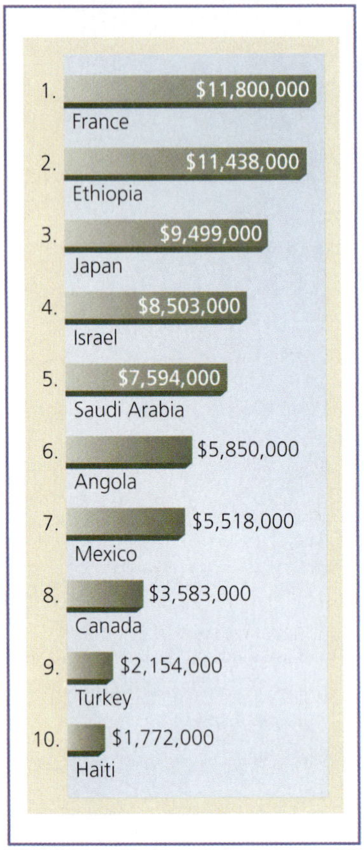

Note: Because the report is for a 6-month period, to get an annual total I doubled the items that referred to legislation.
Source: By the author. Based on Foreign Agents Registration Act, 2002.

"honorariums" to senators who agree to say a few words at a breakfast. A few PACs represent broad social interests such as protecting the environment. Most, however, stand for the financial interests of specific groups, such as the dairy, oil, banking, and construction industries. Those PACs with the most clout in terms of money and votes gain the ear of Congress. To politicians, the sound of money talking apparently sounds like the voice of the people.

PACs in U.S. Elections

Suppose that you want to run for the Senate. To have a chance of winning, not only do you have to shake hands around the state, be photographed hugging babies, and eat a lot of chicken dinners at local civic organizations, but also you must send out hundreds of thousands of pieces of mail to solicit votes and financial support. During the home stretch, television ads may run $700,000 a week (Harwood 1994). If you are an *average* candidate for the Senate, you will spend about $5 million on your campaign. To run for the House will cost a paltry $800,000 (*Statistical Abstract* 2002:Tables 381, 403).

Now suppose that it is only a few weeks from the election, the polls show you and your opponent neck and neck, and your war chest is empty. The representatives of a couple of PACs pay you a visit. One says that his organization will pay for a mailing, while the other offers to buy television and radio ads. You feel somewhat favorable toward their positions anyway, and you accept. Once elected, you owe them. When legislation that affects their interests comes up for vote, their representatives call you—on your private cell phone or at your unlisted number at home—and tell you how they want you to vote. It would be political folly to double-cross them.

It is said that the first duty of a politician is to get elected—and the second duty is to get reelected. If you are an average senator, to finance your reelection campaign you must raise $2,400 *every single day* of your six-year term. It is no wonder that money has been dubbed the "mother's milk of politics."

Criticism of Lobbyists and PACs The major criticism leveled against lobbyists and PACs is that their money, in effect, buys votes. Rather than representing the people who elected them, legislators support the special interests of groups that have the ability to help them stay in power. The influence of foreign lobbyists has been a target of especially harsh criticism. As shown in Figure 15.2, the top ten foreign lobbyists spend $67 million annually to protect their interests and influence votes.

Even if the United States were to outlaw PACs, special-interest groups would not disappear from U.S. politics. Lobbyists walked the corridors of the Senate long before PACs, and since the time of Alexander Graham Bell they have carried the unlisted numbers of members of Congress. For good or ill, lobbyists play an essential role in the U.S. political system.

Who Rules the United States?

With lobbyists and PACs holding such influence, just whom do U.S. senators and representatives really represent? This question has led to a lively debate among sociologists.

The Functionalist Perspective: Pluralism

Functionalists view the state as having arisen out of the basic needs of the social group. To protect themselves from oppressors, people formed a government and gave it the monopoly on violence. The risk is that the state can turn that force against its own citizens. To return to the example used earlier, states have a tendency to become muggers. Thus, people must find a balance between having no government—which would lead to **anarchy**, a condition of disorder and violence—and having a government that protects them from violence, but that also may itself turn against them. When functioning well, then, the state is a balanced system that protects its citizens both from one another *and* from government.

What keeps the U.S. government from turning against its citizens? Functionalists say that **pluralism**, a diffusion of power among many special-interest groups, prevents any one

anarchy a condition of lawlessness or political disorder caused by the absence or collapse of governmental authority

pluralism the diffusion of power among many interest groups that prevents any single group from gaining control of the government group from gaining control of the government and using it to oppress the people (Polsby 1959; Dahl 1961, 1982; Engeman 2001). To keep the government from coming under the control of any one group, the founders of the United States set up three branches of government: the executive branch (the president), the judiciary branch (the courts), and the legislative branch (the Senate and House of Representatives). Each is sworn to uphold the Constitution, which guarantees rights to citizens, and each can nullify the actions of the other two. This system, known as **checks and balances,** was designed to ensure that power remains distributed and that no one branch of government dominates.

Our pluralist society has many parts—women, men, racial-ethnic groups, farmers, factory and office workers, religious organizations, bankers, bosses, the unemployed, the retired—as well as such broad categories as the rich, middle class, and poor. No group dominates. Rather, as each group pursues its own interests, it is balanced by other groups that are pursuing theirs. To attain their goals, groups must negotiate and compromise with one another. This minimizes conflict. Because these groups have political muscle to flex at the polls and politicians need votes, politicians try to design policies that please as many groups as they can. This, say functionalists, makes the political system responsive to the people, and no one group rules.

The Great Depression transformed Americans' attitudes about government intervention in economic matters. Shown here is a poster that in the 1930s was displayed in post offices and other public buildings throughout the country.

The Conflict Perspective: The Power Elite, or Ruling Class

Conflict theorists disagree. If you focus on the lobbyists scurrying around Washington, they say, you get a blurred image of superficial activities. What really counts is the big picture, not its fragments. The important question is who holds the power that determines the country's overarching policies. For example, who determines interest rates—and their impact on the price of our homes? Who sets policies that transfer jobs from the United States to countries where labor costs less? And the ultimate question of power: Who is behind the decision to go to war?

Sociologist C. Wright Mills (1956) took the position that the country's most important matters are not decided by lobbyists or even by Congress. Rather, the decisions that have the greatest impact on the lives of Americans—and people across the globe—are made by a **power elite.** As depicted in Figure 15.3, the power elite consists of the top leaders of the

Figure 15.3 Power in the United States: The Model Proposed by C. Wright Mills

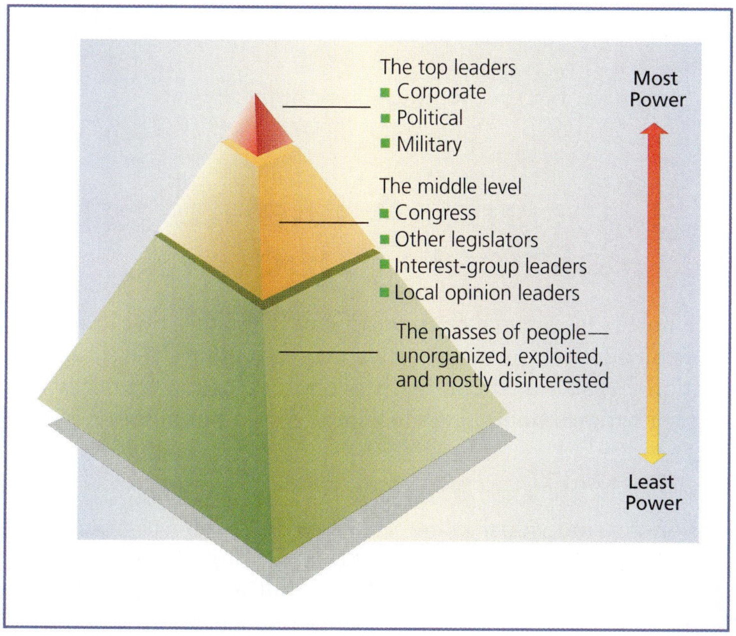

Source: Based on Mills 1956.

checks and balances the separation of powers among the three branches of U.S. government—legislative, executive, and judicial—so that each is able to nullify the actions of the other two, thus preventing the domination of any single branch

power elite C. Wright Mills' term for the top people in U.S. corporations, military, and politics who make the nation's major decisions largest corporations, the most powerful generals and admirals of the armed forces, and certain elite politicians—the president, his cabinet, and select senior members of Congress who chair the major committees. It is they who wield power, make the decisions that direct the country and shake the world.

Are the three groups that make up the power elite—the top business, political, and military leaders—equal in power? Mills said they were not, but he didn't point to the president and his staff or even to the generals and admirals as the most powerful. The most powerful, he said, are the corporate leaders. Because all three segments of the power elite view capitalism as essential to the welfare of the country, business interests, Mills said, come foremost in setting national policy. (Remember the incident mentioned in the previous chapter (page 404) of a U.S. president selling airplanes.)

Sociologist William Domhoff (1990, 1999b) uses the term **ruling class** to refer to the power elite. He focuses on the 1 percent of Americans who belong to the super rich, the powerful capitalist class analyzed in Chapter 10 (pages 268-269). Members of this class control our top corporations and foundations, even the boards that oversee our major universities. It is no accident, says Domhoff, that from this group the president chooses most members of his cabinet and appoints ambassadors to the most powerful countries of the world.

Conflict theorists point out that we should not think of the power elite (or ruling class) as some secret group that meets together in order to agree on specific matters. Rather, their unity springs from the similarity of their backgrounds and orientations to life. All have attended prestigious private schools, they belong to exclusive clubs, and they are millionaires many times over. There is no grand conspiracy to control the country, but, instead, decisions flow from their mutual interest in solving the problems that face big business. Because their political connections extend to the top centers of power, this elite determines the economic and political conditions under which the rest of the country operates (Domhoff 1990, 1998). We shall return to this line of inquiry later.

Which View Is Right?

The functionalist and conflict views of power in U.S. society cannot be reconciled. Either competing interests block any single group from being dominant, as functionalists assert, or a power elite oversees the major decisions of the United States, as conflict theorists maintain. The answer may have to do with the level you look at. Perhaps at the middle level of power depicted in Figure 15.3, the competing groups do keep each other at bay, and none is able to dominate. If so, the functionalist view would apply to this level. But which level holds the key to U.S. power? Perhaps the functionalists have not looked high enough, and activities at the peak remain invisible to them. On that level, does an elite dominate? In order to protect its mutual interests, does a small group make the major decisions of the United States?

The answer is not yet conclusive. For this, we must await more research.

War and Terrorism: A Means to Implement Political Objectives

As we have noted, an essential characteristic of the state is that it claims a monopoly on violence. At times, a state may direct that violence against other nations. **War**, armed conflict between nations (or politically distinct groups), is often part of national policy. Let's look at this aspect of politics.

ruling class another term for the power elite

war armed conflict between nations or politically distinct groups

Is War Universal?

Although human aggression and individual killing characterize all human groups, war does not. War is simply *one option* that groups may choose for dealing with disagreements, but not all societies choose this option. The Mission Indians of North America, the Arunta of Australia, the Andaman Islanders of the South Pacific, and the Eskimos of the Arctic, for example, had procedures to handle aggression and quarrels, but they did not have organized battles that pitted one tribe or group against another. These groups do not even have a word for war (Lesser 1968).

How Common Is War?

One of the contradictions of humanity is that people long for peace while at the same time they glorify war. The glorification of war can be seen by noting how major battles hog the center of a country's retelling of its history and how monuments to generals, patriots, and battles are scattered throughout the land. From May Day parades in Moscow's Red Square to the Fourth of July celebrations in the United States and the Cinco de Mayo victory marches in Mexico, war and revolution are interwoven into the fabric of daily life.

War is so common that a cynic might say it is the normal state of society. Sociologist Pitirim Sorokin (1937) counted the wars in Europe from 500 B.C. to A.D. 1925. He documented 967 wars, an average of one war every two to three years. Counting years or parts of a year in which a country was at war, at 28 percent Germany had the lowest record of warfare. Spain's 67 percent gave it the dubious distinction of being the most war-prone. Sorokin found that Russia, the land of his birth, had experienced only one peaceful quarter-century during the entire previous thousand years. Since the time of William the Conqueror, who took power in 1066, England was at war an average of 56 out of each 100 years. Spain fought even more often. It is worth noting the history of the United States in this regard: Since 1850, it has intervened militarily around the world about 160 times, an average of *once a year* (Kohn 1988; current events).

Why Nations Go to War

Why do nations choose war as a means to handle disputes? Sociologists answer this question not by focusing on factors *within* humans, such as aggressive impulses, but by looking for *social* causes—conditions in society that encourage or discourage combat between nations.

Sociologist Nicholas Timasheff (1965) identified three essential conditions of war. The first is a cultural tradition of war. Because their nation has fought wars in the past, the leaders of a group see war as an option for dealing with serious disputes with other nations. The second is an antagonistic situation in which two or more states confront incompatible objectives. For example, each may want the same land or resources. The third is a "fuel" that heats the antagonistic situation to a boiling point, so that politicians cross the line from thinking about war to actually waging it.

Timasheff identified seven such "fuels." He found that war is likely if a country's leaders see the antagonistic situation as an opportunity to achieve one or more of these objectives:

1. Revenge: settling "old scores" from previous conflicts
2. Power: dictating their will to a weaker nation
3. Prestige: saving the nation's "honor"
4. Unity: uniting rival groups within their country
5. Position: the leaders protecting or exalting their own position
6. Ethnicity: bringing under their rule "our people" who are living in another country
7. Beliefs: forcibly converting others to religious or political beliefs

Timasheff's analysis is excellent, and you can use these three essential conditions and seven fuels to analyze any war. They will help you understand why the politicians at any given time chose this political action.

Costs of War

One side effect of the new technologies stressed in this text is a higher capacity to inflict death. During World War I, bombs claimed fewer than 3 of every 100,000 people in England and Germany. With World War II's more powerful airplanes and bombs, these deaths increased a hundredfold, to 300 of every 100,000 civilians (Hart 1957). With today's higher killing capacity, if a war were fought with nuclear bombs, the death rate could run 100 percent. War is also costly in terms of money. As shown in Table 15.3, the United States has spent $4 trillion on nine major wars.

Table 15.3 What U.S. Wars Cost

American Revolution	$1,918,000,000
War of 1812	$615,000,000
Mexican War	$1,076,000,000
Civil War	$45,990,000,000
Spanish-American War	$5,961,000,000
World War I	$369,580,000,000
World War II	$2,953,716,000,000
Korean War	$262,062,000,000
Vietnam War	$553,088,000,000
Persian Gulf War I	$80,000,000,000
Persian Gulf War II	$?
Total	$4,274,006,000,000

Note: The source lists the costs in 1967 dollars. To account for inflation, I increased these amounts by 350 percent, and added the costs of service-connected benefits. Where a range was listed, I used the mean. The cost for the Persian Gulf War I, from the *New York Times* source, is in 2002 dollars.

The military costs for the U.S. involvement in Grenada, Panama, Kuwait, Somalia, Haiti, Kosovo, Afghanistan, and Persian Gulf War II are not listed in the source. Also not included are interest payments on war loans. Nor are these costs reduced by the financial benefits to the United States, such as the acquisition of California and Texas in the Mexican War. Also not included are ongoing expenditures by the military, currently about $350 billion a year.

Source: Statistical Abstract 1993:Table 553; 2002:Table 485; "In Perspective" 2003.

Despite its massive costs in lives and property, warfare remains a common way to pursue political objectives. For about seven years, the United States fought in Vietnam—at a cost of 59,000 American and about 2 million Vietnamese lives (Herring 1989; Hellinger and Judd 1991). For nine years, the Soviet Union waged war in Afghanistan—with a death toll of about 1 million Afghans and perhaps 50,000 Soviet soldiers (Armitage 1989; Binyon 2001). An eight-year war between Iran and Iraq cost about 400,000 lives. Cuban mercenaries in Africa and South America brought an unknown number of deaths. Civil wars in Africa, Asia, and South America claimed hundreds of thousands of lives, mostly of civilians. Also unknown is how many lives were lost in the two wars against Iraq and the terrorists in Afghanistan.

Sowing the Seeds of Future Wars

Selling advanced war technology to the Least Industrialized Nations sows the seeds of future wars. When a Least Industrialized Nation buys high-tech weapons, its neighbors get nervous, which sparks an arms race among them (Cole and Lubman 1994; Ricks 1994). Table 15.4 shows that the United States is the chief merchant of death. Great Britain and France place a distant second and third. This table also shows the major customers in the business of death. Two matters are of interest. First, Egypt, a country so poor that it can hardly keep its people from starving, is one of the biggest spenders. Either its power elite is drastically insecure (and seeks to bolster its power through these tremendous expenditures) or else it is incredibly secure because of the weapons it has purchased. Second, the purchases of arms by Saudi Arabia, Kuwait, and United Arab Emirates indicate that U.S. dollars spent on oil tend to return to the United States. There is, in reality, an exchange of arms and oil.

The seeds of future wars are also sown by nuclear proliferation. Some Least Industrialized Nations, such as India, Pakistan, China, and North Korea have nuclear weapons. Iran and Libya are furiously trying to develop their own nuclear arsenals. In the hands of a terrorist or a dictator who uses them to settle nationalistic—or even personal—grudges, these weapons can mean nuclear blackmail or nuclear attack.

After the cold war ended in about 1986, the United States and Russia began to cooperate with one another, although they also continued to eye each other suspiciously. The United States formed an organization called G-7 (*the* Group of 7), consisting of the seven richest, most powerful, and most technologically advanced nations (Canada, France, Germany, Great Britain, Italy, Japan, and the United States). Their goal was to perpetuate their global dominance, divide up the world's markets, and regulate global economic activity. Although Russia did not qualify for membership on the basis of wealth, power, or technology, the other nations feared Russia's nuclear arsenal and invited Russia as an observer at its annual summits. Russia became a full member in 2002, and the organization is now called G-8. Because China has increased both its economic clout and its nuclear arsenal, it has been invited to be an observer—a form of trial membership.

G-8, soon to be G-9, may be a force for peace—if these nations can agree on how to divide up the world's markets. Dissension became apparent in 2003, however, when the United States launched military action against Iraq, with only the support of Great Britain and Italy from this group. Later, however, G-8 showed unity by threatening North Korea and Iran with force if they continue their nuclear weapons programs (Tagliabue and Bumiller 2003).

Nuclear, Biological, and Chemical Terrorism

Hatred between ethnic groups spans generations, sometimes continuing for centuries. Groups nurture their bitterness by endlessly chronicling the atrocities committed by their archenemy. One consequence is armed conflict, which continuously erupts somewhere in the world as one group seizes an opportunity to attack its enemy—or to try to remove its yoke of oppression.

Nourished hatreds also make terrorism a danger. If a weaker group seeks to attack a more powerful group, one of its few—and very inviting—options is suicide terrorism. This tactic shocks the world and captures headlines, as it has done time after time when Palestinians use it against Israelis. The most dramatic example of suicide terrorism, of course, was the attack on the World Trade Center and the Pentagon under the direction of Osama bin Laden. These attacks have created a major civil rights issue, the topic of the Down-to-Earth Sociology box on the next page.

As shown in our opening vignette, the real danger lies in weapons of mass destruction—biological, nuclear, and chemical weapons. Unleashed against a civilian population, such weapons could cause millions of deaths. In 2001, Americans caught a glimpse of how easily such weapons can be unleashed when anthrax was mailed to a few select victims. The availability of nuclear, chemical, and biological weapons because of the breakup of the Soviet empire makes further terrorism on U.S. soil a chilling possibility. This topic is discussed in the Down-to-Earth Sociology box on page 441.

War and Dehumanization

> Proud of his techniques, the U.S. trainer was demonstrating to the South American soldiers how to torture a prisoner. As the victim screamed in anguish, the trainer was interrupted by a phone call from his wife. His students could hear him say, "A dinner and a movie sound nice. I'll see you right after work." Hanging up the phone, he then continued the lesson. (Stockwell 1989)

War exacts many costs in addition to killing people and destroying property. One is its effect on morality. Exposure to brutality and killing often causes **dehumanization,** the process of reducing people to objects that do not deserve to be treated as humans.

As we review findings on dehumanization and see how it breeds callousness and cruelty, perhaps we can better understand why "good people" can

Table 15.4 The Business of Death

The 5 Largest Arms Sellers	
1. United States	$31.8 billion
2. Great Britain	$6.6 billion
3. France	$5.9 billion
4. Russia	$2.3 billion
5. China	$1.1 billion

The 10 Largest Arms Consumers	
1. Saudi Arabia	$11.6 billion
2. Taiwan	$9.2 billion
3. Japan	$2.6 billion
4. Great Britain	$2.1 billion
5. Kuwait	$2.0 billion
6. Egypt	$1.6 billion
7. Turkey	$1.6 billion
8. United States	$1.6 billion
9. United Arab Emirates	$1.4 billion
10. South Korea	$1.1 billion
11. Israel	$1.1 billion

Source: Statistical Abstract 2000:Table 571.

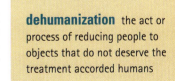

Viewed from the outside, it is difficult to fathom the depth and complexity of the mutual hatreds that enmesh some groups. From their perspective, however, nourishing the hatreds and planning revenge makes sense. The Palestinian parents who dressed this baby as a suicide bomber said they did it as a joke.

dehumanization the act or process of reducing people to objects that do not deserve the treatment accorded humans

DOWN TO EARTH SOCIOLOGY

Is Big Brother Standing on Our Doorstep? Civil Liberties and Homeland Security

THERE IS NO QUESTION THAT WE MUST have security. Our nation cannot be at risk, and we cannot live in peril. But does security have to come at the price of our civil liberties?

Balancing security and civil liberties has always been a sensitive issue in the history of the United States. Never has there been a simple answer. In times of war, the U.S. government has curtailed certain freedoms. During the War Between the States, as the Civil War is called in the South, Abraham Lincoln even banned the right of *habeas corpus* (Neely 1992). This took away people's right to appear in court to determine if they had been unlawfully arrested and imprisoned, and thus should be released from custody.

After the terrorist attacks on New York and Washington in 2001, Congress authorized the formation of the Department of Homeland Security. Other than beefed-up security at airports, few citizens noticed a difference in their everyday lives. Those suspected of terrorism, however, felt a major impact. They were imprisoned without charges being lodged against them in a court, and they were denied the right to consult lawyers or to have a hearing in court.

People shrugged this off. "Those are probably terrorists," they said. What ordinary citizens didn't realize, however, was that behind the scenes their own liberties were being curtailed. FBI agents began to place listening devises on cars, in buildings, and on streets, using Nightstalkers, aircraft outfitted with electronic surveillance equipment, to listen to conversations. All this was done without warrants (Hentoff 2003).

Then there is the "no-fly list" of the Transportation Security Agency. Anyone who *might* have some kind of connection with some kind of terrorist is not allowed on an airplane. This agency has also developed CAPPS II (Computer Assisted Passenger Pre-Screening System). Each traveler will be labeled as a 'green,' 'yellow,' or 'red' security risk. Red is reserved for known terrorists.

But what about those stamped with the yellow code? These people are suspect. They are not "clear, Okay, good," as are those who are marked by green. As the American Civil Liberties Union says, anyone could get caught up in this system, with no way to get out. You might be stamped yellow simply for reading the wrong books—because agents at the Department of Homeland Security now have the right to keep records on the books we buy or check out at libraries. They can now legally even record the Internet sites we visit at libraries.

If such surveillance continues, the government will eventually maintain an intelligence file on each of us. If a yellow code goes in your file, that information could be shared with other government agencies. This, in turn, could affect your chances of getting a job or government benefits, and even a college scholarship.

How far do government officials want to go? The Homeland Security Bill passed by Congress comes with a Total Information Awareness (TIA) program. This allows government officials to track our telephone conversations, credit card purchases, e-mails, medical histories, and travel history (O'Malley 2003). Congress refused to approve a program called Terrorism Information and Prevention System (TIPS), which would have used volunteer spies. Mail carriers, truck drivers, cable installers, and utility employees would have been recruited to be on the lookout for any suspicious behavior.

A dossier on each of us? Government watchdogs looking over our shoulders, noting with whom we associate, even the books and magazine we read? Microphones planted to eavesdrop on our conversations?

Security we must have. But at what cost? Will we eventually be required to have a computer chip installed in our right hand or in our forehead for added surveillance?

For Your CONSIDERATION

What civil liberties do you think we should give up in order to be secure from terrorists? Are you willing to have the government keep track of your everyday affairs in the name of homeland security? What is your opinion of the government keeping a list of the books you check out at the library? Listening to your conversations? Keeping a list of people you associate with?

torture political prisoners. Consider the four characteristics of dehumanization (Bernard et al. 1971):

1. *Increased emotional distance from others.* People stop identifying with others, no longer seeing them as having qualities similar to themselves. They often perceive them as "the enemy," or as objects of some sort, and sometimes as subhuman, not as people at all.
2. *An emphasis on following procedures.* Regulations are not questioned, for they are seen as a means to an end. People are likely to say, "I don't like doing this, but I have to follow rules," or "We all have to die some day. What difference does it make if these people die now?"
3. *Inability to resist pressures.* One's own ideas of morality take a back seat to fears of losing one's job, losing the respect of one's peers, or having one's integrity and loyalty questioned.

DOWN TO EARTH SOCIOLOGY

Biological Terrorism

THIS CHAPTER OPENED WITH A REPORT ON biological terorism. Now, let's consider the following scenario, which presents a different way that such an attack might unfold:

> Over a period of years, agents of a nation whose leaders hate the United States and want to settle a grudge have quietly infiltrated the country. Most were admitted as students at universities. All have been highly trained by their country's secret police. On a predetermined day, at a specified hour, they release anthrax and smallpox into the air of 20 major cities. Within weeks, a third of Americans are dead.

This scenario haunts U.S. officials. There will be no warning, no attempt to hold the United States hostage in order to extort billions of dollars. Money is not the goal. The motive is revenge for humiliation suffered at U.S. hands. The goal will be no less than to wipe out the United States itself.

As you saw in the opening vignette, the military has conducted exercises to play out what might happen if terrorists, armed with genetically modified germs, decided to strike. So has the White House (Broad and Miller 1998). In both exercises, officials were shocked at how easily such an attack could be carried out and at the millions who would die. In response, government officials have stockpiled vaccines around the country and have trained emergency medical teams in major cities (Broad and Petersen 2001). Military personnel, public health workers, and emergency room doctors are being vaccinated against anthrax (Buckley and Cohen 2002).

This is one of the most incredible photos in this text, and one of the most alarming that I have ever seen. This technician in Almaty, Kazakhstan (a former Soviet republic), is holding vials of plague germs that have been stored in an old pea can.

How seriously are officials taking this threat? Even before the 9/11 attacks, President Clinton made a "secret" directive that if such an attack were to occur, the inhabitants of a city would *not* be evacuated. Instead, the military would block the roads. At gunpoint, they would prevent people from fleeing the cities and spreading the disease. The likely result would be chaos and a military takeover of state and local governments (Miller and Broad 1999). This may explain why the U.S. military has openly discussed the legality of martial law (Davies 2000). It may also explain the strange event that occurred after the attack on the World Trade Center—the roads and bridges leading to and from Manhattan were blocked. For several hours, the people who were already in Manhattan, including those who had escaped the World Trade Center, were not allowed to leave the island. In the meantime, specialists were dispatched to the rubble to determine if biological agents had been released in the attack.

An ancient Chinese proverb says: "May you live in exciting times." This seemingly innocuous saying is actually a curse; it expresses the hope that an enemy's life will be upset. We do live in exciting times. Let's hope that the curse that envelops us—proliferating nuclear, chemical, and biological weapons, interstate and interethnic rivalries and domination, aspiring nationalism, and the growing threat of terrorism—does not mean our destruction.

4. *A diminished sense of personal responsibility.* People come to see themselves as only small cogs in a large machine. They are not responsible for what they do, for they are simply following orders. The higher-ups who give the orders are thought to have more complete or even secret information that justifies what is being done. They think, "The higher-ups are in a position to judge what is right and wrong, but in my humble place, who am I to question these acts?"

A Vietnam vet who read this section remarked, "You missed the major one we used. We killed kids. Our dehumanizing technique was a saying, 'The little ones are the soldiers of tomorrow.' " Such sentiments may be more common than we suppose. A good Spanish friend, a mild-mannered man, said that we should kill even the children of terrorists. "It's like weeds," he told me. "You have to pull up the little ones, too, or they'll grow into big weeds."

Dehumanization numbs the conscience. As in the vignette that opened this section, even acts of torture become dissociated from one's "normal self." Brutality and killing, though regrettable, are seen as tools that help to get a job done. Torturing and killing somehow fit into the larger scheme of things—and someone has to do the "dirty work" (Hughes 1962/1993). The individual clothes such acts in patriotic language: They are "the soldier's duty." Those who make the decisions are the ones who are responsible—soldiers simply follow orders.

As sociologist Tamotsu Shibutani (1970) stressed, dehumanization is aided by the tendency for prolonged conflicts to be transformed into a struggle between good and evil.

nationalism a strong identity with a nation, accompanied by the desire for that nation to be dominant

The enemy, of course, represents evil in the equation. To fight against absolute evil sometimes requires the suspension of moral standards—for one is dealing with an abnormal situation, opposing an enemy that is less than human, and fighting for the precarious survival of good. War, then, exalts treachery, cruelty, and killing—and medals are given to glorify actions that would be condemned in every other context of social life.

As soldiers participate in acts that they, too, would normally condemn, they neutralize their morality. This insulates them from acknowledging their behaviors as evil, which would threaten their self-concept and mental adjustment. Surgeons, highly sensitive to patients' needs in ordinary medical situations, become capable of mentally removing an individual's humanity. By thinking of Jews as "lower people (Untermenschen) who are going to die anyway," German surgeons during World War II were able to mutilate Jews just to study the results.

Dehumanization does not always insulate the self from guilt, however, and its failure to do so can bring severe personal consequences. During the war, while soldiers are surrounded by army buddies who agree that the enemy is less than human and deserves inhuman treatment, it is easier for such definitions to remain intact. After returning home, however, the dehumanizing definitions more easily break down. Many soldiers then find themselves disturbed by what they did during the war. Although most eventually adjust, some cannot, such as this soldier from California who wrote this note before putting a bullet through his brain (Smith 1980):

> I can't sleep anymore. When I was in Vietnam, we came across a North Vietnamese soldier with a man, a woman, and a three- or four-year-old girl. We had to shoot them all. I can't get the little girl's face out of my mind. I hope that God will forgive me . . . I can't.

A New World Order?

The globalization of capitalism, accompanied by the worldwide flow of information, capital, and goods discussed in the previous chapter, is little affected by national boundaries. The United States, Canada, and Mexico have formed a North American Free-Trade Association (NAFTA), to which all of South America may eventually belong. Some South American countries have adopted the dollar as an official currency, even as their national currency coexists alongside it. Transcending their national boundaries, most European countries have formed an economic and political unit (the European Union, or EU). They, too, have adopted a cross-national currency, the Euro, which has replaced their marks, francs, liras, and pesetas. The EU is drafting a single constitution (Bruni 2003) and has established a "rapid reaction force" of 60,000 troops under a unified command (Cohen 2001). Transcending national borders, the United Nations has sent out "peace keeping" troops to nations from Korea to Kosovo.

All governments use propaganda to influence public opinion, especially when they are preparing for or waging war. What do you think this poster from North Korea—reminiscent of the anti-Japan posters common in the United States during World War II—is designed to accomplish?

Will this process continue until there is just one state or empire that envelops the earth itself? This is a distinct possibility, deriving perhaps not only from these historical trends but also from a push by a powerful group of capitalists who profit from global free trade (Domhoff 1990). Now that Russia has joined the global capitalist club, it, too, is calling for this change. When Russia was accepted into NATO, the country's prime minister made this remarkable statement: "We must now together build the New World Order" (Purdum 2002).

Although the trend toward one state is in full tilt, we are unlikely to see its conclusion during our lifetimes, for national boundaries and national patriotism die only hard deaths. The Cultural Diversity box on the next page explores this tension between nations and states, which is presenting a stubborn obstacle to the New World Order.

If global political and economic unity does come about, it is fascinating to speculate on what type of government may emerge. Certainly a world order holds potential benefits for human welfare. We could have global peace. And if we have a benevolent government, our lives and participation in politics could be quite sat-

CULTURAL DIVERSITY

around the WORLD

Roadblocks in the Path to the New World Order: The Globalization of Capitalism Versus the Resurgence of Nationalism

The world has about five thousand nations. What makes each one a *nation* is that its people share a language, culture, territory, and political organization. A *state*, in contrast, claims a monopoly on violence over a territory. A state may contain many nations. The Kayapo Indians are but one nation within the state called Brazil. The Chippewa and Sioux are two nations within the state called the United States. The world's five thousand nations have existed for hundreds, some even for thousands, of years. In contrast, most of the world's 194 states have been around only since World War II.

Most modern states are empires; that is, they have incorporated nations into their boundaries—usually by conquest. Some states have far better records than others, but overall, no ideology, left or right, religious or sectarian, has protected nations or promoted pluralism much better or worse than any other. The last century probably saw more genocides and *ethnocides* (the destruction of an ethnic group) than any other.

For nation peoples, group identity transcends political affiliation. Clearly, the Palestinians who live within Israel's borders do not identify themselves as Israelis. But did you know that the Oromos in Ethiopia have more members than do three-quarters of the states in the United Nations, and that they do not think of themselves as Ethiopians? The 22 million Kurds don't consider themselves first and foremost to be Iranians, Iraqis, Syrians, or Turks. There are about 450 nations in Nigeria, 350 in India, 180 in Brazil, 130 in the former USSR, and 90 in Ethiopia. That nations are squeezed into states with which they don't identify is the nub of the problem.

Shown here are Russian troops in what remains of downtown Grozny, the capital of Chechnya. Russia bombed the city in order to stop the former colony from gaining independence.

In most states, power resides in the hands of an elite that operates by a simple credo: Winner takes all. The power elite control foreign investment and aid, and use both to enforce their position. They control exports, levy taxes—and buy the weapons. They confiscate the resources of the nations, whether those take the form of Native American land in North and South America or oil from the Kurds in Iraq. When nations resist, the result is open conflict—and sometimes genocide.

About half of the debt of the least industrialized states and nearly all debt in Africa comes from the purchase of weapons, which the states use to suppress their own citizens. Most of the world's 22 million refugees are victims of such conflicts, as are most of the 100 million internally displaced people who have been uprooted from their homelands.

A vicious cycle forms. The appropriation of a nation's resources leads to conflict, conflict leads to insecurity and the purchase of weapons, weapons purchases lead to debt, and debt leads to the appropriation of more resources. This self-perpetuating cycle helps to ensure that elites of most of the least industrialized states will cooperate with G-8, which supplies the arms, as it divides the globe's resources among its members.

G-8's march to a New World Order has met a serious obstacle, the resurgence of **nationalism**—identity with and loyalty to a nation. Because it promotes loyalty to smaller groups instead of to the regional divisions into which G-8 wants to carve the globe, nationalism threatens the evolving New World Order. The shooting wars increase—fought over issues and animosities that are rooted in history. Such events are only faintly understood by those who are not a party to them, but they have been kept vividly alive in the folklore and collective memory of these nations. These wars threaten the fragile coalitions that G-8 is building as it divides up the world's resources.

G-8 will continue to divide the globe into regional trading blocs, and we will continue to witness this oppositional struggle. We will see seemingly contradictory outcomes: the formation of global coalitions matched by the simultaneous outbreak of local shooting wars as nations struggle for independence.

The end result? It is sufficient to note how greatly the scales are tipped in favor of the most industrialized states and the multinational corporations. David is not likely to defeat Goliath this time. Yet where David had five small stones and needed only one, some nations have discovered the powerful weapon of terrorism. It, too, has become part of the balance of political power.

Sources: Clay 1990; Ohmae 1995; Jáuregui 1996; Marcus 1996; Alter 2000, Hechter 2000; Fletcher 2001; Kaplan 2003; Simons 2004.

isfying. But we must be mindful of Hitler. If his conquests had resulted in world domination, not only would we all be speaking German, but also we would be living under a single dictator in a world totalitarian regime based on racial identification. If the world's resources and people come under the control of a dictatorship or an oligarchy, then, the future for humanity could be bleak.

SUMMARY and REVIEW

Micropolitics and Macropolitics

What is the difference between micropolitics and macropolitics?

The essential nature of politics is **power**, and every group is political. The term **micropolitics** refers to the exercise of power in everyday life. **Macropolitics** refers to large-scale power, such as governing a country. P. 420.

Power, Authority, and Violence

How are authority and coercion related to power?

Authority is power that people view as legitimately exercised over them, while **coercion** is power they consider unjust. The **state** is a political entity that claims a monopoly on violence over some territory. If enough people consider a state's power illegitimate, **revolution** is possible. Pp. 420–421.

What kinds of authority are there?

Max Weber identified three types of authority. In **traditional authority**, power derives from custom—patterns set down in the past serve as rules for the present. In **rational-legal authority** (also called *bureaucratic authority*), power is based on law and written procedures. In **charismatic authority**, power is derived from loyalty to an individual to whom people are attracted. Charismatic authority, which undermines traditional and rational-legal authority, has built-in problems in transferring authority to a new leader. Pp. 421–424.

Types of Government

How are the types of government related to power?

In a **monarchy**, power is based on hereditary rule; in a **democracy**, power is given to the ruler by citizens; and in a **dictatorship**, power is seized by an individual or small group. Pp. 425–427.

The U.S. Political System

What are the main characteristics of the U.S. political system?

The United States has a "winner take all" system, in which a simple majority determines elections. Most European democracies, in contrast, have **proportional representation**; legislative seats are allotted according to the percentage of votes each political party receives. Pp. 427–429.

Voter turnout is higher among people who are more socially integrated—those who sense a greater stake in the outcome of elections, such as the more educated and well-to-do. **Lobbyists** and **special-interest groups**, such as **political action committees** (PACs), play a significant role in U.S. politics. Pp. 430–434.

Who Rules the United States?

Is the United States controlled by a ruling class?

In a view known as **pluralism**, functionalists say that no one group holds power, that the country's many competing interest groups balance one another. Conflict theorists, who focus on the top level of power, say that the United States is governed by a **power elite**, a ruling class made up of the top corporate, political, and military leaders. At this point, the matter is not settled. Pp. 434–436.

War and Terrorism: A Means to Implement Political Objectives

How is war related to politics—and what are its costs?

War is a means of attempting to accomplish political objectives. Because of technological advances in killing, the costs of war in terms of human lives have escalated. The Least Industrialized Nations, which can least afford it, spend huge amounts on technologically advanced weapons. Another cost is **dehumanization**, whereby people no longer see others as worthy of human treatment. This paves the way for torture and killing. Pp. 436–442.

A New World Order?

Is humanity headed toward a world political system?

The global expansion of communications, transportation, and trade, the widespread adoption of capitalism, the retreat of socialism, and the trend toward regional economic and political unions may indicate that a world political system is developing. The oppositional trend is a fierce **nationalism**. If a New World Order develops, the possible consequences for human welfare range from excellent to calamitous. Pp. 442–444.

Where can I read more on this topic?

Suggested Readings for this chapter are at the back of this book.

THINKING Critically ABOUT CHAPTER 15

1. What does biological terrorism have to do with politics?
2. What are the three sources of authority, and how do they differ from one another?
3. Apply the findings on "Why Nations Go to War" (page 437) to some recent war that the United States has waged.

ADDITIONAL RESOURCES for This Chapter

www.ablongman.com/henslin7e

- *Content Select* Research Database for Sociology, with suggested key terms and annotated references
- Link to 2000 Census, with activities
- Flashcards of key terms and concepts
- Practice Tests
- Weblinks
- Interactive Maps

Chapter 16

The Family

Charles H. Alston, *Family,* 1955

Chapter Outline

"Hold still. We're going to be late," said Sharon as she tried to put shoes on 2-year-old Michael, who kept squirming away.

Finally succeeding with the shoes, Sharon turned to 4-year-old Brittany, who was trying to pull a brush through her hair. "It's stuck, Mom," Brittany said.

"Well, no wonder. Just how did you get gum in your hair? I don't have time for this, Brittany. We've got to leave."

Getting to the van fifteen minutes behind schedule, Sharon strapped the kids in, and then herself. Just as she was about to pull away, she remembered that she had not checked the fridge for messages.

"Just a minute, kids. I'll be right back."

Running into the house, she frantically searched for a note from Tom. She vaguely remembered him mumbling something about being held over at work. She grabbed the Post-It and ran back to the van.

"He's picking on me," complained Brittany when her mother climbed back in.

"Oh, shut up, Brittany," Sharon said. "He's only 2. He can't pick on you."

"Yes, he did," Brittany said, crossing her arms defiantly as she stretched out her foot to kick her brother's seat.

Yes, he did," Brittany said, crossing her arms lefiantly as she stretched out her foot to kick her brother's seat.

"Oh, no! How did Mikey get that smudge on his face? Did you do that, Brit?"

Brittany crossed her arms again, pushing out her lips in her classic pouting pose.

As Sharon drove to the day care center, she tried to calm herself. "Only two more days of work this week, and then the weekend. Then I can catch up on housework and have a little relaxed time with the kids. And Tom can finally cut the grass and buy the groceries," she thought. "And maybe we'll even have time to make love. Boy, that's been a long time."

At a traffic light, Sharon found time to read Tom's note. "Oh, no. That's what he meant. He has to work Saturday. Well, there go those plans."

What Sharon didn't know was that her boss also had made plans for Sharon's Saturday. And that their emergency Saturday babysitter wouldn't be available. That Michael was coming down with chicken pox. That Brittany would follow next. That . . .

That there isn't enough time to get everything done is a common complaint of most of us. But it is especially true for working parents of young children. They find themselves without the support systems parents used to take for granted: stay-at-home moms who were the center of the neighborhood, a husband whose sole income was enough to support a wife and several children, a safe neighborhood where even small children could play outside, and a grandma who could pitch in during emergencies.

Those days are gone forever. Today, more and more families are like Sharon's and Tom's. They are harried, working more and seemingly making less, and, certainly, having less time for one another—and for their children. In this chapter, we shall try to understand what is happening to the U.S. family, and to families worldwide.

Marriage and Family in Global Perspective

To better understand U.S. patterns of marriage and family, let's first look at how customs differ around the world. This will give us a context for interpreting our own experience in this vital social institution.

What Is a Family?

"What is a family, anyway?" asked William Sayres (1992) at the beginning of an article on this topic. By this question, he meant that although the family is so significant to humanity that it is universal—every human group in the world organizes its members in families—the world's cultures display so much variety that the term *family* is difficult to define. For example, although the Western world regards a family as a husband, wife, and children, other groups have family forms in which men have more than one wife (**polygyny**) or women more than one husband (**polyandry**). How about the obvious? Can we define the family as the approved group into which children are born? This would overlook the Banaro of New Guinea. In this group, a young woman must give birth before she can marry—and she *cannot* marry the father of her child (Murdock 1949).

polygyny a form of marriage in which men have more than one wife

polyandry a form of marriage in which women have more than one husband

family two or more people who consider themselves related by blood, marriage, or adoption

household people who occupy the same housing unit

nuclear family a family consisting of a husband, wife, and child(ren)

And so it goes. For just about every element you might regard as essential to marriage or family, some group has a different custom. Consider the sex of the bride and groom. Although in almost every instance the bride and groom are female and male, there are exceptions. In some Native American tribes, a man or woman who wanted to be a member of the opposite sex went through a ceremony (*berdache*) and was *declared* a member of the opposite sex. From then on, not only did the "new" man or woman do the tasks associated with his or her new sex, but also the individual was allowed to marry. In this instance, the husband and wife were of the same biological sex. In the 1980s, several European countries legalized same-sex marriages. In 2003, so did the province of Ontario, Canada.

What if we were to say that the family is the unit in which children are disciplined and that parents are responsible for their material needs? This, too, is not universal. Among the Trobriand Islanders, the wife's eldest brother is responsible for making certain that his sister's children have food and for disciplining them when they get out of line (Malinowski 1927). Finally, even sexual relationships don't universally characterize a husband and wife. The Nayar of Malabar never allow a bride and groom to have sex. After a three-day celebration of the marriage, they send the groom packing—and never allow him to see his bride again (La Barre 1954). (In case you're wondering, the groom comes from another tribe. Nayar women are allowed to have sex, but only with approved lovers—who can never be the husband. This system keeps family property intact—along matrilineal lines.)

Such remarkable variety means that we have to settle for a broad definition. A **family** consists of people who consider themselves related by blood, marriage, or adoption. A **household,** in contrast, consists of people who occupy the same housing unit—a house, apartment, or other living quarters.

We can classify families as **nuclear** (husband, wife, and children) and **extended** (including people such as grandparents, aunts, uncles, and cousins in addition to the nuclear unit). Sociologists also refer to the **family of orientation** (the family in which an individual grows up) and the **family of procreation** (the family formed when a couple have their first child). Finally, regardless of its form, **marriage** can be viewed as a group's approved mating arrangements—usually marked by a ritual of some sort (the wedding) to indicate the couple's new public status.

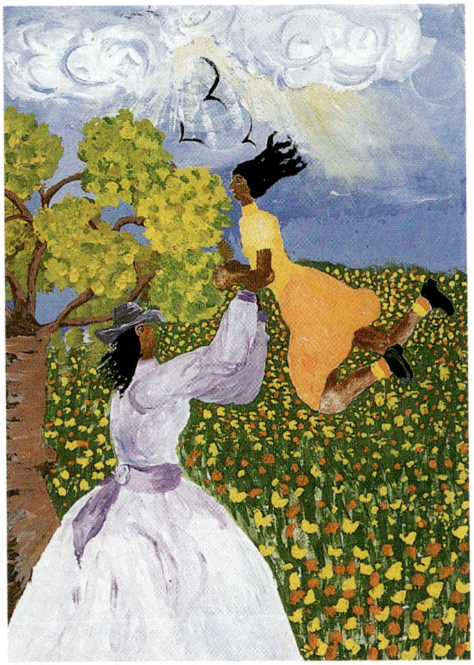

Often one of the strongest family bonds is that of mother–daughter. The young artist, an eleventh grader, wrote: "This painting expresses the way I feel about my future with my child. I want my child to be happy and I want her to love me the same way I love her. In that way we will have a good relationship so that nobody will be able to take us apart. I wanted this picture to be alive; that is why I used a lot of bright colors."

extended family a nuclear family plus other relatives, such as grandparents, uncles, and aunts

family of procreation the family formed when a couple's first child is born

family of orientation the family in which a person grows up

marriage a group's approved mating arrangements, usually marked by a ritual of some sort

Common Cultural Themes

Despite this diversity, several common themes do run through marriage and family. As Table 16.1 illustrates, all societies use marriage and family to establish patterns of mate selection, descent, inheritance, and authority. Let's look at these patterns.

Table 16.1 Common Cultural Themes: Marriage in Traditional and Industrialized Societies

Characteristic	Traditional Societies	Industrialized (and Postindustrial) Societies
What is the structure of marriage?	*Extended* (marriage embeds spouses in a large kinship network of explicit obligations)	*Nuclear* (marriage brings fewer obligations toward the spouse's relatives)
What are the functions of marriage?	Encompassing (see the six functions listed on p. 450)	More limited (many functions are fulfilled by other social institutions)
Who holds authority?	Highly *patriarchal* (authority is held by males)	Although some patriarchal features remain, authority is divided more equally
How many spouses at one time?	Most have one spouse (*monogamy*), while some have several (*polygamy*)	One spouse
Who selects the spouse?	The spouse is selected by the parents, usually the father	Individuals choose their own spouse
Where does the couple live?	Couples usually reside with the groom's family (*patrilocal residence*), less commonly with the bride's family (*matrilocal residence*)	Couples establish a new home (*neolocal residence*)
How is descent figured?	Usually figured from male ancestors (*patrilineal* kinship), less commonly from female ancestors (*matrilineal* kinship)	Figured from male and female ancestors equally (*bilateral kinship*)
How is inheritance figured?	Rigid system of rules; usually patrilineal, but may be matrilineal	Highly individualistic; usually bilateral

endogamy the practice of marrying within one's own group

exogamy the practice of marrying outside one's group

incest taboo the rule that prohibits sex and marriage among designated relatives

system of descent how kinship is traced over the generations

bilateral (system of descent) a system of reckoning descent that counts both the mother's and the father's side

patrilineal (system of descent) a system of reckoning descent that counts only the father's side

matrilineal (system of descent) a system of reckoning descent that counts only the mother's side

patriarchy a society or group in which men dominate women; authority is vested in males

matriarchy a society in which women as a group dominate men as a group

egalitarian authority more or less equally divided between people or groups, in this instance between husband and wife

Mate Selection Each human group establishes norms to govern who marries whom. Norms of **endogamy** specify that people should marry *within* their own group. Groups may prohibit interracial marriage, for example. In contrast, norms of **exogamy** specify that people must marry *outside* their group. The best example of exogamy is the **incest taboo,** which prohibits sex and marriage among designated relatives. In some societies, these norms are written into law, but in most cases they are informal. In the United States most whites marry whites and most African Americans marry African Americans—not because of any laws but because of informal norms.

Descent How are you related to your father's father or to your mother's mother? The explanation is found in your society's **system of descent,** the way people trace kinship over generations. We use a **bilateral system,** for we think of ourselves as related to *both* our mother's and our father's sides of the family. "Doesn't everyone?" you might ask. Interestingly, this is only one logical way to reckon descent. Some groups use a **patrilineal system,** tracing descent only on the father's side; they don't think of children as related to their mother's relatives. Others follow a **matrilineal system,** tracing descent only on the mother's side, and not considering children to be related to their father's relatives. The Naxi of China, for example, don't even have a word for father (Hong 1999).

Inheritance Marriage and family—in whatever form is customary in a society—are also used to compute rights of inheritance. In a bilateral system, property is passed to both males and females, in a patrilineal system only to males, and in a matrilineal system (the rarest form) only to females. No system is natural. Rather, each matches a group of people's ideas of justice and logic.

Authority Historically, some form of **patriarchy,** a social system in which men dominate women, has formed a thread that runs through all societies. Contrary to what many think, there are no historical records of a true **matriarchy,** a social system in which women as a group dominate men as a group. Our marriage and family customs, then, developed within a framework of patriarchy. Although U.S. family patterns are becoming more **egalitarian,** or equal, many of today's customs still reflect their patriarchal origin. One of the most obvious examples is U.S. naming patterns. Despite some changes, the typical bride still takes the groom's last name, and children usually receive the father's last name. For information on a society that systematically promotes equality in marriage, see the Cultural Diversity box on the next page.

Marriage and Family in Theoretical Perspective

A global perspective reveals that human groups have chosen many forms of mate selection, numerous ways to trace descent, and a variety of ways to view parental responsibility to children. Although these patterns are arbitrary, each group sees its own forms of marriage and family as natural. Now let's see what picture emerges when we apply the three sociological perspectives.

The Functionalist Perspective: Functions and Dysfunctions

Functionalists stress that to survive, a society must meet certain basic needs, or functions. When functionalists look at family, they examine how it is related to other parts of society, especially how the family contributes to the well-being of society.

Why the Family Is Universal Functionalists note that although the form of marriage and family varies from one group to another, the family is universal because it fulfills six needs that are basic to the survival of every society. As described on pages 26–28, these needs, or functions, are (1) economic production, (2) socialization of children, (3) care of the sick and aged, (4) recreation, (5) sexual control, and (6) reproduction. To make certain that these functions are performed, every human group adopted some form of the family.

CULTURAL DIVERSITY

around the WORLD

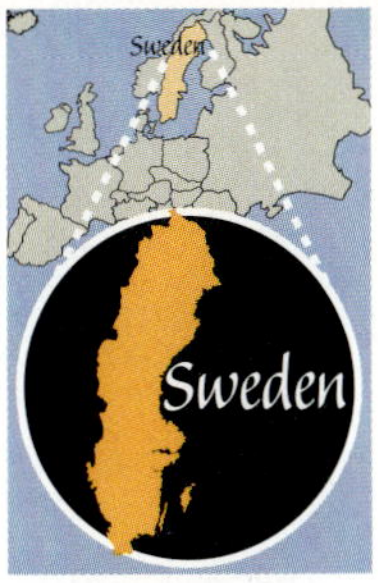

Watching Out for Kids: Gender Equality and Family Life in Sweden

Swedish lawmakers hold a strong image of what makes a good family. Their image centers on equality in marriage and on the welfare of children. They bolster this image with laws designed to put women and men on equal footing in marriage, to give mothers and fathers equal responsibility for the home and children, and to protect the financially weaker party in the event of divorce.

At the center of family law is the welfare of children. Health care for children is free, as is all health care for pregnant women. Maternity centers also offer free courses to help couples prepare for childbirth.

When a child is born, the parents are eligible for fifteen months' paid leave of absence from their jobs. The parents decide how they will split the fifteen months between them, because both cannot receive compensation at the same time. For the first twelve months the state pays 90 percent of gross income, and then a generous fixed rate for the remaining three months. The paid leave can be spread over eight years. Because most mothers take all the leave, the law now includes a "father's month," one month that cannot be transferred to the mother.

The government also guarantees other benefits. When a child is born, the father is entitled to ten days leave of absence with full pay. When a child is sick, either parent can care for the child and receive full pay for missed work—up to sixty days a year per child. Moreover, by law local governments must offer child care. If a husband becomes violent or threatens his wife, the woman can have a security alarm installed in their home free of charge.

Swedish divorce laws have also been drawn up with an eye to what is considered best for the child. Local governments are required to provide free counseling to any parent who requests it. If both parties agree and they have no children under the age of 16, the couple is automatically entitled to a divorce. Otherwise the law requires a six-month cooling-off period so parents can more calmly consider what is best for their children. Joint custody of children is automatic, unless one of the parents opposes it. The children may live with only one of the parents. The parent who does not live with the children is required to pay child support in proportion to his or her finances. If the parent fails to do so, the social security system steps in and makes the payments.

For Your CONSIDERATION

How does the Swedish system compare with that of the United States? What "system" for watching out for the welfare of children does the United States have, anyway?

Sources: Based on The Swedish Institute 1992; Froman 1994; Bernhardt and Goldscheider 2001.

Functions of the Incest Taboo Functionalists note that the incest taboo helps families avoid *role confusion.* This, in turn, facilitates the socialization of children. For example, if father-daughter incest were allowed, how should a wife treat her daughter—as a daughter, as a subservient second wife, or even as a rival? Should the daughter consider her mother as a mother, as the first wife, or as a rival? Would her father be a father or a lover? And would the wife be the husband's main wife, a secondary wife—or even the "mother of the other wife" (whatever role that might be)? Maternal incest would also lead to complications every bit as confusing as these.

The incest taboo also forces people to look outside the family for marriage partners. Anthropologists theorize that *exogamy* was especially functional in tribal societies, for it forged alliances between tribes that otherwise might have killed each other off. Today, exogamy extends a bride's and groom's social networks beyond their nuclear family by building relationships with their spouse's family.

Isolation and Emotional Overload Functionalists also analyze dysfunctions that arise from the relative isolation of the nuclear family. Unlike extended families, which are enmeshed in large kinship networks, members of nuclear families can count on fewer people for material and emotional support. This makes nuclear families vulnerable to "emotional overload." That is, the stress that comes with crises such as the loss of a job—or even the routine pressures of a harried life, as depicted in our opening vignette—is spread among fewer people. This places greater strain on each family member. In addition, the relative isolation of the nuclear family makes it vulnerable to a "dark side"—incest and various other forms of abuse, matters we examine later in this chapter.

The Conflict Perspective: Gender and Power

As you recall, central to conflict theory is the struggle over power. In marriage, the power of wives has been increasing. They are contributing more of the income *and* making more of the marital decisions than they used to (Rogers and Amato 2000). In marriage, husbands and wives maneuver for power in many areas, but due to space limitations, let's focus on housework.

The Power Struggle Over Housework Most men resist doing housework. As Figure 16.1 shows, even wives who work outside the home full time end up doing much more housework than their husbands. The lesser effort that husbands make seems such a strain to them, however, that the husband is likely to see himself as splitting the work fifty-fifty even when his wife does almost all the cooking and cleaning (Galinsky et al. 1993). Things are so one-sided that wives are *eight* times more likely than husbands to feel that the division of housework is unfair (Sanchez 1994).

And no wonder. Wives who put in an eight-hour day of working for wages average 7-1/2 hours more housework each week than their husbands do (Bianchi et al. 2000). If we include child care, the total may come closer to eleven hours a week (Bianchi and Spain 1996). *Incredibly, this is the equivalent of twenty-four 24-hour days a year.* Sociologist Arlie Hochschild (1989) calls this the working wife's "second shift." To stress the one-sided nature of the second shift, she quotes this satire by Garry Trudeau in the *Doonesbury* comic strip:

> A "liberated" father is sitting at his word processor writing a book about raising his child. He types: "Today I wake up with a heavy day of work ahead of me. As Joannie gets Jeffry ready for day care, I ask her if I can be relieved of my usual household

Figure 16.1 In Two-Paycheck Marriages, Who Does the Housework?

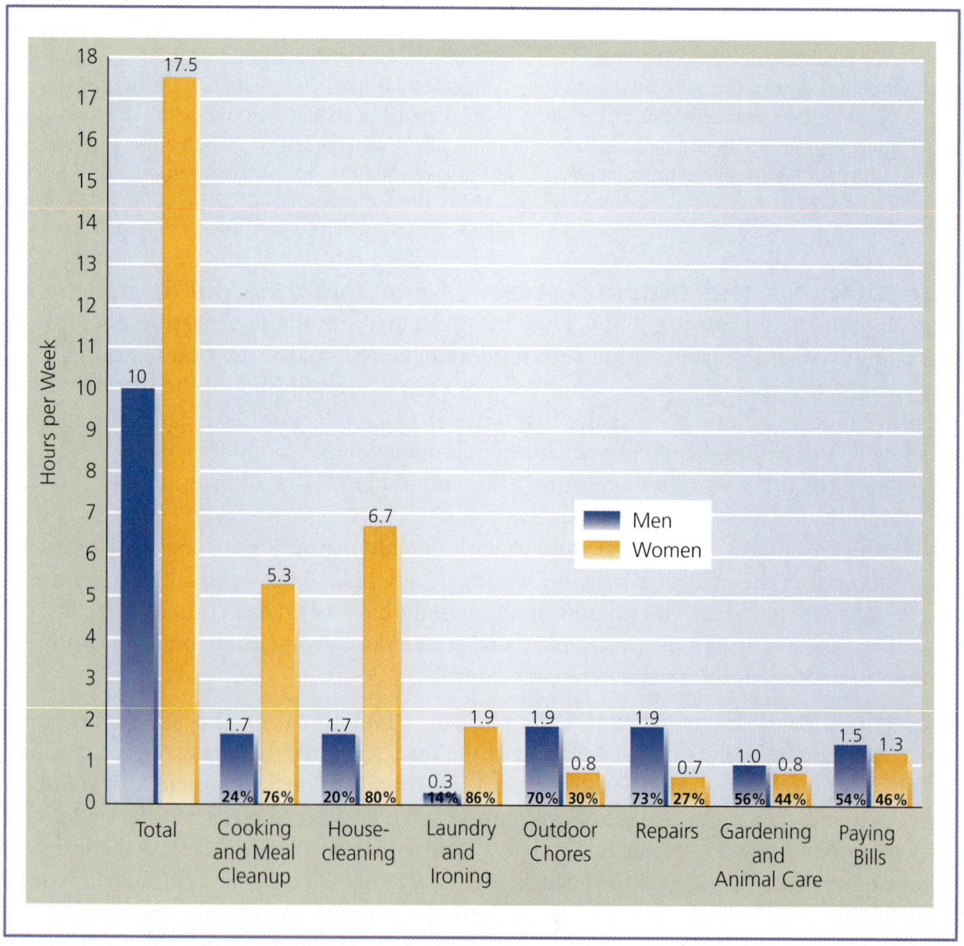

Note: Based on a national sample. Cooking and meal cleanup are combined from the original data.
Source: By the author. Based on Bianchi et al. 2000:Table 1.

responsibilities for the day. Joannie says, 'Sure, I'll make up the five minutes somewhere.' "

Not surprisingly, the burden of the second shift creates deep discontent among wives. These problems, as well as how wives and husbands cope with them, are discussed in the following Thinking Critically section.

THINKING Critically

The Second Shift—Strains and Strategies

To find out what life is like in two-paycheck marriages, for nine years sociologist Arlie Hochschild (1989) and her research associates interviewed and reinterviewed over fifty families. Hochschild also did participant observation with a dozen of them. She "shopped with them, visited friends, watched television, ate with them, and came along when they took their children to day care."

Although men are doing more housework today than they did just a few years ago (Bianchi et al. 2000), most feel that the *second shift*—the household duties that follow the day's work for pay—is the wife's responsibility. But as the wives cook, clean, and take care of the children after their job at the office or factory, many feel tired and emotionally drained. Some pride themselves on being the "supermom" who can do it all, but most just grit their teeth and bear it, doing the extra work, but resenting it. Not uncommonly, these feelings show up in the bedroom, where the wives show a lack of interest in sex.

The strains from working the second shift affect not only the marital relationship, but also the wife's self-concept. Here is how one woman tried to lift her flagging self-esteem:

> After taking time off for her first baby, Carol Alston felt depressed, "fat," and that she was "just a housewife." For a while she became the supermarket shopper who wanted to call down the aisles, "I'm an MBA! I'm an MBA!"

To pick up more of the burden, some husbands cut down on their commitment to a career. Others cut back on movies, seeing friends, doing hobbies. Most men, however, engage in what Hochschild describes as *strategies of resistance*. She identified the following:

Waiting it out. Many men never volunteer to do housework. Since many wives dislike asking, because it feels like "begging," this strategy often works. Some men make this strategy even more effective by showing irritation or becoming glum when they are asked, which discourages the wife from asking again.

Playing dumb. When they do housework, some men become incompetent. They can't cook rice without burning it; when they go to the store, they forget grocery lists; they never can remember where the broiler pan is. Hochschild did not claim that husbands do these things on purpose, but, rather, by withdrawing their mental attention from the task, they "get credit for trying and being a good sport"—but in such a way that they are not chosen next time.

Needs reduction. An example of this strategy is the father of two who explained that he never shopped because he didn't "need anything." He didn't need to iron his clothes because he "[didn't] mind wearing a wrinkled shirt." He didn't need to cook because "cereal is fine." As Hochschild observed, "Through his reduction of needs, this man created a great void into which his wife stepped with her 'greater need' to see him

ARLO & JANIS ® by Jimmy Johnson

The cartoonist has beautifully captured the reduction of needs strategy discussed by Hochschild.

In Hindu marriages, the roles of husband and wife are firmly established. Neither this woman, whom I photographed in Chittoor, India, nor her husband question whether she should carry the family wash to the village pump. Women here have done this task for millennia. As India industrializes, as happened in the West, who does the wash will be questioned—and may eventually become a source of strain in marriage.

wear an ironed shirt . . . and cook his dinner."

Substitute offerings. Expressing appreciation to the wife for being so organized that she can handle both work for wages and the second shift at home can be a substitute for helping—and a subtle encouragement for her to keep on working the second shift.

For Your CONSIDERATION . . .

Hochschild (1991) is confident that the problem of the second shift can be resolved. Based on the materials just presented

1. Identify the underlying *structural* causes of the problem of the second shift.
2. Based on your answer to number 1, identify *structural* solutions to this problem.
3. Determine how a working wife and husband might best reconcile the issues of the second shift.

The Symbolic Interactionist Perspective: Gender and the Meanings of Marriage

As noted in Chapter 1, symbolic interactionists focus on the meanings that people give to their lives. Let's apply this perspective to some surprising findings about husbands and housework.

The first finding is probably what you expect—the closer a husband's and wife's earnings, the more likely they are to share housework. Although husbands in such marriages don't share housework equally, they share more than other husbands. This finding, however, may be surprising: When husbands get laid off, most do *less* housework than before. *And husbands who earn less than their wives do the least housework.*

How can we explain this? It would seem that husbands who get laid off or who earn less than their wives would want to balance things out by doing more around the house, not less. Researchers suggest that the key is *gender role.* If a wife earns more than her husband, it threatens his masculinity—he takes this as a sign that he is failing in his traditional role of provider. To do housework—"women's work" in his eyes—threatens his masculinity even further. By avoiding housework, he "reclaims" his masculinity (Hochschild 1989; Brines 1994).

The Family Life Cycle

We have seen how the forms of marriage and family vary widely, and we have examined marriage and family from the three sociological perspectives. Now let's discuss love, courtship, and the family life cycle.

Love and Courtship in Global Perspective

Until recently, social scientists thought that romantic love originated in western Europe during the medieval period (Mount 1992). When anthropologists William Jankowiak and Edward Fischer (1992) surveyed the data available on 166 societies around the world, however, they found that this was not so. **Romantic love**—people being sexually attracted to one another and idealizing the other—showed up in 88 percent of these groups. The role of love, however, differs sharply from one society to another. As the Cultural Diversity box on the next page details, for example, Indians don't expect love to occur until *after* marriage—if then.

romantic love feelings of erotic attraction accompanied by an idealization of the other

Because love plays such a significant role in Western life—and often is regarded as the *only* proper basis for marriage—social scientists have probed this concept with the tools of the trade: experiments, questionnaires, interviews, and observations. In a fascinating

CULTURAL DIVERSITY

around the WORLD

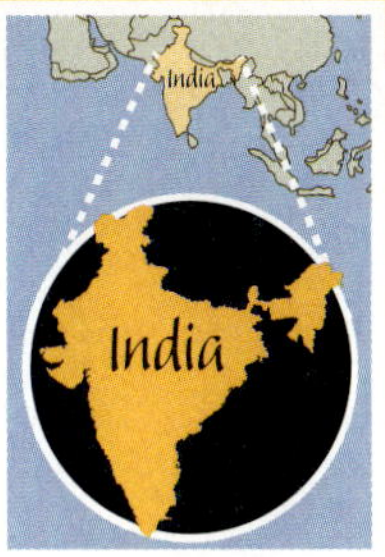

East Is East and West Is West . . . Love and Arranged Marriage in India

After Arun Bharat Ram returned to India with a degree from the University of Michigan, his mother announced that she wanted to find him a wife. Arun would be a good "catch" anywhere: 27 years old, educated, well mannered, intelligent, handsome—and, not incidentally, heir to a huge fortune.

Arun's mother already had someone in mind. Manju came from a solid, middle-class family and was also a college graduate. Arun and Manju met in a coffee shop at a luxury hotel—along with both sets of parents. He found her pretty and quiet. He liked that. She was impressed that he didn't boast about his background.

After four more meetings, one where the two young people met by themselves, the parents asked their children if they were willing to marry. Neither had any major objections.

The Prime Minister of India and fifteen hundred other guests came to the wedding.

"I didn't love him," Manju says. "But when we talked, we had a lot in common." She then adds, "But now I couldn't live without him. I've never thought of another man since I met him."

Although India has undergone extensive social change, Indian sociologists estimate that parents still arrange about 95 percent of marriages. Today, however, as with Arun and Manju, couples have veto power over their parents' selection. Another innovation is that the couple are allowed to talk to each other before the wedding—unheard of just a generation ago.

Why do Indians have arranged marriages? And why does this practice persist today, even among the educated and upper classes? We can also ask why the United States has such an individualistic approach to marriage.

The answers to these questions take us to two sociological principles. First, *a group's marriage practices match its values.* Individual mate selection matches U.S. values of individuality and independence, while arranged marriages match Indian values of children deferring to parental authority. To Indians, allowing unrestricted dating would mean entrusting important matters to inexperienced young people.

Second, *a group's marriage practices match its patterns of social stratification.* Arranged marriages in India affirm caste lines by channeling marriage within the same caste. Unchaperoned dating would encourage premarital sex, which, in turn, would break down family lines. Virginity at marriage, in contrast, assures the upper castes that they know the fatherhood of the children. Consequently, Indians socialize their children to think that parents have superior wisdom in these matters. In the United States, where family lines are less important and caste is an alien concept, the practice of young people choosing their own dating partners matches the relative openness of our social class system.

Even ideas of love differ. For Indians, love is a peaceful emotion, based on long-term commitment and devotion to family. Indians also think of love as something that can be "created" between two people. To do so, one needs to arrange the right conditions. Marriage is one of those right conditions.

These different backgrounds have produced contrasting ideas of love and marriage. Americans perceive love as having a mysterious element, a passion that suddenly seizes an individual. Indians view love as a peaceful feeling that develops when a man and a woman are united in intimacy and share common interests and goals in life. But perhaps the most startling difference is this: *For Americans, love produces marriage—while for Indians, marriage produces love.*

This billboard in Chennai, India, caught my attention. As the text indicates, even though India is industrializing, most of its people still follow traditional customs. This billboard is a sign of changing times.

For Your CONSIDERATION

What advantages do you see to the Indian approach to love and marriage? Do you think that the Indian system could work in the United States? Why or why not? Do you think that love can be created? Or does love suddenly "seize" people? What do you think love is?

Sources: Based on Gupta 1979; Bumiller 1992; Sprecher and Chandak 1992; Whyte 1992; Dugger 1998; Easley 2003.

homogamy the tendency of people with similar characteristics to marry one another

experiment, psychologists Donald Dutton and Arthur Aron discovered that fear breeds love (Rubin 1985). Here's what they did.

> About 230 feet above the Capilano River in North Vancouver, British Columbia, a rickety footbridge sways in the wind. It makes you feel like you won't make it across, that you might fall into the rocky gorge below. A more solid footbridge crosses only ten feet above the shallow stream. The experimenters had an attractive woman approach men who were crossing these bridges. She told them she was studying "the effects of exposure to scenic attractions on creative expression." She showed them a picture, and they wrote down their associations. The sexual imagery in their stories showed that the men on the unsteady, frightening bridge were more sexually aroused than the men on the solid bridge. More of these men also called the young woman afterward—supposedly to get information about the study.

You may have noticed that this research was really about sexual attraction, not love. The point, however, is that romantic love usually begins with sexual attraction. Finding ourselves sexually attracted to someone, we spend time with that person. If we discover mutual interests, we may label our feelings "love." Apparently, then, *romantic love has two components.* The first is emotional, a feeling of sexual attraction. The second is cognitive, a label that we attach to our feelings. If we attach this label, we describe ourselves as being "in love."

Marriage

In the typical case, marriage in the United States is preceded by "love," but, contrary to folklore, whatever love is, it certainly is not blind. That is, love does not hit people willy-nilly, as if Cupid had shot darts blindly into a crowd. If it did, marital patterns would be unpredictable. An examination of who marries whom, however, reveals that love is socially channeled.

Figure 16.2 The Racial Background of Husbands and Wives in Marriages Between Whites and African Americans

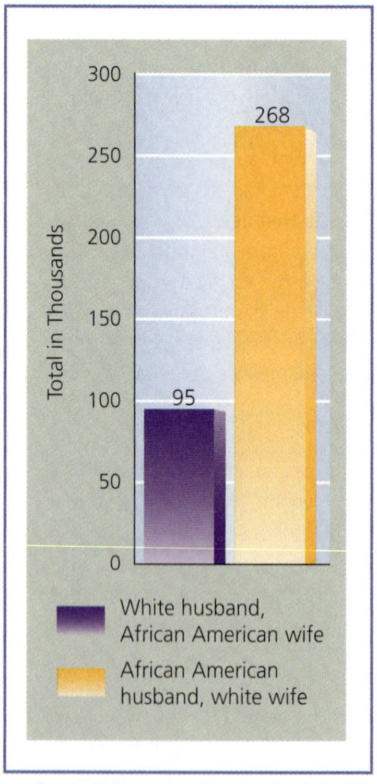

Source: By the author. Based on *Statistical Abstract* 2002:Table 47.

The Social Channels of Love and Marriage

When we marry, we generally think that we have freely chosen our spouse. With few exceptions, however, our choices follow highly predictable social channels, especially those of age, education, social class, and race-ethnicity. For example, a Latina with a college degree whose parents are both physicians is likely to fall in love with and marry a Latino slightly older than herself who has graduated from college. Similarly, a girl who drops out of high school and whose parents are on welfare is likely to fall in love with and marry a man who comes from a background similar to hers.

Sociologists use the term **homogamy** to refer to the tendency of people who have similar characteristics to marry one another. Homogamy occurs largely as a result of *propinquity,* or spatial nearness. That is, we tend to "fall in love" with and marry people who live near us or whom we meet at school, church, or work. The people with whom we associate are far from a random sample of the population, for social filters produce neighborhoods and schools (as well as churches, temples, and mosques) that follow racial-ethnic and social class lines.

As with all social patterns, there are exceptions. Although 94 percent of Americans who marry choose someone of their same racial-ethnic background, 6 percent do not. Because there are 60 million married couples in the United States, those 6 percent add up, totaling three and a half million couples.

One of the more dramatic changes in U.S. marriage is a sharp increase in interracial marriages. We can trace this change back to the norm-shattering 1960s. Among the many changes ushered in during this period was a breaking of the "color line" in courtship. As you can see from Figure 16.2, interracial marriages also show distinct patterns.

Childbirth

Education and income are important in determining how many children women have. Women who graduate from college, for example, are less likely to give birth than those who don't go to college. Even women who drop out of college have fewer children than women who have never taken a college course. It is similar with income. In general, the higher a woman's family income, the fewer children she has (*Statistical Abstract* 2002:Table 82).

What happens when the baby arrives? The popular image is that it makes a couple deliriously happy. The facts are somewhat different.

Marital Satisfaction Sociologists have found that after the birth of a child conflict usually increases while marital satisfaction decreases (Whyte 1992; Bird 1997; Rogers and Amato 2000). To understand why, recall from Chapter 6 that a dyad (just two persons) provides greater intimacy than a triad (after adding a third person, interaction must be shared). In addition, the birth of a child unbalances the roles that the couple have worked out (Knauth 2000). To move from the theoretical to the practical, think about the implications for marriage of coping with a fragile newborn's 24-hour-a-day needs of being fed, soothed, and diapered—while having less sleep and heavier expenses.

Social Class Sociologist Lillian Rubin (1976, 1992b) compared fifty working-class couples with twenty-five middle-class couples. She found that social class made a significant difference in how couples adjust to the arrival of children. For the average working-class couple, the first baby arrived just nine months after marriage. They hardly had time to adjust to being husband and wife before they were thrust into the demanding roles of mother and father. The result was financial problems, bickering, and interference from in-laws. The young husbands weren't ready to "settle down," and they resented getting less attention from their wives. A working-class husband who became a father just five months after getting married made a telling remark to Rubin when he said, "There I was, just a kid myself, and I finally had someone to take care of me. Then suddenly, I had to take care of a kid, and she was too busy with him *to take care of me*" (italics added).

In contrast, the middle-class couples postponed the birth of their first child, which gave them more time to adjust to each other. On average, their first baby arrived three years after marriage. Their greater financial resources also worked in their favor, making life a lot easier and marriage more pleasant.

Child Rearing

Who's minding the kids while the parents are at work? A generation ago such a question would have been ridiculous, for the mother was at home taking care of the children. As with Sharon in our opening vignette, however, that assumption no longer holds. With three of five U.S. mothers working for wages, who is taking care of the children?

Married Couples and Single Mothers Figure 16.3 compares the child care arrangements of married couples and single mothers. As you can see, their overall arrangements are similar. For each group, about one of three preschoolers is cared for in the child's home. The main difference is the role of the child's father while the mother is at work. For married couples, almost one of four children is cared for by the father, while for single mothers this plummets to only one of fourteen. As you can see, grandparents step in to help fill the gap left by the absent fathers.

Day Care As Figure 16.3 shows, about one of six children is in day care. The broad conclusions of research on day care were reported in Chapter 3 (pages 80–81). Apparently only a minority of U.S. day care centers offer high-quality care as measured by stimulating learning activities, safety, and emotional warmth (Bergmann 1995; Blau 2000). A primary reason for this dismal situation is the low salaries paid to day care workers, who average only about $12,000 a year (*Statistical Abstract* 2002:Tables 546, 547).

It is difficult for parents to judge the quality of day care, since they don't know what takes place when they are not there. If you ever look for day care, however, these two factors best predict that children will receive quality care: staff who have taken courses in early childhood development and a small number of children assigned to each day care worker (Blau 2000). If you have nagging fears that your children might be neglected or even abused, choose a center that pipes streaming images from closed circuit cameras onto the Internet. While at work, you can "visit" each room of the day care center via cyberspace, and monitor your toddler's activities and care (Hall 2001).

Nannies For upper-middle-class parents, nannies have become popular. Parents love the one-on-one care. They also like the convenience of in-home care, which reduces

Figure 16.3 Who Takes Care of Preschoolers While Their Mothers Are at Work?

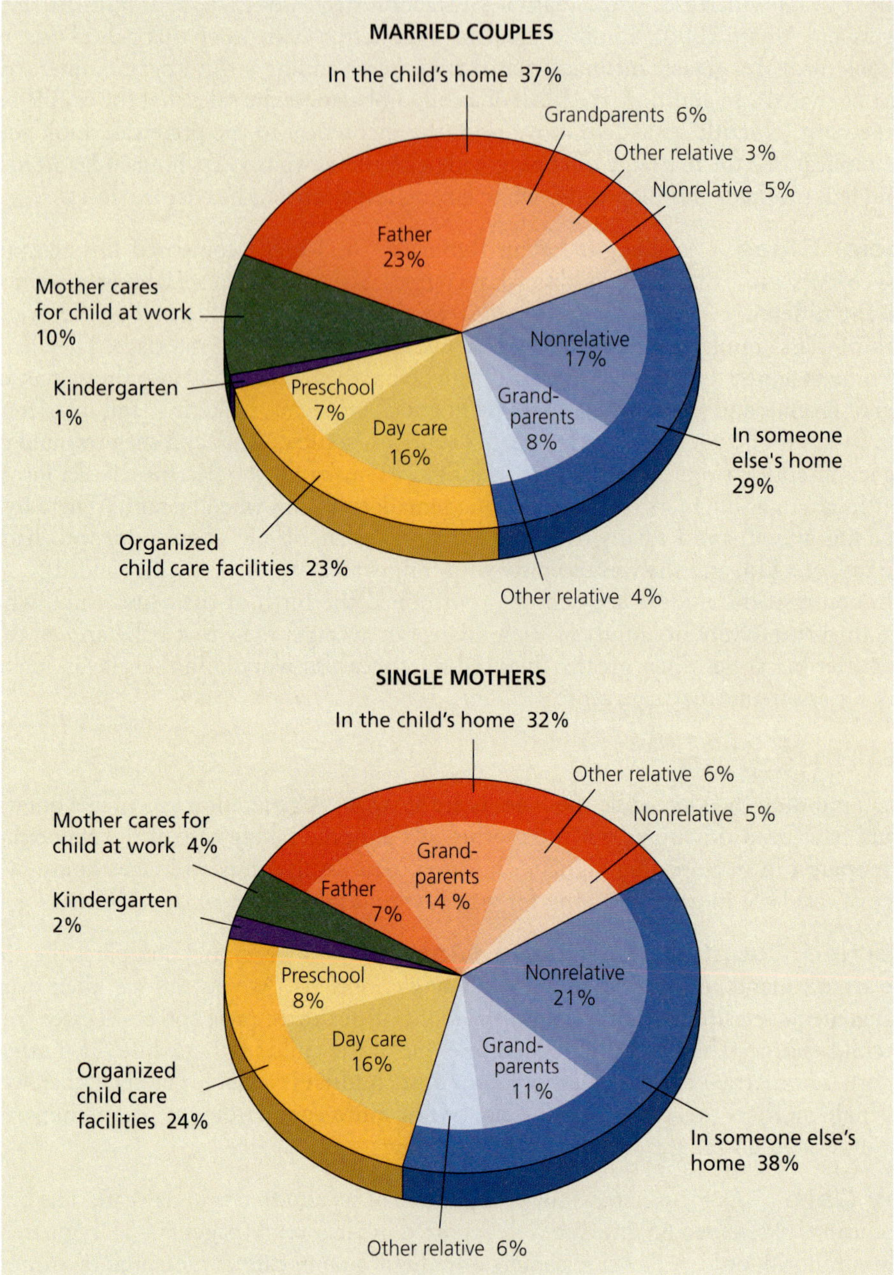

Source: O'Connell 1993.

the chances of their child catching illnesses and eliminates the need to transport the child to an unfamiliar environment. A recurring problem, however, is tensions between the parents and the nanny: jealousy that the nanny may see the first step, hear the first word, or, worse yet, be called mommy. There are also tensions over different discipline styles; disdain on the part of the nanny that the mother isn't staying home with her child; and feelings of guilt or envy as the child cries when the nanny leaves, but not when the mother goes to work.

Social Class Social class makes a huge difference in child rearing. As noted on page 79, sociologist Melvin Kohn found that parents socialize their children into the norms of their work worlds. Because members of the working class are closely supervised and are expected to follow explicit rules, their concern is less with their children's motivation and more with their outward conformity. Thus they are more apt to use physical punishment. In contrast, middle-class parents, who are expected to take more initiative on the job, are more concerned that their children develop curiosity, self-expression, and self-control. They are also more likely to withdraw privileges or affection than they are to use physical punishment.

Social class also makes a difference in how parents view child development (Lareau 2002). Lower-class parents think of children as developing naturally, while middle-class parents think that children need a lot of guidance if they are to develop correctly. Consequently, lower-class parents set limits on their children and then let them choose their own activities while middle-class parents try to involve their children in leisure activities that develop their thinking and social skills.

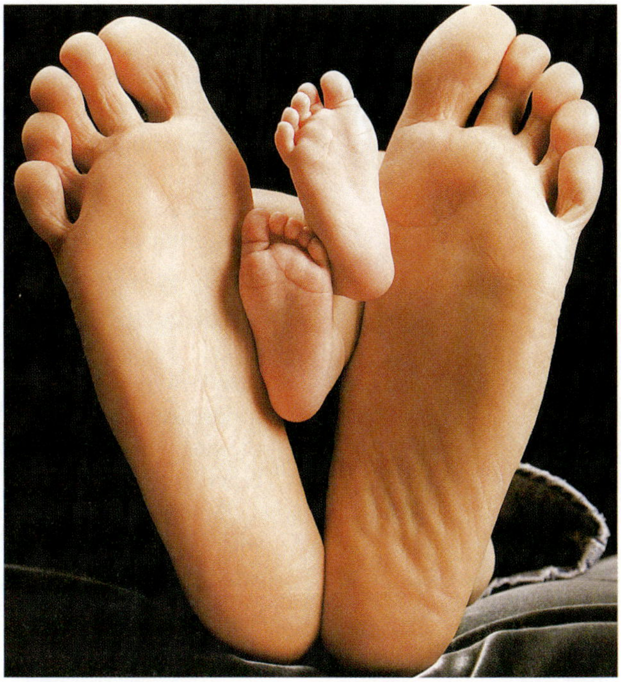

No adequate substitute has been found for the family. Although its form and functions vary around the world, the family remains the primary socializer of children.

Birth Order Birth order is also important. Parents tend to discipline their firstborns more than their later children, and to give them more attention. When the second child arrives, the firstborn competes to remain the focus of attention. Researchers suggest that this instills in firstborns a greater drive for success, which is why they are more likely than their siblings to earn higher grades in school, to attend college, and to go further in college. Firstborns are even more likely to become astronauts, to appear on the cover of *Time* magazine, and to become president of the United States. Although subsequent children may not go as far, most are less anxious about being successful, and are more relaxed in their relationships (Snow et al. 1981; Goleman 1985; Storfer 2000). Firstborns are also more likely to defend the status quo and to support conservative causes, with later-borns tending to upset the apple cart and support liberal causes (Sulloway 1997).

Although such tendencies are strong, they are only that—tendencies. *There are no inevitable outcomes of birth order, social class, or any other social characteristic.*

The Family in Later Life

The later stages of family life bring their own pleasures to be savored and problems to be solved. Let's look at the empty nest, retirement, and widowhood.

The Empty Nest When the last child leaves home, the husband and wife are left, as at the beginning of their marriage, "alone together." This situation, sometimes called the **empty nest,** is thought to signal a difficult time of adjustment for women, because they have devoted so much energy to a child-rearing role that is now gone. Sociologist Lillian Rubin (1992a), who interviewed both career women and homemakers, found that this picture is largely a myth. Contrary to the stereotype, she found that women's satisfaction generally *increases* when the last child leaves home. A typical statement was made by a 45-year-old woman, who leaned forward in her chair as though to tell Rubin a secret:

> To tell you the truth, most of the time it's a big relief to be free of them, finally. I suppose that's awful to say. But you know what, most of the women I know feel the same way. It's just that they're uncomfortable saying it because there's all this talk about how sad mothers are supposed to be when the kids leave home.

Similar findings have come from other researchers, who report that most mothers feel relieved at being able to spend more time pursuing their own interests. Many couples also report a renewed sense of intimacy at this time (Mackey and O'Brien 1995). This closeness appears to stem from four causes: The couple is free of the many responsibilities of child rearing, they have more leisure, their income is at its highest, and they have fewer financial obligations.

empty nest a married couple's domestic situation after the last child has left home

"Boomerang Children" and the Not-So-Empty Nest The empty nest is not as empty as it used to be. With prolonged education and the high cost of establishing a household, U.S. children are leaving home later. Many stay home during college, others move back after college, and some who strike out on their own find the cost or responsibility too great and return to the home nest. As a result, 42 percent of all U.S. 24- to 29-year-olds are still living with their parents (*Statistical Abstract* 2000:Tables 12, 70). Called "boomerang children" by some and "adultolescents" by others, they enjoy the protection of home, but have to work out issues of dependence on their parents while they grapple with concerns and fears about establishing independent lives.

Widowhood Women are more likely than men to become widowed and to have to face the wrenching problems this entails. Not only does the average wife live longer than her husband, but also she has married a man older than herself. The death of a spouse tears at the self, clawing at identities that had merged through the years. Now that the one who had become an essential part of the self is gone, the survivor, as in adolescence, is forced once again to wrestle with the perplexing question "Who am I?"

When death is unexpected, the adjustment is more difficult (Hiltz 1989). Survivors who know that death is impending make preparations that smooth the transition—from arranging finances to psychologically preparing themselves for being alone. Saying goodbye and cultivating treasured last memories help them to adjust to the death of an intimate companion.

Diversity in U.S. Families

It is important to note that there is no such thing as *the* American family. Rather, family life varies widely throughout the United States. The significance of social class, noted earlier, will continue to be evident as we examine diversity in U.S. families.

African American Families

Note that the heading reads African American *families,* not *the* African American family. There is no such thing as *the* African American family any more than there is *the* white family or *the* Latino family. The primary distinction is not between African Americans and other groups, but between social classes. Because African Americans who are members of the upper class follow the class interests reviewed in Chapter 10—preservation of privilege and family fortune—they are especially concerned about the family background of those whom their children marry (Gatewood 1990). To them, marriage is viewed as a merger of family lines. Children of this class marry later than children of other classes.

Middle-class African American families focus on achievement and respectability. Both husband and wife are likely to work outside the home. A central concern is that their children go to college, get good jobs, and marry well—that is, marry people like themselves, respectable and hardworking, who want to get ahead in school and pursue a successful career.

African American families in poverty face all the problems that cluster around poverty (Wilson 1987, 1996; Anderson 2001). Because the men are likely to have few skills and to be unemployed, it is difficult for them to fulfill the cultural roles of husband and father. Consequently, these families are likely to be headed by a woman and to have a high rate of births to single women. Divorce and desertion are also more common than among other classes. Sharing scarce resources and "stretching kinship" are primary survival mechanisms. That is, people who have helped out in hard times are considered brothers, sisters, or cousins to whom one owes obligations as though they were blood relatives (Stack 1974). Sociologists use the term *fictive kin* to refer to this stretching of kinship.

From Figure 16.4, you can see that, compared with other groups, African American families are the least likely to be headed by married couples and the most likely to be headed by women. Because of a *marriage squeeze*—an imbalance in the sex ratio, in this instance fewer unmarried men per 1,000 unmarried women—African American women are more likely than other racial-ethnic groups to marry men who are less educated than themselves (South 1991; Eshleman 2000).

There is no such thing as the African American family, any more than there is the Native American, Asian American, Latino, or Irish American family. Rather, each racial-ethnic group has different types of families, with the primary determinant being social class.

This African American family is observing Kwanzaa, a relatively new festival, that celebrates African heritage. Can you explain how Kwanzaa is an example of ethnic work, *a concept introduced in Chapter 9?*

Latino Families

As Figure 16.4 shows, the proportion of Latino families headed by married couples and women falls in between that of whites and African Americans. The effects of social class on families, which I just sketched, also apply to Latinos. In addition, families differ by

Figure 16.4 Family Structure: The Percentage of U.S. Households Headed by Men, Women, and Married Couples

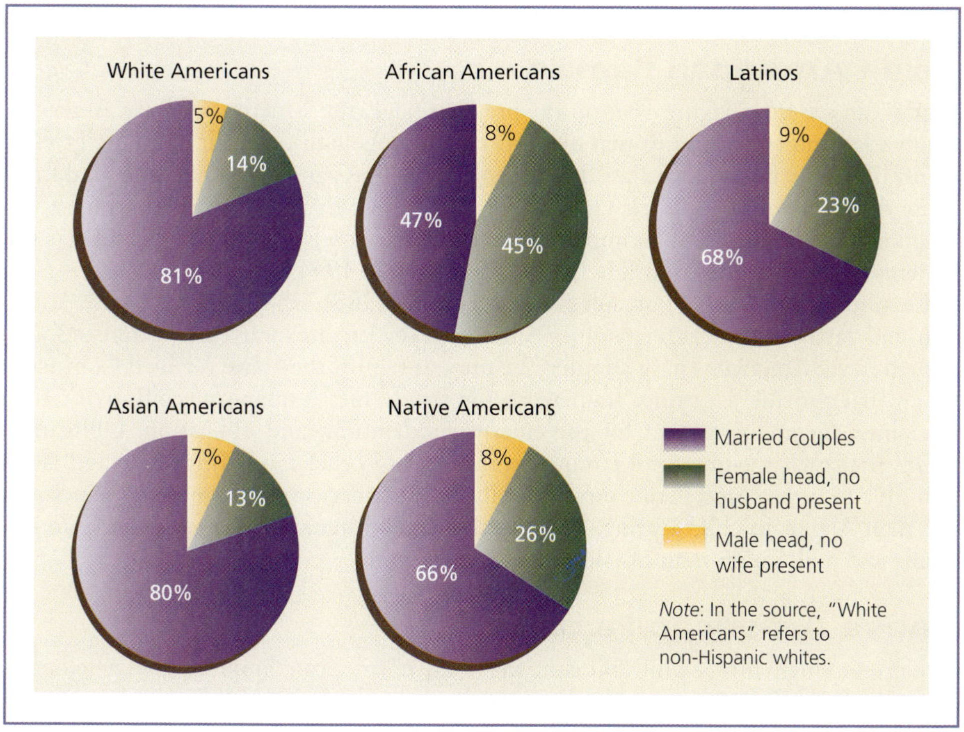

Source: By the author. Based on *Statistical Abstract* 2000: Table 44; 2002:Tables 37, 38, 40.

Although there is no such thing as the *Latino family*, in general, Latinos place high emphasis on extended family relationships.

country of origin. Families from Cuba, for example, are more likely to be headed by a married couple than are families from Puerto Rico (*Statistical Abstract* 2002:Table 40).

What really distinguishes Latino families, however, is culture—especially the Spanish language, the Roman Catholic religion, and a strong family orientation coupled with a disapproval of divorce. Although there is some debate among the experts, another characteristic seems to be ***machismo***—an emphasis on male strength, sexual vigor, and dominance. In Chicano families (those originating from Mexico), the husband-father plays a stronger role than in either white or African American families (Vega 1990). Machismo apparently decreases with each generation in the United States (Hurtado et al. 1992; Wood 2001). The wife-mother is generally in charge of routine matters, making most of the day-to-day decisions for the family and disciplining the children. She is usually more family centered than her husband, displaying more warmth and affection for her children.

Generalizations have limits, of course, and as with other ethnic groups, individual Latino families vary considerably (Baca Zinn 1994; Carrasquillo 1994).

Asian American Families

As you can see from Figure 16.4 on the previous page, the structure of Asian American families is almost identical to that of white families. As with other racial-ethnic groups, family life also reflects social class. In addition, because Asian Americans emigrated from many different countries, their family life reflects those many cultures. As with Latino families, the more recent their immigration, the more closely their family life reflects the patterns in their country of origin (Kibria 1993; Glenn 1994).

Despite such differences, sociologist Bob Suzuki (1985), who studied Chinese American and Japanese American families, identified several distinctive characteristics. Although Asian Americans have adopted the nuclear family, they have retained Confucian values that provide a distinct framework for family life: humanism, collectivity, self-discipline, hierarchy, respect for the elderly, moderation, and obligation. Obligation means that each member of a family owes respect to other family members and is responsible to never bring shame on the family. Asian Americans tend to be more permissive than Anglos in child rearing. To control their children, they are more likely to use shame and guilt rather than physical punishment.

Native American Families

machismo an emphasis on male strength and dominance

Perhaps the single most significant issue that Native American families face is whether to follow traditional values or to assimilate into the dominant culture (Yellowbird and Snipp 1994; Garrett 1999). This primary distinction creates vast differences among families.

To search for the *Native American family would be fruitless. There are rural, urban, single-parent, extended, nuclear, rich, poor, traditional, and assimilated Native American families, to name just a few. Shown here is a Navaho family in Monument Valley, Arizona.*

The traditionals speak native languages and emphasize distinctive Native American values and beliefs. Those who have assimilated into the broader culture do not.

Figure 16.4 depicts the structure of Native American families. You can see how close it is to that of Latinos. In general, Native American parents are permissive with their children and avoid physical punishment. Elders play a much more active role in their children's families than they do in most U.S. families: Elders, especially grandparents, not only provide child care but also teach and discipline children. Like others, Native American families differ by social class.

IN SUM

From this brief review, you can see that race-ethnicity signifies little for understanding family life. Rather, social class and culture hold the keys. The more resources a family has, the more it assumes the characteristics of a middle-class nuclear family. Compared with the poor, middle-class families have fewer children and fewer unmarried mothers. They also place greater emphasis on educational achievement and deferred gratification.

One-Parent Families

Another indication of how extensively the U.S. family is changing is the increase in one-parent families. As you can see from Figure 16.5, the percentage of U.S. children who live with two parents (not necessarily their biological parents) has dropped from 85 percent in 1970 to 69 percent today. The concern often expressed about one-parent families may have more to do with their poverty than with children being reared by one parent. Because women head most one-parent families, these families tend to be poor. Most divorced women earn less than their former husbands, yet about 85 percent of children of divorce live with their mothers ("Child Support" 1995; Aulette 2002).

To understand the typical one-parent family, then, we need to view it through the lens of poverty, for that is its primary source of strain. The results are serious, not just for these parents and their children, but for society as a whole. Children from single-parent families are more likely to drop out of school, to get arrested, to have emotional

Figure 16.5 The Decline of Two-Parent Families

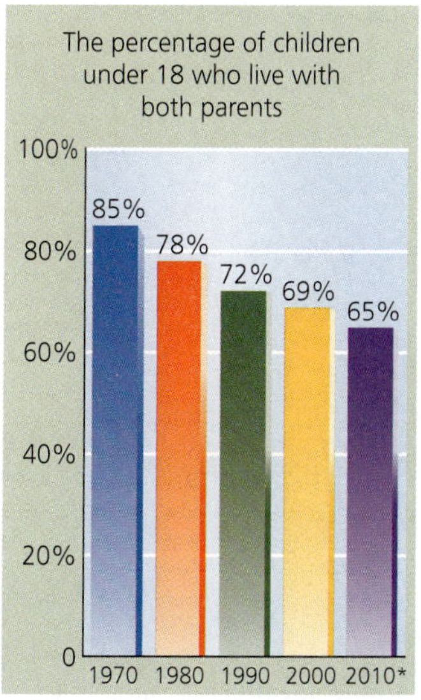

Source: By the author. Based on *Statistical Abstract* 1995:Table 79; 2002:Table 54.
*author's estimate

problems, and to get divorced (McLanahan and Sandefur 1994; Menaghan et al. 1997). If female, they are more likely to bear children while still unmarried teenagers.

Figure 16.6 What Percentage of U.S. Married Women Never Give Birth?

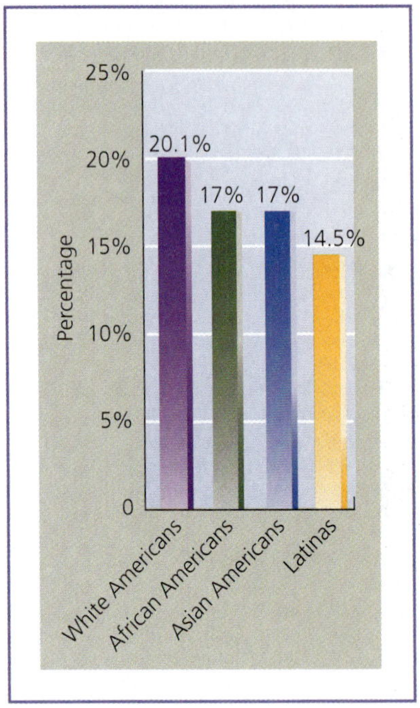

Source: By the author. Based on Bachu and O'Connell 2000:Table A.

Families Without Children

While most married women give birth, about one of five (19 percent) do not. Childlessness has grown so fast that this percentage is *twice* what it was just 20 years ago (Bachu and O'Connell 2000). As you can see from Figure 16.6, this percentage varies by racial-ethnic group, with Latinas standing out the most from the average. Most childless couples have made a choice to not have children. Why? Some simply do not like children, of course, but a main reason is to attain a sense of freedom—to have less stress, to be able to change jobs, or to be able to relax after work (Lunneborg 1999). Some women perceive their marriage as too fragile to withstand the strains a child would bring. Others believe they would be stuck at home—bored, lonely, and with diminishing career opportunities (Gerson 1985). Perhaps the most common reason, though, is summarized by this statement in a newsletter:

> We are DINKS (Dual Incomes, No Kids). We are happily married. I am 43, my wife is 42. We have been married for almost twenty years. . . . Our investment strategy has a lot to do with our personal philosophy: "You can have kids—or you can have everything else!"

With trends firmly in place—more education and careers for women; legal abortion; advances in contraception; the high cost of rearing children; and an emphasis on possessing more and more materials things—the proportion of women who never bear children is likely to increase.

Many childless couples, however, are not childless by choice. Desperately wanting to have children, some adopt, while a few turn to the solutions featured in the Sociology and the New Technology box on the next page.

Blended Families

An increasingly significant type of family in the United States is the **blended family**, one whose members were once part of other families. Two divorced people who marry and each bring their children into a new family unit become a blended family. With divorce common, millions of children spend some of their childhood in blended families. One result is more complicated family relationships. Consider this description written by one of my students:

> I live with my dad. I should say that I live with my dad, my brother (whose mother and father are also my mother and father), my half sister (whose father is my dad, but whose mother is my father's last wife), and two stepbrothers and stepsisters (children of my father's current wife). My father's wife (my current stepmother, not to be confused with his second wife who, I guess, is no longer my stepmother) is pregnant, and soon we all will have a new brother or sister. Or will it be a half brother or half sister?
>
> If you can't figure this out, I don't blame you. I have trouble myself. It gets very complicated around Christmas. Should we all stay together? Split up and go to several other homes? Who do we buy gifts for, anyway?

Gay and Lesbian Families

In 1989, Denmark became the first country to legalize marriage between people of the same sex. Since then, Holland, Norway, Sweden, and the province of Ontario, Canada, have made same-sex marriages legal. In 2000, Vermont became the first state to legalize what they call "gay unions." Except for the name, "gay unions" are marriages. Partners are treated as married couples for purposes of inheritance, property transfers, medical decisions, insurance, and state income taxes. If they want to split up, they must go through "dissolution" proceedings in Family Court. Then in 2003, the supreme court of Massachusetts ruled that to prohibit same-sex marriages was a violation of the state's constitution.

blended family a family whose members were once part of other families

sociology and the **NEW technology**

The Brave New World of High-Tech Reproduction: Where Technology Outpaces Law and Sometimes Common Sense

Jaycee has five parents—or none, depending on how you look at it. The story goes like this. Luanne and John Buzzanca were infertile. Although they spent more than $100,000 on treatments, nothing worked. Then a fertility clinic mixed a man's sperm with a woman's egg. Both the man and the woman remained anonymous. A surgeon implanted the fertilized egg in Pamela Snell, who gave birth to Jaycee (Davis 1998a; Foote 1998).

Her job as surrogate mother completed, Pamela handed Jaycee over to Luanne, who was waiting at her beside. Luanne's husband, John, would have been there, but he had filed for divorce just a month before.

Luanne asked John for child support. John refused, and Luanne sued. The judge ruled that John didn't have to pay. He said that because Jaycee had been conceived in a petri dish with an egg and sperm from anonymous donors, John wasn't the baby's father. The judge added that Luanne wasn't the baby's mother either.

Five parents—or none? Welcome to the brave—and very real—new world of high-tech reproduction. Although most children who are conceived with the aid of high-tech procedures claim only two parents, reproductive technologies have made such scenarios a nightmare for the unsuspecting.

For Your CONSIDERATION

In our new, high-tech world, what is a mother? Is Pamela Snell, who gave birth to Jaycee, a mother? Strangely, she is not. Is the donor of the egg a mother? Biologically, yes, but legally, no. Is Luanne a mother? Fortunately, for Jaycee's sake, a higher court ruled that she is.

What is a father? Consider this case. Elizabeth Higgins of Jacksonville, Indiana, had difficulty conceiving. She gave eggs to Memorial Hospital. Her husband gave sperm. A hospital technician mistakenly mixed someone else's sperm with Mrs. Higgins' eggs. The fertilized eggs were implanted in Mrs. Higgins, who gave birth to twin girls. Mrs. Higgins is white, her husband black. Mr. Higgins was bothered because the girls had only Caucasian features, and he couldn't bond with them. Mr. and Mrs. Higgins separated. They sued the hospital for child support, arguing that the hospital, not Mr. Higgins, is the father (Davis 1998b).

If a hospital can be a father in this brave new world, then what's a grandparent? A man in New Orleans donated sperm to a fertility clinic. He died, and his girlfriend decided to be artificially inseminated with his sperm. The grieved parents of the man were upset that their son, although dead, could still father children. They also feared that those children, who would be their grandchildren, would have a legal claim to their estate (Davis 1998b).

How would you apply common sense to these many cases?

The McCaughey septuplets of Carlisle, Iowa, with their parents, Bobby and Kenny, and their 6 year-old sister, Mikayla.

When same-sex marriages became legal in Canada, additional pressure was placed on U.S. legislators to pass similar laws. In reaction, some groups have proposed a constitutional amendment that would limit marriage to a woman and a man. While this struggle is being resolved, Americans are crossing the border to get married under Canada's new law.

Gay and lesbian families are not evenly distributed throughout the United States. Rather, they are highly urban, with about half concentrated in just 20 cities. The greatest concentrations are in San Francisco, Los Angeles, Atlanta, New York City, and Washington, D.C. About one-fifth of gay and lesbian couples were previously married to heterosexuals. Twenty-two percent of lesbian couples and 5 percent of gay couples have children from their earlier marriages (Bianchi and Casper 2000).

What are gay marriages like? Like everything else in life, same-sex couples cannot be painted with a single brush stroke. As with heterosexual couples, social class is significant, and orientations to life differ with education, occupation, and income. Sociologists Philip Blumstein and Pepper Schwartz (1985) interviewed same-sex couples and found their main struggles to be housework, money, careers, problems with relatives, and sexual adjustment—the same problems that face heterosexual couples. Same-sex couples are more likely to break up, however, and one argument for legalizing gay marriages is that these relationships will become more stable.

Trends in U.S. Families

As is apparent from this discussion, marriage and family life in the United States is undergoing a fundamental shift. Let's examine other indicators of this change.

Postponing Marriage

Figure 16.7 illustrates one of the most significant changes in U.S. marriage. As you can see, the average age of first-time brides and grooms declined from 1890 to about 1950. In 1890 the typical first-time bride was 22, but by 1950 she had just left her teens. For about twenty years, there was little change. Then in 1970 the average age started to increase sharply. *Today's average first-time bride and groom are older than at any time in U.S. history.*

Since postponing marriage is today's norm, it may come as a surprise to many readers to learn that *most* U.S. women used to marry by the age of 24. Figure 16.8 illustrates this change. It shows how the percentage of younger Americans who have not married has soared. The current percentage of unmarried women of this age is now *more than double* what it was in 1970.

Figure 16.7 The Median Age at Which Americans Marry for the First Time

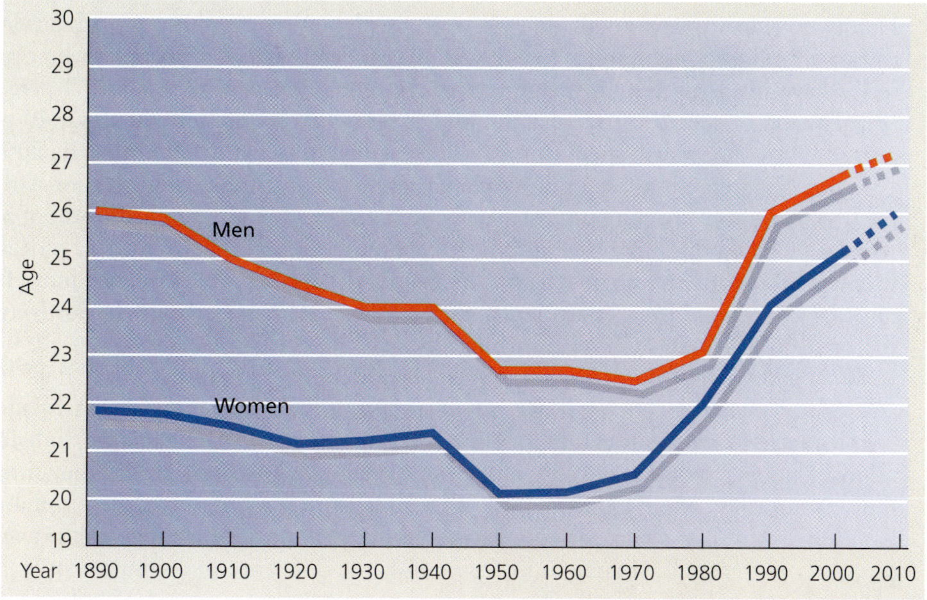

Note: The broken lines indicate the author's estimate.
Source: By the author. Based on *Statistical Abstract* 1999:Table 158; U.S. Bureau of the Census 2003.

Why did this change occur? The reason is cohabitation (Michael et al. 2004). Although Americans have postponed the age at which they first marry, they have *not* postponed the age at which they first set up housekeeping with someone of the opposite sex. Let's look at this trend in cohabitation.

Figure 16.8 Americans Ages 20–24 Who Have Never Married

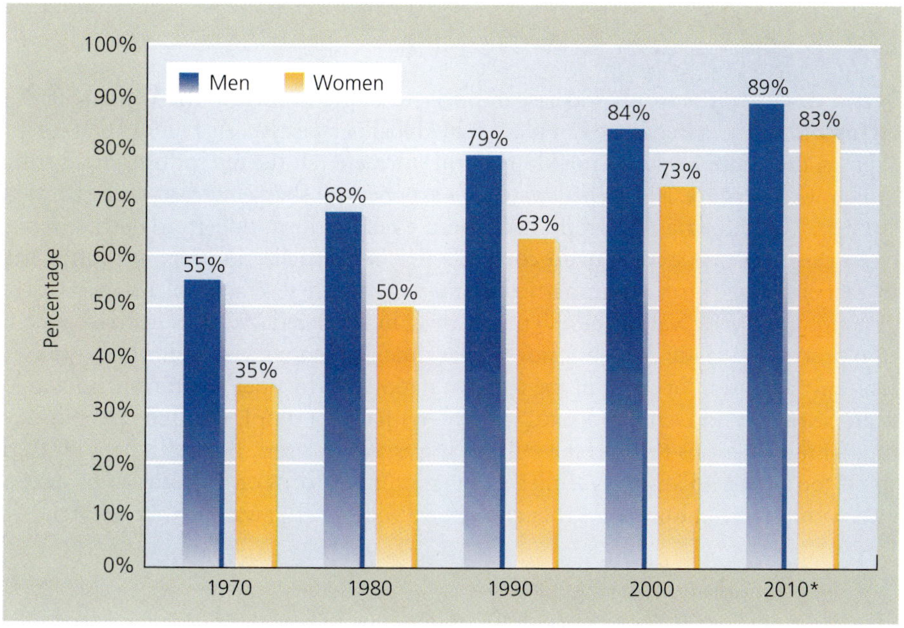

*Author's estimate.
Source: By the author. Based on *Statistical Abstract* 1993:Table 60; 2002:Table 48.

Figure 16.9 Cohabitation in the United States

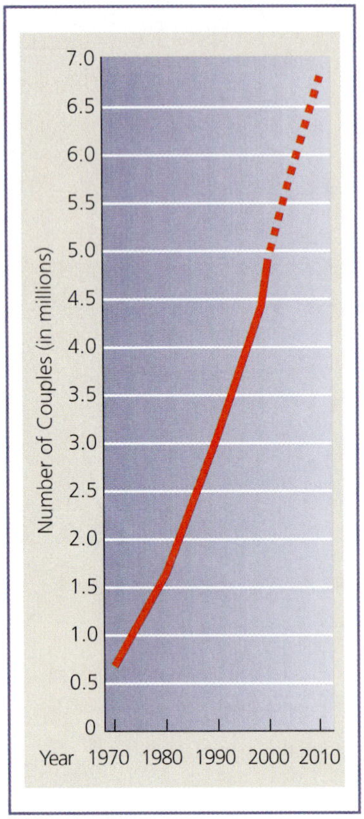

Note: Broken line indicates the author's estimate.
Source: By the author. Based on *Statistical Abstract* 1995:Table 60; 2002:Table 49.

Cohabitation

Figure 16.9 shows the increase in **cohabitation**, adults living together in a sexual relationship without being married. This figure is one of the most remarkable in sociology. Hardly ever do we have totals that rise this steeply and consistently. Cohabitation is *eight times* more common today than it was 30 years ago. Half of the couples who marry today have lived together before marriage. A generation ago, it was just 8 percent (Bianchi and Casper 2000). Cohabitation has become so common that about 40 percent of U.S. children will spend some time in a cohabiting family (Scommegna 2002).

Figure 16.9 represents a significant change in people's attitudes and behavior—from the frowned-upon "shacking up" of a generation ago to a broadly accepted form of premarriage today. From my observations, it is not uncommon for parents to be pleased when a son or daughter begins to cohabit. Some parents help their children move furniture and decorate their apartments. This is a colossal change from the furtiveness that used to surround such relationships.

What is the essential difference between cohabitation and marriage? The single best answer is *commitment.* In marriage, the assumption is permanence; in cohabitation, couples agree to remain together for "as long as it works out." For marriage, individuals make public vows that legally bind them as a couple; for cohabitation, they simply move in together. Marriage requires a judge to authorize its termination; when a cohabiting relationship sours, the couple separate and tell their friends that it didn't work out. Perhaps the single statement that pinpoints the difference in commitment is this: Cohabiting couples are less likely than married couples to have a joint bank account (Brines and Joyner 1999).

Why do some cohabiting couples decide to marry, while others do not? There are many reasons, of course, but sociologists have found that cohabitation means different things to different people, and what it means makes a difference in whether they marry. Let's explore this connection in our Down-to-Earth Sociology box on the next page.

And are the marriages of couples who cohabited stronger than the marriages of couples who did not live together before they married? Have they, perhaps, worked out a lot of problems in advance of marriage? To find out, sociologists compared their divorce rates. They found that couples who cohabited before marriage are *more* likely to divorce. This presented another sociological puzzle. To try to solve it, sociologists Catherine Cohan and Stacy Kleinbaum (2002) videotaped husbands and wives while they worked on marital problems. They found that spouses who had cohabited before marriage were more negative and less supportive of their partners. This certainly nips at the marital bonds.

Unmarried Mothers

Earlier we discussed the steady increase in births to single women in the United States. To better understand this trend, we can place it in global perspective. As Figure 16.10 on page 470 shows, the United States is not alone in this increase. Of the ten industrialized nations for which we have data, all except Japan have experienced sharp increases in births to single women. The U.S. rate is far from the highest; it falls in the middle third of these nations.

From this figure, it seems fair to conclude that industrialization sets in motion social forces that encourage births to unmarried mothers. There are several problems with this conclusion, however. Why was the rate so much lower in 1960 and 1970? Industrialization had been in process for many decades prior to that time. Why are the rates in the bottom four nations only a fraction of those in the top two nations? Why does Japan's rate remain low? Why are Sweden's and Denmark's rates so high? With only a couple of minor exceptions, the ranking of these nations today is the same as it was 40 years ago. By itself, then, industrialization is too simple an answer. A fuller explanation must focus on customs and values embedded within these cultures. For that answer, we will have to await further research.

cohabitation unmarried couples living together in a sexual relationship

Grandparents as Parents

It is becoming increasingly common for grandparents to rear their grandchildren. About 4 percent of white children, 7 percent of Latino children, and 14 percent of African American children are being reared by their grandparents (Waldrop and Weber 2001).

DOWN-TO-EARTH SOCIOLOGY

"You Want Us to Live Together? What Do You Mean By That?"

ONE OF THE MOST REMARKABLE STATISTICS in sociology is the rapid increase of cohabitation in the United States. Hardly any statistic shows such a sharp upward curve as that depicted in Figure 16.9. Two fundamental changes in U.S. culture have led to this surge in cohabitation.

The first is changed ideas of sexual morality. It is difficult for today's college students to grasp the sexual morality that prevailed before the 1960s sexual revolution. Almost everyone used to consider sex before marriage to be immoral. Premarital sex existed, to be sure, but furtively, and often with guilt. To live together before marriage was called "shacking up," and the couple was thought to be "living in sin." A double standard operated. It was the woman's responsibility to say no to sex before marriage. Consequently, she was considered to be the especially sinful one in cohabitation.

The second cultural change is the increase in the U.S. divorce rate. Although the rate has declined slightly since 1980, it still remains at almost the highest level in U.S. history. Youth who reach adulthood today are more likely to have seen their parents divorce than any generation that came before them. This makes marriage seem fragile, something that is not likely to last regardless of what you put into it. This is scary. Cohabitation reduces the threat by offering a relationship of intimacy without the long-term commitment of marriage.

From the outside, all cohabitation may look the same, but not to people who are living together. As you can see from Table 16.2, for about 10 percent of couples, cohabitation is a substitute for marriage. These couples consider themselves married, but for some reason don't want a marriage certificate. Some object to marriage on philosophical grounds ("What difference does a piece of paper make?"); others do not yet have a legal divorce from a spouse. Almost half of cohabitants (46 percent) view cohabitation as a step on the path to marriage. For them, cohabitation is more than "going steady," but less than engagement. Another 15 percent of couples are simply "giving it a try." They want to see what marriage to one another might be like. For the least committed, about 29 percent, cohabitation is a form of dating. It provides a dependable source of sex and emotional support.

Table 16.2 Commitment in Cohabitation: Does It Make a Difference?

		After 5 to 7 Years			
				Of Those Still Together	
Level of Commitment	Percent of Couples	Split Up	Still Together	Married	Cohabitating
Substitute for Marriage	10%	35%	65%	25%	40%
Step toward Marriage	46%	31%	69%	52%	17%
Trial Marriage	15%	51%	49%	28%	21%
Coresidential Dating	29%	46%	54%	33%	21%

Source: Bianchi and Casper 2000.

Do these distinctions make a difference in whether couples marry? Let's look at these couples a half dozen years after they began to live together. As you can see from Table 16.2, couples who view cohabitation as a substitute for marriage are the least likely to marry and the most likely to still be cohabiting a few years later. For couples who see cohabitation as a step toward marriage, the outcome is just the opposite—they are the most likely to marry and the least likely to still be cohabiting. Couples who are the most likely to break up are those who "tried" cohabitation and those for whom cohabitation was a form of dating.

For Your CONSIDERATION

Can you explain why the meaning of cohabitation makes a difference in whether couples marry? Can you classify cohabiting couples you know into these four types? Do you think there are other types? If so, what would they be?

The main reason for these *skipped generation families* is that the parents are incapable of caring for their children (Goldberg-Glen et al. 1998). Other than the death of the parent, the most common reasons are that the parents are ill, homeless, addicted to drugs, or in prison. In other instances, they have neglected and abused their children, and the grandparents have taken them in.

Figure 16.10 Births to Unmarried Women in Ten Industrialized Nations

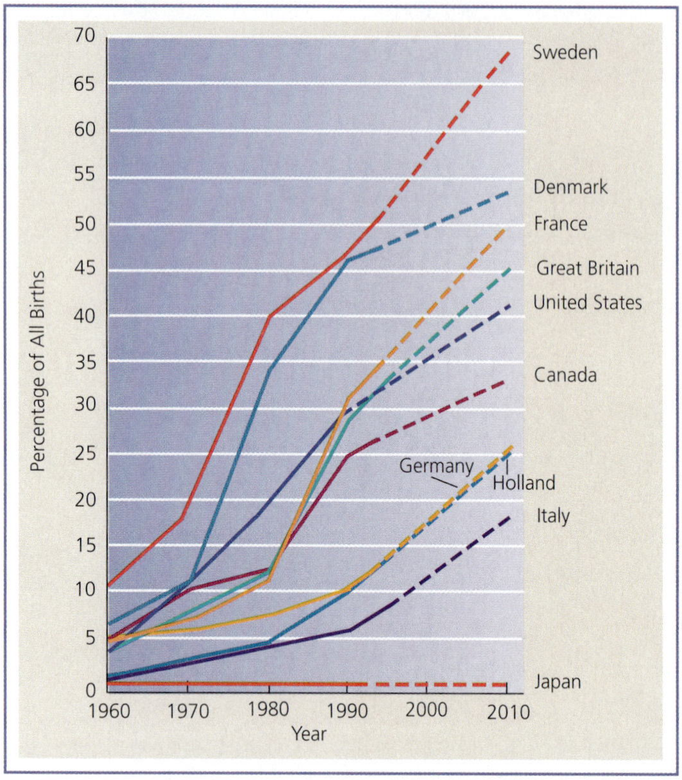

Note: The broken lines indicate the author's estimates.
Source: By the author. Based on *Statistical Abstract* 1993:Table 1380; 1998:Table 1347.

The main stresses faced by the grandparents are additional financial costs, the need to continue working when they expected to be retired, and conflict with the parents of the children (Waldrop and Weber 2001). Their primary satisfactions are knowing that their grandchildren are in loving hands, building strong emotional bonds with the grandchildren, and being able to transmit family values to them.

The "Sandwich Generation" and Elder Care

The *"sandwich generation"* refers to people who find themselves sandwiched between two generations, responsible for both their children and their own aging parents. Typically between the ages of 40 and 55, these people find themselves pulled in two strongly compelling directions. Overwhelmed by two sets of competing responsibilities, they are plagued with guilt and anger because they can only be in one place at a time.

Concerns about elder care have gained the attention of the corporate world, and half of the 1,000 largest U.S. companies offer elder care assistance to their employees (Hewitt Associates 2004). This assistance includes seminars, referral services, and flexible work schedules designed to help employees meet their responsibilities without missing so much work. Why are companies responding more positively to the issue of elder care than to child day care? Most CEOs are older men whose wives stayed home to take care of their children, so they don't understand the stresses of balancing work and child care. In contrast, nearly all have aging parents, and many have faced the turmoil of trying to cope with both their parents' needs and those of work and their own family.

With people living longer, this issue is likely to become increasingly urgent.

Divorce and Remarriage

The topic of family life would not be complete without considering divorce. Let's first try to determine how much divorce there really is.

Problems in Measuring Divorce

You probably have heard that the U.S. divorce rate is 50 percent, a figure that is popular with reporters. The statistic is true in the sense that each year about half as many divorces are granted as there are marriages performed. The totals are roughly 2-1/2 million marriages and 1-1/4 million divorces ("Population Today" 2002).

What is wrong, then, with saying that the divorce rate is 50 percent? The real question is why we should compare the number of divorces and marriages that take place during the same year. The couples who divorced do not—with rare exceptions—come from the group that married that year. The one number has *nothing* to do with the other, so these statistics in no way establish the divorce rate.

What figures should we compare, then? Couples who divorce are drawn from the entire group of married people in the country. Since the United States has 60,000,000 married couples, and only about 1-1/4 million of them obtain divorces in a year, the divorce rate is 2 percent, not 50 percent. A couple's chances of still being married at the end of a year are 98 percent—not bad odds—and certainly much better odds than the mass me-

Figure 16.11 The "Where" of U.S. Divorce

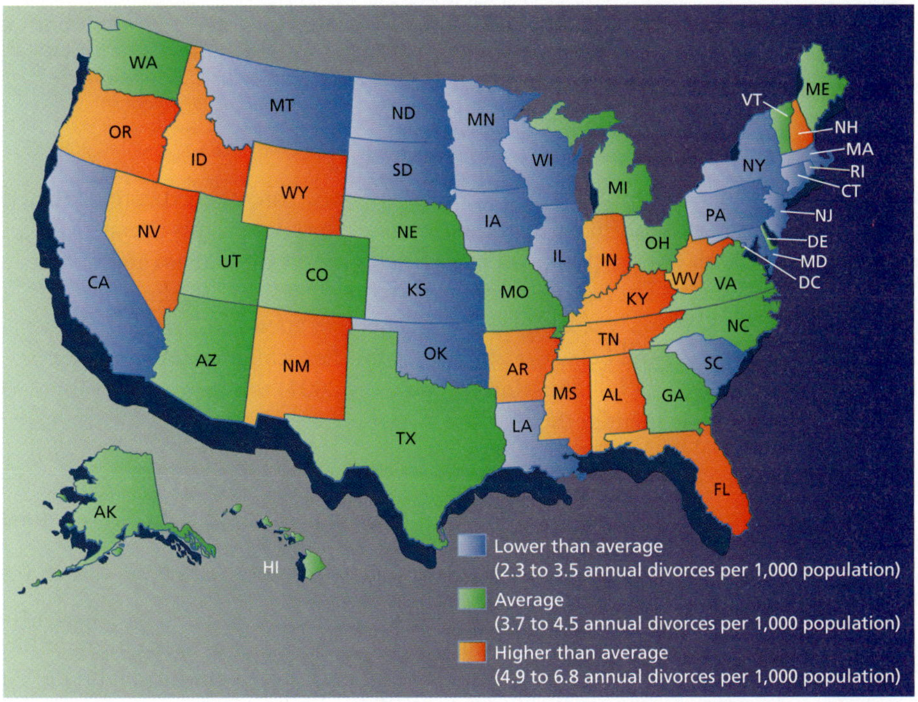

Note: Data for California, Colorado, Indiana, and Louisiana, based on earlier editions, have been decreased by the average decrease in U.S. divorce.
Source: By the author. Based on *Statistical Abstract* 2002:Table 111, and earlier editions.

dia would have us believe. As the Social Map on the next page shows, however, the "odds"—if we want to call them that—change depending on where you live.

Over time, of course, those 2 percent a year add up. A third way of measuring divorce, then, is to ask, "Of all U.S. adults, what percentage are divorced?" Figure 16.12 below answers this question. You can see how divorce has increased over the years. You can also see that people's race-ethnicity makes a difference in the likelihood that they will divorce. In

Figure 16.12 What Percentage of Americans Are Divorced?

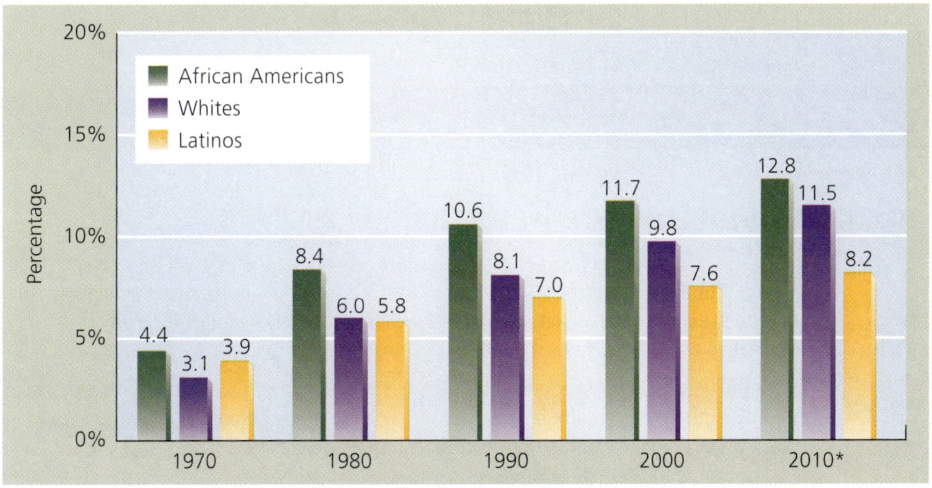

Note: Only these racial-ethnic groups are listed in the source. *author's estimate
Source: By the author. Based on *Statistical Abstract* 1995:Table 58; 2002:Table 46.

addition, you can see that the increase in divorce has been highest among whites and lowest among Latinos. If you look closely, you can also see that the rate of divorce among all groups has slowed up.

The Down-to-Earth Sociology box below reports some "curious" findings about divorce, while factors that make marriage successful are summarized at the end of this chapter.

Children of Divorce

Each year, more than 1 million U.S. children learn that their parents are divorcing (Cherlin 2002). These children are more likely than children reared by both parents to experience psychiatric problems, both during childhood and after they grow up (Amato and Sobolewski 2001; Weitoft et al. 2003). They are also more likely to become juvenile delinquents (Wallerstein et al. 2001), and less likely to complete high school, to attend college, and to graduate from college (McLanahan and Schwartz 2002). Finally, these children of divorce are themselves more likely to divorce (Tallman, Rotolo, and Gray 2001) thus perpetuating the cycle.

Is the greater maladjustment of the children of divorce a serious problem? This question has initiated a lively debate between two well-respected researchers, both psychologists. Judith Wallerstein claims that the scars of divorce afflict children with depression, with their insecurities following them into adulthood (Wallerstein, Blakeslee, and Lewis 2001). Mavis Hetherington replies that 75 percent to 80 percent of children of divorce function as well as children who are reared by both of their parents (Hetherington and Kelly 2003).

Without meaning to weigh in on one side of this debate, it doesn't seem to be a simple case of the glass being half empty or half full. If 75 percent to 80 percent of children of divorce don't suffer long-term harm, this leaves one-fourth to one-fifth who do. Any way you look at it, one-fourth or one-fifth of a million children each year is a lot of kids who are having a lot of problems.

On the other hand, we need better studies. Researchers have generally compared children of divorce with children from average homes. The problem is that children whose parents divorce don't come from average homes. They come from conflict-ridden homes. The real question, then, is how children of divorce compare with children whose parents have high conflict but remain married. When sociologist Susan Jekielek (1998) made this comparison, she found that children whose parents divorce actually are slightly better emotionally adjusted than are children who live with their parents' conflict. Other research supports this finding (Stewart et al. 1997).

What helps children adjust to divorce? Children of divorce who feel close to both parents make the best adjustment, those who feel closest to one parent make the next best adjustment, and those who don't feel intimate with either parent make the worst adjustment (Richardson and McCabe 2001). Other studies show that children adjust very well

DOWN-TO-EARTH SOCIOLOGY

You Be the Sociologist: Curious Divorce Patterns

SOCIOLOGISTS ALEX HECKERT, THOMAS Nowak, and Kay Snyder (1995) did secondary analysis (see page 133) of data gathered from a nationally representative sample of 5,000 U.S. households. Here are three of their findings:

1. If a wife earns more than her husband, the marriage is more likely to break up; if a husband earns more than his wife, divorce is less likely.
2. If the wife's health is poorer than her husband's, the marriage is more likely to break up; if the husband's health is poorer than his wife's, divorce is less likely.
3. The more housework a wife does, the less likely a couple is to divorce.

Can you explain these findings? You be the sociologist. Please develop your own explanations before looking at the answers on the next page.

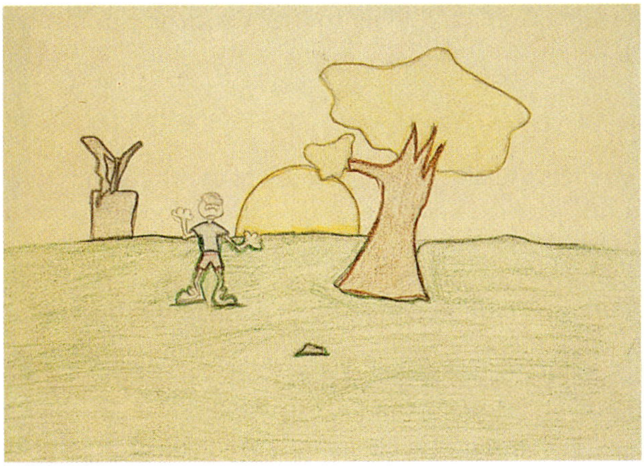

It is difficult to capture the anguish of the children of divorce, but when I read these lines by the fourth-grader who drew these two pictures, my heart was touched:

Me alone in the park . . .
All alone in the park.
My Dad and Mom are divorced
that's why I'm all alone.

This is me in the picture with my son.
We are taking a walk in the park.
I will never be like my father.
I will never divorce my wife and kid.

if their family has adequate money to meet its needs and they experience little conflict, feel loved, live with a parent who is making a good adjustment, and have consistent routines. Preliminary studies also indicate that adjustment is better if the child lives with the parent of the same sex (Lamb 1977; Clingempeel and Repucci 1982; Peterson and Zill 1986; Wallerstein and Kelly 1992). Children also adjust better if a second adult can be counted on for support (Hayashi and Strickland 1998). Urie Bronfenbrenner (1992) says this person is like the third leg of a stool, giving stability to the smaller family unit. Any adult can be the third leg, he says—a relative, friend, mother-in-law, or even co-worker—but the most powerful stabilizing third leg is the father, the ex-husband.

As mentioned, when the children of divorce grow up and marry, they are more likely to divorce than are adults who grew up in intact families. Have researchers found any factors that increase the likelihood that the marriages of the children of divorce will be successful? Actually, they have. Their chances increase if they marry someone whose parents did not divorce. This increases the level of trust and reduces the level of conflict. If both husband and wife came from broken families, however, it is not good news. Their marriages are

DOWN-TO-EARTH SOCIOLOGY

You Be the Sociologist: Curious Divorce Patterns *(continued)*

What do the findings mean? Heckert, Nowak, and Snyder suggest these explanations:

1. A wife who earns more than her husband has more alternatives to an unsatisfying marriage; a wife who earns less is more dependent.
2. Social pressure is greater for a wife to take care of a husband in poor health than it is for a husband to take care of a wife in poor health.
3. Who does the most housework is an indication of a husband's and wife's relative bargaining power. Wives with the most bargaining power do less housework and are the least likely to put up with unsatisfying marriages.

serial fatherhood a pattern of parenting in which a father, after divorce, reduces contact with his own children, serves as a father to the children of the woman he marries or lives with, then ignores these children, too, after moving in with or marrying another woman

likely to be marked by high distrust and conflict, leading to a higher chance of divorce (Tallman, Rotolo, and Gray 2001).

The Absent Father and Serial Fatherhood

With divorce common and with mothers usually granted custody of the children, a new fathering pattern has emerged. In this pattern, known as **serial fatherhood,** a divorced father maintains high contact with his children during the first year or two after the divorce. As the man develops a relationship with another woman, he begins to play a fathering role with the woman's children and reduces contact with his own children. With another breakup, this pattern may repeat. Only about one-sixth of children who live apart from their fathers see their dad as often as every week. Actually, *most* divorced fathers stop seeing their children altogether (Ahlburg and De Vita 1992; Furstenberg and Harris 1992; Seltzer 1994). Apparently, for many men, fatherhood has become a short-term commitment.

The Ex-Spouses

Anger, depression, and anxiety are common feelings at divorce. But so is relief. Women are more likely than men to feel that the divorce is giving them a "new chance" in life. A few couples manage to remain friends through it all—but they are the exception. The spouse who initiates the divorce usually gets over it sooner (Kelly 1992; Wang and Amato 2000). This spouse also usually remarries sooner (Sweeney 2002).

Divorce does not necessarily mean the end of a couple's relationship. Many divorced couples maintain contact because of their children. For others, the "continuities," as sociologists call them, represent lingering attachments (Vaughan 1985; Masheter 1991). The former husband may help his former wife hang a picture and move furniture, or she may invite him over for a meal. Some couples even continue to make love after their divorce.

After divorce, a couple's cost of living increases—two homes, two utility bills, and so forth. But the financial impact is different for men and for women. Divorce usually brings greater economic hardship for women (Smock et al. 1999; Wang and Amato 2000). This is especially true for mothers of small children, whose standard of living drops about a third (Seltzer 1994). The more education a woman has, the better prepared she is to survive financially after the divorce (Dixon and Rettig 1994).

Figure 16.13 The Probability that Divorced Women Will Remarry in Five Years

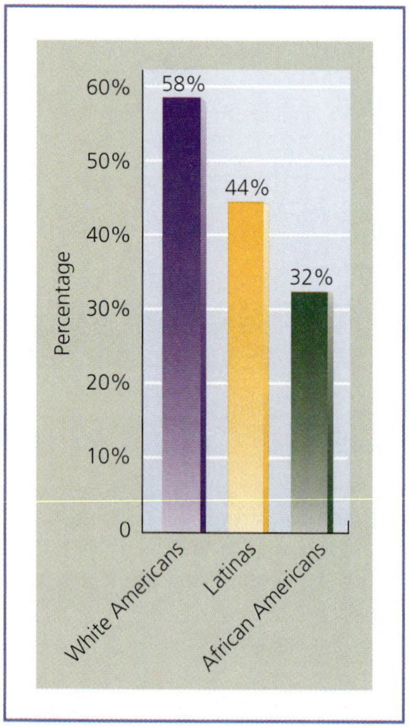

Note: Only these groups are listed in the source.
Source: By the author. Based on Bramlett and Mosher 2002.

Remarriage

Despite the number of people who emerge from the divorce court swearing "Never again!" many do remarry. The rate at which they remarry, however, has dropped remarkably, and today only half of women who divorce remarry (Bramlett and Mosher 2002). Figure 16.13 shows how significant race-ethnicity is in determining whether women remarry. Comparable data are not available for men.

As Figure 16.14 shows, most divorced people marry other divorced people. You may be surprised that the women most likely to remarry are young mothers and those with less education (Glick and Lin 1986; Schmiege, Richards, and Zvonkovic 2001). Apparently women who are more educated and more independent (no children) can afford to be more selective. Men are more likely than women to remarry, perhaps because they have a larger pool of potential mates.

How do remarriages work out? The divorce rate of remarried people *without* children is the same as that of first marriages. Those who bring children into a new marriage, however, are more likely to divorce again (MacDonald and DeMaris 1995). Certainly these relationships are more complicated and stressful. A lack of clear norms to follow may also play a role (Coleman et al. 2000). As sociologist Andrew Cherlin (1989) noted, we lack satisfactory names for stepmothers, stepfathers, stepbrothers, stepsisters, stepaunts, stepuncles, stepcousins, and stepgrandparents. At the very least, these are awkward terms to use, but they also represent ill-defined relationships.

This fanciful depiction of marital trends may not be too far off the mark.

Reprinted with special permission of King Features Syndicate

" I NOW PRONOUNCE YOU SECOND HUSBAND AND FOURTH WIFE."

Figure 16.14 The Marital History of U.S. Brides and Grooms

- First marriage of bride and groom
- Remarriage of bride and groom
- First marriage of bride, remarriage of groom
- First marriage of groom, remarriage of bride

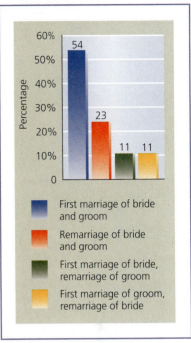

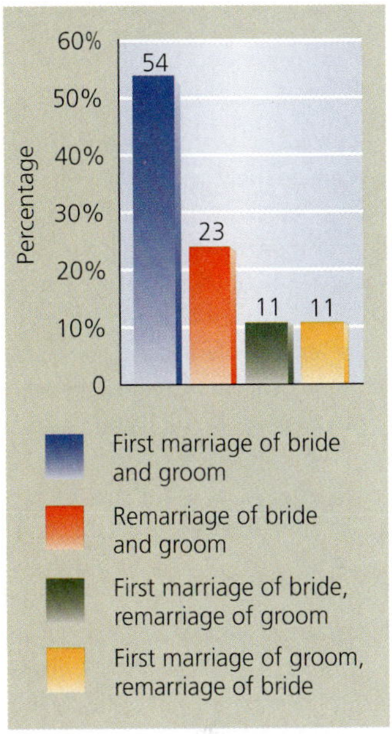

Source: By the author. Based on *Statistical Abstract* 2000:Table 145.

Two Sides of Family Life

et's first look at situations in which marriage and family have gone seriously wrong and then try to answer the question of what makes marriage work.

The Dark Side of Family Life: Battering, Child Abuse, Marital Rape, and Incest

The dark side of family life involves events that people would rather keep in the dark. We shall look at battering, child abuse, rape, and incest.

Battering To study spouse abuse, some sociologists have studied just a few victims in depth (Goetting 2001), while others have interviewed nationally representative samples of U.S. couples (Straus and Gelles 1988; Straus 1992). Although not all sociologists agree (Dobash et al. 1992, 1993; Pagelow 1992), Murray Straus concludes that husbands and wives are about equally likely to attack one another. If gender equality exists here, however, it certainly vanishes when it comes to the effects of violence, where 85 percent of the injured are women (Rennison 2003). A good part of the reason, of course, is that most husbands are bigger and stronger than their wives, putting women at a physical disadvantage in this literal battle of the sexes. The Down-to-Earth Sociology box on the next page discusses why some women remain with their abusive husbands.

Violence against women is related to the sexist structure of society, which we reviewed in Chapter 11, and to the socialization we reviewed in Chapter 3. Because they grew up with norms that encourage aggression and the use of violence, some men feel it is their right to control women. When frustrated in a relationship—or even by events outside it—some men turn violent toward their wives and lovers. The basic sociological question is how to socialize males to handle frustration and disagreements without resorting to violence (Rieker et al. 1997). We do not yet have this answer.

DOWN-TO-EARTH SOCIOLOGY

"Why Doesn't She Just Leave?" The Dilemma of Abused Women

"WHY WOULD SHE EVER PUT UP WITH violence?" is the question on everyone's mind. From the outside, it looks so easy. Just pack up and leave. "I know I wouldn't put up with anything like that."

And yet this is not what typically happens. Women tend to stay with their men after they are abused. Some stay only a short while, to be sure, but others remain in abusive situations for years. Why?

Sociologist Ann Goetting (2001) asked this question, too. To get the answer, she interviewed women who had made the break. She wanted to find out what it was that set them apart. How were they able to leave, when so many women can't seem to? She found these characteristics in the women who made the break:

1. They had a positive self-concept.

   Simply put, they believed that they deserved better.

2. They broke with traditional values.

   They did not believe that a wife had to stay with her husband no matter what.

3. They found adequate finances.

   For some this was easy, but for others it was not. To accumulate enough money to move out, some of the women saved for years, putting away just a little each week.

4. They had supportive family and friends.

   A support network served as a source of encouragement to help them rescue themselves.

If you take the opposite of these four characteristics, you have the answer to why some women put up with abuse: They don't think they deserve anything better, they believe it is their duty to stay, they don't think they can make it financially, and they lack a supportive network. These four factors are not of equal importance for all women, of course. For some, the lack of finances is the most significant, while for others it is their low self-concept. For all, the supportive network—or the lack of one—plays a significant role.

For Your CONSIDERATION

Based on these findings, what would you say to a woman whose husband or partner is abusing her? How do you think battered women's shelters fit into this explanation? What other parts of this puzzle can you think of—such as the role of love?

Child Abuse

> My wife and I answered an ad about a lakeside house in a middle-class neighborhood that was for sale by owner. As the woman showed us through her immaculate house, we were surprised to see a plywood box in the youngest child's bedroom. About 3 feet high, 3 feet wide, and 6 feet long, the box was perforated with holes and had a little door with a padlock. Curious, I asked what it was. The woman replied matter-of-factly that her son had a behavior problem, and this was where they locked him for "time out." She added that other times they would tie him to a float, attach a line to the dock, and put him in the lake.
>
> We left as soon as we could. With thoughts of a terrorized child filling my head, I called the state child abuse hotline.

As you can tell, what I saw upset me. Most of us are bothered by child abuse—helpless children being victimized by their own parents, the very adults who are supposed to love, protect, and nurture them. The most gruesome of these cases make the evening news: The 4-year-old girl who was beaten and raped by her mother's boyfriend, who passed into a coma and then three days later passed out of this life; the 6- to 10-year-old children whose stepfather videotaped them engaging in sex acts. Unlike these cases, which made headlines in my area, most child abuse is never brought to our attention: the children who live in filth, who are neglected—left alone for hours or even days at a time—or who are beaten with extension cords—cases like the little boy I learned about when I went house hunting.

We do know that child abuse is extensive. Each year, about 3 million U.S. children are reported to the authorities as victims of abuse or neglect. About 850,000 of these cases are substantiated (*Statistical Abstract* 2002:Table 321). The excuses that abusive parents make are incredible. Of those I have read, one of the most fantastic is the statement a mother told a Manhattan judge, "I slipped in a moment of anger and my hands accidentally wrapped around my daughter's windpipe" (LeDuff 2002).

Marital or Intimacy Rape Sociologists have found that marital rape is more common than is usually supposed. For example, between one-third and one-half of women who seek help at shelters for battered women are victims of marital rape (Bergen 1996). Women at shelters, however, are not representative of U.S. women. To get a better answer of how common marital rape is, sociologist Diana Russell (1990) used a sampling technique that allows generalization. She found that 14 percent of married women report that their husbands have raped them. Similarly, 10 percent of a representative sample of Boston women interviewed by sociologists David Finkelhor and Kersti Yllo (1985, 1989) reported that their husbands had used physical force to compel them to have sex. Compared with victims of rape by strangers or acquaintances, victims of marital rape are less likely to report the rape (Mahoney 1999).

With the huge numbers of couples who are cohabiting, the term marital rape needs to include sexual assault in these relationships. Perhaps, then, we should use the term *intimacy rape*. And intimacy rape is not limited to men who sexually assault women. In pathbreaking research, sociologist Lori Girshick (2002) interviewed lesbians who had been sexually assaulted by their partners. In these cases, both the victim and the offender are women. Girshick points out that if the pronoun "he" were substituted for "she" in her interviews, a reader would believe that the events were being told by women who had been battered and raped by their husbands (Bergen 2003). Like wives who have been raped by their husbands, these victims, too, suffered from shock, depression, and self-blame.

Incest Sexual relations between certain relatives (for example, between brothers and sisters or between parents and children) constitute **incest.** Incest is most likely to occur in families that are socially isolated (Smith 1992). As with marital rape, sociological research has destroyed assumptions that incest is not common. Sociologist Diana Russell (n.d.) found that incest victims who experience the greatest trauma are those who were victimized the most often, whose assaults occurred over longer periods of time, and whose incest was "more intrusive," for example, sexual intercourse as opposed to sexual touching.

Who are the offenders? Russell found that uncles are the most common offenders, followed by first cousins, fathers (stepfathers especially), brothers, and, finally, other relatives ranging from brothers-in-law to stepgrandfathers. Other researchers report that brother-sister incest is several times more common than father-daughter incest (Canavan et al. 1992). Incest between mothers and sons is rare.

The Bright Side of Family Life: Successful Marriages

Successful Marriages After examining divorce and family abuse, one could easily conclude that marriages seldom work out. This would be far from the truth, however, for about two of every three married Americans report that they are "very happy" with their marriages (Cherlin and Furstenberg 1988; Whyte 1992). To find out what makes marriage successful, sociologists Jeanette and Robert Lauer (1992) interviewed 351 couples who had been married fifteen years or longer. Fifty-one of these marriages were unhappy, but the couples stayed together for religious reasons, family tradition, or "for the sake of the children." Of the others, the 300 happy couples, all:

1. Think of their spouse as their best friend
2. Like their spouse as a person
3. Think of marriage as a long-term commitment
4. Believe that marriage is sacred
5. Agree with their spouse on aims and goals
6. Believe that their spouse has grown more interesting over the years
7. Strongly want the relationship to succeed
8. Laugh together

incest sexual relations between specified relatives, such as brothers and sisters or parents and children

Sociologist Nicholas Stinnett (1992) used interviews and questionnaires to study 660 families from all regions of the United States and parts of South America. He found that happy families:

1. Spend a lot of time together
2. Are quick to express appreciation
3. Are committed to promoting one another's welfare
4. Do a lot of talking and listening to one another
5. Are religious
6. Deal with crises in a positive manner

Other sociologists have found that the better a couple gets along with their in-laws, the happier the marriage is (Bryant et al. 2001).

Symbolic Interactionism and the Misuse of Statistics Many of my students express concerns about their own marital future, a wariness born out of the divorce of their parents, friends, neighbors, relatives—even their pastors and rabbis. They wonder about their chances of having a successful marriage. Because sociology is not just about abstract ideas, but is really about our lives, it is important to stress that you are an individual, not a statistic. That is, if the divorce rate were 33 percent or 50 percent, this would *not* mean that if you marry, your chances of getting divorced are 33 percent or 50 percent. That is a misuse of statistics, and a common one at that. Divorce statistics represent all marriages and have absolutely *nothing* to do with any individual marriage. Our own chances depend on our own situations—and especially the way we approach marriage.

To make this point clearer, let's apply symbolic interactionism. From a symbolic interactionist perspective, we create our own worlds. That is, our experiences don't come with built-in meanings. Rather, we interpret our experiences, and act accordingly. Simply put, if we think of our marriage as likely to fail, we increase the likelihood that it will fail; if we think that our marriage will work out well, our chances of a good marriage increase. In other words, we tend to act according to our ideas, creating a sort of self-fulfilling prophecy. For example, if we think our marriage may fail, we are more likely to run when things become difficult. The folk saying "There are no guarantees in life" is certainly true, but it does help to have a vision that a good marriage is possible and that it is worth the effort to achieve.

The Future of Marriage and Family

What can we expect of marriage and family in the future? Despite its many problems, marriage is in no danger of becoming a relic of the past. Marriage is so functional that it exists in every society. Consequently, the vast majority of Americans will continue to find marriage vital to their welfare.

Certain trends are firmly in place. Cohabitation, births to single women, age at first marriage, and parenting by grandparents will increase. More married women will join the work force, and they will continue to gain marital power. Equality in marriage, however, is not even on the horizon. As the number of elderly increase, more couples will find themselves sandwiched between caring for their parents and rearing their own children.

Our culture will continue to be haunted by distorted images of marriage and family: the bleak ones portrayed in the mass media and the rosy ones painted by cultural myths. Sociological research can help correct these distortions and allow us to see how our own family experiences fit into the patterns of our culture. Sociological research can also help to answer the big question of how to formulate social policy that will support and enhance family life.

To conclude this chapter, in the Down-to-Earth Sociology box on the next page we look at a subtle but fundamental change that may have just begun to affect the family.

DOWN-TO-EARTH SOCIOLOGY

When Work Becomes Home and Home Becomes Work

WORKERS CAN'T STAND THEIR BOSSES, and almost everyone would quit work and stay home if they had the chance, right? Don't be too sure.

Sociologist Arlie Hochschild (1997, 2004) did research on a company she calls Amerco. This company has "family friendly" policies. Workers can work part time, take parental leave, do some of their work at home, and even share a job with another person. What puzzled Hochschild was that hardly anyone took advantage of these policies.

Hochschild was surprised, for she thought that workers were clamoring for relief from job pressures. To check her observation, she decided to participate in a project that sent a questionnaire to 3,000 parents of young children. She found that one third of the fathers and a fifth of the mothers described themselves as "workaholics."

Intrigued, Hochschild probed further. As she did participant observation at Amerco, she found that both work and family have changed. The family has become more harried, with schedules being juggled among two working parents and their children's school and personal lives. As with Sharon and Tom in our opening vignette, family members can feel overwhelmed by responsibilities that come flying at them from several directions at once. As Hochschild puts it:

> [A]t home the divorce rate has risen, and the emotional demands have become more baffling and complex. In addition to teething, tantrums and the normal developments of growing children, the needs of elderly parents are creating more tasks for the modern family—as are the blending, unblending, reblending of new stepparents, stepchildren, exes and former in-laws.

At the same time that pressures at home have increased, for many those at work have lessened. They find work to be less rigorous, less demanding, and more rewarding. As Hochschild says,

> [N]ew management techniques so pervasive in corporate life have helped transform the workplace into a more appreciative, personal sort of social world . . . many companies now train workers to make their own work decisions, and . . . [make them] feel recognized for job accomplishments. Amerco regularly strengthens the familylike ties of co-workers by holding "recognition ceremonies" . . . Amerco employees speak of "belonging to the Amerco family . . . production teams, too, have regular get-togethers. . . . The education-and-training division offers free courses (on company time) in "Dealing with Anger," "How to Give and Accept Criticism," and "How to Cope with Difficult People."

What sort of "appreciation day" do family members have? Or free courses on "How to Cope with Mom" or "How to Understand Your Two-Year-Old–or Unruly Teenager"? With pressures increasing at home and decreasing at work, Hochschild found that some workers put in voluntary overtime "just to get away from the house." As Linda, one of the women Hochschild talked to, said,

> When I get home, and the minute I turn the key, my daughter is right there. Granted she needs somebody to talk to about her day. . . . The baby is still up. He should have been in bed two hours ago, and that upsets me. The dishes are piled in the sink. My daughter comes right up to the door and complains about anything her stepfather said or did, and she wants to talk about her job. My husband is in the other room hollering to my daughter, "Tracy, I don't ever get any time to talk to your mother, because you're always monopolizing her time before I even get a chance!" They all come at me at once.

Reflecting on what she observed, Hochschild says that for many people, the worlds of home and work have begun to reverse places. Home has become more like work, and work has become more like home.

For Your CONSIDERATION

It is difficult to pinpoint changes as they first occur, although some sociologists have been able to do so. As mentioned in Chapter 1, sociologist William Ogburn noted in 1933 that personality was becoming more important in mate selection, and in 1945 sociologists Ernest Burgess and Harvey Locke observed that mutual affection and compatibility were becoming more important in marriage. The change has been so complete that today it is difficult to conceive of getting married apart from affection and compatibility.

Could Hochschild have also put her finger on a fundamental, historical shift just as it has begun to occur? Are the ways we view home and work in the process of reversing? In 50 years or so, will this be the taken-for-granted life for most of us? What do you think?

The cartoonist has aptly picked up the findings of sociologist Arlie Hochschild on the reversal of home and family.

King Features, James Cavett; 800-708-7311 x 246; Orlando, FL

SUMMARY and REVIEW

Marriage and Family in Global Perspective

What is a family—and what themes are universal?

Family is difficult to define. There are exceptions to every element one might consider essential. Consequently, **family** is defined broadly—as people who consider themselves related by blood, marriage, or adoption. Universally, **marriage** and family are mechanisms for governing mate selection, reckoning descent, and establishing inheritance and authority. Pp. 448–450.

Marriage and Family in Theoretical Perspective

What is the functionalist perspective on marriage and family?

Functionalists examine the functions and dysfunctions of family life. Examples include the **incest taboo** and how weakened family functions increase divorce. Pp. 450–452.

What is the conflict perspective on marriage and family?

Conflict theorists examine how marriage and family help perpetuate inequalities, especially men's dominance of women. Power struggles in marriage, such as those over housework, are an example. Pp. 452–454.

What is a symbolic interactionist perspective on marriage and family?

Symbolic interactionists examine how the contrasting experiences and perspectives of men and women are played out in marriage. They stress that only by grasping the perspectives of wives and husbands can we understand their behavior. P. 454.

The Family Life Cycle

What are the major elements of the family life cycle?

The major elements are love and courtship, marriage, childbirth, child rearing, and the family in later life. Most mate selection follows predictable patterns of age, social class, race-ethnicity, and religion. Childbirth and child-rearing patterns also vary by social class. Pp. 454–460.

Diversity in U.S. Families

How significant is race-ethnicity in family life?

The primary distinction is social class, not race or ethnicity. Families of the same social class are likely to be similar, regardless of their racial or ethnic makeup. Pp. 460–463.

What other diversity in U.S. families is there?

Also discussed were one-parent, childless, **blended,** and gay and lesbian families. Each has its unique characteristics, but social class is significant in determining their primary characteristics. Poverty is especially significant for one-parent families, most of which are headed by women. Pp. 463–466.

Trends in U.S. Families

What major changes characterize U.S. families?

Three changes are postponement of first marriage, an increase in **cohabitation,** and more grandparents serving as parents to their grandchildren. With more people living longer, many middle-aged couples find themselves sandwiched between rearing their children and taking care of their parents. Pp. 466–470.

Divorce and Remarriage

What is the current divorce rate?

Depending on what numbers you choose to compare, you can produce almost any rate you wish, from 75 percent to just 2 percent. However you figure it, the U.S. divorce rate is higher than any other industrialized nation. Pp. 470–472.

How do children and their parents adjust to divorce?

Divorce is difficult for children, whose adjustment problems often continue into adulthood. Most divorced fathers do not maintain ongoing relationships with their children. Financial problems are usually greater for the former wives. Although most divorced people remarry, their rate of remarriage has slowed considerably. Pp. 472–474.

Two Sides of Family Life

What are the two sides of family life?

The dark side is abuse—spouse battering, child abuse, marital rape, and **incest,** acts that revolve around the misuse of family power. The bright side is that most people find marriage and family to be rewarding. Pp. 475–478.

The Future of Marriage and Family

What is the likely future of marriage and family?

We can expect cohabitation, births to single women, age at first marriage, and parenting by grandparents to increase. The growing numbers of women in the work force are likely to continue to shift the marital balance of power. Pp. 478–479.

Where can I read more on this topic?

Suggested Readings for this chapter are at the back of this book.

THINKING Critically ABOUT CHAPTER 16

1. Functionalists stress that the family is universal because it provides basic functions for individuals and society. What functions does your family provide? Hint: In addition to the section on The Functionalist Perspective, also consider the section on Common Cultural Themes.
2. Explain why social class is more important than race-ethnicity in determining a family's characteristics.
3. Apply this chapter's contents to your own experience with marriage and family. What social factors affect your family life? In what ways is your family life different from that of your grandparents when they were young?

ADDITIONAL RESOURCES for This Chapter

www.ablongman.com/henslin7e

- *Content Select* Research Database for Sociology, with suggested key terms and annotated references
- Link to 2000 Census, with activities
- Flashcards of key terms and concepts
- Practice Tests
- Weblinks
- Interactive Maps

Chapter 17

Education

Stephen Schildbach, *Students,* 1999

Chapter Outline

There wasn't much for teenagers to do in Littleton, Colorado. Not much happened in this quiet town of 35,000, a middle-class suburb southwest of Denver. Some of the high school kids liked to draw attention to themselves by wearing black trenchcoats and black shirts with swastikas painted on them. They called themselves the Trenchcoat Mafia and tossed around a few phrases in German.

"Just kids. They'll grow out of it," was the typical adult response. "We all went through something ourselves."

The Trenchcoat Mafia had their own table in the cafeteria and their group picture in the yearbook. The caption: "Who says we're different? Insanity's healthy. . . . Stay alive, stay different, stay crazy! Oh, and stay away from CREAM SODA!!"

Just another high school group: jocks, Goths, stoners, geeks, preppies, oddballs. Every school has some.

The jocks despised the Trenchcoat Mafia. They threw them into lockers and called them scumbags, faggots, and inbreeds. They threw rocks and bottles at them from passing cars.

Two seniors, Eric Harris and Dylan Klebold, honors students and members of the Trenchcoat Mafia, talked about killing their classmates, especially the jocks. Eric even had his own Web page, where he described whom he wanted to kill and how he wanted to do it. As a class project, Eric and Dylan made a video in which they pretended to kill the classmates they didn't like. Just talk. But as the killing on *Doom,* the video game they loved, no longer satisfied, the boys hatched a plan for real killing. It was risky. Maybe they would survive, maybe not. But if not, they would go out in a blaze of glory. Hitler's birthday would be perfect.

As bombs went off and shots rang out *students ran in terror,* cowering in closets and under tables.

As bombs went off and shots rang out, students ran in terror, hiding in closets and crawling under tables. Harris and Klebold went from room to room in search of victims. In the library, they found students hiding under a table. "Do you believe in God?" asked one of the shooters. "Yes," replied Cassie Bernall.

"There is no God," the gunman retorted, as he placed a gun against her head and squeezed the trigger.

Before the boys turned their guns on themselves, they killed twelve of their fellow students and one teacher. They wounded another twenty-three students.

—Based on Bai 1999; Gibbs 1999.

The events at Columbine High School are etched into the nation's consciousness. School shootings have confused just about everyone. No one has the full explanation for why they happen, or what we can do to prevent them. When we return to this topic, we are going to find a surprise, but, first, let's take a broad look at education.

The Development of Modern Education

To provide a background for understanding our own educational system better, let's look first at education in earlier societies, then trace the development of universal education.

Education in Earlier Societies

Earlier societies had no separate social institution called education. They had no special buildings called schools, and no people who earned their living as teachers. Rather, as an integral part of growing up, children learned what was necessary to get along in life. If hunting or cooking were the essential skills, then people who already possessed those skills taught them. *Education was synonymous with acculturation,* learning a culture. It still is in today's tribal groups.

In some societies, when a sufficient surplus developed—as in Arabia, China, Greece, and North Africa—a separate institution developed. Some people then devoted themselves to teaching, while those who had the leisure—the children of the wealthy—became

In hunting and gathering societies, there is no separate social institution called education. *As with this Bushman boy in South Africa's Kalahari desert, children learn their adult economic roles from their parents and other kin.*

their students. In ancient China, for example, Confucius taught a few select pupils, while in Greece, Aristotle, Plato, and Socrates taught science and philosophy to upper-class boys. Education, then, came to be something quite distinct from informal acculturation. **Education** is a group's *formal* system of teaching knowledge, values, and skills. Such instruction stood in marked contrast to the learning of traditional skills such as farming or hunting, for it was intended to develop the mind.

Education, which flourished during the period roughly marked by the birth of Christ, slowly died out. During the Dark Ages of Europe, monks kept the candle of enlightenment burning. Except for a handful of the wealthy and some members of the nobility, only the monks could read and write. Although the monks delved into philosophy, they focused on learning Greek, Latin, and Hebrew so that they could study the Bible and writings of early church leaders. The Jews also kept formal learning alive as they studied the Torah.

Formal education remained limited to those who had the leisure to pursue it. (The word *school* comes from the Greek word σχωλή *[scholē]* meaning "leisure.") Industrialization transformed education, for the new machinery and new types of jobs required workers to read, write, and work accurately with figures—the classic three R's of the nineteenth century (Reading, 'Riting, and 'Rithmetic).

education a formal system of teaching knowledge, values, and skills

mandatory education laws laws that require all children to attend school until a specified age or until they complete a minimum grade in school

Industrialization and Universal Education

After the American Revolution, the founders of the new republic were concerned that the country lacked unity, that its many religious and ethnic groups (nationalities) would make the nation unstable. To help create a uniform national culture, Thomas Jefferson and Noah Webster proposed universal schooling. Standardized texts would instill patriotism and teach the principles of representative government (Hellinger and Judd 1991). If this new political experiment were to succeed, they reasoned, it would need educated voters who are capable of making sound decisions. A national culture remained elusive, however, and in the 1800s the country remained politically fragmented. Many states even considered themselves to be near-sovereign nations.

Education reflected this disunity. There was no comprehensive school system, just a hodgepodge of independent schools. Public schools even charged tuition. Lutherans, Presbyterians, and Roman Catholics operated their own schools (Hellinger and Judd 1991). Children of the rich attended private schools. Children of the poor received no formal education—nor did slaves. High school was considered higher education (hence the name *high* school), and only the wealthy could afford it. College, too, was beyond the reach of almost everyone.

Horace Mann, an educator from Massachusetts, found it deplorable that the average family could not afford to send its children even to grade school. In 1837 he proposed that "common schools," supported through taxes, be established throughout his state. Mann's idea spread, and state after state began to provide free public education. It is no coincidence that universal education and industrialization occurred at the same time. The economy was changing, and political and civic leaders recognized the need for an educated work force. They also feared the influx of foreign values and, like the founders of the country, looked on public education as a way to "Americanize" immigrants (Hellinger and Judd 1991).

By 1918, all U.S. states had **mandatory education laws** requiring children to attend school, usually until they had completed the eighth grade or turned 16, whichever came first. In the early 1900s, graduation from the eighth grade marked the end of education for most people. "Dropouts" at that time were students who did not complete grade school.

As industrialization progressed and as fewer people made their living from farming, formal education

This 1893 photo of a school in Hecla, Montana, taught by Miss Blanche Lamont, provides a glimpse into the past, when free public education, pioneered in the United States, was still in its infancy. In these one-room rural schools, a single teacher had charge of grades 1 to 8. Children were assigned a grade not by age but by mastery of subject matter. Occasionally, adults who wished to learn to read, to write, or to add and subtract would join the class. Attendance was sporadic, for the family's economic survival came first.

came to be regarded as essential to the well-being of society. With the distance to the nearest college too far and the cost too great, many high school graduates could not attend college. As discussed in the Down-to-Earth Sociology box below, this gave birth to community colleges. As you can see from Figure 17.1, receiving a bachelor's degree in the United States is now *twice* as common as high school diplomas used to be. Sixty-three percent of all high school graduates enter college (*Statistical Abstract* 2002:Table 255).

One-sixth of Americans still don't make it through high school, however, which condemns most of them to a difficult economic life. As you can see from the Social Map on the next page, the rate of high school graduation is far from evenly distributed across the states. You may wish to compare this Social Map with the one on page 280 that shows how poverty is distributed among the states.

Education in Global Perspective

To further place our own educational system in perspective, let's look at education in three countries. This will help us see how education is directly related to a nation's culture and its economy.

DOWN-TO-EARTH SOCIOLOGY

Community Colleges: Challenges Old and New

I ATTENDED A JUNIOR COLLEGE IN OAKland, California. From there, with my newly minted associate's degree in hand, I transferred to a senior college—a college in Ft. Wayne, Indiana, that had no freshmen or sophomores.

I didn't realize that my experimental college matched the vision of some of the founders of the community college movement. In the early 1900s, they foresaw a system of local colleges that would be accessible to the average high school graduate—a system so extensive that it would be unnecessary for universities to offer courses at the freshman and sophomore levels (Manzo 2001).

An equally strong voice questioned whether preparing high school graduates for entry to four-year colleges and universities should be the goal of junior colleges. They insisted that the purpose of junior colleges should instead be vocational preparation, to equip people for the job market as electricians and other technicians. In some regions, where the proponents of transfer dominated, the admissions requirements for junior colleges were even higher than those of Yale (Pedersen 2001). This debate was never won by either side, and you can still hear its echoes today.

Community colleges have opened higher education to millions of students who would not have access to college due to cost or distance.

The name *junior* college also became a problem. Some felt that the word *junior* made their institution sound as though it weren't quite a real college. A struggle to change the name ensued, and about three decades ago *community* college won out.

The name change didn't settle the debate about whether the purpose was preparing students to transfer to universities or training them for jobs, however. Community colleges continue to serve this dual purpose.

Community colleges have become such an essential part of the U.S. educational system that about *half* of all undergraduates in the United States are enrolled in them (Kim 2002). Most students are what are called *nontraditional* students: Many are age 25 or older, from the working class, have jobs, and attend college part time (Bryant 2001).

To help their students transfer to four-year colleges and universities, many community colleges are making arrangements with top-tier public and private universities (Chaker 2003b). Some provide admissions guidance on how to enter flagship state schools. Others coordinate courses, making sure that they match the university's title and numbering system, as well as its rigor of instruction and grading.

The challenges that community colleges face are the usual ones of securing adequate budgets in the face of declining resources, continuing an open-door policy, meeting changing job markets, and maintaining quality instruction. New challenges include meeting the shifting needs of students, such as the growing need to teach immigrants English as a second language and to provide on-campus day care for parents who no longer enjoy an extensive familial support system.

Figure 17.1 Educational Achievement in the United States

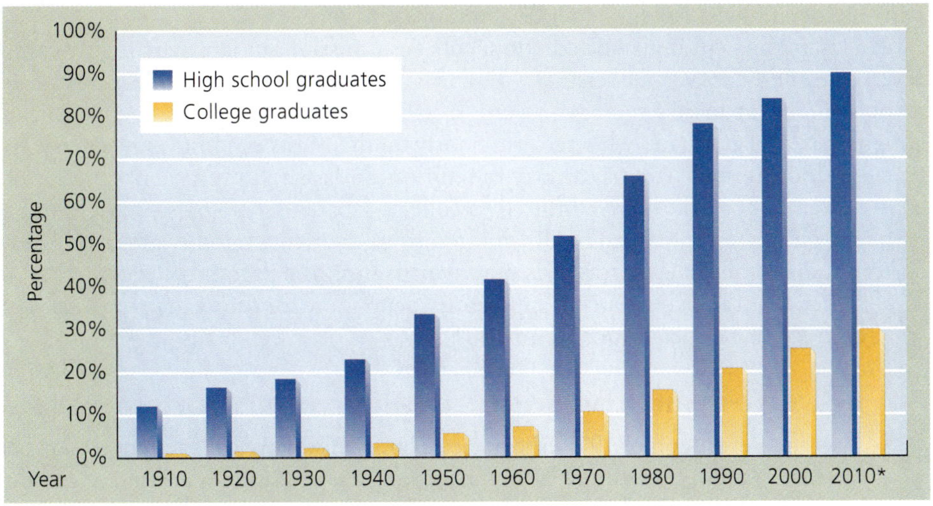

Note: Americans 25 years and over. Asterisk indicates author's estimate.
Sources: By the author. Based on National Center for Education Statistics, 1991:Table 8; *Statistical Abstract* 2002:Table 208.

Figure 17.2 Not Making It: Dropping Out of High School

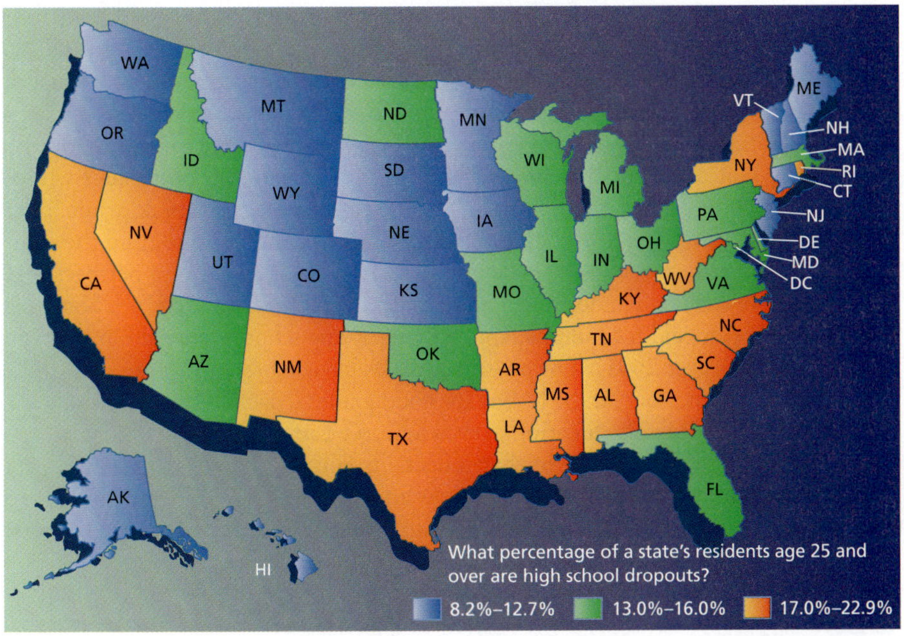

Note: The states vary widely. The extremes range from 8.2 percent in South Dakota and Washington to 22.9 percent in West Virginia.
Source: By the author. Based on *Statistical Abstract* 2002:Table 212.

Education in the Most Industrialized Nations: Japan

A central sociological principle of education is that a nation's education reflects its culture. Because a core Japanese value is solidarity with the group, the Japanese discourage competition among individuals. In the work force, people who are hired together work as a team. They are not expected to compete with one another for promotions, but, instead, they are promoted as a group (Ouchi 1993). Japanese education reflects this group-centered approach to life. Children in grade school work as a group, all mastering the same skills and materials. On any one day, children all over Japan study the same page from the same textbook ("Less Rote . . . " 2000).

In a fascinating cultural contradiction, college admissions in Japan are highly competitive. Like the Scholastic Assessment Test (SAT) required of U.S. college-bound high school seniors, Japanese seniors who want to attend college must also take a national test. U.S. high school graduates who perform poorly on their tests can find some college to attend—as long as their parents can pay the tuition. In Japan, however, only the top scorers—rich and poor alike—are admitted to college. Japanese sociologists have found that even though the tests are open to all, children from the richer families are more likely to be admitted to college. The reason is not favoritism on the part of college officials, but, rather, that the richer parents apparently spend more for tutors to prepare their children for these open exams (Ono 2001).

Figure 17.3 Education in a Most Industrialized (Postindustrial) Nation and a Least Industrialized Nation

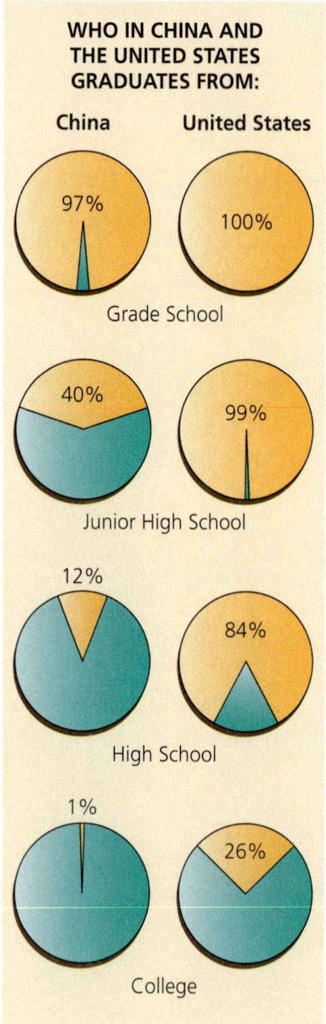

Note: These are initial attendance rates, not completion rates. The U.S. junior high school total is the author's estimate.

Sources: Brauchli 1994; Kahn 2002; *Statistical Abstract* 2002:Table 208.

Education in the Industrializing Nations: Russia

After the Revolution of 1917, the Soviet Communist party changed the nation's educational system. At that time, as in most countries, education was limited to children of the elite. Following the sociological principle that education reflects culture, the new government made certain that socialist values dominated its schools, for it saw education as a means to undergird the new political system. As a result, schoolchildren were taught that capitalism was evil and that communism was the salvation of the world.

Education, including college, was free. Schools stressed mathematics and the natural sciences, and few courses in the social sciences were taught. Just as the economy was directed from central headquarters, so was education. With orders issued out of Moscow, schools throughout the country followed the same state-prescribed curriculum. All students in the same grade used the same textbooks. To prevent the development of thinking that might be contrary to communism, students memorized the materials and were taught to repeat lectures on oral exams (Deaver 2001).

Post-Soviet Russians are in the midst of "reinventing" education. For the first time, private, religious, and even foreign-run schools are allowed, and teachers can encourage students to think for themselves. The problems that Russians confronted are mind-boggling. Not only did they have to retrain tens of thousands of teachers who were used to teaching pat political answers, but also school budgets shrank, while inflation spiraled upward. The average teacher makes just $33 a month, one-third the salary of the average Russian worker ("Saving the . . . " 2001). (To put this in perspective, $17 is the cost of staying in a dormitory for a month [MacWilliams 2001a]). Some teachers haven't been paid for months, and teachers at one school were paid in toilet paper and vodka (Deaver 2001). The abysmal salaries have led to corruption, and students know which professors can be bribed for good grades (MacWilliams 2001b).

Because it is true of education everywhere, we can safely predict that Russia will develop an educational system that reflects its culture. This system will glorify its historical exploits and reinforce its values and world views. The transition to capitalism is transforming basic ideas about profit and private property, and Russia's educational system now reflects those changed values.

Education in the Least Industrialized Nations: Egypt

Education in the Least Industrialized Nations stands in sharp contrast to that in the industrialized world. Even if the Least Industrialized Nations have mandatory attendance laws, they are not enforced. Because most of their people work the land or take care of families, they find little need for education. In addition, formal education is expensive and most of these nations cannot afford it. As we saw from Figure 9.2 (pages 246-247), most people in the Least Industrialized Nations live on less than $1,000 a year. Consequently, in some nations most children do not go to school beyond the first couple of grades. Figure 17.3 contrasts education in China and the United States. As was once common around the globe, it is primarily the wealthy in

The poverty of some of the Least Industrialized Nations defies the imagination of most people who have been reared in the industrialized world. Their educational systems are similarly marked by poverty. This photo shows a village school in Shaanxi Province, China.

the Least Industrialized Nations who have the means and the leisure for formal education—especially anything beyond the basics. As an example, let's look at education in Egypt.

Several centuries before the birth of Christ, Egypt's world-renowned centers of learning produced such acclaimed scientists as Archimedes and Euclid. The primary areas of study during this classic period were physics, astronomy, geometry, geography, mathematics, philosophy, and medicine. The largest library in the world was at Alexandria. Fragments from the papyrus manuscripts of this library, which burned to the ground, have been invaluable in deciphering ancient manuscripts. After Rome defeated Egypt, however, education declined, and has never regained its former prominence.

Although the Egyptian constitution guarantees five years of free grade school for all children, many poor children receive no education at all. For those who do, qualified teachers are few and classrooms are crowded. One result is that half of Egyptians are illiterate, with the rate of illiteracy higher among women (Cook 2001; Zaalouk 2001). Those who go

Within the Least Industrialized Nations are pockets of high quality schools taught by and for Westerners. This bicycle-powered school bus in Nepal transports children to the English Boarding School.

beyond the five years of grade school attend a preparatory school for three years. High school also lasts for three years. During the first two years, all students take the same courses, but during the third year they specialize in arts, science, or mathematics. All high school students take a monthly examination and a national exam at the end of the senior year.

The Functionalist Perspective: Providing Social Benefits

A central position of functionalism is that when the parts of society are working properly, each contributes to the well-being or stability of that society. The positive things that people intend their actions to accomplish are known as **manifest functions.** The positive consequences they did not intend are called **latent functions.** Let's look at the functions of education.

Teaching Knowledge and Skills

Education's most obvious manifest function is to teach knowledge and skills—whether the traditional three R's or their more contemporary counterparts, such as computer literacy. Each generation must train the next to fulfill the group's significant positions. Because our postindustrial society needs highly educated people, the schools supply them.

Often what counts is not the learning, but the *certification* of learning. Sociologist Randall Collins (1979) observed that we have become a **credential society.** By this, he means that employers use diplomas and degrees as *sorting* devices. For example, they assume that college graduates are responsible people, for presumably they have shown up on time for numerous classes, have turned in scores of assignments, and have demonstrated basic writing and thinking skills. The job skills a position requires can then be grafted onto this foundation, which has been certified by the college.

In some cases, job skills must be mastered before an individual is allowed to do certain work. On-the-job training was once adequate for physicians, engineers, and airline pilots, but with changes in information and technology this is no longer the case. This is precisely why doctors display their credentials so prominently. They stand before you certified by an institution of higher learning, their framed degrees declaring that they have completed rigorous training programs and are licensed to work on your body.

Cultural Transmission of Values

Another manifest function of education is the **cultural transmission** of values, a process by which schools pass a society's core values from one generation to the next. Consequently, schools in a socialist society stress values of socialism, while schools in a capitalist society teach values that support capitalism. U.S. schools, for example, stress respect for private property, individualism, and competition.

Regardless of a country's economic system, loyalty to the state is a cultural value, and schools around the world teach patriotism. U.S. schools teach that the United States is the best country in the world; Russians learn that no country is better than Russia; and French, German, Japanese, and Afghani students all learn the same about their respective countries. Grade school teachers in every country extol the virtues of the society's founders, their struggle for freedom from oppression, and the goodness of the country's basic social institutions.

manifest functions intended beneficial consequences of people's actions

latent functions unintended beneficial consequences of people's actions

credential society the use of diplomas and degrees to determine who is eligible for jobs, even though the diploma or degree may be irrelevant to the actual work

cultural transmission in reference to education, the ways in which schools transmit a society's culture, especially its core values

Social Integration

Schools also bring about *social integration;* that is, they help to mold students into a more cohesive unit. When students salute the flag and sing the national anthem, for example, they become aware of the "greater government," and their sense of national identity grows. One of the best indicators of how education promotes political integration is the millions of immigrants who have attended U.S. schools, learned mainstream ideas and values, and

As this photo makes evident, among the major functions of education is the cultural transmission *of values, such as patriotism and good citizenship. Another function of education, social integration, also is apparent from this photo. These students in Los Angeles are learning that despite their individual identities, they all are Americans.*

given up their earlier national and cultural identities as they became Americans (Violas 1978; Rodriguez 1995; Carper 2000).

This integrative function of education goes far beyond making people similar in their appearance or speech. *To forge a national identity is to stabilize the political system.* If people identify with a society's social institutions and *perceive them as the basis of their welfare,* they have no reason to rebel. This function is especially significant when it comes to the lower social classes, from which most social revolutionaries are drawn. The wealthy already have a vested interest in maintaining the status quo, but to get the lower classes to identify with a social system *as it is* goes a long way toward preserving the system in its current state.

mainstreaming helping people to become part of the mainstream of society

People with disabilities often have found themselves left out of the mainstream of society. To overcome this, U.S. schools have added a new manifest function, **mainstreaming,** or inclusion. This means that schools try to incorporate students with disabilities into

In recent years, social integration, a traditional function of public education, has been extended. In a process called mainstreaming *(also known as* inclusion *by educators), children who used to be sent to special schools now attend regular schools. Shown here is a class in Bergen County, New Jersey.*

regular social activities. As a matter of routine policy, students with disabilities used to be placed in special schools. There, however, they learned to adjust to a specialized world; this left them ill prepared to cope with the dominant world. Educational philosophy then changed to one that encourages or even requires students with disabilities to attend regular schools. For people who cannot walk, wheelchair ramps are provided; for those who cannot hear, "signers" (interpreters who use sign language) may attend classes with them. Most students who are blind attend special schools, as do people with severe learning disabilities. Overall, one half of students with disabilities now attend school in regular classrooms ("State of American Education" 2000).

Gatekeeping

Gatekeeping, or determining which people will enter what occupations, is another function of education. One type of gatekeeping is *credentialing*—using diplomas and degrees to determine who is eligible for a job—which opens the doors of opportunity for some and closes it to others. Gatekeeping is often accomplished by **tracking,** sorting students into different educational programs on the basis of their perceived abilities. Some U.S. high schools funnel students into one of three tracks: general, college prep, or honors. Students on the lowest track are likely to go to work after high school, or to take vocational courses. Those on the highest track usually attend prestigious colleges. Those in between usually attend a local college or regional state university. The impact is lifelong, affecting opportunities for jobs, income, and lifestyle. Although schools have retreated from formal tracking, placing students in "ability groups" serves the same purpose (Lucas 1999; Tach and Farkas 2003).

Gatekeeping sorts people on the basis of merit, said functionalists Talcott Parsons (1940), Kingsley Davis, and Wilbert Moore (1945). They pioneered a view known as **social placement,** arguing that some jobs require few skills and can be performed by people of lesser intelligence. Other jobs, however, such as that of physician, require high intelligence and advanced education. To motivate capable people to postpone gratification and to put up with years of rigorous education, rewards of high income and prestige are held out. Thus, functionalists look on education as a system that, to the benefit of society, sorts people according to their abilities and ambition.

Replacing Family Functions

Over the years, the functions of U.S. schools have expanded, and they now rival some family functions. Child care is an example. Grade schools do double duty as babysitters for parents who both work, or for single mothers in the work force. Day care always has been a latent function of formal education, for it was an unintended consequence of schooling. Now, however, because most families have two wage earners, day care has become a manifest function. Some schools even offer child care both before and after formal classes. Another function schools are performing is giving sex education and birth control advice. This has stirred controversy, for some families resent this function being taken from them. Such disagreements over values have fueled a movement for alternative schooling, a topic discussed in the Down-to-Earth Sociology box on the next page.

Other Functions

Education also fulfills other functions. For example, because most students are unmarried, high schools and colleges serve as *matchmaking* institutions. It is at school that many young people find their future spouses. The sociological significance is that schools funnel people into marriage with mates of similar background, interests, and education. Schools also establish *social networks.* Some adults maintain friendships from high school and college; others develop networks that benefit their careers. Finally, schools also help to *stabilize employment.* To keep millions of young people in school is to keep them out of the labor market, protecting the positions of older workers. Schools also *stabilize society* by keeping these millions off the streets, where they might be marching and protesting in search of unskilled jobs long lost to other nations.

gatekeeping the process by which education opens and closes doors of opportunity; another term for the social placement function of education

tracking the sorting of students into different educational programs on the basis of real or perceived abilities

social placement a function of education—funneling people into a society's various positions

DOWN-TO-EARTH SOCIOLOGY

Home Schooling: The Search for Quality and Values

"YOU'RE DOING WHAT? YOU'RE GOING TO teach your kids at home?" is the typical, incredulous response to parents who decide to home school their children. "How can you teach? You're not trained."

The unspoken question is, "What's wrong with you? Do you want your kids to be dumb and social misfits?"

The home schooling movement was small at first, just a trickle of parents who were dissatisfied with the rigidity of the school bureaucracy, the lax discipline, incompetent teachers, low standards, lack of focus on individual needs, and, in some instances, of hostility to their religion.

The trickle has grown. While not yet a raging river, the number of children who are being taught at home is roughly the size of the public school systems of Los Angeles and Chicago combined. The best estimate is that about 1 million children are being home schooled (Hill 2000; Lines 2000; Stevens 2001).

Home schooling seems to have burst onto the U.S. scene, but, surprisingly, it is not new. In the colonial era, home schooling was the *typical* form of education (Carper 2000). Today's home-schooling movement, which is restoring this earlier pattern, reflects a fascinating shift in U.S. politics. Contemporary home schooling was begun by political and religious liberals in the 1950s and 1960s. Their objection was that the schools were too conservative. Shortly after this, the schools grew more liberal, and in the 1970s and 1980s, political and religious conservatives embraced home schooling (Lines 2000; Stevens 2001).

Does home schooling work? Can parents who are not trained as teachers actually teach? The early results of testing

These children in Evanston, Illinois, are being home schooled by their mother. The text reports the surprising results of home schooling.

home schoolers were promising, but they were limited to small groups or to single states. Then in 1990, a national sample of 2,000 home schoolers showed that these students did better than students who were in public schools. Could this really be true?

To find out, researchers tested 21,000 home schoolers across the nation (Rudner 1999). The results are astounding. The median scores for every test at every grade were in the 70th to 80th percentiles. The home schoolers outscored both public and Catholic school students.

The basic reason for the stunning success of home schooling appears to be the parents' involvement in their children's education. Home schoolers receive an intense, one-on-one education. Their curriculum—although it includes the basics that are required by the state—is designed around the student's interests and needs. Ninety percent of students are taught primarily by their mothers, 10 percent by their fathers (Lines 2000). Ninety-eight percent of the fathers are in the labor force, but only 22 percent of the mothers. The parents' income is also above average.

What about the children's socialization? Do home-schooled kids become social misfits? The studies show that they do just fine on this level, too. They actually have fewer behavior problems than children who attend conventional schools (Lines 2000). Home-schooled children are not isolated. As part of their educational experience, their parents take them to libraries, museums, factories, and nursing homes (Medlin 2000). For social activities, many of the children meet with other children who are being home schooled. Home-schooling associations also run conferences for parents and children and even hold sporting events.

What we do not know, of course, is what these home schoolers' test scores would have been if they had been taught in public schools. With their parents' concern and involvement in their education, they likely would have done very well there, too. Finally, although the Rudner study was large, about 21,000 students, it was not a random sample, and we cannot say how the *average* home schooler is doing. But, then, we have no random sample of all public school students, either.

For Your CONSIDERATION

Why do you think home schooling is turning out to be so successful? At current rates of growth, it won't be long before 2 million U.S. children are being taught at home. Do you think this movement may eventually become a threat to U.S. public schools? Would you like to have been home schooled? Would you consider home schooling your children?

Another function of schools is to provide employment. With 53 million students in grade and high schools, and another 15 million enrolled in college, U.S. education is big business. Primary and secondary schools provide jobs for 2.9 million teachers, while another million teach in colleges and universities (*Statistical Abstract* 2002:Tables 200, 239, 257). Millions more work as support personnel—aides, administrators, bus drivers, janitors, and secretaries. Another several million earn their living in industries that service schools—from building schools to manufacturing pencils, paper, desks, and computers.

The Conflict Perspective: Reproducing the Social Class Structure

Unlike functionalists, who look at the benefits of education, conflict theorists examine how education helps the elite to maintain their dominance. They stress that *education reproduces the social class structure.* By this, they mean that education perpetuates a society's social divisions. For example, regardless of abilities, the more well-to-do children are likely to take college preparatory courses and the poor, vocational courses. Both inherit the corresponding life opportunities laid down before they were born.

Let's look, then, at how education reproduces the social class structure.

The Hidden Curriculum

The term **hidden curriculum** refers to the unwritten rules of behavior and attitudes that schools teach in addition to the formal curriculum. Examples are obedience to authority and conformity to mainstream norms. Conflict theorists note how the hidden curriculum helps to perpetuate social inequalities.

To understand this central point, consider the way English is taught. Middle-class schools—whose teachers know where their students are headed—stress "proper" English and "good" manners. In contrast, the teachers in inner-city schools—who also know where *their* students are headed—allow ethnic and street language in the classroom. Each is helping to reproduce the social class structure. That is, each is preparing students to work in positions similar to those of their parents. The social class of some children destines them for higher positions. For these, they need "refined" speech and manners. The social destiny of others is closely supervised, low-status jobs. For these, they need only to obey rules (Bowles and Gintis 1976; 2002). Teaching these students "refined" speech and manners would be needless effort.

From the conflict perspective, even kindergarten has a hidden curriculum, as the Down-to-Earth Sociology box on the next page illustrates.

Conflict theorists stress that education reproduces a country's social class system. To support this position, they point out that the U.S. social classes attend separate schools, where they are taught by teachers of different backgrounds, and where they learn perspectives of the world that match their place in it. Shown here are students lunching with their teacher at St. Alban's School in Washington, D.C.

hidden curriculum the unwritten goals of schools, such as teaching obedience to authority and conformity to cultural norms

DOWN-TO-EARTH SOCIOLOGY

Kindergarten as Boot Camp

AFTER HE DID PARTICIPANT OBSERvation in a kindergarten, sociologist Harry Gracey (2003) concluded that kindergarten is a sort of boot camp for education. Here, tender students from diverse backgrounds are molded into a compliant group that will, on command, follow classroom routines. "Show and tell," for example, does more than allow children to be expressive. It also teaches them to talk only when they are asked to speak. ("It's your turn, Jarmay.") The format also teaches children to request permission to talk ("Who knows what Adela has?") by raising a hand and being acknowledged. This ritual also teaches children to acknowledge the teacher's ideas as superior. She is the one who has the capacity to evaluate students' activities and ideas.

Gracey found a *hidden curriculum* in the other activities he observed. Whether students were drawing pictures, listening to records, eating snacks, or resting, the teachers would scold talkative students and give approval to those who conformed. In short, the children received the message that the teacher—and, by inference, the entire school system—is the authority.

This, Gracey concluded, is not a side issue—it is *the* purpose of kindergarten. The kindergarten teacher's job is to teach children to "follow orders with unquestioning obedience." It is to "create and enforce a rigid social structure in the classroom through which they effectively control the behavior of most of the children for most of the school day."

This produces three kinds of students: (1) "good" students, those who submit to school-imposed discipline and come to identify with it; (2) "adequate" students, those who submit to the school's discipline but do not identify with it; and (3) "bad" students, those who refuse to submit to school routines. Children in the third category are called "problem children." To bring them into line, a tougher drill sergeant—the school psychologist—is called in. If that doesn't work, the problem children are drugged into docility with Ritalin.

These early lessons extend beyond the classroom. As Gracey notes, school serves as a boot camp to prepare students for the routines of the work world, both on the assembly line and at the office. It helps turn children into docile workers who follow the routines imposed by "the company."

Tilting the Tests: Discrimination by IQ

Even intelligence tests play a part in keeping the social class system intact. For example, how would you answer the following question?

A symphony is to a composer as a book is to a(n)__

___ *paper* ___ *sculptor* ___ *musician* ___ *author* ___ *man*

You probably had no difficulty coming up with "author" as your choice. Wouldn't any intelligent person have done so?

In point of fact, this question raises a central issue in intelligence testing. Not all intelligent people would know the answer. This question contains *cultural biases.* Children from some backgrounds are more familiar with the concepts of symphonies, composers, and sculptors than are other children. Consequently, the test is tilted in their favor (Turner 1972; Ashe 1992).

Perhaps asking a different question will make the bias clearer. How would you answer this question?

If you throw dice and "7" is showing on the top, what is facing down?

___ *seven* ___ *snake eyes* ___ *box cars* ___ *little Joes* ___ *eleven*

This question, suggested by Adrian Dove (n.d.), a social worker in Watts, is slanted toward a lower-class experience. It surely is obvious that this *particular* cultural bias tilts the test so that children from some social backgrounds will perform better than others.

It is no different with IQ (intelligence quotient) tests that use such words as *composer* and *symphony.* A lower-class child may have heard about rap, rock, hip hop, or jazz but not about symphonies. In other words, IQ tests measure not only intelligence but also culturally acquired knowledge. Whatever else we can say, the cultural bias built into the IQ tests used in schools is clearly *not* tilted in favor of the lower classes. One consequence is that minorities and the poor, who score lower on these tests, are assigned to less demanding courses to "match" their intelligence (Weiler 1998; Lucas 1999). This destines them for lower-paying jobs in adult life. Thus, conflict theorists view IQ tests as another weapon in an arsenal designed to maintain the social class structure across the generations.

Stacking the Deck: Unequal Funding

To see how funding for education differs by geography, look at the Social Map on this page. You can see that where students live is significant in determining how much is spent on their education. Conflict theorists go beyond this observation, however. They stress that in *all* states the deck is stacked against the poor. Because public schools are largely supported by local property taxes, the richer communities (where property values are higher) have more to spend on their children. The poorer communities end up with much less. Consequently, the richer communities can offer higher salaries and take their pick of the most highly qualified and motivated teachers. They can also afford to buy the latest textbooks, computers, and software, as well as offer courses in foreign language, music, and the arts.

Because U.S. schools reflect the U.S. social class system, the children of the privileged emerge from grade school best equipped for success in high school. In turn, they come out of high school best equipped for success in college. They have been given the tools to maintain their dominance. The children of the poor are blown away in this competition, much as a one-legged runner would be in a race against Marion Jones.

Figure 17.4 The Unequal Funding of Education

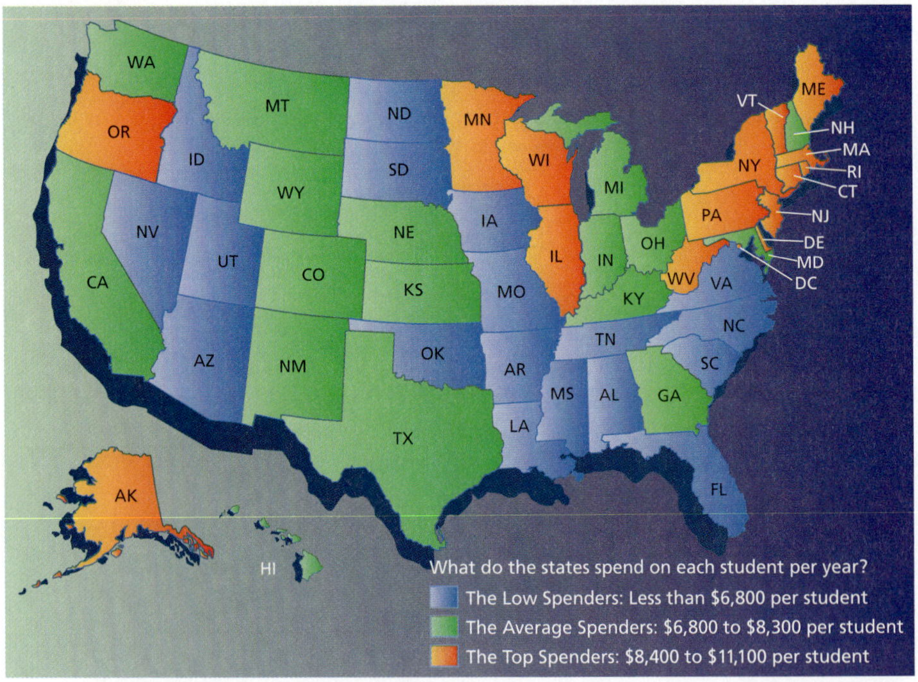

Note: Some states spend more than twice as much on their students. The range is from $4,459 in North Dakota to $11,089 in New York. At $13,525 the District of Columbia is in a class by itself.
Source: By the author. Based on *Statistical Abstract* 2002:Table 235.

In short, because education's doors of opportunity swing wide open for some but have to be pried open by others, conflict theorists say that the educational system reproduces (or perpetuates) the social class structure. In fact, they add, this is one of its primary purposes.

correspondence principle the sociological principle that schools correspond to (or reflect) the social structure of their society

The Correspondence Principle

In a classic analysis, conflict sociologists Samuel Bowles and Herbert Gintis (1976) used the term **correspondence principle** to refer to how schools reflect society. This term means that what is taught in a nation's schools *corresponds* to the characteristics of that society. The following list provides some examples.

Characteristics of Society	Characteristics of Schools
1. Capitalism	1. Promote competition
2. Social inequality	2. Provide unequal funding of schools
3. Racial-ethnic prejudice	3. Funnel minorities into job training programs that demand little intellect
4. Bureaucratic structure of corporations	4. Provide a model of authority in the classroom
5. Need for submissive workers	5. Make students submissive, as in the kindergarten boot camp
6. Need for dependable workers	6. Enforce punctuality in attendance and homework
7. Need to maintain armed forces	7. Promote patriotism (to fight for capitalism)

Thus, conclude conflict theorists, the U.S. educational system is designed to turn most students into dependable workers who will not question their bosses. It also is intended to produce some innovators in thought and action, but who can still be counted on to be loyal to the social system as it exists (Olneck and Bills 1980).

The Bottom Line: Family Background and the Educational System

The end result of unequal funding, IQ tests, and so on is this: Family background is more important than test scores in predicting who attends college. Back in 1977, sociologist Samuel Bowles compared the college attendance of the brightest 25 percent of high school students with the intellectually weakest 25 percent. Figure 17.5 shows the results. Of the *brightest* 25 percent of high school students, 90 percent of those from affluent homes went to college, while only half of those from low-income homes did. Of the *intellectually weakest* students, 26 percent from affluent homes went to college, while only 6 percent from poorer homes did so. Other sociologists, both in the United States and England, have confirmed this: If you rank families from the poorest to the richest, as the family's income increases so does the likelihood that their children will attend college (Manski 1992–1993; Reay et al. 2001). Similarly, sociologist Dalton Conley (2001) found that the wealthier a family is, the more years of schooling their children complete.

Figure 17.5 Who Goes to College? Comparing Social Class and Personal Ability in Determining College Attendance

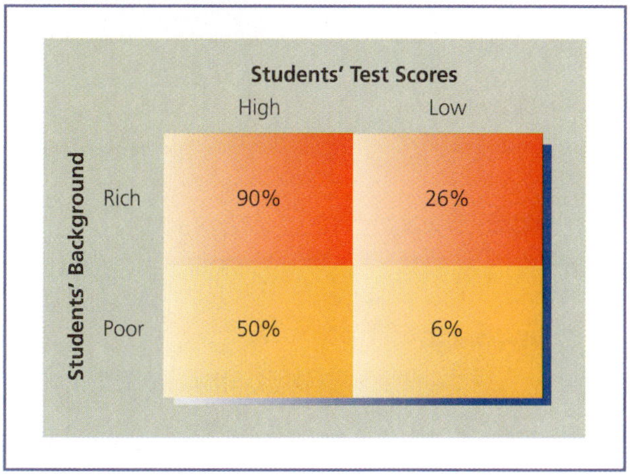

Source: Bowles 1977.

Conflict theorists point out that the educational system reproduces not only the U.S. social class structure, but also its divisions of race and ethnicity. From Figure 17.6, you can see that, compared with whites, African Americans and Latinos are less likely to complete high school and less likely to go to college. The difference is the greatest for Latinos. Because those without college degrees are more likely to end up with low-paying, dead-end jobs, you can see how this supports the

Figure 17.6 The Funneling Effects of Education: Race and Ethnicity

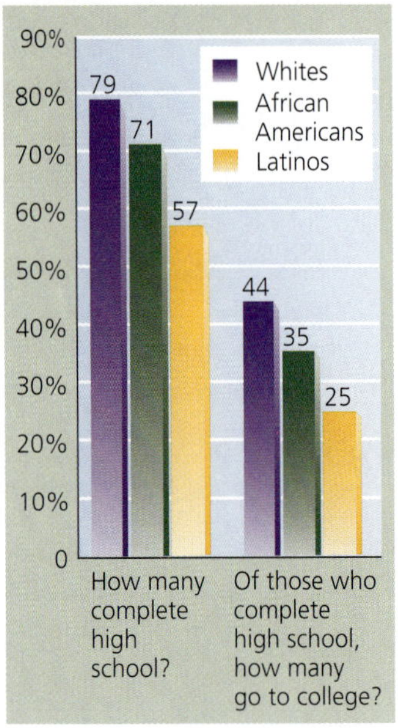

Note: The source gives totals only for these three groups.
Source: By the author. Based on *Statistical Abstract* 2002:Table 252.

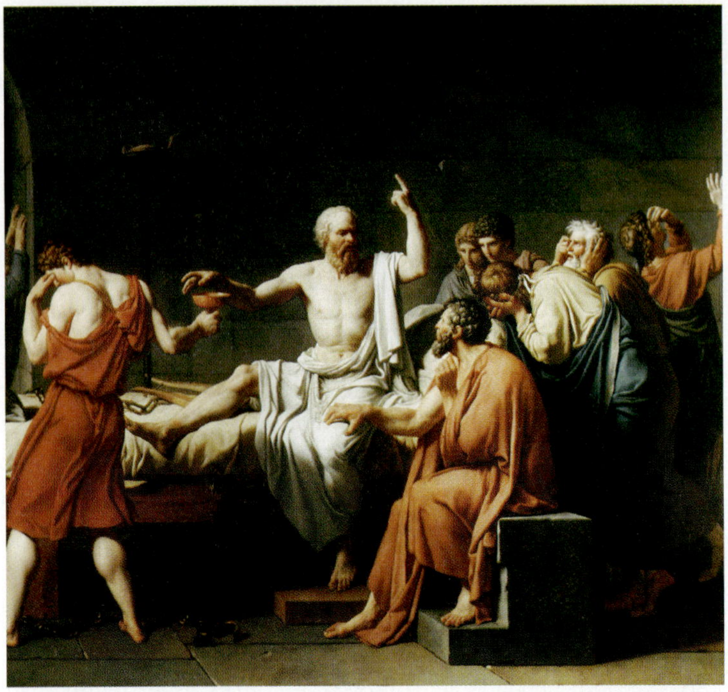

Education can be a dangerous thing. Socrates, who taught in Greece about 400 years before the birth of Christ, was forced to take poison because his views challenged those of the establishment. Usually, however, educators reinforce the perspectives of the elite, teaching students to take their place within the social structure. This 1787 painting of Socrates was done by Jacques Louis David.

conflict view—how education is helping to reproduce the racial-ethnic structure for the next generation.

As you know, the type of college you attend is also important. As Table 17.1 shows, of those who attend college, there isn't much difference in the percentage of whites, African Americans, and Asian Americans who go to four-year private colleges. These totals show growing equality and do not support the conflict view. But look at how much less likely Latinos and Native Americans are to attend private four-year colleges. Coupled with their being less likely to attend college in the first place, you can see how this will help to perpetuate society's racial-ethnic divisions.

Table 17.1 Of Those Who Go to College, What Percentage Attends Each Type of College?

Racial-Ethnic Group	Public College	Private College	2-Year College	4-Year College
Whites	76%	24%	36%	64%
African Americans	76%	24%	41%	59%
Asian Americans	79%	21%	39%	61%
Latinos	83%	17%	56%	44%
Native Americans	85%	15%	50%	50%

Source: Statistical Abstract 2002:Table 258.

IN SUM

Conflict theorists stress that a major purpose of the educational system is to *reproduce social inequality,* to help keep the social class structure intact from one generation to the next. A variety of techniques funnel the children of the poor into community college job training programs and the children of the middle class into state universities and small private colleges. The children of the elite, in contrast, are funneled into exclusive boarding high schools, where they are taught in small classes by well-paid teachers (Persell et al. 1992; Powell 1996). The social networks that these privileged children inherit come with admissions officers who have connections with the nation's most elite colleges. Some of these networks are so efficient that *half* of the graduating classes of these private schools are admitted to Ivy League universities (Persell and Cookson 1986; Golden 2003).

The Symbolic Interactionist Perspective: Fulfilling Teacher Expectations

Functionalists look at how education benefits society, and conflict theorists examine how education perpetuates social inequality. Symbolic interactionists, in contrast, study face-to-face interaction in the classroom. They have found that the expectations of teachers have profound consequences for their students.

The Rist Research

Why do some people get tracked into college prep courses and others into vocational ones? There is no single answer, but in what has become a classic study, sociologist Ray Rist came up with some intriguing findings. Rist (1970) did participant observation in an African American grade school with an African American faculty. He found that after only eight days in the classroom, the kindergarten teacher felt that she knew the children's abilities well enough to assign them to three separate worktables. To Table 1, Mrs. Caplow assigned those she considered to be "fast learners." They sat at the front of the room, closest to her. Those whom she saw as "slow learners," she assigned to Table 3, located at the back of the classroom. She placed "average" students at Table 2, in between the other tables.

This seemed strange to Rist. He knew that the children had not been tested for ability, yet their teacher was certain that she could identify the bright and slow children. Investigating further, Rist found that social class was the underlying basis for assigning the children to the different tables. Middle-class students were separated out for Table 1, children from poorer homes to Tables 2 and 3. The teacher paid the most attention to the children at Table 1, who were closest to her, less to Table 2, and the least to Table 3. As the year went on, children from Table 1 perceived that they were treated better and came to see themselves as smarter. They became the leaders in class activities and even ridiculed children at the other tables, calling them "dumb." Eventually, the children at Table 3 disengaged themselves from many classroom activities. At the end of the year, only the children at Table 1 had completed the lessons that prepared them for reading.

This early tracking stuck. Their first-grade teacher looked at the work they had accomplished and placed students from Table 1 at her Table 1. She treated her tables much as the kindergarten teacher had, and the children at Table 1 again led the class.

The children's reputations continued to follow them. The second-grade teacher reviewed their scores and also divided her class into three groups. The first she named the "Tigers" and, befitting their name, gave them challenging readers. Not surprisingly, the Tigers came from the original Table 1 in kindergarten. The second group she called the "Cardinals." They came from the original Tables 2 and 3. Her third group consisted of children she had failed the previous year, whom she called the "Clowns." The Cardinals and Clowns were given less advanced readers.

Rist concluded that *each child's journey through school was determined by the eighth day of kindergarten!* This research, as with that done on the Saints and Roughnecks (reported in Chapter 4), demonstrates the power of labels. They can set people on courses of action that affect the rest of their lives.

What occurred was a **self-fulfilling prophecy.** This term, coined by sociologist Robert Merton (1949), refers to a false assumption of something that is going to happen but which then comes true simply because it was predicted. For example, if people believe an unfounded rumor that a bank is going to fail, they all rush to the bank to demand their money. The prediction—although originally false—is now likely to come true.

The Rosenthal-Jacobson Experiment

All of us know about teacher expectations—that some teachers have higher standards and expect work of a higher quality. Teacher expectations, however, also work at a subtle level. In what has become a classic experiment, social psychologists Robert Rosenthal and Lenore Jacobson (1968) tried out a new test in a San Francisco grade school. They tested the children's abilities and then told the teachers which students would probably "spurt" ahead during the year. They instructed the teachers to watch these students' progress, but not to let the students or their parents know about the test results. At the end of the year, they tested the students again and found that the IQs of the predicted "spurters" had jumped ten to fifteen points higher than those of the other children.

You might think that Rosenthal and Jacobson became famous for developing such a powerful scholastic aptitude test. Actually, their "test" was another of those covert experiments. Rosenthal and Jacobson had simply given routine IQ tests to the children and had then *randomly* chosen 20 percent of the students as "spurters." These students were *no* different from the others in the classroom. A self-fulfilling prophecy had taken place: The teachers expected more from those particular students, and the students responded. In short, expect dumb and you get dumb. Expect smart, and you get smart.

Although attempts to replicate this experiment have had mixed results (Pilling and Pringle 1978), a good deal of research confirms that, *regardless of their ability,* students who are expected to do better generally do so, and those who are expected to do poorly, do so (Snyder 1993; McKown and Weinstein 2002).

How Do Teacher Expectations Work?

Sociologist George Farkas (1990a, 1990b, 1996) became interested in how teacher expectations affect grades. Using a stratified sample of students in a large school district in Texas, he found that *even though they had the same test scores,* girls averaged higher course grades than did boys. Asian Americans also received higher grades than did African Americans, Latinos, and whites who had the same test scores.

At first, this may sound like more of the same old news—another case of discrimination. But this explanation doesn't fit, which is what makes the finding fascinating. Look who the victims are. It is most unlikely that the teachers would be prejudiced against boys and whites. To interpret these unexpected results, Farkas used symbolic interactionism. He observed that some students "signal" to their teachers that they are "good students." They show an eagerness to cooperate, and they quickly agree with what the teacher says. They also show that they are "trying hard." The teachers pick up these signals and reward these "good students" with better grades. Girls and Asian Americans, the researcher concludes, are better at displaying these characteristics so coveted by teachers.

We do not have enough information on how teachers form their expectations or how they communicate them to students. Nor do we know much about how students "signal" messages to teachers. Perhaps you will become the educational sociologist who will shed more light on this significant area of human behavior.

The Sociology and New Technology box on the next page discusses how technology is producing new forms of "signaling" and of student-teacher interaction.

self-fulfilling prophecy
Robert Merton's term for an originally false assertion that becomes true simply because it was predicted

sociology and the NEW technology

Internet University: No Walls, No Ivy, No All Night Parties

Distance learning, courses taught to students who are not physically present with their instructor, is not new. For decades, we have had correspondence courses. Today, however, telecommunications have transformed distance learning. Satellites, computers, video conferencing, and streaming video are making cyber colleges part of mainstream education. Using video links, students are able to watch the professor on their screen. Clicking a little icon, they can "raise their hands" to ask questions. Eventually, computer-mounted cameras may allow everyone in the class to see everyone else simultaneously. Spider-web diagrams let the instructor know who is e-mailing others—and who is holding back. Tucked deeper in the software is a program to allow deans (supervisors) to scrutinize the instructors. The deans will get reports, for example, that let them know how long it takes instructors to answer e-mail from students.

Distance learning offers tremendous potential for increasing cultural diversity,

to the benefit of both students and professors. It is possible to enjoy a stimulating international experience without ever leaving the country. For example, sociology professors at the State University of New York and the State University of Belarus (Minsk, Russia) jointly taught an online course on Social Control. With their political experiences so different from one another, the American and Russian students found that the course opened their eyes to different realities (Beaman 2003).

Why should formal education be limited to walled classrooms? Think of the possibilities of the Net. We could study human culture and compare notes on eating, dating, or burial customs with fellow students in Thailand, Iceland, South Africa, Germany, Egypt, China, and Australia. We could write a joint paper in which we compare our experiences with one another, within the context of theories taught in the text, and then submit our paper to our mutual instructor.

Will we eventually go from kindergarten to grad school with classmates from around the world? While this may sound intriguing, no walls also means no joking in the hallway or dorm, no flirting after class, no getting together over a cup of coffee. . . .

A different view of distance learning is presented in the Sociology and the New Technology box on the next page.

Problems in U.S. Education—and Their Solutions

To conclude this chapter, let's examine two problems facing U.S. education—and consider their potential solutions.

Problems: Mediocrity and Violence

The Rising Tide of Mediocrity All Arizona high school sophomores took a math test. It covered the math that sophomores should know. Seven of eight failed it. Meanwhile, in New York, to get its students to graduate, the state had to drop its passing sociology and the NEW technology

Capitalism and Distance Learning: Marketing Education in Cyberspace

Always eager for profits and looking for new areas for investment, capitalists saw the potential of advanced communications technology for education. For them, distance learning was a perfect answer. The potential for profit is huge, as distance learning requires little infrastructure—no classrooms, desks, blackboards, or parking lots. In addition, once developed, the course can be repackaged and sold over and over again. Capitalists also want expanding markets, and with the demand for education increasing around the world, distance learning supplied this, too. In many ways, distance learning is a capitalist's dream.

As stressed in this text, one of the main social changes that is enveloping us all is the globalization of capitalism. Distance learning has become part of this fundamental transformation of our world. With the United States being the world's leading capitalist country, it was only natural that U.S. universities would lead the charge, cobble together degrees in cyberspace, and sell them around the world.

But to attract the best-paying customers, marketers need to sell name brands. University of Phoenix—what is that? The name of a bird? A town in Arizona? Is a degree from this virtual school worth anything? The name Cardean University has the same problem.

How then could the marketers get brand names into the virtual market? The promoters of Cardean University, which exists only in cyberspace, hit upon an ingenious solution. Brand name universities were hesitant to venture into this unknown territory as it might sully their ivied reputations. But joining together, they could spread the risk. Stanford, Columbia, Carnegie Mellon, and the University of Chicago decided to participate in offering a joint degree online. The promoters of Cardean were overjoyed, for they could market a degree associated with these hallowed names. And what is more natural for educational capitalists to sell than a masters in business, which is just what their package of courses offers (Pohl 2003)?

It's a global market, and we are still on the frontiers of the Wild West. The new educational capitalists have accurately grasped this, and they envision a student body of *millions* of people around the world. Think of the vast numbers of people in Asia and Africa who don't have access to universities. Of course, most of them don't have any money either—but the children of the elite do. So do the children of the *nouveau riche.* Admittedly, the $24,000 for the Cardean M.B.A. (Pohl 2003) is a bit steep for most of the market, but it is still much less than the $100,000 it costs to get an online M.B.A. from Duke University (Forelle 2003).

grade to 55 out of 100 (Steinberg 2000). Some New York City schools are so bad that officials have given up and turned them over to private, for-profit companies (Wyatt 2000). When test results showed that 1,500 of Michigan's high schools "needed improvement," officials lowered the percentage needed to pass. Overnight, only 200 schools "needed improvement" (Dillon 2003). Perhaps nothing so captures what is wrong with U.S. schools than this event, reported by sociologist Thomas Sowell (1993b):

> [A]n international study of 13-year-olds . . . found that Koreans ranked first in mathematics and Americans last. When asked if they thought they were "good at mathematics," only 23 percent of the Korean youngsters said "yes"—compared to 68 percent of American 13-year-olds. The American educational dogma that students should "feel good about themselves" was a success in its own terms—though not in any other terms.

Figure 17.7, which summarizes the scores on the Scholastic Assessment Test (SAT), indicates how sharply student achievement declined from the 1960s to 1980. At that point, educators—and even Congress—expressed concern and demanded greater accountability. Schools raised their standards, and math scores started to climb. The recovery has been excellent, and, as you can see, today's high school seniors now score higher than seniors did in the 1960s. The verbal scores, however, have not recovered.

Why the SAT scores declined has been a controversy. The president of the American Federation of Teachers said that the lower test scores meant that teachers were doing a *better* job! They were getting more students to stay in high school and to go on to college. Students from poorer academic backgrounds, who used to drop out of high school, had become part of the test results (Sowell 1993b). Perhaps this was the reason. But if so, it did not indicate success, but a severe underlying problem—teachers giving inferior education to disadvantaged students.

Now that the math scores have recovered, we can look to better teaching as the answer. Administrators are requiring more of teachers, and teachers are requiring more of students. Each is performing according to the higher expectations.

Figure 17.7 National Results of the Scolastic Assessment Test (SAT)

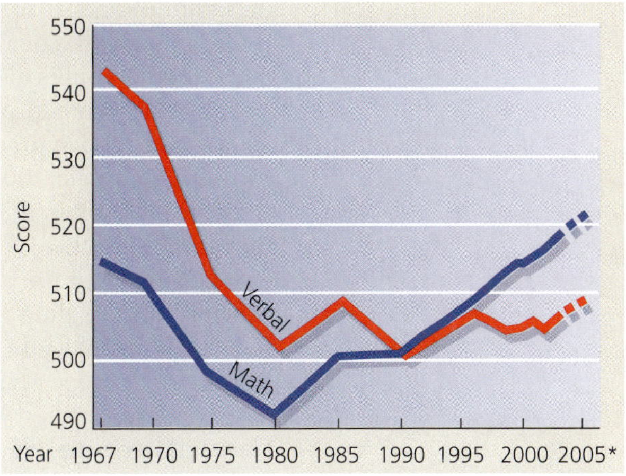

Note: Broken lines indicate the author's estimate.
Source: By the author. Based on *Statistical Abstract* 2002; Table 244; "SAT Scores . . ." 2003.

How about the lower verbal scores? They may have declined because children read less and watch more television and play more video games (Rigdon and Swasy 1990). Students who read little acquire a smaller vocabulary and less rigor in thought and verbal expression. The "Dummied down" textbooks that require little thought certainly haven't helped (Hayes and Wolfer 1993). Nor have lowered teacher expectations—less homework, fewer term papers, grade inflation. Then, too, there are the burned-out teachers who are more interested in collecting paychecks than in educating their students.

How to Cheat on the SATs If you receive poor grades this semester, wouldn't you like to use a magic marker to, presto!, change them into higher grades? I suppose every student would. Now imagine that you had that power. Would you use it?

Some people in authority apparently have found such a magic marker, and they are using it to raise our low national SAT scores. Table 274 of the 1996 edition of the *Statistical Abstract of the United States* reports that in 1995 only 8.3 percent of students earned 600 or more on the verbal portion of the SAT test. The very next edition, in 1997, however, holds a pleasant surprise. Table 276 tells us that it was really 21.9 percent of students who scored 600 or higher in 1995. Later editions of this source retain the higher figure. What a magic marker!

In the twinkle of an eye, we get another bonus. Somehow, between 1996 and 1997 the scores of *everyone* who took the test in previous years improved. Now that's the kind of power we all would like to have. Students, grab your report cards. Workers, change those numbers on your paycheck.

It certainly is easier to give simpler tests than to do better teaching. And this is what has happened to the SAT. The test is now shorter and students have more time to answer fewer questions. To make the verbal part easier, the test on antonyms was dropped (Manno 1995; Stecklow 1995). Results of previous years were then "rescored" to match the easier test. And even with these measures, the national verbal scores remain low.

This "dummying down" of the SAT is yet another form of grade inflation, the topic to which we shall now turn.

Grade Inflation, Social Promotion, and Functional Illiteracy

High school teachers used to be stingy with their *A*'s, reserving them for outstanding performance, but now they give more *A*'s than *C*'s. Since grades went up while learning went down, some of today's *A*'s are the *C*'s of years past. Another sign of **grade inflation** is that *44 percent* of all college freshmen have an overall high school grade point average of A. *Ninety-four percent* have at least a B average (*Statistical Abstract* 2002:Table 264).

Grade inflation has also hit the Ivy League. At Harvard University, *half* of the course grades are *A*'s and *A–*'s. *Ninety percent* of Harvard students graduate with honors. To rein in the "honor inflation," the Harvard faculty voted to limit the number of students who graduate with honors to 60 percent of a class (Hartocollis 2002). To match his colleagues' grading, one Harvard professor gives an official, inflated grade for the student's transcript—and then in private gives a grade that reflects his true evaluation of the student's learning (Mansfield 2001).

Grade inflation in the face of declining standards has been accompanied by **social promotion**, the practice of passing students from one grade to the next even though they have not mastered the basic materials. One result is **functional illiteracy**, people having difficulty with reading and writing even though they have graduated from high school. Some high school graduates cannot fill out job applications; others can't figure out if they get the right change at the grocery store.

The Influence of Peer Groups Two psychologists and a sociologist, who studied 20,000 high school students in California and Wisconsin, found that the peer group is the most important factor on how teenagers do in school (Steinberg et al. 1996). Simply put: Those who hang out with good students tend to do well; those who hang out with friends who do poorly in school do poorly themselves. Student subcultures include informal norms about grades. Some groups have norms of classroom excellence, while others sneer at getting good grades. The applied question that arises from this research, of course, is how to build educational achievement into student culture.

Violence in Schools Some U.S. schools have deteriorated to the point that safety is an issue (Cantor and Wright 2003). To get into some schools, students must pass through metal detectors, and uniformed guards have become a permanent fixture. Some grade schools even supplement their traditional fire drills with "drive-by shooting drills" (Toch 1993; Grossman 1995).

And what about school shootings, such as the event with which we opened this chapter? For a surprising analysis, read the Mass Media box on the next page.

Solutions: Safety, Standards, and Other Reforms

It is one thing to identify problems, and quite another to find solutions for them. Let's consider some solutions to the problems we just reviewed.

A Secure Learning Environment The first step in offering a good education is to make students safe and free from fear. With the high rate of violence in U.S. society, we can expect some violence to spill over into the schools. To minimize that spillover, school administrators can expel all students who threaten the welfare of others. They also can refuse to tolerate threats, violence, and weapons. The zero tolerance policy for guns and other weapons on school property that school boards and adminsitrators have adopted helped to make schools safer.

Higher Standards Within a secure learning environment, then, we can take steps to improve the quality of education. To offer a quality education, we need quality teachers. Don't we already have them? Most teachers are qualified, and if motivated, can do an excellent job. But a large number of teachers are not qualified. Consider just a couple of items. California requires that its teachers pass an educational skills test. California's teachers did so poorly that to get enough teachers to fill their classrooms officials had to drop the passing grade to the 10th grade level. For fifteen of our states, teachers need to be able to read only at the lowest quarter of the national average (Schemo 2002). I don't know about you, but it would seem that this situation is appalling, that it should make

grade inflation higher grades given for the same work; a general rise in student grades without a corresponding increase in learning

social promotion passing students on to the next grade even though they have not mastered basic materials

functional illiterate a high school graduate who has difficulty with basic reading and math

massMEDIA in Social Life

School Shootings: Exploring a Myth

The media sprinkle their reports of school shootings with such dramatic phrases as "alarming proportions," "outbreak of violence," and "out of control." They give us the impression that schools all over the nation are set to erupt in gunfire. The public views the shootings as convincing evidence that something is seriously wrong with society. Parents used to consider schools safe havens, but no longer. Those naïve thoughts have been shattered by the bullets that have sprayed our schools—or at least by the media's portrayal of growing danger and violence in our schools.

Have our schools really become war zones, as the mass media would have us believe? Certainly events such as those at Columbine High School portrayed in this chapter's opening vignette are disturbing, but we need to probe deeper than newspaper headlines and televised images in order to understand their social significance.

When we do, we find that the media's sensationalist reporting has created a myth. Contrary to "what everyone knows," *there is no trend toward greater school violence.* In fact, the situation is just the opposite—*the trend is toward greater safety.* Despite the dramatic school shootings that make headlines, as Table 17.2 shows, shooting deaths at schools are decreasing.

This picture was taken when Drew Golden was 6 years old. Five years later, when Drew was 11, he teamed up with 13-year-old Mitch Johnson. Together, they ambushed their middle school teachers and classmates in Jonesboro, Arkansas. They wounded nine students and one teacher and killed four girls and one teacher.

Table 17.2 Exploding a Myth: Deaths at U.S. Schools[a]

School Year	Shooting Deaths	Other Homicides[b]	Deaths by Gender		Total
			Boys	Girls	
1992–1993	45	11	49	7	56
1993–1994	41	12	41	12	53
1994–1995	16	5	18	3	21
1995–1996	29	7	26	10	36
1996–1997	15	11	18	8	26
1997–1998	36	8	27	17	44
1998–1999	25	6	24	7	31
1999–2000	16	16	26	6	32
2000–2001	18	4	18	4	22
2001–2002	3	1	4	0	4
2002–2003	5	1	5	1	6
Mean, 1992–2003	22.6	7.5	23.3	6.8	30.1

[a]Includes all school-related homicides, even those that occurred on the way to or from school; includes suicides; includes school personnel killed at school by other adults; includes adults who had nothing to do with the school but who were found dead on school property.

[b]Beating, hanging, jumping, stabbing, and strangling.

Source: National School Safety Center, 2003.

This is not to say that school shootings are not a serious problem. Even one student being wounded or killed is too many. But, contrary to the impression fostered by the media, we are seeing a decrease of school shooting deaths.

This is why we need sociology: to quietly, dispassionately search for facts so we can better understand the events that shape our lives. The first requirement for solving any problem is accurate data, for we do not want to create solutions based on hysteria. The information presented in this box may not make for sensational headlines, but it does serve to explode the myth that the media have created.

national headlines and be considered a national disgrace. If we want to improve teaching, we need to insist that teachers meet high standards.

Our schools compete with private industry for the same pool of college graduates. If the starting salary in other fields is higher than it is in education, those fields will attract

Figure 17.8 Starting Salaries of U.S. College Graduates: Public School Teachers Compared with Private Industry

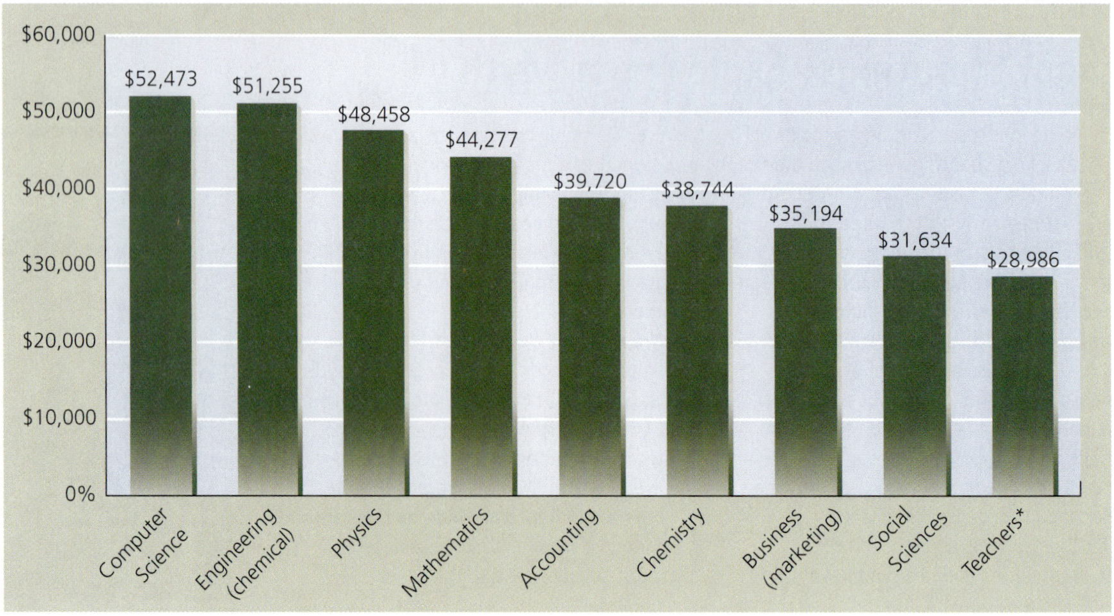

Sources: By the author. Based on *Statistical Abstract* 2002:Table 275; "Survey and . . ." 2003.

brighter, more energetic graduates. Figure 17.8 above highlights the abysmal job we are doing in this competition.

What else can we do to improve the quality of education? A study by sociologists James Coleman and Thomas Hoffer (1987) provides helpful guidelines. They wanted to see why the test scores of students in Roman Catholic schools average 15 to 20 percent higher than those of students in public schools. Is it because Catholic schools attract better students, while public schools have to put up with everyone? To find out, Coleman and Hoffer tested 15,000 students in public and Catholic high schools.

Their findings? From the sophomore through the senior years, students at Catholic schools pull ahead of public school students by a full grade in verbal and math skills. The superior test performance of students in Catholic schools, they concluded, is due not to better students, but to higher standards. Catholic schools have not watered down their curricula as have public schools. The researchers also underscored the importance of parental involvement. Parents and teachers in Catholic schools reinforce each other's commitment to learning.

These findings support the basic principle reviewed earlier about teacher expectations: Students perform better when they are expected to meet higher standards. To this, you might want to reply, "Of course. I knew that. Who wouldn't?" Somehow, however, this basic principle is lost on many teachers, who end up teaching at a low level because they expect little of their students and have supervisors who accept low student performance. The reason, actually, is probably not their lack of awareness of such basics, but, rather, the organization that entraps them, a bureaucracy in which ritual replaces performance. To understand this point better, you may wish to review Chapter 7.

On average, students in Roman Catholic schools score higher on national tests than students in public schools. Is it because Roman Catholic schools have better students, or because they do better teaching? The text reports the sociological findings.

If we raise standards, we can expect protest. It is less upsetting to let standards slip and to tell all students they are doing well than it is to require rigorous teaching and learning. When Florida decided to require its high school seniors to pass an assessment test in order to receive a diploma, 13,000 students failed the test. Parents banded together in protest—not to demand better teaching but to put economic pressure on the state to drop the new test. They asked people to boycott Disney World and to not buy Florida orange juice (Canedy 2003).

Ultimately, then, we must expect more not only of students, but also of teachers and administrators. They, too, must be held accountable to higher standards. One way to do this is to peg their salaries, or at least bonuses, to the performance of their students. Of course, we have to make certain that the test results are legitimate. Unfortunately, some teachers and administrators will cheat for money—giving students the answers and throwing out low test scores (Kantrowitz and McGinn 2000).

Other Reforms—From Vouchers to Charter Schools There is no lack of proposals for improving schools, but perhaps the one that has gained the most media attention—both because it is so controversial and because it holds such potential—is *vouchers.* The state would give the parents of each school-age child a voucher to be spent on the school of the parents' choice. As you can see from Figure 17.4 (page 496), the states have a great deal of money to work with, and the amount available per pupil would be large. Public and private schools—even those operated by individuals and businesses—would compete for the vouchers. With each school's test results published in local newspapers and available online, parents would be able to shop around for the school they like best. One major objection is that vouchers might be used to finance religious schools.

In an attempt to save its inner city schools, Milwaukee, Wisconsin, launched an experimental voucher program in 1990. Officials asked John Witte, a political scientist, to evaluate the results. He knew he was stepping into a minefield, that whether his findings were negative or positive, they would be controversial. His main finding was that some of the schools did well and others did poorly. Overall, the voucher students didn't score any higher than did comparable public school students (Davis 2002).

A second step in school reform is the creation of charter schools. **Charter schools** are public schools that, although financed by tax money, are owned and administered by independent groups. They are *chartered* by the state or some state agency to use innovative techniques in order to improve academic standards. There is no single model. Some charter schools are owned and run by parents, others by for-profit corporations. Some are in the inner city, others in the suburbs. A number are open the entire year. One is operated almost entirely online. A trait they share is freedom from teachers' unions and the public school bureaucracy. As you can imagine, teachers' unions and public school administrators have fought the creation of charter schools. Although these schools have great promise, it is too soon to tell if they will meet their potential (Manno and Finn 1998; Perreault 2000; Anderson et al. 2002).

Many applaud charter schools as a way of bringing educational reform and yet avoiding the political controversy of vouchers—that of funding religious schools. Opponents, however, fear that charter schools, like vouchers, will doom public schools by siphoning off their resources. Proponents of these reforms are unfazed by this objection. They say that public schools need to compete in the marketplace. If they don't produce better results, they *should* fold. It is no wonder that public school teachers and administrators fear reform.

To bring about educational reform, in 2002 the federal government passed the *No Child Left Behind Act.* The law requires each state to improve its schools and to ensure that no child is trapped in a failing school. To evaluate the states' progress, students are tested annually and each school's performance is made public. Students in failing schools are given the opportunity to transfer to better schools. It is too early to evaluate the results of this law, but we can note that practical problems have arisen. For example, Ana Vasquez, the mother of Desiree Lopez, a third grader in a failing school in New York City, wanted to transfer her daughter to a good school. When she found out that the best-performing school on the list the city gave her was an hour and a half from her home, she said, "What kind of choice is that? There is no option I can take." Her daughter remains in the failing school (Medina 2003).

Reform in anything needs a guiding principle. I suggest that this serve as the guiding principle in reforming education: The problem is *not* the ability of the students, but,

charter schools schools that, although financed by taxes, are owned and run by private groups rather, it lies in the nature of the educational system. This principle is illustrated by the following Thinking Critically section, with which we close this chapter.

THINKING Critically

Breaking Through the Barriers: Restructuring The Classroom

Jaime Escalante taught in an East Los Angeles inner-city school that was plagued with poverty, crime, drugs, and gangs. In this self-defeating environment, he taught calculus. His students scored so highly on national tests that officials suspected cheating. They asked his students to retake the test. They did. This time, they earned even higher scores.

How did Escalante do it?

First, Escalante had to open his students' minds to the possibility of success, that they *could* learn. Most Latino students were tracked into craft classes where they made jewelry and birdhouses. "Our kids are just as talented as anyone else. They just need the opportunity to show it," Escalante said. "They just don't think about becoming scientists or engineers."

To say that today's schoolchildren can't learn as well as previous schoolchildren is a case of blaming the victim. As discussed in the text, Jaime Escalante (shown here) demonstrated that teachers can motivate even highly deprived students to study hard and to excel in learning. His experience challenges us to rethink our approach to education.

Students also need to see learning as a way out of the barrio, as the path to good jobs. Escalante arranged for foundations to provide money for students to attend the colleges of their choice. Students learned that if they did well, their poverty wouldn't stop them.

Escalante also changed the system of instruction. He had his students think of themselves as a team, of him as the coach, and the national math exams as a sort of Olympics for which they were preparing. To foster team identity, students wore team jackets, caps, and T-shirts with logos that identified them as part of the math team. Before class, his students did "warm-ups" (hand clapping and foot stomping to a rock song).

Escalante's team had practice schedules as rigorous as a championship football team. Students had to sign a contract that bound them to participate in a summer math program, to complete the daily homework, and to attend Saturday morning and after-school study sessions. To remind students that self-discipline pays off, Escalante covered his walls with posters of sports figures—Michael Jordan, Babe Ruth, Jackie Joyner-Kersee, and Scottie Pippin.

The sociological point is this: The problem was not the ability of the students. Their failure to do well in school was not due to something within them. The problem was the system, the way classroom instruction was designed. When Escalante changed the system of instruction—and brought in hope—both attitudes and performance changed.

For Your CONSIDERATION . . .

What principles discussed in this or earlier chapters did Escalante apply? What changes do you think we can make in education to bring about similar results all over the country?

Sources: Based on Barry 1989; Meek 1989; Escalante and Dirmann 1990; Hilliard 1991.

SUMMARY and REVIEW

The Development of Modern Education

How did modern education develop?

In most of human history, **education** consisted of informal learning, equivalent to **acculturation.** In some earlier societies, centers of formal education did develop, such as among the Arabs, Chinese, Greeks, and Egyptians. Because modern education came about in response to industrialization, formal education is much less common in the Least Industrialized Nations. Pp. 484–486.

Education in Global Perspective

How does education compare among the Most Industrialized, Industrializing, and Least Industrialized Nations?

In general, formal education reflects a nation's economy. Consequently, education is extensive in the Most Industrialized Nations, undergoing vast change in the Industrializing Nations, and spotty in the Least Industrialized Nations. Japan, Russia, and Egypt provide examples of education in countries at three levels of industrialization. Pp. 486–490.

The Functionalist Perspective: Providing Social Benefits

What is the functionalist perspective on education?

Among the functions of education are the teaching of knowledge and skills, providing credentials, **cultural transmission** of values, social integration, **gatekeeping**, and **mainstreaming.** Functionalists also note that education has replaced some traditional family functions. Pp. 490–493.

The Conflict Perspective: Reproducing the Social Class Structure

What is the conflict perspective on education?

The basic view of conflict theorists is that *education reproduces the social class structure;* that is, through such mechanisms as unequal funding and operating different schools for the elite and for the masses, education perpetuates a society's basic social inequalities from one generation to the next. Pp. 494–499.

The Symbolic Interactionist Perspective: Fulfilling Teacher Expectations

What is the symbolic interactionist perspective on education?

Symbolic interactionists focus on face-to-face interaction. In examining what occurs in the classroom, they have found that student performance tends to conform to teacher expectations, whether they are high or low. Pp. 499–501.

Problems in U.S. Education—and Their Solutions

What are the chief problems that face U.S. education?

In addition to violence, the major problems are low achievement as shown by SAT scores, **grade inflation, social promotion,** and **functional illiteracy.** Pp. 501–504.

What are the potential solutions to these problems?

The primary solution is to restore high educational standards, which can be done only after providing basic security for students. Any solution for improving quality must be based on expecting more of *both* students and teachers. Pp. 504–508.

Where can I read more on this topic?

Suggested Readings for this chapter are found at the back of this book.

THINKING Critically ABOUT CHAPTER 17

1. How does education in the United States compare with education in Japan, Russia, and Egypt?
2. Analyze how your experiences in education have influenced your life. What effects have teachers and assignments had on your goals, attitudes, and values? How have your classmates influenced your life? Be specific.
3. How do you think U.S. schools can be improved?

ADDITIONAL RESOURCES for This Chapter

www.ablongman.com/henslin7e

- *Content Select* Research Database for Sociology, with suggested key terms and annotated references
- Link to 2000 Census, with activities
- Flashcards of key terms and concepts
- Practice Tests
- Weblinks
- Interactive Maps

Chapter 18

Religion

Elizabeth Barakah Hodges, *Jerusalem XIX (Ethiopian Boy), 1997*

The first report was stunning. About a hundred armed agents of the Bureau of Alcohol, Tobacco, and Firearms (ATF) attacked the compound of the Branch Davidians, an obscure religious group in Waco, Texas. Four of the agents were shot to death. So were six men who tried to defend the compound. Then came a fifty-one-day standoff, televised to the U.S. public, in which the ATF and FBI did strange things such as bombarding the compound with loud music day and night.

At 6 A.M. on the fifty-first day of the siege, following on-again, off-again negotiations with David Koresh, the 33-year-old leader of the group, a tank rammed the compound's main building. It pumped in gas consisting of chemicals that, by international law, the U.S. military was unable to use against Iraqi soldiers. As a second tank punched holes in the walls, the women and children fled to the second floor. The men shot futilely at the tanks. An explosion rocked the compound, and the buildings burst into flames. Eighty men, women, and children were burned to death. Some of the charred bodies of the twenty-five children were found huddled next to their mothers.

The government removed the bodies, sealed off the area, *and bulldozed the* charred remains of the buildings.

The government removed the bodies, sealed off the area, and bulldozed the charred remains of the buildings. Survivors claimed that the government had set the fire. The government said the Branch Davidians had set it, that they had committed suicide by fire.

Seldom do governments turn this viciously against a religion, but it does happen. One of the topics we shall consider in this chapter is the relationship of the dominant culture to new religions. Let's begin by asking what religion is.

Chapter Outline

What Is Religion?

All human societies are organized by some form of the family, as well as by some kind of economic system and political order. As we have seen, these key social institutions touch on aspects of life that are essential to human welfare. This chapter examines religion, another universal social institution.

Sociologists who do research on religion analyze the relationship between society and religion and study the role that religion plays in people's lives. They do not seek to prove that one religion is better than another. Nor is their goal to verify or disprove anyone's faith. As mentioned in Chapter 1, sociologists have no tools for deciding that one course of action is more moral than another, much less that one religion is "the" correct one. Religion is a matter of faith—and sociologists deal with empirical matters, things they can observe or measure. Thus sociologists study the effects of religious beliefs and practices on people's lives. They also analyze how religion is related to stratification systems. Unlike theologians, however, sociologists cannot evaluate the truth of a religion's teachings.

In 1912 Emile Durkheim published an influential book, *The Elementary Forms of the Religious Life,* in which he tried to identify the elements common to all religions. After surveying religions around the world, Durkheim could find no specific belief or practice that all religions share. He did find, however, that all religions develop a community around whatever their practices and beliefs are. All religions also separate the sacred from the profane. By **sacred,** Durkheim referred to aspects of life having to do with the supernatural that inspire awe, reverence, deep respect, even fear. By **profane,** he meant aspects of life that are not concerned with religion or religious purposes but, instead, are part of the ordinary aspects of everyday life. Durkheim (1912/1965) concluded:

> A religion is a unified system of beliefs and practices relative to sacred things, that is to say, things set apart and forbidden—beliefs and practices which unite into one single moral community called a Church, all those who adhere to them.

Thus, Durkheim said, a **religion** is defined by three elements:

1. *Beliefs* that some things are sacred (forbidden, set apart from the profane)
2. *Practices* (rituals) centering on the things considered sacred
3. *A moral community* (a church) resulting from a group's beliefs and practices

sacred Durkheim's term for things set apart or forbidden, that inspire fear, awe, reverence, or deep respect

profane Durkheim's term for common elements of everyday life

religion according to Durkheim, beliefs and practices that separate the profane from the sacred and unite its adherents into a moral community

From his review of world religions, Durkheim concluded that all religions have beliefs, practices, and a moral community. Shown here is a local Hindu temple that I photographed in Bhubaneswar, India. The figures represent some of the millions of gods that Hindus worship.

Durkheim used the word **church** in an unusual sense, to refer to any "moral community" centered on beliefs and practices regarding the sacred. In Durkheim's sense, *church* refers to Buddhists bowing before a shrine, Hindus dipping in the Ganges River, and Confucianists offering food to their ancestors. Similarly, the term *moral community* does not imply morality in the sense familiar to most of us. A moral community is simply people who are united by their religious practices—and that would include sixteenth-century Aztec priests who each day gathered around an altar to pluck out the beating heart of a virgin.

To better understand the sociological approach to religion, let's see what pictures emerge when we apply the three theoretical perspectives.

The Functionalist Perspective

Functionalists stress that religion is universal because it meets basic human needs. What are some of the functions—and dysfunctions—of religion?

Functions of Religion

Questions About Ultimate Meaning

Around the world, religions provide answers to perplexing questions about ultimate meaning—such as the purpose of life, why people suffer, and the existence of an afterlife. Those answers give people a sense of purpose. Instead of seeing themselves buffeted by random events in an aimless existence, believers see their lives as fitting into a divine plan.

Emotional Comfort

The answers that religion provides about ultimate meaning also comfort people by assuring them that there is a purpose to life, even to suffering. Similarly, religious rituals that enshroud crucial events such as illness and death provide emotional comfort at times of crisis. The individual knows that others care and can find consolation in following familiar rituals.

Social Solidarity

Religious teachings and practices unite believers into a community that shares values and perspectives ("we Jews," "we Christians," "we Muslims"). The religious rituals that surround marriage, for example, link the bride and groom with a broader community that wishes them well. So do other religious rituals, such as those that celebrate birth and mourn death.

Guidelines for Everyday Life

The teachings of religion are not all abstractions. They also provide practical directions on how to live our everyday lives. For example, four of the Ten Commandments delivered by Moses to the Israelites concern God, but the other six contain instructions on how to live everyday life, from how to get along with parents, employers, and neighbors to warnings about lying, stealing, and having affairs.

The consequences for people who follow these guidelines can be measured. People who attend church are less likely to abuse alcohol and illegal drugs than are people who don't go to church (Ostling 2001). This holds true for both adults and teens. In general, churchgoers follow a healthier lifestyle, and they live longer than those who don't go to church. A related function of religion is discussed in the Down-to-Earth Sociology box on the next page.

Social Control

Religion not only provides guidelines for everyday life, but also controls people's behaviors. Most norms of a religious group apply only to its members, but some set limits on nonmembers also. An example is religious teachings that are incorporated into criminal law. In the United States, for example, blasphemy and adultery were once crimes for which people could be arrested, tried, and sentenced. Laws that prohibit the sale of alcohol before noon on Sunday are another example.

church according to Durkheim, one of the three essential elements of religion—a moral community of believers (p. 513); a second definition is the type of religious organization described on page 530, a large, highly organized group with formal, sedate worship services and little emphasis on personal conversion

DOWN-TO-EARTH SOCIOLOGY

Does Prayer Work? An Intriguing Experiment

SELDOM DOES SOCIAL RESEARCH MAKE headlines, but this research did.

The researchers, headed by the chairman of the Department of Obstetrics and Gynecology at Columbia University, were so astounded by their findings that at first they didn't know what to do with them. They didn't even want to report their results, for fear that their scientific colleagues would laugh at or ridicule them.

Their research is so scientifically solid, however, and the results so unambiguous that they decided the only thing they could do was to publish their findings.

What so astounded them?

The setting was a fertility program at Cha General Hospital in Seoul, South Korea. Being treated were women who wanted to have children but who were having difficulty getting pregnant. One of the physicians suggested that prayer might make a difference in whether or not the women became pregnant. The medical researchers knew that prayer could not possibly make a difference. But, after all, what could they lose by trying?

To find out, the researchers set up a research design that would meet the rigorous standards of science (see Figure 18.1). Background information was gathered on the next 219 patients. A statistician in Korea who did not know the purpose of the research sent background data on the women and their photographs to another statistician in the United States. Twenty patients were lost to the sample due to fragmentary e-mail transmission. This second statistician, who also did not know the purpose of the study, matched the remaining 199 women by age, reason for infertility, and length of infertility. The women were then randomly assigned by a computer to either the experimental group (those who would be prayed for) or the control group (those who would not receive prayer).

The U.S. statistician sent photographs of the women who were to be prayed for to members of Christian denominations in the United States, Canada, and Australia. (The statistician sent them just the photographs, not the data.) One group prayed for the women, a second group prayed that the prayers of the first group would be effective, and a third group prayed for the first two groups.

Those who were praying lived continents away from the women who were being prayed for. They prayed for three weeks.

This was a double blind experimental design. The women did *not* know they were being prayed for. (They still don't.) This eliminated the *placebo effect*—the possibility that suggestion or hope or some other emotion might be at work. Even the medical staff that was treating the women did *not* know about the experiment. This eliminated the possibility that the staff might somehow treat some women differently. All women received identical medical treatment, IVT-ET (*in vitro* fertilization-embryo transfer). Finally, the researchers did not work for a religious organization, nor was the study funded by one. This eliminated another possible source of bias (see the box on page 130).

The results?

The women who were prayed for became pregnant *twice* as often as the women who did not have people praying for them.

Based on Cha et al. 2001; Nagourney 2001.

Figure 18.1 The Experimental Outcome of Prayer for Infertile Patients Undergoing *In Vitro* Fertilization—Embryo Transfer

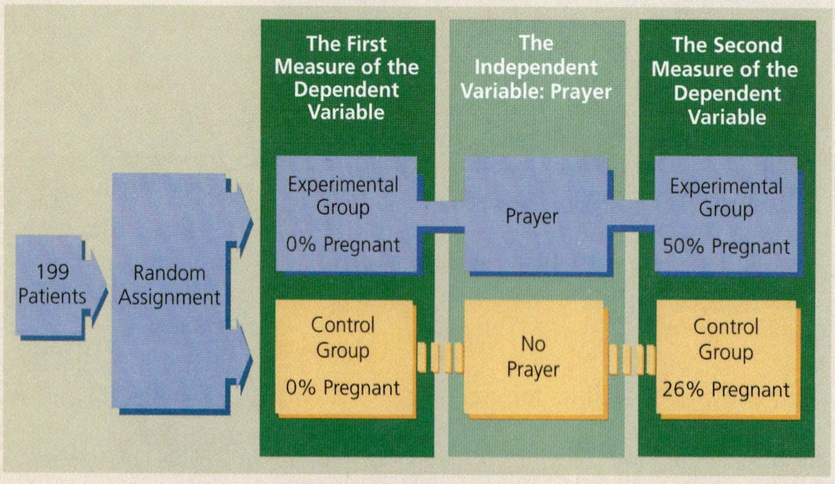

Pregnancy was determined by the presence of a heartbeat detected by ultrasound.

Religion has many functions. Among them are helping people adjust to life's problems. Being able to practice their religion helped earlier immigrants adjust to life in the United States, and it continues to help contemporary immigrants as well.

Adaptation Religion can help people adapt to new environments. For example, it isn't easy for immigrants to adjust to the customs of a new land. By keeping their native language alive and preserving familiar rituals and teachings, religion provides continuity with the immigrants' cultural past. This was the case for earlier immigrants from Europe, and it remains true today for immigrants from the Middle East and other parts of the globe.

Support for the Government Most religions provide support for the government. An obvious example is the way many churches so prominently display the U.S. flag. For their part, governments reciprocate by supporting God—as evidenced by the way U.S. presidents, whether they are believers or not, invariably ask God to bless the nation in their inaugural speeches.

Some governments sponsor a particular religion, ban all others, provide financial support for building churches and seminaries, and even pay salaries to the clergy. These religions are known as **state religions.** During the sixteenth and seventeenth centuries in Sweden, the government sponsored Lutheranism; in Switzerland, Calvinism; and in Italy, Roman Catholicism.

In other instances, even though the government sponsors no particular religion, religious beliefs are embedded in a nation's life. For example, U.S. officials—even those who do not belong to any particular religion—take office by swearing that they will, in the name of God, fulfill their duty. Similarly, Congress opens each session with a prayer led by its own chaplain. The pledge of allegiance includes the phrase "one nation under God," and coins bear the inscription "In God We Trust." To refer to a situation like this, where religion is embedded in a society, sociologist Robert Bellah (1970) uses the term **civil religion.**

state religion a government-sponsored religion; also called *ecclesia*

civil religion Robert Bellah's term for religion that is such an established feature of a country's life that its history and social institutions become sanctified by being associated with God

Social Change Although religion is often so bound up with the prevailing social order that it resists social change, occasionally religion spearheads change. In the 1960s, for example, the civil rights movement, which fought to desegregate public facilities and abolish racial discrimination at southern polls, was led by religious leaders, especially

Religion can promote social change, as was evident in the U.S. civil rights movement. Dr. Martin Luther King, Jr., a Baptist minister, shown here in his famous "I have a dream" speech, was the foremost leader of this movement.

leaders of African American churches such as Martin Luther King, Jr. Churches also served as centers at which demonstrators were trained and rallies were organized.

Functional Equivalents of Religion

If some other component of society answers questions about ultimate meaning, provides emotional comfort and guidelines for daily life, and so on, sociologists call it a **functional equivalent** of religion. Thus, for some people, Alcoholics Anonymous is a functional equivalent of religion (Chalfant 1992). For others, psychotherapy, humanism, transcendental meditation, or even a political party perform similar functions.

Some functional equivalents are difficult to distinguish from a religion (Brinton 1965; Luke 1985). For example, communism had its prophets (Marx and Lenin), sacred writings (everything written by Marx, Engels, and Lenin, but especially the *Communist Manifesto*), high priests (the heads of the Communist party), sacred buildings (the Kremlin), shrines (Lenin's body on display in Red Square), rituals (the annual May Day parade in Red Square), and even martyrs (Cuba's Ché Guevara). Soviet communism was avowedly atheistic and tried to wipe out all traces of Christianity, Judaism, and Islam from its midst. It even replaced baptisms and circumcisions with state-sponsored rituals that dedicated the child to the state. The Communist party also devised its own rituals for weddings and funerals.

As sociologist Ian Robertson (1987) pointed out, however, there is a fundamental distinction between a religion and its functional equivalent. Although the substitute may perform similar functions, its activities are not directed toward God, gods, or the supernatural.

functional equivalent in this context, a substitute that serves the same functions (or meets the same needs) as religion, for example, psychotherapy

Dysfunctions of Religion

Functionalists also examine ways in which religion is *dysfunctional,* that is, how it can bring harmful results. Two main dysfunctions are religious persecution and war and terrorism.

Religion as Justification for Persecution Beginning in the 1200s and continuing into the 1800s, in what has become known as the Inquisition, special commissions of the Roman Catholic Church tortured women to make them confess that they were witches, and then burned them at the stake. In 1692, Protestant leaders in Salem, Massachusetts, executed 21 women and men who were accused of being witches. In 2001, in the Democratic Republic of the Congo, about 1,000 alleged witches were hacked to death in a single "purge" (Jenkins 2002). Similarly, it seems fair to say that the Aztec religion had its dysfunctions—at least for the virgins who were offered to appease

Ein erſchꝛockliche geſchicht/ſo zu Derneburg in der Graff-
ſchafft Reinſtepn·am Hartz gelegen·von dꝛeyen Zauberin·vnnd zwayen
Mañen/Iſt ettlichen tagen des Monats Octobris Im 1 5 5 5. Jare ergangen iſt.

Woodcuts (engraved blocks of wood coated with ink to leave an impression on paper) were used to illustrate books shortly after the printing press was invented. This woodcut commemorates a dysfunction of religion, the burning of witches at the stake. This particular event occurred in 1555 at Derneburg, Germany.

angry gods. In short, religion has been used to justify oppression and any number of brutal acts.

War and Terrorism History is filled with wars based on religion—commingled with politics. Between the eleventh and fourteenth centuries, for example, Christian monarchs conducted nine bloody Crusades in an attempt to wrest control of the Holy Land from the Muslims. Terrorism, too, as discussed in the Down-to-Earth Sociology box on the next page, is often done in the name of religion.

The Symbolic Interactionist Perspective

Symbolic interactionists focus on the meanings that people give their experiences, especially how they use symbols. Let's apply this perspective to religious symbols, rituals, and beliefs to see how they help to forge a community of like-minded people.

Religious Symbols

Suppose that it is about two thousand years ago and you have just joined a new religion. You have come to believe that a recently crucified Jew named Jesus is the Messiah, the Lamb of God offered for your sins. The Roman leaders are persecuting the followers of Jesus. They hate your religion because you and your fellow believers will not acknowledge Caesar as God.

Christians are few in number, and you are eager to have fellowship with other believers. But how can you tell who is a believer? Spies are all over. The government has sworn to destroy this new religion, and you do not relish the thought of being fed to lions in the Coliseum.

You use a simple technique. While talking with a stranger, as though doodling absentmindedly in the sand or dust, you casually trace the outline of a fish. Only

DOWN-TO-EARTH SOCIOLOGY

Terrorism and the Mind of God

WARNING: The "equal time" contents of this box are likely to offend just about everyone.

AFTER 9/11, THE QUESTION ON MANY people's minds was some form of, "How can people do such evil in the name of God?"

Americans are frightened by Islam. Everyone knows that the terrorists who brought down the World Trade Center in New York and attacked the Pentagon in Washington, D.C., were Muslims. The terrorists were convinced that Allah approved what they did.

How can people can do such things in the name of God? To answer this question, we need to broaden the context. The question is fine, but it cannot be directed at Islamic terrorists. If it is, it misses the point.

We need to consider other religions, too. For Christians, we don't have to go back centuries to the Inquisition or to the Children's Crusades. We only have to look at Ireland, and the bombings in Belfast. There, both Protestants and Catholics slaughtered one another in the name of God.

In the United States, we can consider the killing of abortion doctors. Paul Hill, a minister who was executed for killing a doctor in Florida, was convinced that his act was good, that he had saved the lives of unborn babies. Before his execution, he said that he was looking forward to heaven. His friend, Rev. Michael Bray, took no lives. Instead, he burned abortion clinics.

Since I want to give equal time to the major religions, we can't forget the Jews. Dr. Baruch Goldstein was convinced that Yahweh wanted him to take a Galil assault rifle, go to the Tomb of the Patriarchs, and shoot into a crowd of praying Palestinian men and boys. His admirers built a monument on his grave (Juergensmeyer 2000).

Finally, for the sake of equality, let's not let the Hindus, Buddhists, and Sikhs off the hook either. In India, they continue to slaughter one another. In the name of their gods, they attack the houses of worship of the others and blow one another up. (The Hindus are actually equal opportunists—they kill Christians, too. I visited an Indian state where they had doused a jeep with gasoline and burned alive an Australian missionary and his son.)

None of these terrorists—Islamic, Christian, Jew, Sikh, Buddhist, or Hindu—represent the mainstream of their religion, but they do commit violence for religious reasons. How can they do so? Here are five elements that religious terrorists seem to have in common. (I have extrapolated these principles from the acts of individuals and small groups. Terrorism by the state is another matter.)

First, the individuals believe that they are under attack. Evil forces are bent on destroying the good of their world—whether that be their religion, their way of life, or unborn babies.

Second, they become convinced that God wants the evil destroyed.

Third, they conclude that only violence will resolve the situation, and that violence in this case is good.

Fourth, they become convinced that God has chosen them for this task. They don't want to kill or to die, but they reluctantly accept their fate. Dying for God's cause is greater than living as a coward who won't stand up for what is right.

Fifth, these perspectives are nurtured by a community, a group in which the individuals find identity. This smaller group may realize that most members of their faith do not support their views, but that is because the others are uninformed, even brainwashed by the enemy or by the liberal, secularized media. The smaller community holds the truth.

For those groups that have scriptures, there are enough references to violence that they are able to make these selective passages paramount as "God's mandated" solution to the threat they feel.

If these orientations are accompanied by the view that we are in a final confrontation between good and evil, they become even more powerful. If we are in the end times and this is the final battle, there is no retreat. Some Christians, Jews, Muslims, and even Sikhs of India hold such a view (Juergensmeyer 2000).

Under these conditions, morality is turned upside down. Killing becomes a moral act, a good done for a greater cause. This greater good may require self-sacrifice—both in the case of suicide bombers and those who plan to escape but know that authorities will hunt them down.

There is just enough truth in these points of view to keep the delusion alive. After all, wouldn't it have been better for the millions of Jews and the millions of other victims if someone had had the nerve and foresight to kill Hitler? Wouldn't his death and one's own self-sacrifice have been a greater good? Today, there are those bad Protestants, those bad Catholics, those bad Jews, those bad Palestinians, those bad abortionists, those bad Americans—an endless list. And the violence is for the Greater Good, what God wants.

Once people buy into this closed system of thought, discussion in which contrasting views are shared and considered flies out the window. The individuals become convinced that they have access to the mind of God.

Who wants to violate God's will? And when killing and terrorism become equated with God's will, then . . .

fellow believers know the meaning—that, taken together, the first letter of each word in the Greek sentence "Jesus (is) Christ the Son of God" spell the Greek word for *fish.* If the other person gives no response, you rub out the outline and continue the interaction as usual. If there is a response, you eagerly talk about your new faith.

All religions use symbols to provide identity and social solidarity for their members. For Muslims, the primary symbol is the crescent moon and star; for Jews, the Star of

David; for Christians, the cross. For members, these are not ordinary symbols, but sacred emblems that evoke feelings of awe and reverence. In Durkheim's terms, religions use symbols to represent what the group considers sacred and to separate the sacred from the profane.

A symbol is a condensed way of communicating. Worn by a fundamentalist Christian, for example, the cross says, "I am a follower of Jesus Christ. I believe that He is the Messiah, the promised Son of God, that He loves me, that He died to take away my sins, that He rose from the dead and is going to return to earth, and that through Him I will receive eternal life."

That is a lot to pack into one symbol—and it is only part of what the symbol means to a fundamentalist believer. To people in other traditions of Christianity, the cross conveys somewhat different meanings—but to all Christians, the cross is a shorthand way of expressing many meanings. So it is with the Star of David, the crescent moon and star, the cow (expressing to Hindus the unity of all living things), and the various symbols of the world's many other religions.

Symbolic interactionists stress that a basic characteristic of humans is that they attach meaning to objects and events and then use representations of those objects or events to communicate with one another. Some religious symbols are used to communicate feelings of awe and reverence. Michaelangelo's Pietà, depicting Mary tenderly holding her son, Jesus, after his crucifixion, is one of the most acclaimed symbols in the Western world. It is admired for its beauty by believers and nonbelievers alike.

Rituals

Rituals, ceremonies or repetitive practices, are also symbols that help unite people into a moral community. Some rituals, such as the bar mitzvah of Jewish boys and the Holy Communion of Christians, are designed to create in the devout a feeling of closeness with God and unity with one another. Rituals include kneeling and praying at set times, bowing, crossing oneself, singing, lighting candles and incense, scripture readings, processions, baptisms, weddings, funerals, and so on.

Beliefs

Symbols, including rituals, develop from beliefs. The belief may be vague ("God is") or highly specific ("God wants us to prostrate ourselves and face Mecca five times each day"). Religious beliefs include not only *values* (what is considered good and desirable in life—how we ought to live) but also a **cosmology**, a unified picture of the world. For example, the Jewish, Christian, and Muslim belief that there is only one God, the Creator of the universe, who is concerned about the actions of humans and who will hold us accountable for what we do, is a cosmology. It presents a unifying picture of the universe.

One of the functions of religion is to create community—a sense of being connected with one another and, in this case, also a sense of being connected with God. To help accomplish this, religions often use rituals. Shown here are Javanese Muslim women in Aramaribo as they celebrate Id al Fatr at the end of Rammadan.

rituals ceremonies or repetitive practices; in this context, religious observances or rites, often intended to evoke a sense of awe of the sacred

cosmology teachings or ideas that provide a unified picture of the world

religious experience a sudden awareness of the supernatural or a feeling of coming in contact with God

born again a term describing Christians who have undergone a life-transforming religious experience so radical that they feel they have become new persons

Religious Experience

The term **religious experience** refers to a sudden awareness of the supernatural or a feeling of coming in contact with God. Some people undergo a mild version, such as feeling closer to God when they look at a mountain or listen to a certain piece of music. Others report a life-transforming experience. St. Francis of Assisi, for example, said that he became aware of God's presence in every living thing.

Some Protestants use the term **born again** to describe people who have undergone such a life-transforming religious experience. These people say they came to the realization that they had sinned, that Jesus had died for their sins, and that God wants them to live a new life. Their worlds become transformed. They look forward to the Resurrection and to a new life in heaven, and they see relationships with spouses, parents, children, and even bosses in a new light. They also report a need to make changes in how they interact with others so that their lives reflect their new, personal commitment to Jesus as their "Savior and Lord." They describe a feeling of beginning life anew, hence the term *born again.*

Community

Finally, the shared meanings that come through symbols, rituals, and beliefs (and for some, a religious experience) unite people into a moral community. People in a moral community feel a bond with one another, for their beliefs and rituals bind them together while at the same time separating them from those who do not share their unique symbolic world. Mormons, for example, feel a "kindred spirit" (as it is often known) with other Mormons. Baptists, Jews, Jehovah's Witnesses, and Muslims feel the same bonds with members of their respective faiths.

As a symbol of their unity, members of some religious groups address one another as "brother" or "sister." "Sister Luby, we are going to meet at Brother and Sister Maher's on Wednesday" is a common way of expressing a message. The terms *brother* and *sister* are intended to symbolize a relationship so close that the individuals consider themselves members of the same family.

Community is powerful, not only because it provides the basis for mutual identity, but also because it establishes norms that govern the behavior of its members. Members either conform or they lose their membership. In Christian churches, for example, an individual whose adultery becomes known, and who refuses to ask forgiveness, may be banned from the church. He or she may be formally excommunicated, as in the Catholic tradition, or more informally "stricken from the rolls," as is the usual Protestant practice.

Removal from the community is a serious matter for people whose identity is bound up in that community. Sociologists John Hostetler (1980), William Kephart, and William Zellner (2001) describe the Amish practice of *shunning*—ignoring an offender in all situations. Persons who are shunned are treated as though they do not exist (for if they do not repent by expressing sorrow for their act, they have ceased to exist as members of the community). The shunning is so thorough that even family members, who themselves remain in good standing in the congregation, are not allowed to talk to the person being shunned. This obviously makes for some interesting times at the dinner table.

The Conflict Perspective

The conflict perspective has an entirely different focus. Conflict theorists examine how religion supports the status quo and helps to maintain social inequalities.

Opium of the People

In general, conflict theorists are highly critical of religion. Karl Marx, an avowed atheist who believed that the existence of God was impossible, set the tone for conflict theorists with his most famous statement on this subject: "Religion is the sigh of the oppressed creature, the sentiment of a heartless world. . . . It is the opium of the people" (Marx 1844/1964). By this statement, Marx meant that oppressed workers find escape in religion. For them, religion is

Conflict theorists stress that religion reflects and legitimates social inequalities. In this 1941 photo from a Methodist congregation in White Plains, Georgia, what inequalities of the time do you see legitimated?

like a drug that helps them forget their misery. By diverting their thoughts toward future happiness in an afterlife, religion takes their eyes off their suffering in this world, thereby greatly reducing the possibility that they will rebel against their oppressors.

A Legitimation of Social Inequalities

Conflict theorists say that religion legitimates the social inequalities of the larger society. By this, they mean that religion teaches that the existing social arrangements of a society represent what God desires. For example, during the Middle Ages, Christian theologians decreed the "divine right of kings." This doctrine meant that God determined who would become king, and set him on the throne. The king ruled in God's place, and it was the duty of a king's subjects to be loyal to him (and to pay their taxes). To disobey the king was to disobey God.

In what was perhaps the supreme technique of legitimating the social order (and one that went even a step farther than the "divine right of kings"), the religion of ancient Egypt held that the Pharaoh was a god. The Emperor of Japan was similarly declared divine. If this were so, who could ever question his decisions? Today's politicians would give their right arm for such a religious teaching. Deification endorsed by religion!

Conflict theorists point to many other examples of how religion legitimates the social order. In India, Hinduism supports the caste system by teaching that an individual who tries to change caste will come back in the next life as a member of a lower caste—or even as an animal. In the decades before the American Civil War, Southern ministers used scripture to defend slavery, saying that it was God's will—while Northern ministers legitimated *their* region's social structure by using scripture to denounce slavery as evil (Ernst 1988; Nauta 1993; White 1995).

Religion and the Spirit of Capitalism

Max Weber disagreed with the conflict perspective that religion merely reflects and legitimates the social order, and that religion impedes social change by encouraging people to focus on the afterlife. In contrast, Weber saw religion's focus on the afterlife as a source of profound social change.

Like Marx, Weber observed the industrialization of European countries. Weber became intrigued with the question of why some societies embraced capitalism while others clung to their traditional ways. Tradition is strong and tends to hold people in check, yet some societies had been transformed by capitalism, while others remained untouched. As he explored this puzzle, Weber concluded that religion held the key to **modernization**—the transformation of traditional societies to industrial societies.

To explain his conclusions, Weber wrote *The Protestant Ethic and the Spirit of Capitalism* (1904–1905/1958). Because Weber's argument was presented in Chapter 7 (pages 177–178), it is only summarized here.

1. Capitalism is not just a superficial change. Rather, capitalism represents a fundamentally different way of thinking about work and money. *Traditionally, people worked just enough to meet their basic needs, not so that they could have a surplus to invest.* To accumulate money (capital) as an end in itself, not just to spend it, was a radical departure from traditional thinking. People even came to consider it a duty to invest money in order to make profits, which, in turn, they reinvested to make more profits. Weber called this new approach to work and money the **spirit of capitalism.**
2. Why did the spirit of capitalism develop in Europe, and not, for example, in China or India, where the people had similar material resources, education, and so on? According to Weber, *religion was the key.* The religions of China and India, and indeed Roman Catholicism in Europe, encouraged a traditional approach to life, not thrift and investment. Capitalism appeared when Protestantism came on the scene.
3. What was different about Protestantism, especially Calvinism? John Calvin taught that God had predestined some people to go to heaven, others to hell. Neither church membership nor feelings about your relationship with God could assure you that you were saved. You wouldn't know your fate until after you died.
4. This doctrine created intense anxiety among Calvin's followers: "Am I predestined to hell or to heaven?" they wondered. As Calvinists wrestled with this question, they concluded that church members have a duty to prove that they are one of God's elect, and to live as though they are predestined to heaven—for good works are a demonstration of salvation.
5. This conclusion motivated Calvinists to lead moral lives *and* to work hard, to not waste time, and to be frugal—for idleness and needless spending were signs of worldliness. Weber called this self-denying approach to life the **Protestant ethic.**
6. As people worked hard and spent money only on necessities (a pair of earrings or a second pair of dress shoes would have been defined as sinful luxuries), they had money left over. Because it couldn't be spent, this capital was invested—which led to a surge in production.
7. Thus, a change in religion (from Catholicism to Protestantism, especially Calvinism) led to a fundamental change in thought and behavior (the *Protestant ethic*). The result was the *spirit of capitalism.* Thus capitalism originated in Europe, and not in places where religion did not encourage capitalism's essential elements: the accumulation of capital and its investment and reinvestment.

Although Weber's analysis has been influential, it has not lacked critics (Kalberg 2002). Hundreds of scholars have attacked it, some for overlooking the lack of capitalism in Scotland (a Calvinist country), others for failing to explain why the Industrial Revolution was born in England (not a Calvinist country).

Hundreds of other scholars have defended Weber's argument. There is currently no historical evidence that can definitively prove or disprove Weber's thesis.

At this point in history, the Protestant ethic and the spirit of capitalism are not confined to any specific religion or even to any one part of the world. Rather, they have become cultural traits that have spread to societies around the globe (Greeley 1964; Yinger 1970). U.S. Catholics have about the same approach to life as do U.S. Protestants. In addition, Hong Kong, Japan, Malaysia, Singapore, South Korea, and Taiwan—not exactly Protestant countries—have embraced capitalism (Levy 1992).

modernization the transformation of traditional societies into industrial societies

spirit of capitalism Weber's term for the desire to accumulate capital as a duty—not to spend it, but as an end in itself—and to constantly reinvest it

Protestant ethic Weber's term to describe the ideal of a self-denying, highly moral life accompanied by hard work and frugality

The World's Major Religions

The largest of the thousands of religions in the world are listed in Table 18.1. Let's briefly review six of them.

Table 18.1 The World's Largest Religions[a]

Religion	Number of Followers
Christians	1,900,000,000
Muslims	1,100,000,000
Hindus	781,000,000
Chinese folk religions	379,000,000
Buddhists	324,000,000
Sikhs	19,000,000
Jews	14,000,000
Spiritualists	12,000,000
Baha'is	6,100,000
Confucians	5,300,000
Jains	4,900,000
Shintoists	2,800,000

[a] *Note:* The classification of religions is often confusing. Animists, for example, although numerous, are not listed as a separate group in the source. It is often difficult to tell what groups are encompassed in what categories.

Sources: Statistical Abstract 1999:Table 1348; *World Almanac* 2003.

Judaism

The origin of Judaism is traced to Abraham, who lived about four thousand years ago in Mesopotamia. Jews believe that God (Jahweh) made a covenant with Abraham, selecting his descendants as a chosen people and promising to make them "as numerous as the sands of the seashore" and to give them a special land that would be theirs forever. The sign of this covenant was the circumcision of males, which was to be performed when a boy was eight days old. Descent is traced through Abraham and his wife, Sarah, their son Isaac, and their grandson Jacob (also called Israel).

Joseph, a son of Jacob, was sold by his brothers into slavery and taken to Egypt. Following a series of hair-raising adventures, Joseph became Pharaoh's right-hand man. When a severe famine hit Canaan, where Jacob's family was living, Jacob and his eleven other sons fled to Egypt. Under Joseph's leadership, they were welcome. A subsequent Pharaoh, however, enslaved the Israelites. After about four hundred years, Moses, an Israelite who had been adopted by Pharaoh's daughter, confronted Pharaoh. He persuaded Pharaoh to release the slaves, which at that time numbered about 2 million. Moses led them out of Egypt, but before they reached their Promised Land, the Israelites spent forty years wandering in the desert. Sometime during those years, Moses delivered the Ten Commandments from Mount Sinai. Abraham, Isaac, Jacob, and Moses hold revered positions in Judaism. The events of their lives and the recounting of the early history of the Israelites are contained in the first five books of the Bible, called the Torah.

monotheism the belief that there is only one God

polytheism the belief that there are many gods

animism the belief that all objects in the world have spirits, some of which are dangerous and must be outwitted

The founding of Judaism marked a fundamental change in religion, for it was the first religion based on **monotheism,** the belief that there is only one God. Prior to Judaism, religions were based on **polytheism,** the belief that there are many gods. In Greek religion, for example, Zeus was the god of heaven and earth, Poseidon the god of the sea, and Athena the goddess of wisdom. Other groups followed **animism,** believing that all objects in the world have spirits, some of which are dangerous and must be outwitted.

Contemporary Judaism in the United States comprises three main branches: Orthodox, Reform, and Conservative. Orthodox Jews adhere to the laws espoused by Moses. They eat only foods prepared in a designated manner (kosher), observe the Sabbath in a traditional way, and segregate males and females in their religious services. During the 1800s, a group that wanted to make their practices more compatible with U.S. culture broke from this tradition. This liberal group, known as Reform Judaism, mostly uses English in its religious ceremonies and has reduced much of the ritual. The third branch, Conservative Judaism, falls somewhere between the other two. No branch has continued polygyny (allowing a man to have more than one wife), the original marriage custom of the Jews, which was outlawed by rabbinic decree about a thousand years ago.

Religion, which provides community and identification, is passed from the older to the younger. Shown here are older orthodox Jews in Miami Beach as they bind prayers around the arms of adolescent boys. The boys, in turn, will replace their elders and transmit their religion to the next generation.

The history of Judaism is marked by conflict and persecution. The Israelites were conquered by Babylon, and were again made slaves. After returning to Israel and rebuilding the temple, they were later conquered by Rome, and after their rebellion at Masada in A.D. 70 failed, they were exiled for almost two thousand years into other nations. During those centuries, they faced prejudice, discrimination, and persecution (called **anti-Semitism**) by many peoples and rulers. The most horrendous example was the Nazi Holocaust of World War II, when Hitler attempted to eliminate the Jews as a people. Under the Nazi occupation of Europe and North Africa, about 6 million Jews were slaughtered. Many died in gas ovens that were constructed for just this purpose.

Central to Jewish teaching is the requirement to love God and do good deeds. Good deeds begin in the family, where each member has an obligation toward the others. Sin is a conscious choice to do evil, and must be atoned for by prayers and good works. Jews consider Jerusalem their holiest city and believe that the Messiah will one day appear there, bringing redemption for them all.

Christianity

Christianity, which developed out of Judaism, is also monotheistic. Christians believe that Jesus Christ is the Messiah whom God promised the Jews.

Jesus was born in poverty, and traditional Christians believe he was born to a virgin. Within two years of his birth, Herod, named king of Palestine by Caesar, who had conquered Israel, was informed that people were saying a new king had been born. When Herod sent soldiers to kill Jesus, Jesus' parents fled with him to Egypt. After Herod died, they returned, settling in the small town of Nazareth.

At about the age of 30, Jesus began a preaching and healing ministry. His teachings challenged the contemporary religious establishment, and as his popularity grew the religious leaders plotted to have him killed by the Romans. Christians interpret the death of Jesus as a blood sacrifice made to atone for their sins. They believe that through his death they have peace with God and will inherit eternal life.

The twelve main followers of Jesus, called *apostles,* believed that Jesus rose from the dead. They preached the need to be "born again," that is, to accept Jesus as Savior, give up selfish ways, and live a devout life. The new religion spread rapidly, and after an initial period of hostility on the part of imperial Rome—during which time believers were fed to the lions in the Coliseum—in A.D. 317 Christianity became the empire's official religion.

During the first thousand years of Christianity, there was only one church organization, directed from Rome. During the eleventh century, after disagreement over doctrine and politics, Greek Orthodoxy was established. It was headquartered in Constantinople (now Istanbul, Turkey). During the Middle Ages, the Roman Catholic Church, which was aligned with the political establishment, became corrupt. Some Church offices, such as that of bishop, were sold for a set price, and, in a situation that touched off the Reformation led by Martin Luther in the sixteenth century, the forgiveness of sins (including those not yet committed) could be purchased by buying an "indulgence."

Although Martin Luther's original goal was to reform the Church, not divide it, the Reformation began a splintering of Christianity. It coincided with the breakup of feudalism, and as the ancient political structure came apart, people clamored for independence not only in political ideology but also in religious thought. Today, Christianity is the most popular religion in the world, with about 2 billion adherents. Christians are divided into hundreds of groups, some with doctrinal differences so slight that only members of the group can appreciate the extremely fine distinctions that, they feel, significantly separate them from others. The Social Map on the next page shows how some of these groups are distributed in the United States.

Islam

Islam, whose followers are known as Muslims, began in the same part of the world as Judaism and Christianity. Islam, the world's third monotheistic religion, has over a billion followers. It was founded by Muhammad, who was born in Mecca (now in Saudi Arabia) in about A.D. 570. Muhammad married Khadija, a wealthy widow. About the age of 40, he reported that he had had visions from God. These, and his teachings, were later written down in a book called the Koran. Few paid attention to Muhammad, although Ali,

anti-Semitism prejudice, discrimination, and persecution directed against Jews

Figure 18.2 Church Membership: Dominant Religion, by County

When no religious group has 25 percent of the total membership in a county, that county is left blank. When two or more religious groups have 25–49 percent of the membership in a county, the largest is shown.

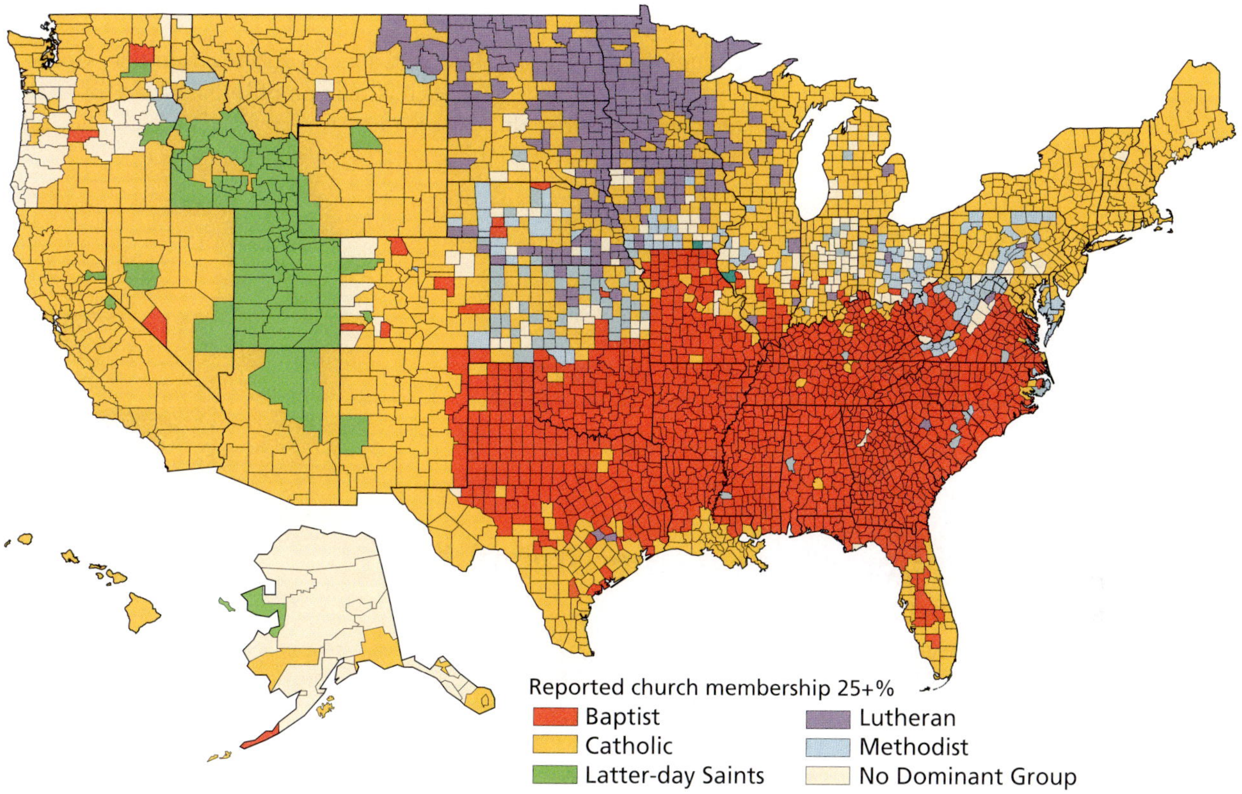

Source: Reprinted with permission from *Religious Congregations and Membership in the United States: 2000.* (Nashville: Glenmary Research Center, 2002). © Association of Statisticians of American Religious Bodies. All rights reserved.

his son-in-law, believed him. When he found out that there was a plot to murder him, Muhammad fled to Medina, where he found a more receptive audience. There he established a *theocracy* (a government based on the principle that God is king, God's laws are the statutes of the land, and priests are the earthly administrators of God). In A.D. 630 he returned to Mecca, this time as a conqueror (Bridgwater 1953).

After Muhammad's death, a struggle for control over the empire he had founded split Islam into two branches that remain today, the Sunni and the Shi'ite. The Shi'ites believe that the *imam* (the religious leader) is inspired as he interprets the Koran. They are generally more conservative and are inclined to **fundamentalism,** the belief that modernism threatens religion and that the faith as it was originally practiced should be restored. The Sunni, who do not share this belief, are generally more liberal, more accepting of social change.

Like the Jews, Muslims trace their ancestry to Abraham. Abraham fathered a son, Ishmael, by Hagar, his wife Sarah's Egyptian maid (Genesis 25:12). Ishmael had twelve sons, from whom a good portion of today's Arab world is descended. For them also, Jerusalem is a holy city. The Muslims consider the Bibles of the Jews and the Christians to be sacred but take the Koran as the final word. They believe that the followers of Abraham and Moses (Jews) and Jesus (Christians) changed the original teachings and that Muhammad restored these teachings to their initial purity. It is the duty of each

fundamentalism the belief that true religion is threatened by modernism and its values and that the faith as it was originally practiced should be restored

Muslim to make a pilgrimage to Mecca during his or her lifetime. Unlike the Jews, the Muslims continue to practice polygyny. They limit a man to four wives, however.

Because of immigration from the Mideast and conversions of African Americans, Islam has grown rapidly in the past few decades in the United States. This topic is explored in the Cultural Diversity box below.

Hinduism

Unlike the other religions described, Hinduism has no specific founder. Going back about four thousand years, Hinduism was the chief religion of India. The term *Hinduism,* however, is Western, and in India the closest term is *dharma* (law). Unlike Judaism,

CULTURAL DIVERSITY in the UNITED STATES

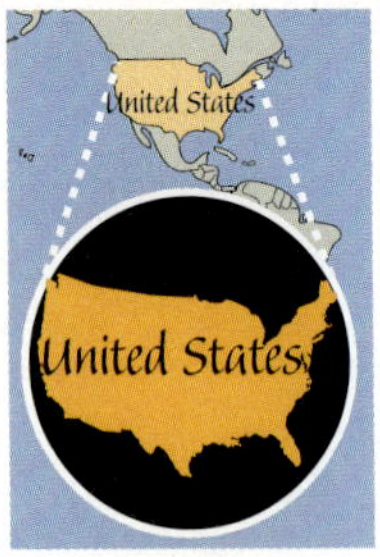

The New Neighbor: Islam in the United States

In a scene that is growing increasingly familiar, instead of going into a church or synagogue to pray and worship, many Americans take off their shoes, face Mecca, and kneel with their faces to the floor.

Called by some the fastest growing religion in the United States, Islam is making its presence felt. Islam's growth is fueled by two main sources. The primary source is the millions of immigrants from the Middle East and Asia who have arrived in the United States since the 1980s. Like the European immigrants who brought Lutheranism, Roman Catholicism, and other branches of Christianity with them, these refugees from Muslim countries brought along their religion as part of their culture. The second source is African Americans. Although African American followers of Islam come from all social classes, the call of Islam is heard most loudly in the inner city (Peart 1993). Overall, U.S. Muslims are about 42 percent African American, 25 percent South Asian, 12 percent Arab, and the remainder from a mix of backgrounds (Power 1998).

The appeal of Islam to African Americans is the message of black pride, self-improvement, and black power. Although African American Muslims are divided among about twenty groups, the appeal is similar: morality (no drugs, crime, or extramarital sex), respect for women, and black empowerment. Among all groups, modest clothing is required. Among some, ultraconservative codes govern behavior: Men and women sit apart in public, women wear robes that cover them from head to toe, and one-on-one dating is prohibited (Tapia 1994). Many men embrace the authority that Islam ascribes to them. For both men and women, Islam is a way to connect with African roots.

Universally, children are socialized into the religion of their group. The kindergarten students shown here at the Al-Ghazaly Islamic school in Jersey City, New Jersey, are learning how to pray.

For many Americans, Louis Farrakhan is synonymous with U.S. Islam. Although he is the most visible and vocal Muslim leader, the group he heads, the Nation of Islam, has only about 10,000 members (Brooke 1995). The Chicago-based Muslim American Society, formerly headed by W. Dean Mohammed, has 200,000 members (Miller 1999).

Just as their organizations are diverse, so their opinions are wide-ranging. With regard to race, for example, some believe the races are equal; others believe African Americans are superior and whites are devils. Similarly, some groups stress black separatism, while others emphasize the need to start businesses and run for office (Miller 1999).

Alarmed that Islam has gained so many converts, some African American Christians are counterattacking. They hold Muslim Awareness seminars in order to warn Christians away from Islam (Tapia 1994). A former Black Muslim who is now a Christian evangelist and who sees it as his duty to counter Islam, says the difference is grace. "Islam is a works-oriented religion, but Christianity is built on God's grace in Jesus."

"His is just a slave religion," retort some Muslims.

The many mosques that are taking their place in the midst of churches and synagogues can be taken as a sign of a maturing multicultural society.

Christianity, and Islam, Hinduism has no canonical scripture, that is, no texts thought to be inspired by God. Instead, several books, including the *Brahmanas, Bhagavad-Gita,* and *Upanishads,* expound on moral qualities that people should strive to develop. They also delineate the sacrifices people should make to the gods.

Hindus are *polytheists;* that is, they believe that there are many gods. They believe that one of these gods, Brahma, created the universe. Brahma, along with Shiva (the Destroyer) and Vishnu (the Preserver), form a triad that is at the center of modern Hinduism. A central belief is *karma,* spiritual progress. There is no final judgment, but, instead, **reincarnation,** a cycle of life, death, and rebirth. Death involves only the body, and each person's soul comes back in a form that matches the individual's moral progress in the previous life (which centers on proper conduct in following the rules of one's caste). If an individual reaches spiritual perfection, he or she has attained *nirvana.* This marks the end of the cycle of death and rebirth, when the soul is reunited with the universal soul. When this occurs, *maya,* the illusion of time and space, has been conquered.

reincarnation in Hinduism and Buddhism, the return of the soul (or self) after death in a different form

Some Hindu practices have been modified as a consequence of social protest—especially child marriage and *suttee,* the practice of cremating a surviving widow along with her deceased husband (Bridgwater 1953). Other ancient rituals remain unchanged, such as *kumbh mela,* a purifying washing in the Ganges River, which takes place every twelve years, and in which many millions participate.

Buddhism

In about 600 B.C., Siddhartha Gautama founded Buddhism. (Buddha means the "enlightened one," a term Gautama was given by his disciples.) Gautama was the son of an upper-caste Hindu ruler in an area north of Benares, India. At the age of 29, he renounced his life of luxury and became an ascetic. Through meditation, he discovered the "four noble truths," which emphasize self-denial and compassion.

1. Existence is suffering.
2. The origin of suffering is desire.
3. Suffering ceases when desire ceases.
4. The way to end desire is to follow the "noble eightfold path."

Depictions of Buddha are found throughout the world. Many Buddhists keep small statues in their homes and businesses, at which they make daily offerings of food. These statues at Wat Chang Hom in Thailand were made in the 13th century.

The noble eightfold path consists of

1. Right belief
2. Right resolve (to renounce carnal pleasure and to harm no living creature)
3. Right speech
4. Right conduct
5. Right occupation or living
6. Right effort
7. Right-mindedness (or contemplation)
8. Right ecstasy

The central symbol of Buddhism is the eight-spoked wheel. Each spoke represents one aspect of the path. As with Hinduism, the ultimate goal of Buddhism is the cessation of rebirth and thereby of suffering. Buddhists teach that all things are temporary, even the self. Because all things are destined to pass away, there is no soul (Reat 1994).

Buddhism spread rapidly. In the third century B.C., the ruler of India adopted Buddhism and sent missionaries throughout Asia to spread the new teaching (Bridgwater 1953). By the fifth century A.D., Buddhism reached the height of its popularity in India, after which it died out. Buddhism, however, had been adopted in Ceylon, Burma, Tibet, Laos, Cambodia, Thailand, China, Korea, and Japan, where it flourishes today. Vigorous communities of Buddhists have also developed in the United States.

Confucianism

About the time that Gautama lived, K'ung Fu-tsu (551–479 B.C.) was born in China. Confucius (his name strung together in English), a public official, was distressed by the corruption that he saw in government. Unlike Gautama, who urged withdrawal from social activities, Confucius urged social reform and developed a system of morality based on peace, justice, and universal order. His teachings were incorporated into writings called the *Analects.*

The basic moral principle of Confucianism is to maintain *jen,* sympathy or concern for other humans. The key to jen is to sustain right relationships—being loyal and placing morality above self-interest. In what is called the "Confucian Golden Rule," Confucius stated a basic principle for jen: to treat those who are subordinate to you as you would like to be treated by people superior to yourself. Confucius taught that right relationships within the family (loyalty, respect) should be the model for society. He also taught the "middle way," an avoidance of extremes.

Confucianism was originally atheistic, simply a set of moral teachings without reference to the supernatural. As the centuries passed, however, local gods were added to the teachings, and Confucius himself was declared a god. Confucius' teachings became the basis for the government of China. About A.D. 1000, the emphasis on meditation gave way to a stress on improvement through acquiring knowledge. This emphasis remained dominant until the twentieth century. By this time, the government had become rigid, and respect for the existing order had replaced respect for relationships (Bridgwater 1953). Following the Communist revolution of 1949, political leaders attempted to weaken the people's ties with Confucianism. They partially succeeded, but Confucianism remains embedded in Chinese culture.

Types of Religious Groups

Sociologists have identified four types of religious groups: cult, sect, church, and ecclesia. The summary presented here is a modification of analyses by sociologists Ernst Troeltsch (1931), Liston Pope (1942), and Benton Johnson (1963). Figure 18.3 illustrates the relationship between each of these four types of groups.

Figure 18.3 Religious Groups: From Hostility to Acceptance

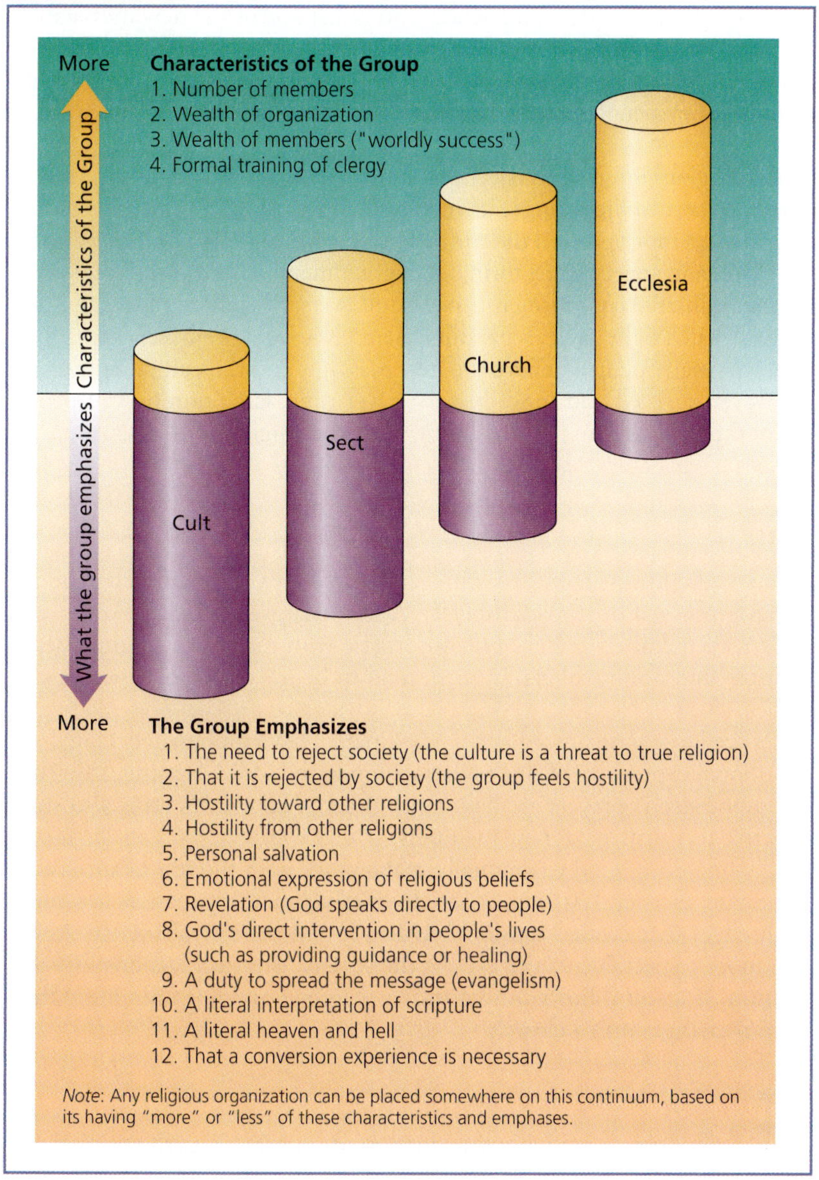

More
Characteristics of the Group
1. Number of members
2. Wealth of organization
3. Wealth of members ("worldly success")
4. Formal training of clergy
What the group emphasizes
Characteristics of the Group
Ecclesia
Church
Sect
Cult
More
The Group Emphasizes
1. The need to reject society (the culture is a threat to true religion)
2. That it is rejected by society (the group feels hostility)
3. Hostility toward other religions
4. Hostility from other religions
5. Personal salvation
6. Emotional expression of religious beliefs
7. Revelation (God speaks directly to people)
8. God's direct intervention in people's lives (such as providing guidance or healing)
9. A duty to spread the message (evangelism)
10. A literal interpretation of scripture
11. A literal heaven and hell
12. That a conversion experience is necessary
Note: Any religious organization can be placed somewhere on this continuum, based on its having "more" or "less" of these characteristics and emphases.

Sources: Based on Troeltsch 1931; Pope 1942; and Johnson 1963.

Cult

The word *cult* conjures up bizarre images—shaven heads, weird music, brainwashing—even ritual suicide may come to mind. Cults, however, are not necessarily weird, and few practice "brainwashing" or bizarre rituals. In fact, *all religions began as cults* (Stark 1989). A **cult** is simply a new or different religion whose teachings and practices put it at odds with the dominant culture and religion. Because the term cult arouses such negative meanings in the public mind, however, some scholars prefer to use *new religion* instead.

Cults often begin with the appearance of a **charismatic leader,** an individual who inspires people because he or she seems to have extraordinary qualities. **Charisma** refers to an outstanding gift or to some exceptional quality. People feel drawn to both the person and the message because they find something highly appealing about the individual—in some instances, almost a magnetic charm.

The most popular religion in the world began as a cult. Its handful of followers believed that an unschooled carpenter who preached in remote villages in a backwater country was the Son of God, that he was killed and came back to life. Those beliefs made

cult a new religion with few followers, whose teachings and practices put it at odds with the dominant culture and religion

charismatic leader literally, someone to whom God has given a gift; more commonly, someone who exerts extraordinary appeal to a group of followers

charisma literally, an extraordinary gift from God; more commonly, an outstanding, "magnetic" personality the early Christians a cult, setting them apart from the rest of their society. Persecuted by both religious and political authorities, these early believers clung to one another for support. Many cut off associations with their friends who didn't accept the new message. To others, the early Christians must have seemed deluded and brainwashed.

So it was with Islam. When Muhammad revealed his visions and said that God's name was really Allah, only a few people believed him. To others, he must have seemed crazy, deranged.

Each cult (or new religion) is met with rejection on the part of society. Its message is considered bizarre, its approach to life strange. Its members antagonize the majority, who are convinced that they have a monopoly on the truth. The new message may claim revelation, visions, visits from God and angels, some form of enlightenment, or seeing the true way to God. The cult demands intense commitment, and its followers, who are confronting a hostile world, pull together in a tight circle, separating themselves from nonbelievers.

Most cults fail. Not many people believe the new message, and the cult fades into obscurity. Some, however, succeed and make history. Over time, large numbers of people may come to accept the message and become followers of the religion. If this happens, the new religion changes from a cult to a sect.

Sect

A **sect** is larger than a cult, but its members still feel tension between their views and the prevailing beliefs and values of the broader society. A sect may even be hostile to its society. At the very least, its members remain uncomfortable with many of the emphases of the dominant culture, and nonmembers, in turn, tend to be uncomfortable with members of the sect.

Ordinarily, sects are loosely organized and fairly small. They emphasize personal salvation and an emotional expression of one's relationship with God. Clapping, shouting, dancing, and extemporaneous prayers are hallmarks of sects. Like cults, sects also stress **evangelism,** the active recruitment of new members.

If a sect grows, its members tend to gradually make peace with the rest of society. To appeal to a broader base, the sect shifts some of its doctrines, redefining matters to remove some of the rough edges that created tension between it and the rest of society. As the members become more respectable in the eyes of the society, they feel less hostility and little, if any, isolation. If a sect follows this course, as it grows and becomes more integrated into society, it changes into a church.

Church

At this point, the religious group is highly bureaucratized—probably with national and international headquarters that give direction to the local congregations, enforce rules about who can be ordained, and control finances. The relationship with God has grown less intense. The group is likely to have less emphasis on personal salvation and emotional expression. Worship services are likely to be more sedate, with sermons more formal, and written prayers read before the congregation. Rather than being recruited from the outside by fervent, personal evangelism, most new members now come from within, from children born to existing members. Rather than joining through conversion—seeing the new truth—children may be baptized, circumcised, or dedicated in some other way. At some designated age, children may be asked to affirm the group's beliefs in a confirmation or bar mitzvah ceremony.

sect a religious group larger than a cult that still feels substantial hostility from and toward society

evangelism an attempt to win converts

ecclesia a religious group so integrated into the dominant culture that it is difficult to tell where the one begins and the other leaves off; also called a *state religion*

Ecclesia

Finally, some groups become so well integrated into a culture, and so strongly allied with their government, that it is difficult to tell where one leaves off and the other takes over. In these *state religions,* also called **ecclesia,** the government and religion work together to try to shape society. There is no recruitment of members, for citizenship makes everyone a member. The majority of the society, however, may belong to the religion in name only. The religion is part of a cultural identification, not an eye-opening experience. How extensively religion and government intertwine in an ecclesia is illustrated by Sweden. In the 1860s, all citizens had to memorize Luther's *Small Catechism* and be tested on it yearly (Anderson 1995). Today, Lutheranism is still the state religion, but most Swedes come to church only for baptisms, marriages, and funerals.

While cults and sects see God as personally involved with and concerned about an individual's life, requiring an intense and direct response, ecclesias envision God as more impersonal and remote. Church services reflect this view of the supernatural, for they tend to be highly formal, directed by ministers or priests who, after undergoing rigorous training in approved schools or seminaries, follow prescribed rituals.

Examples of ecclesia include the Church of England (whose very name expresses alignment between church and state), the Lutheran church in Sweden and Denmark, Islam in Iran and Iraq, and, during the time of the Holy Roman Empire, the Roman Catholic Church, which was the official religion for the region that is now Europe.

denomination a "brand name" within a major religion, for example, Methodist or Baptist

Variations in Patterns

Obviously, not all religious groups go through all these stages—from cult to sect to church to ecclesia. Some die out because they fail to attract enough members. Others, such as the Amish, remain sects. And, as is evident from the few countries that have state religions, very few religions ever become ecclesias.

In addition, these classifications are not perfectly matched in the real world. For example, although the Amish are a sect, they place little or no emphasis on recruiting others. The early Quakers, another sect, shied away from emotional expressions of their beliefs. They would quietly meditate in church, with no one speaking, until God gave someone a message to share with others. Finally, some groups that become churches may retain a few characteristics of sects, such as an emphasis on evangelism or a personal relationship with God.

Although all religions began as cults, not all varieties of a particular religion begin that way. For example, some **denominations**—"brand names" within a major religion, such as Methodism or Reform Judaism—may begin as splinter groups. A group within a church may disagree with *some* aspects of the church's teachings (not its major message) and break away to form its own organization. An example is the Southern Baptist Convention, which was formed in 1845 to defend the right to own slaves (Ernst 1988; Nauta 1993; White 1995).

When Religion and Culture Conflict

As we have seen, cults and sects represent a break with the past. Consequently, they challenge the social order. Three major patterns of adaptation occur when religion and the culture in which it is embedded find themselves in conflict.

First, the members of a religion may reject the dominant culture and have as little as possible to do with nonmembers of their religion. Like the Amish, they may withdraw into closed communities. As noted in the Cultural Diversity box on page 105, the Amish broke away from Swiss-German Mennonites in 1693. They try to preserve the culture of their ancestors, who lived in a simpler time when there were no televisions, movies, automobiles, or even electricity. To do so, they emphasize family life and traditional male and female roles. They continue to wear the style of clothing that their ancestors wore three hundred years ago, to light their homes with oil lamps, and to speak German at home and in church. They also continue to reject radio, television, motorized vehicles, and education beyond the eighth grade. They do mingle with non-Amish when they shop in town—where they are readily distinguishable by their form of transportation (horse-drawn carriages), clothing, and speech.

In the *second* pattern, a cult or sect rejects only specific elements of the prevailing culture. For example, religious teachings may dictate that immodest clothing—short skirts, skimpy swimsuits, low-cut dresses, and so

Americans are a religious people, and one cannot understand them or their history unless one takes this into account. Most Americans consider religion to be a private matter, but some violate this background assumption and take to the streets with their message.

on—is immoral, or that wearing makeup or going to the movies is wrong. Most elements of the main culture, however, are accepted. Although specific activities are forbidden, members of the religion are able to participate in most aspects of the broader society. They resolve this mild tension either by adhering to the religion or by "sneaking," doing the forbidden acts on the sly.

In the *third* pattern, the society rejects the religious group. In the extreme, as with the early Christians, political leaders may even try to destroy it. The Roman emperor declared the followers of Jesus to be enemies of Rome and ordered them to be hunted down and destroyed. In the United States, after mobs hounded the new Mormons out of several communities, and then killed Joseph Smith, the founder of their religion, the Mormons decided to escape the dominant culture altogether. In 1847, they settled in a wilderness, in what is today Utah's Great Salt Lake Valley (Bridgwater 1953). Our opening vignette focused on another example, the destruction of the Branch Davidians by the U.S. government.

Religion in the United States

With its hundreds of denominations and sects, how can we generalize about religion in the United States? What do these many religious groups have in common? It certainly isn't doctrine (church teaching), but doctrine is not the focus of sociology. Sociologists, rather, are interested in the relationship between society and religion, and the role that religion plays in people's lives. To better understand religion in U.S. society, then, we shall focus first on the people who belong to religious groups, and then on the groups they belong to.

Characteristics of Members

About 70 percent of Americans belong to a church, synagogue, or mosque. Let's look at the characteristics of people who hold formal membership in a religion.

Social Class Religion in the United States is stratified by social class. As can be seen from Figure 18.4 below, each religious group draws members from all social classes, but some are "top-heavy" and others "bottom-heavy." The most top-heavy are the Episcopalians and Jews, the most bottom-heavy are the Baptists and Evangelicals (pente-

Figure 18.4 Income and Religious Affiliation

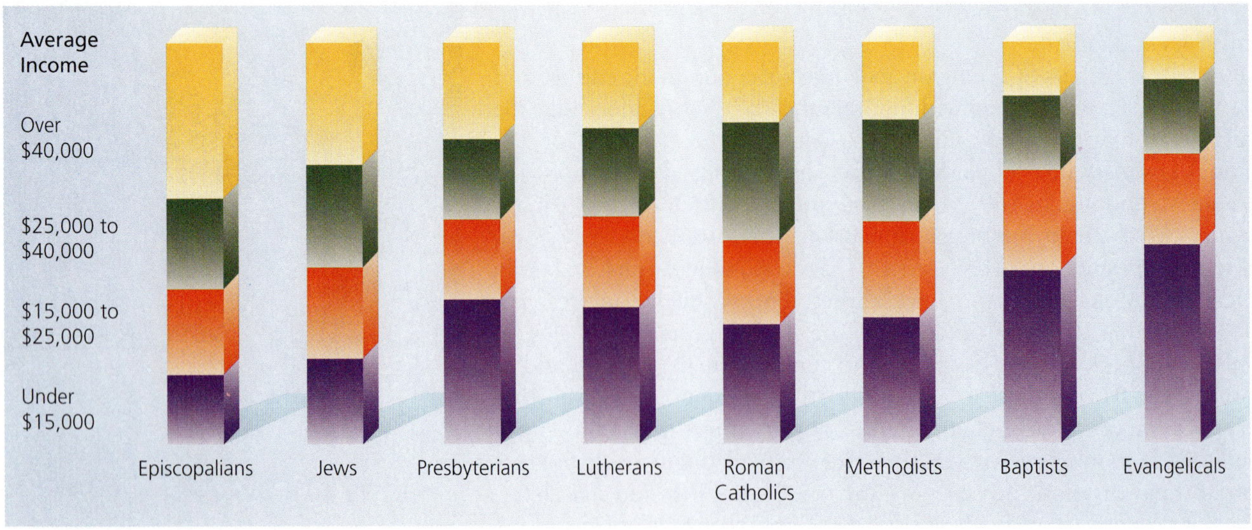

Source: Compiled from data in *Gallup Opinion Index*, 1987:20–27, 29.

costal and holiness groups). This figure is further confirmation that churchlike groups tend to appeal more to the successful, while the more sectlike groups appeal to the less successful.

Americans have a tendency to change their religion. About 40 percent of Americans belong to a denomination that is different from the one in which they were reared (Sherkat and Wilson 1991). People who change their social class are also likely to change their denomination. Upwardly mobile people are likely to seek a religion that draws more people from their new social class. An upwardly mobile Baptist, for example, may become a Methodist or a Presbyterian. For Roman Catholics, the situation is somewhat different. Because each parish is a geographical unit, an upwardly mobile individual who moves into a more affluent neighborhood is likely to automatically transfer into a congregation that has a larger proportion of affluent members.

Race and Ethnicity It is common for religions around the world to be associated with race and ethnicity: Islam with Arabs, Judaism with Jews, Hinduism with Indians, and Confucianism with Chinese. Sometimes, as with Hinduism and Confucianism, a religion and a particular country are almost synonymous. Christianity is not associated with any one country, although it is associated primarily with Western culture.

In the United States, all major religious groups draw from the nation's many racial and ethnic groups. Like social class, however, race and ethnicity tend to cluster. People of Latino or Irish descent are likely to be Roman Catholics, those of Greek origin to belong to the Greek Orthodox Church. African Americans are likely to be Protestants, more specifically Baptists, or to belong to fundamentalist sects.

Although many churches are integrated, it is with good reason that Sunday morning between 10 and 11 A.M. has been called "the most segregated hour in the United States." African Americans tend to belong to African American churches, while most whites see only whites in theirs. The segregation of churches is based on custom, not on law.

Age As shown in Table 18.2, the chances that an American belongs to a church or synagogue generally increase with age. The surveys on which this table is based usually show a smaller percentage of membership among those between the ages of 18 and 29. It could be that this latest survey is tapping a resurgence of religion among younger Americans. A possible—and intriguing—explanation for the large increases after age 50 is that religious people tend to outlive those who do not affiliate with a church or synagogue. Each year, as alcohol and nicotine abuse and other forms of unhealthy lifestyles take their toll, there remains a larger percentage of church members—whose more sedate lifestyles are conducive to better health and longer lives.

Table 18.2 Church and Synagogue Membership

Percentage of Population, by Age

Age	Membership
18–29	68%
30–49	64%
50–64	72%
65+	82%

Note: The source does not have totals for mosque membership.

Source: Statistical Abstract 2000:Table 75.

Table 18.3 The Largest U.S. Religious Groups[a]

Protestants 92,100,000
- Baptist 36,500,000
- Pentecostal 11,800,000
- Methodist 8,700,000
- Lutheran 8,400,000
- Mormon 5,400,000
- Churches of Christ 5,000,000
- African (and Christian) Methodist 4,500,000
- Presbyterian 3,900,000
- Episcopal Church 2,300,000
- Jehovah's Witness 1,000,000
- Seventh Day Adventist 900,000
- Church of the Nazarene 600,000
- Reformed Churches 500,000
- Salvation Army 500,000
- Armenian Church 400,000
- Church of the Brethren 400,000
- Christian Missionary Alliance 300,000
- Evangelical Church 300,000
- Community Churches 200,000
- Congregationalist 200,000
- Unitarian Universalist 200,000
- Mennonite 100,000

Roman Catholic 63,700,000
Jews 6,000,000
Eastern Orthodox 3,600,000
Islamic 1,800,000
Buddhist 400,000
Hindu 200,000

[a]All totals must be taken as approximate. Some groups ignore reporting forms. Totals are rounded to the nearest 100,000.

Sources: Niebuhr 2001 (for Muslim total); *Statistical Abstract* 2000:Table 74; 2002:Table 630.

Characteristics of Religious Groups

Let's examine features of the religious groups in the United States.

Diversity With its 350,000 congregations and hundreds of denominations, no religious group even comes close to being a dominant religion in the United States (*Statistical Abstract* 2002:Table 63). Table 18.3 illustrates some of this remarkable diversity, as did the box on U.S. Islam on page 526.

Pluralism and Freedom It is the U.S. government's policy not to interfere with religions. The government's position is that its obligation is to ensure an environment in

On April 19, 1993, the U.S. Bureau of Alcohol, Tobacco, and Firearms attacked the Branch Davidian compound in Waco, Texas. The leader of the cult and over 80 followers, including children, died in this fire.

which people can worship as they see fit. Religious freedom is so extensive that anyone can start his or her own church and proclaim himself or herself a minister, revelator, or any other desired term. At times, however, if officials feel threatened by a religious group, the government grossly violates its hands-off policy, as with the Branch Davidians featured in our opening vignette. Today, it is almost certain that the government has infiltrated mosques to monitor the activities of Arab immigrants in this country.

Competition and Recruitment The many religious groups of the United States compete for clients. They even advertise in the Yellow Pages of the telephone directory and insert appealing advertising—under the guise of news—in the religious section of the Saturday or Sunday edition of the local newspapers. Because of this intense competition, some groups modify their message, making it closer to what their successful competitors are offering (Greeley and Hout 1999).

Commitment Americans are a religious people, and about 44 percent report that they attend religious services each week (*Statistical Abstract* 2002:Table 64). Sociologists have questioned this statistic, suggesting that the high totals are due to an *interviewer effect.* Because people want to please interviewers, they stretch the truth a bit. To find out, sociologists Stanley Presser and Linda Stinson (1998) examined people's written reports (no interviewer present) on how they spend their Sundays. They concluded that actually about 30 percent or so attend church during a given week.

Whether the percentage of weekly church attendance is 30 or 44, religious people back up their commitment with generous support for religion and its charities. Each year Americans donate about $80 billion to religious causes (*Statistical Abstract* 2002:Table 554). To appreciate the significance of this huge figure, keep in mind that, unlike a country in which there is an ecclesia, those billions of dollars are not forced taxes but money that people give away.

Toleration The general religious toleration of Americans can be illustrated by three prevailing attitudes: (1) "All religions have a right to exist—as long as they don't try to brainwash or hurt anyone." (2) "With all the religions to choose from, how can anyone tell which one—if any—is true?" (3) "Each of us may be convinced about the truth of our religion—and that is good—but to try to convert others is a violation of the individual's dignity."

Fundamentalist Revival The fundamentalist Christian churches are undergoing a revival. They teach that the Bible is literally true and that salvation comes only through a personal relationship with Jesus Christ. They also denounce what they see as the degeneration of U.S. culture: sex on television, in movies, and in videos; abortion; corruption in public office; premarital sex, cohabitation; and drug use. Their answer to these problems is firm, simple, and direct: People whose hearts are changed through religious conversion will change their lives. The mainstream churches, which offer a more remote God and less emotional involvement, fail to meet the basic religious needs of large numbers of Americans. The Down-to-Earth Sociology box below describes a group whose needs are not met by mainstream religious groups.

DOWN TO EARTH SOCIOLOGY

Bikers and Bibles

The Bible Belt churchgoers in Eureka Springs, Arkansas, stare as Herbie Shreve, unshaven, his hair hanging over the collar of his denim vest, roars into town on his Harley Davidson. With hundreds of other bikers in town, it is going to be a wild weekend of drinking, nudity, and fights.

But not for Herbie. After pitching his tent, he sets up a table at which he offers other bikers free ice water and religious tracts. "No hard sell. They seek us out when it's the right time," says Herbie.

The ministry began when Herbie's father, a pastor, took up motorcycling to draw closer to his rebellious teenage son. As the pair rode around the heartland of America, they often were snubbed by fellow Christians when they tried to attend church. So Herbie's father hatched plans for a motorcycle ministry. "Jesus said, 'Go out to the highways and hedges,' and that always stuck with me," says the elder Shreve. "I felt churches ought to be wherever the people are."

They founded the Christian Motorcyclists' Association (CMA), headquartered in Hatfield, Arkansas. It now has about 35,000 members in more than 300 chapters in the United States, Canada, and the United Kingdom. Members of the CMA call themselves "redeemed riders" and "weekend warriors." "Riding for the Son" is emblazoned on their T-shirts and jackets—something that would make them stand out almost anywhere, but especially in the midst of the nudity and drunkenness.

Some Christian groups make evangelism, the conversion of others, a primary goal. One such group is the Christian Motorcyclists' Association. Its members say that they want to get people "to reverse direction, from the highway to hell to the highway to heaven." Mainstream churchgoers often find the appearance of CMA members offensive.

No CMA member has ever been harmed by a biker. But they have come close. In the early days, bikers at a rally surrounded Herbie's tent and threatened to burn it down. "Some of those same people are friends of mine today," says the elder Shreve.

Stepping over a biker who has passed out in front of his tent, Herbie walks through the campground urging last night's carousers to join them by a lake for a Sunday service. Four years ago no one took him up on it. Today twenty bikers straggle down to the dock.

Herbie's brief sermon is plain-spoken. He touches on the biker's alienation—the unpaid bills, the oppressive bosses, the righteous church ladies "who are always mad and always right." He tells them that Jesus loves them, and that they can call him anytime. "I'll help fix your life," he says.

CMA has several conversions this weekend. "You just stay at it. You don't know when their hearts are touched. Look at these guys," Herbie says, pointing to fellow CMA members. "They were all bikers headed for hell, too. Now they follow the Son."

Herbie gets on his Harley. In town, the traditional churchgoers stare as he roars past, his long hair sweeping behind him.

Sources: Based on Graham 1990; Shreve 1991.

Figure 18.5 U.S. Churches: Gains and Losses in Ten Years

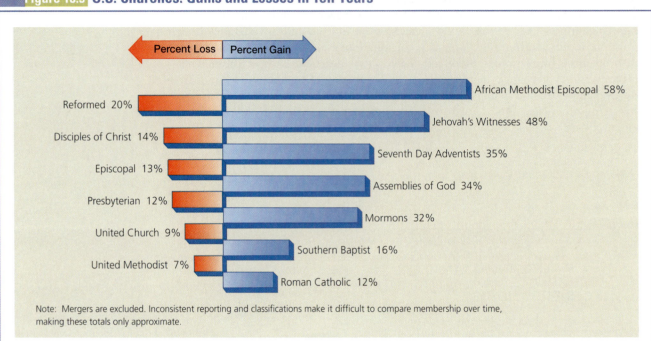

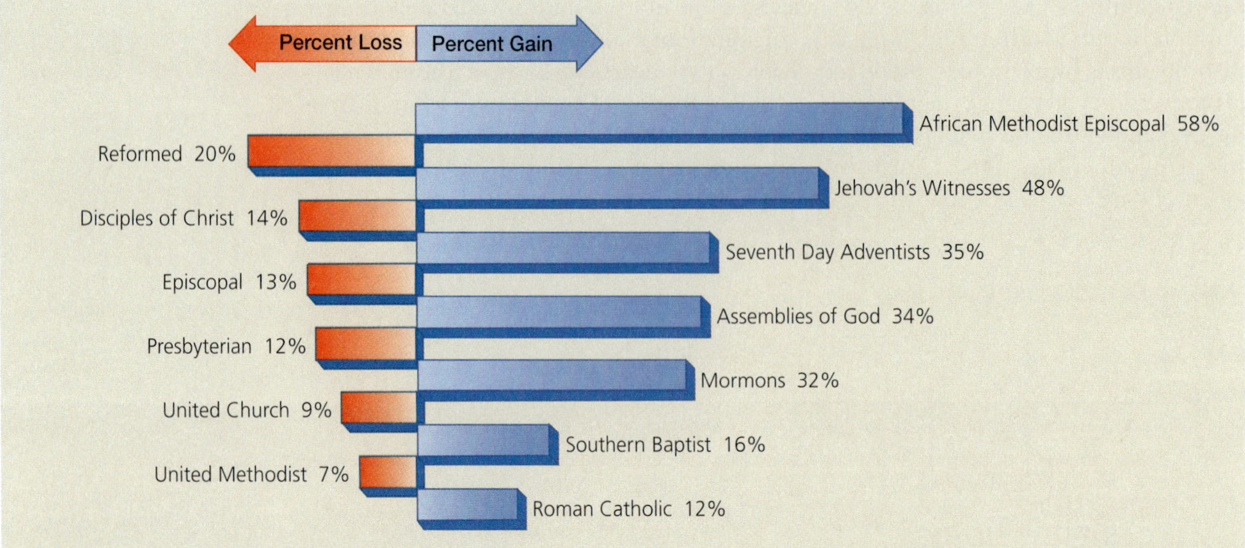

Note: Mergers are excluded. Inconsistent reporting and classifications make it difficult to compare membership over time, making these totals only approximate.

Source: By the author. Recomputed from Jones et al. 2002.

One result is that mainstream churches are losing members while the fundamentalists are gaining. Figure 18.5 above depicts this change. The exception is the Roman Catholic Church, whose growth in North America is due primarily to heavy immigration from Mexico and other Roman Catholic countries.

The Electronic Church What began as a ministry to shut-ins and those who do not belong to a church has blossomed into its own type of church. Its preachers, called "televangelists," reach millions of viewers and raise millions of dollars. Some of its most famous ministries are those of Robert Schuller (the "Crystal Cathedral") and Pat Robertson (the 700 Club).

Many local ministers view the electronic church as a competitor. They complain that it competes for the attention and dollars of their members. The electronic church replies that its money goes to good causes and that through its conversions it feeds members into the local churches, strengthening, not weakening them.

The Internet and Religion As with so many aspects of life, the Internet is having an impact on religion. We will focus on this change in the concluding section.

Secularization of Religion and Culture

The term *secularization* refers to the process by which worldly affairs replace spiritual interests. (The term **secular** means "belonging to the world and its affairs.") As we shall see, both religions and cultures can become secularized.

secular belonging to the world and its affairs

The Secularization of Religion

As the model, fashionably slender, paused before the head table of African American community leaders, her gold necklace glimmering above the low-cut bodice of her emerald-green dress, the hostess, a member of the Church of God in Christ, said, "It's now OK to wear more revealing clothes—as long as it's done in good taste." Then she added, "You couldn't do this when I was a girl, but now it's OK—and you can still worship God." (Author's files)

secularization of religion the replacement of a religion's spiritual or "otherworldly" concerns with concerns about "this world"

When I heard these words, I grabbed a napkin and quickly jotted them down, my sociological imagination stirred by their deep implication. As strange as it may seem, this simple event pinpoints the essence of why the Christian churches in the United States have splintered. Let's see how this could possibly be.

The simplest answer to why Christians don't have just one church, or at most several, instead of the hundreds of sects and denominations that dot the U.S. landscape, is disagreements about doctrine (church teaching). As theologian and sociologist Richard Niebuhr pointed out, however, there are many ways of settling doctrinal disputes besides splintering off and forming other religious organizations. Niebuhr (1929) suggested that the answer lies more in *social* change than it does in *religious* conflict.

The explanation goes like this. As noted earlier, when a sect becomes more churchlike, tension between it and the mainstream culture lessens. Quite likely, when a sect is first established, its founders and first members are poor, or at least not very successful in worldly pursuits. Feeling like strangers in the dominant culture, they derive a good part of their identity from their religion. In their church services and lifestyle, they stress how different their values are from those of the dominant culture. They are also likely to emphasize the joys of the coming afterlife, when they will be able to escape from their present pain.

As time passes, the group's values—such as frugality and the avoidance of gambling, alcohol, and drugs—help later generations become successful. As they attain more education and become more middle class, the group's members grow more respectable in the eyes of society. They no longer experience the alienation that was felt by the founders of their group. Life's burdens don't seem as heavy, and the need for relief through an afterlife becomes less pressing. Similarly, the pleasures of the world no longer appear as threatening to the "truth." As illustrated by the woman at the fashion show, people then attempt to harmonize their religious beliefs with their changing ideas about the culture.

This process is called the **secularization of religion**—shifting the focus from spiritual matters to the affairs of this world. Anyone familiar with today's mainstream Methodists would be surprised to know they once were a sect. Methodists used to ban playing cards, dancing, and theater attendance. They even considered circuses to be sinful. As Methodists grew more middle-class, however, they began to change their views on sin. They began to dismantle the barriers that they had constructed between themselves and the outside world (Finke and Stark 1992).

PEANUTS® by Charles M. Schulz

In its technical sense, to evangelize means to "announce the Good News" (that Jesus is the Savior). In its more common usage, to evangelize means to make converts. As Peanuts *so humorously picks up, evangelization is sometimes accomplished through means other than preaching.*

Secularization leads to a splintering of the group, for accommodation with the secular culture displeases some of the group's members, especially those who have had less worldly success. These people still feel a gulf between themselves and the broader culture. For them, tension and hostility continue to be real. They see secularization as a desertion of the group's fundamental truths, a "selling out" to the secular world.

After futile attempts by die-hards to bring the group back to its senses, the group splinters. Those who protested the secularization of Methodism, for example, were kicked out—even though *they* represented the values around which the group had organized in the first place. The dissatisfied—who by now are viewed as complainers—then form a sect that once again stresses its differences from the world, the need for more personal, emotional religious experiences, and salvation from the pain of living in this world. As time passes, the cycle repeats—adjustment to the dominant culture by some, continued dissatisfaction by others, and further splintering.

This process is not limited to sects, but also occurs in churches. When U.S. Episcopalians elected an openly gay bishop in 2003, some pastors and congregations splintered from the U.S. church and affiliated with the more conservative African archbishops. In an ironic twist, this made them mission congregations from Africa. No studies exist of the relative income/wealth of those who stayed with the group that elected the gay bishop and those who joined the splinter groups. If such a study is done and it turns out that there is no difference, we will have to modify the secularization thesis.

The Secularization of Culture Just as religion can secularize, so can culture. Sociologists use the term **secularization of culture** to refer to a culture that was once heavily influenced by religion, but no longer retains much of that influence. The United States provides an example.

Despite attempts to reinterpret history, the Pilgrims and most of the founders of the United States were highly religious people. The Pilgrims were even convinced that God had guided them to found a new community, while many of the framers of the U.S. constitution felt that God had guided them to develop a new form of government.

The clause in the Constitution that mandates the separation of church and state was *not* an attempt to keep religion out of government, but a (successful) device to avoid the establishment of a state religion like that in England. Here, people were to have the freedom to worship as they wished. The assumption of the founders was even more specific—that Protestantism represented the true religion.

The phrase in the Declaration of Independence, "All men are created equal," refers to a central belief in God as the creator of humanity. A member of the clergy opened Congress with prayer. Many colonial laws were based on principles derived explicitly from the Old and New Testaments. In some colonies, blasphemy was a crime, as was failing to observe the Sabbath. Similarly, adultery was a crime; in some places it even carried the death penalty. Even public kissing between husband and wife was considered an offense, punishable by placement in the public stocks (Frumkin 1967). In other words, religion permeated U.S. culture. It was part and parcel of how the Colonists saw life. Their lives, laws, and other aspects of the culture reflected their religious beliefs.

Today, U.S. culture has been secularized; the influence of religion on public affairs has greatly diminished. No longer are laws based on religious principles. It has even become illegal to post the Ten Commandments in civic buildings. In general, ideas of what is "generally good" have replaced religion as an organizing principle for the culture.

Underlying the secularization of culture is *modernization,* a term that refers to a society industrializing, urbanizing, developing mass education, and adopting science and advanced technology. The significance of modernization goes far beyond these surface changes. Science and advanced technology bring with them a secular view of the world that begins to permeate society. They provide explanations for many aspects of life that people traditionally attributed to God. As a consequence, people come to depend much less on religion to explain life events. Its satisfactions and problems—from births to deaths—are attributed to natural causes. When a society has secularized thoroughly, even religious leaders may turn to answers provided by biology, philosophy, psychology, sociology, and so on.

secularization of culture
the process by which a culture becomes less influenced by religion

Although the secularization of its culture means that religion has become less important in U.S. public life, *personal* religious involvement among Americans has not diminished. Rather, it has increased (Finke and Stark 1992). About 94 percent believe there is a God, and 77 percent believe there is a heaven. Not only do 68 percent claim membership in a church or synagogue, but, as we saw, on any given weekend somewhere between 30 and 44 percent of all Americans attend a worship service (Woodward 1989; Gallup 1990; *Statistical Abstract* 2002:Table 64).

Table 18.4 underscores the paradox. Look at how religious participation has increased while the culture has secularized. The proportion of Americans who belong to a church or synagogue is now *four* times higher than it was when the country was founded. Church membership, of course, is only a rough indicator of how significant religion is in people's lives. Some church members are not particularly religious, while many intensely religious people—Lincoln, for one—never join a church.

Table 18.4 Growth in Religious Membership

The Percentage of Americans Who Belong to a Church or Synagogue

Year	Percentage Who Claim Membership
1776	17%
1860	37%
1890	45%
1926	58%
1975	71%
2000	68%

Sources: Finke and Stark 1992; *Statistical Abstract* 2002:Table 64.

Note: The sources do not contain data on mosque membership.

The Future of Religion

A group of prominent intellectuals once foresaw an end to religion. As science advanced, they said, it would explain everything. It would transform human thought and replace religion, which was merely mistaken prescientific or superstitious thinking. In 1966 Anthony Wallace, one of the world's best-known anthropologists at the time, made the following observation:

> The evolutionary future of religion is extinction. Belief in supernatural beings . . . will become only an interesting historical memory. . . . doomed to die out, all over the world, as a result of the increasing adequacy and diffusion of scientific knowledge.

Wallace and the many other social analysts who took this position were wrong. Religion thrives in the most advanced scientific nations, in capitalist and in socialist countries. It is evident that these analysts did not understand the fundamental significance of religion in people's lives.

Humans are inquiring creatures. They are aware that they have a past, a present, and a future. They reflect on their experiences to try to make sense of them. One of the questions people develop as they reflect on life concerns the purpose of it all. Why are we born? Is there an afterlife? If so, where are we going, and what will it be like when we get there? Out of these concerns arises this question: If there is a God, what does God want of us in this life? Does God have a preference about how we should live?

There is no doubt that religion will last as long as humanity lasts, for science, including sociology, cannot answer such questions. By its very nature, science cannot tell us about four main concerns that many people have: (1) *The existence of God.* For this, science has nothing to say. No test tube has either isolated God or refuted God's existence. (2) *The purpose of life.* Although science can provide a definition of life and describe the characteristics of living organisms, it has nothing to say about ultimate purpose. (3) *An afterlife.* Science can offer no information on this at all, for it has no tests to prove or disprove a "hereafter." (4) *Morality.* Science can demonstrate the consequences of behavior, but not the moral superiority of one action compared with another. This means that science cannot even prove that loving your family and neighbor is superior to hurting and killing them. Science can describe death and measure consequences, but it cannot determine the moral superiority of any action, even in such an extreme example.

There is no doubt that religion will last as long as humanity lasts, for what could replace it? And if something did, and answered such questions, would it not be religion under a different name?

To glimpse the cutting edge of religious change, we'll close with a look at the online marketing of religion.

A basic principle of symbolic interactionism is that meaning is not inherent in an object or event, but is determined by people as they interpret the object or event. Old bones and fossils are an excellent illustration of this principle. Does this skull of homo erectus *"prove" evolution? Does it "disprove" creation? Such "proof" and "disproof" lie in the eye of the beholder, as evidenced by the recent rise of "scientific creationism," now gaining adherents in U.S. universities.*

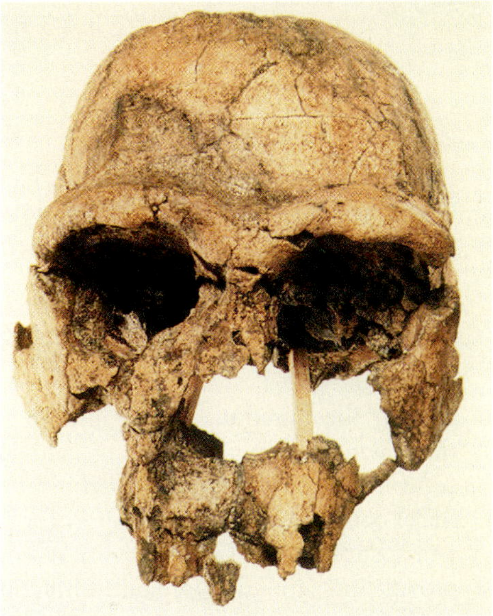

massMEDIA in Social Life

God on the Net: The Online Marketing of Religion

Erin Polzin, a 20-year-old college student, listens to a Lutheran worship service on the radio, confesses online, and uses PayPal to tithe. "I don't like getting up early," she says. "This is like going to church without really having to" (Bernstein 2003).

Going to church in your pajamas without even having to comb your hair does have a certain appeal. And this bothers some religious leaders. They are concerned about what they call the "faithful but lazy." But then, they always have been. The Internet is just changing the form of the "laziness."

But the Internet is doing much more than this. Some say that the Net has put us on the verge of a religious reformation as big as the one set off by Gutenberg's invention of the printing press. This does sound like an exaggeration, but perhaps it is true. The Net certainly has become popular for spiritual pursuits. More people have sought religious information online than have gambled online or used Web auction sites (Larsen 2001).

Muslims in France now download sermons and join an invisible community of worshipers at virtual mosques. Jews in Sweden type messages that fellow believers in Jerusalem download and insert in the Western Wall. Christians in California make digital donations to the Crystal Cathedral. Buddhists in Japan seek enlightenment online. The Internet helps to level the pulpit: On the Net, the leader of a pagan group can compete directly with the Pope.

The Internet is also making religious rebellion easier—and harder for organizations to punish their rebels. Jacques Gaillot is a French Roman Catholic bishop who upset the church hierarchy. He takes the position that the clergy should marry and that homosexual partnerships should be blessed. The Pope exiled him to the Saharan desert of North Africa, a strategy that used to work well. Instead of being silenced in his remote outpost, however, Gaillot logged onto the Internet, where he preaches to a virtual congregation via Real Audio (Huffstutter 1998; Wiliams 2003).

The Net poses a spiritual risk, too. There's always the chance that while you are surfing for religious answers, you'll come across one of those ubiquitous porn sites. But not if you are in the Philippines and using its largest Internet service provider (Sindayen 2001). It is run by the Catholic Bishops' Conference. If someone gives in to temptation and tries to tap into one of the forbidden destinations, up pops this message: "Thank God you're not able to access that bad site."

No one knows the outcome, but the times, they are a-changin'. Because of the Net, we now have:

- New churches that exist only in cyberspace
- Chat rooms directed by rabbis, priests, ministers, imans, and leaders of witchcraft
- Online donations by credit card and PayPal
- Online counseling for spiritual problems
- E-mailing of prayers

Will virtual religion satisfy? Can it replace the warm embrace of fellow believers? Will it bring comfort to someone in mourning in the same way that a sympathetic touch can? For some, yes. For others, not at all. We are gazing into the future. The extent to which this new medium will affect our religious lives—and perhaps even alter the face of religion—remains to be seen.

SUMMARY and REVIEW

What Is Religion?

Durkheim identified three essential characteristics of **religion:** beliefs that set the **sacred** apart from the **profane,** **rituals,** and a moral community (a **church**). Pp. 512–513.

The Functionalist Perspective

What are the functions and dysfunctions of religion?

Among the functions of religion are answering questions about ultimate meaning, providing emotional comfort, social solidarity, guidelines for everyday life, social control, adaptation, support for the government, and fostering social change. Groups or activities that provide these functions are called **functional equivalents** of religion. Among the dysfunctions of religion are religious persecution and war and terrorism. Pp. 513–517.

The Symbolic Interactionist Perspective

What aspects of religion do symbolic interactionists study?

Symbolic interactionists focus on the meanings of religion for its followers. They examine religious symbols, **rituals,** beliefs, **religious experiences,** and the sense of community that religion provides. Pp. 517–520.

The Conflict Perspective

What aspects of religion do conflict theorists study?

Conflict theorists examine the relationship of religion to social inequalities, especially how religion reinforces a society's stratification system. Pp. 520–521.

Religion and the Spirit of Capitalism

What does the spirit of capitalism have to do with religion?

Max Weber saw religion as a primary source of social change. He analyzed how Protestantism gave rise to the **Protestant ethic,** which stimulated what he called the **spirit of capitalism.** The result was capitalism, which transformed society. Pp. 521–522.

The World's Major Religions

What are the world's major religions?

Judaism, Christianity, and Islam, all **monotheistic** religions, can be traced to the same Old Testament roots. Hinduism, the chief religion of India, has no specific founder, but Judaism (Abraham), Christianity (Jesus), Islam (Muhammad), Buddhism (Gautama), and Confucianism (K'ung Fu-tsu) do. Specific teachings and history of these six religions are received in the text. Pp. 523–528.

Types of Religious Groups

What types of religious groups are there?

Sociologists divide religious groups into cults, sects, churches, and ecclesias. All religions began as **cults.** Those that survive tend to develop into **sects** and eventually into **churches.** Sects, often led by **charismatic leaders,** are unstable. Some are perceived as threats and are persecuted by the state. **Ecclesias,** or state religions, are rare. Pp. 528–532.

Religion in the United States

What are the main characteristics of religion in the United States?

Membership varies by social class, age, and race-ethnicity. The major characteristics are diversity, pluralism and freedom, competition, commitment, toleration, a fundamentalist revival, and the electronic church. Pp. 532–536.

What is the connection between secularization of religion and the splintering of churches?

Secularization of religion, a change in a religion's focus from spiritual matters to concerns of "this world," is the key to understanding why churches divide. Basically, as a cult or sect changes to accommodate its members' upward social class mobility, it changes into a church. Left dissatisfied are members who are not upwardly mobile. They tend to splinter off and form a new cult or sect, and the cycle repeats itself. Cultures permeated by religion also secularize. This, too, leaves many members dissatisfied and promotes social change. Pp. 536–539.

The Future of Religion

Although industrialization led to the **secularization of culture,** this did not spell the end of religion, as many social analysts assumed it would. Because science cannot answer questions about ultimate meaning, the existence of God or an afterlife, or provide guidelines for morality, the need for religion will remain. In any foreseeable future, religion will prosper. The Internet is likely to have far-reaching consequences on religion. Pp. 539–540.

Where can I read more on this topic?

Suggested Readings for this chapter are found at the back of this book.

THINKING Critically ABOUT CHAPTER 18

1. Since 9/11, many people have wondered how religion can be used to defend or promote terrorism. What materials in this chapter help answer this question? How do the analyses of groupthink in Chapter 6 and that of dehumanization in Chapter 15 fit into the analysis of terrorism in the Down-to-Earth Sociology box on Terrorism and the Mind of God (p. 518)?
2. How has secularization affected religion and culture in the United States (or of your country of birth)?
3. Why is religion likely to remain a strong feature of U.S. life—and remain strong in people's lives around the globe?

ADDITIONAL RESOURCES for This Chapter

www.ablongman.com/henslin7e

- *Content Select* Research Database for Sociology, with suggested key terms and annotated references
- Link to 2000 Census, with activities
- Flashcards of key terms and concepts
- Practice Tests
- Weblinks
- Interactive Maps

Chapter 19

Medicine and Health

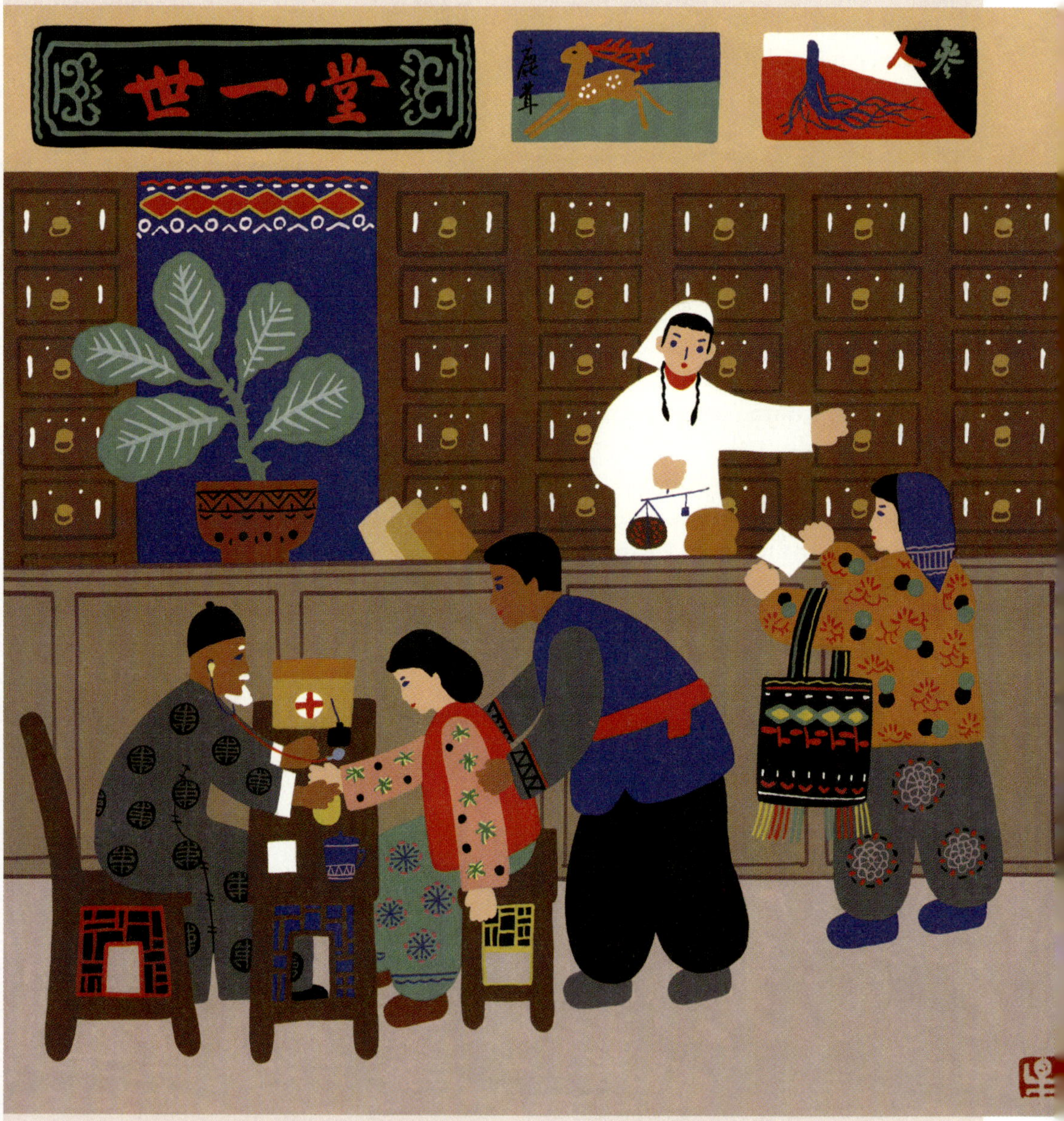

Chen Lian Xing, *Chinese Doctor*, 1998

I had decided that it was not enough to just study the homeless—I had to help them. I learned that a homeless shelter in St. Louis was planning to help poor people save on utilities by installing free wood stoves in their homes. This would help keep them from being forced onto the streets. It wasn't exactly applied sociology, but I volunteered.

I was a little anxious about the coming training session on how to install stoves, as I had never done anything like this. As I entered the homeless shelter on that Saturday morning, I found the building in semi-darkness. "They must be saving on electricity," I thought to myself. Then I was greeted with an unnerving sight. Two police officers were chasing a nude man, who was running through the halls. They caught him. I watched as the elderly man, looking confused, struggled to put on his clothing. From the police, I learned that he had ripped the wires out of the shelter's main electrical box; that was why there were no lights on.

I asked the officers where they were going to take the man, and they replied, "To Malcolm Bliss" (the state hospital). When I said, "I guess he'll be in there for quite a while," they replied, "Probably just a day or two. We picked him up last week—he was crawling under cars at a traffic light—and they let him out in two days."

Ve picked him up last week—

ne was crawling

under cars at a traffic light—

and they let him out in two days.

The police then explained that one must be a danger to others or to oneself in order to be admitted to the hospital as a long-term patient. Visualizing this old man crawling under stopped cars at an intersection, and considering how he had risked electrocution by ripping out the electrical wires with his bare hands, I marveled at the definition of "danger" that the psychiatrists must be using.

Chapter Outline

Sociology and the Study of Medicine and Health

This incident points to a severe problem with U.S. medical care. In this chapter, we will examine why the poor often receive second-rate medical care and, in some instances, abysmal treatment. We'll also look at how skyrocketing costs have created ethical dilemmas such as whether medical care should be rationed.

medicine one of the major social institutions that sociologists study; a society's organized ways of dealing with sickness and injury

shaman the healing specialist of tribal groups who attempts to control the spirits thought to cause a disease or injury; commonly called a witch doctor

health a human condition measured by four components: physical, mental, social, and spiritual

As we consider these issues, the role of sociology in studying **medicine**—a society's standard ways of dealing with illness and injury—will become apparent. For example, because U.S. medicine is a profession, a bureaucracy, and a big business, sociologists study how it is influenced by self-regulation, the bureaucratic structure, and the profit motive. Sociologists also study how illness and health are much more than biological matters—how, for example, they are related to cultural beliefs, lifestyle, and social class. Because of these emphases, the sociology of medicine is one of the applied fields of sociology, and many medical schools and even hospitals have sociologists on their staffs.

The Symbolic Interactionist Perspective

Let's begin, then, by examining how culture influences health and illness. This takes us to the heart of the symbolic interactionist perspective.

The Role of Culture in Defining Health and Illness

Suppose that one morning you look in the mirror and see strange blotches covering your face and chest. Hoping against hope that it is not serious, you rush to a doctor. If the doctor said that you had "dyschromic spirochetosis," your fears would be confirmed.

Now, wouldn't everyone around the world draw the conclusion that your spots are symptoms of a disease? No, not everybody. In one South American tribe, this skin condition is so common that the few individuals who *aren't* spotted are seen as the unhealthy ones. They are even excluded from marriage because they are "sick" (Ackernecht 1947; Zola 1983).

Consider mental "illness" and mental "health." People aren't automatically "crazy" because they do certain things. Rather, they are defined as "crazy" or "normal" according to cultural guidelines. If an American talks aloud to spirits that no one else can see, he or she is likely to be defined as insane—and, for everyone's good, locked up. In some tribal societies, in contrast, someone who talks to invisible spirits might be honored for being in close contact with the spiritual world—and, for everyone's good, be declared a **shaman,** or spiritual intermediary. He or she would then diagnose and treat medical problems.

"Sickness" and "health," then, are not absolutes, as we might suppose. Rather, they are matters of definition. Around the world, each culture provides guidelines that its people use to determine whether they are "healthy" or "sick." As discussed in the Cultural Diversity box, those guidelines also tell you what your illness is. This is another example of how the social construction of reality plays a vital role in our lives.

We define health and illness according to our culture. If almost everyone in a village had this skin disease, the villagers might consider it normal—and those without it the unhealthy ones. I photographed this infant in a jungle village in Orissa, India, so remote that it could be reached only by following a foot path.

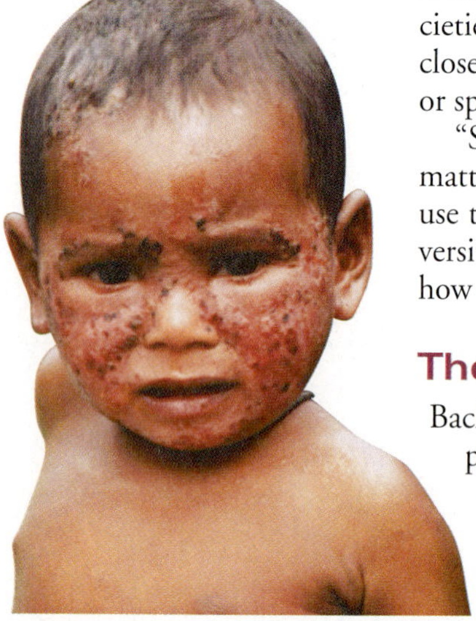

The Components of Health

Back in 1941, international "health experts" identified three components of **health:** physical, mental, and social (World Health Organization 1946). They missed the focus of our previous chapter, however, and I have added a spiritual component to Figure 19.1. Even the dimensions of health, then, are subject to debate.

If we were to agree on the components of health, we would still be left with the question of what makes someone physically, mentally, socially, or spiritually

CULTURAL DIVERSITY in the UNITED STATES

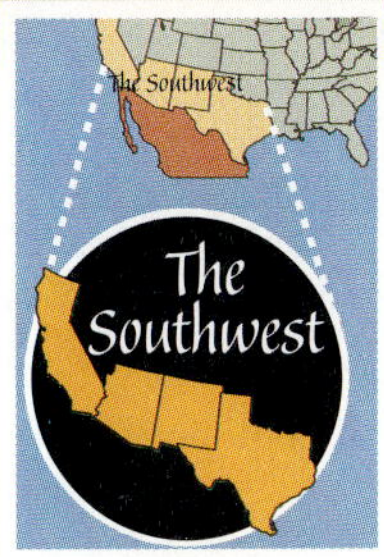

"You Don't Know What *Empacho* Is? What Kind of a Doctor Are You?"

How do you know what illness you have when you don't feel good? Your culture gives you the answer. It gives you a word to apply to your symptoms, such as flu, fever, or cold. Not surprisingly, the same symptoms have different names in different cultures. This is to be expected, for languages differ. The significance of there being different names for the same symptoms, however, extends far beyond the terms that are used. The name can imply different causes of the problem and the need for different cures. The difference can be so great that some illnesses exist in one culture and not another.

Mexicans, for example, suffer from *empacho,* but U.S. physicians haven't even heard of this health problem. *Empacho* is food stuck in the intestines. It leads to severe stomach aches. Massage sometimes relieves *empacho,* helping to get the food unstuck and moving along. So do teas and herbs.

So what happens when immigrants from Mexico go to U.S. doctors who have never heard of *empacho*? The doctor thinks the patient is dumb for thinking that food gets stuck in the intestines, and the patient thinks the doctor is dumb for not knowing about such a common sickness.

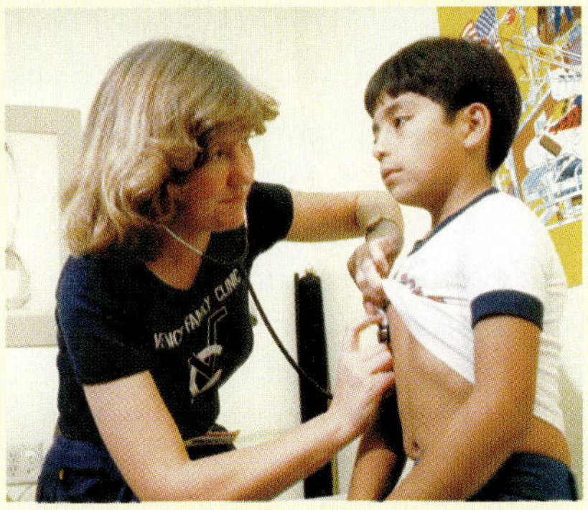

How do you think this doctor's assumptions of the cause and proper treatment of illness might contrast with those of the immigrant parents of her patient?

As these immigrants make a gradual transition to U.S. ways, they will adopt a new way of thinking about illness. In the meantime, in order to adequately treat these patients, physicians need to understand the immigrant culture. *Empacho* is not just a different name for a common ailment. It is about a different way of thinking. *Empacho* is real for these immigrants. To dismiss *empacho* as folklore and useless knowledge is to show disdain for the patient.

The dismissal of empacho also creates suspicion. If the doctor doesn't even know about *empacho*—which *everyone* knows about—how can he or she be trusted to treat other ailments?

For Your CONSIDERATION

The culture conflict is clear. Both patient and doctor have learned different ways of viewing reality. The symptoms are evident to both, but the meaning is entirely different to the Mexican immigrant and the U.S. physician. How do you think the physician can use *empacho* to treat the patient—and to build trust?

healthy. Again, as symbolic interactionists stress, these are not objective matters; rather, what is considered "health" or "illness" varies from culture to culture. In a pluralistic society, they also differ from one group to another.

As with religion in the previous chapter, then, the concern of sociologists is not to define "true" health or "true" illness. Instead, it is to analyze the effects that people's ideas about health and illness have on their lives, and even the ways in which people determine that they are sick.

Figure 19.1 A Continuum of Health and Illness

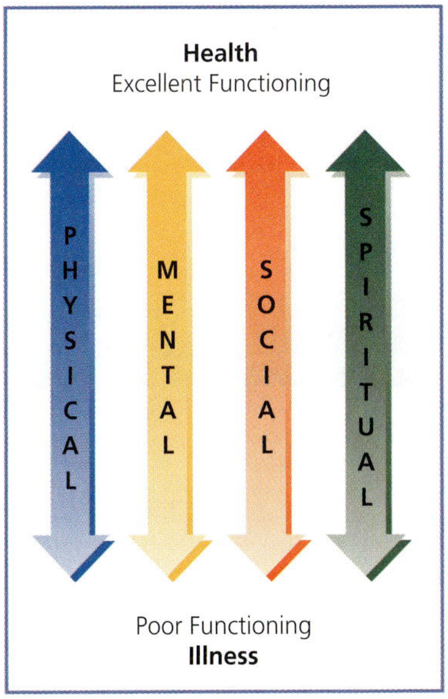

The Functionalist Perspective

Functionalists begin with an obvious point: If society is to function well, its people need to be healthy enough to perform their normal roles. This means that societies must set up ways to control sickness. One way they do this is to develop a system of medical care. Another way is to make rules to keep too many people from "being sick." Let's look at how this works.

The Sick Role

Do you remember when your throat began to hurt, and when your mom or dad took your temperature the thermometer registered 102°F? Your parents took you to the

sick role a social role that excuses people from normal obligations because they are sick or injured, while at the same time expecting them to seek competent help and cooperate in getting well

doctor, and despite your protests that tomorrow was the first day of summer vacation (or some other important event), you had to spend the next three days in bed taking medicine. You were forced to play what sociologists call the "sick role." What do they mean by this term?

Elements of the Sick Role Talcott Parsons, the functionalist who first analyzed the **sick role,** pointed out that it has four elements—you are not held responsible for being sick, you are exempt from normal responsibilities, you don't like the role, and you will get competent help so you can return to your routines. If people don't seek competent help, they are considered responsible for being sick. They are denied the right to claim sympathy from others and permission to be excused from their normal routines. People who seek help are given sympathy and encouragement; the others are given the cold shoulder for wrongfully claiming the sick role.

Ambiguity in the Sick Role Instead of a fever of 102°F, suppose the thermometer registers 99.5°F. Do you then "become" sick or not? That is, do you decide to claim the sick role? Because most instances of illness are not as clear-cut as, say, a heart attack or a limb fracture, decisions to claim the sick role often are based more on social considerations than on physical conditions. Let's also suppose that you are facing a midterm, you are unprepared for it, and you are allowed to make it up if you are ill. The more you think about the test, the worse you are likely to feel—which makes the need to claim the sick role seem more legitimate. Now assume that the thermometer still shows 99.5, but you have no test and your friends are coming over to take you out to celebrate your twenty-first birthday. You are not likely to play the sick role. Note that in both cases your physical condition is the same.

Gatekeepers to the Sick Role Parents and physicians are the primary gatekeepers to the sick role. That is, they mediate between children's feelings of illness and their claim to being sick. Before parents call the school to excuse a child's absence, they decide whether the child is faking or has genuine symptoms that are serious enough to warrant keeping him or her home from school. For adults, physicians are gatekeepers of the sick role. If employers and teachers receive a "doctor's excuse" (official permission for someone to play the sick role), they have no need to pass judgment on the individual's claim.

Gender Differences in the Sick Role Try to figure out this riddle. On average, women are healthier than men, and they live longer. Yet they are also sick more often and go to doctors more frequently (*Statistical Abstract* 2002:Tables 149, 151, 152, 153). How can both statements be true? Apparently, the answer is that women are more willing than men to claim the sick role when they don't feel well (Klonoff and Landrine 1992). The sick role does not match the *macho* image that most boys and men try to project. Most men try to follow the cultural ideal that they should be strong, keep pain to themselves, and "tough it out." Women, in contrast, are given a model that they should share their feelings and seek help from others. Gender roles, then, apparently underlie this riddle of why women can be healthier than men and yet be sick and go to doctors more often.

The Conflict Perspective

As stressed in earlier chapters, the primary focus of conflict theorists is how people struggle over scarce resources. Since medical treatment is one of those resources, let's examine this competition in global perspective and then see how one group developed a monopoly on U.S. health care.

Effects of Global Stratification on Health Care

In Chapter 9 (pages 249–252), we saw how the nations that industrialized first obtained the economic and military power that brought them riches and allowed them to dominate the globe. This also led to global stratification of medical care, a matter of life and death for people around the world. For example, open heart surgery has become routine in the Most Industrialized Nations. The Least Industrialized Nations, however, cannot afford the technology that open heart surgery requires. The photo on this page goes a long way to explaining why. So it is with AIDS. In the United States and other rich nations, those who suffer from AIDS have had their lives extended by expensive medicines. People with AIDS in the Least Industrialized Nations can't afford these medicines. For them, AIDS is a death sentence.

Life expectancy and infant mortality rates tell the story. Most people in the industrialized world can expect to live to about age 75, but *most* people in Angola, Malawi, Mozambique, and Zimbabwe die before they reach 40. As Figure 19.2 shows, in many rich countries fewer than 7 of every 1,000 babies die before they are a year old. In some countries, in contrast, infant mortality runs almost *thirty* times higher. In Angola, for example, of every 1,000 babies, 195 never reach their first birthday (*Statistical Abstract* 2002:Table 1312).

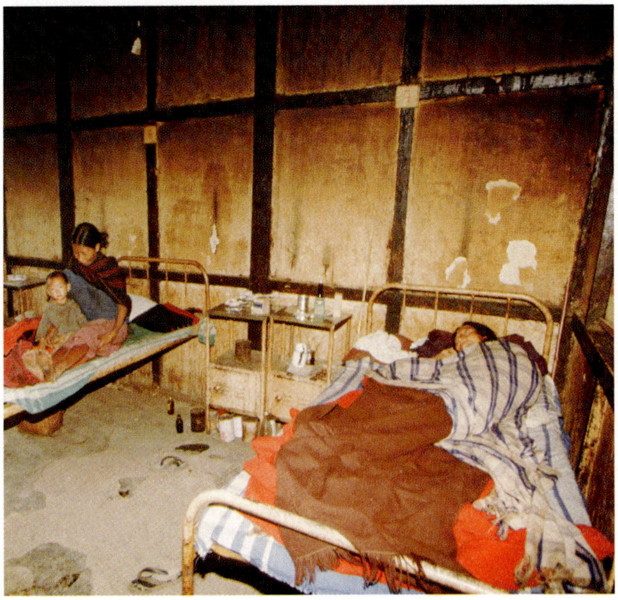

It is difficult to believe, but this is a hospital room. As you would expect, the tuberculosis patients in this hospital have a high rate of mortality. This photo was taken in Nagaland, India.

Global stratification even helps to determine what diseases we get. Suppose that you had been born in a Least Industrialized Nation located in the tropics. During your much shorter life, you would face illness and death from four major sources: malaria (from mosquitoes), internal parasites (from contaminated water), diarrhea (from food and soil contaminated with human feces), and malnutrition. You would not face heart disease and cancer, for they are "luxury" diseases; that is, they characterize the industrialized world where people live long enough to get them. As nations industrialize, they improve health care and nutrition, and their people live longer. The diseases that used to be their primary killers decline, and residents begin to worry about cancer and heart attacks instead.

There is also the matter of social stratification *within* the Least Industrialized Nations. Many diseases that ravage the poor people in these countries could be brought under control if more funds were spent on public health. Cheap drugs can prevent malaria, while safer water supplies and higher food production would go a long way toward eliminating the other major killers. The meager funds that these countries have at their disposal are not spent this way, however. Instead, having garnered the lion's share of the country's

Figure 19.2 **How Many Babies Die Before Their First Birthday?**

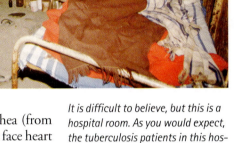

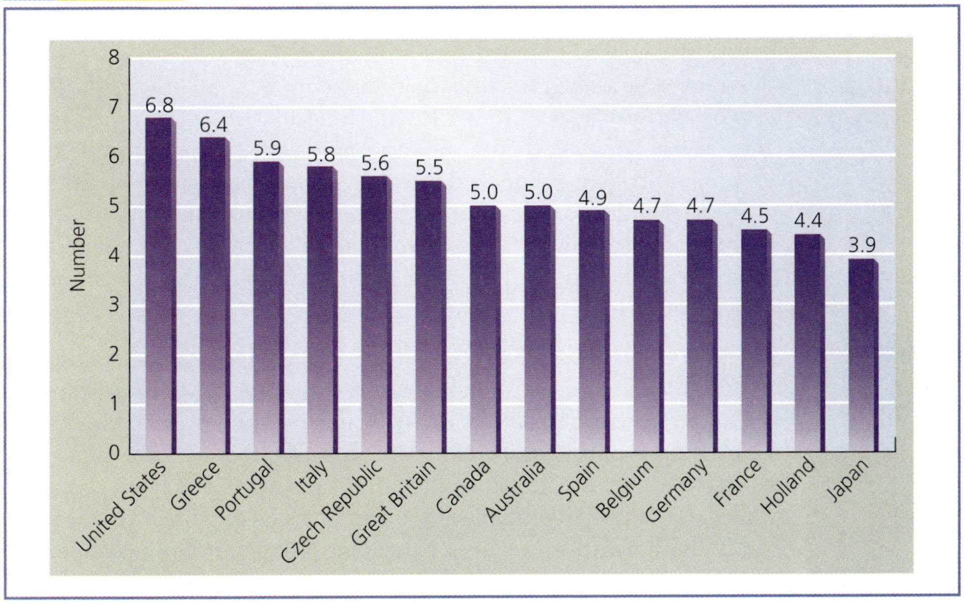

Note: All countries listed in the source with an infant mortality rate below that of the United States. That this is not a complete list is evident from Austria, Switzerland, Hong Kong, and Sweden being dropped from the source, all of which had lower rates in the 1997 edition. Infant mortality is defined as the number of babies that die before their first birthday, per 1,000 live births.
Source: By the author. Based on *Statistical Abstract* 2002:Table 1312.

professionalization of medicine the development of medicine into a specialty in which education becomes rigorous, and in which physicians claim a theoretical understanding of illness, regulate themselves, claim to be doing a service to society (rather than just following self-interest), and take authority over clients

resources, the elite lavish it on themselves. They even send a few students to top medical schools in the West. This gives them access to advanced technology—from X-rays to life support systems. In contrast, the poor of these nations go without even basic medical services and continue to die at an early age.

Establishing a Monopoly on U.S. Health Care

Let's turn our focus to medicine in the United States. How did medicine become the largest business in the country? How did it become the only legal monopoly in the United States? To find the answers, we need to understand how medicine became professionalized.

The Professionalization of Medicine Imagine that you are living in the American colonies in the 1700s and that you want to become a physician. There are no required courses. No entrance exams. In fact, you won't need *any* formal education at all, for there are no medical schools. You can simply ask a physician to train you. In return for the opportunity to learn, you'll be his assistant and will help him with menial tasks. When *you* think that you have learned enough, you'll hang out a shingle and proclaim yourself a doctor. The process is much the same as what an automobile mechanic goes through today. In fact, you can even skip the apprenticeship if you wish, and simply hang out your shingle—just like a mechanic. If you can convince people you are good, you'll make a living. If not, you'll turn to something else.

In the 1800s, things began to change. A few medical schools opened, and there was some licensing of physicians. The medical schools of this period were like religions are today: They competed for clients and made different claims to the truth. One medical school would teach a particular idea about what caused illness and how to treat it, while another medical school would teach something else. Training was short, and often not even a high school diploma was required. There was no clinical training, and lectures went unchanged from year to year. The medical school at Harvard University took only two school years to complete—and the school year lasted only four months (Starr 1982; Rosenberg 1987; Riessman 1994).

Then came the 1900s. In 1906, the United States had 160 medical schools. The Carnegie Foundation asked Abraham Flexner, a renowned educator, to evaluate them. Even the most inadequate schools opened their doors to Flexner, for they thought that gifts from the Carnegie Foundation would follow (Rodash 1982). In some schools, the laboratories consisted only of "a few vagrant test tubes squirreled away in a cigar box." Other schools had libraries with no books. Flexner advised that to raise standards, philanthropies should fund the most promising schools. They did, and the schools that were funded upgraded their facilities and were able to attract more capable faculty and students. In the face of higher standards and greater competition, most of the other schools had to close their doors.

As hard as it is to believe, doctors used to be available at the beck and call of patients. They would come to a patient's home, diagnose the illness, prescribe medication, and even sit up all night with the critically ill—all for a modest fee. This photo is from the 1950s.

The Flexner report (1910) led to the **professionalization of medicine.** When sociologists use the term *profession,* they mean something quite specific. What happened was that physicians began to (1) undergo a rigorous education; (2) claim a theoretical understanding of illness; (3) regulate themselves; (4) assert that they were performing a service for society (rather than just following self-interest); and (5) take authority over clients (Goode 1960; Freidson 2001).

The Monopoly of Medicine When medicine became a profession, it also became a monopoly, and this is the key to understanding our current situation. The group that gained control over U.S. medicine set itself up as *the* medical establishment. This group was able to get laws passed to restrict medical licensing only to graduates of schools they controlled. By controlling the education and licensing of physicians, the medical establishment silenced most competing philosophies of medicine. The WASP males who took control also either refused to admit women and minorities to medical schools or severely limited their enrollment.

Eliminating the competition paved the way for medicine to become big business. The monopoly was so thorough that by law only a select group of men—a sort of priesthood of medicine—was allowed to diagnose and treat medical problems. Only they knew what was right for people's health. Only they could scribble the secret language (Latin) on special pieces of parchment (prescription forms) for translators (pharmacists) to decipher (Miner 2003). This select group was able to shape itself into the most lucrative profession in the country—for its members set their own fees and had little competition. This group of men became so powerful that it was even able to take childbirth away from midwives—the focus of the Down-to-Earth sociology box below.

fee-for-service payment to a physician to diagnose and treat a patient's medical problems

This approach, called **fee-for-service** (payment to a physician in exchange for diagnosis and treatment), which made medicine a *business,* usually went unquestioned. Then, as monopolies do, the medical monopoly drove up the price of health care. This led to a

DOWN-TO-EARTH SOCIOLOGY

To Establish a Monopoly, Eliminate Your Competition: How Physicians Defeated Midwives

A STUDY OF THE HISTORY OF midwifery helps us understand the professionalization of medicine and provides insight into the founding of the U.S. medical establishment. In the United States, as in Europe and elsewhere, pregnancy and childbirth were considered natural events, and women were thought best equipped to help other women deal with them. Consequently, midwives delivered babies. Some midwives were trained; others were neighborhood women who had experience in childbirth. In many European countries, midwives were licensed by the state—as they still are.

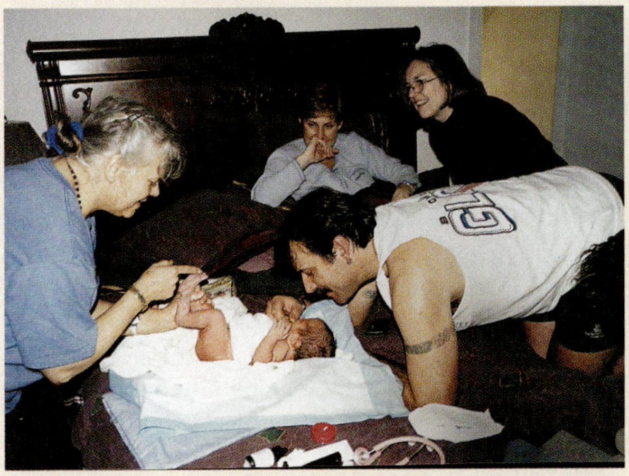

The text discusses how physicians were able to eliminate their competition in delivering babies. In some states, midwives have made a comeback. Shown here is a midwife after she delivered a baby at the parents' home.

As medicine became professionalized, physicians wanted to expand their business. Their desire for expansion, however, ran up against two major obstacles. The first was the midwives, who didn't want physicians to cut into their business. The second was ignorance. Physicians didn't know anything about delivering babies. It was considered indecent for a man to know much about pregnancy, and unheard of for a man to help a woman give birth.

The physicians bribed midwives to sneak them into the bedrooms where women were giving birth. To say "sneaked" is no exaggeration, for some physicians crawled on their hands and knees so that the mother-to-be wouldn't know a man was present. Most physicians, however, weren't fortunate enough to find such cooperative midwives, and they had to train with mannequins. After physicians were able to attend childbirths, a veil of indecency persisted; doctors had to fumble blindly under a sheet in a darkened room, their head decorously turned aside.

As physicians gained political power, they launched a ruthless campaign against their competitors. They attacked midwives as "dirty, ignorant, and incompetent," even calling them a "menace to the health of the community." Using their new political clout in the American Medical Association, physicians succeeded in persuading many states to pass laws that made it illegal for anyone but physicians to deliver babies. Some states, however, continued to allow nurse-midwives to practice. The struggle is not yet over, and nurse-midwives and physicians sometimes still clash over who has the right to deliver babies.

Conflict theorists emphasize that this was a gender struggle—men sought to take control over what had been women's work. They stress that political power was central to the way physicians expanded their domain. Symbolic interactionists, without denying the political aspect, stress the social construction of reality. The key, they say, is the information campaign that physicians launched to eliminate midwives, convincing the public that pregnancy and childbirth were not natural processes, but medical conditions that required the assistance of an able man. This new definition, which flew in the face of the millennia-old tradition of women helping women to have babies, turned childbirth into "men's work." The prestige of the work went up—and so did the price.

Sources: Wertz and Wertz 1981; Rodash 1982; Danzi 1989; Rothman 1994.

public outcry: Because the poor couldn't afford medical treatment, the government should pay for it. The AMA fought every proposal for the government to fund medical care. Physicians were convinced that government funding would "socialize" medicine—that it would eliminate the fee-for-service system and turn doctors into government employees.

In the 1960s, proponents of government funding won. *Medicaid* (government-paid medical care for the poor) and *Medicare* (government-sponsored medical care for the elderly) were established. Physicians' fears proved groundless. Instead of leading to the socialization of medicine, these programs gave physicians millions of additional customers. People who previously could not afford medical services now had their medical expenses paid by the government. As Figure 13.8 on page 377 illustrates, these costly programs have put billions of dollars into physicians' pockets.

From its humble origins, medicine has grown into the largest business in the United States. This business consists not only of physicians, but also of nurses, physician extenders, hospital personnel, pharmacists, insurance companies, corporations that own hospitals and nursing homes, and the huge research, manufacturing, and sales force that lies behind our drugs and medical technology. The medical monopoly is so powerful that it lobbies all the state legislatures and the U.S. Congress. Like sports, some hospitals even pay sign-up bonuses to lure big-name surgeons (McCartney 1993).

Historical Patterns of Health

Let's look at how health and illness in the United States have changed. This will take us into the field of **epidemiology,** the study of how medical disorders are distributed throughout a population.

Physical Health

Leading Causes of Death One way to see how the physical health of Americans has changed is to compare the leading causes of death in two time periods. To get an idea of how dramatic this change is, look at Figure 19.3. Note that half of the leading causes of death in 1900 don't even appear on today's list. Heart disease and cancer, which placed fourth and eighth in 1900, have now jumped to the top of the list, while tuberculosis and diarrhea, which were the number one and number three killers in 1900, don't even show up in today's top ten. Similarly, murder and suicide didn't make the top ten in 1900, but they do now. These shifts indicate that extensive changes have occurred in society. Health, disease, and death, then, are not only biological events. They are also *social,* following the contours of social change.

Were Americans Healthier in the Past? A second way to see how the physical health of Americans has changed is to ask if they are healthier—or sicker—than they used to be. This question brings us face to face with the definitional problem discussed earlier. "Healthy" by whose standards? An additional problem is that many of today's diseases went unrecognized in the past. One way around these problems is to look at mortality rates. If Americans used to live longer, we can assume they were healthier. Because most people today live longer than their ancestors, however, we can conclude that contemporary Americans are healthier.

Some may think this conclusion flies in the face of abundant evidence to the contrary: We all know about our polluted air and water. Then, too, there are the high rates of heart disease and cancer shown in Figure 19.3. And it does. Sometimes older people say, "When I was a kid, hardly anyone died from cancer, and now it seems almost everyone does." What they overlook is that most cancers strike older people, and when life expectancy is shorter, there is less chance that people will die from cancer. Also, in the past most cancer went unrecognized. People were simply said to have died of "old age" or "heart failure."

Mental Health

When it comes to mental health, we have no way to make good comparisons. We may picture a past in which the elderly had lower suicide rates, less mental illness, and so on, but to know if this is true we need solid measures of mental illness or mental health, not stories of

epidemiology the study of disease and disability patterns in a population how things used to be. The idyllic past—where everyone grew up in happy homes with two loving parents, married for life, and lived in harmony in close-knit families with everyone helping one another—never existed. These images are myths that make current life look worse than it is (Coontz 2000). All groups have their share of mental problems—and commonsense beliefs that mental illness is worse today represent a perception, not measured reality. Such perceptions may be true, of course, but the *opposite* could also be true. Since we don't even know how extensive mental illness is today (Scheff 1999), we certainly can't judge how much there was in the past.

Issues in Health Care

Let's turn to issues in health care in the United States.

Medical Care: A Right or a Commodity?

A primary controversy in the United States is whether medical care is a right or a privilege. If it is a right, then all citizens should have access to good medical care. If it is a privilege, then, as with automobiles, clothing, and other commodities, the rich will have access to one type of care, and the poor to another. Currently, medical care is *not* the right of citizens. It is a commodity to be sold at the highest price. Those with the money can buy better quality health care, while the poor and uninsured must go without—or wait for handouts. The attempts to address this disparity with some system of national medical care have been futile.

Related to this issue is the skyrocketing cost of medical care. As shown in Figure 19.4, in 1960 the average American spent $150 a year on health care. Today the average American spends about $4,500. To grasp what this means, consider this. In

Figure 19.4 The Soaring Cost of Medical Care: What the Average American Pays Each Year

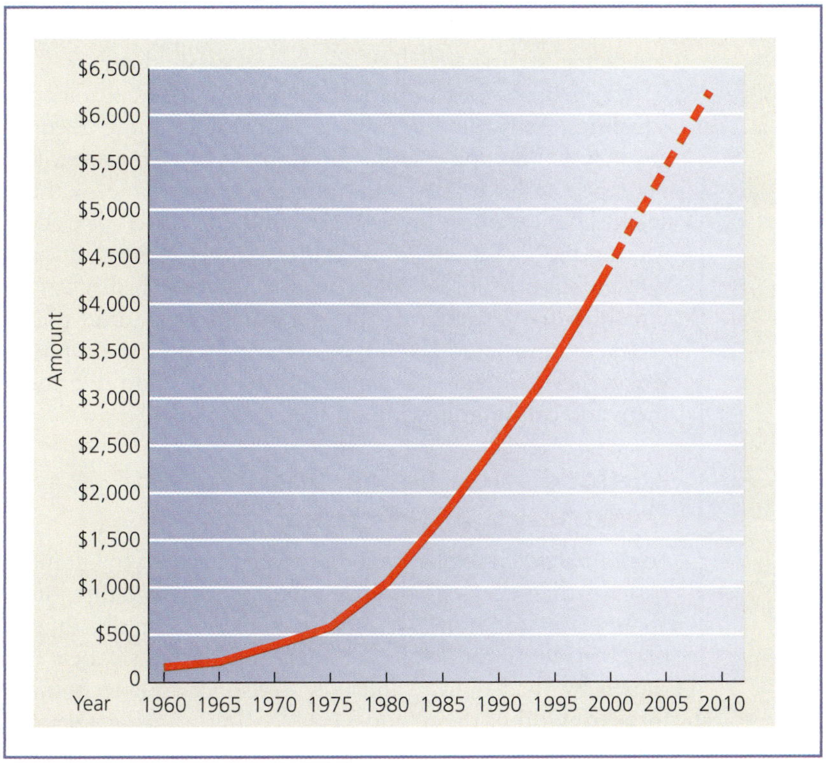

Source: By the author. Based on *Statistical Abstract* 2002:Table 115, and earlier years.

Figure 19.3 The Top Ten Causes of Death in the United States, 1900 and 2000

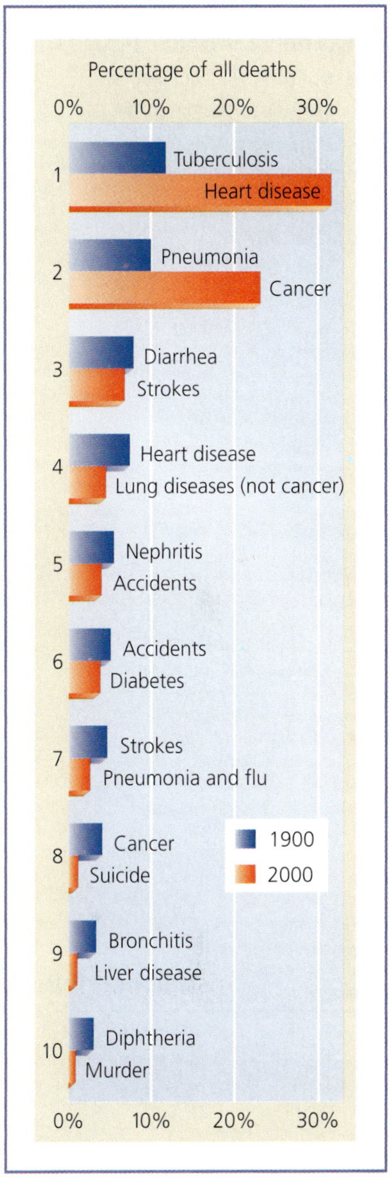

Sources: By the author. Based on National Center for Health Statistics; *Statistical Abstract* 2002:Table 100.

two-tier system of medical care a system of medical care in which the wealthy receive superior medical care and the poor inferior medical care

deinstitutionalization the release of patients from mental hospitals into the community, supposedly while receiving treatment from outpatient services

1960, a 17-inch black-and-white television also cost about $150. If the cost of televisions had risen at the same rate as that of health care, a 17-inch *black-and-white* television would now cost about $4,500. The reasons for this increase in medical costs include the growing numbers of elderly and the new medical technology.

Because health care is a commodity—and a costly one—we have a **two-tier system of medical care.** That is, there is superior care for those who can afford the cost, and inferior care for those who cannot. In short, medical care is like other commodities, such as new sports cars for the wealthy and worn out used cars for the poor.

Social Inequality

The opening vignette, which described the nude man in the homeless shelter who was being taken to the state mental hospital, lays bare the two-tier system of medical care. A middle-class or rich person who had mental problems would visit a private psychiatrist, not be sent to a state mental hospital. Of course, he or she would not have been in that shelter in the first place.

Since 1939, sociologists have found an inverse correlation between mental problems and social class. In other words, the lower the social class, the more mental problems there are. This finding has been confirmed in numerous studies (Faris and Dunham 1939; Hudson 1988; Ross and van Willigen 1997; Croudace et. al 2000). It is not difficult to understand why people in the lower social classes have greater mental problems, for these people bear the many stresses that come with poverty. Compared with middle- and upper-class Americans, the poor have less job security, lower wages, and more unpaid bills and insistent bill collectors. They are also more likely to divorce, to be victims of violent crime, and to abuse alcohol. Such conditions deal severe blows to emotional well-being.

In the 1960s, politicians and psychiatrists came up with a policy that brought shame to the mental health establishment. Called **deinstitutionalization,** the plan was to open the locked wards of state mental hospitals, release the patients, and give them counseling and medications on the outside. The patients were released, but the outpatient services were not put in place. As a result, U.S. streets were flooded with former mental patients who had no money and nowhere to go. The streets became their home.

Needless to say, it was poor people who were abandoned on the streets. Members of the middle and upper classes who had mental problems were counseled by private psychiatrists and, if hospitalized, went to expensive private mental hospitals. The rich were treated with "talk" therapy (various forms of psychotherapy), while the poor were given "medicinal straitjackets" (medication to sedate them).

Figure 19.5 Number of Days Sick

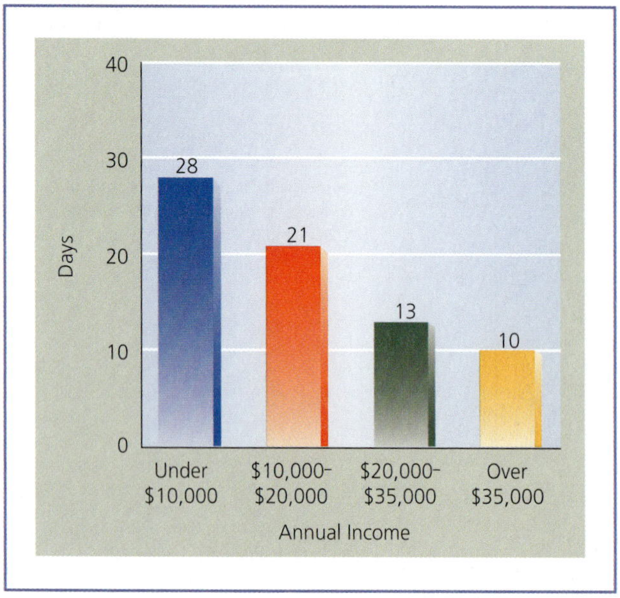

Note: Number of days people were so sick or injured that they cut down on their usual activities for more than half a day; includes days off work and school.
Source: By the author. Based on *Statistical Abstract* 2000:Table 211

When it comes to physical illnesses, we find similar inequalities. As Figure 19.5 shows, the poor are more likely to get sick. Unlike the middle and upper classes, however, few poor people have a personal physician, and some of them spend hours waiting in crowded public health clinics. After waiting most of a day, some don't even get to see a doctor; they are simply told to come back the next day (Fialka 1993). Finally, when hospitalized, the poor are likely to find themselves in understaffed and underfunded public hospitals, where they are treated by rotating interns who do not know them and cannot follow up on their progress.

Malpractice Suits and Defensive Medicine

Some analysts have observed that physicians used to kill more patients than they cured. Given that physicians didn't know about germs and didn't wash before surgery or childbirth, this may be true. In the 1800s, doctors thought that sickness was caused by "bad fluids," and they developed four techniques for getting rid of these fluids: (1) bleeding (cutting a vein or using leeches to drain out "bad" blood); (2) blistering (applying packs so hot they burned the skin, causing "bad pus" to drain); (3) vomiting (feeding patients liquids that made them vomit up the bad fluids); and (4) purging (feeding patients substances that caused diarrhea).

In light of today's superior treatment, one might think malpractice suits would be a thing of the past. The opposite, however, is true. Back then, the law didn't allow patients to recover damages. The thinking was, "People make mistakes," and that included doctors. Today, physicians are held to much higher standards—and not excused for making mistakes. Damage awards are high, and doctors are anxious. One physician told me, "I'm looking for something else to do, because medicine is no longer fun. Every time I treat a patient, I wonder if this is the one who is going to turn around and sue me."

defensive medicine medical practices done not for the patient's benefit but in order to protect a physician from malpractice suits

To protect themselves, physicians practice **defensive medicine.** They consult with colleagues and order lab tests not because the patient needs them but because they want to leave a paper trail in case they are sued. These consultations and tests—done for the doctor's benefit, not the patient's—are one of the major reasons for the increase in the nation's annual medical bill (Volti 1995; Hammerstein 2000). To reduce the costs of defensive medicine, the state of Maine created physician checklists. If doctors follow them, malpractice suits are dismissed (Felsenthal 1993). Although physicians complain about a "paint-by-numbers" approach to medicine, many prefer this to the threat of lawsuits.

Medical Incompetence

My own father was dying of diabetes. He had a large open sore on his foot that wouldn't heal. Dad lived in Minnesota and was taken to the Mayo Clinic in Rochester. While I was visiting him there—and the last time that I saw him alive—orderlies wheeled him out to X-ray his back. Later, my dad complained that his back hurt because he had to lie for a long time on a hard surface.

Something didn't seem right about this. Why would they X-ray his back for either diabetes or a sore on his foot? When I saw the additional pain that my dad was going through, I reported the situation to the head doctor. He examined the records and said that the attending physician had X-rayed the wrong patient. Charts had been bunched together, and my dad's had been pulled instead of the one next to it.

There are a lot worse cases. A woman entered a hospital because of a problem with her lungs—and her doctor did a hysterectomy. No, I'm not making this up. It happened in New York City (Steinhauer and Fessenden 2001). Another doctor operated on the wrong side of a patient's brain, and yet another removed the wrong kidney—leaving the cancerous one intact. Still other physicians operate on the wrong patient altogether (Steinhauer 2001). Although not an everyday event, these things do happen.

Few would disagree that if a surgeon removes the wrong breast, the patient has the right to sue her doctor. But are some malpractice suits unfair? Certainly. Some patients sue doctors for trivial matters, others for matters over which physicians have no control. Yet, despite the rigors of medical education, medical incompetence is extensive. As the photo on this page shows, doctors also accidentally leave tools inside patients. In only 55 percent of cases do doctors correctly diagnose their patients' illnesses (McGlynn et al. 2003). In most cases, this isn't really serious, but in many cases it is. The Institute of Medicine, a branch of the National Academy of Sciences, reports that each year between 44,000 and 98,000 Americans die at the hands of doctors. *If the number of Americans killed by medical errors were an official classification of death, it would rank as one of the top ten leading causes of death* (Steinhauer and Fessenden 2001).

In our age of scientific medicine, the errors by doctors and nurses are astounding. As the text explains, if medical mistakes were listed as a cause of death, they would rank in the top ten.

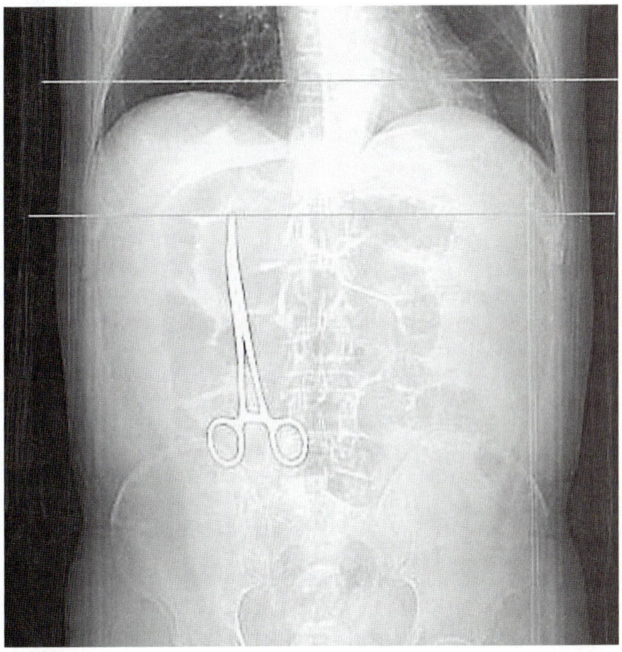

To reduce these needless errors and deaths (what the medical profession calls "adverse events"), in some hospitals the patient and doctor sign their names in ink at the point where an incision is to be made, so no doctor will remove the wrong body part. Because many patients die from cross-reactions of prescription drugs, some suggest that doctors enter all prescriptions

depersonalization dealing with people as though they were objects; in the case of medical care, as though patients were merely cases and diseases, not people

online. A computer program would check patient records, causing the monitor to flash a warning if a doctor tries to prescribe a drug that can interfere with other medications.

A more radical proposal, which gets at the heart of the matter, was made by the Institute of Medicine. The Institute recommends that we establish a Federal Center for Patient Safety. All medical deaths and injuries would be reported to the Center. Just as the Federal Aviation Agency investigates each plane crash, the Center would investigate each medical injury and death. Based on the cause it pinpointed, the Center would set up guidelines designed to reduce the number of similar events. Then, before you are admitted to a hospital, you could check to see how many patients at that hospital have been injured or killed through incompetence.

Depersonalization: The Medical Cash Machine

Sociologist Sue Fisher (1986), who was examined for an ovarian mass, gives this account:

> On my initial visit a nurse called me into an examination room, asked me to undress, gave me a paper gown to put on and told me the doctor would be with me soon. I was stunned. Was I not even to see the doctor before undressing? . . . How could I present myself as a competent, knowledgeable person sitting undressed on the examining table? But I had a potentially cancerous growth, so I did as I had been told.
>
> In a few minutes the nurse returned and said, "Lie down. The doctor is coming." Again I complied. The doctor entered the examining room, nodded in my direction while reading my chart, and proceeded to examine me without ever having spoken to me.

One of the main criticisms leveled against the medical profession is **depersonalization,** the practice of dealing with people as though they were cases and diseases, not individuals. Many patients have the impression that they are being treated by a cash machine—a physician who, while talking to them, is impatiently counting minutes and tabulating dollars so that he or she can move on to the next customer and make more money. After all, any extra time spent with a patient is money down the drain.

Some students start medical school with lofty motives. They want to "treat the whole person," yet they, too, learn to depersonalize patients. Sociologists Jack Haas and William Shaffir (1993), who did participant observation at McMaster University in Canada, discovered how this happens. As vast amounts of material are thrown at medical students, their feelings for patients are overpowered by the need to be efficient. Consider this student's report:

> Somebody will say, "Listen to Mrs. Jones's heart. It's just a little thing flubbing on the table." And *you forget about the rest of her* . . . and it helps in learning in the sense that you can go in to a patient, put your stethoscope on the heart, listen to it, and walk out. . . . The advantage is that *you can go in a short time and see a patient, get the important things out of the patient, and leave* (italics added).

This student's statement to the researchers reveals the extent to which patients become objects.

> You don't know the people that are under anesthesia—just practice putting the tube in, and the person wakes up with a sore throat, and well, it's just sort of a part of the procedure. . . . Someone comes in who has croaked (and you say), "Well, come on. Here is a chance to practice your intubation" (inserting a tube in the throat).

Conflict of Interest

> Sandy was surprised when her doctor brought another person with him to her examination. She would have been even more surprised to learn that this other person was a pharmaceutical sales representative who had paid the doctor to be present at the examination (Petersen 2002).

It turns out that the representative had paid to be present so he could recommend his company's drugs to treat Sandy. Although this representative carried things a little farther than most, drug companies often pay doctors to prescribe their brands of drugs. One doctor received $300,000 for recommending to other doctors that they prescribe a particular drug to their patients (Petersen 2003). Cancer specialists generate *most* of their income by selling drugs to patients. They buy the drugs for chemotherapy at a low price and charge a much higher price when they administer the drugs to their patients (Abelson 2003).

You can see the conflict of interest. If doctors tell patients to stop chemotherapy when they see that it is doing no good, their profits stop, but if they continue the treatment, so do their profits. Another example is when drug companies give bonuses or free vacations to doctors who prescribe their drugs. Is a doctor basing a course of treatment on the patient's best interest—or on the best interest of the doctor's bank account?

Medical Fraud

With 2 million Medicare claims filed every day, physicians with Medicare patients are not likely to be audited. Many have not been able to resist the temptation to cheat. The following are not isolated incidents—they are just some of the most outrageous.

> One doctor wrote so many prescriptions for a patient for OxyContin that to use them the patient would have had to take 31 tablets a day. The patient was a drug dealer (Meier 2001). Another billed Medicare for multiple services on a patient's eye—the only problem was that the patient was missing that eye (Levy 2003). A psychiatrist in California had sex with his patient—and charged Medicaid for the time (Geis et al. 1995).

Worse yet is medical fraud that endangers people's lives. One pharmacist sold expired pacemakers (Schatz 1995). Another, a highly respected pharmacist in Kansas City who was worth $10 million, couldn't resist piling up just a few more bucks. He diluted the drugs he provided for patients in chemotherapy (Belluck 2001).

Sexism in Medicine

In Chapter 11 (page 305), we saw that physicians don't take women's health complaints as seriously as they do those of men. As a result, women with heart disease are operated on at a later stage, making it more likely that they will die from their surgery.

The sexism involving heart disease was so subtle that the physicians were not even aware that they were discriminating against women. Some sexism in medicine, in contrast, is blatant. One of the best examples is bias *against* women's reproductive organs. Sue Fisher (1986), whose encounter with depersonalized medicine was cited earlier, did participant observation in a hospital. When she heard doctors recommend total hysterectomy (removal of both the uterus and the ovaries) even when no cancer was present, she asked why. The doctors explained that the uterus and ovaries are "potentially disease-producing" organs. They also said that these organs are unnecessary after the childbearing years, so why not remove them?

Since few women feel the same way, in order to make money, surgeons have to "sell" the operation. Here is how one doctor explained his "hard sell" to sociologist Diana Scully (1994):

> You have to look for your surgical procedures; you have to go after patients. Because no one is crazy enough to come and say, "Hey, here I am. I want you to operate on me." You have to sometimes convince the patient that she is really sick—if she is, of course [laughs], and that she is better off with a surgical procedure.

To "convince" a woman to have this surgery, the doctor tells her that, unfortunately, the examination has turned up fibroids in her uterus—and they *might* turn into cancer. This statement is often sufficient, for it frightens women, who picture themselves dying from cancer. To clinch the sale, the surgeon withholds the rest of the truth—that the fibroids probably will not turn into cancer and that she has several alternatives to surgery.

Underlying this sexism is male dominance of medicine in the United States. The sex ratio is changing rapidly, however. In 1970, only 8 percent of U.S. medical degrees went to women. Today it is 43 percent (*Statistical Abstract* 2002:Table 281). This change should reduce sexism in medical practice.

The Medicalization of Society

As we have seen, childbirth and women's reproductive organs have come to be defined as medical matters. Sociologists use the term **medicalization** to refer to the process of turning something that was not previously considered a medical issue into a medical matter. "Bad" behavior is an example. If a psychiatric model is followed, crime becomes not willful behavior that should be punished, but a symptom of unresolved mental problems that were created during childhood. These problems need to be treated by doctors. The human body is a favorite target of medicalization. Characteristics that once were taken for granted—such as acne, balding, sagging buttocks and chins, small breasts, and wrinkles—have become medical problems, also in need of treatment by physicians.

As usual, the three theoretical perspectives give us three views of the medicalization of these human conditions. Symbolic interactionists would stress that there is nothing inherently medical about acne, balding, sagging chins, and so on. It is all a matter of definition: People used to consider such matters as normal problems of life; now they are starting to redefine them as medical problems. Functionalists would stress that the medicalization of such conditions helps the medical establishment by broadening its customer base. They would also point out another functional aspect of medicalization—that it provides people with someone who will listen to their problems and this sometimes helps them. Conflict sociologists would argue that this process indicates the growing power of the medical establishment: The more conditions of life that physicians can medicalize, the greater their profits and power.

Medically Assisted Suicide

> I started the intravenous dripper, which released a salt solution through a needle into her vein, and I kept her arm tied down so she wouldn't jerk it. This was difficult as her veins were fragile. And then once she decided she was ready to go, she just hit the switch and the device cut off the saline drip and through the needle released a solution of thiopental that put her to sleep in ten to fifteen seconds. A minute later, through the needle flowed a lethal solution of potassium chloride. (Jack Kevorkian, as quoted in Denzin 1992)

The topic of suicide fascinates the U.S. public. A how-to book on suicide, *Final Exit,* sold more than a half million copies. End-of-Life Choices (formerly the Hemlock Society), a group that advocates voluntary **euthanasia** (mercy killing) for terminally ill people, has grown to eighty chapters. In 1997, Oregon passed a law allowing medically assisted suicide. Opponents called it legalized murder. The controversy continues, and for any physician who participates in a suicide the U.S. Attorney General has threatened to revoke that person's right to prescribe controlled drugs.

Oregon's law and the acts of Kevorkian have brought us face to face with matters of death that are both disturbing and difficult to resolve. Should "medically assisted suicide" be legal? The following Thinking Critically section explores these issues.

medicalization the transformation of something into a matter to be treated by physicians

euthanasia mercy killing

THINKING Critically

Should Doctors Be Allowed to Kill Patients?

Except for the name, this is a true story:

> Bill Simpson, who was in his seventies, had battled leukemia for years. After doctors removed his spleen, he developed an abdominal abscess. It took another operation to drain it. A week later, the abscess filled, and Bill required more surgery. Again the abscess returned. Simpson began to drift in and out of consciousness. His brother-in-law suggested euthanasia. The surgeon injected a lethal dose of morphine into Simpson's intravenous feeding tubes.

At a medical conference, a cancer specialist who had treated thousands of patients announced that he had kept count of those who had asked him to help them die. "There were 127 men and women," he said. Then he added, "And I saw to it that 25 of them got their wish." Thousands of other physicians have done the same (Nuland 1999).

The public seems to hold two dominant images of people who undergo euthanasia. One impression is of an individual who is devastated by chronic pain. The doctor mercifully helps to end that pain by performing euthanasia. The second is of a brain-dead individual—a human vegetable—who lies in a hospital bed, kept alive only by machines. How accurate are these images?

We have the example of Holland. There, along with Belgium, euthanasia is legal, Incredibly, in about 1,000 cases a year, physicians kill their patients without the patients' express consent. In one instance, a doctor ended the life of a nun because he thought she would have wanted him to but was afraid to ask because it was against her religion. In another case, a physician terminated a patient with breast cancer who said that she did *not* want euthanasia. In the doctor's words, "It could have taken another week before she died. I just needed this bed" (Hendin 1997, 2000).

Some Dutch are concerned that they could be euthanized if they have a medical emergency. They carry "passports" that instruct medical personnel that they wish to live. Most Dutch, however, support euthanasia. Many carry another "passport," one that instructs medical personnel to carry out euthanasia (Shapiro 1997).

Jack Kevorkian, the physician who assisted with the suicide mentioned on the previous page, gave the authorities a rough time. He helped 120 people commit suicide. He even taunted the authorities, sometimes dumping bodies off at motels or leaving them in vans. Kevorkian was careful. He provided the "death machine" and the drugs, but he never touched the lever that released the drugs. Michigan prosecutors tried Kevorkian for murder four times, but juries refused to convict him. Then, Kevorkian went too far. He played a videotape on national television, showing him giving a lethal injection to a man who was dying from Lou Gehrig's disease. Prosecutors put Kevorkian on trial again. He was convicted of second degree murder and was sentenced to 10 to 25 years in prison.

For Your CONSIDERATION . . .

Do you think that physicians should have the right to assist in suicides? In addition to what is reported here, Dutch doctors also kill newborn babies who have serious birth defects (Smith 1999). Their justification is that these children would not have "quality of life." Would you support this?

Sources: Gomez 1991; Markson 1992; Angell 1996; Smith 1999; Naik 2002.

health maintenance organization (HMO) a health care organization that provides medical treatment to its members for a fixed annual cost

Curbing Costs: Issues in Health Insurance

We have seen some of the reasons why the price of medical care in the United States has soared: advanced—and expensive—technology for diagnosis and treatment, a growing elderly population, tests performed as defensive measures rather than for medical reasons, and health care that is regarded as a commodity to be sold to the highest bidder. As long as these conditions are in place, the price of medical care will continue to outpace inflation. Let's look at some attempts to reduce costs.

HMOs **Health Maintenance Organizations**, or HMOs, are medical companies that charge an annual fee in exchange for providing medical care for a corporation's employees. Prices are lower because HMOs bid against one another. Whatever money is left over at the end of the year is the HMO's profit. While this arrangement eliminates unnecessary medical treatment, it also puts pressure on doctors to reduce *necessary* treatment.

The results are anything but pretty. Over her doctor's strenuous objections, a friend of mine was discharged from the hospital even though she was still bleeding and running a fever. Her HMO representative said he would not authorize another day in the hospital. A lung specialist in Washington Heights, New York, fought with his HMO for three hours to get permission to do a procedure on a woman who was coughing up life-threatening

FRANK & ERNEST by ® Bob Thaves

The cartoonist has captured an unfortunate reality of U.S. medicine.

dumping the practice of sending unprofitable patients to public hospitals

amounts of blood (Steinhauer 1999). After suffering a heart attack, a man in Kansas City, Missouri, needed surgery that could be performed only at Barnes Hospital in St. Louis, Missouri. The HMO said, "Too bad. That hospital is out of our service area." The man died while appealing the HMO decision (Spragins 1996).

The basic question, of course, is: At what human cost do we reduce spending on medical treatment?

Diagnosis-Related Groups To curb spiraling costs, the federal government has classified all illnesses into diagnosis-related-groups (DRGs) and has set an amount that it will pay for the treatment of each illness. Hospitals make a profit if they move patients through the system quickly—if they discharge patients before the allotted amount is spent. As a consequence, some patients are discharged before they are fully ready to go home. Others are refused admittance because they appear to have a "worse than average" case of a particular illness. In other words, they might take longer to treat and would cost the hospital money instead of making it a profit.

National Health Insurance

> A young woman who was five months pregnant was taken to a hospital complaining of stomach pains. The hospital refused to admit her, because she had no money or credit. As they were about to transfer her to a hospital for the poor, she gave birth. The baby was stillborn. The hospital went ahead and transferred the woman—dead baby, umbilical cord, and all (Ansberry 1988).

Dumping, the practice of refusing to treat unprofitable patients and sending them to public hospitals, is one consequence of a system that puts profit ahead of patient care. Most cases are less dramatic than that of the woman and her stillborn baby, but the same principle applies. With 30 million Americans uninsured (*Statistical Abstract* 2002:Table 137), pressure has grown for the government to provide national health insurance. The Social Map below shows how the uninsured are distributed among the states.

Advocates of national health insurance point out that centralized, large-scale purchases of medical and hospital supplies will reduce costs. They also stress how inadequate medical care is for the poor. Such horror stories as the one I just related make their point. Opponents stress the red tape of national health insurance. They ask if federal agencies—such as those

Figure 19.6 Who Lacks Medical Insurance?

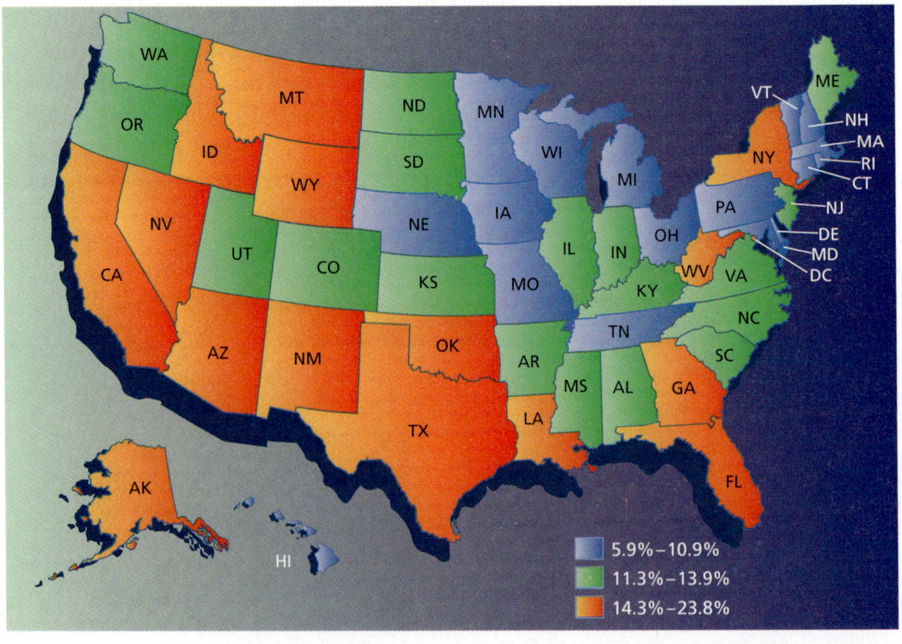

Note: The range is broad, from a low of 5.9 percent who lack medical insurance in Rhode Island to a high of 23.8 percent in New Mexico.
Source: By the author. Based on *Statistical Abstract* 2002:Table 138.

that run the post office—inspire so much confidence that they should be entrusted with administering something so vital as the nation's health care. This debate is not new, and even if some form of national health insurance is adopted, the argument is likely to continue.

Rationing Medical Care The most controversial suggestion for how to reduce medical costs is to ration medical care. We cannot afford to provide all the available technology to everyone, goes the argument, so we have to ration it. No easy answer has been found for this pressing matter, which is becoming the center of a national debate. This dilemma is the focus of the Sociology and the New Technology box.

sociology and the NEW technology

Who Should Live, and Who Should Die? The Dilemma of Rationing Medical Care

Visiting a doctor or a hospital is not without risk. We have seen that doctors kill somewhere between 50,000 and 100,000 patients a year. But today's risk is small compared to that of earlier times, when physicians bled and purged their patients in an effort to cure them. Today's physicians are well trained, and medical care is based on scientific studies. Our new technology even allows us to cure medical conditions that just a short time ago doomed people to early deaths. In other instances, the medical condition can't be cured, but, with treatment, the patient is able to live a longer life.

And therein lies the rub. Even though some particular medical technology is essential for treatment, there isn't enough of it to go around to everyone who needs it. Other technology is so costly that it could bankrupt society if it were made available to everyone who had a particular condition. Who, then, should receive the benefits of our new medical technology?

Consider dialysis, the use of machines to cleanse the blood of people who are suffering from kidney disease. Currently, dialysis is available to anyone who needs it, and the cost runs several billion dollars a year. Four percent of all Medicare goes to pay for the dialysis of just one-fourth of 1 percent of Medicare patients. Great Britain, which faces this same problem, rations dialysis to people under the age of 55 (Volti 1995).

Open heart surgery is a technological wonder, but its costs are astounding. One percent of all the money the nation spends on its medical bills goes to pay for the bypass surgeries of just four-hundredths of 1 percent of the population. Medical treatment at the end of people's lives also helps us understand the issue. Of all Medicare money, about one-fourth is spent to maintain patients during just the last year of their lives. Almost a third of this amount is spent during just the last month of life (Volti 1995).

The situation will worsen. Medical technology—and its spiraling costs—continue to advance. So does the number of elderly people, who need medical treatment the most.

The dilemma is harsh: If we ration medical treatment, many sick people will die. If we don't, we may go bankrupt.

For Your CONSIDERATION

At the heart of this issue lie questions not only of cost, but also of fairness—-of how to distribute advanced medical technology in an equitable manner. Use ideas, concepts, and principles from this and other chapters to develop a proposal for solving this pressing issue. Also note how this dilemma changes if you view it from the contrasting perspectives of conflict theory, functionalism, and symbolic interactionism.

Should wealth or fame be part of the decision? Here is a real example. The liver of Mickey Mantle, one of baseball's legends, had been ravaged by years of hard drinking, by hepatitis C, and by cancer, which had spread to other parts of his body. Mantle waited just two days for a new liver, and he died less than 3 months after receiving it. If the liver had been put in a healthy individual, that person would probably still be alive.

How about the medical treatment of prisoners? As we reviewed in Chapter 8, the number of U.S. prisoners has climbed to an all-time high. These prisoners, too, are growing older and need more medical care. Should they be treated the same as regular citizens when being considered for expensive care? For example, should they be given heart transplants at a million dollars each? If so, when a heart becomes available, should they be given the same consideration as others, perhaps winning out over citizens who have not committed crimes?

How about age? Should it be a factor? If so, should the younger get preferred treatment? Or perhaps the older? Why?

Should race-ethnicity be a factor? Sex? Social class?

Threats to Health

Let's look at six threats to health both in the United States and worldwide: AIDS, obesity, drugs, disabling environments, misguided, foolish, and callous experiments, and the globalization of disease.

HIV/AIDS

In 1981, the first case of AIDS (acquired immune deficiency syndrome) was documented. Since then, this virus that attacks the human immune system has killed almost 500,000 Americans. As you can see from Figure 19.7, in the United States this disease has been brought under control. New cases peaked in 1993, and deaths peaked in 1995. For Americans, AIDS has turned into a chronic disease that you live with, rather than die of. Today, about 375,000 Americans are living with AIDS (or HIV, the virus that causes AIDS) (Centers for Disease Control 2003). The average cost to treat a U.S. AIDS patient is $20,000 a year, making the nation's AIDS medical bill about $7 billion a year.

Globally, in contrast, AIDS has not been brought under control. About 25 million people have died from this disease, but the worst is yet to come. As Figure 19.8 illustrates, Africa is the hardest hit region of the world. Almost 3 million Africans die of AIDS each year. In sub-Saharan Africa, AIDS is the leading cause of death. In some counties there, AIDS is expected to wipe out half the teenagers. Botswana has the highest rate of AIDS in the world, with two of every five adults (39 percent) infected (United Nations 2002a). Incredibly, 45 percent of all pregnant women in Botswana have AIDS (United Nations 2002b).

Throughout the world, each day about 14,000 people (12,000 adults and 2,000 children) become infected with HIV. This is about ten new cases each minute. Ninety-five percent of the infections occur in the Least Industrialized Nations, most of them in Africa (Lamptey et al. 2002).

Figure 19.7 The Growth of AIDS in the United States

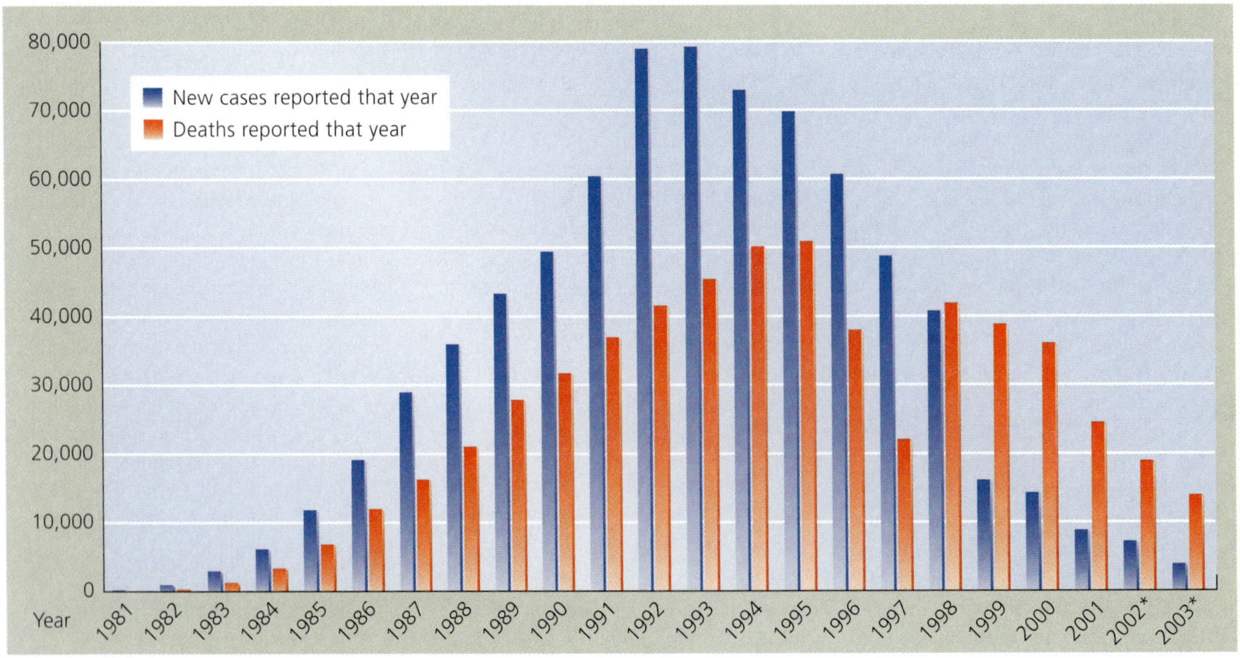

*Author's projections

Source: By the author. Based on *Centers for Disease Control 2003.*

Let's look at some of the major characteristics of this disease.

Origin The question of how AIDS originated baffled scientists for two decades, but it appears to be solved (Kolata 2001). They have traced genetic sequences back to the Congo. Apparently, the virus was present in chimpanzees and was then transmitted to humans. How this occurred is not known, but the best guess is that hunters were exposed to the animals' blood as they slaughtered them for meat.

The Transmission of AIDS The only way a person can become infected with AIDS is if bodily fluids pass from one person to another. AIDS is most commonly transmitted through the exchange of blood and semen, but nursing babies can also get AIDS through the milk of their infected mothers. Since the AIDS virus is present in all bodily fluids (including sweat, tears, spittle, and urine), some people think that AIDS can also be transmitted in these forms. The U.S. Centers for Disease Control, however, say that AIDS cannot be transmitted by casual contact in which traces of these fluids would be exchanged.

Patterns of transmission vary from one society to another. In some, for example, most people get AIDS from heterosexual sex, while in others most victims get the disease from

Figure 19.8 AIDS: A Global Glimpse

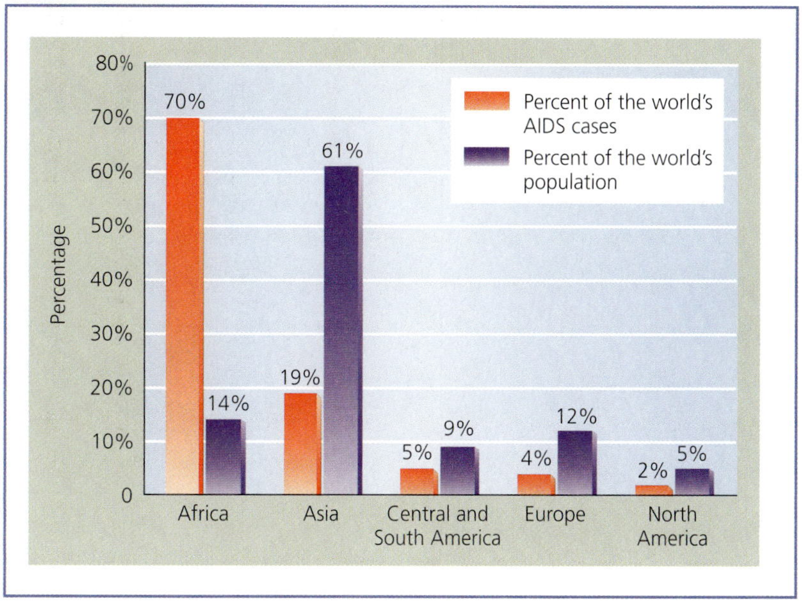

Source: By the author. Based on Haub 2003.

AIDS is devastating huge areas of Africa. In some countries, one-third or more of the population has AIDS. Millions of children have been orphaned. Governments that first ignored the problem are now trying to battle AIDS. This anti-AIDS billboard is posted in Kampala, Uganda.

Figure 19.9 How Americans Get AIDS

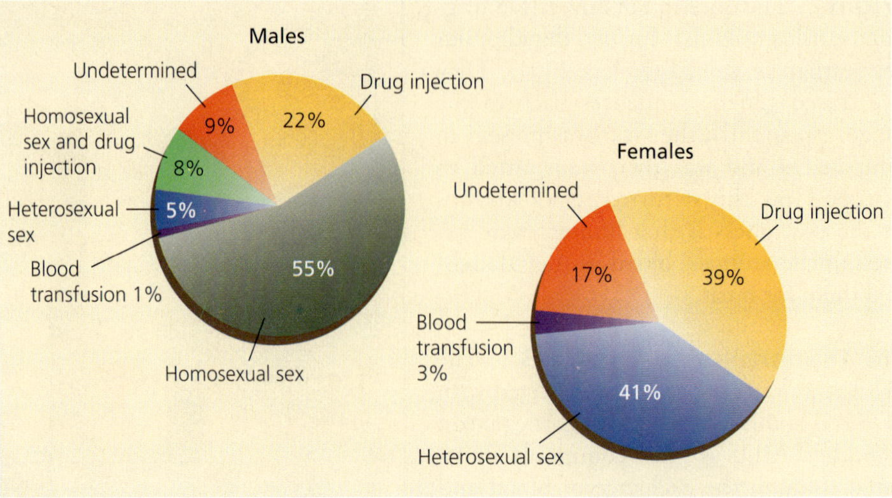

Source: By the author. Based on *Centers for Disease Control 2003.*

homosexual sex. Patterns also differ for men and women within the same society. Figure 19.9 compares the patterns for men and women in the United States.

Gender, Race-Ethnicity, and AIDS Although many people think of AIDS as a man's disease, in sub-Saharan Africa AIDS is more common among women (United Nations 2002b). In the United States, although AIDS hits men the hardest, each year women make up a larger proportion of new cases. In 1982, only 6 percent of AIDS cases were women, but today women account for 26 percent of all new cases (Centers for Disease Control 1997:Tables 3, 10; 2002:Table 5). AIDS is the tenth leading cause of death of both U.S. men and women ages 15 to 24 (*Statistical Abstract* 2002:Table 104).

As shown in Table 19.1 below, the risk of AIDS is also related to race-ethnicity. The reason for this is not genetic; that is, no racial-ethnic group is more susceptible to AIDS because of biological factors. Rather, risks differ because of *social* factors, such as rates of intravenous drug use and the use of condoms.

The Stigma of AIDS One of the most significant sociological aspects of AIDS is its stigma. This provides another example of how social factors are essential to health and illness. Some people refuse even to be tested because they fear the stigma they would bear if they tested HIV-positive. One unfortunate consequence is the continuing spread of AIDS by people who "don't want to know." Even some governments put their heads in the sand. Chinese officials, for example, formerly refused to admit the extent of AIDS in their country, but they now are becoming more open about it. If this disease is to be brought under control, its stigma must be overcome: AIDS must be viewed like any other lethal disease—as the work of a destructive biological organism.

Table 19.1 AIDS and Race-Ethnicity

	Percentage of AIDS Cases	Percentage of U.S. Population
Whites	42.2%	68.2%
African Americans	38.4%	12.2%
Latinos	18.4%	13.5%
Asian Americans	1.2%	4.1%
Native Americans	0.3%	0.8%

Source: Centers for Disease Control 2003.

Is There a Cure for AIDS? Figure 19.7 on page 560 shows how the number of AIDS cases in the United States increased dramatically, reached a peak, and then declined. With such a remarkable decline, have we found a cure for AIDS?

With thousands of scientists conducting research, the media have heralded each new breakthrough as a possible cure.

A controversy surrounding AIDS is the "semilegal" marijuana clubs in San Francisco. Here marijuana is sold to people seeking to combat the side effects of AIDS treatments.

The most promising treatment to date, the one that lies behind the drop in deaths, was spearheaded by David Ho, a virologist (virus researcher). If patients in the early stages of the disease take a "cocktail" of drugs (a combination of protease inhibitors, AZT, and 3TC), all signs of the virus can be erased from their bodies. Their immune systems then rebound (Gorman 1997). No one is calling this a cure, however, for apparently the virus lingers undetected, ready to flourish if the drugs are withdrawn.

While most praise this new treatment, some researchers have issued a dire warning (Rotello 1996). They suggest that the cocktail may become this decade's penicillin. When penicillin was introduced, everyone was ecstatic about its effectiveness. However, over the years, the microbes that penicillin targets mutated, producing "super germs" against which we have no protection. If this is the case with AIDS, then a new, "super-AIDS" virus could hit the world with more fury than its first devastating wave.

Medical researchers are still hopeful that they will be able to develop an effective vaccine. The best estimate, however, is that this will take at least another seven years (Lamptey et al. 2002).

Obesity

It may seem like quite a jump to move from something as unusual and life-threatening as AIDS to a topic as common and seemingly routine as extra pounds on the body. But let's see if it really is. First, we need to note that obesity has increased (Ware 2003). As our lifestyles have become more sedentary, Americans have added pounds. Obesity, weighing more than 25 pounds over one's ideal body weight, is now more common than ever before in our history. About 31 percent of all adults are obese (Tarmann 2002). We have become the fattest nation on earth. Health experts are calling this an obesity epidemic.

Perhaps we should just shrug our shoulders and say, "So what?" Is obesity really anything more than someone's idea of how much we should weigh? It is a great deal more than this. Obesity is more life-threatening to Americans than AIDS or even alcohol abuse. Health experts estimate that 300,000 U.S. adults die each year of obesity-related causes (Tarmann 2002). Obese people are more likely than thinner people to get a variety of diseases that shorten their lives. They are more likely to have strokes (Bonow and Eckel 2003), suffer heart attacks (Kenchaiah et al. 2002), and come down with diabetes (Troiano 2002). In addition, compared with thinner people, they are more likely to die from the diseases they get (Calle et al. 2003). We'll return to this topic when we deal with preventing medical problems.

Drugs: Alcohol and Nicotine

Many drugs, both legal and illegal, harm their users. Let's examine some of the health consequences of alcohol and nicotine, the two most frequently used legal drugs in the United States.

Alcohol Alcohol is *the* standard recreational drug of Americans. The *average* adult American consumes 25 gallons of alcoholic beverages per year—about 22 gallons of beer, 2 gallons of wine, and 1 gallon of whiskey, vodka, or other distilled spirits. Beer is so popular that Americans drink more of it than they do tea, fruit juices, or bottled water (*Statistical Abstract* 2002:Table 2197).

As you know, despite laws that ban alcohol consumption before the age of 21, underage drinking is common. Table 19.2 shows that about seven out of ten high school students drink alcohol during their senior year. Half of them have done so during just the past month. If getting drunk is the abuse of alcohol, then, without doubt, among high school students abusing alcohol is popular. As Table 19.2 shows, about half of all high school seniors have been drunk during the past year, thirty percent during just the past month.

In Table 19.3, we turn to college students. Among them, too, alcohol is the most popular drug, and more than four of five of all college students have drunk alcohol during the past year. Seven out of ten have done so in the past month. As this table shows, men and women are about equally as likely to drink alcohol. Women, however, are considerably less likely to smoke cigarettes. As you can see from this table, in general, men college students use and abuse drugs more than do women, with Ecstasy being the notable exception. Why Ecstasy is more popular among women than men college students is not known.

Is alcohol bad for health? This beverage cuts both ways. About two drinks a day for men and one drink a day for women *reduces* the risk of heart attacks and strokes (Hommel and Jaillard 1999; Mukamal 2003). (Women weigh less on average and produce

Table 19.2 What Drugs Have High School Seniors Used . . .

	In the Past Month?	In the Past Year?
Alcohol	48.6%	71.5%
Nicotine (cigarettes)	26.7%	NA
Marijuana	21.5%	36.2%
Amphetamines	5.5%	11.1%
Barbiturates	3.2%	6.7%
MDMA (Ecstasy)	2.4%	7.4%
Cocaine	2.3%	5.0%
Hallucinogens[a]	2.0%	5.4%
LSD	0.7%	3.5%
Heroin	0.5%	1.0%
How many have been drunk?	30.3	50.4

[a]Other than LSD

Source: Johnston et al. 2002:Table 2.

Table 19.3 What Drugs Have Full-Time College Students Used?

	In the Past Month?		In the Past Year?	
	Men	Women	Men	Women
Alcohol	70.2%	68.0%	83.6%	82.4%
Nicotine (cigarettes)	30.0%	24.6%	42.7%	35.5%
Marijuana	23.7%	17.2%	37.1%	33.1%
Amphetamines	3.2%	2.8%	7.4%	6.7%
MDMA (Ecstasy)	0.9%	0.7%	6.4%	7.1%
Cocaine	2.2%	1.2%	5.7%	4.2%
LSD	0.4%	0.1%	2.8%	1.6%
Heroin	0.0%	0.0%	0.3%	0.1%

Source: Johnston et al. 2003:Tables 8–2, 8–3.

fewer enzymes that metabolize alcohol.) Moderate alcohol consumption also helps people survive heart attacks. Beyond these amounts, however, alcohol consumption *increases* the risk of several diseases, from cancer to stroke. It also increases the likelihood of birth defects. Each year, 700,000 Americans seek treatment for alcohol problems, and about 20,000 die from alcohol abuse (*Statistical Abstract* 2000:Table 142; 2002:Table 181).

Nicotine

Let's suppose that you have a ticket to fly to some exotic destination. There will be 200 passengers plus crew on board your plane. You are excited about your trip, but on the way to the airport, the radio program you are listening to is interrupted by an announcement that five U.S. jets will be hijacked that day. All will crash—and all passengers and crew will die. There is no doubt that five planes will go down, that 1,000 terrified passengers and crew will plunge to their deaths. The reporter adds that the airlines have decided to stay open for business.

Do you still fly? After all, the chances are good that *yours* will not be one of the five planes.

My best guess is that you turn around and go home, that U.S. airports will be eerily silent that day.

The death toll due to alcohol comes not only from disease, as evidenced by this 3 a.m. wreck in Wisconsin that claimed the lives of two teachers. Driving under the influence of any drug, including marijuana, can be fatal.

Nicotine—with its progressive emphysema and several types of cancer—kills about 400,000 Americans each year (Surgeon General 2003). This is the equivalent of five fully loaded, 200-passenger jets with full crews crashing each and every day—leaving no survivors. Who in their right mind would take the risk that *their* plane will not be among those that crashed? Yet this is the risk that smokers take.

Nicotine is, by far, the most lethal of all recreational drugs. Smokers are more likely to have heart attacks, develop cancers, and even to become blind in old age (Goode 1989; Lagnado 1996). About 25 million Americans (including 5 million of today's children) will die prematurely of smoking-related diseases (Surgeon General 2003).

Figure 19.10 Who Is Still Smoking?

The Percentage of Americans Who Smoke Cigarettes

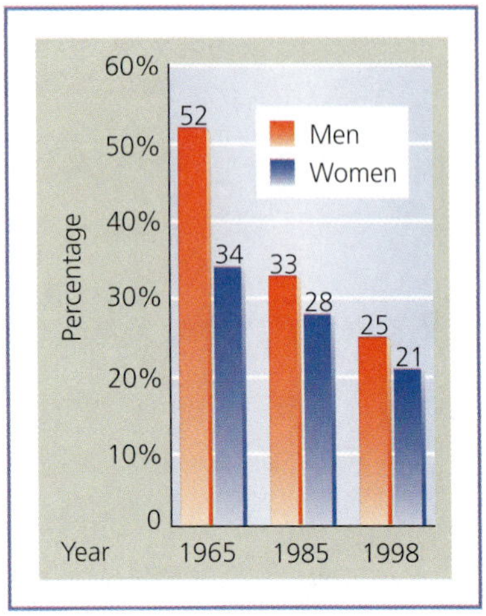

Source: By the author. Based on *Statistical Abstract* 2002:Table 184.

An antitobacco campaign that stresses the health hazards of smoking has been successful. When the campaign began, it was weak and ineffectual in the face of so many smokers and the powerful tobacco lobby in Washington. Gradually, however, the movement gained adherents and political power, and it has now ended smoking on U.S. airlines and in many offices, restaurants, and even bars. Figure 19.10 shows how this antismoking message has hit home. In three decades, cigarette smoking has been cut in *half* among U.S. men, and it has dropped by a third among U.S. women.

Yet millions of Americans—who wouldn't think of flying if they knew that even one jet were going to crash—continue to smoke. Why? The two major reasons are addiction and advertising. Nicotine may be as addictive as heroin (Tolchin 1988). While this may sound far-fetched, consider Buerger's disease:

> In this disease, the blood vessels, especially those supplying the legs, become so constricted that circulation is impaired whenever nicotine enters the bloodstream.
>
> If a patient continues to smoke, gangrene may eventually set in. First a toe may have to be amputated, then the foot at the ankle, then the leg at the knee, and ultimately at the hip. . . . Patients are informed that if they will only stop smoking, it is virtually certain that the otherwise inexorable march of gangrene up the legs will be curbed. Yet surgeons report that some patients with Buerger's disease vigorously puff away in their hospital beds following a second or third amputation. (Brecher et al. 1972)

The second reason is advertising. Even though cigarette ads were banned from television in the 1980s, cigarettes continue to be advertised in newspapers and magazines and on billboards. The tobacco industry has a huge advertising budget, spending about $7 billion a year to encourage people to smoke. This is more than $18 million a day (National Center for Chronic Disease 2001). The industry targets youth, often by associating cigarette smoking with success, high fashion, and independence. With the tobacco industry's political clout and 40,000 Americans depending on the industry for their livelihood, attempts to stop cigarette advertising have failed (*Statistical Abstract* 2002:Table 1254).

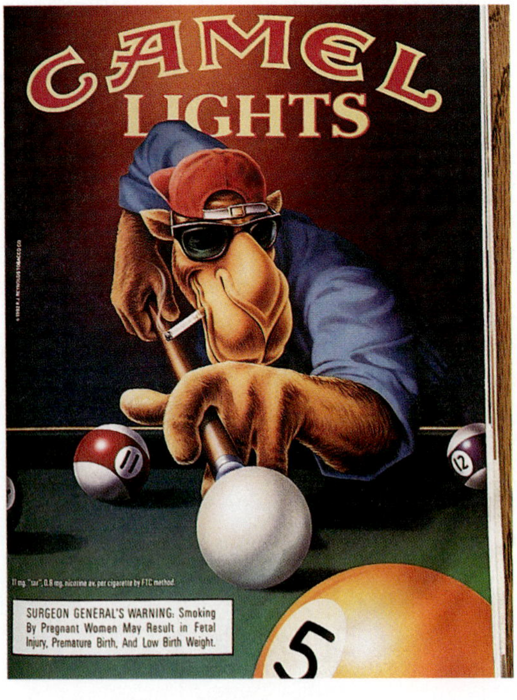

Do you think this magazine ad is designed to make cigarettes appealing to male youth? Although tobacco industry officials denied that they were trying to entice youth to smoke, the evidence such as this ad is overwhelmingly against them. Due to pressure from the U.S. Congress, Camel stopped its Joe Camel ads.

However, Joe Camel, the industry's most blatant attempt to lure children to smoke, has been banned. (See the photo on the facing page.)

Disabling Environments

A **disabling environment** is one that is harmful to people's health. The health risk of some occupations is evident: Lumberjacking, riding rodeo bulls, and taming lions are obvious examples. In many occupations, however, people become aware of the risk only years after they worked at jobs they thought were safe. For example, several million people worked with asbestos during and after World War II. The federal government estimates that one-quarter of them will die of cancer from having breathed asbestos dust. It is likely that many other substances that we have not yet identified also cause slowly developing cancers—including, ironically, some asbestos substitutes (Meier 1987; Hawkes 2001).

disabling environment an environment that is harmful to health

Industrialization increased the world's standard of living and brought better health to hundreds of millions of people. Ironically, it also threatens to disable the basic environment of the human race, posing what may be the greatest health hazard of all time. The burning of carbon fuels is leading to the *greenhouse effect,* a warming of the earth that may change the globe's climate, melt the polar ice caps, and flood the earth's coastal shores. Chlorofluorocarbon gases used in refrigerators and air conditioners have punched a hole in the *ozone shield,* the protective layer of the earth's upper stratosphere that screens out most of the sun's ultraviolet rays. High-intensity ultraviolet radiation is harmful to most forms of life. In humans, it causes skin cancer and cataracts. The pollution of land, air, and water, especially through nuclear waste, pesticides, herbicides, and other chemicals, poses additional risks to life on our planet.

Identifying environmental threats to world health is only the first step. The second is to introduce short- and long-term policies to reduce such problems. The sociology of the environment is discussed on pages 658–664.

Misguided, Foolish, and Callous Experiments

At times, physicians and government officials behave so arrogantly that they callously disregard the health of the people they are sworn to protect. Let's look at two notorious instances.

The Tuskegee Syphilis Experiment

To review this horrible experiment conducted by the U.S. Public Health Service, read the opening vignette for Chapter 15 (page 419). To summarize here, the U.S. Public Health Service did not tell 399 African American men in Mississippi that they had syphilis. Doctors examined them once a year, recording their symptoms, and letting the disease kill them.

In a mind-boggling attempt to justify cigarette smoking, Philip Morris reported that the Czech government saves $1,227 in pensions and health care every time a smoker dies. Following this reasoning, to reduce government deficits we might want to require smoking classes in kindergarten—for the sooner that people begin to smoke, the sooner they get sick and die, and the more the government saves.

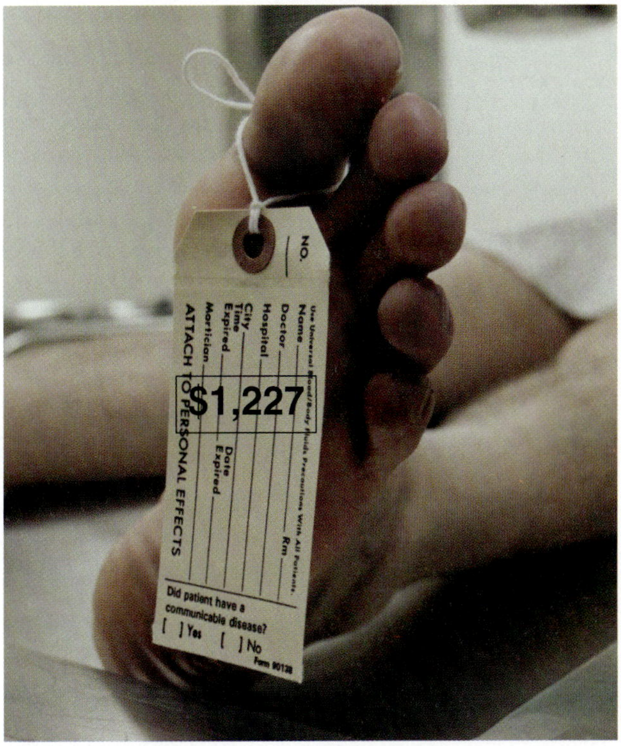

The Cold War Experiments

Now assume that you are a soldier stationed in Nevada, and the U.S. Army orders your platoon to march through an area in which an atomic bomb has just been detonated. Because you are a soldier, you obey. Nobody knows much about radiation, and you don't know that the army is using you as a guinea pig: It wants to see if you'll be able to withstand the fallout—without any radiation equipment. Or suppose you are a patient at the University of Rochester in 1946, and your doctor, whom you trust implicitly, says he is going to give you something "to help you." You are pleased. But the injection, it turns out, is uranium (Noah 1994). He and a team of other doctors are conducting an experiment to find out how much uranium it will take to damage your kidneys ("U.S. Department of Energy, Advisory Committee").

Like the Tuskegee experiment, radiation experiments like these were conducted on unsuspecting subjects simply because government officials wanted information. There were others, too. Some soldiers were given LSD. And in Palmetto, Florida, officials released whooping cough viruses into the air, killing a dozen innocent children (Conahan 1994). In other tests, deadly chemical and biological agents, such as sarin, were sprayed onto naval ships to see if they were vulnerable. The sailors in these tests wore protective clothing, but were unaware that they had become white mice (Shanker 2002). In 2003, congress approved a bill to provide health care for 5,842 soldiers harmed by these secret tests.

Playing God To most of us, it is incredible that government officials and medical personnel would so callously disregard human life, but it obviously happens. Those in official positions sometimes reach a point where they think they can play God and determine who shall live and who shall die. And, obviously, the most expendable citizens are the poor and powerless. *It is inconceivable that an experiment such as the syphilis study would have been forced on the wealthy and powerful.* The elite are protected from such callous disregard of human rights and life. The only way the poor can be protected against such gross abuse of professional positions is if we publicize each known instance of abuse and insist on vigorous prosecution of those who direct and carry out such experiments.

Do such things still happen? You can decide for yourself. Consider how medical researchers developed fetal surgery. The idea of operating on unborn children was intriguing. It held the possibility of extending medical knowledge and getting the names of the pioneers in prestigious medical journals. But would such surgery even be possible? Finding out could cost lives. To reduce the risk, the researchers first experimented with animals. Their next stop in refining their skills was surgery on pregnant Puerto Rican women. Now that the procedures are proven, the main patients are the unborn of the white and affluent (Casper 1998). The steps taken in this process expose an underlying assumption about the value of life. It is almost as though the researchers viewed themselves as climbing an evolutionary ladder.

The Globalization of Disease

> The year was 1918. Men and women, seemingly healthy the day before, collapsed and quickly died. In the morning, men wheeled carts down the streets to pick up corpses that were left on porches like last night's trash. In a matter of months, a half million Americans died. Worldwide, the death toll reached between 20 million and 40 million. (Phillips 1998)

What silent killer had so abruptly hit the United States and most of the world? Incredibly, it was the flu. For some reason, still unknown, a particularly lethal variety of the common flu bug had suddenly appeared.

Medical researchers fear that something like this will happen again. If it does, today's global jet travel, unknown in 1918, may make it even more deadly. Global travel has destroyed the natural frontiers that used to contain diseases. Today, in a matter of just hours, airline passengers can spread a disease around the world. Because older diseases have mutated and have produced "super bugs" that are immune to antibiotics, the resulting number of deaths could make the 1918 death toll seem puny by comparison.

Such are the fears. New diseases do appear on the world scene, and antibiotics are ineffective against many of them. Because some of these new diseases are lethal, we may have to resort to an old remedy—isolating people in asylums. When the Ebola virus made its surprise appearance in 1976, with its particularly hideous form of death, the only way it could be contained was to isolate an entire region of Zaire (Olshansky, et al. 1997). When SARS (Severe Acute Respiratory Syndrome) suddenly appeared in 2003, the World Health Organization of the United Nations called emergency meetings, as did the Centers for Disease Control in the United. States. The fear was that SARS would encircle the globe, killing untold millions of people in a short time. Each person with SARS was isolated, and cities and regions were declared dangerous to visit. Tourism dropped, and the disease was contained. World health officials breathed a collective sigh of relief, while still fearing another outbreak.

The Search for Alternatives

Let's turn our attention again to the U.S. medical system. What alternatives are there to the way U.S. medicine is usually practiced? One promising alternative is to change the focus from the treatment of disease to the prevention of disease. Another is something called alternative medicine. After considering these approaches to medical care, we will look at the health care systems of other countries. Perhaps these three closing topics will suggest new ideas for you to follow—or to avoid.

Treatment or Prevention?

Effects of Values and Lifestyles The impact of values and lifestyle on health becomes apparent if we contrast Utah (home of the Mormons, who disapprove of alcohol, caffeine, tobacco, and extramarital sex) with its adjacent state of Nevada (home of a gambling industry that fosters a rather different lifestyle). Although these two states have similar levels of income, education, urbanization, and medical care, Nevadans are more likely to die from cancer, strokes, heart attacks, lung disease, and AIDS. They also are more likely to die in car wrecks, to be murdered, and to commit suicide (*Statistical Abstract* 2002:Table 104). In short—as mentioned earlier when we discussed obesity, nicotine use, and alcohol consumption—many threats to health are preventable.

Even though it is well known that life style affects health, the message of "wellness" and prevention is not getting through to many millions of Americans. Our schools and the mass media publicize the message that healthy living—exercising regularly, eating nutritious food, maintaining an optimal weight, not smoking, avoiding alcohol abuse, and not having a lot of sexual partners—leads to better health and a longer life. They let us know that the foods we eat are a significant factor in many types of cancer. It doesn't take much reading to know that fatty, low-fiber foods bring disease and that a diet rich in fruits, green tea, and leafy, green vegetables stimulates health.

Unfortunately, we are seeing the public divide into those who exercise regularly and watch their diet and weight, and those who gorge on potato chips, cookies, and soft drinks during their mesmerized hours of television watching. A shorter life and the misery of sickness are simply not on people's minds while snacks, reruns, and video games beckon. Prevention requires work, while illness requires only a doctor's prescription.

This brings us to a related concern: how to get doctors to turn from writing prescriptions to focusing on preventive medicine and "wellness." To do this, it is obvious that "wellness" has to be made profitable, for if doctors and hospitals prevent illness, they lose money. One proposal that seems to have merit is for doctors and hospitals to be paid an annual fee for keeping people well (Cooper 1993). Some HMOs are realizing the benefits of "wellness" to their bottom line, and instead of focusing on getting sick patients out of hospitals faster, they are trying to keep people healthy so they don't become patients. Some HMOs are even calling members and encouraging them to exercise (Marcus 2003).

There is also the broader scale of comprehensive prevention—trying to reduce disabling environments and decrease the use of harmful drugs. Stronger legal action can be taken against businesses that spew industrial waste into the air and use our rivers and oceans as industrial sewers, as well as those that use advertising to seduce youths to use deadly drugs. Finally, since we live in a global village, the creation and maintenance of a health-producing environment requires international controls and cooperation.

Alternative Medicine

Alternative medicine refers to nontraditional medicine, often to medical practices imported from Asian nations. From the perspective of traditional Western medical theory and practice, most alternative medicine does not make sense. Western doctors have

alternative medicine medical treatment other than that of standard Western medicine; often refers to practices that originate in Asia, but may also refer to taking vitamins not prescribed by a doctor

Each culture makes basic assumptions about the causes and cures of health problems. The traditional assumptions of Eastern medical practitioners, usually ridiculed by Western physicians, are now being taken seriously by some. Acupuncture, for example, is gradually gaining acceptance in the West, although it does not fit Western assumptions of cause and cure.

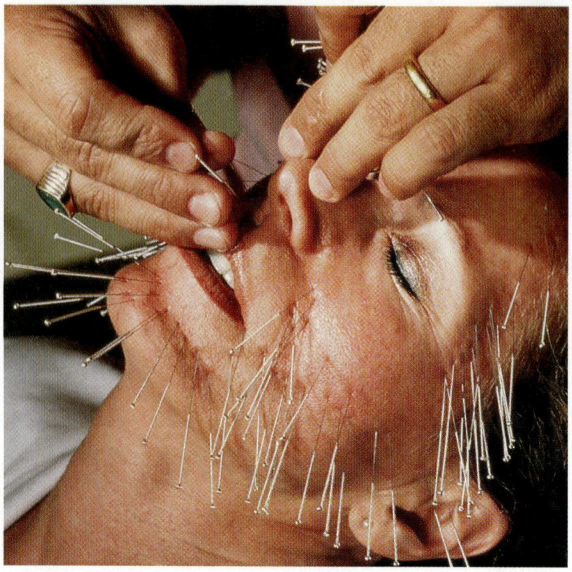

turned a scornful and hostile eye at alternative medicine, considering it superstitious practices of ignorant people. The most well known alternative medicine is acupuncture. Western doctors at first ridiculed acupuncture because it violated their understanding of how the body works. They had no theory to explain its results, but patients began to swear by it. Over the objection of most physicians, acupuncture is slowly gaining an acknowledged place in U.S. medical practice.

As patients have read about alternative medicine and have begun to seek alternative healers instead of AMA physicians, interest in alternative medicine among physicians has grown. Some U.S. physicians, trained in Western theory and practice, are studying alternative medicine. We have even come to the point that in some places the Western and Eastern approaches to medical care are being combined. In two hospitals in Savannah, Georgia, standard and alternative doctors work alongside one another. Patients are given traditional treatment accompanied by yoga, meditation, and Shirodhara, in which warm herbalized sesame oil is slowly dripped onto the patient's forehead. Patients may also choose polarity therapy (to unblock energy), biofeedback, Chinese face-lifting, and aromatherapy (Abelson and Brown 2002). A sign of the changing times is that Stanford University and the University of Maryland School of Medicine have opened hospitals where patients can get a touch of alternative medicine (Keates 2003).

Alternative medicine in the United States is too new to evaluate, but eventually medical researchers will produce solid evaluative studies. Apart from any evaluation, what is sociologically significant is that alternative medicine has begun to make inroads into an exclusive club, the U.S. medical establishment.

Health Care in Global Perspective

The search for alternatives also leads us to examine health care in other nations. Consequently, we shall close this chapter with a comparison of health care in the three worlds of industrialization. As with education (see pages 486–490), no one country can adequately illustrate the varieties of medicine that are practiced in nations in a particular stage of industrialization. Nevertheless, the countries highlighted in the Cultural Diversity box on the next page do illustrate major characteristics of health care around the world. Examining their practices helps us place both positive and negative aspects of the U.S. health care system in cultural perspective.

CULTURAL DIVERSITY

around the WORLD

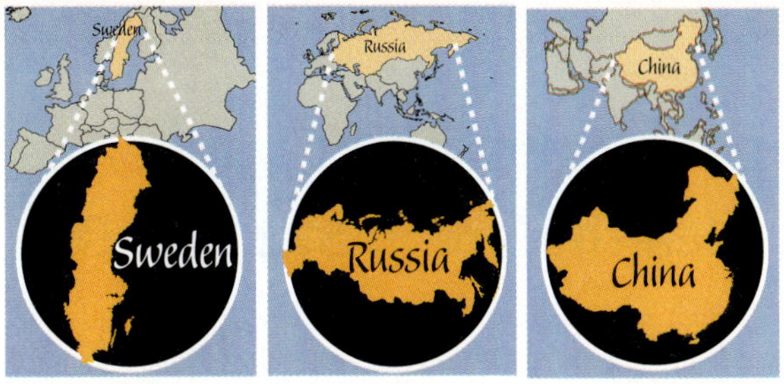

Health Care in Sweden, Russia, and China

Health Care in the Most Industrialized Nations: Sweden

Sweden has the most comprehensive health care system in the world. National health insurance is financed by contributions from both the state and employers. It covers all Swedish citizens and alien residents. Most physicians work for the government, and, except for a small consultation fee, medical and dental treatment is free. The government reimburses travel expenses for patients. Only minimal fees are charged for prescriptions and hospitalization (Swedish Institute 1990).

Medical treatment is just one component of Sweden's cradle-to-grave system of social welfare. For example, people who are sick or who must stay home with sick children receive 90 percent of their salaries. Swedes are given parental leave upon the birth of a child, and are guaranteed a pension.

Sweden's system of socialized medicine is inefficient, however. Swedes have not solved the twin problems of eliminating waiting lines and motivating physicians to "get down to work." Because the salaries of medical personnel are guaranteed, regardless of how many patients they see, physicians are unmotivated and the system has poor productivity. When reporters visited Sweden's largest hospital on a weekday morning, when 80 of 120 surgeons were on duty, they found 19 of 24 operating rooms idle. Their photos of empty operating rooms—at a time when there was a one- to two-year waiting period for hip replacements and cataract surgery—provoked a public outcry (Bergström 1992).

With public pressure to change the situation, in 1999, Swedish lawmakers made a U-turn. They decided that competition creates efficiency and they should abandon the socialized model. They have begun to do this, and they are gradually turning the health care system over to the private sector. The government has sold some hospitals to private companies and is contracting out services instead of providing them through government employees ("Social Darwinism . . . " 2001). We don't yet know what the Swedish medical system will look like by the time this transition is complete.

Health Care in the Industrializing Nations: Russia

Russia's painful transition to capitalism has brought its economic and political system to the verge of collapse. It can't pay its debts, and it is barely being kept afloat by emergency loans from the World Bank—and this only because the Most Industrialized Nations fear a nuclear holocaust should Russia dissolve into anarchy.

Russia's health care system is similarly in tatters. Under the communists, Russia had established a system that made health care available to most people. Like the rest of the nation's systems of production, the health care system was centralized. The state owned the medical schools and determined how many doctors would be trained and in what specialties. The state set the salaries for doctors, paid them, and determined where they would practice.

This medical system has fallen apart, and the health of the population has declined. An example is Moscow's ambulance system. It used to be efficient—dial 03 and an ambulance would arrive within minutes. Now an ambulance can take eight to twelve *hours* to arrive, because drivers are using the ambulances as freelance cabs, and they keep emergency cases waiting (Field 1998).

The only hospitals comparable to those in the United States are reserved for the elite (Light 1992). In the rest, conditions are deplorable. Patients must bring their own linens, medicines, and syringes with them to the hospital. Some hospitals do not even have a doctor on staff. Surgical scalpels are resharpened until they break. Sometimes even razor blades are used for surgery (Donelson 1992). Some doctors face the choice of operating without anesthetic or not operating at all (Paddock 1999). Physicians are paid so little that in order to have food, they have to grow potatoes. They walk to work because they cannot afford the equivalent of a dime to take a bus (Goldberg and Kishkovsky 2000).

The bright spot is that physicians continue to work despite their low status and miserable pay. Many are motivated by idealism and the desire to help, coupled with the hope that things will get better. A second bright spot is that some doctors are making the transition to private practice, which could be the beginning of a new medical system built on the rubble of the old (Goldberg and Kishkovsky 2000).

In the meantime, Russia's medical system remains shattered. Perhaps no event more pinpoints the disarray than this:

> Three patients lay unconscious in the intensive care unit, kept alive only by the Siberian hospital's life support system. Two were elderly; one was 39.
>
> On Wednesday, the hospital received a telegram from the local power company: "You haven't paid your bill for five years. You owe us $94,931. Pay up, or we'll shut off your electricity." The next morning, at 6 A.M., the company shut off the power. Forty minutes later, all three patients were dead. (Paddock 1999)

The years of environmental degradation under the communists have also taken their toll. Serious birth defects have jumped to four times the U.S. rate. A likely

(continued)

CULTURAL DIVERSITY around the WORLD

Health Care in Sweden, Russia, and China *(continued)*

culprit is radiation pollution from decades of nuclear irresponsibility (Specter 1995). Table 19.4 shows what is perhaps the single best indicator of the deterioration of Russian health, the drop in life expectancy that began in the 1960s (Cockerham 1997). Life expectancy is not only a medical issue, but also a barometer of a society's health.

Health Care in the Least Industrialized Nations: China

Because this nation of 1.2 billion people has a vast shortage of trained physicians, hospitals, and medicine, most Chinese see "barefoot doctors," people who have only a basic knowledge of medicine, are paid low wages, and travel from village to village. With its emphases on medicinal herbs and acupuncture, Chinese medicine differs from that of the West. Although Westerners have scoffed at the Chinese approach, some have found reason to change their minds. For example, one of the herbs that the Chinese have used for a thousand years or more to treat liver disease has been tested by Western societies; it reduces liver cancer (Tanouye 1995).

As China makes its transition to capitalism, its medical system, like Russia's, is in tatters (Rosenthal 2001d). There are doctors who make so little that they have to take other jobs to survive. Some hospitals demand a huge deposit before they will admit a patient. In fact, one demands $724. While this may not sound that high, in China the average yearly income is $286 (Wonacott 2003). Some surgeons also demand payment before they will operate, as in the case of the surgeons who, arms scrubbed and held high in the air, refused to enter the operating room until the patient's relatives had stuffed their pockets with cash (Sampson 1992).

Table 19.4 Indicators of Health

	Sweden	United States	Russia	China
Life expectancy	79.2 years	77.3 years	67.3 years	71.6 years
Infant mortality[a]	3.9	6.8	20.1	28.1
Birth rate[b]	11.7	14.2	9.4	16.0
Death rate[b]	10.8	8.7	13.9	6.7
Health costs as a percent of Gross Domestic Product	8.6	12.9	2.3	NA

[a]Per 1,000 live births.
[b]Per 1,000 population.

Sources: Field 1998; *Statistical Abstract* 1998:Tables 1345, 1348; 2000:Tables 1355, 1358; 2002:Table 1312.

For Your CONSIDERATION

No country has discovered the perfect medical system, and each country faces a medical crisis of "too much demand at too great a cost" (Moore and Winslow 1993). In what ways do you think that the U.S. medical system is superior—and inferior—to those of Sweden, Russia, and China? Is there one that you would pick over the U.S. system? Why? Short of instituting socialized medicine, which goes against the U.S. value system, propose changes that will overcome the deficiencies of the U.S. medical system reviewed in this chapter—and that will maintain its strengths.

The Future of Medicine

It is always risky to predict the future, for unexpected events cause twists and turns in the path we are following. Some trends are strong however, and we can expect U.S. medicine to continue its fee-for-service approach, to be marked by social inequalities, and that even larger numbers of women will become doctors. The use of the Internet for self-diagnosing and self-prescribing will become more popular, as will the search for alternative treatment. Despite widespread knowledge of their health risks, alcohol and nicotine will continue to be abused. Cigarette smoking, however, will continue to decrease.

These trends, firmly in place, will be overshadowed by rapid advances in our knowledge of human genes and the development of new technologies to apply that knowledge to benefit human health. These changes in knowledge and technology are going to transform the face of medicine, and, with it, our expectations of health and medical treatment. Some of the implications of these changes are discussed in the Sociology and the New Technology box on the next page, with which we close this chapter.

genomics the study of genes and how they relate to health and illness

sociology and the **NEW technology**

Genetic Profiling: Medicine in the Coming Bioeconomy

You and a friend come down with the same disease. You both go to the same doctor. After examining the two of you, she uploads your genetic charts to a pharmaceutical company that formulates a medicine to match each of your unique genetic structures. When you get to the drug store, waiting for you are separate designer medicines, made to attack the disease at the molecular level.

Your doctor gives you the bad news. You have an incurable heart disease—at least it used to be incurable. Now, however, you pop over to the New Organ Clinic, where you place an order for a new heart. The heart will be a perfect match, since it will be grown from your own cells. You've just extended your life by another 50 years or so.

Are these scenarios far-fetched? Not at all. **Genomics**, the study of genes and how they relate to health and illness, is destined to change the face of medicine. That pivotal event in 2001, the mapping of the human genome system, combined with stem cell research, is expected to make these scenarios a reality during our lifetimes.

And there is more. At birth, the genetic sequence of each child will be recorded on discs. These records will allow physicians to fix health problems *before* they show up. Instead of waiting for symptoms to appear, doctors will examine your genetic record to discover the diseases that are your biological destiny—and then snip out the bad molecules and splice in new ones so you never suffer those problems.

At least this is how it might be if you are wealthy.

No new technology comes without its downside. Not only will genetic discs feed social inequality, but also they will be a treasure trove of information for insurers and future employers. Being able to predict future medical conditions will bring *genetic profiling*. Who wants to insure someone if they know they are going to come down with a debilitating disease? Who wants to hire them? In fact, who wants to marry them?

For Your CONSIDERATION

Assume that you have just graduated from college. With fresh BA in hand, you go for your first job interview. The interviewer says you seem perfect for the job, and then asks for a copy of your genetic disc. Do you think prospective employers should have access to your genetic structure? You can apply symbolic interactionism to this question. How would your answer change if you are the employer? Doesn't it only seem fair that employers should be able to hire healthier workers?

Assume that you have just applied for health insurance. The insurer not only wants your medical history, but also asks for your medical disc. Do you think you should have to comply? Why or why not?

Assume that you have fallen in love and you are thinking about marriage. One evening, as you are discussing plans for the future, your loved one turns to you and says, "I love you dearly, but we can't get married until we have our medical discs examined by bioresearchers. And if we have no unique health risks, then . . ." Do you agree to this?

Based on Cowley and Underwood 2000; Licata 2001; Wilensky 2001.

SUMMARY and REVIEW

Sociology and the Study of Medicine

What is the role of sociology in the study of medicine?

Sociologists study **medicine** as a social institution. As practiced in the United States, three of its primary characteristics are professionalization, bureaucracy, and the profit motive. P. 544.

The Symbolic Interactionist Perspective

What is the symbolic interactionist perspective on health and illness?

Health is not only a biological matter; but also it is intimately related to society. Illness is also far from an objective matter, for illness is always viewed from the framework of culture. The definitions applied to physical and mental conditions vary from one group to another. Pp. 544–545.

The Functionalist Perspective

What is the functionalist perspective on health and illness?

Functionalists stress that in return for being excused from their usual, responsible activities, people have to accept the **sick role.** They must assume responsibility for seeking competent medical help and cooperate in getting well so they can quickly resume normal activities. Pp. 545–546.

The Conflict Perspective

What is the conflict perspective on health and illness?

Health care is one of the scarce resources over which groups compete. On a global level, health care follows the stratification that we studied in Chapter 9. The best health care is available in the Most Industrialized Nations, the worst in the Least Industrialized Nations.

In the American colonies, no training or licensing was necessary to become a doctor. Until the early 1900s, medical training was a hit-or-miss affair. In 1910, the education of physicians came under the control of a group of men who eliminated most of their competition and turned medicine into a monopoly that became the largest business in the United States. Pp. 546–550.

Historical Patterns of Health

How have health patterns changed over time?

Patterns of disease in the United States have changed so extensively that of today's top ten killers, five did not even show up on the 1900 top ten list. Because most Americans live longer than their ancestors did, we can conclude that contemporary Americans are healthier. For mental illness, we have no idea how today compares with the past, for we have no baselines from which to make comparisons. Pp. 550–551.

Issues in Health Care

How does treating health care as a commodity lead to social inequalities?

Because health care is a commodity to be sold to the highest bidder, the United States has a **two-tier system of medical care** in which the poor receive inferior health care for both their mental and physical illnesses. Pp. 551–552.

What are some other problems in U.S. health care?

One problem is **defensive medicine,** which refers to medical procedures that are done for the physician's benefit, not for the benefit of the patient. Intended to protect physicians from lawsuits, these tests and consultations add huge amounts to the nation's medical bill. Other problems are incompetence, **depersonalization,** conflict of interest, medical fraud, and sexism. Pp. 552–556.

Why is medically assisted suicide an issue now?

Due to advanced technology, people can be kept technically alive even when they have no brain waves. Physicians who openly assist in suicides have come under severe criticism. Research findings on **euthanasia** in Holland have fueled this controversy. Pp. 556–557.

What attempts have been made to cut medical costs?

Health maintenance organizations (**HMOs**) and diagnosis-related groups (DRGs) are among the measures that have been taken to reduce medical costs. National health insurance, which has run into immense opposition, has been proposed. The most controversial proposal is to ration medical care. Pp. 557–559.

Threats to Health

What are some threats to the health of Americans?

Discussed here are AIDS, which is declining in the United States but is devastating sub-Saharan Africa; obesity; alcohol and nicotine; **disabling environments;** unethical experiments, of which the Tuskegee syphilis experiments and the Cold War radiation experiments are two examples; and the globalization of disease. Pp. 560–568.

The Search for Alternatives

Are there alternatives to our current health care system?

Two primary alternatives were discussed: a change in focus from treatment to prevention, and alternative medicine. For comparison, we examined the health care systems in Sweden, Russia, and China. Pp. 569–572.

The Future of Medicine

How will the practice of medicine change?

Genomics is going to change the face of medical practice. Knowledge of our genetic structure will allow designer medicines, the treatment of diseases before they appear, and the growth of replacement organs, including hearts. Pp. 572–573.

Where can I read more on this topic?

Suggested Readings for this chapter are found at the back of this book.

THINKING Critically ABOUT CHAPTER 19

1. A major issue in this chapter is the tension between medicine as a right and medicine as a commodity. What arguments support each side of this issue?
2. How do values and lifestyle affect health? What does this have to do with sociology?
3. Have you had an experience with alternative medicine? Or do you know someone who has? If so, how did the treatment (and theory underlying the cause of the medical problem) differ from standard medical practice?

ADDITIONAL RESOURCES for This Chapter

www.ablongman.com/henslin7e

- *Content Select* Research Database for Sociology, with suggested key terms and annotated references
- Link to 2000 Census, with activities
- Flashcards of key terms and concepts
- Practice Tests
- Weblinks
- Interactive Maps

Chapter 20

Population and Urbanization

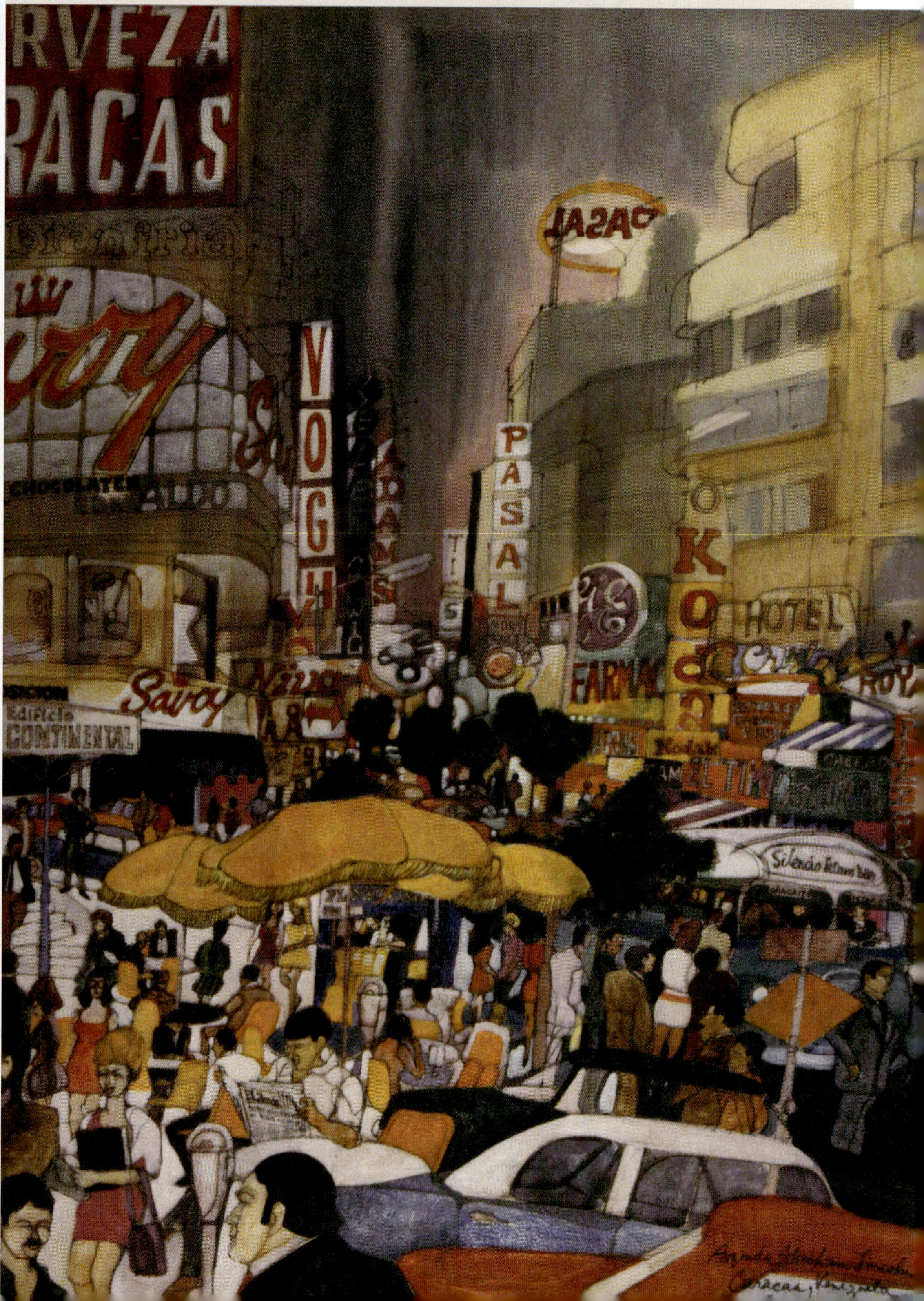

Franklin McMahon,
Avenida Abraham Lincoln

The image still haunts me. There stood Celia, age 30, her distended stomach visible proof that her thirteenth child was on its way. Her oldest was only 14 years old! A mere boy by our standards, he had already gone as far in school as he ever would. Each morning, he joined the men to work in the fields. Each evening around twilight, I saw him return home, exhausted from hard labor in the subtropical sun.

I was living in Colima, Mexico, and Celia and Angel had invited me for dinner. Their home clearly reflected the family's poverty. A thatched hut consisting of only a single room served as home for all fourteen members of the family. At night, the parents and younger children crowded into a double bed, while the eldest boy slept in a hammock. As in many homes in the village, the other children slept on mats spread on the dirt floor.

The home was meagerly furnished. It had only a gas stove, a table, and a cabinet where Celia stored her few cooking utensils and clay dishes. There were no closets; clothes were hung on pegs in the walls. There also were no chairs, not even one. I was used to the poverty in this village, but this really startled me. The family was so poor that they could not afford even a single chair.

here stood Celia, age 30,

her distended stomach

isible proof that

her thirteenth child was on its way.

Celia beamed as she told me how much she looked forward to the birth of her next child. Could she really mean it? It was hard to imagine that any woman would want to be in her situation.

Yet Celia meant every word. She was as full of delightful anticipation as she had been with her first child—and with all the others in between.

Chapter Outline

How could Celia have wanted so many children—especially when she lived in such poverty? That question bothered me. I couldn't let it go until I had the solution.

This chapter helps provide an answer.

Population in Global Perspective

Celia's story takes us into the heart of **demography,** the study of the size, composition, growth, and distribution of human populations. It brings us face to face with the question of whether we are doomed to live in a world so filled with people that there will be practically no space for anybody. Will our planet be able to support its growing population? Or are chronic famine and mass starvation the sorry fate of most earthlings? Let's look at how this concern began, and then at what today's demographers say about it.

A Planet with No Space for Enjoying Life?

The story begins with the lowly potato. When the Spanish conquistadors found that people in the Andes ate this vegetable, which was unknown in Europe, they brought it home with them. At first, Europeans viewed it suspiciously, but gradually the potato became the main food of the lower classes. With more abundant food, fertility increased, the death rate dropped, and Europe's population soared, almost doubling during the 1700s (McKeown 1977; McNeill 1999).

Thomas Malthus (1766–1834), an English economist, saw this surging growth as a sign of doom. In 1798, he wrote a book that became world famous, *First Essay on Population 1798.* In it, Malthus proposed what became known as the **Malthus theorem.** He argued that while population grows geometrically (from 2 to 4 to 8 to 16 and so forth), the food supply increases only arithmetically (from 1 to 2 to 3 to 4 and so on). This meant, he claimed, that if births go unchecked, the population of a country, or even of the world, will outstrip its food supply.

In earlier generations, large farm families were common. Having many children was functional—there were many hands to help with crops, food production, and food preparation. As the country industrialized and urbanized, this changed to a dysfunction—children became expensive and nonproducing. Consequently, the size of families shrank as we entered Stage 3 of the demographic transition, *and today U.S. families of this size are practically nonexistent. (Note the trousers that the boy on the far left is wearing. They used to be his father's.)*

Figure 20.1 How Fast Is the World's Population Growing?

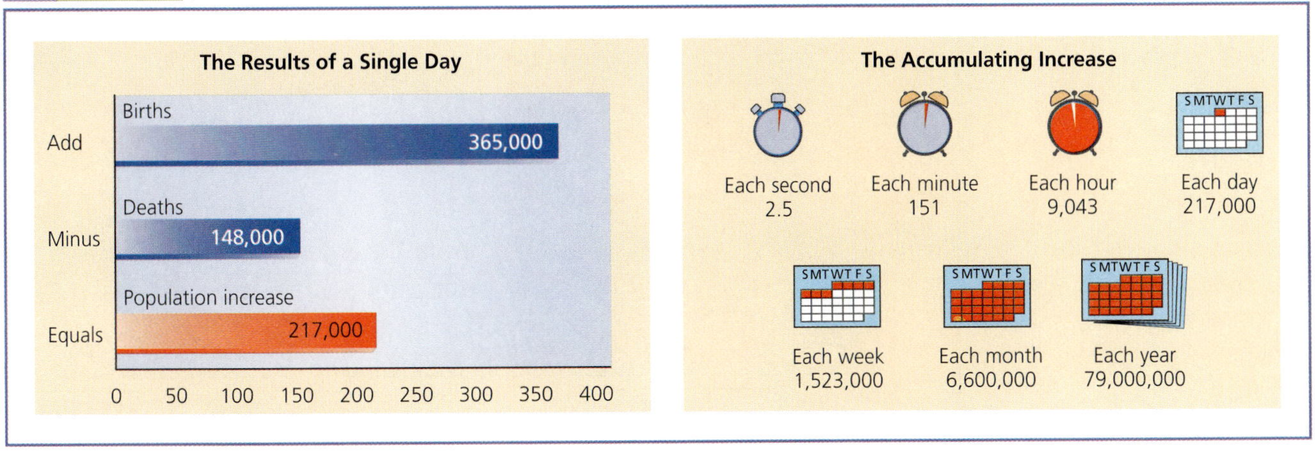

Source: By the author. Based on Haub 2002c.

The New Malthusians

Was Malthus right? This question became a matter of heated debate among demographers. One group, which can be called the *New Malthusians,* is convinced that today's situation is at least as grim, if not grimmer, than anything Malthus ever imagined. For example, *the world's population is growing so fast that in just the time it takes you to read this chapter, another fifteen to twenty thousand babies will be born!* By this time tomorrow, the earth will have almost another quarter of a million people to feed. This increase goes on hour after hour, day after day, without letup. For an illustration of this growth, see Figure 20.1.

The New Malthusians point out that the world's population is following an **exponential growth curve.** This means that if growth doubles during approximately equal intervals of time, it suddenly accelerates. To illustrate the far-reaching implications of exponential growth, sociologist William Faunce (1981) told a parable about a poor man who saved a rich man's life. The rich man was grateful and said that he wanted to reward the man for his heroic deed.

> The man replied that he would like his reward to be spread out over a four-week period, with each day's amount being twice what he received on the preceding day. He also said he would be happy to receive only one penny on the first day. The rich man immediately handed over the penny and congratulated himself on how cheaply he had gotten by. At the end of the first week, the rich man checked to see how much he owed and was pleased to find that the total was only $1.27. By the end of the second week he owed only $163.83. On the twenty-first day, however, the rich man was surprised to find that the total had grown to $20,971.51. When the twenty-eighth day arrived the rich man was shocked to discover that he owed $1,342,177.28 for that day alone and that the total reward had jumped to $2,684,354.56!

This is precisely what alarms the New Malthusians. They claim that humanity has just entered the "fourth week" of an exponential growth curve. Figure 20.2 on the next page shows why they think the day of reckoning is just around the corner. They point out that it took all of human history for the world's population to reach its first billion around 1800. It then took about one hundred thirty years (until 1930) to add the second billion. Just thirty years later (1960), the world population hit 3 billion. The time it took to reach the fourth billion was cut in half, to only fifteen years (1975). It then took just twelve more years (1987) for the total to hit 5 billion, and another twelve for it to reach 6 billion (in 1999).

To illustrate this increase, the New Malthusians have come up with some mind-boggling statistics. They note that before the Industrial Revolution, it took 1,600 years for the world's population to double, but the most recent doubling took just forty years—*forty* times as fast (Cohen 1996). They also point out that between 8000 B.C. and A.D. 1750 the

demography the study of the size, composition, growth, and distribution of human populations

Malthus theorem an observation by Thomas Malthus that although the food supply increases arithmetically (from 1 to 2 to 3 to 4 and so on), population grows geometrically (from 2 to 4 to 8 to 16 and so forth)

exponential growth curve a pattern of growth in which numbers double during approximately equal intervals, thus accelerating in the latter stages

Figure 20.2 **World Population Growth Over 2,000 Years**

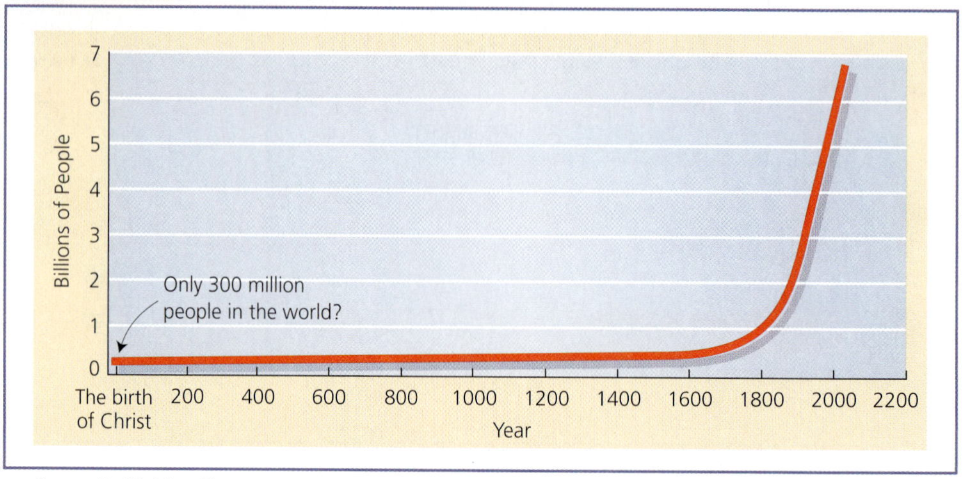

Sources: Modified from Piotrow 1973:4; Haub 2002a.

world added an average of only 67,000 people a year—but now that many people are being added *every seven hours* (Weeks 1994).

It is obvious, claim the New Malthusians, that there are going to be fewer and fewer resources for more and more people.

The Anti-Malthusians

All of this seems obvious, and no one wants to live shoulder-to-shoulder and fight for scraps. How, then, can anyone argue with the New Malthusians?

An optimistic group of demographers, whom we can call the *Anti-Malthusians,* see a far different picture. They believe that Europe's **demographic transition** provides a more accurate glimpse into the future. This transition is diagrammed in Figure 20.3. During most of

Figure 20.3 **The Demographic Transition**

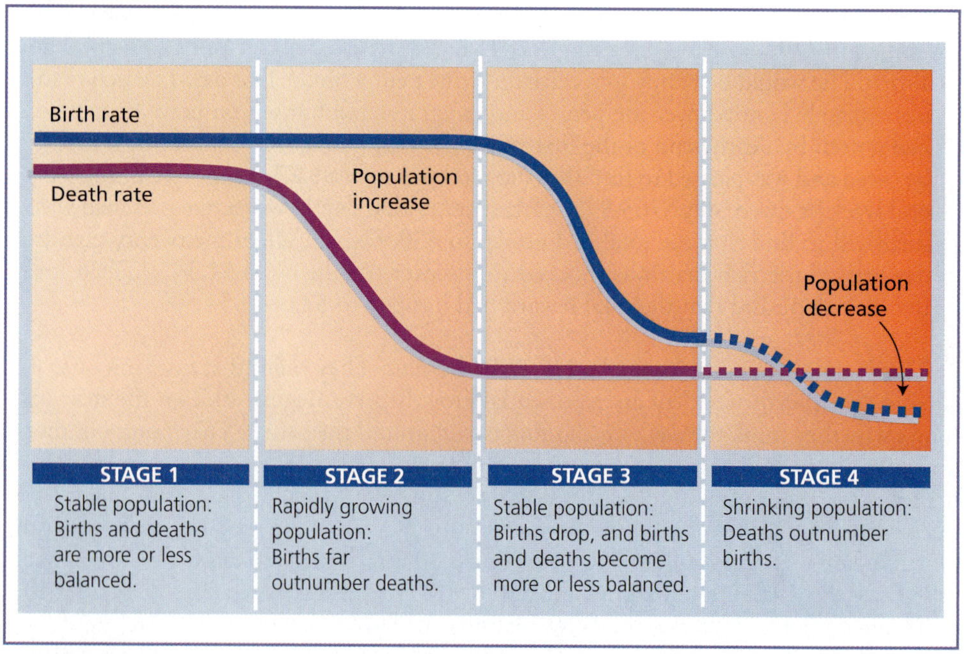

Note: The standard demographic transition is depicted by Stages 1–3. Stage 4 has recently been suggested by some Anti-Malthusians.

Source: By the author.

demographic transition a three-stage historical process of population growth: first, high birth rates and high death rates; second, high birth rates and low death rates; and third, low birth rates and low death rates; a fourth stage has begun to appear in the Most Industrialized Nations, as depicted in Figure 20.3

its history, Europe was in Stage 1. Its population remained about the same from year to year, for high death rates offset the high birth rates. Then came Stage 2, the "population explosion" that so upset Malthus. Europe's population surged because birth rates remained high while death rates went down. Finally, Europe made the transition to Stage 3: The population stabilized as people brought their birth rates into line with their lower death rates.

This, say the Anti-Malthusians, is precisely what will happen in the Least Industrialized Nations. Their current surge in growth simply indicates that they have reached Stage 2 of the demographic transition. Hybrid seeds and medicine imported from the Most Industrialized Nations have cut their death rates, but their birth rates remain high. When they move into Stage 3, as surely they will, we will wonder what all the fuss was about. In fact, you can already see that growth is slowing.

Who Is Correct?

As you can see, both the New Malthusians and the Anti-Malthusians have looked at historical trends and projected them onto the future. The New Malthusians project continued world growth and are alarmed. The Anti-Malthusians project Stage 3 of the demographic transition onto the Least Industrialized Nations and are reassured.

There is no question that the Least Industrialized Nations are in Stage 2 of the demographic transition. The question is, will these nations enter Stage 3? After World War II, the West exported its hybrid seeds, herbicides, and techniques of public hygiene around the globe. Death rates plummeted in the Least Industrialized Nations as their food supply increased and health improved. Their birth rates stayed high, however, and their populations mushroomed. Just as Malthus had done 200 years before, demographers predicted worldwide catastrophe if something were not done immediately to halt the population explosion (Ehrlich and Ehrlich 1972, 1978).

We can use the conflict perspective to understand what happened when this message reached the leaders of the industrialized world. They saw the mushrooming populations of the Least Industrialized Nations as a threat to the balance of power they had so carefully worked out. With swollen populations, the poorer countries might demand a larger share of the earth's resources. The leaders found the United Nations to be a willing tool, and they used it to spearhead efforts to reduce world population growth. The results have been remarkable. The birth rates of the Least Industrialized Nations have dropped from an average of 2.1 percent a year in the 1960s to 1.6 percent today (Haub and Yinger 1994; Haub 2003).

The New Malthusians and Anti-Malthusians have greeted this news with significantly different interpretations. For the Anti-Malthusians, this slowing of growth is the signal they had been waiting for—Stage 3 of the demographic transition is on its way. First the death rate in the Least Industrialized Nations fell—now, just as they predicted, their birth rates are also falling. Did you notice, they say, that it took 12 years to add the fifth billion to the world's population—and also 12 years to add the sixth billion? The New Malthusians reply that a slower growth rate still spells catastrophe—it just takes longer for it to hit (Ehrlich and Ehrlich 1997).

The Anti-Malthusians also argue that our future will be the opposite of what the New Malthusians worry about: There are going to be too few children in the world, not too many. The world's problem will not be a population explosion, but **population shrinkage**—populations getting smaller. They point out that births in 65 countries have already dropped so low that those countries no longer produce enough children to maintain their populations. Of the 42 countries of Europe, *all* of them are in this situation (Haub 2003). They all fill more coffins than cradles.

Some Anti-Malthusians even predict a "demographic free fall" (Mosher 1997). As more nations enter Stage 4 of the demographic transition, the world's population will peak at about 8 or 9 billion, then begin to grow smaller. Two hundred years from now, they say, we will have a lot fewer people on earth.

Who is right? It simply is too early to tell. Like the proverbial pessimists who see the glass of water half empty, the New Malthusians interpret changes in world population growth negatively. And like the optimists who see the same glass half full, the Anti-Malthusians view the totals positively. Sometime during our lifetime we should know the answer.

population shrinkage the process by which a country's population becomes smaller because its birth rate and immigration are too low to replace those who die and emigrate

Photos of starving people, such as this mother and her child, haunt Americans and other members of the Most Industrialized Nations. Many of us wonder why, when some are starving, we should live in the midst of such abundance, often overeating and even casually scrapping excess food into the garbage. The text discusses reasons for such unconscionable disparities.

Why Are People Starving?

Pictures of starving children gnaw at our conscience. We live in such abundance, while these children and their parents starve before our very eyes. Why don't they have enough food? Is it because there are too many of them, or simply that the abundant food produced around the world does not reach them?

The Anti-Malthusians make a point that seems irrefutable. As Figure 20.4 shows, *there is now more food for each person in the world than there was in 1950.* Although the world's population is now two and a half times larger than it was in 1950, improved seeds and fertilizers have made more food available for *each* person on earth. Even more food

Figure 20.4 How Much Food Does the World Produce Per Person?

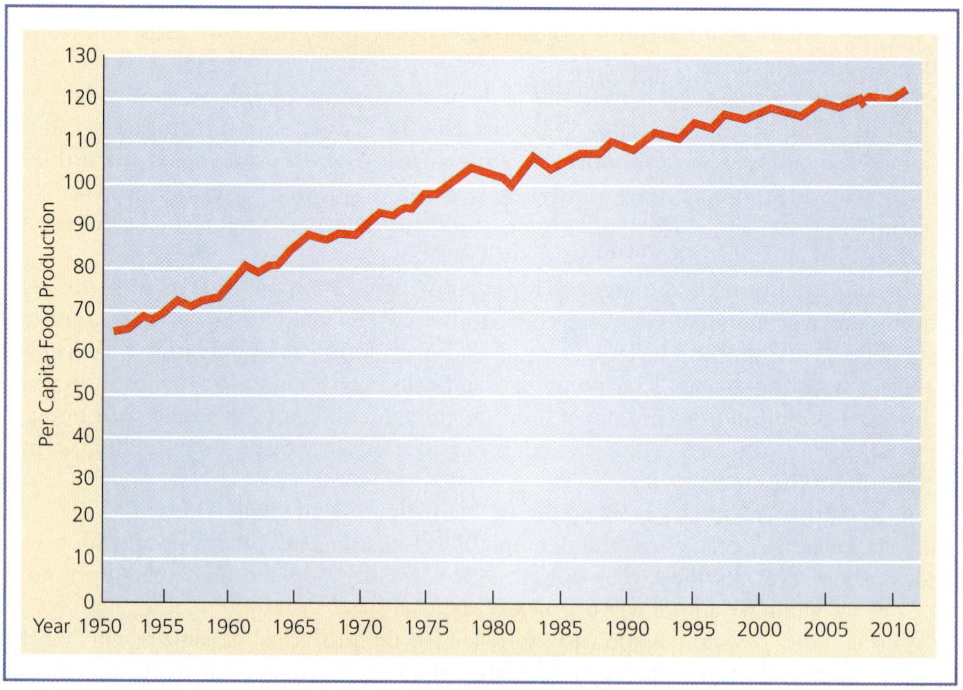

Note: 1979–1981 = 100. Years 1975 to 1991 are U.N. figures; years prior to 1975 have been recomputed from Simon to 1979–1981 base; years beyond 1998 are the author's projections.

Sources: By the author. Based on Simon 1981:58; United Nations Statistical Yearbook: 1985–1986:Table 7; and 1990–1991:Table 4, *Statistical Abstract* 1999:Table 1394, and earlier years.

may be on the way, for bioengineers are making breakthroughs in agriculture. The United Nations estimates that even without agricultural gains through bioengineering, there will be ample food to keep up with the world's growing population for at least the next 30 years (United Nations 2000).

Then why do people die of hunger? From Figure 20.4, we can conclude that starvation does not occur because the earth produces too little food, but because particular places lack food. Droughts and wars are the main reasons. Just as droughts slow or stop food production, so does war. In nations ravaged by civil war, guerillas either confiscate or burn crops, and farmers flee to the cities. While some countries have their food supply disrupted, others are producing more food than their people can consume. At the same time that countries of Africa are hit by drought and civil wars—and millions starve to death—the U.S. government pays farmers to *reduce* their crops. The United States' problem is too much food; West Africa's is too little.

The New Malthusians counter with the argument that the world's population is still growing and that we do not know how long the earth will continue to produce enough food. They remind us of the penny doubling each day. It is only a matter of time, they say, until the earth no longer produces enough food—not "if," but "when."

Both the New Malthusians and the Anti-Malthusians have contributed significant ideas, but theories will not eliminate famines. Starving children are going to continue to peer out at us from our televisions and magazines, their tiny, shriveled bodies and bloated stomachs nagging at our conscience and calling for us to do something. Regardless of the underlying causes of this human misery, it has a simple solution: food can be transferred from nations that have a surplus.

These pictures of starving Africans leave the impression that Africa is overpopulated. Why else would all those people be starving? The truth, however, is far different. Africa has 22 percent of the earth's land, but only 14 percent of the earth's population (Nsamenang 1992; Haub 2003b). The reason for famines in Africa, then, *cannot* be too many people living on too little land. On the contrary, Africa actually contains vast areas of fertile land that have not yet been farmed.

Population Growth

Even if starvation is due to a maldistribution of food rather than to overpopulation, the fact remains that the Least Industrialized Nations are growing about *sixteen times faster* than the Most Industrialized Nations—1.6 percent a year compared with 0.1 percent. At these rates, it will take 800 years for the average Most Industrialized Nation to double its population, but just 42 years for the average Least Industrialized Nation to do so (Haub and Cornelius 2001). Figure 20.5 puts the matter in stark perspective. As you can see, the population is mushrooming in the Least Industrialized Nations, and hardly growing at all in the Most Industrialized Nations

Figure 20.5 World Population Growth, 1750–2150

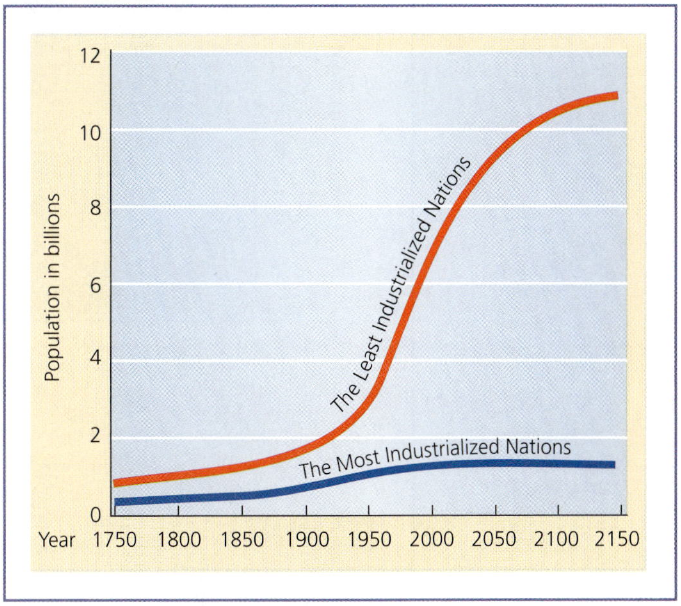

Source: "The World of the Child 6 Billion," 2000.

Why Do the Least Industrialized Nations Have So Many Children?

Why do people in the countries that can least afford it have so many children? To understand, let's figure out why Celia is so happy about having her thirteenth child. Here, we need to apply the symbolic interactionist perspective. We must take the role of the other so we can understand the world of Celia and Angel as *they* see it. As our culture does for us, their culture provides a perspective on life that guides their choices. Celia's and Angel's culture tells them that twelve children are *not* enough, that they ought to have a thirteenth—as well as a fourteenth and fifteenth. How can this be? Let's consider three reasons why bearing many children plays a central role in their lives—and in the lives of millions upon millions of poor people around the world.

First is the status of parenthood. In the Least Industrialized Nations, motherhood is the most prized status a woman can achieve. The more children a woman bears, the more she is thought to have achieved the purpose for which she was born. Similarly, a man proves his manhood by fathering children. The more children he fathers, especially sons, the better—for through them his name lives on.

Second, the community supports this view. Celia and those like her live in *Gemeinschaft* communities, where people share values and closely identify with one another. In their community, children are viewed as a sign of God's blessing. Accordingly, a couple should have many children. By producing children, people reflect the values of their community and achieve status. The barren woman, not the woman with a dozen children, is to be pitied.

These factors certainly provide strong motivations for bearing many children. Yet, there is a third incentive. For poor people in the Least Industrialized Nations, children are economic assets. These people have no Social Security or medical and unemployment insurance. This motivates them to bear *more* children, not fewer, for when parents become sick or too old to work—or when no work is to be found—they rely on their children to take care of them. The more children they have, the broader their base of support. Moreover, like the eldest son of Celia and Angel, children begin contributing to the family income at a young age. See Figure 20.6.

To those of us who live in the Most Industrialized Nations, it seems irrational to have many children. And *for us it would be.* Understanding life from the framework of people

Figure 20.6 Why the Poor Need Children

Surviving children are an economic asset in the Least Industrialized Nations. Based on a survey in Indonesia, this figure shows that boys and girls can be net income earners for their families by the age of 9 or 10.

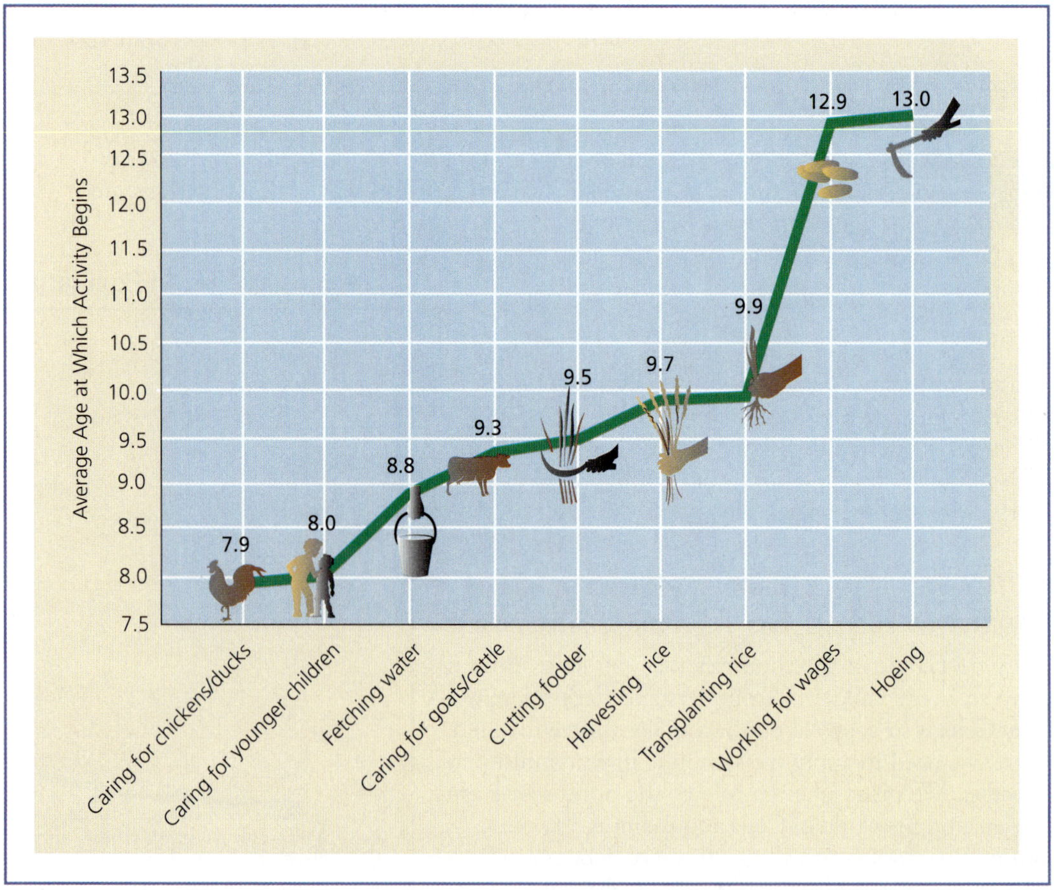

Source: U.N. Fund for Population Activities.

who are living it, however—the essence of the symbolic interactionist perspective—reveals how it makes perfect sense to have many children. For example, consider the following incident, reported by a government worker in India:

> Thaman Singh (a very poor man, a water carrier) . . . welcomed me inside his home, gave me a cup of tea (with milk and "market" sugar, as he proudly pointed out later), and said: "You were trying to convince me that I shouldn't have any more sons. Now, you see, I have six sons and two daughters and I sit at home in leisure. They are grown up and they bring me money. One even works outside the village as a laborer. *You told me I was a poor man and couldn't support a large family. Now, you see, because of my large family I am a rich man."* (Mamdani 1973, italics added)

Conflict theorists offer a different view of why women in the poor nations bear so many children. They would argue that Celia has internalized values that support male dominance. In Latin America, *machismo*—an emphasis on male virility and dominance—is common. To father many children, especially sons, demonstrates virility, giving a man valued status in the community. From a conflict perspective, then, the reason poor people have so many children is that men control women's reproductive choices.

Implications of Different Rates of Growth

The result of Celia's and Angel's desire for many children—and of the many millions of Celias and Angels like them—is that Mexico's population will double in thirty-seven years. In contrast, Spain's population is growing so slowly that it will take 6,931 years to double (Haub and Cornelius 2001). To illustrate population dynamics, demographers use **population pyramids.** These depict a country's population by age and sex. Figure 20.7 compares the population pyramids of the United States, Mexico, and the world.

You can see how important age structure is. If by some miracle Mexico were transformed overnight into a nation as industrialized as the United States and the average

Figure 20.7 Three Population Pyramids

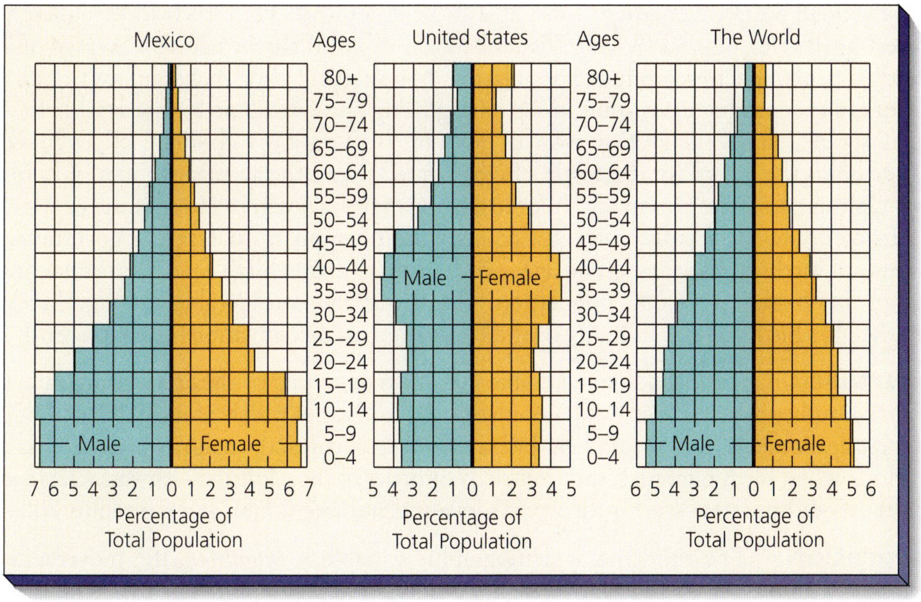

Source: Population Today, 26, 9, September 1998:4, 5.

population pyramid a graphic representation of a population, divided into age and sex number of children per woman dropped to 2.0, the same as in the United States, the population of Mexico would continue to soar. Mexico has *population momentum* because a much higher percentage of Mexican women are in their childbearing years.

The implications of a doubling population are mind-boggling. *Just to stay even,* within thirty-seven years Mexico must double its jobs, food production, and factories; hospitals and schools; transportation, communication, water, gas, sewer, and electrical systems; housing, churches, civic buildings, theaters, stores, and parks. If Mexico fails to double them, its already meager standard of living will drop even further.

Conflict theorists point out that a declining standard of living poses the threat of political instability—protests, riots, even revolution, and, in response, repression by the government. Political instability in one country can spill over into others, threatening an entire region's balance of power. Fearing this, leaders of the Most Industrialized Nations are using the United Nations to direct a campaign of worldwide birth control. With one hand they give agricultural aid, IUDs, and condoms to the masses in the Least Industrialized Nations—while, with the other, they sell weapons to the elites in these countries. Both actions, say conflict theorists, serve the same purpose of promoting political stability and the dominance of the Most Industrialized Nations in global stratification.

The Three Demographic Variables

How many people will live in the United States fifty years from now? What will the world's population be then? These are important questions. Educators want to know how many schools to build. Manufacturers want to anticipate changes in demand for their products. The government needs to know how many doctors, engineers, and executives to train. Politicians want to know how many people will be paying taxes—and how many young people will be available to fight a war.

To project the future of populations, demographers use three **demographic variables:** fertility, mortality, and migration. Let's look at each.

Fertility

The **fertility rate** is the number of children the average woman bears. A term sometimes confused with fertility is **fecundity,** the number of children women are *capable* of bearing. The fecundity of women around the world is about twenty children each. Their fertility rate, however (the actual number of children they bear), is much lower. The world's overall fertility rate is 2.8, which means that the average woman in the world bears 2.8 children during her lifetime. At 2.0, the fertility rate of U.S. women is considerably less.

The region of the world that has the highest fertility rate is sub-Saharan Africa, where the average woman gives birth to 5.2 children; the lowest is Eastern Europe, where the average woman bears 1.2 children. Table 20.1 lists the countries with the world's highest and lowest birth rates. As you look at this table, keep in mind that it takes an average of 2.1 children per couple to reproduce a population. (The extra .1 child makes up for those who die or fail to reproduce.) As you can see, Hong Kong and Macao tie for the world's lowest fertility rate. There, the average woman gives birth to only 0.9 children. Niger in West Africa holds the record for the world's highest rate. There, the average woman gives birth to 8 children, *nine* times as many children as the average woman in Hong Kong or Macao.

To compute the fertility rate of a country, demographers analyze the government's records of births. From these, they figure the country's **crude birth rate,** the annual number of live births per 1,000 population. There may be considerable slippage here, of course. The birth records in many of the Least Industrialized Nations are haphazard.

Mortality

The second demographic variable is measured by the **crude death rate,** the annual number of deaths per 1,000 population. It, too, varies widely around the world. The highest death rate is 24, a record held by Niger in West Africa, the country that also has the world's highest birth rate. At 2, three oil-rich countries in the Mideast—Kuwait, Qatar, and United Arab Emirates—tie for the world's lowest death rate (Haub and Cornelius 2001).

Migration

The third major demographic variable is *migration,* the movement of people from one area to another. There are two types of migration. The first type is people moving from one region to another within the same country. The Social Map on the next page shows this type of migration. Although there is two-way movement among U.S.

demographic variables the three factors that influence population growth: fertility, mortality, and net migration

fertility rate the number of children that the average woman bears

fecundity the number of children that women are capable of bearing

crude birth rate the annual number of live births per 1,000 population

crude death rate the annual number of deaths per 1,000 population

Table 20.1 Extremes in Childbirth

Where Do Women Give Birth to the Fewest Children? Country	Number of Children	Where Do Women Give Birth to the Most Children? Country	Number of Children
1. Hong Kong	0.9	1. Niger	8.0
2. Macao	0.9	2. Somalia	7.2
3. Czech Republic	1.1	3. Liberia	7.0
4. Georgia	1.1	4. Mali	7.0
5. Ukraine	1.1	5. Yemen	7.0
6. Bulgaria	1.2	6. Congo, Democratic Republic of	6.9
7. Greece	1.2	7. Uganda	6.9
8. Italy	1.2	8. Angola	6.8
9. Russia	1.2	9. Comoros	6.8
10. Spain	1.2	10. Chad	6.6

Note: Other countries that tie at 1.2 children per woman are Estonia, Latvia, Lithuania, Romania, Slovakia, and Slovenia.
Source: Haub 2003.

regions, at the end of the year each region has a net loss or gain. As you can see, Americans are migrating to the South, which is in the midst of tremendous growth in economic and political power. During the period shown on this Social Map, the South is the only region to gain population from migration. In all the other regions, more people moved out than moved in. The Northeast lost the most people, most of whom moved to the South.

Part of the South's gain is from African Americans who are returning to the South. During and after World War II, in what is known as "The Great Migration," millions of African Americans moved from the South to the North. In a historical shift, many are returning to the South to participate in its growing economy, to enjoy its warmer climate, and to renew ties with family roots (Frey 2001).

Figure 20.8 Net Migration Between Regions, 1997–2001

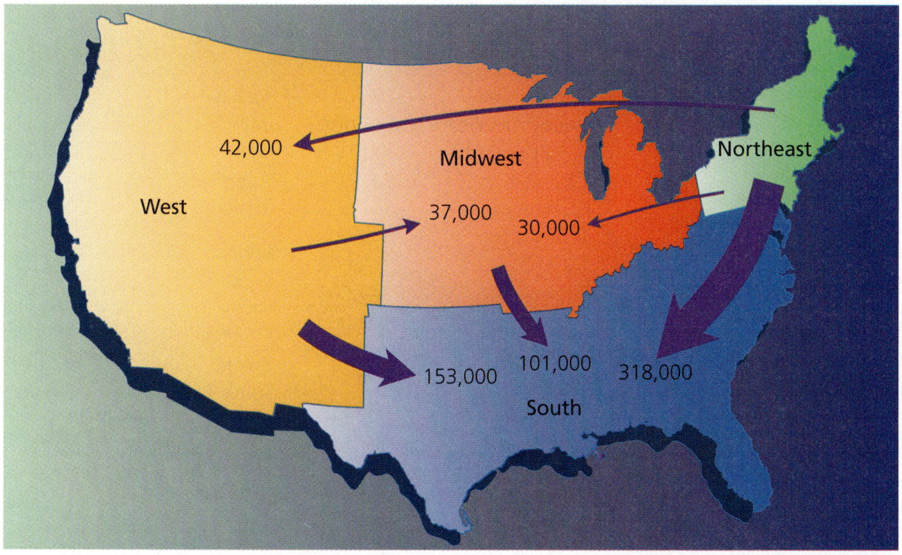

Source: U.S. Census Bureau 1998, 1999, 2000, 2001, 2002:Table 20.

Current immigration shows greater diversity of origin. These contemporary immigrants are Sikhs, members of a religion centered in Punjab, India.

The second type of migration is people moving from one country to another. Demographers use the term **net migration rate** to refer to the difference between the number of *immigrants* (people moving into a country) and *emigrants* (people moving out of a country) per 1,000 population. Unlike fertility and mortality rates, migration does not affect the global population, for people are simply shifting their residence from one country or region to another.

As you know, immigrants are seeking a better life. They are willing to give up the security of their family and friends to move to a country with a strange language and unfamiliar customs. What motivates people to embark on such a venture? To understand migration, we need to look at both push and pull factors. The *push* factors are what people want to escape—poverty, the lack of religious and political freedoms, political persecution. The *pull* factors are the magnets that draw people to a new land, such as a chance for higher wages and better jobs.

Around the world, the flow of migration is from the Least Industrialized Nations to the industrialized countries. After "migrant paths" are established, immigration often accelerates as networks of kin and friends become additional magnets that attract more people from the same nation—and even from the same villages.

By far, the United States is the world's number one choice of immigrants. The United States admits more immigrants each year than all the other nations of the world combined. Thirty-one million residents—one of every nine Americans—were born in other countries (*Statistical Abstract* 2002:Table 41). Table 20.2 shows where U.S. immigrants were born. To escape grinding poverty, such as that which surrounds Celia and Angel, millions of people also enter the United States illegally, most of them from Mexico and

Table 20.2 Place of Birth of Immigrants to the United States, by Region and Country, 1981–2000

North America	**5,906,000**	Thailand	113,000	Argentina	50,000
Mexico	3,950,000*	Japan	105,000	Venezuela	48,000
Dominican Republic	592,000	Lebanon	85,000	Chile	40,000
Jamaica	387,000	Bangladesh	81,000	**Europe**	**1,419,000**
Cuba	340,000	Jordan	72,000	Great Britain	278,000
Haiti	322,000	Israel	68,000	Poland	267,000
Canada	257,000	Iraq	60,000	Russia	149,000
Trinidad and Tobago	103,000	Syria	47,000	Ukraine	141,000
Asia	**5,564,000**	Turkey	47,000	Germany	138,000
Philippines	1,001,000	Afghanistan	44,000	Romania	97,000
Vietnam	823,000	Indonesia	30,000	Ireland	92,000
China	712,000	**Central and South America**	**1,874,000**	Portugal	63,000
India	645,000	El Salvador	432,000	Italy	55,000
Korea	510,000	Colombia	255,000	France	51,000
Iran	267,000	Guatemala	191,000	Yugoslavia	45,000
Taiwan	207,000	Peru	170,000	Greece	43,000
Laos	189,000	Guyana	169,000	**Africa**	**347,000**
Pakistan	186,000	Nicaragua	142,000	Nigeria	103,000
Hong Kong	137,000	Ecuador	132,000	Egypt	78,000
Cambodia	135,000	Honduras	116,000	Ethiopia	77,000
		Brazil	76,000	Ghana	51,000
		Panama	53,000	South Africa	38,000

*This total does not include the estimated 7 million to 9 million illegal immigrants in the United States, about 70 percent of whom are from Mexico (Martin and Midgley 2003).

Note: Because only the countries with the largest immigration to the United States are listed, the total for each region is larger than the total of the countries from that region. Data for 1981–1990 for Taiwan and Russia are based on their proportions of China's and the Soviet Union's immigration for 1991–1998.

Source: By the author. Based on *Statistical Abstract* 2002:Table 7.

net migration rate the difference between the number of immigrants and emigrants per 1,000 population many others from Central and South America. The government estimates the number of illegal immigrants to be between 7 million and 9 million.

Experts cannot agree whether immigrants are a net contributor to the U.S. economy or a drain on it. Economist Julian Simon (1986, 1993) claimed that immigrants benefit the economy. After subtracting what immigrants collect in welfare and adding what they produce in jobs and taxes, he concluded that immigrants produce more than they cost. Other economists such as Donald Huddle (1993) use figures showing that immigrants are a drain on taxpayers. The fairest conclusion seems to be that the more educated immigrants produce more than they cost, while the less educated cost more than they produce.

growth rate the net change in a population after adding births, subtracting deaths, and either adding or subtracting net migration

basic demographic equation growth rate equals births minus deaths plus net migration

Problems in Forecasting Population Growth

The total of the three demographic variables—fertility, mortality, and net migration—gives us a country's **growth rate,** the change after people have been added to and subtracted from a population. What demographers call the **basic demographic equation** is quite simple:

Growth rate = births – deaths + net migration

If population increase depended only on biology, the demographer's job would be simple. But social factors—wars, economic booms and busts, plagues, and famines—push rates of birth and death and migration up or down. As shown in the Cultural Diversity box below, even infanticide can affect population growth. Government programs also

CULTURAL DIVERSITY

around the WORLD

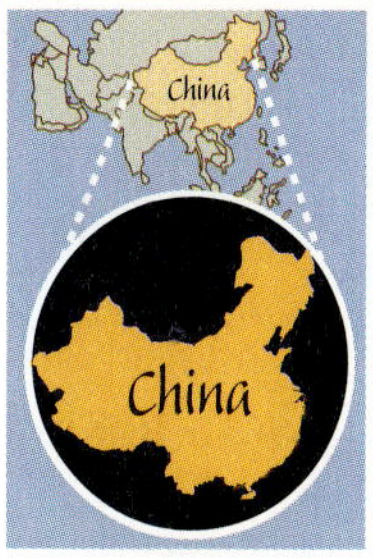

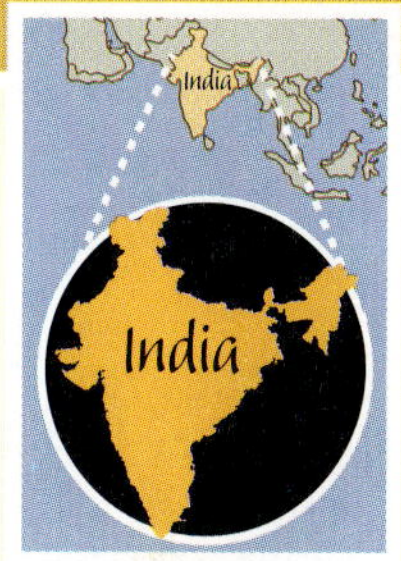

Killing Little Girls: An Ancient and Thriving Practice

"The Mysterious Case of the Missing Girls" could have been the title of this box. Around the globe, for every 100 girls born, about 105 boys are born. In China, however, for every 100 baby girls, there are 111 baby boys. Given China's huge population, this means China has about 400,000 fewer baby girls than one would expect. Why?

The answer is female infanticide, the killing of baby girls. When a Chinese woman goes into labor, village midwives sometimes grab a bucket of water. If the newborn is a girl, she is plunged into the water before she can draw her first breath.

At the root of China's sexist infanticide is economics. The people are poor, and they have no pensions. When parents can no longer work, sons support them. In contrast, a daughter must be married off, at great expense, and at that point her obligations transfer to her husband and his family.

In the past few years, the percentage of boy babies has grown. The reason, again, is economics, but this time it has a new twist. As China opened the door to capitalism, travel and trade opened up—but primarily to men, for it is not thought appropriate for women to travel alone. Thus men find themselves in a better position to bring profits home to the family—giving parents one more reason to desire male children.

Female infanticide is also common in India. Many Indian women use ultrasound to learn the sex of their child, and then abort the fetus if it is a girl. Doctors take portable ultrasound machines from village to village, charging $11 for the test and $44 for the abortion. Although the use of ultrasound for this purpose is illegal, this practice accounts for the abortion of about 3 million girls a year.

One test for sex selection led to a public outcry in India. The outrage was not about female infanticide, however, nor was it due to an antiabortion movement. Rather, the public became incensed when a physician mistakenly gave the parents wrong information and aborted a *male* baby!

It is likely that the preference for boys, and the resulting female infanticide, will not disappear until the social structures that perpetuate sexism are dismantled. This will not take place until women hold as much power as men, a development that, should it ever occur, apparently lies far in the future.

Sources: Lagaipa 1990; McGowan 1991; Polumbaum 1992; Renteln 1992; Greenhalgh and Li 1995; Jordan 2000; Dugger 2001; Raghunathan 2003.

Due to the Chinese government's policy of "one couple, one child," the birth rate of China has dropped sharply. As discussed in the text, this policy is carried out ruthlessly, including forcing abortions on protesting women.

complicate projections. Some governments try to persuade women to bear fewer—or more—children. When Hitler decided that Germany needed more "Aryans," the German government outlawed abortion and offered cash bonuses to women who gave birth. The population increased. Today European leaders have become alarmed that their birth rates have dropped so low that their populations will shrink without immigration. The commissioner of social affairs for the European Union has declared that "Europeans must have more children" (Population Today 2002). Declarations, however, are unlikely to accomplish anything.

In China, we find the opposite situation. Chinese leaders are trying to get their people to limit childbearing. Many people know that China has a "One couple, one child" national policy, but few know how ruthlessly this policy is enforced. Steven Mosher, an anthropologist who did fieldwork in China, revealed that—whether she wants it or not—after the birth of her first child, each woman is fitted with an IUD (intrauterine device). If a woman has a second child, she is sterilized. If a woman gets pregnant without government permission (yes, you read that right), she is aborted. If she does not consent to an abortion, one is performed on her anyway—even if she is nine months pregnant (Erik 1982). The government even has its agents check sanitary napkins to make sure that women are having their menstrual periods and are not pregnant.

Letting such policies pass without comment, we can see that a government's efforts to change a country's growth rate complicate the demographer's task of projecting future populations.

The primary factor that influences a country's growth rate is industrialization. *In every country that industrializes, the birth rate declines.* Not only does industrialization open up economic and educational opportunities, but also it makes children more expensive. They require more education and remain dependent longer. Significantly, the basis for conferring status also changes—from having children to attaining education and displaying material wealth. People like Celia and Angel begin to see life differently, and their motivation to have many children drops sharply. Not knowing how rapidly industrialization will progress or how quickly changes in reproductive behavior will follow adds to the difficulty of making accurate projections.

Because of these many complications, demographers play it safe by making several projections of a country's population growth. For example, what will the U.S. population be in the year 2050? Will there be **zero population growth,** with every 1,000 women giving birth to 2,100 children? (The extra 100 children make up for those who do not survive or reproduce.) Will a larger proportion of women go to college? (The more education women have, the fewer children they bear.) How will immigration change during the coming years? Will AIDS rage out of control? Will some other devastating disease appear? What will happen to the new global economy? With such huge unknowns, it is easy to see why demographers make the three projections of the U.S. population shown in Figure 20.9.

Figure 20.9 Looking Toward the Future: Population Projections of the United States

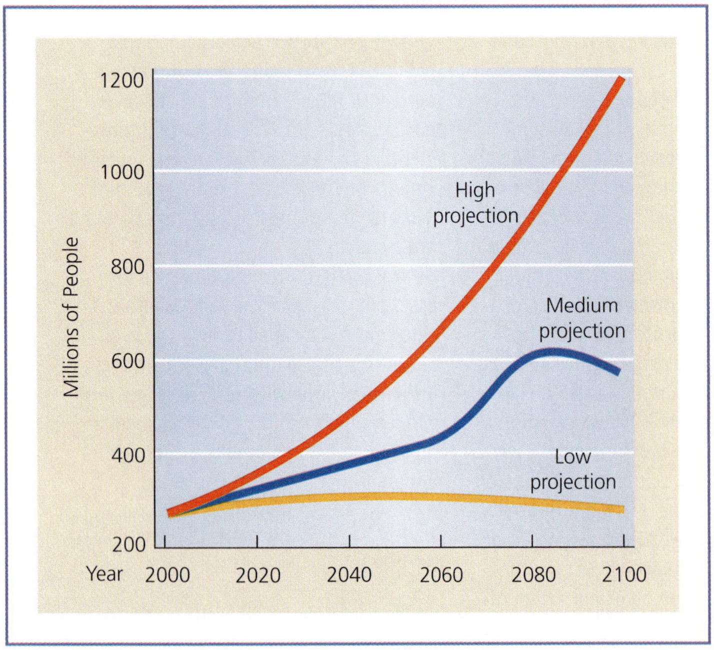

Note: The projections are based on different assumptions of fertility, mortality, and, especially, immigration.
Source: By the author. Based on *Statistical Abstract* 2002:Table 3.

Let's look at a different aspect of population, where people live. Because more and more people around the world are living in cities, we shall concentrate on urban trends and urban life.

URBANIZATION

As I was climbing a steep hill in Medellin, Colombia, in a district called El Tiro, my informant, Jaro, said, "This used to be a garbage heap." I stopped to peer through the vegetation alongside the path we were on, and sure enough, I could see bits of refuse still sticking out of the dirt. The "town" had been built on top of garbage.

This was just the first of my many revelations that day. The second was that El Tiro was so dangerous that the Medellin police refused to enter it. I shuddered for a moment, but I had good reason to trust Jaro. He had been a pastor in El Tiro for several years, and he knew the people well. I knew that if I stayed close to him I would be safe.

Actually, the town had become much safer in recent years. A group of young men had banded together to make it so, Jaro told me. A sort of frontier justice prevailed. The vigilantes told the prostitutes and drug dealers that there would be no prostitution or drug dealing in town, and to "take it elsewhere." They killed anyone who robbed or killed someone. And they even made families safer—they would beat up any man who got drunk and beat "his" woman. With the threat of instant justice, the area had become much safer.

Jaro then added that each household had to pay the group a monthly fee, which turned out to be less than a dollar in U.S. money. Each business had to pay a little more. For this, they received security.

As we wandered the streets of El Tiro, it did look safe—but I still stayed close to Jaro. And I wondered about this group of men who had made the area safe. What kept them from turning on the residents? Jaro had no answer. When Jaro pointed to two young men, whom he said were part of the ruling group, I asked if I could take their picture. They refused. I did not try to snap one on the sly.

My final revelation was El Tiro itself. On the next two pages, you can see some of the things I saw that day.

In this final part of the chapter, I will try to lay the context for understanding urban life—and El Tiro. Let's begin by first finding out how the city itself came about.

The Development of Cities

Cities are not new to the world scene. Perhaps as early as seven to ten thousand years ago people built small cities, surrounding them with defensive walls. An example is biblically famous Jericho (Homblin 1973). About 3500 B.C., around the time that writing was invented, larger cities appeared in Iran (Mesopotamia) (Chandler and Fox 1974; Hawley 1981). Later cities developed in the Nile, Indus, and Yellow River valleys, in West Africa, along the shores of the Mediterranean, in Central America, and in the Andes (Fischer 1976; Flanagan 1990). The first city in the Americas was Caral, in what is now Peru (Fountain 2001).

The key to the origin of cities is the development of more efficient agriculture (Lenski and Lenski 1987). Only when farming produces a surplus can some people stop being food producers and gather in cities to spend time in other pursuits. A **city**, in fact, can be defined as a place in which a large number of people are permanently based and do not produce their own food. The invention of the plow between five and six thousand years ago created widespread agricultural surpluses, stimulating the development of towns and cities (Curwin and Hart 1961).

zero population growth a demographic condition in which women bear only enough children to reproduce the population

city a place in which a large number of people are permanently based and do not produce their own food

THROUGH THE **AUTHOR'S LENS**

A Walk Through El Tiro in
Medellin, Colombia

This is the "richer" area below El Tiro. As you can see, some of the residents own cars.

Kids are kids the world over. These children don't know they are poor. They are having a great time playing on a pile of dirt in the street.

Almost at the top of the garbage heap, I saw this boy in front of his house. His mother hung out the family's wash to dry.

This is one of my favorite photos. The woman is happy that she has a home—and proud of what she has done with it. What I find remarkable is the flower garden she so carefully tends, and has taken great effort to protect from children and dogs. I can see the care she would take of a little suburban home.

The road to El Tiro. On the left, going up the hill, is a board walk. To the right is a meat market (carniceria). Note the structure above the meat market, where the family that runs the store lives.

El Tiro has home delivery.

An infrastructure has developed to serve El Tiro. This woman is waiting in line to use the only public telephone.

"What does an El Tiro home look like inside?," I kept wondering. Then Jaro, my guide at the left, took me inside the home of one of his parishioners. Amelia keeps a neat house, with everything highly organized.

It doesn't take much skill to build your own house in El Tiro. A hammer and saw, some nails and used lumber will provide most of what you need. This man is building his house on top of another house. You can see why so many people are killed in earth tremors in the Least Industrialized Nations.

What do the people do to make a living in El Tiro? Anything they can. This man is sharpening a saw in front of his home. The child looks quite secure behind the barricade the father built.

Early cities were small economic centers surrounded by walls designed to keep out enemies. These cities, built like fortresses, were constantly threatened by armed, roving tribesmen and by the leaders of nearby city-states who raised armies in an effort to enlarge their domain and enrich their coffers by sacking neighboring cities. Pictured here is the fabled Forbidden City in Beijing, where China's rulers lived. Soldiers patrolled the top of the wall. From here, they could shoot arrows onto any enemy that tried to penetrate the city.

Most early cities were tiny in comparison with those of today, merely a collection of a few thousand people in agricultural centers or on major trade routes. The most notable exceptions are two cities that reached 1 million for a brief period of time before they declined—Changan in China about A.D. 800 and Baghdad in Persia (Iraq) about A.D. 900 (Chandler and Fox 1974). Even Athens at the peak of its power in the fifth century B.C. had less than 200,000 inhabitants. Rome, at its peak, may have had a million or more (Flanagan 1990).

Even 200 years ago, the only city in the world that had a population of more than a million was Peking (now Beijing), China (Chandler and Fox 1974). Then in just 100 years, by 1900, the number of such cities jumped to sixteen. The reason was the Industrial Revolution, which drew people to cities by providing work. The Industrial Revolution also stimulated rapid transportation and communication, and allowed people, resources, and products to be moved efficiently—all essential factors (called *infrastructure*) on which large cities depend. Today about 300 cities have a million or more people. As Figure 20.10 shows, this number is continuing to grow (Brockerhoff 2000).

Figure 20.10 The Growth of Cities over 1 Million Residents

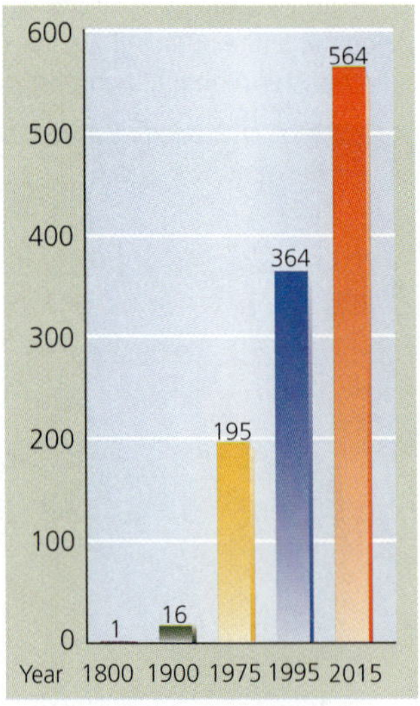

Sources: Chandler and Fox 1974; Brockerhoff 2000.

The Process of Urbanization

Although cities are not new to the world scene, urbanization is. **Urbanization** refers to masses of people moving to cities, and these cities having a growing influence on society. Urbanization is worldwide. In 1800, only 3 percent of the world's population lived in cities (Hauser and Schnore 1965). Today it is 47 percent: 75 percent of people in the industrialized world and 40 percent of those who live in the Least Industrialized Nations (Haub 2003). The year 2007 is expected to mark the historic moment when more than half of all humanity will live in cities (Massey 2001). Without the Industrial Revolution this remarkable growth could not have taken place, for an extensive infrastructure is needed to support hundreds of thousands and even millions of people in a relatively small area.

To understand the city's attraction, we need to consider the "pulls" of urban life. Due to its exquisite division of labor, the city offers incredible variety—music ranging from rock and salsa to country and classic, diets for vegetarians and diabetics as well as imported delicacies from around the world for everyone else. Cities also offer anonymity, which so many find refreshing in light of the tighter controls of village and small-town life. And, of course, the city offers work.

Some cities have grown so large and have so much influence over a region that the term *city* is no longer adequate to describe them. The term **metropolis** is used instead. This term refers to a central city surrounded by smaller cities and their suburbs.

They are linked by transportation and communication and connected economically, and sometimes politically, through county boards and regional governing bodies.

St. Louis is an example. Although this name, St. Louis, properly refers to a city of fewer than 400,000 people in Missouri, it also refers to another 2 million people who live in more than a hundred separate towns in both Missouri and Illinois. Altogether, the region is known as the "St. Louis or Bi-State Area." Although these towns are independent politically, they form an economic unit. They are linked by work (many people in the smaller towns work in St. Louis, or are served by industries from St. Louis), by communications (they share the same area newspaper and radio and television stations), and by transportation (they use the same interstate highways, "Bi-State Bus" system, and international airport). As symbolic interactionists would note, the residents' shared symbols (the Arch, the Mississippi River, Busch Brewery, the Cardinals, the Rams, the Blues—both the hockey team and the music) provide a common identity. Most of the towns run into one another, and if you were to drive through this metropolis you would not know you were leaving one town and entering another—unless you had lived there for some time and were aware of the fierce small-town identifications and rivalries that coexist within this larger identity.

Some metropolises have grown so large and influential that the term **megalopolis** is used to describe them. This term refers to an overlapping area consisting of at least two metropolises and their many suburbs. Of the twenty or so megalopolises in the United States, the three largest are the Eastern seaboard running from Maine to Virginia, the area in Florida between Miami, Orlando, and Tampa, and California's coastal area between San Francisco and San Diego. The California megalopolis extends into Mexico and includes Tijuana and its southern suburbs.

This process of urban areas turning into a metropolis, and a metropolis developing into a megalopolis occurs worldwide. When a city's population hits 10 million, it is called a **megacity**. In 1950, New York City was the only megacity in the world. Today there are 19 megacities, and by the year 2015 there will be 21 (Zwingle 2002). Figure 20.11 shows the ten largest megacities in the world. Note that most megacities are located in the Least Industrialized Nations.

urbanization the process by which an increasing proportion of a population lives in cities and has a growing influence on the culture

metropolis a central city surrounded by smaller cities and their suburbs

megalopolis an urban area consisting of at least two metropolises and their many suburbs

megacity a city of 10 million or more residents

Figure 20.11 **The Urban Giants: The Population of the World's Ten Largest Megacities, in Millions**

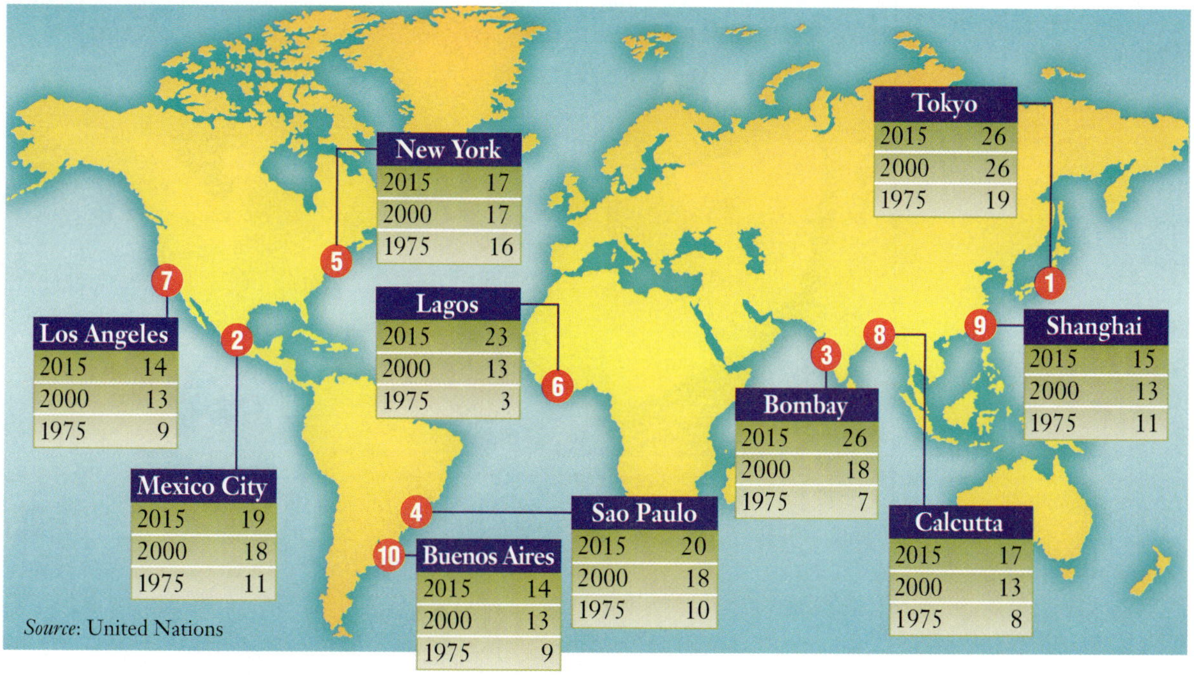

Source: United Nations 2000.

metropolitan statistical area (MSA) a central city and the urbanized counties adjacent to it

edge city a large clustering of service facilities and residential areas near highway intersections that provides a sense of place to people who live, shop, and work there

gentrification middle class people moving into a rundown area of a city, displacing the poor as they buy and restore homes

U.S. Urban Patterns

In its early years, the United States was almost exclusively rural. In 1790, only about 5 percent of Americans lived in cities. By 1920, this figure had jumped to 50 percent. Urbanization has continued without letup, and today 80 percent of Americans live in cities. As you can see from the Social Map below, like our other social patterns, urbanization is uneven across the United States.

The U.S. Census Bureau has divided the country into 274 **metropolitan statistical areas (MSAs).** Each MSA consists of a central city of at least 50,000 people and the urbanized areas linked to it. About three of every five Americans live in just fifty or so MSAs.

As Americans migrate in search of work and better lifestyles, most cities gain population, but a few shrink. Table 20.3 on the next page lists both the cities that have lost population and those that have been the fastest growing. This table reflects the migration patterns we discussed earlier. All of the fastest growing cities are in the West and the South, while all of the declining cities are in the Northeast (and Ohio, which borders the northeastern section of the United States).

As Americans migrate, **edge cities** have developed to meet their needs. This term refers to clusters of shopping malls, hotels, office parks, and residential areas that are located near the intersection of major highways. Although these clusters may overlap the boundaries of several cities or towns, they provide a sense of place to those who live, work, or shop there.

Another major U.S. urban pattern is **gentrification,** the movement of middle-class people into rundown areas of a city. They are attracted by the low prices for quality housing that, although deteriorated, can be restored. One consequence is an improvement in the appearance of some urban neighborhoods—freshly painted buildings, well-groomed lawns, and the absence of boarded-up windows. Another consequence is that the poor residents are displaced as the more well-to-do newcomers move in and drive up prices. Tension often arises between these groups (Anderson 1990, 1999).

A common pattern is for the gentrifiers to be whites and the displaced to be minorities. As discussed in the Down-to-Earth Sociology box on the next page, in Harlem, New

Figure 20.12 How Urban Is Your State? The Rural-Urban Makeup of the United States

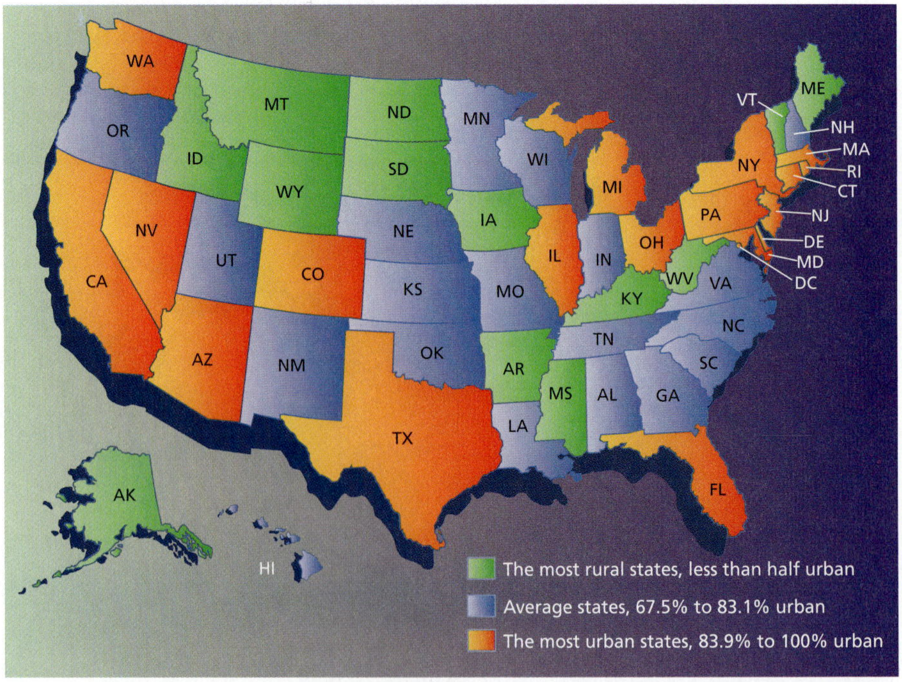

Note: The most urban state is New Jersey; the source reports that it is now 100 percent urban. The most rural state is Vermont, where 72.2 percent live in rural areas.
Source: By the author. Based on *Statistical Abstract* 2002:Table 29.

Table 20.3 The Shrinking and Fastest-Growing U.S. Cities

The Shrinking Cities		The Fastest-Growing Cities	
1. −5.3%	Utica-Rome, NY	1. 83.3%	Las Vegas, NV
2. −4.6%	Binghamton, NY	2. 65.3%	Naples, FL
3. −2.2%	Scranton-Wilkes Barre-Hasleton, PA	3. 49.7%	West Palm Beach–Boca Raton, FL
4. −1.6%	Buffalo-Niagara Falls, NY	4. 48.5%	McAllen-Edinburg-Mission, TX
5. −1.5%	Pittsburgh, PA	5. 47.7%	Austin-San Marcos, TX
6. −1.4%	Syracuse, NY	6. 47.5%	Fayetteville-Springdale-Rogers, AR
7. −1.0%	Youngstown-Warren, OH	7. 46.1%	Boise City, ID
8. −0.3%	New Bedford, MA	8. 45.3%	Phoenix-Mesa, AZ
9. −0.1%	Dayton-Springfield, OH	9. 39.8%	Provo-Orem, UT

Note: The totals indicate the percentage of population change from 1990–2000. A minus sign indicates a loss of population.

Source: Statistical Abstract 2002:Table 30.

York, both the gentrifiers and the displaced are African Americans. As middle-class and professional African Americans reclaim this area, an infrastructure—which includes everything from Starbucks coffee houses to dentists—follows. So do soaring real estate prices.

DOWN-TO-EARTH SOCIOLOGY

Reclaiming Harlem: "It Feeds My Soul"

THE STORY IS WELL KNOWN. THE INNER city is filled with crack, crime, and corruption. It stinks from foul, festering garbage strewn on the streets and piled up around burned-out buildings. Only those who have no choice live in this desolate, despairing environment where danger lurks around every corner.

What is not so well known is that affluent African Americans are reclaiming some of these blighted areas.

Howard Sanders was living the American Dream. After earning a degree from Harvard Business School, he took a position with a Manhattan investment firm. He lived in an exclusive apartment on Central Park West, but he missed Harlem, where he had grown up. He moved back, along with his wife and daughter.

African American lawyers, doctors, professors, and bankers are doing the same.

What's the attraction? The first is nostalgia, a cultural identification with the Harlem of legend and folklore. It was here that black writers and artists lived in the 1920s, here that the blues and jazz attracted young and accomplished musicians.

The second reason is a more practical one. Harlem offers housing value. Five-bedroom homes with 6,000 square feet are available. Some feature Honduran mahogany. Some brownstones are only shells and have to be renovated; others are in perfect condition.

What is happening is the rebuilding of a community. Some people who "made" it want to be role models. They want children in the community to see them going to and returning from work.

When the middle class moved out of Harlem, so did its amenities. Now that young professionals are moving back in, the amenities are returning, too. There were no coffee shops, restaurants, jazz clubs, florists, bakeries, copy centers, dentist and optometrist offices, or art galleries—the types of things urbanites take for granted. Now there are.

The same thing is happening on Chicago's West Side and in other U.S. cities.

The drive to find community—to connect with others and with one's roots—is strong. As an investment banker who migrated to Harlem said, "It feeds my soul."

Sources: Based on Cose 1999; McCormick 1999; Waldman 2000; Scott 2001; Taylor 2002; Leland 2003.

Models of Urban Growth

As I mentioned in the first chapter, in the 1920s sociologists at the University of Chicago studied the contrasting ways of urban life. One of these sociologists, Robert Park, coined the term **human ecology** to describe how people adapt to their environment (Park and Burgess 1921; Park 1936). (This concept is also known as *urban ecology.*) The process of urban growth is of special interest to human ecologists. Let's look at the four main models they developed.

The Concentric Zone Model

To explain how cities expand, sociologist Ernest Burgess (1925) proposed a *concentric-zone model.* As shown in part A of Figure 20.13, Burgess noted that a city expands outward from its center. Zone 1 is the central business district. Zone 2, which encircles the downtown area, is in transition. It contains rooming houses and deteriorating housing, which Burgess said breed poverty, disease, and vice. Zone 3 is the area to which thrifty workers have moved in order to escape the zone in transition and yet maintain easy access to their

Figure 20.13 How Cities Develop: Models of Urban Growth

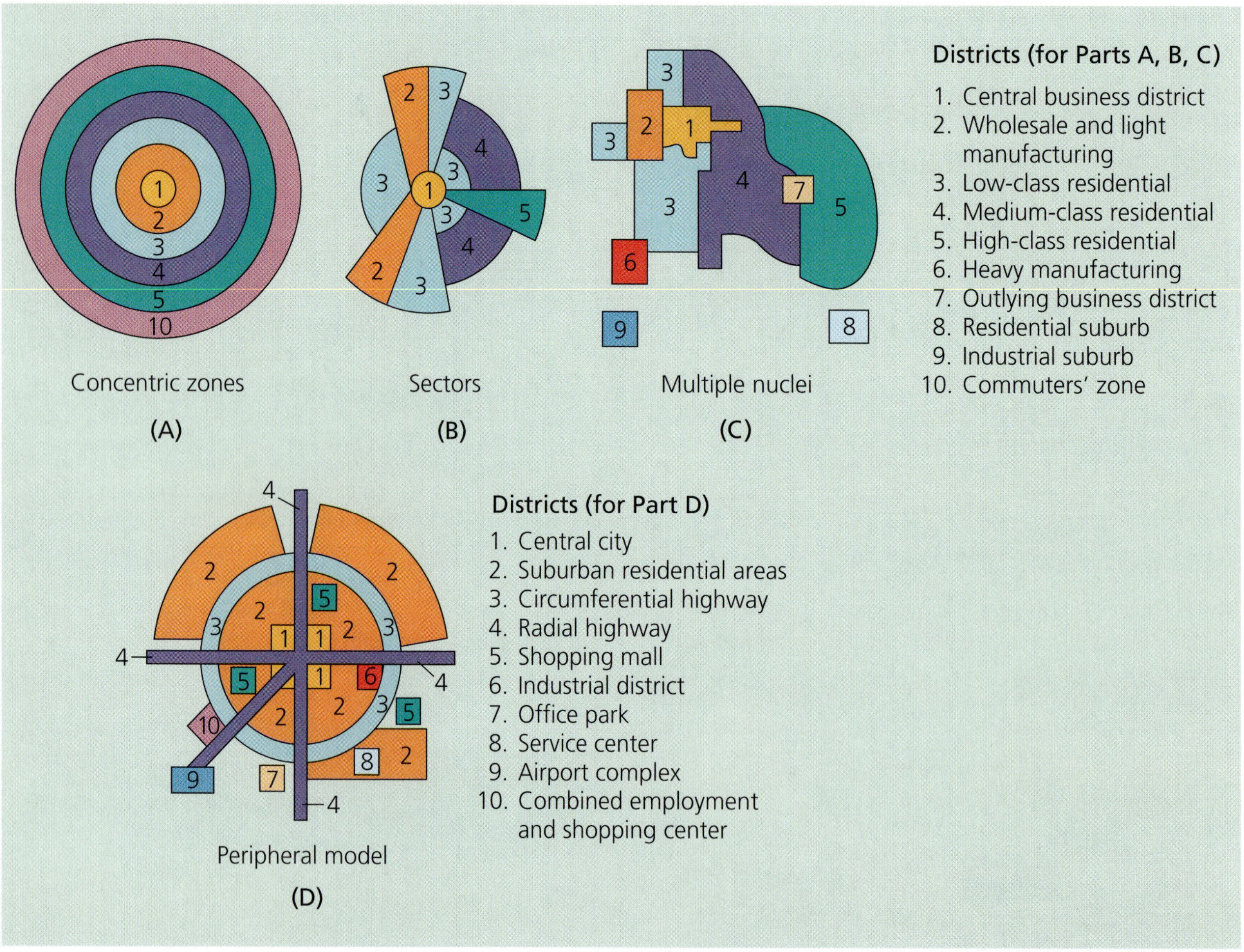

Source: Cousins and Nagpaul 1970; Harris 1997.

work. Zone 4 contains more expensive apartments, residential hotels, single-family homes, and exclusive areas where the wealthy live. Commuters live in Zone 5, which consists of suburbs or satellite cities that have grown up around transit routes.

Burgess intended this model to represent "the tendencies of any town or city to expand radially from its central business district." He noted, however, that no "city fits perfectly this ideal scheme." Some cities have physical obstacles such as a lake, river, or railroad, which cause their expansion to depart from the model. Burgess also noted that businesses had begun to deviate from the model by locating in outlying zones. This was in 1925, and Burgess was seeing the first stage of a major shift that led businesses away from downtown areas to suburban shopping malls. Today, these malls account for most of the country's retail sales.

The Sector Model

Sociologist Homer Hoyt (1939, 1971) noted that a city's concentric zones do not form a complete circle, and he modified Burgess' model of urban growth. As shown in part B of Figure 20.13, a concentric zone can contain several sectors—one of working-class housing, another of expensive homes, a third of businesses, and so on—all competing for the same land.

An example of this dynamic competition is what sociologists call an **invasion-succession cycle.** Poor immigrants and rural migrants look for low-rent areas. As their numbers swell, they spill over into adjacent areas.

Upset by their presence, the middle class moves out, which expands the sector of low-cost housing. The invasion-succession cycle is never complete, for later another group will replace this earlier one. The cycle, in fact, can go full circle, for with gentrification, the "invaders" can be the middle and upper middle classes.

The Multiple-Nuclei Model

Geographers Chauncey Harris and Edward Ullman noted that some cities have several centers or nuclei (Harris and Ullman 1945; Ullman and Harris 1970). As shown in part C of Figure 20.13, each nucleus contains some specialized activity. A familiar example is the clustering of fast-food restaurants in one area and automobile dealerships in another. Sometimes similar activities are grouped together because they profit from cohesion; retail districts, for example, draw more customers if there are more stores. Other clustering occurs because some types of land use, such as factories and expensive homes, are incompatible with one another. One result is that services are not spread evenly throughout the city.

The Peripheral Model

Chauncey Harris (1997) also developed the peripheral model shown in part D of Figure 20.13. This model portrays the impact of radial highways on the movement of people and services away from the central city to the city's periphery, or outskirts. It also shows the development of industrial and office parks.

Critique of the Models

These models tell only part of the story. They are time bound, for ancient cities didn't follow these patterns (see the photo on page 594). In addition, they do not account for urban planning policies. England, for example, has planning laws that preserve green belts (trees and farmlands) around the city. This prevents urban sprawl: Wal-Mart cannot buy land outside the city and put up a store; instead, it must locate in the downtown area with the other stores. Norwich has 250,000 people—yet the city ends abruptly, and on its

human ecology Robert Park's term for the relationship between people and their environment (such as land and structures); also known as *urban ecology*

invasion-succession cycle the process of one group of people displacing a group whose racial-ethnic or social class characteristics differ from their own green belt pheasants skitter across plowed fields while sheep graze in verdant meadows (Milbank 1995).

The models also fall short when it comes to the cities of the Least Industrialized Nations. U.S. visitors are surprised when they visit one of these cities. The wealthy often claim the inner city, where fine restaurants and other services are readily accessible. There, tucked behind tall walls and protected from public scrutiny, they enjoy luxurious homes and gardens. The poor, in contrast, especially rural migrants, settle in areas outside the city—or, as in the case of El Tiro, on top of garbage heaps in what used to be the outskirts of a city. This topic is discussed in the Cultural Diversity box.

CULTURAL DIVERSITY around the WORLD

The World

Why City Slums Are Better than the Country: Urbanization in the Least Industrialized Nations

In the Least Industrialized Nations, rural people have flocked to the cities in such numbers that, as we saw in Figure 20.11 (page 595), these nations now contain most of the world's largest cities. Each year, the cities of the Least Industrialized Nations swell by about 50 million people (Brockerhoff 2000). That's more than all the Spaniards who live in Spain. During the next six years, this is equivalent to the entire population of the United States.

The Least Industrialized Nations are facing massive upheaval as they rapidly urbanize, resulting in disparities such as those depicted here. Lacking the infrastructure to support their many newcomers, cities in the Least Industrialized Nations, already steeped in poverty, face the daunting task of developing jobs, housing, sewage and electrical systems, roads, schools, and so on. This photo was taken in Ulaanbaatar, Mongolia.

When rural migrants and immigrants move to U.S. cities, they usually settle in areas of deteriorating housing near the city's center. In the Least Industrialized Nations, the wealthy live near the downtown area, and migrants establish squatter settlements outside the city. This is the typical pattern, but as we saw with El Tiro (pages 592–593), they move to any area available, even garbage dumps. As you saw from the photos, there they build shacks from scrap boards and bits of corrugated metal. In some areas, even flattened tin cans are scavenged for building material. At first, the squatters enjoy no city facilities—roads, transportation lines, water, sewers, or garbage pickup. After a while, officials acknowledge the squatters' right to live there by adding bus service and minimal electric and water lines. Hundreds of people may use a single spigot.

Why this vast rush to live in the city under such difficult conditions? First, there are "push" factors. The rural way of life is breaking down. The second leg of the demographic transition has kicked in—death rates are dropping while birth rates remain high—and rural populations are multiplying. No longer is there enough land to divide up among children. There also are "pull" factors that draw people to the city—jobs, schools, housing, and even a more stimulating life.

Up to now, industrialization generally preceded urbanization. Now, in contrast, *urbanization is preceding industrialization.* The limited technology of the Least Industrialized Nations makes it difficult to support this substantial migration to their cities.

Will the Least Industrialized Nations adjust to this vast, unwanted migration? They have no choice. Authorities in Brazil, Guatemala, Venezuela, and other countries have sent in the police, even the army, to evict the settlers. It doesn't work. This just leads to violence—and the settlers keep streaming in anyway. The adjustment will be painful. The infrastructure (roads, water, sewers, electricity, and so on) must be built, but these poor countries don't have the resources to build them. As the desperate continue to flock to the cities, the problems will worsen.

For Your CONSIDERATION

What solutions do you see to the vast migration to the cities of the Least Industrialized Nations?

City Life: Alienation and Community

Just as cities provide opportunities, they also create problems. We humans are complex beings. Certainly we have needs of food, shelter, and safety, and satisfying them is important. But this is only part of who we are. We also have a deep need for **community,** a feeling that we belong—the sense that others care about what happens to us and that we can depend on the people around us. Some people find this sense of community in the city; others find its opposite, **alienation,** a sense of not belonging and a feeling that no one cares what happens to you:

> Twenty-eight-year-old Catherine Genovese, who was called Kitty by almost everyone in her Queens neighborhood, was returning home from work. After she had parked her car, a man grabbed her. She screamed, "Oh, my God, he stabbed me! Help me! Please help me!"
>
> For more than half an hour, thirty-eight respectable, law-abiding citizens looked out their windows and watched as the killer stalked and stabbed Kitty in three separate attacks. Twice the sudden glow from their bedroom lights interrupted him and frightened him off. Each time he returned, sought her out, and stabbed her again. Not one person telephoned the police during the assault. (*New York Times,* March 26, 1964)

When the police interviewed them, some witnesses said, "I didn't want to get involved." Others said, "We thought it was a lovers' quarrel." Some simply said, "I don't know." People throughout the country were shocked. It was as though Americans awoke one morning to discover that the country had changed overnight. They took this event as a sign that people could no longer trust one another, that the city was a cold, lonely place.

Why should the city be alienating? In a classic essay, "Urbanism as a Way of Life," sociologist Louis Wirth (1938) argued that the city undermines kinship and neighborhood, which are the traditional sources of social control and social solidarity. Urban dwellers live in anonymity. As they go from one superficial encounter with strangers to another, they grow aloof from one another and indifferent to other people's problems—as did the neighbors of Kitty Genovese. In short, the price of the personal freedom that the city offers is alienation—in some cases a distancing so vast that people can sit by while someone else is being murdered.

The city, however, is more than a mosaic of strangers who feel disconnected and distrustful of one another. It also consists of a series of smaller worlds, within which people find community. People become familiar with the smaller areas of the city where they live, work, shop, and play. Even slums, which to outsiders seem so threatening, can provide a sense of belonging. In a classic study, sociologist Herbert Gans (1962:12) noted,

> After a few weeks of living in the West End (of Boston), my observations—and my perceptions of the area—changed drastically. The search for an apartment quickly indicated that the individual units were usually in much better condition than the outside or the hallways of the buildings. Subsequently, in wandering through the West End, and in using it as a resident, I developed a kind of selective perception, in which my eye focused only on those parts of the area that were actually being used by people. Vacant buildings and boarded-up stores were no longer so visible, and the totally deserted alleys or streets were outside the set of paths normally traversed, either by myself or by the West Enders . . .
>
> Since much of the area's life took place on the street, faces became familiar very quickly. I met my neighbors on the stairs and in front of my building. And, once a shopping pattern developed, I saw the same storekeepers frequently, as well as the area's "characters" who wandered through the streets every day on a fairly regular route and schedule. In short, the exotic quality of the stores and the residents also wore off as I became used to seeing them.

community a place people identify with, where they sense that they belong and that others care about what happens to them

alienation used in several senses; in this context, it refers to feelings of isolation, that you are not a part of something or that no one cares about you

As he lived in the West End, Gans gradually gained an insider's perspective of the area. Despite the narrow streets, substandard buildings, and even piled-up garbage, most West Enders had chosen to live there: *To them the West End was a low-rent district, not a slum.* Within the deteriorated area was a community, people who visited back and forth with relatives and were involved in networks of friendships and acquaintances. Gans therefore titled his book *The Urban Villagers* (1962).

Then came well-intentioned urban planners, who drew up plans to get rid of the "slum." The residents of the West End were upset when they heard about the coming urban renewal, and distrustful that the improvements would benefit them. Their distrust proved well founded, for the urban renewal brought with it another invasion-succession cycle. Along with the gleaming new buildings came people with more money who took over the area. The former residents were dispossessed, their intimate patterns destroyed.

Who Lives in the City?

Whether you find alienation or community in the city depends on many factors, but consider the five types of urban dwellers that Gans (1962, 1968, 1991a) identified. Which type are you? How does this affect your chances of finding alienation or community?

The first three types live in the city by choice; they find a sense of community.

The Cosmopolites The cosmopolites are the city's students, intellectuals, professionals, musicians, artists, and entertainers. They have been drawn to the city because of its conveniences and cultural benefits.

The Singles Young, unmarried people come to the city seeking jobs and entertainment. Businesses and services such as singles bars, singles apartment complexes, and computer dating companies cater to their needs. Their stay in the city is often temporary, for most move to the suburbs after they marry and have children.

The city dwellers whom Gans identified as ethnic villagers find community in the city. Living in tightly knit neighborhoods, they know many other residents. Some first-generation immigrants have even come from the same village in the "old country." Shown here is a Korean neighborhood in Los Angeles.

The Ethnic Villagers United by race-ethnicity and social class, these people live in tightly knit neighborhoods that resemble villages and small towns. Their close circle of family and friends helps to isolate them from what they view as the harmful effects of city life.

The next two groups, the deprived and the trapped, have little choice about where they live. As alienated outcasts of industrial society, they are always skirting the edge of disaster.

The Deprived The deprived live in blighted neighborhoods that are more like urban jungles than urban villages. Consisting of the very poor and the emotionally disturbed, the deprived represent the bottom of society in terms of income, education, social status, and work skills. Some of them stalk their jungle in search of prey, their victims usually deprived people like themselves. Their future holds little chance for anything better in life.

The Trapped The trapped can find no escape either. Some could not afford to move when their neighborhood was "invaded" by another ethnic group. Others in this group are the elderly who are not wanted elsewhere, alcoholics and other drug abusers, and the downwardly mobile. Like the deprived, the trapped also suffer high rates of assault, mugging, robbery, and rape.

Urban Sentiment: Finding a Familiar World

Sociologists note that *the city is divided into little worlds* that people come to know down to their smallest details. City peo-

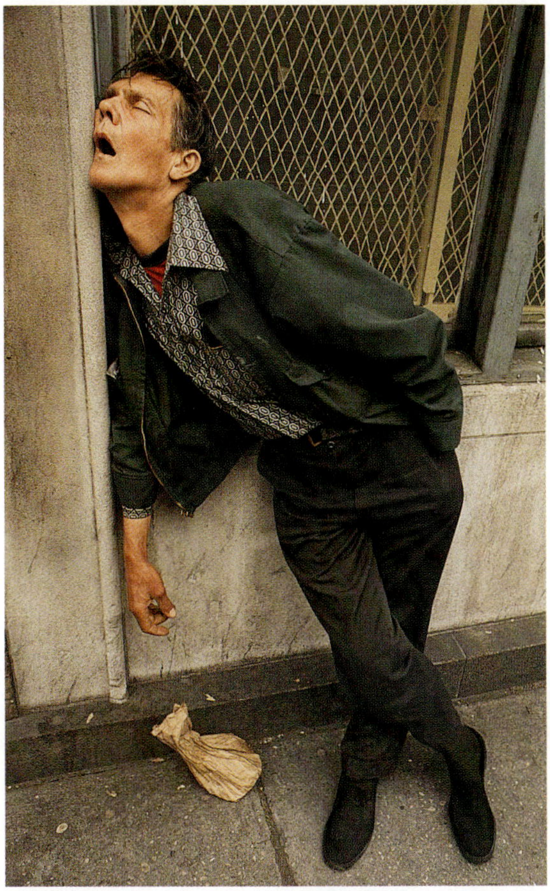

Men like this one, who has drunk himself into a stupor, are not an unfamiliar sight in some parts of U.S. cities. The text describes several types of urban dwellers. What type is this man?

ple create a sense of intimacy by *personalizing* their shopping (Stone 1954; Gans 1970). They shop in the same stores, and after a period of time, customers and clerks greet each other by name. Certain bars, restaurants, and shops are more than just buildings in which they make purchases. They become places where neighborhood residents build social relationships with one another and share informal news about the community.

Spectator sports also help urban dwellers find a familiar world (Hudson 1991). When Mark McGwire of the Cardinals hit the 61st home run that broke Roger Maris' long-standing record, fans around the country celebrated, but for the St. Louis area the celebration was special: It was for "our" man on "our" team—even though fewer than one in seven of the area's 2.5 million people live in the city. Sociologists David Karp and William Yoels (1990) note that such identification is so intense that long after moving to other parts of the country, many people maintain an emotional allegiance to the sports teams of the city in which they grew up.

The Norm of Noninvolvement and the Diffusion of Responsibility

Urban dwellers try to avoid intrusions from strangers. As they go about their everyday lives in the city, they follow a *norm of noninvolvement.*

> To do this, we sometimes use props such as newspapers to shield ourselves from others and to indicate our inaccessibility for interaction. In effect, we learn to "tune others out." In this regard, we might see the Walkman as the quintessential urban prop in that it allows us to be tuned in and tuned out at the same time. It is a device that allows us to enter our own private world and thereby effectively to close off encounters with others. The use of such devices protects our "personal space," along

with our body demeanor and facial expression (the passive "mask" or even scowl that persons adopt on subways). (Karp et al. 1991)

Recall Kitty Genovese, whose story was recounted on page 601. Her story troubled social psychologists John Darley and Bibb Latané (1968), who ran the series of experiments featured in Chapter 6, page 165. In their experiments, Darley and Latané found that the more bystanders there are, the less likely people are to help. As a group grows, people's sense of responsibility becomes diffused, with each person assuming that *another* will do the responsible thing. "With these other people here, it is not *my* responsibility," they reason.

This *diffusion of responsibility,* along with the norm of noninvolvement, helps explain the response to Kitty Genovese's murder. The bystanders at her death were *not* uncaring people. They *did* care that a woman was being attacked. They simply were following an urban norm, one that is helpful for getting them through everyday city life but, unfortunately, dysfunctional in some crucial situations. This norm, combined with the fears nurtured by the city's killings, rapes, and muggings, underlies the desire many have to retreat to a safe haven. This topic is discussed in the Down-to-Earth Sociology box.

DOWN-TO-EARTH SOCIOLOGY

Urban Fear and the Gated Fortress

The U.S. economic system has proven highly beneficial to most citizens, but it also has left many in poverty. To protect themselves, primarily from the poor, the upper middle class increasingly seeks sanctuary behind gated residential enclaves like this one in Seattle, Washington.

GATED NEIGHBORHOODS—where wrought-iron gates open and close to allow or prevent access to a neighborhood—are not new. They always have been available to the rich. What is new is the rush of the upper middle class to towns where they pay high taxes to keep all of the town's facilities, including its streets, private.

Towns cannot discriminate on the basis of religion or race-ethnicity, but they can—and do—discriminate on the basis of social class. Klahanie, Washington, is an excellent example. Begun in 1985, it was supposed to take twenty years to develop. With its safe streets and 300 acres of open space—and with its ban on satellite dishes, flagpoles, and even basketball hoops on garages—demand for the $300,000-plus homes nestled by a lake in this private community exceeded supply (Egan 1995).

The future will bring more private towns as the upper middle class flees urban areas and attempts to build a bucolic dream. A strong sign of the future is Celebration, a town of 20,000 people planned and built by the Walt Disney Company just five minutes from Disney World. Celebration, which won't be completed until 2014, boasts the usual school, hospital, and golf course, but in addition, it offers paths for walking and bicycling, a hotel with a lighthouse tower and bird sanctuary, and a health and fitness center with a rock climbing wall. The median price of homes is $300,000 (Wilkening 2000, Snyder 2001). With advanced fiber-optic technology, the residents of private communities such as these will be able to communicate with the outside world while remaining securely locked within their sanctuaries.

For Your CONSIDERATION

Community involves a feeling of togetherness, a sense of identifying with one another. Can you explain how this concept also contains the idea of separateness from others (not just in the example of gated communities)? What will our future be if we become a nation of gated communities, where middle-class homeowners withdraw into private domains, separating themselves from the rest of the nation?

Urban Problems and Social Policy

suburbanization the movement from the city to the suburbs

suburb a community adjacent to a city

The primary problems of urban life today are poverty, decay, and a general decline of U.S. cities. Let's examine some underlying reasons for these conditions and consider how to develop social policy to solve urban problems.

Suburbanization

Suburbanization, which refers to people moving from cities to **suburbs,** the communities located just outside a city, is not new. Archaeologists recently found that the Mayan city of Caracol (in what is now Belize) had suburbs, perhaps even with specialized subcenters, the equivalent of today's strip malls (Wilford 2000). The extent to which people have left U.S. cities in search of a better life is remarkable. Fifty years ago, about 20 percent of Americans lived in the suburbs (Karp et al. 1991). Today, over half of all Americans live in them (Palen 2002).

The automobile was a major impetus for suburbanization. Beginning about one hundred years ago, whites began to move to small towns near the cities in which they worked. After the racial integration of U.S. schools in the 1950s and 1960s, suburbanization picked up pace as whites fled the cities. Minorities began to suburbanize about 1970. In some of today's suburbs, minorities are the majority.

A new development is bands of suburbs becoming so thick that they merge into one another. In some places, suburbs have merged so completely that they form their own large cities (Firestone 2001). In the area from Atlanta, Georgia, to Raleigh, North Carolina, this filling in is so great that unbroken chains of suburbs stretch for hundreds of miles. This development is so new that we don't yet have a name for it.

The U.S. city has been the loser in this transition. As people moved out of the city, businesses and jobs followed. White-collar corporations, such as insurance companies, first moved their offices to the suburbs, followed by manufacturing firms. This process has continued so relentlessly that today twice as many manufacturing jobs are located in the suburbs than in the city (Palen 2002). As the city's tax base shrank, it left a budget squeeze that

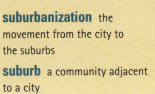

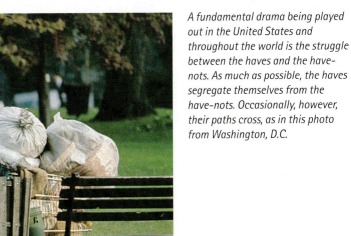

A fundamental drama being played out in the United States and throughout the world is the struggle between the haves and the have-nots. As much as possible, the haves segregate themselves from the have-nots. Occasionally, however, their paths cross, as in this photo from Washington, D.C.

affected not only parks, zoos, libraries, and museums, but also the city's basic services—its schools, streets, sewer and water systems, and police and fire departments.

This shift in population and resources left behind people who had no choice but to stay in the city. As we reviewed in Chapter 12, sociologist William Julius Wilson (1987) says that the net result was to transform the inner city into a ghetto. Left behind were families and individuals who, lacking training and skills, were trapped by poverty, unemployment, and welfare dependency—along with people who prey on others through street crime. The term *ghetto,* says Wilson, "suggests that a fundamental social transformation has taken place . . . that groups represented by this term are collectively different from and much more socially isolated from those that lived in these communities in earlier years" (quoted in Karp et al. 1991).

City Versus Suburb Having made the move out of the city—or having been born in a suburb and preferring to live there—suburbanites want the city to keep its problems to itself. They reject proposals to share suburbia's revenues with the city and oppose measures that would allow urban and suburban governments joint control over what has become a contiguous mass of people and businesses. Suburban leaders generally believe it is in their best interests to remain politically, economically, and socially separate from their nearby city. They do not mind going to the city to work, or venturing there on weekends for the diversions it offers, but they do not want to help pay the city's expenses.

It is likely that the mounting bill will come due ultimately, however, and that suburbanites will have to pay for their uncaring attitude toward the urban disadvantaged. Karp et al. (1991) put it this way:

> It may be that suburbs can insulate themselves from the problems of central cities, at least for the time being. In the long run, though, there will be a steep price to pay for the failure of those better off to care compassionately for those at the bottom of society.

Our occasional urban riots may be part of that bill—perhaps just the down payment.

Suburban Flight In some places, the bill is coming due quickly. As they age, some suburbs are becoming a mirror image of the city their residents so despise, with ris-

Suburbs were once unplanned, taking irregular shapes as people moved from the city in search of bucolic dreams. Some are still unplanned as population spills over from the city. Others, however, as this photo of Sun City, Arizona, a surburb of Phoenix, shows, are planned to precise details even before the first foundation is dug. If you look carefully, you can see the jogging trails.

redlining the officers of a financial institution deciding not to make loans in a particular area

disinvestment the withdrawal of investments by financial institutions, which seals the fate of an urban area

deindustrialization industries moving out of a country or region ing crime, flight of the middle class, a shrinking tax base, and eroding services. This, in turn, creates a spiraling sense of insecurity, more middle-class flight, and a further reduction of property values. Figure 20.14 illustrates this process, which is new to the urban-suburban scene.

Disinvestment and Deindustrialization

As the cities' tax base shrank and their services declined, neighborhoods deteriorated, and banks began **redlining:** Afraid of loans going bad, bankers drew a line on a map around a problem area and refused to make loans for housing or businesses there. This **disinvestment** (withdrawal of investment) pushed these areas into further decline. Youth gangs, murders, and muggings are common in these areas, while good jobs are not—factors that are not unconnected to this process of disinvestment.

The globalization of capitalism has also left a heavy mark on U.S. cities. As we reviewed in Chapter 14, to compete in the global market, many U.S. industries abandoned local communities. In search of lower labor costs, they moved their factories overseas and south of the border. This process, called **deindustrialization,** made U.S. industries more competitive, but it eliminated millions of U.S. manufacturing jobs. Lacking training in the new information technologies, many poor people are locked out of the benefits of the postindustrial economy that is engulfing the United States. Left behind in the inner cities, many live in despair.

The Rural Rebound

The United States is now undergoing a trend that is without precedent in its history: In the 1970s, people began to move from cities and suburbs to rural areas. During the 1990s, seven of every ten U.S. rural counties grew in population. The only losses occurred in the Great Plains and the Mississippi Delta (K. Johnson 1999). Little farming towns are making a comeback, their boarded-up stores and schools once again open for business and learning.

The "push" factors for this fundamental shift are fears of urban crime and violence. The "pull" factors are safety, lower cost of living, recreation, and more space. Facilitating this movement are improvements in transportation and communication. Interstate highways make airports—and the city itself—accessible from longer distances. With satellite communications, cell phones, fax machines, and the Internet, people can be connected with people in the city—and around the world—even though they live in what just a short time ago were remote areas.

Listen to the wife of a former student of mine describe why she and her husband moved to a rural area, three hours from the international airport that they fly out of each week:

> I work for a Canadian company. Paul works for a French company, with headquarters in Paris. He flies around the country doing computer consulting. I give motivational seminars to businesses. When we can, we drive to the airport together, but we often leave on different days. I try to go with my husband to Paris once a year.
>
> We almost always are home together on the weekends. We often arrange three- and four-day weekends, because I can plan seminars at home, and Paul does some of his consulting from here.
>
> Sometimes shopping is inconvenient, but we don't have to lock our car doors when we drive, and the new Wal-Mart superstore has most of what we need. E-commerce is a big part of it. I just type in www—whatever, and they ship it right to my door. I get make-up and books online. I even bought a part for my stove.

Figure 20.14 Urban Growth and Urban Flight

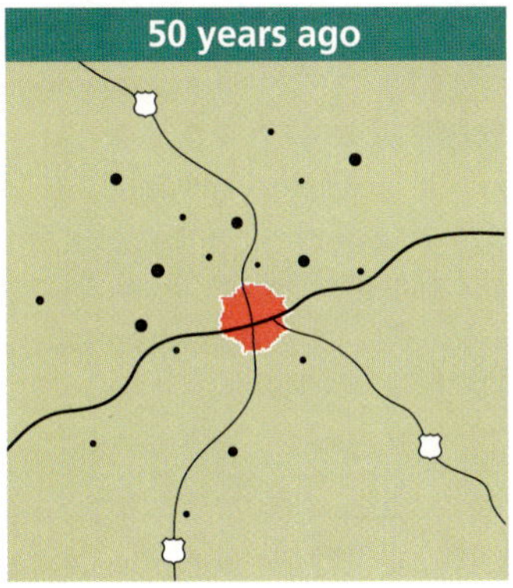

At first, the city and surrounding villages grew independently.

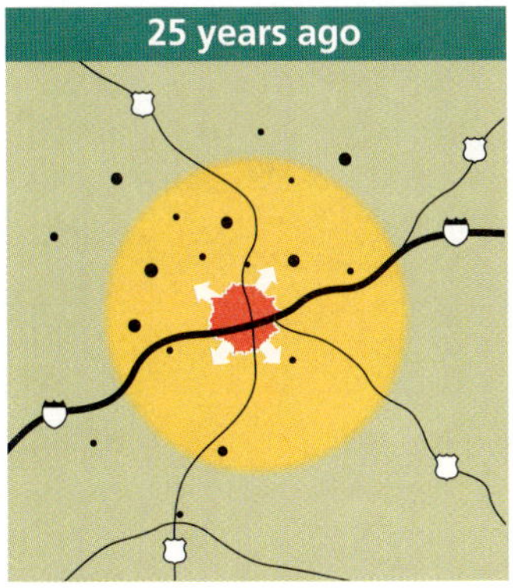

As city dwellers fled urban decay, they created a ring of suburbs.

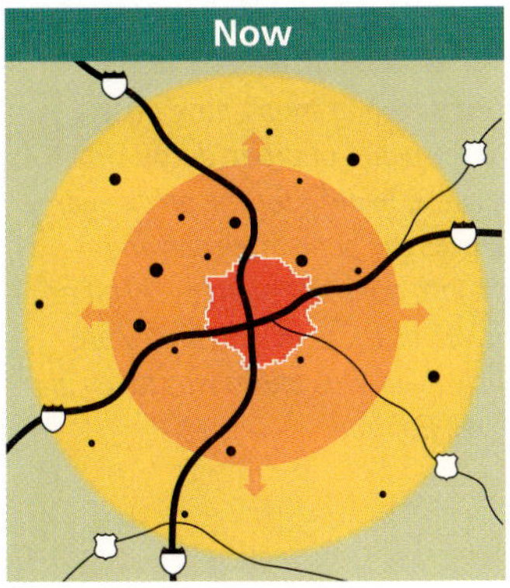

As middle-class flight continues outward, urban problems are arriving in the outer rings.

urban renewal the rehabilitation of a rundown area, which usually results in the displacement of the poor who are living in that area

enterprise zone the use of economic incentives in a designated area with the intention of encouraging investment there

> Why do we live here? Look at the lake. It's beautiful. We enjoy boating and swimming. We love to walk in this park-like setting. We see deer and wild turkeys. We love the sunsets over the lake. (author's files)

She added, "I think we're ahead of the learning curve," referring to the idea that their lifestyle is a wave of the future.

The Potential of Urban Revitalization

Social policy usually takes one of two forms. The first is to tear down and rebuild—something that is fancifully termed **urban renewal.** The result is the renewal of an area—but *not* for the benefit of its inhabitants. Stadiums, high-rise condos, luxury hotels, and boutiques replace run-down, cheap housing. Outpriced, the area's inhabitants are displaced into adjacent areas.

The second is some sort of **enterprise zone,** a designated area of the city that offers economic incentives, such as reduced taxes, to businesses that move into it. Although the intention is good, failure is usually the result. Most businesses refuse to locate in high-crime areas. Those that do relocate pay a high price for security and losses from crime, which can run higher than the tax savings. If workers are hired from within the problem area, and the jobs pay a decent wage, which most do not, the workers move to better neighborhoods—which doesn't help the area (Lemann 1994). After all, who chooses to live with the fear of violence?

A form of the enterprise zone, which has seen some success, is *Federal Empowerment Zones.* In addition to tax breaks, this program offers low-interest loans targeted for redeveloping an area. It is, in effect, the opposite of disinvestment, which devastates areas. The Down-to-Earth Sociology box on page 597 featured the renaissance of Harlem. Stimulating this change was the designation of Harlem as a Federal Empowerment Zone. The economic incentives lured grocery stores, dry cleaners, and video stores, attracting urbanites who expect such services. As the middle-classes moved back in, the demand for more specialty shops followed. A self-feeding cycle of development has begun,

Like the phoenix, luxury hotels and apartments, along with exclusive restaurants and shops, have arisen from the ashes of urban decay. Urban renewal, *a benefit for the privileged, displaces the poor, often shoving them into adjacent areas every bit as deprived as those in which they previously lived. This photo was taken in Denver, Colorado.*

replacing the self-feeding cycle of despair, crime, and drug use that accompanies disinvestment.

U.S. cities can be revitalized and made into safe and decent places to live. There is nothing in the nature of cities that turns them into dangerous slums. Most European cities, for example, are both safe and pleasant. If U.S. cities are to change, they need to become top agenda items of the U.S. government. Adequate resources in terms of money and human talents must be focused on overcoming urban woes. That we have begun to see success in Harlem, Chicago's North Town, and even in formerly riot-torn East Los Angeles indicates that the transformation can be brought about.

What we may need is a *Manhattan Project on Urban Problems.* During World War II, the United States and the Allies faced a triumphant Hitler in Europe and a victorious Tojo in Asia. The United States gathered its top scientific minds and ordered them to produce the atomic bomb. "Manhattan Project" was the code name for that effort. It involved 37 installations across the country, at least 37 university laboratories, and more than 100,000 people, including several Nobel prize-winning physicists. If the federal government were to focus similar resources on our urban ills, why couldn't we see a similar triumph?

Replacing old buildings with new ones is not the answer. Instead, sociological principles of building community need to be followed. Here are guiding principles suggested by sociologist William Flanagan (1990):

Scale. Regional and national planning is necessary. Local jurisdictions, with their many rivalries, competing goals, and limited resources, end up with a hodgepodge of mostly unworkable solutions. A positive example is Portland, Oregon, where a regional government prohibits urban sprawl and ensures a greenbelt.

Livability. Cities must be appealing and meet human needs, especially the need of community, which we discussed earlier. This will attract the middle classes into the city, which will increase its tax base. In turn, this will help finance the services that make the city more livable.

Social justice. In the final analysis, social policy must be evaluated by how it affects people. "Urban renewal" programs that displace the poor for the benefit of the middle class and wealthy do not pass this standard. The same would apply to solutions that create "livability" for select groups but neglect the poor and the homeless.

Finally, and very important: Unless we address the *root* causes of urban problems—poverty, substandard housing, poor schools, and lack of jobs—any solutions we come up with will be, at best, only Band-Aids that cover them up. Such fixes will be window dressings for politicians who want to *appear* as though they are doing something constructive about the problems that affect our quality of life.

SUMMARY and REVIEW

A Planet with No Space for Enjoying Life?

What debate did Thomas Malthus initiate?

In 1798, Thomas Malthus analyzed the surge in Europe's population. His conclusion, called the **Malthus theorem,** was that because the population grows geometrically but the food supply increases only arithmetically, the world's population will outstrip its food supply. The debate between today's New Malthusians and those who disagree, the Anti-Malthusians, continues. Pp. 578–581.

Why are people starving?

Starvation is not due to a lack of food in the world, for there is now *more* food for each person in the entire world than there was fifty years ago. Starvation, rather, is due to a maldistribution of food, which is primarily due to drought and civil war. Pp. 582–583.

Population Growth

Why do the poor nations have so many children?

In the Least Industrialized Nations, children often are viewed as gifts from God, they cost little to rear, they contribute to the family income at an early age, and they represent the parents' social security. Consequently, people are motivated to have large families. Pp. 583–586.

What are the three demographic variables?

To compute population growth, demographers use *fertility, mortality,* and *migration.* The **basic demographic equation** is births minus deaths plus net migration equals the growth rate. Pp. 586–589.

Why is forecasting population difficult?

A nation's growth rate is affected by unanticipated variables—from economic cycles, wars, and famines to industrialization and government policies. Pp. 589–591.

Urbanization

What is the relationship of cities to farming and the Industrial Revolution?

Cities can develop only if there is a large agricultural surplus, which frees people from food production. The primary impetus to the development of cities was the invention of the plow about five or six thousand years ago. Almost without exception, throughout history, cities have been small. After the Industrial Revolution stimulated rapid transportation and communication, cities grew quickly and became much larger. Today **urbanization** is so extensive that some cities have become **metropolises,** dominating the area adjacent to them. The areas of influence of some metropolises have merged, forming a **megalopolis.** Pp. 593–597.

Models of Urban Growth

What models of urban growth have been proposed?

The primary models are concentric zone, sector, multiple-nuclei, and peripheral. These models fail to account for ancient and medieval cities, many European cities, cities in the Least Industrialized Nations, and urban planning. Pp. 598–600.

City Life: Alienation and Community

Is the city inherently alienating?

Although some people experience **alienation** in the city, others find **community** in it. Five types of people who live in cities are cosmopolites, singles, ethnic villagers, the deprived, and the trapped. Pp. 601–604.

Urban Problems and Social Policy

Why have U.S. cities declined?

Three primary reasons for their decline are **suburbanization** (as people moved to the suburbs, the tax base of cities eroded and services deteriorated), **disinvestment** (banks withdrawing their financing), and **deindustrialization** (which caused a loss of jobs). Pp. 605–607.

What is the rural rebound?

As people flee cities and suburbs, the population of most U.S. rural counties is growing. This is a fundamental departure from a trend that had been in place for a couple of hundred years. Pp. 607–608.

What social policy can salvage U.S. cities?

A Manhattan Project on Urban Problems could likely produce workable solutions. Three guiding principles for developing urban social policy are scale, livability, and social justice. Pp. 608–609.

Where can I read more on this topic?

Suggested Readings for this chapter are at the back of this book.

THINKING Critically ABOUT CHAPTER 20

1. Do you think that the world is threatened by a population explosion? Use data from this chapter to support your position.
2. Why can't demographers make accurate predictions about the future of a country's population?
3. What are the causes of urban problems, and what can we do to solve those problems?

ADDITIONAL RESOURCES for This Chapter

www.ablongman.com/henslin7e

- *Content Select* Research Database for Sociology, with suggested key terms and annotated references
- Link to 2000 Census, with activities
- Flashcards of key terms and concepts
- Practice Tests
- Weblinks
- Interactive Maps

Chapter 21

Collective Behavior and Social Movements

Isaak Brodskij, *Demonstration,* 1930

The news spread like wildfire. A police officer had been killed. In just twenty minutes, the white population was armed and heading for the cabin. Men and mere boys, some not more than 12 years old, carried rifles, shotguns, and pistols.

The mob, now swollen to about four hundred, surrounded the log cabin. Tying a rope around the man's neck, they dragged him to the center of town. While the men argued about the best way to kill him, the women and children shouted their advice—some to hang him, others to burn him alive.

Someone pulled a large wooden box out of a store and placed it in the center of the street. Others filled it with straw. Then they lifted the man, the rope still around his neck, and shoved him head first into the box. One of the men poured oil over him. Another lit a match.

As the flames shot upward, the man managed to lift himself out of the box, his body a mass of flames. Trying to shield his face and eyes from the fire, he ran the length of the rope, about twenty feet, when someone yelled, "Shoot!" In an instant, dozens of shots rang out. Men and boys walked to the lifeless body and emptied their guns into it.

They dragged the man's body back to the burning box, then piled on more boxes from the stores, and poured oil over them. Each time someone threw more oil onto the flames, the crowd roared shouts of approval.

One of the men poured oil over him. *Another lit a match.*

Standing about seventy-five feet away, I could smell the poor man's burning flesh. No one tried to hide their identity. I could clearly see town officials help in the burning. The inquest, dutifully held by the coroner, concluded that the man met death "at the hands of an enraged mob unknown to the jury." What else could he conclude? Any jury from this town would include men who had participated in the man's death.

They dug a little hole at the edge of the street, and dumped in it the man's ashes and what was left of his body.

The man's name was Sam Pettie, known by everybody to be quiet and inoffensive. I can't mention my name. If I did, I would be committing suicide.

(Based on a May 1914 letter to *The Crisis*)

Chapter Outline

U.S. race relations have gone through many stages, some of them very tense. They sometimes have even exploded into violence, as with the many lynchings in the South in the early 1900s. This photo was taken in Rayston, Georgia, on April 28, 1936. Earlier in the day, the 40-year-old victim, Lint Shaw, accused of sexually assaulting a white girl, had been rescued from a mob by the National Guard. After the National Guard left, the mob forced their way into the jail.

Collective Behavior

Why did the people in this little town "go mad"? These men—and the women who watched in agreement—were ordinary, law-abiding citizens. Even some of the "pillars of the community" joined in the vicious killing of Sam Pettie, who may have been innocent.

Lynching is a form of **collective behavior,** actions by a group of people who bypass the usual norms governing their behavior and do something unusual (Turner and Killian 1987; Harper and Leicht 2002). Collective behavior is a broad term. It includes not only such violent acts as lynchings and riots, but also panics, rumors, fads, and fashions. Before examining its specific forms, let's look at theories that seek to explain collective behavior.

Early Explanations: The Transformation of the Individual

When people can't figure something out, they often resort to using "madness" as an explanation. People may say, "She went 'off her rocker'—that's why she drove her car off the bridge." "He must have 'gone nuts,' or he wouldn't have shot into the crowd." Early explanations of collective behavior were tied in to such assumptions. Let's look at how these ideas developed.

How the Crowd Transforms the Individual

The field of collective behavior began when Charles Mackay (1814–1889), a British journalist, noticed that "country folks," who ordinarily are reasonable sorts of people, sometimes "went mad" and did "disgraceful and violent things" when they formed a crowd. The best explanation Mackay (1852) could come up with was that people had a "herd mentality"—they were like a herd of cows that suddenly stampede.

About fifty years later, Gustave LeBon (1841–1931), a French psychologist, built on this initial idea. In an 1895 book, LeBon stressed how people feel anonymous in crowds, less accountable for what they do. Some even develop feelings of invincibility and come to think that they can do virtually anything. A **collective mind** develops, he said, and people are swept up by almost any suggestion. Then contagion, something like mass hypnosis, takes over, releasing the destructive instincts that society had so carefully repressed.

Robert Park (1864–1944), a U.S. sociologist who studied in Germany and wrote a 1904 dissertation on the crowd, was influenced by LeBon (McPhail 1991). After Park

collective behavior extraordinary activities carried out by groups of people; includes lynchings, rumors, panics, urban legends, and fads and fashions

collective mind Gustave LeBon's term for the tendency of people in a crowd to feel, think, and act in extraordinary ways joined the faculty at the University of Chicago, he added the ideas of social unrest and circular reaction. He said,

> Social unrest . . . is transmitted from one individual to another . . . so that the manifestations of discontent in A [are] communicated to B, and from B reflected back to A. (Park and Burgess 1921)

circular reaction Robert Park's term for a back-and-forth communication between the members of a crowd whereby a "collective impulse" is transmitted

Park used the term **circular reaction** to refer to this back-and-forth communication. Circular reaction, he said, creates a "collective impulse" that comes to "dominate all members of the crowd." If "collective impulse" sounds just like LeBon's "collective mind," that's because it really is. As noted, Park was influenced by LeBon, and his slightly different term did not change the basic idea at all.

The Acting Crowd

Herbert Blumer (1900–1987), who studied under Park, synthesized LeBon's and Park's ideas. As you can see from Figure 21.1, Blumer (1939) identified five stages that precede what he called an **acting crowd,** an excited group that moves toward a goal. This model still dominates today's police manuals on crowd behavior (McPhail 1989). Let's apply it to the killing of Sam Pettie.

1. *Tension or unrest.* At the root of collective behavior is a background condition of tension or unrest. Disturbed about some condition of society, people become apprehensive. This makes them vulnerable to rumors and suggestions. Sam Pettie was lynched during the early 1900s. At this time, traditional southern life was in upheaval. Due to industrialization, millions of Americans were moving from farm to city in search of jobs, and from South to North. Left behind were many poor, rural southerners, white and black, who faced a bleak future. In addition, African Americans were questioning the legitimacy of their low status and deprivation.
2. *Exciting event.* An exciting event occurs, one so startling that people become preoccupied with it. In this instance, that event was the killing of a police officer.

Figure 21.1 Blumer's Model of How an Acting Crowd Develops

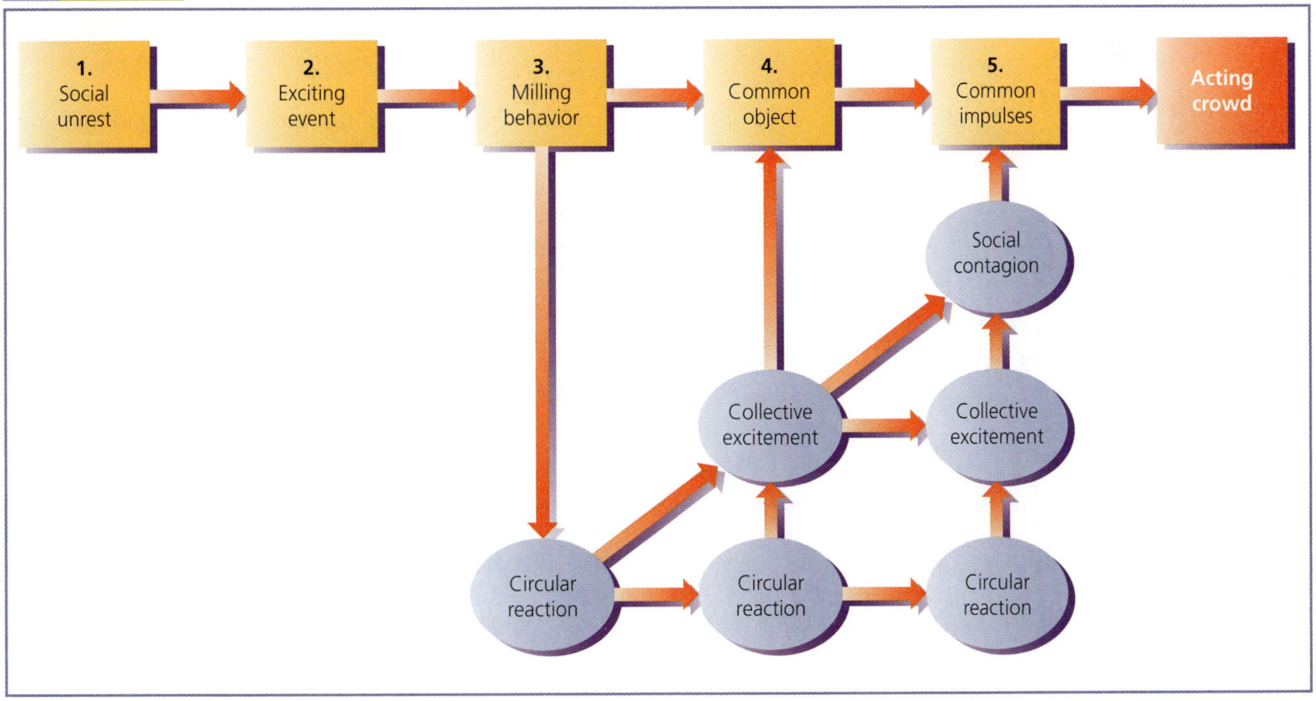

Source: Based on McPhail 1991:11.

3. *Milling.* Next comes **milling,** people standing or walking around, talking about the exciting event. A circular reaction then sets in. As people pick up cues as to the "right" way of thinking and feeling, they reinforce them in one another. During the short period in which Sam Pettie's lynch mob milled, the white residents of this small town became increasingly agitated as they discussed the officer's death.
4. *A common object of attention.* In this stage, people's attention becomes riveted on some aspect of the event. They get caught up in the collective excitement. In this case, people's attention turned to Sam Pettie. Someone may have said that he had been talking to the officer or that they had been arguing.
5. *Common impulses.* People get the feeling that they are in agreement about what should be done. These common impulses are stimulated by *social contagion,* a sense of excitement that is passed from one person to another. In this instance, people concluded that only the killer's immediate, public death would be adequate vengeance—and would serve as a warning for other African Americans who might even think about getting "out of line."

Acting crowds aren't always negative or destructive, as this one was. Some involve spontaneous demonstrations directed against oppression. Nor are they all serious, for students engaging in food fights are also acting crowds.

The Contemporary View: The Rationality of the Crowd

If we were to see a lynching—or a screaming mob or a prison riot—most of us might agree with LeBon that some sort of "madness" had swept over the crowd. Sociologists today, however, point out that beneath this chaotic surface, crowds are actually quite rational (Yamaguchi 2000; Horowitz 2001). They point out that crowds take deliberate steps to reach some goal. As sociologist Clark McPhail (1991) says, even a lynch mob is cooperative—someone gets the rope while others hold the victim, some tie the knot, and others hoist the body. This is exactly what you saw in Pettie's execution—the men working together: the rope, the boxes, the straw, and the oil.

The Minimax Strategy

A general principle of human behavior is that we try to minimize our costs and maximize our rewards. Sociologist Richard Berk (1974) called this a **minimax strategy.** The fewer costs and the more rewards we anticipate from something, the more likely we are to do it. For example, if we believe that others will approve an act, the likelihood increases that we will do it. Whether someone is yelling for the referee's blood after a bad call in a football game, or shouting for real blood as a member of a lynch mob, this principle applies. In short, whether people are playing cards with a few friends or are part of a mob, the principles of human behavior remain the same.

milling a crowd standing or walking around as they talk excitedly about some event

minimax strategy Richard Berk's term for the efforts people make to minimize their costs and maximize their rewards

emergent norms Ralph Turner and Lewis Killian's term for the idea that people develop new norms to cope with a new situation; used to explain crowd behavior

Emergent Norms

Since collective behavior is unusual behavior, however, could it also involve unusual norms? Sociologists Ralph Turner and Lewis Killian (1987) use the term **emergent norms** to express this idea. They point out that life usually proceeds pretty much as we expect it to, and our usual norms are adequate for dealing with everyday life. If our usual ways of doing things are disrupted, however, our ordinary norms may not cover the new situation. To deal with this new situation, people may develop *new* norms. They may even produce new definitions of right and wrong, feeling that the new circumstances justify actions that they otherwise consider wrong.

To understand how new norms emerge, we need to keep in mind that not everyone in a crowd shares the same point of view (Snow et al. 1993b; Rodríguez 1994). As Turner and Killian (1987) point out, crowds have at least five kinds of participants:

1. The *ego-involved* feel a personal stake in the unusual event.
2. The *concerned* also have a personal interest in the event, but less so than the ego-involved.
3. The *insecure* care little about the matter, but they join the crowd because it gives them a sense of power, security, or feeling of belonging.
4. The *curious spectators* also care little about the issue, but they are inquisitive about what is going on.
5. The *exploiters* don't care about the event, but they use it for their own purposes, such as hawking food or T-shirts. For them, a rock concert would serve just as well.

To set the crowd on a particular course of action, the most important role goes to the "ego-involved." Some of them make suggestions about what should be done; others simply take action. As the "concerned" join in, they, too, influence the crowd. If things get heated up, the "insecure" and the "curious spectators" may also join in. Although the "exploiters" are unlikely to participate, they do lend the crowd passive support. A common mood completes the stage for new norms to emerge: Activities that are "not OK" in everyday life now may seem "OK"—whether they involve throwing bottles at the cops or shouting obscenities at the college president.

This analysis of emergent norms helps us see that collective behavior is *rational.* The crowd, for example, does not consider all suggestions made by the ego-involved to be equal: To be acceptable, suggestions must match predispositions that the crowd already has. This analysis, then, is a far cry from earlier interpretations that people were so transformed by a crowd that they went out of their minds.

Forms of Collective Behavior

Sociologists analyze collective behavior the same way they do other forms of behavior. They view collective behavior as the actions of ordinary people who are responding to extraordinary situations. They ask their usual questions about interaction, such as, How do people influence one another? What is the significance of the participants' age, gender, race-ethnicity, and social class? What were their preexisting attitudes? How did they perceive the situation? How did their perceptions get translated into action?

In addition to lynchings, collective behavior includes riots, rumors, panics, mass hysteria, moral panics, fads, fashions, and urban legends. Let's look at each.

Riots

The nation watched in horror. White Los Angeles police officers had been caught on videotape beating an African American traffic violator with their nightsticks. The videotape showed the officers savagely bringing their nightsticks down on a man prostrate at their feet. Television stations around the United States—and the world—broadcast the pictures to stunned audiences.

When the officers went on trial for beating the man identified as Rodney King, how could the verdict be anything but guilty? Yet a jury consisting of eleven whites and one Asian American found the officers innocent of using excessive force. The result was a **riot**—violent crowd behavior aimed against people and property. Within minutes of the verdict, angry crowds began to gather in Los Angeles. That night, mobs set fire to businesses, and looting and arson began in earnest. The rioting

riot violent crowd behavior directed at people and property

As the text explains, people have different reasons for taking part in a riot. In the 1992 L.A. riots, precipitated by the Rodney King verdict, some people rioted because they were incensed at the verdict, others because they were angry at what they themselves had experienced at the hands of the police. For still others, however, the riot simply provided an opportunity to loot stores.

spread to other cities, including Atlanta, Tampa, Las Vegas, and even Madison, Wisconsin. Whites and Koreans were favorite targets of violence.

Americans sat transfixed before their television sets as they saw parts of Los Angeles go up in flames and looters carrying television sets and lugging sofas in full view of the Los Angeles Police Department, which took no steps to stop them. Seared into the public's collective consciousness was the sight of Reginald Denny, a 36-year-old white truck driver who had been yanked from his truck. As he sat dazed in the street, Damian Williams, laughing, broke Denny's skull with a piece of concrete.

On the third night, after 4,000 fires had been set and more than 30 people killed, President George Bush announced on national television that the U.S. Justice Department had appointed prosecutors to pursue federal charges against the police officers. The president stated that he had ordered the Seventh Infantry, SWAT teams, and the FBI into Los Angeles. He also federalized the California National Guard and placed it under the command of Gen. Colin Powell, the chairman of the Joint Chiefs of Staff. Rodney King went on television and tearfully pleaded for peace.

The Los Angeles riot was the bloodiest since the Civil War. Before it was over, 54 people lost their lives, 2,328 people were treated in hospital emergency rooms, thousands of businesses were burned, and about $1 billion of property was destroyed. Two of the police officers were later sentenced to 2 years in prison on federal charges, and King was awarded several million dollars in damages. (Rose 1992; Stevens and Lubman 1992; Holden and Rose 1993; Cannon 1998)

The *background conditions* of urban riots are frustration and anger brought on by feelings of deprivation. Frustration and anger simmer in people who are kept out of mainstream society—limited to a meager education and denied jobs and justice. Then a *precipitating event* brings those pent-up feelings to a boiling point, and they erupt in collective violence. All these conditions existed in the Los Angeles riot, with the jury's verdict being the precipitating event.

Sociologists have found that it is not only the deprived that participate in riots. The first outbursts over the Rodney King verdict didn't come from the poorest neighborhoods but from the most stable neighborhoods. Similarly after the assassination of Dr. Martin Luther King, Jr., in 1968, when many U.S. cities erupted in riots, even people with good jobs participated (McPhail 1991). Why would middle-class people participate in riots? The answer, says sociologist Victor Rodríguez (1994), is the same: frustration and anger. Even though they are employed and living stable lives, middle-class minorities resent being treated as second-class citizens.

rumor unfounded information spread among people

The event that precipitates a riot is less important than the riot's general context. The precipitating event is only the match that lights the fuel. The fuel is the background of tension and unrest—feelings that there is no justice, or that officials condone or encourage unfairness. Beneath what may seem a placid surface lies seething rage. To erupt, it takes but a match, such as the Rodney King verdict. Tension and resentment are felt not only by the poor but also by those who are materially better off. The precipitating event brings these feelings to the surface, and both groups become involved. Also participating in the riots are opportunists—people who feel neither rage at their general condition nor outrage at the precipitating event. For them, the riot simply provides an opportunity for looting—or even for sharing a sense of excitement.

Rumors

> In *Aladdin,* the handsome young title character murmurs, "All good children, take off your clothes." In *The Lion King,* Simba, the cuddly lion star, stirs up a cloud of dust that, floating off the screen, spells S-E-X. Then there is the bishop in *The Little Mermaid,* who, presiding over a wedding, becomes noticeably aroused.
>
> Ann Runge, a mother of eight who owned stacks of animated Disney films, said she felt betrayed when she heard that the Magic Kingdom was sending obscene, subliminal messages. "I felt as though I had entrusted my kids to pedophiles," she said. (Bannon 1995)

A **rumor** is unverified information about some topic of interest that is passed from one person to another. Thriving on conditions of ambiguity, rumors fill in missing information (Turner 1964; Shibutani 1966; Fine and Turner 2001). In response to this particular rumor, Disney reported that Aladdin really says "Scat, good tiger, take off and go." The line is hard to understand, however, leaving enough ambiguity for others to hear what they want to hear, and even to insist that the line is an invitation to a teenage orgy. Similar ambiguity remains with Simba's dust and the aroused bishop.

Rumors *have swirled around the Magic Kingdom's supposed plots to undermine the morality of youth. Could Mickey Mouse be a dark force, and these children his victims? As humorous as this may be, some have taken these rumors seriously.*

Most rumors are short-lived. They arise in a situation of ambiguity, only to dissipate when they are replaced by factual information—or by another rumor. Occasionally, however, a rumor has a long life.

> In the eighteenth and nineteenth centuries, for no known reason, healthy people would grow weak and slowly waste away. No one understood the cause and people said they had *consumption* (now called tuberculosis). People were terrified as they saw their loved ones wither into shells of their former selves. With no one knowing when the disease would strike, or who its next victim would be, the rumor began that some of the dead had turned into vampire-like beings. At night, they were coming back from the grave and draining the life out of the living. The evidence was irrefutable—loved ones who wasted away before people's very eyes.
>
> To kill these ghoulish "undead," people began to sneak into graveyards. They would dig up a grave, remove the leg bones and place them on the skeleton's chest, then lay the skull at the feet, forming a skull and crossbones. Having thus killed the "undead," they would rebury the remains. These rumors and the resulting mutilations of the dead continued off and on in New England until the 1890s. (Associated Press, November 30, 1993)

Most rumors are not only short-lived but also of little consequence. Occasionally, however, as discussed in the Down-to-Earth Sociology box below, rumors severely affect people's lives and even entire communities.

Why do people believe rumors? Three main factors have been identified. Rumors deal with a subject that is important to an individual, and they replace ambiguity with some form of certainty. They also are attributed to a credible source. An office rumor may be preceded by "Jane has it on good authority that . . . " or "Bill overheard the boss say that . . . "

Rumors thrive on ambiguity or uncertainty, for where people know the facts about a situation a rumor can have no life. Surrounded by unexplained illnesses and deaths, however, the New Englanders speculated about why people wasted away. Their rather bizarre conclusions gave them certainty in the face of bewildering events. The uncertainty that sparked the Disney rumor may have been feelings among some that the moral fabric of modern society is decaying.

Rumors usually pass directly from one person to another, although, as we saw with the Tulsa riot, they can originate from the mass media. As the Down-to-Earth Sociology box on the next page illustrates, the Internet, too, has become a source of rumors.

Panics and Mass Hysteria

In 1938, on the night before Halloween, a radio program of dance music was interrupted by a report that explosions had been observed on the surface of Mars. The announcer added that a cylinder of unknown origin had been discovered embedded

DOWN-TO-EARTH SOCIOLOGY

Rumors and Riots: An Eyewitness Account to the Tulsa Riot

IN 1921, TULSA, OKLAHOMA, WAS RIPPED apart by a race riot. And it all began with a rumor. Up to this time, Tulsa's black community had been vibrant and prosperous. Many blacks owned their own businesses, and competed successfully with whites. Then on May 31, everything changed after a black man was accused of assaulting a white girl.

Buck Colbert Franklin (Franklin and Franklin 1997), a black attorney in Tulsa at the time, was there. Here is what he says:

> Hundreds of men with drawn guns were approaching from every direction, as far I could see as I stood at the steps of my office, and I was immediately arrested and taken to one of the many detention camps. Even then, airplanes were circling overhead dropping explosives upon the buildings that had been looted, and big trucks were hauling all sorts of furniture and household goods away.

Unlike later riots, these were white looters who were breaking in and burning the homes and businesses of blacks.

Franklin continues:

> Soon I was back upon the streets, but the building where I had my office was a smoldering ruin, and all my lawbooks and office fixtures had been consumed by flames. I went to where my roominghouse had stood a few short hours before, but it was in ashes, with all my clothes and the money to be used in moving my family. As far as one could see, not a Negro dwellinghouse or place of business stood. . . . Negroes who yesterday were wealthy, living in beautiful homes in ease and comfort, were now beggars, public charges, living off alms.

The rioters had burned all black churches, including the imposing Zion Baptist church, which had just been completed. The homes, businesses, and churches had been destroyed by arson and bombs. Block after block lay in ruins, as through a tornado had swept through the area.

And the young man who had been accused of assault, the event that precipitated the riot? Franklin says that the police investigated, and found that there had been no assault. All the man had done was accidentally step on a lady's foot in a crowded elevator, and, as Franklin says, "She became angry and slapped him, and a fresh, cub newspaper reporter, without any experience and no doubt anxious for a byline, gave out an erroneous report through his paper that a Negro had assaulted a white girl."

For Your CONSIDERATION

It is difficult to place ourselves in such an historical mindset to imagine that stepping on someone's foot could lead to such destruction, but it did. Can you apply the sociological findings on both rumors and riots to explain the riot at Tulsa? Why do you think that so many whites believed this rumor and that some of them were so intent on destroying this thriving black community? What was the "seething rage" that sociologists say underlie these types of riots?

DOWN-TO-EARTH SOCIOLOGY

Danger Lurks Everywhere: The Internet and the Uncertainty of Life

LIFE IN OUR MASS SOCIETY IS FILLED with uncertainty. That new neighbor who just moved in across the street could be a child molester, the guy next door a rapist. Evil lurks everywhere, and, who knows, maybe you'll be the next victim.

Or so it seems. And within this sea of uncertainty comes the Net to feed on our gnawing suspicions. Here is an e-mail that I received:

> Please, read this very carefully. . . . then send it out to all the people online that you know. Something like this is nothing to take casually; this is something that you do want to pay attention to.
>
> If a guy with a screen-name of Slave-Master contacts you, do not answer. DO NOT TALK TO THIS PERSON. DO NOT ANSWER ANY OF HIS/HER INSTANT MESSAGES/E-MAIL.
>
> He has killed 56 women (so far) that he has talked to on the Internet.
>
> PLEASE SEND OUT TO ALL THE WOMEN ON YOUR BUDDY LIST. ALSO ASK THEM TO PASS THIS ON.
>
> He has been on Yahoo and AOL and Excite so far. This is no joke!!!
>
> PLEASE SEND THIS TO MEN TOO . . . JUST IN CASE!!!

For Your CONSIDERATION

How do the three main factors associated with rumors—importance, ambiguity, and source—apply to this note? In what ways do they not apply?

> in the ground on a farm in New Jersey. The radio station then switched to the farm, where a breathless reporter gave details of horrible-looking Martians coming out of the cylinder. Their death-ray weapons had destructive powers unknown to humans. An astronomer then confirmed that Martians had invaded the Earth.

Perhaps six million Americans heard this broadcast. About one million were frightened by it. Thousands panicked, grabbed their weapons, and hid in their basements or ran into the streets. Hundreds bundled up their families and jumped into their cars, jamming the roads as they headed to who knows where.

Of course, there was no invasion. This was simply a dramatization of H. G. Wells' *War of the Worlds,* starring Orson Welles. There had been an announcement at the beginning of the program and somewhere in the middle that the account was fictional, but apparently many people missed it. Although the panic reactions to this radio program may appear humorous to us, the situation is far from humorous to anyone who is in a panic. **Panic** occurs when people become so fearful that they cannot function normally, and may even flee the situation.

Why did people panic in this instance? Psychologist Hadley Cantril (1941) attributed the reaction to widespread anxiety about world conditions. The Nazis were marching in Europe, and millions of Americans (correctly, as it turned out) were afraid that the United States would get involved. War jitters, he said, created fertile ground for the broadcast to touch off a panic.

Contemporary analysts, however, question whether there even was a panic. Sociologist William Bainbridge (1989) acknowledges that some people did become frightened, and that a few actually did get in their cars and drive like maniacs. But he says that most of this famous panic was an invention of the news media. Reporters found a good story, and they milked it, exaggerating as they went along.

Bainbridge points to a 1973 event in Sweden. To dramatize the dangers of atomic power, Swedish Radio broadcast a play about an accident at a nuclear power plant. Knowing about the 1938 broadcast in the United States, Swedish sociologists were waiting to see what would happen. Might some people fail to realize that it was a dramatization and panic at the threat of ruptured reactors spewing out radioactive gasses? The sociologists found no panic. A few people did become frightened. Some telephoned family members and the police; others shut windows to keep out the radioactivity—reasonable responses, considering what they thought had occurred.

panic the condition of being so fearful that one cannot function normally, and may even flee

The Swedish media, however, reported a panic! Apparently, a reporter had telephoned two police departments and learned that each had received calls from concerned citizens. With a deadline hanging over his head, the reporter decided to gamble. He reported that police and fire stations were jammed with citizens, people were flocking to the shelters, and others were fleeing south (Bainbridge 1989).

Panics do occur, of course.

> On December 31, 1999, a rumor spread through Bissau, the capital of Guinea-Bissau, that the "black death" was going to hit at midnight, when the world entered the new millennium. Bissau's 250,000 residents fled the city ("Fears of . . . " 2000).

Nobody has the right to shout "Fire!" in a public building when no such danger exists. If people fear immediate death, they will lunge toward the nearest exit in a frantic effort to escape. Such a panic occurred on Memorial Day weekend in 1977 at the Beverly Hills Supper Club in Southgate, Kentucky.

> About half of the Club's 2,500 patrons were crowded into the Cabaret Room. A fire, which began in a small banquet room near the front of the building, burned undetected until it was beyond control. When employees discovered the fire, they warned patrons. People began to exit in orderly fashion, but when flames rushed in, they trampled one another in a furious attempt to reach the exits. The exits were blocked by masses of screaming people trying to push their way through all at once. The writhing bodies at the exits created further panic among the remainder, who pushed even harder to force their way through the bottlenecks. One hundred sixty-five people died. All but two were within thirty feet of two exits in the Cabaret Room.

Table 21.1 Employees' First Action After Learning of the Fire

Action	Percentage
Left	29%
Helped others to leave	41%
Fought or reported the fire	17%
Continued routine activities	7%
Other (e.g., looked for a friend or relative)	5%

Note: These figures are based on interviews with 95 of the 160 employees present at the time of the fire: 48 males and 47 females, ranging in age from 15 to 59.

Source: Based on Johnston and Johnson 1989.

Sociologists who studied this panic found what other researchers have discovered in analyzing other disasters. *Not everyone panics.* In disturbances, many people continue to act responsibly (Clarke 2002). Especially important are primary group bonds. Parents help their children, for example (Morrow 1995). Gender roles also persist, and more men help women than women help men (Johnson 1993). Even work roles continue to guide some behavior. Sociologists Drue Johnston and Norris Johnson (1989) found that only 29 percent of the employees of the Beverly Hills Supper Club left when they learned of the fire. As noted in Table 21.1, most of the workers helped customers, fought the fire, or searched for friends and relatives.

When the fireworks used by the band Great White set a fire on February 21, 2003, the patrons of The Station in West Warwick, Rhode Island, panicked. Of the 412 people inside the night club, 100 were killed and over 200 were injured.

Sociologists use the term **role extension** to describe the actions of most of these employees. By this, they mean that the workers incorporated other activities into their occupational roles. For example, servers extended their role to include helping people to safety. How do we know that giving help was an extension of the occupational role, and not simply a general act of helping? Johnston and Johnson found that servers who were away from their assigned stations returned to them in order to help *their* customers. For a fascinating and related type of collective behavior, see the Down-to-Earth Sociology box below.

In some life-threatening situations in which we might expect panic, we find, instead, that a sense of order prevails. This seems to be the case during the attack on the World Trade Center when, at peril to their own lives, people helped injured friends and even strangers escape down many floors. These people, it would seem, were highly socialized into the collective good, and had a highly developed sense of empathy.

role extension the incorporation of additional activities into a role

mass hysteria an imagined threat that causes physical symptoms among a large number of people

DOWN-TO-EARTH SOCIOLOGY

Mass Hysteria

LET'S LOOK AT FIVE EVENTS.

Several hundred years ago, a strange thing happened near Naples, Italy. When people were bitten by tarantulas, not only did they feel breathless and have fast-beating hearts, but also they felt unusual sexual urges. As though that weren't enough, they also felt an irresistible urge to dance—and to keep dancing to the point of exhaustion.

The disease was contagious. Even people who hadn't been bitten came down with the same symptoms. The situation got so bad that whole villages would dance in a frenzy instead of gathering the summer harvest.

A lot of remedies were tried, but nothing seemed to work except music. Bands of musicians traveled from village to village, providing relief to the victims of *tarantism by* playing special "tarantula" music (Bynum 2001).

• • •

In the year 2001, in New Delhi, the capital of India, a "monkey-man" stalked people who were sleeping on rooftops during the blistering summer heat. He clawed and bit a hundred victims. Fear struck the capital. People would wake up screaming that the monkey-man was after them. To escape this phantom, some people jumped off two-story buildings. One man was killed when he jumped off the roof of his house during one of the monkey-man's many attacks ("'Monkey'..." 2001).

There was no ape-like killer.

• • •

At the United Arab Emirates University in Al-Ain, twenty-three female students rushed to the hospital emergency room after escaping from a fire in their dormitory. As you might expect, they were screaming, weeping, shaking, and fainting (Amin et al. 1997).

But here was no fire. A student had been burning incense in her room. The fumes of the burning incense had been mistaken for the smell of a fire.

• • •

People across France and Belgium became sick after drinking Coca-Cola. A quick investigation was held, and the experts diagnosed the problem as "bad carbon dioxide and a fungicide." Coke recalled 15 *million* cases of its soft drink ("Coke..." 1999).

Later investigations revealed that there was nothing wrong with the drink.

• • •

In McMinville, Tennessee, a teacher smelled a "funny odor." Students and teachers began complaining of headaches, nausea, and a shortness of breath. The school was evacuated, and doctors treated more than 100 people at the local hospital. Authorities found nothing.

A few days later, a second wave of illness struck. This time, the Tennessee Department of Health shut the high school down for two weeks. They dug holes in the foundation and walls and ran snake cameras through the ventilation and heating ducts. They even tested the victims' blood (Adams 2000).

Nothing unusual was found.

• • •

"It's all in their heads," we might say. In one sense, we would be right. There was no external, objective cause of the illnesses from tarantism or Coca-Cola. There was no "monkey-man," no fire, nor any chemical contaminant at the school.

In another sense, however, we would be wrong to say that it is "all in their heads." The symptoms these people experienced were real. They had real headaches and stomach aches. They did vomit and faint. And they did experience unusual sexual urges and the desire to dance until they could no longer stand.

There is no explanation for **mass hysteria**—an imagined threat that causes physical symptoms among a large group of people—except suggestibility. Experts might use fancy words to try to explain mass hysteria, but once you cut through their terms, you find that they are really simply saying, "It happens."

Perhaps one day we will know more about the causes of mass hysteria, but for now we have to be content with not knowing the specifics. We do know that such events occur in many cultures. This would indicate that mass hysteria follows basic principles of human behavior. Someday, we will understand these principles.

Moral Panics

Moral panics occur when large numbers of people become concerned, even fearful, about some behavior that they believe threatens morality, and when the fear is out of proportion to any supposed danger (Cauthen and Jasper 1994; Goode and Ben-Yehuda 1994; Jenkins 1998; Jenness 2001). The threat is perceived as enormous, and hostility builds toward those deemed responsible. The most famous moral panic was the fear of witches in Europe between 1400 and 1650. It resulted in the Inquisition—investigations, torture, and burning at the stake of people accused of witchcraft. As mentioned in Chapter 18, a recent moral panic in the Democratic Republic of the Congo led to the deaths of about 1,000 alleged witches.

Moral panics today are often fueled by the mass media. During the 1980s, the fear that children were being sexually abused in day care centers spread across the United States. The media reported bizarre rituals with devil worshippers and naked priests and weird sex. The situation grew so bad that almost every day care worker became suspect in someone's eyes. Only fearfully did parents leave their children in day care centers. Although sexual abuse at day care centers has occurred, intensive investigations never substantiated the stories of children subjected to bizarre sexual rituals.

Like other panics, moral panics center around a sense of danger. The supposed thousands of U.S. children who are snatched by strangers from playgrounds, city streets, and their own backyards are part of a moral panic. Parents are fearful, and others are perplexed, at how U.S. society could have gone to hell in a handbasket. This moral panic is destined to meet the same fate as others. The fear and hysteria will subside, and people will feel less danger as they drop children off at school or let them play outside. The actual number of stranger kidnappings in the United States per year is between 200 and 300 (Bromley 1991).

Moral panics are fed by rumor. In the 1990s, a rumor swept the country that some of these supposedly thousands of missing children were being sold to Satanists who abused them sexually and then ritually murdered them. Even though this rumor was outlandish, many believed it because of the rumor that was already circulating about the thousands of abducted children. Stories about the Satanist molesters and killers filled in missing information: who was abducting and doing what to those children. People also appeared who claimed to be eyewitnesses to such sacrifices. The police investigated, but uncovered no evidence to substantiate the rumor.

Moral panics thrive on uncertainty and anxiety. Changes in the nature of the family give rise to a great deal of anxiety. Concerns that children are receiving inadequate care because so many mothers have joined the work force have become linked with fears—that dangers to children are lurking almost everywhere.

Fads and Fashions

A **fad** is a novel form of behavior that briefly catches people's attention. The new behavior appears suddenly and spreads by imitation and identification with people who are already involved in the fad. Reports by the mass media help to spread the fad. After a short life, the fad fades into oblivion, although it may reappear from time to time (Aguirre et al. 1993).

Fads come in many forms. Very short, intense fads are called *crazes.* They appear suddenly, and are gone almost as quickly. "Tickle Me Elmo dolls" and Beanie Babies were object crazes. There also are behavior crazes, as with streaking, which lasted only a couple of months in 1974; as a joke, an individual or a group would run nude in some public place. "Flash mobs," a behavior craze that appeared in 2003, is likely to go the way of streaking and Elmo dolls—relegated to a bit of arcane trivia.

Even the administrators of businesses, colleges, and universities get caught up in fads. For about ten years, quality circles were a fad; these were supposedly an effective way of getting workers and management to cooperate and develop innovative techniques to increase production. This administrative fad peaked in 1983, then quickly dropped from sight (Strang and Macy 2001). Fads also affect child rearing—permissive versus directive, spanking versus non-spanking. Our food is subject to fads: tofu, power drinks, and or-

moral panic a fear that grips a large number of people that some evil threatens the well-being of society, followed by hostility, sometimes violence, toward those thought responsible

fad a temporary pattern of behavior that catches people's attention ganic this and that. Fads in dieting also come and go, with many seeking the perfect diet, and practically all leaving the fad diet disillusioned.

Some fads involve millions of people but still die out quickly. In the 1950s, the Hula Hoop was so popular that stores couldn't keep them in stock. Children cried and pleaded for these brightly colored plastic hoops. Across the nation, children—and even adults—held contests to see who could keep the hoops up the longest or who could rotate the most hoops at one time. Then, in a matter of months it was over, and parents wondered what to do with these items, which seemed useless for any other purpose.

Fads that die out can even have a comeback. Hula hoops have again become a children's toy, although they have not reached the feverish, crazed level they once had.

When a fad lasts, it is called a **fashion.** Some fashions, as with clothing and furniture, are the result of a coordinated international marketing system that includes designers, manufacturers, advertisers, and retailers. By manipulating the tastes of the public, they sell billions of dollars of products. Fashion, however, also refers to hairstyles, to the design and colors of buildings, and even to the names parents give their children (Lieberson 2000). Sociologist John Lofland (1985) pointed out how fashion also applies to common expressions, as demonstrated by these roughly comparable terms: "Neat!" in the 1950s, "Right on!" in the 1960s, "Really!" in the 1970s, "Awesome!" in the 1980s, "Bad!" in the 1990s, "Sweet" in the early 2000s, and, recurringly, "Cool."

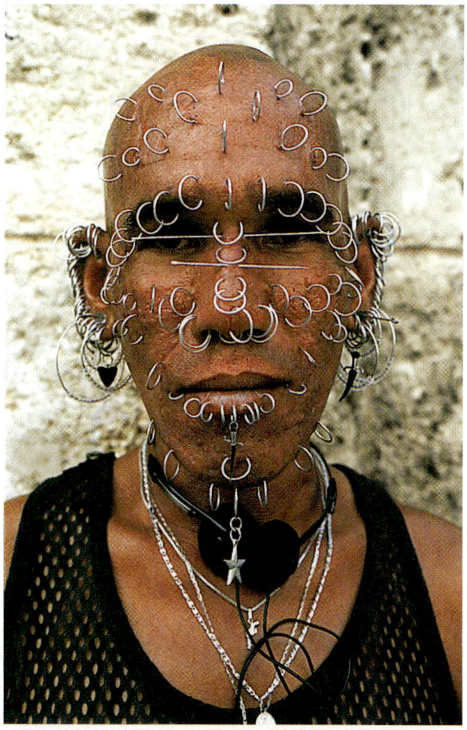

Fads *are one of the fascinating aspects of social life that sociologists study. Body piercing, whose origins reach back into antiquity, has become popular in the Western world. It is unlikely, however, that body piercing will enter the mainstream culture. Certainly its extremes won't.*

Urban Legends

> Did you hear about Lauren and Paul? They were parked at Regatta Bay, listening to the radio, when the music was interrupted by an announcement that a rapist-killer had escaped from prison. Instead of a right hand, he had a hook. Lauren said they should leave, but Paul laughed and said there wasn't any reason to go. When they heard a strange noise, Paul agreed to take her home. When Lauren opened the door, she heard something clink. It was a hook hanging on the door handle!

For decades, some version of "The Hook" has circulated among Americans. It has appeared as a "genuine" letter in "Dear Abby," and some of my students heard it in grade school. **Urban legends** are stories with an ironic twist that sound realistic but are false. Although untrue, they usually are told by people who believe that they happened.

Here is another one:

> A horrible thing happened. This girl in St. Louis kept smelling something bad. The smell wouldn't leave even when she took showers. She finally went to the doctor, and it turned out that her insides were rotting. She had gone to the tanning salon too many times, and her insides were cooked.

Folklorist Jan Brunvand (1981, 1984, 1986, 1999) reports that urban legends are passed on by people who often think that the event happened just one or two people down the line of transmission, sometimes to a "friend of a friend." These stories have strong appeal and gain their credibility by naming specific people or citing particular events. Note the details of where Lauren and Paul were. Brunvand views urban legends as "modern morality stories"; each one teaches a moral lesson about life.

If we apply Brunvand's analysis to these two urban legends, three principles emerge. First, these stories serve as warnings. "The Hook" warns young people that they should be careful about where they go, with whom they go, and what they do when they get there. The tanning salon story warns people about the dangers of new technology. Second, these stories are related to social change: "The Hook" to changing sexual morality, the tanning salon to changing technology. Third, each is calculated to instill fear: We should all be afraid, for dangers abound. They lurk in the dark countryside, or even at our neighborhood tanning salon.

fashion a pattern of behavior that catches people's attention and lasts longer than a fad

urban legend a story with an ironic twist that sounds realistic but is false

These principles can be applied to an urban legend that made the rounds in the late 1980s. I heard several versions of this one; each narrator swore that it had just happened to a friend of a friend.

> Jerry (or whoever) went to a nightclub last weekend. He met a good-looking woman, and they hit it off. They spent the night in a motel. When he got up the next morning, the woman was gone. When he went into the bathroom, he saw a message scrawled on the mirror in lipstick: "Welcome to the wonderful world of AIDS."

Social Movements

When the Nazis, a small group of malcontents in Bavaria, first appeared on the scene in the 1920s, the world found their ideas laughable. This small group believed that the Germans were a race of supermen (*Übermenschen*) and that they would launch a Third Reich (reign or nation) that would control the world for a thousand years. Their race destined them for greatness; lesser races were meant for their service and exploitation.

The Nazis started as a little band of comic characters who looked as though they had stepped out of a grade B movie (see the photo on page 325). From this inauspicious start, the Nazis gained such power that they threatened the existence of Western civilization. How could a little man with a grotesque moustache, surrounded by a few sycophants in brown shirts, ever come to threaten the world? Such things don't happen in real life—only in novels or movies. They are the deranged nightmare of some imaginative author. Only this was real life. The Nazis' appearance on the human scene caused the deaths of millions of people and changed the course of world history.

social movement a large group of people who are organized to promote or resist some social change

proactive social movement a social movement that promotes some social change

reactive social movement a social movement that resists some social change

social movement organization an organization people develop to further the goals of a social movement

alterative social movement a social movement that seeks to alter only some specific aspects of people

redemptive social movement a social movement that seeks to change people totally

reformative social movement a social movement that seeks to change only some specific aspects of society

transformative social movement a social movement that seeks to change society totally

millenarian social movement a social movement based on the prophecy of coming social upheaval

cargo cult a social movement in which South Pacific islanders destroyed their possessions in the anticipation that their ancestors would ship them new goods

Social movements, the second major topic of this chapter, hold the answer to Hitler's rise to power. **Social movements** consist of large numbers of people who organize to promote or resist social change. Members of social movements hold strong ideas about what is wrong with the world—or some part of it—and how to make things right. Examples include the abolitionist (anti-slavery) crusade, the civil rights movement, the white supremacist movement, the women's movement, the animal rights movement, and the environmental movement.

At the heart of social movements lies a sense of injustice (Klandermans 1997). Some find a particular condition of society intolerable, and their goal is to promote social change. Theirs is called a **proactive social movement.** Others, in contrast, feel threatened because some condition of society is changing, and they *react* to resist that change. Theirs is a **reactive social movement.**

To further their goals, people develop **social movement organizations.** Those whose goal is to promote social change develop such organizations as the National Association for the Advancement of Colored People (NAACP). In contrast, those who are trying to resist these particular changes form the Ku Klux Klan. To recruit followers and publicize their grievances, leaders of social movements use attention-getting devices, from marches and protest rallies to sit-ins and boycotts.

Social movements are like a rolling sea, observes sociologist Mayer Zald (1992). During one period, few social movements may appear, but shortly afterward, a wave of them rolls in, each competing for the public's attention. Zald suggests that a *cultural crisis* can give birth to a wave of social movements. By this, he means that there are times when a society's institutions fail to keep up with social change. Then many people's needs go unfulfilled, massive unrest follows, and social movements spring into action to bridge this gap.

Types and Tactics of Social Movements

Let's see what types of social movements there are and then examine their tactics.

Social movements *involve large numbers of people who, upset about some condition in society, organize to do something about it. Shown here is Carrie Nation, a temperance leader who in 1900 began to break up saloons with a hatchet. Her social movement eventually became so popular that it resulted in Prohibition.*

Types of Social Movements

Since social change is their goal, we can classify social movements according to their *target* and the *amount of change* they seek. Look at Figure 21.2. If you read across, you will see that the target of the first two types of social movements is *individuals.* **Alterative social movements** seek only to *alter* some specific behavior. An example is the Women's Christian Temperance Union, a powerful social movement of the early 1900s. Its goal was to get people to stop drinking alcohol. Its members were convinced that if they could shut down the saloons such problems as poverty and wife abuse would go away. **Redemptive social movements** also target individuals, but here the aim is for *total* change. An example is a religious social movement that stresses conversion. In fundamentalist Christianity, for example, when someone converts to Christ, the entire person is supposed to change, not just some specific behavior. Self-centered acts are to be replaced by loving behaviors toward others as the convert becomes, in their terms, a "new creation."

The target of the next two types of social movements is *society.* **Reformative social movements** seek to *reform* some specific aspect of society. The civil rights movement, for example, seeks to reform the ways society treats the minorities, from their place in education and politics to their opportunities in the job market. **Transformative social movements,** in contrast, seek to *transform* the social order itself. Its members want to replace the current social order with their version of the good society. Revolutions, such as those in the American colonies, France, Russia, and Cuba, are examples.

One of the more interesting examples of transformative social movements is **millenarian social movements,** which are based on prophecies of coming calamity. Of particular interest is a type of millenarian movement called a **cargo cult** (Worsley 1957). About one hundred years ago, Europeans colonized the Melanesian Islands of the South Pacific. Ships from the home countries of the colonizers arrived one after another, each loaded with items the Melanesians had never seen. As the Melanesians watched the cargo being unloaded, they expected some of it to go to them. Instead, it all went to the Europeans. Melanesian prophets then revealed the secret of this exotic merchandise. Their own ancestors were manufacturing and sending the cargo to them, but the colonists were intercepting the merchandise. Since the colonists were too strong to fight and too selfish to share the cargo, there was little the Melanesians could do.

Then came a remarkable self-fulfilling prophecy. Melanesian prophets revealed that if the people would destroy their crops and food and build harbors, their ancestors would see their sincerity and send the cargo directly to them. The Melanesians did so. When the colonial administrators of the island saw that the natives had destroyed their crops and were just sitting in the hills waiting for the cargo ships to arrive, they informed the home government. The prospect of thousands of islanders patiently starving to death was too horrifying to allow. The British government fulfilled the prophecy by sending ships to the islands with cargo earmarked for the Melanesians.

As Figure 21.2 indicates, some social movements have a global orientation. As with many aspects of life in our new

Figure 21.2 Types of Social Movements

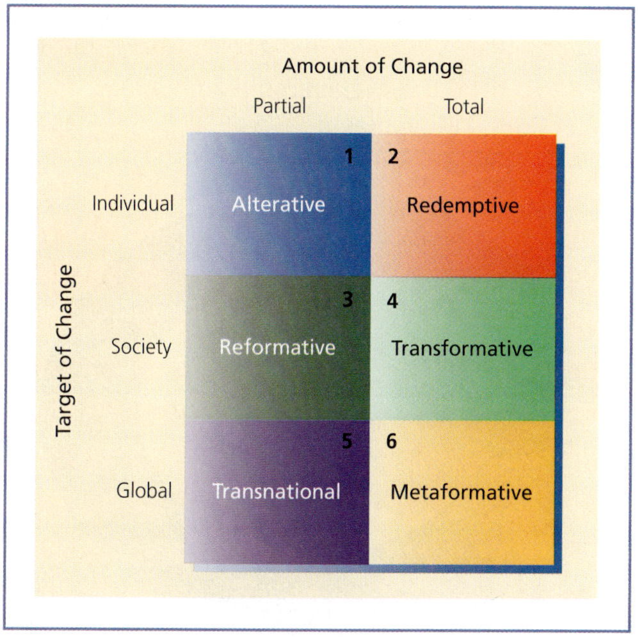

Amount of Change
Partial
Total
Target of Change
Individual
Society
Global
1 Alterative
2 Redemptive
3 Reformative
4 Transformative
5 Transnational
6 Metaformative

Sources: The first four types are from Aberle 1966; the last two are from the author.

transnational social movement a social movement whose emphasis is on some condition around the world, instead of on a condition in a specific country; also known as *new social movements*

metaformative social movement a social movement that has the goal to change the social order not just of a society or two, but of the entire world

global economy, numerous issues that bother people transcend national boundaries. Participants of **transnational social movements** (also called *new social movements*) want to change some condition that exists not just in their society, but also throughout the world. These social movements often center on improving the quality of life (Melucci 1989). Examples are the women's movement, labor movement, environmental movement, and animal rights movement (McAdam et al. 1988; Smith et al. 1997; Walter 2001). As you can see from these examples, transnational social movements still focus on some specific condition, but that condition is global.

Cell number 6 in Figure 21.2 represents a rare type of social movement. The goal of **metaformative social movements** is to change the social order itself—not just of a society or two, but of the entire world. Metaformative social movements strive to reformulate concepts and practices of race-ethnicity, class, gender, religion, government, and the global stratification of nations. Examples include the communist and fascist social movements of the early to middle parts of the twentieth century. (The fascists consisted of the Nazis in Germany, the Black Shirts of Italy, and groups throughout Europe and the United States.) Because these metaformative social movements posed a threat to the existing social order of the time, nations with even opposing ideologies banded together to fight them.

Today, we are witnessing another metaformative social movement, that of international terrorism. Like other social movements before it, this movement is not united, but consists of many separate groups with differing goals. The version of which al-Qaeda is a part wants to cleanse Islamic societies of Western influences, which they contend are demonic and degrading to men, women, and morality. To bring about their goals, they want to transform civilization itself. They want to replace Western civilization with their version of the good society, which consists of an extremist brand of Islam. This frightens both non-Muslims and Muslims, who hold sharply differing views of what constitutes quality of life. If the Islamic international terrorists—or the communists or fascists before them—have their way, they will usher in a new world order.

Tactics of Social Movements

The leaders of a social movement can choose from a variety of tactics. Should they peacefully boycott, stage a march, or hold an all-night candlelight vigil? Or should they bomb a building, burn down a research lab, or assassinate a key figure? To understand why the leaders of social movements choose their tactics, we need to examine a group's levels of membership, the publics it addresses, and its relationship to authorities.

Levels of Membership Figure 21.3 shows the composition of social movements. Beginning at the center and moving outward are three levels of membership. At the center is the inner core, those most committed to the movement. The inner core sets the group's goals, timetables, and strategies. People at the second level are also committed to the movement, but somewhat less so than the inner core. They can be counted on to show up for demonstrations and to do the grunt work—help with mailings, pass out petitions and leaflets, make telephone calls. The third level consists of a wider circle of people who are less committed and less dependable. Their participation depends on convenience—if an activity doesn't interfere with something else they want to do, they participate.

Figure 21.3 The Membership and Publics of Social Movements

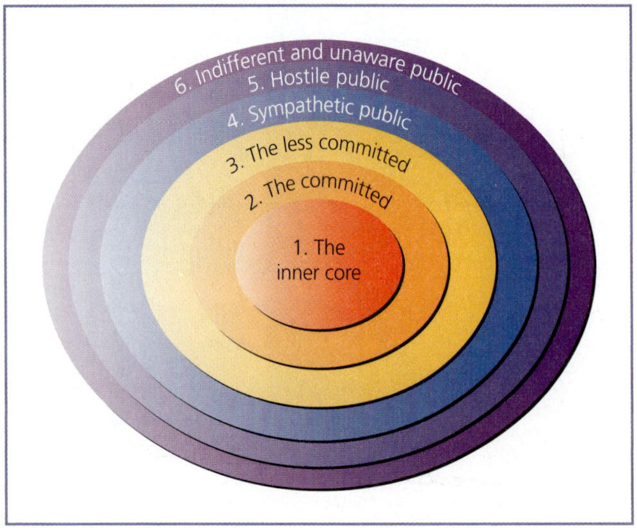

The tactics chosen largely depend on the predispositions and backgrounds of the inner core. Because of their differing backgrounds, some members of the inner core may be predisposed to use peaceful, quiet demonstrations, or even placing ads in newspapers. Others may prefer heated, verbal confrontations. Still others may tend toward violence. Tactics also depend on the number of committed members. Different tactics are called for depending on whether the inner core can count on seven hundred—or only seven—committed members to show up.

The Publics Outside the group's membership is the **public,** a dispersed group of people who may have an interest in the issue. As you can see from Figure 21.3, there are three types of publics. Just outside the third circle of members, and blending into it, is the sympathetic public. Although their sympathies lie with the movement, these people have no commitment to it. Their sympathies with the movement's goals, however, make them fertile ground for recruitment. The second public is hostile. The movement's values go against its own, and it wants to stop the social movement. The third public consists of disinterested people. They are either unaware of the social movement or, if aware, indifferent to it.

public in this context, a dispersed group of people relevant to a social movement; the sympathetic and hostile publics have an interest in the issues on which a social movement focuses; there is also an unaware or indifferent public

In selecting tactics, the leadership pays attention to these publics. The sympathetic public is especially significant, because it is the source of new members and support at the ballot box. Leaders avoid tactics that they think might alienate the sympathetic public. They look for tactics that will create even more sympathy from this group. To make themselves appear to be victims—people whose rights are being trampled on—leaders may even force a confrontation with the hostile public. Tactics directed toward the indifferent or unaware public are designed to neutralize their indifference and increase their awareness.

Relationship to Authorities In determining tactics, the movement's relationship to authorities is also significant. This is especially so when it comes to choosing between peaceful and violent tactics. If a social movement is *institutionalized*—accepted by authorities—violence will not be directed against the authorities, for they are on the movement's side. This, however, does not rule out violence directed against the opposition. In contrast, if authorities are hostile to a social movement, aggressive or even violent tactics may be directed against them. For example, because the goal of a transformative (revolutionary) social movement is to replace the government, the movement and the government are clearly on a collision course.

Other Factors Sociologist Ellen Scott (1993), who studied the movement to stop rape, discovered that friendship, race-ethnicity, and even size of town are important in determining tactics. Women in Santa Cruz, California, chose to directly confront accused rapists—to publicly humiliate them. In a town of 41,000, the tactic worked. In Washington, D.C., women rejected confrontation as ineffective because of the anonymity

The social movement to stop violence against women has had a major impact on our thinking about gender relations, laws, and law enforcement. Discussed in the text are social factors that underlie the choice of tactics used by women's centers. Shown here are the Purple Berets in Santa Rosa, California, who are protesting against county officials for wanting to treat spouse abuse with counseling instead of in the courts.

public opinion how people think about some issue

propaganda in its broad sense, the presentation of information in the attempt to influence people; in its narrow sense, one-sided information used to try to influence people

that comes with a city of 640,000. Another factor was race–ethnicity. Both groups of women were white, but in Santa Cruz, it was white women confronting white men, while in Washington, D.C., it would have been white women confronting black men. Friendships were also important. Public confrontations require a closely working team of people who will back each other up. In Santa Cruz, the women had lived together for years, while the group in Washington, D.C., was a more formal organization.

No matter how carefully the leaders choose their tactics, they may backfire. All around Santa Cruz, women from the center hung pictures of a man accused of rape. He sued the center. The long litigation that followed sapped the women's energy, and the Santa Cruz center folded.

Propaganda and the Mass Media

The leaders of social movements try to manipulate the mass media in order to influence **public opinion,** how people think about some issue. The right kind of publicity enables the leaders to arouse the sympathetic public and to lay the groundwork for recruiting more members. Pictures of bloodied, dead baby seals, for example, go a long way toward getting a group's message across. The photo essay on pages 632–633 reports on the demonstrations that accompanied the execution of Timothy McVeigh. When I interviewed demonstrators who wanted McVeigh killed and those who wanted his life spared, I was stuck by their use of propaganda. I think this will strike you, too, as you look at these photos.

A key to understanding social movements, then, is **propaganda.** Although this word often evokes negative images, it actually is a neutral term. Propaganda is simply the presentation of information in the attempt to influence people. Its original meaning was positive. *Propaganda* referred to a committee of cardinals of the Roman Catholic Church whose assignment was the care of forcign missions. (They were to *propagate*—multiply or spread—the faith.) The term has traveled a long way since then, however, and today it usually refers to a presentation of information so one-sided that it distorts reality.

Propaganda, in the sense of organized attempts to influence public opinion, is a regular part of everyday life. Our news is filled with propaganda, as various interest groups—from retailers to the government—try to manipulate our perceptions of the world. Our movies, too, although seemingly intended as simply entertainment devices, are actually propaganda vehicles, but even more blatantly so during times of war. Underlying effective propaganda are seven basic techniques, discussed in the Down-to-Earth Sociology box on the next page. Perhaps by understanding these techniques, you will be able to re-

The use of propaganda is popular among those committed to the goals of a social movement. They can see only one side to the social issue about which they are so upset. What attention-getting devices have these activists in the animal rights social movement chosen? Are they effective?

DOWN-TO-EARTH SOCIOLOGY

"Tricks of the Trade"—The Fine Art of Propaganda

SOCIOLOGISTS ALFRED AND ELIZABETH Lee (1939) found that propaganda relies on seven basic techniques, which they termed "tricks of the trade." To be effective, the techniques should be subtle, with the audience unaware that their minds and emotions are being manipulated. If propaganda is effective, people will not know why they support something, but they'll fervently defend it.

- *Name calling.* This technique aims to arouse opposition to the competing product, candidate, or policy by associating it with a negative image. By comparison, one's own product, candidate, or policy is attractive. Political candidates who call an opponent "soft on crime" or "insensitive to the poor" are using this technique.
- *Glittering generality.* Essentially the opposite of the first technique, this one surrounds the product, candidate, or policy with images that arouse positive feelings. "She's a real Democrat" has little meaning, but it makes the audience feel that something substantive has been said. "He stands for individualism" is so general that it is meaningless, yet the audience thinks that it has heard a specific message about the candidate.
- *Transfer.* In its positive form, this technique associates the product, candidate, or policy with something the public respects or approves. You might not be able to get by with saying "Coors is patriotic," but surround a beer with images of the country's flag, and beer drinkers will get the idea that it is more patriotic to drink this brand of beer than to drink some other kind. In its negative form, this technique associates the product, candidate, or policy with something the public disapproves of.
- *Testimonials.* Famous individuals endorse a product, candidate, or policy. Michael Jordan lends his name to cologne, Nike products, and even underwear, while Britney Spears touts the merits of Pepsi, and Tiger Woods tells you that Buicks make fine SUVs. Candidates for political office solicit the endorsement of movie stars who may know next to nothing about the candidate or even about politics. In the negative form of this technique, a despised person is associated with the competing product. If propagandists (called "spin doctors" in politics) could get by with it, they would show Saddam Hussein or Osama bin Laden announcing support for an opposing candidate.
- *Plain folks.* Sometimes it pays to associate the product, candidate, or policy with "just plain folks." "If Mary or John Q. Public likes it, you will, too." A political candidate who kisses babies, puts on a hard hat, and has lunch at McDonald's while photographers "catch him (or her) in the act" is using the "plain folks" strategy. "I'm just a regular person" is the message of the presidential candidate who poses for photographers in jeans and work shirt—while making certain that the chauffeur-driven Mercedes does not show up in the background.
- *Card stacking.* The aim of this technique is to present only positive information about what you support, and only negative information about what you oppose. The intent is to make it sound as though there is only one conclusion a rational person can draw. Falsehoods, distortions, and illogical statements are often used.
- *Bandwagon.* "Everyone is doing it" is the idea behind this technique. Emphasizing how many others buy the product or support the candidate or policy conveys the message that anyone who doesn't join in is on the wrong track.

The Lees (1939) added, "Once we know that a speaker or writer is using one of these propaganda devices in an attempt to convince us of an idea, we can separate the device from the idea and see what the idea amounts to on its own merits."

sist one-sided appeals—whether they come from social movements or from hawkers of jeans, running shoes, or perfumes.

The mass media play such a crucial role that we can say they are the gatekeepers to social movements. If those who control and work in the mass media—from owners to reporters—are sympathetic to some particular "cause," you can be sure that it will receive sympathetic treatment. If the social movement goes against their views, however, it likely will be ignored or receive unfavorable treatment. If you ever get the impression that the media are trying to manipulate your opinions and attitudes—even your feelings—on some particular issue or social movement, you probably are right. Far from doing unbiased reporting, the media are under the control and influence of people who have an agenda to get across. To the materials in the Down-to-Earth Sociology box on propaganda, then, we need to add the biases of the media establishment—the issues it chooses to give publicity to, those it chooses to ignore, and its favorable and unfavorable treatment of issues and movements.

THROUGH THE AUTHOR'S LENS

Social Movements and Propaganda:

The Execution of Timothy McVeigh

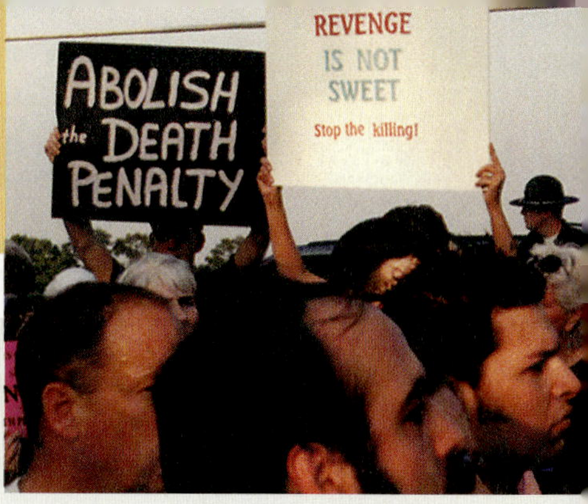

There is so much sociology to do, and so little time to do it! Some events seem irresistible, however.

The execution of Timothy McVeigh, the Oklahoma bomber who claimed more victims than any single individual in U.S. history, was one such event. The media highlighted the possibility of protests and riots at this first federal execution in 38 years. I know that I could never get inside the prison to do research. Yet, there would be all those public activities, so readily accessible.

When I arrived in Terre Haute, Indiana, I found that the city had been turned into an armed camp. The federal, state, and local authorities had prepared for an attack on the prison. The local police had been trained in riot control. The state had sent in its Emergency Management Agency. And the federal government had been active, too. Military sharpshooters were present, ready to act in case any group tried to prevent the execution.

To prevent confrontation, demonstrators were separated on the basis of their sentiment (pro- and anti-execution) and sent to parks on opposite sides of town. The anti-execution people showed up in full force. As you can see from these photos, so few pro-execution protesters appeared that I was able to interview them all.

Sequestered on one side of town, in a small park, were the pro-execution demonstrators. As is evident from this photo, they were not a large, organized group. These demonstrators had simply used a marking pen to print messages on cardboard.

The pro-execution demonstrators placed their focus on the victims. Some told me that a lethal injection was too good for McVeigh, that he should be made to suffer before he died. The demonstrators in this photo are expressing their feelings that McVeigh's death is not adequate payment for 168 victims.

The anti-execution demonstrators expressed mixed motives for their position. These two, isolated from the organized anti-execution crowd—both physically and in their point of view—were not against the death penalty. They felt that McVeigh should not be executed because he had been railroaded by the government in an unfair trial. For them, McVeigh had become a folk hero.

The anti-execution demonstrators displayed professionally made signs that they take from one protest site to another. They were hosted by a local Roman Catholic church. After a rally there, they marched as a group to the prison where the execution took place.

The anti-execution demonstrators—and anti-death penalty to the extreme—were so well organized that they sent busloads of people to protest McVeigh's execution.

Demonstrators also gathered outside the prison where McVeigh was to be executed. They were kept on the opposite side of the road, where they were constantly scrutinized by armed personnel on the prison side of the road. I was told that inside the prison were hundreds of armed troops—in case anyone tried to rescue McVeigh.

Demonstrators often use attention-getting devices. This individual carried a cross to the federal prison. He said that he was convinced that God wanted him to be at the scene. His attention-getting device was effective, as you can see from the individual who is interviewing him.

The huge puppets of the anti-execution demonstrators were an effective attention-getting device. If you look closely, you can see a reporter interviewing the demonstrators.

Sociology can be a liberating discipline (Berger 1963/2003). Sociology sensitizes us to *multiple realities;* that is, for any single point of view on some topic, there are competing points of view. Each represents reality as people see it, their distinct experiences having led them to different perceptions. Consequently, different people find each point of view equally compelling. Although the committed members of a social movement are sincere—and perhaps even make sacrifices for "the cause"—theirs is but one view of the world. If other sides were presented, the issue would look quite different.

Why People Join Social Movements

As we have seen, social movements are fed by a sense of injustice. They stem from widespread, deeply felt discontent—the conviction that some condition of society is no longer tolerable. However, not everyone who feels dissatisfied with an issue joins a social movement. Why some, and not others? Sociologists have found that recruitment generally follows channels of social networks. That is, people most commonly join a social movement because they have friends and acquaintances already in it (McCarthy and Wolfson 1992; Snow et al. 1993a).

Let's look at three explanations for why people join social movements.

Mass Society Theory

To explain why people are attracted to social movements, sociologist William Kornhauser (1959) proposed **mass society theory.** Kornhauser argued that many people feel isolated because they live in a **mass society**—an impersonal, industrialized, highly bureaucratized society. Social movements fill this void by offering a sense of belonging. In areas where social ties are supposedly weaker, such as the western United States, one would expect to find more social movements than in areas where ties are supposedly stronger, such as in the Midwest and South.

This theory seems to match commonsense observations. Certainly, social movements proliferate on the West Coast. But when sociologist Doug McAdam and his colleagues (McAdam et al. 1988) interviewed people who had risked their lives in the civil rights movement, they found that these people were firmly rooted in families and communities. Their strong desire to right wrongs and to overcome injustices, not their isolation, had motivated their participation. Even the Nazis attracted many people who were firmly rooted in their communities (Oberschall 1973). Finally, the most isolated of all, the homeless, generally do not join anything—except food lines.

Deprivation Theory

A second explanation to account for why people join social movements is *deprivation theory.* According to this theory, people who feel deprived—whether it be of money, justice, status, or privilege—join social movements with the hope of redressing their grievances. This theory may seem so obvious as to need no evidence. Don't the thousands of African Americans who participated in the civil rights movement of the 1950s and the World War I soldiers who marched on Washington after Congress refused to pay their promised bonuses provide ample evidence that the theory is true?

Deprivation theory does provide a starting point. But there is more to the matter than this. Almost 150 years ago, Alexis de Tocqueville (1856/1955) made a telling observation. Both the peasants of Germany and the peasants of France were living under deprived conditions. According to deprivation theory, if revolution were to occur we would expect it to take place in both countries. Only the French peasants rebelled and overthrew their king, however. The reason, said de Tocqueville, is *relative* deprivation. The living conditions of the French peasants had been improving, and they could foresee even better circumstances

mass society theory an explanation for why people participate in a social movement based on the assumption that the movement offers them a sense of belonging

mass society industrialized, highly bureaucratized, impersonal society ahead. German peasants, in contrast, had never experienced anything but depressed conditions, and they had no comparative basis for feeling deprived.

According to **relative deprivation theory**, then, it is not people's actual deprivation that matters. Rather, the key to participation in social movements is *relative* deprivation—what people *think* they should have relative to what others have, or relative to their own past or even their perceived future. Relative deprivation theory, which has provided insight into revolutions, holds a surprise. Because improving conditions fuel human desire for even better conditions, *improving* conditions can spark revolutions. As Figure 21.4 shows, this occurs when people's expectations outstrip the actual change they experience. It is likely that we can also apply this to riots.

Figure 21.4 Relative Deprivation and Revolution

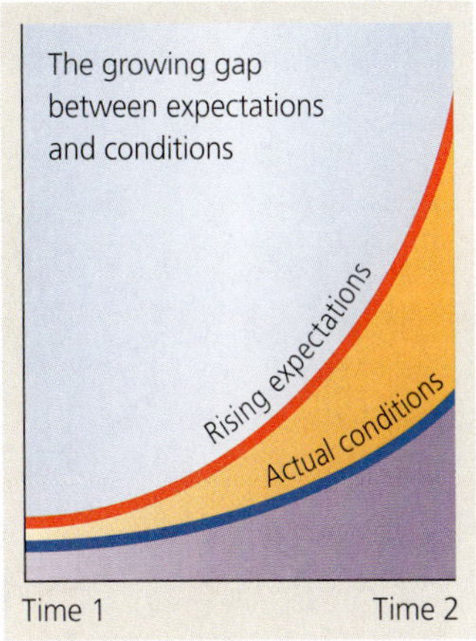

Relative deprivation also explains an interesting aspect of the civil rights movement. Relatively well-off African Americans—college students and church leaders—were at the center of the sit-ins, marches, and boycotts in the South during the 1950s and 1960s. They went to restaurants and lunch counters that were reserved for whites. When refused service, they sat peacefully while curses and food were heaped on them (Morris 1993). Why did they subject themselves to such treatment? Remember that according to relative deprivation theory, what is significant is not what we have or don't have, but with whom we compare ourselves. The African American demonstrators compared themselves with whites of similar status, and they perceived themselves as deprived.

How about the white, middle-class college students and church leaders from the North? They, too, risked their lives when they joined the Southern protesters. They weren't comparing themselves with people whose situation was better than their own. Nor was their own personal welfare at stake. Relative deprivation theory doesn't help us here. We need to look at the *moral* reasons for their involvement (McAdam 1988; Fendrich and Lovoy 1993). Let's consider that motivation in social movements.

relative deprivation theory in this context, the belief that people join social movements based on their evaluations of what they think they should have compared with what others have

Moral Issues and Ideological Commitment

As sociologists James Jasper and Dorothy Nelkin (1993) point out, we will miss the *basic* reason for many people's involvement in social movements if we overlook the moral issue—people sensing injustice and wanting to do something about it. Some people join because of *moral shock*—a sense of outrage at finding out what is "really" going on (Jasper and Poulsen 1995). For people who view a social movement in moral terms, great issues hang

Militias—citizens who arm themselves and form paramilitary organizations—have sprung up across the United States. Although all the theories discussed in the text may apply to members of these militias, those that deal with moral issues and ideological commitment are especially relevant. These two are members of the Michigan Militia, the country's largest militia.

in the balance. They feel they must choose sides and do what they can to help right wrongs. As sociologists put it, they join because of *ideological commitment* to the movement.

Many members on *both* sides of the abortion issue, for example, see their involvement in such terms. Similarly, activists in the animal rights movement are convinced that there can be no justification for making animals suffer in order to make safer products for humans. Activists in the peace movement, the environmental movement, and those who protest against global capitalism see nuclear weapons, pollution, and power in similar moral terms. It is for moral reasons that they risk arrest and ridicule for their demonstrations. For them, to *not* act would be an inexcusable betrayal of future generations. The *moral* component of a social movement, then, is a primary reason for many people's involvement.

A Special Case: The Agent Provocateur

Agent provocateurs are a unique type of participant in social movements. These are agents of the government or even of the opposing sides of a social movement whose job is to spy on the leadership and perhaps to sabotage its activities. Some are recruited from the membership itself, people who are willing to betray their friends in the organization for a few Judas dollars. Others are police or members of a rival group who go underground and join the movement.

The radical social change advocated by some social movements poses a threat to the power elite. In such cases, the use of agent provocateurs is not surprising. What may be surprising, however, is that some agents convert to the social movement on which they are spying. Sociologist Gary Marx (1993) explains that to be credible, agents must share at least some of the class, age, gender, racial-ethnic, or religious characteristics of the group. This background makes the agents more likely to sympathize with the movement's goals, making them disenchanted with trying to harm the group. To be effective, agents must also work their way into the center of the group. This requires that they spend time with the group's committed members. A basic sociological principle is that the more we interact with people, the more we tend to like them. In addition, as these agents build trust, they often are cut off from their own group. The point of view they represent can start to recede in their minds, and be replaced with concerns about betraying and deceiving people who now trust them as friends.

What also may be surprising is how far some agents go. During the 1960s, when a wave of militant social movements rolled across the United States, the FBI recruited agent provocateurs to sabotage groups. These agents provoked illegal activities that otherwise would not have occurred: They set the leadership up for arrest and, in some instances, set them up for death. Two examples will let us see how agent provocateurs operate (Marx 1993). In a plot by a group called the Black Liberation Front to blow up the Statue of Liberty, one of the four men involved was an undercover agent. It was he who drew up the plans and even provided funds to pay for the dynamite and rent the car. In another instance, the FBI paid $36,500 to two members of the White Knights of the Ku Klux Klan to arrange for the Klan to bomb a Jewish businessman's home. A trap was set in which one Klansman was killed and another was arrested in the unsuccessful attempt.

IN SUM

People most commonly join a social movement because they have friends and acquaintances already in it. Motivations are mixed. Some join because of moral convictions, others to further their own careers. Still others join because they find a valued identity, or even because it is fun. Some participate even though they *don't want to.* The Cuban government, for example, compels people to turn out for mass demonstrations to show support of the Communist regime (Aguirre 1993). As we just saw, police agents may join social movements in order to spy on them and sabotage their activities. In no social movement, then, is there a single cause for people joining. As in all other activities in life, people remain a complex bundle of motivations—and this provides a challenge for sociologists to unravel.

agent provocateur someone who joins a group in order to spy on it and to sabotage it by provoking its members to commit extreme acts

On the Success and Failure of Social Movements

Social movements have brought about extensive change. The women's movement, for example, has led not only to new legislation but also to a different way of thinking about relations between women and men. Most social movements, however, are not successful. Let's look at the reasons for their success or failure.

The Stages of Social Movements

Sociologists have identified five stages in the growth and maturity of social movements (Lang and Lang 1961; Mauss 1975; Spector and Kitsuse 1977; Tilly 1978; Jaspar 1991). They are

1. *Initial unrest and agitation.* During this first stage, people are upset about some condition in society and want to change it. Leaders emerge who verbalize people's feelings and crystallize issues. Most social movements fail at this stage. Unable to gain enough support, after a brief flurry of activity, they quietly die.
2. *Resource mobilization.* A crucial factor that enables social movements to make it past the first stage is **resource mobilization.** By this term, sociologists mean the mobilization of resources—time, money, people's skills, and the ability to get the attention of the mass media. Those resources may also include access to churches to organize protests (Mirola 2003). Technology and mailing lists are also key resources: direct mailing, faxing, and e-mailing.

   In some cases, an indigenous leadership arises to mobilize resources. Other groups, lacking capable leadership, turn to "guns for hire," outside specialists who sell their services. As sociologists John McCarthy and Mayer Zald (1977; Zald and McCarthy 1987) point out, even though large numbers of people may be upset over some condition of society, without resource mobilization they are only upset people, perhaps even agitators, but they do not constitute a social movement.
3. *Organization.* A division of labor is set up. The leadership makes policy decisions, and the rank and file carry out the daily tasks necessary to keep the movement going. There is still much collective excitement about the issue, the movement's focal point of concern.
4. *Institutionalization.* At this stage, the movement has developed a bureaucracy, the type of formal hierarchy described in Chapter 7. Control lies in the hands of career officers, who may care more about their own position in the organization than the movement for which the organization's initial leaders made sacrifices. The collective excitement diminishes.
5. *Organizational decline and possible resurgence.* During this phase, managing the day-to-day affairs of the organization dominates the leadership. A change in public sentiment may even have occurred, and there may no longer be a group of committed people who share a common cause. The movement is likely to wither away. Decline is not inevitable, however, as we shall see.

The Rocky Road to Success

These stages, especially resource mobilization and institutionalization, help us understand why social movements seldom solve social problems. To mobilize resources, a movement must appeal to a broad constituency. This means that the group must focus on things that a lot of people are concerned about. For example, if workers at one particular plant are upset about their working conditions, their discontent is not adequate for recruiting the broad support necessary for a social movement. At best, it will result in local agitation.

resource mobilization a theory that social movements succeed or fail based on their ability to mobilize resources such as time, money, and people's skills

Unsafe working conditions of millions of workers, however, have a chance of becoming the focal point of a social movement.

Broad problems, however, are deeply embedded in society. This, of course, means that minor tinkering will not be adequate. Just as the problem touches many interrelated components of society, so the solutions must be broad. With no quick fix available, the social movement must stay around. But longevity brings its own danger of failure. When social movements become institutionalized, they tend to turn inward and focus their energies on running the organization (see stage 4 on page 637).

Many social movements do vitally affect society, however. Some, such as the civil rights and the women's movement, become powerful forces for social change. They draw the public's attention to problems and turn the society on a path that leads toward solutions. Others become powerful forces for resisting the social change that their members consider undesirable. In either case, social movements are highly significant for contemporary society, and we can anticipate that new ones will be a regular feature of our social landscape.

As we saw, the fifth and final stage of social movement is decline. However, decline is not inevitable. More idealistic and committed leaders may emerge and reinvigorate the movement. Or, as in the case of abortion, conflict between groups on opposite sides of the issue may invigorate each side and prevent the movement's decline. Let's close this chapter by focusing on abortion activists.

THINKING **Critically**

Which Side of the Barricades? Prochoice and Prolife as a Social Movement

No issue so divides Americans as abortion. Although most Americans take a more moderate view, on one side are some who feel that abortion should be permitted under any circumstance, even during the last month of pregnancy. They are matched by some on the other side who are convinced that abortion should never be allowed for any circumstances, not even during the first month of pregnancy. This polarization constantly breathes new life into the movement.

When the U.S. Supreme Court made its 1973 decision, *Roe* v. *Wade*, that states could not restrict abortion, the prochoice side relaxed. Victory was theirs, and they thought their opponents would quietly disappear. Instead, large numbers of Americans were disturbed by what they saw as the legal right to murder unborn children.

The views of the two sides could not be more incompatible. Those who favor choice view the 1.3 million abortions performed annually in the United States as examples of women exercising their basic reproductive rights. Those who gather under the prolife banner see these acts as legalized murder. To the prochoice side, those who oppose abortion are blocking women's rights—they would force women to continue pregnancies they want to terminate. To the prolife side, those who advocate choice are seen as condoning murder—they would sacrifice their unborn children for the sake of school, career, or convenience.

There is no way to reconcile these contrary views. Each sees the other as unreasonable and extremist. And each uses propaganda by focusing on worst-case scenarios: prochoice images of young women raped at gunpoint, forced to bear the children of rapists; prolife images of women who are eight months pregnant killing their babies instead of nurturing them.

With no middle ground, these views remain in perpetual conflict. As each side fights for what it considers basic rights, it reinvigorates the other. When in 1989 the U.S. Supreme Court decided in *Webster* v. *Reproductive Services* that states could restrict abortion, one side mourned it as a defeat and the other hailed it as a victory. Seeing the political battle going against them, the prochoice side regrouped for a determined struggle. The prolife side, sensing judicial victory within its grasp, gathered forces for a push to complete the overthrow of *Roe* v. *Wade*.

This goal of the prolife side almost became reality in *Casey* v. *Planned Parenthood*. On June 30, 1992, in a 6-to-3 decision the Supreme Court upheld the right

Activists in social movements become committed to "the cause." The social movement around abortion, currently one of the most dynamic in the United States, has split Americans, is highly visible, and has articulate spokespeople on both sides.

of states to require women to wait 24 hours between the confirmation of pregnancy and getting an abortion; to require girls under 18 to obtain the consent of one parent; and to require that women be given materials that describe the fetus and be informed about alternatives to abortion. In the same case, by a 5-to-4 decision, the Court ruled that a wife does not have to inform her husband if she intends to have an abortion.

Because the two sides do not see the same reality, this social movement cannot end unless the vast majority of Americans commit to one side or the other. Otherwise, every legislative and judicial outcome—including the extremes of a constitutional amendment that declares abortion to be either murder or a woman's right—is a victory to one and a defeat to the other. To committed activists, then, no battle is ever complete. Rather, each action is only one small part of a hard-fought, bitter, moral struggle.

For Your CONSIDERATION . . .

Typically, the last stage of a social movement is decline. Why hasn't this social movement declined? Under what conditions will it decline?

The longer a woman is pregnant, the fewer the people who approve abortion. How do you feel about abortion during the second month versus the eighth month? Or partial-birth abortion? What do you think about abortion in cases of rape and incest? Can you identify some of the social reasons that underlie your opinions?

Sources: Neikirk and Elsasser 1992; McKenna 1995; Williams 1995; *Statistical Abstract* 2002:Table 88; Henslin 2003d.

SUMMARY and REVIEW

Early Explanations: The Transformation of the Individual

How did early theorists explain how crowds affect people?

Early theorists of **collective behavior** argued that crowds transform people. Charles Mackay used the term *herd mentality* to explain why people did wild things when they were in crowds. Gustave LeBon said that a **collective mind** develops, and people are swept away by suggestions. Robert Park said that collective unrest develops, which, fed by a **circular reaction,** leads to collective impulses. Pp. 614–615.

What are the five stages of crowd behavior?

Herbert Blumer identified five stages that crowds go through before they become an **acting crowd:** social unrest, an exciting event, **milling,** a common object of attention, and common impulses. Pp. 615–616.

The Contemporary View: The Rationality of the Crowd

What is the current view of crowd behavior?

Current theorists view crowds as rational. Richard Berk suggested a **minimax strategy;** that is, people try to minimize their costs and maximize their rewards, regardless of whether they are in crowds. In **emergent norm theory,** Ralph Turner and Lewis Killian suggest that new norms emerge that allow people to do things in crowds that they otherwise would not do. Pp. 616–617.

Forms of Collective Behavior

What forms of collective behavior are there?

Forms of **collective behavior** include lynchings, **riots, rumors, panics, moral panics, mass hysteria, fads, fashions,** and **urban legends.** Conditions of discontent or uncertainty provide fertile ground for collective behavior, and each form provides a way of dealing with these conditions. Pp. 617–626.

Types and Tactics of Social Movements

What types of social movements are there?

Social movements consist of large numbers of people who organize to promote or resist social change. Depending on their target (individuals or society) and the amount of social change desired (partial or complete), social movements can be classified as **alterative, redemptive, reformative, transformative, transnational** and **metaformative.** Pp. 626–628.

How do social movement leaders select their tactics?

Leaders choose tactics on the basis of a group's levels of membership, its **publics,** and its relationship to authorities. The three levels of membership are *the inner core, the committed,* and *the less committed.* The predispositions of the inner core are crucial in choosing tactics, but so is the public they wish to address. If relationships with authorities are bad, the chances of aggressive or violent tactics increase. Friendship, size of city, and the race-ethnicity of movement participants and their targets may also be significant. Pp. 628–630.

How are the mass media related to social movements?

The mass media are gatekeepers for social movements. Because the media's favorable or unfavorable coverage affects **public opinion,** leaders choose tactics with the media in mind. Social movements also make use of **propaganda** to further their causes. Pp. 630–634.

Why People Join Social Movements

Why do people join social movements?

A primary reason people join social movements is they know others in the movement. According to **mass society theory,** social movements relieve feelings of isolation created by an impersonal, bureaucratized society. According to **relative deprivation theory,** people join movements to address their grievances. A sense of justice, morality, values, and ideological commitment also motivates people to join social movements. The **agent provocateur** illustrates that even people who oppose a cause may participate in it. Pp. 634–636.

On the Success and Failure of Social Movements

Why do social movements succeed or fail?

Social movements go through several stages—initial unrest and agitation, mobilization, organization, institutionalization, and, finally, decline. Resurgence is also possible. Groups that appeal to few people cannot succeed. To appeal broadly in order to accomplish **resource mobilization,** the movement must focus on broad concerns. These concerns are embedded deeply in society, which makes success difficult. Pp. 637–639.

Where can I read more on this topic?

Suggested Readings for this chapter are at the back of this book.

THINKING Critically ABOUT CHAPTER 21

1. Can you describe the different forms of collective behavior, and explain why people participate in collective behavior?
2. Use sociological findings to analyze a rumor or an urban legend you have heard or a fad you've participated in.
3. Pick a social movement and analyze it according to the sociological principles and findings reviewed in this chapter.

ADDITIONAL RESOURCES for This Chapter

www.ablongman.com/henslin7e

- *Content Select* Research Database for Sociology, with suggested key terms and annotated references
- Link to 2000 Census, with activities
- Flashcards of key terms and concepts
- Practice Tests
- Weblinks
- Interactive Map

Chapter 22

Social Change and the Environment

Jose Orega, *Hand and Environments* (Digital) 1995

Chapter Outline

The morning of January 28, 1986, dawned clear but near freezing—strange weather for subtropical Florida. At the Kennedy Space Center, icicles 6 to 12 inches long hung like stalactites from launch pad 39B. Shortly after 8 A.M., the crew entered the crew module. By 8:36 A.M., the seven members of the crew were strapped in their seats. They were understandably disappointed when liftoff, scheduled for 9:38 A.M., was delayed because of the ice.

Due to a strong public relations campaign, public interest in the flight ran high. Attention focused on Christa McAuliffe, a 37-year-old high school teacher from Concord, New Hampshire, the first private citizen to fly aboard a space shuttle. Mrs. McAuliffe had been selected from thousands of applicants (including the author of this text). She was to give a televised lesson during the flight about life aboard a spacecraft, and across the nation, schoolchildren watched with anticipation.

Eagerly awaiting the launch at the viewing site were the families and friends of the crew, as well as thousands of spectators. After two hours of delays, they were delighted to see *Challenger's* two solid-fuel boosters ignite, and they broke into cheers as this product of technical innovation thundered majestically into space. The time was 11:38 A.M.

Screams of horror arose *from the crowd*

Seventy-three seconds later, the *Challenger* was 7 miles from the launch site, racing skyward at 2,900 feet per second. Suddenly a brilliant glow appeared on one side of the external tank. In seconds, the glow blossomed into a gigantic fireball. Screams of horror arose from the crowd as the *Challenger,* now 19 miles away, exploded, and bits of debris began to fall from the sky.

In classrooms across the country, children burst into tears. Adults stared at their televisions in stunned disbelief.

Sources: Based on Broad 1986; Magnuson 1986; Lewis 1988; Maier 1993.

If any characteristic describes social life today, it is rapid social change. As we shall see in this chapter, technology, such as that which made the *Challenger* first a reality and then a disaster, is a driving force behind this change. To understand social change is to better understand today's society—and our own lives.

How Social Change Transforms Social Life

The Four Social Revolutions

The rapid, far-reaching social change that the world is currently experiencing did not "just happen." Rather, it is the result of forces that were set in motion thousands of years ago, beginning with the domestication of plants and animals. This first social revolution allowed hunting and gathering societies to develop into horticultural and pastoral societies (see pages 149–154). The plow brought about the second social revolution, from which agricultural societies emerged. The third social revolution, prompted by the invention of the steam engine, ushered in the Industrial Revolution. Now we are in the midst of the fourth social revolution, stimulated by the invention of the microchip. The process of change has speeded up so greatly that we may also be seeing the beginning of the bioeconomy, brought about by the mapping of the human genome system.

From *Gemeinschaft* to *Gesellschaft*

Although so many aspects of our lives have already changed, we have seen only the tip of the iceberg. By the time this fourth—and perhaps fifth—social revolution is full-blown, little of our way of life will be left untouched. We can assume this because that is how it was with the earlier social revolutions. For example, the change from agricultural to industrial society meant not only that people moved from villages to cities but also that many intimate, lifelong relationships were replaced by impersonal, short-term associations. Paid work, contracts, and money replaced the reciprocal obligations (such as helping one another) essential to kinship, social status, and friendship. As reviewed on pages 103–105, sociologists use the terms *Gemeinschaft* and *Gesellschaft* to indicate this fundamental shift in society.

Traditional, or *Gemeinschaft,* societies are small, rural, and slow-changing. They are dominated by men, and have firm divisions between the sexes. People look to the past for guidelines on how to deal with the present. They live in extended families, have little formal education, and treat most illnesses at home. People tend to see life and morals in absolute terms. Modern, or *Gesellschaft,* societies, in contrast, are large, more urbanized, and fast-changing. Divisions between the sexes are more fluid. People stress formal education and are more future-oriented. In the third stage of the demographic transition, they have smaller families and low rates of infant mortality. They live longer lives, have higher incomes, and enjoy vastly more material possessions.

Capitalism, Modernization, and Industrialization

Just why did societies change from *Gemeinschaft* to *Gesellschaft?* Karl Marx pointed to a social invention called *capitalism.* He analyzed how the breakup of feudal society threw people off the land, creating a surplus of labor. These masses moved to cities, where they were exploited by the owners of the means of production (factories, machinery, tools). This set in motion antagonistic relationships between capitalists and workers that remain today.

Max Weber, in contrast, traced capitalism to the Protestant Reformation (see pages 177–178). He noted that the Reformation stripped Protestants of the assurance that church membership saved them. As they agonized over heaven and hell, they concluded that God did not want the elect to live in uncertainty. God would surely give a sign to assure them that they were predestined to heaven. That sign, they decided, was prosperity.

Table 22.1 Comparing Traditional and Modern Societies

Characteristics	Traditional Societies	Modern Societies
General Characteristics		
Social change	Slow	Rapid
Size of group	Small	Large
Religious orientation	More	Less
Formal education	No	Yes
Place of residence	Rural	Urban
Demographic transition	First stage	Third stage (or Fourth)
Family size	Larger	Smaller
Infant mortality	High	Low
Life expectancy	Short	Long
Health care	Home	Hospital
Temporal orientation	Past	Future
Material Relations		
Industrialized	No	Yes
Technology	Simple	Complex
Division of labor	Simple	Complex
Income	Low	High
Material possessions	Few	Many
Social Relationships		
Basic organization	*Gemeinschaft*	*Gesellschaft*
Families	Extended	Nuclear
Respect for elders	More	Less
Social stratification	Rigid	More open
Statuses	More ascribed	More achieved
Gender equality	Less	More
Norms		
View of reality, life, and morals	Absolute	Relativistic
Social control	Informal	Formal
Tolerance of differences	Less	More

Social change comes in many forms. Shown here is a Chinese peasant in 1911, whose pigtail is being cut off by the revolutionary army. To retain the custom of never cutting one's hair was considered a sign of allegiance to warlords and of resistance to the new regime.

An unexpected consequence of the Reformation, then, was to make Protestants work hard and be thrifty. This created an economic surplus, which stimulated capitalism. In this way, Protestantism laid the groundwork for the Industrial Revolution that transformed the world.

The sweeping changes ushered in by the Industrial Revolution are called **modernization.** Table 22.1 summarizes these changes. The traits listed on this table are *ideal types* in Weber's sense of the term, for no society exemplifies all of them to the maximum degree. Our new technology has also created unevenness within nations. For example, in Uganda, a traditional society, the elite have computers. Thus the characteristics shown in Table 22.1 should be interpreted as "more" or "less" rather than "either-or."

When technology changes, societies change. Consider how technology from the industrialized world is transforming traditional societies. When the West exported medicine to the Least Industrialized Nations, for example, death rates dropped while birth rates remained high. As a result, the population exploded. This second stage of the demographic transition upset traditional balances of family, property, and inheritance. It brought hunger and led to mass migration to cities that have little industrialization to support the masses of people moving into them. The photo essay on pages 592–593 and the Cultural Diversity box on page 600 discuss some of these problems.

modernization the transformation of traditional societies into industrial societies

The Protestant Reformation ushered in not only religious change but also, as Max Weber analyzed, fundamental social-economic change. This painting by Hans Holbein, the Younger, shows the new prosperity of the merchant class. Previously, only the nobility and higher clergy could afford such possessions.

Social Movements

Social movements reveal the cutting edge of change in society. People band together to express their feelings about something that upsets them. They organize to demand change, or to resist some change they don't like. Because social movements form around issues that bother large numbers of people, they indicate areas of society in which there is great pressure for change. With globalization, these issues increasingly cut across international boundaries, indicating areas of discontent and sweeping change that affect millions of people in different cultures (see pages 626–639).

Conflict, Power, and Global Politics

With all the changes surrounding us, it is impossible to pinpoint the most significant one. Among the contenders, however, would be one that often lies below our vision—the arrangement of power among nations. By the sixteenth century, today's global divisions had begun to emerge. Those nations that had the most advanced technology (at that time, the swiftest ships and the most powerful cannons) became wealthy by conquering other nations and exploiting their resources. Then, as capitalism emerged, some nations industrialized. The newly industrialized nations exploited the resources of those that had not industrialized. According to *world system theory,* this made the nonindustrialized nations dependent and unable to develop their own resources (see pages 249–252).

Today's information revolution, including the new bioeconomics, will also have far-reaching consequences for global stratification. Those nations that make the fastest, most significant advances in these areas are destined to dominate in the coming generation. Obviously, this will be a continuation of the dominance of the Most Industrialized Nations.

Since World War II, a realignment of the world's powers (called *geopolitics*) has resulted in a triadic division of the globe: a Japan-centered East, a Germany-centered Europe, and a United States-centered western hemisphere. These three powers, along with five lesser ones—Canada, France, Great Britain, Italy, and Russia—dominate the globe today. They first called themselves G-7, meaning the "Group of 7." The fear of Russia's nuclear arsenal and appreciation that Russia is cooperating in global affairs prompted G-7 nations to let Russia join its elite club. It is now known as G-8.

These industrial giants hold annual meetings at which they decide how to divide up the world's markets and regulate global economic policy, such as interest rates, tariffs, and currency exchanges. Their goal is to perpetuate their global dominance, which includes keeping prices down on the raw materials they buy from the Least Industrialized Nations. Cheap oil is essential for this goal, which requires that they dominate the Middle East, not letting it become an independent power to upset their planned order.

Threatening the global divisions so carefully constructed by G-8 is the resurgence of ethnic conflicts. The breakup of the Soviet empire unleashed the centuries-old hatreds and frustrated nationalistic ambitions of many ethnic groups. With the Soviet military and the KGB in disarray, these groups turned violently on one another. In Africa, similar seething hatreds brought warfare to ethnic groups that the European powers had lumped together, drawing arbitrary political boundaries on maps and calling them countries. In Europe, the former Yugoslavia split apart, with ethnic groups turning violently against one another. Ethnic conflicts threaten to erupt in Germany, France, Italy, the United States, and Mexico. At what point these resentments and hatreds will play themselves out, if ever, is unknown.

The growing wealth and power of China poses another threat to G-8. China wants to recapture its glory of centuries past, and as it expands its domain of influence it increasingly infringes on the interests of G-8. Bowing to the inevitable, to reduce the likelihood of conflict, G-8 has allowed China to become an observer at its annual summits. As mentioned in Chapter 15, if China follows G-8's rules, the next step will be to incorporate China into this exclusive club.

For global control, G-8 must be able to depend on political and economic stability, both in its own back yard and in those countries that provide the raw materials essential for G-8's industrial machine. This explains why the Most Industrialized Nations have cared little when African nations self-destruct in ethnic slaughter but have refused to tolerate interethnic warfare in their own neighborhoods. For example, to let interethnic warfare in Bosnia and Kosovo go unchecked would be to tolerate conflict that could spread and engulf Europe. The deaths of hundreds of thousands of Tutsis in Rwanda, in contrast, had little or no political significance for G-8.

Each year, the leaders of the world's eight most powerful nations meet in a secluded place to make world-controlling decisions. And each year, protesters demonstrate near the site. Shown here are protesters at G-8's 2003 meeting at Evian, France.

The Most Industrialized Nations have begun to perceive connections between Africa and their own interests, however, and their actions and attitudes have begun to change. African poverty, they are realizing, can provide fertile breeding ground for terrorists. In addition, as the world's last largely untapped market, Africa could provide a huge outlet for their underutilized economic machinery. Then, too, there are Africa's huge oil reserves, which could counterbalance those of the unstable Middle East. As a result, the United States has initiated aid for AIDS and, as with Liberia, has begun to intervene in African governments.

Theories and Processes of Social Change

Social change has fascinated theorists. We shall consider just four of the many explanations of why societies change: cultural evolution, cycles, conflict theory, and the pioneering views of sociologist William Ogburn.

Cultural Evolution

Evolutionary theories of how societies change are of two types, unilinear and multilinear. *Unilinear* theories assume that all societies follow the same path. Each society evolves from simpler to more complex forms, and each goes through uniform sequences (Barnes 1935). Of the many versions of this theory, the one proposed by Lewis Morgan (1877) once dominated Western thought. Morgan said that all societies go through three stages: savagery, barbarism, and civilization. In Morgan's eyes, England, his own society, was the epitome of civilization. All others were destined to follow it.

Multilinear views of evolution replaced unilinear theories. Instead of assuming that all societies follow the same sequence, multilinear theorists proposed that different routes lead to the same stage of development. Although the path leads to industrialization, societies need not pass through the same sequence of stages on their journey (Sahlins and Service 1960; Lenski and Lenski 1987).

Central to evolutionary theories, whether unilinear or multilinear, is the assumption of *cultural progress.* Tribal societies are assumed to have a primitive form of human culture. As they evolve, they will reach a higher state—the supposedly advanced and superior form that characterizes the Western world. Growing appreciation of the rich diversity—and complexity—of tribal cultures has discredited this idea. In addition, Western culture is now in crisis (poverty, racism, discrimination, war, terrorism, alienation, sexual assaults, unsafe streets) and is no longer regarded as the apex of human culture. Consequently, the idea of cultural progress has been cast aside, and evolutionary theories have been rejected (Eder 1990; Smart 1990).

Despite the globe's vast social change, people all over the world continue to make race a fundamental distinction. Shown here is a Ukrainian being measured to see if he is really "full lipped" enough to be called a Tartar.

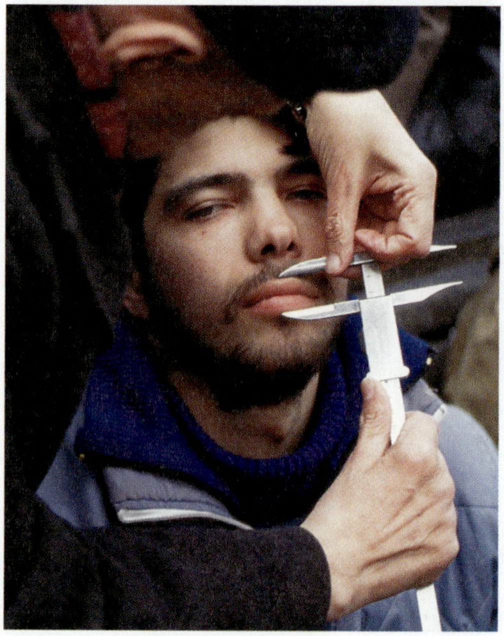

Natural Cycles

Cyclical theories attempt to account for the rise of entire civilizations. Why, for example, did Egypt, Greece, and Rome wield such power and influence, only to crest and fall into a decline? Cyclical theories assume that civilizations are like organisms: They are born, see an exuberant youth, come to maturity, then decline as they reach old age, and finally die (Hughes 1962).

Why do civilizations go through this cycle? Historian Arnold Toynbee (1946) said that each civilization faces challenges to its existence. The solutions to these challenges are not accepted by all, and oppositional forces remain. The ruling elite manages to keep these forces under control, but at a civilization's peak, when it has become an empire, the ruling elite loses its capacity to keep the masses in line "by charm rather than by force." The fabric of society is eventually ripped apart. Force may hold the empire together for hundreds of years, but the civilization is doomed.

In a book that provoked widespread controversy, *The Decline of the West* (1926–1928), Oswald Spengler, a high school teacher in Germany, proposed that Western civilization had passed its peak and was in decline. Although the West succeeded in overcoming the crises provoked by Hitler and Mussolini, as Toynbee noted, civilizations don't end in sudden collapse. Because the decline can last hundreds of years, perhaps the crisis in Western civilization mentioned earlier (poverty, rape, murder, and so on) indicates that Spengler was right, and we are now in decline. If so, it appears that China is waiting on the horizon to be the next global power and to forge a new civilization.

Figure 22.1 Marx's Model of Historical Change

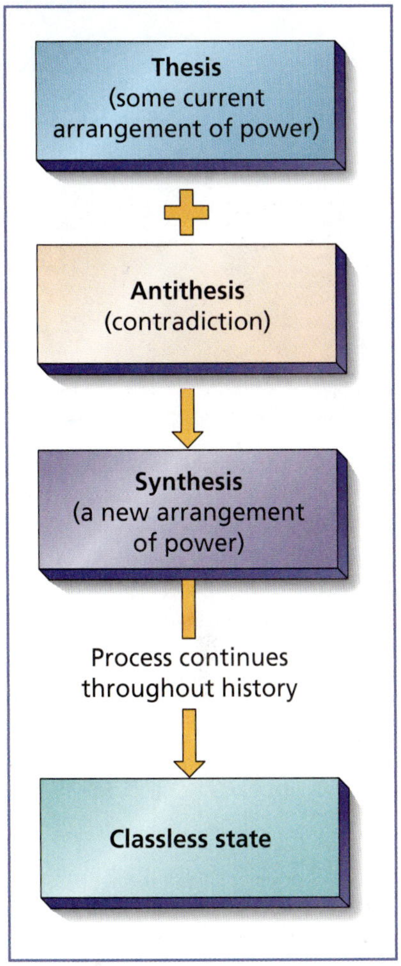

Source: By the author.

Conflict Over Power

Long before Toynbee, Karl Marx identified a recurring process in human history. He said that each *thesis* (a current arrangement of power) contains its own *antithesis* (contradiction or opposition). A struggle develops between the thesis and its antithesis, leading to a *synthesis* (a new arrangement of power). This new social order, in turn, becomes a thesis that will be challenged by its own antithesis, and so on. Figure 22.1 gives a visual summary of this process.

According to Marx's view (called a **dialectical process** of history), each ruling group sows the seeds of its own destruction. Consider capitalism. Marx said that capitalism (the thesis) is built on the exploitation of workers (an antithesis, or built-in opposition). With workers and owners on a collision course, the dialectical process will not stop until workers establish a classless state (the synthesis).

The analysis of G-8 in the previous section follows conflict theory. G-8's current division of the globe's resources and markets is a thesis. Resentment on the part of have-not nations is an antithesis. If one of the Least Industrialized Nations gains in military power, that nation will press for a redistribution of resources. China, India, Pakistan, and North Korea, with their nuclear weapons, fit this scenario. So do the efforts of al-Qaeda to change the balance of power between the Middle East and the industrialized West. Any new arrangement, or synthesis, will contain its own antitheses. These may be ethnic hostilities, or leaders feeling that their country has been denied its fair share of resources. These antitheses will haunt the arrangement of power and must at some point be resolved into a synthesis. The process repeats itself.

Ogburn's Theory

Sociologist William Ogburn (1922, 1961, 1964) proposed a view of social change that is based on technology. Technology, he said, changes society by three processes: invention, discovery, and diffusion. Let's consider each.

Invention

Ogburn defined **invention** as a combining of existing elements and materials to form new ones. We usually think of inventions as being only material, such as computers, but there also are *social inventions*. We have considered three social inventions in this text: capitalism (pages 177–178, 394–396), bureaucracy (pages 179–185), and the corporation (pages 187–195, 401–405). As we saw in these instances, social inventions can have far-reaching consequences on society and people's relationship to one another. So can material inventions, and in this chapter we will examine how the automobile and the computer have transformed society.

Discovery

Ogburn identified **discovery**, a new way of seeing reality, as a second process of change. The reality is already present, but people now see it for the first time. An example is Columbus' "discovery" of North America, which had consequences so huge that they altered the course of human history. This example also illustrates another principle: A discovery brings extensive change only when it comes at the right time. Other groups, such as the Vikings, had already "discovered" North America in the sense of learning that a new land existed—obviously no discovery to the Native Americans already living in it. Viking settlements disappeared into history, however, and Norse culture was untouched by the discovery.

dialectical process (of history) each arrangement, or thesis, contains contradictions, or antitheses, which must be resolved; the new arrangement, or synthesis, contains its own contradictions, and so on

invention the combination of existing elements and materials to form new ones; identified by William Ogburn as one of three processes of social change

discovery a new way of seeing reality; identified by William Ogburn as one of three processes of social change

Culture contact is the source of diffusion, *the spread of an invention or discovery from one area to another. Shown here are two children of the Huli tribe in Papua New Guinea. They are amused by a Polaroid photo of themselves.*

diffusion the spread of an invention or a discovery from one area to another; identified by William Ogburn as one of three processes of social change

cultural lag Ogburn's term for human behavior lagging behind technological innovations

Diffusion Ogburn stressed how **diffusion,** the spread of an invention or discovery from one area to another, can have extensive effects on people's lives. Consider a simple object such as the axe. When missionaries introduced steel axes to the Aborigines of Australia, it upset their whole society. Before this, the men controlled axe-making. They used a special stone, available only in a remote region, and they passed axe-making skills from father to son. Women had to request permission to use the axe. When steel axes became common, women also possessed them, and the men lost both status and power (Sharp 1995).

Diffusion also includes the spread of ideas. As we saw in Chapter 11, the idea of citizenship changed political structure around the world; subsequently, it removed monarchs as an unquestioned source of authority. The concept of gender equality is now circling the globe. Although taken for granted in a few parts of the world, the idea that it is wrong to withhold rights on the basis of someone's sex is revolutionary. Like citizenship, this idea is destined to transform basic human relationships and entire societies.

Cultural Lag Ogburn coined the term **cultural lag** to refer to how some elements of a culture lag behind the changes that come from invention, discovery, and diffusion. Technology, he suggested, usually changes first, with culture lagging behind. In other words, we play catch-up with changing technology, adapting our customs and ways of life to meet its needs.

Evaluation of Ogburn's Theory Some find Ogburn's analysis too one-directional, saying that it makes technology the cause of almost all social change. They point out that the way people adapt to technology is only one part of the story. The other part consists of the way people take control over technology. People develop the technology they need, and they selectively use it. Some groups, such as the Amish (see page 105), reject technologies they perceive as threatening to their culture. Other resistance to technology is discussed in the Sociology and the New Technology box on the next page.

Technology and social change actually form a two-way street: Just as technology stimulates social change, so social change stimulates technology. For example, a major social change is the growing number of elderly in our society. Their needs have spurred new medical technologies, such as those used to treat Alzheimer's disease. Another example is our changing ideas about people with disabilities, that they should not be shunted aside but should participate in the mainstream. This has triggered the development of new types of wheelchairs and prosthetic devices that allow people who cannot move their legs to play basketball, participate in the Special Olympics, and even enter rigorous downhill wheelchair races.

In fairness to Ogburn, we must note that he never said technology is the only force for social change. He did not assert that people are passive pawns in the face of overwhelming technological forces. He did stress, though, that the material culture (technology) usually changes first, and the symbolic culture (people's ideas and ways of life) follows. This direction still holds, as you can see with the many changes that are following on the heels of the development of computers.

Let's consider, then, how technology changes society.

How Technology Changes Society

As you may recall from Chapter 2, *technology* has a double meaning. It refers to both the *tools,* the items used to accomplish tasks, and the skills or procedures needed to make and use those tools. Technology refers to tools as simple as a comb and as complicated as a computer. Technology's second meaning—the

sociology and the NEW technology

From the Luddites to the Unabomber: Opposition to Technology

In the early 1800s in Great Britain, a machine was invented that could make stockings. The owners of the stocking-making factories were delighted. The workers were not. Seeing their livelihood, such as it was, jerked from beneath them, they picked up axes and hammers and smashed the machines to bits. The local police were ineffective against this uprising, and the government had to call out twelve thousand army troops to restore order. Some of the workers were executed. Others were shipped off to Australia.

One of the apprentice stocking makers who destroyed his machine was Ned Ludlum. Since this time, people who oppose new technology have been called *Luddites* (Volti 1995).

New technology always poses threats and creates fears. Because every new technology replaces some existing technology, it always threatens someone. Opposition to new technology, then, is common. Antagonism is usually directed at a specific new technology, but it sometimes becomes a protest against technology in general.

Jacques Ellul (1912–1994), a French sociologist, became upset at technological change. He warned that technology was destroying traditional values. He (1965) said that humans were becoming "a single tightly integrated and articulated component" of technology. He feared that technology would produce a monolithic world culture in which "variety is mere appearance." Ellul's message, and that of others, such as Neil Postman (1992), garnered the attention of only a few intellectuals who discussed the matter in faculty seminars and wrote obscure papers on the subject.

Ted Kaczynski after his arrest in Helena, Montana.

In the 1980s, the Unabomber sent a message that was far from subdued. His warning signals came thundering into the public's consciousness, not in the form of books and articles, but as mailed explosives that maimed and killed their unsuspecting recipients. For seventeen years, the man sent bombs to addresses in Michigan, Utah, and California.

There was no apparent message behind his seemingly random attacks. Then unexpectedly, in 1995, the Unabomber delivered a verbal message. He promised to stop his terror if his 35,000-word essay against technology were published. The *New York Times* and the *Washington Post* duly printed it. His message, in its essence, was similar to Ellul's: Technology is destroying us.

A recluse in the mountains of Montana was eventually identified as the Unabomber. Ted Kaczynski, who had an undergraduate degree from Harvard and a Ph.D. from the University of Michigan, was arrested and found guilty.

For Your CONSIDERATION

What do the Luddites, Jacques Ellul, and the Unabomber have in common? Use concepts presented in this and earlier chapters to analyze the effects of technology on society. Given your conclusions, should we fear new technologies?

skills or procedures needed to make and use tools—refers in this case not only to the procedures used to manufacture combs and computers but also to those required to "produce" an acceptable hairdo or to gain access to the Internet. Apart from its particulars, technology always refers to *artificial means of extending human abilities.*

All human groups make and use technology, but the chief characteristic of postindustrial societies (also called **postmodern societies**) is technology that greatly extends our abilities to analyze information, communicate, and travel. These *new technologies,* as they are called, allow us to do what had never been done before in history: to probe space; to

postmodern society another term for postindustrial society; a chief characteristic is the use of tools that extend human abilities to gather and analyze information, to communicate, and to travel communicate almost instantaneously anywhere on the globe; to travel greater distances faster; and to store, retrieve, and analyze vast amounts of information.

Change is rapid. Desktop computers are giving way to laptops—and some laptops are being replaced by handheld devices that contain keyboards and cameras. And this is just the beginning. In our coming bioeconomic society, we may even "wear" computers, storing data on holograms located in our own proteins (bacteriorhodopsin) (Ferraro 2001). With the many twists and turns yet to come on our journey to the future, no one knows what our life will be like, but it is infinitely challenging and enjoyable to peer over the edge of the present.

The Extent of the Transformation

Technology, as impressive as it is, actually is rather superficial. Its sociological significance is deeper—how technology changes our way of life. When a technology is introduced into a society, it forces other parts of society to give way. In fact, *new technologies can reshape society.* Let's look at four ways that technology changes social life.

Changes in Social Organization Technology changes how people organize themselves. In Chapter 6, we discussed how prior to machine technology, most workers worked alongside their families at home, but that the new power-driven machinery required them to leave their families and go to a place called a factory. In the first factories, each worker still made an entire item. Then it was discovered that workers could produce more if each person did a specialized task. One worker would hammer on a single part, or turn a certain number of bolts, and then someone else would take the item and do some other repetitive task before a third person took over, and so on. Henry Ford built on this innovation by developing the assembly line: Instead of workers moving to the parts, machines moved the parts to the workers. In addition, the parts were made interchangeable and easy to attach (Womack et al. 1991).

Changes in Ideology Technology also spurs ideology. Karl Marx noted that when workers did repetitive tasks on just a small part of a product, they did not feel connected to the finished product. No longer did they think of the product as "theirs." Workers had become *alienated* from the product of their labor. Marx stressed how **alienation** bred dissatisfaction and unrest.

In the photo on the left, Henry Ford proudly displays his 1905 car, the latest in automobile technology. As is apparent, especially, from the spokes on the car's wheels, new technology builds on existing technology. At the time this photo was taken, who could have imagined that this vehicle would transform society?

The photo on the right illustrates today's latest automobile technology. This experimental car, built at the University of Missouri at Rolla, runs by solar power.

Marx also noted that capitalists treated workers like machines and tools—just another replaceable part. Before factories came on the scene, workers owned their tools and were independent. If they didn't like something, they could pack up their hammers and saws and leave. Someone else would hire them to build a wagon or make a harness. The factory was a great contrast, for there the capitalists owned the tools and machinery. With this ownership came power, which the capitalists used to extract every ounce of sweat and blood they could. The workers had to submit, for if they left, other workers would take their place. Marx believed that this exploitation would lead to a workers' revolution—that workers would unite, violently take over the means of production, and establish a workers' state.

alienation Marx's term for workers' lack of connection to the product of their labor; caused by their being assigned repetitive tasks on a small part of a product—this leads to a sense of powerlessness and normlessness; others use the term in the general sense of not feeling a part of something

These historical events led to changes not only in behavior but also in ideology. As they built their factories, capitalists developed a new ideology: that maximizing profits was a moral—and even spiritual—endeavor. It benefited society and pleased God as well. Followers of Marx, in turn, built ideologies of socialism to attack capitalism: that profit comes only by exploiting workers and that workers are the true owner's of society's resources. As we shall see shortly, just as changes in technology stimulated the development of communism, changes in technology have been crucial in bringing about its end.

Changes in Values Just as ideology follows technology, so do values. If technology is limited to clubbing animals, then strength and cunning are valued. So are animal skins. No doubt primitive men and women who wore the skins of some especially unusual or dangerous animal walked with their heads held high—while their neighbors, wearing the same old sheepskins, looked on in envy. Today's technology, in contrast, produces an abundance of synthetic fabrics. Americans brag about cars, boats, vacations, and second homes—and make certain that their jeans and pullovers have trendy labels prominently displayed. In short, while envy and pride may be basic to human nature, the particular emphasis on materialism depends on the state of technology.

Changes in Social Relationships Technology also changes how people relate to one another. When men left home to work in factories, they grew isolated from many of the day-to-day affairs of the family. One consequence of becoming relative strangers to their wives and children was more divorce. Later changes in technology drew more women away from the home to offices and factories. This has had similar consequences—greater isolation from husbands and children, and one more impetus toward fragile marriages. A counter-trend is now in force, as applications of our new technology allow millions of workers to work at home. One consequence may be a strengthening of families.

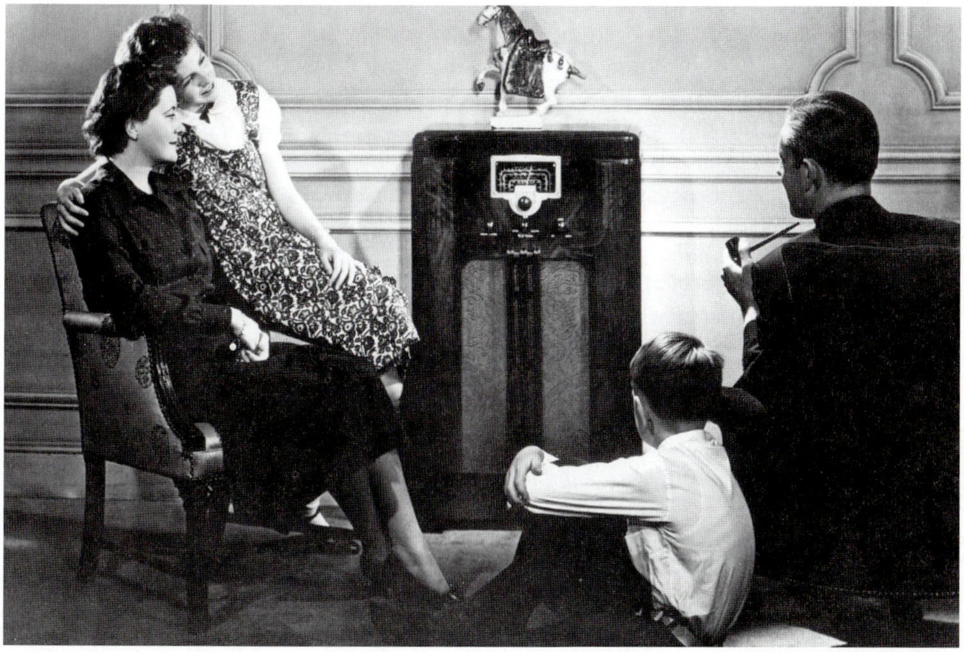

That big piece of furniture that this 1950s family is looking at is a radio. Before television became dominant, middle-class families would eat dinner together, seated at the dining room table. After dinner, they sometimes would gather in the living room to listen to their favorite programs: Jack Benny, Amos and Andy, Hopalong Cassidy, and so on. Can you see how technology is related to values and social relationships?

To get a better idea of how technology shapes our way of life, let's consider the changes ushered in by the automobile and the computer.

When Old Technology Was New: The Impact of the Automobile

If we were to pick out the new technology of 100 years ago that had the greatest impact on social life—and that continues to influence our lives today—it would be the automobile. Let's look at some of the ways in which this invention shaped U.S. society.

Displacement of Existing Technology In a process that began in earnest when Henry Ford began to mass-produce the Model T in 1908, the automobile gradually pushed aside the old technology. People found automobiles to be cleaner, safer, more reliable, and more economical than horses (Flink 1990). People even thought that cars would lower their taxes, for no longer would the public have to pay to clean up the tons of horse manure that accumulated on city streets each day. Humorous as it sounds now, they also thought that automobiles would eliminate the cities' parking problems, for an automobile took up only half as much space as a horse and buggy.

The automobile also replaced a second technology. The United States had developed a vast system of urban transit, with electric streetcar lines radiating outward from the center of the city. As the automobile became more affordable and dependable, Americans found it to be more convenient than public transportation. Instead of walking to the streetcar and waiting for it in the cold and rain, people were able to travel directly from home on their own schedules.

Effects on Cities The decline in the use of streetcars changed the shape of U.S. cities. U.S. cities had been web-shaped, for residences and businesses had located along the streetcar lines. When automobiles freed people from having to live so close to the tracks, they filled in the areas between the "webs."

The automobile also stimulated mass suburbanization. By the 1920s, Americans had begun to leave the city. They found that they could commute to work in the city from outlying areas where they enjoyed more space and lower taxes (Preston 1979). Eventually, this exodus to the suburbs reduced the cities' tax base, contributing, as discussed in Chapter 20, to many of the problems that U.S. cities experience today.

Effects on Farm Life and Villages The automobile had a profound impact on farm life and villages. Before the 1920s, most farmers were isolated from the city. Because using horses for a trip to town was slow and cumbersome, they made such trips infrequently. By the 1920s, however, the popularity and low price of the Model T made the "Saturday trip to town" a standard event. There, farmers would market products, shop, and visit with friends. This changed farm life. Mail-order catalogs stopped being the primary source of shopping, and access to better medical care and education improved (Flink 1990). Farmers also began to travel to bigger towns, where they found more variety of goods. As farmers began to use the nearby villages only for immediate needs, these flourishing centers of social and commercial life dried up.

Changes in Architecture The automobile's effects on commercial architecture are clear—from the huge parking lots that surround shopping malls to the drive-up windows at banks and fast food restaurants. Not so apparent is how the automobile altered the architecture of U.S. homes (Flink 1990). Before the car, each home had a stable in the back where the family kept its horse and buggy. As first, people parked their cars here, as it required no change in architecture. Then, in three steps, architectural change occurred. First, new homes were built with a detached garage. It was located, like the stable, at the back of the home. As the automobile became more essential to the U.S. family, the garage was incorporated into the home. It was moved from the backyard to the side of the house, and was connected by a breezeway. In the final step the breezeway was removed, and the garage was integrated into the home. This allowed people to enter their automobiles without even going outside.

Changed Courtship Customs and Sexual Norms By the 1920s, the automobile was used extensively for dating. This removed children from the watchful eye of parents and undermined parental authority. The police began to receive complaints about "night riders" who parked their cars along country lanes, "doused their lights, and indulged in orgies" (Brilliant 1964). Automobiles became so popular for courtship that by the 1960s about 40 percent of marriage proposals took place in them (Flink 1990).

In 1925 Jewett introduced cars with a foldout bed, as did Nash in 1937. The Nash version became known as "the young man's model" (Flink 1990). Since the 1970s, mobile lovemaking has declined, primarily because changed sexual norms made bedrooms more accessible.

Effects on Women's Roles The automobile may also lie at the heart of the changed role of women in U.S. society. To see how, we first need to see what a woman's life was like before the automobile. Historian James Flink (1990) described it this way:

> Until the automobile revolution, in upper-middle-class households groceries were either ordered by phone and delivered to the door or picked up by domestic servants or the husband on his way home from work. Iceboxes provided only very limited space for the storage of perishable foods, so shopping at markets within walking distance of the home was a daily chore. The garden provided vegetables and fruits in season, which were home-canned for winter consumption. Bread, cakes, cookies, and pies were home-baked. Wardrobes contained many home-sewn garments.
>
> Mother supervised the household help and worked alongside them preparing meals, washing and ironing, and housecleaning. In her spare time she mended clothes, did decorative needlework, puttered in her flower garden, and pampered a brood of children. Generally, she made few family decisions and few forays alone outside the yard. She had little knowledge of family finances and the family budget. The role of the lower-middle-class housewife differed primarily in that far less of the household work was done by hired help, so that she was less a manager of other people's work, more herself a maid-of-all-work around the house.

Because automobiles required skill rather than strength, women were able to drive as well as men. This new mobility freed women physically from the narrow confines of the home. As Flink (1990) observed, the automobile changed women "from producers of food and clothing into consumers of national-brand canned goods, prepared foods, and ready-made clothes. The automobile permitted shopping at self-serve supermarkets outside the neighborhood and in combination with the electric refrigerator made buying food a weekly rather than a daily activity." When women began to do the shopping, they gained greater control over the family budget, and as their horizons extended beyond the confines of the home, they also gained different views of life.

In short, the automobile changed women's roles at home, including their relationship with their husbands. It altered their attitudes, transformed their opportunities, and stimulated them to participate in areas of social life not connected with the home.

IN SUM

With changes this extensive, it would not be inaccurate to say that the automobile also shifted basic values and changed the way we look at life. Because they were no longer isolated, women, teenagers, and farmers began to see the world differently. So did husbands and wives, whose marital relationship had also been altered. The automobile even transformed views of courtship, sexuality, and gender relations.

No one attributes such fundamental changes solely to the automobile, of course, for many historical events, as well as many other technological changes, occurred during this same period, and each made its own contribution to social change. Even this brief overview of the social effects of the automobile, however, illustrates that technology is not merely an isolated tool but exerts a profound influence on social life.

The second candidate for bringing about the greatest social change is that technological marvel, the computer. Let's consider its impact on society.

The Cutting Edge of Change

The ominous wail seemed too close for comfort. Angela looked in her rear-view mirror and realized that the flashing lights and screaming siren might be for her. She felt confused. "I'm just on my way to Soc," she thought. "I'm not speeding or anything." After she pulled over, an angry voice over a loudspeaker ordered her out of the car.

As she got out, someone barked the command, "Back up with your hands in the air!" Bewildered, Angela stood frozen for a moment. "Put 'em up now! Right now!" She did as she was told.

The officer crouched behind his open door, his gun drawn. When Angela reached the police car—still backing up—the officer grabbed her, threw her to the ground, and handcuffed her hands behind her back. She heard words she would never forget, "You are under arrest for murder. You have the right to remain silent. Anything you say can and will be used against you in a court of law. You have the right to an attorney. If you cannot afford one, one will be provided for you."

Traces of alarm still flicker across Angela's face when she recalls her arrest. She had never even had a traffic ticket, much less been arrested for anything. Angela's nightmare was due to a "computer error." With the inversion of two numbers, her car's license number had been entered into the police database instead of the number belonging to a woman wanted for a brutal killing earlier that day.

None of us is untouched by the computer, but it is unlikely that many of us have felt its power as directly and dramatically as Angela did. For most of us, the computer's control lies quietly behind the scenes. Although the computer has intruded into our daily lives, most of us never think about it. Our grades are computerized, and our paychecks probably are as well. When we buy groceries, a computer scans our purchases and presents a printout of the name, price, and quantity of each item.

Many people rejoice over the computer's capacity to improve their quality of life. They are pleased with the higher quality of manufactured goods and the reduction of drudgery. With e-mail, we can type just one letter, and with the press of a button that letter will be delivered in seconds to everyone in our address book.

Most of us take computers for granted, but they are new to the world scene—as are their effects on our lives. This photo captures a significant change in the evolution of computers. The laptop held by the superimposed model has more *power than the room-size ENIAC of 1946.*

Some people, however, have serious reservations about our computerized society. They worry about errors that can creep into computerized records, fearing that something similar to Angela's misfortune could happen to them. For others, identity theft and privacy are the issues. Then there is the matter of political control. With terrorists and other criminals freely moving about our society, there are serious proposals to inject into our bodies a chip the size of a grain of rice ("Microchips Under . . . " 2001). The chip could store not only our name, address, age, weight, height, hair and skin color, race-ethnicity, where we went to school, our grades, and our work and medical history, but also the names and addresses of our friends and associates, even any suspected acts of disloyalty. The chips would be activated by radio, without any of us knowing that our activities were under surveillance. Such computerized techniques could allow Orwell's Big Brother to achieve total control.

At this point, let's consider how the computer is changing education, the workplace, business, and war and terrorism. We'll then consider its likely effects on social inequality.

Technology, *which drives much social change, is at the forefront of our information revolution. This revolution, based on the computer chip, allows reality to cross with fantasy, a merging that sometimes makes it difficult to tell where one ends and the other begins. This example of morphing is taken from* The Matrix Reloaded.

Computers in Education Computers have become a standard item in education, including our grade schools. Students who attend schools that have no teachers knowledgeable in foreign languages are able to take courses in Russian, German, and Spanish. Even though they have no sociology instructors, they can take courses in the sociology of gender, race, social class, or even sex, and sports. (The comma is important. It isn't sex and sports. That course isn't offered yet.).

The unequal funding we discussed in Chapter 17 is significant in this context. Schools that can afford the latest technology are able to better prepare their students for the future. That advantage, of course, goes to students who attend private schools and live in the richest public school districts. This continuing inequality in technology and education helps to perpetuate the social inequalities that arise from the chance of birth. But to gain an historical perspective, we can note that at one point in our history, some schools could not afford textbooks. It is likely that education's digital divide will also become a distant memory.

Computers will transform teaching. Now that we can transform the electrical wiring of buildings into Internet connections, each student can be connected to his or her professor—and to the world. Professors can transmit entire books directly from their office to a student, or back the other way, in *less* time than it took you to read this sentence. To help students and professors do research or prepare reports, computers search millions of pages of text. Digital textbooks will replace printed versions such as this one. As the research capacities of the Internet develop, you will be able to key in the terms *social interaction* and *gender,* select your preference of historical period, geographical area, age, and ethnic group—and the computer will spew out text, maps, moving images, and sounds. You will be able to do the same with almost any topic. You will be able to examine sexual discrimination in the military in 2000, or compare the current price of marijuana and cocaine in Los Angeles and New Orleans. If you wish, the computer will give you a test—geared to the level of difficulty you choose—so you can check your mastery of the material.

Computers in the Workplace The computer is also transforming the workplace. At the simplest level, it affects how we do our work. For example, I wrote the first two editions of this book on a computer, which commanded a printer to produce a copy of the manuscript. Even in this electronic age, a series of archaic, precomputer processes followed: I sent the printed copy via the postal service to an editor, who physically handled the manuscript and sent it to others who did the same. The manuscript, marked up in red pencil, was then returned to me, and I mailed back a corrected copy. The process was primitive, much the same as would have occurred during Benjamin Franklin's day—only without the quill and pony.

Practice finally caught up with potential. My editors and I now zap text back and forth electronically. I may be in the United States or in Spain, while they are in Oregon and

Massachusetts. It makes no difference. I print nothing, and send no papers. Although the distances are greater, the time lapse has shrunk. For me, the process is marvelous testimony of our changing world—and, perhaps, unsettling confirmation of our steady steps into a brave new world.

The computer is also bringing changes on a deeper level, for it alters social relationships. I used to take my manuscript to a university secretary, wait several days for her to type it, and then retrieve it. Now, because my editor and I correct the electronic manuscript, the secretary is bypassed entirely. In this instance, the computer enhanced social relationships, for I made fewer demands on the department secretary. It also reduced tensions, for it eliminated the necessity of the secretary making excuses when she didn't have the manuscript ready on time and I had seen her attending to personal matters instead of working.

For some, including myself, the computer has also reversed the change in work location that industrialization ushered in. As discussed earlier, due to industrialization, work shifted from home to factory and office. Several million workers now remain at home while computers and modems connect them with their bosses and fellow workers at locations around the country—or even on the other side of the globe. We could be seeing the beginning of another historical shift, one that may bring families closer together.

On the negative side are increased surveillance of workers and depersonalization. As a telephone information operator said,

> The computer knows everything. It records the minute I punch in, it knows how long I take for each call. . . . I am supposed to average under eighteen seconds per call. . . . Everything I do is reported to my supervisor on his computer, and if I've missed my numbers I get a written warning. I rarely see the guy. . . . It's intense. It's me and the computer all day. I'm telling you, at the end of the day I'm wiped out (Mander 1992:57)

Computers in Business and Finance Not long ago, the advanced technology of businesses consisted of cash registers and adding machines. Connection to the outside world was by telephone. Today, those same businesses are electronically "wired" to suppliers, salespeople, and clients around the country—and around the world. Computers record changes in inventory and set in motion the process of reordering and restocking. They produce detailed reports of sales that alert managers to changes in their customers' tastes or preferences.

National borders have become meaningless as computers instantaneously transfer billions of dollars from one country to another. No "cash" changes hands in these transactions. The money consists of digits in computer memory banks. In the same day, this digitized money can be transferred from the United States to Switzerland, from there to the Grand Cayman Islands, and then to the Isle of Mann. Its zigzag, instantaneous path leaves few traces for sleuths to follow. "Where's my share?" governments around the world are grumbling, as they consider how to control—and tax—this new technology.

Changes in War and Terrorism: The Beginning of Star Wars
Gulf War I was a prelude. Americans watched at home as guided missiles hit targets with precision. Only a handful of U.S. soldiers was lost. Then the war in Afghanistan and Gulf War II let us know that we were truly involved in a new type of warfare.

The Predator, an unmanned plane, flies thousands of feet above enemy lines. From there, it beams streaming video back to the base. At the bottom of every image it relays, sensors from the Global Positioning System report the Predator's precise location. When operators at the base see a target they want to hit, they press a button, and the Predator beams a laser onto the target. The operators then launch guided bombs, striking the precise target (Barry 2001).

Enemy ground troops don't know what hit them. They don't see the Predator, they are unaware of the laser, but, perhaps just before they are blown to bits, they do hear the sound of an incoming bomb.

There are still ground troops, but many of them have become high-tech, too. Special Forces wear goggles that let them see at night. They use lasers to measure a target's exact distance and to transmit the coordinates to the base. Again, satellite-guided weapons are launched against the target.

On its way is Warfighter I, a camera that uses hyperspectral imaging, a way of identifying objects by detecting their "light signatures." From space, it is able to distinguish between a field of oats and field of barley. It is so precise that it can report whether the fields contain natural or genetically altered oats or barley, and whether they have adequate nitrogen. And the use of this new camera? It can also pick out tanks that are camouflaged or even hiding under trees (Hitt 2001).

And yet all this is but a prelude. The U.S. Defense Department is planning to "weaponize" space. Those plans include a "microwave pill." Concerned that other nations will also launch military information devices and space weapons, the United States is set to launch microsatellites that are the size of a suitcase and weigh just 200 pounds. These satellites will be able to pull alongside an enemy satellite and, using a microwave gun, fry its electronic system. In addition, ground soldiers will be able to fire a laser, the beam will bounce off a mirror in space, and the night battlefield will become visible to soldiers who are wearing special goggles. Also on their way is a series of Star Wars-type weapons: kinetic energy rods, space-based lasers, pyrotechnic electromagnetic pulsers, holographic decoys, suppression clouds, oxygen suckers, robo-bugs—and whatever else the feverish imaginations of military planners can devise.

As a congressional commission reported, "Every medium—air, land and sea—has seen conflict. Reality indicates that space will be no different" (Hitt 2001). The space arsenal is on its way.

These technological marvels bring us a surrealistic world. We watch war and the campaign against terrorism from the comfort of our living rooms, as though the battles and bombings were a video game. It is one thing, however, to fight an enemy that uses technology from decades past, but quite another to face an enemy that possesses similar technology. If this happens, as is inevitable at some point, no longer will our technology make war seem like a bloodless game.

Cyberspace and Social Inequality

About 300 million people around the world communicate on the Internet. Servers such as America Online, CompuServe, and Prodigy allow electronic access to libraries of information. Programs sift, sort, and transmit images, sound, and video. We use e-mail to zap messages and images to people on the other side of the globe. This is the future, a world linked by almost instantaneous communications, with information readily accessible around the globe and few places that can still be called "remote."

The implications of this new technology for national and global stratification are severe. On the national level, as discussed in the box on the digital divide (page 276), this technology may perpetuate present inequalities. We could end up with information have-nots, primarily inner-city residents. On the global level, the question is: How will access to the Internet's information system differ between the citizens of the Least and Most Industrialized nations? This takes us to one of the more profound issues of this century: Will unequal access destine the Least Industrialized Nations to a perpetual pauper status? Or will their access to this new technology be their passport to affluence?

IN SUM

Technology is changing our society, our culture, and our everyday lives. While some welcome new technology, others, who have vested interests in current arrangements, resist it. Apart from the disruptions that technology brings, there are two primary issues: Will the technology that is transforming the face of war come back to haunt us? And will the new technology perpetuate or alleviate social inequalities on both the national and global levels?

The Growth Machine Versus the Earth

Of all the changes swirling around us, other than global war, those that affect the natural environment seem to hold the most serious implications for human life.

Underlying today's environmental decay is the globalization of capitalism, which I have stressed throughout this text. To maintain their dominance and increase their wealth, the Most Industrialized Nations, spurred by multinational corporations, continue to push for economic growth. At the same time, the Industrializing Nations, playing catch-up, are striving to develop their economies. Meanwhile, the Least Industrialized Nations are anxious to enter the race: Because they start from even farther behind, they have to push for even faster growth.

sustainable environment a world system that takes into account the limits of the environment, produces enough material goods for everyone's needs, and leaves a heritage of a sound environment for the next generation

corporate welfare the financial incentives (tax breaks, subsidies, and even land and stadiums) given to corporations in order to attract them to an area or induce them to remain

Many are convinced that the earth cannot withstand such an onslaught. Global economic production creates extensive pollution, and faster-paced production means faster-paced destruction of our environment. The photos below illustrate just the tip of the iceberg. In this relentless pursuit of economic development, many animal species are endangered or on the verge of extinction. If the goal is a **sustainable environment,** a world system in which we use our physical environment to meet our needs without destroying humanity's future, we cannot continue to trash the earth. In short, the ecological message is incompatible with an economic message that it is OK to rape the environment for the sake of profits.

Before looking at the social movement that has emerged about this issue, let's examine major environmental problems. We'll begin with pollution in the Most Industrialized Nations.

Environmental Problems in the Most Industrialized Nations

Sumatran Tiger
Fewer than 400, Indonesia

Texas Ocelot
Fewer than 250, southern United States, northern Mexico

Gaur
About 36,000, Southeast Asia

Mountain Bongo
About 50, Kenya

Although even tribal groups produced pollution, the frontal assault on the natural environment did not begin in earnest until nations industrialized. Industrialization was equated with progress and prosperity. For the Most Industrialized Nations, the slogan has been "Growth at any cost."

Industrial growth did come, but at a high cost to the natural environment. Today, for example, formerly pristine streams are polluted sewers, and the water supply of many cities is unfit to drink. When Los Angeles announces "smog days," schoolchildren are kept inside during recess and everyone is warned to stay indoors. Nuclear wastes, which we knew would remain lethal for thousand of years, have been stored in rusting containers (Wald 2002). We simply don't know what to do with this deadly garbage. The accumulation of industrial wastes is a special problem. Despite the danger it poses, in many cases companies simply dumped toxic wastes onto the ground. The Social Map on the next page shows how the worst hazardous waste sites are distributed throughout the United States. Most of these sites have come from corporate garbage, some of it subsidized by corporate welfare, the topic of the Down-to-Earth Sociology box on the next page.

The major polluters of the earth are the Most Industrialized Nations. Our follies include harming the ozone layer in order to have the convenience of air conditioners and aerosol spray bottles. With limited

Figure 22.2 How Does Your State Rank?

The Location of the Worst Hazardous Waste Sites

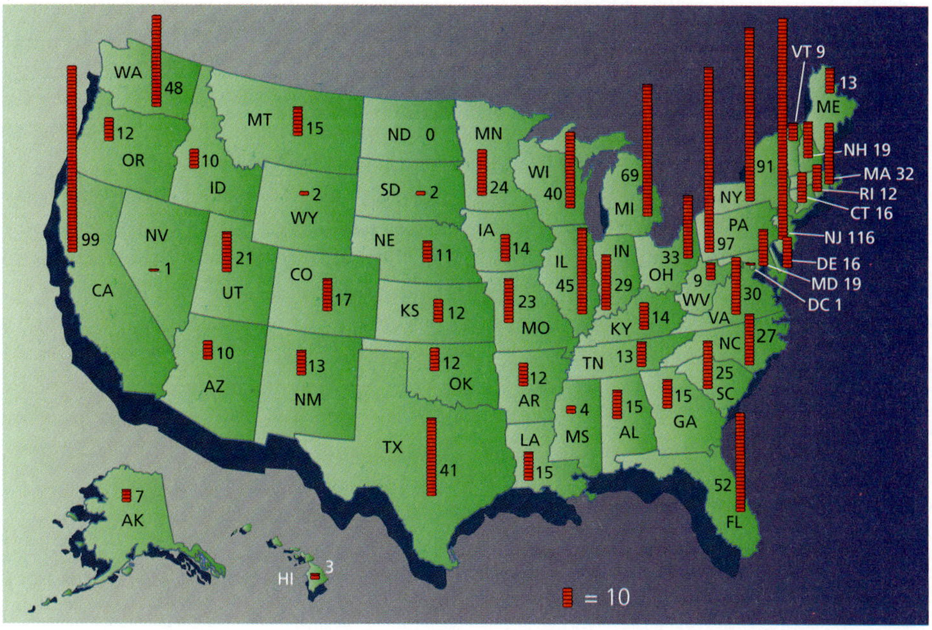

Source: By the author. Based on *Statistical Abstract* 2002:Table 357.

DOWN-TO-EARTH SOCIOLOGY

Corporations and Big Welfare Bucks: How to Get Paid to Pollute

WELFARE IS ONE OF THE MOST CONTROversial topics in the United States. It arouses the ire of many wealthy and middle-class Americans, who view the poor who collect welfare as parasites. But have you heard about *corporate welfare*?

Corporate welfare refers to handouts given to corporations. A state may reduce a company's taxes if it will locate within the state, or remain if it has threatened to leave. A state may even provide land and factories at bargain prices. The reason: jobs.

Corporate welfare even goes to companies that foul the land, water, and air. Borden Chemicals in Louisiana has buried hazardous wastes without a permit and released clouds of hazardous chemicals so thick that to protect drivers, the police have sometimes had to shut down the highway that runs near the plant. Borden even contaminated the groundwater beneath its plant, threatening the aquifer that provides drinking water for residents of Louisiana and Texas.

Borden's pollution has cost the company dearly: $3.6 million in fines, $3 million to clean up the groundwater, and $400,000 for local emergency response units. That's a hefty $7 million. But if we add corporate welfare, the company didn't make out so badly. With $15 million in reduced and cancelled property taxes, Borden has enjoyed a net gain of $8 million (Bartlett and Steele 1998). And that's not counting the savings the company racked up by not having to properly dispose of its toxic wastes in the first place.

Louisiana has added a novel twist to corporate welfare. It offers an incentive to help start-up companies. This itself isn't novel; the owners of that little "mom and pop" grocery store on your corner may have gotten some benefits when they first opened. Louisiana's twist is what it counts as a start-up operation. One of these little start-up companies is called Exxon Corp. Although Exxon opened for business about 125 years ago, it had $213 million in property taxes canceled under this start-up program. Another little company that the state figured could use a nudge to help it get started was Shell Oil Co., which had $140 million slashed from its taxes (Bartlett and Steele 1998). Then there were International Paper, Dow Chemical, Union Carbide, Boise Cascade, Georgia Pacific, and another tiny one called Procter and Gamble.

For Your Consideration

Apply the functionalist, symbolic interactionist, and conflict perspectives to corporate welfare. Which do you think provides the best explanation of corporate welfare? Why?

Figure 22.3 **Acid Rain**

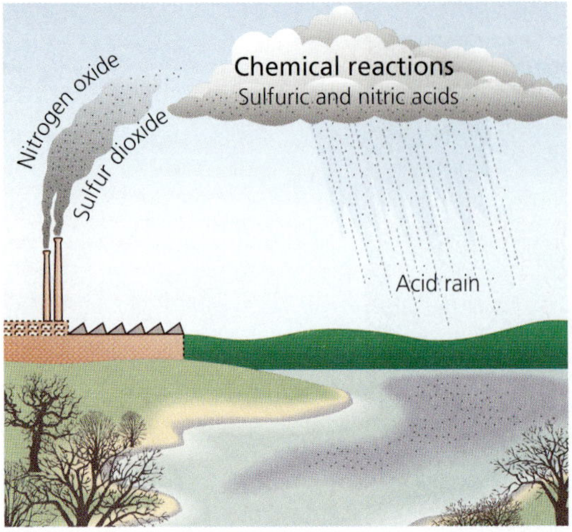

space to address this issue, I would like to focus on an overarching aspect of the pollution of our environment, the burning of fossil fuels.

Fossil Fuels and the Environment

Burning fossil fuels for factories, motorized vehicles, and power plants has been especially harmful. Fish can no longer survive in some lakes in Canada and the northeastern United States because of **acid rain:** As Figure 22.3 illustrates, the burning of fossil fuels releases sulfur dioxide and nitrogen oxide, which react with moisture in the air to become sulfuric and nitric acids (Sawyer 2001).

An invisible but infinitely more serious consequence is the **greenhouse effect.** Like the glass of a greenhouse, the gases emitted from burning fossil fuels allow sunlight to enter the earth's atmosphere freely, but inhibit the release of heat. It is as though the gases have closed the windows in the atmosphere through which our planet breathes. Scientists are increasingly convinced that we face **global warming.** They warn us that polar ice caps may melt and flood the world's shorelines, the climate boundaries may move north several hundred miles, and many animal and plant species may become extinct (Brown 2001; Parmesan and Yohe 2003). They disagree, however, on whether the warming is due to natural or human causes (McFarling 2000). In 1997, 160 nations approved an environmental treaty to reduce "greenhouse gases," but the United States, which contributes about a quarter of the world's emissions, withdrew from the treaty.

The Energy Shortage and Multinational Corporations

If you ever read about an energy shortage, you can be sure that what you read is false. There is no energy shortage, nor can there ever be. We can produce unlimited low-cost power, which can help raise the living standards of humans across the globe. The sun, for example, produces more energy than humanity could ever use. Boundless energy is also available from the tides and the winds. In some cases, we need better technology to harness these sources of energy; in others, we need only to apply the technology we already have.

Burning fossil fuels in internal combustion engines is the main source of pollution in the Most Industrialized Nations. With vast sources of alternative energy available to us, why don't we develop the technology to use them? From a conflict perspective, these abundant sources of energy present a threat to the multinational oil companies. It is in their interest to keep the gasoline-powered engine dominant. Competition is on the way, however, with the gas-electric hybrid cars that have appeared on the market. The hybrid is a bridge until cars powered by fuel cells become practical (Mateja 2001). Fuel cells convert hydrogen into electricity; water, instead of carbon monoxide, will come out of a car's exhaust pipe.

Environmental Injustice

Conflict and unequal power have led to **environmental injustice**—with minorities and the poor being the ones who suffer the most from the effects of pollution (Fitzpatrick and LaGory 2000; Hines 2001). Polluting industries locate where land is cheaper, which is *not* where the wealthy live. Nor will the rich allow factories to spew pollution near their homes. As a result, low-income communities, which are often inhabited by minorities, are exposed to more pollution. Sociologists have studied, formed, and joined *environmental justice* groups that fight to close polluting plants and block construction of polluting industries.

Environmental Problems in the Industrializing and Least Industrialized Nations

Severe consequences of industrialization, such as ozone depletion, the greenhouse effect, and global warming, cannot be laid solely at the feet of the Most Industrialized Nations. With their rush to be contenders in the global competition, along with a lack of funds to

acid rain rain containing sulfuric and nitric acids (burning fossil fuels release sulfur dioxide and nitrogen oxide that become sulfuric and nitric acids when they react with moisture in the air)

greenhouse effect the buildup of carbon dioxide in the earth's atmosphere that allows light to enter but inhibits the release of heat; believed to cause global warming

global warming an increase in the earth's temperature due to the greenhouse effect

environmental injustice refers to the pollution of our environment affecting minorities and the poor the most pay for pollution controls and few anti-pollution laws, the Industrializing Nations have made enormous contributions to this problem. The air of Mexico City, for example, is so bad that the lungs of *most* children living there have been harmed ("Study . . ." 2001).

The former Soviet Union is a special case. Until this empire broke up, pollution had been treated as a state secret. Scientists and journalists were forbidden to mention pollution in public. Even peaceful demonstrations to call attention to pollution could net participants two years in prison (Feshbach 1992). With protest stifled and no environmental protection laws, pollution was rampant: Almost half of Russia's arable land has been made unsuitable for farming, about a third of Russians live in cities where air pollution is *ten* times greater than permissible levels in the United States, and half of Russia's tap water is unfit to drink. Pollution is so severe that it may be partially responsible for the drop in the life expectancy of Russians. If so, it is a lesson that should not be lost on the rest of us as we make decisions on how to treat our environment.

With their greater poverty and swelling populations, the Least Industrialized Nations have an even greater incentive to industrialize at any cost. With these pressures, combined with almost nonexistent environmental regulations, the Least Industrialized Nations have become major sources of pollution (Fialka 2003).

Their lack of environmental protection laws has not gone unnoticed by opportunists in the Most Industrialized Nations, who export their dirty industries to these countries and produce chemicals there that their own people will no longer tolerate (Smith 1995; Mol 2001). Alarmed at the growing environmental destruction, the World Bank, the monetary arm of G-8, has pressured the Least Industrialized Nations to reduce pollution and soil erosion (Lachica 1992). When New Delhi officials tried to comply, workers blocked traffic and set fires, closing down the city for several days (Freund 2001). Understandably, the basic concern of workers is to provide food for their families first, and to worry about the environment later.

Although the rain forests cover just 7 percent of the earth's land area, they are home to *one-third to one-half* of all plant and animal species. Despite our knowledge that the rain forests are essential for humanity's welfare, we seem bent on destroying them. For the sake of timber and farms, we clear the rain forests at a rate of 2,500 acres *each hour* (McCuen 1993). In the process, we extinguish thousands of plant and animal species. Some

One strategy business leaders in the Most Industrialized Nations use to satisfy environmental laws is to move production to the Least Industrialized Nations where laws are less strict. When a tank at the Union Carbide chemical plant at Bhopal, India, ruptured in 1984, it spewed chemical death, claiming 3,800 lives. Thousands of others were permanently disabled. Union Carbide paid $3,300 for each loss of life and $800 for each permanent disability.

estimate that we destroy 10,000 species each year—about 1 *per hour* (Durning 1990). Others say that this number is conservative, that we extinguish 100 plant and animal species a day, *4* per hour (Wolfensohn and Fuller 1998). Whatever the number, as biologists remind us, once a species is lost, it is gone forever.

As the rain forests disappear, so do the Indian tribes who live in them. With their extinction goes their knowledge of the environment, the topic of the Cultural Diversity box. Like Esau who traded his birthright for a bowl of porridge, we are exchanging our future for some lumber, farms, and pastures.

CULTURAL DIVERSITY around the WORLD

The Rain Forests: Lost Tribes, Lost Knowledge

Since 1900, 90 of Brazil's 270 Indian tribes have disappeared. Other tribes have moved to villages as settlers have taken over their lands. With village life comes a loss of tribal knowledge.

Tribal groups are not just "wild" people who barely survive despite their ignorance. On the contrary, they have intricate forms of social organization and possess knowledge that has accumulated over thousands of years. The 2,500 Kayapo Indians, for example, belong to one of the Amazon's endangered tribes. The Kayapo use 250 types of wild fruit and hundreds of nut and tuber species. They cultivate thirteen types of bananas, eleven kinds of manioc (cassava), sixteen strains of sweet potato, and seventeen kinds of yams. Many of these varieties are unknown to non-Indians. The Kayapo also use thousands of medicinal plants, one of which contains a drug that is effective against intestinal parasites.

Until recently, Western scientists dismissed tribal knowledge as superstitious and worthless. Now, however, some have come to realize that to lose tribes is to lose valuable knowledge. In the Central African Republic, a man whose chest was being eaten away by an amoeboid infection lay dying because he did not respond to drugs. Out of desperation, the Roman Catholic nuns who were treating him sought the advice of a native doctor. He applied crushed termites to the open wounds. To the amazement of the nuns, the man made a remarkable recovery.

Along Sega is the headman of the Penan tribe of the Sarawak rain forests in Malaysia. With their way of life threatened, the Penan are among the last rain forest nomads in the world.

The disappearance of the rain forests means the destruction of plant species that may hold healing properties. Some of the discoveries from the rain forests have been astounding. The needles from a Himalayan tree in India contain taxol, a drug that is effective against ovarian and breast cancer. A flower from Madagascar is used in the treatment of leukemia; a frog in Peru produces a painkiller more powerful, but less addictive, than morphine (Wolfensohn and Fuller 1998).

On average, one tribe of Amazonian Indians has been lost each year for the past century—because of violence, greed for their lands, and exposure to infectious diseases against which they have little resistance. Ethnocentrism underlies much of this assault. Perhaps the extreme is represented by the cattle ranchers in Colombia who killed eighteen Cueva Indians. The cattle ranchers were perplexed when they were put on trial for murder. They asked why they should be charged with a crime, since everyone knew that the Cuevas were animals, not people. They pointed out that there was even a verb in Colombian Spanish, *cuevar*, which means "to hunt Cueva Indians." So what was their crime, they asked? The jury found them innocent because of "cultural ignorance."

Sources: Durning 1990; Gorman 1991; Linden 1991; Stipp 1992; Nabhan 1998; Simons 2004.

The Environmental Movement

Concern about environmental problems has produced a worldwide social movement. One result is *green parties,* political parties whose central issue is the environment. In some European countries, these parties are politically successful. In Germany, for example, the Green Party has won seats in the national legislature. Green parties have had little success in the United States, but in the 2000 election, a green party headed by Ralph Nader tipped the balance and gave the presidential election to George W. Bush.

Activists in the environmental movement generally seek solutions in politics, education, and legislation. Despairing that pollution continues, that the rain forests are still being cleared, and that species are becoming extinct, some activists are convinced that the planet is doomed unless immediate steps are taken. Choosing a more radical course, they use extreme tactics to try to arouse indignation among the public and thus force the government to act. Convinced that they stand for true morality, many are willing to break the law and go to jail for their actions. Such activists are featured in the following Thinking Critically section.

THINKING Critically

Ecosabotage

Chaining oneself to a giant Douglas fir slated for cutting; tearing down power lines and ripping up survey stakes; driving spikes into redwood trees, sinking whaling vessels, and torching SUVs and Hummers—are these the acts of dangerous punks who are intent on vandalizing and who have little understanding of the needs of modern society? Or are they the acts of brave men and women who are willing to put their freedom, and even their lives, on the line on behalf of the earth itself?

To understand why **ecosabotage**—actions taken to sabotage the efforts of people thought to be legally harming the environment—is taking place, consider the Medicine Tree, a 3,000-year-old redwood in the Sally Bell Grove near the northern California coast. Georgia Pacific, a lumber company, was determined to cut down the Medicine Tree, the oldest and largest of the region's redwoods, which rests on a sacred site of the Sinkyone Indians. Members of Earth First! chained themselves to the tree. After they were arrested, the sawing began. Other protesters jumped over the police-lined barricade and planted themselves in front of the axes and chain saws. A logger swung an axe and barely missed a demonstrator. At that moment, the sheriff radioed a restraining order, and the cutting stopped.

Twenty-four-year-old David Chain's dedication cost him his life. The federal government and the state of California were trying to purchase 10,000 acres of pristine redwoods for half a billion dollars. As last-minute negotiations dragged on, loggers from the Pacific Lumber Company kept felling trees, and Earth First! activists kept trying to stop them. David Chain died of a crushed skull when a felled tree struck him.

How many 3,000-year-old trees remain on this planet? Do fences and picnic tables for backyard barbecues justify cutting them down? Issues like these—as well as the slaughter of seals, the destruction of the rain forests, and the drowning of dolphins in mile-long drift nets—spawned Earth First! and other organizations devoted to preserving the environment, such as Greenpeace, Sea Shepherds, and the Ruckus Society.

"We feel like there are insane people who are consciously destroying our environment, and we are compelled to fight back," explains a member of one of the militant groups. "No compromise in defense of Mother Earth!" says another. "With famine and death approaching, we're in the early stages of World War III," adds another.

Radical environmentalists represent a broad range of activities and purposes. They are united neither on tactics nor goals. Most espouse a simpler lifestyle that will consume less energy and reduce pressure on the earth's resources. Some want to stop a specific action, such as the killing of whales. Others want to destroy all nuclear weapons and dismantle nuclear power plants. Some want everyone to become vegetarians. Still others want the earth's population to drop to one billion, roughly what it was in 1800. Some even want humans to return to hunting and gathering societies. These groups are so splintered that the founder of Earth First!, Dave Foreman, quit his own organization when it became too confrontational for his tastes.

Radical groups have had some successes. They have brought a halt to the killing of dolphins off Japan's Iki Island, achieved a ban on whaling, established

ecosabotage actions taken to sabotage the efforts of people who are thought to be legally harming the environment trash recycling programs, and saved hundreds of thousands of acres of trees, including, of course, the Medicine Tree.

For Your CONSIDERATION . . .

Should we applaud ecosaboteurs or jail them? As symbolic interactionists stress, it all depends on how you view their actions. And as conflict theorists emphasize, your view likely depends on your location in the economy. That is, if you own a lumber company you will see ecosaboteurs differently from the way a camping enthusiast will. How does your own view of ecosaboteurs depend on your life situation? What effective alternatives to ecosabotage are there for people who are convinced that we are destroying the very life support system of our planet?

Sources: Carpenter 1990; Eder 1990; Foote 1990; Parfit 1990; Reed and Benet 1990; Courtney 1995; Satchell 1998; Skow 1998; Nieves 1999; Knickerbocker 2003.

Environmental Sociology

About 1970, a subdiscipline of sociology emerged called **environmental sociology.** Its focus is the relationship between human societies and the environment (Dunlap and Catton 1979, 1983; Buttel 1987; Freudenburg and Gramling 1989; Laska 1993; Redclift and Woodgate 1997; Pfirman 2003). Its main assumptions are:

1. The physical environment should be a significant variable in sociological investigation.
2. Human beings are but one species among many that depend on the natural environment.
3. Because of feedback to nature, human actions have many unintended consequences.
4. The world is finite, so there are physical limits to economic growth.
5. Economic expansion requires increased extraction of resources from the environment.
6. Increased extraction of resources leads to ecological problems.
7. These ecological problems place restrictions on economic expansion.
8. Governments create environmental problems by encouraging the accumulation of capital.

The goal of environmental sociology is not to stop pollution or nuclear power but, rather, to study how humans (their cultures, values, and behavior) affect the physical environment and how the physical environment affects human activities. Environmental sociologists, however, generally are also environmental activists, and the Section on Environment and Technology of the American Sociological Association tries to influence governmental policies (American Sociological Association n.d.).

Technology and the Environment: The Goal of Harmony It is inevitable that humans will continue to develop new technologies. But the abuse of our environment by those technologies is not inevitable. To understate the matter, the destruction of our planet is an unwise choice.

If we are to live in a world that is worth passing on to coming generations, we must seek harmony between technology and the natural environment. This will not be easy. At one extreme are people who claim that to protect the environment we must eliminate industrialization and go back to some sort of a tribal way of life. At the other extreme are people who are blind to the harm being done to the natural environment, who want the entire world to industrialize at full speed. Somewhere, there must be a middle ground, one that recognizes not only that industrialization is here to stay but also that we *can* control it, for it is our creation. Industrialization, controlled, can enhance our quality of life; uncontrolled, it will destroy us.

It is essential, then, that we develop ways to reduce or eliminate the harm that technology does to the environment. This includes mechanisms to monitor the production, use, and disposal of technology. The question, of course, is whether we have the resolve to take the steps to preserve the environment for future generations. What is at stake is nothing less than the welfare of planet Earth. Surely that is enough to motivate us to make wise choices.

environmental sociology
a specialty within sociology where the focus is the relationship between human societies and the environment

SUMMARY and REVIEW

How Social Change Transforms Society

What major trends have transformed the course of human history?

The primary changes in human history are the four social revolutions (domestication, agriculture, industrialization, and information); the change from *Gemeinschaft* to *Gesellschaft* societies; capitalism and industrialization; **modernization;** and global stratification. Social movements indicate cutting edges of social change. Ethnic conflicts threaten the global divisions G-8 is working out. We may also be on the cutting edge of a new bioeconomy. Pp. 644–648.

Theories and Processes of Social Change

Besides technology, capitalism, modernization, and so on, what other theories of social change are there?

Evolutionary theories presuppose that societies move from the same starting point to some similar ending point. *Unilinear* theories, which assume the same evolutionary path for everyone, were replaced with *multilinear* theories, which assume that different paths lead to the same stage of development. In *cyclical* theories, civilizations are viewed as going through a process of birth, youth, maturity, decline, and death. Conflict theorists view social change as inevitable, for each *thesis* (basically an arrangement of power) contains an *antithesis* (contradictions). A new *synthesis* develops to resolve these contradictions, but it, too, contains contradictions that must be resolved, and so on. This is called a **dialectical** process. Pp. 648–649.

What is Ogburn's theory of social change?

Ogburn identified technology as the basic cause of social change, which comes through three processes: **invention, discovery,** and **diffusion.** The term **cultural lag** refers to symbolic culture lagging behind changes in technology. Pp. 649–650.

How Technology Changes Society

How does new technology affect society?

Because **technology** is an organizing force of social life, changes in technology can have profound effects. The computer was used as an extended example. It is changing the way we learn, work, do business, and fight wars. Control and access to the Internet are major issues that will determine whether this new technology helps to perpetuate or to reduce social inequalities on both a national and a global level. Pp. 650–659.

The Growth Machine Versus the Earth

What are the environmental problems of the Most Industrialized Nations?

The environmental problems of the Most Industrialized Nations range from smog and acid rain to the **greenhouse effect.** The greenhouse effect may cause **global warming** that will fundamentally affect our lives. Burning fossil fuels in internal combustion engines lies at the root of many environmental problems. It is in the interest of the oil companies to keep the internal combustion engine dominant, but alternatives are on the way. The location of factories and hazardous waste sites creates **environmental injustice** where environmental problems have a greater impact on minorities and the poor. Pp. 660–662.

What are the environmental problems of the Industrializing and Least Industrialized Nations?

The worst environmental problems are found in the former Soviet Union, a legacy of the unrestrained exploitation of resources by the Communist party. The rush of the Least Industrialized Nations to industrialize is adding to our environmental decay. The world is facing a conflict between the lust for profits through the exploitation of the earth's resources and the need to produce a **sustainable environment.** Pp. 662–664.

What is the environmental movement?

The environmental movement is an attempt to restore a healthy environment for the world's people. This global social movement takes many forms, from peaceful attempts to influence the political process to **ecosabotage.** Pp. 665–666.

What is environmental sociology?

Environmental sociology is not an attempt to change the environment, but a study of the relationship between humans and the environment. Environmental sociologists are generally also environmental activists. P. 666.

Where can I read more on this topic?

Suggested Readings for this chapter are at the back of this book.

THINKING Critically ABOUT CHAPTER 22

1. What social changes have you experienced? How have they changed your life? Does Ogburn's theory help to explain your experiences or not?
2. In what ways does technology change society?
3. Do you think that a sustainable environment should be a goal of the world's societies? Why or why not? If so, what practical steps do you think we can take to produce a sustainable environment?

ADDITIONAL RESOURCES for This Chapter

www.ablongman.com/henslin7e

- *Content Select* Research Database for Sociology, with suggested key terms and annotated references
- Link to 2000 Census, with activities
- Flashcards of key terms and concepts
- Practice Tests
- Weblinks
- Interactive Maps

Appendix: Why Major in Sociology?

As you explored social life with me in this textbook, I hope that you found yourself thinking along with me. If so, you should have gained much greater understanding of why people think, feel, and act as they do—as well as insights into why *you* view life the way you do. Developing your sociological imagination was my intention in writing this book. I have sincerely wanted to make sociology come alive for you.

Majoring in Sociology

If you feel a passion for peering beneath the surface, for seeking out the social influences in people's lives—and for seeing these influences in your own life—this is the first and best reason to major in sociology. As you take more courses in sociology, you will continue this enlightening process of social discovery. As your sociological imagination continues to grow, you will increasingly become aware of how social factors underlie human behavior.

In addition to people who have a strong desire to continue this fascinating process of social discovery, there is a second type of person whom I also urge to major in sociology. Let's suppose that you have a strong, almost unbridled sense of wanting to explore many aspects of life. Let's furthermore assume that because you have so many interests you can't make up your mind about what you want to do with your life. You can think of so many things you'd like to try, but for each one there are others things equally as compelling. Let me share what one student who read this text wrote me:

> I'd love to say what my current major is—if only I truly knew. I know that the major you choose to study in college isn't necessarily the field of work you'll be going into. I've heard enough stories of grads who get jobs in fields that are not even related to their majors to believe it to a certain extent. My only problem is that I'm not even sure what it is I want to study, or what I truly want to be in the future for that matter.
>
> The variety of choices I have left open for myself are very wide, which creates a big problem, because I know I have to narrow it down to just one, which isn't something easy at all for me. It's like I want to be the best and do the best (medical doctor), yet I also wanna do other things (such as being a paramedic, or a cop, or firefighter, or a pilot), but I also realize I've only got one life to live. So the big question is: What's it gonna be?

This note reminded me of myself. In my reply, I said:

> You sound so much like myself when I was in college. In my senior year, I was plagued with uncertainty about what would be the right course for my life. I went to a counselor and took a vocational aptitude test. I still remember the day when I went in for the test results. I expected my future to be laid out for me, and I hung on every word. But then I heard the counselor say, "Your tests show that mortician should be one of your vocational choices."
>
> Mortician! I almost fell off my chair. That was far removed from anything that I wanted. I immediately gave up on such tests.
>
> I like your list of possibilities: physician, cop, firefighter, and paramedic. In addition to these, mine included cowboy, hobo, and beach bum. One day, I was at the dry cleaners (end of my sophomore year in college), and the guy standing next to me was a cop. We talked about his job, and when I left the dry cleaners, I immediately went to the police station to get an application. I found out that I had to be 21, and I was just 20. I went back to college.
>
> I'm very happy with my choice. As a sociologist, I am able to follow my interests. I was able to become a hobo (or at least a traveler and able to experience different cultural settings). As far as being a cop, I developed and taught a course in the sociology of law.

> One of the many things I always wanted to be was an author. I almost skipped graduate school to move to Greenwich Village and become a novelist. The problem was that I was too timid, too scared of the unknown—and I had no support at all—to give it a try. My ultimate choice of sociologist has allowed me to fulfill this early dream of being an author.

It is sociology's breadth that is so satisfying to those of us who can't seem to find the limit to our interests, who can't pin ourselves down to just one thing in life. Sociology covers *all* of social life. Anything and everything that people do is part of sociology. For those of us who feel such broad, and perhaps changing interests, sociology is a perfect major.

But what if you already have a major picked out, yet you really like thinking sociologically? You can *minor* in sociology. Take sociology courses that continue to pique your sociological imagination. Then after college, continue to stimulate your sociological interests through your reading, including novels. This ongoing development of your sociological imagination will serve you well as you go through life.

But What Can You Do With a Major in Sociology?

I can just hear someone saying: "That's fine for you, since you became a sociologist. I don't want to go to graduate school, though. I just want to get my bachelor's degree and get out of college and get on with life. So, how can a bachelor's in sociology help me?"

This is a fair question. Just what can you do with a bachelor's degree in sociology?

A few years ago, in my sociology department we began to develop a concentration in applied sociology. At that time, since this would be a bachelor's degree, I explored this very question. I was surprised at the answer: *Almost anything*!

It turns out that most employers don't care what you major in. (Exceptions are some highly specific fields such as nursing, computers, and engineering.) *Most* employers, however, just want to make certain that you have completed college, and for most of them one degree is the same as another. *College provides the base on which the employer builds.*

Because you have your bachelor's degree—no matter what it is in—employers assume that you are a responsible person. This credential, employers assume, means that you have proven yourself: You were able to stick with a four-year course, you showed up for classes, listened to lectures, took notes, passed tests, and carried out whatever assignments you were given. On top of this base of presumed responsibility, employers add the specifics necessary for the performance of their particular work, whether that be in sales or service, in insurance, banking, retailing, marketing, product development, or whatever.

If you major in sociology, then, you don't have to look for a job as a sociologist. If you ever decide to go on for an advanced degree, that's fine. But such plans are not necessary. The bachelor's in sociology can be your passport to most types of work in society.

Final Note

I want to conclude by stressing the reason to major in sociology that goes far beyond how you are going to make a living. It is the sociological perspective itself, the way of thinking and understanding that sociology provides. Wherever your path in life may lead, the sociological perspective will accompany you.

You are going to live in a society that is fast-changing that, indeed, with all its conflicting crosscurrents, is going to be in turmoil. The sociological perspective, will cast a different light on life's events, allowing you to perceive them in more insightful ways. As you watch television, attend a concert, visit with a friend, listen to a boss or coworker—you will be more aware of the context that underlies such human behavior. The sociological perspective that you develop as you major in sociology will enable you to view the social change that immerses your life differently from someone who does not have your sociological background. Even events in the news will look different to you.

The final question that I want to leave you with, then, is, "If you enjoy sociology, why not major in it?"

With my best wishes for your success in life,

Glossary

achieved statuses positions that are earned, accomplished, or involve at least some effort or activity on the individual's part

acid rain rain containing sulfuric and nitric acids (burning fossil fuels release sulfur dioxide and nitrogen oxide that become sulfuric and nitric acids when they react with moisture in the air)

activity theory the view that satisfaction during old age is related to a person's amount and quality of activity

age cohort people born at roughly the same time who pass through the life course together

ageism prejudice, discrimination, and hostility directed against people because of their age; can be directed against any age group, including youth

agent provocateur someone who joins a group in order to spy on it and to sabotage it by provoking its members to commit extreme acts

agents of socialization people or groups that affect our self-concept, attitudes, behaviors, or other orientations toward life

aggregate individuals who temporarily share the same physical space but who do not see themselves as belonging together

agricultural revolution the second social revolution, based on the invention of the plow, which led to agricultural society

agricultural society a society based on large-scale agriculture, dependent on plows drawn by animals

alienation There are two primary meanings. The first is Marx's term for workers' lack of connection to the product of their labor; caused by their being assigned repetitive tasks on a small part of a product—this leads to a sense of powerlessness and normlessness. The second meaning refers to feelings of isolation, that you are not a part of something or that no one cares about you

alterative social movement a social movement that seeks to alter only some specific aspects of people

alternative medicine medical treatment other than that of standard Western medicine; often refers to practices that originate in Asia, but may also refer to taking vitamins not prescribed by a doctor

anarchy a condition of lawlessness or political disorder caused by the absence or collapse of governmental authority

animism the belief that all objects in the world have spirits, some of which are dangerous and must be outwitted

anomie Durkheim's term for a condition of society in which people become detached from the norms that usually guide their behavior

anticipatory socialization because one anticipates a future role, one learns parts of it now

anti-Semitism prejudice, discrimination, and persecution directed against Jews

apartheid the separation of racial-ethnic groups as was practiced in South Africa

applied sociology the use of sociology to solve problems—from the micro level of family relationships to the macro level of crime and pollution

ascribed statuses positions an individual either inherits at birth or receives involuntarily later in life

assimilation the process of being absorbed into the mainstream culture

authoritarian leader a leader who leads by giving orders

authoritarian personality Theodor Adorno's term for people who are prejudiced and rank high on scales of conformity, intolerance, insecurity, respect for authority, and submissiveness to superiors

authority power that people consider legitimate, as rightly exercised over them; also called *legitimate power*

back stage where people rest from their performances, discuss their presentations, and plan future performances

background assumptions deeply embedded common understandings, or basic rules, concerning our view of the world and of how people ought to act

barter the direct exchange of one item for another

basic demographic equation growth rate equals births minus deaths plus net migration

bilateral (system of descent) a system of reckoning descent that counts both the mother's and the father's side

bioeconomic society an economy that centers around the application of genetics— human genetics for medicine, and plant and animal genetics for the production of food.

blended family a family whose members were once part of other families

bonded labor, or indentured service a contractual system in which someone sells his or her body (services) for a specified period of time in an arrangement very close to slavery, except that it is voluntarily entered into

born again a term describing Christians who have undergone a life-transforming religious experience so radical that they feel they have become new persons

bourgeoisie Karl Marx's term for capitalists, those who own the means of production

bureaucracy a formal organization with a hierarchy of authority, a clear division of labor; emphasis on written rules, communications, and records; and impersonality of positions

capital punishment the death penalty

capitalism an economic system characterized by the private ownership of the means of production, the pursuit of profit, and market competition

capitalist class the wealthy who own the means of production and buy the labor of the working class

cargo cult a social movement in which South Pacific islanders destroyed their possessions in the anticipation that their ancestors would ship them new goods

caste system a form of social stratification in which one's status is determined by birth and is lifelong

category people who have similar characteristics

centrist party a political party that represents the center of political opinion

charisma literally, an extraordinary gift from God; more commonly, an outstanding, "magnetic" personality

charismatic authority authority based on an individual's outstanding traits, which attract followers

charismatic leader literally, someone to whom God has given a gift; more commonly, someone who exerts extraordinary appeal to a group of followers

charter schools schools that, although financed by taxes, are owned and run by private groups

checks and balances the separation of powers among the three branches of U.S. government—legislative, executive, and judicial—so that each is able to nullify the actions of the other two, thus preventing the domination of any single branch

church according to Durkheim, one of the three essential elements of religion—a moral community of believers (p. 513); a second definition is the type of religious organization described on page 530, a large, highly organized group with formal, sedate worship services and little emphasis on personal conversion

circular reaction Robert Park's term for a back-and-forth communication between the members of a crowd whereby a "collective impulse" is transmitted

citizenship the concept that birth (and residence) in a country impart basic rights

city a place in which a large number of people are permanently based and do not produce their own food

city-state an independent city whose power radiates outward, bringing the adjacent area under its rule

civil religion Robert Bellah's term for religion that is such an established feature of a country's life that its history and social institutions become sanctified by being associated with God

class conflict Marx's term for the struggle between capitalists and workers

class consciousness Karl Marx's term for awareness of a common identity based on one's position in the means of production

class system a form of social stratification based primarily on the possession of money or material possessions

clique a cluster of people within a larger group who choose to interact with one another; an internal faction

closed-ended questions questions that are followed by a list of possible answers to be selected by the respondent

coalition the alignment of some members of a group against others

coalition government a government in which a country's largest party aligns itself with one or more smaller parties

coercion power that people do not accept as rightly exercised over them; also called *illegitimate power*

cohabitation unmarried couples living together in a sexual relationship

collective behavior extraordinary activities carried out by groups of people; includes lynchings, rumors, panics, urban legends, and fads and fashions

collective mind Gustave LeBon's term for the tendency of people in a crowd to feel, think, and act in extraordinary ways

colonialism the process by which one nation takes over another nation, usually for the purpose of exploiting its labor and natural resources

common sense those things that "everyone knows" are true

community a place people identify with, where they sense that they belong and that others care about what happens to them

compartmentalize to separate acts from feelings or attitudes

conflict theory a theoretical framework in which society is viewed as composed of groups competing for scarce resources

conspicuous consumption Thorstein Veblen's term for a change from the Protestant ethic to an eagerness to show off wealth by the consumption of goods

continuity theory the focus of this theory is how people adjust to retirement by continuing aspects of their earlier lives

contradictory class locations Erik Wright's term for a position in the class structure that generates contradictory interests

control group the group of subjects not exposed to the independent variable

control theory the idea that two control systems—inner controls and outer controls—work against our tendencies to deviate

convergence theory the view that as capitalist and socialist economic systems each adopt features of the other, a hybrid (or mixed) economic system will emerge

corporate capitalism the domination of the economic system by giant corporations

corporate crime crimes committed by executives in order to benefit their corporation

corporate culture the orientations that characterize corporate work settings

corporate welfare the financial incentives (tax breaks, subsidies, and even land and stadiums) given to corporations in order to attract them to an area or induce them to remain

corporation the joint ownership of a business enterprise, whose liabilities and obligations are separate from those of its owners

correspondence principle the sociological principle that schools correspond to (or reflect) the social structure of their society

cosmology teachings or ideas that provide a unified picture of the world

counterculture a group whose values, beliefs, and related behaviors place its members in opposition to the broader culture

credential society the use of diplomas and degrees to determine who is eligible for jobs, even though the diploma or degree may be irrelevant to the actual work

credit card a device that allows its owner to purchase goods and to be billed later

crime the violation of norms written into law

criminal justice system the system of police, courts, and prisons set up to deal with people who are accused of having committed a crime

crude birth rate the annual number of live births per 1,000 population

crude death rate the annual number of deaths per 1,000 population

cult a new religion with few followers, whose teachings and practices put it at odds with the dominant culture and religion

culture the language, beliefs, values, norms, behaviors, and even material objects that are passed from one generation to the next

cultural diffusion the spread of cultural characteristics from one group to another

cultural goals the legitimate objectives held out to the members of a society

cultural lag Ogburn's term for human behavior lagging behind technological innovations

cultural leveling the process by which cultures become similar to one another; especially refers to the process by which U.S. culture is being exported and diffused into other nations

cultural relativism not judging a culture but trying to understand it on its own terms

cultural transmission in reference to education, the ways in which schools transmit a society's culture, especially its core values

cultural universal a value, norm, or other cultural trait that is found in every group

culture of poverty the assumption that the values and behaviors of the poor make them fundamentally different from other people, that these factors are largely responsible for their poverty, and that parents perpetuate poverty across generations by passing these characteristics to their children

culture shock the disorientation that people experience when they come in contact with a fundamentally different culture and can no longer depend on their taken-for-granted assumptions about life

currency paper money

debit card a device that allows its owner to charge purchases against his or her bank account

defensive medicine medical practices done not for the patient's benefit but in order to protect a physician from malpractice suits

deferred gratification forgoing something in the present in the hope of achieving greater gains in the future

degradation ceremony a term coined by Harold Garfinkel to describe an attempt to remake the self by stripping away an individual's self-identity and stamping a new identity in its place

dehumanization the act or process of reducing people to objects that do not deserve the treatment accorded humans

deindustrialization industries moving out of a country or region

deinstitutionalization the release of patients from mental hospitals into the community, supposedly while receiving treatment from outpatient services

democracy a system of government in which authority derives from the people; the term comes from two Greek words that translate literally as "power to the people"

democratic leader a leader who leads by trying to reach a consensus

democratic socialism a hybrid economic system in which capitalism is mixed with state ownership

demographic transition a three-stage historical process of population growth: first, high birth rates and high death rates; second, high birth rates and low death rates; and third, low birth rates and low death rates; a fourth stage has begun to appear in the Most Industrialized Nations, as depicted in Figure 20.3

demographic variables the three factors that influence population growth: fertility, mortality, and net migration

demography the study of the size, composition, growth, and distribution of human populations

denomination a "brand name" within a major religion, for example, Methodist or Baptist

dependency ratio the number of workers required to support each dependent person—those 65 and older and those 15 and under

dependent variable a factor that is changed by an independent variable

depersonalization dealing with people as though they were objects; in the case of medical care, as though patients were merely cases and diseases, not people

deposit receipts a receipt stating that a certain amount of goods is on deposit in a warehouse or bank; the receipt is used as a form of money

deviance the violation of rules or norms

dialectical process (of history) each arrangement, or thesis, contains contradictions, or antitheses, which must be resolved; the new arrangement, or synthesis, contains its own contradictions, and so on

dictatorship a form of government in which power has been seized by an individual

differential association Edwin Sutherland's term to indicate that associating with some groups results in learning an "excess of definitions" of deviance, and, by extension, in a greater likelihood that one will become deviant

diffusion the spread of an invention or a discovery from one area to another; identified by William Ogburn as one of three processes of social change

direct democracy a form of democracy in which the eligible voters meet together to discuss issues and make their decisions

disabling environment an environment that is harmful to health

discovery a new way of seeing reality; identified by William Ogburn as one of three processes of social change

discrimination an *act of unfair treatment directed against an individual or a group*

disengagement theory the view that society prevents disruption by having the elderly vacate (or disengage from) their positions of responsibility so the younger generation can step into their shoes

disinvestment the withdrawal of investments by financial institutions, which seals the fate of an urban area

divine right of kings the idea that the king's authority comes directly from God

division of labor the splitting of a group's or a society's tasks into specialties

documents in its narrow sense, written sources that provide data; in its extended sense, archival material of any sort, including photographs, movies, CD disks, and so on

domestication revolution the first social revolution, based on the domestication of plants and animals, which led to pastoral and horticultural societies

dominant group the group with the most power, greatest privileges, and highest social status

downward social mobility movement down the social class ladder

dramaturgy an approach, pioneered by Erving Goffman, in which social life is analyzed in terms of drama or the stage; also called *dramaturgical analysis*

dumping the practice of sending unprofitable patients to public hospitals

dyad the smallest possible group, consisting of two persons

e–cash digital money that is stored on computers

ecclesia a religious group so integrated into the dominant culture that it is difficult to tell where the one begins and the other leaves off; also called a *state religion*

economy a system of distribution goods and services

ecosabotage actions taken to sabotage the efforts of people who are thought to be legally harming the environment

edge city a large clustering of service facilities and residential areas near highway intersections that provides a sense of place to people who live, shop, and work there

education a formal system of teaching knowledge, values, and skills

egalitarian authority more or less equally divided between people or groups, in this instance between husband and wife

ego Freud's term for a balancing force between the id and the demands of society

electronic community individuals who regularly interact with one another on the Internet and who think of themselves as belonging together

emergent norms Ralph Turner and Lewis Killian's term for the idea that people develop new norms to cope with a new situation; used to explain crowd behavior

empty nest a married couple's domestic situation after the last child has left home

endogamy the practice of marrying within one's own group

enterprise zone the use of economic incentives in a designated area with the intention of encouraging investment there

environmental injustice refers to the pollution of our environment affecting minorities and the poor the most

environmental sociology a specialty within sociology where the focus is the relationship between human societies and the environment

epidemiology the study of disease and disability patterns in a population

estate stratification system the stratification system of medieval Europe, consisting of three groups or estates: the nobility, clergy, and commoners

ethnic cleansing a policy of population elimination, including forcible expulsion and genocide

ethnic work activities designed to discover, enhance, or maintain ethnic and racial identification

ethnicity (and ethnic) having distinctive cultural characteristics

ethnocentrism the use of one's own culture as a yardstick for judging the ways of other individuals or societies, generally leading to a negative evaluation of their values, norms, and behaviors

ethnomethodology the study of how people use background assumptions to make sense out of life

euthanasia mercy killing

evangelism an attempt to win converts

exchange mobility about the same numbers of people moving up and down the social class ladder, such that, on balance, the social class system shows little change

exogamy the practice of marrying outside one's group

experiment the use of control and experimental groups and dependent and independent variables to test causation

experimental group the group of subjects exposed to the independent variable

exponential growth curve a pattern of growth in which numbers double during approximately equal intervals, thus accelerating in the latter stages

expressive leader an individual who increases harmony and minimizes conflict in a group; also known as a socioemotional leader

extended family a nuclear family plus other relatives, such as grandparents, uncles, and aunts

face-saving behavior techniques used to salvage a performance that is going sour

fad a temporary pattern of behavior that catches people's attention

false consciousness (or false class consciousness) Karl Marx's term to refer to workers identifying with the interests of capitalists

family two or more people who consider themselves related by blood, marriage, or adoption

family of orientation the family in which a person grows up

family of procreation the family formed when a couple's first child is born

fashion a pattern of behavior that catches people's attention and lasts longer than a fad

fecundity the number of children that women are capable of bearing

fee-for-service payment to a physician to diagnose and treat a patient's medical problems

feminism the philosophy that men and women should be politically, economically, and socially equal; organized activities on behalf of this principle

(the) feminization of poverty a trend in U.S. poverty whereby most poor families are headed by women

feral children children assumed to have been raised by animals, in the wilderness, isolated from other humans

fertility rate the number of children that the average woman bears

fiat money currency issued by a government that is not backed by stored value

folkways norms that are not strictly enforced

formal organization a secondary group designed to achieve explicit objectives

front stage where performances are given

functional analysis a theoretical framework in which society is viewed as composed of various parts, each with a function that, when fulfilled, contributes to society's equilibrium; also known as functionalism and structural functionalism

functional equivalent in this context, a substitute that serves the same functions (or meets the same needs) as religion, for example, psychotherapy

functional illiterate a high school graduate who has difficulty with basic reading and math

functional requisites the major tasks that a society must fulfill if it is to survive

fundamentalism the belief that true religion is threatened by modernism and its values and that the faith as it was originally practiced should be restored

gatekeeping the process by which education opens and closes doors of opportunity; another term for the social placement function of education

Gemeinschaft a type of society in which life is intimate; a community in which everyone knows everyone else and people share a sense of togetherness

gender the behaviors and attitudes that a society considers proper for its males and females; masculinity or femininity

gender age the relative value placed on men's and women's ages

gender role the behaviors and attitudes considered appropriate because one is a female or a male

gender socialization the ways in which society sets children onto different courses in life *because* they are male or female

gender stratification males' and females' unequal access to power, prestige, and property on the basis of their sex

generalizability the extent to which the findings from one group (or sample) can be generalized or applied to other groups (or populations)

generalization a statement that goes beyond the individual case and is applied to a broader group or situation

generalized other the norms, values, attitudes, and expectations of people "in general"; the child's ability to take the role of the generalized other is a significant step in the development of a self

genetic predisposition inborn tendencies; in this context, to commit deviant acts

genocide the systematic annihilation or attempted annihilation of a people based on their presumed race or ethnic group

genomics the study of genes and how they relate to health and illness

gentrification middle class people moving into a rundown area of a city, displacing the poor as they buy and restore homes

gerontocracy a society (or some other group) run by the elderly

Gesellschaft a type of society that is dominated by impersonal relationships, individual accomplishments, and self-interest

gestures the ways in which people use their bodies to communicate with one another

glass ceiling the mostly invisible barrier that keeps women from advancing to the top levels at work

glass escalator the mostly invisible accelerators that push men into higher-level positions, more desirable work assignments, and higher salaries

global warming an increase in the earth's temperature due to the greenhouse effect

globalization the extensive interconnections among nations due to the expansion of capitalism

globalization of capitalism capitalism (investing to make profits within a rational system) becoming the globe's dominant economic system

goal displacement the adoption of new goals by an organization; also known as goal replacement

gold standard paper money backed by gold

grade inflation higher grades given for the same work; a general rise in student grades without a corresponding increase in learning

graying of America refers to the growing percentage of older people in the U.S. population

greenhouse effect the buildup of carbon dioxide in the earth's atmosphere that allows light to enter but inhibits the release of heat; believed to cause global warming

gross domestic product (GDP) the amount of goods and services produced by a nation

group people who have something in common and who believe that what they have in common is significant; also called a social group

group dynamics the ways in which individuals affect groups and the ways in which groups influence individuals

groupthink Irving Janis' term for a narrowing of thought by a group of people, leading to the perception that there is only one correct answer, in which to even suggest alternatives becomes a sign of disloyalty

growth rate the net change in a population after adding births, subtracting deaths, and either adding or subtracting net migration

hate crime crimes to which more severe penalties are attached because they are motivated by hatred (dislike, animosity) of someone's race-ethnicity, religion, sexual orientation, disability, or national origin

health a human condition measured by four components: physical, mental, social, and spiritual

health maintenance organization (HMO) a health care organization that provides medical treatment to its members for a fixed annual cost

hidden curriculum the unwritten goals of schools, such as teaching obedience to authority and conformity to cultural norms

homogamy the tendency of people with similar characteristics to marry one another

Horatio Alger myth the belief that due to limitless possibilities anyone can get ahead if he or she tries hard enough

horticultural society a society based on cultivating plants by the use of hand tools

hospice a place, or services brought into someone's home, for the purpose of bringing comfort and dignity to a dying person

household people who occupy the same housing unit

human ecology Robert Park's term for the relationship between people and their environment (such as land and structures); also known as *urban ecology*

humanizing a work setting organizing a workplace in such a way that it develops rather than impedes human potential

hunting and gathering society a human group dependent on hunting and gathering for its survival

hypothesis a statement of how variables are expected to be related to one another, often according to predictions from a theory

id Freud's term for our inborn basic drives

ideal culture the ideal values and norms of a people; the goals held out for them

ideology beliefs about the way things ought to be that justify social arrangements

illegitimate opportunity structure opportunities for crimes that are woven into the texture of life

impression management people's efforts to control the impressions that others receive of them

incest sexual relations between specified relatives, such as brothers and sisters or parents and children

incest taboo the rule that prohibits sex and marriage among designated relatives

income money received from a job, business, or assets

independent variable a factor that causes a change in another variable, called the dependent variable

individual discrimination the negative treatment of one person by another on the basis of that person's perceived characteristics

Industrial Revolution the third social revolution, occurring when machines powered by fuels replaced most animal and human power

industrial society a society based on the harnessing of machines powered by fuels

inflation an increase in prices

in-groups groups toward which one feels loyalty

institutional discrimination negative treatment of a minority group that is built into a society's institutions; also called *systemic discrimination*

institutionalized means approved ways of reaching cultural goals

instrumental leader an individual who tries to keep the group moving toward its goals; also known as a *task-oriented leader*

intergenerational mobility the change that family members make in social class from one generation to the next

interlocking directorates the same people serving on the board of directors of several companies

internal colonialism the policy of economically exploiting minority groups

interview direct questioning of respondents

interviewer bias effects that interviewers have on respondents that lead to biased answers

invasion-succession cycle the process of one group of people displacing a group whose racial-ethnic or social class characteristics differ from their own

invention the combination of existing elements and materials to form new ones; identified by William Ogburn as one of three processes of social change

the iron law of oligarchy Robert Michels' term for the tendency of formal organizations to be dominated by a small, self-perpetuating elite

labeling theory the view, developed by symbolic interactionists, that the labels people are given affect their own and others' perceptions of them, thus channeling their behavior either into deviance or into conformity

laissez-faire capitalism unrestrained manufacture and trade (literally "hands off" capitalism)

laissez-faire leaders an individual who leads by being highly permissive

language a system of symbols that can be combined in an infinite number of ways and can represent not only objects but also abstract thought

latent functions unintended beneficial consequences of people's actions

leader someone who influences other people

leadership styles ways in which people express their leadership

leisure time not taken up by work or required activities

life course the stages of our life as we go from birth to death

life expectancy the number of years that an average person at any age, including newborns can expect to live

life span the maximum length of life of a species; for humans, the longest that a human has ever lived

lobbyists people who influence legislation on behalf of their clients

looking-glass self a term coined by Charles Horton Cooley to refer to the process by which our self develops through internalizing others' reactions to us

machismo an emphasis on male strength and dominance

macro-level analysis an examination of large-scale patterns of society

macropolitics the exercise of large-scale power, the government being the most common example

macrosociology analysis of social life that focuses on broad features of society, such as social class and the relationships of groups to one another; an approach usually used by functionalists and conflict theorists

mainstreaming helping people to become part of the mainstream of society

Malthus theorem an observation by Thomas Malthus that although the food supply increases arithmetically (from 1 to 2 to 3 to 4 and so on), population grows geometrically (from 2 to 4 to 8 to 16 and so forth)

mandatory education laws laws that require all children to attend school until a specified age or until they complete a minimum grade in school

manifest functions the intended beneficial consequences of people's actions

marginal working class the most desperate members of the working class, who have few skills, little job security, and are often unemployed

market forces the law of supply and demand

market restraints laws and regulations that limit the capacity to manufacture and sell products

marriage a group's approved mating arrangements, usually marked by a ritual of some sort

mass hysteria an imagined threat that causes physical symptoms among a large number of people

mass media forms of communication, such as radio, newspapers, and television that are directed to mass audiences

mass society industrialized, highly bureaucratized, impersonal society

mass society theory an explanation for why people participate in a social movement based on the assumption that the movement offers them a sense of belonging

master status a status that cuts across the other statuses that an individual occupies

material culture the material objects that distinguish a group of people, such as their art, buildings, weapons, utensils, machines, hairstyles, clothing, and jewelry

matriarchy a society in which women as a group dominate men as a group

matrilineal (system of descent) a system of reckoning descent that counts only the mother's side

the McDonaldization of society the process by which ordinary aspects of life become rationalized and efficiency comes to rule them, including such things as food preparation

means of production the tools, factories, land, and investment capital used to produce wealth

mechanical solidarity Durkheim's term for the unity (a shared consciousness) that people feel as a result of performing the same or similar tasks

medicalization of deviance to make deviance a medical matter, a symptom of some underlying illness that needs to be treated by physicians

medicalization the transformation of something into a matter to be treated by physicians

medicine one of the major social institutions that sociologists study; a society's organized ways of dealing with sickness and injury

medium of exchange the means by which people place a value on goods and services in order to make an exchange, for example, currency, gold, and silver

megacity a city of 10 million or more residents

megalopolis an urban area consisting of at least two metropolises and their many suburbs

melting pot the view that Americans of various backgrounds would blend into a sort of ethnic stew

meritocracy a form of social stratification in which all positions are awarded on the basis of merit

metaformative social movement a social movement that has the goal to change the social order not just of a society or two, but of the entire world

metropolis a central city surrounded by smaller cities and their suburbs

metropolitan statistical area (MSA) a central city and the urbanized counties adjacent to it

micro-level analysis an examination of small-scale patterns of society

micropolitics the exercise of power in everyday life, such as deciding who is going to do the housework or control the remote

microsociology analysis of social life that focuses on social interaction; an approach usually used by symbolic interactionists

millenarian social movement a social movement based on the prophecy of coming social upheaval

milling a crowd standing or walking around as they talk excitedly about some event

minimax strategy Richard Berk's term for the efforts people make to minimize their costs and maximize their rewards

minority group people who are singled out for unequal treatment and who regard themselves as objects of collective discrimination

modernization the transformation of traditional societies into industrial societies

monarchy a form of government headed by a king or queen

money any item (from seashells to gold) that serves as a medium of exchange; today, currency is the most common form

monopoly the control of an entire industry by a single company

monotheism the belief that there is only one God

moral panic a fear that grips a large number of people that some evil threatens the well-being of society, followed by hostility, sometimes violence, toward those thought responsible

mores norms that are strictly enforced because they are thought essential to core values or the well-being of the group

multiculturalism (also called pluralism) a philosophy or political policy that permits or encourages ethnic difference

multinational corporations companies that operate across national boundaries; also called *transnational corporations*

nationalism a strong identity with a nation, accompanied by the desire for that nation to be dominant

natural sciences the intellectual and academic disciplines designed to comprehend, explain, and predict events in our natural environment

negative sanction an expression of disapproval for breaking a norm, ranging from a mild, informal reaction such as a frown to a formal reaction such as a prison sentence or an execution

neocolonialism the economic and political dominance of the Least Industrialized Nations by the Most Industrialized Nations

net migration rate the difference between the number of immigrants and emigrants per 1,000 population

networking using one's social networks for some gain

new technology the emerging technologies of an era that have a significant impact on social life

noncentrist party a political party that represents marginal ideas

nonmaterial culture (also called *symbolic culture*) a group's ways of thinking (including its beliefs, values, and other assumptions about the world) and doing (its common patterns of behavior, including language and other forms of interaction)

nonverbal interaction communication without words through gestures, use of space, silence, and so on

norms the expectations, or rules of behavior, that develop to reflect and enforce values

nuclear family a family consisting of a husband, wife, and child(ren)

objectivity total neutrality

oligarchy a form of government in which power is held by a small group of individuals; the rule of the many by the few

oligopoly the control of an entire industry by several large companies

open-ended questions questions that respondents are able to answer in their own words

operational definition the way in which a researcher measures a variable

organic solidarity Durkheim's term for the interdependence that results from the division of labor; people needing others to fulfill their jobs

out-groups groups toward which one feels antagonism

panic the condition of being so fearful that one cannot function normally, and may even flee

pan-Indianism a movement that focuses on common elements in the cultures of Native Americans in order to develop a cross-tribal self-identity and to work toward the welfare of all Native Americans

participant observation (or fieldwork) research in which the researcher participates in a research setting while observing what is happening in that setting

pastoral society a society based on the pasturing of animals

patriarchy a society or group in which men dominate women; authority is vested in males

patrilineal (system of descent) a system of reckoning descent that counts only the father's side

patterns recurring characteristics or events

peer group a group of individuals of roughly the same age who are linked by common interests

personality disorders the view that a personality disturbance of some sort causes an individual to violate social norms

Peter principle a tongue-in-cheek "law" according to which the members of an organization are promoted for good work until they reach their level of incompetence, the level at which they can no longer do good work

pluralism the diffusion of power among many interest groups that prevents any single group from gaining control of the government

pluralistic society a society made up of many different groups

police discretion the practice of the police, in the normal course of their duties, to either arrest or ticket someone for an offense or to overlook the matter

political action committee (PAC) an organization formed by one or more special-interest groups to solicit and spend funds for the purpose of influencing legislation

polyandry a form of marriage in which women have more than one husband

polygyny a form of marriage in which men have more than one wife

polytheism the belief that there are many gods

population the target group to be studied

population pyramid a graphic representation of a population, divided into age and sex

population shrinkage the process by which a country's population becomes smaller because its birth rate and immigration are too low to replace those who die and emigrate

population transfer forcing a minority group to move

positive sanction a reward or positive reaction for following norms, ranging from a smile to a prize

positivism the application of the scientific approach to the social world

postindustrial (information) society a society based on information, services, and high technology, rather than on raw materials and manufacturing

postmodern society another term for postindustrial society; a chief characteristic is the use of tools that extend human abilities to gather and analyze information, to communicate, and to travel

poverty line the official measure of poverty; calculated to include those incomes that are less than three times a low-cost food budget

power elite C. Wright Mills' term for the top people in U.S. corporations, military, and politics that make the nation's major decisions

power the ability to carry out your will, even over the resistance of others

prejudice an *attitude or prejudging, usually in a negative way*

prestige respect or regard

primary group a group characterized by intimate, long-term, face-to-face association and cooperation

proactive social movement a social movement that promotes some social change

profane Durkheim's term for common elements of everyday life

professionalization of medicine the development of medicine into a specialty in which education becomes rigorous, and in which physicians claim a theoretical understanding of illness, regulate themselves, claim to be doing a service to society (rather than just following self-interest), and take authority over clients

proletariat Marx's term for the exploited class, the mass of workers who do not own the means of production

propaganda in its broad sense, the presentation of information in the attempt to influence people; in its narrow sense, one-sided information used to try to influence people

proportional representation an electoral system in which seats in a legislature are divided according to the proportion of votes each political party receives

Protestant ethic Weber's term to describe the ideal of a self-denying, highly moral life accompanied by hard work and frugality

public in this context, a dispersed group of people relevant to a social movement; the sympathetic and hostile publics have an interest in the issues on which a social movement focuses; there is also an unaware or indifferent public

public opinion how people think about some issue

pure or basic sociology sociological research whose purpose is to make discoveries about life in human groups, not to make changes in those groups

qualitative research methods research in which the emphasis is placed on observing, describing, and interpreting people's behavior

quantitative research methods research in which the emphasis is placed on precise measurement, the use of statistics and numbers

questionnaires a list of questions

quiet revolution the fundamental changes in society that follow when vast numbers of women enter the work force

race physical characteristics that distinguish one group from another

racism prejudice and discrimination on the basis of race

random sample a sample in which everyone in the target population has the same chance of being included in the study

rapport (ruh-pour) a feeling of trust between researchers and subjects

rationality using rules, efficiency, and practical results to determine human affairs

(the) rationalization of society a widespread acceptance of rationality and social organizations that are built largely around this idea

rational-legal authority authority based on law or written rules and regulations; also called *bureaucratic authority*

reactive social movement a social movement that resists some social change

real culture the norms and values that people actually follow

recidivism rate the proportion of released convicts who are rearrested

redemptive social movement a social movement that seeks to change people totally

redlining the officers of a financial institution deciding not to make loans in a particular area

reference group Herbert Hyman's term for the groups we use as standards to evaluate ourselves

reformative social movement a social movement that seeks to change only some specific aspects of society

reincarnation in Hinduism and Buddhism, the return of the soul (or self) after death in a different form

relative deprivation theory in this context, the belief that people join social movements based on their evaluations of what they think they should have compared with what others have

reliability the extent to which research produces consistent or dependable results

religion according to Durkheim, beliefs and practices that separate the profane from the sacred and unite its adherents into a moral community

religious experience a sudden awareness of the supernatural or a feeling of coming in contact with God

replication repeating a study in order to test its findings

representative democracy a form of democracy in which voters elect representatives to govern and make decisions on their behalf

research method (or research design) one of six procedures that sociologists use to collect data: surveys, participant observation, secondary analysis, documents, experiments, and unobtrusive measures

reserve labor force the unemployed; unemployed workers are thought of as being "in reserve"—capitalists take them "out of reserve" (put them back to work) during times of high production and then lay them off (put them back in reserve) when they are no longer needed

resocialization the process of learning new norms, values, attitudes, and behaviors

resource mobilization a theory that social movements succeed or fail based on their ability to mobilize resources such as time, money, and people's skills

respondents people who respond to a survey, either in interviews or by self-administered questionnaires

revolution armed resistance designed to overthrow and replace a government

riot violent crowd behavior directed at people and property

rising expectations the sense that better conditions are soon to follow, which, if unfulfilled, increases frustration

rituals ceremonies or repetitive practices; in this context, religious observances or rites, often intended to evoke a sense of awe of the sacred

role the behaviors, obligations, and privileges attached to a status

role conflict conflicts that someone feels *between* roles because the expectations attached to one role are incompatible with the expectations of another role

role exit refers to the ending of a role, including the adjustments people make when they face not "being" what they formerly were

role extension the incorporation of additional activities into a role

role performance the ways in which someone performs a role within the limits that the role provides; showing a particular "style" or "personality"

role strain conflicts that someone feels *within* a role

romantic love feelings of erotic attraction accompanied by an idealization of the other

routinization of charisma the transfer of authority from a charismatic figure to either a traditional or a rational-legal form of authority

ruling class another term for the power elite

rumor unfounded information spread among people

sacred Durkheim's term for things set apart or forbidden, that inspire fear, awe, reverence, or deep respect

sample the individuals intended to represent the population to be studied

sanction expressions of approval or disapproval given to people for upholding or violating norms

Sapir-Whorf hypothesis Edward Sapir's and Benjamin Whorf's hypothesis that language creates ways of thinking and perceiving

scapegoat an individual or group unfairly blamed for someone else's troubles

science the application of systematic methods to obtain knowledge and the knowledge obtained by those methods

scientific method (the) using objective, systematic observations to test theories

secondary analysis the analysis of data that have been collected by other researchers

secondary group compared with a primary group, a larger, relatively temporary, more anonymous, formal, and impersonal group based on some interest or activity, whose members are likely to interact on the basis of specific roles

sect a religious group larger than a cult that still feels substantial hostility from and toward society

secular belonging to the world and its affairs

secularization of culture the process by which a culture becomes less influenced by religion

secularization of religion the replacement of a religion's spiritual or "otherworldly" concerns with concerns about "this world"

segregation the policy of keeping racial or ethnic groups apart

selective perception seeing certain features of an object or situation, but remaining blind to others

self the unique human capacity of being able to see ourselves "from the outside"; the view we internalize of how others see us

self-administered questionnaires questionnaires filled out by respondents

self-fulfilling prophecy Robert Merton's term for an originally false assertion that becomes true simply because it was predicted

serial fatherhood a pattern of parenting in which a father, after divorce, reduces contact with his own children, serves as a father to the children of the woman he marries or lives with, then ignores these children, too, after moving in with or marrying another woman

sex biological characteristics that distinguish females and males, consisting of primary and secondary sex characteristics

sexual harassment the abuse of one's position of authority to force unwanted sexual demands on someone

shaman the healing specialist of tribal groups who attempts to control the spirits thought to cause a disease or injury; commonly called a witch doctor

sick role a social role that excuses people from normal obligations because they are sick or injured, while at the same time expecting them to seek competent help and cooperate in getting well

significant other an individual who significantly influences someone else's life

sign-vehicles the term used by Goffman to refer to how people use social setting, appearance, and manner to communicate information about the self

slavery a form of social stratification in which some people own other people

small group a group small enough for everyone to interact directly with all the other members

social class according to Weber, a large group of people who rank close to one another in wealth, power, and prestige; according to Marx, one of two groups: capitalists who own the means of production or workers who sell their labor

social cohesion the degree to which members of a group or a society feel united by shared values and other social bonds

social construction of reality the use of background assumptions and life experiences to define what is real

social control a group's formal and informal means of enforcing its norms

social environment the entire human environment, including direct contact with others

social facts Durkheim's term for a group's patterns of behavior

social inequality a social condition in which privileges and obligations are given to some but denied to others

social institution the organized, usual, or standard ways by which society meets its basic needs

social integration the degree to which people feel a part of social groups

social interaction what people do when they are in one another's presence

social location the group memberships that people have because of their location in history and society

social mobility movement up or down the social class ladder

social movement a large group of people who are organized to promote or resist some social change

social movement organization an organization people develop to further the goals of a social movement

social network the social ties radiating outward from the self that link people together

social order a group's usual and customary social arrangements, on which its members depend and on which they base their lives

social placement a function of education—funneling people into a society's various positions

social promotion passing students on to the next grade even though they have not mastered basic materials

social sciences the intellectual and academic disciplines designed to understand the social world objectively by means of controlled and repeated observations

social stratification the division of large numbers of people into layers according to their relative power, property, and prestige; applies to both nations and to people within a nation, society, or other group

social structure the framework that surrounds us, consisting of the relationships of people and groups to one another, which give direction to and set limits on behavior

socialism an economic system characterized by the public ownership of the means of production, central planning, and the distribution of goods without a profit motive

socialization the process by which people learn the characteristics of their group—the knowledge, skills, attitudes, values, and actions thought appropriate for them

society people who share a culture and a territory

sociobiology a framework of thought that views human behavior as the result of natural selection and considers biological factors to be the fundamental cause of human behavior

sociological perspective understanding human behavior by placing it within its broader social context

sociology the scientific study of society and human behavior

special-interest group a group of people who support a particular issue and who can be mobilized for political action

spirit of capitalism Weber's term for the desire to accumulate capital as a duty—not to spend it, but as an end in itself—and to constantly reinvest it

split labor market workers split along racial, ethnic, gender, age, or any other lines; this split is exploited by owners to weaken the bargaining power of workers

state a political entity that claims monopoly on the use of violence in some particular territory; commonly known as a country

state religion a government-sponsored religion; also called *ecclesia*

status consistency ranking high or low on all three dimensions of social class

status social ranking; the position that someone occupies in society or a social group

status inconsistency ranking high on some dimensions of social class and low on others

status set all the statuses or positions that an individual occupies

status symbols items used to identify a status

stereotype assumptions of what people are like, whether true or false

stigma "blemishes" that discredit a person's claim to a "normal" identity

stockholders' revolt the refusal of a corporation's stockholders to rubber-stamp decisions made by its managers

stored value the goods that are stored and held in reserve that back up (or provide the value for) a currency

strain theory Robert Merton's term for the strain engendered when a society socializes large numbers of people to desire a cultural goal (such as success) but withholds from many the approved means to reach that goal; one adaptation to the strain is crime, the choice of an innovative means (one outside the approved system) to attain the cultural goal

stratified random sample a sample of specific subgroups of the target population and in which everyone in the subgroups has an equal chance of being included in the study

street crime crimes such as mugging, rape, and burglary

structural mobility movement up or down the social class ladder that is due to changes in the structure of society, not to individual efforts

structured interviews interviews that use closed-ended questions

subculture the values and related behaviors of a group that distinguish its members from the larger culture; a world within a world

subjective meanings the meanings that people give their own behavior

subsistence economy a type of economy in which human groups live off the land and have little or no surplus

suburb a community adjacent to a city

suburbanization the movement from the city to the suburbs

superego Freud's term for the conscience, the internalized norms and values of our social groups

survey the collection of data by having people answer a series of questions

sustainable environment a world system that takes into account the limits of the environment, produces enough material goods for everyone's needs, and leaves a heritage of a sound environment for the next generation

symbol something to which people attach meanings and then use to communicate with others

symbolic culture another term for nonmaterial culture

symbolic interactionism a theoretical perspective in which society is viewed as composed of symbols that people use to establish meaning, develop their views of the world, and communicate with one another

system of descent how kinship is traced over the generations

taboo a norm so strong that it often brings revulsion if violated

taking the role of the other putting oneself in someone else's shoes; understanding how someone else feels and thinks and thus anticipating how that person will act

teamwork the collaboration of two or more people to manage impressions jointly

techniques of neutralization ways of thinking or rationalizing that help people deflect (or neutralize) society's norms

technology in its narrow sense, tools; its broader sense includes the skills or procedures necessary to make and use those tools

theory a general statement about how some parts of the world fit together and how they work; an explanation of how two or more facts are related to one another

Thomas theorem William I. and Dorothy S. Thomas' classic formulation of the definition of the situation: "If people define situations as real, they are real in their consequences."

total institution a place in which people are cut off from the rest of society and are almost totally controlled by the officials who run the place

totalitarianism a form of government that exerts almost total control over people

tracking the sorting of students into different educational programs on the basis of real or perceived abilities

traditional authority authority based on custom

traditional orientation the idea that the past is the best guide for the present; characteristic of tribal, peasant, and feudal societies

transformative social movement a social movement that seeks to change society totally

transnational social movement a social movement whose emphasis is on some condition around the world, instead of on a condition in a specific country; also known as *new social movements*

triad a group of three people

two-tier system of medical care a system of medical care in which the wealthy receive superior medical care and the poor inferior medical care

underclass a group of people for whom poverty persists year after year and across generations

underemployment the condition of having to work at a job beneath one's level of training and abilities, or of being able to find only part-time work

underground economy exchanges of goods and services that are not reported to the government and thereby escape taxation

universal citizenship the idea that everyone has the same basic rights by virtue of being born in a country (or by immigrating and becoming a naturalized citizen)

unobtrusive measures ways of observing people who do not know they are being studied

unstructured interviews interviews that use open-ended questions

upward social mobility movement up the social class ladder

urban legend a story with an ironic twist that sounds realistic but is false

urban renewal the rehabilitation of a rundown area, which usually results in the displacement of the poor who are living in that area

urbanization the process by which an increasing proportion of a population lives in cities

validity the extent to which an operational definition measures what it was intended to measure

value cluster values that fit together form a larger whole

value contradiction values that contradict one another; to follow the one means to come into conflict with the other

value free the view that a sociologist's personal values or biases should not influence social research

values the standards by which people define what is desirable or undesirable, good or bad, beautiful or ugly

variable a factor thought to be significant for human behavior, which varies from one case to another

Verstehen a German word used by Weber that is perhaps best understood as "to have insight into someone's situation"

voluntary association a group made up of people who voluntarily organize on the basis of some mutual interest; also known as voluntary memberships

voter apathy indifference and inaction on the part of individuals or groups with respect to the political process

war armed conflict between nations or politically distinct groups

WASP White Anglo-Saxon Protestant; narrowly, an American of English descent; broadly, an American of western European ancestry

wealth property and income

welfare (or state) capitalism an economic system in which individuals own the means of production but the state regulates many economic activities for the welfare of the population

white ethnics white immigrants to the United States whose cultures differ from that of WASPs

white-collar crime Edwin Sutherland's term for crimes committed by people of respectable and high social status in the course of their occupations; for example, bribery of public officials, securities violations, embezzlement, false advertising, and price fixing

working class those people who sell their labor to the capitalist class

world system theory economic and political connections that tie the world's countries together

zero population growth a demographic condition in which women bear only enough children to reproduce the population

Suggested Readings

CHAPTER 1 The Sociological Perspective

Bartos, Otomar J., and Paul Wehr. *Using Conflict Theory.* New York: Cambridge University Press, 2002. In this application of the conflict perspective, the author's primary concerns are the causes of social conflicts and how to manage or resolve conflict.

Berger, Peter L. *Invitation to Sociology: A Humanistic Perspective.* New York: Doubleday, 1972. This is a delightful analysis of how sociology applies to everyday life.

Best, Joel. *Damned Lies and Statistics: Untangling Numbers from the Media, Politicians, and Activists.* Berkeley: University of California Press, 2001. The author shows how special-interest groups manipulate and misrepresent statistics in order to promote their agendas.

Charon, Joel M. *Symbolic Interactionism: An Introduction, an Interpretation, an Integration,* 7th ed. Englewood Cliffs, N.J.: Prentice Hall, 2003. The author lays out the main points of symbolic interactionism, providing an understanding of why this perspective is important in sociology.

Henslin, James M., ed. *Down to Earth Sociology: Introductory Readings,* 12th ed. New York: Free Press, 2003. This collection of readings about everyday life and social structure is designed to broaden the reader's understanding of society, and of the individual's place within it.

Mills, C. Wright. *The Sociological Imagination.* New York: Oxford University Press, 2000. First published in 1960, this classic work provides an overview of sociology from the framework of the conflict perspective.

Ritzer, George. *Classic Sociological Theory,* 3rd ed. New York: McGraw-Hill, 2004. To help understand the personal and historical context of how theory develops, the author includes biographical sketches of the theorists.

Ruane, Janet M., and Karen A. Cerulo. *Second Thoughts: Seeing Conventional Wisdom Through the Sociological Eye,* 2nd ed. Thousand Oaks, Calif.: Pine Forge Press, 2000. If you want to see how enjoyable sociology can be—and have a few common stereotypes and myths exploded at the same time—read this book.

Steele, Stephen F., and Jammie Price. *Applied Sociology: Topics, Terms, Tools, and Tasks.* Belmont, Calif.: Wadsworth, 2003. This overview of applied sociology illustrates the wide variety of areas in which sociology is being applied.

Journals

Applied Behavioral Science Review, Clinical Sociology Review, International Clinical Sociology, Journal of Applied Sociology, The Practicing Sociologist, Sociological Practice: A Journal of Clinical and Applied Sociology, and *Sociological Practice Review* report the experiences of sociologists who work in applied settings, from peer group counseling and suicide prevention to recommending changes to school boards.

Contexts, published by the American Sociological Association, uses a magazine format to present sociological research in a down-to-earth fashion.

Humanity & Society, the official journal of the Association for Humanist Sociology, publishes articles intended "to advance the quality of life of the world's people."

Electronic Journals

Electronic Journal of Sociology (http://www.sociology.org) and *Sociological Research Online* (http://www.socresonline.org.uk) publish articles on various sociological topics. Access is free.

About a Career in Sociology

What can you do with sociology? You like the subject and would like to major in it, but. . . . The American Sociological Association (ASA) offers three pamphlets free of charge. You can obtain them by contacting the ASA: 1307 New York Avenue NW, Suite 700, Washington, D.C. 20005-4701. Tel. (202) 383-9005. Fax (202) 638-0882. E-mail: Executive.Office@asanet.org

The pamphlets are *Careers in Sociology, Majoring in Sociology: A Guide for Students,* and *The Sociology Major as Preparation for Careers in Business and Organizations.*

The ASA also sells the next three brochures.

Ferris, Abbott L. *How to Join the Federal Workforce and Advance Your Sociological Career.* American Sociological Association. This pamphlet gives tips on how to find employment in the federal government, including information on how to prepare a job application.

Huber, Bettina J. *Embarking Upon a Career in Sociology with an Undergraduate Sociology Major.* American Sociological Association. Designed for undergraduate sociology majors who are seeking employment, this brochure discusses how to identify interests and skills, pinpoint suitable jobs, prepare a resumé, and survive an employment interview.

Miller, Delbert C. *The Sociology Major as Preparation for Careers in Business.* American Sociological Association. What careers can a sociology major pursue in business or industry? This brochure includes sections on job prospects, graduate education, and how to practice sociology in business careers.

Stephens, W. Richard, Jr. *Careers in Sociology,* 4th ed. Boston: Pearson Education, 2004. How can you make a living with a major in sociology? The author explores careers in sociology, from business and government to health care and the law.

CHAPTER 2 Culture

Berger, Arthur Asa. *Video Games: A Popular Culture Phenomenon.* New Brunswick, N.J.: Transaction Publishers, 2002. An analysis of sociological implications of this form of play.

Berger, Peter L., and Samuel P. Huntington, eds. *Many Globalizations: Cultural Diversity in the Contemporary World.* New York: Oxford University Press, 2002. One of the recurring themes of this book is how globalization is changing cultures.

Chagnon, Napoleon A. *Yanomamo: The Fierce People,* 5th ed. New York: Harcourt, Brace, Jovanovich, 1997. This fascinating account of a tribal people whose customs are extraordinarily different from ours will help you to see how arbitrary the choices are that underlie human culture.

Cohen, Mark Nathan. *Culture of Intolerance: Chauvinism, Class, and Racism in the United States.* New Haven: Yale University Press, 2000. The author analyzes how ideas of race, intelligence, and competence permeate U.S. culture.

Cross, Gary S. *An All-Consuming Century: Why Commercialism Won in Modern America.* New York: Columbia University Press, 2001. An analysis of how consumerism (the desire and drive to consume material goods) came about and reshaped U.S. culture.

Edgerton, Robert B. *Sick Societies: Challenging the Myth of Primitive Harmony.* New York: Free Press, 1993. The author's thesis is that cultural relativism is misinformed, that we have the obligation to judge cultures that harm its members as inferior to those that do not.

Lieberson, Stanley. *A Matter of Taste: How Names, Fashions, and Culture Change.* New Haven: Yale University Press, 2000. It is difficult to imagine a more thorough analysis of how patterns change in the naming of children.

Smith, Shawn Michelle. *American Archives: Gender, Race, and Class in Visual Culture.* Princeton, N.J.: Princeton University Press, 2000. The photos in this book show how gender, race, and class have been portrayed in U.S. history and how these portrayals have helped to maintain white dominance.

Stinson, Kandi M. *Women and Dieting Culture: Inside a Commercial Weight Loss Group.* New Brunswick: Rutgers University Press, 2001. Through participant observation, the author provides an insider's perspective on women and dieting.

Sullivan, Nikki. *Tattooed Bodies: Subjectivity, Textuality, Ethics, and Pleasure.* Westport, Conn.: Praeger, 2001. A sociological analysis of this very old and very new custom.

Zellner, William W. *Countercultures: A Sociological Analysis.* New York: St. Martin's Press, 1995. The author's analysis of skinheads, the Ku Klux Klan, survivalists, satanists, the Church of Scientology, and the Unification Church (Moonies) helps us understand why people join countercultures.

CHAPTER 3 Socialization

Ariès, Philippe. *Centuries of Childhood: A Social History of Family Life.* New York: Vintage Books, 1972. The author analyzes how childhood in Europe during the Middle Ages differs from childhood today.

Blumer, Herbert. *George Herbert Mead and Human Conduct.* Lanham, Md.: AltaMira Press, 2004. An overview of symbolic interactionism by a sociologist who studied and taught Mead's thought all of his life.

Cohen, Mark. *Lara Croft: The Art of Virtual Seduction.* New York: Prime Publishing, 2000. Interviews with the creators of Lara Croft and her programmers provide insight into Lara's popularity and the "cult" phenomenon centering on this virtual person.

Duncan, Greg J., and Jeanne Brooks-Gunn, eds. *Consequences of Growing Up Poor.* New York: Russell Sage, 2000. Examines how neighborhoods and families influence children's intellectual development and adolescent behavior.

Messner, Steven F., and Richard Rosenfeld. *Crime and the American Dream,* 3rd ed. Belmont, Calif.: Wadsworth, 2001. Explains how the "American Dream" produces a strong desire to make money but fails to instill adequate desires to play by the rules.

Rymer, Russ. *Genie: A Scientific Tragedy.* New York: HarperPerennial Library, 1994. This moving account of Genie includes the battles to oversee Genie among linguists, psychologists, and social workers, all of whom claimed to have Genie's best interests at heart.

Sociological Studies of Child Development: A Research Annual. Greenwich, Conn.: JAI Press, published annually. Along with theoretical articles, this publication reports on sociological research on the socialization of children.

Van Hoorn, Judith, Elzbieta Suchar, Akos Komlosi, and Doreen A. Samuelson, eds. *Adolescent Development and Rapid Social Change: Perspectives from Eastern Europe.* Albany: State University of New York Press, 2000. Based on the premise that when society changes, we change, this book examines the effects of social change on adolescents in eastern Europe.

Walters, Glenn D. *Criminal Belief Systems: An Integrated-Interactive Theory of Lifestyles.* Westport, Conn.: Greenwood Publishing Group, 2003. The author analyzes how five belief systems (self-view, world-view, past-view, present-view, future-view) explain crime initiation and maintenance.

CHAPTER 4 Social Structure and Social Interaction

Goffman, Erving. *The Presentation of Self in Everyday Life.* New York: Peter Smith, Publisher, 1999. First published in 1959. This classic statement of dramaturgical analysis provides a different way of looking at everyday life. As a student, this was one of the best books I read.

Helmreich, William B. *The Things They Say Behind Your Back: Stereotypes and the Myths Behind Them.* New Brunswick, N.J.: Transaction Books, 1984. Sprinkled with anecdotes and jokes, yet sensitively written, the book explores the historical roots of stereotypes. The author also illustrates how stereotypes help produce behaviors that reinforce the stereotypes.

Lennon, Sharron J., and Kim K. Johnson, eds. *Appearance and Power.* Oxford, England: Berg Publishers, Ltd., 2000. The authors of these articles analyze how significant appearance, especially clothing, is for what happens to us in social life.

Schmidt, Kimberly D., Diane Zimmerman Umble, and Steven D. Reschly, eds. *Strangers at Home: Amish and Mennonite Women in History.* Baltimore: Johns Hopkins University Press, 2002. The accounts of life in this group provide a window onto history and insight into how social structure influences social interaction.

Sobal, Jeffery, and Donna Maurer, eds. *Interpreting Weight: The Social Management of Fatness and Thinness.* New York: Aldine de Gruyter, 1999. The authors of these articles examine the strategies people use to give meaning to their weight, including how they interpret fatness and thinness and how they become involved in weight-related organizations.

Tönnies, Ferdinand. *Community and Society (Gemeinschaft und Gesellschaft).* New York: Dover Publications, 2003. Originally published in 1887, this classic work, focusing on social change, provides insight into how society influences personality. Rather challenging reading.

Vinitzky-Seroussi, Vered. *After Pomp and Circumstance: High School Reunions as an Autobiographical Occasion.* Chicago: University of Chicago Press, 1998. In this analysis of high school reunions, the author examines the relationships between the self and the past and future.

Whyte, William Foote. *Street Corner Society: The Social Structure of an Italian Slum,* 4th ed. Chicago: University of Chicago Press, 1993. Originally published in 1943. The author's analysis of interaction in a U.S. Italian slum demonstrates how social structure affects personal relationships.

Journals

Qualitative Sociology, Symbolic Interaction, and *Urban Life* feature articles on symbolic interactionism and analyses of everyday life.

CHAPTER 5 How Sociologists Do Research

Creswell, John W. *Research Design: Qualitative, Quantitative, and Mixed Methods Approaches.* Beverly Hills, Calif.: Sage, 2003. This introduction to research methods walks you through the research experience and helps you understand when to use a particular method.

Gosselin, Denise Kindschi. *Heavy Hands: An Introduction to the Crimes of Family Violence,* 2nd ed. Upper Saddle River, N.J.: Prentice Hall, 2003. Explores causes, consequences, and prevalence of domestic violence, with an additional emphasis on law enforcement.

Kelley, D. Lynn. *Measurement Made Accessible: A Research Approach Using Qualitative, Quantitative, and Quality Improvement Methods.* Lanham, Md.: AltaMira Press, 2000. In this analysis of both quantitative and qualitative methods for gathering data, the author explains how to develop questionnaires and improve reliability and validity.

Lee, Raymond M. *Unobtrusive Methods in Social Research.* Philadelphia: Open University Press, 2000. This overview of unobtrusive ways of doing social research summarizes many interesting studies.

May, Tim. *Social Research: Issues, Methods, and Process.* Philadelphia: Open University Press, 2001. An introduction to the ways sociologists do research.

Neuman, W. Lawrence. *Social Research Methods: Qualitative and Quantitative Approaches,* 5th ed. Boston: Allyn and Bacon, 2003. This "how-to" book of sociological research describes how sociologists gather data and the logic that underlies each method.

Scully, Diana. *Understanding Sexual Violence: A Study of Convicted Rapists.* New York: Routledge, 1994. The author examines how rapists rationalize their acts, helping us to understand why some men rape.

Whyte, William Foote. *Creative Problem Solving in the Field: Reflections on a Career.* Lanham, Md.: AltaMira Press, 1997. Focusing on his extensive field experiences, the author provides insight into the researcher's role in participant observation.

Wysocki Diane Kholos, ed. *Readings in Social Research Methods,* 2nd ed. Belmont, Calif.: Wadsworth, 2004. These articles provide an excellent overview of research methods.

Writing Papers for Sociology

Richlin-Klonsky, Judith, and Ellen Strenski, eds. The Sociology Writing Group. *A Guide to Writing Sociology Papers,* 5th ed. New York: St. Martin's Press, 2001. The guide walks students through the steps in writing a sociology paper, from choosing the initial assignment to doing the research and turning in a finished paper. Also explains how to manage time and correctly cite sources.

Cuba, Lee J. *A Short Guide to Writing about Social Science,* 4th ed. Boston: Pearson Longman, 2002. The author summarizes the types of social science literature, presents guidelines on how to organize and write a research paper, and explains how to prepare an oral presentation.

CHAPTER 6 Societies to Social Networks

Fleisher, Mark S. *Beggars and Thieves: Lives of Urban Street Criminals.* Madison: University of Wisconsin Press, 1996. Based on years of participant observation, the author presents an inside view of thieves, gangs, addicts, and lifelong criminals.

Forschi, Martha, and Edward J. Lawler, eds. *Group Processes: Sociological Analysis.* New York: Nelson-Hall, 1994. How do your associates, friends, family—and even strangers—influence you? Among other topics, the authors of these articles explore such influences.

Homans, George C. *The Human Group.* New Brunswick, N.J.: Transaction Publishers, 2001. First published in 1950. In this classic work, Homans develops the idea that all human groups share common activities, interactions, and sentiments.

Hughes, Richard L., Robert C. Ginnett, and Gordon J. Curphy. *Leadership: Enhancing the Lessons of Experience,* 4th ed. New York: McGraw-Hill, 2002. Based on both empirical studies and anecdotes, the authors focus on what makes effective leaders.

Janis, Irving L. *Groupthink: Psychological Studies of Policy Decisions and Fiascoes,* 2nd ed. New York: Houghton Mifflin, 1982. Janis analyzes how groups can become cut off from alternatives, interpret evidence in light of their preconceptions, and embark on courses of action that they should have seen as obviously incorrect.

Stewart, Greg L., Charles C. Manz, and Henry P. Sims. *Team Work and Group Dynamics.* New York: John Wiley, 2000. Based on theoretical research and case studies, the authors try to pinpoint how to work effectively in groups.

Wilson, Gerald L. *Groups in Context: Leadership and Participation in Small Groups,* 6th ed. New York: McGraw-Hill, 2001. An overview of principles and processes of interaction in small groups, with an emphasis on how to exercise leadership.

CHAPTER 7 Bureaucracy and Formal Organizations

Altheide, David L. *Creating Fear: News and the Construction of Crisis.* New York: Aldine de Gruyter, 2002. The author analyzes how the news media not only report but also create reality.

Brown, Rupert. *Group Processes: Dynamics Within and Between Groups.* Boston: Blackwell, 2000. Among the group dynamics analyzed here is how groups are a primary source of our identity.

Cyr, Donald. *The Art of Global Thinking: Integrating Organizational Philosophies of East and West.* West Lafayette, In: Ichor Business Books, 2002. The author compares Western and Eastern organizations and their underlying philosophies and suggests ways of extracting and applying the best of both worlds.

Drucker, Peter F. *The Frontiers of Management: Where Tomorrow's Decisions Are Being Shaped Today.* New York: Penguin, 1999. An analysis of global trends and management practices in business, including hostile takeovers and career gridlocks.

Freidson, Eliot. *Professionalism: The 3rd Logic.* Chicago: University of Chicago Press, 2001. The author distinguishes between professions, technical occupations, and crafts, analyzing how they differ by knowledge, education, career, organization, and ideology.

Parkinson, C. Northcote. *Parkinson's Law.* Boston: Buccaneer Books, 1997. Although this exposé of the inner workings of bureaucracies is delightfully satirical, if what Parkinson analyzes were generally true, bureaucracies would always fail.

Ritzer, George. *The McDonaldization of Society: An Investigation into the Changing Character of Contemporary Life,* 3rd ed. Thousand Oaks, Calif.: Pine Forge Press, 2000. The author examines how Durkheim's predictions about the rationalization of society are coming true in everyday life.

Wilson, James Q. *Bureaucracy: What Government Agencies Do and Why They Do It.* New York: Basic Books, 2001. The author analyzes how bureaucracies develop an organizational culture, and how this sometimes leads to irrational behavior.

Yiannis, Gabriel, Stephen Fineman, and David Sims. *Organizing and Organizations: An Introduction,* 2nd ed. Newbury Park, Calif.: Sage, 2000. The authors draw on many first-hand accounts to help make the study of formal organizations come alive.

CHAPTER 8 Deviance and Social Control

Conklin, John E. *Why Crime Rates Fell.* Boston: Allyn and Bacon, 2003. The author analyzes the reasons that experts have suggested for why crime rates have fallen: changes in policing, imprisonment, drugs and gun usage, age, and social institutions.

Curra, John. *The Relativity of Deviance.* Beverly Hills, Calif.: Sage, 2000. The author uses provocative examples to illustrate how deviance varies from place to place, time to time, and situation to situation.

Fleisher, Mark. S. *Dead End Kids: Gang Girls and the Boys They Know.* Madison: University of Wisconsin Press, 2001. This fascinating participant observation study provides an insider's perspective on gang life.

Girshick, Lori B. *No Safe Haven: Stories of Women in Prison.* Boston: Northeastern University Press, 2001. Do women occupy a special status in the criminal justice system? The author analyzes the life stories of forty imprisoned women to help find the answer.

Goffman, Erving. *Stigma: Notes on the Management of Spoiled Identity.* New York: Simon & Schuster, 1986. First published in 1968. The author outlines the social and personal reactions to "spoiled identity," appearances that—due to disability, weight, ethnicity, birth marks, and so on—do not match dominant expectations.

Goode, Erich. *Deviance in Everyday Life: Personal Accounts of Unconventional Lives.* Prospect Heights, Il.: Waveland Press, 2002. Provides insight into the process of becoming deviant and an understanding of how people justify their norm violations.

Jankowski, Martín Sánchez. *Islands in the Street: Gangs and American Urban Society.* Berkeley: University of California Press, 1992. The author's report on his participant observation of street gangs provides insightful understanding into their lives.

Kleinknecht, William. *The New Ethnic Mobs: The Changing Face of Organized Crime in America.* New York: Free Press, 1996. Like ethnic groups before them, the predators among the new immigrants victimize both outsiders and their own groups.

Lott, John R., Jr. *More Guns, Less Crime.* Chicago: University of Chicago Press, 2000. After reviewing state data on crime and right-to-carry gun laws, the author comes to the surprising conclusion that more guns mean less crime.

Lowney, Jeremiah. *What Were Your Parents Doing Back Then?: Youth and Drugs in a Southern California Beach Community from 1970 into the 21st Century.* Lanham, Md.: University Press of America, 2001. The author reports on his participant observation study with high school drug users and his follow-up after they were adults.

Rafter, Nicole Hahn. *Shots in the Mirror: Crime Films and Society.* New York: Oxford University Press, 2000. Explores how the portrayal of criminals in films has changed over time and how their portrayal influences our perception of real-world crime.

Reiman, Jeffrey. *The Rich Get Richer and the Poor Get Prison: Ideology, Class, and Criminal Justice.* Boston: Allyn and Bacon, 2001. An analysis of how social class works to produce different types of criminals and different types of justice.

Scott, Kody (Sanyika Shakur). *Monster: The Autobiography of an L.A. Gang Member.* New York: Addison Wesley, 1998. This intriguing insider's view of gang life provides a rare glimpse of the power of countercultural norms.

Journals

Criminal Justice Review: Issues in Criminal, Social, and Restorative Justice and *Journal of Law and Society* examine the social forces that shape law and justice.

CHAPTER 9 Global Stratification

Burawoy, Michael, Joseph A. Blum, Sheba George, Zsuzsa Gille, Teresa Gowan, Lynne Haney, Maren Klawiter, Steve H. Lopez, Sean Riain, and Millie Thayer. *Global Ethnography: Forces, Connections, and Imaginations in a Postmodern World.* Berkeley, Calif.: University of California Press, 2001. The authors illustrate how our emerging global society affects the everyday lives of people around the world—from feminists in Brazil to homeless can pickers in the United States.

Carpenter, Ted Galen, ed. *NATO's Empty Victory.* Washington, D.C.: Cato Institute, 2000. The author analyzes why NATO invaded Kosovo, although no NATO country had been attacked and the U.N. Security Council was divided on the issue.

Cotton, Samuel. *Silent Terror: A Journey into Contemporary African Slavery.* New York: Writers and Research, 1999. An account of slavery in Mauritania, based on the author's visit to that country.

Deliege, Robert. *The Untouchables of India.* Oxford, U.K.: Berg, 2001. An overview of India's caste system, with an emphasis on the *Dalits,* or untouchables.

Hajnal, Peter I., and Sian Meikle. *The G7/G8 System: Evolution, Role, and Documentation.* Burlington, Vt.: Ashgate Publishing, 1999. An analysis of the development of G7 (G8) and its role in world affairs.

Huggins, Martha K., Mika Haritos-Fatouros, and Philip G. Zimbardo. *Violence Workers: Police Torturers and Murderers Reconstruct Brazilian Atrocities.* Berkeley: University of California Press, 2002. If you want an insider's perspective in order to understand how ordinary people can rape, torture, and kill, this book will provide it.

Kempadoo, Mamala, ed. *Sun, Sex, and God: Tourism and Sex Work in the Caribbean.* Lanham, Md.: Rowman and Littlefield, 2000. The authors analyze connections between the global economy and the women, men, and children who sell sex; contains suggestions for changing the situation.

Sklair, Leslie. *The Transnational Capitalist Class.* Malden, Mass.: Blackwell Publishers, 2001. The author's thesis is that a transnational capitalist class is emerging. Based on the transnational corporation, it is more or less in control of the globalization of capitalism.

Wilkins, David E., and K. Tsianina Lomawaima. *Uneven Ground: American Indian Sovereignty and Federal Law.* Norman: University of Oklahoma Press, 2002. The author traces the relationship of Native Americans and the U.S. government.

Zakarta, Farred. *From Wealth to Power: The Unusual Origins of America's World.* Princeton, N.J.: Princeton University Press, 2000. The author analyzes how growing wealth and the passing of power from the states to the federal government are keys to understanding how the United States became a world power.

CHAPTER 10 Social Class in the United States

Brooks, David. *Bobos in Paradise: The New Upper Class and How They Got There.* New York: Touchstone Books, 2001. A lighthearted analysis of bourgeois bohemians (bobos), a supposed new class orientation that combines both affluent success and a rebellious spirit.

Cottle, Thomas J. *Hardest Times: The Trauma of Long Term Unemployment.* Westport, Conn.: Praeger, 2001. The author's interviews provide a good understanding of the complications that come to people who lose their jobs and cannot find another.

Dent, David J. *In Search of Black America: Discovering the African-American Dream.* New York: Simon and Schuster, 2000. The author, a journalist, examines the life of middle-class African Americans who live in what is largely a segregated world.

Ehrenreich, Barbara. *Nickel and Dimed: On (Not) Getting By in America.* New York: Metropolitan Books, 2001. The author, a sociologist, takes a series of unskilled, minimum-wage jobs—and tries to live on her earnings.

Gatewood, Willard B. *Aristocrats of Color: The Black Elite, 1880–1920.* Fayetteville: University of Arkansas Press, 2000. Analyzing the rise and decline of the African American upper class that developed after the Civil War, the author focuses on marriage, occupations, education, religion, clubs, and relationships with whites and with African Americans of lower classes.

Liebow, Elliot. *Tally's Corner: A Study of Negro Streetcorner Men.* Boston: Little, Brown, 1999. First published in 1968. The author's participant observation with a group of Washington, D.C., African American men provides insight into the dynamics of their decision making and relationships.

Newman, Katherine S. *Falling from Grace: Downward Mobility in the Age of Affluence.* Berkeley: University of California Press, 1999. The focus of this analysis of downward social mobility is on what happens to people who lose their jobs and are unable to find decent work.

Oliver, Melvin L., and Thomas M. Shapiro. *Black Wealth/White Wealth: A New Perspective on Racial Inequality.* New York: Routledge, 1997. This book, which makes the first comparison of the wealth (not income) of African Americans and whites, shows how deep the divide is.

Perucci, Robert, and Earl Wyson. *The New Class Society,* 2nd ed. Lanham, Md.: Rowman and Littlefield, 2003. An overview of the U.S. social class structure, with the suggestion that there no longer is a middle class.

Richardson, Chad. *Batos, Bolillos, Pochos, & Pelados: Class and Culture on the South Texas Border.* Austin: University of Texas Press, 1999. An analysis of class, conflict, cooperation, and identity among Mexican Americans, Anglos, African Americans, and immigrants in the Valley of South Texas.

Schram, Sanford F. *Praxis for the Poor: Piven and Cloward and the Future of Social Science in Social Welfare.* Albany: New York University Press, 2003. The author's thesis is that politically engaged scholarship can contribute to the struggle for social justice.

Wilson, William Julius. *When Work Disappears: The World of the New Urban Poor.* New York: Knopf, 1997. The author analyzes consequences of the disappearance of unskilled jobs near the inner city: the destruction of inner-city businesses, the flight of the middle class, and the stranding of poor people who have few alternatives.

Journals

Journal of Children and Poverty and *Journal of Poverty* analyze issues that affect the quality of life of people who live in poverty.

Race, Gender, and Class publishes interdisciplinary articles on the topics listed in its title.

CHAPTER 11 Sex and Gender

Anderson, Margaret L. *Thinking about Women: Sociological Perspectives on Sex and Gender,* 6th ed. New York: Allyn and Bacon, 2003. An overview of the main issues of sex and gender in contemporary society, ranging from sexism and socialization to work and health.

Beynon, John. *Masculinities and Culture.* Philadelphia: Open University Press, 2002. The author's thesis is that because masculinity is shaped by society and culture, differing from place to place and time to time, the term "masculinities" is more appropriate.

Colapinto, John. *As Nature Made Him: The Boy Who Was Raised as a Girl.* New York: HarperCollins, 2001. A detailed account of the event summarized in this chapter of the boy whose penis was accidentally burned off.

Ferree, Myra Marx, and Beth B. Hess, *Controversy and Coalition: New Feminist Movement across Four Decades of Change,* 3rd ed. New York: Routledge, 2001. An overview of the U.S. women's movement from the 1960s to the 1990s.

Gilman, Charlotte Perkins. *The Man-Made World or, Our Androcentric Culture.* New York: Charlton, 1911. Reprinted in 1971 by Johnson Reprint. This early book on women's liberation provides an excellent view of female–male relations at the beginning of the last century.

Goldberg, Steven. *Why Men Rule: A Theory of Male Dominance.* Chicago: Open Court, 1994. A detailed explanation of the author's theory of male dominance featured in this chapter.

Johnson, Allan G. *Privilege, Power, and Difference.* New York: McGraw-Hill, 2003. The author helps us see the nature and consequences of privilege and our connection to it.

Kimmel, Michael S., and Michael A. Messner, eds. *Men's Lives,* 5th ed. Boston: Allyn and Bacon, 2001. The authors of these articles examine major issues of sex and gender as they affect men. An excellent companion, and often counterpoint, to the Anderson book.

Lorber, Judith, and Lisa Jean Moore. *Gender and the Social Construction of Illness,* 2nd ed. Lanham, Md.: Rowman and Littlefield, 2003. Taking the position that both gender and medicine are social institutions, the author examines their interrelationships.

McKay, Jim, Michael A. Messner, and Donald F. Sabo, eds. *Masculinities, Gender Identities, and Sport.* Beverly Hills, Calif.: Sage, 2000. The authors of these articles provide an overview of major topics in gender relations, with a focus on the relationship between sport and gender.

Renzetti, Claire, and Daniel J. Curran. *Women, Men, and Society,* 5th ed. Boston: Allyn and Bacon, 2003. A basic text that summarizes major issues in the sociology of gender.

Sabo, Don, Terry Kupers, and Willie London, eds. *Prison Masculinities.* Philadelphia: Temple University Press, 2001. The prisoners and former prisoners who have written these articles focus on how men construct their masculinities within the prison subculture that condones rape.

Wymard, Ellie. *Conversations with Uncommon Women: Insights from Women Who've Risen above Life's Challenges to Achieve Extraordinary Success.* New York: AMACOM, 2000. The author, an English professor, interviewed 100 highly successful women to discover their understanding of how they overcame the obstacles they faced.

Zinn, Maxine Baca, Pierrette Handagneu-Sotelo, and Michael A. Messner, eds. *Gender Through the Prism of Difference,* 2nd ed. Boston: Allyn and Bacon, 2000. The authors of these articles explore how the social construction of gender is related to bodies, sexualities, identity, families, the workplace, culture, and politics.

Zweigenhaft, Richard L. *Diversity in the Power Elite: Have Women and Minorities Reached the Top?* New Haven: Yale University Press, 2000. The author examines the rise of women and minorities in the power establishment and analyzes the obstacles that prevent them from reaching the top rung of power.

Journals

These journals focus on the role of gender in social life: *Feminist Studies; Gender and Society; Gender, Place and Culture: A Journal of Feminist Geography; Journal of Gender, Culture, and Health; Sex Roles;* and *Signs: Journal of Women in Culture and Society.*

CHAPTER 12 Race and Ethnicity

Acosta, Teresa Palomo, and Ruthe Winegarten. *Los Tejanas: 300 Years of History.* Austin: University of Texas Press, 2003. An account of how Tejanas in the colonial period and from the Republic of Texas up to 1900 overcame obstacles to their success.

Allen, James, ed. *Without Sanctuary: Lynching Photography in America.* Santa Fe, N.M.: Twin Palms Publishers, 2000. Apart from its gruesomeness, this collection of nearly 100 postcards and photographs from the late nineteenth and early twentieth centuries provides remarkable insight into the mindset of that period.

Blee, Kathleen M. *Inside Organized Racism: Women in the Hate Movement.* Berkeley: University of California Press, 2002. Why and how do people join hate groups? The author's research provides answers to this troubling question.

Deutscher, Irwin. *Accommodating Diversity: National Policies That Prevent Ethnic Conflict.* Lanham Md.: Rowman and Littlefield Publishers, 2003. Instead of focusing on what doesn't work, the author examines positive ethnic relationships around the world.

Du Bois, W. E. B. *Black Reconstruction in America: An Essay Toward a History of the Part Which Black Folk Played in the Attempt to Reconstruct Democracy in America, 1860–1880.* New York: Harcourt, Brace 1935; London: Frank Cass, 1966. This analysis of the role of African Americans in the Civil War and during the years immediately following provides a glimpse into a neglected part of U.S. history.

Hilberg, Raul. *The Destruction of the European Jews,* 3rd ed. New Haven: Yale University Press, 2003. The focus of this book is the machinery of death that the Nazis put together to annihilate the Jewish community of Europe.

Klinkner, Philip A., and Roger M. Smith. *The Unsteady March: The Rise and Decline of Racial Equality in America.* Chicago: University of Chicago Press, 2002. Examines the conditions under which racial equality increases and decreases, and proposes steps to increase racial equality.

Mander, Jerry. *In the Absence of the Sacred: The Failure of Technology and the Survival of the Indian Nations.* New York: Pete Smith, Publisher, 1999. With a focus on the impact of technology, the author analyzes past and present relations of Native Americans and the U.S. government.

Mueller, Timothy, and Sarah Sue Goldsmith. *Nations Within: The Four Sovereign Tribes of Louisiana.* Baton Rouge: University of Louisiana Press, 2004. Analyzes the relationship of four sovereign nations to the dominant, colonizing governmental power.

Patillo-McCoy, Mary. *Black Picket Fences: Privilege and Peril among the Black Middle Class.* Chicago: University of Chicago Press, 2001. The author focuses on the obstacles and pressures faced by the black middle class.

Perry, Pamela. *Shades of White: White Kids and Racial Identities in High School.* Durham: Duke University Press, 2002. The author's research illustrates the complexities of racial self identification, and how social location underlies the meaning of being white.

Roediger, David R. *Colored White: Transcending the Racial Past.* Berkeley: University of California Press, 2002. Racial-ethnic self identification is a complicated, and sometimes troubling, endeavor, as this author makes clear.

Walker, Samuel, Cassia Spohn, and Miriam Delone. *The Color of Justice: Race, Ethnicity, and Crime in America,* 3rd ed. Belmont, Calif.: Wadsworth, 2003. The authors analyze racial, ethnic, and gender discrimination in the criminal justice system.

Wilson, William Julius. *The Bridge over the Racial Divide: Rising Inequality and Coalition Politics.* Berkeley: University of California Press, 2000. The author analyzes how monetary, trade, and tax policies increase social inequality; includes recommendations to increase multiracial political cooperation.

CHAPTER 13 The Elderly

Dychtwald, Ken. *Age Power: How the 21st Century Will Be Ruled by the New Old.* Los Angeles: J. P. Tarcher, 2000. Speculates on how the growing numbers of elderly will affect society, and suggests how we should prepare for the coming change.

Furman, Frida Kerner. *Facing the Mirror: Older Women and Beauty Shop Culture.* New York: Routledge, 1997. This ethnography of Julie's, a beauty parlor, illustrates how women come face to face with and adjust to the realities of aging.

Gubrium, Jaber F. *Living and Dying at Murray Manor.* Charlottesville: University of Virginia Press, 1998. In this ethnography of a nursing home, the author analyzes how staff and patients relate to one another, how patients pass time, and how they react to death.

Gubrium, Jaber F., and James A. Holstein, eds. *Ways of Aging.* Malden, Mass.: Blackwell Publishers, 2003. The authors of these articles examine how people construct their self definitions as they adjust to the realities of aging bodies.

Hatch, Laurie Russell. *Beyond Gender Differences: Adaptation to Aging in Life Course Perspective.* Amityville, N.Y.: Baywood Publishing Company, 2000. The author reviews the research on how men and women adapt to growing old.

Quadagno, Jill S. *Aging and the Life Course: An Introduction to Social Gerontology.* New York: McGraw-Hill, 2002. In this review of major issues in gerontology, the author examines how the quality of life that people experience in old age is the result of earlier choices, opportunities, and constraints.

Roszak, Theodore. *The Longevity Revolution: As Boomers Become Elders.* Berkeley, Calif.: Berkeley Hills Books, 2001. The author's thesis is that the elderly are not a burden to society, but a great resource.

Rubin, Lillian B. *Tangled Lives: Daughters, Mothers, and the Crucible of Aging.* Boston: Beacon Press, 2001. The author reflects on her own experiences with illness and death to try to come to grips with the meaning of growing old—and of life.

Stoller, Eleanor Palo, and Rose Campbell Gibson. *Worlds of Difference: Inequality in the Aging Experience,* 3rd ed. Thousand Oaks, Calif.: Pine Forge Press, 2000. The authors document inequalities borne by the U.S. elderly and explain the social conditions that create those inequalities.

Journals

The Gerontologist, Journal of Aging and Identity, Journal of Aging and Social Policy, Journal of Aging Studies, Journal of Cross-Cultural Gerontology, Journal of Elder Abuse and Neglect, Journal of Gerontology, and *Journal of Women and Aging* focus on issues of aging, while *Youth and Society* and *Journal of Youth Studies* examine adolescent culture.

CHAPTER 14 The Economy

Amott, Teresa. *Caught in the Crisis: Women and the U.S. Economy Today.* New York: Monthly Review Press, 2000. An analysis of how the transformation of the economy is affecting women.

Bales, Kevin. *Disposable People: New Slavery in the Global Economy.* Berkeley: University of California Press, 2000. The author documents the relationship between the globalization of capitalism and current slavery in Brazil, India, Mauritania, Pakistan, and Thailand.

Bluestone, Barry, Bennett Harrison, and Richard C. Leone. *Growing Prosperity: The Battle for Growth and Equity in the Twenty-First Century.* Berkeley: University of California Press, 2001. New York: Houghton Mifflin, 1999. Emphasizes how we can continue economic growth and also have a more just distribution of wealth.

Blumenberg, Werner. *Karl Marx.* New York: VideoBooks, 1999. Written by a member of the underground that fought against Hitler, this classic biography of Marx explores both his personal and public life.

Bonilla, Frank, Edwin Melendez, Maria de Los Angeles Torres, and Rebecca Morales, eds. *Borderless Borders: U.S. Latinos, Latin Americans, and the Paradox of Interdependence.* Philadelphia: Temple University Press, 1998. Analyzes how the globalization of capitalism is affecting U.S. Latinos, their identity, and their relationship to their home country.

Chua, Amy. *World on Fire: How Exporting Free Market Democracy Breeds Ethnic Hatred and Global Instability.* New York: Doubleday, 2003. The author's thesis is that the globalization of capitalism has brought economic devastation, ethnic hatreds, and genocidal violence throughout the Least Industrialized Nations.

Katz, Richard. *Japanese Phoenix: The Long Road to Economic Revival.* New York: M. E. Sharpe, 2003. The author explains why the Japanese economy faltered and suggests reforms to restore economic growth.

Sennett, Richard, and Bob Sennett. *The Corrosion of Character: The Personal Consequences of Work in the New Capitalism.* New York: W. W. Norton, 2000. An examination of how the "new efficiencies" of the multinational corporations affect workers; contains case studies.

Stiglitz, Joseph E. *Globalization and Its Discontents.* New York: W. W. Norton, 2002. The author, who served as Chair of the President's Council of Economic Advisors, documents how politicians put the interests of Wall Street ahead of the needs of the Least Industrialized Nations.

CHAPTER 15 Politics

Amnesty International. *Amnesty International Report.* London: Amnesty International Publications, published annually. This report summarizes human rights violations around the world, listing specific instances, including names, country by country.

Barstow, Anne Llewellyn, ed. *Wars Dirty Secret: Rape, Prostitution, and Other Crimes Against Women.* New York: Pilgrim Press, 2003. The authors of these articles document how sexual violence against women accompanies war in Africa, Asia, Europe, and the Americas.

Castro, Fidel. *Capitalism in Crisis: Globalization and World Politics Today.* New York: Ocean Press, 2001. This collection of speeches by one of the few remaining communist rulers provides a conflict perspective on geopolitical change.

Chirot, Daniel, and E. P. Seligman, eds. *Ethnopolitical Warfare: Causes, Consequences, and Possible Solutions.* New York: American Psychological Association, 2001. The authors of these articles analyze ethnic conflicts around the world to see why they escalate or de-escalate.

Domhoff, G. William. *Who Rules America?: Power and Politics,* 4th ed. New York: McGraw-Hill, 2001. An analysis of how the multinational corporations dominate the U.S. government.

Ginzburg, Eugenia Semyonovna. *Journey into the Whirlwind.* New York: Harvest Books, 2003. The autobiographical and moving account of a woman who spent 18 years in Stalin's prison camps.

McFaul, Michael. *Russia's Unfinished Revolution: Political Change from Gorbachev to Putin.* Ithaca, New York: Cornell University Press, 2003. An account of Russia's transition to capitalism, including the modification of its social institutions.

Mills, C. Wright. *The Power Elite,* 2nd ed. New York: Getty Center for Education in the Arts, 2000. Originally published in 1956. This classic analysis elaborates the conflict thesis summarized in this chapter—that U.S. society is ruled by the nation's top corporate leaders, together with an elite from the military and political institutions.

Osiel, Mark J. *Obeying Orders: Atrocity, Military Discipline, and the Law of War.* New Brunswick, N.J.: Transaction Publishers, 2002. The author examines the social basis of constraint and freedom in the military and how orders can lead to atrocities.

Research in Political Sociology: A Research Annual. Greenwich, Conn.: JAI Press. This annual publication is not recommended for beginners, as the findings and theories are often difficult and abstract. It does, however, analyze political topics of vital concern to our well-being.

Zweigenhaft, Richard L., and G. William Domhoff. *Diversity in the Power Elite: Have Women and Minorities Reached the Top?* New Haven: Yale University Press, 2000. The authors explore the extent to which Jews, women, African Americans, Latinos, Asian Americans, and homosexuals have joined the power elite.

Journals

Many sociology journals publish articles on politics. Three that focus on this area of social life are *American Political Science Review, Journal of Political and Military Sociology,* and *Social Policy.*

CHAPTER 16 The Family

Aulette, Judy Root. *Changing American Families.* Boston: Allyn and Bacon, 2002. A basic text that summarizes the major issues in the sociology of marriage and family.

Contreras, Josefina M., Kathryn A. Kerns, and Angela M. Neal-Barnett. *Latino Children and Families in the United States: Current Research and Future Directions.* New York: Praeger, 2003. The authors consider how parenting beliefs and practices of Latinos differ by socioeconomic and cultural backgrounds and try to identify family values that can be considered "Latino."

Goetting, Ann. *Getting Out: Life Stories of Women Who Left Abusive Men.* New York: Columbia University Press, 2001. Why don't women leave when their husbands abuse them? The author uses the statements of women who were abused to explore this question—and to examine the situations of those who got out.

Hackstaff, Karla B. *Marriage in a Culture of Divorce.* Philadelphia: Temple University Press, 2000. Through in-depth interviews with couples who married in the 1950s and 1970s, the author examines how the meaning of marriage and divorce has changed.

Hochschild, Arlie Russell. *The Time Bind: When Work Becomes Home and Home Becomes Work.* New York: Owl Books, 2001. Do parents really want to spend more time with their families and less at work? Or do parents flee families, finding work a respite from family pressures? The author presents some surprising answers.

Plane, Ann Marie. *Colonial Intimacies: Indian Marriage in Early New England.* Ithaca: Cornell University Press, 2000. Based on legal records, travel narratives, and missionary tracts, the author analyzes Native American-white marriages during the first century and a half of Native American contact with Europeans.

Romano, Renee Christine. *Race Mixing: Black-White Marriage in Postwar America.* Cambridge, Mass.: Harvard University Press, 2003. Provides the legislative background on these marriages, plus social trends, accompanied by first person accounts.

Staples, Robert, ed. *The Black Family: Essays and Studies,* 6th ed. Belmont Calif.: Wadsworth, 1999. The authors of these articles analyze black families—from the times of slavery to postindustrial society—reviewing gender roles, marriage and divorce, family life, parenthood, adolescence, health, violence, sexual relationships, and public policy.

Strasser, Mark. *The Challenge of Same-Sex Marriages: Federalist Principles and Constitutional Protection.* New York: Praeger, 2000. Based on challenges to state laws that limit marriage to people of the opposite sex, the author analyzes same-sex marriages in light of the U.S. Constitution.

Journals

Family Relations, The History of the Family, International Journal of Sociology of the Family, Journal of Comparative Family Studies, Journal of Divorce, Journal of Divorce and Remarriage, Journal of Family and Economic Issues, Journal of Family Issues, Journal of Family Violence, Journal of Marriage and the Family, and *Marriage and Family Review* publish articles on almost every aspect of marriage and family life.

CHAPTER 17 Education

Corwin, Miles. *And Still We Rise: The Trials and Triumphs of 12 Gifted Inner City Students.* New York: HarperPerennial Library, 2001. The author, a journalist who spent a year in a South Los Angeles high school, details the lives of twelve students in an advanced placement program.

Garrod, Andrew, and Colleen Larimore, eds. *First Person, First Peoples: Native American College Graduates Tell Their Life Stories.* Ithaca: Cornell University Press, 1997. Written by graduates of Dartmouth College, these essays recount the anguish minority students often feel in a predominantly white college.

Ibarra, Robert A. *Beyond Affirmative Action: Reframing the Context of Higher Education.* Madison: University of Wisconsin Press, 2001. The author does go beyond affirmative action, as the title suggests, criticizing higher education, and suggesting a new approach, "multi-contextuality."

Kozol, Jonathan. *Ordinary Resurrections: Children in the Years of Hope.* New York: Crown Publishers, 2001. To listen as these children from a dismal neighborhood in South Bronx talk about life is to become aware of the potential that schools have to transform the lives of children in poverty.

Lopez, Nancy. *Hopeful Girls, Troubled Boys: Race and Gender Disparity in Urban Education.* New York: Rutledge, 2003. Building on her thesis that education is failing boys of color, the author suggests ways to improve education.

Patterson, James T. *Brown v. Board of Education: A Civil Rights Milestone and Its Troubled Legacy.* New York: Oxford University Press, 2001. A detailed analysis of the U.S. Supreme Court's 1954 epoch-making decision.

Schiell, Timothy C. *Campus Hate Speech on Trial.* Lawrence: University of Kansas Press, 2000. An analysis of free speech, which lies at the center of personal freedom, and its limits on the college campus.

Spring, Joel H. *Deculturalization and the Struggle for Equality: A Brief History of the Education of Dominated Cultures in the United States.* New York: McGraw-Hill 2003. The author examines how Anglos have used their control of schools to strip away the cultures of minorities and replace them with Anglo culture.

Stevens, Michael L. *Kingdom of Children: Culture and Controversy in the Homeschooling Movement.* Princeton: Princeton University Press, 2001. This analysis of the homeschooling movement, based on interviews and participant observation, contains numerous quotations that provide insight into why parents homeschool their children.

Weiler, Jeanne Drysdale. *Codes and Contradictions: Race, Gender Identity, and Schooling.* New York: State University of New York Press, 2000. After studying girls of African American, Latina, Puerto Rican, and European backgrounds who are at risk of failing in school, the author concludes that schools are able to reorient young women so they perceive educational success as crucial to their future well-being.

Journals

The following journals contain articles that examine almost every aspect of education: *Education and Urban Society, Harvard Educational Review, Sociology and Education,* and *Sociology of Education.*

CHAPTER 18 Religion

Christiano, Kevin J., William H. Swatos, Jr., and Peter Kivisto. *Sociology of Religion: Contemporary Developments.* Lanham, Md.: AltaMira Press, 2002. A basic text that summarizes the major issues in the sociology of religion.

Gilman, Sander. *Jewish Frontiers: Essays on Bodies, Histories, and Identities.* New York: Macmillan, 2003. Analyzes Jewish identity from the framework of living on a frontier, and the representation of this identity in the mass media.

Juergensmeyer, Mark. *Terror in the Mind of God: The Global Rise of Religious Violence.* Berkeley: University of California Press, 2000. The author's summaries of religious violence provide a rich background for understanding this behavior.

Lewis, David C. *After Atheism: Religion and Ethnicity in Russia and Central Asia.* New York: St. Martin's Press, 2000. The author reports on changes in religion since the downfall of communism in Russia.

Mazur, Eric Michael. *The Americanization of Religious Minorities: Confronting the Constitutional Order.* Baltimore: Johns Hopkins University Press, 2000. What happens when religious beliefs conflict with U.S. law? The author analyzes the experiences of Jehovah's Witnesses, Mormons, and Native Americans.

McRoberts, Omar M. *Streets of Glory: Church and Community in a Black Urban Neighborhood.* Chicago: University of Chicago Press, 2003. Four Corners, one of the toughest areas of Boston, contains twenty-nine mostly storefront churches. The author finds most of them are attended and run by people who do not live in the neighborhood and who have little or no attachment to the surrounding area.

Thibodeau, David, and Leon Whiteson. *A Place Called Waco: A Survivor's Story.* New York: Public Affairs, 2000. A first-person account of life inside the Branch Davidian compound, written by one of only four survivors of the fire who were not sentenced to prison.

Wilson, David Sloan. *Darwin's Cathedral: Evolution, Religion, and the Nature of Society.* Chicago: University of Chicago Press, 2002. The author's evolutionary approach to religion comes surprisingly close to a functional analysis of religion.

Wolfe, Alan. *The Transformation of American Religion: How We Actually Live Our Faith.* New York: The Free Press, 2004. The author's thesis is that individualism is changing the shape and substance of religion in the United States, minimizing doctrine and maximizing feelings and personal satisfactions.

Zellner, William W., and William M. Kephart. *Extraordinary Groups: An Examination of Unconventional Lifestyles,* 7th ed. New York: Worth, 2001. This sketch of the history and characteristics of eight groups (the Old Order Amish, Oneida Community, Gypsies, Church of Christ Scientist, Hasidim, Father Divine Movement, Mormons, and Jehovah's Witnesses) illustrates how groups can maintain unconventional beliefs and practices.

Journals

These journals publish articles that focus on the sociology of religion: *Journal for the Scientific Study of Religion, Review of Religious Research,* and *Sociological Analysis: A Journal in the Sociology of Religion.*

CHAPTER 19 Medicine

Cockerham, William C., and Michael Glasser. *Readings in Medical Sociology,* 2nd ed. Upper Saddle River, N.J.: Prentice Hall, 2001. The authors of these articles discuss the social causes and consequences of health and illness.

Eaton, William W. *The Sociology of Mental Disorders,* 3rd ed. New York: Praeger, 2001. From this account of "bizarre" behaviors, including unusual thinking, you will be able to see the differences between sociological and psychological analyses.

Fox, Renee C., and Judith P. Swazey. *The Courage to Fail: A Social View of Organ Transplants and Dialysis.* New Brunswick, N.J.: Transaction Publishers, 2002. The authors examine moral and ethical aspects of organ replacement, a social issue destined to grow in importance as medical technology continues to advance.

Grob, Gerald N. *The Deadly Truth: A History of Disease in America.* Cambridge, Mass.: Harvard University Press, 2003. In this history of disease in the United States, the author stresses relationships among society, environment, and human health.

Karp, David A. *Speaking of Sickness: Depression, Disconnection, and the Meaning of Illness.* New York: Oxford University Press, 1997. Written by a sociologist who has suffered from depression for many years, this book provides deep insight into people's experience with this illness.

Kolata, Gina Bari. *Flu: The Story of the Great Influenza Pandemic of 1918 and the Search for the Virus That Caused It.* New York: Farrar, Straus, and Giroux, 2000. The author recounts the worst pandemic of the twentieth century, in which perhaps 40 million people died within a year.

Reverby, Susan M., ed. *Tuskegee's Truths: Rethinking the Tuskegee Syphilis Study.* Chapel Hill: University of North Carolina Press, 2000. Analyses of the syphilis experiments conducted by the U.S. Public Health Service at Tuskegee Institute, which were carried out on unwitting African Americans.

Smedley, Brian D., Adrienne Y. Stith, and Alan R. Nelson, eds. *Unequal Treatment: Confronting Racial and Ethnic Disparities in Health Care.* Washington, D.C.: National Academies Press, 2003. The authors of these articles examine how stereotyping and biases on the part of healthcare providers, accompanied by barriers of language, geography, and culture, contribute to inequality in healthcare.

Journals

Health: An Interdisciplinary Journal for the Social Study of Health, Illness and Medicine, Journal of Health and Social Behavior, Research in the Sociology of Health Care, Social Science and Medicine, and *Sociological Practice: A Journal of Clinical and Applied Sociology* publish research articles and essays in the field of medical sociology.

CHAPTER 20 Population and Urbanization

Department of Agriculture. *Yearbook of Agriculture.* Washington, D.C.: Department of Agriculture, published annually. This yearbook focuses on specific aspects of U.S. agribusiness, especially international economies and trade.

Duany, Andres, Elizabeth Plater-Zyberk, and Jeff Speck. *Suburban Nation: The Rise of Sprawl and the Decline of the American Dream.* San Francisco: North Point Press, 2001. Lays out a vision of how to plan cities and suburbs so they meet human needs and become inviting places to live.

Duneier, Mitchell. *Sidewalk.* New York: Farrar, Straus, Giroux, 2000. This analysis of city streets provides insight into how the urban mosaic works.

Meller, Helen Elizabeth. *European Cities, 1890–1930s: History, Culture and the Built Environment.* New York: John Wiley, 2002. This background on European urbanization contains principles for improving cities.

Mosher, Steven W. *A Mother's Ordeal: One Woman's Fight Against One-Child China.* New York: HarperCollins, 1994. This book puts a human face on China's coercive family planning policies.

Orfield, Myron. *American Metropolitics: The New Suburban Reality.* Washington, D.C.: Brookings Institution Press, 2002. Explains why regionalism is needed in order to meet the needs of urban areas.

Palen, John J. *The Urban World,* 6th ed. New York: McGraw-Hill, 2002. A short, basic text that summarizes major issues in urban sociology.

Ross, Andrew. *The Celebration Chronicles: Life, Liberty and the Pursuit of Property Values in Disney's New Town.* New York: Ballantine Books, 2000. An analysis of Disney's planned utopian community in Florida, written by a social scientist who lived in Celebration for a year.

Taylor, Monique M. *Harlem: Between Heaven and Hell.* Minneapolis: University of Minnesota Press, 2002. A history and analysis of contemporary Harlem, with many quotes from current residents.

Yaukey, David, and Douglas L. Anderton. *Demography: The Study of Human Population.* Bellevue, Wash.: Waveview Press, 2001. Focusing on both the United States and the world, the authors analyze major issues in population.

Journals

City and Community and *Urban Studies* publish articles whose focus is the city, suburbs, immigration, and community.

CHAPTER 21 Collective Behavior and Social Movements

Brunvand, Jan Harold. *Too Good to Be True: The Colossal Book of Urban Legends.* New York: W. W. Norton, 2002. In this collection of over 200 urban legends, you'll probably find some that you heard and thought were true.

Buechler, Steven M. *Social Movements in Advanced Capitalism: The Political Economy and Cultural Construction of Social Activism.* New York: Oxford University Press, 2000. An analysis of why our current state of economic and political development produces social movements.

Cohen, Stanley. *Folk Devils and Moral Panics: Thirtieth Anniversary Edition,* 3rd ed. New York: Rutledge, 2003. The author's thesis is that the mass media create moral panics and stifle rational discussion about social problems.

Fine, Gary Alan, and Patricia A. Turner. *Whispers on the Color Line: Rumor and Race in America.* Berkeley: University of California Press, 2001. In private, people say things about race that they won't utter in public. What they say in private tells us a great deal about how they understand race.

Goode, Erich. *Paranormal Beliefs: A Sociological Introduction.* Bellevue, Wash.: Waveland Press, 2000. An examination of how the acceptance or rejection of belief in paranormal events is related to social structure.

Gupta, Dipak K. *Path to Collective Madness: A Study in Social Order and Political Pathology.* New York: Praeger, 2002. The author analyzes the process by which people participate in "collective madness"—such events as parents poisoning their children in Jonestown and the genocide of Rwanda.

Jasper, James M. *The Art of Moral Protest: Culture, Biography, and Creativity in Social Movements.* Chicago: University of Chicago Press, 2000. A primary thrust of this book is how protest movements shape moral thinking.

Luker, Kristin. *Abortion and the Politics of Motherhood.* Berkeley: University of California Press, 2000. Based on documents and interviews with pro-choice and pro-life advocates, the author demonstrates how people's moral positions on abortion are related to their views on sexual behavior, the care of children, and family life.

Meyer, David S., Nancy Whittier, and Belinda Robnett, eds. *Social Movements: Identity, Culture, and the State.* New York: Oxford University Press, 2002. Examining wide-ranging social movements, the authors analyze mobilization, organization, strategies, identities, and the culture of social movements.

Tilly, Charles. *The Politics of Collective Violence.* New York: Cambridge University Press, 2003. The author analyzes causes, combinations, and settings that underlie collective violence and tries to identify ways to reduce violence.

Journal

Social Movement Studies examines the origins, development, organization, context, and impact of social movements.

CHAPTER 22 Social Change and the Environment

Allen, Irwin. *Sociology and the Environment: A Critical Introduction to Society, Nature and Knowledge.* Malden, Mass.: Blackwell Publishers, 2001. Presents competing sociological perspectives on the construction of a sustainable environment.

Breton, Mary Joy. *Women Pioneers for the Environment.* Boston: Northeastern University Press, 2000. The stories of 40 women who stepped out of their traditional roles to spearhead environmental campaigns.

Brown, Lester R., ed. *State of the World.* New York: Norton, published annually. Experts on environmental issues analyze environmental problems throughout the world; a New Malthusian perspective.

Council on Environmental Quality. *Environmental Quality.* Washington, D.C.: U.S. Government Printing Office, published annually. Each report evaluates the condition of some aspect of the environment.

Gottlieb, Robert. *Environmentalism Unbound: Exploring New Pathways for Change.* Cambridge, Mass.: MIT Press, 2001. The main emphases are food politics or eco-farming and controlling chemical pollution.

Homer-Dixon, Thomas F. *Environment, Scarcity, and Violence.* Princeton: Princeton University Press, 2002. The author argues that the growth in population and production will create environmental scarcities, which, in turn, will lead to insurrections, ethnic clashes, urban unrest, and other forms of violence.

Howard, Russell D., and Reid L. Sawyer, eds. *Terrorism and Counterterrorism: Understanding the New Security Environment, Readings and Interpretations.* New York: McGraw-Hill, 2003. These analyses stress causes of terrorism and suggest steps to take to combat terrorism; a militaristic emphasis runs through the articles.

Inglehart, Ronald L., ed. *Human Values and Social Change: Findings from the World Values Surveys.* Boston: Brill Academic Publishers, 2003. An overview of how values are changing around the world.

Markell, David L. *Greening NAFTA: The North American Commission for Environmental Cooperation.* Stanford, Calif: Stanford University Press, 2003. As this book makes evident, without winning elections, green politics is having tremendous influence in international affairs and on our lives.

Rogers, Everett M. *Diffusion of Innovations,* 5th ed. New York: The Free Press, 2003. The author will take you on a tour of the world, examining the acceptance and rejection of innovations, and the success and failure of each.

Journals

Earth First! Journal and *Sierra,* magazines published by Earth First! and the Sierra Club respectively, are excellent sources for keeping informed of major developments in the environmental movement.

References

Abelson, Reed. "Drug Sales Bring Huge Profits, and Scrutiny, to Cancer Doctors." *New York Times,* January 26, 2003.

Abelson, Reed, and Patricia Leigh Brown. "Alternative Medicine Is Finding Its Niche in Nation's Hospitals." *New York Times,* April 14, 2002.

Aberle, David. *The Peyote Religion Among the Navaho.* Chicago: Aldine, 1966.

Aberle, David F., A. K. Cohen, A. K. David, M. J. Leng, Jr., and F. N. Sutton. "The Functional Prerequisites of a Society." *Ethics, 60,* January 1950:100–111.

Ackernecht, Erwin H. "The Role of Medical History in Medical Education." *Bulletin of the History of Medicine, 21,* 1947:135–145.

Adams, Noah. "All Things Considered." *New England Journal of Medicine* report. January 12, 2000.

Addams, Jane. *Twenty Years at Hull-House.* New York: Signet, 1981. First published in 1910.

Adler, Patricia A., and Peter Adler. *Peer Power: Preadolescent Culture and Identity.* New Brunswick, N.J.: Rutgers University Press, 1998.

Adler, Patricia A., Steven J. Kless, and Peter Adler. "Socialization to Gender Roles: Popularity Among Elementary School Boys and Girls." *Sociology of Education, 65,* July 1992:169–187.

Adorno, Theodor W., Else Frenkel-Brunswick, D. J. Levinson, and R. N. Sanford. *The Authoritarian Personality.* New York: Harper & Row, 1950.

Aeppel, Timothy. "More Amish Women Are Tending to Business." *Wall Street Journal,* February 8, 1996:B1, B2.

Aguirre, Benigno E. "The Conventionalization of Collective Behavior in Cuba." In *Collective Behavior and Social Movements,* Russell I. Curtis, Jr., and Benigno E. Aquirre, eds. Boston: Allyn and Bacon, 1993: 413–428.

Aguirre, Benigno E., E. L. Quarantelli, and Jorge L. Mendoza. "The Collective Behavior of Fads: The Characteristics, Effects, and Career of Streaking." In *Collective Behavior and Social Movements,* Russell L. Curtis, Jr., and Benigno E. Aguirre, eds. Boston: Allyn and Bacon, 1993:168–182.

Ahlburg, Dennis A., and Carol J. De Vita. "New Realities of the American Family." *Population Bulletin, 47,* 2, August 1992:1–44.

Akol, Jacob. "Slavery in Sudan." *New African,* September 1998.

Alarid, Leanne Fiftal, Velmer S. Burton, Jr., and Francis T. Cullen. "Gender and Crime among Felony Offenders: Assessing the Generality of Social Control and Differential Association Theories." *Journal of Research in Crime and Delinquency, 37,* 2, May 2000:171–199.

Albert, Ethel M. "Women of Burundi: A Study of Social Values." In *Women of Tropical Africa,* Denise Paulme, ed. Berkeley: University of California Press, 1963:179–215.

Aldrich, Nelson W., Jr. *Old Money: The Mythology of America's Upper Class.* New York: Vintage Books, 1989.

Allport, Floyd. *Social Psychology.* Boston: Houghton Mifflin, 1954.

Alter, Jonathan. "From the Prison of the 'Isms.' " *Newsweek,* January 1, 2000:31.

Amato, Paul R., and Juliana M. Sobolewski. "The Effects of Divorce and Marital Discord on Adult Children's Psychological Well-Being." *American Sociological Review, 66,* 6, December 2001:900–921.

Amenta, Edwin, Drew Halfmann, and Michael P. Young. "The Strategies and Contexts of Social Protest: Political Mediation and the Impact of the Townsend Movement in California." *Mobilization, 4,* 1, April 1999:1–23.

American Fact Finder. Washington D.C.: U.S. Bureau of the Census, 2003.

American Sociological Association. "Code of Ethics." Washington, D.C.: American Sociological Association, August 14, 1989; Spring 1997.

American Sociological Association, "Section on Environment and Technology." Pamphlet, no date.

"Americans Work More." Associated Press, September 1, 2001.

Amin, Yousreya, Emad Hamdi, et. al. "Mass Hysteria in an Arab Culture." *International Journal of Social Psychiatry, 43,* 4, Winter 1997:303–306.

Andersen, Margaret L. *Thinking About Women: Sociological Perspectives on Sex and Gender.* New York: Macmillan, 1988.

Anderson, Chris. "NORC Study Describes Homeless." *Chronicle,* 1986:5, 9.

Anderson, Elijah. *A Place on the Corner.* Chicago: University of Chicago Press, 1978.

Anderson, Elijah. *Streetwise.* Chicago: University of Chicago Press, 1990.

Anderson, Elijah. "Streetwise." In *Down to Earth Sociology: Introductory Readings,* 10th ed., James M. Henslin, ed. New York: Free Press, 1999:193–202.

Anderson, Elijah. "Selling Crack." In *Down to Earth Sociology: Introductory Readings,* 11th ed., James M. Henslin, ed. New York: The Free Press, 2001:247–256.

Anderson, Lee, et al. "A Decade of Public Charter Schools." Washington, D.C.: SRI, 2002.

Anderson, Nels. *Desert Saints: The Mormon Frontier in Utah.* Chicago: University of Chicago Press, 1966. First published in 1942.

Anderson, Philip. "God and the Swedish Immigrants." *Sweden and America,* Autumn 1995:17–20.

Anderson, Stephen A., and Ronald M. Sabatelli. *Family Interaction: A Multigenerational Developmental Perspective,* 3rd ed. Boston: Allyn and Bacon, 2003.

Anderson, Teresa A. "The Best Years of Their Lives." *Newsweek,* January 7, 1985:6.

Angell, Marcia. "Euthanasia in the Netherlands—Good News or Bad?" *New England Journal of Medicine, 335,* 22, November 28, 1996.

Angell, Robert C. "The Sociology of Human Conflict." In *The Nature of Human Conflict,* Elton B. McNeil, ed. Englewood Cliffs, N.J.: Prentice Hall 1965.

Angler, Natalie. "Do Races Differ? Not Really, DNA Shows." *New York Times,* August 22, 2000.

Annin, Peter. "Big Money, Big Trouble." *Newsweek,* April 19, 1999:59.

Annin, Peter, and Kendall Hamilton. "Marriage or Rape?" *Newsweek,* December 16, 1996:78.

Ansberry, Clare. "Despite Federal Law, Hospitals Still Reject Sick Who Can't Pay." *Wall Street Journal,* November 29, 1988:A1, A4.

"Anybody's Son Will Do." National Film Board of Canada, KCTS, and Films, Inc. 1983.

Aptheker, Herbert. "W.E.B. Du Bois: Struggle Not Despair." *Clinical Sociology Review, 8,* 1990:58–68.

Archbold, Ronna, and Mary Harmon. "International Success: Acceptance." Online: The Five O'clock Club, 2001.

Arenson, Karen W. "(Big) Red Faces at Cornell Over E-Mail Error." *New York Times,* February 28, 2003.

Arías, Jesús. "La Junta rehabilita en Grenada casas que deberá tirar por ruina." *El Pais,* January 2, 1993:1.

Ariés, Philippe. *Centuries of Childhood.* R. Baldick, trans. New York: Vintage Books, 1965.

Arlacchi, P. *Peasants and Great Estates: Society in Traditional Calabria.* Cambridge, England: Cambridge University Press, 1980.

Armitage, Richard L. "Red Army Retreat Doesn't Signal End of U.S. Obligation." *Wall Street Journal,* February 7, 1989:A20.

Arndt, William F., and F. Wilbur Gingrich. *A Greek-English Lexicon of the New Testament and Other Early Christian Literature.* Chicago: University of Chicago Press, 1957.

Asch, Solomon. "Effects of Group Pressure Upon the Modification and Distortion of Judgments." In *Readings in Social Psychology,* Guy Swanson, Theodore M. Newcomb, and Eugene L. Hartley, eds. New York: Holt, Rinehart and Winston, 1952.

Ashe, Arthur. "A Zero-Sum Game That Hurts Blacks." *Wall Street Journal,* February 27, 1992:A10.

Ashley, Richard. *Cocaine: Its History, Uses, and Effects.* New York: St. Martin's, 1975.

Associated Press. "Future Medicine Looks Futuristic." December 2, 1995.

Aulette, Judy Root. *Changing American Families.* Boston: Allyn and Bacon, 2002.

Ayittey, George B. N. "Black Africans Are Enraged at Arabs." *Wall Street Journal,* interactive edition, September 4, 1998.

Baca Zinn, Maxine. "Adaptation and Continuity in Mexican-Origin Families." In *Minority Families in the United States: A Multicultural Perspective,* Ronald L. Taylor, ed. Englewood Cliffs, N.J.: Prentice Hall, 1994:64–81.

Bachu, Amara, and Martin O'Connell. "Fertility of American Women: Population Characteristics." *Current Population Reports.* Washington, D.C.: U.S. Bureau of the Census, September 2000.

Badgett, M. V. Lee, and Heidi Hartmann. "The Effectiveness of Equal Employment Opportunity Policies." In *Economic Perspectives in Affirmative Action,* Margaret C. Simms, ed. Washington, D.C.: Joint Center for Political and Economic Studies 1995:55–83.

Bai, Matt. "Anatomy of a Massacre." *Newsweek,* May 3, 1999:25–31.

Bainbridge, William Sims. "Collective Behavior and Social Movements." In *Sociology,* Rodney Stark. Belmont, Calif.: Wadsworth, 1989:608–640.

Bales, Kevin. "The Social Psychology of Modern Slavery." *Scientific American, 286,* 4, April 2002.

Bales, Robert F. *Interaction Process Analysis.* Reading, Mass.: Addison-Wesley, 1950.

Bales, Robert F. "The Equilibrium Problem in Small Groups." In *Working Papers in the Theory of Action,* Talcott Parsons et al., eds. New York: Free Press, 1953:111–115.

Baltzell, E. Digby. *Puritan Boston and Quaker Philadelphia.* New York: Free Press, 1979.

Baltzell, E. Digby, and Howard G. Schneiderman. "Social Class in the Oval Office." *Society, 25,* Sept/Oct, 1988:42–49.

Banerjee, Neela. "Rape (and Silence About It) Haunts Baghdad." *New York Times,* July 16, 2003.

Bannon, Lisa. "How a Rumor Spread About Subliminal Sex in Disney's 'Aladdin'." *Wall Street Journal,* October 24, 1995:A1, A6.

Barber, D. A. "The 'New' Economy?" *Tucson Weekly,* January 8, 2003.

Barlett, Donald L., and James B. Steele. "Wheel of Misfortune." *Time,* December 16, 2002:44–58.

Barnes, Fred. "How to Rig a Poll." *Wall Street Journal,* June 14, 1995:A14.

Barnes, Harry Elmer. *The History of Western Civilization,* Vol. 1. New York: Harcourt, Brace, 1935.

Barnes, Helen. "A Comment on Stroud and Pritchard: Child Homicide, Psychiatric Disorder and Dangerousness." *British Journal of Social Work, 31,* 3, June 2001.

Barnes, Julian E. "A Bicycling Mystery: Head Injuries Piling Up." *New York Times,* July 29, 2001.

Baron, Robert, and Gerald Greenberg. *Behavior in Organizations.* Boston: Allyn and Bacon, 1990.

Baron, Stephen W. "Street Youth: Labour Market Experiences and Crime." *Canadian Review of Sociology and Anthropology, 38,* 2, May 2001:189–215.

Barry, John. "A New Breed of Soldier." *Newsweek,* December 10, 2001:24–31.

Barry, Paul. "Strong Medicine: A Talk with Former Principal Henry Gradillas." *College Board Review,* Fall 1989:2–13.

Barstow, David, and Lowell Bergman. "Death on the Job, Slaps on the Wrist." *Wall Street Journal,* January 10, 2003.

Bartlett, Donald L., and James B. Steele. "Paying a Price for Polluters." *Time,* November 23, 1998:72–80.

Bartos, Otomar J., and Paul Wehr. *Using Conflict Theory.* New York: Cambridge University Press, 2002.

Baskin, D. R., and I. B. Sommers. *Casualties of Community Disorder: Women's Careers in Violent Crime.* Boulder: Westview Press, 1998.

Bates, Marston. *Gluttons and Libertines: Human Problems of Being Natural.* New York: Vintage Books, 1967. Quoted in Crapo, Richley H. *Cultural Anthropology: Understanding Ourselves and Others,* 5th ed. Boston: McGraw Hill, 2002.

Beals, Ralph L., and Harry Hoijer. *An Introduction to Anthropology,* 3rd ed. New York: Macmillan, 1965.

Beaman, Jean. "New York to Belarus: Sociology in International Distance-learning." *Footnotes,* February 2003:7.

Beck, Allen J., Susan A. Kline, and Lawrence A. Greenfeld. "Survey of Youth in Custody, 1987." Washington, D.C.: U.S. Department of Justice, September 1988.

Beck, Scott H., and Joe W. Page. "Involvement in Activities and the Psychological Well-Being of Retired Men." *Activities, Adaptation, & Aging, 11,* 1, 1988:31–47.

Becker, Howard S. *Outsiders: Studies in the Sociology of Deviance.* New York: Free Press, 1966.

Beckett, Paul. "Even Piñatas Sold in Mexico Seem to Originate in Hollywood Now." *Wall Street Journal,* September 11, 1996:B1.

Beghley, Leonard. *The Structure of Social Stratification in the United States,* 3rd ed. Boston: Allyn and Bacon, 2000.

Begley, Sharon. "Twins: Nazi and Jew." *Newsweek, 94,* December 3, 1979:139.

Bell, Daniel. *The Coming of Post-Industrial Society: A Venture in Social Forecasting.* New York: Basic Books, 1973.

Bell, David A. "An American Success Story: The Triumph of Asian-Americans." In *Sociological Footprints: Introductory Readings in Sociology,* 5th ed., Leonard Cargan and Jeanne H. Ballantine, eds. Belmont, Calif.: Wadsworth, 1991:308–316.

Bellah, Robert N. *Beyond Belief.* New York: Harper & Row, 1970.

Belluck, Pam. "Prosecutors Say Greed Drove Pharmacist to Dilute Drugs." *New York Times,* August 18, 2001.

Benales, Carlos. "70 Days Battling Starvation and Freezing in the Andes: A Chronicle of Man's Unwillingness to Die." *New York Times,* January 1, 1973:3.

Bender, Sue, "Everyday Sacred: A Journey to the Amish." *Utne Reader,* September–October 1990:91–97.

Benet, Sula. "Why They Live to Be 100, or Even Older, in Abkhasia." *New York Times Magazine, 26,* December 1971.

Bennet, James. "Palestinian Mob Attacks Pollster Over Study on 'Right to Return.' " *New York Times,* July 14, 2003.

Bergen, Raquel Kennedy. *Wife Rape: Understanding the Response of Survivors and Service Providers.* Newbury Park, Calif.: Sage, 1996.

Bergen, Raquel Kennedy. Review of Lori B. Girshick, *Woman-To-Woman Sexual Violence: Does She Call It Rape?* In *Contemporary Sociology, 32,* 2, March 2003:173–174.

Berger, Arthur Asa. *Video Games: A Popular Culture Phenomenon.* New Brunswick, N.J.: Transaction Publishers, 2002.

Berger, Peter L. *The Capitalist Revolution: Fifty Propositions About Prosperity, Equality, and Liberty.* New York: Basic Books, 1991.

Berger, Peter L. *Invitation to Sociology: A Humanistic Perspective.* New York: Doubleday, 1963.

Berger, Peter L. "Invitation to Sociology." In *Down to Earth Sociology: Introductory Readings,* 12th ed., James M. Henslin, ed. New York: The Free Press, 2003: 3-7.

Bergmann, Barbara R. "The Future of Child Care." Paper presented at the 1995 meetings of the American Sociological Association.

Bergström, Hans. "Pressures Behind the Swedish Health Reforms." *Viewpoint Sweden, 12,* July 1992:1–5.

Berk, Richard A. *Collective Behavior.* Dubuque, Iowa: Brown, 1974.

Berle, Adolf, Jr., and Gardiner C. Means. *The Modern Corporation and Private Property.* New York: Harcourt, Brace and World, 1932. As cited in Useem 1980:44.

Bernard, Jessie. "The Good-Provider Role." In *Marriage and Family in a Changing Society,* 4th ed., James M. Henslin, ed. New York: Free Press, 1992:275–285.

Bernard, Viola W., Perry Ottenberg, and Fritz Redl. "Dehumanization: A Composite Psychological Defense in Relation to Modern War." In *The Triple Revolution Emerging: Social Problems in Depth,* Robert Perucci and Marc Pilisuk, eds. Boston: Little, Brown, 1971:17–34.

Bernhardt, Eva M., and Frances K. Goldscheider. "Men, Resources, and Family Living: The Determinants of Union and Parental Status in the United States and Sweden." *Journal of Marriage and the Family, 63,* 3, August 2001:793–803.

Bernstein, Elizabeth. "More Prayer, Less Hassle." *Wall Street Journal,* June 27, 2003:W3, W4.

Bernstein, Nina. "Studies Dispute 2 Assumptions About Welfare Overhaul." *New York Times,* December 12, 2000.

Bernstein, Richard. "Play Penn." *New Republic,* August 2, 1993.

Bernstein, Robert, and Mike Bergman. "Hispanic Population Reaches All-Time High of 38.8 Million, New Census Bureau Estimates Show." *U.S. Department of Commerce News,* June 18, 2003.

Berreby, David. "Scanning Brains for Insights on Racial Perception." *New York Times,* September 5, 2000.

Bertrand, Marianne, and Sendhil Mullainathan. "Are Emily and Brendan More Employable than Lakish and Jamal? A Field Experiment on Labor Market Discrimination." Unpublished paper, November 18, 2002.

Beynon, John. *Masculinities and Culture.* Philadelphia: Open University Press, 2002.

Bianchi, Suzanne M., and Daphne Spain. "Women Work, and Family in America." *Population Bulletin, 51,* 3, December 1996:1–47.

Bianchi, Suzanne M., and Lynne M. Casper. "American Families." *Population Bulletin, 55,* 4, December 2000:1–42.

Bianchi, Suzanne M., Melissa A. Milkie, Liana C. Sayer, and John P. Robinson. "Is Anyone Doing the Housework? Trends in the Gender Division of Household Labor." *Social Forces, 79,* 1, September 2000:191–228.

Binyon, Michael. "The Graveyard of Invading Armies." *The Times,* September 14, 2001.

Bird, Chloe E. "Gender Differences in the Social and Economic Burdens of Parenting and Psychological Distress." *Journal of Marriage and the Family, 59,* August 1997:1–16.

Bird, Chloe E., and Patricia P. Rieker. "Gender Matters: An Integrated Model for Understanding Men's and Women's Health." *Social Science and Medicine, 48,* 6, March 1999:745–755.

Bishop, Jerry E. "Study Finds Doctors Tend to Postpone Heart Surgery for Women, Raising Risk." *Wall Street Journal,* April 16, 1990:B4.

Bjerklie, David, Andrea Dorfman, Wendy Cole, Jeanne DeQuine, Helen Gibson, David S. Jackson, Leora Moldofsky, Timothy Roche, Chris Taylor, Cathy Booth Thomas, and Dick Thompson. "Baby, It's You: And You, and You…" *Time,* February 19, 2001:47–57.

Blassi, Joseph, and Michael Conte. "Employee Stock Ownership and Corporate Performance Among Public Companies." *Industrial and Labor Relations Review, 50,* 1, October 1996:60–79.

Blau, David M. "The Production of Quality in Child-Care Centers: Another Look." *Applied Developmental Science, 4,* 3, 2000:136–148.

Blau, Peter M., and Otis Dudley Duncan. *The American Occupational Structure.* New York: John Wiley, 1967.

Blauner, Robert. "Death and Social Structure." *Psychiatry, 29,* 1966:378–394.

Blee, Kathleen M. *Inside Organized Racism: Women in the Hate Movement.* Berkeley: University of California Press, 2002.

Blumer, Herbert George. "Collective Behavior." In *Principles of Sociology,* Robert E. Park, ed. New York: Barnes and Noble, 1939: 219–288.

Blumer, Herbert George. *Industrialization as an Agent of Social Change: A Critical Analysis,* David R. Maines and Thomas J. Morrione, eds. Hawthorne, N.Y.: Aldine de Gruyter, 1990.

Blumstein, Philip, and Pepper Schwartz. *American Couples: Money, Work, Sex.* New York: Pocket Books, 1985.

Bobo, Lawrence, and James R. Kluegel. "Modern American Prejudice: Stereotypes, Social Distance, and Perceptions of Discrimination Toward Blacks, Hispanics, and Asians." Paper presented at the 1991 annual meetings of the American Sociological Association.

Bonow, Robert O., and Robert H. Eckel. "Diet, Obesity, and Cardiovascular Risk." *New England Journal of Medicine, 348,* 17, May 22, 2003:2057–2058.

Booth, Alan, and James M. Dabbs, Jr. "Testosterone and Men's Marriages." *Social Forces, 72,* 2, December 1993:463–477.

Bosman, Ciska M., et al. "Business Success and Businesses' Beauty Capital." National Bureau of Economic Research Working Paper: 6083, July 1997.

"The Boss's Pay." *Wall Street Journal,* April 14, 2003.

Boulding, Elise. *The Underside of History.* Boulder, Colo.: Westview Press, 1976.

Bourgois, Philippe. "Crack in Spanish Harlem." In *Haves and Have-Nots: An International Reader on Social Inequality,* James Curtis and Lorne Tepperman, eds. Englewood Cliffs, N.J.: Prentice Hall, 1994:131–136.

Bowles, Samuel. "Unequal Education and the Reproduction of the Social Division of Labor." In *Power and Ideology in Education,* J. Karabel and A. H. Halsely, eds. NY: Oxford University Press, 1977.

Bowles, Samuel, and Herbert Gintis. *Schooling in Capitalist America.* New York: Basic Books, 1976.

Bowles, Samuel, and Herbert Gintis. "*Schooling in Capitalist America* Revisited." *Sociology of Education, 75,* 2002:1–18.

Boxer, Sarah. "When Emotion Worms Its Way Into Law." *New York Times,* April 7, 2001.

Boyle, Elizabeth Heger, Fortunata Songora, and Gail Foss. "International Discourse and Local Politics: Anti-Female-Genital-Cutting Laws in Egypt, Tanzania, and the United States," *Social Problems, 48,* 4, November 2001:524–544.

Bradley, Martin B., Norman M. Green, Jr., Dale E. Jones, Mac Lynn, and Lou McNiel. *Churches and Church Membership in the United States 1990.* Atlanta: Glenmary Research Center, 1992.

Brajuha, Mario, and Lyle Hallowell. "Legal Intrusion and the Politics of Fieldwork: The Impact of the Brajuha Case." *Urban Life, 14,* 4, January 1986:454–478.

Bramlett, M. D., and W. D. Mosher. "Cohabitation, Marriage, Divorce, and Remarriage in the United States." Hyattsville, Md.: National Center for Health Statistics, Vital Health Statistics, Series 23, Number 22, July 2002.

Brannon, Linda. *Gender: Psychological Perspectives,* 2nd ed. Boston: Allyn and Bacon, 1999.

Brauchli, Marcus W. "Wary of Education But Needing Brains, China Faces a Dilemma." *Wall Street Journal,* November 15, 1994:A1, A10.

Bray, Rosemary L. "Rosa Parks: A Legendary Moment, a Lifetime of Activism. *Ms., 6,* 3, November–December 1995:45–47.

Brecher, Edward M., and the Editors of Consumer Reports. *Licit and Illicit Drugs.* Boston: Little, Brown, 1972.

Breen, Richard, and Christopher T. Whelan. "Gender and Class Mobility: Evidence from the Republic of Ireland." *Sociology, 29,* 1, February 1995:1–22.

Bretos, Miguel A. "Hispanics Face Institutional Exclusion." *Miami Herald,* May 22, 1994.

Bridgwater, William, ed. *The Columbia Viking Desk Encyclopedia.* New York: Viking Press, 1953.

Brilliant, Ashleigh E. *Social Effects of the Automobile in Southern Califronia during the 1920s.* Unpublished doctoral disertation U. of C. at Berkeley, 1964.

Brines, Julie. "Economic Dependency, Gender, and the Division of Labor at Home." *American Journal of Sociology, 100,* 3, November 1994:652–688.

Brines, Julie, and Kara Joyner. "The Ties That Bind. Principles of Cohesion in Cohabitation and Marriage." *American Sociological Review, 64,* June 1999:333–355.

Brinton, Crane. *The Anatomy of Revolution.* New York: Vintage Books, 1965.

Broad, William J. "The Shuttle Explodes." *New York Times,* January 29, 1986, A1, A5.

Broad, William J., and Judith Miller. "Rocky Start for U.S. Plan to Stockpile Vaccines to Fight Germ Warfare." *New York Times,* August 7, 1998.

Broad, William J., and Melody Petersen. "The Biological Threat." *New York Times,* September 23, 2001.

Brockerhoff, Martin P. "An Urbanizing World." *Population Bulletin, 55,* 3, September 2000:1–44.

Bromley, David G. "The Satanic Cult Scare." *Culture and Society,* May–June 1991:55–56.

Bronfenbrenner, Urie. "Principles for the Healthy Growth and Development of Children." In *Marriage and Family in a Changing Society,* 4th ed., James M. Henslin, ed. New York: Free Press, 1992:243–249.

Brooke, James. "Amid U.S. Islam's Growth in the U.S., Muslims Face a Surge in Attacks." *New York Times,* August 28, 1995:A1, B7.

Brooks-Gunn, Jeanne, Greg. J. Duncan, and Lawrence Aber, eds. *Neighborhood Poverty, Volume 1: Context and Consequences for Children.* New York: Russell Sage Foundation, 1997.

Brown, Donald A. "The Ethical Dimensions of Global Environmental Issues." *Daedalus, 130,* 4, Fall 2001:59–69.

Browne, Beverly A. "Gender Stereotypes in Advertising on Children's Television in the 1990s: A Cross-National Analysis." *Journal of Advertising, 27,* 1, Spring 1998:83–96.

Browning, Christopher R. *Ordinary Men: Reserve Police Battalion 101 and the Final Solution in Poland.* New York: HarperPerennial, 1993.

Bruni, Frank. "Leaders Broadly Back a Draft Charter for the European Union." *New York Times,* June 21, 2003.

Brunvand, Jan Harold. *The Vanishing Hitchhiker: American Urban Legends and Their Meanings.* New York: Norton, 1981.

Brunvand, Jan Harold. *The Choking Doberman and Other "New" Urban Legends.* New York: Norton, 1984.

Brunvand, Jan Harold. *The Study of American Folklore.* New York: Norton, 1986.

Brunvand, Jan Harold. "Introduction." *Skeptical Inquirer,* May–June 1999:29.

Bryant, Alyssa N. "Community College Students: Recent Findings and Trends." *Community College Review, 29,* 3, 2001:77–93.

Bryant, Chalandra M., Rand D. Conger, and Jennifer M. Meehan. "The Influence of In-Laws on Changes in Marital Success." *Journal of Marriage and the Family, 63, 3,* August 2001:614–626.

Bryant, Clifton D. "Cockfighting: America's Invisible Sport." In *Down to Earth Sociology: Introductory Readings,* 7th ed., James M. Henslin, ed. New York: Free Press, 1993.

Brzezinksi, Matthew. "Where Cash Isn't King: Barter Lines Pockets in Ex-Soviet States." *Wall Street Journal,* May 1, 1997:A14.

Buckley, Frank, and Elizabeth Cohen. "Bush Orders Smallpox Vaccination for Military, Himself." CNN.Com, December 16, 2002.

Bumiller, Elisabeth. "First Comes Marriage—Then, Maybe, Love." In *Marriage and Family in a Changing Society,* 4th ed., James M. Henslin, ed. New York: Free Press, 1992:120–125.

Buraway, Michael. "Public Sociologies: Reply to Hausknecht." *Footnotes,* January 2003:8.

Burgess, Ernest W. "The Growth of the City: An Introduction to a Research Project." In *The City,* Robert E. Park et al., eds. Chicago: University of Chicago Press, 1925:47–62.

Burgess, Ernest W., and Harvey J. Locke. *The Family: From Institution to Companionship.* New York: American Book, 1945.

Burnham, Walter Dean. *Democracy in the Making: American Government and Politics.* Englewood Cliffs, N.J.: Prentice Hall, 1983.

Burris, Val. "The Myth of Old Money Liberalism: The Politics of the *Forbes* 400 Richest Americans." *Social Problems, 47,* 3, August 2000:360–378.

Bus, David M., Todd K. Shakelford, Lee A. Kirkpatrick, and Randy L. Larsen. "A Half Century of Mate Preferences: The Cultural Evolution of Values." *Journal of Marriage and Family, 63,* May 2001:491–503.

Bush, Diane Mitsch, and Robert G. Simmons. "Socialization Processes Over the Life Course." In *Social Psychology: Sociological Perspectives,* eds. Morris Rosenberger and Ralph H. Turner. New Brunswick, N.J.:Transaction, 1990:133–164.

Butler, Robert N. "Ageism: Another Form of Bigotry." *Gerontologist, 9,* Winter 1980:243–246.

Butler, Robert N. *Why Survive? Being Old in America.* New York: Harper & Row, 1975.

Buttel, Frederick H. "New Directions in Environmental Sociology." *Annual Review of Sociology, 13,* W. Richard Scott and James F. Short, Jr., eds. Palo Alto, Calif.: Annual Reviews, 1987:465–488.

Butterfield, Fox. "Prison Rates Among Blacks Reach a Peak, Report Finds." *New York Times,* April 7, 2003.

Bynum, Bill. "Discarded Diagnoses." *Lancet, 358,* 9294, November 17, 2001:1736.

Callahan, Daniel. *Setting Limits: Medical Goals in an Aging Society.* New York: Simon & Schuster, 1987.

Calle, Eugenia E., Carmen Rodriguez, Kimberly Walker-Thurmond, and Michael J. Thun. "Overweight, Obesity, and Mortality from Cancer in a Prospectively Studied Cohort of U.S. Adults." *New England Journal of Medicine, 348,* 17, April 24, 2003.

Canavan, Margaret M., Walter J. Meyer, III, and Deborah C. Higgs. "The Female Experience of Sibling Incest." *Journal of Marital and Family Therapy, 18,* 2, 1992:129–142.

Cancian, Maria, Marieka M. Klawitter, Daniel R. Meyer, Ann Rangarajan, Geoffrey Wallace, and Robert G. Wood. "Income and Program Participation Among Early TRANF Recipients: The Evidence from New Jersey, Washington, and Wisconsin." *Focus, 22,* 3, Summer 2003:2–10.

Canedy, Dana. "Critics of Graduation Exam Threaten Boycott in Florida." *New York Times,* May 13, 2003.

Cannon, Lou. *Official Negligence: How Rodney King and the Riots Changed Los Angeles and the LAPD.* New York: Times Books, 1998.

Cantor, David, and Mareena McKinley Wright. "School Crime Patterns: A National Profile of U.S. Public High Schools Using Rates of Crime Reported to Police." Washington, D.C.: U.S. Department of Education, 2003.

Cantril, Hadley. *The Psychology of Social Movements.* New York: Wiley, 1941.

Caplow, Theodore. "The American Way of Celebrating Christmas." In *Down to Earth Sociology: Introductory Readings,* 6th ed., James M. Henslin, ed. New York: Free Press, 1991:88–97.

Carlson, Lewis H., and George A. Colburn. *In Their Place: White America Defines Her Minorities, 1850–1950.* New York: Wiley, 1972.

Carpenito, Lynda Juall. "The Myths of Acquaintance Rape." *Nursing Forum, 34,* 4, October–December 1999:3.

Carpenter, Betsy. "Redwood Radicals." *U.S. News & World Report, 109,* 11, September 17, 1990:50–51.

Carper, James C. "Pluralism to Establishment to Dissent: The Religious and Educational Context of Home Schooling." *Peabody Journal of Education, 75,* 1–2, 2000:8–19.

Carr, Deborah, Carol D. Ryff, Burton Singer, and William J. Magee. "Bringing the 'Life' Back into Life Course Research: A 'Person-Centered' Approach to Studying the Life Course." Paper presented at the 1995 meetings of the American Sociological Association.

Carrasquillo, Hector. "The Puerto Rican Family." In *Minority Families in the United States: A Multicultural Perspective,* Ronald L. Taylor, ed. Englewood Cliffs, N.J.: Prentice Hall, 1994:82–94.

Carrington, Tim. "Developed Nations Want Poor Countries to Succeed on Trade, But Not Too Much." *Wall Street Journal,* September 20, 1993:A10.

Cartwright, Dorwin, and Alvin Zander, eds. *Group Dynamics,* 3rd ed. Evanston, Ill.: Peterson, 1968.

Case, Robbie, and Yukari Okamoto. "The Role of Central Conceptual Structures in the Development of Children's Thought." *Monographs of the Society for Research on Child Development, 61,* 1996:1–2.

Casper, Monica J. *The Making of the Unborn Patient: A Social Anatomy of Fetal Surgery.* New Brunswick, N.J.: Rutgers University Press, 1998.

Cassel, Russell N. "Examining the Basic Principles for Effective Leadership." *College Student Journal, 33,* 2, June 1999:288–301.

Cauthen, Nancy K., and James M. Jasper. "Culture, Politics, and Moral Panics." *Sociological Forum, 9,* 3, September 1994: 495–503.

Centers for Disease Control. *HIV/AIDS Surveillance Report,* 1997.

Centers for Disease Control. *HIV/AIDS Surveillance Report, 12,* 2, June 2001.

Centers for Disease Control, National Center for Injury Prevention and Control. "2000 United States Suicide." Online, 2002.

Centers for Disease Control. "AIDS." Online, 2003.

Cerulo, Karen A., and Janet M. Ruane. "Death Comes Alive: Technology and the Re-Conception of Death." In *Science as Culture,* 1996.

Cerulo, Karen A., Janet M. Ruane, and Mary Chayko. "Technological Ties That Bind: Media-Generated Primary Groups." *Communication Research, 19,* 1, February 1992:109–129.

Cha, Kwang Y., Daniel P. Wirth, and Rogerio A. Lobo. "Does Prayer Influence the Success of In Vitro Fertilization-Embryo Transfer? Report of a Masked, Randomized Trial." *Journal of Reproductive Medicine, 46,* 9, September 2001:781–787.

Chafetz, Janet Saltzman. *Masculine/Feminine or Human? An Overview of the Sociology of Sex Roles.* Itasca, Ill: F. E. Peacock, 1974.

Chafetz, Janet Saltzman. *Gender Equity: An Integrated Theory of Stability and Change.* Newbury Park, Calif.: Sage, 1990.

Chafetz, Janet Saltzman, and Anthony Gary Dworkin. *Female Revolt: Women's Movements in World and Historical Perspective.* Totowa, N.J.: Rowman & Allanheld, 1986.

Chagnon, Napoleon A. *Yanomamo: The Fierce People,* 2nd ed. New York: Holt, Rinehart and Winston, 1977.

Chaker, Anne Marie. "For Antidepressant Makers, Shopaholics Are New Market." *Wall Street Journal,* January 2, 2003.

Chalfant, H. Paul. "Stepping to Redemption: Twelve-Step Groups as Implicit Religion." *Free Inquiry in Creative Sociology, 20,* 2, November 1992:115–120.

Chalker, Anne Marie. "A Backdoor Route to a College Dream." *Wall Street Journal,* June 26, 2003b.

Chalkley, Kate. "Female Genital Mutilation: New Laws, Programs Try to End Practice." *Population Today, 25,* 10, October 1997:4–5.

Chamberlain, Claudine. "Implicit Association Test." ABCNews Online, September 30, 1998.

Chambliss, Daniel F. "The World of the Hospital." In *Down to Earth Sociology: Introductory Readings,* 12th ed., James M. Henslin, ed. New York: The Free Press, 2003:434–446.

Chambliss, William J. *Power, Politics, and Crime.* Boulder: Westview Press, 2000.

Chambliss, William J. "The Saints and the Roughnecks." In *Down to Earth Sociology: Introductory Readings,* 12th ed., James M. Henslin, ed. New York: The Free Press, 2003:271–286. First published in *Society,* 11, 1973.

Chambliss, William J. "A Sociological Analysis of the Law of Vagrancy." *Social Problems, 12,* Summer 1964:67–77.

Chandler, Tertius, and Gerald Fox. *3000 Years of Urban Growth.* New York: Academic Press, 1974.

Chandra, Vibha P. "Fragmented Identities: The Social Construction of Ethnicity, 1885–1947." Unpublished paper, 1993.

Chang, Leslie. "Confucius Said: Sons, Care for Your Elders; Elders Say: We Sue." *Wall Street Journal,* April 3, 2000:A1, A15.

Charles, Camille Zubrinsky. "Neighborhood Racial-Composition Preferences: Evidence from a Multiethnic Metropolis." *Social Problems, 47,* 3, August 2000:379–407.

Chayko, Mary. *Connecting: How We Form Social Bonds and Communities in the Internet Age.* Albany: State University of New York Press, 2002.

Chen, Edwin. "Twins Reared Apart: A Living Lab." *New York Times Magazine.* December 9, 1979:112.

Chen, Kathy. "China's Women Face Obstacles in Workplace." *Wall Street Journal,* August 28, 1995:B1, B5.

Cherlin, Andrew J. "A 'Quieting' of Change." *Contexts, 1,* 1, Spring 2002:67–68.

Cherlin, J. Andrew. "Remarriage as an Incomplete Institution." In *Marriage and Family in a Changing Society,* 3rd ed., James M. Henslin, ed. New York: Free Press, 1989:492–501.

Cherlin, J. Andrew, and Frank F. Furstenberg, Jr. "The American Family in the Year 2000." In *Down to Earth Sociology,* 5th ed., James M. Henslin, ed. New York: Free Press, 1988:325–331.

"Child Support for Custodial Mothers and Fathers." *Current Population Reports,* Series P60-187. Washington, D.C.: U.S. Bureau of the Census, 1995.

Chin, Nancy P., Alicia Monroe, and Kevin Fiscella. "Social Determinants of (Un)Healthy Behaviors." *Education for Health: Change in Learning and Practice, 13,* 3, November 2000:317–328.

Chivers, C. J. "Officer Resigns Before Hearing in D.W.I. Case." *New York Times,* August 29, 2001.

Chodorow, Nancy J. "What Is the Relation Between Psychoanalytic Feminism and the Psychoanalytic Psychology of Women?" In *Theoretical Perspectives on Sexual Difference,* Deborah L. Rhode, ed. New Haven, Conn.: Yale University Press, 1990:114–130.

Churchill, Ward. *A Little Matter of Genocide: Holocaust and Denial in the Americas, 1492 to the Present.* San Francisco: City Lights Books, 1997.

Clair, Jeffrey Michael., David A. Karp, and William C. Yoels. *Experiencing the Life Cycle: A Social Psychology of Aging,* 2nd ed. Springfield, Ill.: Thomas, 1993.

Clark, Candace. *Misery and Company: Sympathy in Everyday Life.* Chicago: University of Chicago Press, 1997.

Clark, Candace. "Sympathy in Everyday Life." In *Down to Earth Sociology: Introductory Readings,* 6th ed., James M. Henslin, ed. New York: Free Press, 1991:193–203.

Clark, Robert L., and Naohiro Ogawa. "Transition from Career Jobs to Retirement in Japan." *Industrial Relations, 36,* 2, April 1997:255–270.

Clarke, Lee. "Panic: Myth or Reality?" *Contexts,* Fall 2002:21–26.

Clarke, Robyn D. "Has the Glass Ceiling Really Been Shattered?" *Black Enterprise, 30,* 7, February 2000:145–148.

Clay, Jason W. "What's a Nation?" *Mother Jones,* November–December 1990:28, 30.

Cleeland, Nancy. "Slowdown's Silent Victims." *Los Angeles Times,* October 21, 2001.

Clingempeel, W. Glenn, and N. Dickon Repucci. "Joint Custody After Divorce: Major Issues and Goals for Research." *Psychological Bulletin, 9,* 1982:102–127.

Cloud, John. "For Better or Worse." *Time,* October 26, 1998:43–44.

Cloward, Richard A., and Lloyd E. Ohlin. *Delinquency and Opportunity: A Theory of Delinquent Gangs.* New York: Free Press, 1960.

Cnaan, Ram A. "Neighborhood-representing Organizations: How Democratic Are They?" *Social Science Review,* December 1991:614–634.

Cockerham, William C. "The Social Determinants of the Decline of Life Expectancy in Russia and Eastern Europe: A Lifestyle Explanation." *Journal of Health and Social Behavior, 38,* June 1997:117–130.

Cohan, Catherine L., and Stacey Kleinbaum. "Toward Greater Understanding of the Cohabitation Effect: Premarital Cohabitation and Marital Communication." *Journal of Marriage and Family, 64,* February 2002:180–192.

Cohen, Joel E. "How Many People Can the Earth Support?" *Population Today,* January 1996:4–5.

Cohen, Roger. "Europe's Shifting Role Poses Challenge to U.S." *New York Times,* February 11, 2001.

Cohen, Steven M. "Hey NCR—We're the Shareholders, You Work for Us." *Wall Street Journal,* December 19, 1990:A16.

"Coke Adds Life, But It Cannot Always Explain It." *Lancet, 354,* 9174, July 17, 1999:173.

Colapinto, John. *As Nature Made Him: The Boy Who Was Raised as a Girl.* New York: HarperCollins, 2001.

Cole, Jeff, and Sarah Lubman. "Weapons Merchants Are Going Great Guns in Post-Cold War Era." *Wall Street Journal,* January 28, 1994:A1, A4.

Coleman, James S., and Thomas Hoffer. *Public and Private Schools: The Impact of Communities.* New York: Basic Books, 1987.

Coleman, James William. "Politics and the Abuse of Power." In *Down to Earth Sociology: Introductory Readings,* 8th ed., James M. Henslin, ed. New York: Free Press, 1995:442–450.

Coleman, Joseph "The Son of North Korean Leader Had a Plan." Associated Press, May 4, 2001.

Coleman, Marilyn, Lawrence Ganong, and Mark Fine. "Reinvestigating Remarriage: Another Decade of Progress." *Journal of Marriage and the Family, 62,* 4, November 2000:1288–1307.

Collins, Huntly. "AIDS Activists Join Gray Panthers Against Drug Company." *Philadelphia Inquirer,* February 15, 2001.

Collins, Randall. *The Credential Society: An Historical Sociology of Education.* New York: Academic Press, 1979.

Collins, Randall. *Theoretical Sociology.* San Diego, Calif.: Harcourt, Brace Jovanovich, 1988.

Collins, Randall. "Socially Unrecognized Cumulation." *American Sociologist, 30,* 2, Summer 1999:41–61.

Collins, Randall, Janet Saltzman Chafetz, Rae Lesser Blumberg, Scott Coltrane, and Jonathan H. Turner. "Toward an Integrated Theory of Gender Stratification." *Sociological Perspectives, 36,* 3, 1993:185–216.

Collymore, Yvette. "Conveying Concerns: Women Report on Gender-Based Violence." Washington, D.C.: Population Reference Bureau, 2000.

"Coming to a Neighborhood Near You." *Economist, 360,* 8220, May 5, 2001:23–24.

Conahan, Frank C. "Human Experimentation: An Overview on Cold War Era Programs." Washington, D.C.: U.S. General Accounting Office, September 28, 1994:1–11.

Conklin, John E. *Why Crime Rates Fell.* Boston: Allyn and Bacon, 2003.

Conley, Dalton. "Capital for College: Parental Assets and Postsecondary Schooling." *Sociology of Education, 74,* 1, January 2001:59–68.

Conley, Dalton. "Forty Acres and a Mule: What If America Pays Reparations?" *Contexts,* Fall 2002:13–20.

Connors, L. "Gender of Infant Differences in Attachment: Associations with Temperament and Caregiving Experiences." Paper presented at the Annual Conference of the British Psychological Society, Oxford, England, 1996.

Conrad, Peter. "Public Eyes and Private Genes: Historical Frames, New Constructions, and Social Problems." *Social Problems, 44,* 2, May 1997:139–154.

Cook, Bradley J. "Islam and Egyptian Higher Education: Student Attitudes." *Comparative Education Review, 45,* 3, August 2001:379–403.

Cooley, Charles Horton. *Human Nature and the Social Order.* New York: Scribner's, 1902.

Cooley, Charles Horton. *Social Organization.* New York: Schocken Books, 1962. First published by Scribner's, 1909.

Coontz, Stephanie. *The Way We Never Were: American Families and the Nostalgia Trap.* New York: Basic Books, 2000.

Cooper, Helene. "Offering Aerobics, Karate, Aquatics, Hospitals Stress Business of 'Wellness.'" *Wall Street Journal,* August 9, 1993:B1, B3.

Cose, Ellis. "The Good News About Black America." *Newsweek,* June 7, 1999:29–40.

Cose, Ellis. "What's White Anyway?" *Newsweek,* September 18, 2000:64–65.

Coser, Lewis A. *Masters of Sociological Thought: Ideas in Historical and Social Context,* 2nd ed. New York: Harcourt Brace Jovanovich, 1977.

Cottin, Lou. *Elders in Rebellion: A Guide to Senior Activism.* Garden City, N.Y.: Anchor Doubleday, 1979.

Coughlin, Ellen K. "Studying Homelessness: The Difficulty of Tracking a Transient Population." *Chronicle of Higher Education,* October 19, 1988:A6–A12.

"Couple Plan to Clone a Baby." CNN Online, August 13, 2002.

Courtney, Kelly. "Two Sides of the Environmental Movement: Radical Earth First! and the Sierra Club." Paper presented at the 1995 meetings of the American Sociological Association.

Cousins, Albert, and Hans Nagpaul. *Urban Man and Society.* New York: McGraw-Hill, 1970.

Cowen, Emory L., Judah Landes, and Donald E. Schaet. "The Effects of Mild Frustration on the Expression of Prejudiced Attitudes." *Journal of Abnormal and Social Psychology.* January 1959:33–38.

Cowgill, Donald. "The Aging of Populations and Societies." *Annals of the American Academy of Political and Social Science, 415,* 1974:1–18.

Cowley, Geoffrey. "Attention: Aging Men." *Newsweek,* November 16, 1996:66–75.

Cowley, Geoffrey. "Sobering Up About AIDS." *Newsweek,* June 26, 1998.

Cowley, Geoffrey, and Anne Underwood. "A Revolution in Medicine." *Newsweek,* April 10, 2000:58–62.

Cowley, Joyce. *Pioneers of Women's Liberation.* New York: Merit, 1969.

Cran, Christina, "Ten Years After the Mass Suicide the Memory of Koresh Lives On." *The Scotsman.* April 19, 2003.

Crosbie, Paul V., ed. *Interaction in Small Groups.* New York: Macmillan, 1975.

Crossen, Cynthia. "Margin of Error: Studies Galore Support Products and Positions, But Are They Reliable?" *Wall Street Journal,* Nov 14, 1991:A1.

Crossen, Cynthia. "Deja Vu." *Wall Street Journal,* March 5, 2003.

Crossette, Barbara. "U.N. Documents Inequities for Women as World Forum Nears." *New York Times,* August 18, 1995a.

Crossette, Barbara. "Worldwide Study Finds Decline in Election of Women Legislators." *New York Times,* August 27, 1995b.

Crossette, Barbara. "Caste May Be India's Moral Achilles' Heel." *New York Times,* October 20, 1996.

Croudace, T. J., R. Kayne, P. B. Jones, and G. L. Harrison. "Non-Linear Relationship Between an Index of Social Deprivation, Psychiatric Admission Prevalence and the Incidence of Psychosis." *Psychology of Medicine, 30,* 1, January 2000:177–185.

Cumming, Elaine. "Further Thoughts on the Theory of Disengagement." In *Aging in America: Readings in Social Gerontology,* Cary S. Kart and Barbara B. Manard, eds. Sherman Oaks, Calif.: Alfred Publishing, 1976:19–41.

Cumming, Elaine, and William E. Henry. *Growing Old: The Process of Disengagement.* New York: Basic Books, 1961.

Curtin, Sharon. "Nobody Ever Died of Old Age: In Praise of Old People." In *Growing Old in America.* Beth Hess, ed. New Brunswick, N.J.: Transaction, 1976:273–284.

Curwin, E. Cecil, and Gudmond Hart. *Plough and Pasture.* New York: Collier Books, 1961.

Dabbs, James M., Jr., Marian F. Hargrove, and Colleen Heusel. "Testosterone Differences Among College Fraternities: Well-Behaved vs. Rambunctious." *Personality and Individual Differences, 20,* 1996:157–161.

Dabbs, James M., Jr., and Robin Morris. "Testosterone, Social Class, and Antisocial Behavior in a Sample of 4,462 Men." *Psychological Science, 1,* 3, May 1990:209–211.

Dabbs, James M., Jr., Timothy S. Carr, Robert L. Frady, and Jasmin K. Riad. "Testosterone, Crime, and Misbehavior Among 692 Male Prison Inmates." *Personality and Individual Differences, 18,* 1995:627–633.

Dahl, Robert A. *Who Governs?* New Haven, Conn.: Yale University Press, 1961.

Dahl, Robert A. *Dilemmas of Pluralist Democracy: Autonomy vs. Control.* New Haven, Conn.: Yale University Press, 1982.

Dahrendorf, Ralf. *Class and Class Conflict in Industrial Society.* Palo Alto, Calif.: Stanford University Press, 1959.

Dalrymple, Theodore. *Life at the Bottom: The Worldview That Makes the Underclass.* Chicago: Ivan R. Dee, 2001.

Danzi, Angela D. "Savaria, The Midwife: Childbirth and Change in the Immigrant Community." In *Contemporary Readings in Sociology,* Judith N. DeSena, ed. Dubuque, Iowa: Kendall/Hunt, 1989:47–56.

Darden, Christoper. *Contempt.* New York: HarperCollins, 1997.

Darley, John M., and Bibb Latané. "Bystander Intervention in Emergencies: Diffusion of Responsibility." *Journal of Personality and Social Psychology, 8,* 4, 1968:377–383.

Darweesh, Suzanne. "Use Your Buying Power to Promote Ethics." *Los Angeles Times,* November 5, 2000.

Darwin, Charles. *The Origin of Species.* Chicago: Conley, 1859.

Dasgupta, Nilanjana, Debbie E. McGhee, Anthony G. Greenwald, and Mahzarin R. Banaji. "Automatic Preference for White Americans: Eliminating the Familiarity Explanation." *Journal of Experimental Social Psychology, 36,* 3, May 2000:316–328.

Davies, Kirk L. "The Imposition of Martial Law in the United States." *Air Force Law Review, 49,* 2000:67–112.

Davis, Ann. "Artificial Reproduction Arrangers Are Ruled Child's Legal Parents." *Wall Street Journal,* March 11, 1998a:B2.

Davis, Ann. "High-Tech Births Spawn Legal Riddles." *Wall Street Journal,* January 26, 1998b:B1.

Davis, Fred. "The Cabdriver and His Fare: Facets of a Fleeting Relationship." *American Journal of Sociology, 65,* September 1959:158–165.

Davis, Kingsley. "Extreme Social Isolation of a Child." *American Journal of Sociology, 45,* 4 Jan. 1940:554–565.

Davis, Kingsley. "Extreme Isolation." In *Down to Earth Sociology: Introductory Readings,* 12th ed., James M. Henslin, ed. New York: Free Press, 2003:133–142.

Davis, Kingsley, and Wilbert E. Moore. "Some Principles of Stratification." *American Sociological Review, 10,* 1945:242–249.

Davis, Kingsley, and Wilbert E. Moore. "Reply to Tumin." *American Sociological Review, 18,* 1953:394–396.

Davis, Nancy J., and Robert V. Robinson. "Class Identification of Men and Women in the 1970s and 1980s." *American Sociological Review, 53,* February 1988:103–112.

Davis, Scott. Review of John J. Witte's *The Market Approach to Education: An Analysis of America's First Voucher Program.* Princeton, N.J.: Princeton University Press, 2000. *Contemporary Sociology, 31,* 6, 2002:781–782.

Davis, Stan, and Christopher Meyer. "What Will Replace the Tech Economy?" *Time,* May 22, 2000.

Davis, Stan. *Lessons From the Future: Making Sense of a Blurred World.* New York: Capstone Publishers, 2001.

Dawley, Richard Lee. *Amish in Wisconsin.* New Berlin, Wis.: Amish Insight, 2003.

Deaver, Michael V. "Democratizing Russian Higher Education." *Demokratizatsiya, 9,* 3, Summer 2001:350–366.

Deck, Leland P. "Buying Brains by the Inch." *Journal of the College and University Personnel Association, 19,* 1968:33–37.

Deegan, Mary Jo. "W. E. B. Du Bois and the Women of Hull-House, 1895–1899." *American Sociologist,* Winter 1988:301–311.

DeFrancis, Marc. "U.S. Elder Care Is in a Fragile State." *Population Today, 30,* 1, January 2002:1–3.

DeGraaf, John. "Workweek Woes." *New York Times,* April 12, 2003.

Del Castillo, Daniel. "A Sociology Professor in Mauritania Fights Its Slave System." *The Chronicle of Higher Education,* May 31, 2002:A39-A40.

Deliege, Robert. *The Untouchables of India.* New York: Berg Publishers, 2001.

DeMartini, Joseph R. "Basic and Applied Sociological Work: Divergence, Convergence, or Peaceful Co-existence?" *The Journal of Applied Behavioral Science, 18,* 2, 1982:203–215.

DeMause, Lloyd. "Our Forebears Made Childhood a Nightmare." *Psychology Today 8,* 11, April 1975:85–88.

D'Emilio, Frances. "Amato Asked to Lead Italy Coalition." Associated Press, April 22, 2000.

Denney, Nancy W., and David Quadagno. *Human Sexuality,* 2nd ed. St. Louis: Mosby, 1992.

Dentler, Robert A. *Practicing Sociology: Selected Fields.* Westport, Conn.: Praeger Publishers, 2002.

Denzin, Norman K. "The Suicide Machine." *Society,* July–August, 1992:7–10.

DeParle, Jason. "Report to Clinton Sees Vast Extent of Homelessness." *New York Times,* February 17, 1994:A1, A10.

DeParle, Jason. "Bold Effort Leaves Much Unchanged for the Poor." *New York Times,* December 30, 1999.

Derber, Charles, and William Schwartz. "Toward a Theory of Worker Participation." In *The Transformation of Industrial Organization: Management, Labor, and Society in the United States,* Frank Hearn, ed. Belmont, Calif.: Wadsworth, 1988:217–229.

Deutscher, Irwin. *Accommodating Diversity: National Policies that Prevent Ethnic Conflict.* Lanham, Md.: Lexington Books, 2002.

Diamond, Edwin, and Robert A. Silverman. *White House to Your House: Media and Politics in Virtual America.* Cambridge, Mass.: MIT Press, 1995.

Diamond, Milton, and Keith Sigmundson. "Sex Reassignment at Birth: Long-term Review and Clinical Implications." *Archives of Pediatric and Adolescent Medicine, 151,* March 1997:298–304.

Dietz, Tracy L. "An Examination of Violence and Gender Role Portrayals in Video Games." *Women and Language, 23,* 2, Fall 2000:64–77.

Dillon, Sam. "States Cut Test Standards to Avoid Sanctions." *New York Times,* May 21, 2003.

Dixon, Celvia Stovall, and Kathryn D. Rettig. "An Examination of Income Adequacy for Single Women Two Years After Divorce." *Journal of Divorce and Remarriage, 22,* 1–2, 1994:55–71.

Doane, Ashley W., Jr. "Dominant Group Ethnic Identity in the United States: The Role of 'Hidden' Ethnicity in Intergroup Relations." *The Sociological Quarterly, 38,* 3, Summer 1997:375–397.

Dobash, Russell P., R. Emerson Dobash, Margo Wilson, and Martin Daly. "The Myth of Sexual Symmetry in Marital Violence." *Social Problems, 39,* 1, February 1992:71–91.

Dobash, Russell P., R. Emerson Dobash, Margo Wilson, and Martin Daly. "Marital Violence Is Not Symmetrical: A Response to Campbell." *SSSP Newsletter, 24,* 3, Fall 1993:26–30.

Dobriner, William M. "The Football Team as Social Structure and Social System." In *Social Structures and Systems: A Sociological Overview.* Pacific Palisades, Calif.: Goodyear, 1969a:116–120.

Dobriner, William M. *Social Structures and Systems.* Pacific Palisades, California: Goodyear, 1969b.

Dobyns, Henry F. *Their Numbers Became Thinned: Native American Population Dynamics in Eastern North America.* Knoxville: University of Tennessee Press, 1983.

Dollard, John, et al. *Frustration and Aggression.* New Haven, Conn.: Yale University Press, 1939.

Domhoff, G. William. *The Powers That Be.* New York: Random House, 1979.

Domhoff, G. William. *The Power Elite and the State: How Policy Is Made in America.* Hawthorne, N.Y.: Aldine de Gruyter, 1990.

Domhoff, G. William. *Who Rules America? Power and Politics in the Year 2000,* 3rd ed. Mountain View, Calif: Mayfield Publishing, 1998.

Domhoff, G. William. "The Bohemian Grove and Other Retreats." In *Down to Earth Sociology: Introductory Readings,* 10th ed., James M. Henslin, ed. New York: Free Press, 1999a:391–403.

Domhoff, G. William. "State and Ruling Class in Corporate America (1974): Reflections, Corrections, and New Directions." *Critical Sociology, 25,* 2–3, July 1999b:260–265.

Donaldson, Stephen. "A Million Jockers, Punks, and Queens: Sex Among American Male Prisoners and Its Implications for Concepts of Sexual Orientation." February 4, 1993. Online.

Donelson, Samuel. "World News Tonight." Television broadcast. May 25, 1992.

Dottridge, Mike. "Dollars and Sense." *New Internationalist,* 337, August 2001:16–17.

Dove, Adrian. "Soul Folk 'Chitling' Test or the Dove Counterbalance Intelligence Test." no date. (Mimeo)

Dowd, Maureen. "The Knife Under the Tree." *New York Times,* December 5, 2002.

Drucker, Peter F. "There's More Than One Kind of Team." *Wall Street Journal,* February 11, 1992:A16.

Du Bois, W.E.B. *The Souls of Black Folk: Essays and Sketches.* Chicago: McClurg, 1903.

Du Bois, W.E.B. *Black Reconstruction in America: An Essay Toward a History of the Part Which Black Folk Played in the Attempt to Reconstruct Democracy in America, 1860–1880.* New York: Frank Cass, 1966. New York: Atheneum, 1992. First published 1935.

Du Bois, W.E.B. *The Philadelphia Negro: A Social Study.* New York: Schocken Books, 1967. First published in 1899.

Du Bois, W.E.B. *The Autobiography of W. E. B. Du Bois: A Soliloquy on Viewing My Life from the Last Decade of Its First Century.* New York: International, 1968.

Dudenhefer, Paul. "Poverty in the Rural United States." *Focus, 15,* 1, Spring 1993:37–46.

Duff, Christina. "Superrich's Share of After-Tax Income Stopped Rising in Early '90s, Data Show." *Wall Street Journal,* November 22, 1995:A2.

Dugger, Celia W. "Wedding Vows Bind Old World and New." *New York Times,* July 20, 1998.

Dugger, Celia W. "Abortion in India Is Tipping Scales Sharply Against Girls." *New York Times,* April 22, 2001.

Duneier, Mitchell. *Sidewalk.* New York: Farrar, Straus and Giroux, 1999.

Dunlap, Riley E., and William R. Catton, Jr. "Environmental Sociology." *Annual Review of Sociology, 5,* 1979:243–273.

Dunlap, Riley E., and William R. Catton, Jr. "What Environmental Sociologists Have in Common Whether Concerned with 'Built' or 'Natural' Environments." *Sociological Inquiry, 53,* 2–3, 1983:113–135.

Durkheim, Emile. *The Division of Labor in Society.* George Simpson, trans. New York: Free Press, 1933. First published in 1893.

Durkheim, Emile. *The Rules of Sociological Method.* Sarah A. Solovay and John H. Mueller, trans. New York: Free Press, 1938, 1958, 1964. First published in 1895.

Durkheim, Emile. *The Elementary Forms of the Religious Life.* New York: Free Press, 1965. First published in 1912.

Durkheim, Emile. *Suicide: A Study in Sociology.* John A. Spaulding and George Simpson, trans. New York: Free Press, 1966. First published in 1897.

Durning, Alan. "Cradles of Life." In *Social Problems 90/91,* LeRoy W. Barnes, ed. Guilford, Conn.: Dushkin, 1990:231–241.

Dyer, Gwynne. "Anybody's Son Will Do." In *Down to Earth Sociology: Introductory Readings,* 12th ed., James M. Henslin, ed. New York: The Free Press, 2003:458–469.

Easley, Hema. "Indian Families Continue to Have Arranged Marriages." *The Journal News,* June 9, 2003.

Ebaugh, Helen Rose Fuchs. *Becoming an EX: The Process of Role Exit.* Chicago: The University of Chicago Press, 1988.

Ebomoyi, Ehigie. "The Prevalence of Female Circumcision in Two Nigerian Communities." *Sex Roles, 17,* 3/4, 1987:139–151.

Eder, Donna. *School Talk: Gender and Adolescent Culture.* New Brunswick, N.J.: Rutgers University Press, 1995.

Eder, Donna. "On Becoming Female: Lessons Learned in School." In *Down to Earth Sociology: Introductory Readings,* 12th ed., James M. Henslin, ed. New York: The Free Press, 2003:155–161.

Eder, Klaus. "The Rise of Counter-Culture Movements Against Modernity: Nature as a New Field of Class Struggle." *Theory, Culture & Society, 7,* 1990:21–47.

Edgerton, Robert B. *Deviance: A Cross-Cultural Perspective.* Menlo Park, Calif.: Benjamin/Cummings, 1976.

Edgerton, Robert B. *Sick Societies: Challenging the Myth of Primitive Harmony.* New York: Free Press, 1992.

Edwards, Richard. *Contested Terrain: The Transformation of the Workplace in the Twentieth Century.* New York: Basic Books, 1979.

Egan, Timothy. "Many Seek Security in Private Communities." *New York Times,* September 3, 1995:1, 22.

Ehrenreich, Barbara, and Deidre English. *Witches, Midwives, and Nurses: A History of Women Healers.* Old Westbury, N.Y.: Feminist Press, 1973.

Ehrlich, Paul R., and Anne H. Ehrlich. *Population, Resources, and Environment: Issues in Human Ecology,* 2nd ed. San Francisco: Freeman, 1972.

Ehrlich, Paul R., and Anne H. Ehrlich. "Humanity at the Crossroads." *Stanford Magazine,* Spring–Summer 1978:20–23.

Ehrlich, Paul R., and Anne H. Ehrlich. *Betrayal of Science and Reason: How Anti-Environmental Rhetoric Threatens Our Future.* Washington, D.C.: Island Press, 1997.

Eibl-Eibesfeldt, Irrenäus. *Ethology: The Biology of Behavior.* New York: Holt, Rinehart, and Winston, 1970.

Eichler, Margrit. *Nonsexist Research Methods: A Practical Guide.* Winchester, Mass.: Unwin Hyman, 1988.

Eisenhart, R. Wayne. "You Can't Hack It, Little Girl: A Discussion of the Covert Psychological Agenda of Modern Combat Training." *Journal of Social Issues, 31,* Fall 1975:13–23.

Eisenstadt, Shmuel Noah. *Paradoxes of Democracy: Fragility, Continuity, and Change.* Washington, D.C.: Woodrow Wilson Center Press, 1999.

Ekman, Paul. *Faces of Man: Universal Expression in a New Guinea Village.* New York: Garland Press, 1980.

Ekman, Paul, Wallace V. Friesen, and John Bear. "The International Language of Gestures." *Psychology Today,* May 1984:64.

Elder, Glen H., Jr. "Age Differentiation and Life Course." *Annual Review of Sociology, 1,* 1975:165–190.

Elder, Glen H., Jr. *Children of the Great Depression: Social Change in Life Experience.* Boulder: Westview Press, 1999.

Elias, Paul. " 'Molecular Pharmers' Hope to Raise Human Proteins in Crop Plants." *St. Louis Post-Dispatch,* October 28, 2001:F7.

Elkins, Stanley M. *Slavery: A Problem in American Institutional and Intellectual Life,* 2nd ed. Chicago: University of Chicago Press, 1968.

Ellul, Jacques. *The Technological Society.* New York: Knopf, 1965.

Engeman, Thomas S. "Religion and Politics the American Way: The Exemplary William Dean Howells." *Review of Politics, 63,* 1, Winter 2001:107–127.

England, Paula. "The Impact of Feminist Thought on Sociology." *Contemporary Sociology: A Journal of Reviews,* 2000:263–267.

Englund, Will, and Gary Cohn. "A Third World Dump for America's Ships." *Baltimore Sun,* December 9, 1997.

Epstein, Cynthia Fuchs. "Inevitabilities of Prejudice." *Society,* September–October 1986:7–15.

Epstein, Cynthia Fuchs. *Deceptive Distinctions: Sex, Gender, and the Social Order.* New Haven, Conn.: Yale University Press, 1988.

Epstein, Cynthia Fuchs. Letter to the author, January 26, 1989.

Erickson, Kristan Glasgow, Robert Crosnoe, and Sanford M. Dornbusch. "A Social Process Model of Adolescent Deviance: Combining Social Control and Differential Association Perspectives." *Journal of Youth and Adolescence, 29,* 4, 2000:395–425.

Erik, John. "China's Policy on Births." *New York Times,* January 3, 1982:19.

Ernst, Eldon G. "The Baptists." In *Encyclopedia of the American Religious Experience: Studies of Traditions and Movements,* Vol. 1, Charles H. Lippy and Peter W. Williams, eds. New York: Scribners, 1988:555–577.

Escalante, Jaime, and Jack Dirmann. "The Jaime Escalante Math Program." *Journal of Negro Education, 59,* 3, Summer 1990:407–423.

Eshleman, J. Ross. *The Family,* 9th ed. Boston: Allyn and Bacon, 2000.

Evans, Peter, and James E. Rauch. "Bureaucracy and Growth: A Cross-National Analysis of the Effects of 'Weberian' State Structures on Economic Growth." *American Sociological Review, 64,* October 1999:748–765.

"Executive Pay." *Wall Street Journal,* April 14, 2003.

Ezekiel, Raphael S. *The Racist Mind: Portraits of American Neo-Nazis and Klansmen.* New York: Viking, 1995.

Fagot, Beverly I., Richard Hagan, Mary Driver Leinbach, and Sandra Kronsberg. "Differential Reactions to Assertive and Communicative Acts of Toddler Boys and Girls." *Child Development, 56,* 1985:1499–1505.

Faris, Robert E. L., and Warren Dunham. *Mental Disorders in Urban Areas.* Chicago: University of Chicago Press, 1939.

Farkas, George. *Human Capital or Cultural Capital?: Ethnicity and Poverty Groups in an Urban School District.* New York: Walter DeGruyter, 1996.

Farkas, George, Daniel Sheehan, and Robert P. Grobe. "Coursework Mastery and School Success: Gender, Ethnicity, and Poverty Groups Within an Urban School District." *American Educational Research Journal, 27,* 4, Winter 1990b:807–827.

Farkas, George, Robert P. Grobe, Daniel Sheehan, and Yuan Shuan. "Cultural Resources and School Success: Gender, Ethnicity, and Poverty Groups Within an Urban School District." *American Sociological Review, 55,* February 1990a:127–142.

"Fat Is a Financial Issue." *Economist, 357,* 8198, November 25, 2000:93.

Faunce, William A. *Problems of an Industrial Society,* 2nd ed. New York: McGraw-Hill, 1981.

Feagin, Joe R. "The Continuing Significance of Race: Antiblack Discrimination in Public Places." In *Majority and Minority: The Dynamics of Race and Ethnicity in American Life,* 6th ed., Norman R. Yetman, ed. Boston: Allyn and Bacon, 1999:384–399.

"Fears of Millennium 'Black Death' Leaves Bissau a Ghost Town." Associated Press Worldstream, January 1, 2000.

Featherman, David L. "Opportunities Are Expanding." *Society, 13,* 1979:4–11.

Featherman, David L., and Robert M. Hauser. *Opportunity and Change.* New York: Academic Press, 1978.

Feldman, Saul D. "The Presentation of Shortness in Everyday Life—Height and Heightism in American Society: Toward a Sociology of Stature." Paper presented at the 1972 meetings of the American Sociological Association.

Felsenthal, Edward. "Maine Limits Liability for Doctors Who Meet Treatment Guidelines." *Wall Street Journal,* May 3, 1993:A1, A9.

Felsenthal, Edward. "Justices' Ruling Further Defines Sex Harassment." *Wall Street Journal,* March 5, 1998:B1, B2.

Felton, Lee Ann, Andrea Gumm, and David J. Pittenger. "The Recipients of Unwanted Sexual Encounters Among College Students." *College Student Journal, 35,* 1, March 2001:135–143.

Fendrich, James Max, and Kenneth L. Lovoy. "Back to the Future: Adult Political Behavior of Former Student Activists." In *Collective Behavior and Social Movements,* Russell L. Curtis, Jr., and Benigno E. Aguirre, eds. Boston: Allyn and Bacon, 1993:429–434.

Ferraro, Susan. "Future Fighters: How Military Technology is Advancing Medical Science." *Daily News,* July 11, 2001.

Feshbach, Murray. "Russia's Farms, Too Poisoned for the Plow." *Wall Street Journal,* May 14, 1992:A14.

Fialka, John J. "Demands on New Orleans's 'Big Charity' Hospital Are Symptomatic of U.S. Health-Care Problem." *Wall Street Journal,* June 22, 1993:A18.

Fialka, John J. "A Dirty Discovery Over Indian Ocean Sets Off a Fight." *Wall Street Journal,* May 6, 2003:A1, A6.

Field, Mark G. "The Health Crisis in the Former Soviet Union: A Report from the 'Post-War' Zone." In *Readings in Medical Sociology,* William C. Cockerham, Michael Glasser, and Linda S. Heuser, eds. Englewood Cliffs, New Jersey: Prentice Hall, 1998:506–519.

"Fighting Illiteracy Is Only Way to Development." Xinhua News Agency, September 8, 2000.

Filkins, Dexter. "61 Slain as Violence Rocks the Caste System in India." *Seattle Times,* December 3, 1997.

Fine, Gary Alan, and Patricia A. Turner. *Whispers on the Color Line: Rumor and Race in America.* Berkeley: University of California Press, 2001.

Finke, Roger, and Roger Stark. *The Churching of America, 1776–1990: Winners and Losers in Our Religious Economy.* New Brunswick, N.J.: Rutgers University Press, 1992.

Finkelhor, David, and Kersti Yllo. *License to Rape: Sexual Abuse of Wives.* New York: Henry Holt, 1985.

Finkelhor, David, and Kersti Yllo. "Marital Rape: The Myth Versus the Reality." In *Marriage and Family in a Changing Society,* 3rd ed., James M. Henslin, ed. New York: Free Press, 1989:382–391.

Firestone, David. "The New-Look Suburbs: Denser or More Far-Flung?" *New York Times,* April 17, 2001.

Fischer, Claude S. *The Urban Experience.* New York: Harcourt, 1976.

Fish, Jefferson M. "Mixed Blood." *Psychology Today, 28,* 6, November–December 1995:55–58, 60, 61, 76, 80.

Fisher, Julie. "Is the Iron Law of Oligarchy Rusting Away in the Third World?" *World Development, 22,* 2, February 1994: 129–143.

Fisher, Marla Jo. "California College Grapples with Title IX Compliance." *Community College Week, 14,* 20, May 13, 2002:18.

Fisher, Sue. *In the Patient's Best Interest: Women and the Politics of Medical Decisions.* New Brunswick, N.J.: Rutgers University Press, 1986.

Fitzpatrick, Kevin, and Mark LaGory. *Unhealthy Places: The Ecology of Risk in the Urban Landscape.* New York: Routledge, 2000.

Flanagan, William G. *Urban Sociology: Images and Structure.* Boston: Allyn and Bacon, 1990.

Flavel, John H., et al. *The Development of Role-Taking and Communication Skills in Children.* New York: Wiley, 1968.

Flavel, John, Patricia H. Miller, and Scott A. Miller. *Cognitive Development,* 4th ed. Upper Saddle River, N.J.: Prentice Hall, 2002.

Fletcher, June. "Address Envy: Fudging to Get the Best." *Wall Street Journal,* April 25, 1997:B10.

Fletcher, Martin. "Jolie Takes Up Plight of World's Refugees." *The Times,* August 28, 2001.

Flexner, Abraham. *Medical Education in the United States and Canada: A Report to the Carnegie Foundation for the Advancement of Teaching.* Bulletin No. 4. Boston: Merrymount Press, 1910.

Flexner, E. *Century of Struggle.* Cambridge, Mass.: Belknap, 1971. In Claire M. Renzetti and Daniel J. Curran, *Women, Men, and Society,* 4th ed. Boston: Allyn and Bacon, 1999.

Flink, James J., *The Automobile Age.* Cambridge, Mass.: MIT Press, 1990.

Flippen, Annette R. "Understanding Groupthink From a Self-Regulatory Perspective." *Small Group Research, 30,* 2, April 1999:139–165.

Flippen, Chenoa. "Neighborhood Transition and Social Organization: The White to Hispanic Case." *Social Problems, 48,* 3, August 2001:299–321.

Foley, Douglas E. "The Great American Football Ritual." In *Down to Earth Sociology: Introductory Readings,* 10th ed., James M. Henslin, ed. New York: Free Press, 2001:454–467.

Foote, Donna. "And Baby Makes One." *Newsweek,* February 2, 1998:68–69.

Foote, Jennifer. "Trying to Take Back the Planet." *Newsweek, 115,* 6, February 5, 1990:24–25.

Foreign Agents Registration Act. Washington, D.C.: Report to the U.S. Dept. of Justice, June 30, 2002.

Forelle, Charles. "Ivy League Schools Begin to Offer Online Courses." *Wall Street Journal,* January 15, 2003.

Form, William. "Comparative Industrial Sociology and the Convergence Hypothesis." In *Annual Review of Sociology, 5,* 1, 1979, Alex Inkeles, James Coleman, and Ralph H. Turner, eds.

Fountain, Henry. "Archaeological Site in Peru Is Called Oldest City in Americas." *New York Times,* April 27, 2001.

Fox, Elaine, and George E. Arquitt. "The VFW and the 'Iron Law of Oligarchy.'" In *Down to Earth Sociology,* 4th ed., James M. Henslin, ed. New York: Free Press, 1985:147–155.

Franklin, John Hope, and John Whittington Franklin. *My Life and an Era: The Autobiography of Buck Colbert Franklin.* Baton Rouge: Louisiana State University, 1997.

Franks, David D., and Viktor Gecas. *Social Perspectives on Emotion: A Research Annual.* Greenwich, Conn.: JAI Press,1992.

Fraser, Graham. "Fox Denies Free Trade Exploiting the Poor in Mexico." *Toronto Star,* April 20, 2001.

Freedman, Jane. *Feminism.* Philadelphia: Open University Press, 2001.

Freidson, Eliot. *Professionalism: The Third Logic.* Chicago: University of Chicago Press, 2001.

French, Howard W. "North Korea to Let Capitalism Loose in Investment Zone." *New York Times,* September 25, 2002.

Freudenburg, William R., and Robert Gramling. "The Emergence of Environmental Sociology: Contributions of Riley E. Dunlap and William R. Catton, Jr." *Sociological Inquiry, 59,* 4, November 1989:439–452.

Freund, Charles Paul. "A Riot of Our Own." *Reason, 32,* 10, March 2001:10.

Frey, William H. "Migration to the South Brings U.S. Blacks Full Circle." *Population Today, 29,* 4, May–June 2001:1, 2.

Friedl, Ernestine. "Society and Sex Roles." In *Conformity and Conflict: Readings in Cultural Anthropology.* James P. Spradley and David W. McCurdy, eds. Glenview, Ill.: Scott, Foresman, 1990:229–238.

Fritz, Jan M. "The History of Clinical Sociology." *Sociological Practice, 7,* 1989:72–95.

Froman, Ingmarie. "Sweden for Women." *Current Sweden,* 407, November 1994:1–4.

Frumkin, Robert M. "Early English and American Sex Customs." In *Encyclopedia of Sexual Behavior,* Vol. 1. New York: Hawthorne Books, 1967.

Fuller, Rex, and Richard Schoenberger. "The Gender Salary Gap: Do Academic Achievement, Internship Experience, and College Major Make a Difference?" *Social Science Quarterly, 72,* 4, December 1991:715–726.

Furstenberg, Frank F., Jr., and Kathleen Mullan Harris. "The Disappearing American Father? Divorce and the Waning Significance of Biological Fatherhood." In *The Changing American Family: Sociological and Demographic Perspectives,* Scott J. South and Stewart E. Tolnay, eds. Boulder, Colo.: Westview Press, 1992:197–223.

Galbraith, John Kenneth. *The Nature of Mass Poverty.* Cambridge Mass.: Harvard University Press, 1979.

Galinsky, Ellen, James T. Bond, and Dana E. Friedman. *The Changing Workforce: Highlights of the National Study.* New York: Families and Work Institute, 1993.

Galliher, John F. *Deviant Behavior and Human Rights.* Englewood Cliffs, N.J.: Prentice Hall, 1991.

Gallmeier, Charles P. "Methodological Issues in Qualitative Sport Research: Participant Observation among Hockey Players." *Sociological Spectrum, 8,* 1988:213–235.

Gallup, George, Jr. *The Gallup Poll: Public Opinion 1989.* Wilmington, Dela.: Scholarly Resources, 1990.

Gallup Opinion Index. *Religion in America, 1987.* Report 259, April 1987.

Gallup Poll. "Poll Analyses." April 13, 2001.

Gans, Herbert J. *The Urban Villagers.* New York: Free Press, 1962.

Gans, Herbert J. *People and Plans: Essays on Urban Problems and Solutions.* New York: Basic Books, 1968.

Gans, Herbert J. "Urbanism and Suburbanism." In *Urban Man and Society: A Reader in Urban Ecology,* Albert N. Cousins and Hans Nagpaul, eds. New York: Knopf, 1970:157–164.

Gans, Herbert J. *People, Plans, and Policies: Essays on Poverty, Racism, and Other National Urban Problems.* New York: Columbia University Press, 1991.

Gans, Herbert. J., "Public Sociologies: Reply to Hausknecht." *Footnotes,* January 2003:8.

Garfinkel, Harold. "Conditions of Successful Degradation Ceremonies." *American Journal of Sociology, 61,* 2, March 1956:420–424.

Garfinkel, Harold. *Studies in Ethnomethodology.* Englewood Cliffs, N.J.: Prentice Hall, 1967.

Garrett, Laurie. "Global Warning." *Los Angeles Times,* March 1, 1999.

Garrett, Michael Tlanusta. "Understanding the 'Medicine' of Native American Traditional Values: An Integrative Review." *Counseling and Values, 43,* 2, January 1999:84–98.

Gatewood, Willard B. *Aristocrats of Color: The Black Elite, 1880–1920.* Bloomington, Ind.: Indiana University Press, 1990.

Gaviak, Dale. "In Sudan, Childhoods of Slavery." *Christian Science Monitor,* August 22, 2000:6.

Geis, Gilbert, Robert F. Meier, and Lawrence M. Salinger. *White-Collar Crime: Classic and Contemporary Views,* 3rd ed. New York: Free Press, 1995.

Genetski, Robert. "Privatize Social Security." *Wall Street Journal,* May 21, 1993.

Gerhard, Jane. "Revisiting 'The Myth of the Vaginal Orgasm': The Female Orgasm in American Sexual Thought and Second Wave Feminism." *Feminist Studies, 26,* 2, Fall 2000:449–477.

Gerson, Kathleen. *Hard Choices: How Women Decide about Work, Career, and Motherhood.* Berkeley: University of California Press, 1985.

Gerth, H. H., and C. Wright Mills. *From Max Weber: Essays in Sociology.* New York: Galaxy, 1958.

Gerth, Jeff. "Two Companies Pay Penalties for Improving China Rockets." *New York Times,* March 3, 2003.

Gibbs, Nancy. "The Littleton Massacre." *Time,* May 3, 1999:25–36.

Giele, Janet Zollinger. *Women and the Future: Changing Sex Roles in Modern America.* New York: Free Press, 1978.

Gilbert, Dennis L. *The American Class Structure in an Age of Growing Inequality,* 6th ed. Belmont, Calif.: Wadsworth Publishing, 2003.

Gilbert, Dennis, and Joseph A. Kahl. *The American Class Structure: A New Synthesis.* 4th ed. Belmont, Calif.: Wadsworth Publishing, 1998.

Gilligan, Carol. *In a Different Voice: Psychological Theory and Women's Development.* Cambridge, Mass.: Harvard University Press, 1982.

Gilligan, Carol. *Making Connections: The Relational World of Adolescent Girls at Emma Willard School.* Cambridge, Mass.: Harvard University Press, 1990.

Gilligan, Carol. *The Birth of Pleasure.* New York: Knopf, 2002.

Gilman, Charlotte Perkins. *The Man-Made World or, Our Androcentric Culture.* New York: 1971. First published 1911.

Gilmore, David D. *Manhood in the Making: Cultural Concepts of Masculinity.* New Haven, Conn.: Yale University Press, 1990.

Girshick, Lori B. *Woman-To-Woman Sexual Violence: Does She Call It Rape?* Boston: Northeastern University Press, 2002.

Gitlin, Todd. *The Twilight of Common Dreams: Why America Is Wracked by Culture Wars.* New York: Metropolitan Books, 1997.

Glascock, Jack. "Gender Roles on Prime-Time Network Television: Demographics and Behaviors." *Journal of Broadcasting and Electronic Media, 45,* Fall 2001:656–669.

Glenn, Evelyn Nakano. "Chinese American Families." In *Minority Families in the United States: A Multicultural Perspective,* Ronald L. Taylor, ed. Englewood Cliffs, N.J.: Prentice Hall, 1994:115–145.

Glick, Paul C., and S. Lin. "More Young Adults Are Living with Their Parents: Who Are They?" *Journal of Marriage and Family, 48,* 1986:107–112.

Goetting, Ann. *Getting Out: Life Stories of Women Who Left Abusive Men.* New York: Columbia University Press, 2001.

Goffman, Erving. *Asylums: Essays on the Social Situation of Mental Patients and Other Inmates.* Chicago: Aldine, 1961.

Goffman, Erving. *The Presentation of Self in Everyday Life.* New York: Doubleday, 1959.

Goffman, Erving. *Stigma: Notes on the Management of Spoiled Identity.* Englewood Cliffs, N.J.: Prentice Hall, 1963.

Gold, Ray. "Janitors Versus Tenants: A Status–Income Dilemma." *American Journal of Sociology, 58,* 1952:486–493.

Goldberg, Carey, and Sophia Kishkovsky. "Russia's Doctors Are Beggars at Work, Paupers at Home." *New York Times,* December 16, 2000.

Goldberg, Steven. *The Inevitability of Patriarchy,* rev. ed. New York: Morrow, 1974.

Goldberg, Steven. "Reaffirming the Obvious." *Society,* September–October 1986:4–7.

Goldberg, Steven. *Why Men Rule: A Theory of Male Dominance.* Chicago: Open Court, 1993.

Goldberg, Susan, and Michael Lewis. "Play Behavior in the Year-Old Infant: Early Sex Differences." *Child Development, 40,* March 1969:21–31.

Goldberg-Glen, Robin, Roberta G. Sands, Ralph D. Cole, and Carolyn Cristofalo. "Multigenerational Patterns and Internal Structures in Families in Which Grandparents Raise Grandchildren." *Families in Society: The Journal of Contemporary Human Services, 79,* 5, September 1998:477–489.

Golden, Daniel. "For Groton Grads, Academics Aren't the Only Keys to Ivy Schools." *Wall Street Journal,* April 25, 2003.

Goldman, Kevin. "Seniors Get Little Respect on Madison Avenue." *Wall Street Journal,* September 20, 1993:B6.

Goldsborough, Margaret. "Cybertimes Education." *New York Times,* February 13, 2001.

Goleman, Daniel. "Spacing of Siblings Strongly Linked to Success in Life." *New York Times,* May 28, 1985:C1, C4.

Goleman, Daniel. "Pollsters Enlist Psychologists in Quest for Unbiased Results." *New York Times,* September 7, 1993:C1, C11.

Gomez, Carlos F. *Regulating Death: Euthanasia and the Case of the Netherlands.* New York: Free Press, 1991.

Goode, Erica. "Study Says 20% of Girls Reported Abuse by a Date." *New York Times,* August 1, 2001.

Goode, Erich. *Drugs in American Society,* 3rd ed. New York: Knopf, 1989.

Goode, Erich, and Nachman Ben-Yehuda. "Moral Panics: Culture, Politics, and Social Construction." *Annual Review of Sociology, 20,* 1994:149–171.

Goode, William J. "Encroachment, Charlatanism, and the Emerging Profession: Psychology, Sociology, and Medicine." *American Sociological Review, 25,* 6, December 1960:902–914.

Gorman, Christine. "The Disease Detective." *Time,* January 6, 1997:56–65.

Gorman, Peter. "A People at Risk: Vanishing Tribes of South America." *The World & I.* December 1991:678–689.

Gorman, Thomas J. "Cross-Class Perceptions of Social Class." *Sociological Spectrum, 20,* 2000:93–120.

Gottfredson, Michael R., and Travis Hirschi. *A General Theory of Crime.* Stanford, Calif.: Stanford University Press, 1990.

Gourevitch, Philip. "After the Genocide." *New Yorker,* December 18, 1995:78–94.

Gourevitch, Philip. *We Wish to Inform You That Tomorrow We Will Be Killed with Our Families: Stories from Rwanda.* New York: Farrar, Straus, and Giroux, 1998.

Gracey, Harry L. "Kindergarten as Academic Boot Camp" In *Down to Earth Sociology: Introductory Readings,* 12th ed., James M. Henslin, ed. New York: The Free Press, 2003:390–404.

Graham, Ellen. "Christian Bikers Are Holy Rollers of a Different Kind." *Wall Street Journal,* September 19, 1990:A1, A6.

Greeley, Andrew M. "The Protestant Ethic: Time for a Moratorium." *Sociological Analysis, 25,* Spring 1964:20–33.

Greeley, Andrew M. "A Religious Revival in Russia." *Journal for the Scientific Study of Religion, 33,* 3, September 1994:253–272.

Greeley, Andrew M., and Michael Hout. "Americans' Increasing Belief in Life After Death: Religious Competition and Acculturation." *American Sociological Review, 64,* December 1999:813–835.

Greengard, Samuel. "The High Cost of Cyberslacking." *Workforce, 79,* 12, December 2000:22–23.

Greenhalgh, Susan, and Jiali Li. "Engendering Reproductive Policy and Practice in Peasant China: For a Feminist Demography of Reproduction." *Signs, 20,* 3, Spring 1995:601–640.

Greenhouse, Linda. "Justices Uphold Long Prison Terms in Repeat Crimes." *New York Times,* March 6, 2003.

Greider, William. "Pro Patria, Pro Mundus." *Nation, 273,* 15, November 12, 2001:22–24.

Gross, Jan T. *Neighbors.* New Haven: Yale University Press, 2001.

Gross, Jane. "In the Quest for the Perfect Look, More Girls Choose the Scalpel." *New York Times,* November 29, 1998.

Gross, Jane. "Right School for a 4-Year-Old? Find an Adviser." *New York Times,* May 28, 2003.

Grossman, Lawrence K. *The Electronic Republic: Reshaping Democracy in the Information Age.* New York: Viking, 1995.

Guarente, Leonard. *Ageless Quest: One Scientist's Search for Genes That Prolong Youth.* Cold Spring Harbor, New York: Cold Spring Harbor Laboratory, 2003.

Guensburg, Carol. "Bully Factories." *American Journalism Review, 23,* 6, 2001:51–59.

Guernsey, Lisa. "Cyberspace Isn't So Lonely After All." *New York Times,* July 26, 2001:E1, E5.

Guice, Jon. "Sociologists Go to Work in High Technology." *Footnotes,* November 1999:8.

Gupta, Giri Raj. "Love, Arranged Marriage, and the Indian Social Structure." In *Cross-Cultural Perspectives of Mate Selection and Marriage,* George Kurian, ed. Westport, Conn.: Greenwood Press, 1979.

Guru, Gopal, and Shiraz Sidhva. "India's 'Hidden Apartheid.' " *UNESCO Courier,* September 2001:27.

Haas, Jack. "Binging: Educational Control Among High-Steel Iron Workers." *American Behavioral Scientist, 16,* 1972:27–34.

Haas, Jack, and William Shaffir. "The Cloak of Competence." In *Down to Earth Sociology: Introductory Readings,* 7th ed. New York: Free Press, 1993:432–441.

Hacker, Helen Mayer. "Women as a Minority Group." *Social Forces, 30,* October 1951:60–69.

Hafner, Katie. "Mounting an Online Posse." *New York Times,* December 19, 2002.

Hale, Robert. "Motives of Reward Among Men who Rape." In *Sexual Deviance: A Reader,* Christopher Hensley and Richard Tewksbury, eds. Boulder, Colo.: Lynnr Rienner, 2003:91–103.

Hall, Anthony T. "Who's Watching the Children?" *Greater Baton Rouge Business Report, 20,* September 25, 2001:14–15.

Hall, Edward T. *The Silent Language.* New York: Doubleday, 1959.

Hall, Edward T. *The Hidden Dimension.* Garden City, N.Y.: Anchor Books, 1969.

Hall, Edward T., and Mildred R. Hall. "The Sounds of Silence." In *Down to Earth Sociology: Introductory Readings,* 12th ed., James M. Henslin, ed. New York: The Free Press, 2003:100–108.

Hall, G. Stanley. *Adolescence: Its Psychology and Its Relations to Physiology, Anthropology, Sociology, Sex, Crime, Religion, and Education.* New York: Appleton, 1904.

Hall, Richard H. "The Concept of Bureaucracy: An Empirical Assessment." *American Journal of Sociology, 69,* July 1963:32–40.

Hall, Ronald E. "The Tiger Woods Phenomenon: A Note on Biracial Identity." *The Social Science Journal, 38,* 2, April 2001:333–337.

Hamermesh, Daniel S., and Jeff E. Biddle. "Beauty and the Labor Market." *American Economic Review, 84,* 5, December 1994:1174–1195.

Hammerstein, J. "Auswirkungen der Defensiven Medizin auf die Kosten." *Arztl Fortbild Qualitatssich, 94,* 10, December 2000:800–804.

Hardy, Dorcas. *Social Insecurity: The Crisis in America's Social Security and How to Plan Now for Your Own Financial Survival.* New York: Villard Books, 1991.

Hardy, Quentin. "Death at the Club Is Par for the Course in Golf-Crazed Japan." *Wall Street Journal,* June 16, 1993:A1, A8.

Harlow, Harry F., and Margaret K. Harlow. "The Affectional Systems." In *Behavior of Nonhuman Primates: Modern Research Trends,* Vol. 2, Allan M. Schrier, Harry F. Harlow, and Fred Stollnitz, eds. New York: Academic Press, 1965:287–334.

Harlow, Harry F., and Margaret K. Harlow. "Social Deprivation in Monkeys." *Scientific American, 207,* 1962:137–147.

Harper, Charles L., and Kevin T. Leicht. *Exploring Social Change: America and the World.* Upper Saddle River, N.J.: Prentice Hall, 2002.

Harrington, Michael. *The Other America: Poverty in the United States.* New York: Macmillan, 1962.

Harrington, Michael. *The Vast Majority: A Journey to the World's Poor.* New York: Simon & Schuster, 1977.

Harris, Chauncey D. "The Nature of Cities and Urban Geography in the Last Half Century." *Urban Geography, 18,* 1997.

Harris, Chauncey D., and Edward Ullman. "The Nature of Cities." *Annals of the American Academy of Political and Social Science, 242,* 1945:7–17.

Harris, Diana K. *The Sociology of Aging.* New York: Harper, 1990.

Harris, Marvin. "Why Men Dominate Women." *New York Times Magazine,* November 13, 1977:46, 115, 117–123.

Harrison, Paul. *Inside the Third World: The Anatomy of Poverty,* 3rd ed. London: Penguin Books, 1993.

Hart, Charles W. M., and Arnold R. Pilling. *The Tiwi of North Australia.* New York: Holt, Rinehart, and Winston, 1970.

Hart, Hornell. "Acceleration in Social Change." In *Technology and Social Change,* Francis R. Allen, Hornell Hart, Delbert C. Miller, William F. Ogburn, and Meyer F. Nimkoff. New York: Appleton, 1957:27–55.

Hart, Paul. "Groupthink, Risk-Taking and Recklessness: Quality of Process and Outcome in Policy Decision Making." *Politics and the Individual, 1,* 1, 1991:67–90.

Hartley, Eugene. *Problems in Prejudice.* New York: King's Crown Press, 1946.

Hartocollis, Anemona. "Harvard Faculty Votes to Put the Excellence Back in the A." *New York Times,* May 22, 2002.

Harwood, John. "For California Senator, Fund Raising Becomes Overwhelming Burden." *Wall Street Journal,* March 2, 1994:A1, A13.

Harwood, John, and Geraldine Brooks. "Other Nations Elect Women to Lead Them, So Why Doesn't U.S.?" *Wall Street Journal,* December 14, 1993:A1, A9.

Haslick, Leonard. *Gerontologist, 14,* 1974:37–45.

Hatch, Laurie Russell. *Beyond Gender Differences: Adaptation to Aging in Life Course Perspective.* Amityville, N.Y.: Baywood Publishing Company, 2000.

Haub, Carl. "How Many People Have Ever Lived on Earth?" *Population Today, 30,* 8, November–December, 2002a:3–4.

Haub, Carl. "2002 World Population Data Sheet of the Population Reference Bureau." Washington, D.C.: Population Reference Bureau, 2002b.

Haub, Carl. "Has Global Growth Reached Its Peak?" *Population Today, 30,* 6, August–September 2002c:6.

Haub, Carl. "2003 World Population Data Sheet of the Population Reference Bureau." Washington, D.C.: Population Reference Bureau, 2003.

Haub, Carl, and Diana Cornelius. "World Population Data Sheet." Washington, D.C.: Population Reference Bureau, 2001.

Haub, Carl, and Nancy Yinger. "The U.N. Long-Range Population Projections: What They Tell Us." Washington, D.C.: Population Reference Bureau, 1994.

Hauser, Philip, and Leo Schnore, eds. *The Study of Urbanization.* New York: Wiley, 1965.

Hawkes, Nigel. "Asbestos-Related Diseases Will Rise for 20 Years." *The Times,* September 25, 2001.

Hawley, Amos H. *Urban Society: An Ecological Approach.* New York: Wiley, 1981.

Hayashi, Gina M., and Bonnie R. Strickland. "Long-Term Effects of Parental Divorce on Love Relationships: Divorce as Attachment Disruption." *Journal of Social and Personal Relationships, 15,* 1, February 1998, 23–38.

Hayes, Donald P., and Loreen T. Wolfer. "Have Curriculum Changes Caused SAT Scores to Decline?" Paper presented at the annual meetings of the American Sociological Association, 1993.

Haynes, Richard M., and Donald M. Chalker. "World Class Schools." *American School Board Journal,* May 1997:20, 22–25.

Hechter, Michael. *Containing Nationalism.* New York: Oxford University Press, 2000.

Heckert, D. Alex, Thomas C. Nowak, and Kay A. Snyder. "The Impact of Husbands' and Wives' Relative Earnings on Marital Dissolution." Paper presented at the 1995 meetings of the American Sociological Association.

Hehir, Grainne. "Female Managers Struggle to Break the Glass Ceiling." *Wall Street Journal,* March 1, 2001.

Heilbrun, Alfred B. "Differentiation of Death-Row Murderers and Life-Sentence Murderers by Antisociality and Intelligence Measures." *Journal of Personality Assessment, 64,* 1990:617–627.

Heilman, Madeline E. "Description and Prescription: How Gender Stereotypes Prevent Women's Ascent Up the Organizational Ladder." *Journal of Social Issues, 57,* 4, Winter 2001:657–674.

Hellinger, Daniel, and Dennis R. Judd. *The Democratic Facade.* Pacific Grove, Calif.: Brooks/Cole, 1991.

Hemmings, Annette. "The 'Hidden' Corridor Curriculum." *High School Journal, 83,* December 1999:1–12.

Hendin, Herbert, "Euthanasia and Physician-Assisted Suicide in the Netherlands." *New England Journal of Medicine, 336,* 19, May 8, 1997:1385–1387.

Hendin, Herbert. "Suicide, Assisted Suicide, and Medical Illness." *Harvard Mental Health Letter, 16,* 7: January 2000, 4–7.

Hendrix, Lewellyn. "What Is Sexual Inequality? On the Definition and Range of Variation." *Gender and Society, 28,* 3, August 1994:287–307.

Henley, Nancy, Mykol Hamilton, and Barrie Thorne. "Womanspeak and Manspeak." In *Beyond Sex Roles.* Alice G. Sargent, ed. St. Paul, Minn.: West, 1985.

Henriques, Diana B. "Review of Nissan Car Loans Finds That Blacks Pay More." *New York Times,* July 4, 2001.

Henslin, James M. *The Cab Driver: An Interactional Analysis of an Occupational Culture.* Washington University Ph.D. dissertation, September 1967.

Henslin, James M. *Introducing Sociology: Toward Understanding Life in Society.* New York: Free Press, 1975.

Henslin, James M. "It's Not a Lovely Place to Visit, and I Wouldn't Want to Live There." In *Studies in Qualitative Methodology, A Research Annual: Reflections on Field Experiences,* Robert G. Burgess, ed. Greenwich, Conn: JAI Press, 1990a:51–76.

Henslin, James M. "When Life Seems Hopeless: Suicide in American Society." In *Social Problems Today: Coping with the Challenges of a Changing Society.* Englewood Cliffs, N.J.: Prentice Hall, 1990b:99–107.

Henslin, James M. "Centuries of Childhood." In *Marriage and Family in a Changing Society,* 4th ed., James M. Henslin, ed. New York: Free Press, 1992:214–225.

Henslin, James M. "Trust and Cabbies." In *Down to Earth Sociology: Introductory Readings,* 7th ed., James M. Henslin, ed. New York: Free Press, 1993:183–196.

Henslin, James M. "How Sociologists Do Research." In *Down to Earth Sociology: Introductory Readings,* 11th ed., James M. Henslin, ed. New York: Free Press, 2001:33–44.

Henslin, James M. "What Is Sociology? Comparing Sociology and the Social Sciences." In *Down to Earth Sociology: Introductory Readings,* 11th ed., James M. Henslin, ed. New York: The Free Press, 2001a:8–18.

Henslin, James M. "On Becoming Male: Reflections of a Sociologist on Childhood and Early Socialization." In *Down to Earth Sociology: Introductory Readings,* 11th ed., James M. Henslin, ed. New York: The Free Press, 2001c:138–148.

Henslin, James M. "Eating Your Friends Is the Hardest: The Survivors of the F-227." In *Down to Earth Sociology: Introductory Readings,* 12th ed., James M. Henslin, ed. New York: The Free Press, 2003b:261–270.

Henslin, James. *Social Problems.* Upper Saddle River, N.J.: Prentice Hall, 2003d.

Henslin, James M., and Mae A. Biggs. "Behavior in Pubic Places: The Sociology of the Vaginal Examination." In *Down to Earth Sociology: Introductory Readings,* 12th ed., James M. Henslin, ed. New York: The Free Press, 2003:202–214.

Hentoff, Nat. "Fifth Grade Freedom Fighters." *Washington Post,* August 1, 1998:A15.

Hentoff, Nat. "Bush-Ashcroft Versus Homeland Security." *The Village Voice,* April 18, 2003.

Herring, Cedric. "Is Job Discrimination Dead?" *Contexts.* Summer 2002:13–18.

Herring, George C. "Vietnam War." *World Book Encyclopedia, 20.* Chicago: World Book, 1989:389–393.

Hetherington, Mavis, and John Kelly. *For Better or For Worse: Divorce Reconsidered.* New York: W. W. Norton, 2003.

Hewitt Associates. *Worklife Benefits Provided by Major U.S. Employers, 2003–2004.* Lincolnshire, Ill.: Hewitt Associates, 2004.

Higginbotham, Elizabeth, and Lynn Weber. "Moving with Kin and Community: Upward Social Mobility for Black and White Women." *Gender and Society, 6,* 3, September 1992:416–440.

Hill, Mark E. "Skin Color and the Perception of Attractiveness Among African Americans: Does Gender Make a Difference?" *Social Psychology Quarterly, 65,* 1, 2002:77–91.

Hill, Paul T. "Home Schooling and the Future of Public Education." *Peabody Journal of Education, 75,* 1–2, 2000:20–31.

Hilliard, Asa, III. "Do We Have the *Will* to Educate All Children?" *Educational Leadership, 49,* September 1991:31–36.

Hiltz, Starr Roxanne. "Widowhood." In *Marriage and Family in a Changing Society,* 3rd ed., James M. Henslin, ed. New York: Free Press, 1989:521–531.

Himes, Christine L. "Elderly Americans." *Population Bulletin, 56,* 1, December 2001:1–40.

Hines, Revathi I. "African Americans' Struggle for Environmental Justice and the Case of the Shintech Plant: Lessons Learned from a War Waged." *Journal of Black Studies, 31,* 6, July 2001:777–789.

Hippler, Fritz. Interview in a television documentary with Bill Moyers in *Propaganda,* in the series "Walk Through the 20th Century," 1987.

Hirschi, Travis. *Causes of Delinquency.* Berkeley: University of California Press, 1969.

Hitt, Jack. "The Next Battlefield May Be in Outer Space." *New York Times,* August 5, 2001.

Hochschild, Arlie Russell. *The Managed Heart: Commercialization of Human Feeling.* Chicago: University of Chicago Press, 1983.

Hochschild, Arlie Russell. *The Second Shift: Working Parents and the Revolution at Home.* New York: Viking, 1989.

Hochschild, Arlie Russell. "Note to the Author." 1991.

Hochschild, Arlie Russell. "The Sociology of Feeling and Emotion: Selected Possibilities." In *Another Voice: Feminist Perspectives on Social Life and Social Science,* Marcia Millman and Rosabeth Moss Kanter, eds. Garden City, N.Y.: Anchor Books, 1975.

Hochschild, Arlie Russell. *The Time Bind: When Work Becomes Home and Home Becomes Work.* New York: Henry Holt, 1997.

Hochschild, Arlie Russell. "When Work Becomes Home and Home Becomes Work." In *Exploring Social Life: Readings to Accompany Essentials of Sociology: A Down-to-Earth Approach* 5th ed., James M. Henslin, ed. Boston: Allyn and Bacon, 2004:127–136.

Hofferth, Sandra. "Did Welfare Reform Work? Implications for 2002 and Beyond." *Contexts,* Spring 2002:45–51.

Holden, Benjamin A., and Frederick Rose. "Two Policemen Get 2 1/2-Year Jail Terms on U.S. Charges in Rodney King Case." *Wall Street Journal,* August 5, 1993:B2.

Holloway, Andy. "Welcome to the Bioeconomy." *Canadian Business. Com,* September 2, 2002.

Holtzman, Abraham. *The Townsend Movement: A Political Study.* New York: Bookman, 1963.

Homblin, Dora Jane. *The First Cities.* Boston: Little, Brown, Time-Life Books, 1973.

Hommel M., and A. Jaillard. "Alcohol for Stroke Prevention?" *New England Journal of Medicine, 341,* 21, November 18, 1999:1605–1606.

Honeycutt, Karen. "Disgusting, Pathetic, Bizarrely Beautiful: Representations of Weight in Popular Culture." Paper presented at the 1995 meetings of the American Sociological Association.

Hong, Lawrence. "Marriage in China." In *Til Death Do Us Part: A Multicultural Anthology on Marriage,* Sandra Lee Browning and R. Robin Miller, eds. Stamford, Conn.: JAI Press, 1999.

Horowitz, Donald L. *The Deadly Ethnic Riot.* Berkeley: University of California Press, 2001.

Horowitz, Ruth. *Honor and the American Dream: Culture and Identity in a Chicano Community.* New Brunswick, N.J.: Rutgers University Press, 1983.

Horowitz, Ruth. "Community Tolerance of Gang Violence." *Social Problems, 34,* 5, December 1987:437–450.

Hossfeld, Karen J. " 'Their Logic Against Them': Contradictions in Sex, Race, and Class in Silicon Valley." In *Gender Through the Prism of Difference,* 2nd ed., Maxine Baca Zinn, Pierrette Hondagneu-Sotelo, and Michael A. Messner, eds. Boston: Allyn and Bacon, 2000:388–400.

Hostetler, John A. *Amish Society,* 3rd ed. Baltimore: Johns Hopkins University Press, 1980.

"House Divided." *People Weekly,* May 24, 1999:126.

Houtman, Dick. "What Exactly Is a 'Social Class'?: On the Economic Liberalism and Cultural Conservatism of the 'Working Class'." Paper presented at the 1995 meetings of the American Sociological Association.

Howe, Henry, John Lyne, Alan Gross, Harro VanLente, Aire Rip, Richard Lewontin, Daniel McShea, Greg Myers, Ullica Segerstrale, Herbert W. Simons, and V. B. Smocovitis. "Gene Talk in Sociobiology." *Social Epistemology, 6,* 2, April–June 1992:109–163.

Howells, Lloyd T., and Selwyn W. Becker. "Seating Arrangement and Leadership Emergence." *Journal of Abnormal and Social Psychology, 64,* February 1962:148–150.

Hoyt, Homer. *The Structure and Growth of Residential Neighborhoods in American Cities.* Washington, D.C.: Federal Housing Administration, 1939.

Hoyt, Homer. "Recent Distortions of the Classical Models of Urban Structure." In *Internal Structure of the City: Readings on Space and Environment,* Larry S. Bourne, ed. New York: Oxford University Press, 1971:84–96.

Hsu, Francis L. K. *The Challenge of the American Dream: The Chinese in the United States.* Belmont, Calif.: Wadsworth, 1971.

Huber, Joan, and William H. Form. *Income and Ideology.* New York: Free Press, 1973.

Huber, Joan. "Micro-Macro Links in Gender Stratification." *American Sociological Review, 55,* February 1990:1–10.

Huddle, Donald. "The Net National Cost of Immigration." Washington, D.C.: Carrying Capacity Network, 1993.

Hudson, Christopher G. "The Social Class and Mental Illness Correlation: Implications of the Research for Policy and Practice." *Journal of Sociology and Social Welfare, 15,* 1, March 1988:27–54.

Hudson, James R. "Professional Sports Franchise Locations and City, Metropolitan and Regional Identities." Paper presented at the annual meetings of the American Sociological Association, 1991.

Hudson, Robert B. "The 'Graying' of the Federal Budget and Its Consequences for Old-Age Policy." *Gerontologist, 18,* October 1978:428–440.

Huffstutter, P. J. "God Is Everywhere on the Net." *Los Angeles Times,* December 14, 1998.

Huggins, Martha K. "Lost Childhoods: Assassinations of Youth in Democratizing Brazil." Paper presented at the annual meetings of the American Sociological Association, 1993.

Huggins, Martha K. "Urban Violence and Police Privatization in Brazil: Blended Invisibility." *Social Justice, 27,* 2, 2000:113–134.

Huggins, Martha K., Mika Haritos-Fatouros, and Philip G. Zimbardo. *Violence Workers: Police Torturers and Murderers Reconstruct Brazilian Atrocities.* Berkeley: University of California Press, 2002.

Hughes, Everett. C. "Good People and Dirty Work." In *Down to Earth Sociology: Introductory Readings,* 7th ed., James M. Henslin, ed. New York: The Free Press, 1993:365–375. First published in 1962.

Hughes, H. Stuart. *Oswald Spengler: A Critical Estimate,* rev. ed. New York: Scribner's, 1962.

Hughes, Kathleen A. "Even Tiki Torches Don't Guarantee a Perfect Wedding." *Wall Street Journal,* February 20, 1990:A1, A16.

Hundley, Greg. "Why Women Earn Less Than Men in Self-Employment." *Journal of Labor Research, 22,* 4, Fall 2001:817–827.

Hurtado, Aída, David E. Hayes-Bautista, R. Burciaga Valdez, and Anthony C. R. Hernández. *Redefining California: Latino Social Engagement in a Multicultural Society.* Los Angeles: UCLA Chicano Studies Research Center, 1992.

Huttenbach, Henry R. "The Roman *Porajmos:* The Nazi Genocide of Europe's Gypsies." *Nationalities Papers, 19,* 3, Winter 1991: 373–394.

"In Perspective: America's Conflicts." *New York Times,* April 20, 2003:B16.

Iori, Ron. "The Good, the Bad and the Useless." *Wall Street Journal,* June 10, 1988:18R.

Isikoff, Michael. "The Waco Flame-Up." *Newsweek,* September 6, 1999:30.

Ismail, M. Asif. "The Clinton Top 100: Where Are They Now?" Washington, D.C.: The Center for Public Integrity, 2003.

Itard, Jean Marc Gospard. *The Wild Boy of Aveyron.* Translated by George and Muriel Humphrey. New York: Appleton-Century-Crofts, 1962.

Jacobs, Jerry A. "Detours on the Road to Equality: Women, Work and Higher Education." *Contexts,* Winter 2003:32–41.

Jacobs, Margaret A. "'New Girl' Network Is Boon for Women Lawyers." *Wall Street Journal,* March 4, 1997:B1, B7.

Jaffee, Sara, and Janet Shibley Hyde. "Gender Differences in Moral Orientation: A Meta-Analysis." *Psychological Bulletin, 126,* 5, 2000:703–726.

Jaggar, Alison M. "Sexual Difference and Sexual Equality." In *Theoretical Perspectives on Sexual Difference,* Deborah L. Rhode, ed. New Haven, Conn.: Yale University Press, 1990:239–254.

James, Daniel. "To Cut Spending, Freeze Immigration." *Wall Street Journal,* June 24, 1993:A13.

Janis, Irving. L. *Groupthink: Psychological Studies of Policy Decisions and Fiascoes.* Boston: Houghton Mifflin, 1982.

Janis, Irving L. *Victims of Groupthink.* Boston, Mass.: Houghton Mifflin, 1972.

Jankowiak, William R., and Edward F. Fischer. "A Cross-Cultural Perspective on Romantic Love." *Journal of Ethnology, 31,* 2, April 1992:149–155.

Jankowski, Martín Sánchez. *Islands in the Street: Gangs and American Urban Society.* Berkeley: University of California Press, 1991.

Jarley, Paul, Jack Fiorito, and John T. Delaney. "National Union Governance: An Empirically-Grounded Systems Approach." *Journal of Labor Research, 21,* 2, Spring 2000:227–246.

Jasper, James M. "Moral Dimensions of Social Movements." Paper presented at the annual meetings of the American Sociological Association, 1991.

Jasper, James M., and Dorothy Nelkin. *Animal Crusade.* New York: The Free Press, 1993.

Jasper, James M., and Jane D. Poulsen. "Recruiting Strangers and Friends: Moral Shocks and Social Networks in Animal Rights and Anti-Nuclear Protests." *Social Problems, 42,* 4, November 1995:493–512.

Jáuregui, Gurutz. "El poder y la soberana en la aldéa global." *El Pais.* July 19, 1996:11.

Jekielek, Susan M. "Parental Conflict, Marital Disruption, and Children's Emotional Well-Being." *Social Forces, 76,* 3, March 1998:905–936.

Jenkins, Philip. *Changing Concepts of the Child Molester in Modern America.* New Haven: Yale University Press, 1998.

Jenkins, Philip. "The Next Christianity." *Atlantic Monthly,* October 2002:53–68.

Jenness, Valerie. "Moral Panic." *Social Forces, 79,* 3, March 2001:1208–1212.

Jerrome, Dorothy. *Good Company: An Anthropological Study of Old People in Groups.* Edinburgh, England: Edinburgh University Press, 1992.

Johansson, Perry. "Consuming the Other: The Fetish of the Western Woman in Chinese Advertising and Popular Culture." *Postcolonial Studies, 2,* 3, November 1999.

Johnson, Benton. "On Church and Sect." *American Sociological Review, 28,* 1963:539–549.

Johnson, Kenneth M. "The Rural Rebound." *Reports on America, 1,* 3, Population Reference Bureau, September 1999.

Johnson, Norris R. "Panic at 'The Who Concert Stampede': An Empirical Assessment." In *Collective Behavior and Social Movements,* Russell L. Curtis, Jr., and Benigno E. Aguirre, eds. Boston: Allyn and Bacon, 1993:113–122.

Johnson, Paul. *A History of the American People.* New York: HarperCollins, 1998.

Johnston, Drue M., and Norris R. Johnson. "Role Extension in Disaster: Employee Behavior at the Beverly Hills Supper Club Fire." *Sociological Focus, 22,* 1, February 1989:39–51.

Johnston, Lloyd D., Patrick M. O'Malley, and Jerald G. Bachman. *Monitoring the Future: National Results on Adolescent Drug Use.* Bethesda, Md.: National Institute on Drug Abuse, 2002.

Johnston, Lloyd D., Patrick M. O'Malley, and Jerald G. Bachman. *Monitoring the Future: National Survey Results on Drug Use, 1975–2003, Volume 2, College Students and Adults Ages 19–40.* Bethesda, Md.: National Institute on Drug Abuse, 2003.

Jones, Dale E., et al. "Religious Congregations and Membership in the United States 2000: An Enumeration by Region, State and County. Based on Data Reported by 149 Religious Bodies." Nashville, Tenn.: Glenmary Research Center, 2002.

Jones, James H. *Bad Blood: The Tuskegee Syphilis Experiment,* 2nd ed. New York: Free Press, 1993.

Jones, Steve. "Let the Games Begin: Gaming Technology and Entertainment Among College Students." Washington, D.C.: PEW Internet and American Life Project, 2003.

Jordan, Miriam. "Among Poor Villagers, Female Infanticide Still Flourishes in India." *Wall Street Journal,* May 9, 2000:A1, A12.

Jordon, Mary. "College Dorms Reflect Trend of Self-Segregation." In *Ourselves and Others,* 2nd ed., The Washington Post Writer's Group, eds. Boston: Allyn and Bacon, 1996:85–87.

Josephson, Matthew. "The Robber Barons." In *John D. Rockefeller: Robber Baron or Industrial Statesman?,* Earl Latham, ed. Boston: Heath, 1949:34–48.

Juergensmeyer, Mark. *Terror in the Mind of God: The Global Rise of Religious Violence.* Berkeley: University of California Press, 2000.

Kaebnick, Gregory E. "On the Sanctity of Nature." *Hastings Center Report, 30,* 5, September–October 2000:16–23.

Kaelber, Lutz. "Comment." *Sociological Footnotes, 30,* 4, July 2001:429.

Kagan, Jerome. "The Idea of Emotions in Human Development." In *Emotions, Cognition, and Behavior,* Carroll E. Izard, Jerome Kagan, and Robert B. Zajonc, eds. New York: Cambridge University Press, 1984:38–72.

Kahn, Joseph. "Some Chinese See the Future, and It's Capitalist." *New York Times,* May 4, 2002.

Kalberg, Stephen. *Introduction to Max Weber, The Protestant Ethic and the Spirit of Capitalism,* 3rd ed. Los Angeles: Roxbury Publishing, 2002.

Kalof, Linda. "Vulnerability to Sexual Coercion Among College Women: A Longitudinal Study." *Gender Issues, 18,* 4, Fall 2000:47–58.

Kanabayashi, Masayoshi. "Work Week." *Wall Street Journal,* August 20, 1996:A1.

Kanter, Rosabeth Moss. *Men and Women of the Corporation.* New York: Basic Books, 1977.

Kanter, Rosabeth Moss. *The Change Masters: Innovation and Entrepreneurship in the American Corporation.* New York: Simon & Schuster, 1983.

Kanter, Rosabeth Moss, Fred Wiersema, and John J. Kao, eds. *Innovation: Breakthrough Thinking at 3M, DuPont, GE, Pfizer, and Rubbermaid.* New York: Harper, 1997.

Kantrowitz, Barbara, and Daniel McGinn. "When Teachers Are Cheaters." *Newsweek,* June 19, 2000.

Kaplan, Robert D. "A Tale of Two Colonies." *Atlantic Monthly,* April 2003.

Karp, David A., Gregory P. Stone, and William C. Yoels. *Being Urban: A Sociology of City Life,* 2nd ed. New York: Praeger, 1991.

Karp, David A., and William C. Yoels. "Sport and Urban Life." *Journal of Sport and Social Issues, 14,* 2, 1990:77–102.

Kart, Cary S. *The Realities of Aging: An Introduction to Gerontology,* 3rd ed. Boston: Allyn and Bacon, 1990.

Katz, Sidney. "The Importance of Being Beautiful." In *Down to Earth Sociology: Introductory Readings,* 12th ed., James M. Henslin, ed. New York: The Free Press, 2003:313–320.

Kaufman, Joanne. "Married Maidens and Dilatory Domiciles." *Wall Street Journal,* May 7, 1996:A16.

Kazman, Sam. "Here's to Honesty in Liquor Sales." *Wall Street Journal,* February 18, 1999.

Keates, Nancy. "Alternative Care Crops Up At 'Traditional' Hospitals." *Wall Street Journal,* March 28, 2003.

Keith, Jennie. *Old People, New Lives: Community Creation in a Retirement Residence,* 2nd ed. Chicago: University of Chicago Press, 1982.

Kelly, Joan B. "How Adults React to Divorce." In *Marriage and Family in a Changing Society,* 4th ed., James M. Henslin, ed. New York: Free Press, 1992:410–423.

Kemp, Alice Abel. "Estimating Sex Discrimination in Professional Occupations with the *Dictionary of Occupational Titles.*" *Sociological Spectrum, 10,* 3, 1990:387–411.

Kenchaiah, Satish, et. al. "Obesity and the Risk of Heart Failure." *New England Journal of Medicine, 347,* August 1, 2002:305–313.

Keniston, Kenneth. *Youth and Dissent: The Rise of a New Opposition.* New York: Harcourt, Brace, Jovanovich, 1971.

"Kenya: Girls Score Court Victory Against Genital Mutilation." *Women's International Network News, 27,* 2, Spring 2001:64.

Kephart, William M., and William W. Zellner. *Extraordinary Groups: An Examination of Unconventional Life-Styles,* 7th ed. New York: Worth Publishing, 2001.

Kerr, Clark. *The Future of Industrialized Societies.* Cambridge, Mass.: Harvard University Press, 1983.

Kerr, Clark, et al. *Industrialism and Industrial Man: The Problems of Labor and Management in Economic Growth.* Cambridge, Mass.: Harvard University Press, 1960.

Kibria, Nazli. *Family Tightrope: The Changing Lives of Vietnamese Americans.* Princeton, N.J.: Princeton University Press, 1993.

Kifner, John. "Building Modernity on Desert Mirages." *New York Times,* February 7, 1999.

Kilbourne, Jean. "Beauty and the Beast of Advertising." In *Down to Earth Sociology: Introductory Readings,* 12th ed., James M. Henslin, ed. New York: The Free Press, 2003:421–424.

Kim, Karen A. "Exploring the Meaning of 'Nontraditional' at the Community College." *Community College Review, 30,* 1, 2002:74–89.

Kingston, Maxine Hong. *The Woman Warrior.* New York: Vintage Books, 1975:108. Quoted in Frank J. Zulke, and Jacqueline P. Kirley. *Through the Eyes of Social Science,* 6th ed. Prospect Heights, Ill.: Waveland Press, 2002.

Kinsella, Kevin, and Cynthia M. Taeuber. *An Aging World.* Washington, D.C.: U.S. Bureau of the Census, 1993.

Klandermans, Bert. *The Social Psychology of Protest.* Cambridge, Mass.: Blackwell, 1997.

Kleinfeld, Judith S. "Gender and Myth: Data about Student Performance." In *Through the Eyes of Social Science,* 6th ed., Frank J. Zulke and Jacqueline P. Kirley, eds. Prospect Heights, Ill.: Waveland Press, 2002a:380–393.

Kleinfeld, Judith S. "The Small World Problem." *Society,* January–February, 2002b:61–66.

Klonoff, Elizabeth A., and Hope Landrine. "Sex Roles, Occupational Roles, and Symptom-Reporting: A Test of Competing Hypotheses on Sex Differences." *Journal of Behavioral Medicine, 15,* 4, August 1992:355–364.

Kluegel, James R., and Eliot R. Smith. *Beliefs About Inequality: America's Views of What Is and What Ought to Be.* Hawthorne, N.Y.: Aldine de Gruyter, 1986.

Knauth, Donna G. "Predictors of Parental Sense of Competence for the Couple During the Transition to Parenthood." *Research in Nursing and Health, 23,* 2000:496–509.

Knickerbocker, Brad. "Firebrands of 'Ecoterrorism' Set Sights on Urban Sprawl." *Christian Science Monitor,* August 6, 2003.

Kohlberg, Lawrence. "Moral Education for a Society in Moral Transition." *Educational Leadership, 33,* 1975:46–54.

Kohlberg, Lawrence. *The Psychology of Moral Development: Moral Stages and the Life Cycle.* San Francisco: Harper and Row, 1984.

Kohlberg, Lawrence. "A Current Statement on Some Theoretical Issues." In *Lawrence Kohlberg: Consensus and Controversy,* Sohan Modgil and Celia Modgil, eds. Philadelphia: Falmer Press, 1986:485–546.

Kohlberg, Lawrence, and Carol Gilligan. "The Adolescent as a Philosopher: The Discovery of the Self in a Postconventional World." *Daedalus, 100,* 1971:1051–1086.

Kohn, Alfie. "Make Love, Not War." *Psychology Today,* June 1988:35–38.

Kohn, Melvin L. "Social Class and Parental Values." *American Journal of Sociology, 64,* 1959:337–351.

Kohn, Melvin L. "Social Class and Parent–Child Relationships: An Interpretation." *American Journal of Sociology, 68,* 1963:471–480.

Kohn, Melvin L., and Carmi Schooler. "Class, Occupation, and Orientation." *American Sociological Review, 34,* 1969:659–678.

Kohn, Melvin L. "Occupational Structure and Alienation." *American Journal of Sociology, 82,* 1976:111–130.

Kohn, Melvin L. *Class and Conformity: A Study in Values,* 2nd ed. Homewood, Ill.: Dorsey Press, 1977.

Kohn, Melvin L., Kazimierz M. Slomczynski, and Carrie Schoenbach. "Social Stratification and the Transmission of Values in the

Family: A Cross-National Assessment." *Sociological Forum, 1,* 1, 1986:73–102.

Kolata, Gina. "The Genesis of an Epidemic: Humans, Chimps and a Virus." *New York Times,* September 4, 2001.

Korda, Michael. *Male Chauvinism: How It Works.* New York: Random House, 1973.

Kornhauser, William. *The Politics of Mass Society.* New York: Free Press, 1959.

Kramer, Josea B. "Serving American Indian Elderly in Cities: An Invisible Minority." *Aging Magazine,* Winter–Spring 1992:48–51.

Krane, Vikki, Julie A. Stiles-Shipley, Jennifer Waldron, and Jennifer Michalenok. "Relationships Among Body Satisfaction, Social Physique Anxiety, and Eating Behaviors in Female Athletes and Exercisers." *Journal of Sport Behavior, 24,* 3, September 2001:247–264.

Kraybill, Donald B. *The Riddle of Amish Culture.* Revised edition. Baltimore, Md.: Johns Hopkins University Press, 2002.

Kristoff, Nicholas D. "Interview With a Humanoid." *New York Times,* July 23, 2002.

Krueger, Alan B. "The Apple Falls Close to the Tree, Even in the Land of Opportunity." *New York Times,* November 14, 2002.

Krueger, Robert F., and Avshalom Caspi. *Journal of Personality, 68,* 6, December 2000:967–998.

Krugman, Paul. "White Man's Burden." *New York Times,* September 24, 2002.

Kübler-Ross, Elisabeth. *On Death and Dying.* New York: Macmillan, 1969.

Kübler-Ross, Elisabeth. *Living with Death and Dying.* New York: Macmillan, 1981.

Kubrin, Charis E., and Ronald Weitzer. "Retaliatory Homicide: Concentrated Disadvantage and Neighborhood Culture." *Social Problems, 50,* 2, May 2003:157–180.

Kuhn, Margaret E. "The Gray Panthers." In *Social Problems,* 2nd ed., James M. Henslin, Englewood Cliffs, N.J.: Prentice Hall, 1990:56–57.

La Barre, Weston. *The Human Animal.* Chicago: University of Chicago Press, 1954.

Lacayo, Richard. "In the Grip of a Psychopath." *Time,* May 3, 1993:34–36, 39–43.

Lacey, Marc. "African Activists Urge End to Female Mutilation." *International Herald Tribune,* February 7, 2003:10.

Lachica, Eduardo. "Third World Told to Spend More on Environment." *Wall Street Journal,* May 18, 1992:A2.

Lagaipa, Susan J. "Suffer the Little Children: The Ancient Practice of Infanticide as a Modern Moral Dilemma." *Issues in Comprehensive Pediatric Nursing, 13,* 1990:241–251.

Lagnado, Lucette. "Another Peril: Smoking Doubles Risk of Old-Age Blindness, Two Studies Say." *Wall Street Journal,* October 9, 1996:B8.

Lalumiere, Martin L., and Vernon Quinsey. "Good Genes, Mating Effort, and Delinquency." *Behavioral and Brain Sciences, 23,* 4, August 2000:608–609.

Lamb, Michael E. "The Effect of Divorce on Children's Personality Development." *Journal of Divorce, 1,* Winter 1977:163–174.

Lamptey, Peter, Merywen Wigley, Dara Carr, and Yvette Collymore. "Facing the HIV/AIDS Pandemic." *Population Bulletin, 57,* 3, September 2002:1–40.

Landler, Mark. "Hi, I'm in Bangalore (But I Dare Not Tell)." *New York Times,* March 21, 2001.

Landtman, Gunnar. *The Origin of the Inequality of the Social Classes.* New York: Greenwood Press, 1968. First published in 1938.

Lane, Kristina. "Moving On Up." *Community College Week, 14,* 15, March 4, 2002:6–9.

Lang, Kurt, and Gladys E. Lang. *Collective Dynamics.* New York: Crowell, 1961.

Langan, Patrick A., and David J. Levin. "Recidivism of Prisoners Released in 1994." Bureau of Justice Statistics Special Report. Washington, D.C.: U.S. Department of Justice, June 2002.

Langley, Alison. "Geneva Suburb Casts Ballots on the Internet in a Test Project." *New York Times,* January 12, 2003.

Lannoy, Richard. *The Speaking Tree: A Study of Indian Culture and Society.* New York: Oxford University Press, 1975.

Lareau, Annette. "Invisible Inequality: Social Class and Childrearing in Black Families and White Families." *American Sociological Review, 67,* October 2002:747–776.

Larsen, Elena. "CyberFaith: How Americans Pursue Religion Online." Washington, D.C.: Pew Internet and American Life Project., December 23, 2001.

Larson, Jeffry H. "The Marriage Quiz: College Students' Beliefs in Selected Myths About Marriage." *Family Relations,* January 1988:3–11.

Larson, Mary Strom. "Interactions, Activities and Gender in Children's Television Commercials: A Content Analysis." *Journal of Broadcasting and Electronic Media, 45,* Winter 2001:41–51.

Lasch, Christopher. *Haven in a Heartless World: The Family Besieged.* New York: Basic, 1977.

Laska, Shirley Bradway. "Environmental Sociology and the State of the Discipline." *Social Forces, 72,* 1, September 1993:1–17.

Lauer, Jeanette, and Robert Lauer. "Marriages Made to Last." In *Marriage and Family in a Changing Society,* 4th ed., James M. Henslin, ed. New York: Free Press, 1992:481–486.

Lawler, Steph. "'Getting Out and Getting Away': Women's Narratives of Class Mobility." *Feminist Review,* 63, Autumn 1999:3–24.

Lazarsfeld, Paul F., and Jeffrey G. Reitz. "History of Applied Sociology." *Sociological Practice, 7,* 1989:43–52.

Leacock, Eleanor. *Myths of Male Dominance.* New York: Monthly Review Press, 1981.

LeBon, Gustave. *Psychologie des Foules (The Psychology of the Crowd).* Paris: Alcan, 1895. Various editions in English.

LeDuff, Charlie. "Handling the Meltdowns of the Nuclear Family." *New York Times,* May 28, 2003.

Lee, Alfred McClung, and Elizabeth Briant Lee. *The Fine Art of Propaganda: A Study of Father Coughlin's Speeches.* New York: Harcourt Brace, 1939.

Lee, Nick. *Childhood and Society: Growing Up in an Age of Uncertainty.* Buckingham: Open University Press, 2001.

Lee, Raymond M. *Unobtrusive Methods in Social Research.* Philadelphia: Open University Press, 2000.

Lee, Sharon M. "Asian Americans: Diverse and Growing." *Population Bulletin, 53,* 2, June 1998:1–39.

Leland, John. "A New Harlem Gentry in Search of Its Latte." *New York Times,* August 7, 2003.

Leland, John, and Gregory Beals. "In Living Colors." *Newsweek,* May 5, 1997:58–60.

Lemann, Nicholas, "The Myth of Community Development." *New York Times Magazine,* January 9, 1994, p. 27.

Lenski, Gerhard. *Power and Privilege: A Theory of Social Stratification.* New York: McGraw-Hill, 1966.

Lenski, Gerhard. "Status Crystallization: A Nonvertical Dimension of Social Status." *American Sociological Review, 19,* 1954:405–413.

Lenski, Gerhard, and Jean Lenski. *Human Societies: An Introduction to Macrosociology,* 5th ed. New York: McGraw-Hill, 1987.

Leonhardt, David. "Wide Racial Disparities Found in Costs of Mortgages." *New York Times,* May 1, 2002.

Lerner, Gerda. *Black Women in White America: A Documentary History.* New York: Pantheon Books, 1972.

Lerner, Gerda. *The Creation of Patriarchy.* New York: Oxford, 1986.

"Less Rote, More Variety: Reforming Japan's Schools." *The Economist,* December 16, 2000:8.

Lesser, Alexander. "War and the State." In *War: The Anthropology of Armed Conflict and Aggression,* Morton Fried, Marvin Harris, and Robert Murphy, eds. Garden City, N.Y.: Natural History, 1968:92–96.

Lester, David. *Suicide in American Indians.* New York: Nova Science Publishers, 1997.

Levine, John M. "Solomon Asch's Legacy for Group Research." *Personality and Social Psychology Review, 3,* 4, 1999:358–364.

Levinson, D. J. *The Seasons of a Man's Life.* New York: Knopf, 1978.

Levy, Clifford J. "Doctor Admits He Did Needless Surgery on the Mentally Ill." *New York Times,* May 20, 2003.

Levy, Marion J., Jr. "Confucianism and Modernization." *Society, 24,* 4, May–June 1992:15–18.

Lewin, Tamar. "Children's Computer Use Grows, But Gaps Persist, Study Says." *New York Times,* January 22, 2001a.

Lewin, Tamar. "Little Sympathy or Remedy for Inmates Who Are Raped." *New York Times,* April 15, 2001b.

Lewis, Oscar. "The Culture of Poverty." *Scientific American, 115,* October 1966a:19–25.

Lewis, Oscar. *La Vida.* New York: Random House, 1966b.

Lewis, Richard S. *Challenger: The Final Voyage.* New York: Columbia University Press, 1988.

Licata, Jane Massey. "Genetic NonDiscrimination: Implications for Employer Sponsored Heath Care Plans." Testimony before the House Committee on Education and the Workforce, *FDCH Congressional Testimony,* September 6, 2001.

Lichter, Daniel T., and Martha L. Crowley. "Poverty in America: Beyond Welfare Reform." *Population Bulletin, 57,* 2, June 2002:1–36.

Lieberson, Stanley. *A Matter of Taste: How Names, Fashions, and Culture Change.* New Haven: Yale University Press, 2000.

Liebow, Elliot. "Tally's Corner." In *Down to Earth Sociology: Introductory Readings,* 9th ed., James M. Henslin, ed. New York: Free Press, 1997:330–339.

Liebow, Elliott. *Tally's Corner: A Study of Negro Streetcorner Men.* Boston: Little, Brown, 1999. Originally published in 1967.

Light, Donald W. "Perestroika for Russian Health Care?" *Footnotes, 20,* 3, March 1992:7, 9.

Light, Richard J. *Making the Most of College.* Cambridge: Harvard University Press, 2001.

Lightfoot-Klein, A. "Rites of Purification and Their Effects: Some Psychological Aspects of Female Genital Circumcision and Infibulation (Pharaonic Circumcision) in an Afro-Arab Society (Sudan)." *Journal of Psychological Human Sexuality, 2,* 1989:61–78.

Lind, Michael. *The Next American Nation: The New Nationalism and the Fourth American Revolution.* New York: Free Press, 1995.

Linden, Eugene. "Lost Tribes, Lost Knowledge." *Time,* September 23, 1991:46, 48, 50, 52, 54, 56.

Lines, Patricia M. "Homeschooling Comes of Age." *Public Interest,* Summer 2000:74–85.

Linton, Ralph. *The Study of Man.* New York: Appleton-Century-Crofts, 1936.

Lippitt, Ronald, and Ralph K. White. "An Experimental Study of Leadership and Group Life." In *Readings in Social Psychology,* 3rd ed., Eleanor E. Maccoby, Theodore M. Newcomb, and Eugene L. Hartley, eds. New York: Holt, Rinehart and Winston, 1958: 340–365. (As summarized in Olmsted and Hare 1978:28–31.)

Lipset, Seymour Martin. "Democracy and Working-Class Authoritarianism." *American Sociological Review, 24,* 1959:482–502.

Lipset, Seymour Martin. "The Social Requisites of Democracy Revisited." Presidential address to the American Sociological Association, Boston, Massachusetts, 1993.

Lofland, John F. *Protest: Studies of Collective Behavior and Social Movements.* New Brunswick, New Jersey: Transaction Books, 1985.

Logue, John, and Jacquelyn Yates. "Modeling an Employee Ownership Sector." *Peace Review, 12,* 2, June 2000:243–249.

Lombroso, Cesare. *Crime: Its Causes and Remedies,* H. P. Horton, trans. Boston: Little, Brown, 1911.

Lorber, Judith. *Paradoxes of Gender.* New Haven, Conn.: Yale University Press, 1994.

Lublin, Joann S. "Trying to Increase Worker Productivity, More Employers Alter Management Style." *Wall Street Journal,* February 13, 1991:B1, B7.

Lublin, Joann S. "Women at Top Still Are Distant from CEO Jobs." *Wall Street Journal,* February 28, 1996:B1.

Lublin, Joann S. "Living Well." *Wall Street Journal,* April 8, 1999.

Lucas, Samuel Roundfield. *Tracking Inequality: Stratification and Mobility in American High Schools.* New York: Teachers College Press, 1999.

Luke, Timothy W. *Ideology and Soviet Industrialization.* Westport, Conn.: Greenwood Press, 1985.

Lunneborg, Patricia. *Chosen Lives of Childfree Men.* Westport, Conn.: Bergin and Garvey, 1999.

Lurie, Nicole, Jonathan Slater, Paul McGovern, Jacqueline Ekstrum, Lois Quam, and Karen Margolis. "Preventive Care for Women: Does the Sex of the Physician Matter?" *New England Journal of Medicine, 329,* August 12, 1993:478–482.

Mabry, Marcus. "The Price Tag on Freedom." *Newsweek,* May 3, 1999:50–51.

MacDonald, William L., and Alfred DeMaris. "Remarriage, Stepchildren, and Marital Conflict: Challenges to the Incomplete Institutionalization Hypothesis." *Journal of Marriage and the Family, 57,* May 1995:387–398.

Mack, Raymond W., and Calvin P. Bradford. *Transforming America: Patterns of Social Change,* 2nd ed. New York: Random House, 1979.

Mackay, Charles. *Memories* of *Extraordinary Popular Delusions and the Madness of Crowds.* London: Office of the National Illustrated Library, 1852.

Mackey, Richard A., and Bernard A. O'Brien. *Lasting Marriages: Men and Women Growing Together.* Westport, Conn.: 1995.

MacWilliams, Bryon. "Corruption, Conflict, and Budget Cuts Afflict Academe in Former Soviet Republics." *The Chronicle of Higher Education,* December 14, 2001a:A43, A45.

MacWilliams, Bryon. "For Russia's Universities, a Decade of More Freedom and Less Money." *The Chronicle of Higher Education,* December 14, 2001b:A42–44.

Magnuson, E. "A Cold Soak, a Plume, a Fireball." *Time,* February 17, 1986:25.

Maher, Sarah. *Salvadorans in Suburbia: Symbiosis and Conflict.* Boston: Allyn and Bacon, 1996.

Mahoney, John S., Jr., and Paul G. Kooistra. "Policing the Races: Structural Factors Enforcing Racial Purity in Virginia (1630–1930)." Paper presented at the 1995 meetings of the American Sociological Association.

Mahoney, Patricia. "High Rape Chronicity and Low Rates of Help-Seeking Among Wife Rape Survivors in a Nonclinical Sample: Implications for Research and Practice." *Violence Against Women, 5,* 9, September 1999:993–1016.

Mahran, M. *Proceedings of the Third International Congress of Medical Sexology.* Littleton, Mass.: PSG Publishing, 1978.

Mahran, M. "Medical Dangers of Female Circumcision." *International Planned Parenthood Federation Medical Bulletin, 2,* 1981:1–2.

Maier, Mark. "Teaching from Tragedy: An Interdisciplinary Module on the Space Shuttle *Challenger.*" *T.H.E. Journal,* September 1993:91–94.

Main, Jackson Turner. *The Social Structure of Revolutionary America.* Princeton, N.J.: Princeton University Press, 1965.

Malinowski, Bronislaw. *Sex and Repression in Savage Society.* Cleveland, Ohio: World, 1927.

Malmberg, Bo, and Gerdt Sundström. "Age Care Crisis in Sweden?" *Current Sweden, 412,* January 1996:1–6.

Malson, Lucien. *Wolf Children and the Problem of Human Nature.* New York: Monthly Review Press, 1972.

Malthus, Thomas Robert. *First Essay on Population 1798.* London: Macmillan, 1926. Originally published in 1798.

Mamdani, Mahmood. "The Myth of Population Control: Family, Caste, and Class in an Urban Village." New York: Monthly Review Press, 1973.

Manavalan, Theresa. "Why Science Is Sexy Now." *New Straits Times-Management Times,* June 26, 2001.

Mander, Jerry. *In the Absence of the Sacred: The Failure of Technology and the Survival of the Indian Nations.* San Francisco, Calif.: Sierra Club Books, 1992.

Manno, Bruno V. "The Real Score on the SATs." *Wall Street Journal,* September 13, 1995:A14.

Manno, Bruno V., and Chester E. Finn. "Do the Right Thing for Marcus Garvey and All Charter Schools." *Phi Delta Kappan, 79,* 7, March 1998:489–500.

Mansfield, Harvey C. "Grade Inflation: It's Time to Face the Facts." *Chronicle of Higher Education, 47,* 30, April 6, 2001:824.

Manski, Charles F. "Income and Higher Education." *Focus, 14,* 3, Winter 1992–1993:14–19.

Manzo, Kathleen Kennedy. "History in the Making." *Community College Week, 13,* 15, March 5, 2001:6–8.

Marable, Manning. "Whites Have an Obligation to Recognize Slavery's Legacy." *Newsweek,* August 27, 2001:22.

Marcus, Amy Dockser. "Mideast Minorities: Kurds Aren't Alone." *Wall Street Journal,* September 5, 1996:A12.

Marcus, Amy Dockser. "Careful, Your HMO Is Watching." *Wall Street Journal,* June 17, 2003.

Markson, Elizabeth W. "Moral Dilemmas." *Society,* July–August, 1992:4–6.

Markusen, Eric. "Genocide in Cambodia." In *Down to Earth Sociology,* 8th ed., James M. Henslin, ed. New York: Free Press, 1995:355–364.

Marolla, Joseph, and Diana Scully. "Attitudes Toward Women, Violence, and Rape: A Comparison of Convicted Rapists and Other Felons." *Deviant Behavior, 7,* 4, 1986:337–355.

Marshall, Samantha. "It's So Simple: Just Lather Up, Watch the Fat Go Down the Drain." *Wall Street Journal,* November 2, 1995:B1.

Marshall, Samantha. "Vietnamese Women Are Kidnapped and Later Sold in China as Brides." *Wall Street Journal,* August 3, 1999.

Martin, Philip, and Elizabeth Midgley. "Immigration: Shaping and Reshaping America." *Population Bulletin, 58,* 2, June 2003:1–44.

Martin, William G., and Mark Beittel. "Toward a Global Sociology: Evaluating Current Conceptions, Methods, and Practices." *Sociological Quarterly, 39,* 1, 1998:139–161.

Martineau, Harriet. *Society in America.* Garden City, N.Y.: Doubleday 1962. First published in 1837.

Marx, Gary T. "Thoughts On a Neglected Category of Social Movement Participant: The Agent Provocateur and the Informant." In *Collective Behavior and Social Movements,* Russell L. Curtis, Jr., and Benigno E. Aguirre, eds. Boston: Allyn and Bacon, 1993:242–258.

Marx, Gary T. "The Road to the Future." In *Triumph of Discovery: A Chronicle of Great Adventures in Science.* New York: Holt, 1995:63–65.

Marx, Karl. "Contribution to the Critique of Hegel's Philosophy of Right." In *Karl Marx: Early Writings,* T. B. Bottomore, ed. New York: McGraw-Hill, 1964:45. First published in 1844.

Marx, Karl, and Friedrich Engels. *Communist Manifesto.* New York: Pantheon, 1967. First published in 1848.

Masheter, Carol. "Postdivorce Relationships Between Ex-spouses: The Role of Attachment and Interpersonal Conflict." *Journal of Marriage and the Family, 53,* February 1991:103–110.

Massey, Douglas S. As quoted in *Footnotes,* September/October 2001:6.

Massey, Douglas S., and Garvey Lundy. "Use of Black English and Racial Discrimination in Urban Housing Markets: New Methods and Findings." *Urban Affairs Review, 36,* 2001:451–468.

Mateja, Jim. "Toyota Mulls Next Move After Success with Gas/Electric Hybrid Car." *Chicago Tribune,* September 6, 2001.

Mateju, Petr, and Martin Kreidl. "Rebuilding Status Consistency in a Post-Communist Society: The Czech Republic." *Innovation: The European Journal of Social Sciences, 14,* 1, March 2001:17–34.

Mauss, Armand. *Social Problems as Social Movements.* Philadelphia, Penn.: Lippincott, 1975.

Maybury-Lewis, David. "Tribal Wisdom." In *Sociology 95/96,* Kurt Finsterbusch, ed. Sluice Dock, Conn.: Dushkin, 1995:16–21.

Mayo, Elton. *Human Problems of an Industrial Civilization.* New York: Viking, 1966.

Mazur, Allan, and Joel Michalek. "Marriage, Divorce, and Male Testosterone." *Social Forces, 77,* 1, September 1998:315–330.

McAdam, Doug, John D. McCarthy, and Mayer N. Zald. "Social Movements." In *Handbook of Sociology,* Neil J. Smelser, ed. Newbury Park, Calif.: Sage, 1988:695–737.

McCabe, J. Terrence, and James E. Ellis. "Pastoralism: Beating the Odds in Arid Africa." In *Conformity and Conflict: Readings in Cultural Anthropology,* James P. Spradley and David W. McCurdy, eds. Glenview, Ill.: Scott, Foresman, 1990:150–156.

McCall, Michael. "Who and Where Are the Artists?" In *Fieldwork Experience: Qualitative Approaches to Social Research,* William B. Shaffir, Robert A. Stebbins, and Allan Turowetz, eds. New York: St. Martin's, 1980:145–158.

McCarthy, John D., and Mark Wolfson. "Consensus Movements, Conflict Movements, and the Cooperation of Civic and State Infrastructures." In *Frontiers in Social Movement Theory,* Aldon D. Morris and Carol McClurg Mueller, eds. New Haven, Conn.: Yale University Press, 1992:273–297.

McCarthy, John D., and Mayer N. Zald. "Resource Mobilization and Social Movements: A Partial Theory." *American Journal of Sociology, 82,* 6, 1977:1212–1241.

McCarthy, Michael J. "James Bond Hits the Supermarket: Stores Snoop on Shoppers' Habits to Boost Sales." *Wall Street Journal,* August 25, 1993:B1, B8.

McCartney, Scott. "People Most Needing Transplantable Livers Now Often Miss Out." *Wall Street Journal,* April 1, 1993:A1, A7.

McCormick, John. "Change Has Taken Place." *Newsweek,* June 7, 1999:34.

McCoy, Elin. "Childhood Through the Ages." In *Marriage and Family in a Changing Society,* 2nd ed., James M. Henslin, ed. New York: Free Press, 1985:386–394.

McCuen, Gary E., ed. *Ecocide and Genocide in the Vanishing Forest: The Rainforests and Native People.* Hudson, Wis.: GEM Publications, 1993.

McFarling, Usha Lee. "Climate Is Warming at Steep Rate, Study Says." *Los Angeles Times,* February 23, 2000.

McGee, Glenn. "Cloning, Sex, and New Kinds of Families." *Journal of Sex Research, 37,* 3, August 2000:266–272.

McGlynn, Elizabeth A., Steven M. Asch, John Adams, Joan Keesley, Jennifer Hicks, Allison deCristofaro, and Eve A. Kerr. "The Quality of Health Care Delivered to Adults in the United States." *New England Journal of Medicine,* June 26, 2003:2635–2645.

McGowan, Jo. "Little Girls Dying: An Ancient & Thriving Practice." *Commonweal,* August 9, 1991:481–482.

McIntosh, Peggy. "White Privilege and Male Privilege: A Personal Account of Coming to See Correspondences through Work in Women's Studies." Working Paper #189. Wellesley College Center for Research on Women, 1988.

McIntyre, Jamie. "Army Rape Case Renews Debate on Coed Training." April 30, 1997: CNN Internet article.

McKenna, George. "On Abortion: A Lincolnian Position." *Atlantic Monthly,* September 1995:51–67.

McKeown, Thomas. *The Modern Rise of Population.* New York: Academic Press, 1977.

McKown, Clark, and Rhona S. Weinstein. "Modeling the Role of Child Ethnicity and Gender in Children's Differential Response to Teacher Expectations." *Journal of Applied Social Psychology, 32,* 1, 2002:159–184.

McLanahan, Sara, and Dona Schwartz. "Life Without Father: What Happens to the Children?" *Contexts, 1,* 1, Spring 2002:35–44.

McLanahan, Sara, and Gary Sandefur. *Growing Up with a Single Parent: What Hurts, What Helps.* Cambridge, Mass.: Harvard University Press, 1994.

McLemore, S. Dale. *Racial and Ethnic Relations in America.* Boston: Allyn and Bacon, 1994.

McNeill, William H. "How the Potato Changed the World's History." *Social Research, 66,* 1, Spring 1999:67–83.

McPhail, Clark. "Blumer's Theory of Collective Behavior: The Development of a Non-Symbolic Interaction Explanation." *Sociological Quarterly, 30,* 3, 1989:401–423.

McPhail, Clark. *The Myth of the Madding Crowd.* Hawthorne, N.Y.: Aldine de Gruyter, 1991.

Mead, George Herbert. *Mind, Self and Society.* Chicago: University of Chicago Press, 1934.

Mead, Margaret. *Sex and Temperament in Three Primitive Societies.* New York: New American Library, 1950. First published in 1935.

Medina, Jennifer. "Often, a Bitter School Choice: Almost as Bad or Far Away." *New York Times,* April 13, 2003.

Medlin, Richard G. "Home Schooling and the Question of Socialization." *Peabody Journal of Education, 75,* 1–2, 2000:107–123.

Meek, Anne. "On Creating 'Ganas': A Conversation with Jaime Escalante." *Educational Leadership, 46,* 5, February 1989:46–47.

Meier, Barry. "Health Studies Suggest Asbestos Substitutes Also Pose Cancer Risk." *Wall Street Journal,* May 12, 1987:1, 21.

Meier, Barry. "Doctor to Face U.S. Charges in Drug Case." *New York Times,* December 23, 2001.

Melloan, George. "Italy 'Steps into the Tunnel' Toward Change." *Wall Street Journal,* April 26, 1993b:A15.

Melucci, Alberto. *Nomads of the Present: Social Movements and Individual Needs in Contemporary Society.* Philadelphia: Temple University Press, 1989.

Menaghan, Elizabeth G., Lori Kowaleski-Jones, and Frank L. Mott. "The Intergenerational Costs of Parental Social Stressors: Academic and Social Difficulties in Early Adolescence for Children of Young Mothers." *Journal of Health and Social Behavior, 38,* March 1997:72–86.

Menzel, Peter. *Material World: A Global Family Portrait.* San Francisco: Sierra Club, 1994.

Mersereau, Adam G. "The Military Should Fight Wars, Not Sexism." *Wall Street Journal,* March 17, 1998:A18.

Merton, Robert K. *Social Theory and Social Structure.* Glencoe, Ill.: Free Press, 1949, Enlarged ed., 1968.

Merton, Robert K. "The Social-Cultural Environment and *Anomie.*" In *New Perspectives for Research on Juvenile Delinquency,* Helen L. Witmer and Ruth Kotinsky, eds. Washington, D.C.: U.S. Department of Health, Education, and Welfare, 1956:24–50.

Merwine, Maynard H. "How Africa Understands Female Circumcision." *New York Times,* November 24, 1993.

Messner, Michael. "Boyhood, Organized Sports, and the Construction of Masculinities." *Journal of Contemporary Ethnography, 18,* 4, January 1990:416–444.

Mezentseva, E. *Russian Social Science Review, 42,* 4, July–August 2001:4–21.

Michael, Robert T. "Measuring Poverty: A New Approach." *Focus, 17,* 1, Summer 1995:2–13.

Michael, Robert T., John H. Gagnon, Edward O. Laumann, and Gina Kolata. "How Many Sexual Partners Do Americans Have?" In *Exploring Social Life: Readings to Accompany Essentials of Sociology: A Down-to-Earth Approach* 5th ed., James M. Henslin, ed. Boston: Allyn and Bacon, 2004:166–174.

Michalowski, Raymond J. *Order, Law, and Crime: An Introduction to Criminology.* New York: Random House, 1985.

Michels, Robert. *Political Parties.* Glencoe, Ill.: Free Press, 1949. First published in 1911.

"Microchips Under the Skin Offer ID, Raise Questions." *New York Times,* December 22, 2001.

Milbank, Dana. "Guarded by Greenbelts, Europe's Town Centers Thrive." *Wall Street Journal,* May 3, 1995:B1, B4.

Milbank, Dana. "Working Poor Fear Welfare Cutbacks Aimed at the Idle Will Inevitably Strike Them, Too." *Wall Street Journal,* August 9, 1995:A10.

Milgram, Stanley. "Behavioral Study of Obedience." *Journal of Abnormal and Social Psychology, 67,* 4, 1963:371–378.

Milgram, Stanley. "The Small World Problem." *Psychology Today, 1,* 1967:61–67.

Milgram, Stanley. "Some Conditions of Obedience and Disobedience to Authority." *Human Relations, 18,* February 1965:57–76.

Milkie, Melissa A. "Social World Approach to Cultural Studies." *Journal of Contemporary Ethnography, 23,* 3, October 1994:354–380.

Miller, Dan E. "Milgram Redux: Obedience and Disobedience in Authority Relations." In *Studies in Symbolic Interaction,* Norman K. Denzin, ed. Greenwich, Conn.: JAI Press, 1986:77–106.

Miller, Judith, and William J. Broad. "Clinton Describes Terrorism Threat for 21st Century." *New York Times,* January 22, 1999.

Miller, Laura L. "Women in the Military." In *Down to Earth Sociology: Introductory Readings,* 11th ed., James M. Henslin, ed. New York: The Free Press, 2001:481–496.

Miller, Lisa. "Son of Elijah Muhammad Preaches Gentler Islam in Tune With the Times." *Wall Street Journal,* July 9, 1999.

Miller, Michael W. "Survey Sketches New Portrait of the Mentally Ill." *Wall Street Journal,* January 14, 1994: B1, B10.

Miller, Walter B. "Lower Class Culture as a Generating Milieu of Gang Delinquency." *Journal of Social Issues, 14,* 3, 1958:5–19.

Miller-Loessi, Karen. "Toward Gender Integration in the Workplace: Issues at Multiple Levels." *Sociological Perspectives, 35,* 1, 1992:1–15.

Mills, C. Wright. *The Power Elite.* New York: Oxford University Press, 1956.

Mills, C. Wright. *The Sociological Imagination.* New York: Oxford University Press, 1959.

Mills, Karen M., and Thomas J. Palumbo. *A Statistical Portrait of Women in the United States: 1978.* U.S. Bureau of the Census, *Current Population Reports,* Series P-23, no. 100, 1980.

Minchin, Timothy J. *Hiring the Black Worker: The Racial Integration of the Southern Textile Industry, 1960–1980.* Chapel Hill, N.C.: University of North Carolina Press, 1999.

Miner, Horace. "Body Ritual Among the Nacirema." In *Down to Earth Sociology: Introductory Readings,* 12th ed., James M. Henslin, ed. New York: The Free Press, 2003:79–83.

Mintz, Beth A., and Michael Schwartz. *The Power Structure of American Business.* Chicago: University of Chicago Press, 1985.

Mirola, William A. "Asking for Bread, Receiving a Stone: The Rise and Fall of Religious Ideologies in Chicago's Eight-Hour Movement." *Social Problems, 50,* 2, May 2003:273–293.

Mitchell, G., Stephanie Obradovich, Fred Harring, Chris Tromborg, and Alyson L. Burns. "Reproducing Gender in Public Places: Adults' Attention to Toddlers in Three Public Locales." *Sex Roles, 26,* 7–8, 1992:323–330.

Mizruchi, Mark S., and Thomas Koenig. "Size, Concentration, and Corporate Networks: Determinants of Business Collective Action." *Social Science Quarterly, 72,* 2, June 1991:299–313.

Mohawk, John C. "Indian Economic Development: An Evolving Concept of Sovereignty." *Buffalo Law Review, 39,* 2, Spring 1991:495–503.

Mol, Arthur P. *Globalization and Environmental Reform: The Ecological Modernization of the Global Economy.* Cambridge, Mass.: MIT Press, 2001.

Money, John, and Anke A. Ehrhardt. *Man and Woman, Boy and Girl.* Baltimore: Johns Hopkins University Press, 1972.

" 'Monkey' Gives Delhi Claws for Alarm." *The Australian,* May 17, 2001.

Monk-Turner, Elizabeth, and Charlie G. Turner. "The Relative Pay of Men and Women in South Korea." *Journal of Asian Economics, 11,* 2, Summer 2000:223–236.

Montagu, M. F. Ashley, ed. *Race and IQ: Expanded Edition.* New York: Oxford University Press, 1999.

Montagu, M. F. Ashley. *Introduction to Physical Anthropology,* 3rd ed. Springfield, Ill.: Thomas, 1960.

Montagu, M. F. Ashley. *The Concept of Race.* New York: Free Press, 1964.

Moore, Stephen D., and Ron Winslow. "Health-Care Systems in 12 Countries Near Crisis, Drug Maker Study Says." *Wall Street Journal,* September 15, 1993:B6.

Morgan, Lewis Henry. *Ancient Society.* New York: Holt, 1877.

Morin, Monte. "$1.7 Million Awarded in Retirement Home Death." *Los Angeles Times,* October 17, 2001.

Morris, Aldon. "Black Southern Student Sit-In Movement: An Analysis of Internal Organization." In *Collective Behavior and Social Movements,* Russell L. Curtis, Jr., and Benigno E. Aguirre, eds. Boston: Allyn and Bacon, 1993:361–380.

Morris, J. R. "Racial Attitudes of Undergraduates in Greek Housing." *College Student Journal, 25,* 1, March 1991:501–505.

Morrow, Betty Hearn. "Urban Families as Support after Disaster: The Case of Hurricane Andrew." Paper presented at the 1995 meetings of the American Sociological Association.

Mosca, Gaetano. *The Ruling Class.* New York: McGraw-Hill, 1939. First published in 1896.

Moscos, Charles, C., and Sydney Butler. *All That We Can Be: Black Leadership and Racial Integration the Army Way.* New York: Basic Books, 1997.

Mosher, Steven W. "Why Are Baby Girls Being Killed in China?" *Wall Street Journal,* July 25, 1983:9.

Mosher, Steven W. "Too Many People? Not by a Long Shot." *Wall Street Journal,* February 10, 1997:A18.

Mount, Ferdinand. *The Subversive Family: An Alternative History of Love and Marriage.* New York: Free Press, 1992.

Moynihan, Daniel Patrick. "Social Justice in the *Next* Century." *America,* September 14, 1991:132–137.

Muir, Donald E. " 'White' Fraternity and Sorority Attitudes Toward 'Blacks' on a Deep-South Campus." *Sociological Spectrum, 11,* 1, January–March, 1991:93–103.

Mukamal, K. J., et al. "Roles of Drinking Pattern and Type of Alcohol Consumed in Coronary Heart Disease in Men." *New England Journal of Medicine, 348,* 2, January 9, 2003.

Murdock, George Peter. "The Common Denominator of Cultures." In *The Science of Man and the World Crisis,* Ralph Linton, ed. New York: Columbia University Press, 1945.

Murdock, George Peter. "Comparative Data on the Division of Labor by Sex." *Social Forces, 15,* 4, May 1937:551–553.

Murdock, George Peter. *Social Structure.* New York: Macmillan, 1949.

Murray, Charles, and R. J. Herrnstein. "What's Really Behind the SAT-score Decline?" *Public Interest, 106,* Winter 1992:32–56.

Murray, G. W. *Sons of Ishmael.* London: Routledge, 1935.

Nabhan, Gary Paul. *Cultures in Habitat: On Nature, Culture, and Story.* New York: Counterpoint, 1998.

Nachman, Sharon. "Elder Abuse and Neglect Substantiations: What They Tell Us About the Problem." *Journal of Elder Abuse and Neglect, 3,* 3, 1991:19–43.

Nagourney, Eric. "Fertility: A Study Links Prayer and Pregnancy." *New York Times,* October 2, 2001.

Naik, Gautam. "Travelers From All Over Seek Assistance From Dignitas to End Pain and Suffering." *New York Times,* November 22, 2002.

Nakao, Keiko, and Judith Treas. "Updating Occupational Prestige and Socioeconomic Scores: How the New Measures Measure Up." *Sociological Methodology, 24,* 1994:1–72.

Narayan, Shoba. "A First in Child Care." *Boston Globe,* December 5, 1994:19–20.

Nash, Gary B. *Red, White, and Black.* Englewood Cliffs, N.J.: Prentice Hall, 1974.

Nathan, John. *Sony: The Private Life.* New York: Houghton Mifflin, 1999.

National Center For Chronic Disease Prevention and Health Promotion. "Tobacco Advertising and Promotion." Athens, Ga.: Centers for Disease Control and Prevention, April 11, 2001.

National Institute of Child Health and Human Development. "Child Care and Mother-Child Interaction in the First 3 Years of Life." *Developmental Psychology, 35,* 6, November 1999:1399–1413.

National School Safety Center. "The School Associated Violent Death Report," Westlake Village, Calif.: 2002.

National School Safety Center. "School Associated Violent Deaths." Westlake Village, Calif.: 2003.

National Women's Political Caucus. "Factsheet on Women's Political Progress." Washington, D.C., June 1998.

National Women's Political Caucus. "News and Opinions; 1998 Election Results." Washington, D.C. November 5, 1998.

Naughton, Keith. "Cyberslacking." *Newsweek,* November 29, 1999:62–65.

Nauta, André. "That They All May Be One: Can Denominationalism Die?" Paper presented at the annual meetings of the American Sociological Association, 1993.

Navarro, Mireya. "For New York's Black Latinos, a Growing Racial Awareness." *New York Times,* April 28, 2003.

Navarro, Vicente, ed. *The Political Economy of Social Inequalities: Consequences for Health and Quality of Life.* Amityville, N.Y.: Baywood Publishing, 2002.

Neeley, Mark E., Jr. *The Fate of Liberty: Abraham Lincoln and Civil Liberties.* New York: Oxford University Press, 1992.

Neikirk, William, and Glen Elsasser. "Ruling Weakens Abortion Right." *Chicago Tribune,* June 30, 1992:1, 8.

Neugarten, Bernice L. "Middle Age and Aging." In *Growing Old in America,* Beth B. Hess, ed. New Brunswick, N.J.: Transaction, 1976:180–197.

Neugarten, Bernice L. "Personality and Aging." In *Handbook of the Psychology of Aging,* James E. Birren and K. Warren Schaie, eds. New York: Van Nostrand Reinhold, 1977:626–649.

Neuman, W. Lawrence. *Social Research Methods: Qualitative and Quantitative Approaches,* 4th ed. Boston: Allyn and Bacon, 2000.

Niebuhr, Gustav. "Studies Suggest Lower Count for Number of U.S. Muslims." *New York Times,* October 25, 2001.

Niebuhr, H. Richard. *The Social Sources of Denominationalism.* New York: Holt, 1929.

Nieves, Evelyn. "Lumber Company Approves U.S. Deal to Save Redwoods." *New York Times,* March 3, 1999.

Nisbett, Richard E. *The Geography of Thought: How Asians and Westerners Think Differently…and Why.* New York: The Free Press, 2003.

Noah, Timothy. "White House Forms Panel to Investigate Cold War Radiation Tests on Humans." *Wall Street Journal,* January 4, 1994:A12.

Nsamenang, A. Bame. *Human Development in Cultural Context: A Third World Perspective.* Newbury Park, Calif.: Sage, 1992.

Nuland, Sherwin B. "Immortality and Its Discontents." *Wall Street Journal,* July 2, 1999.

Nullis, Clare. "U. N.: Worst of AIDS Epidemic Is Still Ahead." Associated Press, June 28, 2000.

Nusbaum, Marci Alboher. "New Kind of Snooping Arrives at the Office." *New York Times,* July 13, 2003.

Oberschall, Anthony. *Social Conflict and Social Movements.* Englewood Cliffs, N.J.: Prentice Hall, 1973.

O'Connell, Martin. "Where's Papa? Father's Role in Child Care." Population Trends and Public Policy No. 20. Washington, D.C.: Population Reference Bureau, September 1993.

Offen, Karen. "Feminism and Sexual Difference in Historical Perspective." In *Theoretical Perspectives on Sexual Difference,* Deborah L. Rhode, ed. New Haven, Conn.: Yale University Press, 1990:13–20.

Ogburn, William F. *Social Change with Respect to Culture and Human Nature.* New York: W. B. Huebsch, 1922. (Other editions by Viking in 1927, 1938, and 1950.)

Ogburn, William F. "The Hypothesis of Cultural Lag." In *Theories of Society: Foundations of Modern Sociological Theory,* Vol. 2, Talcott Parsons, Edward Shils, Kaspar D. Naegele, and Jesse R. Pitts, eds. New York: Free Press, 1961:1270–1273.

Ogburn, William F. *On Culture and Social Change: Selected Papers,* Otis Dudley Duncan, ed. Chicago: University of Chicago Press, 1964.

O'Hare, William P. "A New Look at Poverty in America." *Population Bulletin, 51,* 2, September 1996a:1–47.

O'Hare, William P. "U.S. Poverty Myths Explored: Many Poor Work Year-Round, Few Still Poor After Five Years." *Population Today: News, Numbers, and Analysis, 24,* 10, October 1996b:1–2.

Ohmae, Kenichi. *The End of the Nation State: The Rise of Regional Economies.* New York: Free Press, 1995.

Olmsted, Michael S., and A. Paul Hare. *The Small Group,* 2nd ed. New York: Random House, 1978.

Olneck, Michael R., and David B. Bills. "What Makes Sammy Run? An Empirical Assessment of the Bowles-Gintis Correspondence Theory." *American Journal of Education, 89,* 1980:27–61.

Olshansky, S. Jay, Bruce Carnes, Richard G. Rogers, and Len Smith. "Infectious Diseases—New and Ancient Threats to World Health." *Population Bulletin, 52,* 2, July 1997:1–51.

O'Malley, Michael. "Ashcroft's Agenda: Civil Liberties Take a Back Seat to the Fight on Terrorism." *Orbis,* August, 2003.

Ono, Hiroshi. "Who Goes to College? Features of Institutional Tracking in Japanese Higher Education." *American Journal of Education, 109,* 12, February 2001:161–195.

Ono, Yumiko. "By Dint of Promotion Japanese Entrepreneur Ignites a Soccer Frenzy." *Wall Street Journal,* September 17, 1993:A1, A6.

O'Rand, Angela M., and John C. Henretta. *Age and Inequality: Diverse Pathways Through Later Life.* Boulder: Westview Press, 1999.

Orme, Nicholas. *Medieval Children.* New Haven: Yale University Press, 2002.

Osborne, Lawrence. "Got Silk." *New York Times Magazine,* June 15, 2002.

Ostling, Richard N. "Faith May Prevent Drug Abuse." *New York Times,* November 14, 2001.

Ouchi, William. *Theory Z: How American Business Can Meet the Japanese Challenge.* Reading, Mass.: Addison-Wesley, 1981.

Ouchi, William. "Decision-Making in Japanese Organizations." In *Down to Earth Sociology: Introductory Readings,* 7th ed., James M. Henslin, ed. New York: Free Press, 1993:503–507.

Paddock, Richard C. "Russians Bank on Bartering." *Los Angeles Times,* December 28, 1998.

Paddock, Richard C. "Patient Deaths Point to Depth of Russian Crisis." *Los Angeles Times,* March 13, 1999.

Pagelow, Mildred Daley. "Adult Victims of Domestic Violence: Battered Women." *Journal of Interpersonal Violence, 7,* 1, March 1992:87–120.

Palen, John J. *The Urban World,* 6th ed. Boston: McGraw Hill, 2002.

Parfit, Michael, "Earth First!ers Wield a Mean Monkey Wrench." *Smithsonian, 21,* 1, April 1990:184–204.

Park, Robert Ezra. "Human Ecology." *American Journal of Sociology, 42,* 1, July 1936:1–15.

Park, Robert Ezra, and Ernest W. Burgess. *Human Ecology.* Chicago: University of Chicago Press, 1921.

Parmesan, Camille, and Gary Yohe. "A Globally Coherent Fingerprint of Climate Change Impacts Across Natural Systems." *Nature,* January 2003:37–42.

Parsons, Talcott. "An Analytic Approach to the Theory of Social Stratification." *American Journal of Sociology, 45,* 1940:841–862.

Partington, Donald H. "The Incidence of the Death Penalty for Rape in Virginia." *Washington and Lee Law Review, 22,* 1965:43–75.

Passell, Peter. "Race, Mortgages and Statistics." *New York Times,* May 10, 1996:D1, D4.

Patel, Pragna. "Third Wave Feminism and Black Women's Activism." In *Black British Feminism: A Reader,* Heidi Safia Mirza, ed. London: Routledge, 1997.

Pauken, Tom. Personal communication, January 10, 2003.

Pauken, Tom. Personal research for the author. August 2003.

Pear, Robert. "9 of 10 Nursing Homes Lack Adequate Staff, Study Finds." *New York Times,* February 18, 2002b.

Pear, Robert. "Federal Welfare Rolls Shrink, But Drop Is Smallest Since '94." *New York Times,* May 21, 2002a.

Pearlin, L. I., and Melvin L. Kohn. "Social Class, Occupation, and Parental Values: A Cross-National Study." *American Sociological Review, 31,* 1966:466–479.

Peart, Karen N. "Converts to the Faith." *Scholastic Update, 126,* 4, October 22, 1993:16–18.

Pedersen, R. P. "How We Got Here: It's Not How You Think." *Community College Week, 13,* 15, March 15, 2001:4–5.

Pennar, Karen, and Christopher Farrell. "Notes from the Underground Economy." *Business Week,* February 15, 1993:98–101.

Perreault, George. "Saving the Neighborhood School: The Hometown Story." *High School Journal, 83,* 4, April–May 2000:40–45.

Perrin, Kathleen. "Rationing Health Care: Should It Be Done?" In *Perspectives in Social Gerontology,* Robert B. Enright, Jr., ed. Boston: Allyn and Bacon, 1994:309–314.

Perrow, Charles. "A Society of Organizations." *Theory and Society, 20,* 6, December 1991:725–762.

Persell, Caroline Hodges, and Peter W. Cookson, Jr. "Where the Power Starts." *Signature,* August 1986:51–57.

Persell, Caroline Hodges, Sophia Catsambis, and Peter W. Cookson, Jr. "Family Background, School Type, and College Attendance: A Conjoint System of Cultural Capital Transmission." *Journal of Research on Adolescence, 2,* 1, 1992:1–23.

Peter, Laurence J., and Raymond Hull. *The Peter Principle: Why Things Always Go Wrong.* New York: Morrow, 1969.

Petersen, Melody. "Suit Says Company Promoted Drug in Exam Rooms." *New York Times,* May 15, 2002.

Petersen, Melody. "Court Papers Suggest Scale of Drug's Use." *New York Times,* May 30, 2003.

Peterson, Iver. "1993 Deal for Indian Casino Is Called a Model to Avoid." *New York Times,* June 30, 2003.

Peterson, James L., and Nicholas Zill. "Marital Disruption, Parent–Child Relationships, and Behavior Problems in Children." *Journal of Marriage and the Family, 48,* 1986:295–307.

Peterson, Janice. "Welfare Reform and Inequality: The TANF and UI Programs." *Journal of Economic Issues, 34,* 2, June 2000:517–526.

Pfann, Gerard A., et al. "Business Success and Businesses' Beauty Capital." *Economics Letters, 67,* 2, May 2000:201–207.

Pfirman, S. *Complex Environmental Systems: Synthesis for Earth, Life, and Society in the 21st Century.* Arlington, Va.: National Science Advisory Committee for Environmental Research and Education, January 2003.

Phillips, Barbara D. "America's Forgotten Plague." *Wall Street Journal,* February 9, 1998:A15.

Phillips, John L., Jr. *The Origins of Intellect: Piaget's Theory.* San Francisco: Freeman, 1969.

Piaget, Jean. *The Psychology of Intelligence.* London: Routledge & Kegan Paul, 1950.

Piaget, Jean. *The Construction of Reality in the Child.* New York: Basic Books, 1954.

Pillemer, Karl, and Beth Hudson. "A Model Abuse Prevention Program for Nursing Assistants." *Gerontologist, 33,* 1, 1993:128–131.

Pillemer, Karl, and J. Jill Suitor. "Violence and Violent Feelings: What Causes Them Among Family Caregivers?" *Journal of Gerontology, 47,* 4, 1992:165–172.

Pillemer, Karl, and Rosalie S. Wolf. *Elder Abuse: Conflict in the Family.* Dover, Mass.: Auburn House, 1987.

Pilling, D., and M. Kellmer Pringle. *Controversial Issues in Child Development.* London: Paul Elek, 1978.

Pines, Maya. "The Civilizing of Genie." *Psychology Today, 15,* September 1981:28–34.

Piotrow, Phylis Tilson. *World Population Crisis: The United States' Response.* New York: Praeger, 1973.

Platt, Tony. " 'Street' Crime—A View from the Left." *Crime and Social Justice: Issues in Criminology,* 9, 1978:26–34.

"Playing House: New Data on Unmarried Couples." *Forecast, 21,* 11, July 16, 2001.

Pohl, Otto. "Universities Exporting B.A. Programs Via the Internet." *New York Times,* March 26, 2003.

Polsby, Nelson W. "Three Problems in the Analysis of Community Power." *American Sociological Review, 24,* 6, December 1959:796–803.

Polumbaum, Judy. "China: Confucian Tradition Meets the Market Economy." *Ms.,* September–October 1992:12–13.

Pope, Liston. *Millhands and Preachers: A Study of Gastonia.* New Haven, Conn.: Yale University Press, 1942.

Population Reference Bureau. "World Information Data Sheet." Washington, D.C., May 1995.

"Population Today." Washington, D.C.: Population Reference Bureau, *30,* 1, January-February, 2002.

"Population Today." Washington, D.C.: Population Reference Bureau, May/June 2002:7.

"Population Update." *Population Today, 28,* 1, January 2000.

Portés, Alejandro, and Ruben G. Rumbaut. *Immigrant America.* Berkeley: University of California Press, 1990.

Postman, Neil. *Technopoly: The Surrender of Culture to Technology.* New York: Knopf, 1992.

Powell, Arthur. *Lessons from Privilege: The American Prep School Tradition.* Cambridge: Mass.: Harvard University Press, 1996.

Powell, Bill. "Yeltsin's Legacy." *Newsweek,* January 4, 1999:72.

Power, Carla. "The New Islam." *Newsweek,* March 16, 1998:34–37.

Prashad, Vijay. "Tolerance Arabia." *Colorlines Magazine, 5,* 1, Spring 2002:18–23.

Presley, Cheryl A., Philip W. Meilman, and Rob Lyerla. *Alcohol and Drugs on American College Campuses.* Carbondale, Ill.: Southern Illinois University, 1993.

Presser, Stanley, and Linda Stinson. "Data Collection Mode and Social Desirability Bias in Self-Reported Religious Attendance." *American Sociological Review, 63,* February 1998:137–145.

Pressley, Sue Anne. "The Curious Continue Waco Siege." *Washington Post,* August 28, 1993:A1, A12.

Preston, Howard L. *Automobile Age Atlanta: the Making of a Southern Metropolis, 1900-1935.* Athens U. of Georgia Press, 1979.

Prud'Homme, Alex. "Getting a Grip on Power." *Time,* July 29, 1991:15–16.

Purdum, Todd S. "NATO Strikes Deal to Accept Russia in a Partnership." *New York Times,* May 15, 2002.

Raghunathan, V. K. "Millions of Baby Girls Killed in India." *The Straits Times,* February 8, 2003.

Raney, Rebecca Fairley. "Study Warns of Risks in Internet Voting." *New York Times,* March 8, 1999.

Ray, J. J. "Authoritarianism Is a Dodo: Comment on Scheepers, Felling and Peters." *European Sociological Review, 7,* 1, May 1991:73–75.

Read, Piers Paul. *Alive. The Story of the Andes Survivors.* Philadelphia: Lippincott, 1974.

Reat, Noble Ross. *Buddhism: A History.* Berkeley, Calif: Asian Humanities Press, 1994.

Reay, Diane, Jacqueline Davies, Miriam David, and Stephen J. Ball. "Choice of Degree or Degrees of Choice? Class, 'Race,' and the Higher Education Choice Process." *Sociology, 35,* 4, November 2001:855–876.

Recer, Paul. "Gene Mutation Doubles Life Span." Associated Press, December 14, 2000.

Reckless, Walter C. *The Crime Problem,* 5th ed. New York: Appleton, 1973.

Redclift, Michael, and Graham Woodgate, eds. *The International Handbook of Environmental Sociology.* Cheltenham, England: Edward Elgar, 1997.

"Redefining the Income Gap." *Training, 37,* 9, September 2000:38.

Reed, Susan, and Lorenzo Benet. "Ecowarrior Dave Foreman Will Do Whatever It Takes in His Fight to Save Mother Earth." *People Weekly, 33,* 15, April 16, 1990:113–116.

Reibstein, Larry. "Managing Diversity." *Newsweek,* 11/25/96:50.

Reich, Robert B. *Good for Business: Making Full Use of the Nation's Human Capital, The Environmental Scan.* Washington, D.C.: U.S. Department of Labor, March 1995.

Reiman, Jeffrey. *The Rich Get Richer and the Poor Get Prison: Ideology, Class, and Criminal Justice.* Boston: Allyn and Bacon, 2001.

Reiser, Christa. *Reflections on Anger: Women and Men in a Changing Society.* Westport, Conn.: Praeger Publishers, 1999.

Reitman, Valerie, and Oscar Suris. "In a Cultural U-Turn, Mazda's Creditors Put Ford Behind the Wheel." *Wall Street Journal,* November 21, 1994:A1, A4.

Rennison, Callie Marie. "Intimate Partner Violence, 1993–2001." Washington, D.C.: Bureau of Justice Statistics, February 2003.

Renteln, Alison Dundes. "Sex Selection and Reproductive Freedom." *Women's Studies International Forum, 15,* 3, 1992:405–426.

Reskin, Barbara F. *The Realities of Affirmative Action in Employment.* Washington, D.C.: American Sociological Association, 1998.

Resnik, David B. "Financial Interests and Research Bias." *Perspectives on Science, 8,* 3, Fall 2000:255–283.

Reuters. "Fake Tiger Woods Gets 200-Years-To-Life in Prison." April 28, 2001.

Rhone, Nedra. "Widespread Violations Found at Care Homes." *Los Angeles Times,* April 18, 2001.

Rich, Spencer. "Number of Elected Hispanic Officials Doubled in a Decade, Study Shows." *Washington Post,* September 19, 1986:A6.

Richardson, Stacey, and Marita P. McCabe. "Parental Divorce During Adolescence and Adjustment in Early Adulthood." *Adolescence, 36,* Fall 2001:467–489.

Ricks, Thomas E. "Pentagon Considers Selling Overseas a Large Part of High-Tech Weaponry." *Wall Street Journal,* 2/14/94:A16.

Ricks, Thomas E. "'New' Marines Illustrate Growing Gap Between Military and Society." *Wall Street Journal,* July 27, 1995:A1, A4.

Rieker, Patricia P., Chloe E. Bird, Susan Bell, Jenny Ruducha, Rima E. Rudd, and S. M. Miller, "Violence and Women's Health: Toward a Society and Health Perspective." Unpublished paper, 1997.

Riesman, David. *The Lonely Crowd.* New Haven, Conn.: Yale University Press, 1950.

Riessman, Catherine Kohler. "Women and Medicalization: A New Perspective." In *Dominant Issues in Medical Sociology,* 3rd ed., Howard D. Schwartz, ed. New York: McGraw-Hill, 1994:190–211.

Rifkin, Jeremy. *The End of Work: The Decline of the Global Labor Force and the Dawn of the Post-Market Era.* New York: Putnam, 1995.

Rigdon, Joan E., and Alecia Swasy. "Distractions of Modern Life at Key Ages Are Cited for Drop in Student Literacy." *Wall Street Journal,* October 1, 1990:B1, B3.

Rimer, Sara. "Colleges Find Diversity Is Not Just Numbers." *New York Times,* November 11, 2002.

Risen, James, and David Johnston. "Bush Has Widened Authority of C.I.A. to Kill Terrorists." *New York Times,* December 15, 2002.

Rist, Ray C. "Student Social Class and Teacher Expectations: The Self-Fulfilling Prophecy in Ghetto Education." *Harvard Educational Review, 40,* 3, August 1970:411–451.

Ritzer, George. *The McDonaldization of Society: An Investigation into the Changing Character of Contemporary Life.* Thousand Oaks, Calif.: Pine Forge Press, 1993.

Ritzer, George. *The McDonaldization Thesis: Explorations and Extensions.* Thousand Oaks, Calif.: Sage Publications, 1998.

Ritzer, George. "The McDonaldization of Society." In *Down to Earth Sociology: Introductory Readings,* 11th ed., James M. Henslin, ed. New York: The Free Press, 2001:459–471.

Robertson, Ian. *Sociology,* 3rd ed. New York: Worth, 1987.

Rodash, Mary Flannery. "The College of Midwifery: A Sociological Study of the Decline of a Profession." Unpublished doctoral dissertation, Southern Illinois University at Carbondale, 1982.

Rodriguez, Richard. "The Education of Richard Rodriguez." *Saturday Review,* February 8, 1975:147–149.

Rodriguez, Richard. *Hunger of Memory: The Education of Richard Rodriguez.* Boston: Godine, 1982.

Rodriguez, Richard. "The Late Victorians: San Francisco, AIDS, and the Homosexual Stereotype." *Harper's Magazine,* October 1990:57–66.

Rodriguez, Richard. "Mixed Blood." *Harper's Magazine, 283,* November 1991:47–56.

Rodriguez, Richard. "Searching for Roots in a Changing Society." In *Down to Earth Sociology: Introductory Readings,* 8th ed., James M. Henslin, ed. New York: Free Press, 1995:486–491.

Rodríguez, Victor M. "Los Angeles, U.S.A. 1992: 'A House Divided Against Itself . . .'?" *SSSP Newsletter,* Spring 1994:5–12.

Roediger, David R. *Colored White: Transcending the Racial Past.* Berkeley: University of California Press, 2002.

Roethlisberger, Fritz J., and William J. Dickson. *Management and the Worker.* Cambridge, Mass.: Harvard University Press, 1939.

Rogers, Joseph W. *Why Are You Not a Criminal?* Englewood Cliffs, N.J.: Prentice Hall, 1977.

Rogers, Stacy J., and Paul R. Amato. "Have Changes in Gender Relations Affected Marital Quality?" *Social Forces, 79,* December 2000:731–748.

Rohter, Larry. "For Chilean Coup, Kissinger Is Numbered Among the Hunted." *New York Times,* March 28, 2002.

Romero, Simon. "Tribes Seeking Phone Systems as Step to Web." *New York Times,* October 2, 2000.

Rosaldo, Michelle Zimbalist. "Women, Culture and Society: A Theoretical Overview." In *Women, Culture, and Society,* Michelle Zimbalist Rosaldo, and Louise Lamphere, eds. Stanford: Stanford University Press, 1974.

Rose, Frederick. "Los Angeles Tallies Losses; Curfew Is Lifted." *Wall Street Journal,* May 5, 1992:A3, A18.

Rosenbaum, David E. "U.S. Breaks a Ring That Smuggled in Thousands of Workers." *New York Times,* November 21, 1998.

Rosenberg, Charles E. *The Care of Strangers: The Rise of America's Hospital System.* New York: Basic Books, 1987.

Rosenfeld, Richard. "Crime Decline in Context." *Contexts, 1,* 1, Spring 2002:25–34.

Rosenthal, Elisabeth. "China's Chic Waistline: Convex to Concave." *New York Times,* December 9, 1999.

Rosenthal, Elisabeth. "For a Fee, Chinese Firm Will Beg Pardon for Anyone." *New York Times,* January 3, 2001a.

Rosenthal, Elisabeth. "Without 'Barefoot Doctors,' China's Rural Families Suffer." *New York Times,* March 14, 2001d.

Rosenthal, Elisabeth. "Harsh Chinese Reality Feeds a Black Market in Women." *New York Times,* June 25, 2001b.

Rosenthal, Robert, and Lenore Jacobson. *Pygmalion in the Classroom: Teacher Expectation and Pupils' Intellectual Development.* New York: Holt, Rinehart, and Winston, 1968.

Ross, Catherine E., and Marieke van Willigen. "Education and the Subjective Quality of Life." *Journal of Health and Social Behavior, 38,* 3, September 1997:275–297.

Ross, Emma. "Social Life Helps Prevent Dementia." Associated Press, April 23, 2000.

Rossi, Alice S. "A Biosocial Perspective on Parenting." *Daedalus, 106,* 1977:1–31.

Rossi, Alice S. "Gender and Parenthood." *American Sociological Review, 49,* 1984:1–18.

Rossi, Peter H. *Down and Out in America: The Origins of Homelessness.* Chicago: University of Chicago Press, 1989.

Rossi, Peter H. "Going Along or Getting It Right?" *Journal of Applied Sociology, 8,* 1991:77–81.

Rossi, Peter H. "Half Truths with Real Consequences: Journalism, Research, and Public Policy." *Contemporary Sociology,* 1999:1–5.

Rossi, Peter H., Gene A. Fisher, and Georgianna Willis. *The Condition of the Homeless of Chicago.* Amherst: University of Massachusetts, September 1986.

Rossi, Peter H., James D. Wright, Gene A. Fisher, and Georgianna Willis. "The Urban Homeless: Estimating Composition and Size." *Science, 235,* March 13, 1987:1136–1140.

Rotello, Gabriel. "The Risk in a 'Cure' for AIDS." *New York Times,* July 14, 1996.

Rothman, Barbara Katz. "Midwives in Transition: The Structure of a Clinical Revolution." In *Dominant Issues in Medical Sociology,* 3rd ed. Howard D. Schwartz, ed. New York: McGraw-Hill, 1994:104–112.

Rothschild, Joyce, and J. Allen Whitt. *The Cooperative Workplace: Potentials and Dilemmas of Organizational Democracy and Participation.* Cambridge, England: Cambridge University Press, 1986.

Rubin, Lillian Breslow. "The Empty Nest." In *Marriage and Family in a Changing Society,* 4th ed., James M. Henslin, ed. New York: Free Press, 1992a:261–270.

Rubin, Lillian Breslow. "Worlds of Pain." In *Marriage and Family in a Changing Society,* 4th ed., James M. Henslin, ed. New York: Free Press, 1992b:44–50.

Rubin, Lillian Breslow. *Worlds of Pain: Life in the Working-Class Family.* New York: Basic Books, 1976.

Rubin, Zick. "The Love Research." In *Marriage and Family in a Changing Society,* 2nd ed., James M. Henslin, ed. New York: Free Press, 1985.

Rudner, Lawrence M. "The Scholastic Achievement of Home School Students." *ERIC/AE Digest,* September 1, 1999.

Ruffenbach, Glenn. "Nursing-Home Care as a Work Benefit." *Wall Street Journal,* June 30, 1988:23.

Ruggles, Patricia. "Short and Long Term Poverty in the United States: Measuring the American 'Underclass.' " Washington, D.C.: Urban Institute, June 1989.

Russell, Diana E. H. "Preliminary Report on Some Findings Relating to the Trauma and Long-Term Effects of Intrafamily Childhood Sexual Abuse." Unpublished paper.

Russell, Diana E. H. *Rape in Marriage.* Bloomington: Indiana University Press, 1990.

Sadler, Anne G., Brenda M. Booth, Brian L. Cook, and Bradley N. Doebbeling. "Factors Associated With Women's Risk of Rape in the Military Environment." *American Journal of Industrial Medicine, 43,* 2003:252–273.

Sahlins, Marshall D. *Stone Age Economics.* Chicago: Aldine, 1972.

Sahlins, Marshall D., and Elman R. Service. *Evolution and Culture.* Ann Arbor: University of Michigan Press, 1960.

Salholz, Eloise. "The Push for Power." *Newsweek,* April 9, 1990:19–20.

Salopek, Paul. "Shattered Sudan: Drilling for Oil, Hoping for Peace." *National Geographic, 203,* 2, February 2003:30–66.

Sampat, Jyothi. "My Marriage Was Arranged." *Good Housekeeping, 228,* 2, February 1999:76–77.

Sampson, Catherine. "Corrupt Care." *World Press Review, 39,* 5 May 1992:46.

Sampson, Robert J., Gregory D. Squires, and Min Zhou. *How Neighborhoods Matter: The Value of Investing at the Local Level.* Washington, D.C.: American Sociological Association, 2001.

Sampson, Robert J., Jeffrey D. Morenoff, and Felton Earls. "Beyond Social Capital: Spatial Dynamics of Collective Efficacy for Children." *American Sociological Review, 64,* October 1999:633–660.

Samuelson, Paul Anthony, and William D. Nordhaus. *Economics,* 17th ed. New York: McGraw Hill, 2000.

Samuelson, Robert J. "The Elderly Aren't Needy." *Newsweek,* March 21, 1988:68.

Sanchez, Laura. "Gender, Labor Allocations, and the Psychology of Entitlement Within the Home." *Social Forces, 13,* 2, December 1994:533–553.

Sandefur, Gary D. "Children in Single-Parent Families: The Roles of Time and Money." *Focus, 17,* 1, Summer 1995:44–45.

Sapir, Edward. *Selected Writings of Edward Sapir in Language, Culture, and Personality.* David G. Mandelbaum, ed. Berkeley, Calif.: University of California Press, 1949.

"SAT Scores Hold Steady, State's 2003 Graduates Among the Tops in the Nation." *Education Forum, 6,* 44, August 28–September 5, 2003.

Satchell, Michael. "A Whale of a Protest." *U.S. News Online,* October 5, 1998.

Savells, Jerry. "Social Change Among the Amish." In *Down to Earth Sociology: Introductory Readings,* 12th ed., James M. Henslin, ed. New York: The Free Press, 2003:486–495.

"Saving the Schools." *Business Week,* November 12, 2001:59.

Sawyer, Richard. "Dire New Acid Rain Study." *Conservation Matters, 8,* 1, Summer 2001.

Sayres, William. "What Is a Family Anyway?" In *Marriage and Family in a Changing Society,* 4th ed., James M. Henslin, ed. New York: Free Press, 1992:23–30.

Scarr, Sandra, and Marlene Eisenberg. "Child Care Research: Issues, Perspectives, and Results." *Annual Review of Psychology, 44,* 1993:613–644.

Schaefer, Naomi. "Slavery in Africa Is Largely Ignored by U.S. Black Leaders and Major Media." *Massachusetts News,* May 12, 1999.

Schaeffer, Richard T. *Racial and Ethnic Groups,* 9th ed. Upper Saddle River, N.J.: Prentice Hall, 2004.

Schatz, Thomas A. "Medicare Fraud: Tales from the Gypped." *Wall Street Journal,* August 25, 1995:A8.

Scheff, Thomas J. *Being Mentally Ill: A Sociological Theory,* 3rd ed. New York: Aldine de Gruyter, 1999.

Schellenberg, James A. *Conflict Resolution: Theory, Research, and Practice.* Albany: New York University Press, 1996.

Schemo, Diana Jean. "Education Dept. Says States Have Lax Standard for Teachers." *New York Times,* June 13, 2002.

Schemo, Diana Jean. "Women at West Point Face Tough Choices on Assaults." *New York Times,* May 22, 2003.

Schlesinger, Jacob M., and Jathon Sapsford. "Japan, Shaken by Plunging Stocks, Mulls Further Economic Measures." *Wall Street Journal,* December 1, 1993:A14.

Schmemann, Serge. "Russia's Precapitalist Economy: How Can You Have a Bust If You Never Had a Boom?" *New York Times,* December 27, 1998.

Schmiege, Cynthia J., Leslie N. Richards, and Anisa M. Zvonkovic. "Remarriage: For Love or Money?" *Journal of Divorce and Remarriage,* May–June 2001:123–141.

Schottland, Charles I. *The Social Security Plan in the U.S.* New York: Appleton, 1963.

Schwartz, Felice N. "Management Women and the New Facts of Life." *Harvard Business Review, 89,* 1, January–February 1989:65–76.

Schwartz, Mildred A. *A Sociological Perspective on Politics.* Englewood Cliffs, N.J.: Prentice Hall, 1990.

Scommegna, Paola. "Increased Cohabitation Changing Children's Family Settings." *Population Today, 30,* 7, October 2002:3, 6.

Scott, Ellen Kaye. "How to Stop the Rapists: A Question of Strategy in Two Rape Crisis Centers." *Social Problems, 40,* 3, August 1993:343–361.

Scott, Janny. "White Flight, This Time Toward Harlem." *New York Times,* February 25, 2001.

Scott, Monster Cody. *Monster: The Autobiography of an L. A. Gang Member.* New York: Penguin Books, 1994.

Scully, Diana. *Understanding Sexual Violence: A Study of Convicted Rapists.* Boston: Unwin Hyman, 1990.

Scully, Diana. "Negotiating to Do Surgery." In *Dominant Issues in Medical Sociology,* 3rd ed., Howard D. Schwartz, ed. New York: McGraw-Hill, 1994:146–152.

Scully, Diana, and Joseph Marolla. "Convicted Rapists' Vocabulary of Motive: Excuses and Justifications." *Social Problems, 31,* 5, June 1984:530–544.

Scully, Diana, and Joseph Marolla. "'Riding the Bull at Gilley's': Convicted Rapists Describe the Rewards of Rape." In *Down to Earth Sociology: Introductory Readings,* 12th ed., James M. Henslin, ed. New York: The Free Press, 2003:48–64.

Seaver, W. J. "Effects of Naturally Induced Teacher Expectancies." *Journal of Personality and Social Psychology, 28,* 1973:333–342.

Seib, Gerald F. *Wall Street Journal,* "Click Here for Democracy." *Wall Street Journal,* January 1, 2000:R45–R46.

Selingo, Jeffrey. "It's the Cars, Not the Tires, That Squeal." *New York Times,* October 25, 2001.

Seltzer, Judith A. "Consequences of Marital Dissolution for Children." *Annual Review of Sociology, 20,* 1994:235–266.

Sennett, Richard, and Jonathan Cobb. "Some Hidden Injuries of Class." In *Down to Earth Sociology: Introductory Readings,* 5th ed., James M. Henslin ed. New York: Free Press, 1988:278–288. Excerpts from Richard Sennett and Jonathan Cobb. *The Hidden Injuries of Class.* New York: Knopf, 1972.

Shanker, Thom. "U.S. Troops Were Subjected to a Wider Toxic Testing." *New York Times,* October 8, 2002.

Shapiro, Joseph P. "Euthanasia's Home." *U.S. News and World Report, 122,* 1, January 13, 1997:24–27.

Sharp, Deborah. "Miami's Language Gap Widens." *USA Today,* April 3, 1992:A1, A3.

Sharp, Lauriston. "Steel Axes for Stone-Age Australians." In *Down to Earth Sociology: Introductory Readings,* 8th ed., James M. Henslin, ed. New York: Free Press, 1995:453–462.

Shelden, Randall G. *Controlling the Dangerous Classes: A Critical Introduction to the History of Criminal Justice.* Boston: Allyn and Bacon, 2001.

Shellenbarger, Sue. "When Caring for Aging Relatives Stirs Up Unwelcome Emotions." *New York Times,* July 17, 2003.

Shenon, Philip. "Arguments Conclude in Army Sex Hearing." *New York Times,* August 26, 1997.

Sherif, Muzafer, and Carolyn Sherif. *Groups in Harmony and Tension.* New York: Harper & Row, 1953.

Sherkat, Darren E., and John Wilson. "Status, Denomination, and Socialization: Effects on Religious Switching and Apostasy." Presented at the annual meetings of the American Sociological Association, 1991.

Sherman, Spencer. "The Hmong in America." *National Geographic,* October 1988:586–610.

Shibutani, Tamotsu. *Improvised News: A Sociological Study of Rumor.* Indianapolis, Ind.: Bobbs-Merrill, 1966.

Shibutani, Tamotsu. "On the Personification of Adversaries." In *Human Nature and Collective Behavior,* Tamotsu Shibutani, ed. Englewood Cliffs, N.J.: Prentice Hall, 1970.

Shirouzu, Norhiko. "Driven by Necessity, and Ford, Mazda Downsizes, U.S.-Style." *Wall Street Journal,* January 5, 2000.

Shirouzu, Norihiko, and Michael Williams. "Pummeled by Giants, Japan's Small Firms Struggle with Change." *Wall Street Journal,* July 25, 1995:A1, A5.

Shively, JoEllen. "Cultural Compensation: The Popularity of Westerns Among American Indians," Paper presented at the annual meetings of the American Sociological Association, 1991.

Shively, JoEllen. "Cowboys and Indians: Perceptions of Western Films Among American Indians and Anglos." *American Sociological Review, 57,* December 1992:725–734.

Shreve, Herbie. Personal communication, 1991.

Signorielli, Nancy. "Television and Conceptions About Sex Roles: Maintaining Conventionality and the Status Quo." *Sex Roles, 21,* 5–6, 1989:341–360.

Signorielli, Nancy. "Children, Television, and Gender Roles: Messages and Impact." *Journal of Adolescent Heath Care, 11,* 1990:50–58.

Sills, David L. *The Volunteers.* Glencoe, Ill.: Free Press, 1957.

Sills, David L. "Voluntary Associations: Sociological Aspects." In *International Encyclopedia of the Social Sciences, 16,* David L. Sills, ed. New York: Macmillan, 1968:362–379.

Simmel, Georg. *The Sociology of Georg Simmel,* Kurt H. Wolff, ed. and trans. Glencoe, Ill.: Free Press, 1950. First published between 1902 and 1917.

Simmons, Ann M. "Survivors of Rwandan Genocide Fear Guilty Will Get Away With Murder." *Los Angeles Times,* December 26, 1998.

Simon, Julian L. *Theory of Population and Economic Growth.* New York: Blackwell, 1986.

Simon, Julian L. "The Nativists Are Wrong." *Wall Street Journal,* August 4, 1993:A10.

Simons, Lewis M. "Weapons of Mass Destruction: An Ominous New Chapter Opens on the Twentieth Century's Ugliest Legacy." *National Geographic,* November 2002:3–35.

Simons, Marlise. "Social Change and Amazon Indians." In *Exploring Social Life: Readings to Accompany Essentials of Sociology,* 5th ed., James M. Henslin, ed. Boston: Allyn and Bacon, 2004:158–165.

Simpson, George Eaton, and J. Milton Yinger. *Racial and Cultural Minorities: An Analysis of Prejudice and Discrimination,* 4th ed. New York: Harper & Row, 1972.

Sindayen, Nelly. "I Once Was Lost. But Now I'm Wired." *Time, 157,* 22, June 4, 2001:80–83.

Skeels, H. M. *Adult Status of Children with Contrasting Early Life Experiences: A Follow-up Study.* Monograph of the Society for Research in Child Development, *31,* 3, 1966.

Skeels, H. M., and H. B. Dye. "A Study of the Effects of Differential Stimulation on Mentally Retarded Children." *Proceedings and Addresses of the American Association on Mental Deficiency, 44,* 1939:114–136.

Skiba, Katherine M. "U.S. Slowdown Affects Glendale, Wis.-Based Employment Firm's Mexico Arm." *Milwaukee Journal Sentinel,* July 23, 2001.

Sklair, Leslie. *Globalization: Capitalism and Its Alternatives,* 3rd ed. New York: Oxford: University Press, 2001.

Skow, John. "The Redwoods Weep." *Time,* September 28, 1998:70–72.

Sloan, Allan. "A Lot of Trust, But No Funds." *Newsweek,* July 30, 2001:34.

Smart, Barry. "On the Disorder of Things: Sociology, Postmodernity and the 'End of the Social.'" *Sociology, 24,* 3, August 1990:397–416.

Smedley, Brian D., Adrienne Y. Stith, and Alan R. Nelson eds. *Unequal Treatment: Confronting Racial and Ethnic Disparities in Health Care.* Washington, D.C.: The National Academies Press, 2003.

Smith, Beverly A. "An Incest Case in an Early 20th-Century Rural Community." *Deviant Behavior, 13,* 1992:127–153.

Smith, Clark. "Oral History as 'Therapy': Combatants' Account of The Vietnam War." In *Strangers at Home: Vietnam Veterans Since the War,* Charles R. Figley and Seymore Leventman, eds. New York: Praeger, 1980:9–34.

Smith, Craig S. "China Becomes Industrial Nations' Most Favored Dump." *Wall Street Journal,* October 9, 1995:B1.

Smith, Daniel Scott, and Michael Hindus. "Premarital Pregnancy in America, 1640–1971: An Overview and Interpretation." *Journal of Interdisciplinary History, 4,* Spring 1975:537–570.

Smith, Harold. "A Colossal Cover-Up." *Christianity Today,* December 12, 1986:16–17.

Smith, Jackie, Charles Chatfield, and Ron Pagnucco. *Transnational Social Movements and Global Policy: Solidarity Beyond the State.* Syracuse, N.Y.: Syracuse University Press, 1997.

Smith, Lee. "The War Between the Generations." *Fortune,* July 20, 1987:78–82.

Smith, Simon C. "The Making of a Neo-Colony? Anglo-Kuwaiti Relations in the Era of Decolonization." *Middle Eastern Studies, 37,* 1, January 2001:159–173.

Smith, Wesley J. "Dependency or Death? Oregonians Make a Chilling Choice." *Wall Street Journal,* February 25, 1999.

Smith-Lovin, Lynn, and Charles Brody. "Interruptions in Group Discussions: The Effects of Gender and Group Composition." *American Sociological Review, 54,* 1989:424–435.

Smock, Pamela J., Wendy D. Manning, and Sanjiv Gupta. "The Effect of Marriage and Divorce on Women's Economic Well-Being." *American Sociological Review, 64,* December 1999:794–812.

Snow, David A., Louis A. Zurcher, and Robert Peters. "Victory Celebrations as Theater: A Dramaturgical Approach to Crowd Behavior." In *Collective Behavior and Social Movements,* Russell L. Curtis, Jr., and Benigno E. Aguirre, eds. Boston: Allyn and Bacon, 1993b:194–208.

Snow, David A., Louis A. Zurcher, Jr., and Sheldon Ekland-Olson. "Social Networks and Social Movements: A Microstructural Approach to Differential Recruitment." In *Collective Behavior and Social Movements,* Russell L. Curtis, Jr., and Benigno E. Aguirre, eds. Boston: Allyn and Bacon, 1993a:323–334.

Snow, Margaret E., Carol Nagy Jacklin, and Eleanor E. Maccoby. "Birth-Order Differences in Peer Sociability at Thirty-Three Months." *Child Development, 52,* 1981:589–595.

Snyder, Jack. "Disney's Town of Celebration, Fla., Still Suffers Growing Pains." *Orlando Sentinel,* June 18, 2001.

Snyder, Mark. "Self-Fulfilling Stereotypes." In *Down to Earth Sociology: Introductory Readings,* 7th ed., James M. Henslin, ed. New York: Free Press, 1993:153–160.

"Social Darwinism in Sweden." *Report* (Alberta Edition), *28,* 14, July 9, 2001:4.

Solomon, Charlene Marmer. "Cracks in the Glass Ceiling." *Workforce, 79,* 9, September 2000:87–91.

Solomon, Jolie. "Companies Try Measuring Cost Savings from New Types of Corporate Benefits." *Wall Street Journal,* December 29, 1988:B1.

Sorokin, Pitirim A. *Social and Cultural Dynamics.* 4 vols. New York: American Book Company, 1937–1941.

Soss, Joe. "Lessons of Welfare: Policy Design, Political Learning, and Political Action." *American Political Science Review, 93,* 1999:363–380.

Sourcebook of Criminal Justice Statistics. Washington, D.C.: U.S. Government Printing Office, published annually.

"South African Government Lifts Moratorium on Crime Stats." Associated Press, May 31, 2001.

South, Scott J. "Sociodemographic Differentials in Mate Selection Preferences." *Journal of Marriage and the Family, 53,* November 1991:928–940.

Sowell, Thomas. *Inside American Education: The Decline, the Deception, the Dogmas.* New York: Free Press, 1993.

Spector, Malcolm, and John Kitsuse. *Constructing Social Problems.* Menlo Park, Calif.: Cummings, 1977.

Spencer, Herbert. *Principles of Sociology.* 3 vols. New York: Appleton, 1884.

Spengler, Oswald. *The Decline of the West,* 2 vols. Charles F. Atkinson, trans. New York: Knopf, 1926–1928. First published in 1919–1922.

Spickard, P. R. S. *Mixed Blood: Intermarriage and Ethnic Identity in Twentieth Century America.* Madison: University of Wisconsin Press, 1989.

Spitzer, Steven. "Toward a Marxian Theory of Deviance." *Social Problems, 22,* June 1975:608–619.

Spivak, Gayatri Chakravorty. "Feminism 2000: One Step Beyond." *Feminist Review, 64,* Spring 2000:113.

Spragins, Ellyn E. "To Sue or Not to Sue?" *Newsweek,* December 9, 1996:50.

Sprecher, Susan, and Rachita Chandak. "Attitudes About Arranged Marriages and Dating Among Men and Women from India." *Free Inquiry in Creative Sociology, 20,* 1, May 1992:59–69.

Srole, Leo, et al. *Mental Health in the Metropolis: The Midtown Manhattan Study.* Albany, N.Y.: New York University Press, 1978.

Stack, Carol B. *All Our Kin: Strategies for Survival in a Black Community.* New York: Harper, 1974.

Stampp, Kenneth M. *The Peculiar Institution: Slavery in the Ante-Bellum South.* New York: Vintage Books, 1956.

Stark, Rodney. *Sociology,* 3rd ed. Belmont, Calif.: Wadsworth, 1989.

Starna, William A., and Ralph Watkins. "Northern Iroquoian Slavery." *Ethnohistory, 38,* 1, Winter 1991:34–57.

Starr, Paul. *The Social Transformation of American Medicine.* New York: Basic Books, 1982.

Starrels, Marjorie. "The Evolution of Workplace Family Policy Research." *Journal of Family Issues, 13,* 3, September 1992:259–278.

State of American Education: A 5-Year Report Card on American Education." U.S. Department of Education, February 22, 2000.

"State of the World's Children 2001." *Reading Today, 18,* 4, February–March 2001:24.

Statham, Anne, Eleanor M. Miller, and Hans O. Mauksch. "The Integration of Work: Second-Order Analysis of Qualitative Research." In *The Worth of Women's Work: A Qualitative Synthesis.* Statham, Anne, Eleanor M. Miller, and Hans O. Mauksch, eds. Albany, N.Y.: State University of New York Press, 1988:11–35.

Statistical Abstract of the United States. Washington D.C.: Bureau of the Census, published annually.

Stecklow, Steve. "SAT Scores Rise Strongly after Test Is Overhauled." *Wall Street Journal,* August 24, 1995:B1, B12.

Steele, Shelby. "Reparations Enshrine Victimhood, Dishonoring Our Ancestors." *Newsweek,* August 27, 2001:23.

Steinberg, Jacques. "Student Failure Causes States to Retool Testing Programs." *New York Times,* December 22, 2000.

Steinberg, Laurence, Stanford Dornbusch, and Bradford Brown. *Beyond the Classroom.* New York: Simon & Shuster, 1996.

Steinhauer, Jennifer. "Angry at Managed Care, Doctors Start Fighting Back." *New York Times,* January 10, 1999.

Steinhauer, Jennifer. "So, the Tumor is on the Left, Right?" *New York Times,* April 1, 2001.

Steinhauer, Jennifer, and Ford Fessenden. "Medical Retreads: Doctor Punished by State But Prized at the Hospitals." *New York Times,* March 27, 2001.

Stephens, W. Richard, Jr. *Careers in Sociology,* 3rd ed. Boston: Allyn and Bacon, 2004.

Stevens, Amy, and Sarah Lubman. "Deciding Moment of the Trial May Have Been Five Months Ago." *Wall Street Journal,* May 1, 1992:A6.

Stevens, Mitchell L. *Kingdom of Children: Culture and Controversy in the Homeschooling Movement.* Princeton: Princeton University Press, 2001.

Stevenson, Richard W. "U.S. Debates Investing in Stock for Social Security." *New York Times,* July 27, 1998.

Stewart, Abigail J., Anne P. Copeland, Nia Lane Chester, Janet E. Malley, and Nicole B. Barenbaum. *Separating Together: How Divorce Transforms Families.* New York: Guilford Press, 1997.

Stewart, Elizabeth A. *Exploring Twins: Towards a Social Analysis of Twinship.* New York: St. Martin's Press, 2000.

"Sticky Ticket: A New Jersey Mother Sues Her Son Over a Lottery Jackpot She Claims Belongs to Them Both." *People Weekly,* February 9, 1998:68.

Stinnett, Nicholas. "Strong Families." In *Marriage and Family in a Changing Society,* 4th ed., James M. Henslin, ed. New York: Free Press, 1992:496–507.

Stinson, Kandi M. *Women and Dieting Culture: Inside a Commercial Weight Loss Group.* New Brunswick, N.J.: Rutgers University Press, 2001.

Stipp, David. "Himalayan Tree Could Serve as Source of Anti-cancer Drug Taxol, Team Says." *Wall Street Journal,* April 20, 1992:B4.

Stockard, Jean, and Miriam M. Johnson. *Sex Roles: Sex Inequality and Sex Role Development.* Englewood Cliffs, N.J.: Prentice Hall, 1980.

Stockwell, John. "The Dark Side of U.S. Foreign Policy." *Zeta Magazine,* February 1989:36–48.

Stodgill, Ralph M. *Handbook of Leadership: A Survey of Theory and Research.* New York: Free Press, 1974.

Stolberg, Sheryl Gay. "Blacks Found on Short End of Heart Attack Procedure." *New York Times,* May 10, 2001.

Stone, Gregory P. "City Shoppers and Urban Identification: Observations on the Social Psychology of City Life." *American Journal of Sociology, 60,* November 1954:276–284.

Storfer, Miles D. "Intelligence and Giftedness." In *Sociology: Windows on Society,* 5th ed., John W. Heeren, Marylee Requa, Robert H. Lauer, and Jeanette C. Lauer, eds. Los Angeles: Roxbury Publishing Company, 2000:27–32.

Stouffer, Samuel A., Arthur A. Lumsdaine, Marion Harper Lumsdaine, Robin M. Williams, Jr., M. Brewster Smith, Irving L. Janis, Shirley A. Star, and Leonard S. Cottrell, Jr. *The American Soldier: Combat and Its Aftermath,* Vol. 2. New York: Wiley, 1949.

Strang, David, and Michael W. Macy. "In Search of Excellence: Fads, Success Stories, and Adaptive Emulation." *American Journal of Sociology, 197,* 1, July 2001:147–182.

Strategic Energy Policy: Challenges for the 21st Century. New York: Council on Foreign Relations, 2001.

Straus, Murray A., and Richard J. Gelles. "Violence in American Families: How Much Is There and Why Does It Occur?" In *Troubled Relationships,* Elam W. Nunnally, Catherine S. Chilman, and Fred M. Cox, eds. Newbury Park, Calif.: Sage, 1988:141–162.

Straus, Murray A. "Victims and Aggressors in Marital Violence." *American Behavioral Scientist, 23,* May–June 1980:681–704.

Straus, Murray A. "Explaining Family Violence." In *Marriage and Family in a Changing Society,* 4th ed., James M. Henslin, ed. New York: Free Press, 1992:344–356.

Straus, Roger A. "The Sociologist as a Marketing Research Consultant." *Journal of Applied Sociology, 8,* 1991:65–75.

Strauss, Neil. "Critic's Notebook: A Japanese TV Show That Pairs Beauty and Pain." *New York Times,* July 14, 1998.

Stryker, Sheldon. "Symbolic Interactionism: Themes and Variations." In *Social Psychology: Sociological Perspectives,* Morris Rosenberg and Ralph H. Turner, eds. New Brunswick, N.J.: Transaction, 1990.

"Study Suggests Lungs Damaged in Healthy Kids Exposed to High Levels of Air Pollution." *Canadian Press,* November 28, 2001.

Sullivan, Andrew. "What We Look Up to Now." *New York Times,* November 15, 1998.

Sullivan, Andrew. "What's So Bad about Hate?" *New York Times Magazine,* September 26, 1999.

Sulloway, Frank J. *Born to Rebel: Birth Order, Family Dynamics, and Creative Lives.* New York: Vintage Books, 1997.

Sumner, William Graham. *Folkways: A Study in the Sociological Importance of Usages, Manners, Customs, Mores, and Morals.* New York: Ginn, 1906.

Sun, Lena H. "China Seeks Ways to Protect Elderly." *Washington Post,* October 23, 1990:A1.

Surgeon General of the United States. "Surgeon General's Report: A Call for Action." Washington, D.C.: Centers for Disease Control, April 3, 2003.

"Survey and Analysis of Teacher Salary Trends 2001." Washington, D.C.: American Federation of Teachers, 2003.

Sutherland, Edwin H. *Criminology.* Philadelphia: Lippincott, 1924.

Sutherland, Edwin H. *Principles of Criminology,* 4th ed. Philadelphia: Lippincott, 1947.

Sutherland, Edwin H. *White Collar Crime.* New York: Dryden Press, 1949.

Sutherland, Edwin H., Donald R. Cressey, and David F. Luckenbill. *Principles of Criminology,* 11th ed. Dix Hills, N.Y.: General Hall, 1992.

Suzuki, Bob H. "Asian-American Families." In *Marriage and Family in a Changing Society,* 2nd ed., James M. Henslin, ed. New York: Free Press, 1985:104–119.

Swedish Institute, The. "Fact Sheets on Sweden." February 1992.

Swedish Institute, The. "Health and Medical Care in Sweden." July 1990:1–4.

Sweeney, Megan M. "Remarriage and the Nature of Divorce: Does It Matter Which Spouse Chose to Leave?" *Journal of Family Issues, 23,* 3, April 2002:410–440.

Sweezy, Paul M., and Harry Magdoff. "Globalization—to What End? Part II." *Monthly Review, 43,* 10, March 1992:1–19.

Sykes, Gresham M., and David Matza. "Techniques of Neutralization." In *Down to Earth Sociology: Introductory Readings,* 5th ed., James M. Henslin, ed. New York: Free Press, 1988:225–231. First published in 1957.

Szasz, Thomas S. *The Myth of Mental Illness,* rev. ed. New York: Harper & Row, 1986.

Szasz, Thomas S. "Mental Illness Is Still a Myth." In *Deviant Behavior 96/97,* Lawrence M. Salinger, ed. Guilford, Conn.: Dushkin, 1996:200–205.

Szasz, Thomas S. *Cruel Compassion: Psychiatric Control of Society's Unwanted.* Syracuse: Syracuse University Press, 1998.

Tach, Laura, and George Farkas. "Ability Grouping and Educational Stratification in the Early School Years." Unpublished paper, 2003.

Tagliabue, John, and Elisabeth Bumiller. "G-8 Leaders Talk Tough on Spread of Nuclear Arms." *New York Times,* June 3, 2003.

Tallman, Irving, Thomas Rotolo, and Louis N. Gray. "Continuity or Change? The Impact of Parents' Divorce on Newly Married Couples." *Social Psychology Quarterly, 64,* 4, 2001:333–346.

Tandia, Bakary. "The Plight of Black Mauritanians." *Black Renaissance, 3,* 3, Summer–Fall 2001.

Tannen, Deborah. *You Just Don't Understand: Women and Men in Conversation.* New York: Morrow, 1990.

Tannen, Deborah. "But What Do You Mean? Women and Men in Conversation." In *Down to Earth Sociology: Introductory Readings,* 12th ed., James M. Henslin, ed. New York: The Free Press, 2003:175–181.

Tanouye, Elyse. "Researchers Say Chinese Medicine May Aid in Prevention of Liver Cancer." *Wall Street Journal,* September 6, 1995:B1.

Tapia, Andres. "Churches Wary of Inner-City Islamic Inroads." *Christianity Today, 38,* 1, January 10, 1994:36–38.

Tarman, Allison. "Obesity in the United States: Reaching a Critical Mass." *Population Bulletin, 57,* Population Reference Bureau, December 2002:17.

Tavernise, Sabrina. "Gathering News in the New Russia Can Be Fatal." *New York Times,* April 16, 2002.

Taylor, Chris. "The Man Behind Lara Croft." *Time,* December 6, 1999:78.

Taylor, Howard F. "The Structure of a National Black Leadership Network: Preliminary Findings." Unpublished manuscript, 1992. As cited in Margaret L. Andersen and Howard F. Taylor, *Sociology: Understanding a Diverse Society.* Belmont, Calif.: Wadsworth, 2000.

Taylor, Monique M. *Harlem: Between Heaven and Hell.* Minneapolis: University of Minnesota Press, 2002.

Terry, Don. "Getting Under My Skin." *New York Times,* July 16, 2000.

Thayer, Stephen. "Encounters." *Psychology Today,* March 1988:31–36.

Thomas, Paulette. "Boston Fed Finds Racial Discrimination in Mortgage Lending Is Still Widespread." *Wall Street Journal,* October 9, 1992:A3.

Thompson, Ginger. "Chasing Mexico's Dream into Squalor." *New York Times,* February 11, 2001.

Thompson, Ginger. "Mexico Is Attracting a Better Class of Factory in its South." *New York Times,* June 29, 2002.

Thornton, Russell. *American Indian Holocaust and Survival: A Population History Since 1492.* Norman: University of Oklahoma Press, 1987.

Tilly, Charles. *From Mobilization to Revolution.* Reading, Mass.: Addison-Wesley, 1978.

Timasheff, Nicholas S. *War and Revolution.* Joseph F. Scheuer, ed. New York: Sheed & Ward, 1965.

Timerman, Jacobo. *Prisoner Without a Name, Cell Without a Number.* New York: Knopf, 1981.

Tobias, Andrew. "The 'Don't Be Ridiculous' Law." *Wall Street Journal,* May 31, 1995:A14.

Toch, Thomas. "Violence in Schools." *U.S. News & World Report, 115,* 18, November 8, 1993:31–36.

Tocqueville, Alexis de. *The Old Regime and the French Revolution.* Stuart Gilbert, trans. Garden City, N.Y.: Doubleday Anchor, 1955. First published in 1856.

Tocqueville, Alexis de. *Democracy in America,* J. P. Mayer and Max Lerner, eds. New York: Harper & Row, 1966. First published in 1835.

Tolchin, Martin. "Surgeon General Asserts Smoking Is an Addiction." *New York Times,* May 17, 1988:A1, C4.

Tolchin, Martin. "Mildest Possible Penalty Is Imposed on Neil Bush." *New York Times,* April 19, 1991:D2.

Tönnies, Ferdinand. *Community and Society (Gemeinschaft und Gesellschaft),* with a new introduction by John Samples. New Brunswick, N.J.: Transaction, 1988. First published in 1887.

Toynbee, Arnold. *A Study of History,* D. C. Somervell, abridger and ed. New York: Oxford University Press, 1946.

Treas, Judith. "Older Americans in the 1990s and Beyond." *Population Bulletin, 50,* 2, May 1995:1–46.

Treiman, Donald J. *Occupational Prestige in Comparative Perspective.* New York: Academic Press, 1977.

Tresniowski, Alex. "Payday Or Mayday?" *People Weekly,* May 17, 1999:128–131.

Trice, Harrison M., and Janice M. Beyer. "Cultural Leadership in Organization." *Organization Science, 2,* 2, May 1991:149–169.

Troeltsch, Ernst. *The Social Teachings of the Christian Churches.* New York: Macmillan, 1931.

Troiano, R. P. "Physical Activity Among Young People." *New England Journal of Medicine, 347,* September 5, 2002:706–707.

Tumin, Melvin M. "Some Principles of Social Stratification: A Critical Analysis." *American Sociological Review 18,* August 1953:394.

Turkle, Sherry. *Life on the Screen: Identity in the Age of the Internet.* New York: Simon and Schuster, 1995.

Turnbull, Colin M. "The Mountain People." In *Sociology 95/96,* Kurt Finsterbusch, ed. Sluice Dock, Conn.: Dushkin, 1995:6–15. First published in 1972.

Turner, Bryan S. "Outline of a Theory of Citizenship." *Sociology, 24,* 2, May 1990:189–217.

Turner, Jonathan H. *American Society: Problems of Structure.* New York: Harper & Row, 1972.

Turner, Jonathan H. *The Structure of Sociological Theory.* Homewood, Ill.: Dorsey, 1978.

Turner, Jonathan H. *On the Origins of Human Emotions: A Sociological Inquiry into the Evolution of Human Affect.* Stanford: Stanford University Press, 2000.

Turner, Ralph H. "Collective Behavior." In *Handbook of Modern Sociology,* Robert E. L. Faris, ed. Chicago: Rand McNally, 1964:382–425.

Turner, Ralph H., and Lewis M. Killian. *Collective Behavior,* 2nd ed. Englewood Cliffs, N.J.: Prentice Hall, 1987.

Tye, Larry. "After Waco, the Focus Shifts to Other Cults." *The Boston Globe,* April 30, 1993:1, 22.

Tyler, Patrick E. "A New Life for NATO? But It's Sidelined for Now." *New York Times,* November 20, 2002.

Uchitelle, Louis. "How to Define Poverty? Let Us Count the Ways." *New York Times,* May 28, 2001.

Udry, J. Richard. "Biological Limits of Gender Construction." *American Sociological Review, 65,* June 2000:443–457.

Udy, Stanley H., Jr. "Bureaucracy and Rationality in Weber's Organizational Theory: An Empirical Study." *American Sociological Review, 24,* December 1959:791–795.

Ullman, Edward, and Chauncey Harris. "The Nature of Cities." In *Urban Man and Society: A Reader in Urban Ecology,* Albert N. Cousins and Hans Nagpaul, eds. New York: Knopf, 1970:91–100.

UNESCO: Institute for Statistics, 2000.

UNICEF. *The State of the World's Children.* New York: Oxford University Press, 1995.

Uniform Crime Reports. Washington D.C.: FBI, published annually.

United Nations Statistical Yearbook 1985–1986. New York: The United Nations, 1987.

United Nations Statistical Yearbook 1990–1991. New York: The United Nations, 1992.

United Nations Statistical Yearbook 1995–1996. New York: The United Nations, 1997.

United Nations. "Fact Sheet: The Impact of HIV/AIDS." 2002a.

United Nations. "Fact Sheet: Sub-Saharan Africa." 2002b.

United Nations. "World Urbanization Prospects: The 1999 Revision." New York: United Nations, 2000.

United Nations. "Agriculture: Towards 2015/30." Technical Interim Report, Food and Agriculture Organization (FAO) of the United Nations, Economic and Social Department. April 2000.

U.S. Bureau of the Census. *Statistical Abstract of the United States: The National Data Book.* Washington, D.C.: U.S. Government Printing Office. Published annually.

U.S. Bureau of the Census. *The Current Population Survey.* "Geographic Mobility, Migration Flows Between Regions, by Race and Hispanic Origin and by Selected Characteristics." 1998, 1999, 2000, 2001, 2002.

U.S. Bureau of the Census. *Annual Demographic Supplement to the March 2002 Current Population Survey, Current Population Reports, Series P20-547.* "Estimated Median Age at First Marriage, by Sex: 1890 to Present," Table MS-2. June 12, 2003.

U.S. Department of Energy, Advisory Committee on Human Radiation Experiments. Final Report, 1995. Washington, D.C.: U.S. Government Printing Office, 1995.

U.S. Department of Health and Human Services, Public Health Service. *Healthy People 2000.* Washington, D.C.: U.S. Government Printing Office, 1990.

Usdansky, Margaret L. "English a Problem for Half of Miami." *USA Today,* April 3, 1992:A1, A3, A30.

Useem, Michael. *The Inner Circle: Large Corporations and the Rise of Business Political Activity in the U.S. and U.K.* New York: Oxford University Press, 1984.

Vartabedian, Ralph, and Scott Gold. "New Questions on Shuttle Tile Safety Raised." *Los Angeles Times,* February 27, 2003.

Vaughan, Diane. "Uncoupling: The Social Construction of Divorce." In *Marriage and Family in a Changing Society,* 2nd ed., James M. Henslin, ed. New York: Free Press, 1985:429–439.

Veblen, Thorstein. *The Theory of the Leisure Class.* New York: Macmillan, 1912.

Vega, William A. "Hispanic Families in the 1980s: A Decade of Research." *Journal of Marriage and the Family, 52,* November 1990:1015–1024.

Violas, P. C. *The Training of the Urban Working Class: A History of Twentieth Century American Education.* Chicago: Rand McNally, 1978.

Volti, Rudi. *Society and Technological Change,* 3rd ed. New York: St. Martin's Press, 1995.

Von Hoffman, Nicholas. "Sociological Snoopers." *Transaction 7,* May 1970:4, 6.

Wagley, Charles, and Marvin Harris. *Minorities in the New World.* New York: Columbia University Press, 1958.

Wald, Matthew L. "Government Reversal Adds to Rift in South Carolina." *New York Times,* May 11, 2002.

Wald, Matthew L., and John Schwartz. "Alerts Were Lacking, NASA Shuttle Manager Says." *New York Times,* July 23, 2003.

Waldholz, Michael. "Computer Brain Outperforms Doctors in Diagnosing Heart Attack Patients." *Wall Street Journal,* December 2, 1991:7B.

Waldman, Amy. "Homes and Shops to Rise on Abandoned Harlem Properties." *New York Times,* December 27, 2000.

Waldman, Peter. "Riots in Bahrain Arouse Ire of Feared Monarchy as the U.S. Stands By." *Wall Street Journal,* June 12, 1995:A1, A8.

Waldrop, Deborah P., and Joseph A. Weber. "From Grandparent to Caregiver: The Stress and Satisfaction of Raising Grandchildren." *Families in Society: The Journal of Contemporary Human Services,* 2001:461–472.

Walker, Alice, and Pratibha Parmar. *Warrior Marks: Female Genital Mutilation and the Sexual Blinding of Women.* New York: Harcourt Brace, 1993.

Wallace, Anthony F. C. *Religion: An Anthropological View.* New York: Random House, 1966.

Wallace, L. J. David, Alice D. Calhoun, Kenneth E. Powell, Joann O'Neil, and Stephen P. James. *Homicide and Suicide Among Native Americans, 1979–1992.* Atlanta, Ga.: National Center for Injury Prevention and Control, 1996.

Wallerstein, Immanuel. *The Modern World System: Capitalist Agriculture and the Origins of the European World-Economy in the Sixteenth Century.* New York: Academic Press, 1974.

Wallerstein, Immanuel. *The Capitalist World-Economy.* New York: Cambridge University Press, 1979.

Wallerstein, Immanuel. "Culture as the Ideological Battleground of the Modern World-System." In *Global Culture: Nationalism, Globalization, and Modernity,* Mike Featherstone, ed. London: Sage, 1990:31–55.

Wallerstein, Immanuel. *The Politics of the World-Economy: The States, the Movements, and the Civilizations.* Cambridge, England: Cambridge University Press, 1984.

Wallerstein, Judith S., and Joan B. Kelly. "How Children React to Parental Divorce." In *Marriage and Family in a Changing Society,* 4th ed., James M. Henslin, ed. New York: Free Press, 1992:397–409.

Wallerstein, Judith S., Sandra Blakeslee, and Julia M. Lewis. *The Unexpected Legacy of Divorce: A 25-Year Landmark Study.* Concord, N.H.: Hyperion Press, 2001.

Walsh, Catherine. "The Life and Legacy of Lawrence Kohlberg." *Society, 37,* 2, January–February 2000:38–44.

Walter, Lynn. *Women's Rights: A Global View.* Westport, Conn.: Greenwood Press, 2001.

Wang, Hongyu, and Paul R. Amato. "Predictors of Divorce Adjustment: Stressors, Resources, and Definitions." *Journal of Marriage and the Family, 62,* 3, August 2000:655–668.

Ware, James H. "Interpreting Incomplete Data in Studies of Diet and Weight Loss." *New England Journal of Medicine, 348,* 17, May 22, 2003:2136–2137.

Wark, Gillian R., and Dennis L. Krebs. "Gender and Dilemma Differences in Real-Life Moral Judgment." *Developmental Psychology, 32,* 1996:220–230.

Watson, J. Mark. "Outlaw Motorcyclists." In *Down to Earth Sociology: Introductory Readings,* 5th ed., James M. Henslin, ed. New York: Free Press, 1988:203–213.

Watts, Duncan J. *Six Degrees: The Science of a Connected Age.* New York: W. W. Norton, 2003.

Wayne, Julie Holliday, Christine M. Riordan, and Kecia M. Thomas. "Is All Sexual Harassment Viewed the Same? Mock Juror Decisions in Same- and Cross-Gender Cases." *Journal of Applied Psychology, 86,* 2, April 2001:179–187.

Wayne, Leslie. "Lucrative Lobbying Jobs Await Many Leaving Government Service." *New York Times,* December 16, 2000.

Wayne, Leslie. "Foreigners Extract Trade-Offs From U.S. Contractors." *New York Times,* February 16, 2003.

Weber, Max. *From Max Weber: Essays in Sociology.* Hans Gerth and C. Wright Mills, trans. and ed. New York: Oxford University Press, 1946.

Weber, Max. *The Theory of Social and Economic Organization,* A. M. Henderson and Talcott Parsons, trans., Talcott Parsons, ed. Glencoe, Ill.: Free Press, 1947. First published in 1913.

Weber, Max. *The Protestant Ethic and the Spirit of Capitalism.* New York: Scribner's, 1958. First published in 1904–1905.

Weber, Max. *Economy and Society.* Ephraim Fischoff, trans. New York: Bedminster Press, 1968. First published in 1922.

Weber, Max. *Economy and Society,* G. Roth and C. Wittich, eds. Berkeley: University of California Press, 1978. First published in 1922.

Weeks, John R. *Population: An Introduction to Concepts and Issues,* 5th ed. Belmont, Calif.: Wadsworth, 1994.

Weiler, Jeanne. "Recent Changes in School Desegregation." *ERIC/CUE Digest,* April 1, 1998.

Weitoft, Gunilla Ringback, Anders Hjern, Bengt Haglund, and Mans Rosen. "Mortality, Severe Morbidity, and Injury in Children Living with Single Parents in Sweden: A Population-Based Study." *Lancet, 361,* January 25, 2003:289–295.

Wells, Susan J. "Making Telecommuting Work." *HR Magazine, 46,* 10, October 2001:34–45.

Wertz, Richard W., and Dorothy C. Wertz. "Notes on the Decline of Midwives and the Rise of Medical Obstetricians." In *The Sociology of Health and Illness: Critical Perspectives,* Peter Conrad and Rochelle Kern, eds. New York: St. Martin's Press, 1981:165–183.

Wessel, David. "As Populations Age, Fiscal Woes Deepen." *Wall Street Journal,* September 11, 1995:A1.

West, Candace, and Angela Garcia. "Conversational Shift Work: A Study of Topical Transitions Between Women and Men." *Social Problems, 35,* 1988:551–575.

White, Jack E. "Forgive Us Our Sins." *Time,* July 3, 1995:29.

White, James A. "When Employees Own Big Stake, It's a Buy Signal for Investors." *Wall Street Journal,* February 13, 1991:C1, C19.

White, Joseph B., Stephen Power, and Timothy Aeppel. "Death Count Linked to Failures of Firestone Tires Rises to 203." *Wall Street Journal,* June 19, 2001:A4.

White, Richard D., Jr. "Are Women More Ethical? Recent Findings on the Effects of Gender Upon Moral Development." *Journal of Public Administration Research and Theory, 9,* 3, July 1999:459–471.

Whitley, Bernard E., Jr., and Stefania A. Egisdottir. "The Gender Belief System, Authoritarianism, Social Dominance Orientation, and Heterosexuals' Attitudes Toward Lesbians and Gay Men." *Sex Roles: A Journal of Research,* June 2000.

Whorf, Benjamin. *Language, Thought, and Reality,* J. B. Carroll, ed. Cambridge, MA: MIT Press, 1956.

Whyte, Martin King. "Choosing Mates—The American Way." *Society,* March–April 1992:71–77.

Whyte, William Foote. "Street Corner Society." In *Down to Earth Sociology: Introductory Readings,* 11th ed., James M. Henslin, ed. New York: The Free Press, 2001:61–69.

Whyte, William H. *The City: Rediscovering the Center.* New York: Doubleday, 1989.

Wilensky, Joe. "Rethinking Policy in a Brave New World." *Human Ecology, 29,* 2, Spring 2001:17–19.

Wilford, John Noble. "In Maya Ruins, Scholars See Evidence of Urban Sprawl." *New York Times,* December 19, 2000.

Wilkening, David. "Celebration Hotel Offers a Quiet Reprieve for Disney Visitors." *Travel Weekly, 59,* 57, July 17, 2000:51.

Williams, Christine L. *Still a Man's World: Men Who Do Women's Work.* Berkeley: University of California Press, 1995.

Williams, Robin M., Jr. *American Society: A Sociological Interpretation,* 2nd ed. New York: Knopf, 1965.

Williams, Thomas D. "The Year of Tolerance." Rome: Anteneo Pontificio, 2003.

Willie, Charles V. "Caste, Class, and Family Life Experiences." *Research in Race and Ethnic Relations, 6,* 1991:65–84.

Wilson, Edward O. *Sociobiology: The New Synthesis.* Cambridge, Mass.: Harvard University Press, 1975.

Wilson, James Q. "Lock 'Em Up and Other Thoughts on Crime." *New York Times Magazine,* March 9, 1975:11, 44–48.

Wilson, James Q., and Richard J. Herrnstein. *Crime and Human Nature.* New York: Simon & Schuster, 1985.

Wilson, James Q. "Is Incapacitation the Answer to the Crime Problem?" In *Taking Sides: Clashing Views on Controversial Social Issues,* 7th ed., Kurt Finsterbusch and George McKenna, eds. Guilford, Conn.: Dushkin, 1992:318–324.

Wilson, William Julius. *The Declining Significance of Race: Blacks and Changing American Institutions.* Chicago: University of Chicago Press, 1978.

Wilson, William Julius. *The Truly Disadvantaged: The Inner City, the Underclass, and Public Policy.* Chicago: University of Chicago Press, 1987.

Wilson, William Julius. *When Work Disappears: The World of the New Urban Poor.* Chicago: University of Chicago Press, 1996.

Wilson, William Julius. *The Bridge over the Racial Divide: Rising Inequality and Coalition Politics.* Berkeley: University of California Press, 2000.

Wines, Michael. "Muckraking Governor Slain by Sniper on Moscow Street." *New York Times,* October 19, 2002.

Wirth, Louis. "Urbanism as a Way of Life." *American Journal of Sociology, 44,* July 1938:1–24.

Wirth, Louis. "The Problem of Minority Groups." In *The Science of Man in the World Crisis,* Ralph Linton, ed. New York: Columbia University Press, 1945.

Witt, Susan D. "The Influence of Television on Children's Gender Role Socialization." *Childhood Education, 76,* 2000:322–328.

Wolfensohn, James D., and Kathryn S. Fuller. "Making Common Cause: Seeing the Forest for the Trees." *International Herald Tribune,* May 27, 1998:11.

Wolff, Michael, et al. *Where We Stand: Can America Make It in the Global Race for Wealth and Happiness?* New York: Bantam Books, 1992.

Wolinsky, Frederic D., Timothy E. Stump, and Christopher M. Callahan. "Does Being Placed in a Nursing Home Make You Sicker and More Likely to Die?" In *Societal Mechanisms for Maintaining Competence in Old Age,* Sherry L. Willis, K. Warner Schaie, and Mark Hayward, eds. New York: Springer Publishing Company, 1997:94–130.

Womack, James P., Daniel T. Jones, and Daniel Roos. *The Machine That Changed the World: The Story of Lean Production.* New York: Harper Perrenial, 1991.

"Women of Our World." Washington, D.C.: Population Reference Bureau, 2002.

Wonacott, Peter. "In Rural China, Health Care Grows Expensive, Elusive." *Wall Street Journal,* May 19, 2003:A1, A12.

Wood, Daniel B., "Latinos Redefine What It Means to Be Manly." *Christian Science Monitor, 93,* 161, July 16, 2001.

Wood, Scott Small. "The Price Professors Pay for Teaching at Public Universities." *Chronicle of Higher Education, 2001, 46,* 32, A18-A24.

Woodward, Kenneth L. "Heaven." *Newsweek, 113,* 13, March 27, 1989:52–55.

The World Factbook of the CIA. Washington, D.C.: U.S. Government Printing Office, 2003.

World Health Organization. *Constitution of the World Health Organization.* New York: World Health Organization. Washington, D.C.: Interim Commission, 1946.

"The World of the Child 6 Billion." Population Reference Bureau, 2000.

Worsley, Peter. *The Trumpet Shall Sound.* London: MacGibbon and Kee, 1957.

Wren, David J. "School Culture: Exploring the Hidden Curriculum." *Adolescence, 34,* Fall 1999:593–596.

Wright, Erik Olin. *Class.* London: Verso, 1985.

Wright, Lawrence. "One Drop of Blood." *New Yorker,* July 25, 1994:46–50, 52–55.

Wright, Lawrence. "Double Mystery." *New Yorker,* August 7, 1995:45–62.

Wyatt, Edward. "City Plans to Let Company Run Some Public Schools in a First." *New York Times,* December 21, 2000.

Yamaguchi, Kazuo. "Subjective Rationality of Initiators and of Threshold-Theoretical Behavior of Followers in Collective Action." *Rationality and Society, 12,* 2, May 2000:185–225.

Yat-ming Sin, Leo, and Hon-ming Yau, Oliver. "Female Role Orientation and Consumption Values: Some Evidence from Mainland China." *Journal of International Consumer Marketing, 13,* 2, 2001:49–75.

Yellowbird, Michael, and C. Matthew Snipp. "American Indian Families." In *Minority Families in the United States: A Multicultural Perspective,* Ronald L. Taylor, ed. Englewood Cliffs, N.J.: Prentice Hall, 1994:179–201.

Yinger, J. Milton. *Toward a Field Theory of Behavior: Personality and Social Structure.* New York: McGraw-Hill, 1965.

Yinger, J. Milton. *The Scientific Study of Religion.* New York: Macmillan, 1970.

Young, Laurie E. "The Overlooked Contributions of Women to the Development of American Sociology: An Examination of AJS Articles from 1895–1926." Paper presented at the 1995 meetings of the American Sociological Association.

Zaalouk, Malak. "Community Schools: Egypt's Celebrity Model." *UNESCO Courier,* May 2001:15–16.

Zachary, G. Pascal. "Behind Stocks' Surge Is an Economy in Which Big U.S. Firms Thrive." *Wall Street Journal,* November 22, 1995:A1, A5.

Zald, Mayer N. "Looking Backward to Look Forward: Reflections on the Past and the Future of the Resource Mobilization Research Program." In *Frontiers in Social Movement Theory,* Aldon D. Morris and Carol McClurg Mueller, eds. New Haven, Conn.: Yale University Press, 1992:326–348.

Zald, Mayer N., and John D. McCarthy, eds. *Social Movements in an Organizational Society.* New Brunswick, N.J.: Transaction, 1987.

Zarakhovich, Yuri. "Closing the Door." *Time Atlantic, 157,* 8, February 26, 2001:25.

Zaslow, Jeffrey. "Will You Still Need Me When I'm…84? More Couples Divorce After Decades." *Wall Street Journal,* June 17, 2003:D1.

Zellner, William W. *Countercultures: A Sociological Analysis.* New York: St. Martin's, 1995.

Zernike, Kate. "The Harvard Guide to Happiness." *New York Times,* April 8, 2001.

Zerubavel, Eviatar. *The Fine Line: Making Distinctions in Everyday Life.* New York: Free Press, 1991.

Zeune, Gary D. "Are You Teaching Your Employees to Steal?" *Business Credit, 103,* 4, April 2001:16.

Zielbauer, Paul. "Study Finds Pequot Businesses Lift Economy." *New York Times,* November 29, 2000.

Zola, Irving K. *Socio-Medical Inquiries.* Philadelphia: Temple University Press, 1983.

Zuckerman, Laurence. "Management Employee-Ownership Experiment Unravels at United." *New York Times,* March 14, 2001.

Name Index

Subject Index

Credits

Chapter Opener Art Credits *(continued)*:

Chapter 13: *The Soyer Brothers* by Alice Neel (1900-1984), 1973. Oil on canvas, 60 × 46 in. (152.4 × 116.84 cm.). Whitney Museum of American Art, New York; purchase, with funds from Arthur M. Bullowa, Sydney Duffy, Stewart R. Mott and Edward Rosenthal 74.77. © Estate of Alice Neel. Courtesy of Robert Miller Gallery, New York.

Chapter 14: *Paperworkers* by Douglass Crockwell, 1934. Oil on canvas, 48 ¼ × 36 ⅛ in. (91.7 × 122.4 cm.). © Smithsonian American Art Museum, Washington, DC/Art Resource, NY.

Chapter 15: *The Fourth of July (The Greatest Display of the American Flag Ever Seen in New York, Climax of the Preparedness Parade in May)* by Frederick Childe Hassam, 1916. Oil on canvas, 36 × 26 in. © Christie's Images/SuperStock

Chapter 16: *Family* by Charles H. Alston (1907-1977), 1955. Oil on canvas, 48 ¼ × 35 ¾ in. (122.56 × 90.81 cm.). Whitney Museum of American Art, New York; purchase, with funds from the Artists and Students Assistance Fund 55.47. © The Estate of Charles Alston; Courtesy of Michael Rosenfeld Gallery, LLC, New York, NY.

Chapter 17: *Students* by Stephen Schildbach, 1999. Acrylic, 16 × 13 in. © Stephen Schildbach/Images.com, Inc.

Chapter 18: *Jerusalem XIX (Ehtiopian Boy)* by Elizabeth Barakah Hodges, 1997. Mixed media, 11 ½ × 12 ⅓ in. Private Collection. © Elizabeth Barakah Hodges/SuperStock

Chapter 19: *Chinese Doctor* by Chen Lian Xing, 1998. Watercolor, 14 × 14 in. © Red Lantern Folk Art/The Mukashi Collection/SuperStock

Chapter 20: *Avenida Abraham Lincoln* by Franklin McMahon. © Franklin McMahon/CORBIS.

Chapter 21: *Demonstration* by Isaak Brodskij, 1930. © The State Russian Museum/CORBIS

Chapter 22: *Hand And Environments (Digital)* by Jose Ortega, 1995. Mixed media and digital, 8.5 × 11 in. © Jose Ortega/Images.com, Inc.

Photo Credits:

Chapter 1: p. 4 © Herve Collart Odinetz/Corbis Sygma; **p. 9** Mary Evans Picture Library; **p. 10** © Hulton-Deutsch Collection/CORBIS; **p. 11 (top)** © Gianni Dagli Orti/CORBIS; **(right)** North Wind Picture Archive; **p. 12 (top)** © Bettmann/CORBIS; **(bottom left)** © Bill Lai/Index Stock Imagery; **(bottom right)** © Robert Leon. All rights Reserved. www.robertleon.com; **p. 13** The Granger Collection, New York; **p. 15** AP/Wide World Photos; **p. 16** © John M. Greim. www.mira.com; **p. 18** The Granger Collection, New York; **p. 19 (left)** AP/Wide World Photos; **(top right)** North Wind Picture Archive; **(center right)** Photographs and Prints Division, Schomburg Center for Research in Black Culture/The New York Public Library, Astor, Lenox, and Tilden Foundations; **p. 21** Photo by Yaroslava Mills; **p. 23** University of Chicago Library; **p. 25** © Ronnie Kaufman/CORBIS; **p. 26** The Art Archive/Bergen Library; **p. 27** Culver Pictures. **Chapter 2: p. 38** © Charles Kennard/Stock, Boston; **p. 39 (top left to right)** © SuperStock; © Richard Lord/The Image Works; **(center left to right)** © SuperStock; © Lindsay Hebberd/Woodfin Camp & Associates; © Ben Mangor/SuperStock, Inc.; **(bottom left to right)** © James M. Henslin; © Art Wolfe, www.artwolfe.com; © 2002 Stuart McClymont/Stone/Getty Images; **p. 41 (top)** dog and boy, © 2002 PhotoDisc/Getty Images; **p. 42** © James M. Henslin; **p. 45** AFP/CORBIS; **p. 47 (top)** © Bob Daemmrich/The Image Works; **(bottom)** © Mirror Syndication International; **p. 50** © Catherine Lerov/Sipa Press; **p. 51 (top left to right)** © Cary Wolinsky/IPN/Aurora; © Mike Segar/Reuters/Landov; © West Rock/Taxi/Getty Images; **(center left to right)** AP/Wide World Photos; © Alex Wong/Getty Images; **(bottom left to right)** © Jeff Greenberg/Index Stock Imagery; © William Allard/National Geographic Collection; © Owen Franken/Stock, Boston; **p. 52** Photofest; **p. 53** © Roger Yager/Stone/Getty Images; **p. 54** © Anton Vengo/SuperStock; **p. 55** Clarke Memorial Museum, Eureka, California; **p. 58** © Moshe shai Photography; **p. 59** © Mattel, Inc./Reuters-Archive Photos/Getty Images. **Chapter 3: p. 64** © Laura Dwight/PhotoEdit, Inc.; **p. 65** © James M. Henslin **p. 66** © Kate Brooks/Corbis Saba; **p. 67** © Harlow Primate Laboratory/University of Wisconsin; **p. 69 (top)** © Myrleen Ferguson Cate/PhotoEdit, Inc.; **(bottom)** © Charles Thatcher/Stone/Getty Images; **p. 75** © Karen Ballard/Corbis Sygma; **p. 78 (left)** AP/Wide World Photos; **(right)** © Eidos Interactive Ltd.; **p. 79** Lannis Waters/The Palm Beach Post; **p. 83** © Michael Newman/PhotoEdit, Inc.; **p. 84** © Ellen Senisi/The Image Works; **p. 86** © Ewing Galloway/Index Stock Imagery; **p. 87** The Bridgeman Art Library; **p. 88** © Michael MacIntyre/The Hutchison Library; **p. 89** AP/Wide World Photos. **Chapter 4: p. 94** © Bettmann/CORBIS; **p. 98** AP/Wide World Photos; **p. 101** © James M. Henslin; **p. 102** © Francois Perri/GIMR/Liaison/Getty Images; **p. 104 (left)** © Dominic Arizona Bonuccelli/Photographersdirect.com; **(right)** © Ryan McVay/PhotoDisc/Getty Images; **p. 105** AP/Wide World Photos; **p. 107 (left)** © Powerstock/

SuperStock; **(right)** © David Frazier Photography; **p. 108 (left)** © Alain Evrard/Photo Researchers. Inc.; **(right)** © Frans Lanting/Minden Pictures; **p. 109 (top)** © Nick Dolding/Stone/Getty Images; **(bottom)** ABC Photo Archive; **p.110** © Kelvin Jones/MPTV; **p. 112 (left)** AP/Wide World Photos; **(right)** © Robert Daly/Stone/Getty Images; **p. 115** © Heidi Levine/Sipa Press; **p. 118–119** © James M. Henslin. **Chapter 5: p. 125** © AFP/CORBIS; **p. 129** © Jouanneau Thomas/Corbis Sygma; **p. 132** © Bob Krist/CORBIS; **p. 133** © Lannis Waters/The Palm Beach Post; **p. 134** © Rob Crandall/The Image Works; **p. 138** © Peter Hvizdak/The Image Works; **p. 141** © Jeff Greenberg/Index Stock Imagery. **Chapter 6: p. 148** ©2003 World Wrestling Entertainment, Inc. All Rights Reserved; **p. 150** © Carlos Humberto/Contact Press Images; **p. 152** The Museum of Modern Art/Film Stills Archive; **p. 155** © Tony Freeman/PhotoEdit, Inc.; **p. 157** AP/Wide World Photos; **p. 158 (left)** © Tony Freeman/PhotoEdit, Inc.; **(right)** © George Azar/The Image Works; **p. 159** © Ron McKenzie/Courtesy American Sociological Association; **p. 161** © Fujifotos/The Image Works; **p. 165** © Laura Dwight/PhotoEdit, Inc.; **p. 166** © CORBIS; **p. 169** © 1965 by Stanley Milgram. From the film *Obedience*, distributed by Pennsylvania State University, Audio Visual Services. **Chapter 7: p. 176** © David Butow/Corbis Saba; **p. 178** © Bob Krist/CORBIS; **p. 179** © Alexander Burkatowski/ CORBIS; **p. 181 (top)** Courtesy MetLife Archives; **(bottom)** © AFP/CORBIS; **p. 182** © Earl & Nazima Kowall/CORBIS; **p. 183** © Corbis Sygma; **p. 184** © March of Dimes; **p. 187** AP/Wide World Photos; **p. 190** © Steve Winter/Black Star; **p. 194** © Michael Wolf/Visum/Corbis Saba. **Chapter 8: p. 200** © James M. Henslin; **p. 202 (top)** © Mark Mirko/The Palm Beach Post; **(bottom)** © UPI/Bettmann/CORBIS; **p. 204** © James M. Henslin; **p. 206** © A. Ramey/PhotoEdit, Inc.; **p. 207** AP/Wide World Photos; **p. 208** © Ralf-Finn Hestoft/Corbis Saba; **p. 211** Matt Mahurin; **p. 212** AP/Wide World Photos; **p. 213** The Granger Collection, New York; **p. 214** © J. Michael Short/Loredo Morning Times; **p. 220** © The Californian/Barrios Henry/Corbis Sygma; **p. 223** © Max Whittaker/Getty Images; **p. 224** AP/Wide World Photos; **p. 225** © Monica Almeida, The New York Times. **Chapter 9: p. 230 (left)** © Shawn G. Henry; **(right)** © Peter Ginter/Material World; **p. 231** Library of Congress, Image #LC-B811-3608; **p. 232** © James M. Henslin; **p. 233** C.S.I./Liaison Agency/Getty Images; **p. 234** © James M. Henslin; **p. 236** The Granger Collection, New York; **p. 237 (left)** © Jacob Riis/Bettmann/CORBIS; **(right)** © Bettmann/CORBIS; **p. 238** AP/Wide World Photos; **p. 242** © Archivo Iconografico, SA/CORBIS; **p. 244** © Amelia Kunhardt/The Image Works; **p. 249, 250–251** © James M. Henslin; **p. 253 (top)** © Bob Daemmrich/The Image Works; **(bottom)** © Lisa Quinones/Black Star. **Chapter 10: p. 261** George Burns/Harpo Production/Getty Images; **p. 262** © Rommel Pecson/The Image Works; **p. 263** © Russell Turiak/Getty Images; **p. 264** Jean Clouet, *Elizabeth of Austria, Queen of France.* Musée du Louvre, Paris. Photo © Erich Lessing/Art Resource, NY; **p. 267** © Doral Chenoweth III/Columbus Dispatch/Corbis Sygma; **p. 270 (clockwise from top left)** © Reuters NewMedia, Inc./CORBIS; Carlos Alvarez/Getty Images; Lisa Blumenfeld/Getty Images; Vince Bucci/Getty Images; **p. 272 (left)** © John Maier/The Image Works; **(right)** © Peter Turnley/CORBIS; **p. 276** © Ariel Skelley/CORBIS; **p. 277** © UPI/Bettmann/CORBIS; **p. 281** © Jean-Yves Rabeuf/The Image Works. **Chapter 11: p. 291 (top left to right)** © Jim Zuckerman/CORBIS; © Victor Englebert; **(center left to right)** © Jorgen Schytte/Still Pictures; © David R. Frazier Photolibrary; © Art Wolfe, www.artwolfe.com; **(bottom left to right)** © Owen Franken/Stock, Boston; © SuperStock, Inc.; © Ingrid Moorjohn/Still Pictures; **p. 292** Courtesy of Cynthia Fuchs Epstein; **p. 293** Courtesy of Steven Goldberg; **p. 294** Archive Photos/Getty Images; **p. 295 (top)** © Dave G. Houser/CORBIS; **(bottom)** © Alon Reininger/Contact Press Images; **p. 296–297** © James M. Henslin; **p. 299** © UPI/Bettmann/CORBIS; **p. 301** © Michael Wolf/Aurora; **p.302** © Reuters NewMedia, Inc./CORBIS; **p. 303** Culver Pictures; **p. 308** AP/Wide World Photos; **p. 313** AP/Wide World Photos. **Chapter 12: p. 324 (left)** © Robert Mora/Getty Images; **(right)** © Reuters/Landov; **p. 325** © Adrian Dennis/AFP/Getty Images; **p. 326 (both)** © Time/Getty Images; **p.328** © Jim Hollander/Reuters-Archive Photos/Getty Images; **p. 330** © UPI/Bettmann/CORBIS; **p. 339** © Bob Daemmrich/The Image Works; **p. 344** AP/Wide World Photos; **p. 346** AP/Wide World Photos; **p. 348** Courtesy of William Julius Wilson. © Jon Chase/Harvard News Office; **p. 351** AP/Wide World Photos; **p. 353** North Wind Picture Archives; **p. 357** © Jim Cooper/Stone/Getty Images. **Chapter 13: p. 362** © John Launois/Black Star; **p. 363** Charles P. Mountford. © National Geographic Society; **p. 367** AP/Wide World Photos; **p. 368** © James M. Henslin; **p. 371** © Jon Kopaloff/Getty Images; **p. 372** © Karen Kasmauski/National Geographic Society; **p. 376** Courtesy of Pfizer Corporation; **p. 379** © Jeff Greenberg/PhotoEdit, Inc.; **p. 380** AP/Wide World Photos; **p. 383 (left)** © Bob Daemmrich/Stone/Getty Images; **(righ ht)** © Darren Modricker/CORBIS; **p. 384** © Nathan Benn/Woodfin Camp & Associates. **Chapter 14: p. 390** © James M. Henslin; **p. 391 (left)** © Lewis Hine/Bettmann/CORBIS; **(right)** © Lindsay Hebberd/Woodfin Camp & Associates; **p. 395** The Granger Collection, New York; **p. 396** © AFP/CORBIS; **p. 397 7** © AKG London; **p. 399** © Bruce Dale/National Geographic Society; **p. 400** © David Burnett/Contact Press Images; **p. 402** © Matthew Farruggio; **p. 410** © Ursula Markus/Photo Researchers, Inc.; **p. 413** © Jeffrey Aaronson/Network Aspen; **p. 414** © A. Aarhus/Sipa Press. **Chapter 15: p. 421** Brown Brothers; **p. 422** © Stephanie Maze/Woodfin Camp & Associates; **p. 423 (top)** Jean-Auguste-Dominique Ingres, *Jeanne d'Arc.* 1854. Musée du Louvre, Paris. Photo © AKG London; **(bottom)** © AKG London; **p. 424** © Reuters NewMedia, Inc./CORBIS; **p. 425** AP/Wide World Photos; **p. 426** Supplied by Globe Photos, Inc.; **p. 429** AP/Wide World Photos; **p. 431** © Bettmann/CORBIS; **p. 435** © Hulton Collection/Getty Images; **p. 439** IDF/Getty Images; **p. 441** © Lynn Johnson/Aurora; **p. 442, 443** AP/Wide World Photos. **Chapter 16: p. 449** Courtesy of the National Parenting Association (NPA), N.Y. Copyright © 1994 by the NPA; **p. 454, 455** © James M. Henslin; **p. 459** General Motors Corporation, used with permission; **p. 461** © John Burke/Index Stock Imagery; **p. 462** © Ty Allison/Taxi/Getty Images; **p. 463** © SuperStock; **p. 465** Ambassador/Corbis Sygma; **p. 466** © Peter Jones for Reuters/Landov; **p. 473** Courtesy of the National Parenting Association (NPA), N.Y. Copyright © 1994 by the NPA. **Chapter 17: p. 484** © Nichole Duplaix/National Geographic Image Collection; **p. 485** The Granger Collection, New York; **p. 486** © Bill Aron/PhotoEdit, Inc.; **p. 489 (top)** © Michael Wolf/Aurora; **(bottom)** Courtesy of Lisa Pearce; **p. 491 (top)** © Michael Newman/PhotoEdit, Inc.; **(bottom)**; © Jeff Greenberg/Index Stock Imagery; **p. 493** © Tannen Maury/Landov; **p. 494**

© Catherine Karnow/Woodfin Camp & Associates; **p. 495** © Bob Daemmrich/The Image Works; **p. 498** © Francis G. Mayer/ CORBIS; **p. 501** © Stephen D. Cannerelli/The Image Works; **p. 505** © The Golden Family/Corbis Sygma; **p. 506** © Mary Kate Denny/PhotoEdit, Inc.; **p. 508** © Andy Freeberg. **Chapter 18:** **p. 512** © James M. Henslin; **p. 515** Bill Aron/PhotoEdit, Inc.; **p. 516** © Bob Henriques/Magnum Photos; **p. 517** The Granger Collection, New York; **p. 519 (top)** © Scala/Art Resource, NY; **(bottom)** © Robert Caputo/Aurora; **p. 521** Library of Congress. Photograph by Jack Delano; **p. 523** © Christopher Brown/Stock, Boston; **p. 526** © Monika Graff/The Image Works; **p. 527** © CORBIS; **p. 531** © Paul Almasy/CORBIS; **p. 534** © Greg Smith/Corbis Saba; **p. 535** © Porter Gifford/Liaison/Getty Images; **p. 539** © National Museum of Kenya/Visuals Unlimited. **Chapter 19:** **p. 544** © James M. Henslin; **p. 545** © Alan Oddie/PhotoEdit, Inc.; **p. 547** © Earl & Nazima Kowall/CORBIS; **p. 548** Lambert/ Archive Photos/Getty Images; **p. 549** © Patti Ramos Photography; **p. 553** The New England Journal of Medicine, 1/16/03; Vol. 348, page 228. Copyright © 2003 Massachusetts Medical Society. All rights reserved.; **p. 561** © Malcolm Linton/Liaison/Getty Images; **p. 563** © Rick Gerharter Photography; **p. 565** AP/Wide World Photos; **p. 566** © David Young-Wolff/PhotoEdit, Inc.; **p. 567** © Shuji Kobayashi/Stone/Getty Images; **p. 570** © J. P. Laffong/ Corbis Sygma. **Chapter 20:** **p. 578** © Key Color/Index Stock Imagery/PictureQuest; **p. 582 (left)** © Reuters-Archive Photos/Getty Images; **(right)** © PhotoDisc/Getty Images; **p. 588** © A. Ramey/ Woodfin Camp & Associates; **p. 590** © Owen Franken/Stock, Boston; **p. 592–593** © James M. Henslin; **p. 594** © Stuart Franklin/Magnum Photos; **p. 597** © Bernard Boutrit/Woodfin Camp & Associates; **p. 600** © Noboru/Photo Researchers, Inc.; **p. 602** © John Nordell/The Image Works; **p. 603** © Bill Stanton/Magnum Photos; **p. 604** © Dan Lamont/CORBIS; **p. 605** © Larry Downing/ Woodfin Camp & Associates; **p. 606** © Georg Gerster/Photo Researchers, Inc.; **p. 608** © George Lepp/Stone/Getty Images. **Chapter 21:** **p. 614** AP/Wide World Photos; **p. 618** AP/Wide World Photos; **p. 619** © A. Ramey/PhotoEdit, Inc.; **p. 622** © Reuters NewMedia, Inc./CORBIS **p. 625** © Sean Sprague/Stock, Boston; **p. 627** AP/Wide World Photos; **p. 629** Jeff Vendsel/Santa Rosa Press Democrat; **p. 630** © Seth Joel/Corbis Saba; **p. 632–633** © James M. Henslin; **p. 635** © Cynthia Howe/Corbis Sygma; **p. 639** Jose Traver/Gamma-Liaison/Getty Images. **Chapter 22:** **p. 645** © Roger-Viollet; **p. 646** Hans Holbein the Younger, *The Ambassadors,* 1553. The National Gallery, London. Photo © Erich Lessing/Art Resource, NY; **p. 647** AP/Wide World Photos; **p. 648** © Transit Leipzig/ Sovfoto; **p. 650** © Kevin Schafer/Stone/Getty Images; **p. 651** © Tom Treick, The Oregonian/Corbis Sygma; **p. 652 (left)** © George Eastman House/Archive/Getty Images; **(right)** © Mark Zimmerman/ Getty Images; **p. 653** © Bettmann/CORBIS; **p. 654** Courtesy The Computer Museum History Center/Model photo © Dennis Bourke; **p. 655** Photo by Warner Bros. Pictures/Zuma Press. © 2003 by Warner Bros. Pictures; **p. 658 (clockwise from top left)** © Klein/ Hubert-Bios/Peter Arnold, Inc.; © Terry Whittaker/Photo Researchers, Inc.; © Anup Shah/Animals Animals; © Tom McHugh/ Photo Researchers, Inc.; **p. 661** © Raghu Rai/Magnum Photo; **p. 662** AP/Wide World Photos.

What readers are saying about

Thanks to your book, I'm considering continuing my study of Sociology

... engaging and easy to follow...

I FOUND YOUR BOOK TO BE INCREDIBLY INTERESTING - SO MUCH THAT I AM NOW READING THE CHAPTERS WE SKIPPED OVER IN CLASS.

Your book rocks!
It is the most fun I have ever had reading any text-book in my life!

I seriously believe that reading your book has made me a better person.